Intersections of Gender, Race, and Class

Readings for a Changing Landscape

Marcia Texler Segal
Indiana University Southeast

Theresa A. Martinez
University of Utah

Roxbury Publishing Company
Los Angeles, California

Library of Congress Cataloging-in-Publication Data

Intersections of gender, race, and class: readings for a changing landscape/edited by Marcia Texler Segal and Theresa A. Martinez.—1st ed.
p. cm.
Includes bibliographical references.
ISBN 1-933220-01-5 (alk. paper)
1. Social structure 2. Sexual orientation 3. Ethnic relations I. Segal, Marcia Texler, 1940– II. Martinez, Theresa A., 1960–.

HM706.I57 2007
305.30973—dc22   2007017711

Publisher: Claude Teweles
Managing Editor: Dawn VanDercreek
Production Editor: Monica K. Gomez
Typography: Jerry Lenihan
Cover Design: Marnie Kenney

Printed on acid-free paper in the United States of America. This book meets the standards for recycling of the Environmental Protection Agency.

ISBN 1-933220-01-5

ROXBURY PUBLISHING COMPANY
P.O. Box 491044
Los Angeles, California 90049-9044
Voice: (310) 473-3312 • Fax: (310) 473-4490
E-mail: roxbury@roxbury.net
Website: www.roxbury.net

Contents

About the Editors ix
About the Contributors xi
Introduction 1
Subject Listing of Topics Covered by Chapter 5

Section 1. Framing the Past

1. The Lady and the Mill Girl: Changes in the Status of
    Women in the Age of Jackson 7
    Gerda Lerner

2. Why Irish Became Domestics and Italians and Jews Did Not 16
    Stephen Steinberg

3. Society of Strangers 23
    Graham Robb

4. Congressional Record—House (67 Cong., 2nd Sess.) 31

5. 'Gone With the Wind': The Invisibility of Racism in
    American History 36
    James W. Loewen

6. The Logic of Nonstandard English 57
    William Labov

*7. Double-Consciousness and *Mestiza* Consciousness Raising:
    Linking Du Bois and Anzaldúa 69
    Theresa A. Martinez

Section 2. Story Sharing

8. 1965 80
    Malcolm X

9. A Letter to Harvey Milk 89
    Lesléa Newman

10. Background (From *Tea That Burns:
    A Family Memoir of Chinatown*) 98
    Bruce Edward Hall

11. He Defies You Still: The Memoirs of a Sissy 109
    Tommi Avicolli Mecca

*Indicates chapters written for this volume.

12. With No Immediate Cause.............................114
    Ntozake Shange

13. Working in Other People's Houses 116
    Mpho 'M'atsepo Nthunya

14. Woman Hollering Creek 123
    Sandra Cisneros

15. Yellow Woman and a Beauty of the Spirit 131
    Leslie Marmon Silko

16. From the Margins.................................137
    Stephen Paul Whitaker

17. Long Hours, Starvation Wages 145
    Lorreta Schwartz-Nobel

18. Report from the Bahamas.............................153
    June Jordan

Section 3. Framing Family and Community Relationships

19. The Gendered Politics and Violence of Structural Adjustment:
    A View From Jamaica 161
    Faye V. Harrison

20. Asymmetries: Women and Men Talking at Cross-Purposes 175
    Deborah Tannen

21. Cuban Jewish Women in Miami: A Triple Identity 184
    Hannah Schiller Wartenberg

22. 'Not All Differences Are Created Equal': Multiple Jeopardy
    in a Gendered Organization 194
    Jane Ward

23. When You're a Credit to Your Race, the Bill Will Come Due:
    O. J. Simpson and Our Trial by Fire.......................209
    Michael Eric Dyson

24. Breaking the Silence 220
    Henry Louis Gates, Jr.

25. In the Closet 222
    Steven Seidman

Section 4. Framing Institutions

26. Stories From the Field..............................239
    Wendy Luttrell

27. Schools Struggle Shielding Gay Kids 249
    Nicole Ziegler Dizon

28. Gender and Class Stereotypes: A Comparison of U.S. and
    Taiwanese Magazine Advertisements 251
    Chia-Wen Chi and Cecelia Baldwin

29. Race and Criminalization: Black Americans and the
    Punishment Industry 265
    Angela Y. Davis

30. A Higher Power of Their Understanding: Cheyenne Women
    and Their Religious Roles 274
    Martha Garcia

31. Religious Identity and Mobility 281
    Pamela Paul

32. What's in a Name? 285
    Kendra Hamilton

33. The Return of the Sweatshop 289
    Edna Bonacich and Richard P. Appelbaum

34. Recasting our Understanding of Gender and Work
    During Global Restructuring. 300
    Jean L. Pyle and Kathryn B. Ward

35. Legal Scholars of Gay Rights Offer Strategies to Combat
    the 'Apartheid of the Closet' 318
    D. W. Miller

*36. SES, Race/Ethnicity, and Health. 323
    Melanie L. Johnston

*37. The Illness Experience Among Mexico City's Older Adults:
    The Effect of Gender, Class, and Race/Ethnicity 336
    *Diana Torrez, Roberto Campos-Navarro, and
    Elia Nora Arganis Juárez*

Section 5. On Privilege

38. White Privilege and Male Privilege: A Personal Account of
    Coming to See Correspondences Through Work in
    Women's Studies. 344
    Peggy McIntosh

39. White Views of Civil Rights: Color Blindness and
    Equal Opportunity 353
    Nancy DiTomaso, Rochelle Parks-Yancy, and Corinne Post

*Indicates chapters written for this volume.

40. Growing Up White: The Social Geography of Race 362
    Ruth Frankenberg

41. Women's Employment Among Blacks, Whites, and Three
    Groups of Latinas: Do More Privileged Women Have
    Higher Employment? 368
    *Paula England, Carmen Garcia-Beaulieu, and
    Mary Ross*

42. Rethinking Official Measures of Poverty: Consideration of Race,
    Ethnicity, and Gender 380
    Angela Gardner Roux

43. Characteristics of the Foreign Born in the United States:
    Results From Census 2000 390
    Elizabeth Grieco

*44. Race and Ethnicity: Images of Difference in South Africa 393
    Edwin S. Segal

45. The Haves, The Have-Nots 403
    Christopher Reynolds

Section 6. On Activist Thinking and Activism

46. *La conciencia de la mestiza*/Towards a New Consciousness 405
    Gloria Anzaldúa

47. A Place in the Rainbow: Theorizing Lesbian and Gay Culture 411
    Janice M. Irvine

48. Women of Color on the Front Line 428
    Celene Krauss

49. Angry Women Are Building: Issues and Struggles Facing
    American Indian Women Today 437
    Paula Gunn Allen

50. The Political Is Personal: The Influence of White Supremacy
    on White Antiracists' Personal Relationships 441
    Eileen O'Brien

51. 'If It Wasn't for the Women . . .': African American Women,
    Community Work, and Social Change 453
    Cheryl Townsend Gilkes

52. Liberia's Female Warriors—Fierce, Feared 464
    Glenn McKenzie

53. The Heterosexual Questionnaire 467
    Martin Rochlin

*Indicates chapters written for this volume.

Section 7. On New Perspectives

54. Race Lessons 469
    Dalton Conley

55. Lunch With My 'Enemy': Exploring the Roots of Ethnic Strife 477
    Amitava Kumar

56. 'New Racism,' Color-Blind Racism, and the Future of Whiteness
    in America 483
    Eduardo Bonilla-Silva

57. Buried Alive: The Concept of Race in Science 497
    Troy Duster

58. Playing in the Gender Transgression Zone: Race, Class, and
    Hegemonic Masculinity in Middle Childhood 501
    C. Shawn McGuffey and B. Lindsay Rich

59. Puerto Rican Wannabes: Sexual Spectacle and the Marking of
    Race, Class, and Gender Boundaries 517
    Amy C. Wilkins

60. All Men Are *Not* Created Equal: Asian Men in U.S. History 532
    Yen Le Espiritu

61. LGBT Parents and Their Children 542
    Kristin E. Joos

*62. Color-Blind Racism and Post-Feminism: The Contemporary
    Politics of Inequality 551
    Abby L. Ferber

*63. Systems of Oppression: Ten Principles 557
    **Vasilikie Demos and Anthony J. Lemelle, Jr., with
    Solomon Gashaw**

64. Broken Levees, Unbroken Barriers 565
    Jason DeParle

*Indicates chapters written for this volume.

About the Editors

Marcia Texler Segal is a Professor of Sociology and Dean for Research Emerita at Indiana University Southeast. Her research and teaching focus on the relationships among gender, race, ethnicity, sexualities, and class in the United States and on gender and international development in sub-Saharan Africa. Professor Segal has won many honors and awards in academic and community circles. She co-edits the influential series *Advances in Gender Research* and has just completed Volume X.

Theresa A. Martinez is an Associate Professor of Sociology and Assistant Vice President of Academic Affairs for Outreach at the University of Utah. Her research focuses on the intersection of race, class, and gender; racial and ethnic relations; deviant behavior; juvenile delinquency; and popular culture. Recent works include the 1997 article "Popular Culture as Oppositional Culture: Rap as Resistance" published in *Sociological Perspectives*, the 2002 article "The Double-Consciousness of Du Bois and the 'Mestiza Consciousness' of Anzaldúa" published in *Race, Gender & Class: An Interdisciplinary Journal*, and the 2005 article "Making Oppositional Culture, Making Standpoint: A Journey Into Gloria Anzaldúa's Borderlands" published in *Sociological Spectrum*. ✦

About the Contributors

Gerda Lerner is the Robinson-Edwards Professor of History, Emerita, at the University of Wisconsin–Madison. A prize-winning historian and past president of the Organization of American Historians, she pioneered the study of women's history and was among the first to include a focus on Black women in her scholarship. She was born in Austria, fled the Nazis, and came to the United States as a teenager. A nontraditional student, she was age 38 and a wife and mother when she began her academic study of history.

Stephen Steinberg is a sociologist and is described on his website *http://qcpages.qc.cuny.edu/UBST/DEPT/FACULTY/sstein.htm* as "an internationally renowned authority on race and ethnicity in the United States." His most recent book, *Turning Back: The Retreat From Racial Justice in American Thought and Policy*, received the Oliver Cromwell Cox Award for Distinguished Anti-Racist Scholarship. He is also well known for his previous work, including *The Ethnic Myth*, *The Academic Melting Pot*, and *The Tenacity of Prejudice*.

Graham Robb, a British author, lives in Oxford, England, and has published widely in French literature and history. His publications include biographies of Balzac (1996), Victor Hugo (1999), and Rimbaud (2000). *New York Review of Books* has published reviews of his work as well as his reviews of work by other authors. *Strangers* is based on archives, diaries, and letters.

James W. Loewen earned his Ph.D. in sociology from Harvard University. He taught race relations and related subjects at Tougaloo College in Mississippi and later at the University of Vermont. In 1980, when a textbook he coauthored was rejected for use in Mississippi schools, he sued the state and won an important decision on First and Fourteenth Amendment grounds. He now lives in Washington, DC, and is a popular speaker at universities, conferences, libraries, and other venues.

William Labov is Professor of Linguistics and Director of the Linguistics Laboratory, University of Pennsylvania. His major work is on linguistic change and variation, and he has carried out a number of studies of African American vernacular English and other minority dialects. His books include *The Social Stratification of English in New York City* (1966), *Sociolinguistic Patterns* (1972), *Language in the Inner City* (1972), *Principles of Linguistic Change* (1994, 2000), and the *Atlas of North American English* (with S. Ash and C. Boberg, 2005). He is the Director of the Urban Minorities Reading Project and coauthor (with B. Baker) of the *Individualized Reading Program*. He is coeditor of *Language Variation and Change*, has served as president of the Linguistic Society of America (1979), and is a member of the National Academy of Science. Homepage: *http://www.ling.upenn.edu/~labov/*.

Malcolm X, an activist, charismatic speaker, and the voice for a generation of young Blacks, was born Malcolm Little on May 19, 1925, in Omaha, Nebraska. He became an activist and leader within the Nation of Islam but would later break away and found his own organization, the Muslim Mosque, Inc. According to the official website for Malcolm X, *http://www.cmgww.com/historic/malcolm/about/bio.htm*, "the legacy of Malcolm X has moved through generations as the subject of numerous documentaries, books and movies. A tremendous resurgence of interest occurred in 1992 when director Spike Lee released the acclaimed movie, *Malcolm X*." The website notes that Malcolm X was buried in Hartsdale, New York.

Lesléa Newman is an award-winning author of books and articles for people of all ages from preschool through adult. She began her publishing career right after high school with poems in *Seventeen* magazine. Her work frequently addresses issues of gender, race/ethnicity, class, and sexuality. She teaches creative writing in workshops at colleges and other institutions. Learn more about her at *www.lesleakids.com*.

Bruce Edward Hall died of cancer on October 31, 2003, at the age of 49. Hall studied drama at Syracuse University and even worked with children's shows such as *Romper Room* as well as with Jim Henson and the Muppets. Eventually, however, Hall would find his niche as an author, focusing his historical prose on New York's Chinatown, which his ancestors helped to found, a history recounted in his 1999 book, *Tea That Burns*.

Tommi Avicolli Mecca is a writer, performer, and activist. He grew up Southern Italian, working class, and queer in South Philly in the 1950s and 1960s. He has written and performed issue-oriented and autobiographical shows solo and with multi-racial groups. In addition to writing and performing, he works as a tenant's rights advocate. Excerpts of his work can be found on his website at *www.avicollimecca.com*.

Ntozake Shange attended Barnard College, receiving her B.A. degree in 1970, and the University of Southern California, receiving her M.A. degree in 1973. Between 1972 and 1975, she taught women's studies and Afro-American studies at various California colleges. According to the African American Literature Book Club website, *http://aalbc.com/authors/ntozake.htm*, her 1975 "theatre piece *For Colored Girls Who Have Considered Suicide/When the Rainbow Is Enuf* quickly brought her fame." The website notes that *Ntozake* means "she who comes with her own things," and *Shange* means "who walks like a lion."

Mpho 'M'atsepo' Nthunya was born in Lesotho in 1930. When she was age 8, she went with her mother and brothers to South Africa to live with her father, who had found work there. She attended a Catholic mission school. After she married, she moved back to Lesotho, where she and her husband farmed. To support her family after his death, she became a domestic worker in Lesotho and later in South Africa.

Sandra Cisneros has won popular success as well as critical acclaim for her collections of short stories and books of poetry. Her writing focuses on childhood characters or characters drawn from Latina/o culture as she weaves distinctly ethnic vignettes about life outside of, and often isolated from, mainstream American society. She is perhaps best known for her book *The House on Mango Street*, but has also won praise for *Woman Hollering Creek and Other Stories* and *Loose Woman*.

Leslie Marmon Silko grew up on the Laguna Pueblo located west of Albuquerque, New Mexico. The National Women's History Project website, *http://www.nwhp.org/tlp/biographies/silko/bio.html*, suggests that Silko's "goal has been to use her gift of story telling to promote the cultural survival of her people." She is perhaps best known for her first major novel, *Ceremony*, but has also won praise for her other writings including *Laguna Women Poems*, *Yellow Woman and a Beauty of the Spirit Essays*, and *Gardens in the Dunes*.

Stephen Paul Whitaker comes from rural Kentucky and received his B.A. degree at Morehead State University. He worked as a journalist before returning to college for his undergraduate degree. He completed his M.A. degrees in women's studies and sociology at the University of Cincinnati and is now completing a Ph.D. in women's studies at Emory University.

Loretta Schwartz-Nobel is a writer and journalist residing in Philadelphia. She has won several awards for her outstanding contributions to journalism, including the Women in Communications Award, the Society of Professional Journalists Award, the Columbia Graduate School of Journalism Award, and the Robert F. Kennedy Memorial Award, which she has won twice for recognition of her outstanding work covering issues related to the disadvantaged in America.

June Jordan died of breast cancer in 2002. The website created by her estate, *www.junejordan.com*, describes her as a "moral witness." "Poet, activist, teacher, and essayist, she was a prolific, passionate, and influential voice for liberation." She received numerous grants, awards, and fellowships, including one from the National Endowment for the Arts. She taught at the University of California, Berkeley.

Faye V. Harrison is Professor of Anthropology and African American Studies at the University of Floriday–Gainesville. She is a former Lindsay Young Professor of Anthropology at the University of Tennessee. Her interests include comparative forms of inequality and the intersections of race, gender, class, and nation as well as the African diaspora and the Caribbean. In addition to authoring publications based on her field work, she has edited important volumes on postcolonial and African American anthropology.

Deborah Tannen is University Professor and Professor of Linguistics at Georgetown University. Perhaps her best known work is the book *You Just Don't Understand: Women and Men in Conversation*, which achieved acclaim on *The New York Times* Bestseller List. She has published 19 books, including *That's Not What I Meant!*, *Talking Voices*, and *I Only Say This Because I Love You*.

Hannah Schiller Wartenberg is retired from teaching positions in New York State and later in Miami, but is still an active participant in Sociologists for Women in Society and the American Sociological Association. American Jewry is among her many interests.

Jane Ward is Assistant Professor of Sociology at the University of California, Riverside. The book she is currently working on, *Doing Diversity in Queer L.A.: How the Mainstream Obsession With Diversity Is Transforming Social Movements*, reflects her interest in the impact of sociopolitical currents on identities and social movements. In her work she uses qualitative research methods and feminist, critical race, and social movement theories.

Michael Eric Dyson is the Avalon Foundation Professor in the Humanities at the University of Pennsylvania. His work offers a critical assessment of sociocultural issues facing poor African Americans living in America's inner cities. His most recent book, *Is Bill Cosby Right?*, reads as a challenge to confront issues that civil rights failed to solve. Dyson is the author of numerous books, including *I May Not Get There With You: The True Martin Luther King, Jr.*; *Race Rules: Navigating the Color Line*; and *Making Malcolm: The Myth and Meaning of Malcolm X*.

Henry Louis Gates, Jr. is the W.E.B. Du Bois Professor of the Humanities, Chair of the Department of African and African American Studies, and Director of the W.E.B. Du Bois Institute for African and African American Research at Harvard University. He is the author of important books on Africans and African Americans, works of literary criticism, a personal memoir, and articles in popular and literary magazines. Among his awards are a MacArthur Foundation "genius grant" and a National Humanities Medal. His complete curriculum vitae can be found at *www.fas.harvard.edu*.

Steven Seidman is Professor of Sociology at the State University of New York at Albany, where he specializes in sexuality and social theory. His books include *Beyond the Closet: The Transformation of Gay and Lesbian Life* and *The Social Construction of Sexuality*.

Wendy Luttrell is the Nancy Pforzheimer Aronson Associate Professor in Human Development and Education at the Harvard Graduate School of Education. Her first book, *School-Smart and Mother-Wise: Working-Class Women's Identity and Schooling*, which won an American Sociological Association (ASA) book award, described the life stories of Black and White working class women's lives in relationship to schooling. Her second book, *Pregnant Bodies, Fertile Minds: Gender, Race, and the Schooling of Pregnant Teens*, describes the experiences of urban, African American, low-income girls who must face both shaming and discrimination in the school environment.

Nicole Ziegler Dizon began as an intern in the Associated Press Illinois Statehouse Bureau in 1996. She worked for the Associated Press in St. Louis and Chicago and on special projects, and was recently appointed news editor for Illinois. She earned a bachelor's degree from the University of

Illinois at Urbana-Champaign and a master's from the University of Illinois at Springfield.

Chia-Wen Chi is an account executive at BridgeOne Consultants—a public relations agency in Taiwan, China. She is on the hi-tech PR team serving hardware, software, components, telecom, and related clients.

Cecelia Baldwin is Professor and Chair of the Advertising Program at the School of Journalism and Mass Communications at San Jose State University. Her research focuses on race, class, and gender in relation to media portrayals of men and women. She has published in journals such as *Race, Gender & Class: An Interdisciplinary Journal* and *Visual Communication Quarterly*.

Angela Y. Davis, in 1970, was placed on the FBI's Ten Most Wanted List as a result of false charges and fired from her faculty position at UCLA by then governor Ronald Reagan. Today she holds the University of California Presidential Chair, is a professor in the History of Consciousness Department and chairs the Women's Studies Department at the University of California, Santa Cruz. Her wide-ranging academic interests include feminism, African American studies, critical theory, popular music culture and social consciousness, and philosophy of punishment. She is the author of five books. Read a summary of her life and activities at *en.wikipedia.org/wiki/Angela Davis*.

Martha Garcia was born and raised in Massachusetts. She moved to Colorado, where she met her husband, who exposed her to new cultural perspectives and reawakened her early interest in American Indians. She became fascinated with the varying effects that communities of different sizes and degrees of openness have on their residents. Her master's thesis, which she wrote while working her way up to an executive secretary position at General Electric, is the first contemporary study of Cheyenne women. She has presented her research at professional meetings. She believes her education, research, and day-to-day contacts with people in American Indian communities have had reciprocal benefits.

Pamela Paul was formerly a senior editor at *American Demographics*. Her most recent book is *Pornified: How the Culture of Pornography Is Transforming Our Lives, Our Relationships, and Our Families*. She also wrote *The Starter Marriage and the Future of Matrimony* and is a contributor to *Time* and other magazines.

Kendra Hamilton's work often appears in *Black Issues in Higher Education* (now *Diverse Issues in Higher Education*), where she has written on a wide range of topics from the college aspirations of women in prison to the teaching of Ebonics, and from the education of college athletes to teaching about campus activism.

Edna Bonacich is Professor of Sociology and Ethnic Studies at the University of California, Riverside. Her major research interest is the study of class and race, with special emphasis on racial divisions in the working class. She has studied the garment industry, coauthoring *Behind the Label: Inequality in the Los Angeles Apparel Industry* with Richard Appelbaum. She is currently pursuing research on the Ports of Los Angeles and Long Beach as important nodes in the global economy, which has led her to examine Wal-Mart's role as the premier importer through the ports. She tries to link her teaching and research to efforts to produce progressive social change, especially by working with the labor movement.

Richard P. Appelbaum is Professor of Sociology and Global & International Studies at the University of California, Santa Barbara, where he directs the Institute for Social, Behavioral, and Economic Research and is head of graduate studies and director of the M.A. Program in Global & International Studies. His major research interests are in the rise of large transnational contractors and their implications for labor, changing relations in the global economy, and the social impact of nanotechnology. He has studied the garment industry, coauthoring *Behind the Label: Inequality in the Los Angeles Apparel Industry* with Edna Bonacich. He is active in the anti-sweatshop movement and chairs the Advisory Council of the Worker Rights Consortium.

Jean L. Pyle is Professor Emerita in the Department of Regional Economic and Social Development at the University of Massachusetts, Lowell, and Senior Associate at the Center for Women and Work. Her interests are reflected in the titles of the volumes she recently coedited: *Globalization, Universities, and Issues of Sustainable Human Development* (2003) and *Approaches to Sustainable Development: The Public University in the Regional Economy* (2001).

Kathryn B. Ward is Professor of Sociology and Women's Studies at Southern Illinois University at Carbondale. She is interested in women's work, empowerment, and ending domestic violence in Bangladesh and among immigrant women in the United States. Her ongoing goal is to retheorize gender in the global economy. She is also working on a book on race in Cairo, IL, over the past century.

D. W. Miller was a senior writer at the *Chronicle of Higher Education* who covered scholarly research in the social sciences.

Melanie L. Johnston is Assistant Clinical Professor in the Department of Preventive Medicine and Biometrics at the University of Colorado Health Sciences Center in Denver, Colorado. She is also an epidemiologist with the El Paso County Department of Health and Environment in Colorado Springs, Colorado.

Diana Torrez received her Ph.D. from the University of New Mexico in 1990. Her first tenure track job was at the University of North Texas, where she began her career in aging. She was awarded a postdoctoral fellowship at the University of California, San Francisco, to study aging and health policy. Dr. Torrez also worked in Mexico City, where she conducted research on how older Mexicans with chronic diseases treat and manage their illnesses. She recently took a position with the University of Colorado at Colorado Springs, where she teaches in the Sociology and Gerontology Departments. She is currently developing a research proposal to examine diabetes among different ethnic groups in Colorado Springs.

Roberto Campos-Navarro is a physician with a specialty in family medicine. He also holds a master's degree and a doctorate in social anthropology. He has researched in the area of folk (popular) medicine in Mexico and Latin America. His research focuses on urban and indigenous *curanderismo*. He is a researcher and teaching faculty member at UNAM's School of Medicine in the Department of History and Philosophy and in the Center of Medical Anthropology. He has published numerous articles in journals throughout Latin America and is the author of *Nostros los Curanderos* (1998).

Elia Nora Arganis Juárez is Professor of Social Anthropology with expertise in the area of medical sociology. She is employed as Professor of Anthropology at the National School of Anthropology and History. She is also a research professor at UNAM's Medical School in the Department of History and Philosophy. Since 1984, as a graduate student (a.b.d), she has been employed as a teaching faculty at various private and public universities, and has taught in the areas of anthropological theory, magic and religion, myths and legends, ethnography, and medical anthropology. She has conducted research in the areas of traditional medicine, chronic illnesses, and aging. She has also presented at various Congresses in the following areas: use of herbs and plants in the treatment of diabetes, social support for the chronically ill, and the illness experience of the chronically ill patient.

Peggy McIntosh is the associate director of the Center for Research on Women at the Wellesley Centers for Women and the cofounder and codirector of S.E.E.D. (Seeking Educational Equity and Diversity) Project on Inclusive Curriculum. The project helps K–12 teachers create school-based seminars. She also directs the Gender, Race, and Inclusive Education Project, which provides workshops on privilege systems and related matters. In addition to an earned doctorate and two honorary degrees, she is the recipient of the Klingenstein Award for Distinguished Educational Leadership from Columbia Teachers College.

Nancy DiTomaso is Professor of Management and Global Business at Rutgers Business School–Newark and New Brunswick. Her research specialties include the management of diversity and change, the management of knowledge-based organizations, and the management of scientists and engineers. Her Ph.D. is from the University of Wisconsin–Madison. She has co-authored and coedited five books and has had articles published in such journals as *Academy of Management Journal, Sex Roles, Leadership Quarterly, California Management Review*, and the *Journal of Engineering-Technology Management*. She is currently completing a forthcoming book, entitled *The American Non-dilemma*, about how people think about issues of inequality. In addition, she is analyzing survey data on the career experiences of 3,200 scientists and engineers from 25 major companies. Her work on the transformation of organizations into "organizations of the future" has addressed the changes in the structure of organizations, work and careers, and the management skills needed for the coming decades.

Rochelle Parks-Yancy is Assistant Professor of Management at the Jesse H. Jones School of Business at Texas Southern University. She earned her Ph.D. in Organization Management from Rutgers University Business School–Newark and New Brunswick. Her research expertise includes social capital and the career trajectories of diverse social groups. She has published papers in the *Journal of Experimental Social Psychology, Sociological Spectrum, Sociological Imagination, Management Communication Quarterly, Michigan Sociological Review*, and *Research in the Sociology of Work: Diversity in the Workforce*. Dr. Parks-Yancy won a best paper award from the Careers Division of the Academy of Management, organized a professional development workshop, titled "What To Do When You Don't Get Tenure: Strategies for Success," which was accepted at the Academy of Management, and has presented numerous papers at the Academy of Management, American Sociological Association, and Society for the Advancement of Socio-Economics.

Corinne Post is Assistant Professor of Management at Lubin School of Business at Pace University. She earned her B.S. in organization management and master's in international management in Switzerland from HEC, University of Geneva, and HEC, University of Lausanne, respectively. She received her Ph.D. in organization management from Rutgers University. Dr. Post's recent publications have appeared in the *Journal of Applied Psychology* and *Management Communication Quarterly*. She co-edited *Workforce Diversity* (Elsevier). Her professional affiliations include the Academy of Management, the American Sociological Association, the Society for Human Resource Management, and the Organizational Behavior Teaching Society.

Ruth Frankenberg is a British-born cultural studies scholar. In her most recent book, *Living Spirit, Living Practice: Poetics, Politics, Epistemology* (2004), she turned her attention to religious diversity with the same intensity that she previously studied the social geography of race. Her book is based on in-depth interviews about religion in America across lines of gender, race, ethnicity, class, sexuality, age, and national origin.

Paula England is Professor of Sociology and Faculty Research Affiliate of the Institute for Research on Women and Gender at Stanford University. Her research interests include a focus on gender inequality in labor markets and how changes in family life are affected by the gender and class systems. She has published several books and articles, including *Comparable Worth: Theories and Evidence* and *Households, Employment, and Gender: A Social, Economic, and Demographic View* (with George Farkas). She is a former editor of the *American Sociological Review*.

Carmen Garcia-Beaulieu is Senior Analyst for Decision Support Systems in the Office of Institutional Research at Seminole Community College in Sanford, Florida. She produces ad hoc reports for stakeholders campuswide and is instrumental in data validation for internal purposes and state reporting. She received her master's degree from the University of Arizona in 1998, where her research focused on gender, race, labor, and education. She is currently researching student retention and student perception of the college experience.

Mary Ross is a financial analyst with Network InOne, where she has done research on gender within organizations.

Angela Gardner Roux was a doctoral student in the Department of Sociology at Binghamton University when she wrote the article reprinted here. Her interests include social inequality, poverty, and welfare.

Elizabeth Grieco received her graduate training in the Department of Sociology at Florida State University. She began publishing demographic studies while still a student and is Senior Demographer at the Migration Policy Institute. Her analyses of current population data can be found at *www.migrationinformation.org*.

Edwin S. Segal holds his major appointment in the Department of Anthropology at the University of Louisville. He also holds an associate faculty appointment in the Department of Women's and Gender Studies and is associated with the Department of Pan African Studies. Professor Segal has conducted research in Nigeria, Tanzania, Malawi, Kenya, and South Africa. His major research interests are gender, ethnicity, and national development.

Christopher Reynolds is a frequent contributor to *American Demographics*, compiling, analyzing, and graphically portraying data on a wide range of topics, including Asian Americans, aging Americans, holiday travel plans, saving for college tuition, interest rates, and the housing market.

Gloria Anzaldúa, was a pioneer in Chicana feminist thought in the United States who has influenced the work of her Chicana peers nationwide. Her work is widely recognized among scholars from various fields, including Chicano/Latino, gay and lesbian, gender, postcolonial, cultural, and ethnic studies as well as the disciplines of Sociology, Communication, English, and Psychology and other academic areas. Probably her best known work is *Borderlands/La Frontera: The New Mestiza* published in 1987. She also collaborated with Cherrie Moraga on the groundbreaking *This Bridge Called My Back: Writings by Radical Women of Color*, which came out in 1981.

Janice M. Irvine is Professor of Sociology at the University of Massachusetts. A revised and expanded version of *Disorders of Desire*, her history of American sexology in the twentieth century has just been published. She is also the author of *Talk About Sex: The Battles Over Sex Education in the United States* and editor of *Sexual Cultures and the Construction of Adolescent Sexualities*. In recognition of her leadership in the use of technology in instruction, she was selected to be a TEACHnology Fellow by her university's Center for Teaching. Her research was recognized with the 2005 Simon and Gagnon Award from the Section on Sexualities of the American Sociological Association.

Celene Krauss is Professor of Sociology and Women's Studies at Kean University. Her research has focused primarily on women's involvement in environmental protests through the lens of race, ethnicity, and class issues. She has published work in *Qualitative Sociology* and *Sociological Forum*.

Paula Gunn Allen is Laguna, Sioux, and Lebanese. She grew up on the Laguna Pueblo. Author of novels and volumes of poetry and criticism, and widely anthologized, she earned her Ph.D. from the University of New Mexico. She taught Native American studies, English, and creative writing at several universities before retiring from her last teaching position at the University of California, Los Angeles, in 1999. She is the recipient of a Lifetime Achievement Award from the Native Writer's Circle of the Americas, the American Book Award from the Before Columbus Foundation, the Susan Koppelman Award from the Popular and American Culture Associations, and the Native American Prize for Literature.

Eileen O'Brien earned a B.A. degree in sociology from the College of William and Mary in 1994, an M.A. degree in sociology in 1996 from the Ohio State University, and a Ph.D. in sociology from the University of Florida in 1999. Her research focus can be best summarized as "critical white studies," that is, the study of Whites from an antiracist perspective. Her doctoral dissertation was an in-depth interview and participant observation study of White antiracist activists and their organizations. These findings became the topic of her first book, *Whites Confront Racism: Antiracists and Their Paths to Action*. Her second book, coauthored with Joe R. Feagin, *White Men on Race: Power, Privilege, and the Shaping of Cultural Consciousness*, is based on 100 in-depth interviews with elite White men about their racial views.

The Rev. Cheryl Townsend Gilkes, Ph.D., is the John D. and Catherine T. MacArthur Professor of Sociology and African American Studies at Colby College and Assistant Pastor of the Union Baptist Church (Cambridge, MA). Her work has focused on the contributions of African American women to social change and on the roles of Black women within Christian churches. The results of her research appear in the article reprinted here and more fully in her book, *If It Wasn't for the Women: Black Women's Experience and Womanist Culture in Church and Community* (2001).

Glenn McKenzie is an Associated Press writer who covers areas of the African continent, including Liberia, Nigeria, and the Congo.

Martin Rochlin, who is generally acknowledged to be the author of the widely reprinted Heterosexual Questionnaire, was the first openly gay psychologist in Los Angeles. He founded the Society for the Psychological Study of Lesbian, Gay, and Bisexual Issues (American Psychological Association Division 44) and was a recipient of its award for Distinguished Professional Contribution. He was an accomplished pianist and became a psychologist after a 25-year career in the entertainment industry. He died in 2004 at the age of 75.

Dalton Conley is Professor of Sociology and Public Policy at New York University, Director of NYU's Center for Advanced Social Science Research, and Adjunct Professor of Community Medicine at Mount Sinai School of Medicine. His research publications include *Being Black, Living in the Red: Race, Wealth, and Social Policy in America* and *Honky*, both published by University of California Press. His research focuses on how socioeconomic status is transmitted across generations and on the public policies that affect that process. In this vein, he studies sibling differences in socioeco-

nomic success; racial inequalities; the measurement of class and social status; and how health and biology affect (and are affected by) social position.

Amitava Kumar is the author of *Passport Photos* (2000), *Bombay-London-New York* (2002), and *Husband of a Fanatic* (2005). He is also the editor of several anthologies on pedagogy as well as postcolonial writing. Kumar is currently Professor of English at Vassar College.

Eduardo Bonilla-Silva is a research professor of sociology at Duke University. His 1997 article in the *American Sociological Review*, titled "Rethinking Racism: Toward a Structural Interpretation," challenged sociologists to analyze racial matters from a structural perspective rather than from the typical prejudice problematic. His research has appeared in journals such as *Sociological Inquiry*, *Racial and Ethnic Studies*, *Race and Society*, *Discourse and Society*, *Journal of Latin American Studies*, and *Research in Politics and Society*, among others. To date he has published three books, *White Supremacy and Racism in the Post-Civil Rights Era* (co-winner of the 2002 Oliver Cox Award given by the American Sociological Association), *Racism Without Racists: Color-Blind Racism and the Persistence of Racial Inequality in the United States*, and *White Out: The Continuing Significance of Racism* (with Ashley Doane). He is currently working on two books: *Anything but Racism: How Social Scientists Minimize the Significance of Racism* (Routledge) and *White Logic, White Methods: Racism and Methodology*.

Troy Duster served as President of the American Sociological Association during the 2004–2005 academic year. He is Professor of Sociology and Director of the Institute for the History of the Production of Knowledge at New York University as well as Chancellor's Professor of Sociology at the University of California, Berkeley. The grandson of famed journalist Ida B. Wells, he seems to have been destined to write about race, gender, and class. His biography on the American Sociological Association website (*www.asanet.org*) calls him a "public intellectual with a rich private life."

He is the author of several books and recipient of numerous awards.

C. Shawn McGuffey is Assistant Professor of Sociology at Boston College. His research interests include race, class, and gender, childhood, family, and qualitative methods. His publications include work in the journal *Gender & Society* and the book *Men's Lives*. He received his Ph.D. from the University of Massachusetts, Amherst, in 2005 and has won several teaching and research awards.

B. Lindsay Rich is Associate Professor of Sociology at Transylvania University in Lexington, Kentucky. He received his Ph.D. in sociology for the University of California, Berkeley, in 1984. His work currently focuses on ethnoracial and class dynamics with regard to multiculturalism as a social practice. He is interested in examining these dynamics empirically with regard to the process of Latino immigration to unique destinations in the United States, such as Lexington.

Amy C. Wilkins is a graduate student at the University of Massachusetts–Amherst. She is interested in issues of race, gender, class, and sexuality within youth cultures. A second article published in *Gender & Society* in 2004, "'So Full of Myself as a Chick': Goth Women, Sexual Independence, and Gender Egalitarianism," is also drawn from her dissertation on Puerto Rican wannabes, Goths, and evangelical Christians.

Yen Le Espiritu is Professor of Ethnic Studies at the University of California at San Diego. Her research interests include gender and migration, race and U.S. militarism, refugee studies, Asian American studies, and Southeast Asian American studies. She has published three books: *Home Bound: Filipino American Lives Across Cultures, Communities, and Countries* with University of California Press, *Asian American Women and Men: Labor, Laws, and Love* with Sage Publications, and *Asian American Panethnicity: Bridging Institutions and Identities* with Temple University Press.

Kristin E. Joos earned her Ph.D. in sociology with a certificate in Women's Studies and Gender Research at the University of Florida. She continues to teach in the honors, first year, and sociology programs there while serving as Coordinator of Admissions, Preview, and Student Activities, and Honors Advisor. Among her interests are high-school and college aged students, especially those who are gifted and motivated, and college admissions, life goals, and career development.

Abby L. Ferber is Associate Professor of Sociology, Director of Women's Studies, and former Assistant Vice Chancellor for Academic Diversity and Development at the University of Colorado at Colorado Springs. She has published numerous books, including *White Man Falling: Race Gender and White Supremacy*; is coauthor of *Making a Difference: University Students of Color Speak Out*; edited *Home Grown Hate*; and coedited *Privilege: A Reader*. Her articles have been widely published in both journals and news outlets.

Vasilikie Demos is Professor Emerita of Sociology at the University of Minnesota–Morris and Senior Research Fellow at the Center for Conflict Resolution, Salisbury University. She is coeditor of the series *Advances in Gender Research* and of "Race, Gender, and Class for What?" a special issue of *Race, Gender and Class*. Her research is in the areas of race/ethnicity and gender and includes a study of ethnicity and gender in the United States, Greece, and Australia. She is a past president of the North Central Sociological Association and Sociologists for Women in Society.

Anthony J. Lemelle, Jr. is Professor of Sociology and Urban Studies at the University of Wisconsin–Milwaukee. He earned his doctorate from the University of California, Berkeley. His research is widely published. He is concerned with African American cultural studies, Black masculinity studies, and health and aging issues in the Black community, particularly sociobehavioral studies related to the prevention of HIV/AIDS. Professor Lemelle is editor of the *Journal of African American Studies*. He is a member of many professional organizations, where he has frequently demonstrated leadership.

Solomon Gashaw is Associate Professor of Sociology at the University of Minnesota–Morris. His research interest includes

African politics with focus on ethnicity and the State, democracy and political pluralism, globalization and development. His recent publications are the "State and Its Ethnic Policies in Southern Ethiopia" in the *Proceedings of the 15th International Conference on Ethiopia* and also "The Politics of Ethnicity" and the "Ethiopian Polity," forthcoming in the *International Journal of Ethiopian Studies*, Vol. II, No. 1.

Jason DeParle is a senior writer at the *New York Times* and a frequent contributor to the *New York Times Magazine*. A graduate of Duke University, DeParle won a George Polk Award in 1999 for his reporting on the welfare system and was a two-time finalist for the Pulitzer Prize. He lives in Washington, DC, with his wife, Nancy-Ann, and their two sons. ✦

Introduction

This is a collection of readings about the intersections of gender, race, and social class. In some of the readings, intersections with other attributes of individuals and groups (such as sexuality, religion, or place of residence) also appear. The authors represented here show us these intersections as they have occurred in the past and the present, in different communities in the United States, and even in other countries. Some of the readings are the real or fictional experiences of individual women and men, some are journalistic reports of events or compilations of statistics, and some are analyses of empirical data or theoretical discussions by social scientists. The readings represent the many qualitative and quantitative ways that social scientists and their students observe, discuss, and interpret the intersections of gender, race, and class.

Why Focus on Intersections?

Gender, race, and social class are key elements of social structures. We cannot understand social institutions, actors, and forces without taking these elements into account. While it is surely possible to represent gender, race, and class as distinct aspects of social structures or to use them as discrete variables in statistical analyses, people do not experience them separately in their lives or interact with others on the basis of one at a time. For example, in this volume, epidemiologist Melanie Johnston offers explanations for distinctly different health outcomes among African Americans, American Indians, and Hispanic Americans despite their similar economic status. The late Chicana writer and multidisciplinary scholar Gloria Anzaldúa developed the idea of a *mestiza* consciousness to express a way of thinking that comes from occupying a particular intersection of gender, race, class, and sexuality. Reading these and other pieces we come

to understand that to know how society really operates, we must examine the realities at the intersections. Once we begin to observe and analyze from an intersectional perspective, we also become more sensitive to the impact of additional elements of structure, such as religion, sexuality, age, and rural or urban residence. For example, sociologist Steven Seidman shows how race, class, age, and place of residence affected the lives of the gay men he interviewed. In another example, sociologist Angela Gardner Roux uses census data disaggregated by gender, race/ethnicity, and age to rethink how poverty is defined and measured.

Finally, marches and rallies for immigrant rights are taking place all across the country in this the spring of 2006. In Salt Lake City, one of the co-editors of this volume marched with over 25,000 souls down State Street in the heart of Salt Lake in what was a first in Utah's history both in size and scope. These marches and rallies dramatically reveal the lives of millions of Latina and Latino immigrants, mothers and fathers who are struggling to provide for their families, who are caught up in one of the most intense civil rights struggles in our nation's history. These demonstrations bear witness to the tensions surrounding continued American reliance on immigrant labor-men and women of color whose labor is exploited year after year-while some Americans call for their criminalization. These marches and rallies further herald the very real need for comprehensive immigration reform policy reflecting American realities along critical fault lines of gender, race/ethnicity and class.

How the Book is Organized

There are seven sections in this book, each containing a number of original and reprinted articles that have common threads. This may be a convenient way to read through the book. The subject listing that follows this introduction offers alternative approaches by grouping the readings according to different common threads. The editors have provided brief introductions to each of the readings and a series of questions to stimulate thought and discussion at the end of each. Short biographies of all of the authors may be found in the preceeding section.

Section 1 frames the past by presenting seven articles showing the place of gender, race, and class in history. Exploring the intersections of gender, class, and ethnic background in the nineteenth century, Stephen Steinberg asks why some immigrant women took up domestic work while others did not, and Gerda Lerner asks how some became "ladies" who employed domestic workers while others worked in the mills. Graham Robb explores what life was like for men who were sexually attracted to other men in the same period. Readers will learn from the U.S. Congressional Record how lynching was debated in Congress in 1922, while also finding out what high school American history textbooks omit or misrepresent, in the article by James Loewen. Theresa Martinez introduces the work of W. E. B. Du Bois and Gloria Anzaldúa as historically and theoretically related, and William Labov demonstrates how faulty conclusions were reached in older research regarding the language skills of urban Black children.

Section 2 contains fictional and nonfictional stories reflecting individual experiences at the intersection of race, gender, and class. Among the nonfictional reflections are an excerpt from the *Autobiography of Malcolm X*, June Jordan's "Report From the Bahamas," and Loretta Schwartz-Nobel's interview with a woman who was once homeless and now manages a shelter for others who are homeless. Ntozake Shange and Tommi Avicolli Mecca present their experiences in poetry, while Lesléa Newman and Sandra Cisneros offer fictional tales that ring only too true. Bruce Edward Hall and Mpho 'M'atsepo Nthunya take us to other countries to tell stories of their own or their family's lives, while Leslie Marmon Silko from Laguna

Pueblo and Stephen P. Whitaker from rural Kentucky tell their own American stories.

Section 3 explores family and community relationships. Anthropologist Faye V. Harrison puts the life and family of Beulah Brown, a resourceful woman from an improverished community in Jamaica, in context. Deborah Tannen discusses gender differences in patterns of communication, differences that are likely to be compounded by racial/ethnic and class-based patterns of speech and expression. Hannah Schiller Wartenberg looks at the complex interplay of language, ethnicity, religion, and community among Cuban Jewish women living in Miami. Jane Ward reports on research in a gay-oriented Latino health organization in Los Angeles, showing how it tries, but ultimately fails, to meet the needs of the lesbian members of the working-class Latino/a community. Michael Eric Dyson explores how the trial of O. J. Simpson, for a crime with clear gender and class, overtones was viewed by Black and White communities exposing the racial divide in our country. Henry Louis Gates, Jr. asserts that members of African American communities are aware of the behavioral as well as the structural causes of poverty and challenges people to discuss the issues openly. Steven Seidman points to community size and an individual's relationship to family and community as key variables in the lives of the gay men he interviewed.

Section 4 is about social institutions, including schools, the media, religion, criminal justice, the law, the workplace, and health care. In one of the readings in this section, Edna Bonacich and Richard P. Appelbaum look at the apparel industry in Los Angeles and show both how it reflects the intersections of race, gender, and class and how the industry in the United States reaches beyond our borders. Jean L. Pyle and Kathryn B. Ward approach similar issues from the other side of the border examining the connections between gender and work in the context of global restructuring. For her part, Angela Y. Davis demonstrates the connection between prisons in the United States and global restructuring. Chia-Wen Chi and Cecelia Baldwin compare gender and class stereotypes in U.S. and Taiwanese magazines, and Kendra Hamilton, writing in the magazine *Black Issues in Higher Education,* demonstrates the power of stereotypes by showing that both gender and racially stereotypic names impact one's chances of being interviewed for jobs. Wendy Luttrell and Nicole Ziegler Dizon look at aspects of education. Focusing on religion, Pamela Paul provides readers with some demographic information, while Martha Garcia discusses the religious significance of practices of Cheyenne women. Melanie Johnston and Diana Torrez and her co-authors address aspects of health and illness, and D. W. Miller writes about the legal aspects of gay rights.

Section 5 is about privilege, in some ways the central issue in the study of race, gender, and class. It begins with Peggy McIntosh's classic exploration of the personal meanings of White and male privilege. Christopher Reynolds graphically compares America's haves and have-nots, while Elizabeth Grieco describes the foreign-born population. Paula England and her co-authors look at racial/ethnic and class differences in women's employment, and Angela Gardner Roux considers the privilege implied in how we measure poverty. With her co-authors, Nancy DiTomaso considers how Whites view civil rights and Ruth Frankenberg interviews White women to learn how their childhood experiences contributed to their ideas about race. In contrast to the readings reflecting the intersections of gender, race, and class in the United States, Edwin S. Segal looks at the way an individual's race was designated in apartheid South Africa and what this implied for gender and class.

Activism at the intersections of gender, race, and class is the subject of the readings in Section 6. Gloria Anzaldúa's discussion of *mestiza* consciousness begins the section. Cheryl Townsend Gilkes points to the importance of community work by African American women, and Celene Krauss looks at the different ways White women and women of color become environmental activists. Eileen O'Brien's interviews with White anti-racists highlights the diversity within this category. Paula Gunn Allen's essay about the issues American Indian women must ad-

dress is just as compelling today as when it was published two decades ago. Janice M. Irvine explores the controversy among different interests that arose when New York City attempted to introduce a curriculum that included gay and lesbian people in the cultural rainbow, while Martin Rochlin gives readers an opportunity to consider sexuality from a different perspective by taking the "Heterosexual Questionnaire." Glenn McKenzie's news article about Liberia's female warriors introduces an extreme form of activism being used in a civil war where rape was among the weapons of war. It may interest readers to note that in the spring of 2006, as this volume was being readied for publication, Liberia held a free and fair election and elected Ellen Johnson-Sirleaf, Africa's first woman president.

The readings in Section 7 represent new directions and perspectives in the study of race, gender, and class. Dalton Conley and Amitava Kumar use personal experience as a framework for analysis of contemporary intersections. Conley recounts his experience of being the only White child in the class and being Jewish when Santa visits his Brooklyn school. Kumar, a Hindu married to a Muslim, describes his encounter with a militant Hindu over lunch in Queens. Eduardo Bonilla-Silva and Abby L. Ferber both discuss elements of "color-blind" racism, and Ferber links this new form of racism with what she terms "post-feminism." Vasilikie Demos and her co-authors are also interested in the myriad ways oppression is socially constructed and outline the basic principles that govern systems of oppression. Many discussions of race, gender, and class fail to focus on the Asian experience or erroneously depict Asians as a "model minority." Yen Le Espiritu addresses these issues in her article on Asian men in U.S. history. C. Shawn McGuffey and B. Lindsay Rich go to the playground to examine gender, race, and class in middle childhood, and Amy C. Wilkins studies the boundaries of gender, racial/ethnicity, and class identity by talking to young people about Puerto Rican "wannabes." The very studies Kristin E. Joos summarizes in the fact sheet on lesbian, gay, bisexual, and transgender families were the basis of a plot resolution on a recent episode of *Law and Order, SVU*. Troy Duster brings readers to the cutting edges of the social sciences, the humanities, and even the biological sciences in his discussion of the concept of race in the light of contemporary scholarship. The section ends with Jason DeParle's *New York Times* report at the time when the intersections of gender, race, and class in America were exposed by the receding waters of Hurricane Katrina.

Acknowledgements

The authors would like to extend our heartfelt thanks to those without whose help, support, and hard work, the volume would not have made it to press. We would like to acknowledge Jesse Portillo—intrepid theater major and literary critic—who handled an enormous amount of work during the summer of 2004 while we were readying the book for review. Thanks also go out to Teresa Andrews for scanning our many reading choices and Jason Luttrell for his contributions. As far as truly getting the volume to print, we owe our greatest debt of thanks to Karin Abel for her extraordinary work on our behalf in acquiring permissions from numerous publishers to make sure all the readings we wanted to include truly came through.

We would like to acknowledge all the many contributors to this book, whose work spoke to us and who we are honored and grateful to include. We would also like to acknowledge Professors Eduardo Bonilla-Silva, Marlese Durr, Charles Gallagher, and Kathryn Feltey for review of early draft contents of the manuscript as well as the nine blind reviewers whose comments helped us to frame our sections more clearly.

In addition, we would like to thank Ruby Chacón, a Latina artist from Utah, for gracing our volume with her compelling and timeless cover art, "Self-Portrait as a *Mestiza*." We hope this will bring her remarkable work to a larger audience.

No acknowledgement would be complete, of course, without thanks to Claude Teweles, our Publisher from Roxbury Publishing Company, who spoke to each of us back in the 1990s in hopes of bringing out just such a volume. We would also like to thank Scott Carter from Roxbury for his tireless and consistent support as well as Monica Gomez for her assistance through the last stages of publication.

Finally, we wish to thank our husbands and families for all their love and support, especially Ed and Michael, who lived with us through endless reading, phone calls, photocopying, and the stress of putting together a cohesive anthology. ✦

Subject Listing of Topics Covered by Chapter

African Americans: Ch. 4; Ch. 5; Ch. 6; Ch. 7; Ch. 8; Ch. 18; Ch. 23; Ch. 24; Ch. 25; Ch. 26; Ch. 29; Ch. 32; Ch. 36; Ch. 38; Ch. 41; Ch. 42; Ch. 48; Ch. 50; Ch. 51; Ch. 54; Ch. 56; Ch. 57; Ch. 58; Ch. 63; Ch. 64

American Indians: Ch. 15; Ch. 30; Ch. 36; Ch. 48; Ch. 49

Asian Americans: Ch. 10; Ch. 55; Ch. 60

Autobiography/biography: Ch. 8; Ch. 13; Ch. 16; Ch. 18; Ch. 19; Ch. 54

Civil rights: Ch. 8; Ch. 35; Ch. 39

Crime/criminals: Ch. 23; Ch. 29

Education (higher): Ch. 16; Ch. 18

Education (K–12): Ch. 24; Ch. 26; Ch. 27; Ch. 38; Ch. 47; Ch. 58

Family: Ch. 10; Ch. 14; Ch. 15; Ch. 17; Ch. 19; Ch. 23; Ch. 26; Ch. 37; Ch. 46; Ch. 48; Ch. 49; Ch. 51; Ch. 54; Ch. 61

Gender: Ch. 1; Ch. 2; Ch. 7; Ch. 12; Ch. 13; Ch. 14; Ch. 15; Ch. 16; Ch. 17; Ch. 18; Ch. 19; Ch. 20; Ch. 21; Ch. 22; Ch. 23; Ch. 25; Ch. 26; Ch. 28; Ch. 29; Ch. 30; Ch. 32; Ch. 33; Ch. 34; Ch. 36; Ch. 37; Ch. 38; Ch. 40; Ch. 41; Ch. 42; Ch. 46; Ch. 48; Ch. 49; Ch. 51; Ch. 52; Ch. 54; Ch. 58; Ch. 59; Ch. 60; Ch. 62

Historical perspective: Ch. 1; Ch. 2; Ch. 3; Ch. 4; Ch. 5; Ch. 6; Ch. 7; Ch. 8; Ch. 9; Ch. 10; Ch. 15; Ch. 25; Ch. 30; Ch. 33; Ch. 46; Ch. 49

Immigration: Ch. 1; Ch. 2; Ch. 10; Ch. 19; Ch. 33; Ch. 43; Ch. 55; Ch. 60

Industry: Ch. 1; Ch. 19; Ch. 29; Ch. 33; Ch. 34

Inter-/multi-national issues: Ch. 5; Ch. 19; Ch. 29; Ch. 33; Ch. 34

Intersectional/multi-ethnic perspectives: Ch. 7; Ch. 21; Ch. 36; Ch. 40; Ch. 46; Ch. 47; Ch. 54; Ch. 59

Language: Ch. 6; Ch. 20; Ch. 24

Latinos/as: Ch. 7; Ch. 14; Ch. 21; Ch. 22; Ch. 36; Ch. 37; Ch. 43; Ch. 46; Ch. 56; Ch. 59

Legal issues/courts: Ch. 23; Ch. 29; Ch. 35; Ch. 48

Media: Ch. 28; Ch. 64

Medicine/health: Ch. 22; Ch. 36; Ch. 37

Other racial/ethnic groups: Ch. 2; Ch. 9; Ch. 21

Poetry/fiction: Ch. 9; Ch. 11; Ch. 12; Ch. 14

Poverty: Ch. 8; Ch. 13; Ch. 17; Ch. 19; Ch. 24; Ch. 33; Ch. 37; Ch. 42; Ch. 49

Qualitative analyses (systematic interviews/ participant observation): Ch. 21; Ch. 22; Ch. 25; Ch. 26; Ch. 39; Ch. 40; Ch. 48; Ch. 50; Ch. 51; Ch. 58; Ch. 59

Quantitative analyses: Ch. 28; Ch. 31; Ch. 32; Ch. 36; Ch. 37; Ch. 41; Ch. 42; Ch. 43; Ch. 45

Religion: Ch. 9; Ch. 11; Ch. 21; Ch. 30; Ch. 31; Ch. 54; Ch. 55

Sexualities: Ch. 3; Ch. 9; Ch. 11; Ch. 16; Ch. 18; Ch. 22; Ch. 25; Ch. 27; Ch. 35; Ch. 38; Ch. 46; Ch. 47; Ch. 53; Ch. 61

Social class: Ch. 1; Ch. 16; Ch. 17; Ch. 18; Ch. 25; Ch. 28; Ch. 36; Ch. 37; Ch. 40; Ch. 45; Ch. 58; Ch. 64

Social movements: Ch. 8; Ch. 22; Ch. 35; Ch. 48; Ch. 51

Theoretical discussions of race, gender, and class issues: Ch. 56; Ch. 57; Ch. 62; Ch. 63

White privilege: Ch. 38; Ch. 41; Ch. 50

Whites: Ch. 1; Ch. 2; Ch. 5; Ch. 9; Ch. 16; Ch. 23; Ch. 25; Ch. 26; Ch. 27; Ch. 31; Ch. 32; Ch. 33; Ch. 35; Ch. 38; Ch. 39; Ch. 40; Ch. 41; Ch. 42; Ch. 46; Ch. 48; Ch. 50; Ch. 54; Ch. 56; Ch. 57; Ch. 58; Ch. 62

Work/occupations: Ch. 1; Ch. 2; Ch. 13; Ch. 32; Ch. 33; Ch. 34; Ch. 41

World/global issues (Africa/Asia/Europe/ Latin America/Caribbean): Ch. 3; Ch. 9; Ch. 10; Ch. 13; Ch. 18; Ch. 19; Ch. 28; Ch. 37; Ch. 44; Ch. 52 ✦

1

The Lady and the Mill Girl

Changes in the Status of Women in the Age of Jackson

Gerda Lerner

In this article, Gerda Lerner weaves elements of gender, race, and class together to provide an analytical framework of women's lives in the early nineteenth century. Lerner writes about the ways in which demand for labor, changes in technology, and ideas about work and the proper place of women interacted in the years between 1800 and 1840 to change the status and roles of American women dramatically.

Colonial women worked in many professions and trades as well as in their homes and farms. They were not considered equal to men, but everyone's labor was needed and cultural beliefs required that no one should be idle or dependent on others. By 1840 professionalization and industrialization pushed women out of medicine, law, and commerce and into mills, factories, and classrooms. These same trends made it possible for middle-class women to aspire to the status of the lady.

Before the nineteenth century, the practice of medicine was based on reading, apprenticeship, and experience. Both men and women, free and slave, tended the sick and prepared natural remedies. When formal medical training began in the United States, White women and all people of color were excluded. Thus, when graduation from a medical college became the requirement for a license to practice, only White men qualified. The midwives who delivered babies were initially all women, but a new technology, the obstetrical forceps, became the property of physicians, and women were gradually excluded from that profession as well, although the children of poor and immigrant women were still more likely than

those of middle-class women to be delivered at home by women whose training was largely informal. Owing to their association of activities with the housewife role, the professions of nursing and teaching became the domains of women in the face of labor shortages.

There was a shortage of labor in the new factories as well. White women and children from the farms and towns, and later immigrant women, were recruited to work in the textile mills of New England. Industry began to take over much of the work once done in the home. Middle-class women now had more leisure and class distinctions became sharper. By the 1830s, the "piety, purity, domesticity" model of the "cult of true womanhood" dominated popular thinking. Staying at home, wearing fashionable clothes, and engaging in approved activities, wives and daughters became the vehicles through which husbands and fathers affirmed their status.

Some middle- and upper-class women were able to use their resources to become educated. These women began to press for greater equality, creating the initial women's rights movement. However, as Lerner points out, they were largely ignorant of the conditions of women from other social classes. Their demands for such things as property rights and the vote did not speak to the needs of working-class and poverty-stricken women.

The period 1800–1840 is one in which decisive changes occurred in the status of American women. It has remained surprisingly unexplored: With the exception of a recent, unpublished dissertation by Keith Melder and the distinctive work of Elisabeth Dexter, there is a dearth of descriptive material and an almost total absence of interpretation.[1] Yet the period offers essential clues to an understanding of later institutional developments, particularly the shape and nature of the women's rights movement. This analysis will consider the economic, political and social status of women and examine the changes in each area. It will also attempt an interpretation of the ideological shifts which occurred in American society concerning the "proper" role for women.

Periodization always offers difficulties. It seemed useful here, for purposes of comparison, to group women's status before 1800 roughly under the "colonial" heading and ignore the transitional and possibly atypical shifts which occurred during the American Revolution and the early period of nationhood. Also, regional differences were largely ignored. The South was left out of consideration entirely because its industrial development occurred later.

The status of colonial women has been well studied and described and can briefly be summarized for comparison with the later period. Throughout the colonial period there was a marked shortage of women, which varied with the regions and always was greatest in the frontier areas.[2] This (from the point of view of women) favorable sex ratio enhanced their status and position. The Puritan world view regarded idleness as sin; life in an underdeveloped country made it absolutely necessary that each member of the community perform an economic function. Thus work for women, married or single, was not only approved, it was regarded as a civic duty. Puritan town councils expected single girls, widows and unattached women to be self-supporting and for a long time provided needy spinsters with parcels of land. There was no social sanction against married women working; on the contrary, wives were expected to help their husbands in their trade and won social approval for doing extra work in or out of the home. Needy children, girls as well as boys, were indentured or apprenticed and were expected to work for their keep.

The vast majority of women worked within their homes, where their labor produced most articles needed for the family. The entire colonial production of cloth and clothing, and partially that of shoes, was in the hands of women. In addition to these occupations, women were found in many different kinds of employment. They were butchers, silversmiths, gunsmiths, upholsterers. They ran mills, plantations, tan yards, shipyards and every kind of shop, tavern and boarding house. They were gate keepers, jail keepers, sextons, journalists, printers, "doctoresses," apothecaries, midwives, nurses and teachers. Women acquired their skills the same way as did the men, through apprenticeship training, frequently within their own families.[3]

Absence of a dowry, ease of marriage and remarriage and a more lenient attitude of the law with regard to woman's property rights were manifestations of the improved position of wives in the colonies. Under British common law, marriage destroyed a woman's contractual capacity; she could not sign a contract even with the consent of her husband. But colonial authorities were more lenient toward the wife's property rights by protecting her dower rights in her husband's property, granting her personal clothing and upholding pre-nuptial contracts between husband and wife. In the absence of the husband, colonial courts granted women "femme sole" rights, which enabled them to conduct their husband's business, sign contracts and sue. The relative social freedom of women and the esteem in which they were held was commented upon by most early foreign travelers in America.[4]

But economic, legal and social status tell only part of the story. Colonial society as a whole was hierarchical, and rank and standing in society depended on the position of the men. Women did not play a determining role in the ranking pattern; they took their position in society through the men of their own family or the men they married. In other words, they participated in the hierarchy only as daughters and wives, not as individuals. Similarly, their occupations were, by and large, merely auxiliary, designed to contribute to family income, enhance their husbands' business or continue it in case of widowhood. The self-supporting spinsters were certainly the exception. The underlying assumption of colonial society was that women ought to occupy an inferior and subordinate position. The settlers had brought this assumption with them from Europe; it was reflected in their legal concepts, their willingness to exclude women from political life, their discriminatory educational practices. What is remarkable is the extent to which this felt inferiority of women was constantly challenged and modified under the impact of environment, frontier conditions and a favorable sex ratio.

By 1840 all of American society had changed. The Revolution had substituted an egalitarian ideology for the hierarchical concepts of colonial life. Privilege based on ability rather than inherited status, upward mobility for all groups of society and unlimited opportunities for individual self-fulfillment had become ideological goals, if not always realities. For men, that is; women were, by tacit consensus, excluded from the new democracy. Indeed their actual situation had in many respects deteriorated. While, as wives, they had benefitted from increasing wealth, urbanization and industrialization, their role as economic producers and as political members of society differed sharply from that of men. Women's work outside of the home no longer met with social approval; on the contrary, with two notable exceptions, it was condemned. Many business and professional occupations formerly open to women were now closed, many others restricted as to training and advancement. The entry of large numbers of women into low status, low pay and low skill industrial work had fixed such work by definition as "woman's work." Women's political status, while legally unchanged, had deteriorated relative to the advances made by men. At the same time the genteel lady of fashion had become a model of American femininity and the definition of "woman's proper sphere" seemed narrower and more confined than ever.

Within the scope of this article only a few of these changes can be more fully explained. The professionalization of medicine and its impact on women may serve as a typical example of what occurred in all the professions.

In colonial America there were no medical schools, no medical journals, few hospitals and few laws pertaining to the practice of the healing arts. Clergymen and governors, barbers, quacks, apprentices and women practiced medicine. Most practitioners acquired their credentials by reading Paracelsus and Galen and serving an apprenticeship with an established practitioner. Among the semi-trained "physics," surgeons and healers, the occasional "doctoress" was fully accepted and frequently well rewarded. County records of all the colonies contain references to the work of the female physi-

cians. There was even a female Army surgeon, a Mrs. Allyn, who served during King Philip's war. Plantation records mention by name several slave women who were granted special privileges because of their useful service as midwives and "doctoresses."[5]

The period of the professionalization of American medicine dates from 1765, when Dr. William Shippen began his lectures on midwifery in Philadelphia. The founding of medical faculties in several colleges, the standardization of training requirements and the proliferation of medical societies intensified during the last quarter of the eighteenth century. The American Revolution dramatized the need for trained medical personnel, afforded first hand battlefield experience to a number of surgeons and brought increasing numbers of semi-trained practitioners in contact with the handful of European-trained surgeons working in the military hospitals. This was an experience from which women were excluded. The resulting interest in improved medical training, the gradual appearance of graduates of medical colleges and the efforts of medical societies led to licensing legislation. In 1801, Maryland required all medical practitioners to be licensed; in 1806 New York enacted a similar law, providing for an examination before a commission. By the late 1820's, all states except three had set up licensing requirements. Since most of these laws stipulated attendance at a medical college as one of the prerequisites for licensing, women were automatically excluded.[6] By the 1830's the few established female practitioners who might have continued their practice in the old ways had probably died out. Whatever vested interest they had had was too weak to assert itself against the new profession.

This process of pre-emption of knowledge, institutionalization of the profession and legitimation of its claims by law and public acceptance is standard for the professionalization of the sciences, as George Daniels has pointed out.[7] It inevitably results in the elimination of fringe elements from the profession. It is interesting to note that women had been pushed out of the medical profession in sixteenth-century Europe by a similar process.[8] Once the public had come to accept licensing and college training as guarantees of up-to-date practice, the outsider, no matter how well qualified by years of experience, stood no chance in the competition. Women were the casualties of medical professionalization.

In the field of midwifery the results were similar, but the process was more complicated. Women had held a virtual monopoly in the profession in colonial America. In 1646 a man was prosecuted in Maine for practicing as a midwife.[9] There are many records of well trained midwives with diplomas from European institutions working in the colonies. In most of the colonies midwives were licensed, registered and required to pass an examination before a board. When Dr. Shippen announced his pioneering lectures on midwifery, he did it to "combat the widespread popular prejudice against the man-midwife" and because he considered most midwives ignorant and improperly trained.[10]

Yet he invited "those women who love virtue enough, to own their Ignorance, and apply for instruction" to attend his lectures, offering as an inducement the assurance that female pupils would be taught privately. It is not known if any midwives availed themselves of the opportunity.[11]

Technological advances, as well as scientific, worked against the interests of female midwives. In sixteenth-century Europe the invention and use of the obstetrical forceps had for three generations been the well-kept secret of the Chamberlen family and had greatly enhanced their medical practice. Hugh Chamberlen was forced by circumstances to sell the secret to the Medical College in Amsterdam, which in turn transmitted the precious knowledge to licensed physicians only. By the time the use of the instrument became widespread it had become associated with male physicians and midwives. Similarly in America, introduction of the obstetrical forceps was associated with the practice of male mid-wives and served to their advantage. By the end of the eighteenth century a number of male physicians advertised their practice of midwifery. Shortly thereafter female midwives also resorted to advertising, probably in an effort to met the competition. By the early nineteenth century male

physicians had virtually monopolized the practice of midwifery on the Eastern seaboard. True to the generally delayed economic development in the Western frontier regions, female midwives continued to work on the frontier until a much later period. It is interesting to note that the concepts of "propriety" shifted with the prevalent practice. In seventeenth-century Maine the attempt of a man to act as a midwife was considered outrageous and illegal; in mid-nineteenth-century America the suggestion that women should train as midwives and physicians was considered equally outrageous and improper.[12]

Professionalization, similar to that in medicine with the elimination of women from the upgraded profession, occurred in the field of law. Before 1750, when law suits were commonly brought to the courts by the plaintiffs themselves or by deputies without specialized legal training, women as well as men could and did act as "attorneys-in-fact." When the law became a paid profession and trained lawyers took over litigation, women disappeared from the court scene for over a century.[13]

A similar process of shrinking opportunities for women developed in business and in the retail trades. There were fewer female storekeepers and business women in the 1830's than there had been in colonial days. There was also a noticeable shift in the kind of merchandise handled by them. Where previously women could be found running almost every kind of retail shop, after 1830 they were mostly found in businesses which served women only.[14]

The only fields in which professionalization did not result in the elimination of women from the upgraded profession were nursing and teaching. Both were characterized by a severe shortage of labor. Nursing lies outside the field of this inquiry since it did not become an organized profession until after the Civil War. Before then it was regarded peculiarly as a woman's occupation, although some of the hospitals and the Army during wars employed male nurses. These bore the stigma of low skill, low status and low pay. Generally, nursing was regarded as simply an extension of the unpaid services performed by the housewife—a characteristic attitude that haunts the profession to this day.

Education seems, at first glance, to offer an entirely opposite pattern from that of the other professions. In colonial days women had taught "Dame schools" and grade schools during summer sessions. Gradually, as educational opportunities for girls expanded, they advanced just a step ahead of their students. Professionalization of teaching occurred between 1820–1860, a period marked by a sharp increase in the number of women teachers. The spread of female seminaries, academies and normal schools provided new opportunities for the training and employment of female teachers.

This trend which runs counter to that found in the other professions can be accounted for by the fact that women filled a desperate need created by the challenge of the common schools, the ever-increasing size of the student body and the westward growth of the nation. America was committed to educating its children in public schools, but it was insistent on doing so as cheaply as possible. Women were available in great numbers and they were willing to work cheaply. The result was another ideological adaptation: in the very period when the gospel of the home as woman's only proper sphere was preached most loudly, it was discovered that women were the natural teachers of youth, could do the job better than men and were to be preferred for such employment. This was always provided, of course, that they would work at the proper wage differential—30–50% of the wages paid male teachers was considered appropriate. The result was that in 1888 in the country as a whole 63% of all teachers were women, while the figure for the cities only was 90.04%.[15]

It appeared in the teaching field, as it would in industry, that role expectations were adaptable provided the inferior status group filled a social need. The inconsistent and peculiar patterns of employment of black labor in the present-day market bear out the validity of this generalization.

There was another field in which the labor of women was appreciated and which they were urged to enter—industry. From Alexander Hamilton to Matthew Carey and Tench Coxe, advocates of industrialization sang the praises of the working girl and advanced arguments in favor of her employment. The social benefits of female labor particularly stressed were those bestowed upon her family, who now no longer had to support her. Working girls were "thus happily preserved from idleness and its attendant vices and crimes" and the whole community benefitted from their increased purchasing power.[16]

American industrialization, which occurred in an underdeveloped economy with a shortage of labor, depended on the labor of women and children. Men were occupied with agricultural work and were not available or willing to enter the factories. This accounts for the special features of the early development of the New England textile industry: the relatively high wages, the respectability of the job and relatively high status of the mill girls, the patriarchal character of the model factory towns and the temporary mobility of women workers from farm to factory and back again to farm. All this was characteristic only of a limited area and of a period of about two decades. By the late 1830's the romance had worn off; immigration had supplied a strongly competitive, permanent work force willing to work for subsistence wages; early efforts at trade union organization had been shattered and mechanization had turned semiskilled factory labor into unskilled labor. The process led to the replacement of the New England-born farm girls by immigrants in the mills and was accompanied by a loss of status and respectability for female workers.

The lack of organized social services during periods of depression drove ever greater numbers of women into the labor market. At first, inside the factories distinctions between men's and women's jobs were blurred. Men and women were assigned to machinery on the basis of local need. But as more women entered industry the limited number of occupations open to them tended to increase competition among them, thus lowering pay standards. Generally, women regarded their work as temporary and hesitated to invest in apprenticeship training, because they expected to marry and raise families. Thus they remained untrained, casual labor and were soon, by custom, relegated to the lowest paid, least skilled jobs. Long hours, overwork and poor working conditions would characterize women's work in industry for almost a century.[17]

Another result of industrialization was in increasing differences in life styles between women of different classes. When female occupations, such as carding, spinning and weaving, were transferred from home to factory, the poorer women followed their traditional work and became industrial workers. The women of the middle and upper classes could use their newly gained time for leisure pursuits: they became ladies. And a small but significant group among them chose to prepare themselves for professional careers by advanced education. This group would prove to be the most vocal and troublesome in the near future.

As class distinctions sharpened, social attitudes toward women became polarized. The image of "the lady" was elevated to the accepted ideal of femininity toward which all women would strive. In this formulation of values, lower class women were simply ignored. The actual lady was, of course, nothing new on the American scene; she had been present ever since colonial days. What was new in the 1830's was the cult of the lady, her elevation to a status symbol. The advancing prosperity of the early nineteenth century made it possible for middle class women to aspire to the status formerly reserved for upper class women. The "cult of true womanhood" of the 1830's became a vehicle for such aspirations. Mass circulation newspapers and magazines made it possible to teach every woman how to elevate the status of her family by setting "proper" standards of behavior, dress and literary tastes. *Godey's Lady's Book* and innumerable gift books and traces of the period all preach the same gospel of "true womanhood"—piety, purity, domesticity.[18] Those unable to reach the goal of becoming ladies were to be satisfied with the lesser goal—acceptance of their "proper place" in the home.

It is no accident that the slogan "woman's place is in the home" took on a certain aggressiveness and silliness precisely at the time when increasing numbers of poorer women *left* their homes to become factory workers. Working women were not a fit subject for the concern of publishers and mass media writers. Idleness, once a disgrace in the eyes of society, had become a status symbol. Thorstein Veblen, one of the earliest and sharpest commentators on the subject, observed that it had become almost the sole social function of the lady "to put in evidence her economic unit's ability to pay." She was "a means of conspicuously unproductive expenditure," devoted to displaying her husband's wealth.[19] Just as the cult of white womanhood in the South served to preserve a labor and social system based on race distinctions, so did the cult of the lady in an egalitarian society serve as a means of preserving class distinctions. Where class distinctions were not so great, as on the frontier, the position of women was closer to what it had been in colonial days; their economic contribution was more highly valued, their opportunities were less restricted and their positive participation in community life was taken for granted.

In the urbanized and industrialized Northeast the life experience of middle class women was different in almost every respect from that of the lower class women. But there was one thing the society lady and the mill girl had in common—they were equally disfranchised and isolated from the vital centers of power. Yet the political status of women had not actually deteriorated. With very few exceptions women had neither voted nor stood for office during the colonial period. Yet the spread of the franchise to ever wider groups of white males during the Jacksonian age, [and] the removal of property restrictions, the increasing numbers of immigrants who acquired access to the franchise, made the gap between these new enfranchised voters and the disfranchised women more obvious. Quite naturally, educated and propertied women felt this deprivation more keenly. Their own career expectations had been encouraged by widening educational opportunities; their consciousness of their own abilities and of their potential for power had been enhanced by their activities in the reform movements of the 1830's; the general spirit of upward mobility and venturesome entrepreneurship that pervaded the Jacksonian era was infectious. But in the late 1840's a sense of acute frustration enveloped these educated and highly spirited women. Their rising expectations had met with frustration, their hopes had been shattered; they were bitterly conscious of a relative lowering of status and a loss of position. This sense of frustration led them to action; it was one of the main factors in the rise of the woman's rights movement.[20]

The women, who in 1848 declared boldly and with considerable exaggeration that "the history of mankind is a history of repeated injuries and usurpations on the part of man toward woman, having in direct object the establishment of an absolute tyranny over her," did not speak for the truly exploited and abused working woman.[21] As a matter of fact, they were largely ignorant of her condition and, with the notable exception of Susan B. Anthony, indifferent to her fate. But they judged from the realities of their own life experience. Like most revolutionaries, they were not the most downtrodden but rather the most status-deprived group. Their frustrations and traditional isolation from political power funneled their discontent into fairly Utopian declarations and immature organizational means. They would learn better in the long, hard decades of practical struggle. Yet it is their initial emphasis on the legal and political "disabilities" of women which has provided the framework for most of the historical work on women. For almost a hundred years sympathetic historians have told the story of women in America from the feminist viewpoint. Their tendency has been to reason from the position of middle class women to a generalization concerning all American women. This distortion has obscured the actual and continuous contributions of women to American life.[22] To avoid such a distortion, any valid generalization concerning American women after the 1830's should reflect a recognition of class stratification.

For lower class women the changes brought by industrialization were actually advantageous, offering income and advancement opportunities, however limited, and a chance for participation in the ranks of organized labor. They, by and large, tended to join

men in their struggle for economic advancement and became increasingly concerned with economic gains and protective labor legislation. Middle and upperclass women, on the other hand, reacted to actual and fancied status deprivation by increasing militancy and the formation of organizations for women's rights, by which they meant especially legal and property rights.

The four decades preceding the Seneca Falls Convention were decisive in the history of American women. They brought an actual deterioration in the economic opportunities open to women, a relative deterioration in their political status and a rising level of expectation and subsequent frustration in a privileged elite group of educated women. The ideology still pervasive in our present-day society regarding woman's "proper" role was formed in those decades. Later, under the impact of feminist attacks this ideology would grow defensive and attempt to bolster its claims by appeals to universality and pretentions to a history dating back to antiquity or, at least, to *The Mayflower.* Women, we are told, have always played a restricted and subordinate role in American life. In fact, however, it was in mid-nineteenth-century America that the ideology of "woman's place is in the home" changed from being an accurate description of existing reality into a myth. It became the "feminine mystique"—a longing for a lost, archaic world of agrarian family self-sufficiency, updated by woman's consumer function and the misunderstood dicta of Freudian psychology.

The decades 1800–1840 also provide the clues to an understanding of the institutional shape of the later women's organizations. These would be led by middle class women whose self-image, life experience and ideology had largely been fashioned and influenced by these early, transitional years. The concerns of middle class women—property rights, the franchise and moral uplift—would dominate the women's rights movement. But side by side with it, and at times cooperating with it, would grow a number of organizations serving the needs of working women.

American women were the largest disfranchised group in the nation's history, and they retained this position longer than any other group. Although they found ways of making their influence felt continuously, not only as individuals but as organized groups, power eluded them. The mill girl and the lady, both born in the age of Jackson, would not gain access to power until they learned to cooperate, each for her own separate interests. It would take almost six decades before they would find common ground. The issue around which they finally would unite and push their movement to victory was the "impractical and Utopian" demand raised at Seneca Falls—the means to power in American society—female suffrage.

Footnotes

Research for this article was facilitated by a research grant provided by Long Island University, Brooklyn, N.Y , which is gratefully acknowledged.

The generalizations in this article are based on extensive research in primary sources, including letters and manuscripts of the following women: Elizabeth Cady Stanton, Susan B. Anthony, Abby Kelley, Lucretia Mott, Lucy Stone, Sarah and Angelina Grimke, Maria Weston Chapman, Lydia Maria Child and Betsey Cowles. Among the organizational records consulted were those of the Boston Female Anti-Slavery Society, the Philadelphia Female Anti-Slavery Society, Anti-Slavery Conventions of American Women, all the Woman's Eights Conventions prior to 1870 and the records of various female charitable organizations.

1. Keith E. Melder, "The Beginnings of the Women's Rights Movement in the United States 1800–1840" (Diss. Yale, 1963).
    Elisabeth A, Dexter, *Colonial Women of Affairs: Women in Business and Professions in America before 1776* (Boston, 1931).
    ——. *Career Women of America: 1776–1840* (Francestown, N.H., 1950).

2. Herbert Moller, "Sex Composition and Corresponding Culture Patterns of Colonial America," *William and Mary Quarterly*, Ser. 3, II (April, 1945), 113–153.

3. The summary of the status of colonial women is based on the following sources: Mary Benson, *Women in 18th Century America: A Study of Opinion and Social Usage* (New York, 1935); Arthur Calhoun, *A Social History of the American Family*, 3 vols. (Cleveland, 1918); Dexter, *Colonial Women*; Dexter, *Career Women*; Edmund S. Morgan, *Virginians at Home: Family Life in the 18th Century* (Williamsburg, 1952); Julia C. Spruill, *Women's Life and Work in the Southern Colonies* (Chapel Hill, 1938).

4. E. M. Boatwright, "The political and legal status of women in Georgia: 1783–1860," *Georgia Historical Quarterly*, XXV (April, 1941).

Richard B. Morris, *Studies in the History of American Law* (New York, 1930), Chap 3.
A summary of travelers' comments on American women may be found in: Jane Mesick, *The English Traveler in America: 1785–1835* (New York, 1922), 83–99.

5. For facts on colonial medicine the following sources were consulted: Wyndham B. Blanton, *Medicine in Virginia*, 3 vols. (Richmond, 1930); N. S. Davis, M.D., *History of Medical Education and Institutions in the United States. . . .* (Chicago, 1851); Dexter, *Career Women*; K. C. Hurd Mead, M.D., *A History of Women in Medicine: from the earliest Times to the Beginning of the 19th Century* (Haddam, Conn., 1938); Geo. W. Norris, *The Early History of Medicine in Philadelphia* (Philadelphia, 1886); Joseph M. Toner, *Contributions to the Annals of Medical Progress in the United States before and during the War of Independence* (Washington, D.C., 1874).
    The citation regarding Mrs. Allyn is from Hurd-Mead, *Women in Medicine*, 487.

6. Fielding H. Garrison, M.D., *An Introduction to the History of Medicine* (Philadelphia, 1929).
    For licensing legislation: Davis, 88–103.

7. George Daniels, "The Professionalization of American Science: the emergent period, 1820–1860)," paper delivered at the joint session of the History of Science Society and the Society of the History of Technology, San Francisco, December 28, 1965.

8. Hurd-Mead, *Women in Medicine*, 391.

9. *Ibid.*, 486.

10. Betsy E. Corner, *William Shippen Jr.: Pioneer in American Medical Education* (Philadelphia, 1951), 103.

11. *Ibid.*

12. Benjamin Lee Gordon, *Medieval and Renaissance Medicine* (New York, 1959), 689–691.
    Blanton, *Medicine*, II, 23–24; Hurd-Mead, *Women in Medicine*, 487–88; Annie Nathan Meyer, *Woman's Work in America* (New York, 1891).
    Harriot K. Hunt, M.D. *Glances and Glimpses or Fifty Years Social Including Twenty Years Professional Life* (Boston, 1856), 127–140.
    Eleanor Flexner, *Century of Struggle: The Woman's Rights Movement in the United States* (Cambridge, Mass. 1959), 115–119.

13. Sophie H. Drinker, "Women Attorneys of Colonial Times," *Maryland Historical Society Bulletin*, LVI, No. 4 (Dec, 1961).

14. Dexter, *Colonial Women*, 34–35, 162–165.

15. Harriet W. Marr, *The Old New England Academies* (New York, 1959), Chap. 8; Thomas Woody, *A History of Women's Education in the United States*, 2 vols (New York, 1929) H, 100–109, 458–460, 492–493.

16. Matthew Carey, *Essays on Political Economy. . . .* (Philadelphia, 1822), 459.

17. The statements on women industrial workers are based on the following sources: Edith Abbot, *Women in Industry* (New York, 1910), 66–80; Edith Abbot, "Harriet Martineau and the Employment of Women in 1836," *Journal of Political Economy*, XIV (Dec, 1906), 614–626; Matthew Carey, *Miscella-*

neous Essays (Philadelphia, 1830), 153–203; Helen L. Sumner, *History of Women in Industry in the United States*, in *Report on Condition of Woman and Child Wage-Earners in the United States*, 19 vols. (Washington, D.C., 1910), IX.
Also: Elizabeth F. Baker, *Technology and Woman's Work* (New York, 1964), Chaps. 1–5.

18. Emily Putnam, *The Lady: Studies of certain significant phases of her history* (New York, 1910), 319–320.
Barbara Welter, "The Cult of True Womanhood: 1820–1860," *American Quarterly*, XVIII, No. 2, Part 1 (Summer, 1966), 151–174.

19. Veblen generalized from his observations of the society of the Gilded Age and fell into the usual error of simply ignoring the lower class women, whom he dismissed as "drudges . . . fairly content with their lot," but his analysis of women's role in "conspicuous consumption" and of the function of women's fashions is unsurpassed.
For references see: Thorstein Veblen, *The Theory of the Leisure Class* (New York, 1962, first printing, 1899), 70–71, 231–232.
Thorstein Veblen, "The Economic Theory of Woman's Dress," *Essays in Our Changing Order* (New York, 1934), 65–77.

20. Like most groups fighting status oppression women formulated a compensatory ideology of female superiority. Norton Mezvinsky has postulated that this was clearly expressed only in 1874; in fact this formulation appeared in the earliest speeches of Elizabeth Cady Stanton and in the speeches and resolutions of the Seneca Falls Conventions and other pre-Civil War woman's rights conventions. Rather than a main motivating force, the idea was a tactical formulation, designed to take advantage of the popularly held male belief in woman's "moral" superiority and to convince reformers that they needed the votes of women. Those middle class feminists who believed in woman's "moral" superiority exploited the concept in order to win their major goal—female equality.
For references see: Norton Mezvinsky, "An Idea of Female Superiority," *Midcontinent American Studies Journal*, II, No. 1 (Spring, 1961), 17–26.
E. D. Stanton, S. B. Anthony and M. J. Gage, eds., *A History of Woman Suffrage*, 6 vols. (New York, 1881–1922), I, 72, 479, 522, 529 and *passim*.
Alan P. Grimes, *The Puritan Ethic and Woman Suffrage* (New York, 1967), Chaps. 2 and 3.

21. Stanton *et al. History of Woman Suffrage* I, 70.

22. Mary R. Beard, *Woman as Force in History: A Study of Traditions and Realities* (New York, 1946).

Discussion Questions

1. Is the "cult of true womanhood" a thing of the past, or do we see echoes of it in society today?

2. What part does social class play in discussions of goals and methods for achieving gender equality in contemporary society? Are such goals as equal pay for equal work and convenient and affordable childcare more applicable to a particular social class? Is this question also relevant to discussions of racial and ethnic equality?

3. Arguably, the professionalization of certain occupations, including requiring formal education and certification, was a positive step. However, it resulted in effectively excluding from those fields everyone but White men whose families had the economic means to support them through many years of schooling. Some people contend that this explains and justifies affirmative action programs in law and medical schools today. Do you agree or disagree? Why or why not?

4. Lerner writes about the impact of industrialization on the lives and work of women. How did it affect the lives and work of men?

2

Why Irish Became Domestics and Italians and Jews Did Not

Stephen Steinberg

I*n this chapter, Stephen Steinberg asks a question for the ages: Why are the members of one racial/ethnic group willing to accept poorly paid, lower-status employment while the members of other racial/ethnic groups are not? In addition, Steinberg's comparative study focuses not on all members of the racial/ethnic group, but specifically the women from the group. In this chapter, then, gender becomes a significant foreground for a discussion of racial/ethnic and cultural jockeying for subsistence employment. In his essay, Steinberg questions nineteenth-century "culture of poverty" assumptions made about Irish women, prevalent at the time, which assumed a sort of cultural and therefore particularly Irish gendered predisposition and tolerance for cleaning up after others. In a carefully crafted argument, Steinberg takes the time to ask the harder question: Why did so many Irish women wind up in such undesirable positions as domestics in the first place? Instead of proceeding from a limited cultural standpoint on the issue, he wishes to clarify the sociohistorical antecedents of the so-called choices of Irish women, making the answer to his question decidedly more structural.*

Interestingly, the question of why members of one racial/ethnic group willingly take on jobs characterized by poor pay and ill-treatment while others do not, Steinberg's jumping off point, should not be limited to a discussion of nineteenth-century Irish versus Italian and Jewish immigrants. The

self-same attributes said to characterize Irish immigrant women—lack of self-respect and concomitant willingness to submit to servitude—have often been used to describe and demonize women from other racial and ethnic groups over time in American history, from images of Black "welfare queens" to Chicanas/Latinas of "loose habits." Historical memory, in these cases as well as for the Irish women, clearly marks racial/ethnic status as linked to a particular gendered role, all of course leading to inferior class position.

> *"I hate the very words 'service' and 'servant.' We came to this country to better ourselves, and it's not bettering to have anybody ordering you around."*
>
> The Daughter of an Irish Domestic, Quoted in Helen Campbell, *Prisoners of Poverty,* 1889.

The familiar plaint that "it's hard to find good help these days dates back to the earliest days of this country, when American-born women refused to work as domestics. According to one writer in 1904, the servant class was never native American; even in Colonial days domestics came as indentured servants who ultimately moved up to higher-status jobs once their service was over."[1] In the South, of course, domestic work was a "negro job," but even in the North, as one writer commented in 1860, "domestic service certainly is held to be so degrading . . . that no natives will do it."[2] Those native women who did enter the labor market could usually find more attractive employment as teachers, bookkeepers, saleswomen, clerks, secretaries, and nurses.

While native-born Americans were loath to work as domestics, immigrants sometimes viewed domestic work more favorably. As a Norwegian wrote to a newspaper back home in 1868:

> America is an excellent country for capable and moral servant girls, because usually young American women show a decided unwillingness to submit to the kind of restraint connected with the position of a servant. . . . People are constantly looking for Norwegian and Swedish ser-

vant girls; and as they are treated very well, especially in Yankee families, there is no one whom I can so safely advise to emigrate as diligent, moral, and well-mannered young girls.[3]

As can be inferred from this passage, "the service" was not regarded with the same opprobrium in Europe as in America. This can be traced to a number of demographic and economic factors.

As industrialization advanced in England, France, and other European countries, the hiring of servants became an integral part of the life-style of the new middle classes. At the same time, conditions of poverty and overpopulation in the countryside induced marginal peasants to apprentice their excess children to work as domestics in adjacent cities.[4] As one British historian notes, domestic service became "the major setting for female urban labour force participation during the transitional stages of industrialization."[5] It was often viewed as a respectable path for single young women, one that would indoctrinate them into the values and manners of the middle class, provide them with domestic skills, and in both these respects, prepare them for marriage. Thus, the prevailing cultural attitude sanctioned what was at bottom a matter of economic necessity. For poor country girls, domestic service functioned as a channel of social and economic mobility, and especially before there was a demand for female labor in the nascent textile industries, it provided rural women with an important stimulus for migrating to cities. It provided others with their only opportunity to emigrate to the United States.

From the vantage point of their employers, immigrants made ideal servants. In the first place, they could be paid little, since they had few alternative sources of employment. Perhaps for the same reason, or perhaps because they came from societies where rank was taken for granted, foreigners also tended to make more pliable and less disgruntled servants. As one observer wrote in 1904: "Although the immigrant so frequently lacks training, she is strong, asks few privileges, is content with lower wages and long hours, and has no consciousness of a so-

cial stigma attaching to her work."[6] The pariah status of immigrants also meant that their employers ran little risk that compromising details of their lives might be revealed to anyone in their own milieu.

While it is easy to see why immigrant women were in demand as servants, it might seem curious that immigrants in pursuit of the American Dream would accept such low-status employment. Actually, at the end of the nineteenth century there was only one other major avenue of employment open to immigrant women. That was in the needle trades, an industry that includes dressmakers, milliners, seamstresses, and tailoresses, and could be stretched to include workers in textile mills. Both domestic labor and the needle trades were extensions of traditional female roles, in that they involved work that was similar to household tasks. Domestics, of course, were employed to do the household work of other women. In the case of the needle trades, women were engaged in clothing production that once had been carried out in the home, but by the end of the nineteenth century had been mechanized and transferred to small shops and factories. Among immigrant women in the labor force in 1900, a solid majority worked in these two occupations.[7]

However, women of different ethnic backgrounds differed greatly in their propensity to work as domestics or as workers in the needle trades. Though some Irish women were employed in mills scattered across small industrial towns in the Northeast, the vast majority worked as domestics. The proportion varied, depending on time and place, but its high point occurred during the famine migration of the 1850s. Of the 29,470 domestics that show up in the 1855 census of New York City, 23,386 were Irish.[8] Though Irish were about one-quarter of New York's population, they were over three-quarters of the domestic labor force. Germans were the other major immigrant group during this period, but the German proportion in the domestic labor force was exactly the same as in the city population—15 percent. Not only were most domestics Irish but it was also the case that virtually all Irish women who worked did so as domestics.

Of course, the peak of Irish immigration preceded by several decades the burgeoning of the garment industry. However, even after the waves of Jewish and Italian immigration at the end of the century, it was still the Irish who dominated the ranks of domestic workers. According to figures collected by the United States Immigration Commission in 1900, 71 percent of immigrant Irish women in the labor force were classified as "domestic and personal" workers; 54 percent were specifically classified as "servants and waitresses." In contrast, only 9 percent of Italian female workers and 14 percent of Jewish female workers were classified as "servants and waitresses." And whereas 38 percent of Italian women and 41 percent of Jewish women were in the needle trades, the figure for Irish was only 8 percent.[9]

How is this ethnic division to be explained? Why were Italian and Jewish women generally able to avoid working at one of the most menial and low-status jobs in the labor force, and why should so many Irish flock to it? As with occupations connoting success, social scientists have stressed the operation of cultural factors in explaining why some groups were more likely than others to become domestics.

For example, in *Blood of My Blood*, Richard Gambino implies that Italian women never deigned to work as domestics. As he writes:

> No matter how poor, the Italian-American woman to this day does not work as a domestic. For to work in the house of another family (sometimes an absolute economic necessity in the old land) is seen as a usurpation of family loyalty by her family *and by her*. And if one loses one's place in *la via vecchia* there is no self-respect. In American history, there is no Italian counterpart of Irish, German, black, Spanish-speaking, English, Scandinavian, and French maids.[10]

How is it that Italians were able to escape a fate that befell all these other groups? Gambino implies that a stubborn ethnic pride, buttressed by a strong family system, protected Italian women from the indignities of domestic labor. Would he then suggest that other groups were lacking in these traits?

And if domestic labor was "an absolute economic necessity" in Italy, as Gambino says, why was this not so in America? . . .

The reasons why Irish women were far more likely than either Italians or Jews to be single has to do with conditions in their respective countries of origin. In the case of Italians, an economic crisis in agriculture induced men to emigrate in pursuit of industrial labor and higher wages, and there was a preponderance of males in the immigration pool. Between 1899 and 1910, nearly two million Italian men, but fewer than half a million Italian women entered the United States.[11] In some cases the men planned to send for their families once they had accumulated some savings; more often, they planned to return to Italy. An excerpt from a 1903 study on the Italian colonies in New York City describes this immigration pattern:

> The Italian population in this country is predominately male. The reason for this is plainly seen. In nine cases out of ten, the father of a family decides to emigrate to America; he would like to take with him his wife and children, but since the least cost of a steerage ticket is something over $30, it becomes an impossibility for the entire family to come at once. The result is the wife and children are left behind and the father comes. On the other hand, few women indeed come here of their own accord—they are brought or sent for by husband or prospective husband.[12]

Thus, few Italian women immigrated as independent breadwinners. Invariably, a husband or family member preceded them, sometimes by many years, and by the time the women arrived, they were already part of families that had established at least a tenuous economic foothold. Married women generally stayed out of the job market altogether, though some took in lodgers or homework. Those women who did enter the job generally found employment in the manufacturing sectors, especially in the expanding needle trades. In other words, neither economic necessity nor circumstances forced Italian women into domestic labor.

In Italy the situation was different. According to a study of women's employment in Milan in 1881, 23,000 women or 20 percent of all female workers, were employed as domestics.[13] If few Italian women worked as domestics in America, this can hardly be attributed to a distinctively Italian attitude toward women and the home.

Immigrant Jewish women, like their Italian counterparts, rarely immigrated alone, though for very different reasons. Eastern European Jews were refugees from religious persecution and political violence, and unlike Italians, those who left harbored no thoughts of returning. As a consequence, Jews typically immigrated as families. Whereas there were nearly four Italian men for every woman among those who immigrated between 1809 and 1910, Jews had a much more even sexual balance—608,000 men and 467,000 women.[14] That Jews tended to immigrate as families is also indicated by the fact that a quarter of all Jewish immigrants during this period were children under fourteen years of age. Thus, most Jewish women came to America with husbands or fathers. Few were independent breadwinners, and when they did work, they usually found employment in the burgeoning garment industry. Often they worked in small shops with other family members.

The demographic character of Irish immigration was different from that of either Italian or Jews in that it included large numbers of single women. Unfortunately, no data exist on the marital status of immigrants, and consequently, there is no exact measure of how many were unmarried. However, a rough estimate can be gleaned from examining the sex ratios of the various immigrant pools. In contrast to the situation among Italians and Jews, there were actually more women than men among Irish immigrants around the turn of the century. Specifically, among Irish arriving between 1800 and 1910, there were 109 women for every 100 men. Among Jews there were 77 women for every 100 men; among Italians, only 27 women for every 100 men.[15] Not only were Irish women far less likely to be married when they immigrated, but the sex ratio did not favor their finding Irish husbands after they arrived.

A similar situation existed earlier in the century as well. For example, according to the 1860 census, New York's Irish-born population consisted of 87,000 males, but 117,000 females. Not surprisingly, the marriage rates of Irish in American cities were generally lower than those for other groups throughout the nineteenth century. Hence, from a demographic standpoint, Irish women were an ideal source of live-in domestics. That they also spoke English made them all the more desirable.

Further impetus was given to the immigration of Irish domestics by agencies that sprang up on both sides of the Atlantic. Beginning in the 1850s, a number of British emigration societies were organized to encourage and assist the emigration of surplus population, especially single women of childbearing age who were unlikely to emigrate on their own. They bore imposing names like the London Female Emigration Society, the British Ladies Emigration Society, the Girls' Friendly Society, and the Travelers Aid Society for Girls and Women. With philanthropic pretense, these societies recruited indigent women, paid for their steerage, escorted them to the port of embarkation, and dispatched them to the New World where they were commonly placed in private households as domestic servants.[16] Not all the recipients of this dubious largess were Irish, and many were sent to Canada and other British colonies. Nevertheless, the very existence of these societies testifies to the popular currency given to the idea of sending poor young girls across the Atlantic to work as domestic servants.

There were also employment agencies in the United States that recruited and transported young foreign girls to work as domestics in New York. According to one account, in 1904 there were as many as 300 "intelligence offices" in New York City alone.[17] To some extent, then, "Bridget" was the creation of employment agencies that engaged in this human commerce and collected fees for supplying households with Irish domestics.

There is still other evidence that many Irish women emigrated with the express purpose of finding work as domestics. Among immigrants arriving between 1899 and 1910, 40 percent of the Irish were classified as servants; in contrast, the figure for both Italians and Jews was only 6 percent.[18] Only 14 percent of Irish immigrants were classified as having "no occupation," a category that consisted mostly of children and women who considered themselves homemakers. The comparable figure for Southern Italians was 23 percent; for Jews it was 45 percent. From this it is reasonable to assume that most Irish women who immigrated around the turn of the century planned to enter the labor force, presumably in the servant occupation that they named when asked their occupation at the port of entry.

The reasons why so many young women left Ireland just to become servants in America must be traced to a series of economic crises in the nineteenth century, and the social and cultural changes that ensued. The infamous potato famine of the late 1840s was only one such crisis. Almost as important was a process of land consolidation that, between 1849 and 1851 alone, involved the dispossession of some million people from the land and the physical destruction of their homes.[19] To make matters worse, English colonial policy had reduced Ireland to a producer of wool and food, and the island had no industrial base that might have absorbed its surplus population. Irish emigration reached its peak during the potato famine, but it was already gaining momentum before the famine and it continued at substantial levels long after. Incredibly, Ireland's population in 1900 was almost half of what it had been in 1850.[20]

Ireland's prolonged economic depression played havoc with the family system. Traditionally, marriage was bound up with the inheritance of land, and as land became more scarce, there was a tendency to postpone marriage. For nearly a century after the famine, as one recent study has shown, "the average age at marriage increased, the marriage rate decreased, and the percentage who remained permanently celibate increased."[21] In 1891, for example, two-thirds of men and half the women between the ages of 25 and 34 were single. Even among those between 35 and 44, a third of the men and a quarter of the women were single. One out of six of each sex never married.

The impact of these trends was especially harsh on women, since they were forced onto a labor market that was hardly favorable to them. Against this background it is easy to understand why young women, even more often than men, decided to emigrate. And given their vulnerability as single women in an alien country, as well as the limited alternatives that existed, it is also easy to understand why "the service" provided at least a temporary solution to their dilemma. It made emigration possible, provided them with food and lodging, and carried them over until such time as they could find either husbands or more desirable employment.

If historical circumstances and economic necessity forced immigrant Irish women to accept work as domestics, this was not a trend that continued into the second generation. Table 2.1 . . . reports the occupations in 1900 of first- and second-generation Irish, Italian, and Jewish women. The most striking observation is that whereas 71 percent of immigrant Irish women were classified as working in "domestic and personal service," only 25 percent of their children were so classified. Thus, by the second generation, Irish were not much more likely than other groups to work as domestics.

What the female children of Irish immigrants did was to follow in the footsteps of Italian and Jewish immigrants. As can also be seen in Table 2.1, by 1900 they were entering the needle trades and other branches of manufacturing, precisely at the point when second-generation Italian and Jewish women were abandoning these occupations in favor of work as saleswomen, bookkeepers, clerks, and the like. In a sense, Irish women started out on a lower occupational threshold than either Italians or Jews, and remained one generational step behind. But as far as domestic service is concerned, by the second generation few women in any of these groups were so employed.

Conclusion

Culture and family morality have little or nothing to do with explaining why Irish became domestics and Italians and Jews did not. It was not that Irish husbands were less

Table 2.1
Occupations of First- and Second-Generation Irish, Italian,
and Jewish Female Breadwinners, 1900

Ethnic group	Irish		Italian		Jews	
Generation	First	Second	First	Second	First	Second
Occupation*						
Domestic & personal service (includes waitresses)	71%	25%	21%	15%	18%	21%
Needle trades & textiles	16	29	48	33	44	26
Other manufacturing	6	17	20	28	23	17
Saleswomen, bookkeepers, clerks, etc.	5	19	10	20	14	31
Professional	2	10	1	4	1	5
	100%	100%	100%	100%	100%	100%
Number of cases	(245,792)	(388,108)	(20,307)	(5,751)	(35,030)	(5,781)

*The small number of cases whose occupations could not be classified are excluded from the percentages.

Source: Adapted from the *Reports of the United States Immigration Commission*, Vol. 1 (Washington, D. C.: Government Printing Office, 1911), pp. 834–36.

protective of their wives, but rather that immigrant Irish women were less likely to have husbands in the first place. It was not that as a group Irish had less aversion to working in other people's homes, but that their choices were far more limited. For those courageous women who migrated alone to the New World, domestic work was merely a temporary expedient to allow them to forge new lives. That the Irish had no cultural tolerance for domestic work is pointed up by the fact that they fled "the service" just as quickly as they could establish families of their own or gain access to more desirable employment. If other groups were spared the indignities of domestic labor, it is not that they had better cultural defenses or a superior moral code, but because their circumstances did not compel them to place economic survival ahead of their pride.

Notes

1. Frances A. Kellor, "Immigration and Household Labor," *Charities* XII (1904). Reprinted in Lydio F. Tomasi, ed., *The Italian in America* (New York: Center for Migration Studies, 1972), p. 39.

2. Thomas Kettel, *Southern Wealth and Northern Profits* (New York: G. W. & J. A. Wood, 1860), p. 102.

3. Theodore C. Blegen, ed., *Land of Their Choice* (St. Paul: University of Minnesota Press, 1955), pp. 435–36.

4. Theresa M. McBride, *The Domestic Revolution* (New York: Holmes & Meier, 1976), p. 38.

5. Quoted in McBride, op. cit., p. 14.

6. Kellor, op. cit., p. 39.

7. *Report of the United States Immigration Commission*, Vol. I (Washington, D.C.: Government Printing Office, 1911), pp. 830–38.

8. Robert Ernst, *Immigrant Life in New York City, 1825-1863* (Port Washington, N.Y.: Ira J. Friedman, 1949), p. 219.

9. *Report of the United States Immigration Commission*, op. cit., pp. 834–36.

10. Richard Gambino, *Blood of My Blood* (Garden City, N.Y.: Anchor, 1975), p. 14.

11. Report of the United States Immigration Commission, op. cit., p. 97.

12. Antonio Mangano, "The Italian Colonies of New York City," in *Italians in the City* (New York: Arno Press, 1975), p. 13.

13. Louise A. Tilly, "Urban Growth, Industrialization, and Women's Employment in Milan, Italy, 1881–1911," *Journal of Urban History* 3 (August 1977), pp. 476–78.

14. *Report of the United States Immigration Commission*, op. cit., p. 97.

15. Ibid.

16. Stanley C. Johnson, *A History of Emigration from the United Kingdom to North America, 1763–1812* (London: Frank Case, 1966), orig. 1913, chap. XI, p. 264.

17. Kellor, op. cit., p. 39.

18. *Report of the United States Immigration Commission*, op. cit., p. 173.

19. Oscar Handlin, *Boston's Immigrants* (New York: Atheneum, 1968), p. 46.

20. Walter F. Willcox, ed., *International Migrations,* Vol. II (New York: National Bureau of Economic Research, 1931), p. 274.

21. Richard Stivers, *A Hair of the Dog* (University Park: Pennsylvania State University Press, 1976) p. 56.

Discussion Questions

1. When White American women today take on similar poorly treated, low-paid jobs, how are they viewed by media and within your own friendship/family circles? Are they stigmatized or are they considered simply temporarily down on their luck?

2. Is the sort of domestic work that Irish immigrant women performed and were stereotyped for, seen in the same light in contemporary society? Do maids suffer the same social stigma or has this image changed?

3. Undocumented Mexican immigrants share with nineteenth-century Irish immigrant women the willingness to take on thankless low-paid jobs. When others discuss Mexican immigrants, have you heard cultural arguments in the media or friend and family circles similar to those used about Irish immigrant women? If so, what parts of Mexican immigrant culture are thought to predispose them to such employment? Do these arguments often center on Mexican women or are they generally about the entire group?

4. Have you ever taken a poorly paid job where you were treated badly? How did others see you as a result of this? How did this make you feel about yourself?

Reprinted from: Stephen Steinberg, "Why Irish Became Domestics and Italians and Jews Did Not." In *The Ethnic Myth: Race, Ethnicity, and Class in America,* pp. 151–155, 160–166. Copyright © 1981, 1989 by Stephen Steinberg. Reprinted with permission of Scribner, an imprint of Simon & Schuster Adult Publishing Group. ✦

3
Society of Strangers

Graham Robb

This reading is excerpted from a chapter in Graham Robb's book Homosexual Love in the Nineteenth Century. *In this piece he creates a framework that allows us to glimpse how sexuality, gender, race, and class interacted in the lives of nineteenth century men and women. In it he provides readers with a look at what life was like in that era for those who were attracted to persons of the same sex.*

Robb starts by mentioning that American poet Walt Whitman (1819–1892) looked forward to a "Uranian States of America." Uranian was a label used by and about homosexuals in the late nineteenth and early twentieth century. It is derived from Urning, one of the classes of sexual orientation that appeared in the work of Austrian writer Karl Heinrich Ulrichs in the 1860s (for further information go to: www.glbtq.com/social-sciences/Uranianism.html*).*

While nineteenth century people did not think of being gay, lesbian, bisexual, or transgendered as a marker of identity, a substantial number did seek same-sex intimate activity either to satisfy their physical and emotional needs or to earn money. Prostitution, both heterosexual and homosexual, was more common, and more tacitly accepted, than now. For many, the most effective way to find a willing partner was to pay for one. The pairings among homosexual men were fairly casual and ephemeral, but they were egalitarian. Race, religion, and class were not the major considerations that they were in wider society.

The lives and the options for women differed from those of men in those times. Robb notes that there is less information about lesbians than about gay men, but we do know that many of the prostitutes who serviced heterosexual men made their own domestic arrangements with other women. Although Robb does not mention it, it was also fairly common in this time period for respectable single women to share a home. There was even a popular term, "Boston marriage," for these arrangements. We do not know how many of these relationships involved sexual intimacy; however, most involved affection, and the term implies that at least some of them were sexual. Robb's chapter tells us that there is gay history, but he believes that while there were clubs, bathhouses, and balls for gay men in the nineteenth century, there was no real gay community with a set of traditions on which people today can build.

. . . **W**hen Walt Whitman looked forward to a Uranian States of America, the existing forms of homosexual community resembled the rest of society as much as Dodge City and Tombstone resembled Boston and Philadelphia. None of the various homosexual groups and mileux of the 19th century seems to present a model for the future. They tend to confirm the popular impression that homosexuality was inseparable from prostitution and crime.

The main hope for would-be founders of a Uranian society appeared to lie in the sheer extent of the territory.

Anyone who approaches the subject from standard historical and literary sources in which homosexuality is practically non-existent might find the figures almost unbelievable. At the end of the century, homosexual male prostitutes in Berlin accounted for about 20 percent of all prostitutes: a homosexual Berliner had approximately five times as many prostitutes to choose from as a heterosexual Berliner.[1] Lesbian prostitutes in Berlin were said by different writers to represent between about 20 per cent and 25 per cent of the total.[2] In 1836, a quarter of all female prostitutes in Paris were found to he lesbian. Half a century later, the proportion was thought to be even higher.

Some of these women were lesbians who earned a living by having sex with men. In brothels, as in prisons, female solidarity often took the form of lesbian 'marriages.'

But many were catering to what was obviously a lively market. 'Tribade-prostitutes,' were common on the streets of St. Petersburg, where they were known as *koshki* (she-cats).[3] In 1890s Paris, lesbian prostitutes solicited quite openly in the Bois de Boulogne and the Champs-Élysées.[4] Some shops—especially haberdasheries, perfumeries, boulangeries and patisseries—operated as unregistered brothels. There was some concern in the 1890s (though mostly in unsubstantiated newspaper reports) that rival groups of upper-class lesbians were actively recruiting innocent girls from shops and factories.

Homosexual prostitution, both male and female, was often mentioned as a common fact of city life, not only in the big cities but also in places that were not usually thought of as ant-hills of vice: Bordeaux, Toulouse, Turin, Zurich, Breslau, Sofia, Dublin, etc. A wealthy man like Marcel Proust did not have to rely on chance encounters. He funded his own *'maison de garçons'* at 11, rue de l'Arcade in Paris. Tchaikovsky could travel all over Europe and always be sure of finding someone to have sex with. Roger Casement found rent boys in Lisbon, Las Palmas and Buenos Aires. Practically every port, from San Francisco to San Sebastián, was a haven for homosexuals.

Brothels were vulnerable to 'clean-up' campaigns, especially in England. There were more molly houses in London in the early 19th century than there were male brothels in the early 20th. But alternatives were always available. In Europe and America, bathhouses offered sex and companionship and were usually much safer than brothels. According to Dr. Tarnovsky, 'blackmailing by bath-servants is unheard of, as they do the business in partnership, and share the proceeds.'[5] The Bains de Penthievre in Paris, which flourished in the 1890s, remained in business until the late 1960s.[6] Procedures were sufficiently similar from one country to the next to be understood by any visitor. In pre-Revolution St. Petersberg, for example, customers were shown an album of miniature photographs so that they could choose their attendant and his style or dress. The price list gave an additional measure of desirablity.

Just as men in the novels of Balzac and Zola visit brothels to enjoy the sort of easy and intelligent female company that they claim not to find at home, bathhouse customers could relax in a world where secret signs were no longer necessary. In the bathhouse, the normal situation was reversed: it would have taken more ingenuity to *avoid* a homosexual encounter. . . .

There were strenuous attempts to eradicate or regulate prostitution, but it was impossible to prevent the spread of homosexual districts. According to Rictor Norton, it was after the raid on Mother Clap's molly house in 1726 that the crime-infested area including Holborn and Saffron Hill became notorious as 'a molly district.'[7] Certain parts of Manhattan, especially Broadway and Central Park, were known to be frequented by 'sodomites' as early as the 1840s. Before 1910, almost every American city had a community of 'sexual inverts' with its own cafés, dance-halls, clubs and churches, and 'certain streets where, at night, every fifth man is an invert.'[8] By 1922, Earl Lind could talk of the boldness and 'political power' of sexual underworlds even in 'America's smaller cities west of the meridian of Kansas City.'[9] The flourishing communities described in Edmund White's *States of Desire: Travels in Gay America* (1980) had long histories.

Districts often grew up around particular spots: in Paris, the 'tree of love' on the Avenue Gabriel, the wild boar statue in the Tuileries Gardens, the boulevard in front of Tortoni's restaurant, the foyer of the Comédie Francaise; in London, the statue of Achilles in Hyde Park was a favourite meeting place ('the things that go on in front of that work of art are quite appalling,' says Mabel Chiltern in Wilde's *An Ideal Husband*).[10] The appearance of gay communities is a constant feature of urbanization. The first small groups in Sweden (Stockholm in 1883, Gothenburg in 1917) coincided with increased mobility (bicycle and train).[11] Railway stations, public urinals and parks, and more or less anywhere that afforded cover and an escape route, were likely to become cruising grounds and 'trysting places.'

The terms used by early observers—'plague,' 'infestation' and so on—suggest a natural, haphazard development, but these districts were not always unregulated. Visitor's guides to London and shrewd signs in pub windows warning the public to 'Beware of Sods!' suggest some rudimentary attempt to organize the market.[12] In the rural Champs-Élysées of the 1830s, cruising areas were sectioned off by ropes and park chairs, and sentries were posted, as Victor Hugo discovered one evening. A polite voice came from the darkness: 'M. Victor Hugo is requested to pass this time on the other side of the avenue.'[13]

The same effect was hugely magnified in Australia, which must have had the largest gay districts anywhere in the world in the 19th century. In some colonies, heterosexuality was the exception. Sydney had bars, hotels and drag shows for homosexual men several years before there was firm evidence of such things in the United States.[14] The theory that new Australians were corrupted on convict ships and delivered to the continent in a state of sudden homosexuality hardly does justice to what was evidently a buoyant gay society. In 1839, the *Sydney Gazette* revealed—to the horror of some and for the convenience of others—that sodomites were 'obtaining companions' at the Victoria Theatre, 'both during performances and at the intermissions,' and then 'drinking and supping with them at the hostelry across the way.'[15]

***

There is much less evidence of lesbian organization. Early signs of social activity are suspiciously lurid and usually relate to particular individuals. The famous but probably non-existent 'Club des Anandrynes' in Paris (1770s) was a running joke that was used to discredit lesbians like the actress Mlle. Raucourt.[16] There may have been confederations of actresses—there were hundreds of smutty poems on the subject—but actresses had several reasons apart from sexual preference to band together.[17] Most later evidence refers to institutions: brothels, prisons, factories, schools, hospitals and department stores. Almost none of the information comes directly from women, who tend in any case to be far less categorical than the men.

The groups described by Radclyffe Hall in 1928 are either circumstantial (the women's ambulance brigade in the First World War) or remarkably genteel and discreet (Natalie Clifford Barney's Paris salon).

Most lesbians seem to have favoured 'marriages' rather than groups, though this may simply reflect the more restricted social life of women. Berlin prostitutes often shared a home: the 'father' earned money by selling sex to men; the 'mother' stayed at home to cook and clean. In *fin-de-siècle* Paris, lesbian couples were known as *'petites soeurs'* (little sisters) because they declared their bond by wearing identical clothes. It seems, however, that the effect of urbanization on the development of lesbian communities was delayed rather than profoundly different. The evidence for other cities is patchy, but the lesbian quarter in Paris was so well developed by the end of the 19th century that it is hard to believe that it was unique in Europe.

Montmartre—especially the lively zone on the lower slopes—was already popular with lesbians in the 1880s and had some embryonic features of a lesbian community. Lesbian couples 'took over' certain apartment blocks and restaurants.[18] Cafés like the Souris and the Rat Mort were filled at night with noisy crowds of women wearing gaudy hats and oddly assorted clothes.[19] 'One would have thought,' said the novelist Catulle Mendès, 'that they had dressed in a hurry at a secondhand clothes shop while the police were battering down the door.'[20] The fact that they stood rather than sat, wore no gloves and used the argot of artists and pimps was a sign of defiant independence. There was a wide range of ages and classes. The only men were the waiters (usually homosexual), a few sniggering tourists and some special friends of the house, the most famous being Toulouse-Lautrec. . . .

***

Separating exploitation from free exchange can be just as hard for us as it was for 19th-century policemen and novelists. The famously available and beautifully uniformed royal guardsmen in London for instance had a long tradition of prostituting themselves before settling down and marrying or emigrating....[21] In the early 20th century, soldiers in America and Europe could often be hired for sexual entertainment.

These arrangements are probably best described as mutual exploitation. There was an understanding that the customer (usually middle-class and well-off) would show appreciation if the relationship developed into an affair. An ungenerous 'twank' or 'bag,' as London guardsman called their clients, could always be punished or blackmailed into being reasonable....

...Gondoliers, too, had a long tradition of prostitution. The aim of most gondoliers was to support their family by supplementing their wages, especially in the winter. A rigid code of honour and strict rules of conduct allowed them to keep their self-respect (passive intercourse was shameful; active intercourse was a source of income). Boys in most Italian cities also served foreign tourists, as did Tyrolean peasants, who offered special out-of-season rates.

'Subculture' is an inappropriately portentous term for these arrangements. Sex was—and still is in some parts of the world—a holiday trade comparable to giving guided tours and selling ice cream. Some of the young men known to lovers of Venice... were taking advantage of an adventurous libido and a sense of moral freedom to acquire some little luxuries or to avoid what they considered to be more tedious or demanding work. Some of them might even have been gay. Most, however, were trapped by poverty and abused by pimps. The word 'tradition,' applied to gondoliers and guardsmen, does not preclude coercion and victimization.

Exotic scenery helped to maintain the idea of a sexual paradise in the mind of the paying customer, but desperate paupers could be found all over Europe and America....

The difference between prostitution and mutual exchange is sometimes more obvious. It has been suggested that some boys became Post Office messengers in order to enhance their gay life, but most young prostitutes were simply victims of exploitation. Jack Saul's 'happy hooker' narrative, *The Sins of the Cities of the Plain* (1881), is a work of pornography, not a disinterested personal account. Thousands of infant vagrants were recruited by pimps or served a gruesome apprenticeship. The real-life equivalents of Fagin's gang of urchins on Saffron Hill would not have stopped at picking gentlemen's pockets....

***

The close historical ties of homosexual groups with prostitution are misleading. Many heterosexual men with money resorted to prostitutes, but usually with simpler aims. For homosexual men, there were also social, practical and emotional reasons to descend into the underworld.

The only certain way to find a partner was to head for the red-light district. Heterosexual men could dispense with risky expeditions at any social gathering, everyone could be presumed heterosexual and a certain amount of flirting was acceptable. Homosexual men could either rely on a dubious 'sixth sense' or go to places—clubs, brothels or private homes—where the selection of partners had already been made.

Sex was not always the prime motive. Some establishments became regular meeting places, either because the proprietors themselves were homosexual or because they knew how to exploit a special clientele. Profit was always more powerful than prejudice....

The most popular public venues were balls, ranging from semi-private dances to the regular masked balls attended by hundreds of men—and sometimes women—in drag. The biggest European balls were those of Vienna, Berlin and Paris: at carnival time, the usual ban on transvestism was suspended. By the 1900s, 'invert balls' were being held about twice a week in Berlin.

These were not the 'orgies' of popular myth. The 'Viennese balls' in Berlin were held with the permission of the police, who used them to keep an eye on criminals....

By far the commonest type of organization was the club or the coterie. Practically every town seems to have had small groups of homosexual men who either met at someone's home or travelled to the nearest city. Even this was a risky undertaking. A group of Frenchmen in the 1850s went on regular sprees to Lyon, but always on different trains, 'or else we'd be the talk of the town the next day.'[22] Other shared interests could serve as a front. The Eagle Street College in Bolton (from the 1870s) was a reading group of Whitmaniacs.[23] The 'Háfiz Tavern' in St. Petersburg (1900s), which functioned as a private homosexual cabaret, could always claim to be a club for fans of medieval Persian poetry.[24] The 'Lohengrin' in Berlin was ostensibly a Wagner admiration society.[25] Some clubs hid behind euphemisms; the Reunion philanthropique in Brussels, the Club degli Ignoranti in Rome, or the Klub der Vernünftigen in Vienna.[26,27]

The rituals developed by some of these clubs helped to reinforce a sense of social identity. The parodies of childbirth and nursing performed in London molly houses seem to be a mostly 18th-century phenomenon. But marriages continued to be a common expression of love and sociality. A surprising number of priests and vicars were prepared to perform marriages for homosexual men or lesbians, and there were also many private arrangements.[28] Anne Lister and her lover Marianne agreed to 'solemnize' their mutual vows 'by taking the sacrament together.'[29] They routinely used the words 'marriage,' 'mistress,' 'wife' and 'divorce' without inverted commas.

These marriages were not always subterranean affairs. There is evidence from late-19th-century America, Britain, France and Germany of hotels rented for weddings, male brides in gorgeous gowns, exotic honeymoons (sometimes ruined by blackmailers) and bridal bouquets kept under glass in front parlours. These events were the feast days of small communities, dates in an otherwise blank calendar. The fact that they took place at all shows a remarkable degree of organization.

***

The sheer variety of these groups and coteries makes it hard to identify anything like a coherent 'gay community.' Some groups were exclusively working class; many were open to homosexual and bisexual men and women, others were tightly closed. Some of the most influential groups, like the Cambridge 'Apostles' or the coterie at Exeter College, Oxford, that published *The Chameleon* (p. 219), were groups of friends rather than spontaneous expressions of gay culture.

The importance of these groups is easily exaggerated. . . .

The only real homosexual 'subcultures' in which established customs survived from one generation to the next were institutional—prisons, brothels, navies, or the American hobo subculture.[30] These mini-societies had their own initiation ceremonies, well-developed argots, including a language of tattoos (notably hearts and pansies), and recognized types of relationships.[31] But they were also obviously defined by something other than sexuality.

Diversity is far more apparent than uniformity. The idea that gay culture is characterized in certain periods by certain kinds of relationship has proved to be vulnerable to fresh evidence. There are no lasting patterns of sexual activity based on age difference or sexual role. . . .

The one feature that stands out is the relative unimportance of race, religion and class. Some drag balls in America were attended by blacks and whites.[32] Adolfo Canminha's revolutionary novel *Bom-Crioulo* (Rio de Janeiro, 1895), in which a black sailor loves a young white cabin boy, was naturalistic, not fantastic. Throughout Europe and America, it was common for middle-class men to take a working-class lover. But this seems to have been largely a matter of circumstance. Class differences—like differences of religion and race—were overridden rather than abolished by desire. 'Equality' could become desperately tedious. Mikhail Kuzmin longed for a friend who could satisfy him both intellectually and physically: 'a comrade in tastes, reveries and delights.'. . .[33]

Many gays and lesbians still feel marginalized by the notion of a 'gay and lesbian community,' the coherence of which exists primarily in the minds of market researchers. It may be after all that the distinguishing features of homosexual groups will turn out to be more practical than fundamental. At the present rate of change, monogamy will soon be a primarily homosexual phenomenon.

It may be unprofitable in any case to look to the gay past for firm traditions. The most remarkable characteristic of these early forms of homosocial organization is not their coherence but their ability to survive in the diffuse manner of resistance groups or nomads. Some coteries had an astonishingly wide range. When clubs or homes were raided, extensive networks of friends often came to light. Many people had large collections of photographs, either personal or pornographic. Visiting cards with photo-portraits were exchanged like cigarette cards. Clubs corresponded with one another and operated as consulates and tourist information bureaux. Anyone travelling to another city could be given introductions and geographical information of the sort that was supplied in a less precise form by voyeuristic city guides. . . .

The fragile sense of a gay community was based on experiences that seemed to preclude the possiblity of a community. But then why should 'comrades' simply form another society like the old one? This apparent promiscuity was a life outside the society that had caused such grief and shame.

The men who flocked to alleyways and *pissoirs,* who offered themselves to strangers and explored dark *quartiers* they would otherwise never have seen, were being sociable, not subversive. Fleetingness was essential, not just for practical reasons. The poems of Constantine Cavafy celebrate transcience as a liberation. The past could never stick to single, unrepeated moments of physical pleasure. History could be rewritten in the folds of a sheet and then smoothed out again. It was the revenge of chance on inevitability, sudden intimacy instead of endless anonymity, the memory of the body replacing the memory of the educated mind. And when they returned to the everyday world, lovers could be certain in any case, like Cavfy's student Myrtias, in 'Dangerous Thoughts' (1911), to find the spirit as ascetic as before.

Notes

1. 20 per cent of all prostitutes: Prime-Stevenson (1908), ch. 6.

2. 20 per cent and 25 percent of the total: Moll, 309; Chevalier, 233; Prime-Stevenson (1908), ch, 6; Rüling, also in Blashis-Phelan, 149; see also Elisa-beth Dauthendy, in *JfsZ,* VIII (1906), 285–300; Zimmerman.

3. *koshki:* Healey, 53.

4. lesbian prostitution in Paris: Chevalier, 236–7; Corbin, 214; Taxil, 263.

5. 'blackmailing by bath-servants': Tamovsky 146.

6. Bains de Penthièvre: M. Sibalis, in Higgs, 25.

7. Holborn and Saffron Hill: Norton (1992), 72.

8. 'every fifth man is an invert': Ellis, 352.

9. 'meridian of Kansas City': 'Earl Lind' (1922), 6.

10. particular spots: Delcourt, 285–9; Ariès-Duby, 588; Citron, I, 381–2; Coward, 239; Fournier-Verneuil, 281, 314 and 337; Merrick, 288; M. Sibalis, in Higgs, 16–17; McCormick, 356; Wilde, *An Ideal Husband,* II.

11. groups in Sweden: Rydström, and thesis: 'Sinners and Citizens: Bestiality and Homosexuality in Sweden, 1880–1950' (U. of Stockholm).

12. 'Beware of Sods!': Anon, (1850), 405.

13. Victor Hugo: Ashbee (1879), 407–10.

14. Sydney: Norton (1997), 259–60; also Ellis, 185.

15. *Sydney Gazette:* M. Smith, 'Australia's Gay Heritage,' in Bob Hay, 'The Sodomites' Guide to Colonial Sydney:' *http://members.ozemail.com.au/~vombatus*

16. Mlle. Raucourt: e.g. Coward, 246. See also Stambolian-Marks, 359–60.

17. poems on actresses: Robb (1993), 178–82.

18. lesbian apartment blocks: Chevalier, 237.

19. lesbian cafés: Frey, 374–5; Taxil; etc.

20. 'One would have thought': Mendès (1890), 493.

21. London guardsmen: Ackerly, 174–5; Leeves, 27—29 April 1850; also Lorrain (1922), 176; Porter-Weeks, 32.

22. A group of Frenchmen: Carlier, 442–3.

23. Eagle Street College: C. White, 218.

24. 'Háfiz Tavern': Malmstad-Bogomolov, 103-5.

25. The 'Lohengrin': Hirchfeld (1905), 53.

26. Some clubs hid: O. de Joux, in Müller, 80.

27. *'Vernünftig'* (rational) and *'unvernunftig'* (irrational) were insiders' terms for 'homosexual' and 'heterosexual' respectively, as in Platen's poem, 'Was Vernünft'ge hoch verehren . . .'

28. homosexual marriages: e.g. Carlier, 349–50 and 457; Ellis, 250; Norton (1992), 199.

29. 'taking the sacrament': Lister, *I Know,* 160.

30. American hobo subculture: F. Willard, in Ellis, 360–7; Rev. F. C. Laubach, in Chauncey (1994), 397 n. 56.

31. language of tattoos: Lacassagne, 'Tatouage,' 124–5; also Kurella, 112.

32. blacks and whites: Katz (1976), 49, on a 'miscegenation dance' in Saint Louis.

33. 'a comrade in tastes': Malmstad-Bogomolov, 145.

Works Cited

(Unless otherwise indicated, the place of publication is London, New York, or Paris.)

Ackerly, J. R. *My Father and Myself* (1968). Intro. W. H. Auden (1969). New York Review Books, 1999.

Anon. *Yokel's Preceptor, or More Sprees in London! Being a Regular and Curious Show-Up of all the Rigs and Doings of the Flash Cribs in this Great Metropolis* [etc.]. Dugdale, *c.* 1850.

Ariès, Phillipe and Georges Duby, gen. eds. *Historie de la vie privée. IV. De la Révolution à la Grande Guerre.* Seuil, 1987.

Ashbee, H. S. *Centuria librorum absconditorum [etc.].* Privately printed, 1879.

Blasius, Mark and S. Phelan, eds. *We Are Everywhere. A Historical Sourcebook of Gay and Lesbian Politics.* Routledge, 1997.

Carlier, Francois. *Études de pathologie sociale. Les Deux prostitutions.* Dentu, 1887.

Chauncey, G. *Gay New York. The Making of the Gay Male World, 1890–1940.* 1994; Flamingo, 1995.

Chevalier, Julien. *Une maladie de la personnalité: l'inversion sexuelle; psychophysiologie; sociologie; tératologie.* Pref. A. Lacassagne. Storck; Masson, 1893.

Citron, Pierre. *La Poésie de Paris dans la littérature française.* 2 vols. Éditions de Minuit, 1961.

Corbin, Alain. *Les Filles de noce. Misère sexuelle et prostitution (19ᵉ siècle).* 1978; Flammarion, 1982.

Coward, David. 'Attitudes to Homosexuality in 18th-Century France.' *Journal of European Studies,* 10 (1980), 231–55.

Delcourt, Pierre. *Le Vice à Paris.* Piaget, 1888.

'Earl Lind' (a.k.a 'Ralph Werther' and 'Jennie June'). *Autobiography of an Androgyne.* Ed. A. W. Herzog. New York: The Medico-Legal Journal, 1918; Arno Press, 1975.

——. *The Female-Impersonators. A Sequel to the Autobiography of an Androgyne and an account of some of the author's experiences during his six years' career as instinctive female-impersonator in New York's Underworld; together with the life stories of androgyne associates and an outline of his subsequently acquired knowledge of kindred phenomena of human character and psychology.* Ed. A. W. Herzog. New York: The Medico-Legal Journal, 1922; Arno Press, 1975.

Ellis, Havelock. *Studies in the Psychology of Sex.* II. 1910; New York: Random House, 1936.

Fournier-Verneuil. *Paris, tableau moral et philosophique.* Chez les principaux libraires, 1826.

Frey, Julia. *Toulouse-Lautrec. A Life.* Weidenfeld and Nicolson, 1994.

Healey, Dan. *Homosexual Desire in Revolutionary Russia: the Regulation of Sexual and Gender Dissent.* Chicago, 2001.

Higgs, David, ed. *Queer Sites. Gay Urban Histories Since 1600.* Routledge, 1999.

Hirschfeld, Magnus. *Berlins drittes Geschlecht. Schwules and lesbisches Leben in Berlin der Jahrhundertwende.* 1905; ed. M. Herzer. Rosa Winkel, 1991. Tr. *Le Troisième sexe, Les Homosexuels de Berlin* (1908).

Katz, Jonathan. *Gay American History. Lesbians and Gay Men in the U.S.A. A Documentary.* Thomas Y. Crowell, 1976.

Kurella, Hans. *Naturgeschichte des Verbrechers: Grundzüge der criminellen Anthropologie und Criminalpsychologie.* Stuttgart: Enke, 1893.

Lacassagne, Albert. 'Pédérastie.' *Dictionnaire encyclopédique des sciences médicales.* 2nd series (1869–89), XXII, 239–59; 'Tatouage.' 3rd series (1874–87), XVI, 124–5.

Leeves, Edward. *Leaves from a Victorian Diary.* Intro. J. Sparrow. The Alison Press/Secker & Warburg, 1985.

Lister, Anne. *I Know My Own Heart. The Diaries of Anne Lister 1791–1840.* Ed. H. Whitbread. New York UP, 1992. [Excerpts from 1817–1824.]

Lorrain, Jean. *Le Vice errant.* II. *Les Noronsoff.* Ollendorff, 1922.

Malmstad, John E. and N. Bogomolov. *Mikahail Kuzmin. A Life in Art.* Harvard, 1999.

McCormick, Ian. *Sexual Outcasts.* II. Routledge, 2000.

Mendès, Catulle. *La Maison de la vieille. Roman contemporain.* 1894; ed. J.-J. Lefrère et al. Champ Vallon, 2000.

——. *Méphistophéla. Roman contemporain.* Dentu, 1890.

Merrick, Jefferey. 'Commissioner Foucault, Inspector Noël, and the "Pederasts" of Paris, 1780–3.' *Journal of Social History,* XXXII, 2 (1998), 287–307.

Moll, Albert. *Die conträre Sexualempfindung.* 1891; 2nd ed., 1893. Tr. Drs Pactet and Romme. *Les Perversions de l'instinct génital. Étude sur l'inversion sexuelle basée sur des documents officiels.* Carré, 1893.

Müller, Klaus. *Aber in meinem Herzen sprach eine Stimme so laut. Homosexuelle Autobiographien und medizinische Pathographien im neunzehnten Jahrhundert.* Rosa Winkel, 1991.

Norton, Rictor. *Mother Clap's Molly House. The Gay Subculture in England 1700–1830.* GMP, 1992.

Porter, Kevin and J. Weeks, eds. *Between the Acts. Lives of Homosexual Men, 1885–1967.* Routledge, 1991.

Prime-Stevenson, Edward Irenaeus. *The Intersexes. A History of Similisexualism as a Problem in Social Life.* By Xavier Mayne. Naples: privately printed, *c.* 1908.

Robb, Graham. *La Poésie de Baudelaire et la poésie française, 1838–1852.* Aubier, 1993.

Rüling, Anna. 'Welches Interesse hat die Frauenbewegung an der Lösung des homosexuellen Problems?' *JfsZ,* VII, 1 (1905), 129–51.

Rydström, Jens. '"Sodomitical Sins are Threefold": Typologies of Bestiality, Masturbation and Homosexuality in Sweden, 1880–1950.' *Journal of the History of Sexuality,* IX, 3 (July 2000), 240–76.

[Saul, Jack.] *The Sins of the Cities of the Plain, or The Recollections of a Mary-Ann. With Short Essays on Sodomy and Tribadism.* London, Leicester Square, 1881.

Smith, Morton. *The Secret Gospel. The Discovery and Interpretation of the Secret Gospel According to Mark.* 1973; Aquarian Press, 1985.

Stambolian, George and Elaine Marks, eds. *Homosexualities and French Literature. Cultural Contexts/ Critical Texts.* Cornell UP, 1979.

Tarnovsky, Veniamin. *The Sexual Instinct and its Morbid Manifestations from the Double Standpoint of*

Jurisprudence and Psychiatry. 1885; tr. W. C. Costello and A. Allinson. Carrington, 1898.

Taxil, Léo. *La Corruption fin-de-siècle.* Noirot, *c.* 1909.

White, Chris, ed. *Nineteenth-Century Writings on Homosexuality. A Sourcebook.* Routledge, 1999.

White, Edmund. *States of Desire. Travels in Gay America.* 1980; Picador, 1986.

Zimmerman, Bonnie, ed. *Lesbian Histories and Cultures. An Encyclopedia.* Garland, 2000.

Discussion Questions

1. In the nineteenth century, factors such as class, race/ethnicity, and sexuality circumscribed access to potential romantic and sexual partners, and gay men and lesbians were often forced to find partners through prostitution or in places that were not entirely respectable. What means do people have available today to find partners? Are the means different for people of different sexual orientations, genders, racial/ethnic backgrounds, or social class positions?

2. Why is it important to study sexuality as Robb does in historical and geographic context?

3. Why do you think there is less information about lesbians in the nineteenth and early twentieth century than about gay men? What factors about society or about the people who wrote about society in those times would limit recorded knowledge about women and their sexuality?

4. Robb seems to think that what happened in the nineteenth and early twentieth centuries is not relevant for late twentieth and early twenty-first century lesbian, gay, bisexual, and transgendered (LGBT) people trying to find or build community. Why do you agree or disagree with this position?

4

Congressional Record—House (67 Cong., 2nd Sess.)

On June 13, 2005, the U.S. Senate passed a resolution of apology for failing to pass anti-lynching legislation (see http://www.msnbc.msn.com/id/8206697/). American lynchings were horrific public spectacles where mainly Black men (although some victims were Black women and children as well as White men) were subjected to mutilation, torture, castration, and immolation all before crowds of White onlookers, including law enforcement, who took body parts of the victims as well as picture postcards as souvenirs of the event. These almost ritual public executions were found to be "at the hands of persons unknown" since almost no one was prosecuted for these atrocities.

This chapter takes us back to a 1922 debate between two American congressmen—Mr. Dyer from Illinois and Mr. Sumners from Texas. In his argument before the House of Representatives, Mr. Dyer attempts to debunk the gendered and racial characterization of lynching, often used to justify the crime as a fitting form of public and community retribution. Dyer strikes at the heart of the lynching argument—that it is a punishment of Black men for their rape of White women—stating that statistics gathered by the Tuskegee Institute and the NAACP determine this argument to be false.

Mr. Sumners, on the other hand, appeals to the House via two separate fronts. He challenges the anti-lynching bill by appealing to those who favored states' rights, arguing that such a law would allow the federal government undue powers. But his second argument, perhaps, might have carried the most emotional weight. Here he dismisses the sta-

tistical evidence discussed by Dyer and mocks Black activism as mere "agitation" by inferior stock. In fact, Sumners makes it eminently clear that Blacks as a group are inferior and unworthy of consideration, relegated to tenth-class citizenship. Instead, Mr. Sumners paints vivid pictures in the minds of his fellow House members of "evil," "brutish," Black rapists and "chaste," White "virginal" victims—appealing to the worst sort of racial, gendered stereotypes. In addition, in paternalistic tones, he emphasizes that White women epitomize and represent not only purity of body but also purity of blood—women become the gendered embodiment of White racial purity in the face of gendered Black male bestiality.

Mr. Dyer. Mr. Chairman and gentlemen of the committee, my interest in this legislation comes from lynchings that have occurred in my own State. My special attention to this matter came five years ago when at the very doors of my home occurred one of the most disgraceful lynchings and riots known to civilization. That occurred in the city of East St. Louis, Ill. I introduced a resolution at that time asking that the House of Representatives investigate that lynching and ascertain the cause and see if there was something we might do to make such disgraceful events scarce and impossible for the future. In that lynching and in that mob riot there were 100 and more people injured and killed—innocent men and innocent women.

Some of the most outrageous murders known to humanity took place at this time. Little children were taken away from their mother's arms and thrown into the fire.

This affair grew out of a killing that occurred in East St. Louis. There had been race feeling in that city, and there was an automobile containing police officers driven through sections of East St. Louis that were populated largely by colored people, and while they were doing this they were fired upon—fired upon by somebody, presumably, although I do not think it was ever ascertained as a fact, by some Negroes. A man was killed, another was wounded, and this lynching, this murder of more than 100 people, innocent as you and I of any connection with that affair, took place. Some people started out to find the people who had killed this man for the purpose of lynching them.

This legislation, if enacted into law, will cover cases of that kind notwithstanding the statement made by some gentleman previous to the holiday recess that this legislation is aimed at only the Southern States, where lynchings have been promiscuous. Mr. Chairman, I may say in this connection that that thought never entered my mind in what I have done to secure this legislation. I want to make it so that lynchings of the kind that happened in East St. Louis, Ill., will not go unpunished to the fullest extent possible.

***

Lynchings have been going on in this country for these many years without any special effort apparently being made to prosecute or to punish the guilty. It is true that some few of those who participated in that East St. Louis lynching were convicted and sent to the penitentiary. But that is one of the few instances to my knowledge where there has ever been any conviction.

The charge has been made here, Mr. Chairman, that these lynchings are caused by attacks upon women, that they are the result of rape. That is as far from the truth as many of the other extravagant statements that have been made.

I have taken pains to obtain the best possible information regarding lynchings in the last 35 years or more, and I have here a statement prepared by the president of the Tuskegee Institute of Alabama, under date of December 31, 1921. In a word, it says that in this 36-year period, from 1885 to 1921, there [have] been 4,096 lynchings. Of this number 810 were charged with rape or attempted rape. In other words, of the total number of 4,096, only 810 were even charged with this horrible crime or its attempt. I have taken pains to have other statements compiled. I have one here prepared by the National Association for the Advancement and Protection of Colored People stating that during the period from 1889 up until December 1919, there were 3,434 known lynchings in the United States.

Of that number 570 have been charged with rape or attempted rape—570 out of 3,434.

It is especially emphasized in this connection that there have been many lynchings where the victim was not even accused of rape but in which cases the lynchers gave rape as the cause in order to justify their action. They did this, of course, because they felt that a great majority of the American public would not censure them for lynching under those circumstances; and that is, I take it, why some of the gentlemen rise in their seats and say that this bill should be labeled a bill to legalize rape.

***

Mr. Sumners of Texas. Mr. Chairman and gentlemen of the committee, I assume that there is no difference of opinion among men representing the different sections of the country in reference to the fact that the crime of lynching is a crime which nobody can defend, a crime which must be suppressed. The question is how best to proceed to do the thing that ought to be done. Before beginning a discussion of this bill I want to challenge the slanders which have been heaped upon the South by a lot of these hired Negro agitators and white negroettes that have been going over the country falsely representing my people. I received the other day a statement from the Tuskegee Institute. The gentleman who has just taken his seat quoted practically all of his statistics and gave practically all his information from that source. Under the date of December 31, 1921, they sent out broadcast, with release for publication dated January 1, "The lynch record for 1921," from which I quote, "there were 63 persons lynched in 1921. Of those 62 were in the South and one in the North." I do not know how I happened to clip this out, but the *Washington Post* of July 16, 1921, carried a statement under these headlines, which I quote: "Three Negroes hanged by mob in Duluth; 5,000 seize prisoners at police headquarters; troops ordered out. Attack on young white girl rouses crowd's fury." These Negroes were connected with a circus. They took a white girl into the circus grounds and ravished her. This Duluth, Minn., mob hung them all to a telephone pole in the middle of the city. Three at once in one place. And yet we are told that only one person was lynched in the entire North during all of the year 1921. The gentleman who has just taken his seat told you of a killing in East St. Louis of 100 people at one time.

***

Let me tell you something. Suppose this other thing happens—and you can do it under this bill—suppose that a black man takes a little white child and drags her off into seclusion where no voice can hear and no hand can help, and rapes that child, and the father of that child and the brothers of the child come up on him and kill him, and the Federal Government takes them away in the face of public sentiment and places them in the Federal penitentiary, and then has a tax of $10,000 levied against the county for the benefit of the rapist's family, a part of which sum might go to buy that family an automobile to ride by the home of the innocent victim, do you think, as a matter of common sense, with such a policy you could long prevent a condition in that country like those which developed in East St. Louis, Omaha, and Chicago?

***

Mr. Chairman, I am opposed to mob violence, to the armies which provoke mob violence, and to the conditions which permit those crimes to result in mob violence. I am opposed to this bill because it would increase mob violence by encouraging the crimes which are the most provocative of mob violence and which more than all things else combined create the condition out of which mob violence as a punishment for other offenses arises. I am opposed to this bill because the interposition of Federal power would lessen the sense of local responsibility and retard the growth of local purpose to suppress mob violence. I am opposed to this bill because it is unconstitutional and appeals for its support to the very spirit which it denounces—the spirit of disregard for law and for the sacredness of the official oath. This bill can not pass this House unless it is

put through by that same spirit which inspires the mob, when, backed by the courage of numbers, excused in conscience by the law's delays and alleged miscarriage of justice, they crush through by the sheer weight of numbers the legal barriers which deny the right to proceed in the manner undertaken and do an unlawful thing.

You are asked to do a thing contrary to the supreme law of the land in order to make certain and quick a punishment alleged to be deserved. Gentlemen, that is the identical appeal of the leader of the mob. This bill has incorporated therein provisions which no lawyer in this House or elsewhere can defend and but few, if any, have reputations so poor or so well established that they will hazard them in the attempt. Yet you will be asked to pass the bill. They whisper in your ears "political expediency" and ask you to yield to it. That is the same whisper which comes to the ear of the sherriff when the mob is battering at the jail door. Wonderful example they ask you to set to the constabulary of this country.

I am opposed to lynching. If I were at home and I heard that an effort was being made to arouse the mob spirit, I would oppose it.

If I had been in Omaha when they were about to mob the mayor because he had stood beween the mob and its intended victim, I would have opposed that. To-day the Constitution of the United States stands at the door, guarding the governmental integrity of the States, the plan and the philosophy of our system of government, and the gentleman from Missouri, rope in hand, is appealing to you to help him lynch the Constitution. I am opposed to that. If it were not for the tragic possibilities which are involved and the duty imposed, if I were actuated by political considerations, I would merely register a general protest and hope for favorable action. But, gentlemen, this is not a matter with regard to which either side can afford to play politics.

***

This bill, as I say, challenges the efficiency of the government of the States, and here is the difference between this bill and the other bills that we have been enacting here expanding the Federal power: This bill, challenging as it does the relative governmental efficiency of the States and the integrity of purpose of their governmental agencies, placing the Federal Government, as it does, in the attitude of an arbitrary dictator assuming coercive powers over the States, their officers, and their citizens in matters of local police control, would do incomparable injury to the spirit of mutual respect and trustful cooperation between the Federal Government and the States essential to the efficiency of government. As a precedent, this bill, establishing the principles which it embodies and the congressional powers which it assumes to obtain, would strip the States of every element of sovereign power, control, and final responsibility for the personal and property protection of its citizens, and would all but complete the reduction of the States to a condition of governmental vassalage awaiting only the full exercise of the congressional power.

Gentlemen, I do not excuse the sixty-odd lynchings that occurred in the South in a year, but when you consider the millions of black people who live in that country, and when you consider the fact that we do have white men there who are not law-abiding, just as we do have the black men there who are not law-abiding, and you measure what occurs there by what occurred in East St. Louis, Chicago, and Omaha, it shows that the people in that great section of the country are doing the best they can.

***

We are tired of it. We know it is not right. The conscience of the country is revolting against these conditions, and if we could get a little more help from you people, exerted with the black people to encourage them to run out the criminal element from among them while we work on the criminal element of the white people instead of sending these Negro agitators down there to preach social equality among my people, you would aid more than you are aiding now. We might just as well understand ourselves, gentlemen. That day never will come—there is no neces-

sity for anybody mistaking it—that day never will come when the black and the white man will stand upon a plane of social equality in this country, and that day never will come in any section of the United States when you will put a black man in office above the white man. That never will happen. It never can happen on the face of God Almighty's earth. It has not happened in 4,000 years and never will. Oh, you can elect one here and there in communities where you have them in control. You can give him a little recognition to keep the boys lined up, but he is under white control, and you never will surrender the control of your government in any community to the black race. It can not happen.

***

And it is a rather interesting thing, too, that as society has established legislatures and courts, men in my part of the country have never yielded to the courts established by legislatures or to laws established by legislatures the protection of their women. There is just one thing they will not litigate. Nowhere under God Almighty's sky will they yet litigate the issue of a foul wrong committed against their women. They have not yielded that yet. You see, they had that jurisdiction first. The delegated authority to the courts after the courts got there, but they were there first. That will change as pioneer influences and ideals give way. It is changing now. There is another thing that makes the situation more difficult in the South. I do not know why, but somewhere in the great purpose of God Almighty He has determined to preserve, for a while yet, at least, these lines of racial cleavage that He has drawn the races of men.

***

When a white woman is raped by a black man the call to the man is from his two strongest most primitive instincts. No doubt when men lived in caves the strongest instinct of the man was to his woman. The next strongest instinct is to protect the blood. When the call comes from the woman, crying out from the depths of her outraged chastity, there comes to the man a call which reaches back to the days when he was a savage in the cave, and he goes. When that call comes from the woman who has been raped by a man of alien blood, woman, who in every age of the world has been the faithful guardian of the purity of the race—when that call comes it is the call of his woman and the call of his blood, and he he goes. It is not an easy situation to deal with. He goes not alone. His neighbors, whose women live under the same danger, go with him. The impulse is to kill, to kill as a wild beast would be killed.*

Note

* *Congressional Record—House* (67 Cong., 2 Ses.), January 4, 1922.

Discussion Questions

1. Can you find similar views of "evil Black rapists" or "Black male bestiality" in media images of Black men today? Can you find them among your own friendship/family circles? How do you respond to such views? Do these views sometimes encompass all men of color today?

2. It is well-documented historically that White men who were slave masters raped slave women. Has this, in turn, created a cultural view of "evil White male rapists"? Why or why not?

3. Is the view of the "pure, virginal, White woman" who needs male protection and/or embodies the purity of the White race, which was so prevalent in the rhetoric in favor of lynching, still alive today in some form? If so, what forms has it taken and for which constituencies?

4. How did you personally respond to Mr. Sumners' arguments in this chapter? Did they resonate with your own views or differ? Why or why not? ✦

5

'Gone With the Wind'

The Invisibility of Racism in American History Textbooks

James W. Loewen

This reading is taken from James W. Loewen's book, Lies My Teacher Told Me: Everything Your American History Textbook Got Wrong. He dedicated the book to "all American history teachers who teach against their textbooks." To show us what is being taught, he compared twelve widely-used high-school texts with each other and with the facts historians actually know about slavery, the Founding Fathers, the opinions of Lincoln and Douglas, the Civil War, Reconstruction, and the early years of the twentieth century. Loewen believes that much of what is presented in textbooks is distorted, biased, or completely incorrect. He also notes that a good deal has simply been omitted. To understand why history texts contain distortions and omissions, we need to understand the way books are written, the influences of popular culture and politics, and the purposes to which history can be put. In Loewen's piece, gender is framed solely from the standpoints of male historical figures, class is largely a product of slavery and Jim Crow era politics, and race becomes the centerpiece for his analysis.

History books both shape and reflect our images of ourselves. They give us heroes to worship, villains to hate, and explanations and justifications for events past and present. Textbooks show us heroic images of people such as Patrick Henry, George Washington, and Thomas Jefferson. They don't confuse us with the knowledge that these Founding Fathers were slave owners whose personal opinions were conflicted if not outspokenly racist. The authors who write the books and the companies that publish them are products of their times and places, and they hope to make money by having books widely adopted. Texts are selected for schools by local and statewide committees. Therefore, it is not surprising that local and regional politics are reflected in selections. Until the civil rights movement, the influence of the White south prevailed. Slavery was treated as a relatively benign institution and the Civil War was often referred to as "the War between the States." Times change. Loewen points out that the books used today do acknowledge the devastating social and economic impact slavery had on Black Americans. However, what is still missing is an analysis of its impact on White Americans, its legacy of cultural racism. The books do not discuss the causes, forms, or effects of racism.

As a case in point, the influence of slavery and later of racism on our domestic and foreign policies is omitted. Policies toward American Indian nations, for example, were designed to expand slaveholding territories and secure borders to prevent slaves from escaping and joining with indigenous people of color. Policies toward France and Spain were shaped both by a fear of Haiti becoming a model for other racially mixed or predominantly Black colonies seeking independence and a desire to secure borders. The Seminole were originally a collection of various Native American groups that had absorbed runaway slaves and free Blacks. They forged themselves into a nation and defended themselves in the Seminole Wars (1816–1818 and 1835–1842) because they were unwilling to surrender their Black members and move west.

Reconstruction followed the Civil War. The textbook images are largely of ex-slaves, either helpless and destitute, as if they had not been working during the pre-war and war periods and had no skills, or ignorant and arrogant, trying to run communities and legislatures for which they had no background. The books omit White violence and opposition to education for Blacks. Between 1890 and 1920, roughly the same period during which the country experienced mass migrations from Eastern and Central Europe, segregation was imposed everywhere. Blacks and Whites were kept apart wherever they were doing the same things (e.g., in schools, public accommodations, and on sports teams) but together whenever Blacks served Whites (e.g., *in homes or in the fields). This hierarchical separation carried with it the stigma of inferiority and forms part of the legacy of racism today. This was a time of lynchings, riots, revocation of voting rights, and the power of the Ku Klux Klan. It was a time when legislators refused to address the issues and Supreme Court decisions reinforced segregation and racism. These facts are largely missing from the texts. When they are presented, the facts are in neutral or White voices, not those drawn from the Black experience of those times and places.*

. . . Perhaps the most pervasive theme in our history is the domination of black America by white America. Race is the sharpest and deepest division in American life. Issues of black-white relations propelled the Whig Party to collapse, prompted the formation of the Republican Party, and caused the Democratic Party to label itself the "white man's party" for almost a century. The first time Congress ever overrode a presidential veto was for the 1866 Civil Rights Act, passed by Republicans over the wishes of Andrew Johnson. Senators mounted the longest filibuster in U.S. history, more than 534 hours, to oppose the 1964 Civil Rights bill. Thomas Byrne Edsall has shown how race prompted the sweeping political realignment of 1964–72, in which the white South went from a Democratic bastion to a Republican stronghold.[1] . . .

Almost no genre of our popular culture goes untouched by race. From the 1850s through the 1930s, except during the Civil War and Reconstruction, minstrel shows, which derived in a perverse way from plantation slavery, were the dominant form of popular entertainment in America. During most of that period *Uncle Tom's Cabin* was our longest-running play, mounted in thousands of productions. America's first epic motion picture, *Birth of a Nation*; first talkie, *The Jazz Singer*, and biggest blockbuster novel ever, *Gone with the Wind*, were substantially about race relations. The most popular radio show of all time was "Amos 'n' Andy," two white men posing as humorously incompetent African Americans.[2] The most popular

television miniseries ever was "Roots," which changed our culture by setting off an explosion of interest in genealogy and ethnic background, in music, race relations provide the underlying thematic material for many of our spirituals, blues numbers, reggae songs, and rap pieces.

The struggle over racial slavery may be the predominant theme in American history. Until the end of the nineteenth century, cotton—planted, cultivated, harvested, and ginned by slaves—was by far our most important export.[3] Our graceful antebellum homes, in the North as well as in the South, were built largely by slaves or from profits derived from the slave and cotton trades. Black-white relations became the central issue in the Civil War, which killed almost as many Americans as died in all our other wars combined. Black-white relations was the principal focus of Reconstruction after the Civil War; America's failure to allow African Americans equal rights led eventually to the struggle for civil rights a century later.

The subject also pops up where we least suspect it—at the Alamo, throughout the Seminole Wars, even in the expulsion of the Mormons from Missouri.[4] Studs Terke is right: race *is* our "American obsession."[5] Since those first Africans and Spaniards landed on the Carolina shore in 1526, our society has repeatedly been torn apart and sometimes bound together by this issue of black-white relations.

Over the years white America has told itself varying stories about the enslavement of blacks. In each of the last two centuries America's most popular novel was set in slavery—*Uncle Tom's Cabin* by Harriet Beecher Stowe and *Gone with the Wind* by Margaret Mitchell. The two books tell very different stories: *Uncle Tom's Cabin* presents slavery as an evil to be opposed, while *Gone with the Wind* suggests that slavery was an ideal social structure whose passing is to be lamented. Until the civil rights movement, American history textbooks in this century pretty much agreed with Mitchell. In 1959 my high school textbook presented slavery as not such a bad thing. If bondage was a burden for African Americans, well, slaves were a burden on Ole Massa and Ole Miss, too. Besides, slaves were reasonably happy and well fed. Such arguments constitute the "magnolia myth," according to which slavery was a social structure of harmony and grace that did no real harm to anyone, white or black. A famous 1950 textbook by Samuel Eliot Morison and Henry Steele Commager actually said, "As for Sambo, whose wrongs moved the abolitionists to wrath and tears, there is some reason to believe that he suffered less than any other class in the South from its 'peculiar Institution.'"[6] "Peculiar institution" meant slavery, of course, and Morison and Commager here provided a picture of it that came straight from *Gone with the Wind*.

This is not what textbooks say today. Since the civil rights movement, textbooks have returned part of the way toward Stowe's devastating indictment of the institution. The discussion in *American History* begins with a passage that describes the living conditions of slaves in positive terms: "They were usually given adequate food, clothing, and shelter." But the author immediately goes on to point out, "Slaves had absolutely no *rights*. It was not simply that they could not vote or own property. Their owners had complete control over their lives." He concludes, "Slavery was almost literally inhuman." *American Adventures* tells us, "Slavery led to despair, and despair sometimes led black people to take their own lives. Or in some cases it led them to revolt against white slaveholders." *Life and Liberty* takes a flatter view: "Historians do not agree on how severely slaves were treated"; the book goes on to note that whipping was common in some places, unheard of on other plantations. *Life and Liberty* ends its section on slave life, however, by quoting the titles of spirituals—"All My Trials, Lord, Soon Be Over"—and by citing the inhumane details of slave laws. No one could read any of these three books and think well of slavery. Indeed, ten of the twelve books I studied portray slavery as intolerable to the slave.[7]

Today's textbooks also show how slavery increasingly dominated our political life in the first half of the nineteenth century. They tell that the cotton gin made slavery more profitable.[8] They tell how in the 1830s Southern states and the federal government pushed the Indians out of vast stretches of

Mississippi, Alabama, and Georgia, and slavery expanded. And they tell that in the decades between 1830 and 1860, slavery's ideological demands grew shriller, more overtly racist. No longer was it enough for planters and slave traders to apologize for slavery as a necessary evil. Now slavery came to be seen "of positive value to the slaves themselves," in the words of *Triumph of the American Nation*. This ideological extremism was matched by harsher new laws and customs. "Talk of freeing the slaves became more and more dangerous in the South," in the words of *The United States—A History of the Republic*. Merely to *receive* literature advocating abolition became a felony in some slaveholding states. Southern states passed new ordinances interfering with the rights of masters to free their slaves. The legal position of already free African Americans became ever more precarious, even in the North, as white Southerners prevailed on the federal government to make it harder to restrict slavery anywhere in the nation.[9]

Meanwhile, many Northern whites, as well as some who lived below the Mason-Dixon line, grew increasingly unhappy, disgusted that their nation had lost its idealism.[10] The debate over slavery loomed ever larger, touching every subject. In 1848 Thomas Hart Benton, a senator from Missouri, likened the ubiquity of the issue to a biblical plague: "You could not look upon the table but there were frogs. You could not sit down at the banquet table but there were frogs. You could not go to the bridal couch and lift the sheets but there were frogs. We can see nothing, touch nothing, have no measures proposed, without having this pestilence thrust before us."[11]

History textbooks now admit that slavery was the primary cause of the Civil War. In the words of *The United States—A History of the Republic*, "At the center of the conflict was slavery, the issue that would not go away." Before the civil rights movement, many textbooks held that almost anything else—differences over tariffs and internal improvements, blundering politicians, the conflict between the agrarian South and the industrial North—caused the war. This was a form of Southern apologetics.[12] Among the twelve textbooks I reviewed, only *Triumph of the American Nation*, a book that originated in the 1950s, still holds such a position.

Why do textbooks now handle slavery with depth and understanding? Before the 1960s publishers had been in thrall to the white South. In the 1920s Florida and other Southern states passed laws requiring "Securing a Correct History of the U.S., including a True and Correct History of the Confederacy."[13] Textbooks were even required to call the Civil War "the War between the States," as if no single nation had existed which the South had rent apart. In the fifteen years between 1955 and 1970, however, the civil rights movement destroyed segregation as a formal system in America. The movement did not succeed in transforming American race relations, but it did help African Americans win more power on the local level and prompted whites to abandon segregation. Today many school boards, curricular committees, and high school history departments include African Americans or white Americans who have cast off the ideology of white supremacy. Therefore contemporary textbooks can devote more space to the topic of slavery and can use that space to give a more accurate portrayal.[14]

Americans seem perpetually startled at slavery. Children are shocked to learn that George Washington and Thomas Jefferson owned slaves. Interpreters at Colonial Williamsburg say that many visitors are surprised to learn that slavery existed there—in the heart of plantation Virginia! Very few adults today realize that our society has been slave much longer than it has been free. Even fewer know that slavery was important in the North, too, until after the Revolutionary War. The first colony to legalize slavery was not Virginia but Massachusetts. In 1720, of New York City's population of seven thousand, 1,600 were African Americans, most of them slaves. Wall Street was the marketplace where owners could hire out their slaves by the day or week.[15]

Most textbooks downplay slavery in the North, however, so slavery seems to be a sectional rather than national problem. Indeed, even the expanded coverage of slavery comes across as an unfortunate but minor blemish,

compared to the overall story line of our textbooks. James Oliver Horton has pointed out that "the black experience cannot be fully illuminated without bringing a new perspective to the study of American history."[16] Textbook authors have failed to present any new perspective. Instead, they shoehorn their improved and more accurate portrait of slavery into the old "progress as usual" story line. In this saga, the United States is always intrinsically and increasingly democratic, and slaveholding is merely a temporary aberration, not part of the big picture. Ironically, the very success of the civil rights movement allows authors to imply that the problem of black-white race relations has now been solved, at least formally. This enables textbooks to discuss slavery without departing from their customarily optimistic tone.

While textbooks now show the horror of slavery and its impact on black America, they remain largely silent regarding the impact of slavery on white America, North or South. Textbooks have trouble acknowledging that anything might be wrong with white Americans, or with the United States as a whole. Perhaps telling realistically what slavery was like for slaves is the easy part. After all, slavery as an institution is dead. We have progressed beyond it, so we can acknowledge its evils. Even the Museum of the Confederacy in Richmond has mounted an exhibit on slavery that does not romanticize the institution.[17] Without explaining its relevance to the present, however, extensive coverage of slavery is like extensive coverage of the Hawley-Smoot Tariff—just more facts for hapless eleventh graders to memorize.

Slavery's twin legacies to the present are the social and economic inferiority it conferred upon blacks and the cultural racism it instilled in whites. Both continue to haunt our society. Therefore, treating slavery's enduring legacy is necessarily controversial. Unlike slavery, racism is not over yet.

To function adequately in civic life in our troubled times, students must learn what causes racism. Although it is a complicated historical issue, racism in the Western world stems primarily from two related historical processes: taking land from and destroying indigenous peoples and enslaving Africans to work that land. To teach this relationship, textbooks would have to show students the dynamic interplay between slavery as a socioeconomic system and racism as an idea system. Sociologists call these the social structure and the superstructure. Slavery existed in many societies and periods before and after the African slave trade. Made possible by Europe's advantages in military and social technology, the slavery started by Europeans in the fifteenth century was different, because it became the enslavement of one *race* by another. Increasingly, whites viewed the enslavement of whites as illegitimate, while the enslavement of Africans became acceptable. Unlike earlier slaveries, children of African American slaves would be slaves forever and could never achieve freedom through intermarriage with the owning class. The rationale for this differential treatment was racism. As Montesquieu, the French social philosopher who had such a profound influence on American democracy, ironically observed in 1748: "It is impossible for us to suppose these creatures to be men, because, allowing them to be men, a suspicion would follow that we ourselves are not Christian."[18]

Historians have chronicled the rise of racism in the West. Before the 1450s Europeans considered Africans exotic but not necessarily inferior. As more and more nations joined the slave trade, Europeans came to characterize Africans as stupid, backward, and uncivilized. Amnesia set in: Europe gradually found it convenient to forget that Moors from Africa had brought to Spain and Italy much of the learning that led to the Renaissance. Europeans had known that Timbuctu, with its renowned university and library, was a center of learning. Now, forgetting Timbuctu, Europe and European Americans perceived Africa as the "dark continent."[19] By the 1850s many white Americans, including some Northerners, claimed that black people were so hopelessly inferior that slavery was a proper form of education for them; it also removed them physically from the alleged barbarism of the "dark continent."

The superstructure of racism has long outlived the social structure of slavery that generated it. The following passage from Margaret Mitchell's *Gone with the Wind*, written in the 1930s, shows racism alive and well in that decade. The narrator is interpreting Reconstruction: "The former field hands found themselves suddenly elevated to the seats of the mighty. There they conducted themselves as creatures of small intelligence might naturally be expected to do. Like monkeys or small children turned loose among treasured objects whose value is beyond their comprehension, they ran wild—either from perverse pleasure in destruction or simply because of their ignorance."[20] White supremacy permeates Mitchell's romantic bestseller. Yet in 1988, when the American Library Association asked library patrons to name the best book in the library, *Gone with the Wind* won an actual majority against all other books ever published![21]

The very essence of what we have inherited from slavery is the idea that it is appropriate, even "natural," for whites to be on top, blacks on the bottom. In its core our culture tells us—tells all of us, including African Americans—that Europe's domination of the world came about because Europeans were smarter. In their core, many whites and some people of color believe this. White supremacy is not only a residue of slavery, to be sure. Developments in American history since slavery ended have maintained it. Textbooks that do not discuss white involvement in slavery in the period before 1863, however, are not likely to analyze white racism as a factor in more recent years. Only five of the twelve textbooks books list *racism, racial prejudice*, or any term beginning with *race* in their indexes.[22]

Only two textbooks discuss what might have caused racism. The closest any of the textbooks comes to explaining the connection between slavery and racism is this single sentence from *The American Tradition*: "In defense of their 'peculiar institution,' southerners became more and more determined to maintain their own way of life." Such a statement hardly suffices to show today's students the origin of racism in our society—it doesn't even use the word! *The American Adventure* offers a longer treatment: "[African Americans] looked different from members of white ethnic groups. The color of their skin made assimilation difficult. For this reason they remained outsiders." Here *Adventure* has retreated from history to lay psychology. Unfortunately for its argument, skin color in itself does not explain racism. Jane Elliot's famous experiments in Iowa classrooms have shown that children can quickly develop discriminatory behavior and prejudiced beliefs based on eye color. Conversely, the leadership positions that African Americans frequently reached among American Indian nations from Ecuador to the Arctic show that people do not automatically discriminate against others on the basis of skin color.[23]

Events and processes in American history, from the time of slavery to the present, are what explain racism. Not one textbook connects history and racism, however. Half-formed and uninformed notions rush in to fill the analytic vacuum textbooks thus leave. *Adventure's* three sentences imply that it is natural to exclude people whose skin color is different. White students may conclude that *all* societies are racist, perhaps by nature, so racism is all right. Black students may conclude that all whites are racist, perhaps by nature, so to be anti-white is all right. The elementary thinking in *Adventure's* three sentences is all too apparent. Yet this is the *most substantial* treatment of the causes of racism among all twelve textbooks.

In omitting racism or treating it so poorly, history textbooks shirk a critical responsibility. Not all whites are or have been racist. Levels of racism have changed over time.[24] If textbooks were to explain this, they would give students some perspective on what caused racism in the past, what perpetuates it today, and how it might be reduced in the future.

Although textbook authors no longer sugarcoat how slavery affected African Americans, they minimize white complicity in it. They present slavery virtually as uncaused, a tragedy, rather than a wrong perpetrated by some people on others. Textbooks maintain the fiction that planters did the work on the plantations. "There was always much work to be done," according to *Triumph of the American Nation*, "for a cotton grower also raised most of the food eaten by his family and slaves." Although managing a business worth hundreds of thousands of dollars was

surely time-consuming, the truth as to who did most of the work on the plantation is surely captured more accurately by this quotation from a Mississippi planter lamenting his situation after the war: "I never did a day's work in my life, and don't know how to begin. You see me in these coarse old clothes; well, I never wore coarse clothes in my life before the war."[25]

The emotion generated by textbook descriptions of slavery is sadness, not anger. For there's no one to be angry *at*. Somehow we ended up with four million slaves in America but no owners! This is part of a pattern in our textbooks: anything bad in American history happened anonymously. Everyone named in our history made a positive contribution. . . . Or as Frances FitzGerald put it when she analyzed textbooks in 1979, "In all history, there is no known case of anyone's creating a problem for anyone else."[26]

Certainly the Founding Fathers never created one. "Popular modern depictions of Washington and Jefferson are utterly at variance with their lives as eighteenth-century slaveholding planters."[27] Textbooks play their part by minimizing slavery in the lives of the founders. As with Woodrow Wilson, Helen Keller, and Christopher Columbus, authors cannot bear to reveal anything bad about our heroes. Nevertheless, almost half of the signers of the Declaration of Independence were slaveowners.

In real life the Founding Fathers and their wives wrestled with slavery. Textbooks canonize Patrick Henry for his "Give me liberty or give me death" speech. Not one tells us that eight months after delivering the speech he ordered "diligent patrols" to keep Virginia slaves from accepting the British offer of freedom to those who would join their side. Henry wrestled with the contradiction, exclaiming, "Would anyone believe I am the master of slaves of my own purchase!"[28] Almost no one would today, because only two of the twelve textbooks, *Land of Promise* and *The American Adventure*, even mention the inconsistency.[29] Henry's understanding of the discrepancy between his words and his deeds never led him to act differently, to his slaves' sorrow. Throughout the Revolutionary period he added slaves to his holdings, and even at his death, unlike some other Virginia planters, he freed not a one. Nevertheless, *Triumph of the American Nation* quotes Henry calling slavery "as repugnant to humanity as it is inconsistent with the Bible and destructive of liberty," without ever mentioning that he held slaves. *American Adventures* devotes three whole pages to Henry, constructing a fictitious melodrama in which his father worries, "How would he ever earn a living?" *Adventures* then tells how Henry failed at storekeeping, "tried to make a living by raising tobacco," "started another store," "had three children as well as a wife to support," "knew he had to make a living in *some* way," "so he decided to become a lawyer." The student who reads this chapter and later learns that Henry grew wealthy from the work of scores of slaves has a right to feel hoodwinked.

Even more embarrassing is the case of Founding Father Thomas Jefferson. American history textbooks use several tactics to harmonize the contradiction between Jefferson's assertion that everyone has an equal right to "Life, Liberty, and the pursuit of Happiness" and his enslavement of 175 human beings at the time he wrote those words. Jefferson's slaveholding affected almost everything he did, from his opposition to internal improvements to his foreign policy.[30] Nonetheless, half of our textbooks never note that Jefferson owned slaves. *Life and Liberty* offers a half-page minibiography of Jefferson, revealing that he was "shy," "stammered," and "always worked hard at what he did." Elsewhere *Life* contrasts Jefferson's political beliefs with Alexander Hamilton's and supplies six paragraphs about "Jeffersonian Changes" of Federalist policies, noting that Jefferson refused to wear a wig, repealed a whiskey tax, and walked rather than rode in his inaugural parade. *Life and Liberty* says nothing about Jefferson and slavery, however. *American History* offers six different illustrations of the man for us to admire but makes no mention of his slaveholding. *The Challenge of Freedom* mentions Jefferson on sixteen different pages but never in the context of slavery.

Even textbooks that admit that Jefferson owned slaves go out of their way to downplay the fact. *The American Way* buries his complicity with the institution in a paragraph about his opposition to the practice:

> In his *Notes on the State of Virginia*, published in 1787, Thomas Jefferson spoke out against owning slaves. Slavery, he said, made tyrants out of the masters and destroyed the spirit of the slaves. . . . Although Jefferson and others who owned slaves spoke against slavery, many people did not believe that a mixed society of equals could work.

"Jefferson and others who owned slaves" is ambiguous. Only the careful reader will infer that Jefferson was a slaveowner. Also ambiguous is *Notes on the State of Virginia*, which contains lengthy arguments about why blacks and whites can never participate in society equally. The attempt "will probably never end but in the extermination of the one or the other race," Jefferson luridly concluded. *Way* has mischaracterized the source.[31]

The paragraph in *American Adventures* is more forthright:

> The idea of slavery bothered Thomas Jefferson all his life. As an adult, he himself owned many slaves. He depended on their labor for raising tobacco on his plantation. Yet he understood that slavery was wrong, terribly wrong. It was the opposite of the thing he valued most in life—freedom.

Again, the thrust of the treatment, the thing most likely to be remembered, is that Jefferson was an opponent of slavery, not a slaveowner.

Textbooks stress that Jefferson was a humane master, privately tormented by slavery and opposed to its expansion, not the type to destroy families by selling slaves. In truth, by 1820 Jefferson had become an ardent advocate of the expansion of slavery to the western territories. And he never let his ambivalence about slavery affect his private life. Jefferson was an average master who had his slaves whipped and sold into the Deep South as examples, to induce other slaves to obey. By 1822, Jefferson owned 267 slaves. During his long life, of hundreds of different slaves he owned, he freed only three, and five more at his death—all blood relatives of his.[32]

Another textbook tactic to minimize Jefferson's slaveholding is to admit it but emphasize that others did no better. "Jefferson revealed himself as a man of his times," states *Land of Promise*. Well, what were those times? Certainly most white Americans in the 1770s were racist. Race relations were in flux, however, due to the Revolutionary War and to its underlying ideology about the rights of mankind that Jefferson, among others, did so much to spread. Five thousand black soldiers fought alongside whites in the Continental Army, "with courage and skill," according to *Triumph of the American Nation*. In reality, of course, some fought "with courage and skill," like some white recruits, and some failed to fire their guns and ran off, like some white recruits.[33] But because these men fought in integrated units for the most part and received equal pay, their existence in itself helped decrease white racism.[34]

Moreover, the American Revolution is one of those moments in our history when the power of ideas made a real difference. "In contending for the birthright of freedom," said a captain in the army, "we have learned to feel for the bondage of others."[35] Abigail Adams wrote her husband in 1774 to ask how we could "fight ourselves for what we are daily robbing and plundering from those who have as good a right to freedom as we have."[36] The contradiction between his words and his slaveowning embarrassed Patrick Henry, who offered only a lame excuse—"I am drawn along by the general inconvenience of living here without them"—and admitted, "I will not, I cannot justify it."[37] Other options were available to planters. Some, including George Washington, valued consistency more than Henry or Jefferson and freed their slaves outright or at least in their wills. Other slaveowners freed their male slaves to fight in the colonial army, collecting a bounty for each one who enlisted. In the first two decades after the Revolution, the number of free blacks in Virginia soared tenfold, from 2,000 in 1780 to 20,000 in 1800. Most Northern states did away with slavery altogether. Thus Thomas Jefferson lagged behind many whites of his times in the actions he took with regard to slavery.[38]

Manumission gradually flagged, however, because most of the white Southerners who, like Jefferson, kept their slaves, grew rich. Their neighbors thought well of them, as people often do of those richer than themselves. To a degree the ideology of the upper class became the ideology of the whole society, and as the Revolution receded, that ideology increasingly justified slavery. Jefferson himself spent much of his slave-earned wealth on his mansion at Monticello and on books that he later donated to the University of Virginia; these expenditures became part of his hallowed patrimony, giving history yet another reason to remember him kindly.[39]

Other views are possible, however. In 1829, three years after Jefferson's death, David Walker, a black Bostonian, warned members of his race that they should remember Jefferson as their greatest enemy. "Mr. Jefferson's remarks respecting us have sunk deep into the hearts of millions of whites, and never will be removed this side of eternity."[40] For the next hundred years, the open white supremacy of the Democratic Party, Jefferson's political legacy to the nation, would bear out the truth of Walker's warning.

Textbooks are in good company: the Jefferson Memorial, too, white-washes its subject. On its marble walls a carved panel proclaims Jefferson's boast, "I have sworn eternal hostility against every form of tyranny over the mind of men," without ever mentioning his participation in racial slavery. Perhaps asking a marble memorial to tell the truth is demanding too much. Should history textbooks similarly be a shrine, however? Should they encourage students to worship Jefferson? Or should they help students understand him, wrestle with the problems he wrestled with, grasp his accomplishments, and also acknowledge his failures?

The idealistic spark in our Revolution, which caused Patrick Henry such verbal discomfort, at first made the United States a proponent of democracy around the world. However, slavery and its concomitant ideas, which legitimated hierarchy and dominance, sapped our Revolutionary idealism. Most textbooks never hint at this clash of ideas, let alone at its impact on our foreign policy.

After the Revolution, many Americans expected our example would inspire other peoples. It did. Our young nation got its first chance to help in the 1790s, when Haiti revolted against France. Whether a president owned slaves seems to have determined his policy toward the second independent nation in the hemisphere. George Washington did, so his administration loaned hundreds of thousands of dollars to the French planters in Haiti to help them suppress their slaves. John Adams did not, and his administration gave considerable support to the Haitians. Jefferson's presidency marked a general retreat from the idealism of the Revolution. Like other slaveowners, Jefferson preferred a Napoleonic colony to a black republic in the Caribbean. In 1801 he reversed U.S. policy toward Haiti and secretly gave France the go-ahead to reconquer the island. In so doing, the United States not only betrayed its heritage, but also acted against its own self-interest. For if France had indeed been able to retake Haiti, Napoleon would have maintained his dream of an American empire. The United States would have been hemmed in by France to its west, Britain to its north, and Spain to its south. But planters in the United States were scared by the Haitian Revolution. They thought it might inspire slave revolts here (which it did). When Haiti won despite our flip-flop, the United States would not even extend it diplomatic recognition, lest its ambassador inflame our slaves "by exhibiting in his own person an example of successful revolt," in the words of a Georgia senator.[41] Five of the twelve textbooks mention how Haitian resistance led France to sell us its claim to Louisiana, but none tells of our flip-flop, indeed, no textbook ever makes any connection between slavery and U.S. foreign policy.

Racial slavery also affected our policy toward the next countries in the Americas to revolt, Spain's colonies. Haiti's example inspired them to seek independence, and the Haitian government gave Simon Bolivar direct aid. Our statesmen were ambivalent, eager to help boot a European power out of the hemisphere but worried by the racially mixed rebels doing the booting. Some planters wanted our government to replace Spain as the colonial power, especially in Cuba. Jefferson suggested annexing Cuba. Fifty years later, diplomats in the Franklin Pierce administration signed the Ostend Manifesto, which proposed that the United States buy or take the island from Spain. Slaveowners, still obsessed with Haiti as a role model, thus hoped to prevent Cuba's becoming a second Haiti, with "flames [that might] extend to our own neighboring shores," in the words of the Manifesto.[42] In short, slavery prompted the United States to have imperialist designs on Latin America rather than visions of democratic liberation for the region.

Slavery affected our foreign policy in still other ways. The first requirement of a slave society is secure borders. We do not like to think of the United States as a police state, a nation like East Germany that people had to escape from, but the slaveholding states were just that. Indeed, after the *Dred Scott* decision in 1857, which declared "A Negro had no rights a white man was bound to respect," thousands of free African Americans realized they could not be safe even in Northern states and fled to Canada, Mexico, and Haiti.[43] Slaveholders dominated our foreign policy until the Civil War. They were always concerned about our Indian borders and made sure that treaties with Native nations stipulated that Indians surrender all African Americans and return any runaways.[44]

U.S. territorial expansion between 1787 and 1855 was due in large part to slavers' influence. The largest pressure group behind the War of 1812 was slaveholders who coveted Indian and Spanish land and wanted to drive Indian societies farther away from the slaveholding states to prevent slave escapes. Even though Spain was our ally during that war, in the aftermath we took Florida from Spain because slaveholders demanded we do so. Indeed, Andrew Jackson attacked a Seminole fort in Florida in 1816 precisely because it harbored hundreds of runaway slaves, thus initiating the First Seminole War.[45]

The Seminoles did not exist as a tribe or nation before the arrival of Europeans and Africans. They were a triracial isolate composed of Creek Indians, remnants of smaller tribes, runaway slaves, and whites who preferred to live in Indian society. The word

Seminole is itself a corruption of the Spanish *cimarron* (corrupted to *maroons* on Jamaica), a word that came to mean "runaway slaves."[46] The Seminoles' refusal to surrender their African American members led to the First and Second Seminole Wars (1816–1818, 1835–1842). Whites attacked not because they wanted the Everglades, which had no economic value to the United States in the nineteenth century, but to eliminate a refuge for runaway slaves. The Second Seminole War was the longest and costliest war the United States ever fought against Indians.[47] The college textbook *America: Past and Present* tells why we fought it, putting the war in the context of slave revolts:

> The most sustained and successful effort of slaves to win their freedom by force of arms took place in Florida between 1835 and 1842 when hundreds of black fugitives fought in the Second Seminole War alongside the Indians who had given them a haven. The Seminoles were resisting removal to Oklahoma, but for the blacks who took part, the war was a struggle for their own freedom, and the treaty that ended it allowed most of them to accompany their Indian allies to the trans-Mississippi West.

This is apparently too radical for high school: only six of the twelve textbooks even mention the war. Of these, only four say that ex-slaves fought with the Seminoles; not one tells that the ex-slaves were the real reason for the war.

Slavery was also perhaps the key factor in the Texas War (1835–1836). The freedom for which Davy Crockett, James Bowie, and the rest fought at the Alamo was the freedom to own slaves! As soon as Anglos set up the Republic of Texas, its legislature ordered all free black people out of the Republic.[48] Our next major war, the Mexican War (1846–1848), was again driven chiefly by Southern planters wanting to push the borders of the nearest free land farther from the slave states. Probably the clearest index of how slavery affected U.S. foreign policy is provided by the Civil War, for between 1861 and 1865 we had two foreign policies, the Union's and the Confederacy's. The Union recognized Haiti and shared considerable ideological compatibility with postrevolutionary Mexico. The Confederacy threatened to invade Mexico and then welcomed Louis Napoleon's takeover of it as a French colony, because that removed Mexico as a standard bearer of freedom and a refuge for runaway slaves.[49] Confederate diplomats also had their eyes on Cuba, had they won the Civil War.

For our first seventy years as a nation, then, slavery made our foreign policy more sympathetic with imperialism than with self-determination. Textbooks cannot show the influence of slavery on our foreign policy if they are unwilling to talk about ideas like racism that might make whites look bad. When textbook authors turn their attention to domestic policy, racism remains similarly invisible. Thus, although textbooks devote a great deal of attention to Stephen A. Douglas, the most important leader of the Democratic Party at mid-century, they suppress his racism. Recall that Douglas had bulldozed what came to be called the Kansas-Nebraska Act through Congress in 1854. Douglas himself, a senator from Illinois and seeker of the presidency, was neither for nor against slavery. He mainly wanted the United States to organize territorial governments in Kansas and Nebraska, until then Indian land, because he was connected with interests that wanted to run a railroad through the territory.[50] He needed Southern votes. During most of the 1840s and 1850s Southern planters controlled the Supreme Court, the presidency, and at least one house of Congress. Emboldened by their power while worried about their decreasing share of the nation's white population, slaveowners agreed to support the new territories only if Douglas included in the bill a clause opening them to slavery. Douglas capitulated and incorporated what he called "popular sovereignty" in the bill. This meant Kansas could go slave if it chose to, even though it lay north of the Missouri Compromise line, set up in 1820 to separate slavery from freedom. So, for that matter, could Nebraska. The result was civil war in Kansas.

While textbooks do not treat Stephen Douglas as a major hero like Christopher Columbus or Woodrow Wilson, they do discuss him with sympathy. In 1858 Douglas ran for reelection against Abraham Lincoln in a contest that presaged the ideologies that would dominate the two major parties for the next three decades.[51] Accordingly, textbooks give the debates an extraordinary amount of space: an average of seven paragraphs and two pictures.[52] Textbook authors use this space as if they were writing for *Vanity Fair*. . . .

. . . While celebrating the "Little Giant" for his "powerful speech" or "splendid oratory," nine textbooks silence him completely. Instead, the omnipresent authorial voice supplies his side of the debates: "Douglas was for popular sovereignty." This summary from *Life and Liberty* is shorter than most but otherwise representative. Of course, phrased this abstractly, who would oppose popular sovereignty?

Douglas's position was not so vague, however. The debate was largely about the morality of racially based slavery and the position African Americans should eventually hold in our society. . . .

Textbook readers *cannot* see that the issues are distinctly drawn, however, because textbooks give them no access to Douglas's side. *American History* is the only textbook that quotes Stephen Douglas on race: "Lincoln 'thinks the Negro is his brother,' the Little Giant sneered."

Why do textbooks censor Douglas? Since they devote paragraphs to his wardrobe, it cannot be for lack of space. To be sure, textbook authors rarely quote anyone. But more particularly, the heroification process seems to be operating again. Douglas's words might make us think badly of him.

Compared to Douglas, Lincoln was an idealistic equalitarian, but in southern Illinois, arguing with Douglas, he too expressed white supremacist ideas. Thus at the debate in Charleston he said, "I am not, nor ever have been in favor of bringing about the social and political equality of the white and black races (applause)—that I am not nor ever have been in favor of making voters or jurors of Negroes." Textbook authors protect us from a racist Lincoln. By so doing, they diminish students' capacity to recognize racism as a force in American life. For if Lincoln could be racist, then so might the rest of us be. And if Lincoln could transcend racism, as he did on occasion, then so might the rest of us.

During the Civil War, Northern Democrats countered the Republican charge that they favored rebellion by professing to be the "white man's party." They protested the government's emancipation of slaves in the District of Columbia and its diplomatic recognition of Haiti. They claimed Republicans had "nothing except 'nigger on the brain.'" They were enraged when the U.S. army accepted African American recruits. And they made race a paramount factor in their campaigns.

In those days before television, parties held coordinated rallies. On the last Saturday before the election, Democratic senators might address crowds in each major city; local officeholders would hold forth in smaller towns. Each of these rallies featured music. Hundreds of thousands of songbooks were printed so the party faithful might sing the same songs coast to coast. A favorite in 1864 was sung to the tune of "Yankee Doodle Dandy":

THE NEW NATIONAL ANTHEM
"NIGGER DOODLE DANDY"

Yankee Doodle is no more,
Sunk his name and station;
Nigger Doodle takes his place,
And favors amalgamation.

Chorus: *Nigger Doodle's all the go,*
Ebony shins and bandy,
"Loyal" people all must bow
To Nigger Doodle dandy.

The white breed is under par
It lacks the rich a-romy,
Give us something black as tar,
Give us "Old Dahomey."

Chorus: *Nigger Doodle's all the go, etc.*

Blubber lips are killing sweet,
And kinky heads are splendid;
And oh, it makes such bully feet
To have the heels extended.

Chorus: *Nigger Doodle's all the go, etc.*

I have shared these lyrics with hundreds of college students and scores of high school history teachers. To get audiences to take the words seriously, I usually try to lead them in a singalong. Often even all-white groups refuse. They are shocked by what they read. Nothing in their high school history textbooks hinted that national politics was ever like this.

Partly because many party members and leaders did not identify with the war effort, when the Union won Democrats emerged as the minority party. Republicans controlled Reconstruction. Like slavery, Reconstruction is a subject on which textbooks have improved since the civil rights movement. The earliest accounts, written even before Reconstruction ended, portrayed Republican state governments struggling to govern fairly but confronted with immense problems, not the least being violent resistance from racist ex-Confederates. Textbooks written between about 1890 and the 1960s, however, painted an unappealing portrait of oppressive Republican rule in the postwar period, a picture that we might call the Confederate myth of Reconstruction. For years black families kept the truth about Reconstruction alive. The aging slaves whose stories were recorded by WPA writers in the 1930s remained proud of blacks' roles during Reconstruction. Some still remembered the names of African Americans elected to office sixty years earlier. "I know folks think the books tell the truth," said an eighty-eight-year-old former slave, "but they shore don't."[53] As those who knew Reconstruction from personal experience died off, however, even in the black community the textbook view took over.

My most memorable encounter with the Confederate myth of Reconstruction came during a discussion with seventeen first-year students at Tougaloo College, a predominantly black school in Mississippi, one afternoon in January 1970. I was about to launch into a unit on Reconstruction, and I needed to find out what the students already knew. "What was Reconstruction?" I asked. "What images come to your mind about that era?" The class consensus: Reconstruction was the time when African Americans took over the governing of the Southern states, including Mississippi. But they were too soon out of slavery, so they messed up and reigned corruptly, and whites had to take back control of the state governments.

I sat stunned. So many major misconceptions glared from that statement that it was hard to know where to begin a rebuttal. African Americans never took over the Southern states. All governors were white and almost all legislatures had white majorities throughout Reconstruction. African Americans did not "mess up"; indeed, Mississippi enjoyed less corrupt government during Reconstruction than in the decades immediately afterward. "Whites" did not take back control of the state governments; rather, *some* white Democrats used force and fraud to wrest control from biracial Republican coalitions.

For young African Americans to believe such a hurtful myth about their past seemed tragic. It invited them to doubt their own capability, since their race had "messed up" in its one appearance on American history's center stage. It also invited them to conclude that it is only right that whites be always in control. Yet my students had merely learned what their textbooks had taught them. Like almost all Americans who finished high school before the 1970s, they had encountered the Confederate myth of Reconstruction in their American history classes. I, too, learned it from my college history textbook. John F. Kennedy and his ghost writer retold it in their portrait of L. Q. C. Lamar in *Profiles in Courage*, which won the Pulitzer Prize.

Compared to the 1960s, today's textbooks have vastly improved their treatments of Reconstruction. All but three of the twelve textbooks I surveyed paint a very different picture of Reconstruction from *Gone with the Wind*.[54] No longer do histories claim that federal troops controlled Southern society for a decade or more. Now they point out that military rule ended by 1868 in all but three states. No longer do they say that allowing African American men to vote set loose an orgy of looting and corruption. The 1961 edition of *Triumph of the American Nation* condemned Republican rule in the South: "Many of the 'carpetbag' governments were inefficient, wasteful, and corrupt." In stark contrast, the 1986 edition explains that "The southern reconstruction legislatures started many needed and long overdue public improvements . . . strengthened public education . . . spread the tax burden more equitably . . . [and] introduced overdue reforms in local government and the judicial system."

Like their treatment of slavery, textbooks' new view of Reconstruction represents a sea change, past due, much closer to what the original sources for the period reveal, and much less dominated by white supremacy. However, in the way the textbooks structure their discussion, most of them inadvertently still take a white supremacist viewpoint. Their rhetoric makes African Americans rather than whites the "problem" and assumes that the major issue of Reconstruction was how to integrate African Americans into the system, economically and politically. "Slavery was over," says *The American Way*. "But the South was ruined and the Blacks had to be brought into a working society." Blacks were already working, of course. One wonders what the author thinks they had been doing in slavery![55] Similarly, according to *Triumph of the American Nation*, Reconstruction "meant solving the problem of bringing black Americans into the mainstream of national life." *Triumph* supplies an instructive example of the myth of lazy, helpless black folk: "When white planters abandoned their plantations on islands off the coast of South Carolina, black people there were left helpless and destitute." In reality, these black people enlisted in Union armies, operated the plantations themselves, and made raids into the interior to free slaves on mainland plantations. The archetype of African Americans as dependent on others begins here, in textbook treatments of Reconstruction. It continues to the present, when many white Americans believe blacks work less than whites, even though census data show they work more.[56]

In reality, white violence, not black ignorance, was the key problem during Reconstruction. The figures are astounding. The victors of the Civil War executed but one Confederate officeholder, Henry Wirz, notorious commandant of Andersonville prison, while the losers murdered hundreds of officeholders and other Unionists, white and black.[57] In Hinds County, Mississippi, alone, whites killed an average of one African American a day, many of them servicemen, during Confederate Reconstruction—the period from 1865 to 1867 when ex-Confederates ran the governments of most Southern states. In Louisiana in the summer and fall of 1868, white Democrats killed 1,081 persons, mostly African Americans and white Republicans.[58] In one judicial district in North Carolina, a Republican judge counted 700 beatings and 12 murders.[59]

Moreover, violence was only the most visible component of a broader pattern of white resistance to black progress. Attacking education was an important element of the white supremacists' program. "The opposition to Negro education made itself felt everywhere in a combination not to allow the freedmen any room or building in which a school might be taught," said Gen. O. O. Howard, head of the Freedmen's Bureau. "In 1865, 1866, and 1867 mobs of the baser classes at intervals and in all parts of the South occasionally burned school buildings and churches used as schools, flogged teachers or drove them away, and in a number of instances murdered them."[60]

With the exception of *The American Way* and *Discovering American History*, each of the twelve textbooks includes at least a paragraph on white violence during Reconstruction. Six of twelve textbooks tell how that violence, coupled with failure by the United States to implement civil rights laws, played a major role in ending Republican state governments in the South, thus ending Reconstruction.[61] But, overall, textbook treatments of Reconstruction still miss the point: the problem of Reconstruction was integrating *Confederates*, not African Americans, into the new order. As soon as the federal government stopped addressing the problem of racist whites, Reconstruction ended. Since textbooks find it hard to say anything really damaging about white people, their treatments of why Reconstruction failed lack clarity. *Triumph* presents the end of Reconstruction as a failure of African Americans: "Other northerners grew weary of the problems of black southerners and less willing to help them learn their new roles as citizens." *The American Adventure* echoes: "Millions of ex-slaves could not be converted in ten years into literate voters, or successful politicians, farmers, and businessmen." . . .

Focusing on white racism is even more central to understanding the period Rayford Logan called "the nadir of American race relations": the years between 1890 and 1920, when African Americans were again put back into second-class citizenship.[62] During this time white Americans, North and South, joined hands to restrict black civil and economic rights. Perhaps because the period was marked by such a discouraging increase in white racism, ten of the twelve textbooks ignore the nadir. The finest coverage, in *American History*, summarizes the aftermath of Reconstruction in a section entitled "The Long Night Begins." "After the Compromise of 1877 the white citizens of the North turned their backs on the black citizens of the South. Gradually the southern states broke their promise to treat blacks fairly. Step by step they deprived them of the right to vote and reduced them to the status of second-class citizens." *American History* then spells out the techniques—restrictions on voting, segregation in public places, and lynchings—which southern whites used to maintain white supremacy.

Triumph of the American Nation, on the other hand, sums up in these bland words: "Reconstruction left many major problems unsolved and created new and equally urgent problems. This was true even though many forces in the North and the South continued working to reconcile the two sections." These sentences are so vague as to be content-free. . . . Five hundred pages later in *Triumph*, when the authors reach the civil rights movement, race relations again becomes a "problem." The authors make no connection between the failure of the United States to guarantee black civil rights in 1877 and the need for a civil rights movement a century later. Nothing ever causes anything. Things just happen.

In fact, during Reconstruction and the nadir, a battle raged for the soul of the Southern white racist and in a way for that of the whole nation. There is a parallel in the reconstruction of Germany after World War II, a battle for the soul of the German people, a battle which Nazism lost (we hope). But in the United States, as *American History* tells, racism won. Between 1890 and 1907 every Southern and border state "legally" disfranchised the vast majority of its African American voters. Lynchings rose to an all-time high. In 1896 the Supreme Court upheld segregation in *Plessy v. Ferguson*. No textbook explains the rationale of segregation, which is crucial to understanding its devastating effect on black and white psyches. Describing the 1954 Supreme Court decision that would begin to undo segregation, *The American Way* says, "No separate school could truly be equal for Blacks," but offers no clue as to why this would be so.

Textbooks need to offer the sociological definition of segregation: a system of racial etiquette that keeps the oppressed group separate from the oppressor when both are doing equal tasks, like learning the multiplication tables, but allows intimate closeness when the tasks are hierarchical, like cooking or cleaning for white employers. The rationale of segregation thus implies that the oppressed are a pariah people. "Unclean!" was the caste message of every "colored" water fountain, waiting room, and courtroom Bible. "Inferior" was the implication of every school that excluded blacks (and often Mexicans, Native Americans, and "Orientals"). This ideology was born in slavery and remained alive to rationalize the second-class citizenship imposed on African Americans after Reconstruction. This stigma is why separate could never mean equal, even when black facilities might be newer or physically superior. Elements of this stigma survive to harm the self-image of some African Americans today, which helps explain why Caribbean blacks who immigrate to the United States often outperform black Americans.[63]

During the nadir, segregation increased everywhere. Jackie Robinson was *not* the first black player in major league baseball. Blacks had played in the major leagues in the nineteenth century, but by 1889 whites had forced them out. In 1911 the Kentucky Derby eliminated black jockeys after they won fifteen of the first twenty-eight derbies.[64] Particularly in the South, whites attacked the richest and most successful African Americans, just as they had the most acculturated Native Americans, so upward mobility offered no way out for blacks but only made them more of a target. In the North as well as in the South, whites forced African Americans from skilled occupations and even unskilled jobs such as postal carriers.[65] ...

American popular culture evolved to rationalize whites' retraction of civil and political rights from African Americans. The Bronx Zoo exhibited an African behind bars, like a gorilla.[66] Theatrical productions of *Uncle Tom's Cabin* played throughout the nadir, but since the novel's indictment of slavery was no longer congenial to an increasingly racist white society, rewrites changed Uncle Tom from a martyr who gave his life to protect his people into a sentimental dope who was loyal to kindly masters. In the black community, *Uncle Tom* eventually came to mean an African American without integrity who sells out his people's interests. In the 1880s and 1890s, minstrel shows featuring bumbling, mislocuting whites in blackface grew wildly popular from New England to California. By presenting heavily caricatured images of African Americans who were happy on the plantation and lost and incompetent off it, these shows demeaned black ability. Minstrel songs such as "Carry Me Back to Old Virginny," "Old Black Joe," and "My Old Kentucky Home" told whites that Harriet Beecher Stowe got *Uncle Tom's Cabin* all wrong: blacks really liked slavery. Second-class citizenship was appropriate for such a sorry people.[67]

Textbooks abandoned their idealistic presentations of Reconstruction in favor of the Confederate myth, for if blacks were inferior, then the historical period in which they enjoyed equal rights must have been dominated by wrong-thinking Americans. Vaudeville continued the portrayal of silly, lying, chicken-stealing black idiots. So did early silent movies. Some movies made more serious charges against African Americans: D. W. Griffith's racist epic *Birth of a Nation* showed them obsessed with interracial sex and debased by corrupt white carpetbaggers.

In politics, the white electorate had become so racist by 1892 that the Democratic candidate, Grover Cleveland, won the White House partly by tarring Republicans with their attempts to guarantee civil rights to African Americans, thereby conjuring fears of "Negro domination" in the Northern as well as Southern white mind. From the Civil War to the end of the century, not a single Democrat in Congress, representing the North or the South, ever voted in favor of any civil rights legislation. The Supreme Court was worse: its segregationist decisions from 1896 (*Plessy*) through 1927 (*Rice v. Gong Lum*, which barred Chinese from white schools) told the nation that whites were the master race. We have seen how Woodrow Wilson won the presidency in 1912 and proceeded to segregate the federal government. Aided by *Birth of a Nation*, which opened in 1915, the Ku Klux Klan rose to its zenith, boasting over a million members. The KKK openly dominated the state government of Indiana for a time, and it proudly inducted Pres. Warren G. Harding as a member in a White House ceremony. During the Wilson and Harding administrations, perhaps one hundred race riots took place, more than in any other period since Reconstruction. White mobs killed African Americans across the United States. Some of these events, like the 1919 Chicago riot, are well known. Others, such as the 1921 riot in Tulsa, Oklahoma, in which whites dropped dynamite from an airplane onto a black ghetto, killing more than 75 people and destroying more than 1,100 homes, have completely vanished from our history books.[68]

It is almost unimaginable how racist the United States became during and just after the nadir. Mass attacks by whites wiped out or terrorized black communities in the Florida Keys, in Springfield, Illinois, and in the Arkansas Delta, and were an implicit, ever-present threat to every black neighborhood in the nation. Some small communities in the Midwest and West became "sundown" towns, informally threatening African Americans with death if they remained overnight. African Americans were excluded from juries throughout the South and in many places in the North, which usually meant they could forget about legal redress even for obvious wrongs like assault, theft, or arson by whites. Lynchings offer evidence of how defenseless blacks were, for the defining characteristic of a lynching is that the murder takes place in public, so everyone knows who did it, yet the crime goes unpunished. During the nadir, lynchings took place as far north as Duluth. Once again, as *Dred Scott* had proclaimed in 1857, "a Negro had no rights a white man was bound to respect." Every time African Americans interacted with European Americans, no matter how insignificant the contact, they had to be aware of how they presented themselves, lest they give offense by looking someone in the eye, forgetting to say "sir," or otherwise stepping out of "their place." Always, the threat of overwhelming force lay just beneath the surface.[69] . . .

Although formal racial discrimination grows increasingly rare, as young Americans grow up, they cannot avoid coming up against the rift of race relations. They will encounter predominantly black athletic teams cheered by predominantly white cheerleaders on television, self-segregated dining rooms on college campuses, and arguments about affirmative action in the workplace. More than any other social variable (except sex!), race will determine whom they marry. Most of their friendship networks will remain segregated by race, and most churches, lodges, and other social organizations will be overwhelmingly either black or nonblack. The ethnic incidents and race riots of tomorrow will provoke still more agonizing debate.

Since the nadir, the climate of race relations has improved, owing especially to the civil rights movement. But massive racial disparities remain, inequalities that can only be briefly summarized here. In 1990, African American median family income averaged only 57 percent of white family income; Native Americans and Hispanics averaged about 65 percent as much as whites. Money can be used to buy many things in our society, from higher SAT scores to the ability to swim, and African American, Hispanic, and Native American families lag in their access to all those things. Ultimately, money buys life itself, in the form of better nutrition and health care and freedom from danger and stress. It should therefore come as no surprise that in 1990 African Americans and Native Americans had median life expectancies at birth that were six years shorter than whites'.

On average, African Americans have worse housing, lower scores on IQ tests, and higher percentages of young men in jail. The sneaking suspicion that African Americans might be inferior goes unchallenged in the hearts of many blacks and whites. It is all too easy to blame the victim and conclude that people of color are themselves responsible for being on the bottom. Without causal historical analysis, these racial disparities are impossible to explain.

When textbooks make racism invisible in American history, they obstruct our already poor ability to see it in the present. The closest they come to analysis is to present a vague feeling of optimism: in race relations, as in everything, our society is constantly getting better. We used to have slavery; now we don't. We used to have lynchings; now we don't. Baseball used to be all white; now it isn't. The notion of progress suffuses textbook treatments of black-white relations, implying that race relations have somehow steadily improved on their own. This cheery optimism only compounds the problem, because whites can infer that racism is over. "The U.S. has done more than any other nation in history to provide equal rights for all," *The American Tradition* assures us. Of course, its authors have not seriously considered the levels of human rights in the Netherlands, Lesotho, or Canada today, or in Choctaw society in 1800, because they don't mean their declaration as a serious statement of comparative history—it is just ethnocentric cheerleading.

High school students "have a gloomy view of the state of race relations in America today," according to a recent nationwide poll. Students of all racial backgrounds brood about the subject.[70] Another poll reveals that for the first time in this century, young white adults have less tolerant attitudes toward black Americans than those over thirty. One reason is that "the under-30 generation is pathetically ignorant of recent American history."[71] Too young to have experienced or watched the civil rights movement as it happened, these young people have no understanding of the past and present workings of racism in American society.

Educators justify teaching history because it gives us perspective on the present. If there is one issue in the present to which authors should relate the history they tell, the issue is racism. But as long as history textbooks make white racism invisible in the nineteenth century, neither they nor the students who use them will be able to analyze racism intelligently in the present.

Notes

1. Filibuster information in John and Claire Whitecomb, *Oh Say Can You See?* (New York: Morrow, 1987), 116. On Republicans see Richard H. Sewell, *Ballots for Freedom* (New York: Oxford University Press, 1976), 292. On parties, see Thomas Byrne Edsall, *Chain Reaction* (New York: Norton, 1991), and "Willie Horton's Message," *New York Review of Books*, February 13, 1992, 7–11.

2. Minstrelsy was an important mass entertainment from 1850 to 1930 and the dominant form from about 1875 to World War I. *Gone with the Wind* was the largest grossing film ever in constant dollars. When first shown on television, it also won the highest ratings accorded an entertainment program up to that time. Admittedly, it is first a romance, but its larger social setting is primarily about race. *Time*, February 14, 1977, tells of the popularity of *Roots*. For general discussions of black stereotyping in mass media see Michael Rogin, "Making America Home," *Journal of American History* 79, no. 3 (December 1992): 1071–1073; Donald J. Bogle, *Toms, Coons, Mulattoes, Mammies, and Bucks* (New York: Bantam, 1974); and Loewen, "Black Image in White Vermont: The Origin, Meaning, and Abolition of Kake Walk," in Robert V. Daniels, ed., *Bicentennial History of the University of Vermont* (Boston: University Press of New England, 1991).

   An early draft of this paragraph cited racial content I remembered from the first full-length animated movie, *Fantasia*. When I rented the video to check my memory, I found no race relations. Then I learned from Ariel Dorfman (*The Empire's Old Clothes* [New York: Pantheon, 1983], 120) that the Disney company had eliminated all the segments containing racial stereotypes from the video re-release.

3. 1993 Exhibition: *The Cotton Gin and Its Bittersweet Harvest* at the Old State Capitol Museum in Jackson, Miss.

4. The Alamo and the Seminoles will be discussed later in the chapter. The foremost reason why white Missourians drove the Mormons of Missouri into Illinois in the 1830s was the suspicion that they were not "sound" on slavery. Indeed they were not: Mormons admitted black males to the priesthood and invited free Negroes to join them in Missouri. In response to this pressure, Mormons not only fled Missouri but changed their attitudes and policies to resemble those of most white Americans in the 1840s, concluding that blacks were inferior and should not become full members. They did not reverse this policy until 1978. See Ray West, Jr., *Kingdom of the Saints* (New York: Viking, 1957), 45–49, 88; Forrest G. Wood, *The Arrogance of Faith* (New York: Alfred A. Knopf, 1990), 96–97; and Newell Bringhurst, *Saints, Slaves, and Blacks* (Westport, Conn.: Greenwood, 1981).

5. Studs Terkel, *Race: How Blacks and Whites Think and Feel About the American Obsession* (New York: The New Press, 1992).

6. Samuel Eliot Morison and Henry Steele Commager, *The Growth of the American Republic* (New York: Oxford University Press, 1950), 521. In Andrew Rooney and Perry Wolf's film *Black History: Lost, Stolen or Strayed?* (Santa Monica, Calif.: BFA, 1968), Bill Cosby points out that this textbook was written by two northern Pulitzer Prize-winning historians.

7. Nancy Bauer's *The American Way* says little about slavery as experienced by slaves, but she does mention slave revolts and the underground railway. *Discovering American History* tells about slavery, using primary sources, but these are all by whites and contain little about slavery from the slaves' point of view. Considering the many slave narratives, it is surprising that *Discovering* excludes black sources. There is nothing "cutting edge" in any of the books' coverage of slavery. Twenty years ago historians developed the "slave community" interpretation to emphasize how African Americans experienced the institution; no textbook shows any familiarity with that school. Nor do any authors describe the controversies among competing slavery "schools." For a compact discussion of these interpretations, see Loewen, "Slave Narratives and Sociology," *Contemporary Sociology* 11, no. 4 (July 1982): 380–84, reviewing works by Blassingame, Escott, Cenovese, Gutman, and Rawick.

8. Whether slavery was profitable in the nineteenth century spurred a minor historical tempest a few years back. Although it eroded Southern soil, and although the Southern economy grew increasingly dependent on the Northern, evidence indicates planters did find slavery profitable. See, inter alia, Herbert Aptheker, *And Why Not Even Man?* (New York: International, 1961), 191–92.

9. James Currie, review of *The South and Politics of Slavery*, *Journal of Mississippi History* 41 (1979): 389; see also William Cooper, Jr., *The South and the Politics of Slavery, 1828–56* (Baton Rouge: Louisiana State University Press, 1978).

10. Roger Thompson, "Slavery, Sectionalism, and Secession," *Australian Journal of American Studies* 1, no. 2 (July 1981): 3, 5; William R. Brock, *Parties and Political Conscience* (Millwood, NY: KTO Press, 1979).

11. Joseph R. Conlin, ed., *Morrow Book of Quotations in American History* (New York: Morrow, 1984), 38.

12. Frank Owsley, a historian with Confederate sympathies, championed reasons for war other than slavery. When it was fought, however, virtually everyone, including Abraham Lincoln, Oliver Wendell Holmes, and Ulysses S. Grant on the Union side and Jefferson Davis and Alexander H. Stephens, president and vice-president of the Confederacy, thought the war was caused by slavery. See Daniel Aaron, *The Unwritten War* (New York: Oxford University Press, 1973), 28, 180.

13. Bessie L. Pierce, *Public Opinion and the Teaching of History in the United States* (New York: Alfred A. Knopf, 1926), 66–70. Nor was the North a great incubator of progressive textbooks in those decades.

14. Frances FitzGerald, *America Revised* (New York: Vintage, 1980), tells how history textbooks changed their treatment of slavery and Reconstruction in the 1970s. Hillel Black describes the former influence of white segregationist southerners and the new black influence in northern urban school districts, resulting from the civil rights and Black Power movements, in *The American Schoolbook* (New York: Morrow, 1967), chapter 8. "Liberating Our Past," *Southern Exposure*, November 1984, 2–3, tells of the influence of the civil rights movement. The new treatments of slavery are closer to most of those written at the time and to the primary sources.

15. Interviews at Williamsburg; Sloan, *Blacks in America, 1492–1970*, 2; Howard Zinn, *The Politics of History* (Boston: Beacon, 1970), 67.

16. Horton is quoted by Robert Moore in *Stereotypes, Distortions, and Omissions in U.S. History Textbooks* (New York: Council on Interracial Books for Children, 1977), 17.

17. *Before Freedom Came*, which was also a book, edited by E. D. C. Campbell, Jr. (Richmond, Va.: Museum of the Confederacy, 1991).

18. Quoted in Felix Okoye, *The American Image of Africa: Myth and Realty* (Buffalo: Black Academy Press, 1971), 37. Here Montesquieu presages Festinger's idea of cognitive dissonance. See Leon Festinger, *A Theory of Cognitive Dissonance* (Evanston, Ill.: Row, Peterson, 1957).

19. Okoye, *The American Image of Africa*.

20. Margaret Mitchell, *Gone with the Wind* (New York: Avon, 1964 [1936]), 645.

21. In reporting the survey, a journalist added dryly, "The Bible also ranked high."

22. I also searched under "white racism," "white supremacy," and various other headings, to no avail. The five books that mention racism are *Land of Promise*, *A History of the Republic*, *American Adventures*, *The American Adventure*, and *The American Pageant*. *The American Tradition* does include—though not in its index—a small quote from the Kerner Report mentioning the word.

23. On Ecuador, see Ivan von Sertima, *They Came Before Columbia* (New York: Random House, 1976), 30. On blacks' influence among the Seminoles, see Daniel F. Littlefield, Jr., *Africans and Creeks* (Westport, Conn.: Greenwood, 1979). On Elliot's Iowa eye-color experiment, see the PBS Frontline documentary, *A Class Divided* (Videotape, Yale University Films. Alexandria, Virginia: PBS, 1986). On the Arctic, see "Discoverers' Sons Arrive for Reunion," Burlington *Free Press*, May 1, 1987; Susan A. Kaplan, introduction to Matthew Henson, *A Black Explorer at the North Pole* (Lincoln: University of Nebraska Press, 1989); and Irving Wallace, David Wallechinsky, and Amy Wallace, *Significa* (New York: Dutton, 1983), 17–18. Note that *The American Adventure* blithely assumes assimilation to white society as the goal.

24. That racism has varied is a problem for black rhetors who seek to make it always the overwhelming force of history, which of course reduces our ability to recognize other factors.

25. James W. Loewen and Charles Sallis, *Mississippi: Conflict and Change* (New York: Pantheon, 1980), 141.

26. *America Revised*, 158. Matthew Downey makes the same point in "Speaking of Textbooks: Putting Pressure on the Publishers," *History Teacher* 14 (1980), 68.

27. David Lowenthal, *The Past is a Foreign Country* (Cambridge: Cambridge University Press, 1988), 343.

28. Richard R. Beeman, *Patrick Henry* (New York: McGraw-Hill, 1974), 182; Henry quoted; in J. Franklin Jameson, *The American Revolution Considered as a Social Movement* (Boston: Beacon Press, 1965), 23.

29. *The American Adventure*, an inquiry textbook partly assembled from primary sources, includes more of the letter from which the quoted sentence was drawn. Henry went on to write, "Let us transmit to our descendants, together with our slaves, a pity for their unhappy lot, and an abhorrence of slavery." His biographer, Richard R. Beeman, treats Henry's view of slavery drily: "If it was not hypocrisy, then it was at least self-deception on a grand scale." See *Patrick Henry* (New York: McGraw-Hill, 1974), 97.

30. Paul Finkelman, "Jefferson and Slavery," in Peter S. Onuf, ed., *Jefferson Legacies* (Charlottesville: University Press of Virginia, 1993), 181–221, is an extensive analysis of Jefferson's slaveholding and the difference it made on his thought.

31. James M'Cune Smith, "On the Fourteenth Query of Thomas Jefferson's Notes on Virginia," *The Anglo-African Magazine* 1, no. 8 (August 1859): 1–9.

32. Paul Finkelman, "Treason Against the Hopes of the World: Thomas Jefferson and the Problem of Slavery" (Washington D.C.: National Museum of American History colloquium. March 23, 1993); Roger Kennedy, *Mr. Lincoln's Ancient Egypt* (Washington, D.C.: National Museum of American History, 1991, typescript), 93; Ronald Takaki, *A Different Mirror* (Boston: Little, Brown, 1993), 69. William W. Freehling also treats Jefferson's ambivalence about slavery in *The Road to Disunion* (New York: Oxford University Press, 1990) 123–31, 136.

33. Patronizing compliments like this are surely intended to woo African American and liberal white members of textbook adoption committees. Or

perhaps publishers imagine that such praise helps white students think less badly of African Americans today. Showing how the Revolution decreased white racism would be more legitimate historically, however, and probably more relevant to reducing bigotry today.

34. Bruce Glasrud and Alan Smith, *Race Relations in British North America, 1607–1783* (Chicago: Nelson-Hall, 1982), 330.

35. George Imlay, quoted in Okoye, *The American Image of Africa*, 55. See also Glasrud and Smith, *Race Relations in British North Africa*, 278–330.

36. Aptheker, *Essays in the History of the American Negro*, 76.

37. Quoted in J. Franklin Jameson, *The American Revolution Considered as a Social Movement* (Boston: Beacon Press, 1965), 23.

38. Regarding the impact of the Revolution on slavery, see Glasrud and Smith, *Race Relations in British North America*, 278; Richard H. Sewell, *Ballots for Freedom* (New York: Oxford University Press, 1976), 3; Dwight Dumond, *Antislavery* New York: Norton, 1966 [1961]), 27–34, Arthur Zilversmit, *The First Emancipation* (Chicago: University of Chicago Press, 1967); and Paul Finkelman, *An Imperfect Union* (Chapel Hill: University of North Carolina Press, 1981). Virginia data from Finkelman, "Jefferson and Slavery," 187.

39. Finkelman, "Treason Against the Hopes of the World."

40. David Walker quoted in Okoye, *The American Image of Africa*, 45–46. Even as he attacked Jefferson, Walker also quoted with approval from the Declaration of Independence.

41. Piero Gleijesus, "The Limits of Sympathy." *Journal of Latin American Studies* 24, no. 3 (October 1992): 486, 500; Roger Kennedy, *Orders from France* (New York: Alfred A. Knopf, 1989), 140–45, 152–57.

42. Gleijesus, "The Limits of Sympathy," 504; the Ostend Manifesto quoted in Dumond, *Antislavery*, 361. See also Robert May, *The Southern Dream of a Caribbean Empire, 1854–1861*, (Baton Rouge: Louisiana State University Press, 1973).

43. Henry Sterks, *The Free Negro in Antebellum Louisiana* (Rutherford, N.J.: Fairleigh Dickenson University Press, 1972), 301–4.

44. William S. Willis, "Division and Rule: Red, White, and Black in the Southeast," in Leonard Dinnerstein and Kenneth Jackson, eds., *American Vistas, 1607–1877* (New York: Oxford University Press, 1975), 61–64; see also Littlefield, *Africans and Creeks*, 10–100, and Theda Perdue, "Red and Black in the Southern Appalachians," *Southern Exposure* 12, no. 6 (November 1984): 19.

45. Sloan, *Blacks in America, 1492–1970*, 9; Littlefield, *Africans and Creeks*, 72–80.

46. William C. Sturtevant, "Creek Into Seminole," in Eleanor Burke Leacock and Nancy O. Lurie, eds., *North American Indians in Historical Perspective* (Prospect Heights, Ill.: Waveland, 1988 [1971]), 92–128.

47. J. Leitch Wright, Jr., *The Only Land They Knew* (New York: Free Press, 1981), 277; William Loren Katz, *Teachers' Guide to American Negro History* (Chicago: Quadrangle, 1971), 34, 63. See also Scott Thybony, "Against All Odds, Black Seminole Won Their Freedom," *Smithsonian Magazine* 22, no. 5 (August 1991): 90–100; and Littlefield, *Africans and Creeks*, 85–90.

48. Reginald Horsman, "American Indian Policy and the Origins of Manifest Destiny," in Francis Prucha, ed., *The Indian in American History* (New York: Holt, Rinehart and Winston, 1971), 28. Almost every textbook mentions slavery as an issue in Texas, but most bury it within other "rights" Mexicans denied Anglos. On free blacks see Moore, *Stereotypes, Distortions, and Omissions in U.S. History Textbooks*, 24. Readers may also enjoy a brilliant historical novel by R. A. Lafferty, *Okla Hannali* (Garden City, NY: Doubleday, 1972), 100, which declares: "however it be falsified (and the falsification remains one of the classic things), there was only one issue there: slavery."

49. Thomas David Schoonover, *Dollars Over Dominion* (Baton Rouge: Louisiana State University Press, 1978), 41, 78.

50. Patricia N. Limerick, *The Legacy of Conquest* (New York: Norton, 1987), 92–93.

51. The debates were also the first events in American public life to be transcribed verbatim, allowing much fuller and more accurate news coverage.

52. Amazingly, the two inquiry tests gloss over the debates. *The American Adventure* includes only a paragraph of questions, *Discovering American History* only a paragraph of descriptive prose (though it does quote from Lincoln's "House Divided" speech). When treating actions, inquiry texts can have a difficult time incorporating primary sources, which by nature are usually words rather than deeds. Here the action consists of words—yet the textbooks ignore them!

53. Quoted in Paul D. Escott, *Slavery Remembered* (Chapel Hill: University of North Carolina Press, 1979), 153.

54. The exceptions are *The American Pageant*, *The American Way*, and *Discovering American History*. *American Pageant* is a patch job by David Kennedy on Thomas Bailey's original, which dates to 1956! Where Bailey literally embraced Margaret Mitchell—"The moonlight-and-magnolia Old South of ante-bellum days had gone with the wind"—after "days" Kennedy adds "largely imaginary in any case." Despite such new material, the result is still a dated and racist interpretation of "Reconstruction by the Sword," emphasizing its "drastic legislation" and completely downplaying the considerable acceptance Republican policies won among many Southern whites. *The American Way* paints "Radical" Republicans as opportunists who "sent northerners to the South to make sure the Blacks remembered to vote for the party that freed them." (Blacks needed no such aid, of course; many voted Republican through the 1950s!) *The American Way* also claims that "The Radicals felt that it was not enough to give Blacks

the same rights as Whites," so they "managed to pass the Fourteenth Amendment"—but that amendment in fact gave blacks exactly the same rights as whites! In all, *American Way's* treatment is amateurish. Even sparser is the coverage in *Discovering American History*, an inquiry text: it devotes just two pages to all of Congressional Reconstruction, and most of that space is used to reprint the texts of the Fourteenth and Fifteenth Amendments. *Discovering American History* is the only text to avoid the terms "carpetbagger" and "scalawag," but then again it avoids Reconstruction almost entirely.

55. Perhaps Bauer was influenced by Margaret Mitchell's portrait of African Americans who lazed about as soon as slavery ended and white supervision relaxed. Writings and recollections by newly freed people offer no support for this portrait, however. See Paul Escott, *Slavery Remembered* (Chapel Hill: University of North Carolina Press, 1979), which offers valuable information about Reconstruction remembered. See also studies of individual locales, and statewide analyses, such as Roberta Sue Alexander, *North Carolina Faces the Freedmen* (Durham: Duke University Press, 1985).

56. In 1990, for instance, only blacks with less than high school educations participated in the labor force at a lower rate than whites. See U.S. Bureau of the Census: *Statistical Abstract of the United States: 1993* (Washington, D.C.: Government Printing Office, 1993), 394.

57. George C. Rable, *But There Was No Peace* (Athens: University of Georgia Press, 1984), 1.

58. Morgan Kousser, "The Voting Rights Act and the Two Reconstructions" (Washington, D.C.: Brookings Institution, October 19, 1990); Du Bois, *Black Reconstruction*, 681.

59. Foner, *Reconstruction*, as reviewed by C. Vann Woodward in "Unfinished Business," *New York Review of Books*, May 12, 1988, referring to statistics gathered by Albion W. Tourgée. See also Roberta Sue Allen, *North Carolina Faces the Freedmen* (Durham: Duke University Press, 1985).

60. Gen. O. O. Howard quoted in Robert Moore, *Reconstruction: The Promise and Betrayal of Democracy* (New York: CIBC, 1983), 17.

61. The six are *The American Pageant, Life and Liberty, American History, A History of the Republic, Promise of Freedom*, and, being generous, *The American Tradition. Tradition* offers three paragraphs under the heading "Violence"; the longest is a 1906 defense of the KKK by "Pitchfork" Ben Tillman of South Carolina, rather than a first-person description of the violence itself.

62. Logan, *The Betrayal of the Negro* (New York Macmillan, 1970 [1954]). See also Eric Foner, *Reconstruction* (New York: Harper & Row 1988), 604.

63. In *Minority Education and Caste* (New York: Academic Press, 1978), anthropologist John Ogbu uses stigma to explain why members of oppressed minorities typically fare better outside their home societies.

64. Michael L. Cooper, *Playing America's Game* (New York: Lodestar, 1993), 10; Gordon Morgan, "Emancipation Bowl" (Fayetteville: University of Arkansas Department of Sociology, n.d., typescript).

65. Robert Azug and Stephen Maizlish, eds., *New Perspectives on Race and Slavery America* (Lexington: University Press of Kentucky, 1986), 118–21, 125; Loewen and Sallis, *Mississippi: Conflict and Change*, 241.

66. Wallace, Wallechinsky, and Wallace, *Signified*, 26–27, "Man in the Zoo."

67. On the cultural meaning of minstrelsy see Robert Toll, *Blacking Up* (New York: Oxford University Press, 1971), 57, and the introduction to Ike Simond, *Old Slack's Reminiscence and Pocket History of the Colored Profession* (Bowling Green, Ohio; Popular Press, 1974), xxv; Joseph Boskin, *Sambo* (New York: Oxford University Press, 1986), 129; Myrdal, *An American Dilemma*, 989; and Loewen, "Black Image in White Vermont."

68. For Cleveland, see Stanley Hirshson, *Farewell to the Bloody Shirt* (Chicago: Quadrangle, 1968), 239–45. For Democrats, see Kousser, "The Voting Rights Act and the Two Reconstructions," 12. For Harding see Wyn Craig Wade, *The Fiery Cross* (New York: Simon and Schuster, 1987), 165. Harding's induction merely showed the legitimacy of the KKK; his administration was not as racist as Wilson's, although it did not undo Wilson's segregative policies. For *Rice v. Gong Lum*, see James W. Loewen, *The Mississippi Chinese: Between Black and White* (Prospect Heights, Ill.: Waveland Press, 1988), 66–69. For Tulsa, see Wallace Wallechinsky, and Wallace, *Significa*, 60–61. As I was writing this chapter in 1992, Los Angeles erupted in what many reporters called "the worst race riot of the century." Perhaps, having been weaned on our history textbooks, they didn't know of the savage riots of the nadir.

69. Americans who did not experience segregation, which ended in the South in about 1970, may consider these words melodramatic. American history textbooks do not help today's students feel the reality of the period. Please see the last field study of segregation, Loewen, *The Mississippi Chinese*, 45–48, 51, and 131–34.

70. "Racial Division Taking Root in Young America, People For Finds." People for the American Way, *Forum 2*, no. 1 (March, 1992): 1.

71. Cohen, "Generation of Bigots," *Washington Post*, July 23, 1993; Marttila & Kiley, Inc., *Highlights from an Anti-Defamation League Survey on Racial Attitudes in America* (New York: Anti-Defamation League, 1993), 21.

Discussion Questions

1. Loewen discusses the most popular American novels of the nineteenth and twentieth centuries, *Uncle Tom's Cabin* and *Gone With the Wind*. Have you read either or both of these books? Even if

you have not, you probably have images in your mind that derive from them. What are they? Why does *Gone With the Wind* remain popular today despite our knowledge of what plantation life was really like? Have you read any novels by African Americans about the period Loewen calls the nadir (e.g., Richard Wright's *Black Boy*)? What is the value of presenting situations in the voices of people of different racial, class, and gender backgrounds?

2. Loewen claims that while individuals and groups are credited for the good they do, no one in American history is ever presented as being responsible for the bad things, such as slavery, the failure of Reconstruction, or the imposition of segregation; they just seem to happen. He also says that textbooks leave the impression that race relations are improving on their own. Why is this problematic? What might be the causes and consequences of this kind of presentation?

3. Loewen's book was published in 1995. If you are a recent high school graduate or have looked at a high school American history text published in the year 2000 or later, did you find these topics treated differently? Was anything else missing? For example, how were the lives and goals of working class people in the nineteenth and twentieth century portrayed?

4. Loewen writes in a gender-neutral way. What would you add from other readings in the section to fill in the gaps in Loewen's work? Is he guilty of the same kind of omission regarding gender that he accuses others of regarding race?

Reprinted from: James W. Loewen, "Gone With the Wind: The Invisibility of Racism in American History Textbooks." In *Lies My Teacher Told Me: Everything Your American History Textbook Got Wrong* pp. 131–151, 153–159, 332–338. Copyright © 1995 by James W. Loewen. Reprinted with permission of The New Press, New York. ✦

6

The Logic of Nonstandard English

William Labov

In this classic piece by William Labov, the author explores the answers to the question: Why are inner-city children demonstrating such low achievement in American schools? Generously, Labov lays out the arguments of his day from various academic quarters. The two positions on the subject with which Labov most disagrees are those that hold that either heredity or environment are responsible for the deplorable achievement of students in inner-city schools. The heredity argument holds that the inner-city child is inheriting an inferior I. Q., while the environmental stance posits a singularly gendered framework in arguing that inner-city children live in inferior homes where the child's mother has not the wherewithal to provide ample verbal stimulation and experience.

It is a third position to which Labov subscribes. Labov does not believe this lack of school achievement among inner-city children is the result of inherited traits. Nor does he believe that they are the result of inferior, mother-centered environments. Rather, he argues that the low achievement of these children indicates a failure of the school system to respect and reach out to children whose social milieu dramatically differs from the middle-class norm.

As a linguist, Labov takes his cue from modes and nuances of language acquisition and, thereby, makes an argument for the third position by using the very language of inner-city children often vilified by those researchers who judge the inner-city child as suffering from so-called verbal or cultural deprivation, or both. These "culture of poverty" arguments make no

sense to Labov, who takes the very same data—interviews with inner-city youth—used by researchers who adhere to "verbal deprivation" models, making them instances of his own resonant argument. In a fascinating passage, Labov explores the language of the inner-city child versus the middle-class child and finds that the inner-city child's verbal ability indicates more effective debate and reasoning powers. Labov's piece underscores the ignorance of academic arguments that are manifestly race-, class-, and gender-coded as they seek for deprivation in the poor inner-city black child raised by an "inferior" mother, swallowing the camel of systemic school failure on behalf of the nation's neediest children.

Interestingly and tragically, today in the United States inner-city children continue to be marginalized in the American educational system, exhibiting the very same low rates of achievement as the children that Labov described over 30 years ago. Policies such as "No Child Left Behind" (NCLB), sponsored by President George W. Bush's administration, have come under fire from the National Education Association for supporting unfunded mandates and pushing standardized tests as opposed to classroom-based solutions to the achievement gap. Moreover, the very same "culture of poverty," victim-blaming arguments that were used back then—newer versions of the "verbal deprivation" argument—are still used to explain the low scores of inner-city children in our nation.

. . .In the past decade, a great deal of federally-sponsored research has been devoted to the educational problems of children in ghetto schools. In order to account for the poor performance of children in these schools, educational psychologists have attempted to discover what kind of disadvantage or defect they are suffering from. The viewpoint which has been widely accepted, and used as the basis for large-scale intervention programs, is that the children show a cultural deficit as a result of an impoverished environment in their early years. Considerable attention has been given to language. In this area, the deficit theory appears as the concept of "verbal deprivation": Negro children from the ghetto area receive little verbal stimulation, are said to hear very little well-formed language, and as a result are impoverished in their means of verbal expression: they cannot speak complete sentences, do not know the names of common objects, cannot form concepts or convey logical thoughts.

Unfortunately, these notions are based upon the work of educational psychologists who know very little about language and even less about Negro children. The concept of verbal deprivation has no basis in social reality: in fact, Negro children in the urban ghettos receive a great deal of verbal stimulation, hear more well-formed sentences than middle-class children, and participate fully in a highly verbal culture; they have the same basic vocabulary, possess the same capacity for conceptual learning, and use the same logic as anyone else who learns to speak and understand English.

The notion of "verbal deprivation" is a part of the modern mythology of educational psychology, typical of the unfounded notions which tend to expand rapidly in our educational system. In past decades linguists have been as guilty as others in promoting such intellectual fashions at the expense of both teachers and children. But the myth of verbal deprivation is particularly dangerous, because it diverts attention from real defects of our educational system to imaginary defects of the child; and as we shall see, it leads its sponsors inevitably to the hypothesis of the genetic inferiority of Negro children which it was originally designed to avoid. . . .

1. Verbality

The general setting in which the deficit theory has arisen consists of a number of facts which are known to all of us: that Negro children in the central urban ghettos do badly on all school subjects, including arithmetic and reading. In reading, they average more than two years behind the national norm.[1] Furthermore, this lag is cumulative, so that they do worse comparatively in the fifth grade than in the first grade. Reports in the literature show that this bad performance is correlated most closely with socio-economic status. Segregated ethnic groups, however, seem to do worse than others: in particular, Indians, Mexican-Americans, and Negro children. . . .

. . . We are obviously dealing with the effects of the caste system of American society—essentially a "color marking" system. Everyone recognizes this. The question is, by what mechanism does the color bar prevent children from learning to read? One answer is the notion of "cultural deprivation" put forward by Martin Deutsch and others: the Negro children are said to lack the favorable factors in their home environment which enable middle-class children to do well in school. (Deutsch and assoc. 1967; Deutsch, Katz, and Jensen 1968). These factors involve the development of various cognitive skills through verbal interaction with adults, including the ability to reason abstractly, speak fluently, and focus upon long-range goals. In their publications, these psychologists also recognize broader social factors.[2] However, the deficit theory does not focus upon the interaction of the Negro child with white society so much as on his failure to interact with his mother at home. In the literature we find very little direct observation of verbal interaction in the Negro home; most typically, the investigators ask the child if he has dinner with his parents, and if he engages in dinnertable conversation with them. He is also asked whether his family takes him on trips to museums and other cultural activities. This slender thread of evidence is used to explain and interpret the large body of tests carried out in the laboratory and in the school.

The most extreme view which proceeds from this orientation—and one that is now being widely accepted—is that lower-class Negro children have no language at all. The notion is first drawn from Basil Bernstein's writings that "much of lower-class language consists of a kind of incidental 'emotional' accompaniment to action here and now" (Jensen 1968: 118). Bernstein's views are filtered through a strong bias against all forms of working-class behavior, so that middle-class language is seen as superior in every respect—as "more abstract, and necessarily somewhat more flexible, detailed and subtle." One can proceed through a range of such views until one comes to the practical program of Carl Bereiter, Siegfried Engelmann and their associates. (Bereiter et al. 1966; Bereiter and Engelmann 1966). Bereiter's program for an academically oriented preschool is based upon their premise that Negro children must have a language with which they can learn, and their empirical finding that these children come to school without such a language. In his work with four-year-old Negro children from Urbana, Bereiter reports that their communication was by gestures, "single words": and "a series of badly-connected words or phrases," such as *They mine* and *Me got juice*. He reports that Negro children could not ask questions, that "without exaggerating . . . these four-year-olds could make no statements of any kind." Furthermore, when these children were asked "Where is the book?," they did not know enough to look at the table where the book was lying in order to answer. Thus Bereiter concludes that the children's speech forms are nothing more than a series of emotional cries, and he decides to treat them "as if the children had no language at all." He identifies their speech with his interpretation of Bernstein's restricted code: "the language of culturally deprived children . . . is not merely an underdeveloped version of standard English, but is a basically non-logical mode of expressive behavior" (Bereiter et al. 1966: 113). The basic program of his preschool is to teach them a new language devised by Engelmann, which consists of a limited series of questions and answers such as *Where is the squirrel? The squirrel is in the tree*. The children will not be punished if they use their vernacular speech on the playground, but they will not be allowed to use it in the schoolroom. If they should answer the question *Where is the squirrel?* with the illogical vernacular form *In the tree* they will be reprehended by various means and made to say, *The squirrel is in the tree*.

Linguists and psycholinguists who have worked with Negro children are apt to dismiss this view of their language as utter nonsense. Yet there is no reason to reject Bereiter's observations as spurious: they were certainly not made up: on the contrary, they give us a very clear view of the behavior of student and teacher which can be duplicated in any classroom. In our own work outside of the adult-dominated environments of school and home,[3] we do not observe Negro children behaving like this, but on many occasions we have been asked to help analyze the results of research into verbal deprivation in such test situations.

Here, for example, is a complete interview with a Negro boy, one of hundreds carried out in a New York City school. The boy enters a room where there is a large, friendly white interviewer, who puts on the table in front of him a block or a fire engine, and says "Tell me everything you can about this," (The interviewer's further remarks are in parentheses.)

> [12 seconds of silence]
> (What would you say it looks like ?)
> [8 seconds of silence]
> A space ship.
> (Hmmmm.)
> [13 seconds of silence]
> Like a je-et.
> [12 seconds of silence]
> Like a plane.
> [20 seconds of silence]
> (What color is it?)
> Orange. [2 seconds]. An' whi-ite. [2 seconds]. An' green.
> [6 seconds of silence]
> (An' what could you use it for ?)
> [8 seconds of silence]
> A je-et.
> [6 seconds of silence]
> (If you had two of them, what would you do with them?)
> [6 seconds of silence]
> Give one to some-body.
> (Hmmm. Who do you think would like to have it?)
> [10 seconds of silence]
> Cla-rence.
> (Mm. Where do you think we could get another one of these ?)
> At the store.
> (Oh ka-ay!)

We have here the same kind of defensive, monosyllabic behavior which is reported in Bereiter's work. What is the situation that produces it? The child is in an asymmetrical situation where anything he says can literally be held against him. He has learned a number of devices to *avoid* saying anything in this situation, and he works very hard to achieve this end. . . .

If one takes this interview as a measure of the verbal capacity of the child, it must be as his capacity to defend himself in a hostile and threatening situation. But unfortunately, thousands of such interviews are used as evidence of the child's total verbal capacity, or more simply his "verbality"; it is argued that this lack of verbality *explains* his poor performance in school. . . .

The verbal behavior which is shown by the child in the test situation quoted above is not the result of the ineptness of the interviewer. It is rather the result of regular sociolinguistic factors operating upon adult and child in this asymmetrical situation. . . . At one point we began a series of interviews with younger brothers of the "Thunderbirds" in 1390 5th Avenue. Clarence Robins returned after an interview with 8-year-old Leon L., who showed the following minimal response to topics which arouse intense interest in other interviews with older boys.

CR: What if you saw somebody kickin' somebody else on the ground, or was using a stick, what would you do if you saw that?

Leon: Mmmmm.

CR: If it was supposed to be a fair fight—

Leon: I don' know.

CR: You don' know? Would you do anything . . . huh? I can't hear you.

CR: Did you ever see somebody got beat up real bad?

Leon: . . . Nope ? ? ?

CR: Well—uh—did you ever get into a fight with a guy?

Leon: Nope.

CR: That was bigger than you?

Leon: Nope.

CR: You never been in a fight?

Leon: Nope.

CR: Nobody ever pick on you?

Leon: Nope.

CR: Nobody ever hit you?

Leon: Nope.

CR: How come?

Leon: Ah 'on' know.

CR: Didn't you ever hit somebody?

Leon: Nope.

Leon: [incredulous] You never hit nobody?

Leon: Mhm.

CR: Aww, ba-a-a-be, you ain't gonna tell me that. . . .

This nonverbal behavior occurs in a relatively *favorable* context for adult-child interaction; since the adult is a Negro man raised in Harlem, who knows this particular neighborhood and these boys very well. He is a skilled interviewer who has obtained a very high level of verbal response with techniques developed for a different age level, and he has an extraordinary advantage over most teachers or experimenters in these respects. But even his skills and personality are ineffective in breaking down the social constraints that prevail here.

When we reviewed the record of this interview with Leon, we decided to use it as a test of our own knowledge of the sociolinguistic factors which control speech. We made the following changes in the social situation: in the next interview with Leon, Clarence

(1) brought along a supply of potato chips, changing the "interview" into something more in the nature of a party;

(2) brought along Leon's best friend, 8-year-old Gregory;

(3) reduced the height imbalance (when Clarence got down on the floor of Leon's room, he dropped from 6 ft. 2 in. to 3 ft. 6 in.);

(4) introduced taboo words and taboo topics, and proved to Leon's surprise that one can say anything into our microphone without any fear of retaliation.

The result of these changes is a striking difference in the volume and style of speech.

CR: Is there anybody who says *your momma drink pee?*

{ Leon: [rapidly and breathlessly] Yee-ah!
Greg: Yup!

Leon: And your father eat doo-doo for breakfas'!

CR: Ohhh!! [laughs]

Leon: And they say *your father—your father eat doo-doo for dinner!*

Greg: When they sound on me, I say *C. B. M.*

CR: What that mean?

{ Leon: Congo booger-snatch! [laughs]
Greg: Congo booger-snatcher! [laughs]

Greg: And sometimes I'll curse with *B. B.*

CR: What that?

Greg: Black boy! [Leon—crunching on potato chips] Oh that's a *M. B. B.*

CR: M. B. B. What's that?

Greg: 'Merican Black Boy!

CR: Ohh . . .

Greg: Anyway, 'Mericans is same like white people, right?

Leon: And they talk about Allah.

CR: Oh yeah?

Greg: Yeah.

CR: What they say about Allah?

{ Leon: Allah—Allah is God.
Greg: Allah—

CR: And what else?

Leon: I don' know the res'.

Greg: Allah i—Allah is God, Allah is the only God, Allah—

Leon: Allah is the *son* of God.

Greg: But can he make magic?

Leon: Nope.

Greg: I know who can make magic.

CR: Who can?

Leon: The God, the *real* one.

CR: Who can make magic?

Greg: The son of po'— [CR: Hm?] I'm saying the po'k chop God! He only a po'k chop God![4] [Leon chuckles].

The "nonverbal" Leon is now competing actively for the floor; Gregory and Leon talk to each other as much as they do to the interviewer.

. . . The monosyllabic speaker who had nothing to say about anything and cannot remember what he did yesterday has disappeared. Instead, we have two boys who have so much to say they keep interrupting each other, who seem to have no difficulty in using the English language to express themselves. . . .

One can now transfer this demonstration of the sociolinguistic control of speech to other test situations—including I. Q. and reading tests in school. It should be immediately apparent that none of the standard tests will come anywhere near measuring Leon's verbal capacity. On these tests he will show up as very much the monosyllabic, inept, ignorant, bumbling child of our first interview. The teacher has far less ability than Clarence Robins to elicit speech from this child; Clarence knows the community, the things that Leon has been doing, and the things that Leon would like to talk about. But the power relationships in a one-to-one confrontation between adult and child are too asymmetrical. This does not mean that some Negro children will not talk a great deal when alone with an adult, or that an adult cannot get close to any child. It means that the social situation is the most powerful determinant of verbal behavior and that an adult must enter into the right social relation with a child if he wants to find out what a child can do: this is just what many teachers cannot do.

The view of the Negro speech community which we obtain from our work in the ghetto areas is precisely the opposite from that reported by Deutsch, Engelmann and Bereiter. We see a child bathed in verbal stimulation from morning to night. We see many speech events which depend upon the competitive exhibition of verbal skills: sounding, singing, toasts, rifting, louding—a whole range of activities in which the individual gains status through his use of language.[5] We see the younger child trying to acquire these skills from older children—hanging around on the outskirts of the older peer groups, and imitating this behavior to the best of his ability. We see no connection between verbal skill at the speech events characteristic of the street culture and success in the schoolroom.

2. Verbosity

There are undoubtedly many verbal skills which children from ghetto areas must learn in order to do well in the school situation, and some of these are indeed characteristic of middle-class verbal behavior. Precision in spelling, practice in handling abstract symbols, the ability to state explicitly the meaning of words, and a richer knowledge of the Latinate vocabulary, may all be useful acquisitions. But is it true that *all* of the middle-class verbal habits are functional and desirable in the school situation? Before we impose middle-class verbal style upon children from other cultural groups, we should find out how much of this is useful for the main work of analyzing and generalising, and how much is merely stylistic—or even dysfunctional. In high school and college middle-class children spontaneously complicate their syntax to the point that instructors despair of getting them to make their language simpler and clearer. . . .

Our work in the speech community makes it painfully obvious that in many ways working-class speakers are more effective narrators, reasoners and debaters than many middle-class speakers who temporize, qualify, and lose their argument in a mass of irrelevant detail. Many academic writers try to rid themselves of that part of middle-class style that is empty pretension, and keep that part that is needed for precision. But the average middle-class speaker that we encounter makes no such effort; he is enmeshed in verbiage, the victim of sociolinguistic factors beyond his control.

I will not attempt to support this argument here with systematic quantitative evidence, although it is possible to develop measures which show how far middle-class speakers can wander from the point. I would like to contrast two speakers dealing with roughly the same topic—matters of belief. The first is Larry H., a 15-year-old core member of the Jets, being interviewed by John Lewis. Larry is one of the loudest and roughest members of the Jets, one who gives the least recognition to the conventional rules of politeness.[6] . . .

JL: What happens to you after you die? Do you know?

Larry: Yeah, I know.

JL: What?

Larry: After they put you in the ground, your body turns into—ah—bones, an' shit.

JL: What happens to your spirit?

Larry: Your spirit—soon as you die, your spirit leaves you.

JL: And where does the spirit go?

Larry: Well, it all depends . . .

JL: On what?

Larry: You know, like some people say if you're good an' shit, your spirit goin' t' heaven . . . 'n if you bad, your spirit goin' to hell. Well, bullshit! Your spirit goin' to hell anyway, good or bad.

JL: Why ?

Larry: Why? I'll tell you why. 'Cause, you see, doesn' nobody really know that it's a God, y' know, 'cause I mean I have seen black gods, pink gods, white gods, all color gods, and don't nobody know it's really a God. An' when they be sayin' if you good, you goin' t' heaven, tha's bullshit, 'cause you ain't goin' to no heaven, 'cause it ain't no heaven for you to go to.

Larry is a paradigmatic speaker of nonstandard Negro English (NNE) as opposed to standard English (SE). His grammar shows a high concentration of such characteristic NNE forms as negative inversion [*don't nobody know . . .*], negative concord [*you ain't goin' to no heaven . . .*], invariant *be* [*when they be sayin' . . .*], dummy *it* for SE *there* [*it ain't no heaven . . .*], optional copula deletion [*if you're good . . . if you bad . . .*], and full forms of auxiliaries [*I have seen . . .*]! The only SE influence in this passage is the one case of *doesn't* instead of the invariant *don't* of NNE. Larry also provides a paradigmatic example of the rhetorical style of NNE: he can sum up a complex argument in a few words, and the full force of his opinions comes through without qualification or reservation. He is eminently quotable, and his interviews give us many concise statements of the NNE point of view. One can almost say that Larry *speaks* the NNE culture.

It is the logical form of this passage which is of particular interest here. Larry presents a complex set of interdependent propositions which can be explicated by setting out the SE equivalents in linear order. The basic argument is to deny the twin propositions

(A) If you are good,
(B) then your spirit will go to heaven.

(-A) If you are bad,
(C) then your spirit will go to hell. . . .

Larry denies (B), and asserts that *if (A) or (-A), then (C)*. His argument may be outlined as follows:

(1) Everyone has a different idea of what God is like.

(2) Therefore nobody really knows that God exists.

(3) If there is a heaven, it was made by God.

(4) If God doesn't exist, he couldn't have made heaven.

(5) Therefore heaven does not exist.

(6) You can't go somewhere that doesn't exist.

(-B) Therefore you can't go to heaven.

(C) Therefore you are going to hell. . . .

This hypothetical argument is not carried on at a high level of seriousness. It is a game played with ideas as counters, in which opponents use a wide variety of verbal devices to win. There is no personal commitment to any of these propositions, and no reluctance to strengthen one's argument by bending the rules of logic as in the (2–5) sequence. But if the opponent invokes the rules of logic, they hold. In John Lewis' interviews, he often makes this move, and the force of his argument is always acknowledged and countered within the rules of logic. . . .

JL: Well, if there's no heaven, how could there be a hell?

Larry: I mean—ye-eah. Well, let me tell you, it ain't no hell, 'cause this is hell right here, y'know!

JL: This is hell?

Larry: Yeah, this is hell right here!

Larry's answer is quick, ingenious and decisive. The application of the (3-4-5) argument to hell is denied, since hell is here, and therefore conclusion (C) stands. These are not ready-made or preconceived opinions, but new propositions devised to win the logical argument in the game being played. The reader will note the speed and precision of Larry's mental operations. He does not wander, or insert meaningless verbiage. The only repetition is (2), placed before and after (1) in his original statement. It is often said that the nonstandard vernacular is not suited for dealing with abstract or hypothetical questions, but in fact speakers from the NNE community take great delight in exercising their wit and logic on the most improbable and problematical matters. Despite the fact that Larry H. does not believe in God, and has just denied all knowledge of him, John Lewis advances the following hypothetical question:

JL: . . . But, just say that there is a God, what color is he? White or black?

Larry: Well, if it is a God . . . I wouldn' know what color, I couldn' say,—couldn' nobody say what color he is or really *would* be.

JL: But now, jus' suppose there was a God—

Larry: Unless'n they say . . .

JL: No, I was jus' sayin' jus' suppose there is a God, would he be white or black?

Larry: . . . He'd be white, man.

JL: Why?

Larry: Why? I'll tell you why. 'Cause the average whitey out here got everything, you dig? And the nigger ain't got shit, y'know? Y'understan'? So—um—for—in order for *that* to happen, you know it ain't no black God that's doin' that bullshit.

No one can hear Larry's answer to this question without being convinced that they are in the presence of a skilled speaker with great "verbal presence of mind," who can use the English language expertly for many purposes. . . .

Let us now turn to the second speaker, an upper-middle-class, college educated Negro man being interviewed by Clarence Robins in our survey of adults in Central Harlem.

CR: Do you know of anything that someone can do, to have someone who has passed on visit him in a dream?

Chas. M.: Well, I even heard my parents say that there is such a thing as something in dreams some things like that, and sometimes dreams do come true. I have personally never had a dream come true. I've never dreamt that somebody was dying and they actually died, (Mhm) or that I was going to have ten dollars the next day and somehow I got ten dollars in my pocket. (Mhm). I don't particularly believe in that, I don't think it's true. I do feel, though, that there is such a thing as—ah—witchcraft. I do feel that in certain cultures there is such a thing as witchcraft, or some sort of *science* of witchcraft; I don't think that it's just a matter of believing hard enough that there is such a thing as witchcraft. I do believe that there is such a thing that a person can put himself in a state of *mind* (Mhm), or that—er—something could be given them to intoxicate them in a certain—to a certain frame of mind—that—that could actually be considered witchcraft.

Charles M. is obviously a "good speaker" who strikes the listener as well-educated, intelligent and sincere. He is a likeable and attractive person—the kind of person that middle-class listeners rate very high on a scale of of "job suitability" and equally high as a potential friend.[8] His language is more moderate and tempered than Larry's; he makes every effort to qualify his opinions, and seems anxious to avoid any misstatements or over-statements. From these qualities emerge the primary characteristic of this passage—its *ver-*

bosity. Words multiply, some modifying and qualifying, others repeating or padding the main argument. The first half of this extract is a response to the initial question on dreams, basically:

(1) Some people say that dreams sometimes come true.

(2) I have never had a dream come true.

(3) Therefore I don't believe (1).

. . . [T]his much of Charles M.'s response is well-directed to the point of the question. He then volunteers a statement of his beliefs about witchcraft which shows the difficulty of middle-class speakers who (a) want to express a belief in something but (b) want to show themselves as judicious, rational and free from superstitions. The basic proposition can be stated simply in five words:

But I believe in witchcraft.

However, the idea is enlarged to exactly 100 words, and it is difficult to see what else is being said. . . .

Without the extra verbiage and the O.K. words like *science, culture,* and *intoxicate,* Charles M. appears as something less than a first-rate thinker. The initial impression of him as a good speaker is simply our long-conditioned reaction to middle-class verbosity: we know that people who use these stylistic devices are educated people, and we are inclined to credit them with saying something intelligent. . . .

3. Grammaticality

Let us now examine Bereiter's own data on the verbal behavior of the children he dealt with. The expressions *They mine* and *Me got juice* are cited as examples of a language which lacks the means for expressing logical relations—in this case characterized as "a series of badly connected words." (Bereiter 1966: 113 ff.) In the case of *They mine,* it is apparent that Bereiter confuses the notions of logic and explicitness. We know that there are many languages of the world which do not have a present copula, and which conjoin subject and predicate complement without a verb. Russian, Hungarian, and Arabic may be foreign; but they are not by that same token illogical. In the case of nonstandard Negro English we are not dealing with even this superficial grammatical difference, but rather with a low-level rule which carries contraction one step farther to delete single consonants representing the verbs *is*, *have*, and *will*. (Labov, Cohen, Robins & Lewis 1968: sect. 3.4) We have yet to find any children who do not sometimes use the full forms of *is* and *will*, even though they may frequently delete it. . . .

Furthermore, the deletion of the *is* or *are* in nonstandard Negro English is not the result of erratic or illogical behavior: it follows the same regular rules as standard English contraction. Wherever standard English can contract, Negro children use either the contracted form or (more commonly) the deleted zero form. Thus *They mine* corresponds to standard *They're mine*, not to the full form *They are mine*. On the other hand, no such deletion is possible in positions where standard English cannot contract: just as one cannot say *That's what they're* in standard English, *That's what they* is equally impossible in the vernacular we are considering. The internal constraints upon both of these rules show that we are dealing with a phonological process like contraction, sensitive to such phonetic conditions as whether or not the next word begins with a vowel or a consonant. The appropriate use of the deletion rule, like the contraction rule, requires a deep and intimate knowledge of English grammar and phonology. Such knowledge is not available for conscious inspection by native speakers: the rules we have recently worked out for standard contraction (Labov, Cohen, Robins & Lewis 1968: 3.4) have never appeared in any grammar, and are certainly not a part of the conscious knowledge of any standard English speakers. Nevertheless, the adult or child who uses these rules must have formed at some level of psychological organization clear concepts of "tense markers," "verb phrases," "rule ordering," "sentence embedding," "pronoun," and many other grammatical categories which are essential parts of any logical system.

Bereiter's reaction to the sentence *Me got juice* is even more puzzling. If Bereiter believes that *Me got juice* is not a logical expression, it can only be that he interprets the use of the objective pronoun *me* as representing a difference in logical relationship to the verb: that the child is in fact saying that *the juice got him* rather than *he got the juice*! If on the other hand the child means "I got juice," then this sentence form shows only that he has not learned the formal rules for the use of the subjective form *I* and oblique form *me*. . . .

Bereiter shows even more profound ignorance of the rules of discourse and of syntax when he rejects *In the tree* as an illogical, or badly-formed answer to *Where is the squirrel?* Such elliptical answers are of course used by everyone; they show the appropriate deletion of subject and main verb, leaving the locative which is questioned by *wh + there*. The reply *In the tree* demonstrates that the listener has been attentive to and apprehended the syntax of the speaker.[9] Whatever formal structure we wish to write for expressions such as *Yes* or *Home* or *In the tree*, it is obvious that they cannot be interpreted without knowing the structure of the question which preceded them, and that they presuppose an understanding of the syntax of the question. Thus if you ask me "Where is the squirrel?" it is necessary for me to understand the processes of *wh*-attachment, *wh*-attraction to the front of the sentence, and flip-flop of auxiliary and subject to produce this sentence from an underlying form which would otherwise have produced *The squirrel is there*. If the child had answered *The tree*, or *Squirrel the tree*, or *The in tree*, we would then assume that he did not understand the syntax of the full form, *The squirrel is in the tree*. Given the data that Bereiter presents, we cannot conclude that the child has no grammar, but only that the investigator does not understand the rules of grammar. It does not necessarily do any harm to use the full form *The squirrel is in the tree*, if one wants to make fully explicit the rules of grammar which the child has internalized. Much of logical analysis consists of making explicit just that kind of internalized rule. But it is hard to believe that any good can come from a program which begins with so many misconceptions about the input data. Bereiter and Englemann believe that in teaching the child to say *The squirrel is in the tree* or *This is a box* and *This is not a box* they are teaching him an entirely new language, whereas in fact they are not only teaching him to produce slightly different forms of the language he already has. . . .

4. What's wrong with being wrong?

If there is a failure of logic involved here, it is surely in the approach of the verbal deprivation theorists, rather than in the mental abilities of the children concerned. We can isolate six distinct steps in the reasoning which has led to programs such as those of Deutsch, Bereiter and Engelmann:

(1) The lower-class child's verbal response to a formal and threatening situation is used to demonstrate his lack of verbal capacity, or verbal deficit.

(2) This verbal deficit is declared to be a major cause of the lower-class child's poor performance in school.

(3) Since middle-class children do better in school, middle-class speech habits are seen to be necessary for learning.

(4) Class and ethnic differences in grammatical form are equated with differences in the capacity for logical analysis.

(5) Teaching the child to mimic certain formal speech patterns used by middle-class teachers is seen as teaching him to think logically.

(6) Children who learn these formal speech patterns are then said to be thinking logically and it is predicted that they will do much better in reading and arithmetic in the years to follow.

In sections 1–[3] of this paper, I have tried to show that these propositions are wrong, concentrating on (1), (4), and (5). Proposition (3) is the primary logical fallacy which illicitly identifies a form of speech as the *cause* of middle-class achievement in school. Proposition (6) is the one which is most easily shown to be wrong in fact, as we will note below.

However, it is not too naive to ask, "What is wrong with being wrong?" There is no competing educational theory which is being dismantled by this program; and there does not

seem to be any great harm in having children repeat *This is not a box* for twenty minutes a day. We have already conceded that NNE children need help in analyzing language into its surface components, and in being more explicit. But there are serious and damaging consequences of the verbal deprivation theory which may be considered under two headings: [one is] the theoretical bias. . . .

. . . It is widely recognized that the teacher's attitude towards the child is an important factor in his success or failure. The work of Rosenthal on "self-fulfilling prophecies" shows that the progress of children in the early grades can be dramatically affected by a single random labelling of certain children as "intellectual bloomers." (Rosenthal & Jacobson 1968) When the everyday language of Negro children is stigmatized as "not a language at all" and "not possessing the means for logical thought," the effect of such a labelling is repeated many times during each day of the school year. Every time that a child uses a form of NNE without the copula or with negative concord, he will be labelling himself for the teacher's benefit as "illogical," as a "nonconceptual thinker." Bereiter and Engelmann, Deutsch and Jensen are giving teachers a ready-made, theoretical basis for the prejudice they already feel against the lower-class Negro child and his language. When they hear him say *I don't want none* or *They mine*, they will be hearing through the bias provided by the verbal deprivation theory: not an English dialect different from theirs, but the primitive mentality of the savage mind.

But what if the teacher succeeds in training the child to use the new language consistently? The verbal deprivation theory holds that this will lead to a whole chain of successes in school, and that the child will be drawn away from the vernacular culture into the middle-class world. Undoubtedly this will happen with a few isolated individuals, just as it happens in every school system today, for a few children. But we are concerned not with the few but the many, and for the majority of Negro children the distance between them and the school is bound to widen under this approach. . . .

The essential fallacy of the verbal deprivation theory lies in tracing the educational failure of the child to his personal deficiencies. At present, these deficiencies are said to be caused by his home environment. It is traditional to explain a child's failure in school by his inadequacy; but when failure reaches such massive proportions, it seems to us necessary to look at the social and cultural obstacles to learning, and the inability of the school to adjust to the social situation. . . .

That educational psychology should be strongly influenced by a theory so false to the facts of language is unfortunate; but that children should be the victims of this ignorance is intolerable. It may seem that the fallacies of the verbal deprivation theory are so obvious that they are hardly worth exposing; I have tried to show that it is an important job for us to undertake. If linguists can contribute some of their available knowledge and energy toward this end, we will have done a great deal to justify the support that society has given to basic research in our field.

Notes

1. A report of average reading comprehension scores in New York City was published in the *New York Times* on December 3, 1968. The schools attended by most of the peer group members we have studied showed the following scores:

School	Grade	Reading score	National norm
J. H. S. 13	7	5.6	7.7
	9	7.6	9.7
J. H. S. 120	7	5.6	7.7
	9	7.0	9.7
I. S. 88	6	5.3	6.7
	8	7.2	8.7

The average is then more than two full years behind grade in the ninth grade.

2. For example, in Deutsch, Katz and Jensen 1968 there is a section on "Social and Psychological Perspectives" which includes a chapter by Proshansky and Newton on "The Nature and Meaning of Negro Self-Identity" and one by Rosenthal and Jacobson on "Self-Fulfilling Prophecies in the Classroom."

3. The research cited here was carried out in South Central Harlem and other ghetto areas in 1965–1968 to describe structural and functional differences between nonstandard Negro English and standard English of the classroom. It was supported by the Office of Education as Cooperative Research Projects 3091 and 3288. Detailed reports are given in Labov, Cohen and Robins 1965, Labov 1965, and Labov, Cohen, Robins and Lewis 1968.

4. The reference to the *pork chop God* condenses several concepts of black nationalism current in the Harlem community. A *pork chop* is a Negro who has not lost traditional subservient ideology of the South, who has no knowledge of himself in Muslim terms, and the *pork chop God* would be the traditional God of Southern Baptists. He and his followers may be pork chops, but he still holds the power in Leon and Gregory's world.

5. For detailed accounts of these speech events, see Labov, Cohen, Robins and Lewis 1968, section 4.2.

6. A direct view of Larry's verbal style in a hostile encounter is given in Labov, Cohen, Robins and Lewis 1968, Vol. II, pp. 39–43. Gray's Oral Reading Test was being given to a group of Jets on the steps of a brownstone house in Harlem, and the landlord tried unsuccessfully to make the Jets move. Larry's verbal style in this encounter matches the reports he gives of himself in a number of narratives cited in section 4.8.

7. See Labov, Cohen, Robins and Lewis 1968, Volume II, p. 38, 71–73, 281–292.

8. See Labov, Cohen, Robins and Lewis 1968, section 4.6 for a description of subjective reaction tests which utilize these evaluative dimensions.

9. The attention to the speaker's syntax required of the listener is analyzed in detail by Harvey Sacks in his unpublished 1968 lectures.

References

Bereiter, Carl et al. 1966. An Academically Oriented Pre-School for Culturally Deprived Children. In Fred M. Hechinger (ed.) *Pre-school Education Today*. (New York, Doubleday) 105–137.

Bereiter, Carl and Siegfried Engelmann. 1966. Teaching Disadvantaged Children in the Preschool. Englewood Cliffs, N.J., Prentice-Hall.

Caldwell, Bettye M. 1967. What is the Optimal Learning Environment for the Young Child? *American Journal of Orthopsychiatry*, Vol. XXXVII, No. 1, 8–21.

Chomsky, Noam. 1965. *Aspects of the Theory of Syntax*. Cambridge, Mass., M.I.T. Press.

Deutsch, Martin and Associates. 1967. *The Disadvantaged Child*. New York, Basic Books.

Deutsch, Martin, Irwin Katz and Arthur R. Jensen (eds.). 1968. *Social Class, Race, and Psychological Development*. New York, Holt.

Jensen, Arthur. 1968. *Social Class and Verbal Learning*. In Deutsch, Katz, and Jensen 1968.

———. 1969. How Much Can We Boost IQ and Scholastic Achievement? *Harvard Educational Review*, Vol. 39, No. 1.

Labov, William. 1967. Some Sources of Reading Problems for Negro Speakers of Non-Standard English.

In A. Frazier (ed.), *New Directions in Elementary English* (Champaign, Ill., National Council of Teachers of English) 140–167. Reprinted in Joan C. Baratz and Roger W. Shuy. 1969. *Teaching Black Children to Read*. (Washington, D.C., Center for Applied Linguistics) 29–67.

Labov, William, Paul Cohen and Clarence Robins. 1965. *A Preliminary Study of the Structure of English Used by Negro and Puerto Rican Speakers in New York City*. Final Report, Cooperative Research Project No. 3091, Office of Education, Washington, D.C.

Labov, William, Paul Cohen, Clarence Robins and John Lewis. 1968. *A Study of the Non-Standard English of Negro and Puerto Rican Speakers in New York City*. Final Report, Cooperative Research Project No. 3288, Office of Education, Washington, D.C., Vol. I and Vol. II.

Labov, William, and Clarence Robins. 1969. A Note on the Relation of Reading Failure to Peer-Group Status in Urban Ghettos. *The Teachers College Record*, Volume 70, Number 5.

Rosenthal, Robert and Lenore Jacobson. 1968. *Self-Fulfilling Prophecies in the Classroom: Teachers' Expectations as Unintended Determinants of Pupils' Intellectual Competence*. In Deutsch, Katz and Jensen 1968.

Whiteman, Martin and Martin Deutsch. *Social Disadvantage as Related to Intellective and Language Development*. In Deutsch, Katz and Jensen 1968.

Discussion Questions

1. Have you noticed "culture of poverty" arguments as discussed in Labov being used in media and friendship/family circles? If so, what are the latest versions of the "verbal deprivation" argument? How do these arguments explain the achievement gap?

2. What solutions might you offer to the achievement gap? How could we change the scenario now being played out in our nation's schools so that children truly aren't left behind?

3. Have you, or someone you know attended an inner-city school? How was this different or similar to your experience of school when you were growing up?

4. If we could decide now to wave a magic wand and make the American educational system nurturing of the potential of all American youth, would everyone be agreeable to this? Why or why not?

Reprinted from: William Labov, "The Logic of Nonstandard English." In *Georgetown Monograph on Languages and Linguistics* 22 1–9, 11–22, 26–28, 34–39. Copyright © 1970 by William Labov. Published by Georgetown University Press. Reprinted with permission. ◆

7

Double-Conscious-ness and *Mestiza* Consciousness Raising

Linking Du Bois and Anzaldúa

Theresa A. Martinez

Theresa A. Martinez, one of the editors of this volume, examines the writings of W. E .B. Du Bois (African American sociologist, 1868–1963) and Gloria Anzaldúa (Latina writer and poet, 1942–2004). She argues that sociologists have paid little attention to important parallels in the work of Black and Latina/o scholars. Du Bois and Anzaldúa both write about oppositional cultures, forms of consciousness or ways of thinking about the world and one's place in it that derive from a matrix of oppression and humiliation within the broader society. Such cultures, as defined by sociologists Mitchell and Feagin, provide members of subordinated groups the intellectual and behavioral tools that help "to preserve dignity and autonomy." What may be less obvious is that members of the dominant culture are also caught up in and affected by the matrix of oppression and that, because each person has gender, race, class, sexuality, and other characteristics, any individual can be simultaneously oppressor and oppressed. Theories and observations generated from oppositional cultures allow us to view the dominant culture critically.

Du Bois was a Black man born just after the Civil War. He was educated in the United States and Germany and was the first African American to earn a Ph.D. from Harvard University. His dissertation was about the slave trade. When he was a professor, he sent his students out to conduct systematic empirical studies of the African American communities of Philadelphia and Atlanta. After leaving the academic world, he devoted his talents and skills to advocacy as a founder of the NAACP and editor of its journal. Late in his life, he moved to the newly independent African county of Ghana, the ancestral home of many African Americans.

Texas-born Anzaldúa, the daughter of Mexican immigrants, was an award-winning editor and writer of fiction, nonfiction, and poetry. She wrote for children as well as adults and played a major role in redefining Chicana/Latina studies and queer studies. Beginning in 1981, with the anthology This Bridge Called My Back, (edited with Cherrie Moraga) her work emphasized the relationship between racism and homophobia and how identities such as sexuality, race, gender, and class are connected. At the time of her death, she was completing her doctoral dissertation at the University of California, Santa Cruz.

Martinez tells us that Du Bois focused his analysis on issues of race and class, while Anzaldúa dealt more fully with gender and sexuality. Each examines the impacts of history and personal experience and writes of a second sight, an ability or faculty that emerges from experiencing oppression, an empowering double- or mestiza consciousness. This way of thinking places people at a crossroads, in the borderlands, which exemplify the tensions of living in multiple worlds at once. It is living in these very borderlands that can lead to freedom from either/or, majority/minority, gay/straight, White/Black, European/indigenous, male/female models of the world.

Introduction

Sociological theorists have long recognized the contributions of W.E.B. Du Bois to the discipline (Rudwick 1969, 1980). Du Bois, one of the first sociological theorists to emerge in the United States, was the first to utilize a Marxian framework to contextualize the relationship of racial oppression to class oppression (Du Bois 1948; see also Aptheker 1990). In contrast, although the work of Gloria Anzaldúa has been reviewed and discussed widely in other disciplines (Saldívar 1991; Alarcón 1998; Gonzalez 1998; Sandoval 1991, 1998; Hurtado 1999), her work has only been described to a limited extent in the discipline of sociology (Pierce 1982; Segura and Pesquera 1992; Denzin 1997). Moreover, while African Americans and Latinos/as are often linked in sociological research with regard to everything from patterns of residential segregation (Charles 2001) to perceived risk of crime (Chiricos, McEntire, and Gertz 2001), and from health outcomes (Ralls 2001) to the politics of imprisonment rates (Jacobs and Carmichael 2001), sociologists have paid little or no attention to the relationship between African American and Latina/o thinkers and the common threads of Black and Latina/o thought.

This paper suggests that the work of W.E.B. Du Bois—noted African American sociologist—and the work of Gloria Anzaldúa—Chicana feminist writer and poet—are resonant works spanning two centuries of African American and Latina/o thought. Moreover, the writing of each represents a significant form of oppositional culture and consciousness describing intersecting oppressions within a matrix of domination. While Du Bois describes a "vast veil" of racial prejudice, poverty, and systematic sexism (Du Bois 1903/1995: 45, 44), Anzaldúa's stories and poems describe racism, classism, sexism, and homophobia in the "borderlands" (Anzaldúa 1987: 78; see also Martinez 1999).

Oppositional Culture as a Response to Oppression

European invasion and the systematic domination and subjugation of non-European peoples make up our nation's history (Blauner 1972). European hegemony was accomplished through social, economic, and political control and exploitation of non-European groups, including American Indians, Africans and African Americans, and Mexican Americans. European domination began with the near genocide of American Indian peoples in order to procure Indian lands. Later, African men, women, and children would be literally "packed" aboard ships to endure the "middle passage" and cruelly transported to a "new world" to insure slave labor (Zinn 1990). Mexican labor was also necessary to the expansion of industrial development in the southwestern United States. The need for land and labor, then, were central motivating factors for European invaders, colonists, and authors of the new American republic. Moreover, racial domination became embedded over time in the national consciousness. Joe Feagin writes, "[O]nce this system was put into place in the seventeenth century, white privileges soon came to be sensed as usual and natural" (2000: 175).

Patricia Hill Collins expands the discussion of domination of non-European groups in the United States from a discourse of racial oppression to one that encompasses intersecting oppressions. Referencing African American women scholar-activists, such as Angela Davis, the Combahee River Collective, and Audre Lorde, Collins asserts that their pioneering works "called for a new approach to analyzing Black women's experiences" which were "shaped not just by race, but [also] by gender, social class, and sexuality" (2000; see also Davis 1981, Combahee River Collective 1982; Lorde 1984). Collins suggests that this new approach lead to exploration of "intersectionality" as a key concept that "refers to particular forms of intersecting oppressions, for example, intersections of race and gender, or of sexuality and nation" (2000, 18). According to Collins, "intersecting paradigms" remind us "that oppression cannot be reduced to one fundamental type, and that oppressions work together in producing injustice" (2000, 18). Further, Collins suggests that intersecting oppressions "originate, develop, and are contained" within a matrix of domination (2000, 228, 276).

At the same time, those non-Europeans subjected to intersecting oppressions within the matrix of domination—African Americans, American Indians, and Mexican Americans—did not suffer oppression without response. Bonnie Mitchell and Joe Feagin (1995; see also Scott 1990, Hechter 1976,

1978; Rose 1994; Feagin 2000) describe a theory of *oppositional culture or culture of resistance*, which asserts that groups who endure subjugation will develop strategies to resist domination that draw on their own cultural resources. Mitchell and Feagin suggest that oppressed groups will generate a "culture of resistance" or oppositional culture in order

> to preserve dignity and autonomy, to provide an alternative construction of identity (one not based entirely on deprivation), and to give members of the dominant group an insightful critique of their own culture. From this perspective, members of oppressed subordinate groups are not powerless pawns that merely react to circumstances beyond their control, but rather are reflective, creative agents that construct a separate reality in which to survive. (1995, 69)

Mitchell and Feagin argue in addition that an oppositional culture embodies "a coherent set of values, beliefs, and practices which mitigates the effects of oppression and reaffirms that which is distinct from the majority culture" (1995, 68).

Oppositional culture developed by subjugated groups within an environment of intersecting oppressions can mean developing extended family networks to withstand and survive harsh day-to-day economic realities, generating movements that direct collective efforts toward protest and civic demonstrations to redress grievances, exploring artistic and cultural expression via various mediums that serve to reinforce cultural pride or protest, and assigning new meanings to imposed European American cultural products that reflect the values and culture of subjugated groups. Mitchell and Feagin emphasize that much oppositional culture is a people's use of "their own art and music, and their own philosophical and political thinking about oppression and liberation," along with a "critical assessment of the dominant culture" (Mitchell and Feagin 1995, 73).

It is the central argument of this paper that the writing of W.E.B. Du Bois and Gloria Anzaldúa, spanning two centuries of African American and Latina/o thought on intersecting oppressions within a matrix of domina-

tion, each represents a viable form of oppositional culture as they describe the history of their respective peoples, their personal experiences of oppression in the United States, and the emergence of unique perspectives on oppression—the "double-consciousness" and the "*mestiza* consciousness," respectively. In their oppositional framings of the American experience, Du Bois chiefly deals with intersections of race and class with some references to gender, while Anzaldúa adds a more thorough discussion of gender and links this to her discussion of sexuality.

Some Words on Analysis

In the tradition of feminist methods in social science research, the following discussion is a brief qualitative content analysis of W.E.B. Du Bois' writing taken from his influential work *The Souls of Black Folk* (1903/1995), and Gloria Anzaldúa's writing drawn from her pivotal work, *Borderlands/La Frontera: The New* Mestiza (1987). According to Reinharz, feminist content analysis of texts has included works of feminist nonfiction, of which Anzaldúa's work is an example (1992, 146). Though this analysis is viewed through the lens of race relations theory in sociology, the theory of oppositional culture, it is well within feminist tradition in that Anzaldúa's writing "exposes pervasive patriarchal and even misogynist culture"—a hallmark of feminist content analysis of cultural products (1992, 147). As Reinharz asserts, "qualitative sociologists apply an inductive, interpretive framework to cultural artifacts. What differentiates sociologists from historians is simply the use of sociological theory as an aid in the explanation" (1992, 159).

The Souls of Oppositional Consciousness: Du Bois and Anzaldúa

A number of common themes emerge from a reading of Du Bois' and Anzaldúa's writing. Themes include recognition of a historical legacy of oppression that takes root over time, personal experience of discrimination in the United States, and finally, the emergence of a "double-consciousness" and a *mestiza* consciousness." In the following discussion, I will discuss each theme in turn, linking African American and Latina/o thought across two centuries and describing two exceptional examples of oppositional culture.

History's Mark on African American and Latina/o Consciousness

In the writings of W.E.B. Du Bois and Gloria Anzaldúa, one can distinguish clear descriptions of a historical legacy of oppression. Du Bois frames his discussion of Black experience in America to include intersecting oppressions of race, class, and gender. In *The Souls of Black Folk*, Du Bois suggests that the life choices of Blacks in early America became circumscribed by the total racial subjugation of slavery and later by the virtual serfdom that followed slavery when Black opportunities would be circumscribed and their "powers of body and mind" would be "strangely wasted, dispersed, or forgotten" (1903/1995, 46). Blacks would seek first freedom, then the vote, then education, only to learn that all these could be limited goals. For Anzaldúa, the history of Chicanas/os in the "borderlands" includes discussion of intersecting oppressions of race, class, gender, and sexuality. Anzaldúa tells tales of life along the U.S.-Mexican border that include conquering Spaniards, discriminatory U.S. policies, and racist border patrols. Her discussion of racism is linked to classism as she describes people robbed of their homes and land. Moreover, Anzaldúa's writing focuses most strikingly on the treatment of women of color and lesbians of color.

Du Bois on African American History

For Du Bois, race, class, and gender oppression are summed up in the "peculiar institution" of slavery. Du Bois argues that "slavery was indeed the sum of all villainies, the cause of all sorrow, the root of all prejudice" (1903/1995, 47), which included "two centuries of systematic legal defilement of Negro women" (1903/1995, 50). Yet, even with the coming of the long hoped for "Freedom" extolled in the Emancipation Procla-

mation, the experience for Blacks became more complex but not more free. Du Bois suggests emancipation was followed by a decade filled with more war, "the terrors of the Ku-Klux Klan, the lies of carpetbaggers, the disorganization of industry, and the contradictory advice of friends and foes" (1903/1995, 48). Blacks learned that physical freedom was not enough, but that they must seek the vote—the power of the ballot box—to realize their hopes for equality. Yet, this goal also resulted in disappointment, leaving Blacks only half-free. Du Bois writes, "A million black men started with renewed zeal to vote themselves into the kingdom. So the decade flew away, the revolution of 1876 came, and left the half-free serf weary, wondering, but still inspired" (1903/1995, 48).

So Blacks turned to "the ideal of 'book-learning,'" according to Du Bois, struggling "to know and test the power of the cabalistic letters of the white man, longing to know" (1903/1995, 49). Du Bois writes in a moving passage:

> For the first time he sought to analyze the burden he bore upon his back, masked behind a half-named Negro problem. He felt his poverty; without a cent, without a home, without land, tools or savings, he had entered into competition with rich, landed, skilled neighbors. To be a poor man is hard, but to be a poor race in a land of dollars is the very bottom of hardships. He felt the weight of his ignorance,—not simply of letters, but of life, of business, of the humanities. . . . (1903/1995, 49–50)

For Du Bois, "ignorance" and poverty were the direct result of centuries of shackled hands and feet, and to these heavy burdens were added others, including the consequences of two centuries of systematic rape—the "heredity weight of a mass corruption from white adulterers"—which threatened to destroy the Black family (1903/1995, 50). The infamy of slavery, consequent poverty and lack of education, and the aftermath of systematic rape of Black women left a profound stamp on the Black race. Du Bois writes, "A people thus handicapped ought not to be asked to race with the world, but rather allowed to give all its time and thought to its own social problem" (1903/1995, 50).

"Booklearning" in the face of such burdens was clearly not enough. In fact, Du Bois asserts, learned sociologists would use their books against the Black race to "count his bastards and his prostitutes" (1903/1995, 50), never seeking to understand the results of systematic intersecting oppressions of race, class, and gender or bothering to describe the "vast despair" in the Black community. In a poetic passage, Du Bois describes the fallout from America's consistent denial of equal rights to Blacks:

> Lo! we are diseased and dying, cried the dark hosts; we cannot write, our voting is vain; what need of education, since we must always cook and serve? And the Nation echoed and enforced this self-criticism, saying: Be content to be servants and nothing more; what need of higher culture for half-men? Away with the black man's ballot, by force or fraud,—behold the suicide of a race! (1903/1995, 51)

Choice and opportunity are denied Blacks early and late in historical time, according to Du Bois, and result in Black discouragement and hopelessness, as the "shades of the prison-house closed round about us all" (1903/1995, 45).

Finally, Du Bois suggests, Blacks recognized that it was only through harnessing all three in combination—"physical freedom, political power, the training of brains and the training of hands"—that they could achieve full liberty in America and contribute to a very American future. Du Bois suggests that "these ideals must be melted and welded into one," all working together to realize "human brotherhood" in accordance with "the greater ideals of the American Republic" (1903/1995, 52).

Du Bois' discussion of Black history offers an insightful critique of domination (Mitchell and Feagin 1995, 69)—an oppositional stance describing intersecting oppressions of race, class, and gender, where systematic enslavement and rape are followed by systematic disenfranchisement. Du Bois argues that such burdens can be overcome only

when Blacks combine and blend strategies for survival, advancement, and resistance.

Anzaldúa on Latina/o History

Anzaldúa begins her historical journey by describing "gold-hungry" conquistadors, whose subjugation and conquest of Mexico led to the mixture of peoples—the *mestiza/o*, the Mexicana/o, the "people of mixed Indian and Spanish blood" (1987, 5). *Mestizas/os* would follow the conquerors north into the American Southwest, where most of Anzaldúa's story lies, beginning with Texas.

Anzaldúa suggests that the Anglos who migrated to Texas in the nineteenth century committed "all manner of atrocities against" the Mexican people living in Texas, both before and during a brutal war of annexation (1987, 6). Later, Mexicans living in other southwestern states, such as New Mexico, California, Arizona, and Nevada, would also become residents of a conquered territory, as the U.S. would acquire Mexican holdings with the Treaty of Guadalupe Hidalgo. In the poem "We Call Them Greasers," Anzaldúa describes in detail the depredations visited on the Mexicans who dared stand up to Anglo brutality. The poem is written from the standpoint of an Anglo mercenary, who by his own account, steals land from Mexican residents through "legal" and illegal means. It is clear from the poem that this mercenary views Mexicans as an inferior race and class of people—"[t]hey knew their betters" and "they didn't even own the land" (1987, 134). The mercenary then describes the rape of a Mexican woman and the lynching of her husband when this couple "refused to budge" from their land (1987, 134). He orders his men to tie the husband to a tree while he brutally rapes the man's wife, a further tool of brutal domination that encompasses gender and race. Afterward, he allows the woman to live, because he "didn't want to waste a bullet on her," and orders his men to lynch her husband (1987, 135). Through the mercenary's eyes, intersecting oppressions of race, class, and gender become horrifyingly apparent (see also Acuña 1988).

For Anzaldúa, the twentieth century U.S.-Mexican border "*es una herida abierta* (is an open wound) where the Third World grates against the first and bleeds" (1987, 3). Anzaldúa suggests that the Mexicans who cross the border and the Mexican Americans who live in the borderlands have much in common. Mexican immigrants enter the country to find prosperity only to discover their Mexican American cousins enduring longstanding racist practices. Anzaldúa writes:

> Those who make it past the checking points of the Border Patrol find themselves in the midst of 150 years of racism in Chicano barrios in the Southwest and in big northern cities. Living in a no-man's-borderland, caught between being treated as criminals and being able to eat, between resistance and deportation, the illegal refugees are some of the poorest and the most exploited of any people in the U.S. (1987, 12).

Anzaldúa notes that the women who cross the border face both physical and sexual exploitation. "The Mexican woman is especially at risk. Often the coyote . . . doesn't feed her for days or let her go to the bathroom. Often he rapes her or sells her into prostitution" (1987, 12).

Anzaldúa also stresses the racist and sexist nature of both Anglo and Chicana/o culture. She writes, "The dark-skinned woman has been silenced, gagged, caged, bound into servitude with marriage. . . . For 300 years she has been a slave, a force of cheap labor, colonized by the Spaniard, the Anglo, by her own people" (1987, 22). This description of racism and sexism becomes an even more heated discussion of homophobia in both Anglo and Chicana/o culture. Anzaldúa writes, "Most cultures have burned and beaten their homosexuals and others who deviate from the sexual common. The queer are the mirror reflecting the heterosexual tribe's fear: being different, being other and therefore lesser, therefore sub-human, inhuman, non-human" (1987, 18).

Finally, Anzaldúa argues that living on the U.S.-Mexican border creates a borderlands consciousness, born of living in the borderlands, and a method for coping with and combating intersecting oppressions. For it is only through recognizing our capacity to be a crossroads among divergent groups,

Anzaldúa suggests, that we can heal. She writes, "At some point, on our way to a new consciousness, we will have to leave the opposite bank, the split between the two mortal combatants somehow healed so that we are on both shores at once . . ." (1987, 78–79).

Anzaldúa's standpoint on Chicana/o history offers a scathing critique of intersecting oppressions of race, class, gender, and sexuality, providing an oppositional stance in the borderlands where Mexicans and Mexican Americans cope with ongoing injustice. It is through Anzaldúa's oppositional consciousness, her "*mestiza* consciousness," that she discovers a method to struggle and resist intersecting oppressions within the matrix of domination.

Personal Memories of Oppression in America

Du Bois and Anzaldúa both have firsthand experience of the awful realities of intersecting oppressions and describe it in their work. For both, these experiences come early and consequent life lessons are learned quickly. For Du Bois the lesson will be learned in a schoolhouse in his youth, and for Anzaldúa it is also in her youth that she discovers a "rebel" self (Du Bois 1903/1995, 44; Anzaldúa 1987, 16) within a family that experiences oppression but also holds to sexist and homophobic traditions.

Du Bois on the Personal

In his book *The Souls of Black Folk*, Du Bois writes about an early initiation into the "rites" of discrimination. Du Bois was a young boy growing up in New England when "the shadow swept across me" (1903/1995, 44). One day in the schoolhouse, the boys and girls were asked to exchange gift cards. Du Bois describes this as a "merry" experience until a new girl refuses his card—"refused it peremptorily, with a glance" (1903/1995, 44). For Du Bois, this was a first "revelation," that is, he realized that he "was different from the others" (1903/1995, 44). On the heels of his first revelation came another that was even more stunning for him—that he was "shut out from their world by a vast veil" (1995, 44). This was a shattering experience for Du Bois, who saw it as a literal closing of doors to camaraderie and opportunity. Du Bois' initial reaction is a fierce contempt for Whites and an eagerness to beat them at their own game, to "beat their stringy heads" and to "tear down that veil" (1903/1995, 44).

Anzaldúa on the Personal

Anzaldúa writes: "At a very early age I had a strong sense of who I was and what I was about and what was fair. I had a stubborn will" (1987, 16). Anzaldúa's stubborn will developed on the U.S.-Mexico border, as well as in the borderlands of marginality within her own home and culture as a female and a lesbian.

Anzaldúa's life was circumscribed early by racism and poverty. She writes about conversations with her mother about the family history, which described her own grandmother's losses during the land grab of the southwestern states: "A smart *gabacho* [White] lawyer took the land away—*mamá* hadn't paid taxes. No *hablaba inglés* [she didn't speak English], she didn't know how to ask for time to raise the money" (1987, 8). Later, large agribusinesses would buy out the remaining land, which her family and other Mexican American families had "toiled over . . . or had been used communally by them" (1987, 9). Anzaldúa herself witnessed this same land cleared of all vegetation. Meanwhile, her father was forced to become a sharecropper and required to pay 40 percent of his earnings to the Rio Farms. Her family worked "three successive Rio farms," one being a chicken farm, where she and her mother handled eggs. "For years afterwards I couldn't stomach the sight of an egg" (1987, 9).

The borderlands also encompass a family memory of humiliation for Anzaldúa. She writes about the experience of her uncle Pedro, who was working in the fields with his family when the INS came—*la migra*. Pedro's wife, Anzaldúa's aunt, warns him not to run because *la migra* will think he is "del otro lao"—from the other side of the border. Her uncle is terrified and he runs. Even though he is a fifth generation American, he is deported to Guadalajara. Anzaldúa writes, "He tried to smile when he looked back at us, to raise his fist. But I saw the shame pushing

his head down, I saw the terrible weight of shame hunch his shoulders" (1987, 4).

Anzaldúa's memories of discrimination are not limited to stories of Anglos. She writes that she learned early that Chicano/a culture had rigid gender roles, in which "males make the rules and laws" and "women transmit them" (1987, 16). "The culture and the Church insist that women are subservient to males. . . . Women are made to feel like total failures if they don't marry and have children" (1987, 17). If a woman rebels, she is considered a *"mujer mala"*—a bad woman. Anzaldúa recalls that she rebelled early and that even "as a child I would not obey. . . . Instead of ironing my younger brothers' shirts or cleaning the cupboards, I would pass many hours studying, reading, painting, writing" (1987, 16).

Anzaldúa's rebellion would also be focused around her own sexuality, a sexuality that, she suggests, was not accepted by her family or her culture. She writes: "Every bit of self-faith I'd painstakingly gathered took a beating daily. Nothing in my culture approved of me" (1987, 16). At a New England college, she recalls that

the presence of a few lesbians threw the more conservative heterosexual students and faculty into a panic. The two lesbian students and we two lesbian instructors met with them to discuss their fears. One of the students said, "I thought homophobia meant fear of going home after a residency." And I thought, how apt. Fear of going home. And not being taken in. We're afraid of being abandoned by the mother, the culture, *la Raza*, for being unacceptable, faulty, damaged. Most of us unconsciously believe that if we reveal this unacceptable aspect of the self our mother/culture/race will totally reject us. (1987, 20)

Personal experiences for Du Bois center on racist themes, where Whites in his childhood schoolhouse presented him with damaging revelations about racial prejudice deeply embedded in American culture. These are pivotal memories for Du Bois. For Anzaldúa, personal experiences ranged from racist, to classist, to sexist, to homophobic aspects of American and Chicana/o culture.

Her response was to rebel. For both, these personal experiences would generate their own unique brands of consciousness, each an oppositional consciousness.

'Double-Consciousness' and '*Mestiza* Consciousness'

The notion of the "double-consciousness" is arguably one of Du Bois' most discussed ideas in the context of twentieth century thought, a gift to both the "sons of night" and the children of Europe. For Anzaldúa also, the "*mestiza* consciousness" is one of her most discussed concepts in academic writing, a bequest to the multiple faces and voices in the borderlands. For each, the development of the "double-consciousness" and the "*mestiza* consciousness" signifies both profound disquiet and profound potential as their oppositional stands reach culmination.

The Double-Consciousness of Du Bois

Du Bois argues that a "double-consciousness" emerges from the experience of Blacks in America—an experience of dogged survival in the face of overwhelming and intersecting oppressions of race, class, and gender. Du Bois suggests that the double-consciousness reflects a "twoness"—a consciousness that is at once Black and American. Experience of the double-consciousness means to be both split apart from one's self and connected to one's self, to be at tension with one's self and at ease with one's self. The double-consciousness, then, means a constant tension emergent within the self, a fragmented sense of self. As Du Bois so poignantly describes it, the double-consciousness signifies "two warring ideals in one dark body, whose dogged strength alone keeps it from being torn asunder" (1903/1995, 45).

Although Du Bois stresses that the double-consciousness is chiefly characterized by division, he also makes clear that the double-consciousness embraces the divide. Du Bois maintains that in the twoness that is the double-consciousness, neither self is abandoned or rejected. It is within the division, in the tension between two warring selves, that the chance for real potential emerges. He argues that the American Black

would not Africanize America, for America has too much to teach the world and Africa. He would not bleach his Negro soul in a flood of white Americanism, for he knows that Negro blood has a message for the world (1903/1995, 45).

Du Bois stresses that it is existence within the tension of the double-consciousness that fosters a more egalitarian space for understanding and signals the possibility for change.

For Du Bois, the double-consciousness is part of "a vaster ideal . . . the ideal of human brotherhood" (1903/1995, 52). Moreover, "the ideal of human brotherhood" for Du Bois is part of "the greater ideals of the American Republic in order that some day on American soil two world-races may give each to each those characteristics both so sadly lack" (1903/1995, 52). Du Bois stresses that a double-consciousness for Black men and women brings a remarkable contribution to the table of the American Republic for

there are no truer exponents of the pure human spirit of the Declaration of Independence than the American Negroes; there is no true American music but the wild sweet melodies of the Negro slave; the American fairy tales and folklore are Indian and African; and, all in all, we black men seem the sole oasis of simple faith and reverence in a dusty desert of dollars and smartness. (1903/1995, 52)

The double-consciousness that Du Bois describes is an oppositional consciousness, decrying intersecting oppressions of race, class, and gender within a matrix of domination over historical time. Du Bois maintains that this double-consciousness—this oppositional consciousness—is a burden and a gift "in the name of an historic race . . . and in the name of human opportunity" (1903/1995, 53).

The *Mestiza* Consciousness of Anzaldúa

According to Anzaldúa, a *mestiza* consciousness emerges from surviving in the "borderlands." The word *mestiza* literally implies a mixed heritage—Spanish and Indian. In Anzaldúa's writings, the word *mestiza* also takes on multiple meanings—a blending, an amalgam of cultures, sexual orientations, colors, and ideas. Further, it can also indicate learning to cope with and survive within this multi-faceted environment.

The "borderlands" signify Anzaldúa's family history of oppression, her memories of brutal backbreaking work, and her knowledge of history on the border. The "borderlands" are, in fact, the site of Anzaldúa's worst struggles with intersecting oppressions of race, class, gender, and sexuality. Yet, much like in Du Bois' discussion of recognizing strength within the tensions of living with the double-consciousness, Anzaldúa recognizes that these borderlands, this crossroads, is also the site of her greatest strength. This "floundering in uncharted seas," this "swamping of her psychological borders" (1987, 79) creates other ways of coping and viewing the landscape. Anzaldúa writes: "*[L]a mestiza* undergoes a struggle of flesh, a struggle of borders, an inner war. . . . The coming together of two self-consistent but habitually incompatible frames of reference" is what causes "*un choque*, a cultural collision" (1987, 78). This "*choque*" forces the *mestiza* consciousness into existence in a psychic birthing process of sorts to become a reflection of the borderlands themselves—a crossroads and a consciousness of multiple voices and paradigms.

According to Anzaldúa, the *mestiza* consciousness, which emerges from life in the borderlands, signifies a "tolerance for ambiguity" (1987, 79). It is a flexible and inclusive consciousness and indeed synthesizes colliding parts. It is a "crossroads" or link between cultures, genders, and paradigms whether Chicana/o or *gabacha/o* (White), straight or "queer," men or women; it is the psychic border between all worlds. The *mestiza* consciousness, in fact, mandates an inclusive vision advocating for multiple views, peoples, cultures, skin colors, and sexualities, as it makes a "conscious rupture with all oppressive traditions" and "adopts new perspectives toward the darkskinned, women and queers" (1987, 82). The *mestiza*

> has discovered that she can't hold concepts or ideas in rigid boundaries. . . . Rigidity means death. . . . The new *mestiza* copes by developing a tolerance for contradictions, a tolerance for ambiguity. . . . She learns to juggle cultures. . . . She has a

> plural personality, she operates in a pluralistic mode—nothing is thrust out, the good the bad and the ugly, nothing rejected, nothing abandoned. (1987, 79)

Ultimately, the *mestiza* consciousness is Anzaldúa's gift to American culture and consciousness. It is in the borderlands space where she is affirmed in her own humanity and she affirms the humanity of all others. The *mestiza* consciousness, then, is an oppositional consciousness describing and defying intersecting oppressions of race, class, gender, and and sexuality.

Discussion and Conclusions

W. E. B. Du Bois has long been recognized in sociology for his significant contributions to our understanding of racial and ethnic relations in the United States. Gloria Anzaldúa, on the other hand, has not been accorded any substantial attention in the discipline. This paper, while attempting to begin to redress the gap in the sociological literature with regard to Anzaldúa, seeks to address yet another gap as well. While African Americans and Latina/os are often linked in sociological research in discussions of societal ills, such as residential segregation, health outcomes, and rates of incarceration, researchers have paid little if any attention to the linkages between African American and Latino/a thought. This [chapter] provides a brief content analysis of the writing of African American sociologist W.E.B. Du Bois in relation to the work of Chicana feminist writer and poet Gloria Anzaldúa suggesting that their work is related and resonant as they construct significant forms of oppositional culture within the United States (Mitchell and Feagin 1995). For Du Bois, oppositional culture takes the form of the "double-consciousness," embedded in historical knowledge and personal experience of oppression that is directly related to intersecting oppressions of race, class, and gender within the matrix of domination. For Anzaldúa, oppositional culture takes the form of the "*mestiza* consciousness," also embedded in personal and historical memory of oppression, which are directly connected to intersecting oppressions of race, class, gender, and sexuality.

It is hoped that future research will begin to discuss further linkages between African American and Latinoa/o thought across time and geographic space as we seek to explore a broader and more inclusive American experience, whether on the U.S.-Mexican border or in the American South, whether we link discussions of Mexican immigrants or African slaves, and whether we explore lynching in Alabama or lynching in Texas. African American and Latino/a scholars and writers teach us much about who we were, who we are, and what we might become as Americans today.

References

Acuña, Rodolfo. 1988. *Occupied America: A History of Chicanos* (3rd ed.). New York: Harper & Row.

Alarcón, Norma. 1998. "Chicana Feminism: In the Tracks of 'The' Native Woman." Pp. 371–382 in *Living Chicana Theory*, edited by Carla Trujillo. Berkeley, CA: Third Woman Press.

Anzaldúa, Gloria. 1987. *Borderlands/La Frontera: The New Mestiza.* San Francisco: Aunt Lute Books.

Aptheker, Herbert. 1990. "W.E.B. Du Bois: Struggle Not Despair." *Clinical Sociology Review* 8, 58–68.

Blauner, Robert. 1972. *Racial Oppression in America.* New York: Harper & Row.

Charles, Camille Zubrinsky. 2001. "Processes of Racial Residential Segregation." Pp. 217–271 in *Urban Inequality: Evidence From Four Cities*, edited by Alice O'Conner, Chris Tilly, and Lawrence D. Bobo. New York: Russell Sage Foundation.

Chiricos, Ted, Renee McEntire, and Marc Gertz. 2001. "Perceived Racial and Ethnic Composition of Neighborhood and Perceived Risk of Crime." *Social Problems* 48: 322–340.

Collins, Patricia Hill. 2000. *Black Feminist Thought: Knowledge, Consciousness, and the Politics of Empowerment* (2nd ed.). New York: Routledge.

Combahee River Collective. 1982. "A Black Feminist Statement." Pp. 13–22 in *But Some of Us Are Brave*, edited by Gloria T. Hull, Patricia Bell Scott, and Barbara Smith. Old Westbury, New York: Feminist Press.

Davis, Angela Y. 1981. *Women, Race, and Class.* New York: Random House.

Denzin, Norman. 1997. "The Standpoint Epistemologies and Social Theory." *Current Perspectives in Social Theory* 17: 39–76.

Du Bois, W.E.B. 1903/1995. *The Souls of Black Folk.* New York: Penguin Books.

——. 1948. "Is Man Free?" *Scientific Monthly* 66 (May), 432–434.

Feagin, Joe R. 2000. *Racist America: Roots, Current Realities, and Future Reparations.* New York: Routledge.

Gonzalez, Deena J. 1998. "Speaking Secrets: Living Chicano Theory." Pp. 46–77 in *Living Chicana Theory*, edited by Carla Trujillo. Berkeley, CA: Third Woman Press.

Hechter, Michael. 1975. *Internal Colonialism.* Berkeley: University of California Press.

——. 1978. "Group Formation and the Cultural Division of Labor." *American Journal of Sociology* 84, 293–318.

Hurtado, Aida. 1999. *The Color of Privilege: Three Blasphemies on Race and Feminism.* Ann Arbor: University of Michigan Press.

Jacobs, David, and Jason T. Carmichael. 2001. "The Politics of Punishment Across Time and Space: A Pooled Time-Series Analysis of Imprisonment Rates." *Social Forces* 80, 61–89.

Lorde, Audre. 1984. *Sister Outsider.* Trumansberg, NY: The Crossing Press.

Martinez, Theresa A. 1999. "Storytelling as Oppositional Culture: Race, Class, and Gender in the Borderlands." *Race, Gender & Class: An Interdisciplinary and Multicultural Journal* 6, 33–51.

Mitchell, Bonnie L., and Joe R. Feagin. 1995. "America's Racial-Ethnic Cultures: Opposition Within a Mythical Melting Pot." Pp. 65–86 in *Toward the Multicultural University*, edited by B. Bowser, T. Jones, and G. A. Young. Westport, CT: Praeger.

Pierce, Jennifer. 1982. "This Bridge Called My Back: Writings by Radical Women of Color." *Contemporary Sociology* 13, 311–312.

Ralls, Brenda H. 2001. "The Impact of Minority Group Membership on Changes in Selected Health Outcomes Among Midlife Americans With Type 2 Diabetes." Unpublished dissertation.

Reinharz, Shulamit. 1992. *Feminist Methods in Social Research.* New York: Oxford University Press.

Rose, Tricia. 1994. *Black Noise: Rap Music and Black Culture in Contemporary America.* Hanover, MA: Wesleyan University Press.

Rudwick, Elliott. 1969. "Note on a Forgotten Black Sociologist: W.E.B. Du Bois and the Sociological Profession." *American Sociologist* 4 (Nov), 303–306.

——. 1980. "W.E.B. Du Bois on Sociology and the Black Community." *Contemporary Sociology* 9 (Nov), 831–832.

Saldívar, Sonia. 1991. "Feminism on the Border: From Gender Politics to Geopolitic." Pp. 203–220 in *Criticism in the Borderlands: Studies in Chicano Literature, Culture, and Ideology*, edited by Hector Calderón and Jose David Saldívar. Durham, NC: Duke University Press.

Sandoval, Chela. 1991. "U.S. Third World Feminism: The Theory and Method of Oppositional Consciousness in the Postmodern World." *Genders* 10, 1–24.

——. 1998. "*Mestizaje* as Method: Feminists-of-Color Challenge the Canon." Pp. 352–370 in *Living Chicana Theory*, edited by Carla Trujillo. Berkeley, CA: Third Woman Press.

Scott, James C. 1990. *Domination and the Arts of Resistance*. New Haven, CT: Yale University Press.

Segura, Denise A. and Beatriz M. Pesquera. 1992. "Making Face, Making Soul: Haciendo Caras." *Gender and Society* 6(3): 519–522.

Zinn, Howard. 1990. *The People's History of the United States*. New York: HarperCollins.

Discussion Questions

1. Anzaldúa claimed that *mestiza* consciousness is inclusive rather than exclusive and involves a "tolerance for ambiguity." What evidence can we find of this kind of consciousness in current popular culture and fashion? What counter trends are evident? Look at the article by Amy C. Wilkins about Puerto Rican wannabes in Section 7. Do wannabes and those who talked about them with Wilkins reflect *mestiza* thinking or its opposite?

2. Oppositional cultures are also cultures of resistance and vehicles for social change. What are some ways that oppressed groups can resist domination to empower themselves and produce social change?

3. One thing that Du Bois and Anzaldúa have in common is that, even though they had academic credentials, they spent most of their careers working and writing outside the university. Do you think it is easier to adopt a critical position, a border or *mestiza* consciousness, from outside the university or is the university a good place to look critically at society?

4. Sociology is also a kind of borderland. Its perspective, data, and concepts should allow us to view society from the inside and the outside at the same time. Has your study so far allowed you to do that? How does it make you feel? Uncomfortable? Insightful? Angry?

8
1965

Malcolm X

When Malcolm X looks deep within the body of America, he observes the malignant cancer of racism which, he argues, has grown metastatically since the genocidal treatment of American Indians. For Malcolm, the "race issue" is at the core of all U.S. history, informing all sociohistorical interactions and institutions, from politics to religion and from economics to global relations. When the American media ask for Malcolm's endorsement of American political candidates, Malcolm affords us a summary sketch of Black disillusionment with White hypocrisy, decrying both candidates as useless to the Black community—one will talk nicer like the fox and the other will be more open about his racism like the wolf, but neither will do justice to the "race issue."

Subtly and overtly, other issues are intertwined with the core issue of race in Malcolm's piece. In "1965," race is part of an almost invisible, yet measured, gendered reality. Malcolm intones throughout the piece about the history and response to history of Black men; in this instance, men are the arbiters and powerbrokers within the Black community. Yet, Malcolm is speaking about "black brothers and sisters" when he challenges racial injustice. After all, the young White co-ed Malcolm turns away, only to regret he had not shared further ideas with her, is also a representative of what Malcolm terms "sincere white people" who can work separately but in conjunction with Blacks to bring about longed for equality. How much more, then, are Black women, the "sisters" he extols near the end of his life and whose freedom he also seeks.

In addition, it is the "black ghettos" of America where race matters are played out in Malcolm's words—places where youth will turn to the "wrong kinds of heroes, and the wrong kinds of influences" in a ruthless, urban inner-city space lacking the means to a decent education, healthcare, housing, and sometimes even suffrage. As the text reads, "No man is given but so much time to accomplish whatever is his life's work." For Malcolm X, his life's work is the quest for justice, a justice denied in segregated ghettoes across the country, where youth of color such as Malcolm will respond to the long, hot summer of American race, class, and gender relations in ever more complex ways.

I must be honest. Negroes—Afro-Americans—show no inclination to rush to the United Nations and demand justice for themselves here in America. I really had known in advance that they wouldn't. The American white man has so thoroughly brainwashed the black man to see himself as only a domestic "civil rights" problem that it will probably take longer than I live before the Negro sees that the struggle of the American black man is international.

And I had known, too, that Negroes would not rush to follow me into the orthodox Islam which had given me the insight and perspective to see that the black men and white men truly could be brothers. America's Negroes—especially older Negroes—are too indelibly soaked in Christianity's double standard of oppression.

So, in the "public invited" meetings which I began holding each Sunday afternoon or evening in Harlem's well-known Audubon Ballroom, as I addressed predominantly non-Muslim Negro audiences, I did not immediately attempt to press the Islamic religion, but instead to embrace all who sat before me:

"—not Muslim, nor Christian, Catholic, nor Protestant . . . Baptist nor Methodist, Democrat nor Republican, Mason nor Elk! I mean the black people of America—and the black people all over this earth! Because it is as this collective mass of black people that we have been deprived not only of our civil rights, but even of our human rights, the right to human dignity. . . ."

On the streets, after my speeches, in the faces and the voices of the people I met—even those who would pump my hands and want my autograph—I would feel the wait-and-see attitude. I would feel—and I understood—their uncertainty about where I stood. Since the Civil War's "freedom," the black man has gone down so many fruitless paths. His leaders, very largely, had failed him. The religion of Christianity had failed him. The black man was scarred, he was cautious, he was apprehensive.

I understood it better now than I had before. In the Holy World, away from America's race problem, was the first time I ever had been able to think clearly about the basic divisions of white people in America, and how their attitudes and their motives related to, and affected Negroes. In my thirty-nine years on this earth, the Holy City of Mecca had been the first time I had ever stood before the Creator of All and felt like a complete human being.

In that peace of the Holy World—in fact, the very night I have mentioned when I lay awake surrounded by snoring brother pilgrims—my mind took me back to personal memories I would have thought were gone forever . . . as far back, even, as when I was just a little boy, eight or nine years old. Out behind our house, out in the country from Lansing, Michigan, there was an old, grassy "Hectors Hill," we called it—which may still be there. I remembered there in the Holy World how I used to lie on the top of Hector's Hill, and look up at the sky, at the clouds moving over me, and daydream, all kinds of things. And then, in a funny contrast of recollections, I remembered how years later, when I was in prison, I used to lie on my cell bunk—this would be especially when I was in solitary: what we convicts called "The Hole"—and I would picture myself talking to large crowds. I don't have any idea why such previsions came to me. But they did. To tell that to anyone then would have sounded crazy. Even I didn't have, myself, the slightest inkling. . . .

In Mecca, too, I had played back for myself the twelve years I had spent with Elijah Muhammad as if it were a motion picture. I guess it would be impossible for anyone ever to realize fully how complete was my belief in Elijah Muhammad. I believed in him not only as a leader in the ordinary *human* sense, but also I believed in him as a *divine* leader, I believed he had no human weaknesses or faults, and that, therefore, he could make no mistakes and that he could do no wrong. There on a Holy World hilltop, I realized how very dangerous it is for people to hold any human being in such esteem, especially to consider anyone some sort of "divinely guided" and "protected" person.

My thinking had been opened up wide in Mecca. In the long letters I wrote to friends, I tried to convey to them my new insights into the American black man's struggle and his problems, as well as the depths of my search for truth and justice.

"I've had enough of someone else's propaganda," I had written to these friends. "I'm for truth, no matter who tells it, I'm for justice, no matter who it is for or against. I'm a human being first and foremost, and as such I'm for whoever and whatever benefits humanity *as a whole*."

Largely, the American white man's press refused to convey that I was now attempting to teach Negroes a new direction. With the 1964 "long, hot summer" steadily producing new incidents, I was constantly accused of "stirring up Negroes." Every time I had another radio or television microphone at my mouth, when I was asked about "stirring up Negroes" or "inciting violence," I'd get hot.

"It takes no one to stir up the sociological dynamite that stems from the unemployment, bad housing, and inferior education already in the ghettoes. This explosively criminal condition has existed for so long, it needs no fuse; it fuses itself; it spontaneously combusts from within itself. . . ."

They called me "the angriest Negro in America." I wouldn't deny that charge. I spoke exactly as I felt. "I *believe* in anger. The Bible says there is a *time* for anger." They called me "a teacher, a fomentor of violence." I would say point blank, "That is a lie. I'm not for wanton violence, I'm for justice. I feel that if white people were attacked by Negroes—if the forces of law prove unable, or inadequate, or reluctant to protect those whites from those Negroes—then those white people should protect and defend themselves from those Negroes, using arms if necessary. And I feel that when the law fails to protect Negroes from whites' attack, then those Negroes should use arms, if necessary, to defend themselves."

"Malcolm X Advocates Armed Negroes!"

What was wrong with that? I'll tell you what was wrong. I was a black man talking about physical defense against the white man. The white man can lynch and burn and bomb and beat Negroes—that's all right: "Have patience" . . . "The customs are entrenched" . . . "Things are getting better."

Well, I believe it's a crime for anyone who is being brutalized to continue to accept that brutality without doing something to defend himself. If that's how "Christian" philosophy is interpreted, if that's what Gandhian philosophy teaches, well, then, I will call them criminal philosophies.

I tried in every speech I made to clarify my new position regarding white people—"I don't speak against the sincere, well-meaning, good white people. I have learned that there *are* some. I have learned that not all white people are racists. I am speaking against and my fight is against the white *racists*. I firmly believe that Negroes have the right to fight against these racists, by any means that are necessary."

But the white reporters kept wanting me linked with that word "violence." I doubt if I had one interview without having to deal with that accusation.

"I *am* for violence if non-violence means we continue postponing a solution to the American black man's problem—just to *avoid* violence. I don't go for non-violence if it also means a delayed solution. To me a delayed solution is a non-solution. Or I'll say it another way. If it must take violence to get the black man his human rights in this country, I'm *for* violence exactly as you know the Irish, the Poles, or Jews would be if they were flagrantly discriminated against. I am just as they would be in that case, and they would be for violence—no matter what the consequences, no matter who was hurt by the violence." . . .

When the white man came into this country, he certainly wasn't demonstrating any "non-violence." In fact, the very man whose name symbolizes non-violence here today has stated:

"Our nation was born in genocide when it embraced the doctrine that the original American, the Indian, was an inferior race. Even before there were large numbers of Negroes on our shores, the scar of racial hatred had already disfigured colonial society. From the sixteenth century forward, blood flowed in battles over racial supremacy. We are perhaps the only nation which tried as a matter of national policy to wipe out its indigenous population. Moreover, we elevated that tragic experience into a noble crusade. Indeed, even today we have not permitted ourselves to reject or to feel remorse for this shameful episode. Our literature, our films, our drama, our folklore all exalt it. Our children are still taught to respect the violence which reduced a red-skinned people of an earlier culture into a few fragmented groups herded into impoverished reservations."

"Peaceful coexistence!" That's another one the white man has always been quick to cry. Fine! But what have been the deeds of the white man? During his entire advance through history, he has been waving the banner of Christianity . . . and carrying in his other hand the sword and the flintlock. . . .

I believe that God now is giving the world's so-called "Christian" white society its last opportunity to repent and atone for the crimes of exploiting and enslaving the world's non-white peoples. It is exactly as when God gave Pharaoh a chance to repent. But Pharaoh persisted in his refusal to give justice to those whom he oppressed. And, we know, God finally destroyed Pharaoh.

Is white America really sorry for her crimes against the black people? Does white America have the capacity to repent—and to atone? Does the capacity to repent, to atone, exist in a majority, in one-half, in even one-third of American white society?

Many black men, the victims—in fact most black men—would like to be able to forgive, to forget, the crimes.

But most American white people seem not to have it in them to make any serious atonement—to do justice to the black man.

Indeed, how *can* white society atone for enslaving, for raping, for unmanning, for otherwise brutalizing *millions* of human beings, for centuries? What atonement would the God of Justice demand for the robbery of the black people's labor, their lives, their true identities, their culture, their history—and even their human dignity?

A desegregated cup of coffee, a theater, public toilets—the whole range of hypocritical "integration"—these are not atonement.

After a while in America, I returned abroad—and this time, spent eighteen weeks in the Middle East and Africa.

The world leaders with whom I had private audiences this time included President Gamal Abdel Nasser, of Egypt; President Julius K. Nyerere, of Tanzania; President Nnamoi Azikiwe, of Nigeria; Osagyefo Dr. Kwame Nkrumah, of Ghana; President Sekou Touré, of Guinea; President Jomo Kenyatta, of Kenya; and Prime Minister Dr. Milton Obote, of Uganda.

I also met with religious leaders—African, Arab, Asian, Muslim, and non-Muslim. And in all of these countries, I talked with Afro-Americans and whites of many professions and backgrounds.

An American white ambassador in one African country was Africa's most respected American ambassador: I'm glad to say that this was told to me by one ranking African leader. We talked for an entire afternoon. Based on what I had heard of him, I had to believe him when he told me that as long as he was on the African continent, he never thought in terms of race, that he dealt with human beings, never noticing their color. He said he was more aware of language differences than of color differences. He said that only when he returned to America would he become aware of color differences.

I told him, "What you are telling me is that it isn't the American white *man* who is a racist, but it's the American political, economic, and social *atmosphere* that automatically nourishes a racist psychology in the white man." He agreed.

We both agreed that American society makes it next to impossible for humans to meet in America and not be conscious of their color differences. And we both agreed that if racism could be removed, America could offer a society where rich and poor could truly live like human beings.

That discussion with the ambassador gave me a new insight—one which I like: that the white man is *not* inherently evil, but America's racist society influences him to act evilly. The society has produced and nourishes a psychology which brings out the lowest, most base part of human beings. . . .

***

Politics dominated the American scene while I was traveling abroad this time. In Cairo and again in Accra, the American press wire services reached me with trans-Atlantic calls, asking whom did I favor, Johnson—or Goldwater?

I said I felt that as far as the American black man was concerned they were both just about the same. I felt that it was for the black man only a question of Johnson, the fox, or Goldwater, the wolf.

"Conservatism" in America's politics means "Let's keep the niggers in their place." And "liberalism" means "Let's keep the *knee-grows* in their place—but tell them we'll treat them a little better; let's fool them more, with more promises." With these choices, I felt that the American black man only needed to choose which one to be eaten by, the "liberal" fox or the "conservative" wolf—because both of them would eat him.

I didn't go for Goldwater any more than for Johnson—except that in a wolf's den, I'd always known exactly where I stood; I'd watch the dangerous wolf closer than I would the smooth, sly fox. The wolf's very growling would keep me alert and fighting him to survive, whereas I *might* be lulled and fooled by the tricky fox. I'll give you an illustration of the fox. When the assassination in Dallas made Johnson President, who was the first person he called for? It was for his best friend, "Dicky"—Richard Russell of Georgia. Civil rights was "a moral issue," Johnson was declaring to everybody—while his best friend was the Southern racist who *led* the civil rights opposition. How would some sheriff sound, declaring himself so against bank robbery—and Jesse James his best friend?

Goldwater as a man, I respected for speaking out his true convictions—something rarely done in politics today. He wasn't whispering to racists and smiling at integrationists. I felt Goldwater wouldn't have risked his unpopular stand without conviction. He flatly told black men he wasn't for them—and there is this to consider: always, the black people have advanced further when they have seen they had to rise up against a system that they clearly saw was outright against them. Under the steady lullabies sung by foxy liberals, the Northern Negro became a beggar. But the Southern Negro, facing the honestly snarling white man, rose up to battle that white man for his freedom—long before it happened in the North.

Anyway, I didn't feel that Goldwater was any better for black men than Johnson, or vice-versa. I wasn't in the United States at election time, but if I had been, I wouldn't have put myself in the position of voting for either candidate for the Presidency, or of recommending to any black man to do so. It has turned out that it's Johnson in the White House—and black votes were a major factor in his winning as decisively as he wanted to. If it had been Goldwater, all I am saying is that the black people would at least have known they were dealing with an honestly growling wolf, rather than a fox who could have them half-digested before they even knew what was happening.

I kept having all kinds of troubles trying to develop the kind of Black Nationalist organization I wanted to build for the American Negro. Why Black Nationalism? Well, in the competitive American society, how can there ever be any white-black solidarity before there is first some black solidarity? If you will remember, in my childhood I had been exposed to the Black Nationalist teachings of Marcus Garvey—which, in fact, I had been told had led to my father's murder. Even when I was a follower of Elijah Muhammad, I had been strongly aware of how the Black Nationalist political, economic, and social philosophies had the ability to instill within black men the racial dignity, the incentive, and the confidence that the black race needs today to get up off its knees, and to get on its feet, and get rid of its scars, and to take a stand for itself.

One of the major troubles that I was having in building the organization that I wanted—an all-black organization whose ultimate objective was to help create a society in which there could exist honest white-black brotherhood—was that my earlier public image, my old so-called "Black Muslim" image, kept blocking me. I was trying to gradually reshape the image. I was trying to turn a corner, into a new regard by the public, especially Negroes; I was no less angry than I had been, but at the same time the true brotherhood I had seen in the Holy World had influenced me to recognize that anger can blind human vision.

Every free moment I could find, I did a lot of talking to key people whom I knew around Harlem, and I made a lot of speeches, saying; "True Islam taught me that it takes *all* of the religious, political, economic, psychological, and racial ingredients, or characteristics, to make the Human Family and the Human Society complete.

"Since I learned the *truth* in Mecca, my dearest friends have come to include *all* kinds—some Christians, Jews, Buddhists, Hindus, agnostics, and even atheists! I have friends who are called capitalists, Socialists, and Communists! Some of my friends are moderates, conservatives, extremists—some are even Uncle Toms! My friends today are black, brown, red, yellow, and *white!*"

I said to Harlem street audiences that only when mankind would submit to the One God who created all—only then would mankind even approach the "peace" of which so much *talk* could be heard . . . but toward which so little *action* was seen.

I said that on the American racial level, we had to approach the black man's struggle against the white man's racism as a human problem, that we had to forget hypocritical politics and propaganda. I said that both races, as human beings, had the obligation, the responsibility, of helping to correct America's human problem. The well-meaning white people, I said, had to combat, actively and directly, the racism in other white people. And the black people had to build within themselves much greater awareness that along with equal rights there had to be the bearing of equal responsibilities.

I knew, better than most Negroes, how many white people truly wanted to see American racial problems solved. I knew that many whites were as frustrated as Negroes. I'll bet I got fifty letters some days from white people. The white people in meeting audiences would throng around me, asking me, after I had addressed them somewhere, "What *can* a sincere white person do?"

When I say that here now, it makes me think about that little co-ed I told you about, the one who flew from her New England college down to New York and came up to me in the Nation of Islam's restaurant in Harlem, and I told her that there was "nothing" she could do. I regret that I told her that. I wish that now I knew her name, or where I could telephone her, or write to her, and tell her what I tell white people now when they present themselves as being sincere, and ask me, one way or another, the same thing that she asked.

The first thing I tell them is that at least where my own particular Black Nationalist organization, the Organization of Afro-American Unity, is concerned, they can't *join* us. I have these very deep feelings that white people who want to join black organizations are really just taking the escapist way to salve their consciences. By visibly hovering near us, they are "proving" that they are "with us." But the hard truth is this isn't helping to solve America's racist problem. The Negroes aren't the racists. Where the really sincere white people have got to do their "proving" of themselves is not among the black *victims*, but out on the battle lines of where America's racism really *is*—and that's in their own home communities; America's racism is among their own fellow whites. That's where the sincere whites who really mean to accomplish something have got to work.

Aside from that, I mean nothing against any sincere whites when I say that as members of black organizations, generally whites' very presence subtly renders the black organization automatically less effective. Even the best white members will slow down the Negroes' discovery of what they need to do, and particularly of what they can do—for themselves, working by themselves, among their own kind, in their own communities.

I sure don't want to hurt anybody's feelings, but in fact I'll even go so far as to say that I never really trust the kind of white people who are always so anxious to hang around Negroes, or to hang around in Negro communities. I don't trust the kind of whites who love having Negroes always hanging around them. I don't know—this feeling may be a throwback to the years when I was hustling in Harlem and all of those red-faced, drunk whites in the afterhours clubs were always grabbing hold of some Negroes and talking about "I just want you to know you're just as good as I am—" And then they got back in their taxicabs and black limousines and went back downtown to the places where they lived and worked, where no blacks except servants had better get caught. But, anyway, I know that every time that whites join a black organization, you watch, pretty soon the blacks will be leaning on the whites to support it, and before you know it a black may be up front with a title, but the whites, because of their money, are the real controllers.

I tell sincere white people, "Work in conjunction with us—each of us working among our own kind." Let sincere white individuals find all other white people they can who feel as they do—and let them form their own all-white groups, to work trying to convert other white people who are thinking and acting so racist. Let sincere whites go and teach non-violence to white people!

We will completely respect our white co-workers. They will deserve every credit. We will give them every credit. We will meanwhile be working among our own kind, in our own black communities—showing and teaching black men in ways that only other black men can—that the black man has got to help himself. Working separately, the sincere white people and sincere black people actually will be working together.

In our mutual sincerity we might be able to show a road to the salvation of America's very soul. It can only be salvaged if human rights and dignity, in full, are extended to black men. Only such real, meaningful actions as those which are sincerely motivated from a deep sense of humanism and moral responsibility can get at the basic causes that produce the racial explosions in America today. Otherwise, the racial explosions are only going to grow worse. Certainly nothing is ever going to be solved by throwing upon me and other so-called black "extremists" and "demagogues" the blame for the racism that is in America.

Sometimes, I have dared to dream to myself that one day, history may even say that my voice—which disturbed the white man's smugness, and his arrogance, and his complacency—that my voice helped to save America from a grave, possibly even a fatal catastrophe.

The goal has always been the same, with the approaches to it as different as mine and Dr. Martin Luther King's non-violent marching, that dramatizes the brutality and the evil of the white man against defenseless blacks. And in the racial climate of this country today, it is anybody's guess which of the "extremes" in approach to the black man's problems might *personally* meet a fatal catastrophe first—"non-violent" Dr. King, or so-called "violent" me.

***

Anything I do today, I regard as urgent. No man is given but so much time to accomplish whatever is his life's work. My life in particular never has stayed fixed in one position for very long. You have seen how throughout my life, I have often known unexpected drastic changes.

I am only facing the facts when I know that any moment of any day, or any night, could bring me death. This is particularly true since the last trip that I made abroad. I have seen the nature of things that are happening, and I have heard things from sources which are reliable.

To speculate about dying doesn't disturb me as it might some people. I never have felt that I would live to become an old man. Even before I was a Muslim—when I was a hustler in the ghetto jungle, and then a criminal in prison, it always stayed on my mind that I would die a violent death. In fact, it runs in my family. My father and most of his broth-

ers died by violence—my father because of what he believed in. To come right down to it, if I take the kind of things in which I believe, then add to that the kind of temperament that I have, plus the one hundred percent dedication I have to whatever I believe in—these are ingredients which make it just about impossible for me to die of old age.

***

I have given to this book so much of whatever time I have because I feel, and I hope, that if I honestly and fully tell my life's account, read objectively it might prove to be a testimony of some social value.

I think that an objective reader may see how in the society to which I was exposed as a black youth here in America, for me to wind up in a prison was really just about inevitable. It happens to so many thousands of black youth.

I think that an objective reader may see how when I heard "The white man is the devil," when I played back what had been my own experiences, it was inevitable that I would respond positively; then the next twelve years of my life were devoted and dedicated to propagating that phrase among the black people.

I think, I hope, that the objective reader, in following my life—the life of only one ghetto-created Negro—may gain a better picture and understanding than he has previously had of the black ghettoes which are shaping the lives and the thinking of almost all of the 22 million Negroes who live in America.

Thicker each year in these ghettoes is the kind of teen-ager that I was—with the wrong kinds of heroes, and the wrong kinds of influences. I am not saying that all of them become the kind of parasite that I was. Fortunately, by far most do not. But still, the small fraction who do add up to an annual total of more and more costly, dangerous youthful criminals. The F.B.I. not long ago released a report of a shocking rise in crime each successive year since the end of World War II—ten to twelve percent each year. The report did not say so in so many words, but I am saying that the majority of that crime increase is annually spawned in the black ghettoes which the American racist society permits to exist. In the 1964 "long, hot summer" riots in major cities across the United States, the socially disinherited black ghetto youth were always at the forefront.

In this year, 1965, I am certain that more—and worse—riots are going to erupt, in yet more cities, in spite of the conscience-salving Civil Rights Bill. The reason is that the *cause* of these riots, the racist malignancy in America, has been too long unattended.

I believe that it would be almost impossible to find anywhere in America a black man who has lived further down in the mud of human society than I have; or a black man who has been any more ignorant than I have been; or a black man who has suffered more anguish during his life than I have. But it is only after the deepest darkness that the greatest joy can come; it is only after slavery and prison that the sweetest appreciation of freedom can come.

For the freedom of my 22 million black brothers and sisters here in America, I do believe that I have fought the best that I knew how, and the best that I could, with the shortcomings that I have had. I know that my shortcomings are many.

My greatest lack has been, I believe, that I don't have the kind of academic education I wish I had been able to get—to have been a lawyer, perhaps. I do believe that I might have made a good lawyer. I have always loved verbal battle, and challenge. You can believe me that if I had the time right now, I would not be one bit ashamed to go back into any New York City public school and start where I left off at the ninth grade, and go on through a degree. Because I don't begin to be academically equipped for so many of the interests that I have. For instance, I love languages. I wish I were an accomplished linguist. I don't know anything more frustrating than to be around people talking something you can't understand. Especially when they are people who look just like you. In Africa, I heard original mother tongues, such as Hausa, and Swahili, being spoken, and there I was standing like some little boy, waiting for someone to tell me what had been said; I never will forget how ignorant I felt.

Aside from the basic African dialects, I would try to learn Chinese, because it looks as if Chinese will be the most powerful political language of the future. And already I have begun studying Arabic, which I think is going to be the most powerful spiritual language of the future.

I would just like to *study*. I mean ranging study, because I have a wide-open mind. I'm interested in almost any subject you can mention. I know this is the reason I have come to really like, as individuals, some of the hosts of radio or television panel programs I have been on, and to respect their minds—because even if they have been almost steadily in disagreement with me on the race issue, they still have kept their minds open and objective about the truths of things happening in this world. Irv Kupcinet in Chicago, and Barry Farber, Barry Gray and Mike Wallace in New York—people like them. They also let me see that they respected my mind—in a way I know they never realized. The way I knew was that often they would invite my opinion on subjects off the race issue. Sometimes, after the programs, we would sit around and talk about all kinds of things, current events and other things, for an hour or more. You see, most whites, even when they credit a Negro with some intelligence, will still feel that all he can talk about is the race issue; most whites never feel that Negroes can contribute anything to other areas of thought, and ideas. You just notice how rarely you will ever hear whites asking any Negroes what they think about the problem of world health, or the space race to land men on the moon.

***

Every morning when I wake up, now, I regard it as having another borrowed day. In any city, wherever I go, making speeches, holding meetings of my organization, or attending to other business, black men are watching every move I make, awaiting their chance to kill me. I have said publicly many times that I know that they have their orders. Anyone who chooses not to believe what I am saying doesn't know the Muslims in the Nation of Islam.

But I am also blessed with faithful followers who are, I believe, as dedicated to me as I once was to Mr. Elijah Muhammad. Those who would hunt a man need to remember that a jungle also contains those who hunt the hunters.

I know, too, that I could suddenly die at the hands of some white racists. Or I could die at the hands of some Negro hired by the white man. Or it could be some brainwashed Negro acting on his own idea that by eliminating me he would be helping out the white man, because I talk about the white man the way I do.

Anyway, now, each day I live as if I am already dead, and I tell you what I would like for you to do. When I *am* dead—I say it that way because from the things I *know*, I do not expect to live long enough to read this book in its finished form—I want you to just watch and see if I'm not right in what I say: that the White man, in his press, is going to identify me with "hate."

He will make use of me dead, as he has made use of me alive, as a convenient symbol of "hatred"—and that will help him to escape facing the truth that all I have been doing is holding up a mirror to reflect, to show, the history of unspeakable crimes that his race has committed against my race.

You watch. I will be labeled as, at best, an "irresponsible" black man. I have always felt about this accusation that the black "leader" whom white men consider to be "responsible" is invariably the black "leader" who never gets any results. You only get action as a black man if you are regarded by the white man as "irresponsible." In fact, this much I had learned when I was just a little boy. And since I have been some kind of a "leader" of black people here in the racist society of America, I have been more reassured each time the white man resisted me, or attacked me harder—because each time made me more certain that I was on the right track in the American black man's best interests. The racist white man's opposition automatically made me know that I did offer the black man something worthwhile.

Yes, I have cherished my "demagogue" role. I know that societies often have killed the people who have helped to change those societies. And if I can die having brought any light, having exposed any meaningful truth that will help to destroy the racist cancer that is malignant in the body of America—then, all of the credit is due to Allah. Only the mistakes have been mine.

Discussion Questions

1. Do you think this chapter, which was written back in 1965, still has resonance today? How or how not?

2. If this were written by a Black woman, how might the center of the piece pivot, that is, would the issues be the same or different? How or how not?

3. Do you believe that Malcolm X was incorrect in his assessment of America as harboring a "racist cancer" back in 1965? Would his assessment be different today? How or how not?

4. How do you feel personally when you read this sort of rhetoric coming from an author? Does it make you uncomfortable or upset? Does it confirm your own opinions? Does it validate your thinking?

Reprinted from: Malcolm X, "1965." In *The Autobiography of Malcolm X* (pp. 371–375, 377–378, 380–389). Copyright © 1965 by Alex Hayley and Betty Shabazz. Used by permission of Random House, Inc. ✦

9
A Letter to Harvey Milk

Lesléa Newman

Lesléa Newman weaves real and fictional people and events together in her short story "A Letter to Harvey Milk." In the course of the story, the central characters—Harry, a 77-year-old widowed, Jewish man, and the teacher, a 30-year-old Jewish woman who is a lesbian—connect on many levels. This is a story about the intersections of family, friendship, community, ethnicity, age, gender, and sexuality. Harvey Milk was a real person. His murder and the events that followed it are accurately recounted in the story. The use of the pink triangle and treatment of Jewish and gay prisoners in the Nazi concentration camps are also historical facts. The rest is fiction but could easily be true.

The characters in the story speak as people like them would speak, mixing words and phrases from Hebrew and Yiddish with their English. In her dedication, Newman hopes that one grandmother who is dead will rest in peace (literally peace be on her) and that no evil will come to her living grandmother by virtue of having the story dedicated to her and her name mentioned along with her deceased counterpart (literally no evil eye). Harry doesn't want to remember life in the shtetls *or villages of Eastern Europe, and he says the assignment to write a letter is a little crazy. The label he uses for Harvey Milk means "little bird." It is used the way an English speaker might use* fairy, *but he clearly regards Harvey as a friend, and in a poem he describes his late wife's hands using the same word. Dan White, Harvey's assassin, is called a* momzer, *a "bastard."*

This story asks the reader to consider what is important to remember and relate about the past. Perhaps the poverty of the shtetl can be forgotten, but not the meaning of the yellow stars and pink triangles of the Holocaust. The story also asks the reader to reflect on the nature of friendship and family. Harvey and Harry were friends despite differences in age, social class, country of birth, and sexuality; they did have being male and Jewish in common. Izzie and Yussl became lovers in the most perilous of circumstances. The teacher's family rejected her because of her sexuality, though she seems in every other way to be an ideal daughter. She seeks an opportunity to interact with people like her family members, and Harry identifies with her immediately because they share a religious tradition. He criticizes her family for rejecting her, and urges her not to give up on them, but he also recalls that his wife needed time to accept their daughter's marriage outside of their faith.

I.

The teacher says we should write about our life, everything that happened today. So *nu* what's there to tell? Why should today be different than any other day? May 5, 1986, I get up, I have myself a coffee, a little cottage cheese, half an English muffin. I get dressed. I straighten up the house a little, nobody should drop by and see I'm such a slob. I go down to the Senior Center and see what's doing. I play a little cards, I have some lunch, a bagel with cheese. I read a sign in the cafeteria, Writing Class 2:00. I think to myself, why not, something to pass the time. So at two o'clock I go in. The teacher says we should write about our life.

Listen, I want to say to this teacher, I. B. Singer I'm not. You think anybody cares what I did all day? Even my own children, may they live and be well, don't call. You think the whole world is waiting to see what Harry Weinberg had for breakfast?

The teacher is young and nice. She says everybody has something important to say. Yeah, sure, when you're young you believe things like that. She has short brown hair and big eyes, a nice figure, *zaftig* like my poor Fannie, may she rest in peace. She's wearing a Star of David around her neck, hanging from a purple string, that's nice. She gave us all notebooks and told us we're gonna write something every day, and if we want we can even write at home. Who'd a thunk it, me—Harry Weinberg, seventy-seven-years old—scribbling in a notebook like a school-girl. Why not, it passes the time.

II.

Today the teacher tells us something about herself. She's a Jew, this we know from the *Mogen David* she wears around her neck. She tells us she wants to collect stories from old Jewish people, to preserve our history. *Oy* such stories that I could tell her, shouldn't be preserved by nobody. She tells us she's learning Yiddish. For what, I wonder. I can't figure this teacher out. She's young, she's pretty, she shouldn't be with the old people so much. I wonder is she married. She doesn't wear a ring. Her grandparents won't tell her stories, she says, and she's worried that the Jews her age won't know nothing about the culture, about life in the *shtetls*. Believe me, life in the *shtetl* is nothing worth knowing about. Hunger and more hunger. Better off we're here in America, the past is past.

Then she gives us our homework, the homework we write in the class, it's a little *meshugeh*, but alright. She wants us to write a letter to somebody from our past, somebody who's no longer with us. She reads us a letter a child wrote to Abraham Lincoln, like an example. Right away I see everybody's getting nervous. So I raise my hand. "Teacher," I say, "you can tell me maybe how to address such a letter? There's a few things I've wanted to ask my wife for a long time." Everybody laughs. Then they start to write.

I sit for a few minutes, thinking about Fannie, thinking about my sister Frieda, my mother, my father, may they all rest in peace. But it's the strangest thing, the one I really want to write to is Harvey.

Dear Harvey:

You had to go get yourself killed for being a *faygeleh*? You couldn't let somebody else have such a great honor? Alright, alright, so you liked the boys, I wasn't wild about the idea. But I got used to it. I never said you wasn't welcome in my house, did I?

Nu, Harvey, you couldn't leave well enough alone? You had your own camera store, your own business, what's bad? You couldn't keep still about the boys, you weren't satisfied until the whole

world knew? Harvey Milk, with the big ears and the big ideas, had to go make himself something, a big politician. I know, I know, I said, "Harvey, make something of yourself, don't be an old *shmegeggie* like me, Harry the butcher." So now I'm eating my words, and they stick like a chicken bone in my old throat.

It's a rotten world, Harvey, and rotten-er still without you in it. You know what happened to that *momzer*, Dan White? They let him out of jail, and he goes and kills himself so nobody else should have the pleasure. Now you know me, Harvey, I'm not a violent man. But this was too much, even for me. In the old country, I saw things you shouldn't know from, things you couldn't imagine one person could do to another. But here in America, a man climbs through the window, kills the Mayor of San Francisco, kills Harvey Milk, and a couple years later he's walking around on the street? This I never thought I'd see in my whole life. But from a country that kills the Rosenbergs, I should expect something different?

Harvey, you should be glad you weren't around for the trial. I read about it in the papers. The lawyer, that son of a bitch, said Dan White ate too many Twinkies the night before he killed you, so his brain wasn't working right. Twinkies, *nu*, I ask you. My kids ate Twinkies when they were little, did they grow up to be murderers, God forbid? And now, do they take the Twinkies down from the shelf, somebody else shouldn't go a little crazy, climb through a window, and shoot somebody? No, they leave them right there next to the cupcakes and the donuts, to torture me every time I go to the store to pick up a few things, I shouldn't starve to death.

Harvey, I think I'm losing my mind. You know what I do every week? Every week I go to the store, I buy a bag of jellybeans for you, you should have something to *nosh* on, I remember what a sweet tooth you have. I put them in a jar on the table, in case you should come in with another crazy petition for me to sign. Sometimes I think you're gonna just walk through my door and tell me it was another *meshugeh* publicity stunt.

Harvey, now I'm gonna tell you something. The night you died the whole city

of San Francisco cried for you. Thirty
thousand people marched in the street, I
saw it on TV. Me, I didn't go down. I'm an
old man, I don't walk so good, they said
there might be riots. But no, there were
no riots. Just people walking in the street,
quiet, each one with a candle, until the
street looked like the sky all lit up with a
million stars. Old people, young people,
Black people, white people, Chinese people. You name it, they were there. I remember thinking, Harvey must be so
proud, and then I remembered you were
dead and such a lump rose in my throat,
like a grapefruit it was, and then the tears
ran down my face like rain. Can you
imagine, Harvey, an old man like me, sitting alone in his apartment, crying and
carrying on like a baby? But it's the God's
truth. Never did I carry on so in all my
life.

And then all of a sudden I got mad. I
yelled at the people on TV: for getting shot
you made him into such a hero? You
couldn't march for him when he was
alive, he couldn't *shep* a little *naches*?

But *nu*, what good does getting mad do, it
only makes my pressure go up. So I took
myself a pill, calmed myself down.

Then they made speeches for you,
Harvey. The same people who called you
a *shmuck* when you were alive, now you
were dead, they were calling you a *mensh*.
You were a *mensh*, Harvey, a *mensh* with
a heart of gold. You were too good for this
rotten world. They just weren't ready for
you.

Oy Harveleh, alav ha-sholom,

Harry

III.

Today the teacher asks me to stay for a
minute after class. *Oy*, what did I do wrong
now, I wonder. Maybe she didn't like my letter to Harvey? Who knows?

After the class she comes and sits down
next to me. She's wearing purple pants and a
white T-shirt. "*Feh*," I can just hear Fannie
say. "God forbid she should wear a skirt?
Show off her figure a little? The girls today
dressing like boys and the boys dressing like
girls—this I don't understand."

"Mr. Weinberg," the teacher says.

"Call me Harry," I says.

"O.K., Harry," she says. "I really liked the
letter you wrote to Harvey Milk. It was ter-
rific, really. It meant a lot to me. It even made
me cry."

I can't even believe my own ears. My letter
to Harvey Milk made the teacher cry?

"You see, Harry," she says, "I'm gay, too.
And there aren't many Jewish people your
age that are so open-minded. At least that I
know. So your letter gave me lots of hope. In
fact, I was wondering if you'd consider publishing it."

Publishing my letter? Again I couldn't believe my own ears. Who would want to read a
letter from Harry Weinberg to Harvey Milk?
No, I tell her. I'm too old for fame and glory. I
like the writing class, it passes the time. But
what I write is my own business. The teacher
looks sad for a moment, like a cloud passes
over her eyes. Then she says, "Tell me about
Harvey Milk. How did you meet him? What
was he like?" *Nu*, Harvey, you were a pain in
the ass when you were alive, you're still a
pain in the ass now that you're dead. Everybody wants to hear about Harvey.

So I tell her. I tell her how I came into the
camera shop one day with a roll of film from
when I went to visit the grandchildren. How
we started talking, and I said, "Milk, that's
not such a common name. Are you related to
the Milks in Woodmere?" And so we found
out we were practically neighbors forty years
ago, when the children were young, before
we moved out here. Gracie was almost the
same age as Harvey, a couple years older,
maybe, but they went to different schools.
Still, Harvey leans across the counter and
gives me such a hug, like I'm his own father.

I tell her more about Harvey, how he didn't
believe there was a good *kosher* butcher in
San Francisco, how he came to my store just
to see. But all the time I'm talking I'm thinking to myself, no, it can't be true. Such a gorgeous girl like this goes with the girls, not
with the boys? Such a *shanda*. Didn't God in
His wisdom make a girl a girl and a boy a
boy—boom they should meet, boom they
should get married, boom they should have
babies, and that's the way it is? Harvey I
loved like my own son, but this I never could
understand. And *nu*, why was the teacher

telling me this, it's my business who she sleeps with? She has some sadness in her eyes, this teacher. Believe me I've known such sadness in my life, I can recognize it a hundred miles away. Maybe she's lonely. Maybe after class one day I'll take her out for a coffee, we'll talk a little bit, I'll find out.

IV.

It's 3:00 in the morning, I can't sleep. So *nu*, here I am with this crazy notebook. Who am I kidding, maybe I think I'm Yitzhak Peretz? What would the children think, to see their old father sitting up in his bathrobe with a cup of tea, scribbling in his notebook? *Oy, meyn kinder*, they should only live and be well and call their old father once in a while.

Fannie used to keep up with them. She could be such a *nudge*, my Fannie. "What's the matter, you're too good to call your old mother once in a while?" she'd yell into the phone. Then there'd be a pause. "Busy-shmusy" she'd yell even louder. "Was I too busy to change your diapers? Was I too busy to put food into your mouth?" *Oy*, I haven't got the strength, but Fannie could she yell and carry on.

You know sometimes, in the middle of the night, I'll reach across the bed for Fannie's hand. Without even thinking, like my hand got a mind of its own, it creeps across the bed, looking for Fannie's hand. After all this time, fourteen years she's been dead, but still, a man gets used to a few things. Forty-two years, the body doesn't forget. And my little *Faigl* had such hands, little *hentelehs*, tiny like a child's. But strong. Strong from kneading *challah*, from scrubbing clothes, from rubbing the children's backs to put them to sleep. My Fannie, she was so ashamed from those hands. After thirty-five years of marriage when finally, I could afford to buy her a diamond ring, she said no. She said it was too late already, she'd be ashamed. A girl needs nice hands to show off a diamond, her hands were already ruined, better yet buy a new stove.

Ruined? *Feh*. To me her hands were beautiful. Small, with veins running through them like rivers, and cracks in the skin like the desert. A hundred times I've kicked myself for not buying Fannie that ring.

V.

Today in the writing class the teacher read my notebook. Then she says I should make a poem about Fannie. "A poem," I says to her, "now Shakespeare you want I should be?" She says I have a good eye for detail. I says to her, "Excuse me Teacher, you live with a woman for forty-two years, you start to notice a few things."

She helps me. We do it together, we write a poem called "Fannie's Hands"

> Fannies hands are two little birds
> that fly into her lap.
> Her veins are like rivers.
> Her skin is cracked like the desert.
> Her strong little hands
> baked *challah*, scrubbed clothes,
> rubbed the children's backs.
> Her strong little hands
> and my big clumsy hands
> fit together in the night
> like pieces of a jigsaw puzzle
> made in Heaven, by God.

So *nu*, who says you can't teach an old dog new tricks? I read it to the class and such a fuss they made. "A regular Romeo," one of them says. "If only my husband, may he live and be well, would write such a poem for me," says another. I wish Fannie was still alive, I could read it to her. Even the teacher was happy, I could tell, but still, there was a ring of sadness around her eyes.

After the class I waited till everybody left, they shouldn't get the wrong idea, and I asked the teacher would she like to go get a coffee. "*Nu*, it's enough writing already," I said. "Come, let's have a little treat."

So we take a walk, it's a nice day. We find a diner, nothing fancy, but clean and quiet. I try to buy her a piece of cake, a sandwich maybe, but no, all she wants is coffee.

So we sit and talk a little. She wants to know about my childhood in the old country, she wants to know about the boat ride to America, she wants to know did my parents speak Yiddish to me when I was growing up. "Harry," she says to me, "when I hear old people talking Yiddish, it's like a love letter blowing in the wind. I try to run after them, and sometimes I catch a phrase that makes me cry or a word that makes me laugh. Even if I don't understand, it always touches my heart."

Oy, this teacher has some strange ideas. "Why do you want to speak Jewish?" I ask her. "Here in America, everybody speaks English. You don't need it. What's done is done, what's past is past. You shouldn't go with the old people so much. You should go out, make friends, have a good time. You got some troubles you want to talk about? Maybe I shouldn't pry," I say, "but you shouldn't look so sad, a young girl like you. When you're old you got plenty to be sad. You shouldn't think about the old days so much, let the dead rest in peace. What's done is done."

I took a swallow of my coffee, to calm down my nerves. I was getting a little too excited.

"Harry, listen to me," the teacher says. "I'm thirty years old and no one in my family will talk to me because I'm gay. It's all Harvey Milk's fault. He made such an impression on me. You know, when he died, what he said, 'If a bullet enters my brain, let that bullet destroy every closet door.' So when he died, I came out to everyone—the people at work, my parents. I felt it was my duty, so the Dan Whites of the world wouldn't be able to get away with it. I mean, if every single gay person came out—just think of it!—everyone would see they had a gay friend or a gay brother or a gay cousin or a gay teacher. Then they couldn't say things like 'Those gays should be shot.' Because they'd be saying you should shoot my neighbor or my sister or my daughter's best friend."

I never saw the teacher get so excited before. Maybe a politician she should be. She reminded me a little bit of Harvey.

"So *nu*, what's the problem?" I ask.

"The problem is my parents" she says with a sigh, and such a sigh I never heard from a young person before. "My parents haven't spoken to me since I told them I was gay. 'How could you do this to us?' they said. I wasn't doing anything to them. I tried to explain I couldn't help being gay, like I couldn't help being a Jew, but that they didn't want to hear. So I haven't spoken to them in eight years."

"Eight years, *Gottenyu*," I say to her. This I never neard in my whole life. A father and a mother cut off their own daughter like that. Better they should cut off their own hand. I thought about Gracie, a perfect daughter she's not, but your child is your child. When she married the *Goy*, Fannie threatened to put her head in the oven, but she got over it. Not to see your own daughter for eight years, and such a smart, gorgeous girl, such a good teacher, what a *shanda*.

So what can I do, I ask. Does she want me to talk to them, a letter maybe I could write. Does she want I should adopt her, the hell with them, I make a little joke. She smiles. "Just talking to you makes me feel better," she says. So *nu*, now I'm Harry the social worker. She says that's why she wants the old people's stories so much, she doesn't know nothing from her own family history. She wants to know about her own people, maybe write a book. But it's hard to get the people to talk to her, she says, she doesn't understand.

"Listen, Teacher," I tell her. "These old people have stories you shouldn't know from. What's there to tell? Hunger and more hunger. Suffering and more suffering. I buried my sister over twenty years ago, my mother, my father—all dead. You think I could just start talking about them like I just saw them yesterday? You think I don't think about them every day? Right here I keep them," I say, pointing to my heart. "I try to forget them, I should live in peace, the dead are gone. Talking about them won't bring them back. You want stories, go talk to somebody else. I ain't got no stories."

I sat down then. I didn't even know I was standing up, I got so excited. Everybody in the diner was looking at me, a crazy man shouting at a young girl.

Oy, and now the teacher was crying. "I'm sorry," I says to her. "You want another coffee?"

"No thanks, Harry," she says. "I'm sorry, too."

"Forget it. We can just pretend it never happened," I say, and then we go.

VI.

All this crazy writing has shaken me up inside a little bit. Yesterday I was walking home from the diner, I thought I saw Harvey walking in front of me. No, it can't be, I says to myself, and my heart started to pound so, I got afraid I shouldn't drop dead in the street from a heart attack. But then the man turned around and it wasn't Harvey. It didn't even look like him at all.

I got myself upstairs and took myself a pill, I could feel my pressure was going up. All this talk about the past—Fannie, Harvey, Frieda, my mother, my father—what good does it do? This teacher and her crazy ideas. Did I ever ask my mother, my father, what their childhood was like? What nonsense. Better I shouldn't know.

So today is Saturday, no writing class, but still I'm writing in this crazy notebook. I ask myself, Harry, what can I do to make you feel a little better? And I answer myself, make me a nice chicken soup.

You think an old man like me can't make chicken soup? Let me tell you, on all the holidays it was Harry that made the soup. Every *Pesach* it was Harry skimming the *shmaltz* from the top of the pot, it was Harry making the *kreplach*. I ask you, where is it written that a man shouldn't know from chicken soup?

So I take myself down to the store, I buy myself a nice chicken, some carrots, some celery, some parsley—onions I already got, parsnips I can do without. I'm afraid I shouldn't have a heart attack *shlepping* all that food up the steps, but thank God, I make it alright.

I put up the pot with water, throw everything in one-two-three, and soon the whole house smells from chicken soup.

I remember the time Harvey came to visit and there I was with my apron on, skimming the *shmaltz* from the soup. Did he kid me about that! The only way I could get him to keep still was to invite him to dinner. "Listen, Harvey," I says to him. "Whether you're a man or a woman, it doesn't matter. You gotta learn to cook. When you're old, nobody cares. Nobody will do for you. You gotta learn to do for yourself."

."I won't live past fifty, Har," he says, smearing a piece of rye bread with *shmaltz*.

"Nobody wants to grow old, believe me, I know," I says to him. "But listen, it's not so terrible. What's the alternative? Nobody

wants to die young, either." I take off my apron and sit down with him.

"No, I mean it Harry," he says to me with his mouth full. "I won't make it to fifty. I've always known it. I'm a politician. A gay politician. Someone's gonna take a pot shot at me. It's a risk you gotta take."

The way he said it, I tell you, a chill ran down my back like I never felt before. He was forty-seven at the time, just a year before he died.

VII.

Today after the writing class, the teacher tells us she's going away for two days. Everyone makes a big fuss, the class they like so much already. She tells us she's sorry, something came up she has to do. She says we can come have class without her, the room will be open, we can read to each other what we write in our notebooks. Someone asks her what we should write about.

"Write me a letter," she says. "Write a story called 'What I Never Told Anyone'."

So, after everyone leaves, I ask her does she want to go out, have a coffee, but she says no, she has to go home and pack.

I tell her wherever she's going she should have a good time.

"Thanks, Harry," she says. "You'll be here when I get back?"

"Sure," I tell her. "I like this crazy writing. It passes the time."

She swings a big black bookbag onto her shoulder, a regular Hercules this teacher is, and she smiles at me. "I gotta run, Harry. Have a good week." She turns and walks away and something on her bookbag catches my eye. A big shiny pin that spells out her name all fancy-shmancy in rhinestones: Barbara. And under that, right away I see sewn onto her bookbag an upside-down pink triangle.

I stop in my tracks, stunned. No, it can't be, I says to myself. Maybe it's just a design? Maybe she doesn't know from this? My heart is beating fast now, I know I should go home, take myself a pill, my pressure, I can feel it going up.

But I just stand there. And then I get mad, What, she thinks maybe I'm blind as well as old, I can't see what's right in front of my nose? Or maybe we don't remember such things? What right does she have to walk in here with that, that thing on her bag, to remind us of what we been through? Haven't we seen enough?

Stories she wants. She wants we should cut our hearts open and give her stories so she could write a book. Well, alright, now I'll tell her a story.

This is what I never told anyone. One day, maybe seven, eight years ago—no, maybe longer, I think Harvey was still alive—one day Izzie comes knocking on my door. I open the door and there's Izzie, standing there, his face white as a sheet. I bring him inside, I make him a coffee. "Izzie, what is it," I says to him. "Something happened to the children, to the grandchildren, God forbid?"

He sits down, he doesn't drink his coffee. He looks through me like I'm not even there. Then he says, "Harry, I'm walking down the street, you know I had a little lunch at the Center, and then I come outside, I see a young man, maybe twenty-five, a good-looking guy, walking toward me. He's wearing black pants, a white shirt, and on his shirt he's got a pink triangle."

"So," I says. "A pink triangle, a purple triangle, they wear all kinds of crazy things these days."

"*Heshel*," he tells me, "don't you understand? The gays are wearing pink triangles just like the war, just like in the camps."

No, this I can't believe. Why would they do a thing like that? But if Izzie says it, it must be true. Who would make up such a thing?

"He looked a little bit like *Yussl*," Izzie says, and then he begins to cry, and such a cry like I never heard. Like a baby he was, with the tears streaming down his cheeks and his shoulders shaking with great big sobs. Such moans and groans I never heard from a grown man in all my life. I thought maybe he was gonna have a heart attack the way he was carrying on. I didn't know what to do. I was afraid the neighbors would hear, they shouldn't call the police, such sounds he was making. Fifty-eight years old he was, but he looked like a little boy sitting there, sniffling. And who was *Yussl*? Thirty years we'd been friends, and I never heard from *Yussl*.

So finally, I put my arms around him, and I held him, I didn't know what else to do. His body was shaking so, I thought his bones would crack from knocking against each other. Soon his body got quiet, but then all of a sudden his mouth got noisy.

"Listen, *Heshel*, I got to tell you something, something I never told nobody in my whole life. I was young in the camps, nineteen, maybe twenty when they took us away." The words poured from his mouth like a flood. "*Yussl* was my best friend in the camps. Already I saw my mother, my father, my Hannah marched off to the ovens. *Yussl* was the only one I had to hold on to.

"One morning, during the selection, they pointed me to the right, *Yussl* to the left. I went a little crazy, I ran after him. 'No, he stays with me, they made a mistake.' I said, and I grabbed him by the hand and dragged him back in line. Why the guard didn't kill us right then, I couldn't tell you. Nothing made sense in that place.

"*Yussl* and I slept together on a wooden bench. That night I couldn't sleep. It happened pretty often in that place. I would close my eyes and see such things that would make me scream in the night, and for that I could get shot. I don't know what was worse, asleep or awake. All I saw was suffering.

"On this night, *Yussl* was awake, too. He didn't move a muscle, but I could tell. Finally he said my name, just a whisper, but something broke in me and I began to cry. He put his arms around me and we cried together, such a close call we'd had.

"And then he began to kiss me. 'You saved my life,' he whispered, and he kissed my eyes, my cheeks, my lips. And Harry, I kissed him back. Harry, I never told nobody this before. I, we . . . we, you know, that was such a place that hell, I couldn't help it. The warmth of his body was just too much for me and Hannah was dead already and we would soon be dead too, probably, so what did it matter?"

He looked up at me then, the tears streaming from his eyes. "It's O.K., Izzie," I said. "Maybe I would have done the same."

"There's more, Harry," he says, and I got him a tissue, he should blow his nose. What more could there be?

"This went on for a couple of months maybe, just every once in a while when we couldn't sleep. He'd whisper my name and I'd answer with his, and then we'd, you know, we'd touch each other. We were very, very quiet, but who knows, maybe some other boys in the barracks were doing the same.

"To this day I don't know how it happened, but somehow someone found out. One day *Yussl* didn't come back to the barracks at night. I went almost crazy, you can imagine, all the things that went through my mind, the things they might have done to him, those lousy Nazis. I looked everywhere, I asked everyone, three days he was gone. And then on the third day, they lined us up after supper and there they had *Yussl*. I almost collapsed on the ground when I saw him. They had him on his knees with his hands tied behind his back. His face was swollen so, you couldn't even see his eyes. His clothes were stained with blood. And on his uniform they had sewn a pink triangle, big, twice the size of our yellow stars.

"Oy, did they beat him but good. 'Who's your friend?' they yelled at him. 'Tell us and we'll let you live.' But no, he wouldn't tell. He knew they were lying, he knew they'd kill us both. They asked him again and again, 'Who's your friend? Tell us which one he is: And every time he said no, they'd crack him with a whip until the blood ran from him like a river. Such a sight he was, like I've never seen. How he remained conscious I'll never know.

"Everything inside me was broken after that. I wanted to run to his side, but I didn't dare, so afraid I was. At one point he looked at me, right in the eye, as though he was saying, *Izzie, save yourself. Me, I'm finished, but you, you got a chance to live through this and tell the world our story.*

"Right after he looked at me, he collapsed, and they shot him, Harry, right there in front of us. Even after he was dead they kicked him in the head a little bit. They left his body out there for two days, as a warning to us. They whipped us all that night, and from then on we had to sleep with all the lights on and with our hands on top of the blankets. Anyone caught with their hands under the blankets would be shot."

"He died for me, Harry, they killed him for that, was it such a terrible thing? *Oy*, I haven't thought about *Yussl* for twenty-five years maybe, but when I saw that kid on the street today, it was too much." And then he started crying again, and he clung to me like a child.

So what could I do? I was afraid he shouldn't have a heart attack, maybe he was having a nervous breakdown, maybe I should get the doctor. *Vay iss mir*, I never saw anybody so upset in my whole life. And such a story, *Gottenyu*.

"Izzie, come lie down," I says, and I took him by the hand to the bed. I laid him down, I took off his shoes, and still he was crying. So what could I do? I lay down with him, I held him tight. I told him he was safe, he was in America. I don't know what else I said, I don't think he heard me, still he kept crying.

I stroked his head, I held him tight. "Izzie, it's alright," I said. "Izzie, Izzie, *Izzaleh*." I said his name over and over, like a lullaby, until his crying got quiet. He said my name once softly, *Heshel*, or maybe he said *Yussl*, I don't remember, but thank God he finally fell asleep. I tried to get up from the bed, but Izzie held onto me tight. So what could I do? Izzie was my friend for thirty years, for him I would do anything. So I held him all night long, and he slept like a baby.

And this is what I never told nobody, not even Harvey. That there in that bed, where Fannie and I slept together for forty-two years, me and Izzie spent the night. Me, I didn't sleep a wink, such a lump in my throat I had, like the night Harvey died.

Izzie passed on a couple months after that. I saw him a few more times, and he seemed different somehow. How, I couldn't say. We never talked about that night. But now that he had told someone his deepest secret, he was ready to go, he could die in peace. Maybe now that I told, I can die in peace, too?

VIII.

Dear Teacher:

You said write what you never told nobody, and write you a letter. I always did all my homework, such a student I was. So *nu*, I got to tell you something. I can't write in this notebook no more, I can't come no more to the class. I don't want you should take offense, you're a good teacher and a nice girl. But me, I'm an old man, I don't sleep so good at night, these stories are like a knife in my heart. Harvey, Fannie, Izzie, *Yussl*, my father, my mother, let them all rest in peace. The dead are gone. Better to live for today. What good does remembering do, it doesn't bring back the dead. Let them rest in peace.

But Teacher, I want you should have my notebook. It doesn't have nice stories in it, no love letters, no happy endings for a nice girl like you. A bestseller it ain't, I guarantee. Maybe you'll put it in a book someday, the world shouldn't forget.

Meanwhile, good luck to you, Teacher. May you live and be well and not get shot in the head like poor Harvey, may he rest in peace. Maybe someday we'll go out, have a coffee again, who knows? But me, I'm too old for this crazy writing. I remember too much, the pen is like a knife twisting in my heart.

One more thing, Teacher. Between parents and children, it's not so easy. Believe me, I know. Don't give up on them. One father, one mother, it's all you got. If you were my *tochter*, I'd be proud of you.

Harry

Discussion Questions

1. Are there events in your own past or that of an ethnic or other group to which you belong that are painful, but still must be remembered? Are there any that people are reluctant to talk about with the younger generation?

2. Are any of the attributes (religion, sexuality, age, gender) of the characters in this story more important than any of the others? Would their lives be markedly different if one or more of these attributes were different? Would it matter, for example, if Harry and the teacher were Christian or Muslim or if they were both female or nearer to the same age?

3. Germany had once been a place of fairly liberal attitudes toward sexuality, yet the Nazis tried to put all gay men into concentration camps. Those who were not members of ethnic or religious minorities, that is Jews, Gypsies, or Jehovah's Witnesses, were sent to slave labor camps rather than death camps. Why would the Nazis want to eliminate gay men from society? Based on their *Kinder, Kuche, und Kirche* (children, kitchen, and church) policy, they had a different attitude and policy toward lesbians. There was no systematic attempt to eliminate them from society. What do you think it was about gender, sexuality, and gender differences that led to the different ways gay men and lesbians were treated?

4. There is not much said about social class in this story; however, there are clues and underlying assumptions about class. What are they?

From Lesléa Newman: "A Letter to Harvey Milk." In *A Letter to Harvey Milk*, pp. 32–47. Copyright © 2004 by The University of Wisconsin Press. Reprinted with permission. ✦

10
Background

From *Tea That Burns: A Family Memoir of Chinatown*

Bruce Edward Hall

Bruce Edward Hall offers the reader a poetic boyhood vision of panoramic family memories reaching back to a much older time in Imperial China replete with dynastic rulers, to California mining camps that lured Chinese men who became "guests of the Golden Mountain," to a vista of ghosts down Mott Street in the heart of Brooklyn's Chinatown, to New England, where he was a "Connecticut boy, albeit one who could eat with chopsticks." Hall's panoramic journey is played out with significant reference to Chinese men both in their home country and as Chinese immigrants.

For men in China, Chinese economic and political history could make life for the majority of men in the countryside prey to bouts of unemployment, starvation, depredations from armies of bandits or brigands, violence in clan and national wars, and colonizing efforts from foreign powers. For Chinese immigrant men, it is Whites in America whose racist beliefs become the main crippler of their human agency. It was Chinese men who were dangled from sheer cliffs and whose small bodies made it easier for them to plant dynamite in rocky crevasses during the construction of the Transcontinental Railroad; it was, in fact, their labor that made completion of the railroad possible. Yet their stories were silenced by a single famous photograph commemorating the event, which includes not one Chinese face. Moreover, Chinese men were also further stigmatized by White American men for taking on "women's work"—laundering clothes and cooking—in order to survive, further marginalizing them from the standpoint of the White male-dominated West.

Chinese immigrants in general were ignored in their new American homes by political parties and politicians who could have fought for their civil rights. Instead they endured decades of legal discrimination with little recourse. When Hall's great grandfather embarks for New York, at the end of the piece, the immigrant and the American story become one and the same as his father becomes the third generation Chinese American who "made good." Hall's family story is a classic American immigrant story gone awry, as seen when one delves into the gendered, racial, and class overtones.

There are ghosts in Chinatown. They're all there, lined up, waiting to see me whenever I venture down Mott Street, squeezing past the crowds inspecting the sidewalk vendors' fruit or firecrackers or wind up birds that really fly. There are ghosts of men and women, some in exotic clothes, some gambling, bent over little ivory tiles, some eating. No, everyone's eating. Inside a certain shop, there is the ghost of a man in a broad-sleeved jacket, with a long braid, working on an intricate work of art. On a tiny street, a vintage black Cadillac, driven by a little man with a big cigar, careens away from the curb, full of flowers and that day's race receipts. On a narrow sidewalk is the image of a shy young women in magnificent ceremonial clothes, venturing uncertainly into the sunlight. And then there is the ghost of a little boy with a blue blanket, being carted up a staircase to a mysterious place full of dragons and phoenixes and, once, even a bowl of Chinese Cheerios. These are my personal spirits, shadows of my existence reaching out to me from over 125 years. To me they are dollops of magic—magic that can still be found by those who know where to look.

My father knows where the magic is. Even though he began life there, to him the old neighborhood is still a little mysterious. He is actually third-generation Chinese, born in Chinatown, raised in Brooklyn, and sounding remarkably like Walter Cronkite. His was a classic poor-boy-made-good story—youngest of five children, blessed with exquisite good looks and opportunity, graduating from Columbia at nineteen. As a wartime Army Air Corps cadet in Denver, he married the beautiful Southern blonde he met at a church social, a scandalous move in 1944. Chinatown was far behind him when, as an up-and-coming corporate executive in 1950, he Anglicized his name to Hall from Hor, a name many Chinese-Americans modify for obvious reasons. Pronounced "Haw" and written 何 it functions in sentences as a question mark. By itself it could mean "What?" although some say it more accurately translates to "Huh?"

Our house *was* the ethnic neighborhood in Madison, Connecticut, and despite the fact that none of us, my father included, spoke Chinese or engaged in any of the martial arts, we were considered somewhat exotic. When meeting us for the first time, my WASPy mother's new acquaintances from bridge at the country club always assumed we kids were Korean War orphans. But Mrs. Hall, ever the Southern Lady, would always smile sweetly and say, "Guess again!"

My friends all had blue-eyed pedigrees. They had middle names like Williston and Carlton followed by a III, a IV, in one instance a IX. In school the teacher pointed to a map of Europe and spoke confidently of where "our people" were from—England, Ireland, Scandinavia, sometimes Italy. I had "people" from those parts as well, but so many generations distant that I no longer felt any direct connection. No, in that world I was always the Chinese kid. The Chinaman. The Chink who spoke real good English. I was never exactly sure where I was from. The closest thing I could come to it was this tiny corner of New York City.

Yet I couldn't entirely fit in here either. I was an outsider with inside connections. An inside/outsider, perhaps, definitely a Connecticut boy, albeit one who could eat with chopsticks. Yet I knew that even Connecticut only went back three hundred years or so, whereas on Mott Street I could almost smell the beginning of time.

I could sense ghosts back then too, but only dimly. The enchantment I felt was stronger for their being just out of sight, heightened by the fact that we would visit only a few times a year. Months of atmosphere and mystery would be crammed into forays lasting only as long as it took to consume a twelve-course banquet, with insufficient time to explore the shadows behind teakwood dragons and mysterious basement doorways.

Over time, I determined to drag those ghosts into the daylight, and find out more about the Chinatown that was tugging on my sleeve. Of course I am talking about "old" Chinatown, those few blocks of Mott Street from Canal south to Chatham Square, and then up Bowery to Doyers and Pell Streets, then west back to Mott—three little thoroughfares to which a whole universe had been transplanted, in miniature.

***

For my family, that universe is a village of soot-stained mud brick in the waning decades of imperial China—fifty houses in a jumble of streets so narrow you couldn't lie across them without your head and feet knocking against the opposing walls. Every bit of available space is in use, leaving no room for sidewalks or flower gardens or any kind of personal privacy. There are just the houses, squeezed suffocatingly close, with heavy tile roofs that turn up at the corners into dragon-points that are meant to frighten away evil spirits. As further protection, the village's tiny lanes squirm around in curves and sudden, switchback turns, because, of course, evil spirits can only travel in straight lines and so will come to grief against a wall before crossing some family's threshold. Carved screens or miniature goldfish pools just inside doorways take care of any stray demons that manage to penetrate all other defenses. Household gods and smoldering incense stand guard over the ancestors tablets in the parlor. . . .

Ancestors. My ancestors. The family Hor, in the seventh house, fifth row from the head of the village of Hor Lup Chui, in the Toi-Shan district of Kuang Tung Province, southern China. Pretty much everyone is named Hor in this village. A bigger community might have two, or even three surnames represented, but Hor Lup Chui has been home to the Hor clan for countless generations, and besides, there are only 438 surnames in the entire nation of China anyway. Still, just because everyone shares a name doesn't mean they are closely related, and individual family trees are scrupulously kept. People of the same surname are not supposed to marry, so boys get wives from one of the other little villages that dot the horizon. Girls are married away, never to return.

Hor Jick Wah was my great-great-grandfather, the oldest Chinese ancestor that I can put a definite name to. I don't really know what he looked like, but I can pretty well guess. He must have had a square face with heavy brows, like my grandfather had, and he was probably skinny like everyone else in China back then. There just wasn't enough food to make anyone fat. . . .

He was born in Hor Lup Chui during the reign of Emperor Tao Kuang, and family tradition suggests that he was an artisan, probably a woodworker. He built the altars and carved the screens and constructed the intricate window-lattices that regulated demon traffic in and out of people's lives. He also built the coffins in which they took their final journeys. But very likely he hammered out an existence similar to others' in the Toi-shan district during that period—part artisan, part merchant, part farmer of the dry rocky soil that yielded only enough food to sustain the population for four months out of twelve.

He seems to have been a man of modest substance, however, living in a house with a courtyard, and having some education. After all, an artisan was fairly high up on the social scale, higher anyway than people who merely bought and sold things, and certainly his family had enough leisure to allow his son to learn to read and write, no small feat in a complicated language that consists of tens of thousands of unrelated symbols with roots in pictographs created far back in antiquity. . . .

It was in the 29th year of the Emperor's reign, the Year of the Monkey, a.k.a. 1850, that my Great-Grandfather Hor Poa was born. Chinese counted time according to the number of years that the current emperor had been on the throne, and Tao Kuang was sixth in the line of long-reigning monarchs of the Ch'ing or Manchu Dynasty, which had,

until recently, been a period of peace and prosperity for the great Chinese Empire.

But soon after Hor Poa's birth, young Prince Hsien Fêng ascended as Emperor of *Chung Guo*, or the Middle Kingdom, an event that would have been celebrated with feasting and firecrackers all across the nation. The people of Hor Lup Chui may have considered this dawn of a new reign a good omen for the baby Hor Poa's future. But the omens were not so good for China and Toi-shan.

In those days, the country was wracked with chaos and starvation and social upheaval. By 1850, the population had soared to an estimated 410 million from about 150 million in the previous century. The first Opium War had ended only eight years before in 1842, with Great Britain humiliating China into opening her markets to foreign trade and ceding them the island of Hong Kong into the bargain. The British bought up Chinese tea and silk, and built a city on their luxuriant stolen isle. They also made billions by flooding the country with opium produced in British India. China quickly became a nation of addicts, thus making Victoria the world's first international drug Queenpin. The Emperor imposed disastrous taxes on his subjects to pay the costs of losing a war.

Furthermore, just as Hsien Fêng ascended the Peacock Throne in 1851, the Tai-ping or "Great Peace" Rebellion was getting underway in southern China. A messianic maniac named Hong Hsiu-ch'üan fought to set himself up as a rival god-emperor. It would be fourteen long, hungry years before Hong and his movement were finally exterminated by the Chinese army, but the anarchy he generated continued to take its toll.

All across the southern provinces of Kuang Tung and Fukien there was massive unemployment. Armies of bandits from "Secret Societies"—terrorist groups ostensibly formed to restore the Ming Dynasty, out of power for some two hundred years—ravaged the countryside. Travelers were compelled to move about in large groups, and then only at night, with armed guards and lanterns covered by deep shades lest their light attract hungry bands of brigands. Village fought against village in bloody inter-clan feuds.

Sometimes warring villagers would steal out under cover of darkness to dig up hillocks and move giant boulders in an attempt to destroy their rival village's *feng shui*, the spiritual balance determined by the physical arrangement of the landscape. It was just one more way to bring ruin upon their enemies' lives.

Meanwhile in 1856, the fifth year of Hsien Fêngs reign, and the sixth year of Hor Poa's life, the Opium Wars started up again, adding even more devastation to the mix. European invaders ultimately chased Hsien Fêng and his court from the vast splendor of Peking's Forbidden City to a crumbling palace in the hills, where the hapless monarch died in 1861. He was twenty-nine years old.

Hsien Fêng's successor was Tung Chih, a six-year-old boy controlled by his scheming mother, a former minor concubine of the late Emperor, who for the rest of the century would stop at nothing, including royal murder, to hold onto her newfound power. The reeling Chinese Empire was steadily being gnawed away by hunger, war, and drug addiction, afflictions which killed an estimated twenty million people. Some say it was more like sixty million. The swirl of misery created a chasm which foreigners rushed to fill.

***

The people of Hor Lup Chui knew there had been Foreign Barbarians, also known as White Devils, visiting the nearby city of Canton for centuries. But ever since the Emperor had been forced to create "treaty ports" for foreign trade, it seemed that White Devils were everywhere—huge, ugly, pasty-faced men, with big bellies and hair sprouting from all over their bodies. Occasionally, there would be strange straw-haired women, walking brazenly in the street, wearing bizarre gowns that flared out from their waists like giant bells. They all came from barbarian lands far across the sea, in big wooden ships crowned with heaps of white sails or tall smoke-belching chimneys.

All through Hor Poa's growing years these White Devils, also known as Big Noses, told stories of gold—mountains of gold in a country called California, where one could go and become rich by just plucking the stuff off the ground. Chinese middlemen in their employ traveled around the villages, spreading the tales of this land of riches. The Big Noses had ships, they said, that could take a person to their country. The middlemen just needed money—a lot of money—and you could sail away to wealth, guaranteed. Or, if need be, a loan could be arranged. The middlemen would pay the passage in exchange for a little work until the money was repaid. It was easy, they said. You will be rich.

In other parts of the country, people were skeptical of these stories. Every Chinese knew that all other places on earth were beneath the notice of those who lived in the Middle Kingdom. Besides, life was too hard, the burden of tradition too great to allow them to be curious about unknown lands across the sea. But here in Toi-shan, where living had been particularly difficult for so long, people were looking for ways out of their misery. The stories the White Devils told sounded good to hungry men and women. The lure of gold began to ease the disapproval from the spirits of a hundred generations of ancestors and overcome any fear of the unknown.

It had been in the 27th year of Emperor Tao Kuang, a.k.a. 1848, that two men and one woman first went aboard one of the alien ships and disappeared into the mists. Months went by. But eventually, little packets of nuggets and gold dust started to arrive for their families. The following year, nearly eight hundred men and two women followed their compatriots. The year after that, more than three thousand men and five women—and finally by 1852, 27,000 Toi-shan residents were seeking treasure beyond the sea.

Many bought passage and sailed off on their own to try their luck. But some shipowners, under contract to western masters, had their middlemen—or *k'o-t'ou*, who were often returned emigrants themselves—recruiting shiploads of young men for laboring jobs in an assortment of distant places. The Chinese only knew that they were going off into the unknown to make money. But while some jobs were in the California gold fields, many more were on sweltering tropical plantations surrounded by the malarial rain forests of Cuba, or South America, or Malaysia, where the workers, referred to by the Big Noses as "coolies," died like flies.

Then, by the middle 1860s, the White Devils had stopped talking about gold and were actively recruiting men to go to California and work on something called a Rail Road. No one in the village knew exactly what a Rail Road was, but it apparently provided good, steady work, and could make a man rich. Some of the contracts offered by the *k'o-t'ou* to these mostly illiterate laborers promised payment of their passage in exchange for a certain number of years of labor for the sponsoring company, This "credit-ticket" system was nothing more than indentured servitude. Many called it slavery.

Early on, the Imperial Court was suspicious of Chinese mixing with foreigners. Emperor Hsien Fêng didn't want any of his subjects going abroad to work for these uncouth Barbarians who had forced opium upon his nation and more or less hijacked Hong Kong into the bargain. Thus, starting in 1855, the émigrés had to contend with an Imperial decree branding them traitors to the Manchu Dynasty, and mandating death by beheading for anyone trying to leave the Middle Kingdom. Ambitious bureaucrats were promised merit points for every ten illegal emigrants they captured. The heads of one hundred emigrants meant a promotion in rank.

However, the siren call of gold, plus the great "face" or prestige of having a relative working in California, taught families how to elude the authorities. They could sell a water buffalo or pawn some jewelry to come up with the exorbitant fare demanded by the *k'o-t'on*. Some used moneylenders to raise the cash, and many traveled under the credit-ticket system.

But however the money was obtained, there was still the leader of the local garrison to bribe, and maybe a payment to the regional magistrate or government official. It was then a fairly simple matter to take a junk down the Pearl River to one of the big ships standing in Hong Kong harbor and start the long, long voyage to another world. Most thought their sojourn would be a temporary one. For many, their exile is not yet over.

***

It was an arduous journey, especially for country boys—for they were very nearly all young men expecting to return to their women—who had never been out of sight of land before. Three months of being tossed about on the Pacific Ocean ensued, crammed into holds that had carried cargo on the outgoing journey—but then, the passengers were little more than cargo themselves. Everyone was sick on the first days out, made all the worse by the fact that they usually were forced to stay below decks, just like on the African slave traders that had stopped plying the Atlantic only a few decades before. Food, such as it was, consisted of whatever fare could be carried aboard by the passengers themselves and kept for ninety days in the era before refrigeration. Many even had to supply their own water, which they carried in distinctive cylindrical wooden casks. Some captains supplied hardtack and dried peas, which could be boiled down into a gruel, with maybe a piece of saltpork on occasion. Perhaps a load of rice would have been taken aboard before sailing. Of course, rats could fry up to make a special treat.

But nothing could stop the contagious diseases which sometimes ravaged the ships, the close quarters only accelerating the spread of infection. In the 1850s and 1860s, dozens of these vessels met with disaster caused by overcrowding, such as the *Lady Montague*, where 300 of the 450 passengers sickened and died. There were 338 out of 380 who perished on the *Providenza* before she passed Japan. On the *Dolores Ugarte*, desperate Chinese locked below decks started a fire as a ploy to get the crew to open the hatches. Over 600 were burned to death in their floating prison.

Troublemakers were beaten with rods by the Caucasian crews or locked in bamboo cages. Many were chained with iron shackles or even hanged by captains fearing mutiny. Some merely gave up and committed suicide. Yet even so, they sailed. As one Chinese survivor would later write, "To be starved and to be buried in the sea are the same."

For those lucky enough to avoid death from starvation or disease, the devastating seasickness eventually wore off, and the men grew accustomed to sitting with the others in the semi-darkness of their quarters. They had long since sought out those with the same surname or others from the same region. It wasn't family, exactly, but they had grown up in a society where people weren't so much individuals as part of a group and it was essential for them to merge with others. So they passed the time, smoking and gambling, gambling, gambling with their little *pai gao* dominoes, or perhaps they played *fan tan*, where they bet on the number of beans shaken from a cup. "Strings of cash"—Chinese copper coins with holes in the middle, carried on loops of string—began to clutter the winners' pockets.

A stop for revictualing in the Kingdom of the Sandwich Islands, also known as Hawaii, brought a little relief to the passenger-freight below decks in the form of fresh water and maybe some dried fruit or vegetables. They were not allowed to go ashore, of course, but that didn't matter, as all they were interested in was their final destination.

***

The arrival in San Francisco, some ninety-five days after leaving home. The bewildered boys would stumble down the gangplank, two by two, wobbly from their weeks of inactivity and the constant movement of the ship. Customs officials would fall upon their baggage, consisting of wooden boxes, wicker baskets, and rolls of cloth tied with cord. The essentials for a civilized existence in a barbarian world were spilled upon the ground. Chopsticks, porcelain teapots, bamboo steamers, and iron woks; family portraits, scrolls of calligraphy, ivory mah-jongg tiles, and skeins of silk; smoking tobacco, delicate pipes, dried lizards, and live snakes for use as medicine were pawed through by white men looking for boxes and bags of one item and one item only—opium. It wasn't that these Government officials were there to seize contraband. They had to make sure that they collected the very substantial duty which was charged, for opium was not then illegal in this country, nor would it be for decades to come.

Teams of Chinese representing the Six Companies—the Chinese-run benevolent associations that controlled every aspect of Chinese life in San Francisco—met these new immigrants as they reassembled their belongings. Groups of boys would recognize a summons in their own local dialect, and separate from the group to follow the speaker, who would pile them into carts for the trip to "Chinese Street," which the whites called by the name of Jackson. Narrow alleys running off to the sides were crammed with cheap wooden houses and shacks in which hundreds of Chinese men slept on hard wooden bunks. The crowding and sanitation were not much better than in the hulls of the immigrant ships, but the newcomers were largely indifferent to their surroundings as long as they could make money. Their newfound friends from their home district would soon help them slide into jobs in this rapidly expanding frontier town.

The earlier arrivals mostly worked for white prospectors, digging and panning out hastily-staked claims. They were allowed to keep half of whatever gold they found, which sometimes amounted to what seemed like a fortune to these cash-poor peasants. Claims abandoned by their original white prospectors were hastily taken over by Chinese, who hungrily squeezed gold dust out of the discarded tailings.

After 1864, shiploads of Chinese men were imported to work on the Transcontinental Railroad. Called "Crocker's Pets" after Chester Crocker, the railroad mogul who first conceived of this method of amassing cheap labor, ten thousand Chinese were toiling away at any given time. They worked long, backbreaking hours without complaint, their small, lithe bodies perfect for creeping into rocky crevasses to plant dynamite for blowing away obstacles. Often they were dangled down sheer cliffs in order to reach otherwise inaccessible places. The expression "Chinaman's chance" referred to the likelihood of their being killed in a fall or a badly-timed explosion. For all this they were given board and $30 per month in gold.

It was largely due to Chinese labor that the Transcontinental Railroad was finished in an amazing five years, but not a single Chinese face appears in the famous photograph of the ceremony surrounding the driving of the final spike in 1869. It is estimated that between five hundred and a thousand Chinese laborers were killed in those five years. Many believe the numbers were far higher.

Even so, the Chinese were appreciated by their white bosses for their energetic hard work, although some of their habits truly astounded them. At the insistence of their white co-workers, Chinese prospectors and railroad workers alike lived in separate camps; there their own cooks could prepare a semblance of the food they knew at home. American eyes were exposed to the mysteries of chopsticks and stir-frying for the first time. White men were further amazed to see Chinese carefully wash themselves every day—*every day*—coiling their long, braided queues on the tops of their heads to keep them out of the way. And then there was the strange Chinese habit of drinking nothing but tea—sans milk or sugar, no less—with the cooks keeping vats of water constantly on the boil so as to provide a constant supply. No one could figure out why the Chinese seemed never to get sick, while the Big Noses, also known as Round Eyes, who drank cold water directly from streams, were often doubled over with dysentery.

After 1869 the gold mines were getting depleted and the Transcontinental Railroad had been finished. Although thousands of Chinese were kept working on another branch of the railroad, thousands of others suddenly found themselves without work. Long practice in scrambling for subsistence in Toi-shan had taught them nothing if not resourcefulness, however, and the men just joined the swelling ranks of those who worked in various businesses catering to the ballooning Chinese expatriate community.

All sorts of skills were needed, like those of the Chinese immigrants in 1870, among whom were found six herbal doctors, seventy-one carpenters, fourteen stone-cutters, three bakers, seven barbers, and twenty-seven tailors to construct the loose-fitting blouses and trousers for the thousands of their countrymen who had preceded them. Scribes wrote letters for their illiterate compatriots. Troupes of actors entertained with classical Chinese opera. And then there were the importers who provided all that tea and other essentials from home.

Some Chinese were opening restaurants. Of course the cooking was just basic bachelor fare—a dim imitation of what they were used to eating in Toi-shan. Yet it was this plain country, Cantonese food which became the staple of the restaurants that were springing up in cities and towns where the railroad had dumped its men. Whole new dishes were invented to appeal to Round Eye palates. For instance, there is a legend of a group of drunken white miners breaking into a Chinese restaurant after hours and demanding food. The proprietor just scraped together table scraps and garbage and called it "chop suey," which means either "leftovers" or something vastly more rude.

Still others founded laundries, a desperately needed service for the sweaty white men who disdained clothes-washing as an effeminate task fit only for women. But with not very many white women to take care of all those men, some of these newly rich, western pioneers actually sent their laundry all the way to Hong Kong to be washed and pressed, rather than besmirch their manhood by doing it themselves. The Chinese stepped into the breach, and all over the West Chinese men sweated over great tubs of steaming water, boiling and pressing white people's clothes.

Others found work in the rapidly expanding cigar-making factories, where Chinese were favored over "Bohemians" for their dexterity and hard work. Tobacco would be shipped to San Francisco direct from Cuba, with over a million finished cigars per month sent East for $18 to $50 per thousand. The Chinese cigar-maker would earn four to twelve dollars for producing the same amount.

Some Southern plantation owners whose black slaves had run off after Emancipation turned to cheap Chinese labor to work in their fields and live in the old slave quarters. In the Northwest, loggers valued the strong, agile men who could scamper up a tree as well as wield an axe. These qualities made them even more valuable in the silver mines of the Rockies, where they could reach into the narrowest fissure.

Chinese found work as servants, as shoemakers, and in all manner of factories. Many operated their own truck farms, supplying two-thirds of all the vegetables eaten in California by 1872. And all the while, these good Chinese sons hoarded their money and sent a substantial amount to their honored wives and parents back home—for first and foremost, a Chinese son's duty is to his parents. After all, a hundred American dollars could make a family rich in Toi-shan. It could provide for a bride price, or a bigger house, or more farmland, or just food—sumptuous food, like squab, and crabs, and duck, hot and juicy, for everyone to become sleek and fat, the envy of their neighbors.

Besides, none of these men expected to stay in California for long, and they dreamed of the day when they would be able to return to their villages and bask in the honor reaped from their Barbarian-acquired riches. The upshot was that in the 1850s and 1860s so much money was sent back that Toi-shan became the most prosperous region in China. The United States became known as *Mei Guo*, "Superlative Country," while the sons in California were referred to as *Gum Shan Hok*, or "guests of the Golden Mountain."

After 1866, even the Emperor's Government—that is to say, the Emperor's mother—realized the benefits of so much hard cash being sent into Chinese coffers, and in 1868, the thirteen-year-old Sovereign affixed his seal to the Burlingame Treaty, which provided for free emigration between the U.S. and China, and further confirmed the rights of Chinese to use American schools and pursue naturalization. Those were not rights that most Californians thought should be granted, but then Anson Burlingame was a great fan of the Chinese.

Meanwhile, in the little village of Hor Lup Chui, my great-grandfather, Hor Poa, was playing with his friends in the surrounding hills, hunting, fishing, or just plain exploring with one of the village's many pet dogs. Of course the children never went out at night, because that's when demons from the surrounding graveyards roamed, looking for

young inductees to the netherworld. But through daylight and darkness, there was always one thing present—the distant smell of gold in his nostrils.

***

He waited longer than many of the other young men of his region to make the big trip. Perhaps things were good enough at home so that there was no urgency. Perhaps they were so bad that he couldn't afford a ticket. At any rate, in the twelfth year of Emperor Tung Chih, a.k.a. 1873, twenty-three-year-old Hor Poa took the junk down to Hong Kong and there boarded the *Oceanic* with some 725 of his countrymen for passage to San Francisco. His fare: $45.25. The *Oceanic* was one of a new fleet of steamships built specifically for the Pacific passenger trade since 1869. No longer locked below decks in dank holds designed for cargo, immigrants could now sleep in berths and cross the Pacific in about a month. Food, albeit strange Barbarian food, was provided by the line. Richer passengers could even enjoy the comfort of private cabins.

He did well. Family tradition says that Hor Poa worked on the new southern spur of the Central Pacific Railroad, but not as a common laborer, God forbid. We have always been solemnly informed that our Chinese-American Patriarch worked in the somewhat more genteel position of cook to the workmen. Still, whatever he did, Hor Poa sent a steady stream of money home to old Hor Jick Wah, waiting expectantly in his little village. And after fewer than six years, Hor Poa had fulfilled the dream of every immigrant Chinese man in California—he had saved enough money to return home in style. . . .

. . . Hor Poa, [then age 29, married and] could now be formally known by his marriage name, Hor Lup Chut, while the Moy daughter could add the Chinese suffix *She*, for Mrs. or Madame, to her maiden name, thus becoming Moy She. Her own given name, bestowed upon her by her parents, would never again be used, and would remain unknown to almost everyone, including her children. It would not be long until it would be forgotten forever.

The formal worship of Hor Poa's ancestors would come next, a short ritual in front of the ancestral tablets in the parlor with incense and offerings—he first, and she imitating him. In this way she left her own father's family forever, and joined her new husband's line. Now all her obligations would be to Hor Poa, Hor Jick Wah, and the long trail of Hor family predecessors. If she was a traditional Chinese mother-in-law, my great-great grandmother, whose name is lost to my generation, would have made Moy She's life a misery. At least until she provided a grandson—or two—or three.

But that was still in the future as, following the ancestor worship in the parlor, there would have been a day-long celebration of feasting and drinking in the village banquet hall—with the women separated from the men, of course, for a good wife never ate with her husband. And that night, the entire wedding party, spouting astonishingly rude jokes made all the more lewd by the liberal imbibing of rice wine, would have escorted the couple to their wedding bed, a great canopied fantasy of teakwood dragons and lucky birds flying among flowers and vines. It was time for Hor Poa to fulfill his obligation to his ancestors and give them that son they had been clamoring for, so they could brag about him in heaven. Three days later, Hor Jick Wah would send a gift of tender young pigs to the Moy parents in Chung On village, a traditional confirmation that their daughter was, in fact, a virgin. Not to do so would have been a mortal breach of etiquette.

But despite the auspicious omens provided by the Year of the Rabbit, as well as entreaties to dead generations, it seems that Moy She did not conceive. So, not able to wait any longer, Hor Poa agreed to the adoption of a girl-child, very likely from some impoverished widow trying to raise money for her husband's funeral; such an arrangement was very common and simple. This girl, named Yee Sum, or "Good Heart," was provided basically so that his lonely wife would have someone to wait on her. A son would have provided greater face, but there would be time for that later. Adopted daughter waited

on adopted mother who waited on parents-in-law in Hor Jick Wah's house in the fifth row from the head of the village. But the father was long gone. For four months earlier, Hor Poa had returned to the Golden Mountain. It would be years before he saw any of them again.

***

In California, there had been a measure of hostility towards the Chinese almost from the beginning. With the number of immigrants increasing from three to something over 25,000 between 1848 and 1852, the white population of San Francisco feared imminent obliteration by the seeming hordes arriving every day. Granted, at first the educated opinion was that they were good for the country—"Sober, diligent, laborious, orderly people—economical in their habits, and in all respects a desirable population," wrote one observer. Yet as early as 1849, there was mob violence against Chinese gold miners, and by the mid 1850s individual communities started banning Chinese miners altogether. In response to the growing anti-Chinese rallies held in San Francisco and elsewhere, exorbitant taxes were levied on the remaining mine workers, as well as on Chinese laundries, restaurants, and every other kind of Chinese enterprise. An attempt was made to deny the Chinese business licenses of any kind. In 1870, San Francisco prohibited the hiring of Chinese for municipal works. In 1879, an amendment to the California state constitution prohibited any corporation from hiring Chinese at all. Laws were enacted specifically to harass them: prohibiting the use of poles to carry burdens in the street; prohibiting firecrackers and ceremonial gongs; mandating the cutting of queues; and preventing bodies from being shipped to China for burial. The latter two were both cruel dilemmas. For most Chinese men intended someday to return to their native country, where they could be beheaded for *not* wearing a queue, the symbol of loyalty to the Emperor. And all of them believed that if they weren't buried in their home soil, their souls would wander, lost and aimless, forever.

Flouting the 1868 Burlingame Treaty, which promised the Chinese civil rights equal to any other foreign residents, local laws were passed to prevent Chinese from owning real estate, attending white schools, or even fishing, whether commercially or for pleasure. There was even a California law enacted threatening jail for people who slept in a space of less than 800 cubic feet—an obvious attack on the notoriously crowded Chinese neighborhoods. This measure backfired, however, when it was realized not only that tens of thousands of Chinese would have to be incarcerated, but also that the space allotted to them in jail was considerably less than that prescribed by law.

Chinese immigrants were baselessly accused of spreading leprosy and bubonic plague. Between 1854 and 1872, they were forbidden to testify against whites in Californian courts. Since they could not legally protect themselves, this left them open to all sorts of abuse from their Caucasian neighbors. And since Asians did not technically fall into the categories of "white persons, Africans, or those of African descent" specified by the Fourteenth Amendment to the Constitution, Chinese people were denied naturalization. Since they couldn't become citizens, they couldn't vote, Since they couldn't vote, politicians ignored them.

Yet all these were the least of the indignities suffered by Chinese in the American West. The very few Chinese women present were commonly assumed to be prostitutes and liable for deportation, as on the occasion in September of 1874 when some two dozen women were brutally forced onto the China-bound steamer *Japan*, their "screams and wails" filling the quayside air. Whenever they ventured into white neighborhoods, Chinese men could expect streams of abuse from white children, who would pelt them with stones and pull their queues. Chinese mining camps were regularly attacked by whites wielding clubs, rocks, and shotguns. There were wholesale massacres: Twenty-two killed in Los Angeles in 1871, thirty-one miners in one 1887 raid, a "so-called massacre" of "only five or six" laborers by a gang of white thugs in 1877. Despite the fact that the perpetrators were usually well known,

courts could not be found that would even indict them. Communities of Chinese were routed out of towns all over the West. In Seattle and Tacoma their homes were looted and burned by angry white mobs. The Knights of St. Crispin, a rapidly growing anti-Chinese labor group, declared in their founding statement that "one effect of a thorough organization here would be to deter the Chinese from coming, as they would think it unsafe." Led by the St. Crispins, California exerted greater and greater pressure to force Washington to ban Chinese immigration altogether.

The Six Companies pleaded for tolerance in appeals to San Francisco's white population: "We hoped you would, by knowing us, learn to like us, and be willing to protect us from some evils we now suffer . . ." But by 1876, the popular opinion concerning the Chinese was expressed in this typical commentary in a California newspaper ". . . he is a slave, reduced to the lowest forms of beggarly economy, and is no fit competitor for an American freeman . . . his sister is a prostitute from instinct, religion, education, and interest, and degrading to all around her they . . . they defy the law, keep up the manners and customs of China, and utterly disregard all the laws of health, decency and morality . . ."

Once, again, desperate Chinese started looking for a way out. Then, early in 1880, a fare war erupted between the Central Pacific Railroad and the Pacific Mail Steamship Company. The railroad wanted to eliminate competition on transcontinental travel once and for all, and started offering tickets for the unheard-of low price of $35. Frugally-minded Chinese jumped at the opportunity and started to buy. Their destination: New York City.

Discussion Questions

1. How is the experience of Chinese immigrant men gender-coded in relation to White American males in the west? What sorts of patriachal belief systems in the U.S. reinforce this gender-coding?

2. How is the experience of Chinese immigrant men racially-coded and class-

coded with regard to the building of the Transcontinental Railroad? How is this experience similar to or different from that of African American or American Indian men?

3. How much of the history that Bruce Edward Hall shares with the reader were you familiar with? Should discussions of Chinese immigrant history in America be part of the high school curriculum?

4. What was your response to learning what "chop suey" really was? What does this lesson tell us about race, class, and gender relations in our country's history?

Reprinted from Bruce Edward Hall: "Background." In *Tea That Burns: A Family Memoir of Chinatown*, pp. 5–20, 22–26. Copyright © 1998 by The Free Press. Reprinted with permission. ✦

11
He Defies You Still
The Memoirs of a Sissy

Tommi Avicolli Mecca

In this memoir, drawn in part from his poems and plays and originally published in a journal for teachers, Tommi Avicolli Mecca recalls his childhood and teen years. He was a quiet, studious boy who walked differently from other boys and did not like sports. He sensed that he was an embarrassment to his family, and he had few friends. When he was in grade school, a nun told his mother there was something wrong with him because he wore his sweater over his shoulders. In his Catholic high school, the other boys teased him and the teachers ignored what was happening. Homosexuality was an unforgivable sin; there was never any indication that gay people contributed to history or culture. He felt utterly alone, even suicidal. In his epilogue, Avicolli Mecca speaks with what we might today call queer consciousness, expressing his feelings of visibility, pride, and defiance at a gay pride march.

Avicolli Mecca talks about how labels such as "sissy" and especially "faggot" were used, and still are, in high school to control behavior. Faggot was, and is, a power word used to disarm anyone whose actions or attitudes were unacceptable to the group. It carried the implication that the person so labeled was weak, girl-like. A whole variety of totally unrelated, but uncommon or unpopular, attributes (e.g., being smart or opposing a war) come to be associated with cross-gender behavior and homosexuality through the use of this power word. Recently, states and school districts have begun passing legislation to protect children from bullying in schools. Sometimes those mandates include gender and sexuality issues explicitly, sometimes they do not. Some high schools and colleges have encouraged the formation of gay/straight alliances among students and safe-zone campaigns among faculty

and staff members willing to be receptive to the concerns of gay, lesbian, bisexual, and transgendered students. The Dizon article in Section 4 addresses this issue.

Avicolli Mecca mentions that as he began to identify his sexual orientation, he felt that he was totally alone in the world. When sexual relations between people of the same gender were mentioned at all, it was in the context of sin. Neither history nor English classes mentioned that same-sex relationships were common in the armies of classic civilizations and that many of the artists and writers studied were known to have had same-sex desires and relationships. The Robb and Irvine articles in this volume address those issues. Robb (Section 1) writes about the nature of same-sex relationships in the nineteeth and early twentieth centuries, mentioning writers such as Oscar Wilde and Walt Whitman. Irvine (Section 6) discusses the attempt to introduce a multicultural curriculum that included sexual minorities in New York City.

> You're just a faggot
> No history faces you this morning
> A faggot's dreams are scarlet
> Bad blood bled from words that scarred[1]

Scene One

A homeroom in a Catholic high school in South Philadelphia. The boy sits quietly in the first aisle, third desk, reading a book. He does not look up, not even for a moment. He is hoping no one will remember he is sitting there. He wishes he were invisible. The teacher is not yet in the classroom so the other boys are talking and laughing loudly.

Suddenly, a voice from beside him:

"Hey, you're a faggot, ain't you?"

The boy does not answer. He goes on reading his book, or rather pretending he is reading his book. It is impossible to actually read the book now.

"Hey, I'm talking to you!"

The boy still does not look up. He is so scared his heart is thumping madly; it feels like it is leaping out of his chest and into his throat. But he can't look up.

"Faggot, I'm talking to you!"

To look up is to meet the eyes of the tormentor.

Suddenly, a sharpened pencil point is thrust into the boy's arm. He jolts, shaking off the pencil, aware that there is blood seeping from the wound.

"What did you do that for?" he asks timidly.

"Cause I hate faggots," the other boy says, laughing. Some other boys begin to laugh, too. A symphony of laughter. The boy feels as if he's going to cry. But he must not cry. Must not cry. So he holds back the tears and tries to read the book again. He must read the book. Read the book.

When the teacher arrives a few minutes later, the class quiets down. The boy does not tell the teacher what has happened. He spits on the wound to clean it, dabbing it with a tissue until the bleeding stops. For weeks he fears some dreadful infection from the lead in the pencil point.

Scene Two

The boy is walking home from school. A group of boys (two, maybe three, he is not certain) grab him from behind, drag him into an alley and beat him up. When he gets home, he races up to his room, refusing dinner ("I don't feel well," he tells his mother through the locked door) and spends the night alone in the dark wishing he would die. . . .

✳✳✳

These are not fictitious accounts—I *was* that boy. Having been branded a sissy by neighborhood children because I preferred jump rope to baseball and dolls to playing soldiers, I was often taunted with "hey sissy" or "hey faggot" or "yoo hoo honey" (in a mocking voice) when I left the house.

To avoid harassment, I spent many summers alone in my room. I went out on rainy days when the street was empty.

I came to like being alone. I didn't need anyone, I told myself over and over again. I was an island. Contact with others meant pain. Alone, I was protected. I began writing poems, then short stories. There was no reason to go outside anymore. I had a world of my own.

In the schoolyard today
they'll single you out
Their laughter will leave your ears ringing
like the church bells
which once awed you. . . .[2]

School was one of the more painful experiences of my youth. The neighborhood bullies could be avoided. The taunts of the children living in those endless repetitive row houses could be evaded by staying in my room. But school was something I had to face day after day for some two hundred mornings a year.

I had few friends in school. I was a pariah. Some kids would talk to me, but few wanted to be known as my close friend. Afraid of labels. If I was a sissy, then he had to be a sissy, too. I was condemned to loneliness.

Fortunately, a new boy moved into our neighborhood and befriended me; he wasn't afraid of the labels. He protected me when the other guys threatened to beat me up. He walked me home from school; he broke through the terrible loneliness. We were in third or fourth grade at the time.

We spent a summer or two together. Then his parents sent him to camp and I was once again confined to my room.

Scene Three

High school lunchroom. The boy sits at a table near the back of the room. Without warning, his lunch bag is grabbed and tossed to another table. Someone opens it and confiscates a package of Tastykakes; another boy takes the sandwich. The empty bag is tossed back to the boy who stares at it, dumbfounded. He should be used to this; it has happened before.

Someone screams, "faggot," laughing. There is always laughter. It does not annoy him anymore.

There is no teacher nearby. There is never a teacher around. And what would he say if there were? Could he report the crime? He would be jumped after school if he did. Besides, it would be his word against theirs. Teachers never noticed anything. They never heard the taunts. Never heard the word "faggot." They were the great deaf mutes, pillars of indifference; a sissy's pain was not relevant to history and geography and God made me to love, honor and obey him, amen.

Scene Four

High school Religion class. Someone has a copy of *Playboy*. Father N. is not in the room yet; he's late, as usual. Someone taps the boy roughly on the shoulder. He turns. A finger points to the centerfold model, pink fleshy body, thin, and sleek. Almost painted. Not real. The others ask in a mocking voice, "Hey, does she turn you on? Look at those tits!"

The boy smiles, nodding meekly; turns away.

The other [boy] jabs him harder on the shoulder, "Hey, whatsamatter, don't you like girls?"

Laughter. Thousands of mouths; unbearable din of laughter. In the Arena: thumbs down. Don't spare the queer.

"Wanna suck my dick? Huh? That turn you on, faggot!"

The laughter seems to go on forever. . . .

Behind you, the sound of their laughter
echoes a million times
in a soundless place
They watch how you walk/sit/stand/breathe. . . .[3]

What did being a sissy really mean? It was a way of walking (from the hips rather than the shoulders); it was a way of talking (often with a lisp or in a high-pitched voice); it was a way of relating to others (gently, not wanting to fight, or hurt anyone's feelings). It was being intelligent ("an egghead" they called it sometimes); getting good grades. It meant not being interested in sports, not playing football in the street after school; not discussing teams and scores and playoffs. And it involved not showing fervent interest in girls, not talking about scoring with tits or *Playboy* centerfolds. Not concealing naked women in your history book; or porno books in your locker.

On the other hand, anyone could be a "faggot." It was a catch-all. If you did something that didn't conform to what was the acceptable behavior of the group, then you risked being called a faggot. If you didn't get along with the "in" crowd, you were a faggot. It was the most commonly used put-down. It kept guys in line. They became angry when somebody called them a faggot. More fights started over someone calling someone else a faggot than any-thing else. The word had power. It toppled the male ego, shattered his delicate facade, violated the image he projected. He was tough. Without feeling. Faggot cut through all this. It made him vulnerable. Feminine. And feminine was the worst thing he could possibly be. Girls were fine for fucking, but no boy in his right mind wanted to be like them. A boy was the opposite of girl. He was not feminine. He was not feeling. He was not weak.

Just look at the gym teacher who growled like a dog; or the priest with the black belt who threw kids against the wall in rage when they didn't know their Latin. They were men, they got respect.

But not the physics teacher who preached pacifism during lectures on the nature of atoms. Everybody knew what he was—and why he believed in the anti-war movement.

***

My parents only knew that the neighborhood kids called me names. They begged me to act more like the other boys. My brothers were ashamed of me. They never said it, but I knew. Just as I knew that my parents were embarrassed by my behavior.

At times, they tried to get me to act differently. Once my father lectured me on how to walk right. I'm still not clear on what that means. Not from the hips, I guess, don't "swish" like faggots do.

A nun in elementary school told my mother at Open House that there was "something wrong with me." I had draped my sweater over my shoulders like a girl, she said. I was a smart kid, but I should know better than to wear my sweater like a girl!

My mother stood there, mute. I wanted her to say something, to chastise the nun; to defend me. But how could she? This was a nun talking—representative of Jesus, protector of all that was good and decent.

An uncle once told me I should start "acting like a boy" instead of like a girl. Everybody seemed ashamed of me. And I guess I was ashamed of myself, too. It was hard not to be.

Scene Five

Priest: Do you like girls, Mark?

Mark: Uh-huh.

I mean *really* like them?

Mark: Yeah—they're okay.

Priest: There's a role they play in your salvation. Do you understand it, Mark?

Mark: Yeah.

Priest: You've got to like girls. Even if you should decide to enter the seminary, it's important to keep in mind God's plan for a man and a woman. . . .[4]

Catholicism of course condemned homosexuality. Effeminacy was tolerated as long as the effeminate person did not admit to being gay. Thus, priests could be effeminate because they weren't gay.

As a sissy, I could count on no support from the church. A male's sole purpose in life was to father children—souls for the church to save. The only hope a homosexual had of attaining salvation was by remaining totally celibate. Don't even think of touching another boy. To think of a sin was a sin. And to sin was to put a mark upon the soul. Sin—if it was a serious offense against God—led to hell. There was no way around it. If you sinned, you were doomed.

Realizing I was gay was not an easy task. Although I knew I was attracted to boys by the time I was about eleven, I didn't connect this attraction to homosexuality. I was not queer. Not I. I was merely appreciating a boy's good looks, his fine features, his proportions. It didn't seem to matter that I didn't appreciate a girl's looks in the same way. There was no twitching in my thighs when I gazed upon a beautiful girl. But I wasn't queer.

I resisted that label—queer—for the longest time. Even when everything pointed to it, I refused to see it. I was certainly not queer. Not I.

We sat through endless English classes, and History courses about the wars between men who were not allowed to love each other. No gay history was ever taught. No history faces you this morning. You're just a faggot. Homosexuals had never contributed to the human race. God destroyed the queers in Sodom and Gomorrah.

We learned about Michelangelo, Oscar Wilde, Gertrude Stein—but never that they were queer. They were not queer. Walt Whitman, the "father of American poetry," was not queer. No one was queer. I was alone, totally unique. One of a kind. Were there others like me somewhere? Another planet, perhaps?

In school, they never talked of the queers. They did not exist. The only hint we got of this other species was in religion class. And even then it was clouded in mystery—never spelled out. It was sin. Like masturbation. Like looking at *Playboy* and getting a hard-on. A sin.

Once a progressive priest in senior year religion class actually mentioned homosexuals—he said the word—but was into Erich Fromm, into homosexuals as pathetic and sick. Fixated at some early stage; penis, anal, whatever. Only heterosexuals passed on to the nirvana of sexual development.

No other images from the halls of the Catholic high school except those the other boys knew: swishy faggot sucking cock in an alley somewhere, grabbing asses in the bathroom. Never mentioning how much straight boys craved blowjobs, it was part of the secret.

It was all a secret. You were not supposed to talk about the queers. Whisper maybe. Laugh about them, yes. But don't be open, honest; don't try to understand. Don't cite their accomplishments. No history faces you this morning. You're just a faggot faggot no history just a faggot.

Epilogue

The boy marching down the Parkway. Hundreds of queers. Signs proclaiming gay pride. Speakers. Tables with literature from gay groups. A miracle, he is thinking. Tears are coming loose now. Someone hugs him.

You could not control
the sissy in me
nor could you exorcise him
nor electrocute him
You declared him illegal illegitimate
insane and immature
But he defies you still.[5]

Notes

1. From the poem "Faggot" by Tommi Avicolli, published in *GPU News*, September 1979.

2. Ibid.

3. Ibid.

4. From the play *Judgment of the Roaches* by Tommi Avicolli, produced in Philadelphia at the Gay Community Center, the Painted Bride Arts Center, and the University of Pennsylvania; aired over WXPN-FM, in four parts; and presented at the Lesbian/Gay Conference in Norfolk, VA, July 1980.

5. From the poem "Sissy Poem," published in *Magic Doesn't Live Here Anymore* (Philadelphia: Spruce Street Press, 1976).

Discussion Questions

1. Does this memoir remind you of your high school? Was there a boy who was called "faggot" or a girl subjected to some comparable pejorative label? How did you feel about it then? How do you feel about it now? Are your feelings dependent upon your own sexual orientation? Is it worse for a boy's sexuality to be questioned than for a girl's? Why?

2. Is it important to include information about the sexual orientation and behavior of the people we study in history and literature? Does it contribute to our understanding of their actions or their work? Are there other important reasons to include this information in courses and textbooks?

3. Avicolli Mecca grew up in the Catholic Church and mentions what he was taught about same sex relationships in Catholic school. What does your religious tradition teach about this topic? Has that changed recently, or is there ongoing discussion about this topic within your religious community?

12
With No Immediate Cause

Ntozake Shange

In *a poem that reads like the rush of blood from an open wound—immediate, real, raw, painful, and potentially deadly—Ntozake Shange reminds us all of some brutal, homegrown facts of life, the kind your mama does not want to have to tell you when describing what it means to live day-to-day as a woman. All women are at risk in the harsh vision described in Shange's poem. It is the fact of their gender that literally and figuratively binds them one to the other in this "crime clock" litany of depredations against women. In addition, Shange's words make visible women's and girls' bodies in a merciless listing of bodies that are ripped open, shoved, ironed, bloated, torn, murdered, exposed, raped, bruised, and violated in various ways while fluids are naturally evident—from blood, to menses, to semen.*

Shange provides us with a harsh, clear vision of crimes against women without sheltering us in any way from either the brutality of these crimes or the faces of the victims and the perpetrators. When Shange notes that "some woman's innocence/pours from her mouth/like the betsy wetsy dolls have been torn/apart," or that she "bought a paper from a/man who might/have held his old lady onto/a hot pressing iron," it is not difficult to envision real women and real men in these instances. Tellingly, images of neither race nor class surface anywhere in Shange's poetic litany—they are not captured in any nuance. In this, she is also faithful to a true vision of her subject matter. Women and girls universally ride subways, go to parks, take buses, and certainly live in home settings with men. Crimes against women—rape, murder, incest, and abuse—are just that, crimes against women, without respect to race, ethnic status, or class grouping.

every 3 minutes a woman is beaten
every five minutes a
woman is raped/every ten minutes
a lil girl is molested
yet i rode the subway today
i sat next to an old man who
may have beaten his old wife
3 minutes ago or 3 days/30 years ago
he might have sodomized his
daughter but i sat there
cuz the young men on the train
might beat some young women
later in the day or tomorrow
i might not shut my door fast
enuf/push hard enuf
every 3 minutes it happens
some woman's innocence
rushes to her cheeks/pours from her mouth
like the betsy wetsy dolls have been torn
apart/their mouths
menses red & split/every
three minutes a shoulder
is jammed through plaster and the oven door/
chairs push thru the rib cage/hot water or
boiling sperm decorate her body
i rode the subway today
& bought a paper from a
man who might
have held his old lady onto
a hot pressing iron/i dont know
maybe he catches lil girls in the
park & rips open their behinds
with steel rods/i can't decide
what he might have done i only
know every 3 minutes
every 5 minutes every 10 minutes/so
i bought the paper
looking for the announcement
the discovery/of the dismembered
woman's body/the
victims have not all been
identified/today they are
naked and dead/refuse to
testify/one girl out of 10's not
coherent/i took the coffee
& spit it up/i found an
announcement/not the woman's
bloated body in the river /floating
not the child bleeding in the
59th street corridor/not the baby
broken on the floor/
    "there is some concern

that alleged battered women
    might start to murder their
    husbands & lovers with no
        immediate cause"
i spit up i vomit i am screaming
we all have immediate cause
every 3 minutes
every 5 minutes
every 10 minutes
every day
women's bodies are found
in alleys & bedrooms/at the top of the stairs
before i ride the subway/buy a paper/drink
coffee/i must know/
have you hurt a woman today
did you beat a woman today
throw a child across a room
        are the lil girl's panties
        in yr pocket
did you hurt a woman today

i have to ask these obscene questions
the authorities require me to
establish
immediate cause

Discussion Questions

1. What was your immediate response to the poem? Did you like or dislike it? What about the poem did you like or dislike?

2. In the field of criminology within the discipline the sociology, we often refer to "crime clocks," which record how many crimes happen within the context of a single second, hour, minute, or day. How did you respond to the crime clock statistics Shange includes in her poem? Were you aware of these sorts of numbers with regard to abuse and/or rape? Was this an effective method of sharing such information?

3. What other ways are currently being used to share information with the public with regard to crimes against women? Do you think they have been effective?

4. Has anyone you know been the victim of rape or incest? Did that impact your reading of the poem in any way?

13
Working in Other People's Houses

Mpho 'M'atsepo Nthunya

Mpho 'M'atsepo Nthunya is a Sotho woman living in Lesotho, a small nation within the borders of South Africa. In this excerpt from her autobiography, she describes her years as a domestic worker. Her employers are other, more affluent Black families. Her experiences reflect the conditions of life for people from different social classes. Her experiences also reflect complicated gender relationships and a lack of trust between employers and employees. Nthunya is literate and articulate, having attended school off and on for 10 years. She clearly values education, but when she lived in a rural area, school was too far away. Thus, her children, ranging in age from 2 to 16, were able to start school only when she moved in with her mother in an urban area. She tells us that this was not unusual; because many people like her move down from the mountains, children of all ages were enrolled in Standard One (first grade). Still, it is not surprising that Tseliso, her 16 year old, fell in with some other boys and began to skip school.

In her first job, with Mrs. Masongo, she learned how to use electrical appliances and took care of her employer's two daughters while her own six children were cared for by their grandmother. The contrast between her lifestyle and living conditions and those of her employer is great. Her family lives in a rondavel with a thatched roof that is not even big enough for all of the family members to sleep in, while the Masongos can send their older daughters to England and move into a house big enough to include servant's quarters.

The distrust between employer and employee is reflected in the matter of language. Nthunya knows English and Afrikaans as well as Xhosa, Zulu, Tswana, and Pedi in addition to her own Sesotho, but she doesn't let her employer know this. Given the fact that several local and two European languages are spoken by significant numbers of people in Lesotho and neighboring countries, fluency in more than one is common even among people with little or no formal education. Being able to follow conversations in whatever language they happen to occur gives Nthunya a measure of control over her circumstances. Once Mrs. Masongo finds out, however, their relationship begins to deteriorate.

Relations between genders as well as between employer and employee are reflected in what happens when Mrs. Masongo goes to England to visit her daughter. Professor Masongo brings a woman friend home for the night. Nthunya is accused of stealing a pair of earrings that were taken by, or perhaps given to, this woman. She cannot defend herself without accusing the professor of adultery. He apparently felt entitled to bring his lover home in his wife's absence and does nothing to defend Nthunya, who is fired after eight years of service.

When I started to work for Mrs. Masango, at the University, I left all the children with my mother. Tseliso was sixteen, Manraile eleven, Motlatsi nine, Ralibuseng eight, Mofihli four, and Muso two. None of them knew what was a school, because in Marakabei the school was too far away. When they all came together in Roma after Alexis died, I started all of them to school. It was January 1969, and at that time there were no school fees, only ten cents for pencils, so I could send them. They had no uniforms, no shoes, but they all went to Roma Primary School. They were very glad, at first, to go to school. They always saw others going to school, and they were happy to go. Because the people were just learning about what is school, people coming down from the mountains, children would begin Standard One whenever they could do it, and there was no shame from being big. Tseliso was in school with children of all ages in Standard One.

My mother was taking care of the children, and I was making seventeen rand a fortnight, and that is all we had for six children and two adults. It was enough to buy maize meal, paraffin for the stove, soap, and sometimes a few second-hand clothes from the Mission. Everybody had no shoes, so my children were not feeling shame; they only felt the stinging of the stones on their feet, and the ice in winter would make deep cracks in their feet, which would sometimes bleed. I would rub animal fat into those cracks, and they would put their feet close to the fire. It hurt them, but it made the cracks go away.

One of my aunties in Roma was working at the University, cleaning another lady's house, and she told me that somebody arrived who wanted a helper. She told me to go to this new lady and ask for work, but Auntie said I must not say this is my first job. I must say I used to work for another lady who moved away. So I go, I say these things, and Mrs. Masongo tells me I can begin to work.

I work for Mrs. Masongo, a Mosotho who was married with a Xhosa. On my first day she showed me where her things belonged, and she didn't ask me what I know. She just showed me how she liked it done, and I watched. She wanted me to do washing for her and her husband and their children, ironing, house cleaning. I knew how to do these things, but it was hard for me because it was my first time to work in a big house. The work made me tired, and it was strange to me to have to please another lady all the time, when I was just used to pleasing myself.

I knew how to wash, but I didn't know anything about electricity. I was afraid, maybe I will burn the trousers of Professor Masongo. They had four children, two grown ones in England, and two girls living with them, one in primary school and one in high school. Mrs. Masongo taught me how to iron with an electric iron, how to cook meat in an oven, and how to bake cakes and buns. She was nice to me; she spoke Sesotha with me and showed me exactly how to do everything she wanted me to do. At first I work for her from 8 a.m. to 5 p.m.; at five o'clock I go home and find my children at home with my mother. At that time Mrs. Masongo did not give me lunch; I had to bring my little bit of *papa* or bread from home. Later, Mrs. Masongo moved to a bigger house and gave me a little room at the back, and then I could only see my children on the weekends, but from then I could eat all my meals at Mrs. Masongo's house. My room had a narrow bed and a small blue table. I could keep my clothes in a suitcase under the bed and hang a few things on nails on the wall.

Some of my children were proud of their school work; they would show me, and we would talk about it when I came home to be with them. Others did not care so much. Tseliso made friends with some other big boys, and sometimes they did not go to school at all. They would hide in the forest all day and tell us they were in school.

I was just thinking all the time how much I would like to have a house. We were all living in the small rondavel of my mother. There were holes in the wall and in the thatch of the roof. There was not room on the floor for all of us to sleep; when I sleep I go out to another house, to another lady in front of our house. She was my friend, 'M'ampho. She was the same age as me. She and her two children lived in that house alone because she had no husband, and she let me sleep with her.

One day there was a great wind, and a stone fell from the rondavel and hit my mother on the chest. When my mother was hit, we wanted her to go to the hospital. She said, 'I'm not a child. I'm not sick. I'm not going to the hospital.'

But from that time I was always dreaming to have a house for all of us, not this falling-down rondavel. I would cry to see somebody building a house, even if it's a small house. I would be glad for them, but I would cry because I can't see when I can ever have a house. I was just working for *phofo*. That's what we say when a woman works all the time, as hard as she can, and all she can buy is what she needs to eat, and to feed her children, and maybe even sometimes they can't all eat till the end of the month.

One day I said to my mother, 'I think it's better to me to go home to the mountains to my old house.'

My mother says, 'No, you mustn't go there. God will help you. You can't go to the Maluti because your husband told you he doesn't want you to live there alone. You must stay here so that your children can go to school.'

I say, 'No. I'm going.' I was fed up. Even the work did not make me have hope, I say, 'I have to leave this work with Mrs. Masongo and go home to the mountains.' I missed the mountains.

But my mother talked to me, and she prayed, and I could not finally leave her alone in Roma. She was loving the children so much, and me, and she was not even thinking about going to the mountains with me. So I stayed, working in other women's houses.

I started working for Mrs. Masongo while Alexis was still in the hospital. When he passed away, the phone call came from the police station to Mrs. Masongo's house. She took me with her car to my home in Mafikeng, and she was very kind to me. She knew our custom, that I would have to stay away for a time, and so she told me to find her a person to work in her house while I am away, and I could come back to my job. I say she was kind, because another lady would say if I must leave because my husband is passed away, she would find herself another helper and I have to look for work when my mourning time is over.

When Alexis is buried and I go to the Maluti for two months, I asked 'M'anthabiseng to work for me. 'M'anthabiseng was a good friend to me, but she didn't like working for Mrs. Masongo. While I was in the Maluti, 'M'anthabiseng wrote me a letter and told me I should come back to Roma as soon as possible, because she has weak lungs and she doesn't like to work in the house.

So I came back and started my work again. It was good to me to have work, because I needed the money. I liked Mrs. Masongo's house. No complaints. Maybe if I had another kind of work I would have liked it better, but this was all I knew.

One day I answered the phone for Mrs. Masongo. It was a white man. He said, 'Where is Mrs. Masongo? Is she there?'

I call her. After she talks to him she asks me, 'How can this *lekhooa* (white person) talk with you? I thought you said you don't speak English. I thought you could only speak Sesotho, but one day I heard you talking Xhosa, and my children tell me you understand Zulu and speak many languages. I think you are a liar. You say you are a Mosotho from the Maluti Mountains, and you don't know anything. But this is not true.'

I didn't say anything. But she told her children to catch me by talking with me in Xhosa. When I answer them she will know the truth. And this happens. Then another time her sister-in-law comes to visit and speaks Xhosa with me, I answer her, not thinking, and she says, 'Oh, you know how to talk Xhosa!'

She calls Mrs. Masongo and says, 'This lady knows how to talk Xhosa and Afrikaans. Be careful around her. She understands everything you say.'

Mrs. Masongo says, 'This woman is a *tsotsi*. She told me she didn't understand anything but Sesotho, but she lied.'

And it was partly true. She didn't ask me what languages I speak, and I didn't tell her. I didn't want her to know I understand what she says, no matter what language she speaks. If I walk in and she is saying something bad about me to the children, I understand her words. This is necessary, because when you are working with a person, you can't make her always to be happy with you. You will forget to dust the windowsill one day; you will break a cup, or leave some streaks on the floor from mopping. She will say something about you which she doesn't want you to hear. I pretend I don't understand, but I do, and because of that I can know a little bit what is coming, or why she acts angry when she says nothing to me about what makes her angry.

But after she sets the trap for me with the children and her sister-in-law, we sit down and she asks me, 'Where did you learn this Xhosa?' I tell her I was in Benoni Location, many years in school, and we used to speak Xhosa, Zulu, Sesotho, Afrikaans, Tswana, and Pedi. We would talk English in the classroom, and also at times Afrikaans and Sesotho, or even Xhosa. You never knew from day to day what language you would speak that day. Sometimes when you arrive in the morning the teacher will tell you, 'I don't want any more Xhosa. We will talk only Sesotho today.' Other days he will say, 'We are going to talk Afrikaans the whole day.' And so I told Mrs. Masongo that's how I learned these languages. I lived in Benoni ten years; they were the years of my schooling, though I didn't go to school every year the whole time.

After this, Mrs. Masongo was careful when she talked about me. She would go behind a closed door, or whisper, 'Sh! The maid will hear you.'

Mrs. Masongo is dead now, but she would be even more surprised to know the maid is writing a book about everything that happened.

I remember the first time I got money for the work I did, I was very, very glad, because I knew my children were going to eat, and I even bought some sugar for the house. It felt different than when Alexis gave me money, because my pay was seventeen rands; when Alexis gave me money it was thirty pounds. That was a lot of money in the mountains; I could buy anything I like with it. My little money in Roma was not for much besides *phofo*, but I was happy to get it, because for several years I had no money at all. When I began to live in Mrs. Masongo's house, she cut my pay from seventeen rands a fortnight to twenty-two rands a month, and I continued at that pay for eight years, until 1977, when we had the problem with the earrings.

In 1977 Mrs. Masongo went to London for a holiday, to stay six months. Her grown daughter was working there, and she was going to stay with her. She left me with *Ntate* Masongo and the two girls, and she said, 'Be sure you don't ever let anyone in my bedroom except *Ntate*.'

I didn't think anything about this, and we went on living as we always did, no troubles, until *Ntate* brought home a lady he was going to sleep with while his wife was away.

One morning *Ntate* Masongo went to town and bought a fried chicken. He told me that at nine o'clock at night, I should put the chicken in the oven to be warm. He said a lady was coming with *papa*, and I just needed to cook spinach. The lady was a nurse, working in the hospital; that's why dinner was going to be so late. He brought her into the kitchen and introduced her to me when she arrived. I didn't want to meet her, but what could I do? I greeted her nicely, and they passed to the sitting room. *Ntate* said, 'You can go and sleep, 'M'atsepo. It's not your time to be in the kitchen now. I will wash the dishes.'

So I go to my room and sleep. The next day she was gone before I got up, and from then on she always came late at night and left early. I did not have to speak to her again. But I knew she was sleeping in Mrs. Masongo's bedroom, and I remembered Mrs. Masongo told me not to let anyone in her bedroom except *Ntate*. But it was his house. I could not tell him not to take the lady in there.

When Mrs. Masongo came home, a friend of hers told her about the lady who was sleeping with Mr. Masongo while she was away, and she told Mrs. Masongo that I was a *tsotsi* because I let this lady stay there with him. She seemed to think I could stop *Ntate* from doing what he liked in his bedroom when his wife was gone. It was his house. I am a maid. I don't know anything.

Two weeks after Mrs. Masongo came back from London she said a pair of her earrings are lost. I ask her, 'What kind of earrings are they?'

She told me.

I said, 'I don't know anything about them. I think I never saw any earrings like those.'

She says, 'That means that when I was not here, you let somebody come in my house, look in my wardrobe, and take my things.'

I say, 'No, *'M'e*. I never touched the wardrobe since you went away. Even when I washed the clothes of *Ntate* Masongo, I put them on the bed. He takes them and puts them on a hanger in the wardrobe. So I don't know anything about these earrings.' I didn't want to say anything about whether somebody came into her bedroom. What could I say? It was not my business to tell her what her husband was doing.

She was angry. On Friday she told me that I must stay at home for two weeks with no pay and think about those earrings. She said, 'This is a holiday I am giving you for two weeks. You think about those earrings and come back on Monday, two weeks from now.'

I finish my holiday and go back to work on Sunday night, like I used to when I spent the weekend at home, but there was nobody in the house. I had to walk back home in the dark. So on the next morning, Monday, I come very early. I find Mrs. Masongo's daughter in the kitchen. I greet her and ask her, 'Where were you last night?'

She says, 'We were in Maseru. We came back late, at midnight.'

'Why didn't you leave the key for me?'

She says, 'I don't know, *'M'e*. I don't know what is going on.' The child looked very serious and sad. I could see something was wrong. She was preparing her food for going to school. I tried to prepare the food for breakfast for *Ntate* and Mrs. Masongo, but Mrs. Masongo comes in the kitchen and finds me.

'*Lumela*, 'M'atsepo,' she greet me in a big voice, looking very angry.

I answer, '*Lumeta*, *'M'e*.'

She didn't ask how I am. She just passed through the kitchen and went out. Then *Ntate* came and greeted me, asked how are my children these two weeks.

I answered him, 'They are well.' I gave him food. He ate, and he went to work. Mrs. Masongo went out without eating. I thought she was going to her office to work, but in a short time she came back. She called one of the gardeners, *Ntate* Lepota, and she said, 'Come here, 'M'e 'M'atsepo, to my room.'

I go, and she says, '*Ntate* Lepota, sit down here with us.' We all sit, wondering what is happening. She says, '*Ntate* Lepota, I'm sorry, because I have to send 'M'atsepo away. We have worked together for eight years, but today I have to let her go and rest. I think she is tired. So I want you to be the witness. I lost my earrings. I don't say she is stealing.'

Ntate says, 'Maybe the children have taken the earrings.'

She says, 'I can't chase my children away.'

Ntate says, 'Is it because of the earrings, or are you tired of working with 'M'e 'M'atsepo?'

She says, 'I'm not tired, but I see that she is tired.'

I say, 'Thanks, *'M'e*, for working with me so nicely. If you are tired of working with me, I understand.'

'I'm not tired. You are tired.' And her voice is very hard.

I say, 'Thanks, *'M'e*, God bless you.' And I never go to the kitchen again from that time. I go to my room and begin to pack my things.

She says, 'When you are ready, tell me. I can take you home with my car.'

I say, 'Yes,' but I don't do that. I take my time with my packing. I pack, I sit on the bed and remember many things from those eight

years. I was going to say good-bye to her children, who were just like my own. I packed again. At four o'clock, when the people who were working in the offices and the houses started to go home, I asked another lady to help me with my things. When we were taking my things out the back door I saw Mrs. Masongo, and I said, '*Sala hantle*, *'M'e*, stay well.'

She looked ashamed, but I was not angry. I was 'M'e 'M'atsepo, who never changed.

When I arrived at home, I told my mother what happened. She said, 'You and Mrs. Masongo—there must be something which is happening between the two of you. You are not people who will do this. There must be bad luck on one of you.'

But I didn't tell my mother about the nurse who came to sleep with *Ntate* Masongo. I stayed at home for two weeks. After that I found a job again, in Maseru, with Mrs. Mohapi. I got this job because a good friend of Mrs. Masongo found me one day at the bus stop and said, 'M'e 'M'atsepo, I don't want you to stay at home with no work. I don't know what makes you to have trouble with 'M'e Masongo. She is my friend, but I don't understand this. This doesn't feel right to me. You are a person who always works nicely. You don't talk. When she shouts at you, you don't talk back. So I don't know what happened. But I know of a lady in Maseru. She is cruel, but I think you can work for her. Let's go to Maseru, and I will show you where her house is.'

So we went there. She introduced me to Mrs. Mohapi. She seemed to be a nice lady, but her heart was not nice. I worked there for three months, but it seemed like three years. Every day I was tense; I got a headache.

At the beginning, the first two days, everything was OK. After that she said, 'Shame! You were working for Mrs. Masongo eight years?'

I said, 'Yes.'

'I can't work with you. I can't believe it.'

I didn't ask why.

'You don't know how to iron. You don't know how to cook. So I don't know what were you doing those eight years.'

At that same time Mrs. Masongo moved to Maseru, and her children came to see me and showed me their new house. They said, 'We think our mother was wrong to fire you.'

But I heard Mrs. Mohapi go ask Mrs. Masongo, 'How did you work with *'M'e 'M'atsepo?*'

Mrs. Masongo says, 'She was a good lady. We worked nicely together. I can't tell you what happened at the end, but she is good.'

Later Mrs. Masongo tells me, *'M'e 'M'atsepo,* I know this lady. She is cruel. She comes from Johannesburg. You can never please her. She can't ever say anything nice.'

But Mr. Mohapi was very good. He would try to make his wife treat me like a human being. I was eating bread and tea for breakfast, bread and tea for lunch, bread and tea at night. So one day Mr. Mohapi asked his wife, 'What is this *'M'e* eating?'

'Bread and tea.'

'From morning till night?'

'Yes. What can I do? I told her there is cabbage in the garden, if she wants to eat something besides bread and tea.'

Mr. Mohapi says, 'What are you eating? Bread and tea?'

She says, 'No. This is my house. I eat what I like.'

But he says, 'Bread and tea from morning till night can make a person sick. If she gets sick from staying with you, it's not good, really.' He began to be angry, and he said, 'That's why your helpers are always leaving you. You starve them and complain just like a Boer woman. You are cruel. You don't like people. You don't care how they live.'

She was paying me twenty-four rands a month, plus a room to sleep in, and this bread and tea. When I got my money I would bring it to Roma and keep a little bit and buy a little meat, just once a month. Sometimes Mr. Mohapi would come into the kitchen and put a little money into my hand secretly. He said I must not tell his wife. But Mr. Mohapi was not staying at home for long. He would always go to other countries, travelling to Zambia, America, England. He only stayed at home a few days at a time, because he was a diplomat in the government of Leabua Jonathan. Mrs. Mohapi was not working, just staying at home all day, watching me while I work.

One day at Mrs. Mohapi's house was like this: a little before 7 a.m. I wake up. I wash myself in the little bathroom and I go to the kitchen, I knock at the door, and Mrs. Mohapi opens it. We greet each other, and she complains, 'It is five past seven. You are only now waking up?'

I say, 'It's seven.'

She says, 'You're mad, You sleep like a dead thing, as if you are in your own house.'

I don't answer. I just pass her and take my broom and start to clean the veranda. She follows me. I am kneeling down, taking a cloth to wipe the veranda. She says, 'What are you doing? You are trying to cheat me. You think you are cleaning this veranda? I have cleaned it myself. I have been up a long time. I don't sleep like you. I have finished cleaning the veranda and I want my house to be clean. I have a party at seven o'clock this evening.'

The house was always clean. You can't even find a speck of dirt the size of a fingernail. The rug was green like grass, and anything that falls on this rug shows. There is never anything there. But I go in and clean the house where it is already clean. Sometimes I just go up and down, and clean the clean floors so she sees I am busy.

But that day I was working hard to prepare for supper at 7 p.m. for many people. Mr. Mohapi was arriving home from overseas. The soldiers of Leabua Jonathan were there, and twelve more diplomats were coming, and the King was coming too. I saw them when they arrived. Some of them brought their wives, but the Queen did not come. Mrs. Mohapi served them, and then she ate with them. They had very beautiful clothes; I could see when the kitchen door opened. But I did not serve them. I stayed in the kitchen all day and all night, working, with no food. I had to do everything before I could eat, and I worked till 2 a.m.

The dishes were coming in and going out, I was the only one in the kitchen. Mrs. Mohapi did all the cooking, and I was smelling that food all day but could not eat anything. By seven o'clock I was very hungry. The hours pass: 9, 10, 11, 12. By 1 a.m. I was so hungry I took some salad that was left on a plate. It had mayonnaise, and it was warm, and it poisoned me. By three or four o'clock I was vomiting, stomach aching, diarrhoea. But it was no use, because at seven o'clock the next morning I must be knocking at the kitchen door. I was tired, and Mrs. Mohapi greeted me,

'You are always late!'

I said I was not feeling very well.

'Oh well,' she says, 'So what?'

I look at her and think it's a pity. I think, 'When I go from here, she won't see me any more.' Out loud I tell her I have to go home for my daughter's wedding. It was not true; Manraile was married in 1975. But I say I am going, and I will come back after the wedding.

Mr. Mohapi comes for his breakfast, and he hears me talking. He asks me, 'Are you coming back, *'M'e?*'

I say, 'Yes, I will come back. After the wedding.'

When I was packing my things, Mrs. Mohapi comes into my room and says, 'She is taking everything. She will not come back.' Her husband looks sad, but he doesn't say anything.

I packed everything that was mine. I washed my overall dresses which belonged to Mrs. Mohapi, and I left them on the bed, washed and folded nicely. Then Mr Mohapi takes me with his car to the bus stop. He asks again, 'Are you coming back, *'M'e?* I know my wife. People always do this. I told her she will never find a person to work for her who is as good as you.'

I say, 'No, *Ntate*, I will come back. Don't worry.' But in my heart I know I am not coming back. I couldn't tell him the truth because I felt sorry for him. I didn't want him to be angry with his wife. It was the last time I ever saw him. . . .

Discussion Questions

1. In what ways do Nthunya's employers exercise class privilege? In what ways do the men in the families she works for exercise gender privilege? Do you think the exercise of privilege would be very different if these events had taken place in the United States rather than in Lesotho?

2. Her ability to speak several languages gives Nthunya a measure of control over her situation. What other forms of agency or control does she have while working in other people's houses?

3. Does this excerpt make you want to read the rest of Nthunya's autobiography or hear her speak about her life? What questions would you ask her if she came to speak on your campus?

Reprinted from Mpho 'M'atsepo Nthunya, "Working in Other People's Houses." *Singing Away the Hunger: The Autobiography of an African Woman,* pp. 118–129. Copyright © 1997 by Indiana University Press. Reprinted with permission. ✦

14
Woman Hollering Creek

Sandra Cisneros

In "Woman Hollering Creek" by Sandra Cisneros, from her book of the same name, we can discern nuanced outlines of gender, race, and class issues as they dovetail with the lives of her characters. This is the story of a young Mexican immigrant bride, Cleófilas, who crosses borders when she marries Juan Pedro, who comes from el otro lado—the other side—of the U.S. Mexican border. From the outset, the marriage seems ill-advised—a foreshadowing from the point of view of the father of the bride. Perhaps, Don Serafin discerns some level of immaturity or shades of temperamental behavior in his young son-in-law; the author does not let us in on the father's thoughts. What we do know is that Don Serafin's thoughtful foresight is pointedly accurate as Cleófilas—who had hoped for a romantic, passionate relationship with her spouse just like in the telenovelas (Latino soap operas)—does indeed soon long to return to her home in Mexico to get away from an abusive and philandering husband. Juan Pedro, indeed, behaves like many abusers—creating bruises and cuts one day, while honeymooning with his victim the next—yet there is more to this character than his kisses, fists, and belches. Juan Pedro, like the other immigrant men in the story, must work in the "ice house," a place that drives many to depression and drink, in the hopeless struggle to find a way out of endless days of backbreaking work for presumably little pay. Implied in Juan Pedro's story is the exploitation of immigrant Mexican male workers and the strains this places on relationships and marriages—race and class issues that impact gendered relationships.

Interestingly, Cisneros introduces the two lead male characters in the very first sentence of the story; Don Serafin and Juan Pedro Martínez Sánchez are introduced prior to Cleófilas herself—both with claims on this young woman, though with very different approaches to her character. Although Cleófilas performed numerous chores back home for her father and "six good-for-nothing brothers," she is still la consentida (the princess), in her father's house. However, on the U.S. side of the border, in her new life with Juan Pedro, she finds herself confined and isolated with few choices, controlled by her husband in her actions and words, sitting mute beside Juan Pedro at social occasions with his coworkers. Her isolation is compounded by the way U.S. border towns are organized in comparison with those in Mexico—on the U.S. side, "towns are built so that you have to depend on husbands." Gender roles, then, are perhaps livable in her father's house, but grossly abusive and unacceptable in her married home.

In a further fascinating addition to the discussion of gender in the story, Cisneros introduces two mythic female figures as significant to Cleófilas—La Llorona and La Gritona, the weeping woman and the hollering woman—signifying shame and sadness, on the one hand, and pain and anger, on the other. Yet, near the end of her story, Cisneros throws off the old meanings associated with these mythic female figures with the introduction of the character Felice—whose name literally means happy or joyous. Felice is a young Mexican American woman on the U.S. side of the border who introduces Cleófilas to gendered behavior Chicanastyle—outspoken, gutsy, and independent. Felice crosses La Gritona with a raucous, joyful yell. In this, Cleófilas catches a glimpse of the power of La Gritona—the woman hollering creek.

The day Don Serafin gave Juan Pedro Martínez Sánchez permission to take Cleófilas Enriqueta DeLeon Hernandez as his bride, across her father's threshold, over several miles of dirt road and several miles of paved, over one border and beyond to a town en el otro lado—on the other side—already did he divine the morning his daughter would raise her hand over her eyes, look south, and dream of returning to the chores that never ended, six good-for-nothing brothers, and one old man's complaints.

He had said, after all, in the hubbub of parting: I am your father, I will never abandon you. He *had* said that, hadn't he, when he hugged and then let her go. But at the moment Cleófilas was busy looking for Chela, her maid of honor, to fulfill their bouquet conspiracy. She would not remember her father's parting words until later. *I am your father, I will never abandon you.*

Only now as a mother did she remember. Now, when she and Juan Pedrito sat by the creek's edge. How when a man and a woman love each other, sometimes that love sours. But a parent's love for a child, a child's for its parents, is another thing entirely.

This is what Cleófilas thought evenings when Juan Pedro did not come home, and she lay on her side of the bed listening to the hollow roar of the interstate, a distant dog barking, the pecan trees rustling like ladies in stiff petticoats—*shh-shh-shh, shh-shh-shh*— soothing her to sleep.

***

In the town where she grew up, there isn't very much to do except accompany the aunts and godmothers to the house of one or the other to play cards. Or walk to the cinema to see this week's film again, speckled and with one hair quivering annoyingly on the screen. Or to the center of town to order a milk shake that will appear in a day and a half as a pimple on her backside. Or to the girlfriend's house to watch the latest *telenovela* episode and try to copy the way the women comb their hair, wear their makeup.

But what Cleófilas has been waiting for, has been whispering and sighing and giggling for, has been anticipating since she was old enough to lean against the window displays of gauze and butterflies and lace, is passion. Not the kind on the cover of the *¡Alarma!* magazines, mind you, where the lover is photographed with the bloody fork she used to salvage her good name. But passion in its purest crystalline essence. The kind the books and songs and *telenovelas* describe when one finds, finally, the great love of one's life, and does whatever one can, must do, at whatever the cost.

Tú o Nadie. "You or No One." The title of the current favorite *telenovela*. The beautiful Lucía Méndez having to put up with all kinds of hardships of the heart, separation and betrayal, and loving, always loving no matter what, because *that* is the most important thing, and did you see Lucía Méndez on the Bayer aspirin commercials—wasn't she lovely? Does she dye her hair do you think? Cleófilas is going to go to the *farmacía* and buy a hair rinse; her girlfriend Chela will apply it—it's not that difficult at all.

Because you didn't watch last night's episode when Lucia confessed she loved him more than anyone in her life. In her life! And she sings the song "You or No One" in the beginning and end of the show. *Tú o Nadie.* Somehow one ought to live one's life like that, don't you think? You or no one. Because to suffer for love is good. The pain all sweet somehow. In the end.

***

Seguín. She had liked the sound of it. Far away and lovely. Not like *Monclova. Coahuila.* Ugly.

Seguín, Tejas. A nice sterling ring to it. The tinkle of money. She would get to wear outfits like the women on the tele, like Lucía Méndez. And have a lovely house, and wouldn't Chela be jealous.

And yes, they will drive all the way to Laredo to get her wedding dress. That's what they say. Because Juan Pedro wants to get married right away, without a long engagement since he can't take off too much time from work. He has a very important position in Seguin with, with . . . a beer company, I think. Or was it tires? Yes, he has to be back. So they will get married in the spring when he can take off work, and then they will drive off in his new pickup—did you see it?—to their new home in Seguin. Well, not exactly new, but they're going to repaint the house. You know newlyweds. New paint and new furniture. Why not? He can afford it. And later on add maybe a room or two for the children. May they be blessed with many.

Well, you'll see. Cleófilas has always been so good with her sewing machine. A little *rrrr, rrrr, rrrr* of the machine and *¡zas!* Miracles. She's always been so clever, that girl. Poor thing. And without even a mama to advise her on things like her wedding night. Well, may God help her. What with a father with a head like a burro, and those six clumsy brothers. Well, what do you think! Yes, I'm going to the wedding. Of course! The dress I want to wear just needs to be altered a teensy bit to bring it up to date. See, I saw a new style last night that I thought would suit me. Did you watch last night's episode of *The Rich Also Cry*? Well, did you notice the dress the mother was wearing?

***

La Gritona. Such a funny name for such a lovely *arroyo*. But that's what they called the creek that ran behind the house. Though no one could say whether the woman had hollered from anger or pain. The natives only knew the *arroyo* one crossed on the way to San Antonio, and then once again on the way back, was called Woman Hollering, a name no one from these parts questioned, little less understood. *Pues, allá de los indios, quién sabe*—who knows, the townspeople shrugged, because it was of no concern to their lives how this trickle of water received its curious name.

"What do you want to know for?" Trini the laundromat attendant asked in the same gruff Spanish she always used whenever she gave Cleófilas change or yelled at her for something. First for putting too much soap in the machines. Later, for sitting on a washer. And still later, after Juan Pedrito was born, for not understanding that in this country you cannot let your baby walk around with no diaper and his pee-pee hanging out, it wasn't nice, *¿entiendes? Pues*.

How could Cleófilas explain to a woman like this why the name Woman Hollering fascinated her. Well, there was no sense talking to Trini.

On the other hand there were the neighbor ladies, one on either side of the house they rented near the *arroyo*. The woman Soledad on the left, the woman Dolores on the right.

The neighbor lady Soledad liked to call herself a widow, though how she came to be one was a mystery. Her husband had either died, or run away with an ice-house floozie, or simply gone out for cigarettes one afternoon and never came back. It was hard to say which since Soledad, as a rule, didn't mention him.

In the other house lived *la señora* Dolores, kind and very sweet, but her house smelled too much of incense and candles from the altars that burned continuously in memory of two sons who had died in the last war and one husband who had died shortly after from grief. The neighbor lady Dolores divided her time between the memory of these men and her garden, famous for its sunflowers—so tall they had to be supported with broom handles and old boards; red red cockscombs, fringed and bleeding a thick menstrual color; and, especially, roses whose sad scent reminded Cleófilas of the dead. Each Sunday *la señora* Dolores clipped the most beautiful of these flowers and arranged them on three modest headstones at the Seguin cemetery.

The neighbor ladies, Soledad, Dolores, they might've known once the name of the *arroyo* before it turned English but they did not know now. They were too busy remembering the men who had left through either choice or circumstance and would never come back.

Pain or rage, Cleófilas wondered when she drove over the bridge the first time as a newlywed and Juan Pedro had pointed it out. *La Gritona*, he had said, and she had laughed. Such a funny name for a creek so pretty and full of happily ever after.

***

The first time she had been so surprised she didn't cry out or try to defend herself. She had always said she would strike back if a man, any man, were to strike her.

But when the moment came, and he slapped her once, and then again, and again; until the lip split and bled an orchid of blood, she didn't fight back, she didn't break into tears, she didn't run away as she imagined she might when she saw such things in the *telenovelas*.

In her own home her parents had never raised a hand to each other or to their children. Although she admitted she may have been brought up a little leniently as an only daughter—*la consentida*, the princess—there were some things she would never tolerate. Ever.

Instead, when it happened the first time, when they were barely man and wife, she had been so stunned, it left her speechless, motionless, numb. She had done nothing but reach up to the heat on her mouth and stare at the blood on her hand as if even then she didn't understand.

She could think of nothing to say, said nothing. Just stroked the dark curls of the man who wept and would weep like a child, his tears of repentance and shame, this time and each.

***

The men at the ice house. From what she can tell, from the times during her first year when still a newlywed she is invited and accompanies her husband, sits mute beside their conversation, waits and sips a beer until it grows warm, twists a paper napkin into a knot, then another into a fan, one into a rose, nods her head, smiles, yawns, politely grins, laughs at the appropriate moments, leans against her husband's sleeve, tugs at his elbow, and finally becomes good at predicting where the talk will lead, from this Cleófilas concludes each is nightly trying to find the truth lying at the bottom of the bottle like a gold doubloon on the sea floor.

They want to tell each other what they want to tell themselves. But what is bumping like a helium balloon at the ceiling of the brain never finds its way out. It bubbles and rises, it gurgles in the throat, it rolls across the surface of the tongue, and erupts from the lips—a belch.

If they are lucky, there are tears at the end of the long night. At any given moment, the fists try to speak. They are dogs chasing their own tails before lying down to sleep, trying

to find a way, a route, an out, and—finally—get some peace.

***

In the morning sometimes before he opens his eyes. Or after they have finished loving. Or at times when he is simply across from her at the table putting pieces of food into his mouth and chewing. Cleófilas thinks, This is the man I have waited my whole life for.

Not that he isn't a good man. She has to remind herself why she loves him when she changes the baby's Pampers, or when she mops the bathroom floor, or tries to make the curtains for the doorways without doors, or whiten the linen. Or wonder a little when he kicks the refrigerator and says he hates this shitty house and is going out where he won't be bothered with the baby's howling and her suspicious questions, and her requests to fix this and this and this because if she had any brains in her head she'd realize he's been up before the rooster earning his living to pay for the food in her belly and the roof over her head and would have to wake up again early the next day so why can't you just leave me in peace, woman.

He is not very tall, no, and he doesn't look like the men on the *telenovelas*. His face still scarred from acne. And he has a bit of a belly from all the beer he drinks. Well, he's always been husky.

This man who farts and belches and snores as well as laughs and kisses and holds her. Somehow this husband whose whiskers she finds each morning in the sink, whose shoes she must air each evening on the porch, this husband who cuts his fingernails in public, laughs loudly, curses like a man, and demands each course of dinner be served on a separate plate like at his mother's, as soon as he gets home, on time or late, and who doesn't care at all for music or *telenovelas* or romance or roses or the moon floating pearly over the *arroyo*, or through the bedroom window for that matter, shut the blinds and go back to sleep, this man, this father, this rival, this keeper, this lord, this master, this husband till kingdom come.

***

A doubt. Slender as a hair. A washed cup set back on the shelf wrong-side-up. Her lipstick, and body talc, and hairbrush all arranged in the bathroom a different way.

No. Her imagination. The house the same as always. Nothing.

Coming home from the hospital with her new son, her husband. Something comforting in discovering her house slippers beneath the bed, the faded housecoat where she left it on the bathroom hook. Her pillow. Their bed.

Sweet sweet homecoming. Sweet as the scent of face powder in the air, jasmine, sticky liquor.

Smudged fingerprint on the door. Crushed cigarette in a glass. Wrinkle in the brain crumpling to a crease.

***

Sometimes she thinks of her father's house. But how could she go back there? What a disgrace. What would the neighbors say? Coming home like that with one baby on her hip and one in the oven. Where's your husband?

The town of gossips. The town of dust and despair. Which she has traded for this town of gossips. This town of dust, despair. Houses farther apart perhaps, though no more privacy because of it. No leafy *zócalo* in the center of the town, though the murmur of talk is clear enough all the same. No huddled whispering on the church steps each Sunday. Because here the whispering begins at sunset at the ice house instead.

This town with its silly pride for a bronze pecan the size of a baby carriage in front of the city hall. TV repair shop, drugstore, hardware, dry cleaner's, chiropractor's, liquor store, bail bonds, empty storefront, and nothing, nothing, nothing of interest. Nothing one could walk to, at any rate. Because the towns here are built so that you have to depend on husbands. Or you stay home. Or you drive. If you're rich enough to own, allowed to drive, your own car.

There is no place to go. Unless one counts the neighbor ladies. Soledad on one side, Dolores on the other. Or the creek.

Don't go out there after dark, *mi'jita*. Stay near the house. *No es bueno para la salud. Mala suerte*. Bad luck. *Mal aire*. You'll get sick and the baby too. You'll catch a fright wandering about in the dark, and then you'll see how right we were.

The stream sometimes only a muddy puddle in the summer, though now in the springtime, because of the rains, a good-size alive thing, a thing with a voice all its own, all day and all night calling in its high, silver voice. Is it La Llorona, the weeping woman? La Llorona, who drowned her own children. Perhaps La Llorona is the one they named the creek after, she thinks, remembering all the stories she learned as a child.

La Llorona calling to her. She is sure of it. Cleófilas sets the baby's Donald Duck blanket on the grass. Listens. The day sky turning to night. The baby pulling up fistfuls of grass and laughing. La Llorona. Wonders if something as quiet as this drives a woman to the darkness under the trees.

***

What she needs is . . . and made a gesture as if to yank a woman's buttocks to his groin. Maximiliano, the foul-smelling fool from across the road, said this and set the men laughing, but Cleófilas just muttered. *Grosero*, and went on washing dishes.

She knew he said it not because it was true, but more because it was he who needed to sleep with a woman, instead of drinking each night at the ice house and stumbling home alone.

Maximiliano who was said to have killed his wife in an ice-house brawl when she came at him with a mop. I had to shoot, he had said—she was armed.

Their laughter outside the kitchen window. Her husband's, his friends.' Manolo, Beta, Efraín, el Perico. Maximiliano.

Was Cleófilas just exaggerating as her husband always said? It seemed the newspapers were full of such stories. This woman found on the side of the interstate. This one pushed from a moving car. This one's cadaver, this one unconscious, this one beaten blue. Her ex-husband, her husband, her lover, her father, her brother, her uncle, her friend, her co-worker. Always. The same grisly news in the pages of the dailies. She dunked a glass under the soapy water for a moment—shivered.

***

He had thrown a book. Hers. From across the room. A hot welt across the cheek. She could forgive that. But what stung more was the fact it was *her* book, a love story by Corín Tellado, what she loved most now that she lived in the U.S., without a television set, without the *telenovelas*.

Except now and again when her husband was away and she could manage it, the few episodes glimpsed at the neighbor lady Soledad's house because Dolores didn't care for that sort of thing, though Soledad was often kind enough to retell what had happened on what episode of *María de Nadie*, the poor Argentine country girl who had the ill fortune of falling in love with the beautiful son of the Arrocha family, the very family she worked for, whose roof she slept under and whose floors she vacuumed, while in that same house, with the dust brooms and floor cleaners as witnesses, the square-jawed Juan Carlos Arrocha had uttered words of love, I love you, María, listen to me, *mi querida*, but it was she who had to say No, no, we are not of the same class, and remind him it was not his place nor hers to fall in love, while all the while her heart was breaking, can you imagine.

Cleófilas thought her life would have to be like that, like a *telenovela*, only now the episodes got sadder and sadder. And there were no commercials in between for comic relief. And no happy ending in sight. She thought this when she sat with the baby out by the creek behind the house. Cleófilas de . . . ? But somehow she would have to change her name to Topazio or Yesenia, Cristal, Adriana, Stefania, Andrea, something more poetic than Cleófilas. Everything happened to women with names like jewels. But what happened to a Cleófilas? Nothing. But a crack in the face.

***

Because the doctor has said so. She has to go. To make sure the new baby is all right, so there won't be any problems when he's born, and the appointment card says next Tuesday. Could he please take her. And that's all.

No, she won't mention it. She promises. If the doctor asks she can say she fell down the front steps or slipped when she was out in the backyard, slipped out back, she could tell him that. She has to go back next Tuesday, Juan Pedro, please, for the new baby. For their child.

She could write to her father and ask maybe for money, just a loan, for the new baby's medical expenses. Well then if he'd rather she didn't. All right, she won't. Please don't anymore. Please don't. She knows it's difficult saving money with all the bills they have, but how else are they going to get out of debt with the truck payments? And after the rent and the food and the electricity and the gas and the water and the who-knows-what, well, there's hardly anything left. But please, at least for the doctor visit. She won't ask for anything else. She has to. Why is she so anxious? Because.

Because she is going to make sure the baby is not turned around backward this time to split her down the center. Yes. Next Tuesday at five-thirty. I'll have Juan Pedrito dressed and ready. But those are the only shoes he has. I'll polish them, and we'll be ready. As soon as you come from work. We won't make you ashamed.

***

Felice? It's me, Graciela.

No, I can't talk louder. I'm at work.

Look, I need kind of a favor. There's a patient, a lady here who's got a problem.

Well, wait a minute. Are you listening to me or what?

I can't talk real loud cause her husband's in the next room.

Well, would you just listen?

I was going to do this sonogram on her—she's pregnant, right?— and she just starts crying on me. *Hijole*, Felice! This poor lady's got black-and-blue marks all over. I'm not kidding.

From her husband. Who else? Another one of those brides from across the border. And her family's all in Mexico.

Shit. You think they're going to help her? Give me a break. This lady doesn't even speak English. She hasn't been allowed to call home or write or nothing. That's why I'm calling you.

She needs a ride.

Not to Mexico, you goof. Just to the Greyhound. In San Anto. No, just a ride. She's got her own money, All you'd have to do is drop her off in San Antonio on your way home. Come on, Felice. Please? If we don't help her, who will? I'd drive her myself, but she needs to be on that bus before her husband gets home from work. What do you say?

I don't know. Wait.

Right away, tomorrow even.

Well, if tomorrow's no good for you. . . .

It's a date, Felice. Thursday. At the Cash N Carry off I-10. Noon. She'll be ready,

Oh, and her name's Cleófilas.

I don't know. One of those Mexican saints, I guess. A martyr or something.

Cleófilas. C-L-E-O-F-I-L-A-S. Cle. O. Fi. Las. Write it down.

Thanks, Felice. When her kid's born she'll have to name her after us, right?

Yeah, you got it. A regular soap opera sometimes. *Que vida, comadre. Bueno* bye.

***

All morning that flutter of half-fear, half-doubt. At any moment Juan Pedro might appear in the doorway. On the street. At the Cash N Carry. Like in the dreams she dreamed.

There was that to think about, yes, until the woman in the pickup drove up. Then there wasn't time to think about anything but the pickup pointed toward San Antonio. Put your bags in the back and get in.

But when they drove across the *arroyo*, the driver opened her mouth and let out a yell as loud as any mariachi. Which startled not only Cleófilas, but Juan Pedrito as well.

Pues, look how cute. I scared you two, right? Sorry. Should've warned you. Every time I cross that bridge I do that. Because of

the name, you know. Woman Hollering. *Pues*, I holler. She said this in a Spanish pocked with English and laughed. Did you ever notice, Felice continued, how nothing around here is named after a woman? Really. Unless she's the Virgin. I guess you're only famous if you're a virgin. She was laughing again.

That's why I like the name of that *arroyo*. Makes you want to holler like Tarzan, right?

Everything about this woman, this Felice, amazed Cleófilas. The fact that she drove a pickup. A pickup, mind you, but when Cleófilas asked if it was her husband's, she said she didn't have a husband. The pickup was hers. She herself had chosen it. She herself was paying for it.

I used to have a Pontiac Sunbird. But those cars are for *viejas*. Pussy cars. Now this here is a *real* car.

What kind of talk was that coming from a woman? Cleófilas thought. But then again, Felice was like no woman she'd ever met. Can you imagine, when we crossed the *arroyo* she just started yelling like a crazy, she would say later to her father and brothers. Just like that. Who would've thought?

Who would've? Pain or rage, perhaps, but not a hoot like the one Felice had just let go. Makes you want to holler like Tarzan, Felice had said.

Then Felice began laughing again, but it wasn't Felice laughing. It was gurgling out of her own throat, a long ribbon of laughter, like water.

Discussion Questions

1. What was your response to the story of Cleófilas? What was your response to the character of Juan Pedro? Did your attitude towards the characters change at all during the course of reading the story?

2. There are two primary male characters in the life of Cleófilas—Don Serafín and Juan Pedro. How are these characters similar and how are they different in relation to Cleófilas? What are their differences in relationship to their sociocultural environments as men?

3. What is the significance of *La Gritona*—the woman hollering creek in the story of Cleófilas?

4. Have you ever known someone or yourself been in an abusive relationship? Did this experience seem similar to that of Cleófilas? If so, how or in what way did it differ?

15
Yellow Woman and a Beauty of the Spirit

For a Laguna Pueblo Child Who Looked 'Different,' There Was Comfort in the Old Ways—A World in Which Faces and Bodies Could Not Be Separated From Hearts and Souls

Leslie Marmon Silko

In *"Yellow Woman and the Beauty of the Spirit,"* Leslie Marmon Silko shares with her readers a deeply rooted understanding of her Pueblo Indian culture evincing images and pleasant smells gleaned from a girlhood in the New Mexico desert. There is no question that Silko's most poignant memories are of her great-grandmother, with whom she waters roses and for whom she derives a sense of pride and achievement in the simple act of carrying buckets of coal. Her great-grandmother represents the ways of the "old-time people"—traditional Pueblo ways not always shared by modern-day adult Pueblos.

From her great-grandmother, Silko learns that differences should be accepted and even honored. This becomes particularly important to the young Silko, who is a biracial child—half Indian and half White—who has already experienced "modern" ways of thinking, which according to Silko, signify racism from Whites as well as from American Indians. The "old-time people" also have very strong opinions about harmony with one's environment and egalitarian views with regard to individuals. Silko suggests that people from her great-grandmother's time valued individuals without respect to material trappings of wealth or status. Instead, just as they believed that all members of the ecosystem, from plants and animals to earth and water, are meant to exist in union with each other, so human beings should also live in union without disturbing that harmony with unnecessary games of power and control.

This view of all things in harmonious balance also had a profound influence on gendered aspects of life. From the standpoint of her great-grandmother, there would be no separation between women's roles and men's roles, but simply roles taken on by human beings for the good of all and at peace with the group. The "old-time people" admired women for their strength and intelligence, for their ability to take charge of situations. Moreover, since all humans were viewed as a "mixture of male and female" attributes, sexuality was considered fluid and changeable over time. It is Yellow Woman that Silko admires most, a heroine from the old stories known for her bravery, passion, daring, and a "fearless sensuality"—an open honest approach to her sexual self. Some of the most telling lessons from Silko's piece center around the issue of physical appearance. Silko consistently points out the singular lack of importance placed on appearance by the "old-time people." Beauty, they would suggest for the generations, is about one's willingness to face life in all its complexity and realize that each individual is "the only one of its kind," and therefore, "incomparably valuable."

From the time I was a small child, I was aware that I was different, I looked different from my playmates. My two sisters looked different too. We didn't look quite like the other Laguna Pueblo children, but we didn't look quite white either. In the 1880s, my great-grandfather had followed his older brother west from Ohio to the New Mexico territory to survey the land for the U.S. government. The two Marmon brothers came to the Laguna Pueblo Reservation because they had an Ohio cousin who already lived there. The Ohio cousin was involved in sending Indian children thousands of miles away from their families to the War Department's big

Indian boarding school in Carlisle, Pa. Both brothers married "full blood" Laguna Pueblo women. My great-grandfather had first married my great-grandmother's older sister, but she died in childbirth and left two small children. My great-grandmother was 15 or 20 years younger than my great-grandfather. She had attended Carlisle Indian School and spoke and wrote English beautifully.

I called her Grandma A'mooh because that's what I heard her say whenever she saw me. "A'mooh" means "granddaughter" in the Laguna language. I remember this word because her love and her acceptance of me as a small child were so important. I had sensed immediately that something about my appearance was not acceptable to some people, white and Indian. But I did not see any signs of that strain or anxiety in the face of my beloved Grandma A'mooh.

Younger people, people my parents' age, seemed to look at the world in a more "modern" way. The "modern" way included racism. My physical appearance seemed not to matter to the old-time people. They looked at the world very differently; a person's appearance and possessions did not matter nearly as much as a person's behavior. For them, a person's value lies in how that person interacts with other people, how that person behaves toward the animals and the Earth. That is what matters most to the old-time people. The Pueblo people believed this long before the Puritans arrived with their notions of sin and damnation, and racism. The old-time beliefs persist today; thus I will refer to the old-time people in the present tense as well as the past. Many worlds may coexist here.

***

I spent a great deal of time with my great-grandmother. Her house was next to our house, and I used to wake up at dawn, hours before my parents or younger sisters, and I'd go wait on the porch swing or on the back steps by her kitchen door. She got up at dawn, but she was more than 80 years old so she needed a little while to get dressed and to get the fire going in the cookstove. I had been carefully instructed by my parents not to

bother her and to behave, and to try to help her any way I could. I always loved the early mornings when the air was so cool with a hint of rain smell in the breeze. In the dry New Mexico air, the least hint of dampness smells sweet.

My great-grandmother's yard was planted with lilac bushes and iris; there were four o'clocks, cosmos, morning glories and hollyhocks and old-fashioned rose bushes that I helped her water. If the garden hose got stuck on one of the big rocks that lined the path in the yard, I ran and pulled it free. That's what I came to do early every morning: to help Grandma water the plants before the heat of the day arrived.

Grandma A'mooh would tell about the old days, family stories about relatives who had been killed by Apache raiders who stole the sheep our relatives had been herding near Swahnee.

Sometimes she read the Bible stories that we kids liked because of the illustrations of Jonah in the mouth of a whale and Daniel surrounded by lions. Grandma A'mooh would send me home when she took her nap, but when the sun got low and the afternoon began to cool off, I would be back on the porch swing, waiting for her to come out to water the plants and to haul in firewood for the evening. When Grandma was 85, she still chopped her own kindling. She used to let me carry in the coal bucket for her, but she would not allow me to use the ax. I carried armloads of kindling too, and I learned to be proud of my strength.

I was allowed to listen quietly when Aunt Susie or Aunt Alice came to visit Grandma. When I got old enough to cross the road alone, I went and visited them almost daily. They were vigorous women who valued books and writing. They were usually busy chopping wood or cooking but never hesitated to take time to answer my questions. Best of all they told me the "hummah-hah" stories, about an earlier time when animals and humans shared a common language. In the old days, the Pueblo people had educated their children in this manner; adults took time out to talk to and teach young people. Everyone was a teacher, and every activity had the potential to teach the child.

But as soon as I started kindergarten at the Bureau of Indian Affairs day school, I began to learn more about the difference between the Laguna Pueblo world and the outside world. It was at school that I learned just how different I looked from my classmates. Sometimes tourists driving past on Route 66 would stop by Laguna Day School at recess time to take photographs of us kids. One day, when I was in the first grade, we all crowded around the smiling white tourists who peered at our faces. We all wanted to be in the picture because afterward the tourists sometimes gave us each a penny. Just as we were all posed and ready to have our picture taken, the tourist man looked at me. "Not you," he said and motioned for me to step away from my classmates. I felt so embarrassed that I wanted to disappear. My classmates were puzzled by the tourists' behavior, but I knew the tourists didn't want me in their snapshot because I looked different, because I was part white.

***

In the view of the old-time people, we are all sisters and brothers because the Mother Creator made all of us—all colors and all sizes. We are sisters and brothers, clanspeople of all the living beings around us. The plants, the birds, fish, clouds, water, even the clay—they all are related to us. The old-time people believe that all things, even rocks and water, have spirit and being. They understood that all things only want to continue being as they are; they need only to be left as they are. Thus the old folks used to tell us kids not to disturb the earth unnecessarily. All things as they were created exist already in harmony with one another as long as we do not disturb them.

As the old story tells us, Tse'its'i'na-ko, Thought Woman, the Spider, thought of her three sisters, and as she thought of them, they came into being. Together with Thought Woman, they thought of the sun and the stars and the moon. The Mother Creators imagined the earth and the oceans, the animals and the people, and the kat'sina spirits that reside in the mountains. The Mother Creators imagined all the plants that flower and the trees that bear fruit. As Thought Woman and her sisters thought of it, the whole universe came into being. In this universe, there is no absolute good or absolute bad; there are only balances and harmonies that ebb and flow. Some years the desert receives abundant rain, other years there is too little rain, and sometimes there is so much rain that floods cause destruction. But rain itself is neither innocent or guilty. The rain is simply itself.

My great-grandmother was dark and handsome. Her expression in photographs is one of confidence and strength. I do not know if white people then or now would consider her beautiful. I do not know if the old-time Laguna Pueblo people considered her beautiful or if the old-time people even thought in those terms. To the Pueblo way of thinking, the act of comparing one living being with another was silly, because each being or thing is unique and therefore incomparably valuable because it is the only one of its kind. The old-time people thought it was crazy to attach such importance to a person's appearance. I understood very early that there were two distinct ways of interpreting the world. There was the white people's way, and there was the Laguna way. In the Laguna way, it was bad manners to make comparisons that might hurt another person's feelings.

In everyday Pueblo life, not much attention was paid to one's physical appearance clothing. Ceremonial clothing was quite elaborate but was used only for the sacred dances. The traditional Pueblo societies were communal and strictly egalitarian, which means that no matter how well or how poorly one might have dressed, there was no "social ladder" to fall from. All food and other resources were strictly shared so that no one person or group had more than another. I mention social status because it seems to me that most of the definitions of beauty in contemporary Western culture are really codes for determining social status. People no longer hide their face-lifts, and they discuss their liposuctions because the point of the procedures isn't just cosmetic, it is social. It says to the world, "I have enough spare cash that I can afford surgery for cosmetic purposes."

In the old-time Pueblo world, beauty was manifested in behavior and in one's relationships with other living beings. Beauty was as much a feeling of harmony as it was a visual, aural or sensual effect. The whole person had to be beautiful, not just the face or the body; faces and bodies could not be separated from hearts and souls. Health was foremost in achieving this sense of well-being and harmony; in the old-time Pueblo world, a person who did not look healthy inspired feelings of worry and anxiety, not feelings of well-being. A healthy person, of course, is in harmony with the world around her; she is at peace with herself too. Thus an unhappy person or spiteful person would not be considered beautiful.

In the old days, strong, sturdy women were most admired. One of my most vivid preschool memories is of the crew of Laguna women, in their 40s and 50s, who came to cover our house with adobe plaster. They handled the ladders with great ease, and while two women ground the adobe mud on stones and added straw, another woman loaded the hod with mud and passed it up to the two women on ladders, who were smoothing the plaster on the wall with their hands. Since women owned the houses, they did the plastering. At Laguna, men did the basket-making and the weaving of fine textiles; men helped a great deal with the child-care too. Because the Creator is female, there is no stigma on being female; gender is not used to control behavior. No job was a "man's job" or a "woman's job"; the most able person did the work.

My Grandma Lily had been a Ford Model. A mechanic when she was a teen-ager. I remember when I was young, she was always fixing broken lamps and appliances. She was small and wiry, but she could lift her weight in rolled roofing or boxes of nails. When she was 75, she was still repairing washing machines in my uncle's coin-operated laundry.

The old-time people paid no attention to birthdays. When a person was ready to do something, she did it. When she no longer was able, she stopped. Thus the traditional Pueblo people did not worry about aging or about looking old because there were no social boundaries drawn by the passage of years. It was not remarkable for young men

to marry women as old as their mothers. I never heard anyone talk about "women's work" until after I left Laguna for college. Work was there to be done by any able-bodied person who wanted to do it. At the same time, in the old-time Pueblo world, identity was acknowledged to be always in a flux; in the old stories, one minute Spider Woman is a little spider under a yucca plant, and the next instant she is a spritely grandmother walking down the road.

When I was growing up, there was a young man from a nearby village who wore nail polish and women's blouses and permed his hair. People paid little attention to his appearance; he was always part of a group of other young men from his village. No one ever made fun of him. Pueblo communities were, and still are, very interdependent, but they also have to be tolerant of individual eccentricities because survival of the group means everyone has to cooperate.

In the old Pueblo world, differences were celebrated as signs of the Mother Creators' grace. Persons born with exceptional physical or sexual differences were highly respected and honored because their physical differences gave them special positions as mediators between this world and the spirit world. The great Navajo medicine man of the 1920s, the Crawler, had a hunchback and could not walk upright, but he was able to heal even the most difficult cases. Before the arrival of Christian missionaries, a man could dress as a woman and work with the women and even marry a man without any fanfare. Likewise, a woman was free to dress like a man, to hunt and go to war with the men and to marry a woman. In the old Pueblo world view, we are all a mixture of male and female, and this sexual identity is changing constantly. Sexual inhibition did not begin until the Christian missionaries arrived. For the old-time people, marriage was about teamwork and social relationships, not about sexual excitement. In the days before the Puritans came, marriage did not mean an end to sex with people other than your spouse. Women were just as likely as men to have a "si'ash," or lover.

New life was so precious that pregnancy was always appropriate, and pregnancy before marriage was celebrated as a good sign. Since the children belonged to the mother and her clan, and women owned and bequeathed the houses and farmland, the exact determination of paternity wasn't critical. Although fertility was prized, infertility was no problem because mothers with unplanned pregnancies gave their babies to childless couples within the clan in open adoption arrangements. Children called their mother's sisters "mother" as well, and a child became attached to a number of parent figures.

In the sacred kiva ceremonies, men mask and dress as women to pay homage and to be possessed by the female energies of the spirit beings. Because differences in physical appearance were so highly valued, surgery to change one's face and body to resemble a model's face and body would be unimaginable. To be different, to be unique was blessed and was best of all.

***

The traditional clothing of Pueblo women emphasized a woman's sturdiness. Buckskin leggings wrapped around the legs protected her from scratches and injuries while she worked. The more layers of buckskin, the better. All those layers gave her legs the appearance of strength, like sturdy tree trunks. To demonstrate sisterhood and brotherhood with the plants and animals, the old-time people make masks and costumes that transform the human figures of the dancers into the animal beings they portray. Dancers paint their exposed skin; their postures and motions are adapted from their observations. But the motions are stylized. The observer sees not an actual eagle or actual deer dancing, but witnesses a human being, a dancer, gradually changing into a woman/buffalo or a man/deer. Every impulse is to reaffirm the urgent relationships that human beings have with the plant and animal world.

In the high desert plateau country, all vegetation, even weeds and thorns, becomes special, and all life is precious and beautiful because without the plants, the insects and the animals, human beings living here cannot survive. Perhaps human beings long ago noticed the devastating impact human activity can have on the plants and animals; maybe

this is why tribal cultures devised the stories about humans and animals intermarrying, and the clans that bind humans to animals and plants through a whole complex of duties.

We children were always warned not to harm frogs or toads, the beloved children of the rain clouds, because terrible floods would occur. I remember in the summer the old folks used to stick big bolls of cotton on the outside of their screen doors as bait to keep the flies from going in the house when the door was opened. The old folks staunchly resisted the killing of flies because once, long, long ago, when human beings were in a great deal of trouble, green bottle fly carried the desperate messages of human beings to the Mother Creator in the Fourth World below this one. Human beings had outraged the Mother Creator by neglecting the Mother Corn altar while they dabbled with sorcery and magic. The Mother Creator disappeared, and with her disappeared the rain clouds, and the plants and the animals too. The people began to starve, and they had no way of reaching the Mother Creator down below. The green bottle fly took the message to the Mother Creator, and the people were saved. To show their gratitude, the old folks refused to kill any files.

***

The old stories demonstrate the interrelationships that the Pueblo people have maintained with their plant and animal clanspeople. Kochininako, Yellow Woman, represents all women in the old stories. Her deeds span the spectrum of human behavior and are mostly heroic acts, though in at least one story, she chooses to join the secret Destroyer Clan, which worships destruction and death. Because Laguna Pueblo cosmology features a female creator, the status of women is equal with the status of men, and women appear as often as men in the old stories as hero figures. Yellow Woman is my favorite because she dares to cross traditional boundaries of ordinary behavior during times of crisis in order to save the Pueblo; her power lies in her courage and in her uninhibited sexuality, which the old-time

Pueblo stories celebrate again and again because fertility was so highly valued.

The old stories always say that Yellow Woman was beautiful, but remember that the old-time people were not so much thinking about physical appearances. In each story, the beauty that Yellow Woman possesses is the beauty of her passion, her daring and her sheer strength to act when catastrophe is imminent.

In one story, the people are suffering during a great drought and accompanying famine. Each day, Kochininako has to walk farther and farther from the village to find fresh water for her husband and children. One day she travels far, far to the east, to the plains, and she finally locates a freshwater spring. But when she reaches the pool, the water is churning violently as if something large had just gotten out of the pool. Kochininako does not want to see what huge creature had been at the pool, but just as she fills her water jar and turns to hurry away, a strong, sexy man in buffalo skin leggings appears by the pool. Little drops of water glisten on his chest. She cannot help but look at him because he is so strong and so good to look at. Able to transform himself from human to buffalo in the wink of an eye, Buffalo Man gallops away with her on his back. Kochininako falls in love with Buffalo Man, and because of this liaison, the Buffalo People agree to give their bodies to the hunters to feed the starving Pueblo. Thus Kochininako's fearless sensuality results in the salvation of the people of her village, who are saved by the meat the Buffalo people "give" to them.

My father taught me and my sisters to shoot .22 rifles when we were 7; I went hunting with my father when I was 8, and I killed my first mule deer buck when I was 13. The Kochininako stories were always my favorite because Yellow Woman had so many adventures. In one story, as she hunts rabbits to feed her family, a giant monster pursues her, but she has the courage and presence of mind to outwit it. In another story, Kochininako has a fling with Whirlwind Man and returns to her husband 10 months later with twin baby boys. The twin boys grow up to be great heroes of the people. Once again, Kochininako's vibrant sexuality benefits her people.

The stories about Kochininako made me aware that sometimes an individual must act despite disapproval, or concern for "appearances" or "what others may say." From Yellow Woman's adventures, I learned to be comfortable with my differences. I even imagined that Yellow Woman had yellow skin, brown hair and green eyes like mine, although her name does not refer to her color, but rather to the ritual color of the East.

There have been many other moments like the one with the camera-toting tourist in the schoolyard. But the old-time people always say, remember the stories, the stories will help you be strong. So all these years I have depended on Kochininako and the stories of her adventures.

Kochininako is beautiful because she has the courage to act in times of great peril, and her triumph is achieved by her sensuality, not through violence and destruction. For these qualities of the spirit, Yellow Woman and all women are beautiful.

Discussion Questions

1. Yellow Woman is a singular icon in Pueblo Indian culture. Do you know of any similar such female figures in Western culture? If so, who? If not, why do you think Western culture lacks such women figures?

2. How is biracial status viewed today in the United States? Is it accepted or not accepted? Why or why not?

3. What lessons about appearance do young women learn from American media from an early age? Are these lessons different from or similar to those taught by the "old-time people" in Silko's article? If so, how or how not?

4. What were your thoughts on reading Silko's piece? Do you wish we lived in a culture similar to that of the "old-time people"? Why or why not?

16
From the Margins

Stephen Paul Whitaker

Stephen Paul Whitaker describes himself proudly and defiantly as a "White-trash hill-billy faggot," claiming all the labels that others might use to disparage him. He explicitly recognizes both his position on the borderland of the dominant society and the ways in which his statuses intersect. In this essay, he interweaves the story of his personal and academic life with a speech he gave at an honors convocation. Reaching this level of self- and social awareness and achievement was not easy for him. He flunked out of college the first time he enrolled, worked as a journalist, returned to community college, and finally earned a bachelor's degree in sociology and admission to graduate school. By that time, he had overcome his own homophobia and come to believe that rural working-class people should use education as a vehicle for social change rather than as a path to personal mobility.

His comments about his interactions with faculty and staff members and administrators at his local community college and the state university from which he graduated demonstrate the impact that positive support can have on individual students as well as the actions students can take in the face of homophobia, sexism, classism, or racism. He expresses surprise at his ability to establish a warm relationship with an individual whose religious beliefs lead her to regard him as a sinner and at the effectiveness of both collective action and formal complaints in an environment that appears indifferent, if not actively hostile.

Through his coursework in sociology and gender studies, his discussions with members of the faculty, and his participation in student organizations and demonstrations, Whitaker comes to understand the interrelated and intersected nature of social life. He is able to see how his particular working-class and rural background, together with his gender and sexuality, interact to form a pattern of oppression that, once recognized, can be overcome. In seeing his own situation, he is also able to see that of others and to identify patterns of dominance and oppression in the society. In the end, he is able to see what he can do to promote social change and to use his position at the margins to offer a critique of the broader gay rights movement, which he sees as homogeneous, "too urban, White, and middle-class."

I suppose a "typical" or "normal" sort of student speech for this type of event would involve the definition of success—how we as honors students and you as the people who are responsible for our presence here today can measure our worth by our future achievements.

Uh-oh, I said to myself when I noticed the honors program secretary summoning me from across the parking lot. *Maybe I can pretend I didn't see her.* Three weeks earlier I'd walked out of an honors seminar protesting the instructor's sexist, elitist, and homophobic comments. Although I hadn't dropped the class, I was considering it. In a conversation with the honors program director, I'd been frank about the problems I saw with the class. I figured his secretary, Jo, had heard about my latest episode and was going to offer unsolicited advice about "getting along."

Well, those of you who know me know I don't usually participate in what is considered "typical" or "normal" patterns.

"Shit," I muttered. Out of the corner of my eye, I saw Jo jogging toward me. I stopped, waved, and began a self-lecture about being nice to her. Jo took a maternal interest in and approach to many of the honors program students. I think she was particularly interested in my welfare because she too was a nontraditional-aged student from Eastern Kentucky as well as a university employee. She reminded me of my mother and was among the first people on campus in whom I had confided my sexual orientation. A deeply religious woman, she cried when I came out, but we had remained fairly close despite her belief that I was a "sinner."

"Steve, I need to talk to you," she said, slightly out of breath. I knew the honors program committee had met the day before, and I assumed my latest exploit had been discussed. I also figured I was about to get yet another lecture about "learning to play the game."

I do want to discuss success in the context of responsibility, though. I would like for each of us to consider how we—as people who have been privileged with the opportunity to participate in formal education, who have been privileged with having the opportunity to acquire the skills it takes to surmount educational barriers that keep many other people out—are now obligated to use the success we are celebrating today as an instrument of social change rather than a weapon to maintain or increase our social position at the expense of others.

"The committee met yesterday," Jo said. I nodded.

"Well, we're putting together the program for the honors convocation, and we selected the speaker."

I nodded again, thinking the committee had probably selected some conservative jerk and Jo was trying to warn me before I threw a public fit.

"They decided they want you to speak," she added.

I dropped my book bag. "What?" I asked. "This is an April Fool's joke, isn't it?" Many of the professors and administrators whom I'd criticized most were members of the committee.

Jo looked at me quizzically. "No. It was unanimous." She paused. "It's quite an honor, you know. But I want you to remember that I'm going to be right there, and you had better not say anything bad."

"Can I wear a dress?" I grinned irreverently, unable to resist teasing her despite my shock.

Jo rolled her eyes and sighed. "Absolutely not! Can I tell the committee you accept?"

"Yeah," I said, picking up my bag and heading toward class a bit stunned.

Each of us has within our power the ability to disrupt and transform some of the barriers we have overcome. But to do so, we each must recognize the privilege of our positions. We must not only fulfill our own potential but also actively work to foster the potential of our neighbors.

Later that day, I thought back on my arrival at Morehead State University, a small public institution in Appalachian Kentucky. I had walked into the office of the academic honors program at the beginning of my first semester emboldened by the results of my latest ACT scores and asking to be admitted. When classes started the next day I had trudged into the Honors 101 course with none of my earlier bravado. I was scared to death. I was 29 years old, from a working-class background, gay, and Appalachian. I was nontraditional in nearly every sense of the word. *Why do you do these things to yourself?* an inner voice barked. I knew the students who belonged here, the "normal" or "typical" people, had been recruited.

I entered the classroom that day surreptitiously looking for the danger signs: groups of students talking, whispering, laughing in a corner, a holdover from high school. Keeping my eyes averted, I sought the anonymity of the row closest to the window, taking myself out of the line of fire with the other outcasts. Self-awareness operating at hyper levels, I was sure everyone could tell I was poor and gay, that I was an impostor who did not belong in college, much less in an honors program. Nearly sick with misery by the time class began I'd convinced myself of complete failure.

We must re-examine our idea of leadership. Activist Mike Clark says that one of the major problems facing Appalachia is that there are too many leaders, that college-educated Appalachians run the risk of "being the people who will attempt to control the lives of Appalachian poor folks,"[1] those people in this region who are prevented from obtaining the skills necessary to surmount the matrix of obstacles designed to exclude them from success.

My first attempt at college nearly ten years before was a complete failure. I dropped out of school because I didn't see the immediate worth of attending class. People from working-class families, especially those like mine from economically deprived areas like Appalachia, are taught repeatedly that education, "book learnin," is purely recreational. The only thing that counts is hard, honest labor. The kind that makes others rich. The kind that makes us grow old before our time. The kind that deprives us of our cultural heritage, our identity. The value I placed on education was also marred by the stigma associated with my sexuality. I'd been taunted and physically abused in the public school system for being gay even though I wasn't out. From those experiences, I'd learned to associate education with oppression. Looking back, I am not surprised that my first attempt at college was unsuccessful. I flunked out of school at 19 and did what was expected of me. I went to work.

Clark cautioned that education in this society often means control, not freedom, a way to enforce the values of the dominant culture on the rest of us, and a way for some of us to fight our way to the top, achieve success, work to control those at the bottom of the hierarchy, and then blame them for being there.

My desire to do "real" work was thwarted about eight years later, however, when I was fired from my job as a reporter for a small-town newspaper. I had become pretty radical on the job as I explored my sexuality and started to come to terms with it. I was no longer acquiescent. In fact, I was angry, so angry that I was fired over an ideological conflict with the newspaper editor.

At various times in my journalism career, I'd attempted to take college classes and planned to "someday" finish my degree. I was intensely interested in education and maintained a fairly good relationship with Dr. Miller, the president of the local community college. I turned to him when I lost my job. "We'll work something out," he said, advising me to make an appointment for the next day with his secretary. Shortly after I arrived the next morning, I found myself sitting across a conference table from Dr. Miller, talking about my media qualifications in newspaper, radio, and television, hoping for the job as public relations coordinator.

"I've worked all over the state," I said, placing emphasis on my television experience because I knew that the person who had worked in the college's video studio had recently retired.

"We've shut down the studio," Dr. Miller said. "And frankly, Steve, there's no way I can hire you for that job without your having a degree. I can find you work here, though, if you'll make me a deal," he added.

I eyed him suspiciously. Refusing to "make a deal" was precisely what had gotten me fired.

"I've reviewed your transcript" he said, his gentle tone belying his words. "You failed English 101 three times. What was going on in your head?"

I looked at him uncomfortably. "I thought it was boring."

"I guess you thought history, psychology, and algebra were boring too? You failed those as well."

"I was working and didn't have time."

Dr. Miller sighed and settled into his chair. After a moment of silence, he said quietly but forcefully, "I cannot begin to tell you how it disgusts me to see people from this region throwing away their potential." His "deal" involved my enrolling in classes in exchange for a job and making a commitment to complete a degree. "I want you to begin classes next semester and get this transcript straightened out," he said.

To attain lasting change in the educational system, we need people from this region who are willing to do as the students here have done: become educated. But those of us who successfully negotiate the educational system must also be willing to return to Appalachia and use our education to promote a voice within and for the region.

Dr. Miller found me a job with student support services, a federally funded TRIO program that provides support for at-risk students. In my hometown that meant working with mainly nontraditional-aged single mothers returning to school. I was hired as a professional tutor and began work almost immediately. Working with these women helped me put my own life into perspective. As my attitudes toward education changed and my self-esteem improved, I became increasingly open in the workplace about my sexuality. But activism centered on sexuality never occurred to me. My geographic and class positions did not include space for the concept of an "out" homosexual or a politics based on homosexuality. I knew there were gay rights groups, but they were in metropolitan areas on the coasts and far from my sphere of reality. I also had no contact with other gays or lesbians, even people who were closeted. Although I was serving as an advocate both within and outside of the institution for my student-clients, and was involved with an environmental group fighting the expansion of the local landfill, when it came to issues of sexuality I remained silent. I had learned to express myself, but I was still unable to overcome my own homophobia at school, even though the community college system was linked to the University of Kentucky, which had implemented a clause regarding sexual orientation in its nondiscrimination policies a couple of years earlier.

We must also recognize our self-worth and understand that Appalachians have a specialized knowledge and specific methods of resistance. And the people here today who are representative of the educated portion of the Appalachian group, the Appalachian scholars, have a choice to make: We can continue to use the backs and bodies of our brothers and sisters to achieve middle-class "success," or we can use our education to disrupt the status quo.

The emotional progress I'd made at the junior college, however, diminished to a trickle when I transferred to Morehead State University. I hated the city. I hated the school. I constantly felt awkward and out of place. When I had enrolled in the community college, it had been from a position of power. I had the personal interest of the president and a reputation as a journalist and was in familiar territory. My transfer to Morehead forced me to begin again with no influence, no friends, and a lot of bad memories of the educational system despite more recent pleasant ones. I retreated into my shell and remained completely quiet about my sexuality.

In those first few weeks as I scurried around campus lonely and scared, I came to hate my major. Because I was interested in environmental issues and because Kentucky has such a poor environmental protection track record, I had planned to enter MSU's environmental science program with the ultimate goal of completing a law degree. Almost overwhelmingly depressed by the end of that first semester, I started thinking about changing my major. I consulted the coordinator for nontraditional students who suggested I take an interest inventory. After filling in countless bubbles, I turned in the test for scoring. I was shocked to discover I'd scored off the scale in sociology, mainly because I didn't know what it was. My experiences as a reporter were again a valuable asset. I went to the sociology department and asked to talk to a faculty member, where I met Dr. Hardesty, whose areas of expertise were class stratification, racial inequality and gender constructions. I was intrigued since I'd dealt with all these issues as a reporter.

In our quest for change, we can look at some of the faculty and staff members here who utilize the transformative potential of education rather than its punitive nature. That is, they recognize the influence of the educational institution as a potential instrument of empowerment as well as a historical weapon of enslavement.

For days, I agonized over changing my major. I struggled with the practicality of working and paying for a degree in a field I knew was overpopulated. My background—the barrier created by my experiences with gender, class, and regionality—kept cropping up. How could I major in something without any guarantee of a job? On the other hand, I was definitely attracted to the field. Finally, I called Dr. Hardesty and confessed my reluctance.

"But Steve," she said. "What is more important? Do you want to be happy now or do you plan to keep postponing it?"

Wow! Her words hit home! I was depressed because I wasn't enjoying college, but was reluctant to take steps to change my situation. That day, I changed my major and enrolled in two sociology courses for the spring semester. For the first time since I had arrived at MSU, I was excited about being there.

We can also look to the work of philosopher-activist Angela Davis, who writes that "the process of empowerment cannot be simplistically defined in accordance with our own particular class interests. We must learn to lift as we climb."[2]

As I sat in Dr. Hardesty's Sociology 101 class, I was entranced. Here was a whole discipline devoted to studying society, and many of that discipline's theories sang out to me, particularly those dealing with societal conflict and inequality. Dr. Hardesty was giving me the means to define my life and the tools to reconstruct it. To say I was enthusiastic would be an understatement. The conversations I'd had with Dr. Hardesty often extended from after class to time in her office. When I came out to her, she treated my revelation with a nonchalance that tested the fabric of my reality. Here was a virtual stranger, a straight woman, who did not care about my sexual orientation! She also talked about some of her gay academic friends at other institutions, and for the first time I realized there were people who had faced similar barriers who had achieved academic success. As we talked that day and in the days that followed, she encouraged me to apply to graduate school. "Your voice needs to be heard," she said. In class, she was relentless about social justice issues, and approached class, racial, and gender inequality with equal fervor. Her attitudes and opinions were beneficial to my personal growth, but so were the attitudes of my classmates. While they were significantly younger than I, for the most part they came to MSU from similar backgrounds. They were the same kinds of students as those I'd attended school with ten years earlier and who had tormented me. And they were talking openly in class about their gay cousins, brothers, aunts, and friends, and their experiences. I discovered I wasn't the only one, that there are plenty of people who don't hate gay men and lesbians—probably the biggest lesson I learned at MSU.

We must recognize that true educators are people who are truly teachers, people who are working not just at their jobs, but ardently at social change, at education as a process of transformation and empowerment.

As I became involved in my new major, I also began taking women's studies classes. Reading about the history of labor protest in my region; learning about women who had,

decades before I was born, protested the constraints of gender; and discovering the work of theorists such as Audre Lorde, bell hooks, and Gloria Anzaldúa opened a place in my world for protest. Not only was resistance acceptable, but it was also required, a responsibility.

Of course, there was still a real world outside the sociology classroom. The same semester I declared my sociology major, a woman was assaulted on campus because she was a lesbian. All the anger and fear I held aside since my experiences in high school came boiling to the top. I hesitantly agreed to participate in a meeting to organize a march protesting the administration's decision to treat the matter as incidental and not hate-motivated. At that time I was in a quasi-out stage. That is, I didn't deny my sexuality, but I hadn't been broadcasting it. Fear immobilized me briefly. When I arrived at the meeting after much soul-searching, I met a woman with whom I felt an immediate affinity, Dr. Patti Swartz, an English professor who had successfully battled the administration's decision to exclude a gay and lesbian literature course from the curriculum.

When the day of the march arrived, I was terrified. I'd heard several fraternities planned to counter-protest our "Take Back the Night" march, and we were also expecting wide media coverage. I cannot put into words the fear, sadness, and anger I felt while deciding whether to show up. Would anyone else be there? Would I be assaulted? Would I destroy my future by participating? Dozens of questions and unformed (and sometimes unrealistic) fears ran through my mind. I couldn't let down Dr. Swartz, though, so I went.

When I arrived at our starting place, I was surprised to see about 30 people standing around, including several reporters. Then the crowd grew. And grew. Several hundred people were gathered holding signs by the time we began our march down the main street of campus and around the area where the assault had taken place. I'll never forget it. Even though I had come to terms with my sexuality mostly on my own, the march initiated a period of accelerated emotional growth focused on external social relationships. During the march I realized I wasn't alone, that being gay wasn't a solitary "burden."

We had organized the march as an anti-violence demonstration. As a result many straight people were involved, as well as many closeted gays and lesbians. But they were all there: Dr. Hardesty, many of my classmates, and activists from other campuses. In addition to the young woman who had been assaulted, several people spoke that night, among them two students from the University of Kentucky's Lambda organization. "I like to have sex with men," one of the Lambda representatives shouted into the microphone as he began his speech. If the fabric of my reality had been tested in sociology classes and by Dr. Hardesty, this display and its response demolished it.

Ultimately, we don't have to tolerate the second-class status of women, people of color, sexual minorities, people who are differently abled, or our own second-class status as Appalachians, in our classrooms, at our institution, or in our communities. We can use our education, our recognized achievement in the area of scholarship, to effect change.

The way that my heritage as an Appalachian from Eastern Kentucky meshes with my socialization in a working-class family is complex. When those issues become even more complicated by gender and sexuality, the effect is stifling. Particularly potent is the added difficulty that accompanies rurality. Ultimately for me, the oppression created by my different cultural positions was surmountable. I realized this during the march.

Riding high on the success of the march, I began working with another student to organize a gay and lesbian group. The campus newspaper interviewed Dr. Swartz and me, and I appeared on a campus television program. Each of my projects required dealing with that old fear, and each time, like the march, I was surprised when nothing bad happened. I worked with both the GLBT group and Students for Social Justice for about a year. Also following the march I began to focus my energy on gender research and present my work at honors conferences across the country. Taking the cue from the young men who spoke at our march, I began

my presentations by describing myself as a "white-trash hillbilly faggot." My frankness wasn't always appreciated by the honors program director or the various conference organizers, but I was never silenced.

My campus organizing, combined with my work in social inequality, certainly lit a fire of revolt in me. Rather than remaining reticent about my sexuality, my Appalachian origins, or my class background, I was brutally honest. I unsettled several closeted professors by outing myself in classes, petitioned the Board of Regents to include sexual orientation in MSU's nondiscrimination policies, and frequently complained to the campus affirmative action officer and minority affairs director about instances of hate speech.

One day, for example, I had stopped by the registrar's office to fill out a form. As I waited for my appointment, I noticed three men who were clearly not students talking loudly. They were discussing a sexual harassment incident involving two males.

"A real man wouldn't have put up with that," one said.

"They oughta throw those fags to the sharks," added another.

At first I tried to ignore them, but the longer I listened the more pissed I got. I walked over to them. "Excuse me. Are you gentlemen employees of the university?" I asked. Two of them nodded.

"Well, I'm a gay student at this university, and I don't appreciate your remarks," I said.

They looked at each other, and then one of them looked at me and said, "Isn't that interesting?"

Then I got really pissed. "Not as interesting as you're going to find it in five minutes," I said as I walked out the door and to the affirmative action office where I filed a formal affirmative action complaint. I was later told that all three men, one of whom was a fairly high-ranking administrator, were officially reprimanded.

Now, I was never told not to get an education. I do remember being warned to not ever get above my raisin'. I have to admit I have spent years thinking the prohibition on and the suspicion of formal education expressed by that phrase was a direct attack on learning. I know now it wasn't. I realize now that the

*people telling me not to get above my raisin'
were warning me not to use the backs and bodies of my brothers and sisters to achieve someone else's definition of success.*

Dr. Swartz, who is also from a working-class Appalachian background, often talks about the issues of entitlement that have affected us both. "We didn't feel we were entitled to a sexuality any more than we felt we were entitled to an education," she says. For me at least, this is true. As I neared the end of the first semester of my senior year, I began to work on applications for graduate school. I solicited advice from others on the best way to approach the letter of application. Most of them told me to "play the game." So I did. I wrote what I considered to be an "academic" letter.

"You sound like a real prick," Dr. Swartz said after she read my letter.

"What?" I said, taken aback.

"You've taken about 500 words to show off your vocabulary. I think the kind of school that would be excited about this kind of letter is the last kind of school you would want to attend."

Following her advice, I rewrote my letter, discussing the potential for subverting the academic system, and launching a critique from the borderlands. I was also explicit about my sexual orientation, my class background, and my activism. Of the six institutions to which I applied, I received offers from four; three included substantial financial aid and tuition waivers.

We must not allow ourselves to be sentenced to doing things the same old way, and we don't have to. We have the ability to make a difference. And the first crucial step is recognizing the privilege of our positions, understanding precisely how our choices can negatively affect those around us. We must understand that lifting others as we climb does not diminish our status or limit our access to resources or tarnish our success.

The honors convocation at MSU represented more than academic achievement for me. As I recognized that gay students possess a viable voice, I came to the culmination of a personal journey. Of course, I was also a nervous wreck. My parents were traveling from my hometown two hours away. And I knew that much of what I had to say directly attacked the institution, both MSU and the education system. I was scared about the reception too. I was placed in line with both the president of the university and the vice president for academic affairs. By the time we reached the stage, I felt completely nauseous. As I was waiting to be introduced, I scanned the audience and located my parents. I walked to the podium with my speech in hand and began: "I suppose a 'typical' or 'normal' sort of student speech for this type of event would involve the definition of success. . . ."

We can manipulate the educational system and use it as a tool to disrupt the status quo and as an instrument of social change. For that to work, we must look for new ways of doing things, and we must all be ready to lift as we climb. Thank you.

I have been deeply moved just a few times in my life. Giving my speech was one of those times. I don't remember hearing the applause as I walked back to my seat. I do remember the president grabbing my arm.

"They're standing for you," he said in a shocked tone. I looked up and saw the faculty standing and applauding. Numbly, I waved and nodded my head. I'm told I was not only the first openly gay student to speak at the honors convocation but that many also thought I was also the first honors student who had anything worthwhile to say. Perhaps my gender, class, and geographical position allowed me to communicate across those boundaries to a fairly homogenous group of people.

My undergraduate experiences represent an enormous struggle: a fight to overcome the label of "white-trash hillbilly faggot" and to reclaim it, as well as resolve my own homophobia. I cannot say that MSU was the optimal environment. The university's upper administration was insensitive and, in some cases, openly hostile to issues of sexuality despite having many gay and lesbian students. Campus activism in marginalized rural areas is further problematized by the lack of understanding from mainstream and urban gay rights groups. I often think that the gay rights movement has remained too urban, white, and middle-class—too homogenous—to deal effectively with the issues most rural gays and lesbians face. As those of us who speak from the margins can attest, we often feel left behind. To us remains the battle of dealing with the isolation, building connections, and carving out lives in areas where difference often results in stigma and sanction. In the words of Audre Lorde, "There's still work to do."[3] And for many of us in rural areas, this work is as basic as the activism that led the drag queens into the streets at Stonewall.

Ultimately, my greatest hurdle was my own homophobia coupled with a dose of class prejudice and personal disdain for Appalachia. I hated those parts of myself that were truly me. Learning how to combat that self-talk was the outstanding, and almost unbelievable, accomplishment of my undergraduate career.

Notes

1. Excerpts from Mike Clark's speech, "Education and exploitation." In H. Lewis, L. Johnson, and D. Askins, Eds. (1978). *Colonialism in Modern America: The Appalachian Case*. North Carolina: The Appalachian Consortium Press.

2. In Davis, A. (1981). *Women, Race, and Class*. New York: Random House.

3. From "Age, Race, and Class: Women Redefining Difference." (1995). In A. Kesselman, L. McNair, N. Schniedewind, Eds., *Women, Images, and Realities: A Multicultural Anthology*. Mountain View, CA: Mayfield Publishing.

Discussion Questions

1. Whitaker used to think that that the warning not to "get above his raisin'"

meant not to get an education or become middle class. By the end of the essay, he has a very different idea of what this means. How might this apply to people from environments different from Appalachia—people from urban ghettos or barrios, reservations, or immigrant communities, for example?

2. Look around your campus and community. What kinds of advocacy groups exist? What types of social action are present? Have you participated in any such groups or actions? Would you consider demonstrating on behalf of a racial, ethnic, gender, or sexuality group to which you do not belong? Why or why not?

3. Whitaker is White, male, gay, working class, and an older student who is the first in his family to attend college. What characteristics do you have in common with him? In what way(s) are you different? How have some or all of these characteristics affected your experience as a student?

17

Long Hours, Starvation Wages

Loretta Schwartz-Nobel

Cathy Lewis is a young white woman, a single parent who holds down a managerial job to support her family so that she can make a bright future for herself and her children. Her story is not so different from many other Cathys in the United States today. Her aspirations are certainly no different. What sets Cathy and her children apart is the tragic experience of homelessness, something they went through for a period of time in the not so distant past, and tragically something that is becoming more and more common in our nation's cities for young single mothers and even entire nuclear families. Some social scientists might argue that Cathy made "poor" choices in her downward spiral into homelessness. If we review her choices, they list as follows: Cathy enlisted in the military at a young age, fell in love, married, and had children. When that marriage failed, she remarried and that marriage also failed. Afterward, she sought gainful employment only to be turned away for lack of experience—ten years of leadership roles in the military seemingly did little to help her qualify for most jobs. Cathy, in fact, did nothing that tens of thousands of young men and women in America have not done for decades. Yet, Cathy's story points up a glaring reality for single parents who are women. Cathy is vulnerable to homelessness precisely because she lost the financial support that her spouse provided and jobs for women with only a high school diploma do not often provide a living wage, even when they do not have dependents. Interestingly, Cathy is white. She is not a member of a racial/ethnic group overrepresented among those who live below the poverty line and are therefore vulnerable to homelessness; we would not assume that women in Cathy's position could be so vulnerable. Ultimately, it is in Cathy's very ordinariness in terms of race, class, and gender that her story takes on such utterly alarming proportions. How could this happen in America?

... Today, Cathy Lewis is the managing director of a privately run homeless shelter. But once, she too was a homeless resident turned away and humiliated by her local department of social services and her food stamp office. That memory and her continued sense of economic vulnerability makes all the difference.

"I'm not going to kid you," she told me as she led me into her first-floor office. "This is a tough job full of stress. There's always another problem waiting around the corner, but to me it's worth every single migraine. It's worth it because, instead of knocking people down, we get them back on their feet, people like me." She wiped the sweat from her forehead and smiled. "Speaking of stress, I just started on a new prescription for migraines today. So, in a way, this is a good day for an interview, I mean you're getting a chance to talk to me when I'm all relaxed from my happy pills."

She took a gulp of air, smiled again, then grew serious. "I have a fancy title now and I earn a little over twenty-four thousand dollars a year, but that's for me and my two kids. So after taxes come out, we're still pretty poor, or to use the professional term, still 'at risk.' Do you want to know how easy it is for a family at risk to cross that bridge into hunger and homelessness?"

She rolled her dark eyes and swayed a little. I nodded and sat down. "Well, I'll tell you," she said. "The wrong job, the wrong luck, the wrong guy, it's really surprisingly easy. You just kind of S-L-I-D-E into it. It's the downward spiral they all talk about. I never would have thought it could happen to me or my kids, but then, I guess none of us do."

Her eyes hunted for mine and something I saw in her face or heard in her words brought me back, once again, to the day my landlord threatened my children and me with eviction. It was along time ago, more than twenty years, and we were never actually homeless, but that didn't keep my eyes from stinging as the margins between Cathy's life and my own suddenly blurred. I shivered in the August heat, surprised by how quickly she had moved right to the heart of things.

"I enlisted in the Army while I was still in high school. I met my first husband and my second husband there and spent ten years on active duty," Cathy said, leaning forward and letting her chin rest inside her palm. She sat there for a minute forming her thoughts, then said, "I left because I'd injured my back and because my youngest son, my three-year-old, had been diagnosed with childhood leukemia. I wanted to be where I could get him the best treatment. My husband was still enlisted. We had always done all right in the service because there were two of us and we both had salaries.

"When I left the military they gave me a lump sum of about eighteen thousand dollars. At the time it seemed like a lot of money, a huge amount. We rented a nice apartment and bought some furniture and, pretty soon, the money started to go. It was all the things working-class people get into, the car payments, the furniture payments, the rent, the tuition. My children were in a Christian private school and I had enrolled at Anne Arundel Community College. I was still thinking I'd train for something specific first then go out and get a really good job. We were doing fine with that plan until my husband got sent off to Germany and the marriage ended. I guess it was for all the usual reasons, distance, loneliness and a lack of trust. Then came the economic troubles.

"We no longer had his income and there was no child support because he wasn't my children's father. From January to the following February, there was a slow decline, a trickle-down effect as the eighteen thousand dollars whittled down. Then the trickle became a flood. Soon after that, I felt as if the dam had broken.

"I was looking for a job every day but I couldn't find one. I'd been out of the traditional job market for a long time and people kept telling me I wasn't qualified for the positions I applied for. It really upset me and in my head I was saying, 'What do you mean I'm not qualified? What do you mean I can't answer your phones and copy your documents? Why can't I file your mail?' For ten years I ran patrols. I lay in ditches. I shot targets. I had dozens of people working under me. I was just an E-4 but I was in a leadership position. I had major responsibilities. OK, so maybe I hadn't done these kinds of jobs before but I knew I could learn if someone would just give me a chance.

"All that winter I searched but no one hired me and the panic inside kept growing. It roared in my stomach all day and pounded in my heart at night. With every dollar I had to spend and nothing coming in, the pounding got louder. I was trying to quiet it by holding out on the bills. If I had a big gas or electric bill, I'd pay just enough so they wouldn't turn off the heat or the lights. I was trying to make the money last and the food stamps stretch. But no matter what I did, there wasn't enough of either, so we ate beans, dried beans, the cheapest dried beans we could get. I bought them in bulk to save money. When we got sick from the beans and all the gas, we'd have eggs or rice with a little bacon, just enough to add flavor. I'd get the thinnest sandwich meat you could buy. It was like ninety-nine cents a pack, just so my kids could have the taste of meat on their bread.

"We were all under enormous strain. The children's grades dropped. They were hungry all the time but they were bloated. They swore that if they ate another bean they would die. They said, they would rather starve, but soon they got hungry again and begged for something to eat."

As I listened to Cathy, I visualized the huge underclass of families like hers, families who worked hard or wanted to but couldn't find jobs, families with "just barely enough," families who got hit by an unexpected crisis and were struck down. Then, I thought about all their imperiled children, children who didn't know each other but who were bound together by poverty, hunger and destitution, children like Cathy's living mostly on beans, rice or bread, children who could not possibly function like other kids who sat in the same classrooms, often only a desk or two away, but went home to a different world.

As the Center on Hunger, Poverty and Nutrition Policy has pointed out, even moderate undernutrition can have lasting effects on the cognitive development of children. Inadequate nutrition is a major cause of impaired mental development and is associated with increased educational failure among poor children. While this is recognized more and more by child development experts, it is still not well known to the general public.

Compelling new research shows a clear threat to the intellectual development of children who do not get adequate nutrition. "That is because, when children are chronically undernourished, their bodies conserve the limited food energy available, first reserved for maintenance of critical organ function, second for growth and last for social activity and cognitive development."

"Even nutritional deprivation of a relatively short-term nature influences children's capacity to learn. Deficiencies in specific nutrients, such as iron, have an immediate effect on the ability to concentrate. Children who come to school hungry are known to have shorter attention spans. They are unable to perform tasks as well as their peers."

That is why when Meyers, Sampson, et al., examined the effect of the School Breakfast Program on low-income elementary school children in Lawrence, Massachusetts, they found that impoverished children who participated in the School Breakfast Program had significantly higher standardized achievement test scores than impoverished children who did not participate.

The School Breakfast Program is authorized to provide federal funds to schools, but most school districts are not required to offer it and, even when it is offered, many mothers do not know that it exists.

"Going to school without a decent breakfast was real hard on the kids," Cathy said, spreading her fingers across her forehead and rubbing her temples with her thumb and pinky. "Their grades dropped, they became depressed, they also felt different and ashamed. Little things like not being able to afford a hamburger at a fast-food place and having to eat those damn beans really got to them. Let me tell you, this wasn't like eating soul food for fun. I tried to vary our diet.

Once I got a neck bone and they scraped the fat off it and ate pure fat. That's how hungry they were.

"And like I told you, all during this time I was interviewing every day or I was out prowling the streets looking for interviews. Finally, I got an eighteen-hour-a-week, six-dollars-an-hour, part-time, no-benefits job." Cathy tilted her head and smiled a mock smile. "Then guess what happened? Go on. Guess."

I looked up at her over the top of my glasses. "They cut your food stamps," I ventured.

"You got it," she roared, hitting her desk with the flat of her hand. "They cut my food stamps down to eleven dollars because I had a job. Now that I was working, I was worse off than ever. Now we couldn't even afford the beans anymore. People at work began to wonder what was wrong with me. I had these huge shadows under my eyes all the time. If someone touched my hand, I was ready to cry my heart out. That little bit of warmth was all it took. One woman I confided in gave me some of her hours but it still wasn't enough.

"Each month I fell further and further behind in all our payments, including the rent. We began to get eviction notices. When the first one came and I saw what it was, I panicked. After that, I tried not to open them. I let them pile up, I hid them in a drawer so I wouldn't see them every time I walked past. I tried to ignore them as long as I could. Then, when I knew we were actually about to be evicted, I mean put out on the street, I put the furniture in storage and went to the Baltimore Department of Social Services. I walked up to the counter and burst into tears. I was so upset, I couldn't even speak. I couldn't get the words out. I had to walk away and sit down for a while to collect myself. Finally, with my voice still shaking and about to break again, I said we'd lost our apartment and had nowhere to go. The lady who worked there just looked at me. Her eyes were the color of cactus and, I swear to God, there were spikes in them. 'All the shelters are full,' she said very matter-of-factly. 'Do you have a car?' When I said yes, she opened her eyes a little wider and pulled out a spike.

'Then you and your kids can live in your car,' she said, sticking it straight into my heart.

"She gave me some emergency food stamps and sent me back to my car. I was frightened and I was outraged. I felt so naked and so pathetic that I wanted to say keep your damn stamps but I didn't. I took them because, if there was one thing I knew, it was that I was going to feed my kids. If I had to sell my body to a stranger, if I had to steal, if I had to call my kids' father collect from a pay phone and say, 'I'm not doing well'—I was going to feed my kids. You reach a point when you get desperate enough or hungry enough that you will do anything to eat. Now, I'm not talking about selling my body for crack or alcohol. I'm talking about selling it for food for my kids. When people said, 'How'd you get homeless? Was it drugs, was it alcohol or did you have a breakdown?' I'd say, 'No, none of the above. Just hard times and a bad choice of men.' It was that simple. It really was. Anyhow, I knew we had to get to another town where they might have a shelter for us. Don't get me wrong," she said with a quick toss of her head. "Struggling, even hunger, was nothing new to me, but this was a whole different level, a whole new ball game.

"I mean, there we were in our car, me and these kids who I had promised to always protect and take care of, trying to find a safe neighborhood to sleep in where we wouldn't get chased away by the cops. Finally, we drove from Baltimore into Annapolis and parked near the waterfront in the tourist area. I figured we'd get showers and use the bathrooms there but it turned out that all those facilities were only for the people living on boats. People living in cars were outcasts. There were no facilities for them. We were using the food stamps to buy cold cuts and bread and eating sandwiches in the car. We slept in our clothes for three or four days. We were trying to become residents of the county so we could qualify for local benefits. I told my sons that if we couldn't get help soon they'd have to go and live with their father. They cried and said, 'Mommy, even if we're homeless, we want to stay with you.'

"That's when I went to the shelter and asked them for a place to stay. I had always been so proud and it was hard for me to admit I'd run out of ideas. Showing up at a shelter that Monday morning was a big deal for me but it was nothing to the staff. They saw people like me every day. They said they were sorry but they were full. They were kind about it but they were full. They told me to come back on Thursday. They said they'd see what they could do. Those were the longest days of my life.

"Looking back now, I don't know how we lived through it, sleeping in the car, washing up at gas stations and eating nothing but junk food. I never told my family what had happened till four or five years later. I was too ashamed. I guess I still had that Mary Tyler Moore 'I'm gonna make it' mentality."

Cathy took in a deep breath and let out a sigh. "I'm very careful with the choices I make now and the money I spend. I've been badly burned and so have my sons.

"My furniture was auctioned off because I couldn't pay the storage costs of one hundred five dollars a month. I lost everything I had, even the beautiful dining room set that I bought on installments and all the crystal I'd collected on three tours to Germany."

She put her elbows on her desk, then covered her ears and closed her eyes, as if to shut out the world.

"The fear of hunger and homelessness is still very real for me. I can still see myself living in that car. Right now, I'm living with another person, one of the sisters from my church, but before I found her, I was paying seven hundred dollars a month in rent and making eight dollars an hour. I began getting scared again. I began thinking we'd end up just like before. Luckily, this woman saw what was happening to me and opened up her home. She gave us two of her four bedrooms and I shared the rent. We are six people now with only one bathroom but we've managed just fine. We've never had a fight. We just go half on everything. This way my rent is only four hundred seventy-six dollars a month, but even paying only half the rent, it still gets tough. I worked two full-time jobs last year from February to May. I was here at the shelter from seven in the morning until three in the afternoon. Then from four to twelve I worked at the comptroller's office. I did it because my money was getting too low for comfort and I was getting terrified. I was beginning to feel that crazy train racing around in circles on the tracks inside my belly again. I tell you, I can smell the fear in my guts when it starts and I can see it like a ball rolling through the snow and gathering size. I always know when it's going to be a problem. So, right away, I will turn off my cable. I will turn down my heat. I will turn off my lights. I will stop talking on the phone. I will go back to eating beans. I will do whatever it takes."

Cathy shivered. "I haven't been on a vacation since 1991 because I'm too scared to spend the money. I'm also too proud to go to food pantries. I've been on both sides, so I know how demeaning it is to have someone look at me condescendingly and say 'And what do you need today?' It makes me feel like I'm nothing. Right away I see 'big you' and 'little me.'" She held up her hands. "Look at this. Just remembering it makes my hands start shaking, but the fact that I've been there also makes me good at the job I do. I not only know what people are going through, to a lesser degree I'm still going through it myself.

"My oldest son is always hungry. He wants red meat and fresh vegetables and, of course, even now we can't afford them. It's very expensive to buy red meat and fresh vegetables so I go for the coupon sales and the canned goods. I went into Fresh Fields the other day, and when I saw the prices, I just turned around and walked out empty-handed. I watched that automatic door open, then I felt it close behind me. Even now, eating out for us is strictly fast food, like hamburgers at two for ninety-nine cents.

"I hold on to my money very tightly," Cathy said, rolling her fingers into a fist, then plunging them into the palm of her other hand. "It's self-defense. It's a primal reflex because I always want to make sure that we can eat and that my car and rent are paid."

"The men who know me now know how I feel. They know not to mess with my food or my money or my kids."

I watched, as a tremor passed over Cathy's body. For a minute she looked like she wanted to cry, but instead she rolled her chair back on its wheels, then leaned toward me.

"I stash food," she whispered. She opened her eyes wider, waiting for a reaction. I must have looked puzzled or incredulous. "I'm not kidding you, Loretta," she repeated. "I stash food. Look. See, it's there right under my desk."

I stood, up and looked and, sure enough, hidden under her desk was a black plastic crate. It was filled to the brim with hot chocolate mix, tea bags, chocolate chip cookies, oatmeal, canned goods and dried foods. I was about to say, "But you run the emergency food pantry. All you have to do is walk back there and take whatever you need." Then I realized that this had nothing to do with logic. "You're afraid you'll be hungry again?" I said.

"Uh-huh," she answered, clutching the desk. "That's right, and my fear comes from the other place, the dark place under the trees at night, so if I've got nothing I know I can always eat this. I keep another stash in my car trunk. It's like I've been through a war and I've got post-traumatic stress syndrome. This is my bomb shelter.

"If my bank account drops below five hundred dollars, I panic. I freak out because five hundred dollars is what I know I need for gas and other stuff to get me and my sons back home to Texas. I'm not as proud as I used to be. This time I'd go home. I'm never living in my car again. I never want to be in that desperate place where I can't feed myself or my children. For their sake and my own sanity, I can't risk it, I'm too scared. I still have hopes and I still have dreams, big ones," Cathy said, her hand still clutching the edge of her desk. "My goal now is to get my degree and to earn more money. I want a salary of six figures before the decimal point and I want a house with four bedrooms and three baths."

"You do?" I said, surprised by the sudden turn in our conversation. I had assumed that her primary need was just to avoid poverty and hunger. Although it made perfect sense, it hadn't occurred to me that she actually wanted to become part of the middle class or the upper middle class.

"Yes, I do. You bet I do. And I don't want a townhouse either. I want a house with a yard. I've settled for too little for too long. Don't get me wrong, sharing a house with my church sister hasn't been traumatic, it's been wonderful, but I want my own house and I want to go on real vacations someday, not just read a travel book about the places other people go.

"Don't misunderstand," she said. "I'm not sorry about what happened to me because I've learned so much from it. If I had no test, I wouldn't have a testimony. If I had no mess, I wouldn't have a message. Each one of my great strengths is because I've been through a struggle. Before this happened, I didn't feel the way I do now about people who were suffering. Coming through hunger and homelessness has totally changed me. It threw me off my high horse and made me a better person. I want to help other poor people now just as much as I want to help myself. I am still poor in material things but I am no longer poor in spirit. That's because, here at this shelter, I'm doing the work that I feel called to do. I still get scared, sometimes I get very scared, but my biggest fear really isn't for myself anymore, it's for all the others out there without decent jobs or a place to turn. It's for the ones who've been cast out by the new Welfare to Work laws because I know what's going to happen to them. If they're lucky enough to get jobs, they'll join the working poor. A lot of them will be even poorer than they were on welfare. They'll lose their food stamps and many of them will also lose their homes. They'll have nowhere to go and groups like ours just can't house or feed them all."

***

The provisions of the new Welfare to Work legislation that Cathy referred to go on for hundreds of pages, but there are three major changes in public policy that are certain to drastically increase hunger and, indirectly, homelessness in America.

Until now, at least officially, the availability of food stamps was based on the need for food. But under the new welfare reform law, food stamps are limited to three months out of every three years for adults under fifty without children regardless of need. What that really means is that there is no longer a guarantee that people will not starve, even starve to death, in America. While the cuts

do not include families with children, there is no way that existing food pantries and other emergency food providers can meet the suddenly increased needs of adults without having less for children.

The new law also takes food stamps away from immigrants who aren't citizens unless they qualify for specific exemptions. But fear, confusion, adversarial treatment and concern about deportation make many afraid even to ask. In fact, it sent thousands to emergency food pantries instead of food stamp offices even before the law took effect. In addition, the law freezes the standard deduction. It also lowers the Thrifty Food Plan even further than the 1975 level that some of the Department of Agricultures own workers called inadequate for more than short-term emergency use. That means that everyone including the children will now have even less.

As the impact of the cuts continues, the strain on emergency food providers will also continue and increase. They will be forced to turn people away without food because they will have no food left to give them.

The new welfare policy shifts the source of control from the federal government to the individual states and from federal entitlements to states' choices. Federal guidelines have vanished and Aid to Families with Dependent Children has been converted to a block grant called Temporary Assistance for Needy Families (TANF). It too gives discretion to the states without any guarantee that they will be responsive to the needs of hungry children.

The primary emphasis is on work, work as a promised answer, work as a panacea, work as a magic solution to welfare and to poverty. In theory, it's great. In reality, there are many strikes against the welfare recipient. First, relatively little emphasis is actually placed on training people for work that can lift them out of poverty. Second, competition for jobs is increasing. In fact, as huge corporations like Sara Lee, Lucent, CNN, Chrysler, DuPont and others downsize, currently employed blue-collar and professional middle-class workers are losing their jobs and scrambling for a limited number of new ones. Now, poorly trained welfare recipients are suddenly being asked to compete with these higher-skilled and better-educated groups.

Commonly held false beliefs about family size and the kind of people who receive welfare adds another strike and makes it even harder for them to succeed.

Actually, families who receive welfare do not have more children than other families. In fact, more than 70 percent of all AFDC families have two or fewer children and families receiving AFDC are about as likely to be white as black. In addition, more than two-thirds of the 14 million welfare recipients in 1995 were children.

People currently living on welfare, even welfare combined with food stamp benefits, are still living below the poverty levels in every state and below 75 percent of the poverty level in almost four-fifths of the states.

But as inadequate as welfare is, we are not moving most of these people from welfare to well-being. We are moving them from one form of poverty to another that may be even worse.

As the Children's Defense Fund study *Welfare to What?* points out, only a small fraction of former welfare recipients' new jobs actually pay above poverty wages and most of the new jobs pay far below the poverty line, which Census Bureau surveys defined as about $250 a week for a family of three in 1998.

The ability to escape from poverty through work is directly linked to the minimum wage. A national wage floor was first established in the United States during the 1930s Depression. At that time, with the exception of agriculture, business firms were forced to share more of their revenues with workers. For many years, the minimum wage rose in step with the top wages, but by 1997 the minimum wage had declined to the point where it no longer lifted its workers out of poverty. Seven states, including Alaska, California, Connecticut, Massachusetts, Oregon and Vermont had moved toward raising the minimum wage beyond the federally required level, but except for that small amount of progress, the maldistribution of money between the rich and the poor kept growing more and more extreme.

As William Greider pointed out in *One World, Ready or Not*, by 1997, 80 percent of America's wealth belonged to one-fifth of its people. The unspoken assumption was that this gross disparity was the natural, immutable order of things.

While many of the rich were raised in wealth, more than one in five American children was raised in poverty.

According to the Congressional Budget Office, income disparities were greater at the end of the twentieth century than at any time in the previous quarter century. Yet public awareness of the hunger and suffering caused by these disparities remained surprisingly low.

The United States was number one in the world in wealth and number twenty-six in the world in childhood mortality under the age of twelve.

A study done by the Children's Defense Fund found that an American child was two times more likely to be poor than a British child, three times more likely to be poor than a French child and at least six times more likely to be poor than a Belgian, Danish or Swiss child.

At the turn of the century, poverty in contemporary America not only hurt poor children, sometimes it killed them, if not directly through hunger then indirectly through diseases, parasites, inadequate health care and homelessness.

There is still a deeply held belief in the United States that poverty is a choice and that if people are willing to work, they will not be poor. But the reality is that half of America's poor children live with a parent who works. Millions of the families who work the longest hours at the least rewarding jobs never get above the poverty level or earn enough to adequately feed their hungry children.

Discussion Questions

1. Many people have stereotypes about homeless people. Name some of the stereotypes that you have heard in regard to this population.

2. Does Cathy's story break down some of those stereotypes or does it reinforce them? If so, how do they accomplish this? How not?

3. If Cathy were African American or Latina, what other issues might be involved in her experience of homelessness? How might her experience be similar or dissimilar to the Cathy Lewis in this piece?

4. Have you or anyone you know been homeless? How did this experience shape your or their life experiences and chances?

18
Report From the Bahamas

June Jordan

June Jordan, a Black American of West Indian heritage writes about a weekend spent in the Bahamas. As a women traveling alone, she has chosen an expensive hotel of a major chain for safety and comfort. While she is there she becomes acutely conscious of race, class, and gender as they affect her life and as they make her similar to and different from those around her. She thinks about what she has (gender and color) and does not have (class and nationality) in common with the woman who cleans her hotel room, the women who sell handcrafts to tourists, and the woman in the hotel coffee shop. She has been reading a novel by and about a poor Jewish woman set at the start of the twentieth century. Jordan has gender in common with the character in the novel and the character in turn has poverty in common with the Bahamian women. The book was given to Jordan by a student who, unlike Jordan's son, is financially comfortable enough not to need a student loan; further, he is White, male, and Jewish. They have in common the fact that he is doing an independent study project with her and that they both know and love an ethnic language, Yiddish and Black English. She remembers a graduate student, a woman probably close to her own age, who feels oppressed by her position as a middle-class homemaker and thinks Jordan is "lucky" to have a cause—discrimination of various kinds—in her life. Finally, she thinks of Sokuto and Cathy, two students, one Black and South African, one White and Irish. Besides being students and women, they have the effects of the alcoholism of Cathy's father and Sokuto's husband in common.

On this vacation trip, Jordan is acutely aware of gender, race, class, and religion. She understands intersectionality, the ways in which each of our characteristics combine to shape our lives and life chances and give each of us a standpoint from which we experience and act in the world. What she comes to see is that having one or two characteristics in common, race and gender for example, may not mean as much as the ways in which people differ. She realizes that as a middle-class American, she has more in common with the other tourists, White and Black, than with the Black Bahamians. Reflecting on her experiences with students, she sees commonalities with a young White man and profound differences between herself and a more mature woman. These realizations make her wonder if it is possible for people to find common ground with one another. She wonders if the differences are just too many and too deep. Then she recalls the situation involving the two students from very different backgrounds, and she makes a promise to herself to try to connect with others.

This article turns the gender, race, and class perspective of most of the articles in this volume inside out. Jordan recognizes her combination of statuses and the ways in which she is both disadvantaged and privileged. She sees the relationship of her situation to history and to her teaching as well as to everyday life. These realizations cause her to want to get beyond them, to make common cause with others. However, when Bahamians have to debase themselves for tourists in order to have money for food, when a student cannot understand that cut-backs in student loans affect him even if he doesn't personally need one, and when a homemaker thinks that people who have to be concerned with racism in their daily lives are "lucky" because they have "cause," it is difficult to see how meaningful connections can be made.

I am staying in a hotel that calls itself The Sheraton British Colonial. One of the photographs advertising the place displays a middle-aged Black man in a waiter's tuxedo, smiling. What intrigues me most about the picture is just this: while the Black man bears a tray full of "colorful" drinks above his left shoulder, both of his feet, shoes and trouserlegs, up to ten inches above his ankles, stand in the also "colorful" Caribbean salt water. He is so delighted to serve you he will wade into the water to bring you Banana Daquiris while you float! More precisely, he will wade into the water, fully clothed, oblivious to the ruin of his shoes, his trousers, his health, and he will do it with a smile.

I am in the Bahamas. On the phone in my room, a spinning complement of plastic pages offers handy index clues such as CAR RENTAL and CASINOS. A message from the Ministry of Tourism appears among these travellers' tips. Opening with a paragraph of "WELCOME," the message then proceeds to "A PAGE OF HISTORY," which reads as follows:

> New World History begins on the same day that modern Bahamian history begins—October 12, 1492. That's when Columbus stepped ashore—British influence came first with the Eleutherian Adventurers of 1647—After the Revolutions, American Loyalists fled from the newly independent states and settled in the Bahamas. Confederate blockade-runners used the island as a haven during the War between the States, and after the War, a number of Southerners moved to the Bahamas. . . .

There it is again. Something proclaims itself a legitimate history and all it does is track white Mr. Columbus to the British Eleutherians through the Confederate Southerners as they barge into New World surf, land on New World turf, and nobody saying one word about the Bahamian people, the Black peoples, to whom the only thing new in their island world was this weird succession of crude intruders and its colonial consequences.

This is my consciousness of race as I unpack my bathing suit in the Sheraton British Colonial. Neither this hotel nor the British nor the long ago Italians nor the white Delta airline pilots belong here, of course. And every time I look at the photograph of that fool standing in the water with his shoes on I'm about to have a West Indian fit, even though I know he's no fool; he's a middle-aged Blackman who needs a job and this is his job—pretending himself a servile ancillary to the pleasures of the rich. (Compared

to his options in life, I am a rich woman. Compared to most of the Black Americans arriving for this Easter weekend on a three nights, four days' deal of bargain rates, the middle-aged waiter is a poor Black man.)

We will jostle along with the other (white) visitors and join them in the tee shirt shops or, laughing together, learn ruthless rules of negotiation as we, Black Americans as well as white, argue down the price of hand woven goods at the nearby straw market while the merchants, frequently toothless Black women seated on the concrete in their only presentable dress, humble themselves to our careless games:

"Yes? You like it? Eight dollar."

"Five."

"I give it to you. Seven."

And so it continues, this weird succession of crude intruders that, now, includes me and my brothers and sisters from the North.

This is my consciousness of class as I try to decide how much money I can spend on Bahamian gifts for my family back in Brooklyn. No matter that these other Black women incessantly weave words and flowers into the straw hats and bags piled beside them on the burning dusty street. No matter that these other Black women must work their sense of beauty into these things that we will take away as cheaply as we dare, or they will do without food.

We are not white, after all. The budget is limited. And we are harmlessly killing time between the poolside rum punch and "The Native Show on the Patio" that will play tonight outside the hotel restaurant.

This is my consciousness of race and class and gender identity as I notice the fixed relations between these other Black women and myself. They sell and I buy or I don't. They risk not eating. I risk going broke on my first vacation afternoon.

We are not particularly women anymore; we are parties to a transaction designed to set us against each other.

"Olive" is the name of the Black woman who cleans my hotel room. On my way to the beach I am wondering what "Olive" would say if I told her why I chose The Sheraton British Colonial; if I told her I wanted to swim. I wanted to sleep. I did not want to be harassed by the middle-aged waiter, or his nephew. I did not want to be raped by anybody (white or Black) at all and I calculated that my safety as a Black woman alone would best be assured by a multinational hotel corporation. In my experience, the big guys take customer complaints more seriously than the little ones. I would suppose that's one reason why they're big; they don't like to lose money anymore than I like to be bothered when I'm trying to read a goddamned book underneath a palm tree I paid $264 to get next to. A Black woman seeking refuge in a multinational corporation may seem like a contradiction to some, but there you are. In this case it's a coincidence of entirely different self-interests: Sheraton/cash = June Jordan's short run safety.

Anyway, I'm pretty sure "Olive" would look at me as though I came from someplace as far away as Brooklyn. Then she'd probably allow herself one indignant query before righteously removing her vacuum cleaner from my room; "and why in the first place you come down you without your husband?"

I cannot imagine how I would begin to answer her.

My "rights" and my "freedom" and my "desire" and a stew of other New World values; what would they sound like to this Black woman described on the card atop my hotel bureau as "Olive the Maid?" "Olive" is older than I am and I may smoke a cigarette while she changes the sheets on my bed. Whose rights? Whose freedom? Whose desire?

And why should she give a shit about mine unless I do something, for real, about hers?

It happens that the book that I finished reading under a palm tree earlier today was the novel *The Bread Givers* by Anzia Yezierska. Definitely autobiographical, Yezierska lays out the difficulties of being both female and "a person" inside a traditional Jewish family at the start of the 20th century. That any Jewish woman became anything more than the abused servant of her father or her husband is really an improbable piece of news. Yet Yezierska managed such an unlikely outcome for her own life. In *The Bread Givers*, the heroine also manages an important, although partial, escape from traditional Jewish female destiny. And in the unpardonable,

despotic father, the Talmudic scholar of that Jewish family, did I not see my own and hate him twice, again? When the heroine, the young Jewish child, wanders the streets with a filthy pail she borrows to sell herring in order to raise the ghetto rent and when she cries, "Nothing was before me but the hunger in our house, and no bread for the next meal if I didn't sell the herring. No longer like a fire engine, but like a houseful of hungry mouths my heart cried, 'herring—herring! Two cents apiece!'" who would doubt the ease, the sisterhood of conversation possible between that white girl and the Black women selling straw bags on the streets of paradise because they do not want to die? And is it not obvious that the wife of that Talmudic scholar and "Olive," who cleans my room here at the hotel, have more in common than I can claim with either one of them?

This is my consciousness of race and class and gender identity as I collect wet towels, sunglasses, wristwatch, and head towards a shower.

I am thinking about the boy who loaned this novel to me. He's white and he's Jewish and he's pursuing an independent study project with me, at the State University where I teach whether or not I feel like it, where I teach without stint because, like the waiter, I am no fool. It's my job and either I work or I do without everything you need money to buy. The boy loaned me the novel because he thought I'd be interested to know how a Jewish-American writer used English so that the syntax, and therefore the cultural habits of mind expressed by the Yiddish language, could survive translation. He did this because he wanted to create another connection between us on the basis of language, between his knowledge/his love of Yiddish and my knowledge/my love of Black English.

He has been right about the forceful survival of the Yiddish. And I had become excited by this further evidence of the written voice of spoken language protected from the monodrone of "standard" English, and so we had grown closer on this account. But then our talk shifted to student affairs more generally, and I had learned that this student does not care one way or the other about currently jeopardized Federal Student Loan

Programs because, as he explained it to me, they do not affect him. He does not need financial help outside his family. My own son, however, is Black. And I am the only family help available to him and that means, if Reagan succeeds in eliminating Federal programs to aid minority students, he will have to forget about furthering his studies, or he or I or both of us will have to hit the numbers pretty big. For these reasons of difference, the student and I had moved away from each other, even while we continued to talk.

My consciousness turned to race, again, and class.

Sitting in the same chair as the boy, several weeks ago, a graduate student came to discuss her grade. I praised the excellence of her final paper; indeed it had seemed to me an extraordinary pulling together of recent left brain/right brain research with the themes of transcendental poetry.

She told me that, for her part, she'd completed her reading of my political essays. "You are so lucky!" she exclaimed.

"What do you mean by that?"

"You have a cause. You have a purpose to your life."

I looked carefully at this white woman; what was she really saying to me?

"What do you mean?" I repeated.

"Poverty. Police violence. Discrimination in general."

(Jesus Christ, I thought: Is that her idea of lucky?)

"And how about you?" I asked.

"Me?"

"Yeah, you. Don't you have a cause?"

"Me? I'm just a middle-aged woman: a housewife and a mother. I'm a nobody."

For a while, I made no response.

First of all, speaking of race and class and gender in one breath, what she said meant that those lucky preoccupations of mine, from police violence to nuclear wipe-out, were not shared. They were mine and not hers. But here she sat, friendly as an old stuffed animal, beaming good will or more "luck" in my direction.

In the second place, what this white woman said to me meant that she did not believe she was "a person" precisely because she had fulfilled the traditional female func-

tions revered by the father of that Jewish immigrant, Anzia Yezierska. And the woman in front of me was not a Jew. That was not the connection. The link was strictly female. Nevertheless, how should that woman and I, another female, connect beyond this bizarre exchange?

If she believed me lucky to have regular hurdles of discrimination then why shouldn't I insist that she's lucky to be a middle class white Wasp female who lives in such well-sanctioned and normative comfort that she even has the luxury to deny the power of the privileges that paralyze her life?

If she deserts me and "my cause" where we differ, if, for example, she abandons me to "my" problems of race, then why should I support her in "her" problems of housewifely oblivion?

Recollection of this peculiar moment brings me to the shower in the bathroom cleaned by "Olive." She reminds me of the usual Women's Studies curriculum because it has nothing to do with her or her job: you won't find "Olive" listed anywhere on the reading list. You will likewise seldom hear of Anzia Yezierska. But yes, you will find, from Florence Nightingale to Adrienne Rich, a white procession of independently well-to-do women writers. (Gertrude Stein/Virginia Woolf/Hilda Doolittle are standard names among the "essential" women writers.)

In other words, most of the women of the world—Black and First World and white who work because we must—most of the women of the world persist far from the heart of the usual Women's Studies syllabus.

Similarly, the typical Black History course will slide by the majority experience it pretends to represent. For example, Mary McLeod Bethune will scarcely receive as much attention as Nat Turner, even though Black women who bravely and efficiently provided for the education of Black people hugely outnumber those few Black men who led successful or doomed rebellions against slavery. In fact, Mary McLeod Bethune may not receive even honorable mention because Black History too often apes those ridiculous white history courses which produce such dangerous gibberish as The Sheraton British Colonial "history" of the Bahamas. Both Black and white history courses exclude from their central consideration those people who neither killed nor conquered anyone as the means to new identity, those people who took care of every one of the people who wanted to become "a person," those people who still take care of the life at issue: the ones who wash and who feed and who teach and who diligently decorate straw hats and bags with all of their historically unrequired gentle love: the women.

Oh the old rugged cross

on a hill far away

Well I cherish the old rugged cross

It's Good Friday in the Bahamas. Seventy-eight degrees in the shade. Except for Sheraton territory, everything's closed.

It so happens that for truly secular reasons I've been fasting for three days. My hunger has now reached nearly violent proportions. In the hotel sandwich shop, the Black woman handling the counter complains about the tourists; why isn't the shop closed and why don't the tourists stop eating for once in their lives. I'm famished and I order chicken salad and cottage cheese and lettuce and tomato and a hard boiled egg and a hot cross bun and apple juice.

She eyes me with disgust.

To be sure, the timing of my stomach offends her serious religious practices. Neither one of us apologizes to the other. She seasons the chicken salad to the peppery max while I listen to the loud radio gospel she plays to console herself. It's a country Black version of "The Old Rugged Cross."

As I heave much chicken into my mouth tears start. It's not the pepper. I am, after all, a West Indian daughter. It's the Good Friday music that dominates the humid atmosphere.

Well I cherish the old rugged cross

And I am back, faster than a 747, in Brooklyn, in the home of my parents where we are wondering, as we do every year, if the sky will darken until Christ has been buried in the tomb. The sky should darken if God is in His heavens. And then, around 3 p.m., at the conclusion of our mournful church service at the neighborhood St. Phillips, and even while we dumbly stare at the black cloth covering the gold altar and the slender unlit candles, the sun should return through the high gothic windows and vindicate our waiting faith that the Lord will rise again, on Easter.

How I used to bow my head at the very name of Jesus: ecstatic to abase myself in deference to His majesty.

My mouth is full of salad. I can't seem to eat quickly enough. I can't think how I should lessen the offense of my appetite. The other Black woman on the premises, the one who disapprovingly prepared this very tasty break from my fast, makes no remark. She is no fool. This is a job that she needs. I suppose she notices that at least I included a hot cross bun among my edibles. That's something in my favor. I decide that's enough.

I am suddenly eager to walk off the food. Up a fairly steep hill I walk without hurrying. Through the pastel desolation of the little town, the road brings me to a confectionary pink and white plantation house. At the gates, an unnecessarily large statue of Christopher Columbus faces me down, or tries to. His hand is fisted to one hip. I look back at him, laugh without deference, and turn left.

It's time to pack it up. Catch my plane. I scan the hotel room for things not to forget. There's that white report card on the bureau. "Dear Guests:" it says, under the name "Olive." "I am your maid for the day. Please rate me: Excellent. Good. Average. Poor. Thank you."

I tuck this memento from the Sheraton British Colonial into my notebook. How would "Olive" rate *me*? What would it mean for us to seem "good" to each other? What would that rating require?

But I am hastening to leave. Neither turtle soup nor kidney pie nor any conch shell delight shall delay my departure. I have rested, here, in the Bahamas, and I'm ready to return to my usual job, my usual work. But the skin on my body has changed and so has my mind. On the Delta flight home I realize I am burning up, indeed.

So far as I can see, the usual race and class concepts of connection, or gender assumptions of unity, do not apply very well. I doubt that they ever did. Otherwise why would

Black folks forever bemoan our lack of solidarity when the deal turns real. And if unity on the basis of sexual oppression is something natural, then why do we women, the majority people on the planet, still have a problem?

The plane's ready for takeoff. I fasten my seatbelt and let the tumult inside my head run free. Yes: race and class and gender remain as real as the weather. But what they must mean about the contact between two individuals is less obvious and, like the weather, not predictable.

And when these factors of race and class and gender absolutely collapse is whenever you try to use them as automatic concepts of connection. They may serve well as indicators of commonly felt conflict, but as elements of connection they seem about as reliable as precipitation probability for the day after the night before the day.

It occurs to me that much organizational grief could be avoided if people understood that partnership in misery does not necessarily provide for partnership for change: *When we get the monsters off our backs all of us may want to run in very different directions*.

And not only that: even though both "Olive" and "I" live inside a conflict neither one of us created, and even though both of us therefore hurt inside that conflict, I may be one of the monsters she needs to eliminate from her universe and, in a sense, she may be one of the monsters in mine.

I am reaching for the words to describe the difference between a common identity that has been imposed and the individual identity any one of us will choose, once she gains that chance.

That difference is the one that keeps us stupid in the face of new, specific information about somebody else with whom we are supposed to have a connection because a third party, hostile to both of us, has worked it so that the two of us, like it or not, share a common enemy. *What happens beyond the idea of that enemy and beyond the consequences of that enemy?*

I am saying that the ultimate connection cannot be the enemy. The ultimate connection must be the need that we find between us. It is not only who you are, in other words, but what we can do for each other that will determine the connection.

I am flying back to my job. I have been teaching contemporary women's poetry this semester. One quandary I have set myself to explore with my students is the one of taking responsibility without power. We had been wrestling ideas to the floor for several sessions when a young Black woman, a South African, asked me for help, after class.

Sokutu told me she was "in a trance" and that she'd been unable to eat for two weeks.

"What's going on?" I asked her, even as my eyes startled at her trembling and emaciated appearance.

"My husband. He drinks all the time. He beats me up. I go to the hospital. I can't eat. I don't know what/anything."

In my office, she described her situation. I did not dare to let her sense my fear and horror. She was dragging about, hour by hour, in dread. Her husband, a young Black South African, was drinking himself into more and more deadly violence against her.

Sokutu told me how she could keep nothing down. She weighed 90 lbs at the outside, as she spoke to me. She'd already been hospitalized as a result of her husband's battering rage.

I knew both of them because I had organized a campus group to aid the liberation struggles of Southern Africa.

Nausea rose in my throat. What about this presumable connection: this husband and this wife fled from that homeland of hatred against them, and now what? He was destroying himself. If not stopped, he would certainly murder his wife.

She needed a doctor, right away. It was a medical emergency. She needed protection. It was a security crisis. She needed refuge for battered wives and personal therapy and legal counsel. She needed a friend.

I got on the phone and called every number in the campus directory that I could imagine might prove helpful. Nothing worked. There were no institutional resources designed to meet her enormous, multifaceted, and ordinary woman's need.

I called various students. I asked the Chairperson of the English Department for advice. I asked everyone for help.

Finally, another one of my students, Cathy, a young Irish woman active in campus IRA activities, responded. She asked for further details. I gave them to her.

"Her husband," Cathy told me, "is an alcoholic. You have to understand about alcoholics. It's not the same as anything else. And it's a disease you can't treat any old way."

I listened, fearfully. Did this mean there was nothing we could do?

"That's not what I'm saying," she said. "But you have to keep the alcoholic part of the thing central in everybody's mind, otherwise her husband will kill her. Or he'll kill himself."

She spoke calmly, I felt there was nothing to do but to assume she knew what she was talking about.

"Will you come with me?" I asked her, after a silence. "Will you come with me and help us figure out what to do next?"

Cathy said she would but that she felt shy: Sokutu comes from South Africa. What would she think about Cathy?

"I don't know," I said. "But let's go."

We left to find a dormitory room for the young batterred wife.

It was late, now, and dark outside.

On Cathy's VW that I followed behind with my own car, was the sticker that reads BOBBY SANDS FREE AT LAST. My eyes blurred as I read and reread the words. This was another connection: Bobby Sands and Martin Luther King Jr. and who would believe it? I would not have believed it; I grew up terrorized by Irish kids who introduced me to the word "nigga."

And here I was following an Irish woman to the room of a Black South African. We were going to that room to try to save a life together.

When we reached the little room, we found ourselves awkward and large. Sokutu attempted to treat us with utmost courtesy, as though we were honored guests. She seemed surprised by Cathy, but mostly Sokutu was flushed with relief and joy because we were there, with her.

I did not know how we should ever terminate her heartfelt courtesies and address, directly, the reason for our visit: her starvation and her extreme physical danger.

Finally, Cathy sat on the floor and reached out her hands to Sokutu.

"I'm here," she said quietly, "Because June has told me what has happened to you. And I know what it is. Your husband is an alcoholic. He has a disease. I know what it is. My father was an alcoholic. He killed himself. He almost killed my mother. I want to be your friend."

"Oh," was the only small sound that escaped from Sokutu's mouth. And then she embraced the other student. And then everything changed and I watched all of this happen so I know that this happened: this connection.

And after we called the police and exchanged phone numbers and plans were made for the night and for the next morning, the young South African woman walked down the dormitory hallway, saying goodbye and saying thank you to us.

I walked behind them, the young Irish woman and the young South African, and I saw them walking as sisters walk, hugging each other, and whispering and sure of each other and I felt how it was not who they were but what they both know and what they were both preparing to do about what they know that was going to make them both free at last.

And I look out the windows of the plane and I see clouds that will not kill me and I know that someday soon other clouds may erupt to kill us all.

And I tell the stewardess No thanks to the cocktails she offers me. But I look about the cabin at the hundred strangers drinking as they fly and I think even here and even now I must make the connection real between me and these strangers everywhere before those other clouds unify this ragged bunch of us, too late.

Discussion Questions

1. In this essay, Jordan recalls times and places when she was especially conscious of her gender, race, and social class. Interestingly, she was not the victim of racism or sexism at those times. In fact, in some respects she was a member of the privileged class. This consciousness is unset-

tling to her. Can you recall similar times in your own life?

2. Are you optimistic or pessimistic about the ability of people of different backgrounds to recognize where they have common interests? Is it always necessary for people to be personally affected in order to work together in the service of a cause?

3. Jordan thinks working in the tourist industry is demeaning to the Bahamian people, but she also recognizes that such work provides essential income. Have you worked in a service job, such as waiting tables, parking cars, or cleaning hotel rooms? Did you find it demean-

ing? Does it have to be? Does it matter that you had to do it only temporarily, whereas the people Jordan describes will probably have the same jobs all their lives?

4. Can you identify at all with the student who didn't need a loan or the one who envies people who have to face discrimination because they have a "cause"? What is it about people or society that lies beneath such responses?

19

The Gendered Politics and Violence of Structural Adjustment

A View from Jamaica

Faye V. Harrison

Anthropologist Faye V. Harrison uses the life story of a woman she calls Beulah Brown to illustrate the impact of structural adjustment and export-oriented economic development policies on the lives of middle- and working-class people in Jamaica. The details may vary slightly, but similar effects were observable in other countries of the economic South in the 1980s and '90s. During this time period, the creditor nations, led by the United States and international agencies such as the World Bank and the International Monetary Fund (IMF), mandated broad reforms across the developing world. They imposed an investment- and export-oriented development model in which currency would be devalued and resources would be channeled toward enterprises leading toward growth, as gauged by increases in the Gross Domestic Product and other macro-economic measures, and away from social investment in food subsidies, heath care, education, and subsistence activities. These policies were designed to end waste and improper management of loans and donor funds and, through a trickle-down mechanism, eventually lead to economic stability and improve lives. Not incidentally, they were also designed to increase investment by transnational companies whose profits and products are exported and

to increase the chances that debtor nations would be able to repay their loans. These policies failed on almost all counts.

Because a large proportion of Jamaican households are headed by women and women are more likely to be working in the informal sector, the supposedly gender-neutral new economic policies had greater impact on the lives of women than of men. Mrs. Brown was a hard-working, kind, and giving woman with political connections, relatives abroad, and considerable work skills and experience. Despite all this, she was barely able to make ends meet when government services were curtailed. When some people turned to illegal activities such as drug trafficking, Mrs. Brown used personal and church resources to engage in a number of informal sector enterprises, ranging from dressmaking to selling prepared food. She also visited relatives abroad, where she technically violated laws by earning some money babysitting. Conditions such as those in Jamaica encourage both documented and undocumented migration to the economic North.

An Ethnographic Window on a Crisis

"The ghetto not'ing but a sad shanty town now." This is what one of my friends and informants sadly remarked to me upon my 1992 visit to "Oceanview," a pseudonym for an impoverished slum neighborhood with a roughly 74 percent formal unemployment rate in the downtown district of the Kingston Metropolitan Area. Times were so hard that the tenements had deteriorated beyond repair. The conspicuous physical decline was a marker of the deepened socioeconomic austerity accompanying what some critics (e g., *Race & Class* 1992) now consider to be the "recolonization" of Jamaica by "the new conquistadors"—the policies and programs that the International Monetary Fund (IMT), the World Bank, and the Reagan and Bush administrations of the United States government designed to "adjust" and "stabilize" the country's revived export-oriented economy. These strategies for delivering third world

161

societies from collapsing economies are informed by a development ideology that euphemizes the widening social disparities that have been the outcome of policies imposing an unbearable degree of austerity on living conditions. Hence, these policies have sacrificed ordinary people's—especially the poor's—basic needs in health care, housing, education, social services, and employment for those of free enterprise and free trade.

Since 1978, I have observed and conversed with Oceanview residents about the social, economic, and political conditions shaping their lived experiences and struggles for survival in this neighborhood (e.g., Harrison 1987a,b; 1988; 1991a,b). The late 1970s was a time of economic hardship and political turbulence, a time when the People's National Party's (PNP) democratic socialist path to economic development and social transformation was vehemently contested, blocked, and destabilized by political opponents both within and without the country and by the concerted economic force of an international recession, quadrupled oil prices, and a massive flight of both domestic and foreign capital. Life was certainly hard then, but, as one resident commented, "Cho, mahn [sic]; tings worse now." Despite the bright promises of political and economic "deliverance" made by the Jamaica Labour Party (JLP) and its major backer, the Reagan and later Bush administrations of the U.S. government, the 1980s and early 1990s—under the leadership of much more conservative PNP—brought only a deepened poverty to the folk who people the streets and alleys of slum and shantytown neighborhoods like Oceanview. This deepening poverty is reflected, for example, in a serious decline in the conditions of public health. The implementation of structural adjustment policies has brought about alarming reductions in government health-care expenditures and promoted the privatization of more costly and less accessible medical care (Phillips 1994, 157). Those most heavily burdened by the impact of these deteriorating social conditions and capital-centered policies are women (Antrobus 1989) who serve as the major "social shock absorbers" (Sparr 1992, 31; 1994) mediating the crisis at the local level of households and

neighborhoods. Nearly 50 percent of all Kingston's households are female-headed, giving women the major responsibilities for making ends meet out of virtually nothing (Deere et al. 1990, 52–53) Concentrated in the informal sector of the economy, these women along with their children are most vulnerable to the consequences of "malnutrition, hunger, and poor health: rising levels of morbidity and mortality (Phillips 1994, 142; Pan American Health Organization/World Health Organization 1992).

To appreciate and understand the effects, contradictions, and meanings that constitute the reality of a structurally adjusted pattern of production and trade, we must examine the everyday experiences, practices, discourses, and common sense of real people, particularly those encouraged to wait—and wait—for social and economic benefits to trickle down. In the interest of an ethnographically grounded view of Jamaica's current economic predicament, I present the case of Mrs. Beulah Brown, an admirable woman whose life story I collected over several years, to help elucidate the impact the ongoing crisis has on the everyday lives of ordinary Jamaicans, particularly poor urban women and those who depend most on them. A longtime household head and informal-sector worker like so many other Jamaican women, Mrs. Brown was once a community health aide with a government program that provided much needed health services to a population to which such care would not have been available otherwise. Mrs. Brown would not have gotten or held that job for the years that she did without "the right political connections," something, unfortunately, that too few poor people ever obtain. Although visible benefits from membership in the local PNP group may have set her apart from most of her neighbors, the centrality of patronage-clientelism in local and national politics makes a former political client's experience an insightful window on the constraints and vulnerabilities built into Jamaica's political and economic policies.

Highlights from Mrs. Brown's life story lead us to the more encompassing story of postcolonial Jamaica's experience with debt, export-led development, and structural adjustment, and their combined impact on women workers as well as on neighborhood-level negotiations of crisis.

A Hard-Working Woman's Story Within a Story

In the 1970s Beulah Brown, then a middle-aged woman responsible for a two-generation household and extended family, worked as a community health aide under the combined aegis of a government public health program and a local urban redevelopment agency, two projects that owed their existence to the social-policy orientation of the reformist PNP administration. Mrs. Brown had begun her employment history as a worker in a factory manufacturing undergarments. However, she preferred household-based self-employment over the stringent regimentation of factory work. A woman with strong civic consciousness and organizing skills, she had worked her way into the leadership of the PNP group within the neighborhood and wider political division. By the late 1970s, she was no longer an officer; however, her membership in the party was still active.

Mrs. Brown was so effective at working with patients and exhibiting good citizenship that she was widely recognized and addressed as "Nurse Brown," the term "nurse" being a title of utmost respect. When Mrs. Brown made her daily rounds, she did more than expected of a health aide. She treated her patients as whole persons with a range of basic needs she felt obligated to help meet. To this end, she saw to it that they had nutritional food to eat, clean clothes to wear, and neat and orderly rooms in which to live. She was especially devoted to the elderly, but she also invested considerable energy in young mothers who were often merely children themselves. She shared her experiences and wisdom with them, admonishing them to eat healthy foods, read good books, and, given her religious worldview, "pray to the Lord Jesus Christ" so that their babies' characters and personalities would be positively influenced while still in the womb.

When I initially met her, Mrs. Brown was responsible for caring for her elderly father, her handicapped sister, her sister's three daughters, and her own two daughters. At earlier times she had even minded a young niece who eventually joined her other siblings and mother, another of Mrs. Brown's sisters, in Canada. Despite many hardships, Beulah managed her household well enough to see to it that the children were fed, clothed, and schooled. Indeed, one of her nieces, Claudia, is now a nurse in New York City, and—"by the grace of God"—her eldest daughter, Cherry, is a graduate of the University of the West Indies. Unfortunately, Marie, the daughter who still remains at home, had difficulty getting and keeping wage work, whether in an office or factory, so she decided to make and sell children's clothes so she could work at home while minding her children. Despite the economic uncertainty of informal sector work, Marie appreciates its flexibility and the freedom from the "downpressive" (oppressive) industrial surveillance about which a number of former factory workers in Oceanview complain.

Because the community health aide job did not bring in enough income to support the household, Mrs. Brown found ways to augment her income. Mainly she made dresses, a skill and talent she had cultivated over most of her life. Years ago she had even had a small shop in Port Antonio that catered to locals as well as foreign tourists. That was before she gave up everything—her shop and her husband—to return home to Kingston to care for relatives who were going through some hard times. Besides her dressmaking enterprise, Mrs. Brown also baked and sold meat patties, bought and sold cheese, and sold ice from the deep freezer she had purchased with remittances from her twin sister in England and help from her church. Through political party connections gained through her earlier activism in the local PNP group, she also saw to it that her sister got a job cleaning streets in the government Crash Programme. Although her family managed better than most of their neighbors, survival was still an everyday struggle.

In the mid-1980s, Mrs. Brown lost her health aide job. The Community Health Aide Program suffered massive losses due to the retrenchment in public-sector employment stipulated by the structural-adjustment and stabilization measures imposed by the IMF and World Bank. Luckily, the layoff came around the time when the girls she had raised were coming of age and could work to support themselves and their families. By 1988, the household was made up of only Beulah, her second daughter, Marie, and Marie's three small children. Everyone else had moved on to independent residences in Kingston or emigrated to the U.S. and Canada to live with relatives, "a foreign," overseas. This dispersal relieved the household of considerable financial pressure, but to make ends meet Beulah still had to intensify her informal means of generating income. She did more dressmaking and added baking wedding and birthday cakes to her list of money-making activities.

No matter how much work she did, she never seemed to be able to do more than barely make ends meet. With the devaluation of the Jamaican dollar and the removal of subsidies on basic consumer items like food, the costs of living had increased dramatically. What more could she do to keep pace with the inflationary trend designed to make Jamaican exports more competitive on the international market? She knew that she would never resort to the desperate illicit measures some of her neighbors had taken by "tiefing" ("thiefing") or dealing drugs. She simply refused to sell her soul to the devil for some of the "blood money" obtainable from the activities of local gangs—now called posses—that move from Kingston to the U.S. and back trafficking in substances like crack cocaine. Increasingly, especially with political patronage becoming more scarce, drug trafficking has become an important source of local subsistence and small-scale investment. However, the price paid for a life of crime is too high. She lamented that too many "youts" (youths) involved in the drug economy make the return trip home to Jamaica enclosed in deathly wooden crates.

Like most Caribbean people, Mrs. Brown has long belonged to and actively participated in an international family network extending from Jamaica to Great Britain, Canada, and the U.S. (Basch et al. 1994). Her sisters abroad had often invited her to visit them, and they had also encouraged her to migrate so that she, too, could benefit from better opportunities. Before the mid-1980s, Mrs. Brown had been determined to remain at home caring for her family. Moreover, she loved her country, her church, and her party, and she wanted to help shape the direction of Jamaica's future. She strongly felt that someone had to remain in Jamaica to keep it going on the right course. Everyone couldn't migrate. "My home is here in Jamaica," she insisted adamantly.

These were her strong feelings *before* structural adjustment hit the heart of her home: her refrigerator, deep freezer, and kitchen table. In 1990 alone, the cost of chicken—a desirable entree to accompany rice and peas on Sunday—went up three times. The cost of even more basic staples also rose, making items such as fresh milk, cornmeal, and tomatoes (whose price increased 140 percent) more and more unaffordable for many people (Statistical Institute of Jamaica 1991).

Between 1987–92, Mrs. Brown travelled abroad twice for extended visits with relatives in England, Canada, and the U.S. While away for nearly a year at a time, she "did a little babysitting and ting" to earn money that she was able to save for her own purposes. Her family treated her "like a queen," buying her gifts ("good camera, TV, radio, and ting"), not letting her spend her own money for living expenses, and paying for her air transportation from point to point along her international itinerary. The savings she managed to send and bring back home were key to her Oceanview household's survival. Her transnational family network, and the geographical mobility it offered, allowed her to increase her earnings by taking advantage of the marked wage differential between Jamaica and the countries where her relatives live (Ho 1993, 33). This particular financial advantage has led even middle-class Jamaican women to tolerate an otherwise embarrassing and humiliating decline in social status to work as nannies and domestic helpers in North American homes. International migration within the Caribbean region as well as between it and major metropoles has been a traditional survival strategy among Jamaicans since nineteenth century post-emancipation society.

Harsh circumstances forced Mrs. Brown to join the larger wave of female emigrants from the Caribbean who, since the late 1960s, have outnumbered their male counterparts (Deere et al. 1990, 76; Ho 1993, 3). Thus far, Mrs. Brown has remained a "visitor," but she acknowledges the possibility and perhaps even the probability that some day soon she will join her sisters as a permanent resident abroad. Meanwhile, she continues to take care of business at home by informally generating and allocating resources within the kinship-mediated transnational social field within which her local life is embedded.

Mrs. Brown's story and many others similar to it are symptomatic of the current age of globalization, marked by a deepening crisis that policies such as structural adjustment and its complementary export-led development strategy attempt to manage in favor of the mobility and accumulation of transnational capital. Mrs. Brown's story, however, is only a story within a story about the dramatic plot-thickening details of Jamaica's nonlinear struggle for development and decolonization. Let us now place Beulah Brown's lived experience in a broader context, and, in so doing, illuminate the forces and conditions that differentially affect Jamaica's hardworking women, particularly those who work in the informal sector and free trade zone. As we shall see, their dilemmas and struggles are closely interrelated.

Once Upon a Time: Dilemmas of Development

Deep into Debt

Postcolonial Jamaica, like many other third world and southern hemisphere countries, is beset by a serious case of debt bondage. Jamaica is embroiled in a crisis that can be traced back to the economic turmoil of the mid-1970s. By 1980, when the conservative JLP ousted the democratic socialist PNP from power, Jamaica's debt had doubled due to the extensive borrowing undertaken to absorb the impact the receding international economy was having on the country, to offset massive capital flight (a domestic and international panic response to the PNP's move to the left), and to underwrite state-initiated development projects. To stabilize and reinvigorate the collapsed economy, the JLP administration, with the support and guidance of the Reagan administration, relied on the IMF and the World Bank for massive loans to redress its critical balance of payments and fiscal deficits. Consequently, the country's indebtedness grew by leaps and bounds. As a result, Jamaica now owes more than U.S. $4 billion. Its debt servicing exceeds what it receives in loans and grants (Ferguson 1992, 62), and it devours 40 percent of the foreign exchange it earns from its exports, which are supposed to jump start the economy into a pattern of sustained development. The development strategy pursued since 1980—one that privileges private-sector export production—has been underwritten by these relations of indebtedness. The IMF, World Bank, and the U.S. government's Caribbean Basin Initiative (CBI) and USAID have delimited terms for Jamaica's economic restructuring that further integrate the island into a global hierarchy of free-trade relations. This global hierarchy is not only class- and racially biased (Kohler 1978); it is also fundamentally gendered (Antrobus 1989; Enloe 1989; Sparr 1994).

The Path to Economic Growth and Social Crisis

The debt-constrained, export-led, and free trade-based development path that the Jamaican economy is following has failed to deliver the masses of Jamaican people from the dilemmas of persistent poverty and underdevelopment. Benefits from this development strategy have not trickled down the socioeconomic ladder. However, what have trickled down are the adverse effects of drastic austerity measures, which are the strings attached to aid from the IMF and World Bank. These strings stipulate that the government de-nationalize or privatize public sectors of the economy, cut back social services and public employment, devalue the Jamaican dollar, impose restraints on wages, liberalize imports, and remove subsidies and price controls on food and other consumer goods (Antrobus 1989, 20). These measures along with the stipulated focus on export production have resulted in increased unemployment, a decline in real wages for those fortunate enough to have regular incomes, a dramatic rise in the costs of living, and, with these, an increase in malnutrition and hunger, a general deterioration in public health, and an escalating incidence of drug abuse and violence—including violence against women (Antrobus 1989, 23). Conditions are so severe that economist Clive Thomas (1988, 369) poignantly argues that poor people cannot afford to live as well as nineteenth century slaves whose access to protein, carbohydrates, fuel, and work tools was more adequate. Those bearing the heaviest burden in coping with today's social and economic austerity are women, a large proportion of whom have the responsibility—whether they are formally employed or not—to support households and family networks (Bolles 1991).

Although it has sacrificed ordinary people's basic needs, the debt bondage and free trade strategy has successfully restored "the military and economic foundations of U.S. superiority . . . incorporating the Caribbean Basin countries into the U.S. military-industrial complex" (Deere et al. 1990, 157). A central aspect of the CBI has been the increased sale of U.S. exports to the Caribbean (McAfee 1991, 43). Exports from the Caribbean that receive duty-free entry into the U.S. market are produced in foreign, and to a considerable extent, U.S. controlled free-trade zones where items (usually those of apparel and electronics) are assembled from raw materials and capital goods imported from the U.S. In other words, the Caribbean has become an offshore site for branch plants that are not generating the backward linkages and horizontal integration necessary for stimulating the domestic sectors of Jamaica's economy.

Gender Inequality in Globalization

Transnational capital has appropriated the enterprising freedom to repatriate profits without any enforced obligations to invest in the host country's future; it has enjoyed the freedom to employ workers, to a great extent female, whose labor has been politically, legally, and culturally constructed to be cheap and expendable. As Enloe (1989, 160–163) argues, economic globalization depends upon laws and cultural presumptions about femininity, sexuality, and marriage that help to lower women's wages and benefits. For instance, transnational garment production has taken advantage of and reinforced the patriarchal assumptions that activities such as sewing are "natural" women's tasks requiring no special skill, training, or compensation; that jobs defined as skilled belong to men, who deserve to be remunerated for their special physical strength and training; that women are not the major breadwinners in their households and families and are really supported by their fathers or husbands (Safa 1994); and finally that women's needs should not direct the policies and practices of business management and development specialists.

The profitability, capital mobility, and structural power (Wolf 1990) constitutive of globalization are fundamentally gendered phenomena marked by a masculinist logic. Present-day strategies to adjust, stabilize, and facilitate capital accumulation implicate constructions of femininity and masculinity that, in effect, legitimate the super exploitation of the productive and reproductive labor of women, with women of color bearing the heaviest burdens (see Enloe 1989; Deere et al. 1990; Antrobus 1989) and being the most vulnerable targets of structural violence—the symbolic, psychological, and physical assaults against human subjectivities, physical bodies, and sociocultural integrity that emanate from situations and institutions structured in social, political, and economic dominance (Kohler 1978).

The misogynous symbolic assault against women is reflected in the language and images of promotional materials addressed to prospective investors in trade journals and industrial magazines as well as in fliers and posters at trade shows. For instance, a Jamaica Promotions Corporation (JAMPRO) advertisement highlighting investment opportunities on the island features an image of a black woman's shapely lower back, protruding buttocks (in Jockey briefs), and upper thighs (National Labor Committee 1992, 44). Inscribed across the underpants in large white print is the phrase: "A brief example of our work." Below this, under a sentence attesting to the high quality and productivity of Jamaican factories, is found in smaller print the statement: "From jeans to jackets—from suits to shorts—smart apparel manufacturers are *making it* in Jamaica" (emphasis added). "Making it" can be construed as a double or triple entendre evoking manufacture and profitmaking as well as the more risque connotations associated with female anatomy. The implicit set of meanings being manipulated relates to the hypersexuality that historically racist/sexist ideology has attributed to women of African descent. Jamaican female labor is *cheap* in the dual sense of low labor costs and the myth of unrestrained sexual availability. Drawing on stereotypic notions of African-Caribbean "promiscuity," the advertisement informs prospective manufacturers that they can "make it" with Jamaican female workers without any legal strings attached or long-term commitment. The foreign manufacturer can take advantage of this lucrative situation for at most—and often less than—75 cents an hour or anywhere from 13 percent to 24 percent of what is paid to American apparel workers (McAfee 1991, 83). According to a 1988 survey 80 percent of Kingston's free-trade zone workers earn less than U.S. $15 a week (McAfee 1991, 86). Although wonderful incentive for the investor, from the vantage point of the worker, this wage purchases less than 40 percent of a family's food needs (McAfee 1991, 24).

Beyond its decided class bias, Jamaica's current approach to development has a definite gender bias in that women's productive and reproductive roles are expected to bear the brunt and absorb the highest risks of both the export-growth and austerity facets of present-day policies. Caribbean feminist Peggy Antrobus (1989, 19) argues that structural adjustment policies in particular presuppose "a gender ideology [that is] fundamentally exploitative of women's time, labor, and sexuality." Poor women, whether employed in free-trade-zone factories or whether informally eking out a meagre livelihood in their ghetto households and neighborhoods, bear the burden of policies and programs that, in

effect even if not in design, contribute to what George Beckford (1972) called the "persistent poverty" characteristic of plantation and post-plantation societies in the throes of recolonization (*Race & Class* 1992) in late twentieth-century capitalism.

The Trickle-Down Effects of Free Trade Zones

The free-trade or export-processing zones established under JAMPRO and the program organized under section 807 of the U.S. Special Tariff Provisions represent a "type of unregulated trade, investment and employment that the [World] Bank believes ought to be in effect worldwide." The recipients of generous incentives, free trade zones do not pay "import duties and taxes on stock dividends," and they are free to transfer their profits from host countries. A state within a state, the free trade zone is unfriendly to unions (McAfee 1991, 84–85), and it has been given the license to exploit its host country's laborers, who are often forced to work overtime without any notice and denied sufficient time and facilities for rest and lunch breaks. In some cases, workers are frisked before they are allowed to use the restroom and, in the worst situations, are only permitted access to the restroom once a day (Ferguson 1992, 68–69; McAfee 1991, 85).

When export-processing-zone workers contest the free trade zone's cheap labor policy and, consequently, organize for better wages and work conditions, they risk being fired and blacklisted, which precludes their finding work in any other free-trade-zone factory. Despite the severe risks, Jamaican women have not accepted dehumanizing conditions without responding organizationally. For instance, in March 1988 2,000 women from Kingston's free trade zone went on a three-day strike (*Jamaican Weekly Gleaner* 1988a–d). The women complained of verbal and physical abuse, unreasonably low pay, and the lack of union representation. Initially, then Prime Minister Edward Seaga appointed a joint union-management council to investigate the workers' complaints; however, he eventually gave in to pressure from factory owners, who threatened that they would close down their plants if the government failed to live up to promises it made and if workers continued to exhibit "poor work attitudes."

Economic Desperation in the Informal Sector

Seaga's attitude that, no matter how bad the situation, free-trade-zone jobs are better than no free-trade-zone jobs is shared by many workers, who prefer these jobs over the insecure, unstable, and aggressively competitive work found in the informal economic sector (Deere et al. 1990). Free-trade-zone workers, nonetheless, are extremely vulnerable to losing their jobs. If they exhibit behavior that management construes as nonproductive and reflective of poor work attitudes, they face abuse or summary termination. Moreover, they are apt to be made expendable if factory owners decide to move on to more lucrative grounds in a country better able to enforce a cheaper wage labor force.

While wage workers frequently augment their income with informal means of generating additional income, close to 40 percent of Jamaican women—as compared with 12 percent of the male labor force—work primarily in the informal economy, where they predominate in household service and petty commerce (Deere et al. 1990, 67; Bolles 1991; Harrison 1991b). To maximize survival, informal-sector workers have to balance the competitive spirit of "aggressive hustling" with the cooperative spirit sustaining the extended kin and friendship networks through which goods, services, and cash are circulated for the sake of basic survival. In light of the increasing scarcity of cash, these extended exchange networks allow their impoverished participants to meet basic needs outside of formal market transactions.

While many women prefer factory jobs over informal means of subsistence, the reality is that there are few such job opportunities available. Moreover, the built-in expendability of free-trade-zone labor means that the export-processing proletariat cannot enjoy any real distance from the day-to-day reality of the informal sector and the people—like Beulah and Marie Brown—who operate within its sphere. While the full-time informal work force includes those with no recourse but the "underground" economy, there are, nonetheless, petty entrepreneurs for whom small-scale self-employment represents a meaningful source of livelihood preferable to work conditions in the free trade zone. Local residents' social criticism of the factory regime may amount to unemployed workers rationalizing the resentment they feel for being excluded from a wage-work opportunity. On the other hand, their criticism may also be an expression of a local knowledge cognizant of the contradictions and iniquities of the prevailing model of development, and its structure of employment/unemployment.

Many analysts claim that the individuated and present-day-oriented "aggressive hustling" characteristic of informal-sector activities "hinders the development of a sense of collective struggle" and contributes to "the fragmentation of the working class and a deterioration of its institutions" (Deere et al. 1990, 11–12). This predicament, they argue, "further deepens the social crisis." Under what circumstances can a sense of collective struggle emerge among those without any recourse but "hustling" to survive? What role does gender politics play in the development of collective consciousness-of-kind in the sociopolitical space of structural unemployment and informal-sector work? These are questions that inform the following analysis of the structural violence of poverty in the slum where Beulah Brown's story began.

Negotiating Crisis in a Downtown Constituency

Everyday life is literally a struggle against "sufferation" in a place like Oceanview where unemployment is extremely high; the violent rivalry between gang-organized clients of the country's two major political parties, the PNP and JLP, runs rampant; "Babylon," or what the Rastafari call the oppressive society and its repressive state apparatus, reveals the fullness of its terror-provoking face; and (paraphrasing Roger Abraham's [1983] book title) men-and-*women*-of-words engage in verbal performances punctuated by questions concerning the meaning of freedom and sovereignty for "sufferers" and "little people" who struggle to survive in a national context in which independence has represented a redefined legal status unaccompanied by a fundamental social and economic metamorphosis (Lewis 1968). The rising expectations and unfulfilled promises of independence and decolonization have wrought in the folk experience and sociopsychology a deep sense of disappointment, alienation, and anger, which informs agency among Oceanview's sufferers.

No-Man's-Land and Centerwomen's Space

According to most Kingstonians' cognitive maps, the uptown-downtown division is a central dimension in local social class and political geography. Also, within the space of the expansive downtown ghetto zone, partisan boundaries demarcate loci of safety, danger, and neutrality, all of which are contingent and subject to recodification. The neighborhoods that are viewed as "no-man's-lands" to most middle-class people, who are afraid to be "caught dead" most places downtown, are highly contested sites that are often reduced to virtual war zones, especially during election campaigns.

These ghetto zones or "no-man's-lands" are also gendered, as suggested by this figure of speech. Territories within and between neighborhoods have been masculinized and paramilitarized according to a cluster of sociocultural criteria grounded in a popular imagination shaped and promoted by the violence-glorifying, B-rated movies imported from the U.S. during the 1960s and early 1970s. More importantly, local constructions of masculinity are grounded in what Lacey (1977, 159) calls the guns/ganja/organized crime nexus that has internationalized Jamaican marijuana production and distribution since the late 1960s (Harrison 1990). Aided and abetted by the routinized gang-centered political violence through which many politicians expropriate power, the gunman syndrome that has swept across Jamaica's urban ghettoes draws upon and reconfigures traditional notions of lower-class African-Jamaican masculinity that privileges such "reputational" attributes as virility, physical prowess, toughness, and de-

fiance of authority (Wilson [1973] 1995; Whitehead 1986). Accordingly, masculinity is constructed in terms of the ability to be tough and defiant enough to use violence to conquer and control women and weaker men. In light of the salience of achieving a sense of social balance, this militarized manhood is most valued when it is balanced out by the "respectability" of being able to satisfy at least some of the material needs of one's offspring and "babymother" by "living by the gun." If a relative balance between reputation and respectability is not achieved, the gunman is judged to be "wicked"—a form of moral weakness.

Gunman values do not, however, stand uncontested. The paramilitarized masculinity of political gangs, drug posses, and their turfs and war zones is challenged both by peaceful men of street-corner networks, who manage to negotiate political neutrality, and by those women who claim local spaces and convert them into the sanctuaries, safety zones, and neutral interfaces (cf. Feldman 1991) of such nonpartisan fields of power as open markets, schools, churches, mutual-aid associations, and some "yards" or coresidential compounds. Peace-making women, similar in many respects to the "centerwomen" that Sacks (1984) analyzes in the context of workplace struggles in North Carolina, mobilize social power rooted in the familistic values and skills that enable and empower them to engage in effective communication, goal and priority setting, decision making, and conflict mediation and resolution.

In Oceanview, government- and political party-based domains are typically the primary and most visible loci of power, but at certain junctures partisanism and its attendant conflicts have been contained by truces negotiated and sustained for varying (but usually limited) periods of time. During peaceful phases, women-centered networks and associations (particularly the nonpartisan and multipurpose Blessed Sacrament School PTA, to which Beulah Brown belonged) have been visible agents of the microcultural change that has heightened social solidarity and consciousness-of-kind (cf. Velez-Ibanez 1983). However, these periods of calm and collective identity are vulnerable to being subverted by the victimization and violence that accompany electoral campaigns.

The Structure and Meanings of Violence

The worst case of political violence was in 1980 when the heated rivalry between the PNP's democratic socialism and the JLP's free-market strategy set the stage for an unprecedented level of violence. Kingston came to be described as the "Beirut of the Caribbean" and life in Oceanview was "the worst nightmare," as one local resident described to me. More recently, in early 1993, the Jamaican Weekly Gleaner (1993a–c) published numerous articles, some with front-page headlines, on violence and the general election that took place in March of that year. Whether the expected level of violence could be contained was a major concern expressed by journalists, politicians, the police commisioner, and a respected priest who runs a mission in a downtown ghetto.

Violence—whether perpetrated by politicized gangs, criminals, the police, or men against women—is an integral feature of life in Oceanview. It is a phenomenon that conditions the climate affecting not only local and national politics but also economic activities and patterns of association and social interaction. Oceanview residents are forced to live with and against violence that provides a basis, though not the sole one, for the meanings invested in local evaluations of the legitimacy of government and its policies of development and political participation. As an instrument and process in power contests, violence is constitutive of the sociocultural forms and meanings that inform and negotiate the terms of interaction, conflict, and political culture. Throughout Jamaica's history, violence has generated politically and culturally salient meanings since the initial colonization of the island and the subsequent formation of an exploitative plantation slavery society. Violence has not only served as an instrument of domination, it has also been deployed in protest and resistance, as exemplified in the case of slave rebellions and *marronage* in which the moral economy and cultural politics of slavery were forcefully contested (Campbell 1977).

In its duality, violence is salient in Jamaicans' historical memory and present-day experience, and in places like Oceanview its salience is reproduced in a local *realpolitik* that has been buttressed by the growing pattern of militarization affecting the state as well as criminal forces like drug posses. State militarization has been underwritten by CBI aid from the U.S., which has determined that regional security and U.S. dominance be achieved in the Caribbean Basin by any means necessary (see Harrison 1987a, 32; Barry et al. 1984). The broader context within which physical violence in its various forms can be situated is that of structural violence. According to Kohler's (1978) and other peace researchers' conceptualization, structural violence encompasses such assaults and violations against human rights and dignity as food shortages and hunger, pollution and environmental degradation, and police brutality—conditions engendered by the "situations, institutions, and social, political, and economic structures" (Haviland 1990, 458) that characterize the polarized economic growth associated with the concerted IMF/World Bank/CBI strategy for development.

As suggested above, the structural violence of development relies upon constructions of masculinity and femininity that help produce and reproduce the mobility and accumulation of transnational capital. Violence-legitimating constructions of masculinity are implicit in U.S.-supported, military-industrial policies implemented in Jamaica. In either direct or indirect ways, the managers and protectors of the postcolonial—or neocolonial—social order (namely, politicians, policemen, and army officers) are expected to take high, "manly" risks and negotiate danger to ensure such desired outcomes as profitability, law and order, and counter-insurrection. Even tourism advertisements appropriate images of legitimately militarized males in police or army uniforms (and welcoming, available, and compliant females in colorful peasant attire) in order to sell the comfort and safety of Jamaica's beach resorts to prospective foreign tourists (Enloe 1989, 32).

In Jamaica's clientelist political system, a form of "democracy by default" (Edie 1990), the managers of the postcolonial social order commonly expropriate and enforce their power through paramilitary means: deploying ghetto "forces" or partisan street gangs. The success of this tactic depends, of course, on a social construction of ghetto masculinity that privileges the dauntless toughness of living by the gun. Such a value is rooted in the forms of complicity and cooptation embodied in the current hegemonic structure of masculinized power.

Gendered Fields of Regenerative Power

Oceanview's struggle over war and peace, over repressive militarism and people-centered democracy is also a struggle over the reconstruction of both gender and development. On the sociopolitical terrain of peace mobilization, local agents contest and renegotiate the terms and meanings of gender identity, power, work, and development, especially as they apply to local community life.

Sociopolitical agency is constituted in gendered fields of power. Gendered politics, through which dominant gender ideologies are sometimes challenged and refashioned, plays an integral part in the microcultural processes that periodically give rise to emergent forms of class-cognizant solidarity. Such episodes enable wider networks of men and women to coalesce and defy the legitimacy of the state, whose seductively divisive rituals of marginality (Velez-Ibanez 1983) trap clients into vicious cycles of disenfranchisement.

During the 1970s and 1980s, Oceanview's political trajectory encompassed three phases (circa 1975, 1978–79, 1984–85) in which local social relations were marked by peaceful, bilateral, nonsectarian alliances, extra-local cohort formation, and increased inter-local consciousness-of-kind (Harrison 1987b). At these junctures there was a heightened recognition of the local consequences of underdevelopment and polarized economic growth, and a more explicitly articulated awareness of a connection between, on one hand, local poverty and political victimization and, on the other, national (and international) development strategies. At these moments of truce and reconcilia-

tion, the values and social power characteristic of women-centered sanctuaries and safety zones became more widespread.

Through the micro-transformative practices of these phases of reconciliation and solidarity, networks of local women in conjunction with peace-seeking men expressed their opposition to political violence, the politicization of scarce wage-work opportunities (generally public sector controlled), and the cultural construction of violence-glorifying definitions of ghetto manhood. In the process of contesting the paramilitarization of local masculinity as well as the masculinization of power in clientelist and partisan political spheres, these women redefined the meaning and purview of their womanhood. They reinterpreted and extended the meanings of the cultural principles of regeneration and reproduction invested in many African Caribbean notions of womanhood and mothering. According to folk sensibilities, mothering is a shared, co-operative-kin-network-based configuration and set of practices that involves nurturing, counseling, and healing dependents as well as fulfilling the obligations of meeting family needs through participation in the public arenas of work and sociopolitical engagement.

Oceanview's centerwomen applied these traditional principles to the extended, supra-kin public domain of neighborhood redevelopment—the term "redevelopment" signifying the renewal and reconstruction of the locality as a community and fictive kindred. Through their praxis in nonpartisan, multipurpose arenas like the Blessed Sacrament School PTA, these ghetto women asserted their collective familial responsibility and motherlike authority to challenge routinized political and criminal violence and to contest the hegemony of masculinist notions of power in the space of their everyday lives and lived experience. The polluted and violated space of the partisan political constituency was, hence, reclaimed and purified as an extended "yard." At once a space and a cluster of social relationships, a yard—especially as a metaphor for greater inclusiveness and cooperation—is reminiscent of the symbolically charged notion of "family land" that is believed to be the source of cosmopolitical and physical regeneration for both biological reproduction and folk-centered economic development (Carnegie 1987). Through trace-making efforts, centerwomen and their male allies reconstituted their base of survival by reclaiming the contested urban space of no-man's-land and converting it into a shared place of community.

Local articulations of social criticism and community solidarity confront nationwide forces that reduce ghetto sufferers to dispensable clients and pawns sacrificed to the secular deities of what Velez-Ibanez (1983) calls "rituals of marginality." The challenge to the gender and class ideologies embedded in the syndrome of political violence and in current poverty-perpetuating policies is a key element in the grassroots politics of survival and rehumanization found in places like Oceanview. Underpinning this woman-centered praxis is a deep, potentially subversive knowledge of a longstanding tradition of resisting and contesting the status quo and of celebrating the power of the relatively powerless to imagine—and struggle for—a community that privileges freedom. The freedom imagined is not that of capital mobility and accumulation, but that which is wedded to social justice and equality. Oceanview's centerwomen, like their counterparts throughout Jamaica and the Caribbean, are catalysts in grassroots responses to a crisis that reverberates transnationally, affecting both southern and northern hemispheres. Grassroots mobilizations—in the form of action groups, cooperatives, nongovernment organizations, and social movements—are expressing the urgent concerns and grievances of households, communities, and the informal sector in ways that the established political parties and trade unions have not (Deere et al. 1990, 101, 106). It is not at all surprising that in light of "the specific ways in which the crisis impinges upon women" they "have been among the first to protest and organize in new ways. "

End of Story Within a Story—for Now

Tired from feeling the weight of her 63 years, especially the past 10 of them, Mrs.

Brown complained to me about the prohibitive costs of living and the unjust formula being used to devalue the Jamaican dollar so as to make the economy more penetrable for foreign investment. "And all at the people's expense!" As we waited at the airport for my departure time, she remarked that she didn't know how she could have made it through all her trials and tribulations if it weren't for the grace of God who gave her industry, creativity, and a loving family as gifts; her church, upon which she had always been able to depend for both spiritual guidance and material aid; and Blessed Sacrament School, its PTA, and the various other activities and community services based on the grounds of that strategic local sanctuary from political warfare and economic desperation. When she was abroad she raised a respectable sum of money from her relatives and friends for the church and school that have helped sustain her family through plenty of hard times. She insisted that no amount of "gunshot or war" could ever dissuade her from giving back to and continuing to be a part of the vital organs of support and solidarity that have been integral to her sense of moral and sociopolitical agency. While committed to her Oceanview network of support and praxis, Mrs. Brown appreciated the freedom to go as she pleased or needed to and from the various sites of her international family.

It was time for me to go to my exit, so we kissed and hugged each other goodbye as we had done several times before. We promised to write and phone until we were able to meet again—whether in Jamaica or in the U.S. After all, she smiled, she had many other stories to tell me about her life as a hardworking Jamaican woman making her way in a difficult world.

I am back home now, but I can't help but think—and worry—about Beulah and Oceanview in light of the global restructuring that affects life in the Caribbean as well as in the U.S. , where the implementation of first world versions of structural adjustment are being felt and confronted. The economic restructuring occurring in the U.S. is only a variation on a wider structural adjustment theme reverberating across the globe. Policies implemented in the U.S. resemble the austerity measures the IMF and World Bank are imposing on "developing" nations: cutbacks in social spending and public investments in housing, education, and health care; deregulation of airline, trucking, banking, finance, and broadcasting industries; corporate union-busting; currency devaluation; divestment of public enterprises; the increasing privatization of public services; and dramatic alterations of the tax system, shifting the tax burden away from wealthy individuals and large corporations (Sparr 1992, 30–31).

Probing the political and moral economy of poverty in "the field" (cf. D'Amico-Samuels 1991) has led me to reconceptualize analytical units and boundaries in ways that discern and utilize points of articulation and conjuncture between, for instance, Beulah Brown and myself, and Jamaica and the U.S., for a deeper, more broadly situated, and more personally grounded understanding of structural adjustment's gendered assaults—its invidious structural violence.

Works Cited

Abrahams, Roger D. 1983. *The Man-of-Words in the West Indies: Performance and the Emergence of Creole Culture.* Baltimore: The Johns Hopkins University Press.

Antrobus, Peggy. 1989. Crisis, Challenge and the Experiences of Caribbean Women. *Caribbean Quarterly* 35 (1&2): 17–28.

Barry, Tom, et al. 1984. *The Other Side of Paradise: Foreign Control in the Caribbean.* New York: Grove Press.

Basch, Linda, Nina Glick Schiller, and Cristina Szanton Blanc. 1994. *Nations Unbound: Transnational Projects, Postcolonial Predicaments, and Deterritorialized Nation-States.* Langhorne, PA: Gordon and Breach Science Publishers.

Beckford, George. 1972. *Persistent Poverty: Under Development in Plantation Economies of the Third World.* New York: Oxford University Press.

Bolles, A. Lynn. 1991. Surviving Manley and Seaga: Case Studies of Women's Responses to Structural Adjustment Policies. *Review of Radical Political Economy* 23 (3&4): 20–36.

———. 1992. Common Ground of Creativity. *Cultural Survival Quarterly* (Winter): 34–37.

Campbell, Mavis C. 1977. Marronage in Jamaica: Its Origins in the Seventeenth Century. In *Comparative Perspectives on Slavery in New World Plantation Societies.* Ed. Vera Rubin and Arthur Tuden. *Annals of the New York Academy of Sciences* 292: 446–480.

Carnegie, Charles V. 1987. Is Family Land an Institution? In *Afro-Caribbean Villages in Historical Perspective. ACIJ Research Review no 2.* Kingston: African-Caribbean Institute of Jamaica: 83–99.

D'Amico-Samuels, Deborah. 1991. Undoing Fieldwork: Personal, Political, Theoretical, and Methodological Implications. In *Decolonizing Anthropology: Moving Further Toward an Anthropology for Liberation.* Ed. Faye V. Harrison. Washington, D. C.: American Anthropological Association.

Deere, Carmen Diana, et al. 1990. *In the Shadows of the Sun: Caribbean Development Alternatives and U.S. Policy.* Boulder: Westview Press.

Edie, Carlene. 1990. *Democracy by Default: Dependency and Clientelism in Jamaica.* Boulder: Lynne Rienner Publishers.

Enloe, Cynthia. 1989. *Bananas, Beaches, and Bases: Making Feminist Sense of International Politics.* Berkeley: University of California Press.

Feldman, Allen. 1991. *Formations of Violence: The Narrative of the Body and Political Terror in Northern Ireland.* Chicago: University of Chicago Press.

Ferguson, James. 1992. Jamaica: Stories of Poverty. *Race & Class* 34 (1): 61–72.

Harrison, Faye V. 1987a. Crime, Class, and Politics in Jamaica. *TransAfrica Forum* 5 (1): 29–38.

———. 1987b. Gangs, Grassroots Politics, and the Crisis of Dependent Capitalism in Jamaica. In *Perspectives in U.S. Marxist Anthropology.* Ed. David Hakken and Hanna Lessinger. Boulder: Westview Press.

———. 1988. The Politics of Social Outlawry in Urban Jamaica. *Urban Anthropology and Studies in Cultural Systems and World Economic Development* 17 (2&3): 259–277.

———. 1990. Jamaica and the International Drug Economy. *TransAfrica Forum* 7 (3): 49–57.

———. 1991a. Ethnography as Politics. In *Decolonizing Anthropology: Moving Further Toward an Anthropology for Liberation.* Ed. Faye V. Harrison. Washington, D.C.: American Anthropological Association.

———. 1991b. Women in Jamaica's Urban Informal Economy: Insights from a Kingston Slum. In *Third World Women and the Politics of Feminism.* Ed. Chandia T. Mohanty et al. Bloomington: Indiana University Press.

Haviland, William. 1990. *Cultural Anthropology*, 6th ed. Fort Worth: Holt, Rinehart and Winston.

Ho, Christine G. T. 1993. The Internationalization of Kinship and the Feminization of Caribbean Migration: The Case of Afro-Trinidadian Immigrants in Los Angeles. *Human Organization* 52(1): 32–40

Jamaican Weekly Gleaner. 1988a JIC [Joint Industrial Council] for Free Zone Workers. 14 March, 13.

———. 1988b. Textile Workers Strike to Get "a Better Deal." 14 March, 28.

———. 1988c. More Garment Workers Strike. 21 March, 24.

———. 1988d. Free Zone Operators "Going Public" with Grouse. 28 March, 5.

———. 1993a. Peace Treaty Signed. 26 February, 3.

———. 1993b. Nomination Day Violence. 19 March, 2.

———. 1993c. Landslide Election Marred by Bungling, Violence. April 2, 4.

Köhler, Gemot, 1978. Global Apartheid. *World Order Models Project*. Working Paper, No 7. New York: Institute for World Order.

Lacey, Terry. 1977. *Violence and Politics in Jamaica, 1960–70: Internal Security in a Developing Country*. Manchester: Manchester University Press.

Lewis, Gordon K. 1968. *The Growth of the Modern West Indies*. New York: Monthly Review Press.

McAfee, Kathy. 1991 *Storm Signals: Structural Adjustment and Development Alternatives in the Caribbean*. Boston: South End Press.

National Labor Committee. 1992. *Preliminary Report: Paying to Lose Our Jobs*. New York: National Labor Committee Education Fund in Support of Worker and Human Rights in Central America.

Pan American Health Organization/World Health Organization. 1992. *The Health of Women in the English Speaking Caribbean*.

Phillips, Daphene. 1994. The IMP, Structural Adjustment and Health in the Caribbean: Policy Change in Health Care in Trinidad and Tobago. *Twenty-first Century Policy Review* 2 (1&2): 129–149.

Race & Class. 1992. *The New Conquistadors* 34 (1) (July–Sept.): 1–114.

Sacks, Karen Brodkin. 1984. Computers, Ward Secretaries, and a Walkout in a Southern Hospital. In *My Troubles Are Going to Have Trouble with Me: Everyday Trials and Triumphs of Women Workers*. Ed. Karen Brodkin Sacks and Dorothy Remy. New Brunswick: Rutgers University Press.

Safa, Helen. 1994. *The Myth of the Male Breadwinner: Women and Industrialization in the Caribbean*. Boulder: Westview Press.

Sparr, Pamela. 1992. How We Got into This Mess and Ways to Get Out. *Ms.* March/April, 130.

——. 1994. ed. *Mortgaging Women's Lives. Feminist Critiques of Structural Adjustment*. London: Zed Books.

Statistical Institute of Jamaica. 1991. *Statistical Yearbook of Jamaica*. Kingston: Statistical Institute of Jamaica.

Thomas, Clive Y. 1988. *The Poor and the Powerless: Economic Policy and Change in the Caribbean*. New York: Monthly Review Press.

Velez-Ibanez, Carlos. 1983. *Rituals of Marginality: Politics, Process, and Culture Change in Urban Central Mexico, 1969-74*. Berkeley: University of California Press.

Whitehead, Tony Larry. 1986. Breakdown, Resolution, and Coherence: The Fieldwork Experiences of a Big, Brown, Pretty-Talking Man in a West Indian Community. In *Self, Sex, and Gender in Cross-Cultural Fieldwork*. Ed. Tony Larry Whitehead and Mary Ellen Conaway. Urbana: University of Illinois Press.

Wilson, Peter J. [1973] 1995. *Crab Antics: The Social Anthropology of English-Speaking Societies of the Caribbean*. Reprint, Prospect Heights, IL: Waveland Press.

Wolf, Eric. 1990. Distinguished Lecture: Facing Power—Old Insights, New Questions. *American Anthropologist* 92 (3): 586–596.

Discussion Questions

1. The result of late twentieth-century structural adjustment policies was greater poverty and food insecurity in developing nations such as Jamaica. In the end, debtor nations were less, not more, able to sustain economic growth and repay debt. The lives of individuals like Mrs. Brown became more precarious. Who benefited from these policies?

2. How does the life of a single woman such as Mrs. Brown provide insight into the effect of national and international policies on gender, race, and class in other countries and in our own?

3. How does Mrs. Brown's story illustrate the interdependency of families and communities facing economic hardship?

20
Asymmetries
Women and Men Talking at Cross-Purposes

Deborah Tannen

Have you ever wondered why men don't ask for directions and why women do? Or perhaps you would like to know why women tend to offer sympathy and advice when their friend comes to them with a problem, while men tend to dismiss the problem outright, refusing to offer advice of any kind? These are just the sorts of questions Deborah Tannen asks in her article, "Asymmetries: Women and Men Talking at Cross-Purposes." Gender is the solid backdrop and foreground of this piece, yet Tannen's findings suggest implications for issues of race and class as well. Much of Tannen's argument hinges on a sort of White, middle-class model of male-female relations, that is, a "men as problem solvers-women as nurturers" model. However, African American history and culture, to paint a broad stroke, make clear that women have often had to take on men's roles while men have taken on caretaking roles, specifically with children. Latinas as well have been for generations responsible for taking on work as domestics and other low-wage work that White women have not typically been required to do; women's liberation and freedom to work did not mean menial work.

This could of course have ramifications for male-female interactions. In one telling passage from her book, Schoolsmart and Motherwise: Working-Class Women's Identity and Schooling, *Wendy Luttrell notes that White working-class women in her study coded men's work as involving what they called "real intelligence," which meant that the work required specific skills sets that "women's work" did not exhibit (a different chapter from her book is featured in this volume). However, Luttrell notes, working-class Black women respondents believed women and men capable of "real intelli-gence," which fit a more holistic, gendered definition of resolving issues and dealing with children as well. Luttrell notes that this would make sense since Black men were systematically barred from guilds and apprenticeships for many skilled labor positions. It would be fitting, then, for "real intelligence" to differ in its meaning to different racial groups.[1] In addition, such research also points up the significance of social class in male-female conversational forms. Perhaps, as Tannen would suggest, "real men" do not ask for directions; yet, men on the edge financially might also take their insistence on being the competent one who is in control to extremes, as in cases of abuse. In that scenario, it would be the man's desire to show knowledge and superior status in the hierarchy that would lead to his underscoring his wife's inferiority, even with fists. Further, as William Labov's article in this volume points out, communication styles may be viewed through a lens of race and class difference working in combination. In that piece, it is clear that the communication styles of poor ghetto youth are misinterpreted as inferior by White middle-class researchers. Tannen, then, offers an excellent jumping off point from which we can explore how women and men fail to understand each other. And, adding race and class to this primarily gendered framework would add complexity to an already promising field of study.*

Eve had a lump removed from her breast. Shortly after the operation, talking to her sister, she said that she found it upsetting to have been cut into, and that looking at the stitches was distressing because they left a seam that had changed the contour of her breast. Her sister said, "I know. When I had my operation I felt the same way." Eve made the same observation to her friend Karen, who said, "I know. It's like your body has been violated." But when she told her husband, Mark, how she felt, he said, "You can have plastic surgery to cover up the scar and restore the shape of your breast."

Eve had been comforted by her sister and her friend, but she was not comforted by Mark's comment. Quite the contrary, it upset her more. Not only didn't she hear what she wanted, that he understood her feelings, but, far worse, she felt he was asking her to undergo more surgery just when she was telling him how much this operation had upset her. "I'm not having any more surgery!" she protested. "I'm sorry you don't like the way it looks." Mark was hurt and puzzled. "I don't care," he protested. "It doesn't bother me at all." She asked, "Then why are you telling me to have plastic surgery?" He answered, "Because you were saying *you* were upset about the way it looked."

Eve felt like a heel: Mark had been wonderfully supportive and concerned throughout her surgery. How could she snap at him because of what he said—"just words"—when what he had done was unassailable? And yet she had perceived in his words metamessages that cut to the core of their relationship. It was self-evident to him that his comment was a reaction to her complaint, but she heard it as an independent complaint of his. He thought he was reassuring her that she needn't feel bad about her scar because there was something she could do about it. She heard his suggestion that she do something about the scar as evidence that he was bothered by it. Furthermore, whereas she wanted reassurance that it was normal to feel bad in her situation, his telling her that the problem could easily be fixed implied she had no right to feel bad about it.

Eve wanted the gift of understanding, but Mark gave her the gift of advice. He was taking the role of problem solver, whereas she simply wanted confirmation for her feelings.

A similar misunderstanding arose between a husband and wife following a car accident in which she had been seriously injured. Because she hated being in the hospital, the wife asked to come home early. But once home, she suffered pain from having to move around more. Her husband said, "Why didn't you stay in the hospital where you would have been more comfortable?" This hurt her because it seemed to imply that he did not want her home. She didn't think of his suggestion that she should have stayed in the hospital as a response to her complaints about the pain she was suffering; she

thought of it as an independent expression of his preference not to have her at home.

They're My Troubles—Not Yours

If women are often frustrated because men do not respond to their troubles by offering matching troubles, men are often frustrated because women do. Some men not only take no comfort in such a response, they take offense. For example, a woman told me that when her companion talks about a personal concern—for example, his feelings about growing older—she responds, "I know how you feel; I feel the same way. To her surprise and chagrin, he gets annoyed; he feels she is trying to take something away from him by denying the uniqueness of his experience.

A similar miscommunication was responsible for the following interchange, which began as a conversation and ended as an argument:

> HE: I'm really tired. I didn't sleep well last night.
>
> SHE: I didn't sleep well either. I never do.
>
> HE: Why are you trying to belittle me?
>
> SHE: I'm not! I'm just trying to show that I understand!

This woman was not only hurt by her husband's reaction; she was mystified by it. How could he think she was belittling him? By "belittle me," he meant "belittle my experience." He was filtering her attempts to establish connection through his concern with preserving independence and avoiding being put down.

I'll Fix It for You

Women and men are both often frustrated by the other's way of responding to their expression of troubles. And they are further hurt by the other's frustration. If women resent men's tendency to offer solutions to problems, men complain about women's refusal to take action to solve the problems they complain about. Since many men see themselves as problem solvers, a complaint or a trouble is a challenge to their ability to think of a solution, just as a woman presenting a broken bicycle or stalling car poses a challenge to their ingenuity in fixing it. But whereas many women appreciate help in fixing mechanical equipment, few are inclined to appreciate help in "fixing" emotional troubles.

The idea that men are problem solvers was reinforced by the contrasting responses of a husband and wife to the same question on a radio talk show. The couple, Barbara and William Christopher, were discussing their life with an autistic child. The host asked if there weren't times when they felt sorry for themselves and wondered, "Why me?" Both said no, but they said it in different ways. The wife deflected attention from herself: She said that the real sufferer was her child. The husband said, "Life is problem solving. This is just one more problem to solve."

This explains why men are frustrated when their sincere attempts to help a woman solve her problems are met not with gratitude but with disapproval. One man reported being ready to tear his hair out over a girlfriend who continually told him about problems she was having at work but refused to take any of the advice he offered. Another man defended himself against his girlfriend's objection that he changed the subject as soon as she recounted something that was bothering her: "What's the point of talking about it any more?" he said. "You can't do anything about it." Yet another man commented that women seem to wallow in their problems, wanting to talk about them forever, whereas he and other men want to get them out and be done with them, either by finding a solution or by laughing them off.

Trying to solve a problem or fix a trouble focuses on the message level of talk. But for most women who habitually report problems at work or in friendships, the message is not the main point of complaining. It's the metamessage that counts: Telling about a problem is a bid for an expression of understanding ("I know how you feel") or a similar complaint ("I felt the same way when something similar happened to me"). In other words, troubles talk is intended to reinforce rapport by sending the metamessage "We're the same; you're not alone." Women are frustrated when they not only don't get this reinforcement but, quite the opposite, feel dis-

tanced by the advice, which seems to send the metamessage "We're not the same. You have the problems; I have the solutions."

Furthermore, mutual understanding is symmetrical, and this symmetry contributes to a sense of community. But giving advice is asymmetrical. It frames the advice giver as more knowledgeable, more reasonable, more in control—in a word, one-up. And this contributes to the distancing effect.

The assumption that giving advice can be oneupmanship underlies an observation that appeared in a book review. In commenting on Alice Adams' *After You've Gone*, reviewer Ron Carlson explained that the title story is a letter from a woman to a man who has left her for a younger woman. According to Carlson, the woman informs her former lover about her life "and then steps up and clobbers him with sage advice. Here is clearly a superior woman. . . ." Although we do not know the intention of the woman who wrote the story, we see clearly that the man who reviewed it regards giving advice as a form of attack and sees one who gives advice as taking a superior position.

Parallel Tracks

These differences seem to go far back in our growing up, A sixteen-year-old girl told me she tends to hang around with boys rather than girls. To test my ideas, I asked her whether boys and girls both talk about problems. Yes, she assured me, they both do. Do they do it the same way? I asked. Oh, no, she said. The girls go on and on. The boys raise the issue, one of them comes up with a solution, and then they close the discussion.

Women's and men's frustrations with each other's ways of dealing with troubles talk amount to applying interpretations based on one system to talk that is produced according to a different system. Boys and men do not respond to each other the way women respond to each other in troubles talk. The roots of the very different way that men respond to talk about troubles became clear to me when I compared the transcript of a pair of tenth-grade boys talking to each other to the transcripts of girls' conversations from videotapes of best friends talking, recorded as part of a research project by psychologist Bruce Dorval.

Examining the videotaped conversations, I found that the boys and girls, who expressed deep concerns to each other, did it in different ways—ways that explain the differences that come up in daily conversations between women and men. The pairs of girls at both the sixth grade and tenth grade talked at length about one girl's problems. The other girl pressed her to elaborate, said, "I know," and gave supporting evidence. The following brief excerpts from the transcripts show the dramatic difference between the girls and boys.

The tenth-grade girls are talking about Nancy's problems with her boyfriend and her mother. It emerges that Nancy and Sally were both part of a group excursion to another state. Nancy suddenly left the group and returned home early at her mother's insistence. Nancy was upset about having to leave early. Sally reinforces Nancy's feelings by letting her know that her sudden departure was also upsetting to her friends:

NANCY: God, it was *bad*. I couldn't believe she made me go home.

SALLY: I thought it was kind of weird though. I mean, one minute we were going out and the next minute Nancy's going, "Excuse me, gotta be going." [Both laugh] I didn't know what was going *on*, and Judy comes up to me and she whispers (the whole place knows), "Do you know that Nancy's going home?" And I go, "What?" [Both laugh] "Nancy's going home." I go, *"Why?"* She goes, "Her mom's making her." I go [makes a face], "Ah," She comes back and goes, "Nancy's left." Well, I said, "WELL, that was a fine thing TO DO, she didn't even come and say goodbye." And she starts boiling all over me. I go [mimicking yelling], *"All right!"* She was upset, Judy. I was like "God"—

Sally's way of responding to her friend's troubles is to confirm Nancy's feelings of distress that her mother made her leave the trip early, by letting her know that her leaving upset her friends. In contrast, examining the transcript of a conversation between boys of the same

age shows how differently they respond to each other's expressions of troubles.

The tenth-grade boys also express deep feelings. Theirs too is troubles talk, but it is troubles talk with a difference. They don't concentrate on the troubles of one, pursuing, exploring, and elaborating. Instead, each one talks about his own troubles and dismisses the other's as insignificant.

In the first excerpt from these boys' conversation, Richard says he feels bad because his friend Mary has no date for an upcoming dance, and Todd dismisses his concern:

RICHARD: God, I'm going to feel so bad for her if she stays home.

TODD: She's not going to stay home, it's ridiculous. Why doesn't she just ask somebody?

Yet Todd himself is upset because he has no date for the same dance. He explains that he doesn't want to ask Anita, and Richard, in turn, scoffs at his distress:

TODD: I felt so bad when she came over and started talking to me last night.

RICHARD: Why?

TODD: I don't know. I felt uncomfortable, I guess.

RICHARD: **I'll never understand that.** [Laugh]

Far from trying to show that he understands, Richard states flatly that he doesn't, as shown in boldface type.

Richard then tells Todd that he is afraid that he has a drinking problem. Todd responds by changing the subject to something that is bothering him, his feelings of alienation:

RICHARD: When I took Anne home last night she told me off.

TODD: Really?

. . .

RICHARD: You see when she found out what happened last Thursday night between Sam and me?

TODD: Mhm.

RICHARD: She knew about that. And she just said— and then she started talking about drinking. You know? . . . And then she said, you know, "You, how you hurt everybody when you do it. You're always cranky." And she just said, "I don't like it. You hurt Sam. You hurt Todd. You hurt Mary. You hurt Lois."

. . .

I mean, when she told me, you know I guess I was kind of stunned. [Pause] I didn't really drink that much.

TODD: **Are you still talking to Mary, a lot, I mean?**

RICHARD: Am I still talking to Mary?

TODD: Yeah, 'cause that's why—that's why I was mad Friday.

RICHARD: Why?

TODD: Because.

RICHARD: 'Cause why?

TODD: 'Cause I didn't know why you all just wa- I mean I just went back upstairs for things, then y'all never came back. I was going, "Fine. I don't care." I said, "He's going to start this again."

As the lines printed in boldface show when Richard says that he is upset because Anne told him he behaved badly when he was drunk, Todd responds by bringing up his own concern: He feels left out, and he was hurt when Richard disappeared from a party with his friend Mary.

Throughout the conversation, Todd expresses distress over feeling alienated and left out. Richard responds by trying to argue Todd out of the way he feels. When Todd says he felt out of place at a party the night before, Richard argues:

RICHARD: **How could you feel out of place? You knew Lois, and you knew Sam.**

TODD: I don't know. I just felt really out of place and then last night again at the party, I mean, Sam was just running around, he knew everyone from the sorority. There was about five.

RICHARD: **Oh, no, he didn't.**

TODD: He knew a lot of people. He was—I don't know.

RICHARD: **Just Lois. He didn't know everybody.**

. . .

TODD: I just felt really out of place that day, all over the place. I used to feel, I mean—

RICHARD: Why?

TODD: I don't know. I don't even feel right in school anymore.

RICHARD: I don't know, last night, I mean—

TODD: I think I know what Ron Cameron and them feels like now. [Laugh]

RICHARD: [Laugh] **No, I don't think you feel as bad as Ron Cameron feels.**

TODD: I'm kidding.

RICHARD: Mm-mm. **Why should you? You know more people—**

TODD: I can't talk to anyone anymore.

RICHARD: You know more people than me.

By telling Todd that his feelings are unjustified and incomprehensible, Richard is not implying that he doesn't care. He clearly means to comfort his friend, to make him feel better. He's implying, "You shouldn't feel bad because your problems aren't so bad."

Matching Troubles

The very different way that women respond to the telling of troubles is dramatized in a short story, "New Haven" by Alice Mattison. Eleanor tells Patsy that she has fallen in love with a married man. Patsy responds by first displaying understanding and then offering a matching revelation about a similar experience:

"Well," says Patsy, "I know how you feel."
"You do?"
"In a way, I do. Well, I should tell you, I've been sleeping with a married man for two years."

Patsy then tells Eleanor about her affair and how she feels about it. After they discuss Patsy's affair, however, Patsy says:

"But you were telling me about this man and I cut you off. I'm sorry. See? I'm getting self-centered."

"It's OK." But she is pleased again.

The conversation then returns to Eleanor's incipient affair. Thus Patsy responds first by confirming Eleanor's feelings and matching her experience, reinforcing their similarity, and then by encouraging Eleanor to tell more. Within the frame of Patsy's similar predicament, the potential asymmetry inherent in revealing personal problems is avoided, and the friendship is brought into balance.

What made Eleanor's conversation with Patsy so pleasing to Eleanor was that they shared a sense of how to talk about troubles, and this reinforced their friendship. Though Eleanor raised the matter of her affair, she did not elaborate on it until Patsy pressed her to do so. In another story by the same author, "The Knitting," a woman named Beth is staying with her sister in order to visit her sister's daughter Stephanie in a psychiatric hospital. While there, Beth receives a disturbing telephone call from her boyfriend, Alec. Having been thus reminded of her troubles, she wants to talk about them, but she refrains, because her sister doesn't ask. She feels required, instead, to focus on her sister's problem, the reason for her visit:

> She'd like to talk about her muted half-quarrels with Alec of the last weeks, but her sister does not ask about the phone call. Then Beth thinks they should talk about Stephanie.

The women in these stories are balancing a delicate system by which troubles talk is used to confirm their feelings and create a sense of community.

When women confront men's ways of talking to them, they judge them by the standards of women's conversational styles. Women show concern by following up someone else's statement of trouble by questioning her about it. When men change the subject, women think they are showing a lack of sympathy—a failure of intimacy. But the failure to ask probing questions could just as well be a way of respecting the other's need for independence. When Eleanor tells Patsy that she is in love with Peter, Patsy asks, "Are you sleeping with him?" This exploration of Eleanor's topic could well strike many men—and some women—as intrusive, though Eleanor takes it as a show of interest that nourishes their friendship.

Women tend to show understanding of another woman's feelings. When men try to reassure women by telling them that their situation is not so bleak, the women hear their feelings being belittled or discounted. Again, they encounter a failure of intimacy just when they were bidding to reinforce it. Trying to trigger a symmetrical communication, they end up in an asymmetrical one.

A Different Symmetry

The conversation between Richard and Todd shows that although the boys' responses are asymmetrical if looked at separately—each dismisses the other's concerns—they are symmetrical when looked at together: Todd responds to Richard's concern about his drinking in exactly the same way that Richard responds to Todd's feeling of alienation, by denying it is a problem:

RICHARD: Hey, man, I just don't feel—I mean, after what Anne said last night, I just don't feel like doing that.

TODD: **I don't think it was that way. You yourself knew it was no big problem.**

RICHARD: Oh, Anne—Sam told Anne that I fell down the levee.

TODD: **It's a lie.**

RICHARD: I didn't fall. I slipped, slid. I caught myself.

TODD: **Don't worry about it.**

RICHARD: But I do, kind of. I feel funny in front of Sam. I don't want to do it in front of you.

TODD: **It doesn't matter 'cause sometimes you're funny when you're off your butt.**

Todd denies that Richard was so drunk he was staggering ("It's a lie") and then says that even if he was out of control, it wasn't bad; it was funny.

In interpreting this conversation between tenth-grade boys, I initially saw their mutual reassurances and dismissals, and their mutual revelations of troubles, in terms of connection and sameness. But another perspective is possible. Their conversation may be touching precisely because it was based on asymmetries of status—or, more precisely, a deflecting of such asymmetries. When Todd tells his troubles, he puts himself in a potentially one-down position and invites Richard to take a one-up position by disclaiming troubles and asymmetrically offering advice or sympathy. By offering troubles of his own, Richard declines to take the superior position and restores their symmetrical footing, sending the metamessage "We're just a couple of guys trying to make it in a world that's tough on both of us, and both of us are about equally competent to deal with it."

From this perspective, responding as a woman might—for example by saying, "I can see how you feel; you must feel awful; so would I if it happened to me"—would have a totally different meaning for boys, since they would be inclined to interpret it through the lens of status. Such a response would send a metamessage like "Yes, I know, you incompetent jerk. I know how awful you must feel. If I were as incompetent as you, I'd feel the same way. But, lucky for you, I'm not, and I can help you out here, because I'm far too talented to be upset by a problem like that." In other words, refraining from expressing sympathy is generous, insofar as sympathy potentially condescends.

Women are often unhappy with the reactions they get from men when they try to start troubles talk, and men are often unhappy because they are accused of responding in the wrong way when they are trying to be helpful. But Richard and Todd seem satisfied with each other's ways of reacting to their troubles. And their ways make sense. When men and women talk to each other, the problem is that each expects a different kind of response. The men's approach seeks to assuage feelings indirectly by attacking their cause. Since women expect to have their feelings supported, the men's approach makes them feel that they themselves are being attacked.

Don't Ask

Talking about troubles is just one of many conversational tasks that women and men view differently, and that consequently cause trouble in talk between them. Another is asking for information. And this difference too is traceable to the asymmetries of status and connection.

A man and a woman were standing beside the information booth at the Washington Folk Life Festival, a sprawling complex of booths and displays. "You ask," the man was saying to the woman, "I don't ask."

Sitting in the front seat of the car beside Harold, Sybil is fuming. They have been driving around for half an hour looking for a street he is sure is close by. Sybil is angry not because Harold does not know the way, but because he insists on trying to find it himself rather than stopping and asking someone. Her anger stems from viewing his behavior through the lens of her own. If she were driving, she would have asked directions as soon as she realized she didn't know which way to go, and they'd now be comfortably ensconced in their friends' living room instead of driving in circles, as the hour gets later and later. Since asking directions does not make Sybil uncomfortable, refusing to ask makes no sense to her. But in Harold's world, driving around until he finds his way is the reasonable thing to do, since asking for help makes him uncomfortable. He's avoiding that discomfort and trying to maintain his sense of himself as a self-sufficient person.

Why do many men resist asking for directions and other kinds of information? And, it is just as reasonable to ask why is it that many women don't? By the paradox of independence and intimacy, there are two simultaneous and different metamessages implied in asking for and giving information. Many men tend to focus on one, many women on the other.

When you offer information, the information itself is the message. But the fact that you have the information, and the person you are speaking to doesn't, also sends a metamessage of superiority. If relations are inherently hierarchical, then the one who has more information is framed as higher up on the ladder, by virtue of being more knowledgeable and competent. From this perspective, finding one's own way is an essential part of the independence that men perceive to be a prerequisite for self-respect. If self-respect is bought at the cost of a few extra minutes of travel time, it is well worth the price.

Because they are implicit, metamessages are hard to talk about. When Sybil begs to know why Harold won't just ask someone for directions, he answers in terms of the message, the information: He says there's no point in asking, because anyone he asks may not know and may give him wrong directions. This is theoretically reasonable. There are many countries, such as, for example, Mexico, where it is standard procedure for people to make up directions rather than refuse to give requested information. But this explanation frustrates Sybil, because it doesn't make sense to her. Although she realizes that someone might give faulty directions, she believes this is relatively unlikely, and surely it cannot happen every time. Even if it did happen, they would be in no worse shape than they are in now anyway.

Part of the reason for their different approaches is that Sybil believes that a person who doesn't know the answer will say so, because it is easy to say, "I don't know." But Harold believes that saying "I don't know" is humiliating, so people might as well take a wild guess. Because of their different assumptions, and the invisibility of framing, Harold and Sybil can never get to the bottom of this difference; they can only get more frustrated with each other. Keeping talk on the message level is common, because it is the level we are most clearly aware of. But it is unlikely to resolve confusion since our true motivations lie elsewhere.

To the extent that giving information, directions, or help is of use to another, it reinforces bonds between people. But to the extent that it is asymmetrical, it creates hierarchy: Insofar as giving information frames one as the expert, superior in knowledge, and the other as uninformed, inferior in knowledge, it is a move in the negotiation of status.

It is easy to see that there are many situations where those who give information are higher in status. For example, parents explain things to children and answer their questions, just as teachers give information to students. An awareness of this dynamic underlies one requirement for proper behavior at Japanese dinner entertainment, according to anthropologist Harumi Befu. In order to help the highest-status member of the party to dominate the conversation, others at the dinner are expected to ask him questions that they know he can answer with authority.

Because of this potential for asymmetry, some men resist receiving information from others, especially women, and some women are cautious about stating information that they know, especially to men. For example, a man with whom I discussed these dynamics later told me that my perspective clarified a comment made by his wife. They had gotten into their car and were about to go to a destination that she knew well but he did not know at all. Consciously resisting an impulse to just drive off and find his own way, he began by asking his wife if she had any advice about the best way to get there. She told him the way, then added, "But I don't know. That's how I would go, but there might be a better way." Her comment was a move to redress the imbalance of power created by her knowing something he didn't know. She was also saving face in advance, in case he decided not to take her advice. Furthermore, she was reframing her directions as "just a suggestion" rather than "giving instructions."...

The View from a Different Mountain

In a story by Alice Mattison, "The Colorful Alphabet," a man named Joseph invites another man, Gordon, to visit his family in the country because Gordon's wife has just left him. During the visit, they all climb a mountain. On the way down, they stop to rest, and Gordon realizes that he left his beloved old knapsack on the mountaintop. Joseph volunteers to climb back up to get it because Gordon is not used to climbing and his feet are sore. Joseph's wife goes with him, but she is too tired to climb all the way to the top, and he leaves her on the path to complete the mission himself. When he finds her again, he is empty-handed: The bag wasn't there. He says then that he knew it wouldn't be because he had seen a man carrying the bag pass them when they all stopped to rest. He explains why he didn't just say that he had seen someone go by with the bag: "I couldn't tell him I'd seen it and hadn't been smart enough to get it back for him." Instead, he says, "I had to *do* something."

Exhausted and frustrated, the wife is not so much angry as incredulous. She can't understand how he could have preferred reclimbing the mountain (and making her reclimb it too) to admitting that he had seen someone carrying Gordon's bag. "I would never have done that," she says, but she speaks "more in wonder than anger." She explains, "I'd have just blurted it out. I'd have been upset about making the mistake—but not about people *knowing*. That part's not a big deal to me." Her husband says, "Oh, is it ever a big deal to me."

This story supports the view of men's style that I have been proposing. Joseph wanted to help Gordon, and he did not want to let it be known that he had done something he thought stupid. His impulse to do something to solve the problem was stronger than his impulse not to climb a mountain twice. But what struck me most strongly about the story was the wife's reflections on the experience. She thinks:

It was one of the occasional moments when I'm certain I haven't imagined him: I would never have done what he'd done, wouldn't have dreamt it or invented it—Joseph was, simply, *not me*.

This excerpt reflects what may be the subtlest yet deepest source of frustration and puzzlement arising from the different ways that women and men approach the world. We feel we know how the world is, and we look to others to reinforce that conviction. When we see others acting as if the world were an entirely different place from the one we inhabit, we are shaken.

We look to our closest relationships as a source of confirmation and reassurance. When those closest to us respond to events differently than we do, when they say things that we could not imagine saying in the same circumstances, the ground on which we stand seems to tremble and our footing is suddenly unsure. Being able to understand why this

happens—*why* and *how* our partners and friends, though like us in many ways, are *not* us and different in other ways—is a crucial step toward feeling that our feet are planted on firm ground.

Note

1. See Luttrell, W. (1997). *Schoolsmart and Motherwise: Working-Class Women's Identity and Schooling* (pp. 13–36). New York: Routledge.

Discussion Questions

1. Using Tannen's framework, explain why men do not ask for directions and women do? Do you think these findings still apply today, years after Tannen's research was published?

2. Can you think of other ways, beyond those described above, that Tannen's work might be expanded to encompass race and class? How would the model Tannen uses need to be altered to take the other variables of race and class into account with regard to male-female relationships?

3. Can you describe a personal example that illustrates Tannen's arguments? Give examples from your relationships with men and women.

4. Have you ever felt as a male or female that your method of conversing was more attuned to and like that of the opposite sex? In other words, might you be a woman who tends to think in terms of problem-solving, underscoring one's own competence and control, and valuing status and hierarchy? By the same token, might you be a man who tends to think terms of creating harmony and community, being nurturing of and sympathetic toward others? Is it possible to straddle both these modes of understanding the world in your own behavior, or is there too much tension between them?

21

Cuban Jewish Women in Miami

A Triple Identity

Hannah Schiller Wartenberg

Hannah Schiller Wartenberg interviewed a group of Miami women with a triple identity. They are Spanish-speaking Cuban immigrants, but unique among Cuban-Americans and indeed among the vast majority of Spanish-speakers in the United States; they are Jewish. Wartenberg seeks to understand why their religious identity is the most salient and how, despite being American citizens with no desire to return to Cuba, they remain essentially Cuban in their customs and outlook. Studies of groups such as this one can help us to understand the dynamics of the intersections of religion, race, gender, and class as well as the processes of the adjustment of immigrants to life in a new country.

This is a second migration for the families of the women in this study. They came to Cuba from Eastern Europe or Turkey with different economic situations, cultural traditions, and languages. They were part of a minority community in Cuba, which accounts for the salience of religion during the one or two generations they remained there and, perhaps, its continuing importance after their move to the United States. Several factors appear to account for the salience of their Cuban identity in Miami. The cultural traditions of Jewish and non-Jewish Cubans, including gender roles that make home and family the primary focus of women's lives whether they have paid or volunteer work outside the home or not, male dominance, and attitudes toward their children, are apparently congruent. When they arrived in the United States, their American co-religionists were not particularly welcoming. Their relative affluence, and the fact that

they have formed their own school, organizations, and congregations, insulates them from the necessity of interacting with the wider Jewish and secular communities. The class differences that once separated members of their community in Cuba no longer exist, and they now identify as Cuban Jews and mix more freely. On the other hand, they see themselves as quite different from other Jewish people, whether Spanish- or English-speaking, because of their refugee status. Living in a bilingual city and marrying mostly within their own community allows them to continue to speak Spanish at home, thus reinforcing and preserving their Cuban identity.

The fact that the elements of the researcher's own identity can have an impact on the research is often overlooked. Wartenberg shares gender, religion, and immigrant status with those she interviews. This contributes to the sort of trust, rapport, and empathy that can make the interviewing and the interpretation of the data go more smoothly. On the other hand, Wartenberg views the world from a perspective that is not exactly the same as that of her interviewees. Moreover, she comes to her task with her training and interests as a sociologist and seeks to frame that data for readers in terms of her discipline.

Among the Cubans who emigrated to the United States after the Castro revolution of 1959 were a large number of Cuban Jews, most of whom came here in 1960–62. A study of this unique group and a comparison with non-Jewish Cuban and earlier Jewish immigrants offers an opportunity for drawing a profile of these little-known recent immigrants.

The Jewish women who came to the United States from Cuba and now live in the Miami area have created a distinctive lifestyle for themselves and their families, one that blends their three identities. This has been facilitated by their concentration in a single metropolitan area and the presence of a large Cuban community in the same area. Interviews with these women indicate that they regard maintaining the family's Jewish identity as primary. They achieve this by keeping holidays, customs, and food restrictions in their homes and by sending their children to the Hebrew Academy, rather than secular public or private schools. Cuban identity is reinforced by speaking Spanish at home and by conducting organizational and social activities exclusively among family members and other Cuban Jews. Yet they are now American citizens. They intend to remain here, and in the past three decades, they have encouraged their children to pursue higher education and professional lives here. And they have begun to add the customs and cuisines of this culture to those of the other traditions.

Method and Sample

Dade County, Florida,[1] contains the largest concentration of Cuban Jews. The greater Miami area, in Dade County, is said to be home to 85 percent of the Cuban Jews in the United States, or 1200 to 1700 Cuban Jewish families. Since Jews are not a census category, there are no statistics available on Cuban Jews. All these figures are estimates, based in part on number of Temple members; the latest estimate is 8000-10,000 individuals.

I began by interviewing Jewish and non-Jewish Cuban women and Cuban Jewish men in academic and leadership positions in the Miami area about the history of the Cuban Jewish immigration, their background in Cuba, and the nature of the Cuban community in Miami. As Portes (1987) has pointed out, the advantage of verbal testimony gathered from strategic individuals is that it is particularly suited "to find answers to as yet unanswered questions."

I obtained names of Jewish women through informants and employed "snowball sampling"; that is, the women I interviewed in turn referred me to friends, relatives, and leading women in the Miami Jewish community I could interview. I conducted exploratory in-depth interviews of one to two hours with twenty Cuban Jewish women, who are demographically representative of the Cuban Jewish community in Miami: twelve are of Ashkenazic (eastern European: Poland and Russia) background, and eight are Sephardic (Spanish origin, mostly from Turkey).

Owing to the nature of the sampling process, disproportionate numbers of my respondents are prominent, rather than rank-and-file, members of the community. Nevertheless, I think that my findings and interpretations are valid for this group as a whole. Not being a Cuban Jew, I interacted with them as an "outsider." The "insider-outsider" theory "holds that one has privileged access to knowledge, or is wholly excluded from it by virtue of one's group membership or social position" (Merton [1957]: 15). My being Jewish gave me some "insider" status. One woman who asked me if I was Jewish stated, "If you are Jewish, you can understand better why Jews help each other." My not being a native-born American, but a Jewish refugee, albeit from Germany, created a common bond. . . . My female status was probably also helpful in establishing rapport (see Riessman 1987). The women welcomed the opportunity to tell their story to an apparently sympathetic and interested "Anglo," as all nonblack Americans are called in Miami, and they are anxious to have it disseminated.

The women I interviewed can be roughly divided into three age groups, each of whom experienced immigration differently because of the different stages in their life cycles at which they arrived in this country:

1. Five arrived in the United States as children and went to American schools; they are now 29–40 years old.

2. Seven came as teenagers or in their early twenties, many of them alone to complete their education; they are now 41–50 years old.

3. Eight married women came with husbands and children and are now more than 50 years old. One of them is over seventy.

Except for those in the youngest group, attitudes do not vary much by age in this sample. The four who are in their early thirties, especially those sent ahead by their parents to stay with American Jewish families and educated in American schools and colleges, speak fluent American English and are almost indistinguishable from their American peers. Two of this group intermarried with

American Jews and thus speak English in their daily lives. They still know Spanish, though partly, by their own account, it is "Spanglish." There is a strong norm against intermarriage with non-Jews, for both males and females, and it is enforced through strong family, communal, and Conservative or Orthodox religious ties. Intermarriage with American Jews is increasing because of the relatively small pool of Cuban Jews, but I came across only one young woman who had married a non-Jewish Cuban, and he had converted to Judaism, making him acceptable to her family.

These young women generally find employment in positions where their bilingual and bicultural background is an asset. They feel "Americanized," but as one stated: "We're a blend of two cultures; we may speak English, but we do a lot of Cuban things." In this they differ from the second generation of earlier waves of Jewish immigration from Europe who rejected their ethnic culture and tried to assimilate by totally adopting the dominant culture (Weinberg 1988).

The middle-aged as well as the older group have vivid memories of life in Cuba, and they speak English with a Spanish or Yiddish accent. In contrast to some Cubans in the older age group, they are all able to speak English, as demonstrated by my ability to interview them in English. The middle-aged group consists of women (1) who are active in organizations; (2) are working women, some of whom have their own businesses or are in executive positions, and (3) are part of a very wealthy group whose lifestyle is characterized by "conspicuous consumption." Like other first-generation immigrants, because of financial need the oldest group worked outside their homes when they first came here, mostly helping their husbands in business. Some now work for their daughters' businesses or are active in separate Cuban Jewish divisions of Jewish organizations.

In answer to the question "What are you? What do you consider yourself to be?" eighteen of the twenty replied "a Cuban Jew"; some volunteered the nickname "Jewban" or "Juban." All of them emphasized that their primary identity was Jewish. They are Cuban Jewish women because they were born in Cuba and acquired the culture and speak the Spanish language: "I'm a Jew, a Cuban Jew and American by citizenship" was the typical reply. Only two out of the twenty identified themselves as "Cuban American Jews"; that is, Americans of Cuban origin, but primarily Jewish, and they belonged to the youngest group. Even those in this group do not identify with American Jews. The experiences of Jewish families in Cuba and Miami and their lifestyles today help explain why Jewish women who came to the United States from Cuba stress their Cuban origins, rather than their American citizenship, and emphasize their Jewishness but do not identify with the American Jewish community. . . .

Determinants of Identity and Selection of Reference Groups

Sociological theories and concepts that regard human behavior within the context of social structure are useful tools for understanding Cuban Jewish immigrant women. Reference-group theory (Merton 1957; Merton and Rossi 1957), in particular, provides a framework for analyzing the processes that led to the triple identity of the women in this sample. It is a method for determining how individuals take the values and standards of groups as frames of reference for their self-evaluation and attitudes. Groups in which "people interact frequently with one another in accordance with established patterns," and of which they define themselves as members and are so defined by others, are called membership groups. Individuals generally identify with them and take them as normative reference groups, adopting their values and standards, but they may also identify with non-membership groups, which then are positive reference groups for them. From a social-structural perspective, identification, or selection of reference groups, "tends to be patterned by the environing structure of established social relations and by prevailing cultural definitions" (Merton 1957: 302).

Cuban Jews in Miami have multiple reference groups. They have two normative, mutually supporting ethnic reference groups, Jews and Cubans, but their only membership group is Jewish. They consider Americans a non-membership group and are perceived as "outsiders" by Americans. They consider American Jews a negative reference group, because they feel that the Jewish identity of Americans is not as strong as their own. American Jews are also a conflict group for them because their language and culture render Cuban Jews invisible (Merton 1957) to American Jews (as well as to others).

Being Jewish in Cuba

Cuban Jewish identity in Miami is related to the history of the Jewish people in Cuba (Kahn 198[1]). Owing to the legacy of the Spanish Inquisition[2] there were no openly practicing Jews in Cuba until the conclusion of the Spanish-American War in 1898, when Cuba ceased being a Spanish colony. The first to arrive were American Jews, who had business relations with the Cubans but maintained their American identity. The first group who became Cuban Jews were Sephardic Jews, mainly from Turkey, who began to arrive before World War I. In the 1920s when the United States imposed quotas against immigrants from eastern Europe, Jews from Russia and Poland arrived in Cuba, which they hoped would be a way station to the United States. The Sephardim spoke Ladino (a mixture of medieval Spanish and Hebrew), which enabled them to learn Cuban Spanish rather quickly, and they easily adapted to the similar Cuban culture; the Ashkenazim spoke Yiddish (a mixture of Middle High German and Hebrew with an admixture of Slavic languages) and were products of a different culture. Within a generation or less they too had learned Spanish and became acculturated to Cuba and adapted to Cuban culture. Both groups maintained their Jewishness. As the size of the groups grew, they founded Jewish religious, educational, and cultural institutions in Havana, where the largest number of Jews resided.[3]

My seventy-five year old respondent remembers arriving from Russia as a ten year old in 1923, speaking only Yiddish, finding her way to a school and learning Spanish. She also remembers the extreme poverty and economic struggles of that group of immigrants. The other women I interviewed were all born in Cuba and raised in Spanish-speaking families, but many attended the Jewish school. They lived among Cubans, whom they did not perceive as being anti-Semitic because, they say, they were not discriminated against. As individuals, the Cubans were good to them; yet they were "outsiders" and remained marginal (Park [1950]).[4] The Jews associated with native Cubans as neighbors and in business, but their social life was within the Jewish community. The Jewish Community Center was the center of their secular and religious life. Their Jewishness gave them a feeling of belonging, of being less marginal,[5] wherever they lived; it was as true in Cuba as it is in Miami. . . .

Being Jewish and Cuban in Miami

Dade County is the center of Cuban culture. Cubans are in the majority in Miami (Portes et al. 1980), and Spanish rivals English as the language of daily and business discourse. Jews who fled from Cuba to America arrived in Miami, as did all Cubans. The Jews were sent by the HIAS (Hebrew Immigrant Aid Society), just as non-Jews by the U.S. Immigration Service, to sponsors throughout the United States. Eventually most of them returned to Miami, because they have relatives there, they like the climate, and they have friendship ties with Cuban Jews and business connections with Cubans of all faiths. They feel at home in the Latin American environment and in the familiar surroundings they remember from earlier visits. Many wealthy Jewish women came to Miami in pre-Castro times, as illustrated by the remark of one of the older women and confirmed by others: "Every summer we used to come to Miami with my children. I used to bring the maid and spend the summer here." They live in Cuban Jewish enclaves in Miami Beach and North Miami Beach. Some of the younger ones live in mixed suburban neighborhoods, but have family in the enclaves. I have been told that some of them are returning to Miami Beach. Their values and lifestyles are a blend of those of Miami Cubans and Jews.

Despite their strong Jewish identity, most Cuban Jewish women do not identify with the American Jewish community. When they arrived in Miami, members of the American Jewish community were hostile toward them because they spoke Spanish and seemed so foreign. The immigrant Jewish women felt hurt and rejected, which reinforced their tendency to maintain their Cuban Jewish culture, further alienating them from American Jews, many of whom have, in turn, maintained their negative attitude. Because they speak Spanish, others, both Jews and non-Jews, are not even aware of the existence of a group of Cuban Jews. As one woman stated, "They identify me as a Cuban and therefore lower class." One of the younger women explained: "American Jews have some difficulty with Jews who are Cuban; we speak Spanish and have weddings where the rabbi performs the ceremony and the food is kosher and the music is Latin." Or, as one of my informants stated, "they combine Jewish ethics with Cuban customs."

A specific example of their negative reception by the Jewish community in Miami was cited by several women. When the Cuban Jews arrived, they had no money to pay for High Holyday tickets. Temple attendance was very important for them because they are observant Jews, but only one temple on Miami Beach invited them to attend services [for] free.[6] The rabbi (spiritual leader) of that congregation also organized a Sunday school for Cuban Jewish children. To this day, many Cuban Jews, especially the middle aged and older ones, who live in enclaves on Miami Beach, maintain their membership in that temple, and they have more than repaid the free tickets. Now they also belong to the Orthodox Sephardic or the Conservative Ashkenazic Cuban temple on Miami Beach.[7]

Almost all Cuban Jews are affiliated with a temple, and they give strong financial as well as ideological support to Israel, continuing a tradition that started in Cuba, where they were active in Zionist groups. The oldest of my respondents stated: "I gave all my life to Zionist affairs." As a young woman in Cuba she was one of the founders of a Zionist youth group because it gave them "something to hang on to, geared to events in Israel." When their husbands became successful businessmen, these women contributed to Zionist and other Jewish organizations in Cuba and now in Miami. Here they see a difference between themselves and American Jews. One expressed their feeling: "Cuban Jews are very generous; among Americans only the very wealthy give, the middle class does not contribute."

Both Sephardic and Ashkenazic women are ardently pro-Israel and active in fund raising for Jewish and Zionist organizations. One woman said: "Israel lets anyone be a Jew outside of Israel. If there were no Israel, we would have a harder time being Jewish." Despite their devotion to the Jewish state, no one in my sample had visited Israel, though some said they would like go. Only one emigrated first to Israel, but she and her family could not adjust to the style of living there—she called it "too European"—and came to Miami, where they feel "at home.". . .

Triple Identity and the Miami Social Structure

Portes and Back (198[5]), who examined the immigrants' role in the U.S. labor market and their social adaptation patterns, conclude that "structural" variables emerge, in every instance, as the most significant predictors of the nature of social relations that immigrants engage in." (p. 331)

Organizations

Like their non-Jewish counterparts, Jewish Cubans are a cohesive group, and since they are fairly numerous in Miami, they have been able to re-create the social structure of Jewish life in Havana within the larger Miami Cuban environment. Like American Jews, they are active in Jewish organizations, but feeling unwelcome in American Jewish groups, the women formed their own chapters of these groups. One of the older women related: "I got into Hadassah (Women's Zionist Organization), I gave them a speech in my broken English, I joined the group, but I was never in the group. I did not feel rejected, but I did not feel welcome. Eventually I dropped out." She joined the Inter-American chapter of Hadassah on Miami Beach as soon as it was founded. Almost all Cuban women belong to it, and it is the largest Hadassah chapter in Dade County, having 1000 members. To this day meetings are conducted in Spanish. . . .

Unlike Cuban and American women of the same social class, the women described here are not active in political or secular community organizations. One young mother of school-age children told me that she was not active in PTA because "it was not for me." These women avoid political activity in part because they do not define such activity as consistent with the traditional role of Jewish women, but also because, in Cuba, Jews were excluded from wider civic and political life. They vote in American elections, but avoid political discussions, in contrast to other Cubans who engage in them all the time (Didion 19[8]7) and whom they do not want to antagonize. Informants told me that they tend to be somewhat more liberal than other Cubans, but not on the issue of Cuba. They share other Cubans' anticommunist and anti-Castro attitude because Castro took everything away from them and because of his stand on Israel. As one said: "We are mostly anti-Castro, because Cuba never accepted Israel, so for us he [Castro] is taboo."

Family and Friendship

Like other Cubans, members of this group have a large extended family network and close family ties. Even a woman in the youngest age group, who considers herself Americanized, is married to an American Jew, and is career oriented like her American peers, related that she had 150 relatives living in the Miami area and is in close social contact with them. Families meet, as they did in Havana, at the Jewish Cuban Center, which is also the Cuban Hebrew Congregation, for family and other social occasions and for religious services.

Similarly, like other Cubans, both older and younger women associate with their own kind.[8] When asked who their friends were, the vast majority responded "Cuban Jews." Several among the older age group told me that they had old friends with whom they had gone to school in Cuba, so "there is no need to look for new friends" (i. e., American Jews). One middle-aged woman who came to America in her early twenties and worked in New York before returning to Miami explained: "Socially we [Cuban Jews] stay together. We like the same things, we enjoy each other." Even in New York, she said, "I had some Cuban Jews near me." Another one stated, "I must admit, we are cliquish."

Women in their forties who were temporarily brought up by American families in the Midwest became more "Cuban" and spoke more Spanish since they returned to Miami. They have almost exclusively Cuban Jewish friends. "We feel more comfortable when we go out with Cubans . . . my husband finds Americans [Jews] boring," one of them told me. She added, "When we are with American friends we have to speak English because the Americans feel uncomfortable if we make a comment in Spanish and are suspicious that we are talking about them." One of the older women stated, "You start to speak Spanish without realizing it." She, like others, complained that she was forgetting her English, because of lack of opportunity to speak it.

In Miami Sephardim and Ashkenazim mix more with one another than they did in Cuba, where there was a cultural and social class difference between them. Here they are drawn together by their common background as Cuban Jewish refugees,[9] and they cooperate in Cuban branches of Jewish organizations, such as Hadassah and Federation of Jewish Philanthropies. Neither group, however, interacts with other Hispanic Jews, many of whom have come to Miami in recent years from other Latin American countries. They explain that "they are different, they are not refugees, they came with money, and they came voluntarily and can go back." (See Pedraza-Bailey, 1985 for theoretical discussion of this difference.)

As in Cuba, they have no social relations with non-Jewish Cubans but do have business relations with them. Many have become very wealthy in Miami because of the enclave economy and their prior business contacts with Americans (Portes 1987)

Maintenance of Identity and Degree of Acculturation

On the whole, Cuban Jewish women are happy in this country. They are grateful that the United States has afforded them and their families asylum and so many opportu-

nities. In contrast to some other Cuban immigrants, they have no expectation of returning to Cuba to live. In view of this, it may
seem surprising that they identify so
strongly with Cuban culture, especially since
they were only first- or second-generation
Cubans, and for those who arrived in Cuba
in the 1920s, the exodus from Cuba was the
second migration in their lifetime. It seems
to me that there are two reasons for this:
value congruity and nostalgia.

Value Congruity

Although they do not socialize with Cubans, there is a special fit between Jewish
and Cuban values.[10] Both have strong family
ties and traditional values, such as male dominance and in-group marriage, and intense
involvement with and control over their children. They both socialize a great deal with
their children and insist on knowing who
their children's friends are. They adhere to a
double standard, being more protective of
girls than boys, and differ from American
mothers, whom they perceive of as being too
casual. Cuban Jewish mothers differ in some
respects from Cuban mothers by being less
strict. In spite of the double standard, Jewish
girls are not chaperoned, nor were they in
Cuba. There, however, they did not "date,"
but went out in groups. "Jubans" give priority to Jewish values when they conflict with
others. For instance, other Cubans attach
importance to having their children, both
male and female, stay close to home during
the college years. Cuban Jews, in contrast,
place a high value on education. Their determination to have their children get the best
education possible allows Cuban Jews to
send them away from home to attend college.
Moreover, they have accepted some Americans' customs: they celebrate "sweet sixteen," not the Latin Qinze (fifteen), which
has become an even bigger event among up-
wardly mobile Cubans in Miami than it was
in Cuba.

Whether they work outside the home or
not, both Cuban and Jewish women remain
mothers, above all else, adhering to the
"family work ethic" (Perez 1986: 16), working only to help support the family. In sum,
as the author of a study of Cuban women put

it, "Cuban mothers are like Jewish mothers;
they give constant attention to their families" (Boone 1977: 299). This was facilitated
by the affluent lifestyle they enjoyed, especially after World War II, as most of the Jews
became well-off middle-class merchants or
manufacturers. There was no "cult of domesticity" in Cuba (Ferree 1979), since the women
all had maids, which freed them from being
housewives and gave them enough time to be
devoted mothers and ladies of leisure or to
work or to pursue professional careers without guilt.

Nostalgia

Cuban Jewish women enjoyed the relaxed
way of life of the island and long for its ease
and comfort. The middle-aged woman who
owns a business in Miami and had worked in
Havana told me: "I loved Cuba . . . I loved the
way of life, the siesta, the pace was slower,
there was less competition." Most of them no
longer thought of coming to the United States
until after the Castro revolution of 1959. They
had adopted the lifestyle of the host culture:
They spoke Spanish with their children and
dressed in the elegant, not to say flamboyant, style of Cuban women. In outward appearance they did not differ very much from
other Cuban women, who valued personal
grooming and attractiveness and with whom
they shared the love of material things and
visible display of wealth. They maintained
traditional Jewish homes, but their normative reference groups were both Jewish and
Cuban, and their way of life was no longer
European.

Yet Cuban Jews have Americanized more
than the majority of Cubans in Miami. This
is so in part because they are a smaller
group, and there is a smaller pool of marriageable Cuban Jews, so there is considerable intermarriage with American Jews.
This is particularly true of those in their thirties, who are "returnees" from other areas of
the United States. Like their American peers,
many have careers, but they do not identify
with the woman's movement, although they
acknowledge their debt to it. It conflicts with
their traditional values. All of them, however,
even those not in paid work, have adopted

some of the movement's goals, such as equality for women in the family and on the job.[11]

As in Cuba, even those who do not work do not consider themselves "housewives." As one stated, "I am a mother and a wife." Nevertheless, like many American midlife women, she wants to return to work, as a number of Cuban Jewish women with grown children are doing, not out of financial need, but for personal satisfaction.

As I stated at the outset and described earlier, it is the women who maintain the Jewish identity and foster it in their children. They realize, however, that in spite of their efforts, children born in America tend to identify as Americans. They know that by going away to college, their children will become more "Americanized" and the influence of Cuban values and conservative political views, which are based almost exclusively on the effect of policies on and attitudes of politicians toward Cuba, will decline. One woman told me that she fights with her liberal son, who is attending Harvard. Another stated that she and her husband let them go "with fear in our hearts," lest they marry non-Jews.

Cuban Jews may eventually acculturate, and their mix of Cuban, Jewish, and American customs indicates some movement in that direction, but in the Cuban cultural environment of Miami, the model of Anglo conformity, of submerging their ethnicity in the dominant WASP culture, which was the aspiration of earlier immigrants (Gordon 1964), does not apply to them, as it does not to the larger Cuban community in Miami. They are rather striving to achieve ethnic pluralism (Portes 198[7]), the coexistence of different ethnic groups, all respecting each other while maintaining their distinctive cultural values. Those who are dispersed will acculturate more quickly because geographic dispersion facilitates assimilation and acculturation. Sociological studies conducted in cities where Cuban immigrants are a dispersed minority bear this out (Portes 1969; Boone 1977; 1980).

In the unique environment of Miami, Cuban Jewish women are likely selectively to adopt the values of the larger society while maintaining their special blend of Cuban-Jewish-American identity, at least for another generation, as long as there is continued tourism from and trade with Latin America, necessitating the use of Spanish, and as long as the Cuban enclave and its economy continue to exist and Cuban Jewish institutions are preserved.

Notes

1. Dade County is the area generally called Miami; it consists of 20 incorporated cities, of which Miami Beach is one, and some unincorporated areas. One is the City of Miami, which is 56 percent Cuban, about 25 percent Black, and has a small minority of less than 20 percent non-Hispanic Whites or "Anglos," a term commonly used in South Florida; it comprises the downtown business district, Coconut Grove, Liberty City and Overton, and "little Havana," the area of the first settlement of Cuban immigrants and still a Cuban enclave of mostly older and less-well-off people. Hialeah is 75 percent Latin (mostly Cuban), and West Miami, a suburb where the younger Cuban families have moved, is 62 percent Cuban. Figures are from Boswell and Curtis (198[3]: 82) based on the 1980 census.

2. During the Spanish Inquisition, an edict was issued in 1492, expelling all Jews from Spain unless they submitted to baptism and became Christians. This edict was also enforced in the Spanish possessions in the New World. For this reason, Jews were not allowed in Cuba, though a number of the Spaniards who came to Cuba had Jewish blood and were called *conversos* (converted) or, more pejoratively, *marranos* (pigs), who secretly practiced some Jewish rites while outwardly being Christians.

3. I recently met and interviewed a Cuban Jewish women who grew up in Guantánamo where there were only 5-10 Jewish families. The Jews there felt very isolated, had no Jewish organizations or religious institutions, and celebrated the holidays surreptitiously, almost like the *conversos*. She found out about Jewish customs only after arriving in the United States.

4. This term is based on Park's concept of the "marginal man," whose prototype is the immigrant, who belongs to two cultures, the one where he was born and the new one, but is not fully a member of either.

5. The "pain" of being marginal to all three groups is illustrated by the case history of one young woman, who has an executive position in an American organization. She had come with her parents as an eight year old, lived in various parts of the United States with her family, and gone to college in New England. She spoke American English as well as good Spanish and called herself "Cuban American." She did not identify herself as Jewish because she is not involved in Jewish groups, although she went to temple with her parents on special occasions. Cuban Jews are a negative reference group for her; she called them narrow-minded because "nothing but their Jewishness matters to them." Although Americans are a positive membership group for her, in Miami's Cuban environment she is an "outsider" to

them. She related her feelings of marginality to her age group: "We are such a weird lot. We speak Spanish, but we really don't know where we belong. We move in and out of everything. It's just so hard." Those who came here a little older, she felt, are still more attached to Latin values and culture. She had returned to Miami for health reasons, [and] socializes with American Jews and Hispanics. She misses the New England Thanksgiving of her teen years in New Hampshire and has no social relations in Miami with anyone who celebrates it in the traditional American way. The Cubans, she told me, adapt it to their own customs, serving roast pork instead of turkey.

6. Jewish custom forbids the handling of money on the Sabbath and some holidays. Therefore, there are no collection plates at Jewish services. Instead, most congregations collect annual dues and sell tickets for seats in the sanctuary on the High Holy days when attendance is higher than at other times of the year.

7. Orthodox, Conservative, and Reform are main branches of Judaism in North America. They are distinguished by their degree of adherence to written and oral Jewish law and traditional customs and practices. Orthodox people and congregations are the most traditionally observant, Reform the least. Conservative individuals and congregations fall between the others. Each has seminaries and clerical associations and publishes prayer books and other literature consistent with its recommended positions and practices. None of the three is less religious; rather, their interpretations of what it means to be a religious Jew today differ.

8. This may explain why Cuban Jews do not perceive Christian Cubans as anti-Semitic; they do not intermingle socially because each group likes to stay "with their own kind." Several said that when they came to the United States they were shocked by the anti-Semitism, which they perceived as being much more prevalent. One stated that contrary to the restriction against Jews in Miami social and golf clubs, "I could join the Club of the Big Five [top Cuban social club in Miami], if I wanted to, but I don't, because I don't know anybody there." Instead, she is president of the Sisterhood of the Sephardic temple.

9. During my research I attended their joint Cuban Jewish observance of *Yom Hashoa*, the Holocaust Day of Remembrance; the languages used at the service were English, Hebrew, Yiddish, and Spanish.

10. Some of the information about non-Jewish Cubans was provided by a student at the University of Miami, Zina Zinotti, who conducted interviews with five male and seven female Cubans in Miami in the spring of 1988.

11. I have a sense, based on what my informants and some of the respondents told me, that due to my sampling method, the affluent leisure women, who are married to very successful businessmen and who are said to be predominant among Cuban Jews, are under-represented in my sample.

References

Baum, Charlotte, Paula Hyman, and Sonya Michel. 1975. *The Jewish Woman in America*. New York: Dial Press.

Bejarano, Margalit. 1985 "Los Seraradies, Pioneros de la Immigracion Judia a Cuba." *Rumbos en el Judaismo, el Sionismo e Israel* 14: 102–22.

Boone, Margaret S. 1977. "Cubans in City Context: The Washington Case." Ph.D. dissertation, Ohio State University.

——. 1980 "The Use of Traditional Concepts in the Development of New Urban Roles: Cuban Women in the United States." In *World of Women*, edited by Erika Bourgignon. New York: Prager.

Boswell, Thomas D., and James Curtis. 1983. *The Cuban-American Experience: Culture, Images, and Perspectives*. Totowa, N.J.: Rowman and Allenheld.

Boswell, Thomas D., and Manuel Rivero N.D. 1980. *Demographic Characteristics of Pre-Mariel Cubans Living in the United States: 1980* Monograph. Coral Gables: University of Miami. Research Institute for Cuban Studies, Graduate School of International Studies.

Casal, Lourdes, and Andres R. Hernandes. 1980. "Cubans in the U.S.: A Survey of the Literature." In *The Cuban Experience in the United States*, edited by C.E. Cortes. New York: Arno Press.

Clark, Juan M. 1975 "The Exodus from Revolutionary Cuba (1959–1974): A Sociological Analysis." Ph.D. dissertation, University of Florida.

Clark, Juan M., Jose Lasaga, and Rose S. Reque. 1981. *The 1980 Mariel Exodus: An Assessment and Prospect*. Washington, D.C.: Council for Inter-American Security.

Cortes, Carlos E., ed. 1980. *The Cuban Experience in the United States*. New York: Arno Press.

Didion, Joan. 1987. *Miami*. New York: Simon and Schuster.

Egerton, John. 1980. "Cubans in Miami: A Third Dimension in Racial and Cultural Relations." In *The Cuban Experience in the United States*, edited by C.E. Cortes. New York: Arno Press.

Ferree, Myra Marx. 1979. "Employment without Liberation: Cuban Women in the United States." *Social Science Quarterly* 60:35–50.

Gordon, Milton. 1964. *Assimilation in American Life: The Role of Race, Religion and Nation*. New York: Oxford University Press.

Hadassah Jewish Education Guide. 1987. *Bat Kol*, edited by Carol Diament. New York: Hadassah Order Department.

Jorge, Antonio, and Raul Moncarz. 1987. *The Political Economy of Cubans in South Florida*. Monograph. Coral Gables: University of Miami, Graduate School of International Studies.

Kahn, Jeffrey A. 1981. "The History of the Jewish Colony in Cuba." Ph.D. dissertation. Hebrew Union College, Jewish Institute of Religion, Cincinnati.

Liebman, Seymour B. 1977. "Cuban Jewish Community in South Florida." In *A Coat of Many Colors*, edited by Abraham D. Lavender. Westport, Conn.: Greenwood Press.

Llanes, Jose. 1982. *Cuban Americans: Masters of Survival.* Cambridge: AbtBooks.

MacCorkle, Lyn. 1984. *Cubans in the U.S.: A Bibliography for Research in the Social and Behavioral Sciences 1960–1983.* Westport, Conn.: Greenwood Press.

Merton, Robert K. 1957. "Continuities in the Theory of Reference Groups and Social Structure." In *Social Theory and Social Structure,* edited by R. K. Merton. Glencoe, IL: Free Press.

Merton, Robert K. with Alice Rossi. 1957. "Contributions to the Theory of Reference Group Behavior." In *Social Theory and Social Structure,* edited by R. K. Merton. Glencoe, IL: Free Press.

Park, Robert E. 1950. *Race and Culture.* Part 4. Glencoe, IL: Free Press.

Pedraza-Bailey, Silvia. 1985. "Cuba's Exiles: Portrait of a Refugee Migration." *International Migration Review* 19: 4–34.

Perez, Lisandro. 1984. *The Cuban Population of the United States: The Results of the 1980 U.S. Census of Population.* Monograph Miami: Latin American and Caribbean Center, FIU.

———. 1986. "Immigrant Economic Adjustment and Family Organization: The Cuban Success Story Reexamined." *International Migration Review* 20: 4–20.

Portes, Alejandro. 1969. "Dilemmas of a Golden Exile: Integration of Cuban Refugee Families in Milwaukee." *American Sociological Review* 34: 505–18.

———. 1987. "The Social Origins of the Cuban Enclave Economy of Miami." *Sociological Perspectives* 30: 340–72.

Portes, Alejandro, and Robert L. Back. 1985. *Latin Journey: Cuban and Mexican Immigrants in the United States.* Berkeley: University of California Press.

Portes, Alejandro, Robert N. Parker, and Jose A. Cobas. 1980. "Assimilation or Consciousness: Perceptions of U.S. Society Among Recent Latin American Immigrants to the United States." *Social Forces* 59: 220–24.

Prieto, Yolanda. 1986. "Cuban Women and Work in the United States: A New Jersey Case Study." In *International Migration. The Female Experience,* edited by R. J. Simon and C. B. Brettel. New York: Free Press.

———. 1987. "Cuban Women in the U.S. Labor Force: Perspectives on the Nature of Change" *Cuban Studies* 17: 73–91.

Richmond, Marie. 1980. *Immigrant Adaptation and Family Structure Among Cubans in Miami, Florida.* New York: Arno Press.

Rogg, Eleanor M. 1974. *The Assimilation of Cuban Exiles: The Role of Community and Class.* New York: Aberdeen Press.

Stevenson, James M. 1973. "Cuban-Americans: New Urban Class." Ph.D. dissertation, Wayne State University.

University of Miami, Center for Advanced International Studies. 1967. *The Cuban Immigration 1959–1966 and Its Impact on Miami-Dade County.* Coral Gables: University of Miami.

Weinberg, Sydney Stahl. 1988. *The World of Our Mothers: The Lives of Jewish Immigrant Women.* Chapel Hill: University of North Carolina Press.

Discussion Questions

1. Some people feel strongly that people who live in the United States should learn English as quickly as possible and use it exclusively. Others argue that learning a new language is difficult, especially for older people, that there is value in being able to speak another language, and that we should accommodate people who don't know English by having translators available and printing crucial signs and documents in several languages. How do you feel about this debate? Have the Cuban Jews found the best solution in learning English but continuing to use Spanish?

2. Will the next generation of the Miami Cuban Jewish community be able to sustain its current level of isolation from the wider Jewish, secular, or Cuban communities? What factors will affect the outcome?

3. Are there any clues in Wartenberg's discussion to tell us how the lives of the men in the Miami Cuban Jewish community might differ from those of their wives and daughters? Would a male interviewer have asked different questions or learned different things about the community?

4. What other recent immigrant group(s) might have something in common with the Cuban Jews of Miami? In what ways is the Cuban Jews' situation similar to and different from other immigrants?

22

'Not All Differences Are Created Equal'

Multiple Jeopardy in a Gendered Organization

Jane Ward

Jane Ward asserts that "not all differences are created equal," based on participant observation and interviews at Bienestar, a Latino health organization in Los Angeles. The article raises a question about how we frame our understanding and social action around various combinations of gender, race/ethnicity, social class, and sexuality. In the context of this particular organization, where all of the staff and clients are Latino/a and most are gay or lesbian, gender comes to the forefront. All the clients suffer from oppression in the wider society, but this is a gendered environment in which attitudes toward and services provided for men are given priority while those of women are discounted. Ward argues that in some contexts, oppressions are additive and some oppressed people are more oppressed than others.

Bienestar was actually started by Latina lesbians who saw the need for a culturally appropriate way to address the threat of HIV/ AIDS. Despite having grown out of a more general Latino/a gay and lesbian organization and including a queer youth-oriented unit, its funding and mission are as an AIDS service organization (ASO). Ward asks and answers the question of why it is the organization of choice for Latina lesbians: Both men and women at Bienestar agree that they have no other place to go. Men point out that other gay and lesbian organizations are dominated by middle-class Whites and are insensitive to cultural and economic differences. Other Latino/a organizations are homophobic. Women add that they would have chosen a more women-centered organization, but none exists. The men imply that the lesbians are comfortable in this organization because they prioritize culture and sexuality over gender. The women's level of frustration and burn-out and their actions seeking change within the organization indicate that this is not the case. The reasoning used to justify the status quo was both puzzling and difficult to refute. The organization could serve the low-risk lesbian population because of its psychological and cultural approach to AIDS prevention, but it could not justify a fuller program and more lesbian staff members because the majority of HIV/AIDS clients were men. The men's words and actions conveyed their sense of entitlement; women felt they had to be grateful for whatever they received.

This article shows the interplay of ethnicity, sexuality, and gender within an organization. It also shows that organizations operate in a wider context in which funding agencies, community geography, and medical crises have an impact on internal policy and decision making. The location and ethnic program of Bienestar drew people to it. It was able to grow because of the availability of HIV/AIDS-prevention funding, but dependence on that source of funding limited its activities or provided a plausible excuse for doing so.

The triad of race, class, and gender oppression, or "triple jeopardy," continues to be the normative framework used by many scholars to discuss the matrix of oppression. In the essay in which she proposes the more apt term "multiple jeopardy," Deborah King (1990) asserted that identities are not additive "because oppression is about the quality, and not the quantity of one's experiences." In addition to clarifying the relationship between race, class, and gender inequality, King's multiple jeopardy theory has allowed for an expanded understanding of the "matrix of domination," including, for example, a recognition of the multiplicative effects of heterosexism and homophobia for lesbians and gay men already affected by other forms of structural inequality (Anzaldúa 1990; Trujillo 1991). This theory of the intersectional nature of oppressions commonly referred to as intersectional feminist theory developed in the 1980s largely in response to racism in the feminist movement of the 1970s and sexism in the civil rights movement of the 1950s and 1960s. Thus, a critique of "single-identity" social movements that combat one form of oppression while supporting others has also been central to the feminist intersectional approach (Combahee River Collective 1983; hooks 1981: Robnet 1996).

More recently, social movement scholars have applied feminist intersectional theory to demonstrate that single-identity movements are inevitably ineffective because they exclude vast numbers of constituents, support the matrix of domination by addressing one form of inequality and not others, and fail to recognize the complex mechanisms behind the very inequality they intend to address (Kurtz 2002; Stockdill 2001). Yet the application of feminist intersectional theory to social movement work is difficult in part due to unanswered questions within intersectional theory itself about how to recognize and respond to multiple oppressions simultaneously, particularly within organizational contexts in which one or more forms of structural inequality emerge as more salient obstacles than others. An extensive body of intersectional feminist theory has explored how the multiplicative nature of structural inequalities produces "multiple consciousness;" or the consciousness that develops from being at the center of intersecting and mutually reliant systems of oppression (Baca Zinn and Thorton Dill 1996; Hill Collins 1990; King 1990). Multiple consciousness, paired with coalition politics that temporarily unite differently located groups working toward a common goal, has been posited as the corrective to single-identity movements and the problematic practice of counting or ranking oppressions (Kurtz 2002; Stockdill 2001). Multiple consciousness, it has been argued, allows individuals and groups to recognize that no system of domination is more primary than another.

Yet many feminists are still counting and/or ranking oppressions, and the notion that "not all differences are created equally" has developed as a particularly common theme within writing by queer women of color (Takagi 1996, 24). For example, Dana Takagi argued that while some white lesbian and gay activists "think of themselves as patterned on the 'ethnic model'" of identity, there are important ideological discursive, and historical differences between ethnicity and sexuality, particularly with respect to the way that race/ethnicity is "more obviously written on the body" than one's sexual identity (1996, 23–25). According to Takagi, oppression claims by lesbians and gay men raise many questions about whether homosexuality is a form of marginalization that people "choose" and is therefore less urgent than racism given the "quality of volunteerism in being gay/lesbian" (p. 25). Takagi's assertions imply that counting oppressions is problematic for the very reason that it treats oppressions as "equal," or unrankable, by obscuring important contextual differences between them. In contrast Barbara Smith argued that lesbians of color often have been the most astute in their opposition to the "easy way out of choosing a primary oppression" (1993, 100). Yet Smith positioned homophobia as particularly complicated and urgent by explaining that "homophobia is usually the last oppression to be mentioned, the last to be taken seriously, and the last to go" and identifying the "numerous reasons for otherwise sensitive people's reluctance to confront homophobia," such as the misconception that "lesbian and gay oppression is not as serious as other oppressions" (pp. 100–101). Even within queer multicultural feminist theory the tension between efforts not to create a hierarchy of oppressions and the highly contextual sense of urgency that individuals often feel with respect to one or more forms of oppression (and not others) is evident and difficult to avoid.

This article demonstrates that there is a disjuncture between multiple jeopardy theory and the experiences of individuals moving in and out of organizations with different political ideologies, structures, and leadership. These meso-level factors may result in the perception that one form of inequality is more oppressive than others. The dictate to not count oppressions is therefore difficult to reconcile with the experience of many lesbians of color that not all oppressions are created equal inside social movement organizations. I focus on the experiences of lesbian staff and clients at Bienestar, a large, Latino health organization in Los Angeles focusing primarily on HIV/AIDS prevention and education. This study shows that oppression can be experienced as layered, or additive. Counting oppressions may remain a common practice, and an important political strategy, in the context of some social movement organizations. Emphasizing gender oppression, or ranking it as primary, may be an important strategy for women in social movement organizations in which combating other, and multiple, forms of oppression—racism, homophobia, and AIDS phobia—are central to organizational ideology.

This article also responds to Dana Britton's (2000) call for research that builds on Acker's (1990) theory of gendered organizations by describing and explaining the contexts in which organizations are gendered. Feminist scholarship has contributed to the sociology of organizations by offering insight into the gendered nature of bureaucracy (Acker 1990), the domination of particular occupations and workplaces by men of women and the value respectively assigned to them (Reskin 1988), and the gendered symbols or characteristics associated with particular occupations (Moss Kanter 1977). Acker's theory of gendered organizations suggests that gender inequality is an inherent characteristic of bureaucratic organizations, leaving little hope or guidance for the development of egalitarian organizations. Recognizing this limitation, Dana Britton argued that

> The gendered organizations approach remains theoretically and empirically underdeveloped as there have as yet been few clear answers to the question central to the perspective: What does it really mean to say that an organization itself, or a policy, practice, or slot in the hierarchy is "gendered?" (p. 418)

Britton suggested that what is required is a better understanding of the contexts and methods through which organizations are gendered. Britton emphasized the importance of context as a means of discovering

how gendered characteristics of organizations change and develop over time, how members of an organization understand and interact with these characteristics, and how organizations might become less oppressively gendered.

One way to explore context is to examine the ways in which organizations are influenced by other organizations and bureaucracies, social movements, and a vast array of exogenous forces that may have implications for organizational gender ideology. External forces or events may compromise organizational gender ideology and practices or may provide legitimacy and external support for their institutionalization. They can lead an organization to adapt its goals to ensure survival. In nonprofit or social movement organizations, exogenous forces can lead to a willingness of members to allow organizational failure rather than compromise ideology (Ward 2000). This article examines the impact of one exogenous force, the AIDS epidemic, on the evolving gender ideology and practices of an organization founded as a lesbian and gay activist group and transformed by the epidemic.

Institutionalized Sexism and the AIDS Infrastructure

In the late 1980s, gay and lesbian activists began to take notice of the drain of funds from gay-liberation causes to AIDS-related projects perceived by many funding agencies to be more urgent. Many activists became concerned that the political agenda of the gay and lesbian movement was being "de-gayed" and "swallowed by AIDS" (Rofes 1990; Vaid 1995). By the late 1980s, government grants for gay men and lesbians appeared to be earmarked almost exclusively for HIV/ AIDS, and many gay and lesbian organizations shifted their attention to new HIV/AIDS-related components to survive or grow (Vaid 1995). The phenomenal need for HIV-related services, combined with the need to distribute public and private funds to the organizations delivering these services, resulted in the development of a national AIDS infrastructure, including a network of AIDS service organizations (ASOs), AIDS-related government bureaucracies, and a community of natural and social scientists studying the epidemic and the communities it affects (Altman 1994).

Yet the extent to which the AIDS infrastructure has helped or hindered queer organizing and service delivery cannot be generalized, as it has differently affected lesbians and gay men, queer whites and queer people of color. On one hand, the availability of government funds for HIV/AIDS services has been a catalyst for the growth of organizations established by and for queer communities of color. Prior to the epidemic, white lesbian and gay organizations were funded largely by wealthy white gay men, while queer communities of color had fewer wealthy community members from whom to solicit private funding (Clendinen and Nagourney 1999; Vaid 1995). Thus, public HIV/AIDS grants have allowed for the development of organizations that aim to provide culturally sensitive services to queer people of color in general, and particularly gay men of color who are believed to be at high risk for contracting HIV. The now widely accepted epidemiological contention that all gay men are at high risk for HIV infection translates into more and better social services for all gay men, both HIV positive and HIV negative. Most urban ASOs and lesbian, gay, bisexual, transgendered (LGBT) community centers offer a host of publicly funded HIV-prevention programs designed to encourage HIV-negative gay men, and particularly gay men of color who are now understood to be at even higher risk than white gay men, to practice safer sex (Gay and Lesbian Medical Association 2000). Based on the principles of community and individual empowerment, these prevention programs address factors such as culture, communication, and self-esteem through fun, community-building activities that offer alternatives to high-risk behavior.

On the other hand, the AIDS infrastructure has had a different impact on lesbians, lesbians of color specifically. While the link between HIV-prevention and empowerment programs for gay men of color is relatively easy to draw by pointing to data on infection rates, the use of HIV/AIDS money for lesbian empowerment programs, in light of lesbians' reportedly low risk for HIV infection, requires more complicated rationales. Rates of infection among lesbians demonstrate that the threat of HIV/AIDS in the lesbian community has been and continues to be considerably less urgent than the threat to the gay male community. Yet lesbians remain at high risk for a number of psychosocial dangers, such as depression, suicide, and sexual violence—risk categories that are presumably addressed by mental health services in lesbian and gay organizations and funded by non-AIDS-related funding sources (Gay and Lesbian Medical Association 2000).

There are limited comfortable community spaces and service providers for lesbians of color. Few organizations provide an environment that is both queer and culturally familiar. LGBT community centers, generally run by queer whites, are often unknown, too far, too uncomfortable, or too racist to be a realistic alternative for lesbians of color (Stockdill 2001). Instead lesbians of color may meet, socialize, organize, and receive services and support within their racial/ethnic communities even in AIDS organizations not structured to receive lesbians and run by and for gay men (Schwartz 1993). In organizations such as Bienestar lesbians of color may find cultural solidarity in a queer environment yet at the cost of an internal struggle with sexism. According to Stockdill (2001, 208), "AIDS-related inequality . . . emanates not only from dominant social institutions, but from within oppressed communities themselves." This is an important finding not only because racism, homophobia, and sexism "are major obstacles to effective AIDS prevention and intervention" but also because these inequalities structure the opportunities of even those groups presumably least at risk, such as lesbians.

This article is concerned with how the nexus of sexism and racism leads lesbians of color to seek community and identity in AIDS organizations and, second, how the financial and ideological support given to racial, cultural, and queer pride in ASOs run by gay men of color leads lesbians of color to experience gender oppression as a primary obstacle in their organizational lives. Yet it is important to recognize that lesbians of color are not the only group of women affected by the focus on men, or heterosexual focus in the case of notions about women's risk, that has been central to the very structure of local and national AIDS organizations. For example, some research demonstrates that middle-class and male-centered notions about HIV risk have contributed to the failure of health educators to identify and address risky behaviors among young Black women living in poverty (White 1999). Other scholars and activists have suggested that lesbians, across racial groups, engage in AIDS activism even while they perceive it as a distraction from their own health concerns (Schwartz 1993; Stoller 1997). While some historical accounts of the lesbian and gay movement explain this trend by emphasizing the important work done by lesbians to take care of gay men living with AIDS and heal the political divisions between them (Schneider and Stoller 1995), essays such as Schwartz's (1993) and empirical research such as this focus on the limited structural opportunities available to lesbians, particularly lesbians of color outside of AIDS-funded organizations.

Method

Bienestar is headquartered in East Los Angeles, California, and is a Latino health organization focused primarily on HIV prevention and education. It is also home to a queer youth component that includes non-HIV-related services for queer Latinas and is the only organization in Los Angeles that provides geographically accessible, culturally sensitive, and bilingual services for lesbian and bisexual Latinas. At the time I began studying Bienestar in the Spring of 2000, this research project was broadly motivated by my interest in gender discrimination in LGBT organizations. I selected Bienestar because it accurately reflects the ethnic composition of the county. According to the 2000 U.S. Census, Latinos represent the largest population in Los Angeles County. Bienestar is representative of a relatively new organizational field that crystallized in the early 1990s, that of ASOs targeting specific racial/ethnic communities. The rise in HIV infections among

gay men of color in the United States in the 1990s as well as public health research documenting the significance of culturally competent HIV education, has made ASOs targeting queer communities of color not uncommon in metropolitan areas. Los Angeles is home to multiple ASOs targeting Black, Latino, and Asian American gay men, and many of these organizations include some services for both lesbian and heterosexual women and transgender communities.

I gained access to the lesbian program at Bienestar through my partner (we used the term "girlfriend"), who was a Bienestar employee. As a white outsider, I gained access to the Latina lesbian social network at Bienestar by means of the sponsorship of my Latina girlfriend, who introduced me to the women at Bienestar and implicitly vouched for my character through her association with me (Duneier 1999; Liebow 1967). At the same time, she helped to define the boundaries of my participant observation, inviting me only to public events and meetings in which she felt the presence of a white woman would not be threatening or disrespectful. Not only did my girlfriend's sponsorship increase my access to Bienestar, but it is what made this research possible "by facilitating the development of my friendships with key women informants (see Blackwood and Wieringa 1999 for similar examples). In fact, some feminist research suggests that this form of sponsorship is particularly important in the Chicana community in which integrated community members are more likely to elicit reliable interview data (Segura 1989) although this preference for "insider" research has been critiqued by some antiracist field workers (Twine 2000).

I conducted eight in-depth tape-recorded interviews approximately one hour in length with five women employees, one female board member, one male manager, and the organization's male executive director. I told each of the interview respondents that I was studying gender relations in the lesbian and gay community and that Bienestar was one of my research sites. Respondents agreed that they would be given pseudonyms in any publication of my research findings. During interviews, I asked questions about respondents' history of involvement with Bienestar, programs and funding sources, quantity and quality of interaction between gay male and lesbian staff members and clients, and details about organizational conflicts and practices when such subjects were introduced by respondents themselves. In addition, I collected Bienestar's newsletters and other printed materials and took extensive notes at public meetings, such as Bienestar's general town hall meeting, as well as similar town hall meetings held by women staff. While I did not formally request approval to study Bienestar from the organization's board, leaders in the organization, including one board member and the executive director, consented to an interview "for my dissertation" and about gender relations at Bienestar. At the town hall meetings at which all women participants were present, I shared my research interests, asked if women had questions or comments, and explained that women staff and clients would be given pseudonyms in any printed material or publication of the research. This form of anonymity and the use of human subjects in this research was also approved by the University of California's Human Subjects Review Board. In total, I collected data for this project through nine months of participant observation, with a greater emphasis on observation than on participation. Participant observation included being present at women's meetings, events, and social functions and sometimes contributing to games and discussion as I felt was appropriate in the moment. I made these judgments by trying to assess the situations in which my silence, or lack of participation, was respectful and conversely when my failure to participate would draw attention to my presence and distract from the task at hand.

I used a "grounded theory" approach to analyze the data I collected at Bienestar, allowing my hypotheses to surface and transform throughout the research process (Glasner and Strauss 1967). "Diagnostic ethnography" or the metaphor of medical diagnosis, is also a useful way to explain the ethnographic method I employed (Duneier 1999). Armed with some knowledge from the relevant literature, diagnostic ethnographers enter a research setting with general informa-

tion about how such settings function and formulate a preliminary diagnosis based on the factors that appear to have the greatest influence on the observed phenomena. Duneier suggested that this convergence of knowledge gained from the literature, the research participants, and through one's observations is key to avoiding "the ethnographic fallacy" or taking either one's observations or participants' accounts at face value (1999, 343). It was in this way in relation to both the literature reviewed above and the problems I observed and that participants emphasized that I identified analytic themes and formulated theory.

Bienestar: From Lesbian and Gay Organization to ASO

Bienestar began in 1989 as a health subcommittee of the East Los Angeles-based political and social group Gay and Lesbian Latinos Unidos (GLLU). According to Martin, the current and founding executive director of Bienestar, it was the lesbian leadership in GLLU that "forced the discussion about HIV in the Latino community" as early as 1985 while many of the male GLLU members wished not to discuss it due to "denial about AIDS." Similar to lesbian activists in other communities throughout the country, GLLU women led early efforts to develop an organizational infrastructure to address the epidemic (Stoller 1997). Ana, a current Bienestar board member who has been involved with GLLU since 1985, agrees with Martin's account, adding that "women did all the work, and the guys watched." Ana explains that the lesbians in GLLU raised the start-up funds for the Health Committee and later did the manual labor that was required to open an office when the Health Committee became its own organization, named Bienestar. Although lesbians remain present on the organization's current board of directors, Bienestar is now an HIV-focused organization that serves a diversity of Latino communities affected by HIV in Los Angeles—primarily gay men who have sex with men but also HIV-positive heterosexuals, "gang-affiliated" clients, and injection drug users. In 1995, Bienestar became independent from GLLU as GLLU board members recognized that

Bienestar had become a powerful agency in its own right, with a mission statement that no longer possessed a logical connection to the goals of GLLU. Bienestar's mission statement makes no mention of sexual identity and states that it was established to "provide social and support services to enhance the health and well-being of the [Latino] community." In 2000–2001, Bienestar was the largest Latino ASO in the United States and had grown to approximately 80 staff members and six centers across Los Angeles, including its executive office in East Los Angeles.

Yet at the same time that Bienestar is not formally an LGBT organization, it is informally quite well known for its LGBT programs and its leadership in the gay Latino community. Not only do gay men make up the vast majority of the staff and leadership at Bienestar, producing a dominant gay male culture in the organization, but the agency also dedicates one of its East Los Angeles centers, La Casa, exclusively to LGBT youth programs. Bienestar is a regular presence at LGBT community events as well and widely advertises its services in the Los Angeles gay and lesbian press.... During the time of my data collection, lesbian staff produced at least four dance parties for queer women, a women's poetry night called *Café con leche*, a queer women's day-long retreat, and several other social events designed to facilitate the building of a community of young, queer Latinas. . . . [At the start of the research] Bienestar had no funding for the lesbian-specific programs that it offered and advertised. Past funding had been available for queer women based at least in part on the premise that they might be having sex with young gay and bisexual men.

While lesbian staff rarely or never discussed HIV/AIDS in the lesbian support groups they facilitated (and instead focused on topics of interest to their young clients, such as, "Where do you meet women and what do you do once you have met them?"), the gay, male HIV-prevention focus at Bienestar was nevertheless evident in the HIV risk assessment forms that all lesbian clients were asked to complete. Lesbian staff were required to administer these surveys and assessments to their lesbian clients for the organization to meet the contact numbers specified in its contracts. However, the questions asked, or not asked, on these forms seemed to highlight that they had not been intended for lesbians. Risk assessment forms ask respondents to identify as "gay," "bisexual," "heterosexual," or "transgender" prompting many lesbian clients to write in the word "lesbian" on their forms. A survey administered to all clients in the queer youth program also appeared to be targeted at gay men because it focused heavily on condom use without any mention of dental dams, the barrier that lesbian staff at Bienestar had occasionally discussed and handed out to their clients. These sorts of omissions provided some of the more subtle clues to lesbian staff and clients that there was a lack of resonance between the mission of the organization (HIV prevention) and the needs and desires that motivated young lesbian clients to come to the organization.

Why Bienestar? Counting Oppressions and Making Organizational Choices

In the Summer of 2000, the women's program at Bienestar had only 1 employee and no funding and was suffering by comparison to a thriving gay men's component that was staffed by approximately 10 gay men across seven locations. In light of these disparities and the organization's primary identification as an HIV/AIDS organization, it is important to examine the intersection of factors that bring Latina lesbians to Bienestar as opposed to organizations that have funding for lesbian-specific programs, such as the Los Angeles Gay and Lesbian Center. In Los Angeles, a city in which there are dozens of Latino community organizations, several white queer community organizations, and a handful of queer Latino organizations (all ASOs), the Latina lesbians interviewed for this project explained that three layers of inequality prevented them from finding an organization intended for their specific community. For Latina lesbians in Los Angeles, without organizations of their own, triple jeopardy has a practical and rotating meaning—race is the oppressive category in queer white organizations, sexual identity is the oppressive category in Latina organizations, and gender is the oppressive category in gay Latino organizations. It is the experience of being othered in each of these contexts that can make counting one's oppression a relevant practice in the lives of lesbians of color.

According to the organization's male leaders, Bienestar's women's component provides an exclusively Latina environment that fosters *jota* (or queer Latina) pride, community building and romantic relationships among Chicana/Latina lesbians. Martin, the executive director, explains that queer Latinas "choose" Bienestar not only because it produces events and offers programs that are culturally familiar, but also because of the racism that Latinas experience in large gay and lesbian organizations with white leadership. Gay and lesbian resource centers often appear to have achieved racial/ethnic/cultural integration but maintain a white leadership and a European American cultural hegemony that is manifested in the look and feel of the organization and its events (Vaid 1995). Martin argues that Bienestar is needed because staff in gay and lesbian organizations with predominantly white leadership will claim that they "open the door and welcome [Latinos]," but despite this ideological commitment, "the music, the food, the everything, is not really welcome to Latinos." In response to my question about whether a lesbian component is appropriate in an AIDS organization that is managed by gay men and has no funds for lesbians, David, the director of QUE PASA, explains,

It's appropriate [because] it's not just about HIV and AIDS issues: it's about cultural relevancy. I have seen and heard stories from women that go to the agencies that do have lesbian-specific money and because the women are only able to identify along a sexuality basis they still have to deal with issues of racism at those agencies and may not feel comfortable. It's amazing to me even taking into consideration how small the women's program is here, the overwhelming response we get from the community is that it's needed.

Both Martin and David assert that cultural sensitivity and an environment free of racism is often more important to Bienestar's lesbian clients than having a large and well-supported queer women's component. For the gay Latino men in leadership at Bienestar, it was therefore not unexpected that Latina lesbians would seek services at their organization, regardless of whether the organization has made an explicit commitment to hiring queer women or including service to lesbians in its mission.

In contrast the women staff at Bienestar offered a more nuanced explanation for the presence of young Latina lesbians in the organization. According to lesbian staff it is the lack of alternative, more woman-centered political and social organizations for queer Latinas in Los Angeles that brings young Latinas to Bienestar. While some Latino gay and lesbian organizations, such as GLLU, were growing and active in the late 1970s and 1980s, the undeniable impact of the AIDS epidemic on gay Latino men, as well as the availability of AIDS-related funds, led many of these organizations to turn their attention to HIV/AIDS or to disband altogether. Elena, a previous manager of the women's program, suggests that she might have become involved in an organization that was both culturally sensitive and gender sensitive had such an organization existed:

If I wanted to work for something that was more specific to being a jota and being queer identified and female, I couldn't find that. . . . There was Lesbianas Unidas. They kind of have been defunct for a while. I think there has been like a backlash as far as identity politics go . . . anything that [comes] to queer communities of color [is] in the form of AIDS monies.

Similarly, according to Tina, a transgender Latina staff member,

You have to earn your respect there because if we start first with society in general, men are always in the position of power . . . You're a woman so that's not good because you're not in a position of power. Apart from that, you're a lesbian.

And the last part is you're Latina. So you are triple-fucked.

While Martin and David's comments imply that many of Bienestar's lesbian clients prioritize racial/ethnic unity over the greater stability and centrality of lesbian programming offered in non-Latino organizations, Elena and Tina emphasize that it is the limited choices for women of color in general and within the queer Latino community that lead women to Bienestar. If an ideal organization for Latina lesbians is one that offers cultural empowerment and lesbian leadership and programming, the attention of David and Martin to the failings of white organizations distracted from, or overlooked, work that might be done at Bienestar to produce such an environment.

Yet according to Martin, the supportive presence of Latinas in an organization run predominately by and for Latino men is also a reflection of a "comfortable" and "natural" gender division of labor in Latino culture. For example, lesbian board members, he argues, are invested in the success of Bienestar in part because of the cultural role of Latinas as caretakers. . . . While many of the women staff and clients at Bienestar were dissatisfied with the marginal role of the women's program, ultimately leading them to organize against sexism in the organization as described below, it is also important to recognize the partial truth in Martin's assessment that the Latinas at Bienestar were willing to manage their coworkers' machismo in exchange for being accepted as queer in a distinctly Latino/Chicano space. . . .

A gay-male-dominated organization. Lesbian staff members at Bienestar describe examples of inequalities that are well documented in the literature on women working in male-dominated environments and particularly emphasized male coworkers' ignorance of male privilege and their entitlement to conversational and physical space (Lorber 1994; West and Zimmerman 1987). Lesbian staff perceived that they and their clients had been relegated to the least desirable physical space in the centers in which they worked. Fatima, a staff member who was holding a lesbian support group in a makeshift area of one of Bienestar's offices, recalls her supervisor's response to her request that he share the nicer meeting room where the gay men's group was being held:

> He was telling me ". . . I've been facilitating this group with the same men for about two years, and we worked hard to get this . . . nice group discussion room. And I feel, for lack of a better word *offended* that you are even asking me to *share* the room." And I was like, "It's not like I am taking something away from you. I'm asking you to share what we have together within the agency!" And he had to *think* about it!

Fatima adds that the discussion that ensued around sharing the meeting room signaled to her that her supervisor lacked the ability to recognize male privilege or draw connections between systems of oppression. . . .

Fatima and other lesbian staff members assert that they had more or less expected to struggle with sexism of this kind at Bienestar based on its reputation as a gay-male-dominated organization. Yet they found that gender inequality at Bienestar was complicated by the centrality of gay men to the organization's HIV-focused mission, the external legitimacy given to Bienestar's programmatic priorities, the urgency of the AIDS epidemic, and the availability of funding for gay men's programs. If lesbian programs had no funding, did their support groups deserve to use the better meeting room? If the mission of the organization is HIV prevention and most clients are gay men, on what grounds could lesbian staff demand an environment more sensitive to their needs?

Lesbian Programs: Appropriate but Not Necessary

The psychocultural barriers model. Understanding the intersection of clients' racial/ethnic, sexual and cultural identities is central to Bienestar's HIV-prevention model. According to David, HIV-prevention services at Bienestar are guided by the research findings of Rafael Miguel Diaz, a professor at the Center for AIDS Prevention Studies in San Francisco. Diaz's work on HIV-risk-reduction among gay and bisexual Latino men focuses on identifying psychocultural factors (machismo, *familismo,* and taboos about discussing sex) that are barriers to safer sex practices. Diaz (1997) concluded with the assertion that HIV prevention must move beyond sharing facts about transmission and instead provide "culturally relevant" interventions that address the host of cofactors that contribute to unsafe sex. At Bienestar, the application of Diaz's work means providing support groups and social events for gay men that enhance general self-esteem and demonstrate healthy ways for gay Latinos to communicate with one another about sex and relationships. According to this model it may not be necessary to mention HIV/AIDS or safer sex at all for a group meeting to be a successful part of the prevention effort. For the purposes of this article, what is most significant about Bienestar's use of this model is the manner in which it is applied to the queer women's program to justify the provision of services to a nonfundable, low-risk population. . . .

In theory, Bienestar's funding structure necessitated that the queer women's component prioritize the provision of HIV-prevention services to lesbian clients. Given that lesbian clients come to the organization to come out and meet other women this project would likely have failed immediately had staff prioritized HIV prevention in practice or relied on the prevention models David refers to above (i.e., talking about biological risk, handing out condoms, etc.). Thus, the psychocultural barriers model, which David generalizes from Diaz's study at gay Latino men to include the gender-inclusive term "communities of color" justifies the delivery of HIV-prevention services to lesbians because the method de-emphasizes HIV and instead emphasizes issues that are of interest to young Latina lesbians (e.g., family, communication, dating).

If lesbians are being served at Bienestar, then why should it matter who funds these services and with what intention? While Bienestar boasts that it is the only organization in Los Angeles that provides culturally relevant services to Latina lesbians, it does so without an ideological commitment to lesbian programs, lesbian staff, or lesbian clients. Although the use of the psychocultural model validates the importance of

issues that might be important to young Latina lesbians, it is based on accountability to funders and not lesbian clients themselves or the Latina lesbian community. Women staff and clients were therefore simultaneously grateful for the opportunity to be part of the only queer Latino organization that provided lesbian services but also aware that their role in the organization was fragile and auxiliary. Bienestar's financial rationale for queer women's marginalization (i.e. "there just isn't funding for your program") made it difficult for lesbian staff to determine whether lack of support for their programs, and for themselves as employees, stemmed from a funding obstacle that the male leadership could do nothing about or a more personal conflict between gay men and lesbians in the organization. Monica, a queer staff member points out that limited funding is an obstacle for the queer women's program but also emphasizes that gay male staff felt threatened by the program and the possibility that women could be "taking over":

> In an agency that employs 90-plus employees, at any given tune, they are only employing 3 queer women. Part of that I believe is because, as they say, the federal government does not provide funding to educate women on prevention. So they have implemented a queer women's component but every time I think that women try to push the program out there, they are stopped because of funding [but also] they are stopped because of the reality that these men feel that the women are taking over the space when they come in.

Such comments highlight the awareness of lesbian staff that difficulty finding funds to support lesbian youth programs is a real obstacle, likely faced by organizations other than Bienestar. Yet the constant attention to HIV/AIDS funding as a means to explain all disparities between gay men and lesbians in the organization begged other questions for lesbian staff, questions that focused on inequalities between gay and lesbian employees that had little or nothing to do with external funding for lesbian programs.

"We are the population we serve": Hiring and promotions at Bienestar. Lesbian staff suggested that a second philosophy adopted at Bienestar supported gender discrimination in hiring and promotions. Committed to the notion that staff members should represent the population they serve, Bienestar's leaders emphasized the importance of peer-led programs in which the identities of employees closely matched those of their clients. According to Elena, "[David] was always proud to say that, 'We are the population that we serve; we are the ones who have been here before.'". . . While the psychocultural model could be used to explain why a lesbian program was appropriate at Bienestar, the number of AIDS cases could be used to explain why developing the program, and concomitantly hiring and promoting more lesbian staff, was not necessary. Together these logics led lesbian staff to believe that their presence at Bienestar was a privilege or luxury, in contrast with the feeling of entitlement that they perceived in gay men. At Bienestar, the good news of being theoretically at low risk for HIV infection became bad news for lesbians who hoped for job advancement in an organization in which the staff was expected to reflect AIDS demographics.

Collective Resistance: The Town Hall Meetings

While lesbian staff suggested that they experienced an initial "honeymoon period" in which it was exciting and a relief to work in a queer Latino space, most of the women explained that this experience changed within the first year of their employment at Bienestar. Committed to their clients and fearful of being unable to find another queer Latino work environment, the women I interviewed also described a period in which they stayed at Bienestar despite burnout and strategized to accept or improve their working conditions. Some women staff members highlighted the importance of developing personal coping strategies for accepting that the organization would never change; others devised plans to organize women clients and staff and eventually confront the agency's male leadership. In July of 2000, the two queer women staff who remained in the organization, Fatima and Blanca, decided to hold a town hall meeting at a local cafe to inform women clients, past

lesbian staff members, and other Latina lesbians in the community about the structural deterioration of the queer women's program and the lack of emotional and financial support being given to lesbian staff. Fatima explains that planning the town hall meeting was about encouraging queer Latinas to "take the matter into [their] own hands" and that men were not invited to attend. Bienestar's leadership saw the announcements for the women's meeting circulating over e-mail. One week before the women's meeting, Martin, Bienestar's executive director, announced a general town hall meeting for the entire Bienestar community—staff, clients and interested community members. Blanca argues that the general town hall meeting was a "buzz kill for [the women's] town hall event" and expressed anger that it had been scheduled at the same time as a queer women's support group, thus discouraging women staff and clients from attending.

In response, Fatima explains that she called each of her group members and asked them to attend the general town hall meeting instead of the women's support group.

Twenty-five women (and 45 men) attended the general meeting, and several lesbian clients came prepared with questions to ask the facilitators. The meeting was facilitated by two gay Latino men, one Bienestar administrator, and one employee from a second gay Latino organization. Concerns about lesbian representation at Bienestar nearly dominated the discussion. The comments of women attendees produced a long list of demands, and one lesbian community member in the audience addressed gender inequality directly by arguing that there was a "double standard" at Bienestar because "women help the men with their outreach but they are responsible for their own [outreach] and the men don't help." She added that "women need to feel more welcome, but we don't. We have one foot in, one foot out. The women's component needs to be allowed to grow!" In response to this comment and the dialog focused on lesbians at Bienestar, one of the facilitators remarked, "This town hall has been kindly sponsored by Bienestar, but other organizations are here. So let's focus not on a specific program or organization so that this is useful for everyone." Visibly angry, the woman who had made the comment about the double standard stood up and left the meeting.

Consistent with my discussion above about the factors that compel young Latina lesbians to seek services at Bienestar, lesbian clients expressed to the facilitators that they focused on Bienestar because it was the only organization to which they had access. One lesbian client, in her early 20s, explained, "I don't mean to point at Bienestar, but it is the only [queer] place in East L. A. . . . That's why I talk about it."

Later in the meeting, participants were asked to offer ideas about how to address the concerns that had been raised. The tone of the meeting became increasingly tense as both women and men in the audience communicated their suspicion that the strategy session would result in few "real changes." The facilitator from Bienestar responded by shifting accountability to the staff and clients in the audience. "You have all been asked a thousand times what your needs are," he explained, and later, when a gay man suggested that Bienestar should have domestic violence services, he asked in response, "Have you asked for that? We aren't telepathic." Similarly, when a lesbian in the room delivered a passionate speech about the "triple oppression from racism, sexism, and homophobia" faced by lesbians of color and added that lesbians are not encouraged to feel "entitled" to Bienestar's services, the facilitator gestured to a group of young lesbian clients sitting together in one section of the room and asked "What are you doing to better the program?" One lesbian client responded with frustration "Well, I am going to the groups. We are willing to be educated so we can educate others, but that is why we are here!"

The following week, 38 lesbians and bisexual women attended the town hall event facilitated by Fatima and Blanca, including several of the women clients who had attended the general meeting. The women in attendance asked a series of questions, many of which highlighted their distrust of Bienestar and its leadership: Will funds we raise for the women's component actually go to women? How can we raise money for the women's component but keep it independent of Bienestar's control? If we get the funds, will that do anything to change the lack of respect lesbians receive at Bienestar? Why don't we start our own organization? Women clients also appeared to feel more comfortable expressing sadness, in addition to anger at the women's meeting. Rosie, a young lesbian who regularly attended the support group in East Los Angeles asserted while crying, "I never went [to Bienestar] because I heard it was for men. There is no place for me!" Carla, Rosie's girlfriend, added, "Rosie was so in need for services . . . Women are always there for men; it's not fair that they aren't there for us." While all of the women who attended the meeting appeared enthusiastic about effecting change at Bienestar, no one emerged as a leader and no plan was developed to begin the significant work necessary to raise money for the women's component or a new queer women's center. Women staff explained that they were too financially vulnerable to risk losing their jobs by challenging Bienestar's leaders.

Analysis and Conclusions

The data presented here indicate that the external sociopolitical environment and ideological currents within social movements can assist in forming an institutional context in which gender inequality is mystified, legitimized, and/or naturalized. In the case of Bienestar, which began as a subcommittee of a lesbian and gay organization (GLLU), the urgency of the AIDS epidemic resulted in a shift in organizational identity and goals such that the organization's constituency became HIV-positive gay men. While GLLU women struggled with sexism, they were nonetheless central to GLLU's early mission and functioning. As GLLU became Bienestar, it was the new emphasis on HIV paired with external logics about HIV-risk and prevention methods, that institutionalized the marginal position of lesbian staff and lesbian programs in the organization. In conjunction with other research findings (Schwartz 1993; Stockdill 2001; White 1999), the data presented here suggest that public health discourse, the AIDS infrastructure, gendered norms regarding women's caretaking of gay men affected by HIV, and the prioritization of racial/cultural pride over gender equality in the AIDS movement have converged to provide both scientific and political justifications for the marginal position of women in AIDS-funded organizations.

While sexism has divided the gay liberation movement since its inception (D'Emilio 2000; Faderman 1991), lesbian marginalization has witnessed a new level as the centrality of gay men in LGBT organizations has been rendered less visible by a new set of tools and logics made available by the AIDS epidemic. On the surface, the case of Bienestar tells a familiar story of women struggling with sexism in a male-dominated work organization. Yet what is sociologically significant in their accounts is the way in which lesbian staff at Bienestar were compelled to believe in the legitimacy of their own marginalization, based on external logics about risk associated with HIV/AIDS. Conflicts regarding sexism at Bienestar were complicated by the interconnectedness of, on one hand, sexist attitudes and practices that male coworkers could conceivably change and, on the other hand, external obstacles, such as a shortage of funding for women's programs, about which male managers could do little. The interplay of internal organizational dynamics and external forces, micro-level interactions between men and women coworkers and macro-level trends in the national response to an epidemic resulted in additional challenges for women attempting to make sense of and respond to their position within a gendered organization.

These effects are particularly consequential for lesbians of color, whose experience of triple jeopardy is both cause and effect of their limited organizational options. This article has also demonstrated that in the context of multicultural social movement organizations, it is difficult for organizational actors not to count, emphasize, and prioritize particular oppressions for the very reason that the histories and meanings of racism, classism, sexism, homophobia, and other forms of oppression are personally, politically, and organizationally distinct. Several women interviewed for this research referred to their experience of triple jeopardy, or the primary yet rotating significance of three forms of oppression in their lives: sexism, racism, and homophobia. In the context of Bienestar, in which both racism and homophobia received significant ideological attention from male staff, sexism emerged as the most salient form of oppression for women staff. Although racism and homophobia bring queer Latinas to Bienestar to begin with, sexism became the form of oppression with the greatest material consequences given the centrality of Bienestar to their economic security and sense of safety and community. The data presented here support the assertion that oppressions are multiplicative and qualitatively experienced. Yet the case of Bienestar simultaneously, and perhaps paradoxically, suggests the need for an expansion of intersection feminist theory, multiple jeopardy theory specifically, to include an analysis of organizational context and the rotating significance of experientially countable and distinct forms of oppressions.

Britton (2000) has stressed the importance of examining context as a means of discovering how gendered characteristics of organizations change and develop over time, how members of an organization understand and interact with these characteristics, and how organizations might become less oppressively gendered. The organized response of lesbian and gay communities to the AIDS epidemic serves as one example of a sociopolitical context that has produced change in the gendered characteristics of LGBT organizations. The case of Bienestar suggests two directions for further inquiry into how to create less oppressively gendered organizations. First, the goals and mission of organizations are not gender (or race) neutral, even when they may appear so. Research on antiracism education in nonprofit organizations suggests that integrating antiracism into an organization's mission is critical to creating racial equality, no matter what services an organization provides (Luft 2003). Similarly, it is likely that unless gender equality is an integrated part of an organization's mission, organizational goals themselves may be used to support oppressively gendered outcomes (Ostrander 1999). Second, the interaction between organizations and other institutions with power to grant money, grant legitimacy, and stimulate organizational growth influences the gendered characteristics of organizations. Future research on gendered organizations should therefore consider the ways in which some gendered practices and ideologies in organizations are rewarded more than others by outside systems, bureaucracies, and other organizations (Reger 2002).

References

Acker. Joan. 1990. Hierarchies, jobs, bodies: A theory of gendered organizations. *Gender & Society* 4: 139–58.

Altman, Dennis. 1994. *Power and community: Organizational and cultural response to AIDS.* London: Taylor & Francis.

Anzaldúa, Gloria. 1990. Bride, drawbridge, sandbar or island: Lesbians-of-color hacienda alianzas. In *Bridges of power: Women's multicultural alliances,* edited by Lisa Albrecht and Rose M. Brewer. Philadelphia: New Society.

Baca Zinn, Maxine and Bonnie Thorton Dill. 1996. Theorizing differences from multicultural feminism. *Feminist Studies* 22: 321–31.

Blackwood, Evelyn and Saskia Wieringa. 1999. *Female desires: Same-sex relations and transgender practices across culture.* New York: Columbia University Press.

Britton, Dana. 2000. The epistemology of the gendered organization. *Gender & Society* 14: 418–34.

Clendinen Dudley and Adam Nagourney. 1999. *Out for good: The struggle to build a gay rights movement in America.* New York: Simon & Schuster.

Combahee River Collective. 1983. The Combahee River Collective statement. In *Home girls: A Black feminist anthology,* edited by Barbara Smith. New York: Kitchen Table Women of Color Press.

D'Emilio, John. 2000. Cycles of change, questions of strategy: The gay and lesbian movement after fifty years. In *Politics of gay rights,* edited by C. Rimmerman, K. Wald, and C. Wilcox. Chicago: University of Chicago Press.

Diaz Rafael Jorge. 1997. Latino gay men and psycho-cultural barriers to AIDS prevention. In *In changing times: Gay men and lesbians encounter HIV and AIDS,* edited by M. Levine, P. Nardi and J. Gagnon. Chicago: University of Chicago Press.

Duneier, Mitchell. 1999. *Sidewalk.* New York: Farrar, Straus, and Giroux.

Faderman, Lillian. 1991. *Odd girls and twilight lovers: A history of lesbian life in twentieth-century America.* New York: Penguin.

Gay and Lesbian Medical Association. 2000. *Healthy people 2010: A companion document for lesbian, gay, bisexual and transgender health.* San Francisco: Gay and Lesbian Medical Association.

Glasner Barry and Anselm Strauss. 1967. *The discovery of grounded theory.* Chicago: Aldine de Gruyter.

Hill Collins, Patricia. 1990. *Black feminist thought: Knowledge, consciousness, and the politics of empowerment.* Boston: Unwin Hyman.

hooks, bell. 1981. *Ain't I a woman: Black women and feminism.* Boston: South End.

King, Deborah. 1990. Multiple jeopardy, multiple consciousness: The context of a Black feminist ideology. In *Black women in America: Social science perspectives,* edited by M. Malson, Elisabeth Mudimbe-Boyi, Jean F. O'Barr and Mary Wyer. Chicago: University of Chicago Press.

Kurtz, Sharon. 2002. *Workplace justice: Organizing multi-identity movements.* Minneapolis: University of Minnesota Press.

Liebow, Elliot. 1967. *Tally's corner.* Boston: Little Brown.

Lorber, Judith. 1994. *Paradoxes of gender.* New Haven, CT: Yale University Press.

Luft, Rachel. 2003. Race training: Antiracist workshops in a post-civil rights era. Ph.D. diss. University of California, Santa Barbara.

Moss Kanter, Rosabeth. 1977. *Men and women of the corporation.* New York: Basic Books.

Ostrander, Susan. 1999. Gender and race in a pro-feminist, progressive, mixed-gender, mixed-race organization. *Gender & Society* 13: 628–42.

Reger, Jo. 2002. Organizational dynamics and the construction of multiple feminist identities in the national organization for women. *Gender & Society* 16: 710–27.

Reskin, Barbara. 1988. Bringing the men back in: Sex differentiation and the devaluation of woman's work. *Gender & Society* 2: 58–81.

Robnet, Belinda. 1996. African-American women in the civil rights movement, 1954–1965: Gender, leadership, and micromobilization. *American Journal of Sociology* 101 (6): 1661–93.

Rofes, Eric. 1990. Gay lib vs. AIDS: Averting civil war in the 1990s. *OUT/LOOK* 2 (4): 8–17.

Schneider, Beth and Nancy Stoller. 1995. *Woman resisting AIDS: Feminist strategies of empowerment.* Philadelphia: Temple University Press.

Schwartz, Ruth. 1993. New alliances, strange bedfellows: Lesbians, gay men, AIDS. In *Sisters sexperts, queers: Beyond the lesbian nation,* edited by A. Stein. New York: Penguin.

Segura, Denise. 1989. Chicana and Mexican immigrant women at work: The impact of class, race and gender on occupational mobility. *Gender & Society* 3: 37–52.

Smith, Barbara. 1993. Homophobia: Why bring it up? In *The lesbian and gay studies reader,* edited by Henry Abelove, Michile Aina Barale, and David Halperin. New York: Routledge.

Stockdill, Brett. 2001. Forging a multidimensional oppositional consciousness: Lessons from community-based AIDS activism. In *Oppositional consciousness: The subjective roots of social protest,* edited by J. Mansbridge and A. Morris. Chicago: University of Chicago Press.

Stoller, Nancy. 1997. From feminism to polymorphous activism: Lesbians in AIDS organizations. In *In changing times: Gay men and lesbians encounter*

HIV/AIDS, edited by M. Levine, P. Nardi, and S. Gagnon. Chicago: University of Chicago Press.

Takagi, Dana. 1996. Maiden voyage: Excursion into sexuality and identity politics in Asian America. In *Asian American sexualities: Dimensions of the gay and lesbian experience*, edited by Russell Leong. New York: Routledge.

Trujillo, Carla, ed. 1991. *Chicana lesbians: The girls our mothers warned us about*. Berkeley CA: Third Woman Press.

Twine, France, Windance. 2000. Racial ideologies and racial methodologies. In *Racing research, researching race: Methodological dilemmas in critical race studies*, edited by F. Twine and J. Warren. New York: New York University Press.

Vaid, Urvashi. 1995. *Virtual equality: The mainstreaming of gay and lesbian liberation*. New York: Anchor Books.

Ward, Jane. 2000. A new kind of AIDS: Adapting to the success of protease inhibitors in an AIDS care organization. *Qualitative Sociology* 23: 247–66.

West Candace and Don Zimmerman. 1987. Doing gender. *Gender & Society* 1: 125–51.

White, Renee. 1999. *Putting risk in perspective: Black teenage lives in the era of AIDS*. Lanham, MD: Rowman and Littlefield.

Discussion Questions

1. As you read the articles in this volume, pay attention to whether they take an intersectional approach, seeing such characteristics as race, ethnicity, gender, class, or sexuality as a composite or an approach that prioritizes or centers one above others. Have you observed real-life situations where one characteristic is being prioritized or ignored in contrast to others?

2. If you were a staff member or client of Bienestar, how would you deal with the situation Ward describes? What would you say to the men in leadership positions? What would you say to the women who spoke out at the town meetings?

3. The almost unspoken social class issue here is that many, perhaps most, of Bienestar's clients must depend on an organization that has public or grant funding for social services. What alternatives might be available if the clients were more affluent? What alternatives might they pursue given their economic situations?

Reprinted from: Jane Ward, "Not All Differences Are Created Equal: Multiple Jeopardy in a Gendered Organization." In *Gender & Society*, 18 (1), pp. 82–102. Copyright © 2004 by Sociologists for Women in Society. Reprinted by permission of Sage Publications, Inc. ✦

23

When You're a Credit to Your Race, the Bill Will Come Due

O. J. Simpson and Our Trial by Fire

Michael Eric Dyson

On June 17, 1994, I can vividly recall watching along with millions of Americans the strange sight of a Ford Bronco traveling along a freeway in Los Angeles. O. J. Simpson, beloved sports figure and comedic actor, was being followed by police and camera crews in some weirdly staged, hopeless chase in the aftermath of two brutal murders. By October 3, 1995, the world was watching when the O. J. Simpson verdict was reached—not guilty of murdering Nicole Brown Simpson and Ronald Goldman. The trial ripped open for public scrutiny profound issues of race, class, and gender. Michael Eric Dyson explores the wounds in the wake of the Simpson verdict, highlighting for readers the complexity surrounding Orenthal James Simpson's fascinating rise and fall.

Dyson asserts that the case "rudely reminded us of a gigantic and numbing racial divide," drawing back the nice facade of racial harmony to reveal deeply felt fears and rage. O. J. Simpson himself, Dyson suggests, is a paradoxical figure. He is a Black man who chose to ignore the reality of race and racism and aspire to "surrogate whiteness," also called "honorary whiteness," which necessitates playing by the rules and essentially knowing your place. Here also class issues intervene. Whites might have accepted a not guilty verdict for a wealthy White man in this case, Dyson suggests; however, this would not apply to a mere "surrogate white" no matter what his or her wealth, due to the perception that he or she had essentially "reverted back to barbaric blackness." On the other hand, Dyson argues, Black response to the Simpson verdict must be understood through the lens of a brutal African American history also replete with race and class images. Through this lens one can discern, as Dyson points out so convincingly, that the O. J. Simpson verdict was an inevitability once we as Americans had opened the door to legal judgments where considerations of race colored the facts. Blacks, whether enslaved or grudgingly freed to become tenth-class citizens, had coped for centuries with immoral legal decisions with brutal ramifications. In sum, Dyson argues, Whites tasted in the O. J. Simpson trial the same dread that inevitably follows from "the absolute rejection of the faith one has placed in a judicial ruling's power to bring justice." If race is part and parcel of Simpson's trial, so also is gender, albeit again influenced by race. Domestic violence became the headline issue in the Simpson case. Dyson rightly describes Simpson's treatment of Nicole Brown Simpson as "vicious." Yet, at the same time, Dyson does not let White feminists off the hook for their own blind spots—for ignoring the complexity of the issue and using the case as a platform for racist stereotyping. Moreover, Dyson tells us that while domestic abuse is a legitimate cause with regard to Nicole's treatment, the furor over the abuse Nicole experienced as well as her murder underscore the lack of visibility given to brutality against Black women whose graves seemingly go unnoticed and who do not receive the attention from feminists and the public that they rightly deserve.

Now it says here, "And every white man shall be allowed to pet himself a Negro. Yea, he shall take a black man unto himself to pet and to cherish, and this same Negro shall be perfect in his sight...." The appointer has his reasons, personal or political. He can always point to the beneficiary and say, "Look, Negroes, you have been taken care of. Didn't I give a member of your group a big job?"

Zora Neale Hurston "The 'Pet' Negro System," 1943

The studio crackled with excitement. Although I had appeared on Black Entertainment Television (BET) a few times before, this night was special. In fact, it was extraordinary. Former BET anchor Ed Gordon, my Detroit homeboy, had snagged the first televised interview with O. J. Simpson since his acquittal for the murder of his ex-wife, Nicole, and her companion, Ron Goldman. BET asked me to give "color commentary" before and after Simpson's appearance. A large irony, indeed. I'd written about Simpson in my previous book, and I'd discussed his trial on other national television shows. But there was poetic justice in me talking about Simpson's trials and tribulations, and those of black America, on the only television station that caters to black folk.

I must confess that I was an O. J. addict. I watched the trial every day for hours at a time. I was completely mesmerized. I knew it was a vulgar display of American excess. I knew it was the revelation of the gaudiness behind the lifestyles of the rich and famous. (Of course, I took delight in seeing so many rich folk exposed for the shallow people many of us hoped they'd be.) I knew it was the theater of the absurd meets the Twilight Zone. I knew as well that the trial was a painful choreography of black grief—that of O. J. and of every black person who identified with him—before an international audience. I knew it was totally artificial, a sordid drama full of kitsch that fiendishly aspired to the status of morality play. I knew it was the story of a black man who had made good but who had forgotten what made it possible, which made it bad. I knew it was all that and much, much more. And I couldn't stop watching.

Even as questions about O. J.'s guilt or innocence fade from daily debate, we continue to grapple with the wounds the trial exposed, with the trial's revelations of the pernicious rules of race in America, '90s style. That night, as I viewed Simpson on the big screen in BET's green room, I was struck again by how flawless his face is, how smooth his skin is. But I was taken as well by the jagged horrors his eyes never gaze on—how many white folk now hate his name, how they wish he would

disappear. And some wish him dead. And how black folk look at him with a mix of pity and disdain. Like the member of the family you have to recognize but hate to, because the recognition embarrasses him as well. I was struck by the size of the denials by which Simpson lives, as if he must now draw energy from the resentment that he can't afford to acknowledge, though its sheer vehemence defines and confirms his every step. Seeing Simpson so resiliently spiteful that night—not in any way bitter against whites, just against the idea that they might not love him—made it painful for me to have to say anything after he spoke. It was the final step in my loss of a hero who had once thrilled me, as he, in Ralph Ellison's words, "slice[d] through an opposing line with a dancer's slithering grace." A part of me was now gone. It was sad, and sadly disorienting.

Something of the same disorientation gripped America when Simpson was set free. When the not guilty verdicts in the O. J. Simpson double-murder case were handed down, the compass of race went haywire. The Simpson case has made many Americans doubt if we can all get along. The case has rudely reminded us of a gigantic and numbing racial divide. It reminds us, too, that boasting about racial progress often hides racial pain. The response to the verdicts knocked down the floodgates that hold back the waters of racial hostility. The Simpson case also taught us a tough lesson: the more settled race relations seem to be, the more likely they are raging beneath the surface.

Americans have become addicted to the Simpson case for more than its grotesque exaggeration of our secret racial fears. From its very beginning the case was overloaded with huge social meanings we claim not to be able to understand under normal circumstances. We have become dependent on the Simpson case to represent complicated truths that we think can only be illustrated by catastrophe. That dependence shows contempt for ordinary signs of ruin. It ignores the experience of common people, especially blacks, whose silent suffering is the most powerful evidence of decay. What their experience shows us is this: a two-tiered universe of perception rotates around an axis defined by race. While good fortune lights one side, despair darkens the other. It is rarely sunny at the same time in white and black America. In a nutshell, that's what the Simpson case reminds us of.

That O. J. Simpson is at the heart of the most ugly racial spectacle to hit America in decades is a symptom of just how crazy things are. For a quarter century, Simpson symbolized the icon-next-door. His athletic genius was revered by many blacks. His athletic skill and "colorless" image were attractive to millions of whites.

Simpson's sleek form and catlike grace as a running back brought glamour to a brutal sport. Simpson beautifully combined judgment and intuition. His sixth sense for where his pursuers were likely to pounce on him allowed him to chisel arteries of escape around heaving bodies.

As with many famous athletes, Simpson's athletic exploits gave him influence beyond the boundaries of his sport. This is hardly natural. After all, why should athletes receive tons of money and notoriety beyond the recognition and compensation they earn in sports? The absurdity of this is masked by the fact that we take for granted that such things should occur. That's not to say sports don't teach us valuable lessons about life. Sports are often a powerful training ground for moral excellence. Take the case of Willis Reed, the injured center for the 1969–70 New York Knicks who was not expected to play in the seventh and deciding game for the NBA championship. When Reed emerged from the locker room, limping but determined to compete, several virtues were literally embodied: sacrifice of self for the sake of the larger good; the courage to "play through pain"; and the sort of moral leadership that rallies one's teammates and lifts their level of expectation and achievement. These virtues transcend sport. They inspire ordinary people to overcome obstacles in achieving their goals.

There's another way, one wholly beyond his choosing, that the rare athlete has managed to rise beyond the limits of his sport. Some figures have served as heroic symbols of national identity. Others have heroically represented achievement against the artificial restrictions imposed on a group of people. In those cases, a restriction was also placed on competition as an ideal of democratic participation. Joe DiMaggio, of course, fit the first bill. His 56-game hitting streak in baseball thrilled America in 1941, a colossal feat of endurance to which the nation would turn its attention time and again as our preeminence as a world power began to fade after World War II. Jackie Robinson fit the second meaning of heroism. As major league baseball's first black player, Robinson performed gallantly in the face of bitter opposition. His gifted play paved the way for blacks in his sport and beyond the bounds of baseball.

Joe Louis managed the difficult art of fulfilling both sorts of heroism. He existed in a racial era just as complex—if more violent—as the one Robinson faced. As was true of DiMaggio's Italian world, Louis's black community celebrated its ethnic roots while affirming its American identity. Louis captured the genius of American citizenship and the protest of blacks against their exclusion from full citizenship in a single gesture: the punch that sunk German boxer Max Schmeling at the height of Nazism. That punch transformed Louis into an American hero. It also revealed the hidden meaning of Louis's heroic art: beating white men in the ring was a substitute argument for social equality. Louis's prizefighting was an eloquent plea to play the game of American citizenship by one set of rules.

Simpson never aspired to that sort of heroism. In part, that's because the times didn't demand it. Near the start of Simpson's pro career in the late '60s, the tension between the older civil rights establishment and the newer black power movement produced a more acerbic model of black heroism. Instead of integration, many blacks preferred separating from white society to build black institutions. Black antiheroism gave an angry face to the resentment that festered in pockets of black life. To be an American and a Negro—later still, a black man—were not considered flip sides of the same coin. They were different currency altogether.

Judging from Simpson's behavior during the height of his career, he had no interest in claiming whatever remained of Louis's heroic inheritance. Neither was Simpson attracted to the sort of antiheroism championed by his contemporary, Muhammad Ali. Ali's self-promoting verse and brilliant boxing proved to be sparring matches for his real battle: the defiance of white authority because of his religious beliefs. And Simpson certainly wasn't drawn to the plainspoken demeanor of fellow athlete-turned-actor Jim Brown. Brown's militant, studly image had Crazy Negro written all over it. It was the opposite of everything Simpson seemed to stand for. That is, until he was charged with brutally slashing his ex-wife and her companion.

Simpson's appeal beyond sports rested on two related but distinct factors: commerce and the conscious crafting of a whitened image. Simpson came at the beginning of an era when athletes began to make enormous sums of money inside sports. (To be sure, Simpson's highest salary was pittance compared to what even mediocre sports figures now make.) He also helped pioneer the entrepreneurial athlete. Simpson hawked everything from tennis shoes to soft drinks. He turned charisma into cash on television. Now that Michael Jordan has eclipsed everyone who came before him, it's easy to forget that Simpson's Hertz commercials used to be the star athletes aimed for in marketing their fame.

The wide adulation heaped on Simpson beyond his gridiron glory also owed much to his absent, indeed *anti*-racial politics. Simpson soothed white anxieties about the racial turmoil caused by black radicalism. Simpson's Teflon race-lessness assured white citizens and corporations that no negative, that is, exclusively black, racial inference would stick to his image. That is Jordan's charm as well. He is a latter-day Simpson of sorts. His universal appeal derives from a similar avoidance of the entanglements of race. As the old black saying goes, it's alright to *look* black, just don't *act* your color. As Simpson's case suggests, the Faustian bargain of trading color for commercial success may prove devastating in the long run.

Simpson's silence about race didn't necessarily have to be a bad thing. After all, given the history of their relative powerlessness, blacks have a heroic tradition of fighting in ways that cloak their rebellion. They adapt their speech and activity to the language and styles of the dominant society. Silence in the presence of whites was often a crucial weapon in the war to survive. If it looked like blacks were happy to be oppressed, all the better. Such appearances greased the track of covert action on which black freedom rolled. For instance, slaves sang spirituals both to entertain their masters and to send each other coded messages about plans of escape.

Still, Simpson's privileged perch in white America led many blacks to hope that he might cautiously speak about the troubles of ordinary blacks. It soon became clear, however, that Simpson was having none of that. What many blacks wanted from Simpson was no different from what was expected of other blacks. Simpson was not expected to be a politician. At least not in any way that departed from the political behavior required of all blacks in O. J.'s youth, who had to carry themselves with an acute awareness of their surroundings. To do less meant early death. Or, more crushing, it meant a slow, painful surrender of life in gasps of frustrated energy because you just didn't understand the rules of survival in a white world.

***

It's easy to understand how O. J. and other blacks wanted to escape the demands of being representatives of The Race, its shining symbols. Standing in for the group was a burden. It was also risky. You could never be sure that your efforts were taken seriously. In fact, a law of inversion seemed to apply. For most blacks, only the negative acts seemed to count. Even the positive became a negative good: it only counted as a credit against black liability, against all the wrong things black folk inevitably did. The good you did simply meant that you, and, by extension, all blacks, didn't mess up this time. When the good was allowed to count, it only underscored one's uniqueness, that one was not like other black folk. For many whites, excellence made blacks exceptions to, not examples of, their race. Ironically, to be thought of as an exception to the race still denied a pure consideration of individual merit. As long as race colored the yardstick, a real measurement of individual achievement was impossible. It is a bitter paradox that the evaluation of individual achievement that blacks yearned for was subordinated to a consideration of any achievement's impact on, and relation to, the race. Blacks were routinely denied the recognition of individual talent that is supposed to define the American creed. This history is barely mentioned now that blacks are made by many whites to look as if they duck individual assessment while embracing group privilege.

The problem of representing The Race is compounded by whites who protest its injustice to famous blacks. "Why should they be made to represent the race?," well-meaning whites ask, as if anonymous blacks had more choice in the matter than their well-known peers. (Besides, such protest releases these whites from the awful burden of confronting racism in their own world. If the representative of The Race is relieved of duty, everybody can party. It also obscures how the need for racial representation was created by white racism to begin with.) The assumption is that fame makes the burden of representation heavier for some blacks. In many ways, that's true. There is more territory to cover. And there are certainly more folk to deal with in countering or confirming destructive views of black life. On the other hand, visible blacks have routes of escape that ordinary blacks will never know. The well-known black can bask in fortunes of fate most blacks will never be tempted by. They can make lots of money, join elite social clubs, live in exclusive neighborhoods, send their kids to tony schools, enjoy the lifestyles of the rich and famous. Famous blacks can cash in on their complaints about having to represent all blacks. They can enjoy the fruits of a situation created by their being black in the first place.

Simpson took the path of least resistance for those looking to dodge the burden of being black: ignoring race. Although ignoring race is often mistaken for self-hatred, they are not the same. Those who confuse them commit what philosophers call a "category mistake." In such cases, shades of meaning slip off the edges of sloppy distinctions. Those

who ignore race, and those who hate themselves because they can't, do share self-defeating habits: both deny the differences race makes and the lingering effects of racism. But not all blacks who have these habits hate themselves or consciously set out to ignore race. Some blacks are simply nonconformists who seek to defy the bitter boundaries of race, both within and beyond black life.

Simpson has confessed (not exactly, I'm afraid, what millions of Americans were hoping for) that it wasn't until he got hate mail in jail that he admitted racism hadn't gone away. Simpson concedes that he simply ignored or denied racism for most of his adult life. Simpson's denial, combined with his raceless image, entitled him to a derisive honor: White Man's Negro. Simpson earned his crown by avoiding and forgetting about race. He kept it by lusting after white acceptance at any cost. On the face of it—at least the side of his face he showed me on the BET interview—that lust continues to shape his sense of reality. On the BET interview, Simpson said most whites don't believe he's guilty. That suggests more than Simpson's delusional state of mind. It shows how his perception of events squares with the logic of denial that made him useful to the white world. It is a vicious twist of fate for Simpson. The same technique of survival that brought him praise from whites in the past—as he was lauded, no doubt, for bravely resisting the demagogic demand to represent The Race—now causes those same whites to view him as pathological. No wonder O. J. is confused.

Simpson has now been forced to claim his race by default. It is an act that undoubtedly fills him—at least it would the old Simpson—with great regret. And not a little disdain. The blackness Simpson embraced during the trial was foreign to him. Its unfamiliar feel made him clutch it with great desperation. That blackness was molded for Simpson by Johnnie Cochran, who proved to be a shrewd conjurer of a "one size fits all" blackness. After all, it might complicate matters to acknowledge the conflicting varieties of black identity. In Cochran's conjuring, the complexity of race was skillfully shifted to a more narrow, but, on the surface at least, universal meaning of blackness-as-oppression. When applied to Simpson, such a meaning was laughable. It fit him even worse than the gloves prosecutor Christopher Darden tried to make Simpson force over his arthritic joints. But because blackness-as-oppression is often true for most blacks, Simpson benefited from its link to his case.

Darden, on the other hand, was unfairly stigmatized by Cochran's conjuring of blackness during the trial. Darden was viewed by many blacks as a traitor because he dared to call narrow blackness a phony idea in full view of white America. Darden failed because he didn't have Cochran's oratorical or lawyerly skills. (But Darden also had the thankless task of prosecuting a beloved, fallen American hero who was, at the same time, seeking to make a comeback to his black roots. Black folk are too often suckers for this sort of figure. Although blacks resent racial infidelity, we are often open to reconciliation. Even if the forgiven black continues to abuse the privilege of return, as Simpson has done. It's painfully clear that black folk are his fallback, not his first choice.) Darden also goofed when he argued that black jurors would be outdone if they had to hear the dreaded "N" word, particularly if it leapt from the past of star prosecution witness, police detective Mark Fuhrman. Black folk endure that epithet and much worse every day.

Darden's naiveté and strategic mistakes made it easy to believe that he had little understanding of the harsh realities black folk routinely face. Ironically, Darden desperately tried to point out that it was Simpson who had avoided the hardship most blacks confront. In the symbolic war of blackness being waged between Darden and Cochran, Darden tried to make Simpson appear unworthy of the knee-jerk black loyalty he enjoyed but from which Darden had been excluded. But that point was skillfully shredded in rhetorical and legal crossfire with Cochran, both in the courtroom and in the court of public opinion.

Simpson *has* largely sidestepped the indignities imposed on ordinary blacks. His fame and fortune certainly helped. Equally important, Simpson has made a career out of making white folk feel safe. He has been

an emissary of blackness-as-blandness. With O. J. present, there was no threat of black rage careening out of control. He made no unreasonable demands—or any reasonable ones for that matter—for change of any sort. He blessed the civility and rightness of the status quo. Indeed, O. J. got a big bonus by comparing favorably not only to black "hotheads," but to figures like Hank Aaron, the baseball legend whose mellow thunder led him to speak gently but insistently about racism in sports. Once Simpson put away his youthful law-breaking in San Francisco's Potrero Hill projects, he adopted a winning formula: he would play by the rules within the limits of the Given. The Given amounts to whites being on top. To win, you must act and talk white. In many interviews, Simpson has literally said so.

The extraordinary white hostility aimed at Simpson after the verdicts can largely be explained by the equally extraordinary investment O. J. made in the white world. He was a Good Negro who played by the rules. Many whites returned the favor. They invested in Simpson as a surrogate white. That investment explains their sense of betrayal by O. J. once he was charged, then cleared, of murder. According to the rules of surrogate whiteness, Simpson should have confessed his guilt and taken his punishment like a (white) man. Of course, by breaking the rules of surrogate whiteness, Simpson actually followed the rules of the Given: Those on top—wealthy whites—are not accountable to the system of justice in the same way as those on the bottom. The rules—of justice, fairness, equality—work fine for privileged whites as long as they are applied to a world of experience whites are familiar with. Beyond that territory, their sense of how and when the rules should apply is severely limited. That's the supreme paradox of white power Simpson learned up close.

It's not that white people are inherently more unfair or unjust than others. It's just that the rules are often applied in an arbitrary fashion to those outside the realm of their understanding and sympathy. That's why the barbarity of police brutality against blacks didn't faze many whites until the Rodney King beating and the riots that followed his molesters' acquittal. (Even now many whites still don't get it, as the response to the April 1996 beatings of illegal Mexican immigrants by deputies from the Riverside County Sheriff's office in South El Monte, California, proves.) Once O. J. lost his standing as a surrogate white, once he reverted back to a barbaric blackness, all bets were off. All rules were broken. Simpson began to see, perhaps for the first time, that he was worse than "just another nigger." He was a spurned black member of the white elite, an honorary white who had fallen from grace.

Simpson's celebrity, honorary whiteness, and wealth made him largely immune to the treatment shown the run-of-the-mill black male suspect. He was partly exempted by analogy: just the notion that a person *like* Simpson could murder his wife was hard for many of us to believe. The glow of false familiarity that lit his affable screen image helped too. (If one doubts the transfer between screen roles and real life, ask soap stars, who are constantly taken for their television characters, sometimes with disastrous results.) For a long stretch, Simpson made nice on television, both as a sports commentator and in typecast roles in a string of forgettable films that occasionally surface on late-night rotation. Simpson had only recently managed to find a role whose career benefit exceeded his paycheck: the hilariously unlucky Lt. Nordberg in the three *Naked Gun* films highlighted Simpson's comedic talent.

The sum of Simpson's celebrated parts—plus an unnameably perverse addiction to vicarious disintegration—moved his mostly white fans to cheer "the Juice" as he and pal A. C. Cowlings halfheartedly fled the law up I-5 and, later, the I-405 freeway in Cowlings's infamous white Bronco. (Always wanting to be like Simpson but never quite measuring up, Cowlings, this one time, ended up in the driver's seat.) Here privilege intervened. Any other black fugitive would most likely have been shot or otherwise stomped before he could call his mother, or swing by home to get a swig of orange juice. (At the time of Simpson's ungetaway cruise, LA's freeways had been the setting of the blockbuster adventure flick *Speed*. The similarities are eerie: a chase with an uncertain conclusion; a spectacle involving revenge, murder, and obsession; and the freeway itself as a metaphor for both the resolution and realization of urban trauma.)

***

If Simpson's celebrity kept him from trauma, it attracted others to his trial to compete for public attention. Understanding that there's only so much understanding to go around—witness the spread of "compassion fatigue" and the backlash against "p.c."–abused women, blacks, feminists, and others lobbied for the trial to be viewed through the lens of their suffering. While their pain was legitimate, their perspectives were often depressingly narrow. The scamper for the spotlight ruined some. Plain old greed and self-aggrandizement spoiled others.

Still, the Simpson trial and its aftermath reveal how nefarious social forces intersect and collide, how the suffering these forces breed cuts across every imaginable line of social identity, and how the suffering of some groups outweighs the suffering of others. Domestic violence made a cameo appearance at the trial's center stage. It quickly became a bit player in the judicial drama that followed. It was shattered and swept away by a hurricane of legal strategies and tactical maneuvers. It was clear that the bodies of battered women simply don't count where they should matter most—in the public imagination, and in private spaces where women live, work, play, and, too often, where they die.

True enough, the exposure of his ugly treatment of Nicole rightly shamed Simpson. The halo Simpson wore blinded the public to the darker corners of his character. The trial deglamorized Simpson's gentle, happy-go-lucky public demeanor. At the same time, a more telling symptom of our national hypocrisy emerged: The attack on Simpson as a batterer often degenerated into scapegoating. Such a practice eases consciences. It does little, however, to erase harmful attitudes and behaviors. By demonizing Simpson, many felt they were proving the moral enlightenment of a culture that refuses to tolerate such behavior. Such self-congratulation is groundless. The demonization of Simpson amounted to little more than moral posturing. We permit, sometimes condone, the abuse and killing of women every day. We need look no further than countless courtrooms and morgues for proof. Scapegoating allows us to avoid changing the beliefs and behavior that give domestic violence secret vitality.

If we were to really change our cultural habits, calling Simpson's behavior barbaric would ring true. It would be the extension of, not the exception to, our everyday practice. In our present climate, labeling Simpson's behavior barbaric revives, however remotely, ugly stereotypes of black men as beasts. The less sophisticated version of that stereotype has long been demolished. It is reborn, however, in images of young black males as social pariahs and older black males as rootless, ruthless ne'er-do-wells. Plus, the labeling invokes the ancient taboo against interracial love, whispering to all potential Nicoles: "See, that's what happens when you mess around with a black man."

Let's face it. Beating women is a manly sport in America. It is not a widely reviled practice, at least not before the Simpson trial. (It is helpful to remind ourselves that for years many white stars in every major American sport have beat their wives, too. But without a history of stereotypes to support white male beastliness, the wife-beating issue failed to catch on among the cause cèlébre set.) Simpson's treatment of Nicole—manhandling, stalking, surveilling, beating, and tyrannizing her—was vicious. It was the extreme but logical outgrowth of deeply entrenched beliefs about the worth of women's bodies in our culture. Sadly, such beliefs persist in the face of feminist activism.

Part of our problem is that we think we can have it both ways. We think we can detest feminists while lauding the "good" women, those who wouldn't call themselves feminists to save their lives. And often don't. But most men are ignorant of flesh and blood feminism and the lives of the women who fill its ranks. Feminism is what women do when they realize they must struggle to protect the rights and privileges most men take for granted.

Still, Gloria Steinem's appearance on the *Charlie Rose* show immediately after the verdicts—where she recounted taking solace in an apology offered to her, and, presumably, all whites, by an elderly black man who assured her that "not all of us feel this way"—was disappointing. It showed a lack of appreciation for the trial's complexity from a feminist who has heroically struggled for human rights. Steinem's lapse was topped, however, by the pit bull meanness of NOW's Los Angeles head, Tammy Bruce. She was later removed from office because of her relentlessly racist attacks on Simpson.

Steinem's and Bruce's behavior underlines why it is difficult for even battered black women to imagine themselves as feminists. They played the dangerous game of ranking suffering without regard to context. They made their pain, and the greater pain of abused women, the almost exclusive focus of their fiery outrage. Domestic abuse *is* a legitimate and largely neglected plague. But what Steinem and Bruce overlooked was how race gives white women's pain, and the bodies on which that pain is inflicted, more visibility than the suffering bodies of black women. There are thousands of black women who have gone to their graves at the hands of hateful men. Some of their deaths were more heinous than Nicole's. (True, they didn't have the dubious advantage of having a famous man charged with their murder.) But these women remain invisible. Even to folk like Steinem and Bruce, who are bravely committed to keeping the memory of abused women alive.

No doubt some of this resentment of unspoken white privilege—of ranking black bodies lower on the totem pole of distress—slid onto the tongues of black women who claimed the Simpson case was not about domestic violence. Technically, that's true. But neither was it, technically, about race. The important ways this case was about race are the same ways it was about domestic violence. And about the benefits and liabilities of class, wealth, fame, and gender. The disavowal of domestic abuse as an issue in the Simpson case by black women reinforces the tragic refusal of many blacks to face the crushing convergence of issues that shape black life.

Their disavowal was not simply a way these women remained loyal to the script they've been handed—race first, race finally, race foremost. It was a telling example of how that script writes out their lives as well. Often in their own handwriting. The dispute between Clarence Thomas and Anita Hill showcased the futility of thinking about our problems in strictly racial terms.

There is damning evidence, too, that Nicole contributed to the brutality that broke her. And in all likelihood, killed her. I'm not arguing that Nicole should have simply left, got out at the first whiff of trouble. The destructive dance of complicity and shame, of cooperation and resistance, of instigation and retaliation, is too complex to blame victims for the brutal behavior of their abusers. And the psychology of identifying with one's abuser is too well established to mock the difficulty of leaving. But Nicole was also obsessed with O. J. Her huge appetites for cash, cocaine, and convenience tied her to a destructive lifestyle that rivaled her relationship to Simpson.

Equally tragic, Nicole's suffering was partially aided by her family's silence and inaction. Time and again Simpson hurled Nicole's body across the room. He crashed her face with his fists, leaving telltale signs almost as large as his anger. Her family surely knew or suspected that there was big trouble between Nicole and O. J. The Browns' not knowing is just as plausible as Simpson not having murdered Ron and Nicole. After Nicole's death, her sister, Denise, insisted that Nicole wasn't a battered woman. That's an excusable lie if we admit that silence, secrecy, and shame choke domestic abuse victims and their families.

Nicole's martyrdom can certainly aid other victims of domestic abuse. Her martyrdom might also help restore her family to wholeness. The Browns' helplessness and willed ignorance about Nicole's abuse—their neglect of her living body, bought in part by O. J.'s generous patronage—helped to make her a symbol of domestic violence. Her bloodied body obviously gave the Browns the energy they needed to speak up, to act. Martyrdom lifts a person's life beyond her body. Her suffering supports those who draw

strength from her life's purpose—even if that purpose is only fully realized after death. The Browns must now join with others who identify, beyond blood ties or biology, with the fight against domestic violence to which Nicole's life and martyred body have become connected. Without the Browns' acknowledgment of complicity in Nicole's suffering, her martyred body becomes an empty tablet on which her family's guilt is written.

As serious as the Browns' failure was, Simpson's was by far the greater sin. His beating of Nicole marked a vile sexual obsession. Simpson apparently believed he owned Nicole. She was a trophy. She was a commodity O. J. bought with his considerable earnings. Such logic might suggest that Nicole was interchangeable with most of the other women to whom Simpson was attracted. Like her, they had blonde hair and big breasts.

But sexual obsession is not offset by potential—by what one might have or get in the future to replace what one lost or can't have. This makes it difficult to defend Simpson by saying that he didn't have to kill Nicole because he could have had any woman he wanted. Sexual obsession can never be satisfied.

The obsessor fixes on the object of desire as a way of realizing his own desire. Hence, sexual obsession is a disguised form of narcissism. It ultimately refers back to itself. Such self-reference contains the seed of the obsessor's dissatisfaction. By projecting his desire onto an erotic interest, the obsessor surrenders the means of achieving fulfillment to a force outside himself. Hence, the obsessor employs various forms of control, including seduction and violence, to bring the erotic interest in line with his wishes. The obsessor ultimately requires the collapse of the erotic interest into himself. This feat is rarely possible, and certainly not desirable, at least not from the erotic interest's point of view. It means that the erotic interest will have to surrender her self and identity completely to the obsessor. In the obsessor's eye, to be rejected by the erotic interest is to be rejected by himself. This is a narcissist's nightmare. Such rejection is perceived as a form of self-mutilation. Or, more painfully, it is a form of self-denial. Nicole's final rejection of the sickness of her own, and O. J.'s, obsession a month before she died was the doorway to her freedom and her martyrdom. If the same act of independence led to her liberty and her death, it suggests something of the lethal obsession that millions of women live with and die from.

***

A similarly lethal obsession—compounded by an even more sinister and convoluted history—shapes the course of race in this country. The responses to the verdicts were misrepresented in the media as an avalanche of emotion determined exclusively by color. Such simple scribing must never be trusted. Nevertheless, the responses showed just how sick and separate race makes us. O. J.—the figure, the trial, the spectacle, the aftermath—was a racequake. It crumbled racial platitudes. It revealed the fault lines of bias, bigotry, and blindness that trace beneath our social existence. The trial has at least forced us to talk about race. Even if we speak defensively and with giant chips on our shoulders. Race remains our nation's malevolent obsession. Race is the source of our harmony or disfavor with one another. Black and white responses to O. J. prove how different historical experiences determine what we see and color what we believe about race.

For instance, even as many blacks defended O. J., they knew he had never been one of black America's favorite sons. He didn't remember his roots when his fame and fortune carried him long beyond their influence. (Or, as a black woman wrote to me, "O. J. didn't know he had roots until they started digging.") On the surface, the black defense of Simpson can be positively interpreted. It can be viewed as the refusal of blacks to play the race authenticity game, which, in this instance, amounts to the belief that only "real" blacks deserve support when racial difficulties arise. But black responses to O. J. can also be read less charitably. They can be seen as the automatic embrace of a fallen figure simply because he is black. If you buy this line of reasoning, Simpson has a double advantage. He is eligible for insur-

ance against the liability of racism, and he is fully covered for all claims made against him by whites, including a charge of murder. But all of these readings are too narrow. Black responses to Simpson must be viewed in light of the role race and racism have played in our nation's history. Race has been the most cruelly dominant force in the lives of black Americans. Racism exists in its own poisoned and protected world of misinformation and ignorance. Its fires of destruction are stoked by stereotype and crude mythology.

That history may help explain black support for figures like O. J. and Clarence Thomas, who have denied the lingering impact of race. Many black folk know that, in the long run, such figures remain trapped by race. Still, it is unprincipled for blacks like Thomas and Simpson to appeal to race in their defense when they opposed such appeals by other blacks in trouble. Many blacks support such figures because they think they discern, even in their exploitative behavior, a desperation, a possible seed of recognition, a begrudging concession even, that race does make a difference.

The ugly irony is that such figures get into a position to do even more harm to blacks because of the black help they receive. (Look at Thomas's judicial opinions against affirmative action and historically black colleges and universities.) For many whites, the example of race exploiters symbolizes how black Americans use race in bad faith. The problem is many whites see this only when their interests are being undermined. Simpson's offense—allowing race to be used on his behalf—is as obvious to many whites as Thomas's injury to blacks is obscured. By contrast, Thomas looks just fine to many whites. His beliefs and judicial opinions protect conservative white interests. But Thomas's cry of "high-tech lynching" when he was seeking confirmation to the Supreme Court choked off critical discussion of his desperate dishonesty. Thomas's comment was a callous, calculated attempt to win Senate votes and public sympathy by using race in a fashion he had claimed was unjust. Thomas's dishonest behavior—gaining privilege because of his blackness only to unfairly deny the same privilege to other blacks— highlights the absurdity of race for black Americans.

A small sense of the absurdity of race came crashing down on many whites when the not guilty verdicts were delivered. A surreal world prevailed. Clocks melted. Time bent. Cows flew over the moon. The chronology of race was forever split: Before Simpson and After Simpson. October 3, 1995, became a marker of tragedy. For many whites, it is a day that will live in the same sort of infamy that Roosevelt predicted for the day Pearl Harbor was bombed. It is hard to adequately describe the bewilderment many blacks felt at white rage over the verdicts. As difficult, perhaps, as it is for whites to understand how so many blacks could be deliriously gleeful at Simpson's acquittal. For perhaps the first time, the wide gulf between legality and morality became real to many whites. At least real in a way that most blacks could see whites cared about. That gulf is one blacks have bitterly protested for years, with only moderate support from most whites. The day of the verdicts, many white people were forced to think of themselves as a group—one denied special privilege rather than guaranteed it—for the first time. As a group, these whites tasted the dread, common to blacks, that follows the absolute rejection of the faith one has placed in a judicial ruling's power to bring justice. The fact that the decision officially took four hours only heaped insult on the injured souls of white folk.

In reality, however, that decision was much longer in the making. *That jury decision was set in motion the first time an American citizen, acting on behalf of the state and supported by public sentiment, made a legal judgment about a human being where an interpretation of the facts was colored by a consideration of race.* The O. J. verdicts are an outgrowth of the system started in that moment. They are, too, a painful exposure of, and a stinging rebuke to, the unjust operation of the judicial system for blacks throughout the history of our nation. . . .

Discussion Questions

1. What is your immediate reaction to this reading? Do you find Dyson's arguments convincing? Why or why not?

2. Along with many other researchers, Dyson points out the concept of "surrogate whiteness" or "honorary whiteness." Do you think this is a useful concept? Why or why not?

3. Is race still an issue with regard to the criminal justice system in the United States? If so, how is this played out from your understanding? If not, what evidence can you present to argue that point?

4. What was your personal response to the O. J. Simpson verdict? Does the Dyson article shed any light on your personal response? Why or why not?

Reprinted from: Michael Eric Dyson, "When You're a Credit to Your Race, the Bill Will Come Due: O. J. Simpson and Our Trial by Fire." In *Race Rules: Navigating the Color Line*, pp. 10–33. Copyright © 1996 by Michael E. Dyson. Reprinted by permission of Basic Books, a member of Perseus Books, L.L.C. ✦

24
Breaking the Silence

Henry Louis Gates, Jr.

In this guest column from the New York Times, Henry Louis Gates, Jr. asks why it is difficult for Black leaders to raise questions about behavior and life choices that may contribute to Black people being disadvantaged. His answer is that when public figures such as Bill Cosby, politicians like Senator Barack Obama, or professors such as Dena Wallerson point out that dropping out of high school or getting pregnant while still a teenager are counterproductive, they are accused of placing the blame on themselves rather than on the wider society, of blaming the victims of prejudice and discrimination. Gates says that while they hesitate to discuss these matters publicly, people in the Black communities know that speaking standard English, aspiring to be a medical or legal professional rather than a professional athlete, or not becoming a teenage parent increases one's chances of not living in poverty. He advocates breaking the silence by recognizing that the problem of poverty is both structural and behavioral. He calls on society to offer more choices and for individual people to make better choices.

"Go into any inner-city neighborhood," Barack Obama said in his keynote address to the Democratic National Convention, "and folks will tell you that government alone can't teach kids to learn. They know that parents have to parent, that children can't achieve unless we raise their expectations and eradicate the slander that says a black youth with a book is acting white." In a speech filled with rousing applause lines, it was a line that many black Democratic delegates found especially galvanizing. Not just because they agreed, but because it was a home truth they'd seldom heard a politician say out loud.

Why has it been so difficult for black leaders to say such things in public, without being pilloried for "blaming the victim"? Why the huge flap over Bill Cosby's insistence that black teenagers do their homework, stay in school, master standard English and stop having babies? Any black person who frequents a barbershop or beauty parlor in the inner city knows that Mr. Cosby was only echoing sentiments widely shared in the black community.

"If our people studied calculus like we studied basketball," my father, age 91, once remarked as we drove past a packed inner-city basketball court at midnight, "we'd be running M.I.T." When my brother and I were growing up in the 50s, our parents convinced us that the "blackest" thing that we could be was a doctor or lawyer. We admired Hank Aaron and Willie Mays, but our real heroes were people like Thurgood Marshall, Dr. Benjamin Mays and Mary McLeod Bethune.

Yet in too many black neighborhoods today, academic achievement has actually come to be stigmatized. "We are just not the same people anymore" says the mayor of Memphis, Dr. Willie W. Herenton. "We are worse off than we were before *Brown v. Board*" says Dr. James Comer, a child psychiatrist at Yale. "And a large part of the reason for this is that we have abandoned our own black traditional core values, values that sustained us through slavery and Jim Crow segregation."

Making it, as Mr. Obama told me, "requires diligent effort and deferred gratification. Everybody sitting around their kitchen table knows that."

"Americans suffer from anti-intellectualism, starting in the White House," Mr. Obama went on. "Our people can least afford to be anti-intellectual." Too many of our children have come to believe that it's easier to become a black professional athlete than a doctor or lawyer. Reality check: according to the 2000 census, there were more than 31,000 black physicians and surgeons, 33,000 black lawyers and 5,000 black dentists. Guess how many black athletes are playing professional basketball, football and baseball combined[?] About 1,400. In fact, there are more board-certified black cardiologists than there are black professional basketball players. "We talk about leaving no child behind," says Dena Wallerson, a sociologist at Connecticut College. "The reality is that we are allowing our own children to be left behind." Nearly a third of black children are born into poverty. The question is: why?

Scholars such as my Harvard colleague William Julius Wilson say that the causes of black poverty are both structural and behavioral. Think of structural causes as "the devil made me do it," and behavioral causes as "the devil is in me." Structural causes are faceless systemic forces, like the disappearance of jobs. Behavioral causes are self-destructive life choices and personal habits. To break the conspiracy of silence, we have to address both of these factors.

"A lot of us," Mr. Obama argues, "hesitate to discuss these things in public because we think that if we do so it lets the larger society off the hook. We're stuck in an either/or mentality—that the problem is either societal or it's cultural."

It's important to talk about life chances—about the constricted set of opportunities that poverty brings. But to treat black people as if they're helpless rag dolls swept up and buffeted by vast social trends—as if they had no say in the shaping of their lives—is a supreme act of condescension. Only 50 percent of all black children graduate from high school; an estimated 64 percent of black teenage girls will become pregnant. (Black children raised by female "householders" are five times as likely to live in poverty as those raised by married couples.) Are white racists forcing black teenagers to drop out of school or to have babies?

Mr. Cosby got a lot of flak for complaining about children who couldn't speak standard English. Yet it isn't a derogation of the black vernacular—a marvelously rich and inventive tongue—to point out that there's a language of the marketplace, too, and learning to speak that language has generally been a precondition for economic success, whoever you are. When we let black youth become monolingual, we've limited their imaginative and economic possibilities.

These issues can be ticklish, no question, but they're badly served by silence or squeamishness. Mr. Obama showed how to get the balance right. We've got to create as many opportunities as we can for the worst-off and "make sure that every child in America has a decent shot at life." But values matter, too. We can't talk about the choices people have without talking about the choices people make.

Discussion Questions

1. Do you think the issues that Gates raises apply only or especially to poverty in the Black community, or are they relevant for other minority communities and for poor Whites as well?

2. Are there gender issues that Gates does not explore in this brief essay? Are the options and choices faced by young women and young men different? In what ways might they be different but interrelated?

3. Why is it important to use standard English? Some people might argue that doing so is "acting White" or using the language of the oppressor. How does the value Gates places on using standard English relate to the value Labov and Jordan place on Black English? Is there a time and place for each of them?

25

In the Closet

Steven Seidman

Steven Seidman's book Beyond the Closet: The Transformation of Gay and Lesbian Life *is based on interviews conducted between 1996 and 1998 with 30 men and women who responded to ads in newspapers and newsletters or were referred by friends and relatives. Those interviewed were from different races, social classes, and generations. He intended to focus on the experience of being "in the closet." What he discovered is that for many people today, the closet is a thing of the past. Their lives are characterized by episodic concealment rather than by life-shaping concealment. In Seidman's view, the way of life defined by the closet is only necessary at times characterized by "heterosexual domination," or what other authors have called "compulsory heterosexuality." When gays and lesbians are demonized and repressed, they have little choice but to pass as straights, to manage their sexuality so as to hide it.*

The case studies of Lenny, Bill, and Robert in this reading demonstrate clearly how the generation into which one is born as well as race and social class influence the closet and the way people live in it. Seidman notes that other characteristics, especially gender, but also disability, region, religion, and nationality shape closeted lives. Reading the case studies also shows that the experience of homosexuality can vary greatly. Lenny, Bill, and Robert are all gay men, but they do not see or relate to their sexuality in the same way.

Lenny was born in 1935. He is heterosexually married and is a father. He lives in the closet, using business travel to make it possible to be with male partners well away from his home town. He fears being discovered and uses a very conventional masculine gender performance to draw suspicion away from his sexuality. Bill is like Lenny in many ways. He comes from a working-class family and grew up in a small town. He did not go to college, did serve in the military, and married and had a family as expected. He also used a straight-acting masculine gender performance as a way to deflect suspicion. The difference is that, being born in 1958, he grew up when more attention was being paid to sexual orientation. There was a gay and lesbian movement, some people framed their identities around their sexual orientations, and there was an open backlash. Bill eventually divorced and began leading an openly gay lifestyle.

Seidman notes that being working class, Lenny and Bill had fewer options in deciding whether to live in the closet than they would have had if they were middle-class professional men. However, being White gave them more options than Robert, who is Black. Born in 1974, Robert came of age and recognized his sexuality at a time when there were vibrant gay communities in many cities, but organized gay life was dominated by White people. Moreover, out of necessity and desire, being part of a kin group and community is likely to be central to the lives of Black people. White people may decide to trade kin and community of origin for a new home in the gay world. It is difficult for a Black person to leave a supportive environment only to be met with racism or indifference. Much of Robert's life has been characterized by limited social contacts and a separation of his sexuality from his working life and neighborhood. As Jane Ward indicates in another article in this section, when racial/ethnic background is not a factor, gender may be. In "Not All Differences Are Created Equal," she writes about women trying to establish their place in a Los Angeles organization that is supposed to serve Latino/a gay men and lesbians.

Heterosexual domination may have a long history, but the closet does not.[1] As I use the term, the closet will refer to a life-shaping pattern of homosexual concealment. To be in the closet means that individuals hide their homosexuality in the most important areas of life, with family, friends, and at work. Individuals may marry or avoid certain jobs in order to avoid suspicion and exposure. It is the power of the closet to shape the core of an individual's life that has made homosexuality into a significant personal, social, and political drama in twentieth-century America.

The closet may have existed prior to the 1950s, but it was only in the postwar years that it became a fact of life for many gay people.[2] At this time, there occurred a heightened level of *deliberateness and aggressiveness* in enforcing heterosexual dominance. A national campaign against homosexuality grew to an almost feverish pitch in the 1950s and 1960s. Observes Allan Berube, author of *Coming Out under Fire,*

> [Gays came] under heavy attack during the postwar decade. . . . When arrested in gay bar raids, most people pleaded guilty, fretful of publicly exposing their homosexuality during a trial. . . . Legally barred from many forms of private and government employment, from serving their country, from expressing their opinions in newspapers and magazines, from gathering in bars and other public places as homosexuals, and from leading sexual lives, gay men and women were denied civil liberties. . . . Such conditions led to stilled anger, fear, isolation, and helplessness.[3]

The attack on gays accompanied their social visibility. After the war years, many gay individuals moved to cities where they expected to find other people like themselves and at least enough tolerance to put together something like a gay life. My sense is that gay visibility was less the cause than the justification of an anti-gay campaign. A growing public homosexual menace was invoked to fuel an atmosphere of social panic and a hateful politic. But why the panic around homosexuality?

Despite popular images of domestic tranquility on television and in the movies, the 1950s and early 1960s was a period of great anxiety for many Americans.[4] There was a feeling of change in the air that evoked new hopes as well as new dangers. For example, as the war ended America emerged as a true superpower. However, it now faced what many considered to be a growing Soviet threat. Hysteria around the red scare narrowed social tolerance. Dissent and nonconventional lifestyles were associated with political subversion. Communists and homosexuals were sometimes viewed as parallel threats to "the American way of life." As invisible, corrupting forces seducing youth, spreading perversion and moral laxity, and weakening our national will, communists and homosexuals were to be identified and ruthlessly suppressed. And ruthlessly suppressed they were.[5]

Moreover, though the war was over and America was victorious, this nation was changing in ways that were troubling to many of its citizens. For example, women now had some real choices. Their social independence during the war gave many women a sense of having options; some wanted only to return to being wives and mothers, but others wished to pursue a career or remain single. Set against the happy homemaker on television shows such as *I Love Lucy, Leave It to Beaver,* and *Ozzie and Harriet* was the "new woman" in *Cosmopolitan* or Helen Gurly Brown's *Sex and the Single Girl.* The *Cosmo* girl may have been heterosexual, but she was also educated, career-minded, and sexy.

Men were also restless. During the war they had been exposed to different types of people, places, and ideas. While many men wanted little more than a job, wife, and a home, the world they returned to offered them many choices—a bounty of well-paying jobs, free higher education, and "good" women who did not necessarily believe that sex had to lead to marriage. Hugh Hefner's playboy lifestyle may not have expressed men's actual lives, but it tapped into a reality and a wish for expanded sexual choice.

It was not just adults who were restless. There was a growing population of young people who were becoming downright unruly. The popularity of rock-n-roll expressed something of their restless spirit. Many young people wished to fashion lives that expressed their individual desires and wants rather than the social scripts of their parents and society. The panic over "juvenile delinquents" and "loose girls" expressed Americans' fears that the family, church, and neighborhood community had lost control of their youth.

So, while changes in the postwar period created a sense of expanded choice for many

Americans, it also stirred up fears of disorder and social breakdown. Many citizens looked to the government and cultural institutions like television and magazines such as *The Reader's Digest* to be reassured about what this nation stood for. On the global front, protecting what came to be thought of as "the American way of life" meant flexing our military muscle to ward off the communist threat. On the domestic front, moral order was thought to require stable families—and such families were to be built on the exclusive foundation of heterosexuality, marriage, monogamy, and traditional dichotomous gender roles. In this context, the homosexual stepped forward as a menacing figure, invoked to defend a narrow ideal of respectable heterosexuality. In popular culture and in the psychiatric establishment, the homosexual came to symbolize a threat to marriage, the family, and civilization itself; he or she was imagined as predatory, seductive, corrupting, promiscuous, and a gender deviant. The moral message of this campaign against homosexuality was clear: anyone who challenges dominant sexual and gender norms risks homosexual stigma and social disgrace. The homosexual was not alone in symbolizing social disorder and deviance; there was also the "loose woman," "the delinquent," and "the sex offender." All these menacing figures served to reinforce a narrow norm of the respectable sexual citizen—heterosexual, married, monogamous, gender conventional, and family oriented.

By the end of the 1960s, the idea of a rigid division between the pure heterosexual and the polluted, dangerous homosexual began to take hold in American culture. The state and other institutions were given the moral charge to protect America from the homosexual menace. Gay men and lesbians were to be excluded from openly participating in respectable society. They were demonized, and any trace of them in public was to be repressed. The world of the closet was created.

The Closet as Social Oppression

Not all instances of homosexual concealment should be described by the term *the closet*. Consider Lenny (b. 1935), one of the people I interviewed.

Lenny was keenly aware of his homosexuality as a young person. However, he was not clear about what these feelings meant. Growing up in a small town in the 1940s and early 1950s, he was not exposed to any explicit ideas about homosexuality. He never heard the term used in his family, among peers, or in the popular media. Throughout adolescence and even as a young adult, he thought of his homosexuality as a discrete feeling or impulse that could be isolated and managed. His homosexuality did not figure in the way that he defined himself.

Heterosexuality and marriage was so deeply ingrained in the world of his kin and peers that it was never doubted or questioned. Lenny grew up wanting to marry, to have a family, and to be part of a respectable heterosexual society. These heterosexual longings were deeply felt; they were real feelings and wants.

Lenny didn't anguish over his homosexuality through his adolescence and early adulthood. He knew that these feelings were not acceptable and he kept them hidden. He never entertained the idea of a life organized around his homosexuality. Until he was well into his forties (in the 1970s), he had never known an openly gay individual; he had never read about homosexuality; and he doesn't recall having been exposed to images of the homosexual in the movies or on television. Through the 1950s and 1960s, Lenny never knew there were gay political organizations such as the Mattachine Society, a small, secretive organization that focused on educating the public. Lenny felt little pressure to think of his homosexuality as an identity, and there was virtually no social encouragement for him to live an openly gay life.

Lenny eventually married. Even today, after a gay movement has vilified the closet and championed the idea of a proud, public gay self, Lenny doesn't view his straight life as a strategy to pass. "I married because that's what I wanted to do. I wanted that kind of a life." He still enjoys a heterosexual way of life. Lenny doesn't buy into the view that his straight life is a lie or is inauthentic. Lenny's life, at least through early adulthood, should not be described as "in the closet."

If the concept of the closet is to be sociologically useful, it should not be used casually to cover any and all acts of homosexual concealment. The closet is a historically specific social pattern. This concept makes sense only if there is also the idea of homosexuality as a core identity. Viewed as an identity, homosexuality cannot be isolated and minimized as a discrete feeling or impulse; choosing to organize a public heterosexual life would create a feeling of betraying one's true self. The closet may make a respectable social status possible but at a high price: living a lie. Not surprisingly, the closet is often likened to "a prison," "an apartheid," "a coffin-world," or to "lives led in the shadows."[6] It is said to emasculate the self by repressing the very passions that give life richness and vitality. Listen to Paul Monette, author of the award-winning memoir *Becoming a Man*: "Until I was 25, I was the only man I knew who had no [life] story at all. I'd long since accepted the fact that nothing had ever happened to me and nothing ever would. That's how the closet feels, once you've made your nest in it and learned to call it home." Monette's struggle for an authentic self is narrated as a war against the closet, which he variously describes as an "internal exile," an "imprisonment," and as "the gutting of all our passions till we are a bunch of eunuchs."[7]

In short, the closet is about social oppression. Among its defining features are the following. First, to be in the closet means that individuals act to conceal who they are from those that matter most in their lives: family, friends, and sometimes spouses and children. Being in the closet will shape the psychological and social core of an individual's life. Second, the closet is about social isolation. Individuals are often isolated from other homosexually oriented individuals and are often emotionally distant from the people they are closest to—kin and friends.[8] Third, secrecy and isolation are sustained by feelings of shame, guilt, and fear. The closeted individual often internalizes society's hatred of homosexuals; if he or she manages to weaken the grip of shame, the fear of public

disgrace and worse enforces secrecy and isolation. Finally, secrecy, isolation, shame, and fear pressure individuals to conduct a life involving much deception and duplicity.[9] To be in the closet is, then, to suffer systematic harm—to lack basic rights and a spectrum of opportunities and social benefits; to be denied respect and a feeling of social belonging; and more than likely to forfeit the kinds of intimate companionship and love that make personal happiness possible.

This notion of the closet makes sense only in relation to another concept: *heterosexual domination*.[10] The closet is a way of adjusting to a society that aggressively enforces heterosexuality as the preferred way of life. In the era of the closet, heterosexual dominance works not only by championing a norm of heterosexuality but also by demonizing homosexuality. The making of a culture of homosexual pollution is basic to the creation of the closet. Enforcing the exclusion of homosexuals from public life also involves aggressive institutional repression. Homosexuals are suppressed by means of laws, policing practices, civic disenfranchisement, and harassment and violence. The state has been a driving force in the making of the closet. To the extent that heterosexual privilege is enforced by keeping homosexuals silent and invisible, we can speak of a condition of heterosexual domination.

The closet does not, however, create passive victims. Too often, critics emphasize only the way the closet victimizes and strips the individual of any sense of integrity and purposefulness. But closeted individuals remain active, deliberate agents. They make decisions about their lives, forge meaningful social ties, and may manage somewhat satisfying work and intimate lives, even if under strained circumstances.

Passing is not a simple, effortless act; it's not just about denial or suppression. The closeted individual closely monitors his or her speech, emotional expression, and behavior in order to avoid unwanted suspicion. The sexual meaning of the things (for example, clothes, furniture), and acts (for example, styles of walking, talking, posture) of daily life must be carefully read in order to skillfully fashion a convincing public heterosexual identity.

For closeted individuals, daily life acquires a heightened sense of theatricality or performative deliberateness. The discrete, local practices of "sexual identity management" that is the stuff of the closet reveals something of the workings of heterosexual domination but also of how gays negotiate this social terrain.

Accommodating to the closet is only part of the story. Rebellion is the other. For individuals to rebel against the closet they must be seen as active, thoughtful, and risk-taking agents. Passive victims do not rebel; they surrender to things as they are. To reject the closet, individuals must view the disadvantages and indignities of the closet as illegitimate and changeable. They must have the inner resources and moral conviction to contest heterosexual domination. As sociologists have put it, rebellion is propelled less by utter despair and victimization than by "relative deprivation." Individuals rebel when social disadvantages feel unjust but changeable—which is to say, when they don't feel only like victims.

Finally, it is perhaps more correct to speak of multiple closets. The experience and social pattern of being in the closet vary considerably depending on factors such as age, class, gender, race, ability or disability, region, religion, and nationality. In this chapter I convey something of the negotiated and varied texture of the closet through a series of case studies. These examples are not intended to capture the full spectrum of closet experiences, but to show something of its oppressive, negotiated, and varied character.

The Closet Before Stonewall: Lenny's Story

We've already been introduced to Lenny. He grew up in a small town in Massachusetts at a time when few Americans were exposed to clear ideas about homosexuality. Lenny understood that his attraction to men had to be kept secret; no one had to tell him. Heterosexuality pervaded and organized his world. His family, friends, popular music, and peer culture conveyed a simple truth: heterosexuality was the right way to live. There was no need to aggressively enforce heterosexual dominance.

At the age of twenty-two (in 1957), Lenny had his first homosexual experience. It happened in the navy. It was hard for Lenny to forget the pleasure associated with that encounter. Confused and fearful, Lenny initially suppressed his homosexuality. He thought of these feelings as a strange, disturbing part of himself that needed to be controlled. Lenny didn't define himself as a homosexual; this notion was alien to him. He moved forward in his life. He did what was expected of him, which was also what he learned to want. He married and had a family. Lenny and his wife are still married and living in the town he grew up in.

However, between the 1950s, when Lenny was coming of age, and the 1970s, America had changed. Homosexuals were now a part of public life; they were in the news and from time to time the topic of homosexuality surfaced in conversations among family members and peers. His approach to homosexuality also began to change. Lenny learned that his attraction to men was more than a minor impulse; it meant, at least in the eyes of others, that he was a homosexual, something nobody wanted to be.

Lenny's fear of exposure intensified. "I had a wife and a child, and I certainly didn't want anybody to know about it. I had too much to lose. I enjoyed married life. I enjoyed what it gave me by way of security, home, family, children, relatives, and friends." Lenny stepped into the closet and has remained there. "No one knows about my homosexuality—not family, friends, or neighbors, I never thought about telling anybody. I won't tell anybody."

Although closeted, Lenny no longer represses his homosexual feelings. His initial homosexual encounter stirred up passions and pleasures he had not felt with women. He decided to find safe ways to have sex with men. He minimized the risk of exposure by separating these experiences from the rest of his life—geographically, emotionally, and socially. His work allows him to travel, and during his trips he has sex with men. Lenny enjoys homosexual sex and considers it natural and normal, though he is convinced that others don't see it this way. Accordingly, being closeted is, for Lenny, not about denying his homosexuality but regulating it.

Managing his homosexuality means minimizing its importance. Despite a culture that views homosexuality as an identity, he continues to think of it as merely a sexual feeling or impulse. Lenny keeps these feelings separate from the rest of his emotional and social life. Although he acts on these desires, they lack any deeper meaning for his sense of identity. Lenny understands his homosexuality as a sexual impulse that can be psychologically compartmentalized.

Socially speaking, managing his homosexuality involves a twofold practice. On the one hand, Lenny has to successfully perform a public heterosexual identity. Being married and a father makes this easy, he says. On the other hand, he must avoid homosexual suspicion. Lenny says that his marital and parental status, along with a conventional masculine gender status, makes passing relatively effortless.

Yet as Lenny described his daily life it was obvious that avoiding homosexual suspicion involves considerable effort and focus. Fear of exposure is almost constant. "I am always concerned that somehow, some way, I will be found out. I am always suspicious that somebody might pick up something." Accordingly, daily life must be deliberately and carefully managed. For example, Lenny is silent in the face of homophobic comments by family, friends, or coworkers; he will never defend gay or lesbian people for fear of arousing suspicion. He not only avoids the company of openly gay people but will not associate with people who might be suspected of being homosexual. Lenny is especially mindful to avoid staring at men for fear of being noticed. In order to reduce the risk of exposure, Lenny travels about fifty miles from his hometown at least once a week to have sex with men. In fact, he went into his present business in part because it made such travel possible without raising suspicion. Still, fear accompanies these homosexual episodes; he worries that someone will recognize him. Lenny wrestles with feelings of guilt for betraying his wife's trust.

Although safe in a marriage and family where suspicion is greatly minimized, homosexual suspicion is never absent from Lenny's world. For example, he believes that his brother might suspect him. "He may suspect. Any time I say that I've met a male friend, he wants to know if he's married." Also, Lenny is very tolerant toward people who are different. "I'm not prejudiced or bigoted at all and my brother knows that." Lenny thinks that his brother might interpret his tolerant social attitudes as a sign of homosexuality. Moreover, Lenny himself is suspicious of others. He says, "I know of a man who embroiders or crochets and right away I think, He's gay." Gender nonconformity is for Lenny, and, as we'll see, for all those I interviewed, the most telling sign of a gay identity.

For the most part, Lenny says that he likes his life. He enjoys marriage and family life. His standing as a valued part of the community means a lot to him. His business has brought him great success and satisfaction. Yet Lenny is aware that he pays a price for a heterosexually organized life. "Being in the closet limits my life. I have to put constraints on myself." When asked what it feels like to conceal his homosexuality, he says that its "confining." Lenny may wish that this aspect of his life was different but he won't change, because he enjoys a conventional heterosexual life and fears social rejection. "I'll never come out to anybody. I'm going to keep it closeted."

Lenny's decision to be closeted as a condition of maintaining a respectable social status works, in part, because he is a man of his generation. There were few alternatives to heterosexuality for many men and women born in Lenny's time and circumstances. Heterosexuality was simply taken for granted. This was, moreover, a generation that often looked longingly to a peaceful, secure, and happy heterosexual domestic life in the wake of World War II and the Korean War. It was also a generation in which self-satisfaction was tightly linked to social approval. An individual's personal goals often overlapped with social expectations. The tension between self-fulfillment and social approval was heightened in subsequent generations. Indeed, by the 1960s and 1970s the heterosexual dream of marriage and the family as havens of love and intimacy was tarnished by public revelations of the dark side of family life—violence, abuse, divorce, abortions, and gender conflict. Moreover, the baby boomer generation came of age in the midst of the rise of a proud and assertive gay movement. In short Lenny's choices are indicative of a world that is passing—a world where doing what was expected was self-fulfilling, where heterosexuality was taken for granted, and where heterosexuals and homosexuals were rigidly segregated with little or no intermingling. In this world, passing as straight was relatively easy for men and women who were married, had families, were gender conventional, and avoided homosexual associations. This world is still a part of America, but it is less so. Today, self-fulfillment is defined more in terms of subjective satisfaction than gaining social approval. Individuals have more choice about intimate lifestyle. And the texture of life in the closet has also changed.

Social Class and the Closet: Bill's Story

Bill (b. 1958) is a baby boomer. Like Lenny, he grew up in a small town. Bill recalls feeling sexual desire for boys at an early age. "I probably started thinking about my homosexuality around the time I was ten. I guess it was when other boys were becoming interested in girls and dating and I wasn't. That's when I started to see that I've got to hide who I am and I've got to pretend that I like girls." Unlike Lenny, Bill remembers being exposed to a public culture of homophobia. Family and friends referred to homosexuals in demeaning ways. Bill was very religious and quickly learned from his church minister that "God hates homosexuals." Born a generation later than Lenny, Bill grew up in a culture that not only viewed heterosexuality as an ideal, but also aggressively enforced its compulsory status by defiling the homosexual.

Bill felt overwhelming pressure to be heterosexual. His parents encouraged dating and expected him to marry and have a family. Kin, friends, church, and the media likewise celebrated an adult life organized around heterosexuality. For virtually all Americans born after 1950, there was a clear, often explicit expectation that adults should marry and raise a family.

Bill didn't want to disappoint those who mattered to him. While being socialized into an ideal of heterosexuality motivated him to adopt a public heterosexual identity, fear drove Bill into the closet. "Fear is the biggest thing. Fear of the people that might find out, fear of what will happen if they did." Fear, for Bill, translated into an anxiety that he would lose his family, livelihood, and the respect of his community.

The closet provided Bill with a strategy to resolve the conflict between social expectations and his homosexuality. He decided to present a consistently heterosexual public identity. This entailed managing his homosexual feelings and negotiating a public identity that avoided suspicion. From the standpoint of being in the closet, Bill experienced social life as filled with risk, a world where others read the sexual meaning of his behavior. To navigate this scary world, Bill had to learn the skills to successfully project a heterosexual identity.

High school was a frightening time. The term *fag* circulated as the ultimate put-down. "It was the worst thing to call somebody a faggot, even though kids didn't always know what it was." Bill knew what it meant and he saw how individuals were shamed and shabbily treated if suspected of being gay.

Bill, and almost everyone I interviewed, experienced high school as a seamless homophobic social environment. One man I interviewed, Ralph (b. 1962), avoided any behavior that might even remotely raise suspicion. For example, he decided against pursuing cooking and dance in favor of "wood-shopping." And, despite considerable athletic talent and his coach's encouragement to pursue gymnastics, Ralph feared exposure. "In the men's locker room I was panic stricken every time we had to take off our clothes. I was afraid of being aroused by whoever was standing next to me." Pressured by his parents, he joined the library club. This made him very nervous because he feared that his classmates would interpret his bookishness as a sign of being gay. For Ralph, high school meant isolation and surviving by establishing social distance. "Very few people noticed me. I stayed to myself and didn't even like to go outside."

Bill's strategy of passing in high school was different from Ralph's. Bill was more social. His friends mattered a great deal to him. The problem was they all dated, so, Bill followed suit. "I pretended to be interested in girls. I dated and I think these were attempts to hide the fact that I was gay." Bill eventually found a girlfriend, whom he later married. Still, Bill vigilantly monitored his behavior to avoid suspicion. He gradually turned to drugs and drinking to sustain a sexually active heterosexual relationship, even though his desires pulled in the opposite direction. Managing his sexuality also involved maintaining silence in the face of homophobic comments that were pervasive in school culture. Gradually, Bill grew distant from family and many friends, as he feared exposure.

After high school, Bill worked as a middle-level manager. He was very careful. His boss "was very heterosexual. He talked loudly and repeatedly about heterosexual sex. I felt really compelled to conceal." Bill learned to fit into a heterosexual world by accommodating to others' expectations. "I'm like a chameleon. I was attuned to how others felt about gays and would adjust." Bill learned to pass by mastering a public heterosexual persona.

Despite having a girlfriend, Bill couldn't escape an almost paralyzing fear of exposure. His demeanor presented a seamless masculine self. He speaks of "straightening" up his appearance. "I was very practiced in walking very straight and very military-like." Ultimately, anxieties of exposure drove Bill to join the marines. "I thought that if I was in the marines nobody would suspect, that maybe they could teach me to be more masculine."

After the marines, Bill married. All of his friends "knew that I was married and I let them assume things. I was afraid of them finding out. I was scared about it." Bill explains his decision to get married.

I don't think anybody really wants to be homosexual. Who wants to be subjected to the jokes, the harassment, the beatings, the condemnation, having to live your life as an actor? I know I didn't want to be. I knew I was homosexual from the time I was six. I wanted to be whatever normal was. I wanted a family, children. I bought the lie that if I met the right girl that the sexual attraction would be there or develop. If I loved her, it would work. I just didn't think a homosexual life was possible.

Bill married in part because he wanted the life promised by marriage—a companion, family, and social approval. He also married to avoid suspicion. Several people I interviewed were convinced that being a single adult would raise suspicion. Mike, another baby boomer, felt that staying single amounted to virtually coming out. "I knew that I was gay before I married. I was afraid not to be married. I was afraid of what it might indicate if I didn't get married. It felt like I'd be forced to come out. How could I keep hiding, being single? I was just terrified of not being married."

Bill married despite the absence of sexual attraction. "I kept waiting for the sexual attraction to come but it never did. As a result, when we had sex I had to fantasize about men." Throughout his marriage Bill struggled with his homosexual longings. He tried to suppress them. "I wanted to be faithful to my wife." He turned to alcohol. "I drank to not deal with the [homosexual] feelings, to not feel."

From childhood to his coming out in his mid-thirties, Bill relied on several strategies to sustain the closet. At the heart of the closet was self-control. At times, this meant that Bill simply had to suppress any homosexual feeling. "I didn't act on it at all for many years." At other times, Bill threw himself into work and his marriage to control his homosexuality. "I channeled my energies into work and our marriage. I wanted a family, a house. I just worked and worked. I was so closeted." Even after he was married. Bill describes a life of intense self-control to a point of self-estrangement. "I've always been aware of what I say and how I act, how I hold my cigarette, how I laugh, I mean anything. When I was living in the closet, I had a mask that I presented to anybody. It was tailored to the person or people that I was around. I didn't know who I was really." Self-control meant carefully regulating his behavior. Bill dressed to avoid homosexual suspicion. " I didn't wear anything that looked like it could be gay." Finally, self-control involved social distance. Bill had few friends after high school, and they were kept at arm's length to avoid possible exposure. Although his family was close, Bill kept aloof from his parents. "I couldn't be as open to them as I wanted to be."

In Bill's closet world, everyone potentially suspected. Despite his considerable efforts to avoid suspicion, including marriage, enlisting in the marines, and a seamless masculine self-presentation, Bill believed that his wife suspected. Perhaps, he thinks, she interpreted his lack of sexual passion symptomatically. Bill believes that his parents suspected as well. Asked why, Bill referred to a cluster of behaviors that might signal homosexuality. "The people I hung around with, the way I dressed, and [after divorce] the absence of a girl in my life." Bill thought that his mother suspected because he didn't date after his divorce. Bill threw himself into work and parenting in part to avoid suspicion. "I was hoping that my mother would figure that I didn't have time for a relationship, but I think that's when she started to question [my sexual identity]." In this world of pervasive suspicion, Bill began to suspect others. For example, he wondered about his father. "I always had an idea that he might be gay. He was very gentle. He tried real hard to get everybody to like him, and everybody did."

Bill described his closet world in theatrical terms. "My whole life until recently has been being the actor, pretending I'm somebody I'm not." Invoking the image of the actor to describe his life tellingly acknowledges that Bill had in fact acquired considerable social skill in order to succeed at passing. Of course, this heterosexual identity performance meant, as he says, living an inauthentic life. Bill passed successfully, but to do so he married, had children, joined the marines, became dependent on alcohol, and distanced himself from his own inner life as well as from family and friends. In short, the closet was a way to accommodate being the bearer

of a polluted identity but at a considerable psychic and social cost.

Managing homosexuality was somewhat different for Lenny and Bill in part because of their age difference. Lenny came of age in the 1950s and in a small town in the northeast where homosexuals were never seen or talked about; still, he somehow knew it was a defiled status. He accommodated, as did many in his generation, by fashioning a conventional heterosexual life interrupted by furtive homosexual episodes. Bill's coming of age paralleled the rise of a nationally organized gay movement. Heterosexual privilege could no longer be sustained by simply taking heterosexuality for granted. America responded to this new homosexual assertiveness with an aggressive strategy of cultural pollution and social repression. Bill grew up hearing only disparaging remarks about homosexuality from his family, peers, minister, and in newspapers and the movies. Still, as Bill reached adulthood he was aware that there were public spaces (for example, bars and community centers) where being gay was accepted. Bill initially managed these conflicting social currents by fashioning his own closet pattern. However, in contrast to Lenny, Bill eventually decided to live an open, integrated gay life.

Despite their generational differences, it is important to note that Lenny and Bill share a similar class position. They grew up in working-class families and neighborhoods. Their fathers worked in local factories and their siblings and kin were blue-collar workers, clerks, secretaries, and receptionists. No one in their families went to college. Boys were expected to work after high school.

Homosexuality presented a real symbolic and economic threat to Lenny and Bill. In their working-class culture, family was the cornerstone of life. Getting married and having a family was expected and celebrated. Men were expected to present a more or less seamless masculine self. Homosexuality threatened humiliation—for themselves and their families. Exposure risked isolation from their kin and their blue-collar community of kin, peers, and neighbors.

Their fear of exposure was also economically based. The financial interdependence between the individual and family is central to working-class life. For example, as a wage earner Bill was economically independent. Yet he was aware that his material well-being was never secure. Growing up, he had seen adults lose jobs as industry migrated from his hometown. He saw kin sustaining their own when brothers, cousins, aunts, and uncles were out of work for long periods of time. Bill considered his family a potential source of material support; he also expected that at some point his family would ask for his financial help.

Class shapes closet patterns.[11] The extent of economic interdependence between the individual and his or her family wanes between blue- and white-collar workers. This class difference shapes how individuals manage their homosexuality.

For the middle class, economic independence is valued and expected. This provides a material base for coming out and organizing a public gay life. At a minimum, middle-class individuals have options. They can move to avoid exposure; they can afford to establish a workable double life; and they can sustain themselves if estranged from their families. Moreover, because of the high value placed on individualism, middle-class individuals anticipate a considerable disengagement from their family and the community they were brought up in. They can also expect a relatively smooth integration into a middle-class gay life as compensation for any estrangement from family and friends resulting from coming out.

For working-class individuals, economic interdependence with kin is a lifelong expectation. Exiting the closet as a working-class lesbian or gay man carries serious economic risks—for themselves and their kin. Blue-collar workers expect that at some point they will either turn to kin for economic help or their family will turn to them. Additionally, estrangement from kin carries the threat of losing a primary source of community. There is no anticipation of an immediate compensation for lost community because of the middle-class character of the gay institutionalized world.

The closet is not, then, the same experience for all individuals. To understand its workings, we have to pay close attention to age and social class.

Race and the Closet: Robert's Story

Bill's and Lenny's strong economic ties to their families made exiting the closet difficult and potentially more risky than for the economically independent middle class. But their white racial status made it relatively easy for them to identify as gay. The gay world—at least the institutionalized world of bars, social and political organizations, and cultural institutions (newspapers, magazines, publishers, theater groups)—was and still is overwhelmingly white. Moreover, American public cultures, both white and nonwhite, associate being gay with being white. Accordingly, race is a key factor shaping the dynamics of homosexuality, including the closet.

Generalizations are risky. The few interviews I conducted with people of color, and the paucity of relevant social research, gives a somewhat speculative cast to my comments. Still, the evidence suggests what we would expect: race matters.[12]

To illustrate, consider the implications for blacks of an overwhelmingly white gay community. No matter how accepting some individuals may be, blacks often feel like outsiders in the gay community. The culture, the leadership, the organizations, and the political agenda of the institutionalized gay world have been and remain dominated by whites. Blacks often report encountering an inhospitable gay world, one that until recently participated in the racism of straight America. For example, through the early 1990s, black men tell of being carded at gay bars or objectified as exotic sexual selves; black women describe being silenced or ignored in decisions about social events and politics. Despite a deliberate commitment to a multicultural gay community, blacks continue to feel that they have to negotiate a somewhat foreign social terrain.

White privilege in the gay world means that blacks manage their homosexuality somewhat differently than whites. Whites may come out to an unfriendly world of kin and friends, but they anticipate an easy integration into a gay world that will affirm their sense of self and offer an alternative type of community. By contrast, if blacks exit from the closet they expect a struggle for acceptance not only in the straight but also in the gay world. To state the contrast sharply, whites expect a trade-off when they come out: estrangement from the straight world in exchange for social integration and acceptance in the gay community. Blacks do not expect such compensation for their anticipated disapproval and diminished status in the straight world. Given their more ambivalent relationship to the gay community, blacks may be more likely than their white counterparts to manage their homosexuality within the framework of the closet.

If an inhospitable or at least uncertain reception in the gay world gives pause to blacks as they consider coming out, so too does the central role that a race-based community plays in their lives. Many blacks have a fundamental personal and social investment in maintaining integration into a race-based community. This community offers protection and material sustenance in the face of the bodily and economic threats of racism; it provides a positive culture of racial pride and solidarity. Maintaining strong ties with kin and a race-based community is a cornerstone of black identity in a way that is obviously not true for whites. If whites grow up with a sense of racial entitlement and a feeling that it is their America, many blacks experience and expect an inhospitable reception in the larger society. Experience and kin have taught them that their personal and social well-being depends on maintaining solidarity with a black community. For many blacks, America is two nations, and it's only in the black world that they feel a sense of integrity and social belonging.

In short, blacks—straight or gay—are heavily invested in their racial identity and in their membership in the black community in a way that is generally not true of whites. Coming out, then, risks not merely estrangement from kin and community but potentially the loss of a secure sense of identity and social belonging. In other words, leaving the closet threatens social isolation from both the straight and gay worlds. It risks being cast adrift in a society that does not recog-

nize or value being black and gay; it jeopardizes a secure sense of belonging and protection (physical and economic) in exchange for an outsider status.

If a white privileged society creates pressures for blacks to sustain primary lifetime ties to their racial community, the latter pressures individuals to maintain the primacy of their racial identity. And if the individual turns out to be gay, the black community has often demanded that this identity be kept private as a condition of acceptance.

Whites, like blacks, can expect a mixed reception in the straight world. For example, an organized anti-gay opposition led by a white-dominated Christian Right has focused largely on the white gay population. However, at least since the mid-1980s, there is also considerable support for gay rights and respect from "white" elite institutions and public figures—from newspaper editors to intellectuals, writers, and church and political figures. Until fairly recently, black gay men and women could not count on much, if any, support from the elite community. The dominant institutions and leadership in black communities have been routinely in different, if not hostile, to gays. This is a repeated motif in the stories black gay men and women tell of coming of age in the 1980s and 1990s. The late artist and activist Marlon Riggs commented bitterly on the degraded status of black gay men in black communities:

> The terrain black gay men navigate in the quest for self and social identity is, to the say the least, hostile. What disturbs—no enrages me, is not so much the obstacles set before me by whites . . . but by my so-called brothers. . . .
>
> I am a Negro faggot, if I believe what movies, TV, and rap music say of me . . . Because of my sexuality, I cannot be black. A strong, proud, "Afrocentric" black man is resolutely heterosexual. . . . My sexual difference is considered of no value; indeed it's a testament to weakness. Hence, I remain a sissy, punk, faggot. . . . I am game to be used, joked about, put down, beaten, slapped, and bashed, not just by illiterate homophobic thugs in the night, but by black American culture's best and brightest. . . . I believe [that] black America's pervasive cultural homophobia is the desper-

ate need for a convenient Other within the community, yet not truly of the community, an Other to which blame for the chronic identity crises afflicting the black male psyche can be readily displaced.[13]

I am not saying that black communities are more homophobic than other racial or [ethnic] communities. After all, anti-gay movements have largely been affairs of white people—led by whites and largely addressing white publics. Furthermore, there is at least anecdotal evidence suggesting informal tolerance toward gays in black communities. However, tolerance often gives way to aggressive homophobia if being gay is made into a public identity and a political cause. And, as Riggs and many others have insisted, this informal culture of tolerance has often coexisted with an elite culture that has been routinely hostile to gays.[14] This has begun to change in the last decade as academics and public figures like [Jesse] Jackson and Mayor Willy Brown, public intellectuals like Angela Davis, bell hooks, Cornel West, and Henry Louis Gates, and writers like Alice Walker and Toni Morrison, have stepped forward as advocates of gay rights.

If there has been weak institutional support for gays in black communities it is in part because of an underdeveloped black gay culture. While public gay cultures were established in many towns and cities across the country during the post-Stonewall period, this has rarely been the case in black communities. There has been individual- and kin-based support, and informal networks and sometimes bars or baths have evolved that cater to blacks, but there are few public social and political organizations, or groups in black communities. Even in Harlem, where one researcher has argued that there is considerable tolerance and integration of gays, there is no community center, no political club or organization, and no openly-gay leader among Harlem's political elite.[15] Indeed, only in the last decade, as more and more black gay men and women have exited the closet, have loosely formed organizations been created to represent their interests within both gay and straight communities.[16]

The absence, at least until recently, of a politically assertive public gay and straight culture supporting black gay men and women has made the wager of coming out risky and potentially too costly for many individuals. Moreover, as black communities have continued to struggle with a sense of being under assault by racism, poverty, and family instability, tolerance for a public gay life is shaky. The closet presents a credible option, especially if, as some evidence suggests, a more relaxed or flexible closet pattern than that experienced by Lenny or Bill is possible in many black communities. Moreover, as black gay networks developed in the 1980s and 1990s, some blacks now have an alternative to the closet. However, to the extent that these networks remain small and institutionally insecure, establishing an independent gay life remains much more difficult for many blacks than for whites.

Some of these dynamics and dilemmas of being black and gay in America surface in Robert's story. His is a story of a black gay man trying to navigate between a black world that is not seen as particularly hostile nor especially friendly and a somewhat welcoming white-dominated gay world but one that doesn't feel quite like home. In the end, Robert tries to forge a satisfying life by becoming part of a small, fragile black gay world that is not solidly part of a gay or a black community.

Robert was born in 1974 and came of age in the 1990s, when gays were experiencing more personal freedom. He grew up in a large, close, middle-class family in Brooklyn. He was aware of his homosexuality as a child. He accepted these feelings as a natural part of himself. Still, he kept his homosexuality a secret through his teen and early adult years. Unlike Lenny and Bill, Robert's chief closet strategy did not involve a deliberate projection of a public heterosexual identity that included marriage or a hypermasculine self-presentation. Robert sought to avoid suspicion by maintaining a rigid separation between a gay and straight world.

Anticipation of disapproval and rejection underpins Robert's emotional and social distancing from the straight world. Fear prevented Robert from disclosing to his family as a young person. Fear also shaped his public school experience. Although he grew up in a predominantly black community in Brooklyn, Robert went to high school in what he described as a small all-white town in upstate New York. He lived in an almost constant state of fear during these years. Negotiating his racial difference was hard enough. The prospect of being viewed as sexually deviant terrified him. Robert managed by maintaining social distance. He avoided any contact with classmates that might be suspected of being gay. He remained silent in the face of an openly homophobic school culture. Robert tried to fit in by lying about having a girlfriend back home. Despite excelling in sports and enjoying athletics, Robert refused to participate in any school team sports. He was afraid that he'd "get a hard-on in the shower."

Robert spoke of feeling like he was "the only gay person in the world." Isolated and terrified of exposure, Robert felt suicidal through out his high school years. Exercising extreme self-control and social isolation, which entailed the vigilant monitoring of his feelings, self-presentation, and behavior, was how he got by. "I mostly kept to myself. I had few friends and didn't get involved in school life. I could never be relaxed. I always feared someone would find out. I never let anyone get to know me."

After high school, Robert joined the navy, where exposure would have meant a discharge as well as social disgrace. He managed to pass by being a loner and by excessive drinking during his years in the service.

After leaving the navy, Robert worked as an electrician in Los Angeles. Away from home, economically independent, and in a liberal social environment, Robert began to participate in gay life. He dated and soon had a boyfriend.

Robert did not, however, disclose his sexual identity to any of his coworkers. He preferred to keep personal matters out of his work life. Although his coworkers often talked about their boyfriends, girlfriends, marriages, and children, Robert never shared any of his personal life. Robert remained aloof. Although he worked at this job for six years, he did not become friends with any of his coworkers. In order to sustain social distance, Robert avoided any meaningful social ties with his coworkers. As a result of being closeted, Robert's workplace experience resembled the impersonal, dehumanizing world that Karl Marx and Max Weber described in their chilling portraits of modern industrial life.

At the age of twenty-three, Robert came out to his mother, who told his father and his siblings. Robert has never discussed specific aspects of his gay life with any family member. They all know, but it's not talked about. Robert interprets the absence of hostile behavior and rejection on the part of his family as indicating acceptance. Asked why he keeps his gay life separate from his family, Robert says that his homosexuality is personal and doesn't need to be shared. Accordingly, his family knew nothing of his boyfriend or any other aspect of his personal life. Much to his regret, but hardly surprising, Robert speaks of a weakening of his family bond. Today, he's not close to his mother or anyone in his family. His visits with his family are infrequent and lack the emotional spontaneity and richness of past family interactions. For these reasons, Robert has not told his family that he is HIV positive.

Several years ago, Robert moved back east. However, still wanting to sustain social distance from his family, he resides in a mid-sized city in the northeast. He chose this place in part because it has a sizable gay community. His initial visit to the gay community center was telling of his strained, distant relationship to the white gay world. "I went to the community center to see who else in this community is like myself. And I really didn't find anybody . . . because most of the gay community was what it is, it seems to be white. So, I just accepted that to be what gay culture was."

Cheap housing led Robert to live in a predominantly black neighborhood. His contacts with his neighbors are formal and lack emotional depth. In fact, he has never come out to any straight black person, aside from his mother. Robert says matter-of-factly that no black person ever asked him if he was gay, He admits, though, that many blacks disparage being gay. "Many blacks think it's already dangerous out there for a black man, why would you want to add another danger to your life? Besides, being gay was viewed for a long time as equivalent to having AIDS. So, most of the conversations [among blacks] about being gay is about having sex and death. Because they perceive the lifestyle as being very painful . . . not many people are going to be accepting of the lifestyle."

Robert eventually found a small network of black gay men and women. This network is the emotional and social focus of his life.

Today, Robert's life is divided between a gay and a straight world. The former provides emotional and social sustenance; the latter is a somewhat risky terrain he navigates to do what he has to do. He speaks, as is typical of those speaking from a closeted standpoint, of a heterosexual dictatorship. Robert's closetedness entails such a narrowing of his world that intimate expression and bonding are possible only within a very small social circle. His closet world is not built on pretense (as was true of Bill), but a fear and distrust so deeply felt that his social distancing has cost him his family, meaningful ties to a black community, a satisfying work life, and has resulted in a pervasive loneliness.

From Lenny's generation to Robert's, the psychosocial texture of the closet has changed considerably. For Lenny and many of his generation, the closet often meant a double life: a conventional public heterosexual life and a secretive homosexual life. By contrast, coming of age in the 1990s, Robert never married. But if Robert rejected strategies involving deception and disguise, he still lives a double life. Like many individuals who are closeted today, he is both part of a gay world and maintains a clear separation from the straight world. The nongay world remains a world of risk and danger. Roberts avoids suspicion and potential conflict by organizing a life of extreme self-control; sadly, he has paid a steep price for passing. . . .

Notes

1. Consider this description of the world of a middle-class lesbian living in the late 1920s and 1930s: "During the 1920s and 1930s Boyer Reinstein was an active lesbian within a community of lesbian friends. She had few, if any, negative feelings about being a lesbian, and she was 'out' to her immediate family. Yet, she did not publicly disclose being gay. She was always discreet." The author, Elizabeth Kennedy, cautions against using the concept of the closet to depict Reinstein's social world. "I am afraid using the term 'closet' to refer to the culture of the 1920s and 1930s might be anachronistic." Elizabeth Kennedy, "But We Would Never Talk about It: The Structures of Lesbian Discretion in South Dakota, 1928–1933," in *Inventing Lesbian Cultures in America*, ed. Ellen Lewin (Boston: Beacon Press, 1996). Similarly, George Chauncey describes a working-class gay culture in which gays and straights openly mingle in saloons, cafeterias, rent parties, and speak-easies. The gay world before World War I is said to be very different from the era inaugurated by the Stonewall rebellions. For example, the language and concept of "coming out of the closet" was foreign to this gay world. "Gay people in the prewar years did not speak of coming out of what we call the gay closet but rather of coming out into what they called homosexual society or the gay world, a world neither so small, nor so isolated, nor so hidden as closet implies." George Chauncey, *Gay New York: Gender, Urban Culture, and the Making of the Gay Male World, 1890–1940* (New York: Basic Books, 1994).

2. For descriptions of homosexual life in the 1950s and 1960s, *The Mattachine Review* and *The Ladder*, respectively published by the Mattachine Society and the Daughters of Bilitis, are superb sources. For examples of personal testimony, see Peter Nardi, David Sanders, and Judd Marmor, eds., *Growing up before Stonewall: Life Stories of Some Gay Men* (New York: Routledge, 1994); Donald Vining, *A Gay Diary, 5 vols.* (New York: Pepys Press, 1979–93); Martin Duberman, *Cures: A Gay Man's Odyssey* (New York: Dutton, 1991); Robert Reinhart, *A History of Shadows: A Novel* (Boston: Alyson, 1986); Audre Lorde, *Zami: A New Spelling of My Name* (New York: Crossing Press, 1982); Andrea Weiss and Greta Schiller, *Before Stonewall: The Making of the Gay and Lesbian Community* (New York: Naiad Press, 1988); Jonathan Ned Katz, *Gay American History* (New York: Meridian, 1976) and *Gay/Lesbian Almanac* (New York: Harper and Row, 1983); and Eric Marcus, *Making History: The Struggle for Gay and Lesbian Equal Rights: An Oral History* (New York: HarperCollins, 1992). For informative popular and academic works of the time, see Daniel Webster Cory [pseudonym Edward Sagarin], *The Homosexual in America* (New York: Peter Nevill, 1951); Evelyn Hooker, "Male Homosexuals and Their Worlds," in *Sexual Inversion*, ed. J. Marmor (New York: Basic Books, 1965); Martin Hoffman, *The Gay World* (New York: Basic Books, 1968); Del Martin and Phyllis Lyon, *Lesbian/Woman* (San Francisco: Bantam, 1972); Sidney Abbott and Barbara Love, *Sappho Was a Right-On Woman: A Liberated View of Lesbianism* (New York: Stein and Day, 1972); John Gagnon and William Simon, "The Lesbians: A Preliminary Overview," in *Sexual Deviance*, ed. William Simon and John Gagnon (New York: Harper and Row, 1967). For some current scholarly perspectives on gay life in the immediate postwar years, see John D'Emilio, *Sexual Politics, Sexual Communities: The Making of a Homosexual Minority in the United States, 1940–1970* (Chicago: University of Chicago Press, 1983); Lillian Faderman, *Odd*

Girls and Twilight Lovers: A History of Lesbian Life in Twentieth-Century America (New York: Columbia University Press, 1991); Elizabeth Kennedy and Madeline Davis, *Boots of Leather, Slippers of Gold: The History of a Lesbian Community* (New York: Routledge, 1993); Leila J. Rupp, "Imagine My Surprise: Women's Relationships in Mid-Twentieth-Century America," in *Hidden from History*, ed. M. Duberman, M. Vicinus and G. Chauncey Jr. (New York: Meridian, 1990); Rochella Thorpe, "A House where Queers Go: African-American Lesbian Nightlife in Detroit, 1940–1975," in *Inventing Lesbian Cultures in America*, ed. Ellen Lewin (Boston: Beacon Press, 1996); and Marc Stein, *City of Sisterly and Brotherly Loves: Lesbian and Gay Philadelphia, 1945–72* (Chicago: University of Chicago Press, 2000).

3. Allan Berube, *Coming Out under Fire: The History of Gay Men and Women in World War Two* (New York: Macmillan, 1990), p. 271.

4. To understand the social context of the 1950s as a time of both change and anxiety, especially regarding gender and intimate life, I have drawn on the following: Wini Breines, *Young, White, and Miserable: Growing up Female in the Fifties* (Boston: Beacon Press, 1992); Stephanie Coontz, *The Way We Never Were: American Families and the Nostalgia Trap* (New York: Basic Books, 1992); Barbara Ehrenreich, *Hearts of Men: American Dreams and the Flight from Commitment* (Garden City, N.Y.: Anchor Books, 1983); Elaine Tyler May, *Homeward Bound: American Families in the Cold War Era* (New York: Basic Books, 1988); Jessica Weiss, *To Have and to Hold: Marriage, the Baby Boom, and Social Change* (Chicago: University of Chicago Press, 2000); Cynthia Enloe, *The Morning after: Sexual Politics and the End of the Cold War* (Berkeley: University of California Press, 1993); and Robert Corber, *In the Name of National Security: Hitchcock, Homophobia, and the Political Construction of Gender in Postwar America* (Durham, N.C.: Duke University Press).

5. On the making of the closet in the 1950s, see John D'Emilio, "The Homosexual Menace: The Politics of Sexuality in Cold War America," in *Making Trouble: Essays on Gay History, Politics, and the University* (New York: Routledge, 1992), and *Sexual Politics, Sexual Communities*, Allan Berube and John D'Emilio, "The Military and Lesbians during the McCarthy Years" *Signs* 9 (Summer 1984): 759–75; Barbara Epstein, "Anti-Communism, Homophobia, and the Construction of Masculinity in the Postwar U.S." *Critical Sociology* 20 (1994): 21–44; Faderman, *Odd Girls*, Robert Corber, *Homosexuality in Cold War America: Resistance and the Crisis of Masculinity* (Durham, N.C.: Duke University Press, 1997); and Gerard Sullivan, "Political Opportunism and the Harassment of Homosexuals in Florida, 1952–1965," *Journal of Homosexuality* 37 (1999): 57–81.

6. Chauncey, *Gay New York*, p. 6; William Eskridge Jr., *Gaylaw: Challenging the Apartheid of the Closet* (Cambridge, Mass.; Harvard University Press, 1999), p. 13; Paul Monette, *Becoming a Man: Half a Life Story* (New York: HarperCollins, 1992), p. 2; Joseph Beam, "Leaving the Shadows Behind," in *In the Life: A Black Gay Anthology*, ed. Joseph Beam (Boston: Alyson, 1986), p. 16.

7. Monette, *Becoming a Man*, p. 1.

8. In his memoir, Mel White, the former ghostwriter for Billy Graham and Jerry Falwell, movingly describes his experience of isolation: "I was isolated, not by bars or guards in uniforms, but by fear. I was surrounded by my loving family and close friends, but there was no way to explain to them my desperate, lonely feelings even when we were together. I wasn't tortured by leather straps or cattle prods, but my guilt and fear kept me in constant torment. I was starving for the kind of human intimacy that would satisfy my longing, end my loneliness." White says that this isolation made him "feel like an alien who had been abandoned on a strange planet. . . . Living rooms and dining rooms, restaurants and lobbies, became foreign, unfriendly places. [I grew] weary of pretending to be someone I was not, tired of hiding my feelings. . . . My once lively spirit was shriveling like a raisin in the sun. . . . Desperation and loneliness surged. . . . I felt trapped and terrified." Mel White, *Stranger at the Gate: To Be Gay and Christian in America* (New York: Plume, 1995), pp. 123, 177–78.

9. Allan Berube describes the closet as a "system of lies, denials, disguises, and double entendres—that had enabled them to express some of their homosexuality by pretending it didn't exist and hiding it from view." Berube, *Coming Out under Fire*, p. 271.

10. My research suggests that the category of the closet initially appeared in the writing of gay liberationists. The earliest reference I've found was an editorial statement in the short-lived newspaper *Come Out!* in 1969. By the early 1970s the concept of the closet was widely circulating in liberationist writings; e.g., Signo Canceris, "From the Closet," *Fag Rag* 4 (January 1973); Bruce Gilbert "Coming Out," *Fag Rag* 23/24 (1976); Morgan Pinney, "Out of Your Closets," *Gay Sunshine* 1 (October 1970); Ian Young, "Closet Wrecking," *Gay Sunshine* 28 (Spring 1976); Jennifer Woodhul, "Darers Go First," *The Furies* 1 (June/July 1972); and Allen Young, "Out of the Closets, into the Streets," in *Out of the Closets*, ed. Karla Jay and Allen Young. The closet underscored a condition of oppression. Gays were not merely discriminated against but dominated. And the closet was not a product of individual ignorance or prejudice but a social system of heterosexual domination. The core institutions and culture of America were said to be organized to enforce the norm and ideal of heterosexuality. In short, the closet underscored the way a system of compulsory heterosexuality creates a separate and oppressed homosexual existence. By arguing that the very organization of American society compels homosexuals to live socially isolated, inauthentic lives, the category of the closet served both as a way to understand gay life and as a critique of America.

By the mid-1970s, as liberationism gave way to politics of minority rights, the concept of the closet was in wide use. However, its meaning began to change. Within the minority rights discourse that triumphed in the late 1970s, the closet was viewed as an act of concealment in response to actual or anticipated prejudice; it was seen as a matter of individual choice. By the late 1970s and 1980s, some gays were arguing that America had become a much more tolerant nation; the risks of coming out were greatly diminished. Being in or out of the closet was now seen as an individual choice rather than an adjustment to heterosexual domination. In fact, gays began to feel considerable pressure to come out, as many came to believe that visibility was both more possible and a key to challenging prejudice. For example, David Goodstein, the owner and editor of *The Advocate* from roughly the mid-1970s through the mid-1980s, gravitated to a view of the closet as almost self-imposed, as a product of "low self-esteem" or "cowardice." "I truly believe that there is no reason for you to be closeted and hide who you are" *(The Advocate,* 1983, p. 6). Goodstein blamed social intolerance in part on the cowardice of those who choose to be closeted. "I take a dim view of staying in the closet. . . . What brings up my irritation at this time . . . is the price we uncloseted gay people pay for the cowardice and stupidity of our [closeted] brothers and sisters" ("Opening Spaces," *The Advocate,* 1981, p. 6).

I have stated my preference for a liberationist approach. If the concept of the closet is to help us to understand changes in gay life, it should be used in a way that indicates more than an act of concealment. In this regard, the liberationist idea of the closet as a condition of social oppression is persuasive. Explaining gay subordination, at least from the 1950s through the 1980s, as a product of individual prejudice or ignorance makes it hard, if not impossible, to understand its socially patterned character. It was not simply that gays were disadvantaged in one institution or only by isolated acts of discrimination or disrespect, but gay subordination occurred across institutions and culture. Heterosexual privilege was aggressively enforced by the state, cultural practices, daily acts of harassment and violence, and by institutions such as marriage, the wedding industry, and a dense network of laws covering taxes, family, immigration, military policy, and so on. At least during the heyday of the closet, the social risks of exposure were so great that it is naive to speak of the closet as an individual choice. In short, the concept of the closet helps us to understand the way heterosexuality functioned as an "institution" or a "system" that oppressed gay people.

A liberationist approach requires, however, some modification. In particular, the closet should be approached as a product of historically specific social dynamics; in particular, a culture of homosexual pollution and state repression. Furthermore, liberationists tend to read heterosexual domination as so closely and deeply intertwined with a whole system of gender, racial, economic, and political dom-

ination that America is viewed as irredeemably repressive. Such totalizing views are not credible.

11. Class is absent from much of queer social analysis. There are theoretical and rhetorical appeals to the importance of class, but little social research that addresses class patterns of concealment and coming out, gay and lesbian identification, and workplace dynamics. I have made use of the following work: Nicola Field, *Over the Rainbow: Money, Class, and Homophobia* (London: Pluto Press, 1995); Steve Valocchi, "The Class-Inflected Nature of Gay Identity," *Social Problems* 46 (1999): 207–44; Katie Gilmartin, "We Weren't Bar People: Middle Class Identities and Cultural Space," *Gay and Lesbian Quarterly* 3 (1996): 1–5; Roger Lancaster, *Life Is Hard: Machismo Danger, and the Intimacy of Power in Nicaragua* (Berkeley: University of California Press, 1992); and David Evans, *Sexual Citizenship: The Material Construction of Sexualities* (London: Routledge, 1993). Joshua Gamson's *Freaks Talk Back: Tabloid Talk Shows and Sexual Nonconformity* (Chicago University of Chicago Press, 1998) and Chrys Ingraham's *White Weddings: Romancing Heterosexuality in Popular Culture* (New York: Routledge, 1999) weave class into an analysis of sexual identities in interesting ways. Lillian Faderman's *Odd Girls, Twilight Lovers* and Kennedy and Davis's *Boots of Leather, Slippers of Gold* are indispensable sources for understanding the role of class in early postwar lesbian life.

12. Like class, race figures prominently in theoretical statements and in personal testimonies but is lacking when it comes to empirical research. There is an abundance of personal testimonies or interpretive statements; e.g., Cherrie Moraga and Gloria Anzaldúa, eds., *This Bridge Called My Back: Writings by Radical Women of Color* (New York: Kitchen Table, 1981); Joseph Beam, ed., *In the Life: A Black Gay Anthology* (Boston: Alyson, 1986); Essex Hemphill, ed., *Brother to Brother: New Writings by Black Gay Men* (Boston: Alyson, 1991); Keith Boykin, *One More River to Cross: Black and Gay in America* (New York: Anchor Books, 1996); Carla Trujillo, ed., *Chicana Lesbians: The Girls Our Mothers Warned Us About* (Berkeley: Third Woman Press, 1991); Juanita Ramos, ed., *Compañeras: Latina Lesbians* (New York: Latina Lesbian History Project, 1987); Russell Leong, ed., *Asian American Sexualities* (New York: Routledge, 1996). There has also developed a tradition of literary-critical studies of racialized gay identities; e.g., Arthur Flannigan-Saint-Augin, "Black Gay Male Discourse: Reading Race and Sexuality between the Lines," in *American Sexual Politics: Sex, Gender, and Race since the Civil War,* ed. John Fout and Maura Shaw Tantillo (Chicago: University of Chicago Press, 1993); Phillip Brian Harper, "Eloquence and Epitaph: AIDS, Homophobia, and Problematics of Black Masculinity," in *Are We Not Men? Masculine Anxiety and the Problem of African-American Identity* (New York: Oxford University Press, 1996); Isaac Julien and Kobena Mercer, "True Confessions: A Discourse on Images of Black Male Sexuality," in *Male Order: Unwrapping Masculinity,* ed. R. Chapman and J. Rutherford (London: Lawrence and Wishart, 1988); Ann duCille, "Blues Notes

on Black Sexuality: Sex and the Texts of Jessie Fauset and Nella Larsen," in *American Sexual Politics: Sex, Gender, and Race since the Civil War*, ed. Fout and Tantillo; Mason Stokes, *The Color of Sex: Whiteness, Heterosexuality, and the Fictions of White Supremacy* (Durham, N.C. Duke University Press, 2000). There is very little historical, empirical, or ethnographic research on race and gay identities. Regarding patterns of concealment, coming out, and sexual identification among African Americans, I've drawn from the following: Cathy Cohen, *The Boundaries of Blackness: AIDS and the Breakdown of Black Politics* (Chicago: University of Chicago Press, 1999); William Hawkesworth, *One of the Children: Gay Black Men in Harlem* (Berkeley: University of California Press, 1996); John Peterson, "Black Men and Their Same-Sex Desires and Behaviors," in *Gay Culture in America: Essays from the Field*, ed. Gilbert Herdt (Boston: Beacon Press, 1992); Rochella Thorpe, "A House where Queers Go"; "African-American Lesbian Nightlife in Detroit, 1940–1975" in *Inventing Lesbian Culture in America* (Boston: Beacon Press, 1996); Kevin Mumford, "Homosex Changes: Race, Cultural Geography, and the Emergence of the Gay," *American Quarterly* 48 (1996): 220–31; and Lisa Walker, *Looking like What You Are: Sexual Style, Race, and Lesbian Identity* (New York: New York University Press, 2001).

13. Marlon Riggs, "Black Macho Revisited: Reflections of a SNAP! Queen," in *Brother to Brother: New Writings by Black Gay Men*, ed. Essex Hemphill (Boston: Alyson, 1991) p. 254.

14. See Joseph Beam, "Brother to Brother: Words from the Heart," in *In the Life*, ed. Joseph Beam Cf. Essex Hemphill, "Introduction," Charles Nero, "Toward a Black Gay Aesthetic," Ron Simmons, "Some Thoughts on the Challenges Facing Black Gay Intellectuals," and Joseph Beam, "Making Ourselves from Scratch," in *Brother to Brother: New Writings by Black Gay Men*, ed. Essex Hemphill; Barbara Smith and Beverly Smith, "Across the Kitchen Table: A Sister-to-Sister Dialogue," in *This Bridge Called My Back*, ed. Moraga and Anzaldúa; bell hooks, "Reflections on Homophobia and Black Communities," *Outlook* 1 (1988): 22–25; Cheryl Clarke, "The Failure to Transform: Homophobia in the Black Community," in *Home Girls: A Black Feminist Anthology*, ed. Barbara Smith (New York: Kitchen Table, 1983); and Jackie Goldsby, "What It Means to Be Colored Me," *Outlook* 9 (Summer 1990): 8–17.

15. Hawkesworth, *One of the Children*.

16. Cohen, *The Boundaries of Blackness*, pp. 91–95.

Discussion Questions

1. Seidman speaks of gender and sexuality as kinds of performances. Lenny and Bill keep others from suspecting their sexuality by acting out very traditional and stereotyped masculine roles and by behaving the way heterosexual men are expected to behave. What are the key elements of male and female, gay and straight performance? Are they different for Robert's or your generation than for people of Lenny's or Bill's age?

2a. If you are straight, imagine what it would be like to live in a world where homosexuality was the norm and those who were attracted to people of a different gender were the butt of jokes and knowing looks and denied the right to form families. Would you choose to live an openly straight life or would you choose the closet? Would you speak out when someone made a heterophobic remark or would you remain silent?

2b. If you are gay or lesbian, imagine what it would be like to live in the world of 2a. How would your life be different from the way it is now or the way you imagine it might be in 10 years?

2c. If you are bisexual or transgendered or not sure of your sexual orientation, write your own scenario about a world where you did not have to consider the option of the closet.

3. Although all the case studies in this excerpt are of gay men, Seidman does include lesbians in his book. Do you think it would be easier or harder, more or less necessary, for women attracted to women than for men attracted to men to lead closeted lives? Why? Would the social class, race, and size of community issues raised here be the same or different for women than for men?

Reprinted from: Steven Seidman, "In the Closet." In *Beyond the Closet: The Transformation of Gay and Lesbian Life*, pp. 25–49, 214–220. Copyright © 2002. Reproduced by permission of Routledge/Taylor & Francis Group, LLC. ✦

26
Stories From the Field

Wendy Luttrell

In Schoolsmart and Motherwise, *Wendy Luttrell wishes to explore how adult women from different racial groups but similar class backgrounds describe their experiences in the school system. Whether they experienced parochial or public schools, or segregated one-room school houses, Luttrell is interested in how they narrate their lives in relationship to schools. To accomplish her task, she enters two very different settings as a teacher, encountering two very different groups of women. In the Philadelphia setting, Luttrell meets with White ethnic working-class women, all mothers who attended neighborhood schools from the 1940s to the 1960s. In the North Carolina setting, Luttrell encounters Black women, all housekeepers and mothers who had attended school prior to desegregation. The bedrock variables that guide Luttrell's analysis are clearly the variables of race, class, and gender.*

In this study, Luttrell commits from the outset to feminist research strategies in order to best explore the lives of these working class Black and White women. Such strategies ask that the researcher not adopt a distant, so-called value-free, objective stance to the individuals under study as much scientific, positivist research has for centuries. Instead, feminist research strategies insist that the researcher be both self-reflective and respectful of relationships to the respondents in one's study. Far from being distant or value-free, feminist research recognizes the value-laden aspect of dealing with the lives of real human beings and also insists on accountability to one's research respondents. Luttrell truly embraces this process as she attends to the women's stories and responses in all their emotional impact even when this is painful. When, for example, both groups of women open up about their negative

experiences with teachers, Luttrell feels some discomfort about how the women actually see and judge her as a teacher. In her negotiation of the North Carolina setting, to cite another example, Luttrell feels extreme discomfort with the obvious segregation at the university in which she is teaching. Here she sees "stark racial divisions between black and white" in a setting where all the housekeeping staff are people of color, while the administration, students, and faculty are almost all White. She writes, "I resented being caught up in social patterns of dominance and deference that were vestiges of a past time I naively thought was over in the New South." In sum, Luttrell is willing to take the sorts of risks that make for a truly faithful recording of the lives of real people, and this is the strength of her study.

> *Participant-observation begins at home—and not only because we are studying "ourselves"; part of every "us" is "other" too.*
>
> —Anna Tsing, quoted in Behar and Gordon, *Women Writing Culture*

In this chapter I take the reader into each research setting and tell some stories that I use as resources for analyzing the women's narratives. These stories of self and other, empathy and identification, conflict and comfort are common to fieldwork, but all too often are kept out of the official record.[1] I view this gap in research storytelling as unfortunate, because the knowledge of fieldwork grows out of and depends upon what happens between researchers and researched.[2] Feminist research strategies tell us to attend to our own experiences in the field and to be conscious of the research process as a relationship.[3] The challenge is to write about what transpires in such a way that readers can decide for themselves the truthfulness, significance, or usefulness of the knowledge that is produced.

The Philadelphia Setting

The Lutheran Settlement House Women's Program is located in a Philadelphia neighborhood residents refer to as Fishtown. Once stable and vibrant, this historically white, ethnic, and working-class neighborhood had lost its industrial base and was suffering economic decline and rising unemployment when the Women's Program opened its doors in 1976.[4] The neighborhood had long been neglected by city services. Local residents complained about poor health care; nonexistent child-care facilities; a lack of recreational opportunities, especially for teenagers; increased rates of drug and alcohol abuse; environmental hazards; and a rising crime rate (see Luttrell 1988). In the face of city, state, and federal cutbacks, neighborhood women were taking on new or additional roles and responsibilities to make ends meet. Some women were entering the labor force for the first time, others were seeking more lucrative jobs, still others were taking in boarders or doing piecework at home so they could support their families. Reluctantly, many women were seeking welfare assistance. No matter what circumstances people found themselves in, the integrity and quality of community life was being questioned. In response to these changes, the Women's Program offered a wide range of educational opportunities, a counseling service, on-site child care, vocational training, and a battered women's hotline.

The fifteen Philadelphia women I selected to interview had all grown up in the neighborhood surrounding the Lutheran Settlement House.[5] Most lived within blocks of where they had been born and where extended family members still resided. They ranged in age from twenty-three years to forty-eight and had all attended neighborhood schools during the 1940s, 1950s, and 1960s before school integration. One-third had gone to parochial school, and two-thirds had gone to public school.[6] Five of the fifteen women had graduated from high school, and the rest had left either before or during their sophomore year.[7] They had all moved in and out of the work force as factory hands, clerical workers, waitresses, hospital or teachers' aides. Two-thirds of the women were married at the time of the interviews, although over the course of the study more became divorced single mothers. One woman had never married. All of them

were mothers with at least one child still living at home.

The holistic and community-based approach of the Women's Program was crucial to its success. Despite the fact that there were high-school equivalency classes being offered at a nearby community center two elevated-train stops away, and college preparatory classes held at Philadelphia Community College four elevated-train stops away, the women preferred to stay closer to home mostly because they didn't want to feel "uncomfortable" in places they did not "belong."

As will become evident, concerns about not fitting in or feeling at odds with people they viewed as "different" persisted throughout the Philadelphia women's accounts. This was especially the case when speaking about school and their relationships with teachers. Meanwhile, I took note of how often students in the Women's Program classes kept their distance from certain teachers in the program. It wasn't that they didn't like these teachers, I was told; rather, these teachers were just "different." All this talk about difference, often punctuated by the familiar "You know what I mean," made me nervous since I wasn't sure I did know what they meant. And since I too had been their teacher, I wondered how and in what ways the Philadelphia women viewed me as "different." I felt determined to probe this in the interviews.

Mary was especially gracious during our first meeting at her home; she offered me tea and cookies and had bought a small gift for my two-year-old daughter, who accompanied me on this visit. I was feeling particularly at ease as our two toddlers played together. So when Mary started to describe her teachers as having been "different," I took the opportunity to probe more forcefully than I had with others. I asked her to be as specific as she could. First she said the teachers "lived in different neighborhoods—they weren't like the rest of us." When I asked her to explain how the teachers were different, she said, "I saw them as my superiors, I guess. I always saw them as more intelligent. I never saw them as equal." She hesitated and there was a brief silence I sensed some discomfort—I wasn't sure if it was mine or hers. We both shifted a bit in our seats. After a moment she said:

> I always thought of them (I guess I should say you) [she stopped, looked at me] as being real rich. I just didn't think they were like us. They were from a higher class and must have been real smart to go to college in the first place. I just never felt comfortable with them. But now I know better, I mean they are not all alike. They, I mean, you [she smiled at me and we both started laughing], are not all rich, higher-class people who talk down to students.

This exchange crystallized my own discomfort. I was afraid that the Philadelphia women viewed me as "different" in this way—as a "rich, higher-class person" who would likely talk down to them. In light of their somewhat defensive accounts about why they had felt uncomfortable in school or had dropped out of it, I also worried that they thought I was sitting in judgment of them. When I asked Mary about this, she told me the same thing that Sennett and Cobb's white, working-class male interviewees told them—"not to take it personally" and that she liked me (1972: 42).

As did Sennett and Cobb's interviewee Frank Rissarro, the Philadelphia women often treated me as an "emissary from a different way of life" before whom they "spread a justification of their entire life":

> Frank Rissarro did not so much grant an interview as give a confession. . . . Rissarro believes people of a higher class have a power to judge him because they seem internally more developed human beings; and he is afraid, because they are better armed, that they will not respect him (1972: 25).

Nevertheless, not all people of a higher class deserve to be respected by others, a point that was made over and over again by the women I observed and interviewed. While the Philadelphia women viewed formal education as giving people tools for achieving respect, they, like Frank Rissano, had a certain "revulsion against the work of educated people."[8]

My fieldnotes and interview transcripts were riddled with references to who was smart and worthy of respect, in what ways, and why. I was puzzling over all this material and why it made me uncomfortable when a particular event, early in the second year of my research, clarified my thinking. Doreen had invited me to her home, where we talked over coffee about the difficulties of raising children. We swapped strategies, confessed inadequacies, and enlisted each others advice. As we sat in her small, square, brightly painted kitchen, our children played outside on the backyard concrete stoop. The gritty screened door kept slamming as they regularly came in to request snacks or to get help resolving disputes over the toys. We had just settled a dispute over several sand toys when Doreen observed:

> Wendy, your daughter is really bright. Listen to how well she talks. Look, she's even talking about that toy. Tony is older, but he doesn't know half those words. He doesn't talk much—especially when he's playing.

Doreen sounded both congratulatory and somewhat defensive, but I was unsure how to read her remarks. Familiar with Doreen's anxiety that five-year-old Tony was not doing well in school, I felt the need to reassure her (and perhaps myself) about the significance, if any, of my daughter Mikaela's and Tony's different abilities. As I peered through the screen door, I could see my almost-three-year-old daughter struggling to operate a large plastic truck. Tony had moved next to her and quickly manipulated a series of levers, which made the objects he had placed in the shovel drop to the floor. I was amazed by the complexity of the toy and said:

> Look at how Tony figured out how the truck works—it's incredibly complicated. Maybe he doesn't talk yet about it, but he will.

Doreen replied:

> Oh, that just takes common sense. He's good with his hands and figuring out how things work, but he's not smart like Mikaela. Maybe if he had went to daycare. . . .

Interrupted by more requests for apple juice, we left this conversation hanging. For days I felt uneasy about our exchange, unsettled by these distinctions between Mikaela's so-called smarts and Tony's so-called common sense. That Mikaela's verbal abilities had won her the mark of being "bright" and Tony's abilities to "figure things out" had been classified as "just common sense" seemed somewhat at odds with what I was hearing in class and in the interviews. I had often noted the Philadelphia women defend the value of common sense, especially the ability to "make things work," a kind of intelligence they attributed to their fathers, brothers, or husbands, whom they held in great esteem for doing manual labor. Why in this circumstance was Tony's ability to make things work viewed as "just common sense?" Meanwhile, what was it about Mikaela's facility with words, her social and communicative skills, that made her seem "bright" to Doreen?

This exchange was not only intellectually challenging, it also touched me on a deeper, more personal level. For one thing, it evoked my own childhood memories of being told that while I might be doing well in school, I lacked "common sense." This familiar refrain from family members always used to provoke me, making me feel torn about my school accomplishments. In another sense, I identified with Tony, feeling the sting of his mothers comparative and somewhat disparaging remark. But most assuredly I felt uncomfortable with Mikaela's seeming triumph over Tony in the competitive race for respect (otherwise known as intelligence) that characterizes America's class-, race-, and gender-divided society.[9]

There is yet another side to both of these stories. Divided by my own working- and middle-class family roots and loyalties, I found that my conversations with Mary and Doreen evoked in me feelings of envy and guilt about our differences.[10] Put bluntly, I was emotionally bound up in discussions about class. Did these feelings provide insight or distort my ability to narrate and interpret the Philadelphia women's stories and self-understandings? I think both, and one precipitous event confirmed this.

Toward the end of my research in Philadelphia, I submitted a paper abstract about working-class women learners to a regional Women's Studies conference. The paper was accepted, although I felt far from being finished with the analysis. Nevertheless, I knew that presenting some preliminary findings and gathering reactions would be helpful. Two students and two staff members from the Women's Program (two of whom I had interviewed) were also attending the conference as panelists to speak about feminist community-based studies. They all had promised to attend my session to give me moral support.

As I nervously waited in the empty room where I was to deliver the paper, I was grateful to see my four supporters arrive, but no one else appeared. My feelings of disappointment and rejection must have been evident when Joanne, an interviewee, said:

> You know, this is exactly why I don't call myself a feminist. Look at this; you say you're going to talk about working-class women learners and no one shows up. If you were talking about Virginia Woolf or women in the 1800s, there'd be plenty of people here.

Joanne's anger put me in touch with my own. I wanted to go home but the women, especially those I had interviewed, insisted I present the paper to them anyway. The paper, filled with their own words, sparked an animated discussion. They said they agreed with much of my analysis; they recognized themselves and women they knew in what I had said. But I sensed they were disappointed or doubtful, and I asked Joanne what she really thought. She said that I told about her life, but I had not told *her* story. I said that I doubted I could do that—only she could tell her own story. She disagreed and said I could do a better job narrating the individual life of each woman I interviewed than the women themselves could. Tina disagreed, saying she didn't want me to write her story; she preferred her experiences being used to illustrate larger points about "working-class women's lives" (her words). We debated this issue but could come to no consensus.

Looking back, this conversation reminds me of Judith Stacey's (1990: 544) account of an epiphanal exchange she had with one of her interviewees: "While everything I reported was accurate, I had not succeeded in rendering her core sense of self. No one could do that she countered, 'you could never capture me.'"[11] Joanne's and Tina's different views about being "captured," as well as my own discomforts about being the "capturer"—a metaphor that bespeaks the problematic politics of representation—lay at the heart of our debate. I also came away from this conversation with more appreciation for the ambiguity of my role as narrator of the women's stories—understanding better that "accuracy" was not the same as "authenticity." Meanwhile, our debate made me an advocate for the notion of a *relational* rather than a highly differentiated *core* "self." What I would write about the women's storied selves would necessarily represent our mutual engagement and exchange.[12]

The North Carolina Setting

In 1984 I moved to North Carolina. I had a hard time adjusting to the stark racial divisions between white and black. But nothing provoked my discomfort as much as my working at the university, where the housekeeping staff and landscaping crew were people of color and the students, faculty, and administrative staff were predominantly white (with the notable exception of the basketball team). I resented being caught up in social patterns of dominance and deference that were vestiges of a past time I naively thought was over in the New South. Part of my new job included administering a workplace literacy program at the university that offered literacy and high-school equivalency classes to selected members of the maintenance staff who were released from their work duties for four hours a week to attend class. There were four classes of fifteen students, of which I taught two. Over a ten-year period, the program had served close to 200 people, including janitors, housekeepers, painters, electricians, landscapers, and members of the motor pool. I couldn't help noticing, however, that the mainstays of the program were African American female housekeepers.

My first day of class was reminiscent of the Women's Program, except that I was white and everyone else was not. After introductions, Ola said that she hoped I would stay longer than the last teacher, who had only stayed six months. She said all the teachers she had ever liked left before the year was over; she had been "sticking it out" for five years and was getting tired of the teacher turnover. I promised not to leave before the year was finished. Kate asked if I was a "real professor," adding, "We've never had a professor to teach *us*" (her emphasis). With my Ph.D. degree three months new, I was not sure how much of a "real professor" I was. In any case, I was more compelled by the second half of her statement and wondered who *us* meant, though I did not feel comfortable yet to ask her directly.

Ola said she was in school to "better herself"—she was especially proud to announce that her daughter would be graduating high school this year, and her goal was to get her high school diploma alongside her daughter. Others nodded approvingly, and Bessie said she too was in school to "set a good example for my son." Kate said she had graduated high school and attended college for one year before "losing her senses" and marrying; she was in school because she wanted to "become somebody." These parallels between the Philadelphia women and the North Carolina women grabbed my interest, but I felt a new set of qualms about my role as a white, middle-class researcher.

During the first year of teaching, I became acutely aware of myself as a particular kind of white person as the women puzzled over my ethnicity and lack of religious affiliation. For example, Geraldine said she had never met any white person who wasn't Jewish and that still claimed she wasn't a Christian. Lilly speculated that I was of "mixed blood," a cross between one of those Catholic groups (either Italian or Polish) and Jewish. No one could believe I had Irish, "hillbilly" ancestors nor that I had been raised a Methodist, then Presbyterian. I was told I was most unlike *those* white people. Again, I did not yet feel comfortable enough to ask what they meant by "those." Meanwhile, more than a few of the women promised to pray for me and for my return to the church.

I followed the same research protocol as in Philadelphia, surveying present and past program participants about why they had returned to school. In the second year, I selected fifteen women to interview in-depth, and later, when I was no longer a teacher, I observed the women in class.[13]

The North Carolina women I interviewed had all been raised in southern rural communities, although they now resided in neighborhoods close to the university. Most had grown up on tenant farms, and all but two had tended tobacco and picked cotton in their youths. They had all attended school before the 1964 desegregation ruling, often in one-room schoolhouses, and reported sporadic school attendance.... They were all mothers with at least one child still living at home; two-thirds had been single heads of households for most of their lives.[14] These women were all employed as housekeepers at the university and shared similar work histories, including domestic work in white people's homes. Throughout the interviews, they told stories about the tremendous social and political changes in the South that had occurred over the course of their lives and related how these changes had affected them.

Most compelling to me at the time were their stories about working as domestics. In story after story, the North Carolina women recounted in an ironic tone the ineptness or "sorriness" of the "white ladies" they had worked for. Sounding much like the domestic workers Judith Rollins interviewed, the North Carolina women were able to "skillfully deflect the psychological attacks on their personhood" by refusing to accept "employers' definitions of them as inferior" (1985: 212). These stories were told with laughter, and yet I often felt more like crying. I did not know why these stories evoked in me so much emotion. Then one day after a particularly long session with Linda, who had told several stories related to her domestic work experiences, including one where her employer had sprayed her with Lysol, she asked me if I had ever seen anything like what she had described. A long-forgotten memory came to mind, which I shared with her.

In 1963, I was ten years old and my family moved from Chicago to Houston, Texas, for one year. I remember being shocked by the rural and segregated forms of poverty. On a shopping trip with my mother, I encountered

segregation firsthand. Needing to use the bathroom, I ventured into territory where I did not know yet that I didn't belong. As I stood at the sink washing my hands, three black women broke into laughter and one remarked: "You're in the wrong place, honey." I said, "But isn't this the ladies room?" This statement generated even louder laughter as another woman said: "Yes, but we aren't ladies." I quickly dried my hands and as I closed the door behind me, I read the sign: "For colored women only." By the time I located my mother in the store I was crying. I told her my version of the story, including my distress about what I viewed as a terrible injustice. Somewhat distracted by the demands of my younger siblings, she calmly replied that this was how it was in the South. I was unsatisfied with her answer, angry that she seemed not to share my strong feelings about this. I proceeded to find the manager of the store to complain.[15] The red-haired youthful manager smiled briefly as I described my outrage about the separate bathrooms. Without so much as an apology or explanation he patted me on the head and said that he would help me find my mother.

After telling Linda the story, I felt embarrassed and vulnerable, as if she were one of the women in the store bathroom. Here I was, years later, still struggling on both an emotional and intellectual level to discern what these women had meant by saying they weren't ladies and what, exactly, this memory meant to me. I was also concerned about how Linda would respond to my story. I knew this story revealed my privileged protection from all the abuses she had just spoken about. Linda waited a moment before speaking and said, "You should tell that story in your book." Then she asked if I had ever been "cared for by a black woman" or if black women had cleaned our house. She asked, didn't I have any stories to tell of that? I explained that my family didn't have domestic servants of any kind. My mothers philosophy was that people should clean up after themselves (or more accurately that women should clean up after men). Linda was surprised by this and explained that "things were different here," and reiterated an earlier statement: "Like I said, some of the white women I worked for were nice and some weren't." Again, this conversation confirmed the value of mutual engagement and exchange in fieldwork. By listening to and exchanging stories with the women, I developed a clearer picture of what it means to define one's womanhood against controlling gender-, race-, and class-based images, including images that I projected onto the women and they projected onto me.

The same can be said about self-definitions in relation to teachers. I learned that my role as teacher vis-à-vis the North Carolina women evoked an altogether different set of comforts and conflicts than those I had experienced in Philadelphia. One particular event highlighted this. As a teacher, I always made it a point to meet with each student to evaluate her progress at the end of a semester. For some reason, the North Carolina student conferences felt more taxing than those with the Philadelphia students and I was unsure why. The process itself—students filling out a self-assessment form and talking about their own strengths and weaknesses and me writing a narrative evaluation of their progress—seemed fruitful. But I was never sure whether the North Carolina students saw their progress or that they shared my same assessment of their academic skills and achievements.[16] In one conference, Ola said that she hoped I knew that the reason she came to class was because she "loved me" (her words). She reminded me about how earlier in the year I had called her at home because she had missed several classes. It was not unusual for me to call students at home, so I was surprised that this routine teaching practice had so affected her. As the administrator of the program, I had become aware that certain supervisors made it difficult for their employees to come to class and it was within my authority to intervene if necessary. I thought this might be the case with Ola. However, Ola had explained she was waiting for payday so she could buy a new pair of glasses. She was getting headaches from reading and had not yet been able to afford the new prescription. I had asked if she wanted me to lend her the money so that she would not have to miss class. She did not take me up on my offer, but returned to class the next day (without glasses). During our conference Ola said: "I figured if you cared enough to call me at home, then you must really think that I can do the work. Then too, if you cared enough to call me and to loan me the money, then I should care enough about myself to be in class everyday and not give up on myself. I just never had a teacher to call me like that." She then took my hand and said, "So I am going to keep working at it."

In each research setting my role as "teacher/interviewer" proved to be more significant than I had anticipated. Insofar as the women were willing to talk with me because they knew me as their teacher and we had developed trust and rapport, my teacher role was beneficial. At the same time, this role evoked in them certain experiences with and memories about teachers that were projected onto me as a routine feature of our interview discussions.[17] It was not uncommon for women in both the Philadelphia and North Carolina groups, when talking about their teachers in negative ways, to reassure me that "I was not like that." Meanwhile, as part of this exchange I learned that the women in each group had different concerns about and stakes in their relationships with teachers. Whereas the North Carolina women framed their relationships with teachers in terms of care, the Philadelphia women framed their relationships in terms of conflict. . . . The tenacious but different holds that student-teacher relationships have on students' self-understandings and views of school is underestimated in current research about schooling, identity, and social change. I am doubtful that I would have learned as much about this had it not been for my teacher role.

Generally speaking, the women were blind to who I was and held their own fantasies and images about me, as I did of them. This healthy tension between who we are and who we are imagined to be by others is part of all relationships. These tensions can be frustrating and limiting, but they are also what provide us pleasure in making meaningful connections with others.

Notes

1. John Lofland (1971), author of my early fieldwork bible, says that the fieldworker inevitably experiences emotional reactions and that these reactions can compromise the research. As an antidote to this, the author suggests that fieldworkers record and take account of their private feelings. As I recorded my feelings during the fieldwork process, I viewed my activity as a way to minimize, counterbalance, or neutralize the variable of my "self." In writing about the fieldwork, I found Susan Krieger's views most helpful. She says that social scientists "write to protect as much as we write to express the self and to describe the world. Although we speak of protecting others—usually the people our studies are about—the main object of our protective strategies is always our selves" (1991: 32). Hindsight lets me see that this self-protection kept me from representing all that I know about my subject. Many others have written about gaining insight into fieldwork observations vis-à-vis one's own emotional reactions as well as memories and dreams evoked during the research process. See Behar (1993); Briggs (1986); Collins (1990); Ewing (1990); Hunt (1989); Krieger (1991); Paget (1990); Thorne (1993); Williams (1988) for how the self can be a source rather than a contaminant of knowledge for the researcher. An especially helpful guide about emotions and fieldwork is written by Sherryl Kleinman and Martha Copp (1993).

2. Prior to the emergence of what Barbara Tedlock (1991: 69) calls "narrative ethnography," the ethnographer was faced with the choice of writing either an ethnographic memoir "centering on the Self" or a more traditional account "centering on the Other." I have attempted to avoid this either/or choice, and instead, to present both sides as "co-participants" (not the same as equal participants) in the ethnographic encounter. See also Deborah Gordon (1988) and Margery Wolf (1992) for discussions of this dilemma in ethnographic writing.

3. I have been influenced by the work of several feminist scholars writing about the problems and possibilities of feminist research methods, including Anderson and Jacks (1991); Behar and Gordon (1995); Devault (1990); Griffin and Smith (1987); McRobbie (1982); Oakley (1981); Reinharz (1992); Smith (1987); Stacey (1988); Stanley (1990); Stanley and Wise (1983); Strathern (1987).

4. See Peter Binzen (1970) for a portrait of the same neighborhood. His account was not well liked among the women with whom I spoke.

5. These women also represented the basic demographic profile of white women in the community, including marital status, occupation, income, education level, religion, and race. I also selected women who represented the basic profile of Women's Program participants in terms of age, family situation, past attendance and type of school, academic achievement and level of community or civic participation.

6. The Philadelphia women's school careers varied. Five of the women had attended local Catholic grammar schools for some part (not all) of their elementary years. At the time, the cost of attending these grammar schools was minimal, and in some cases, was free depending on whether one's family was a member of the local parish. Two of these women attended a Catholic all-girls high school; they both left (for different reasons) after the first year. Of the remaining women who attended public schools, two had attended the public girls' high school before it had become co-ed. I mention these variations because school context becomes an important factor in the women's identities and stance towards school. I hope my account will spur more research about the contrasts between Catholic and public school contexts and between single-sex and coeducational contexts in shaping student identities in school.

7. This graduation rate reflected the neighborhood educational attainment figures reported in the 1980 census data.

8. I discovered, however, that wrapped up in these views about the dignity or manual work were implicit values about male privilege. . . .

9. At the time I scribbled my reactions on the margins of my fieldnotes. They read, "I wonder about the gender dynamics at play; could this interaction be said to illustrate socialization patterns and developmental differences between boys and girls? Will Mikaela's verbal abilities and her social skills always be viewed so positively? Will they ever be turned against her? Will these social skills always earn her respect and will she come to see her communication skills as evidence of her intelligence?" . . .

10. My relatives on my mother's side are white, proper, Midwestern, Protestant, church-going, business-oriented, middle-class people. My grandmother grew up on a farm. On my father's side are Scottish-Irish, hard-living, urban, blue-collar people. My grandfather left a Kentucky mining town for industrial work in Chicago. As a young girl I often felt torn between the two sides, especially when it came to my educational aspirations. The Philadelphia women often reminded me of my paternal cousin who seemed to have little invested in others' approval. I had always envied this in my cousin and I imagined that she did not feel pressured to perform or achieve in the same ways I did. Still I felt guilty about the discrepancy in our resources and opportunities, as if I had been unfairly bestowed with benefits that should rightfully be hers as well.

11. Stacey acknowledges that while her interviewee's statement is "true enough," as the author she does control the terms and textual forms or representing the women in her study. Stacey calls for a "greater respect for ambivalence as a worthy moral and theoretical stance" (1990: 544) as a result of this exchange. I see my work as a pitch for sustaining the tensions and ambivalences between self and other

in dialogic relationships as a worthy moral and theoretical stance.

12. See Chodorow (1989: 154–162) for her discussion of the progression in psychoanalytic theory from a view of the self as a "pure, differentiated individuality based on rigid notions of autonomous separateness toward a relational individualism" (162).

13. Let me briefly explain my coding procedures. The material gathered in Philadelphia was coded according to recurrent themes that arose in the interview materials and observational notes. I examined what the women said, specifically what they identified as difficult or problematic in their schooling and family lives and how they sought to resolve these problems. I coded each woman's interview text separately (to discern the patterns that emerged in her own life narrative) and then looked across all fifteen texts to determine the patterns. In collecting the interview material in North Carolina, I started with a comparative frame of reference, i.e., the Philadelphia women's material. I noted the different themes raised by the North Carolina women but began to discover a common pattern among women in both groups in how they narrated their stories. Thus, I developed a second coding strategy, whereby I examined the interview materials as school stories that followed certain storytelling patterns. Specifically, these patterns included *who* the women identified as primary actors and the events that characterized the problems they encountered in school; how they *ordered* then stories; and what *themes* tied the various stories together.

14. There were some significant differences between the two groups of women I interviewed. While equal numbers of them had become pregnant as teenagers, a higher proportion of the Philadelphia women had gotten married as a result. Whereas two-thirds of the Philadelphia women were or had been married, two-thirds of the North Carolina women had been single heads of households for most of their lives. Because of life-cycle differences, several of the North Carolina women but none of the Philadelphia women were grandmothers raising school-aged children. Meanwhile, whereas none of the North Carolina women had spent any time out of the labor force since becoming mothers, roughly half of the Philadelphia women had been out of the paid labor force when raising children under school age. The North Carolina women on average earned less than the Philadelphia women, but all the women's family incomes had fluctuated considerably over the previous fifteen years.

15. The directness with which I handled this event is akin to the descriptions of young girls' development that Lyn Mikel Brown and Carol Gilligan (1992) describe. As a fourth grade girl, I was "allowed" this outrage (both internally and by the store manager) because the forces of good girl socialization had not yet set in. Indeed, as I grew older I learned to drive underground certain feelings and thoughts that did not seem appropriate. This story of course (re)presents my view only—in fact, my mother doesn't even remember this event, which I view as being so central to my childhood.

16. It is worth noting here that the reading skills of the Philadelphia and North Carolina women were similar and ranged from roughly third to ninth grade. Yet for reasons that will become clearer later the North Carolina women held a lower opinion of themselves as competent learners.

17. See Jennifer Hunt (1989) about issues of transference and counter-transference in the interviewing process.

References

Anderson, Kathryn, and Dana Jacks. 1991. "Learning to Listen: Interview Techniques and Analyses." In *Women's Words: The Feminist Practice of Oral History*, ed. S. Gluck and D. Patai, 11–27. New York: Routledge.

Behar, Ruth. 1993. *Translated Woman: Crossing the Border With Esperanza's Story*. Boston: Beacon.

Behar, Ruth, and Deborah Gordon. 1995. *Women Writing Culture*. Berkeley: University of California Press.

Binzen, Peter. 1970. *Whitetown, USA*. New York: Random House.

Briggs, Jean. 1986. "Kapluna Daughter." In *Women in the Field: Anthropoligical Experiences*, ed. Peggy Gold, 19–44. Berkeley: University of California Press.

Brown, Lyn Mikel, and Carol Gilligan. 1992. *Meeting at the Crossroads: Women's Psychology and Girls' Development*. Cambridge and London: Harvard University Press.

Chodorow, Nancy. 1989. *Feminism and Psychoanalytic Theory*. New Haven and London: Yale University Press.

Collins, Patricia Hill. 1990. *Black Feminist Thought: Knowledge, Consciousness, and the Politics of Empowerment*. London: Harper Collins Academic.

Devault, Marjorie. 1990. "Talking and Listening from Women's Standpoint: Feminist Strategies for Interviewing and Analysis." *Social Problems* 37 (1): 96–116.

Ewing, Katherine. 1990. "The Illusion of Wholeness: Culture, Self and the Experience of Inconsistency." *Ethos* 18 (3): 251–78.

Gordon, Deborah. 1988. "Writing Culture, Writing Feminism: The Poetics and Politics of Experimental Ethnography." *Inscriptions* 3/4: 7–24.

Griffith, Alison, and Dorothy Smith. 1987. "Constructing Cultural Knowledge: Mothering as Discourse." In *Women and Education: A Canadian Perspective*, ed. Jane Gaskell and Arlene McLaren, 87–103. Calgary, Alberta: Detselig Enterprises.

Hunt, Jennifer. 1989. *Psychoanalytic Aspects of Fieldwork*. Newbury Park, CA: Sage.

Kleinman, Sherryl, and Martha Copp. 1993. *Emotions and Fieldwork*. Newbury Park, CA: Sage.

Krieger, Susan. 1991. *Social Science and the Self: Personal Essays on Art Form*. New Brunswick, NJ: Rutgers University Press.

Lofland, John. 1971. *Analyzing Social Settings: A Guide to Qualitative Observation and Analysis*. Belmont, CA: Wadsworth.

Luttrell, Wendy. 1988. "The Edison School Story: Reshaping Working-Class Education and Women's Consciousness." In *Women and the Politics of Empowerment*, ed. Ann Bookman and Sandra Morgen, 136–156. Philadelphia: Temple University Press.

McRobbie, Angela. 1982. "The Politics of Feminist Research: Between Talk, Text and Action." *Feminist Review* 12: 46–57.

Oakley, Ann. 1981. "Interviewing Women: A Contradiction in Terms." In *Doing Feminist Research*, ed. H. Roberts, 30–61. London: Routledge and Kegan Paul.

Paget, Marianne. 1990. "Life Mirrors Work Mirrors Text Mirrors Life." *Social Problems* 37 (2): 137–148.

Reinharz, Shulamit. 1992. *Feminist Methods in Social Research*. New York and Oxford: Oxford University Press.

Rollins, Judith. 1985. *Between Women: Domestics and Their Employers*. Philadelphia: Temple University Press.

Sennett, Richard, and Jonathan Cobb. 1972. *The Hidden Injuries of Class*. New York: W.W. Norton and Co.

Smith, Dorothy. 1987. *The Everyday World as Problematic: A Feminist Sociology*. Boston: Northeastern University Press.

Stacey, Judith. 1988. "Can There Be a Feminist Ethnography?" *Women's Studies International Forum* 11 (1): 21–27.

———. 1990. "On Resistance, Ambivalence and Feminist Theory: A Response to Carol Gilligan." *Michigan Quarterly Review* 29 (4): 537–46.

Stanley, Liz, ed. 1990. *Feminist Praxis: Theory and Epistemology in Feminist Sociology*. New York and London: Routledge.

Stanley, Liz, and Sue Wise. 1983. *Breaking Out: Feminist Consciousness and Feminist Research*. London: Routledge and Kegan Paul.

Strathern, Marilyn. 1987. "An Awkward Relationship: The Case of Feminism and Anthropology." *Signs: Journal of Women in Culture and Society* 12(2): 276–92.

Tedlock, Barbara. 1991. "From Participant Observation to the Observation of Patricipation: The Emergence of Narrative Ethnography." *Journal of Anthropological Research* 47 (1): 69–94.

Thorne, Barrie. 1993. *Gender Play: Girls and Boys in School*. New Brunswick, NJ: Rutgers University Press.

Williams, Patricia. 1988. "On the Object of Property." *Signs: Journal of Women in Culture and Society* 14 (1): 5–24.

Wolf, Margery. 1992. *A Thrice Told Tale: Feminism, Postmodernism and Ethnographic Responsibility*. Stanford, CA: Stanford University Press.

Discussion Questions

1. Feminist research strategies, according to Luttrell, require the researcher to be both self-reflective and respectful of relationships to the researcher's respondents. Do you think this an effective strategy for research? Why or why not?

2. Would a feminist research approach lend itself to all types of studies? Why or why not?

3. If you were a researcher, would you be interested in the sort of research that involved really getting to know research respondents? Why or why not?

4. A lot of what Luttrell discovers in her research is that issues of race, class, and gender deeply influence an individual's school experience. What experiences did you have in school that related to your race, class, and gender or intersections of these variables?

27

Schools Struggle Shielding Gay Kids

Nicole Ziegler Dizon

This brief Associated Press news article concerns the actions of one school board, but it makes several general points: More high school students are being open about their sexual orientation and are asking schools to establish policies to protect them from harassment. Schools and school districts are giving the matter serious consideration, but they face opposition from groups, such as the Family Research Council (FRC), that believe harassment policies should not single out one group or that such policies are a first step toward curriculum mandates. Teachers may not know how to handle harassment based on sexual orientation, but there are groups, such as Gay, Lesbian & Straight Educational Network (GLSEN), that are able to help. The article refers to a U.S. Supreme Court decision allowing students to sue for failure to take action regarding sexual harassment. Lawyers believe this can be extended to include harassment based on sexual orientation.

Meg Sievers was tired of the teasing, the snickers, the whispered death threats.

So she and other gay students in this suburb west of Chicago asked the school board to include "sexual orientation" in a policy that bars students from harassing other students.

The monthlong battle that ensued reflects the struggles school districts across the country face as more students "come out" during high school and demand the right to express their sexual orientation without fear of abuse.

"We used to get a call once a year. Now it's once a week," said Anthony G, Scariano, a Chicago attorney who fields districts' questions about policies that protect gay students.

Scariano's clients include 200 Illinois school districts and 15 outside the state. He points to several recent court decisions in advising them to include sexual orientation in their anti-harassment codes.

In 1996, for example, school officials in Ashland, WI, agreed to pay $900,000 to former student Jamie Nabozny, who had alleged in a federal lawsuit that school officials failed to stop harassment that ranged from anti-gay slurs to severe beatings.

And last year, a divided U.S. Supreme Court ruled that schools can be sued when officials don't prevent students from sexually harassing each other. That ruling could be interpreted to include harassment based on sexual orientation, Scariano said.

The Gay, Lesbian and Straight Education Network, a gay-rights group meeting in Arlington Heights, IL, this weekend, has discussed ways teachers and administrators can address the needs of gay students. Workshops on the group's agenda included "How to Handle Harassment in the Hallways in Three Minutes" and "Strategies for Effective Anti-Bias Trainings."

Peter LaBarbera, a senior analyst with the Family Research Council, a conservative policy group in Washington, worries that groups like GLSEN have a larger agenda in mind when they try to get sexual orientation clauses included in district policies.

"We think these nondiscrimation policies end up being used in schools for purposes that most parents would object to," such as to teach young children about homosexuality, LaBarbera said.

In Naperville, 27 parents, students and community members spoke passionately on both sides of the issue at an August school board meeting on the proposal. The district includes nearly 19,000 students.

Pastor Brian VanDerway of Cornerstone Church in Naperville said a school policy should ban harassment of any kind instead of singling out a particular group of students.

"No matter who you are, somebody is going to find something about you at that age that they don't like," VanDerway said. "(The policy) should say we as a school refuse to permit harassment of any kind for any reason."

But Sievers, an 18-year-old who has graduated from Naperville Central High School, said teachers need to know that they can and should stand up for gay students.

"I heard name-calling, taunting, teasing. I had some death threats," she said of her junior and senior years, after she told classmates she was gay. "Teachers did nothing. . . I don't think that they thought they could do something about it."

The board eventually approved a compromise version that does not explicitly ban harassment based on sexual orientation, but does point out that gay students in particular may face harassment.

Superintendent Don Weber also said he would make it clear that anti-gay slurs would not be allowed in school.

"We said all along that the policy does not promote a lifestyle," Weber said. "We're saying that students should not be harassed."

Other school districts—most of them large—have adopted similar policies over the past several years.

GLSEN surveyed 42 of the country's largest school districts two years ago and found that 58 percent of them barred discrimination against students based on sexual orientation.

June Million, a spokeswoman for the National Association of Elementary School Principals in Alexandria, VA, said her group has begun holding seminars on including sexual orientation in anti-harassment policies. She's seen more schools adopt such policies, although teachers still may not know how to handle playground slurs or teasing.

"It is awkward," she said. "I just think that they need more examples of how to deal with it."

In Naperville, it's too early to tell what difference, if any, the policy has made, said 18-year-old Audrey Martin, a recent graduate of Naperville Central who pushed for the changes.

"If we made a difference for one student that they won't get harassed," Martin said, "then it's worth it."

On the Net

Naperville School District 203: *http://www.ncusd203.org/*

Gay, Lesbian & Straight Education Network: *http://www.glsen.org/*

Family Research Council: *http://www.frc.org/*

Discussion Questions

1. In your opinion, is there a qualitative difference between harassment based on gender and harassment based on sexual orientation? Should schools or workplaces treat them differently? Why (not)?

2. Some people favor a general policy against harassment between students; others argue for one that identifies specific targets of harassment, such as race, gender, disability, or sexual orientation. What are the advantages and disadvantages of each type of harassment policy?

3. Should citizen's groups, such as FRC and GLSEN, get involved in policy decisions being made by school districts? What type of influence over what kinds of policies should they have? Are there some decisions that are best left to educational authorities or some that really should be made with community input?

28

Gender and Class Stereotypes

A Comparison of U.S. and Taiwanese Magazine Advertisements

Chia-Wen Chi
Cecelia Baldwin

While mass media try to sell us products—from shampoos to cars and from clothing to computers, they also serve two other distinct purposes, according to Chia-Wen Chi and Cecelia Baldwin. They reflect and communicate cultural values as well as shape and influence cultural values. Therefore, gender stereotyping in media will both reflect and have significant impact on societal views. In this chapter, Chi and Baldwin take us into the world of magazine media on a global scale, creating a cross-cultural analysis of gender portrayals in magazine advertisements in the United States and Taiwan. Although gender and class are more explicitly included in the analysis, race is implied in the researchers' choice to make the study cross-cultural and international. Chi and Baldwin assert that such research has added merit in that feminist movements did not take hold at the same time in these two distinct national cultural settings—the United States has a longer history of the women's movement than does Taiwan and would therefore be assumed to have "fewer traditional stereotypes."

The authors' findings are disturbing, to say the least. Chi and Baldwin find that both countries tend to reinforce gender stereotypes by portraying American and Taiwanese women as nonworking, decorative, sex objects despite women's gains in the workplace. More concerning still, these findings hold despite a longer history of U.S. feminism. In fact, the depictions of men working and women non-working were represented in percentages that were higher in U.S. than in Taiwanese magazines, while the tendency to portray "more sexually explicit women" was greater in U.S. than in Taiwanese advertising. Studies like this should give us pause as we realize that it has been forty years since the inception of the women's liberation movement in the United States and almost one hundred and forty years since the beginning of the suffrage movement in our nation's history.

According to Miller (1997), the female portrayals in U.S. advertisements have come under heavy scrutiny since the height of the women's movement in the mid-1970s. Compared with the long history of U.S. feminism, the history of Taiwanese feminism is no longer than three decades, beginning in the 1970s. Given the long history of the women's movement in the United States and the shorter history in Taiwan, the basic assumption of this study is that gender portrayals in the U.S. media utilize fewer traditional stereotypes than those in Taiwan. Therefore, a cross-cultural study of male and female portrayals in the U.S. and Taiwanese media and an interpretation of gender roles in these different countries are worth conducting.

The purpose of this study was to examine how media representations reflect gender stereotypes in U.S. and Taiwanese culture after decades of the women's movement. By reviewing long-term challenges from previous researchers, the present study was trying to reexamine how the magazine advertising portrays both genders at the end of 20th century. In addition, a comparison of U.S. and Taiwanese magazine advertisements was performed to measure how culture impacts gender roles in the media.

Gender roles are global, according to Layng (1995). Despite the great variety of sex roles from one society to another, there are certain behavior patterns and attitudes that appear to be similar in both traditional and modern societies. Sorrels (1983) identified four broad stereotypes that summarize cultural views of female roles: homemaker, servant, sex object, and emotional, unintelligent creature. Doyle (1985) also named five male norms, as portrayed in the media: the anti-feminine element, the success element, the aggressive element, the sexual element, and the self-reliant element. In addition, Ferguson (1978) found a general editorial persuasion in women's magazines embracing the three C's of traditional female roles: cooking, cleaning, and caring. As Doyle (1985) found, most people could hardly deny that men are portrayed as already having it all—the *it* being the three P's of power, position, and privilege. In conclusion, from the moment a girl infant is wrapped in a pink blanket and a boy infant in a blue one, gender role development begins (Lindsey, 1995). Additionally, working roles determine class structures.

Advertising as a mirror of the times is a social guide to our society (Hsu, 1991). Sengupta (1995) suggested that cultures are social settings in which a set of practices produces meanings, while communication refers to the exchange of meanings among members of a culture. Because values lie at the core of culture and advertising is a form of communication, it is logical to expect cultural values to have a significant influence on advertising. Since the mid 1970s, feminist scholars found that the mass media are vitally important as a major potential tool for shaping people's perceptions of reality. Research regarding female as well as male stereotypes, in essence, stemmed from feminists' concerns about the social status and class structures of both genders.

The media has given different treatments to both genders. Synnott (1988) conducted a content analysis of advertisements in the *New York Times Magazine* and concluded that the most general message of the ads was that youth and beauty were essential for women but not for men. Men were still men when they become old and ugly, but women were not. After all, according to Hsu (1997), old, ugly women have no value in the marketplace. It was men's role—but not women's—to work and to be physically active. A woman just had to *be*—to be young and beautiful. There was a clear distinction between men as active and women as passive, between men as doing and women as being. "Aristotle

would have been proud of the *New York Times*" (Synnott, 1988: 440).

This also exists in Chinese culture. The traditional Chinese family was based on Confucian principles, which gave complete authority to males, and especially to the oldest males. Lindsey (1990) noted that the traditional Chinese family was patriarchal, patrilineal, and patrilocal. A woman's marriage was arranged, she could not normally inherit property, she would move into her husband's household at marriage and had to survive under the unquestioned authority of her husband, father, and other assorted male relatives (Chang, 1977; Chang, 1995; Gu, 1991; Lay, 1994; Niou, 1981). Women were valued for their domestic work and were not as likely as men to work outside the home for pay. The only real option for women to gain any semblance of prestige was to produce sons. A woman could gain ancestral status only through her husband and sons. Without male descendents, she could have no afterlife to speak of (Lindsey, 1990). Established in 1912, Taiwan, the Republic of China, had inherited the core of Chinese Confucianism.

Compared with the long history of U.S. feminism, the history of Taiwanese feminism is no longer than three decades, beginning in the 1970s. However, by the 1980s, a rising trend of studies stemming from feminists' concerns about gender roles in culture has challenged portrayals in the Taiwanese media. Furthermore, after the lifting of martial law in 1987, not only has academia started to emphasize women's studies, but many women's organizations and women's magazines have also appeared (Chou & Jiang, 1989). By the late 1990s, people in Taiwan are facing an overwhelmingly changed society after a decade of social liberalization. Therefore, it is worth examining gender portrayals in the modern media to obtain a deeper understanding of the relationships among the culture, the media, the time, and gender roles.

Research Design

The research design is a cross-cultural study of gender stereotypes in magazine advertisements from the United States and Taiwan in 1988 and 1998. Content analysis was used in this cross-cultural study. The selection of magazines from the United States and Taiwan was based on parity of magazine types and target markets in both countries. Three categories of magazines were defined: (a) women's fashion, (b) business, and (c) general interest magazines. The U.S. magazines were *Vogue* (women's fashion), *Fortune* (business), and *Newsweek* (general interest). The Taiwanese magazines were *ViVi* (women's fashion), *Common Wealth* (business), and *Global Views* (general interest). A total sample of 600 male and female models appearing in the advertisements of the 144 magazine issues were randomly selected.

The coding system for the content analysis was adapted from Courtney and Lockeretz (1971) for working/non-working roles in magazine advertisements; coding criteria for the type of dress worn by women derived from Soley and Kurzbard's (1986) study. Levels profess[ed] and/or working class roles were additionally coded. Semiotics was also used to help observe the role playing of men and women in the magazine advertisements.

Category Construction

De Voe's (1984) study was adapted and it defined the models' working roles in magazine advertisements as follows:

1. High Level Business — An individual portrayed as a high-ranking official in a business such as a president, vice president, controller, or operations manager.

2. Professional — A model who was playing an expert in a field such as a nurse, chef, doctor, dentist, journalist, architect, judge, artist, engineer, or an athlete.

3. Entertainment, Sports — A celebrity from the performing arts (theater, TV, music) or sports world (tennis, football, baseball) with fame to promote the product.

4. Middle Level Business — A model who was portraying the local grocer, a sales clerk, or an insurance agent.

5. Non Professional White Collar — A model representing a service role, such as a secretarial or clerical job, an assistant, a steward/stewardess, or a waiter/waitress.

6. Blue Collar Labor — An individual who performed manual labor, such as a ranch hand, a construction worker, a cowboy, a driver, or an oil rig worker.

7. Civil Service — An individual in public service such as a fire fighter, a postman, a police officer, a paramedic, or a representative of the military, etc.

Non-working activities were as follows:

1. Family/ At Home — An individual depicted as a wife/husband, mother/father, grandmother/grandfather, or a daughter/son. The model is at home doing "housewifely tasks" such as cooking, cleaning, childcare, or personal beautification.

2. Recreational — An individual depicted as participating in outdoor [activities] or exercises, such as fishing, hiking, swimming, jogging, walking, picnicking, or camping. Activities of drinking, smoking, relaxing, traveling, having a party, hanging out with friends were also included.

3. Decorative — An individual appearing only as an adornment to an object. For example, a person whose main function was to admire a model's outfit was considered to be in a decorative role. The individual had no real function in the advertisement.

4. Other — Activities other than the above, such as driving, writing, talking, getting married, or simply doing nothing.

The female dress were categorized by Hsiung's (1997) definitions as follows:

1. Typical Dress — Models wearing formal dress, like gowns that do not expose cleavage or back, casual dress like walking shorts, sportswear except swimsuits, loungewear, or company uniforms/work wear/suits.

2. Seductive Dress — Models wearing open blouses or shirts that expose chest areas, mini-skirts, "short shorts," tight clothing that accentuates the figure or middle inseam of trousers, full-length nontranslucent lingerie, evening gowns that expose cleavage or back, "muscle shirts," or hiked-up skirts exposing thighs.

3. Partially Clad — Models wearing bathing suits, under-apparel, and three-quarter length or shorter nontranslucent lingerie; models portrayed in "close-up" shots in which the shoulders were bare or in photographs or illustrations of legs that included the thigh but displayed no clothing.

4. Nudity — Unclothed bodies, or models wearing translucent underapparel or lingerie; "medium shots" in which the models displayed no clothing or had only a towel over their shoulders, and full shots where the model was unclad except for a towel.

5. Can't tell — It was difficult to tell the dress, as with advertisements depicting models' faces only.

It was found that above 97% of the males were wearing *typical dress* and the clustered data were not valid for analysis; therefore, dress worn by male models was excluded in this study.

The Pilot Study and Intercoder Reliablity

A pilot study had been conducted to calculate the intercoder reliability coefficient. The researcher and a colleague who speaks English and Mandarin and has a background in mass communications independently coded 60 out of the total 600 models randomly collected from the magazine advertisements. By applying the Scott's pi formula, 85% of the intercoder reliability was obtained to ensure the consistency and accuracy of the coding process in this study. Thereafter, the chi-

square test was applied in the study to analyze the results and examine the hypotheses.

Results

A total sample of 600 models included 298 males and 302 females, 322 characters from the United States and 278 from Taiwan, and 300 portrayals per year for both 1988 and 1998 (see Table 28.1).

Males from both countries were more often depicted in working roles, whereas females from both countries were more often depicted in non-working roles in ads appearing in 1988. More specifically, in U.S. ads for 1988, 69.4% of the males were portrayed in working roles, compared with only 27.3% of the females. In Taiwanese ads for 1988, 63.2% of the males were portrayed in working roles, compared with only 34.3% of the females. Males were portrayed in working roles slighter frequently in the U.S. advertisements (69.4%) than in the Taiwanese advertisements (63.2%). Females were portrayed in non-working roles more frequently in the U.S. advertisements (72.7%) than in the Taiwanese advertisements (65.7%). In the U.S. ads in 1988, relating the sex of the model to the type of role portrayed, working or non-working, was statistically significant ($p < .05$). In the Taiwanese ads for 1988, there was also a significant relationship between the type of role portrayed and the sex of the model ($p < .05$). [See Table 28.2]

In the United States and Taiwan, what type of role (working/non-working) was depicted more often by males in 1998? By females? Table 28.3 indicates that in both coun-

Table 28.1
The Distributions of Males and Females from the United States and Taiwan for 1988 and 1998

	1988 n = 300		1998 n = 300	
	Male	Female	Male	Female
United States	55.6% (85)	52.4% (77)	51.0% (74)	55.5% (86)
Taiwan	44.4% (68)	47.6% (70)	49.0% (71)	44.5% (69)
Total	100% (153)	100% (147)	100% (145)	100% (155)

Table 28.2
A Comparison of the Type of Role Portrayals in Advertisements from the
United States and Taiwan in 1988

	United States n = 162		Taiwan n = 138	
	Male	Female	Male	Female
Working	69.4% (59)	27.3% (21)	63.2% (43)	34.3% (24)
Non-working	30.6% (26)	72.7% (56)	36.8% (25)	65.7% (46)
Total	100% (85)	100% (77)	100% (68)	100% (70)
Pearson chi-square	$x\_(1) = 28.70$, $p < .05$		$x\_1 = 11.57$, $p < .05$	

Table 28.3
A Comparison of the Type of Role Portrayals in Advertisements from the
United States and Taiwan in 1998

	United States n = 160		Taiwan n = 140	
	Male	Female	Male	Female
Working	70.3% (52)	25.6% (22)	54.9% (39)	26.1% (18)
Non-working	29.7% (22)	74.4% (64)	45.1% (32)	73.9% (51)
Total	100% (74)	100% (86)	100% (71)	100% (69)
Pearson chi-square	$x\_(1) = 31.95$, $p < .05$		$x\_(1) = 12.06$, $p < .05$	

tries, males were more often depicted in working roles, whereas females were shown more often in non-working roles. U.S. males had a higher percentage (70.3%) in the working role category, compared it with 54.9% of Taiwanese men. However, the U.S. and Taiwanese women had only slightly different percentages in non-working roles, with 74.4% and 73.9% respectively. For the U.S. ads in 1998, the results showed a significant relationship between the type of role portrayed and the sex of the model ($p < .05$). Relating the sex of the model to the type of role portrayed in Taiwanese ads appearing in 1998 also revealed a statistical significance ($p < .05$).

In order to avoid small samples in the cells, certain categories were combined to produce Table 28.4 and Table 28.5. The term *ns* stands for a non-significant relationship between the coding variables.

In the United States and Taiwan, what working role was portrayed most often by males in 1988? By females? Working males in the U.S. ads were mostly portrayed in high-level business roles, while working men in Taiwan were mostly depicted as professionals. However, working women from both countries in 1988 were mostly shown in mid-level business/non-professional white-collar roles. (See Table 28.4.)

Table 28.4
A Comparison of Working Role Portrayals in Advertisements from the United States and Taiwan in 1988

	United States n = 80		Taiwan n = 67	
	Male	Female	Male	Female
High-level business	44.1% (26)	33.3% (7)	27.9% (12)	8.3% (2)
Professional	23.7% (14)	14.3% (3)	39.5% (17)	4.2% (1)
Entertainment/Sports	5.1% (3)	14.3% (3)	4.7% (2)	25.0% (6)
Mid-level business/Non-professional white collar	15.3% (9)	38.1% (8)	20.9% (9)	58.3% (14)
Blue-collar labor/Civil Service	11.9% (7)		7.0% (3)	4.2% (1)
Total	100% (59)	100% (21)	100% (43)	100% (24)
Pearson chi-square	*ns*		$x_{(4)} = 21.82, p < .05$	

Table 28.5
A Comparison of Working Role Portrayals in Advertisements from the United States and Taiwan in 1998

	United States n = 74		Taiwan n = 51	
	Male	Female	Male	Female
High-level business	25.0% (13)	13.6% (3)	46.2% (18)	11.1% (2)
Professional	19.2% (10)	27.3% (6)	30.8% (12)	27.8% (5)
Entertamment/Sports	3.8% (2)	18.2% (4)	2.6% (1)	33.3% (6)
Mid-level business/Non-professional white collar	34.6% (18)	27.3% (6)	12.8% (5)	27.8% (5)
Blue-collar labor/Civil Service	17.3% (9)	13.6% (3)	7.7% (3)	
Total	100% (52)	100% (22)	100% (39)	100% (18)
Pearson chi-square	*ns*		*ns*	

In working role portrayals (see Table 28.4), males appeared more frequently in high-level business roles in the U.S. advertisements (44.1%) than in the Taiwanese advertisements (27.9%). The percentage of U.S. females portrayed in high-level business roles was slightly more than four times that of Taiwanese women (33.3% and 8.3% respectively). Looking at professional roles, the research found that U.S. men were shown less frequently in professional roles (23.7%) than were Taiwanese men (39.5%), but U.S. women were shown in professional roles more than three times as often (14.3%) as women in Taiwan (4.2%). Examining the mid-level business/non-professional roles showed that Taiwanese men were presented in these roles more frequently (20.9%) than U.S. men were (15.3%), and women in Taiwan had a higher percentage (58.3%) when compared with the U.S. females (38.1%). In entertainment/sports roles, Taiwanese females appeared in these roles more often (25%) than U.S. women (14.3%).

In comparisons between the sexes, a consistent phenomenon was that high-level business, professional, and blue-collar males in both countries for 1988 all showed higher percentages than did females in identical categories (see Table 28.4). On the other hand, women in advertisements from both countries had much higher percentages than men did in the roles of entertainment/sports and mid-level business/non-professionals. Moreover, in Taiwan, males in high-level business roles were coded more than three times as often as females (27.9% and 8.3% respectively), and males were portrayed in professional roles more than nine times as often as females (39.5% and 4.2% respectively). As for mid-level business roles, U.S. females were depicted more frequently (38.1%) than U.S. males (15.3%), and in Taiwan, women were also portrayed more frequently (58.3%) than men (20.9%). Blue-collar men, however, appeared more often than women in ads appearing in 1988. Taiwanese portrayals in 1988 revealed a significant relationship between the type of working role and the sex of the model ($p < .05$).

In the United States and Taiwan, what working role was portrayed most often by males in 1998? By females? As Table 28.5 indicates, U.S. men were mostly portrayed in mid-level/non-professional roles, while most men in ads from Taiwan were portrayed in high-level business roles. U.S. women were most often portrayed in professional and mid-level/non-professional roles, whereas Taiwanese women were mostly depicted in entertainment/sports roles. (These results [are] listed in Table 28.5.)

In advertisements from both countries in 1998 (see Table 28.5), high-level business roles still ranked higher among males than among females, although Taiwanese men were more frequently presented in this category (46.2%) than U.S. males (25%). On the other hand, 34.6% of U.S. men were portrayed in mid-level/non-professional roles, while only 12.8% of Taiwanese men were portrayed in these roles. U.S. women were shown to be just as likely as Taiwanese women to appear in both professional and mid-level/non-professional white-collar roles in 1998. However, 33.3% of women in Taiwanese advertisements were portrayed in entertainment/sports roles, compared with only 18.2% of U.S. females.

As Table 28.5 shows, men in Taiwan were still shown more frequently in high-level business and professional roles than were women, while U.S. men were shown more often in high-level business roles and less often in professional roles than were U.S. women in 1998. It was found that women in Taiwanese advertisements were portrayed more frequently in mid-level business roles (27.8%) than were men (12.8%). On the other hand, U.S. females were less often depicted in mid-level roles (27.3%) than were males (34.6%). In both countries, females were more likely to be portrayed in entertainment/sports roles than were males, while blue-collar men appeared more often than blue-collar women in ads appearing in 1998.

In the United States and Taiwan, were more females portrayed in high-level business roles in 1998 than in 1988? (See these comparative findings in Table 28.4 and Table 28.5.) The research showed that the percentage of U.S. females appearing in high-level business roles in 1988, 33.3%, had decreased to 13.6% in 1998, while the percentage of women appearing in high-level business roles in advertisements in Taiwan had increased, from 8.3% in 1988 to 11.1% in 1998. However, the difference between 1988 and 1998 did suggest a trend toward more portrayals of female professionals in both countries. It is worth mentioning that in Taiwan, the percentage of females portrayed in professional roles in 1988 (4.2%) had increased to 27.8% in 1998, with a difference of more than six times. Furthermore, women were portrayed in mid-level/non-professional roles less often in both countries after a decade.

In the United States and Taiwan, what non-working role was portrayed most often by males in 1988? By females? (See Table 28.6.) It was found that men in both countries were most often presented in recreational settings, while women in both countries were mostly cast in decorative roles. In the category of recreational activity, U.S. males were shown more frequently (54.2%) than men in Taiwan (40.9%). In both countries in 1988, men were also portrayed in recreational settings more often than were women. Regarding decorative roles, Taiwanese women had a slightly higher percentage (50%) than U.S. females (48%). In both countries, women were portrayed in decorative roles more than two times as often as males. Surprisingly, men from both countries were presented more frequently in the family/at home setting than women were, with per-

centages more than two times higher. Furthermore, men and women in Taiwanese advertisements were found more often in the home settings than were the U.S. characters. The study revealed a significant relationship between the type of non-working role and the sex of the model for U.S. ads appearing in 1988 ($p < .05$).

In the United States and Taiwan, what non-working role was portrayed most often by males in 1998? By females? (See Table 28.7.) In both countries, men were mostly portrayed in recreational settings, while women were mostly cast in decorative roles. Surprisingly, non-working female characters in advertisements from both countries had barely different percentages in the three identical categories. However, Taiwanese men were shown more frequently in decorative roles (33.3%) than were U.S. males (14.3%). In both the family/at home and the recreational settings, U.S. men were more often portrayed in these settings than were men in Taiwan.

Advertisements from both countries revealed a consistent phenomenon (see Table 28.7): more men than women were involved in family/at home and recreational activities, while more women than men were portrayed in decorative roles. Surprisingly, U.S. males were portrayed in family settings more than twice as often as women were (23.8% and 9.5% respectively), and Taiwanese men were also presented more often at

Table 28.6
A Comparison of Non-working Role Portrayals in Advertisements from the United States and Taiwan in 1988

	United States n = 74		Taiwan n = 64	
	Male	Female	Male	Female
Family/At home	29.2% (7)	12.0% (6)	36.4% (8)	16.7% (7)
Recreational	54.2% (13)	40.0% (20)	40.9% (9)	33.3% (14)
Decorative	16.7% (4)	48.0% (24)	22.7% (5)	50.0% (21)
Total	100% (24)	100% (50)	100% (22)	100% (42)
Pearson chi-square	$x_{(2)} = 7.66, p < .05$		*ns*	

Table 28.7
A Comparison of Non-working Role Portrayals in Advertisements from the United States and Taiwan in 1998

	United States n = 84		Taiwan n = 71	
	Male	Female	Male	Female
Family/At home	23.8% (5)	9.5% (6)	12.5% (3)	8.5% (4)
Recreational	61.9% (13)	33.3% (21)	54.2% (13)	34.0% (16)
Decorative	14.3% (3)	57.1% (36)	33.3% (8)	57.4% (27)
Total	100% (21)	100% (63)	100% (24)	100% (47)
Pearson chi-square	$x_{(2)} = 11.86$, $p < .05$		*ns*	

home (12.5%) than were women in Taiwan (8.5%). In U.S. ads appearing in 1998, the type of non-working activities was significantly related to the sex of the model ($p < .05$).

In the United States and Taiwan, were more males portrayed in decorative roles in 1998 than in 1988? (Compare the findings in Table 28.6 and Table 28.7.) The data showed a slight decline from 1988 (16.7%) to 1998 (14.3%) among U.S. males, while the percentage of Taiwanese men portrayed in decorative roles in 1988 (22.7%) had risen to 33.3% in 1998. A consistent phenomenon was found in advertisements from both countries: after a decade, not only males but females were shown less and less often in the home settings. In both the United States and Taiwan, nevertheless, it was disappointing that more and more women were portrayed in decorative roles from 1988 to 1998.

As Table 28.8 shows, it was typical dress that was most often worn by women in U.S. and Taiwanese ads appearing in both years. In the United States and Taiwan, what type of dress worn by women was shown most often in 1988? In 1998? In the 1988 advertisements, 83.8% of Taiwanese women wore typical dress, more than the 76.7% of U.S. females wearing typical dress. In the 1998 advertisements, however, only 54.4% of Taiwanese women wore typical dress, less than the 70.2% of U.S. females wearing typical dress. More-

over, the study found a statistically significant relationship between the type of dress worn by women and the country in which the ad appear[ed] in 1998 ($p < .05$).

For both years, U.S. women were portrayed wearing seductive dress more often than Taiwanese women were (see Table 28.8). In 1988 and 1998, were more women wearing seductive dress in the United States than in Taiwan? It is also noteworthy that in 1998, 27.9% of women in the Taiwanese advertisements were portrayed as partially clad/nude, a percentage more than four times higher than the 6% of U.S. females. In 1988, however, 5.5% of U.S. females were portrayed as partially clad/nude, more than the 4.4% of women in Taiwan.

As demonstrated in Table 28.9, in the United States and Taiwan, more women were portrayed wearing seductive dress in 1998 than in 1988. Surprisingly, the data showed a sharp increase in the percentage of Taiwanese women portrayed as partially clad/nude, from 4.4% in 1988 to 27.9% in 1998, while the percentage of U.S. females in the same category only increased from 5.5% to 6%. And in the categories of typical dress worn by women in both countries, percentages decreased after a decade, with a sharper decline among Taiwanese women, almost 30% (from 83.8% to 54.4%), compared with a 6.5% decline among U.S. women (from

Table 28.8
A Comparison of the Type of Women's Dress in Advertisements from the
United States and Taiwan in 1988 and in 1998

	1988 n = 141		1998 n = 152	
	United States	Taiwan	United States	Taiwan
Typical dress	76.7% (56)	83.8% (57)	70.2% (59)	54.4% (37)
Seductive dress	17.8% (13)	11.8% (8)	23.8% (20)	17.6% (12)
Partially clad/Nudity	5.5% (4)	4.4% (3)	6.0% (5)	27.9% (19)
Total	100% (73)	100% (68)	100% (84)	100% (68)
Pearson chi-square	*ns*		$x_{(2)} = 13.68$, $p < .05$	

76.7% to 70.2%). During this 10-year range, a significant relationship between the type of dress worn by women and the year was found in the Taiwanese ads ($p < .05$).

Discussion

Working and Non-working Portrayals

A growing number of women will make up an estimated 47% of the overall work force by 2006 (Sohn, Wicks, Lacy, & Sylvie, 1999). Quoting recent media research, furthermore, Hsu (1998) stated that *woman power* is the most influential trend for the next century in Asia. However, findings in this study show that advertisements contradict the reality.

This study revealed that in the United States and Taiwan, magazine advertisements portrayed males mainly in working roles and females mainly in non-working roles, stereotyping both genders universally, not only in 1988 but in 1998, when at least 65.7% of women in advertisements were depicted as non-working. By referring to the chi-square result, the researcher consistently found significant relationships between the type of role portrayed and the model's gender (all with $p < .05$) in both the United States and Taiwan for both

Table 28.9
A Comparison of the Type of Women's Dress in Advertisements from the
United States and from Taiwan in 1988 and 1998

	United States n = 157		Taiwan n = 136	
	1988	1998	1988	1998
Typical dress	76.7% (56)	70.2% (59)	83.8% (57)	54.4% (37)
Seductive dress	17.8% (13)	23.8% (20)	11.8% (8)	17.6% (12)
Partially clad/Nudity	5.5% (4)	6.0% (5)	4.4% (3)	27.9% (19)
Total	100% (73)	100% (84)	100% (68)	100% (68)
Pearson chi-square	*ns*		$x_{(2)} = 16.69$, $p < .05$	

years. Moreover, the U.S. media even had higher percentages of working men and non-working women than Taiwanese media did in 1988 and 1998.

Working Roles

In the working universe, high-level business, professional, and blue-collar roles were the preferences of male portrayals in the magazine advertisements for the United States and Taiwan in 1988 and 1998. On the other hand, women were cast more frequently in entertainment/sports roles and mid-level/non-professional white-collar roles for both countries and both years.

There appeared an interesting trend among working women in 1998: Taiwanese females were as likely as U.S. women to be portrayed in both professional and mid-level/non-professional white-collar roles. Working men portrayed in 1998 U.S. advertisements, however, did bring changes, with fewer high-level business and professional roles and with more mid-level/non-professional white-collar roles when compared with advertisements in Taiwan. In brief, some alternatives of models' working portrayals in the advertisements from both countries had occurred in 1998.

During a 10-year range, the rise in the number of professional women and the decrease in the number of non-professional women had brought an expectation that female images in the U.S. and Taiwanese media should change. As for high-level businesswomen, it is disappointing to find a decline among U.S. females from 1988 to 1998, and the insignificant increase among women in Taiwan from 8.3% to 11.1% also suggests the need for efforts to raise female status in media portrayals.

Overall, Taiwanese magazine advertising has more stereotypical portrayals in models' working roles than advertising in the United States, for 1988 as well as 1998. The tendency to represent men in high-level business and professional roles while women are portrayed in mid-level business remains three decades after the women's movement in Taiwan started in 1971.

Non-working Activities

In portrayals of non-working people in both countries, men were consistently represented more often in recreational settings and women in decorative roles for the years of 1988 and 1998. In both years in the United States and Taiwan, decorative females appeared in magazine advertisements much more often than decorative males, reaching the highest variance in 1998, with a 42.8% difference between U.S. males and U.S. females. It was disappointing that in advertisements from both countries, more and more women were portrayed in decorative roles between 1988 and 1998, and the number of decorative males in advertisements from Taiwan also increased.

On the other hand, it was interesting to find that a trend of casting more men than women in the family/at home settings appeared in both years in both the United States and Taiwan. However, this study also revealed a trend in both countries toward fewer and fewer men and women portrayed in home settings, as shown by the decrease in this category between 1988 and 1998. This trend suggests a change in views toward the traditional home-oriented society.

Overall, the two countries were found to be similar when it comes to representations of women in decorative roles during the study decade. Advertisers all over the world continue to stereotype females as *doing nothing* in the late 1990s. In addition, U.S. magazine advertising in both 1988 and 1998 includes more stereotypical portrayals in models' non-working roles than does Taiwanese advertising.

Dress Worn by Women

A trend is apparent between 1988 and 1998: more U.S. women than Taiwanese women were wearing seductive dress. This revealed that the U.S. women were more sexually explicit than women in Taiwan. On the other hand, typical dress was found less and less often in advertisements from both countries between 1988 and 1998. The trend toward more U.S. and Taiwanese women wearing seductive dress or depicted as partially clad/nude suggests a more sexually explicit world after a decade. Surprisingly, 27.9% of female models in the 1998 sample from Taiwan were portrayed as partially clad/nude, showing a 21.9% difference over the 1998 U.S. sample and a 23.5% difference over the 1988 Taiwanese sample. This illustrates a boom of portrayals of sexually explicit females in the Taiwanese media by the late 1990s. According to Tao (1991) and Sengupta (1995), using seductively dressed women to draw attention to the advertisements may be a common strategy practiced by advertisers around the world.

Overall, the significant relationship between the type of dress worn by women and the country in which the ad appeared in 1998 (p .05) suggests that culture does impact female portrayals in the U.S. and Taiwanese media by the 1990s.

Conclusions

Compared with the long history of U.S. feminism, the history of Taiwanese feminism is no longer than three decades, beginning in the 1970s. However, studies stemming from feminists' concerns about gender roles in culture have challenged gender stereotypes in the Taiwanese media as well as in the United States. It is worth while to compare sex portrayals by using the cross-cultural approach, since the two countries are progressing at different stages.

On the other hand, gender roles are global regardless of race, class, or culture (Layng, 1995). Sorrels (1983) defined four broad stereotypes that summarize cultural views of female roles: homemaker, servant, sex object, and emotional, unintelligent creature. Doyle (1985) also identified five male norms: the anti-feminine element, the success element, the aggressive element, the sexual element, and the self-reliant element. Hence, there are certain behavior patterns and attitudes that appear to be the same in both traditional and modern societies despite the great variety of sex roles from one society to another (Layng, 1995).

In summarizing the comparison between genders, this study concludes that women's status in both cultures is inferior to that of men. By ignoring an increase in female work force universally, the U.S. and Taiwanese

media misrepresent female images as non-working in a majority of portrayals in magazine advertisements. Surprisingly, advertising in the United Stales stereotyped men as working and women as non-working in even higher percentages than in Taiwan. Although it held a position of leadership in the world, the U.S. media did not reflect the actual diversity of female roles in modern society.

This study also concludes that women are depicted as inferior to men in the type of work they do. In general, men were frequently portrayed as high-level business and professional people, while women were most likely to be portrayed in entertainment/sports or mid-level/non-professional roles regardless of the country and the year. This confirms the female stereotype as a servant, and it responds to the success element in male identities. For 1998, however, an increase of mid-level/non-professional men in advertisements from the United States and a trend toward more professional women in advertisements from Taiwan represented a nice try in improving working portrayals by the late 1990s. Overall, the U.S. media can reflect a greater variety of gender roles than the Taiwanese media do when it comes to representing the work place in magazine advertisements.

Apparently, the ads were more likely to portray non-working men as mostly involved in recreational settings and more likely to portray non-working women as decorative beings. During the decade of this study, moreover, the increase of women in decorative roles, mainly in apparel advertisements from both countries, is disappointing. Along with the trend toward more and more seductively dressed women in the U.S. and Taiwanese media, this finding leads to the conclusion that the media do stereotype females as sex objects. In general, the U.S. media's attempts to portray more sexually explicit women than the Taiwanese media do leads to accusations of stereotypical female images and consignment of women to non-working roles.

In conclusion, gender stereotypes in the media remain consistent even decades after the women's movement began in the 1960s and the 1970s in both countries. Female inferiority and male superiority have caused difficulties for both genders in both societies. Culture does play a crucial role in the production of stereotypical portrayals in different countries during different stages of the social progress, with the media either reflecting or misrepresenting the real subjects.

Bibliography

Chang, J-H. (1995). Feminism and communication studies. In J-H. Chang, Y-H. Ke, Y-J. Gu, & Y-Y. Chou (eds.), *Media's women; women's media*, Vol. 1, pp. 1–68 . Taipei, Taiwan: suo-Ren.

Chang, Z-Z. (1977). *The changing of women's communication behavior and traditional female roles: study on the subjects of female college students*. Unpublished master's thesis, National Cheng Chih University, Taipei, Taiwan.

Chou, B-E & Jiang, L-H. (1989). The experience of Taiwanese women's movement in the current stage. In C-K. Hsu & W-L. Song (eds.), *The arising social movements in Taiwan*, pp. 79–101 Taipei, Taiwan: Chu-Liou.

Courtney, A. E., & Lockeretz, S. W. (1971). A woman's place: An analysis of the roles portrayed by women in magazine advertisements. *Journal of Marketing Research*, 8 (1): 92–95.

De Voe, J. L. (1984). *An analysis of the roles portrayed by males in magazine advertisements*. Unpublished master's thesis, San Jose State University.

Doyle, J. A. (1985). *Sex and gender: The human experience*. Dubuque, IA: Wm. C. Brown.

Ferguson, M. (1978). Imagery and ideology: The cover photographs of traditional women's magazines. In G. Tuchman, A. Kaplan Daniels, & J. Benet (eds.), *Hearth and home: Images of women in the mass media*, pp. 97–115. New York: Oxford University Press.

Gu, Y-J. (1991). *Interpreting female connotations in television commercials*. Unpublished masters thesis, National Cheng Chih University, Taipei, Taiwan.

Hsiung, S-H. (1997). *A comparison of women's portrayals in U.S. and Taiwanese magazine advertisements*. Unpublished master's thesis, San Jose State University.

Hsu, G.H-L. (1991). *Women's portraits and values as reflected in the late 1980s women's magazine advertisements*. Unpublished master's thesis, Fu Jen Catholic University, Taipei, Taiwan.

Hsu, L. (1998). *A survivor from the dark night*. Taipei, Taiwan: Ping-Ann.

Hsu, S-T. (1997). *Cinderella in the evening gown: Stewardesses who exchange physical beauty for money*. Unpublished master's thesis, National Taiwan University, Taipei, Taiwan.

Lay, P-R. (1994). *An analysis of relationships between women's magazines and the changing of female values*. Unpublished master's thesis, National Cheng Chih University, Taipei, Taiwan.

Layng, A. (1995). Evolution explains traditional gender rofes. In Jonathan S. Petrikin (ed,), *Male/female roles*: Opposing viewpoints, pp. 17–23. San Diego, CA: Greenhaven Press.

Lindsey, L. L. (1990). *Gender roles: A sociological perspective*. Englewood Cliffs, NJ: Prentice-Hall.

——. (1995), Culture determines gender roles. In J. S. Petrikin (ed.), *Male/female roles: Opposing viewpoints*, pp. 74–81. San Diego, CA: Greenhaven Press.

Miller, A. M. (1997). *A content analysis of portrayals of women in magazine advertising from 1975 to 1995*. Unpublished master's thesis, San Jose State University.

Niou, C-F. (1981). *The changing of Chinese women's roles: From a perspective of the soap operas on television*. Unpublished master's thesis, National Cheng Chih University, Taipei, Taiwan.

Sengupta, S. (1995). The influence of culture on portrayals of women in television commercials: A comparison between the United States and Japan. *International Journal of Advertising*, 14: 314–333.

Sohn, A. B., Wicks, J. L., Lacy, S., & Sylvie, G. (1999). *Media management: A casebook approach*. Mahwah, NJ: Lawrence Erlbaum Associates.

Soley, L. & Kurzbard, G. (1986). Sex in advertising: A comparison of 1964 and 1984 magazine advertisements, *Journal of Advertising*, 15 (3): 46–54.

Sorrels, B. D. (1983). *The nonsexist communicator* (Rev. ed.). Englewood Cliffs, NJ: Prentice-Hall.

Synnott, A. (1988). The presentation of gender in advertising. In A. A. Berger (ed.), *Media USA: Process and effect*, pp. 436–444. White Plains, NY: Longman.

Tao, F-Y. (1991). *A content analysis of male and female portrayals in Taiwanese magazine advertisements*. Unpublished master's thesis, National Cheng Chih University, Taipei, Taiwan.

Discussion Questions

1. What differences in American and Taiwanese culture with regard to magazine advertisements emerge from Chi and Baldwin's study?

2. If a study were to be done using Chi and Baldwin's model variables on gender portrayals in magazine advertisements of African Americans and White Americans, what results would you predict?

3. Do you think a magazine can survive in the United States if it does not portray women as described in this study? Why or why not?

4. What have you observed in magazine advertisements? Have you seen the sorts of trends Chi and Baldwin describe? Use examples to back up your statements.

5. Assignment: Take the time to browse magazines at your local bookstore this weekend. While you leaf through the pages, try to get a sense of how many women are portrayed either as decorative objects or sex objects from your point of view. Bring this information to the class next week.

Reprinted from: Chia-Wen Chi and Cecelia Baldwin, "Gender and Class Stereotypes: A Comparison of U.S. and Taiwanese Magazine Advertisements." In *Race, Gender & Class*, 11 (2), pp. 156–175. Copyright © 2004 by *Race, Gender & Class*. Reprinted with permission. ✦

29

Race and Criminalization

Black Americans and the Punishment Industry

Angela Y. Davis

In this discussion of what she calls the "punishment industry," professor and activist Angela Y. Davis shows how race and gender connect such seemingly unrelated matters as the war on drugs, NAFTA, capitalism, welfare, and the manufacturing of electronic equipment. Because our public discourse celebrates the progress that has been made in dealing with racial issues and we treat any evidence of racism that remains as a problem to be solved by changing peoples' hearts and minds, policies and discussions that appear to be race-blind or neutral actually conceal an underlying social structure that is not only racialized, but gendered as well. People talk about the elimination of crime or the economic benefits of using prison labor without addressing the facts that well over five million people are in the criminal justice system, that a disproportionate number of them are African American or Latino/a, or that the increase in rates of imprisonment of women of color far exceeds those of men.

Davis maintains that when prisons are seen as places to protect society, prevent further crime, or keep "undesirables" out of circulation, and those "undesirables" are members of racial and ethnic minorities, racism is both produced and concealed. Instead of seeing crime as an isolated and abstract problem, she locates crime in an economic cycle in which jobs move out of the country in search of cheaper labor, increasing unemployment and leaving communities unable to provide basic services. Under such circumstances, some people will turn to crime. Prisons are needed to house those convicted of crime. Building and operating pris-

ons provides jobs and those who have been incarcerated can, in turn, become a source of cheap labor.

In this post-civil rights era, as racial barriers in high economic and political realms are apparently shattered with predictable regularity, race itself becomes an increasingly proscribed subject. In the dominant political discourse it is no longer acknowledged as a pervasive structural phenomenon, requiring the continuation of such strategies as affirmative action, but rather is represented primarily as a complex of prejudicial attitudes, which carry equal weight across all racial boundaries. Black leadership is thus often discredited and the identification of race as a public, political issue itself called into question through the invocation of, and application of the epithet "black racist" to, such figures as Louis Farrakhan and Khalid Abdul Muhammad. Public debates about the role of the state that once focused very sharply and openly on issues of "race" and racism are now expected to unfold in the absence of any direct acknowledgment of the persistence—and indeed further entrenchment—of racially structured power relationships. Because race is ostracized from some of the most impassioned political debates of this period, their racialized character becomes increasingly difficult to identify, especially by those who are unable—or do not want—to decipher the encoded language. This means that hidden racist arguments can be mobilized readily across racial boundaries and political alignments. Political positions once easily defined as conservative, liberal, and sometimes even radical therefore have a tendency to lose their distinctiveness in the face of the seductions of this camouflaged racism.

President Clinton chose the date of the Million Man March, convened by Minister Louis Farrakhan of the Nation of Islam, to issue a call for a "national conversation on race," borrowing ironically the exact words of Lani Guinier (whose nomination for assistant attorney general in charge of civil rights he had previously withdrawn because her writings focused too sharply on issues of race).[1] Guiniei's ideas had been so easily dismissed because of the prevailing ideological equation of the "end of racism" with the removal of all allusions to race. If conservative positions argue that race consciousness itself impedes the process of solving the problem of race—i.e., achieving race blindness—then Clinton's speech indicated an attempt to reconcile the two, positing race consciousness as a means of moving toward race blindness. "There are too many today white and black, on the left and the right, on the street corners and radio waves, who seek to sow division for their own purposes. To them I say: 'No more. We must be one.'"

While Clinton did acknowledge "the awful history and the stubborn persistence of racism," his remarks foregrounded those reasons for the "racial divide" that "are rooted in the fact that we still haven't learned to talk frankly, to listen carefully and to work together across racial lines." Race, he insisted, is not about government, but about the hearts of people. Of course, it would be absurd to deny the degree to which racism infects in deep and multiple ways the national psyche. However, the relegation of race to matters of the heart tends to render it increasingly difficult to identify the deep structural entrenchment of contemporary racism.

When the structural character of racism is ignored in discussions about crime and the rising population of incarcerated people, the racial imbalance in jails and prisons is treated as a contingency at best as a product of the "culture of poverty," and at worst as proof of an assumed black monopoly on criminality. The high proportion of black people in the criminal justice system is thus normalized and neither the state nor the general public is required to talk about and act on the meaning of that racial imbalance. Thus Republican and Democratic elected officials alike have successfully called for laws mandating life sentences for three-time "criminals," without having to answer for the racial implications of these laws. By relying on the alleged "race-blindness" of such laws, black people are surreptitiously constructed as racial subjects, thus manipulated, exploited, and abused, while the structural persistence of racism—albeit in changed forms—in social and eco-

nomic institutions, and in the national culture as a whole, is adamantly denied.

Crime is thus one of the masquerades behind which "race," with all its menacing ideological complexity, mobilizes old public fears *and* creates new ones. The current anti-crime debate takes place within a reified mathematical realm—a strategy reminiscent of Malthus's notion of the geometrical increase in population and the arithmetical increase in food sources, thus the inevitability of poverty and the means of suppressing it: war, disease, famine, and natural disasters. As a matter of fact, the persisting neo-Malthusian approach to population control, which, instead of seeking to solve those pressing social problems that result in real pain and suffering in people's lives, calls for the elimination of those suffering lives—finds strong resonances in the public discussion about expurgating the "nation" of crime. These discussions include arguments deployed by those who are leading the call for more prisons and employ statistics in the same fetishistic and misleading way as Malthus did more than two centuries ago. Take for example James Wooten's comments in the *Heritage Foundation State Backgrounder*:

> If the 55% of the 800,000 current state and federal prisoners who are violent offenders were subject to serving 85% of their sentence, and assuming that those violent offenders would have committed 10 violent crimes a year while on the street, then the number of crimes prevented each year by truth in sentencing would be 4,000,000. That would be over 2/3 of the 6,000,000 violent crimes reported.[2]

In *Reader's Digest*, Senior Editor Eugene H. Methvin writes:

> If we again double the present federal and state prison population—to somewhere between 1 million and 1.5 million and leave our city and county jail population at the present 400,000, we will break the back of America's 30 year crime wave.[3]

The real human beings—a vastly disproportionate number of whom are black and Latino/a men and women—designated by these numbers in a seemingly race-neutral way are deemed fetishistically exchangeable with the crimes they have or will allegedly commit. The real impact of imprisonment on their lives never need be examined. The inevitable part played by the punishment industry in the reproduction of crime never need be discussed. The dangerous and indeed fascistic trend toward progressively greater numbers of hidden, incarcerated human populations is itself rendered invisible. All that matters is the elimination of crime—and you get rid of crime by getting rid of people who, according to the prevailing racial common sense, are the most likely people to whom criminal acts will be attributed. Never mind that if this strategy is seriously and consistently pursued, the majority of young black women spend a good portion of their lives behind walls and bars in order to serve as a reminder that the state is aggressively confronting its enemy.[4]

While I do not want to locate a response to these arguments on the same level of mathematical abstraction and fetishism I have been problematizing, it is helpful, I think, to consider how many people are presently incarcerated or whose lives are subject to the direct surveillance of the criminal justice system. There are already approximately 1 million people in state and federal prisons in the United States, not counting the 500,000 in city and county jails or the 600,000 on parole or the 3 million people on probation or the 60,000 young people in juvenile facilities. Which is to say that there are presently over 5.1 million people either incarcerated, on parole, or on probation. Many of those presently on probation or parole would be behind bars under the conditions of the recently passed crime bill. According to the Sentencing Project, even before the passage of the crime bill, black people were 7.8 times more likely to be imprisoned than whites.[5] The Sentencing Project's most recent report[6] indicates that 32.2 percent of young black men and 12.3 percent of young Latino men between the ages of twenty and twenty-nine are either in prison, in jail, or on probation or parole. This is in comparison with 6.7 percent of young white men. A total of 827,440 young African-American males are under the supervision of the criminal justice system, at a cost of $6 billion per year. A major strength of the 1995 report, as compared to

its predecessor, is its acknowledgment that the racialized impact of the criminal justice system is also gendered and that the relatively smaller number of African-American women drawn into the system should not relieve us of the responsibility of understanding the encounter of gender and race in arrest and incarceration practices. Moreover, the increases in women's contact with the criminal justice system have been even more dramatic than those of men.

> The 78% increase in criminal justice control rates for black women was more than double the increase for black men and for white women, and more than nine times the increase for white men. . . . Although research on women of color in the criminal justice system is limited, existing data and research suggest that it is the combination of race and sex effects that is at the root of the trends which appear in our data. For example, while the number of blacks and Hispanics in prison is growing at an alarming rate, the rate of increase for women is even greater. Between 1980 and 1992 the female prison population increased 276% compared to 163% for men. Unlike men of color, women of color thus belong to two groups that are experiencing particular dramatic growth in their contact with the criminal justice system.[7]

It has been estimated that by the year 2000 the number of people imprisoned will surpass 4 million, a grossly disproportionate number of whom will be black people, and that the cost will be over $40 billion a year,[8] a figure that is reminiscent of the way the military budget devoured—and continues to devour—the country's resources. This out-of-control punishment industry is an extremely effective criminalization industry, for the racial imbalance in incarcerated populations is not recognized as evidence of structural racism, but rather is invoked as a consequence of the assumed criminality of black people. In other words, the criminalization process works so well precisely because of the hidden logic of racism. Racist logic is deeply entrenched in the nation's material and psychic structures. It is something with which we are all very familiar. The logic, in fact, can persist, even when direct allusions to "race" are removed.

Even those communities that are most deeply injured by this racist logic have learned how to rely upon it, particularly when open allusions to race are not necessary. Thus, in the absence of broad, radical grassroots movements in poor black communities so devastated by new forms of youth-perpetuated violence, the ideological options are extremely sparse. Often there are no other ways to express collective rage and despair but to demand that police sweep the community clean of crack and Uzis, and of the people who use and sell drugs and wield weapons. Ironically, Carol Moseley-Braun, the first black woman senator in our nation's history, was an enthusiastic sponsor of the Senate Anticrime Bill, whose passage in November 1993 paved the way for the August 25, 1994, passage of the bill by the House. Or perhaps there is little irony here. It may be precisely because there is a Carol Moseley-Braun in the Senate and a Clarence Thomas in the Supreme Court—and concomitant class differentiations and other factors responsible for far more heterogeneity in black communities than at any other time in this country's history—that implicit consent to antiblack racist logic (not to speak of racism toward other groups) becomes far more widespread among black people. Wahneema Lubiano's explorations of the complexities of state domination as it operates within and through the subjectivities of those who are the targets of this domination facilitates an understanding of this dilemma.[9]

Borrowing the title of Cornel West's recent work, race *matters*. Moreover, it matters in ways that are far more threatening and simultaneously less discernible than those to which we have grown accustomed. Race matters inform, more than ever, the ideological and material structures of U.S. society. And, as the current discourses on crime, welfare, and immigration reveal, race, gender, and class matter enormously in the continuing elaboration of public policy and its impact on the real lives of human beings.

And how does race matter? Fear has always been an integral component of racism. The ideological reproduction of a fear of black people, whether economically or sexually grounded, is rapidly gravitating toward and being grounded in a fear of crime. A question to be raised in this context is whether and how the increasing fear of crime—this ideologically produced fear of crime—serves to render racism simultaneously more invisible and more virulent. Perhaps one way to approach an answer to this question is to consider how this fear of crime effectively summons black people to imagine black people as the enemy. How many black people present at this conference have successfully extricated ourselves from the ideological power of the figure of the young black male as criminal—or at least seriously confronted it? The lack of a significant black presence in the rather feeble opposition to the "three strikes, you're out" bills, which have been proposed and/or passed in forty states already, evidences the disarming effect of this ideology.

California is one of the states that has passed the "three strikes, you're out" bill. Immediately after the passage of that bill, Governor Pete Wilson began to argue for a "two strikes, you're out" bill. Three, he said, is too many. Soon we will hear calls for "one strike, you're out." Following this mathematical regression, we can imagine that at some point the hardcore anticrime advocates will be arguing that to stop the crime wave, we can't wait until even one crime is committed. Their slogan will be: "Get them before the first strike!" And because certain populations have already been criminalized, there will be those who say, "We know who the real criminals are—let's get them before they have a chance to act out their criminality."

The fear of crime has attained a status that bears a sinister similarity to the fear of communism as it came to restructure social perceptions during the fifties and sixties. The figure of the "criminal"—the racialized figure of the criminal—has come to represent the most menacing enemy of "American society." Virtually anything is acceptable—torture, brutality, vast expenditures of public funds—as long as it is done in the name of public safety. Racism has always found an easy route from its embeddedness in social structures to the psyches of collectives and individuals precisely because it mobilizes deep fears. While explicit, old-style racism may be increasingly socially unacceptable—precisely as a result of antiracist movements over the last forty years—this does not mean that U.S. society has been purged of racism. In fact, racism is more deeply embedded in socioeconomic structures, and the vast populations of incarcerated people of color is dramatic evidence of the way racism systematically structures economic relations. At the same time, this structural racism is rarely recognized as "racism." What we have come to recognize as open, explicit racism has in many ways begun to be replaced by a secluded, camouflaged kind of racism, whose influence on people's daily lives is as pervasive and systematic as the explicit forms of racism associated with the era of the struggle for civil rights.

The ideological space for the proliferations of this racialized fear of crime has been opened by the transformations in international politics created by the fall of the European socialist countries. Communism is no longer the quintessential enemy against which the nation imagines its identity. This space is now inhabited by ideological constructions of crime, drugs, immigration, and welfare. Of course, the enemy within is far more dangerous than the enemy without, and a black enemy within is the most dangerous of all.

Because of the tendency to view it as an abstract site into which all manner of undesirables are deposited, the prison is the perfect site for the simultaneous production and concealment of racism. The abstract character of the public perception of prisons militates against an engagement with the real issues afflicting the communities from which prisoners are drawn in such disproportionate numbers. This is the ideological work that the prison performs—it relieves us of the responsibility of seriously engaging with the problems of late capitalism, of transnational capitalism. The naturalization of black people as criminals thus also erects ideological barriers to an understanding of the connections between late-twentieth-century structural racism and the globalization of capital.

The vast expansion of the power of capitalist corporations over the lives of people of color and poor people in general has been accompanied by a waning anticapitalist consciousness. As capital moves with ease across national borders, legitimized by recent trade agreements such as NATTA and GATT, corporations are allowed to close shop in the United States and transfer manufacturing operations to nations providing cheap labor pools. In fleeing organized labor in the U.S. to avoid paying higher wages and benefits, they leave entire communities in shambles, consigning huge numbers of people to joblessness, leaving them prey to the drug trade, destroying the economic base of these communities, thus affecting the education system, social welfare—and turning the people who live in those communities into perfect candidates for prison. At the same time, they create an economic demand for prisons, which stimulates the economy, providing jobs in the correctional industry for people who often come from the very populations that are criminalized by this process. It is a horrifying and self-reproducing cycle.

Ironically, prisons themselves are becoming a source of cheap labor that attracts corporate capitalism—as yet on a relatively small scale—in a way that parallels the attraction unorganized labor in Third World countries exerts. A statement by Michael Lamar Powell, a prisoner in Capshaw, Alabama, dramatically reveals this new development:

> I cannot go on strike, nor can I unionize. I am not covered by workers' compensation or the Fair Standards Act. I agree to work late-night and weekend shifts. I do just what I am told, no matter what it is. I am hired and fired at will, and I am not even paid minimum wage: I earn one dollar a month. I cannot even voice grievances or complaints, except at the risk of incurring arbitrary discipline or some covert retaliation.
>
> You need not worry about NAFTA and your jobs going to Mexico and other Third World countries. I will have at least five percent of your jobs by the end of this decade.
>
> I am called prison labor. I am The New American Worker.[10]

This "new American worker" will be drawn from the ranks of a racialized population whose historical super exploitation—from the era of slavery to the present—has been legitimized by racism. At the same time, the expansion of convict labor is accompanied in some states by the old paraphernalia of ankle chains that symbolically links convict labor with slave labor. At least three states—Alabama, Florida, and Arizona—have re-instituted the chain gang. Moreover, as Michael Powell so inclusively reveals, there is a new dimension to the racism inherent in this process, which structurally links the super exploitation of prison labor to the globalization of capital.

In California, whose prison system is the largest in the country and one of the largest in the world, the passage of an inmate initiative in 1990 has presented businesses seeking cheap labor with opportunities uncannily similar to those in Third World countries. As of June 1994, a range of companies were employing prison labor in nine California prisons. Under the auspices of the Joint Venture Program, work now being performed on prison grounds includes computerized telephone messaging, dental apparatus assembly, computer data entry, plastic parts fabrication, electronic component manufacturing at the Central California Women's facility at Chowchilla, security glass manufacturing, swine production, oak furniture manufacturing, and the production of stainless steel tanks and equipment. In a California Corrections Department brochure designed to promote the program, it is described as "an innovative public-private partnership that makes good business sense."[11] According to the owner of Tower Communications, whom the brochure quotes,

> The operation is cost effective, dependable and trouble free. . . . Tower Communications has successfully operated a message center utilizing inmates on the grounds of California state prison. If you're a business leader planning expansion, considering relocation because of a deficient labor pool, starting a new enterprise, look into the benefits of using inmate labor.

The employer benefits listed by the brochure include

federal and state tax incentives; no benefit package (retirement pay, vacation pay, sick leave, medical benefits); long term lease agreements at far below market value costs; discount rates on Workers Compensation; build a consistent, qualified work force; on call labor pool (no car breakdowns, no babysitting problems); option of hiring job-ready ex-offenders and minimizing costs; becoming a partner in public safety.

There is a major, yet invisible, racial supposition in such claims about the profitability of a convict labor force. The acceptability of the super exploitation of convict labor is largely based on the historical conjuncture of racism and incarceration practices. The already disproportionately black convict labor force will become increasingly black if the racially imbalanced incarceration practices continue.

The complicated yet unacknowledged structural presence of racism in the U.S. punishment industry also includes the fact that the punishment industry which sequesters ever-larger sectors of the black population attracts vast amounts of capital. Ideologically, as I have argued, the racialized fear of crime has begun to succeed the fear of communism. This corresponds to a structural tendency for capital that previously flowed toward the military industry to now move toward the punishment industry. The ease with which suggestions are made for prison construction costing in the multibillions of dollars is reminiscent of the military buildup: economic mobilization to defeat communism has turned into economic mobilization to defeat crime. The ideological construction of crime is thus complemented and bolstered by the material construction of jails and prisons. The more jails and prisons are constructed, the greater the fear of crime, and the greater the fear of crime, the stronger the cry for more jails and prisons, ad infinitum.

The law enforcement industry bears remarkable parallels to the military industry (just as there are anti-Communist resonances in the anti-crime campaign). This connection between the military industry and the punishment industry is revealed in a *Wall*

Street Journal article entitled "Making Crime Pay: The Cold War of the '90s":

> Parts of the defense establishment are cashing in, too, scenting a logical new line of business to help them offset military cutbacks. Westinghouse, Electric Corp., Minnesota Mining and Manufacturing Co., GDE Systems (a division of the old General Dynamics) and Alliant Techsystems Inc., for instance, are pushing crime-fighting equipment and have created special divisions to retool then defense technology for America's streets.

According to the article, a conference sponsored by the National Institute of Justice, the research arm of the Justice Department, was organized around the theme "Law Enforcement Technology in the 21st Century." The secretary of defense was a major presenter at this conference, which explored topics like "the role of the defense industry, particularly for dual use and conversion":

> Hot topics: defense-industry technology that could lower the level of violence involved in crime fighting. Sandia National Laboratories, for instance, is experimenting with a dense foam that can be sprayed at suspects, temporarily blinding and deafening them under breathable bubbles. Stinger Corporation is working on "smart guns," which will fire only for the owner, and retractable spiked barrier strips to unfurl in front of fleeing vehicles. Westinghouse is promoting the "smart car," in which mini-computers could be linked up with big mainframes at the police department, allowing for speedy booking of prisoners, as well as quick exchanges of information.[12]

Again, race provides a silent justification for the technological expansion of law enforcement, which, in turn, intensifies racist arrest and incarceration practices. This skyrocketing punishment industry, whose growth is silently but powerfully sustained by the persistence of racism, creates an economic demand for more jails and prisons and thus for similarly spiraling criminalization practices, which, in turn fuels the fear of crime.

Most debates addressing the crisis resulting from overcrowding in prisons and jails focus on male institutions. Meanwhile, women's institutions and jail space for women are proportionately proliferating at an even more astounding rate than men's. If race is largely an absent factor in the discussions about crime and punishment, gender seems not even to merit a place carved out by its absence. Historically, the imprisonment of women has served to criminalize women in a way that is more complicated than is the case with men. This female criminalization process has had more to do with the marking of certain groups of women as undomesticated and hypersexual, as women who refuse to embrace the nuclear family as paradigm. The current liberal-conservative discourse around welfare criminalizes black single mothers, who are represented as deficient, manless, drug-using breeders of children, and as reproducers of an attendant culture of poverty. The woman who does drugs is criminalized both because she is a drug user and because as a consequence, she cannot be a good mother. In some states, pregnant women are being imprisoned for using crack because of possible damage to the fetus.

According to the U.S. Department of Justice, women are far more likely than men to be imprisoned for a drug conviction.[13] However, if women wish to receive treatment for their drug problems, often their only option, if they cannot pay for a drug program, is to be arrested and sentenced to a drug program via the criminal justice system. Yet when U.S. Surgeon General Jocelyn Elders alluded to the importance of opening discussion on the decriminalization of drugs, the Clinton administration immediately disassociated itself from her remarks. Decriminalization of drugs would greatly reduce the numbers of incarcerated women, for the 278 percent increase in the numbers of black women in state and federal prisons (as compared to the 186 percent increase in the numbers of black men) can be largely attributed to the phenomenal rise in drug-related and specifically crack-related imprisonment. According to the Sentencing Project's 1995 report, the increase amounted to 828 percent.[14]

Official refusals to even consider decriminalization of drugs as a possible strategy that might begin to reverse present incarceration practices further bolsters the ideological staying power of the prison. In his well-known study of the history of the prison and its related technologies of discipline, Michel Foucault pointed out that an evolving contradiction is at the very heart of the historical project of imprisonment.

> For a century and a half, the prison has always been offered as its own remedy: . . . the realization of the corrective project as the only method of overcoming the impossibility of implementing it.[15]

As I have attempted to argue, within the U.S. historical context, racism plays a pivotal role in sustaining this contradiction. In fact, Foucault's theory regarding the prison's tendency to serve as its own enduring justification becomes even more compelling if the role of race is also acknowledged. Moreover; moving beyond the parameters of what I consider the double impasse implied by his theory—the discursive impasse his theory discovers and that of the theory itself—I want to conclude by suggesting the possibility of radical race-conscious strategies designed to disrupt the stranglehold of criminalization and incarceration practices.

In the course of a recent collaborative research project with U.C. Santa Barbara sociologist Kum-Kum Bhavnani, in which we interviewed thirty-five women at the San Francisco County Jail, the complex ways in which race and gender help to produce a punishment industry that reproduces the very problems it purports to solve become dramatically apparent. Our interviews focused on the women's ideas about imprisonment and how they themselves imagine alternatives to incarceration. Their various critiques of the prison system and of the existing "alternatives," all of which are tied to reimprisonment as a last resort, led us to reflect more deeply about the importance of retrieving, retheorizing, and reactivating the radical abolitionist strategy first proposed in connection with the prison-reform movements of the sixties and seventies.

We are presently attempting to theorize women's imprisonment in ways that allow us to formulate a radical abolitionist strategy departing from, but not restricted in its conclusions to, women's jails and prisons. Our goal is to formulate alternatives to incarceration that substantively reflect the voices and agency of a variety of imprisoned women. We wish to open up channels for their involvement in the current debates around alternatives to incarceration, while not denying our own role as mediators and interpreters and our own political positioning in these debates. We also want to distinguish our explorations of alternatives from the spate of "alternative punishments" or what are now called "intermediate sanctions" presently being proposed and/or implemented by and through state and local correctional systems.

This is a long-range project that has three dimensions: academic research, public policy, and community organizing. In other words, for this project to be successful, it must build bridges between academic work, legislative and other policy interventions, and grassroots campaigns calling, for example, for the decriminalization of drugs and prostitution—and for the reversal of the present proliferation of jails and prisons.

Raising the possibility of abolishing jails and prisons as the institutionalized and normalized means of addressing social problems in an era of migrating corporations, unemployment and homelessness, and collapsing public services, from health care to education, can hopefully help to interrupt the current law-and-order discourse that has such a grip on the collective imagination, facilitated as it is by deep and hidden influences of racism. This late-twentieth-century "abolitionism," with its nineteenth-century resonances, may also lead to a historical recontextualization of the practice of imprisonment. With the passage of the Thirteenth Amendment, slavery was abolished for all except convicts—and in a sense the exclusion from citizenship accomplished by the slave system has persisted within the U.S. prison system. Only three states allow prisoners to vote, and approximately 4 million people are denied the right to vote because of their present or past incarceration. A radical strategy to abolish jails and prisons as the normal way of dealing with the social problems of late capitalism is not a strategy for abstract abolition. It is designed to force a rethinking of the increasingly repressive role of the state during this era of late capitalism and to carve out a space for resistance.

Notes

1. See, for instance, the *Austin-American Statesman,* October 17, 1995.
2. Charles S. Clark, "Prison Overcrowding," *Congressional Quarterly Researcher* 4, no 5 (Feb 4, 1994): 97–119.
3. Ibid.
4. Marc Mauer; "Young Black Men and the Criminal Justice System: A Growing National Problem," Washington, DC: The Sentencing Project, February 1990.
5. Alexander Cockburn, *Philadelphia Inquirer,* August 29, 1994.
6. Marc Mauer and Tracy Huling, "Young Black Americans and the Criminal Justice System: Five Years Later." Washington, DC: The Sentencing Project, October 1995.
7. Ibid., 18
8. See Cockburn.
9. See Lubiano's essay . . . as well as "Black Ladies, Welfare Queens, and State Minstrels: Ideological War by Narrative Means," in *Race-ing Justice, En-gendering Power: Essays on Anita Hill, Clarence Thomas, and the Construction of Social Reality,* ed. Toni Morrison (New York: Pantheon, 1992), 323–63.
10. Unpublished essay, "Modern Slavery American Style," 1995.
11. I wish to acknowledge Julie Brown, who acquired this brochure from the California Department of Correction in the course of researching the role of convict labor.
12. *Wall Street Journal,* May 12, 1994.
13. Lawrence Rence, A. Greenfield, Stephanie Minor-Harper, *Women in Prison* (Washington, DC: U.S. Dept. of Justice, Office of Justice Programs, Bureau of Statistics, 1991).
14. Mauer and Huling, "Young Black Americans," 19.
15. Michel Foucault, *Discipline and Punish: The Birth of the Prison,* trans. Alan Sheridan (New York: Vintage, 1979), 395.

Discussion Questions

1. What social factors might account for the high proportion of young Black and Latino men in jails, prisons, and on parole? Why are the rates of incarceration of women, especially women who are members of minority groups, increasing?

2. What are the costs and benefits of the criminalization of drugs by federal and state laws and of "three strikes you're out" laws passed by some state legislatures?

3. Does Davis connect all of the pieces of her argument fully? What questions would you like to ask her? What further information about the relationships she suggests would you like to have?

4. What does Davis mean when she says that the "punishment industry" produces *and* conceals racism? How can it do both?

30

A Higher Power of Their Understanding

Cheyenne Women and Their Religious Roles

Martha Garcia

In *"A Higher Power of Their Understanding: Cheyenne Women and Their Religious Roles,"* Martha Garcia challenges the limited and clearly inaccurate depictions of Cheyenne women made by White male anthropologists, focusing on religious practices within the Cheyenne tribe. Here religion becomes the foreground for discussions of race, class, and gender. Martha Garcia begins the article by admitting her own honest limitations—she is a European American woman and therefore an outsider looking in on a culture which she has found fascinating for most of her life, yet as an outsider nonetheless. She then attempts to trace a more faithful rendering of the lives of Cheyenne women than those depicted in the writings of White anthropologists, missionaries, and others who came before her. Garcia suggests that these White male observers were not only limited in their access to Cheyenne women but also that the lens of European domination and European gender roles colored their perceptions so much so that they described Cheyenne women as performing only passive and subservient roles.

Garcia's own rendering involves a more nuanced description of Cheyenne women as leaders and honored members of the tribe, as skilled hunters in their own right, as complex individuals who did not just perform berry picking but also gambled, made jokes, and shared gossip during the process. More than any of these indications of Cheyenne women's status,

however, Garcia wishes to focus on two religious practices within the Cheyenne tribe as clear demonstrations of the place of honor that Cheyenne women held: the ritual of menses and the ceremony of the Massaum. With regard to the ritual of menses, simply put, while White male anthropologists viewed the seclusion of women during the ritual of menses as indicative of women's lowered status as *"polluted and unclean,"* Garcia insists that on the contrary, the women's seclusion was about experiencing *"the most sacred and powerful time"* for women. In fact, it was a time when women obtained sacred knowledge. With regard to the ceremony of the Massaum, which commemorated the *"giving of the earth in the four directions to the Cheynennes for their use,"* Garcia takes pains to describe the major role of women in the ceremony, which was of paramount significance in Cheyenne history. In seeking to represent the true nature of these religious practices, and in stark contrast to those offered by White male anthropologists, Martha Garcia attempts a more faithful depiction of spirituality in the lives of Cheyenne women and, as a result, makes visible lines of race, class, and gender.

This chapter deals with the religious and cultural participation of Cheyenne women. My research suggests that traditional Cheyenne culture reflected equality between the genders even to the extent of allowing a woman to perform a man's traditional activities, and vice versa.

First, a disclaimer or two is necessary. This chapter does not reveal any unpublished sacred information; instead it reexamines a few previously published works from a women's perspective. Next, I am a full-blood Euro-American anthropologist. My knowledge, experience, and education began in Boston. In elementary school I developed an interest in American Indians because these people lived in the West, dressed differently (as seen in pictures), and spoke differently from the people in my world at the time. My interest resurfaced when I lived in Colorado. Ultimately I earned an M.A. in anthropology, history, and women's studies. At the present time I sell books on and by American Indians. I take the books to various American Indian functions, and in fact have become a conduit for information to them. I often feel like a trader of the 1800s, but I am a purveyor of information.

I have acquired some of my knowledge through my academic work; however, through direct interaction with American Indians I have developed a fundamental understanding of their beliefs, values, and other aspects of their culture. I am taught continuously by American Indians. Their methods of teaching are as individual as the person. Some people sit with me and explain; others have looked positively angry while giving me a humbling compliment; women, especially, lecture me. Some of the People I am acquainted with remind me, "You know, Indians do. . ." or "Indians don't do. . . ." I have seen a great deal, been taught a great deal, and still have a great deal to learn. If I want to know something, I ask. On a personal level this vocation requires, among other things, a thick skin to fend off some comments, humility, honesty, and openness. With these qualities one can develop a respect for the People, their beliefs and lifeways and can try to maintain friendly relationships.

I want the reader of this chapter to understand clearly that Indian women have always been extremely important within their cultures. In *Indian Women Chiefs* (1954), Carolyn Foreman wrote that many females were the "heads of state" in the seventeenth and eighteenth centuries. Alderman's book *Nancy Ward, Cherokee Chieftainess* (1978) describes the Cherokees of the 1700s and Ward's function as the Beloved Woman and ultimate decision maker for war or peace. The creation myth and stories about North West Coast women told by Anne Cameron reflect their importance in spiritual life (1981). For additional information on the status and activities of Indian women see Albers and Medicine (1983) and Niethammer (1977).

As Euro-Americans moved onto the Plains, anthropologists, travelers, and missionaries, virtually all of whom were men, began to record details of Indian life. Their reports were limited to those aspects of life accessible to them as outsiders and as men, and they imposed their Western conceptions of women's and men's roles on what they observed. American Indian women were seen mainly as they acted within the male realm, carrying out such tasks as loading horses for moving camp. These reporters of culture also noted that women performed what they described as unexciting work, such as group berry picking. What was not noted, because it was not visible, was the gossiping, joking and gambling that usually accompanied the work. (In contrast, see the reports of the field work of Elsie Clews Parsons, an early woman anthropologist, in Babcock 1991.)

Anthropologists and other observers did not realize that Cheyenne women were raised, then and now, to be modest, not to speak to strangers or call attention to themselves. Rosemary and Joseph Agonito (1982) point out that owing to the male-sightedness of the reporters, there is very little information on Cheyenne women's use of weapons, their strategies defending themselves and their communities, their skills with horses or their hunting skills. Further, there is little information on formal women's groups or societies among the Cheyennes. Grinnell's *The Cheyenne [Indians]* (1972), for example, includes very little on the women's quillwork society, which had various levels of skill. Not everyone could decorate usable items. The point is that much information on women was neglected in the older anthropological reports for two reasons: the women were not forthcoming, and the mind set of the white male observers at that time did not motivate them to seek out the women. Therefore the literature must be continuously questioned and reevaluated.

Another neglected subject is Cheyenne women's participation in religion and religious practices. We read about men going on vision quests, but did women? Did women leave family and home to go on this journey? This chapter focuses on women's involvement in two areas of traditional Cheyenne spiritual or religious practice: the ritual surrounding menses and the ceremony of the Massaum.

The ritual surrounding menses. From talking, listening, sharing and learning from Cheyenne women, I have concluded that women had dreams, visions, and insights that demonstrated songs, designs, and ways of creating items. These women put them to use and therefore owned them. They did not have to go to the mountaintop to obtain them. They could give away these intangibles, sell them, or keep them. This also happens today.

Traditionally, Cheyenne women left their families and homes for about four days each month. At the onset of their menses, the women would go to a separate place. As some women said, each month they would get a four-day vacation. This "vacation" is modified today by individual choice but still influenced by tradition and cultural custom. In the old days during this time, women would obtain lessons and knowledge that will never be known by outsiders. If any information is available, it is rarely ever discussed. This was the most sacred and powerful time for Cheyenne women. There were many taboos to which they had to adhere because they were so powerful; in fact, they could negate anybody else's power. This was a natural, sacred power, not one sought after or pleaded for as men had to plead for their power. With this power women could, and often did, become medicine practitioners. With this power women could create children, who are the backbone of any ongoing culture. Then, as now, children assured the Cheyennes they would remain forever.

When white male anthropologists learned of the period of seclusion during menstruation, they associated it with *their* belief, which was that at this time women were polluted and unclean. Not so with the Cheyennes. Menstruating Cheyenne women were considered too powerful to attend the rituals or ceremonies that make up a part of the Cheyenne religious system.... At other times women were a major part of Cheyenne ceremonial life.

The Massaum ceremony. Cheyenne religious structure is very sophisticated; it is neither male oriented nor female oriented. There are several areas of the cosmic universe, and they all have spirits. There is the world below (the deep earth), the middle zone (on which we live), and the world above.

The deepest earth zone contains caverns where animal spirits of all species gather on death. From this place the animal spirits may be released to become physical. The next

zone up contains the sacred caves where powerful spirits instruct humans. The best-known Cheyenne sacred cave is inside Bear Butte in the northeastern section of the Black Hills. Where the tree and grass roots stop is the end of the deep earth and the lowest portion of the middle zone. "Our Grandmother" is the female spirit of the deep earth.

There are four parts to the middle zone. Beginning with the lowest region of this zone is the area of roots, where badgers and rodents live, bears hibernate, and dens are made by coyotes and wolves. The second area up is the area of short grasses and low growing plants, where small animals reside. The third area up is where humans reside; it features large animals, bushes, and tall grasses. The fourth area, of trees and forests, is a transition into the world above.

The world above includes several regions. The first level up is the near-sky space that contains the mountains and clouds. Other things that move in this area are tornadoes, thunderstorms, and high-flying birds. The gift of breath, wind, and air that make physical life possible begins above the clouds and mountains and ends below the roots in the earth. The second level is where the sun, moon, and stars reside. The most sacred area of all is the blue-sky space. Blue represents Maheo, the Supreme Being who created the world and gave it order. From Maheo comes the Cosmic Power that maintains the world. The physical and spiritual life in the universe derives from Maheo. The work of the spirits is in accordance with his plan. Generally, Cheyenne ceremonies celebrate Maheo and this order of the universe.

According to Schlesier in *The Wolves of Heaven* (1987), the Massaum ceremony explained the giving of the earth in the four directions to the Cheyennes for their use. It commemorated the relationship of the Cheyennes to the spirit world of the grasslands, the sacred relationship with animals, and taught the proper approach to hunting plains herd animals by calling them into camps and pounds. In the beginning the ceremony required a group that was able to perform it annually and would accept the land as caretakers and protectors. The consequence of these requirements was to pull together the small Algonquian groups that had migrated west into a single group calling itself *Tsistsistas* (Cheyenne). They located in the Black Hills as a permanent home, with Bear Butte as the center of their religious beliefs. The Cheyennes were not restricted to that area; through the Massaum earth-giving ceremony, they could hunt in the four directions. When the Massaum was performed in a new area, that area accepted Cheyenne guardianship.

The Massaum ceremony has its basis in sacred stories of the Cheyenne. The keepers of the animal spirits are Wolf Man and Old Woman. They were parents of Yellow-haired Woman, a buffalo spirit turned human to help the Cheyenne. She had the power to bring game. Yellow-haired Woman married a Cheyenne, and through this marriage the kin relationship between the spirits and the Cheyenne became established, as well as a kin relationship with the animals under the guardianship of the spirits and Yellow-haired Woman. The Massaum was a renewal of the agreement the Cheyenne made with the spirits.

The annual Massaum ceremony was performed in midsummer and required attendance by all Cheyenne bands. The whole campground represented the grasslands. The wolf lodge represented Bear Butte, the center of the Cheyenne universe, and was placed in the center of the camp. The wolf lodge symbolized the wolves, which are the master hunters of the grasslands, protect other species, are guardians of Bear Butte, and are considered messengers of the spirits. The Cheyennes learned to hunt in the grasslands by watching the wolves hunt. The Cheyennes would leave meat aside for the wolves after dressing the kill. They are represented through the red wolf, male, and the white wolf, female, in the Massaum ceremony.

The Cheyenne lodges circled the wolf lodge in a horseshoe. A second, inside horseshoe of lodges represented the animal spirits impersonated by Cheyenne participants. In this circle each lodge represented a particular species, or collection of species. Each lodge was directed by a shaman whose guardian spirit was of that species. The people dressed as

their species during the ceremony and waited the call of Old Woman for their appearance. The circles opened toward Bear Butte for an uninterrupted line to the spirits. The camp became a spirit camp in which all spirits were present.

The Massaum law required the calling of game into pounds or camps. Women of the Young Wolf Society made a compound with an entrance of brush wings (similar to a corral) that herded the game into the compound. The seven society members raised the sacred tree, then made and raised the wolf lodge. The Young Wolf Society seems to be one of the oldest societies of the Cheyennes, and during the ceremony acted as assistants to Yellow-haired Woman.

A woman usually pledged herself to sponsor the Massaum ceremony and acted as Yellow-haired Woman, the focal point of the ceremony. She did not have to be a member of the Young Wolf Society, but could be. If she was married, her husband pledged with her. If she was single, a man pledged himself as co-sponsor. At the end of the ceremony she qualified to instruct future women pledgers of the Massaum. As a pledger, the woman secured instructors who acted as Wolf Man and Old Woman, and both had to be previous pledgers. As a group, they chose the ceremonial shaman, then they all decided on the location of the ceremony, and messages went out to the bands.

The responsibility of Yellow-haired Woman included receiving instructions, songs, prayers, and the sacred pipe. She reenacted the position of master spirit of animals in the grasslands. A symbolic and sacred hunt occurred four times, and each time the woman offered the pipe to the animal spirits.

This is a simplified description of a ceremony in which women took a major role. The ceremony was important in the cosmology, life way, and especially the history of the Cheyenne. From the perspective of feminist scholarship, this ceremony and the myth associated with it reflect the symbolic importance of women. The myth clearly states that a woman was responsible for bringing the buffalo and other animals to the Cheyenne diet and lifeway. Therefore it was important that a woman pledge the ceremony and that she take the major role in it. The ceremony's religiousness is seen by the participation of all the entities of the universe in the spirit camp. It was as though the whole world stopped during the occurrence of this ceremony.

The last time the ceremony was performed was in 1927 in Oklahoma among the Southern Cheyennes. The Cheyennes can no longer celebrate earth-giving because they no longer control their land; guardianship is under the federal government. Further, many of their sacred animals have been decimated.

Today

The Massaum ceremony was a way of passing on the symbolic history and the values of the Cheyenne. Old Woman and Yellow-haired Woman, a mythical mother and daughter, were central figures in the ceremony. Although the contemporary Northern Cheyennes have adopted the Roman Catholic faith, mothers and grandmothers continue to teach both girls and boys the Cheyenne spiritual philosophy, which is reflected in values, traditions, codes of conduct, and lifeways. Its precepts are taught through myths that have moral endings and through stories based on actual history so that the past is not forgotten.

One of the lifeways of the Cheyenne that children are taught over and over again is that they are to give understanding, not to look for it. When there is contention with a non-Cheyenne, they are expected to look to find similar values. Children are taught to find and know what is good for them, emphasize the good, and recognize what will hurt or destroy them.

Respect is a central value that guides behavior. Respect does not cover just the Cheyenne, but with respect old enemies can communicate together, and many things can be accomplished for the good of the whole. Respect does not have to be serious, it can also be funny. For example, if someone did something that backfired and made him or her feel like a fool, when that person started laughing about it, he or she would receive respect. Respect is encompassing and applies to everyone. It is defined as showing honor

or esteem for someone or something. It can be seen in listening to someone without interruption, accepting people as they are, not putting anyone down or hurting anyone's feelings, not intruding on others, and not touching what is not one's own. One should show respect for Mother Earth and show respect for the religion of others. Love, spirituality, and respect should be shown continuously. These precepts apply equally to women and men. If they are practiced, a person should be able to keep himself or herself in balance between the good and bad sides of self and in harmony with the rest of the family, community, and world. Harmony, for the Cheyenne, is the mouth saying what the heart believes.

If a person—man or woman—gets too far out of harmony, a sweat lodge was, and still is, an appropriate remedy. Sweat lodges can be used for medical treatments or religious ceremonies. According to Grinnell (1972), the construction of lodges required twelve to sixteen willow shoots of approximately six to eight feet in length. They were bent so that each went into the ground in a circular arrangement with an opening. This structure was covered by hides, which eventually gave way to canvas and blankets. From one to twelve people could fit into the very dark lodge. Outside the lodge a fire heated some stones, and the fire tender passed the stones inside using two forked sticks. Water was sprinkled on stones, creating a dense steam and intense heat. This caused the participant's body to sweat profusely and rid itself of impurities. Often herbs and other medicines were administered in the lodge. Usually the sweat was followed by a plunge in the river. If men sweated, women often tended the fire; if women sweated, men often tended the fire.

Marriott and Rachlin (1977) write about the life of Mary Little Bear Inkanish, a Southern Cheyenne woman who was half white and half Cheyenne. Her Cheyenne mother, Mah-hee-yuna (a woman who dedicated her mind, body, and life to benefit her people), took Mary into her first sweat bath at the age of six. She explained to Mary how to use wild sage to scrub and cleanse herself. She also told her that when she grew up, she would have to cleanse herself at least once a month.

When something important is to happen or there is a ceremony, a sweat bath is necessary "to be clean for whatever comes" (p. 8). During pregnancy, Mary's instructions were to take a sweat bath followed by the usual plunge in the river every four days. For everyone, bathing in the sweat lodge was a serious event designed to clean the body and the mind. If anyone spoke or chanted while inside, it was to pray.

In this chapter I have tried to use the example of Cheyenne women to counter the prevailing stereotype that American Indian women of the past were subjugated by the men of their communities and insignificant in their own right. Cheyenne women as a group occupied a special place within their culture. They earned respect through their behavior, deeds, cooperation, and sharing. Some individuals earned honored places through their actions in what whites would call the male realm, but they all spoke their minds when the council decided on something affecting everyone. Not all Cheyenne women, nor all Cheyenne men, made the pages of the history books, but those who were written about were representative of many. We know about one woman who killed four soldiers at Sand Creek (Marriott and Rachlin 1977: 60), but she is not an exception; other women participated in other battles. In various ways, Cheyenne women continued, and continue today, the fight for survival of their children and their culture.

In the past women were active and visible in Cheyenne life and ceremonies. I have described the period of seclusion that protected the community from the power of women during their menses and the important Massaum ceremony that was pledged by a woman and which featured the active participation of women throughout. This ceremony celebrated Yellow-haired Woman bringing the plains animals to the Cheyennes. It also allowed them to hunt in the area where it was held. Menstrual vacations are now a matter of choice, and the Massaum ceremony, though still remembered, is no longer performed. Other traditions, however, such as the use of the sweat lodge for physical and spiritual cleansing and the teaching of the Cheyenne worldview and lifeways by mothers and grandmothers continue into the present. What survives is not gender specific; the teachings and the expectations are the same for Cheyenne women and men.

Notes

1. A pledge was made in times of danger or difficulty. It was a vow or promise that if the higher power (Maheo) gave help in the situation, the person would perform a certain ceremony or make a sacrifice. This commitment had to be acted on within a reasonable time (about one year), or dire consequences would occur for the one who made the promise or a member of his other family (see Grinnell 1972).

References

Agonito, Rosemary, and Joseph Agonito 1982. "Resurrecting History's Forgotten Women: A Case Study from the Cheyenne Indians." *Frontiers* 6 (3).

Albers, Pat, and Bea Medicine, eds. 1983. *The Hidden Half*. Lanham, MD: University Press of America.

Alderman, Pat. 1978. *Nancy Ward, Cherokee Chieftainess*. Johnson City, TN: Overmountain Press.

Babcock, Barbara A., ed. 1991. *Pueblo Mothers and Children: Essays by Elsie Clews Parsons, 1915–1924*. Santa Fe, NM: Ancient City Press.

Bopp, Tudie, Michael Bopp, Lee Brown, and Phil Lane. 1985. *The Sacred Tree*. Alberta, Canada: Four Worlds Development Press.

Cameron, Anne. 1981. *Daughters of Copper Woman*. Vancouver, BC: Press Gang.

Foreman, Carolyn. 1966. *Indian Women Chiefs*. Muskogee, OK: Hoffman Printing.

Grinnell, Georg Bird. 1972. *The Cheyenne Indians: Their History and Ways of Life*, vol. 2. Lincoln: University of Nebraska Press.

Marriott, Alice, and Carol K. Rachlin. 1977. *Dance Around the Sun: The Life of May Little Bear Inkanish*. New York: Crowell.

Niethammer, Carolyn J., ed. 1977. *Daughters of the Earth: Lives and Legends of American Indian Women*. New York: Collier.

Schlesier, Karl H. 1987. *The Wolves of Heaven*. Norman: University of Oklahoma Press.

Discussion Questions

1. Do you think the research Martha Garcia pursued was important? Why or why not?

2. Do you think that anthropologists today are doing a more faithful rendering of the lives of racial/ethnic women? Can you bring any evidence to bear on your argument?

3. Have you heard or read about depictions of religious ceremonies among racial/ethnic groups that you felt were unfair or inaccurate? If so, describe these to the class.

4. Have you ever experienced any religious ceremonies that you have felt were falsely portrayed in research or media?

31
Religious Identity and Mobility

Pamela Paul

It would violate the establishment of religion clause of the First Amendment to the U.S. Constitution if the Census Bureau asked people about their religious membership or beliefs. Thus, this very important demographic variable is not included in the census. Pamela Paul summarizes results from several recent studies of religion in America. In one study, eight out of ten Americans identified themselves with a specific religion and a Gallup poll found that over half the people asked see religion as increasing in influence. According to the CCNY 2001 survey, more than three quarters (77 percent) see themselves as Christians. This percentage has decreased since a similar 1990 study, and there has been a measurable shift away from more liberal denominations, such as Presbyterian and United Church of Christ, and from Roman Catholicism toward more evangelical and conservative denominations. This trend includes Hispanic Americans, about half of whom have moved from Catholicism to one of the more conservative Protestant denominations in recent years. About 16 percent of Americans report having changed their religious identification.

The Barna Research Group asked people some questions about the nature of their beliefs. They found differences among Black, Hispanic, and White Christians. Blacks and Whites are more likely than Hispanics to consider themselves "born again" and to be "absolutely committed to Christian faith." Blacks are more likely than Whites to search for meaning in life and to feel a responsibility to share their religious beliefs. There are also gender and age differences with women being more likely (45 percent) than men (36 percent) to be born again and 35- to 56-year-olds being more likely than older or younger adults to be born again. Except in the

box detailing the characteristics of the Jewish population, no information about social class or related variables is provided in this article. In the past, the Protestant groups that are losing members have tended to have more affluent members, and those that are gaining members have been characterized by lower levels of income and education. It would be interesting to see if these generalizations continue to be valid.

It is more difficult to get demographic data about such minority religions as Islam and Judaism, both because the overall populations are small and because people may define membership differently. Many Jewish people, for example, identify with Judaism as their cultural heritage, but do not practice the religion. Some Muslim communities recognize only some forms of Islam as being genuine. As the number of immigrants from Africa and Asia increases (see the Grieco article in Section 5), the number of minority religions and of people who identify with them will also increase.

The vast majority of Americans identify with a particular religion, practice their faith to some degree and hold strong spiritual beliefs. Although the U.S. Census Bureau does not ask questions about religious affiliation (it's considered a violation of the Constitution), a number of private and academic polling sources do track religious identification. Their counts indicate significant movement across faiths, as people's religious identities shift and our definitions of religious affiliation, particularly among minority faiths, are in flux.

The U.S. remains a predominantly Christian country. According to the Baina Research Group, 40 percent of Americans say they are evangelical Christians, while 39 percent say they are born again. The Barna group also found that about half of Americans say they are "theologically conservative" and 21 percent say they are "charismatic or Pentecostal." A recent study by the Glenmary Research Center, Religious Congregations and Membership: 2000, found that the fastest-growing church denominations in America are conservative Christian churches, with the Mormon church, the Christian churches, the Churches of Christ and the Pentecostal Assemblies of God each growing 19 percent since 1990. Losing the most members were Presbyterian churches and the United Church of Christ, which declined by 12 percent and 15 percent, respectively, since 1990.

But the face of religion in America is changing, due to immigration, waning and waxing denominations and increasing diversity. People are identifying less strongly with a particular religion, and fewer identify themselves as Christian. According to the 2001 American Religious Identification Survey, conducted by the Graduate Center of the City University of New York in 1990, 90 percent of the population identified with a particular religion. By 2001, only 81 percent did so. In 1990, 86 percent of the country identified with a Christian religion; 77 percent did so by 2001.

Change in Allegiance

Several demographic groups have undergone significant shifts in recent years in terms of their religious identification and composition. For example the share of Hispanics who adhere to Roman Catholicism is rapidly declining. According to surveys by the Barna Research Group two-thirds of Hispanic adults considered themselves Catholic a decade ago. Today that figure has fallen to about half (49 percent) as some Hispanics have become part of other Christian denominations. When Hispanics convert to Protestant faiths they are more likely than non-Hispanics to be drawn to charismatic evangelical and Pentecostal churches than to Baptist churches or any of the mainstream Protestant faiths (e. g., Episcopal, Methodist, Lutheran, Presbyterian) which together draw a mere 1 percent of the Hispanic population.

Age differences also emerge. According to Barna, Americans 38 to 56 are most likely to consider themselves born again. Nearly half (49 percent) of 38- to 56-year-olds say they are born again, compared with one-third of people 19 to 37 and about one-third (36 percent) of those born before 1926. Women are more likely to be born again than men: 45 percent say they've "accepted Christ as their savior" compared with 36 percent of men.

The Color of Christianity

Blacks are much more likely to be born again than Hispanics, and Hispanics are less likely to consider themselves "committed Christians," even though Hispanics are commonly perceived as one of the more religious ethnic groups.

Religious Characteristic	Hispanics	Blacks	Non-Hispanic Whites
Considers self "born again"	27%	45%	42%
Considers self "absolutely committed" to Christian faith	30%	51%	51%
Considers moral truth to be absolute	15%	10%	26%

Source: Barna Research Group, 2001

Black and White

More than twice as many blacks as whites are actively searching for meaning and purpose in life.

Religious Characteristic	Blacks	Whites
Am "searching for meaning and purpose in life"	58%	28%
Feel has a responsibility to tell others about their religious beliefs	46%	33%

Source: Barna Research Group, 2001

Changing My Religion

In 2001, more than 33 million adults (approximately 16 percent of the total adult population) reported that they had changed their religious identification or preference at some point in their lives, according to the 2001 American Religious Identification Survey, conducted by the Graduate Center of the City University of New York (CUNY).

Jews and Muslims

The size and relative growth of the Jewish population is unresolved based on several recent studies, because there is much debate over how a Jew is defined—whether by parentage, upbringing, practice, culture or self-identity. One of the most recent and largest studies, the National Jewish Population Survey 2000–2001, commissioned by the United Jewish Communities and released in October 2002, counts the Jewish population at 5.2

Leaving My Religion

Less than 1 percent of Americans are Jehovah's Witnesses, and almost one-third of those born into that religion switch to another faith at some point in their lives.

Religion	Percent of Americans Who Self-Identify	Percent Born into the Denomination Who Switched
Jehovah's Witness	0.6%	32%
Seventh Day Adventist	0.3%	27%
Methodist	6.8%	25%
Presbyterian	2.7%	25%
Episcopalian/Anglican	1.7%	23%
Buddhist	0.5%	23%
Church of God	0.5%	22%
Protestant	2.2%	20%
Lutheran	4.6%	19%
Pentecostal	2.1%	19%
Congregational/UCC	0.7%	18%

Finding My Religion

While Jehovah's Witnesses account for less than 1 percent of Americans, almost 2 in 5 of their membership joined the faith after being born into another religion.

Religion	Percent of Americans Who Self-Identify	Percent Not Born Into the Religion But Switched to it
Jehovah's Witness	0.6%	39%
Evangelical/born-again	0.5%	37%
Seventh Day Adventist	0.3%	34%
Buddhist	0.5%	33%
Pentecostal	2.1%	30%
Nondenominational	1.2%	29%
Episcopalian/Anglican	1.7%	26%
Church of God	0.5%	26%
Presbyterian	2.7%	24%
No religion	14.1%	23%

Source: CUNY 2001 American Religious Identification Survey

million, a lower figure than several other surveys' findings of roughly 6 million. The study also shows the Jewish population in America to be aging and shrinking (by 5 percent in the past decade). However, other studies show slight growth, such as a survey by the Glenmary Research Center also released in October, which put the number of self-described "ethnic" Jews at 6.1 million, an increase of 2.7 percent over the 1990 figure. Falling in between is the 2001 American Jewish Identity Survey, conducted by the Graduate Center of the City University of New York, which counts the number of Jews at 5.5 million—nearly 4 percent of American households, including those that have at least one member who is Jewish by religion, parentage, upbringing or self-identification. This figure has increased from 3.2 million in 1990.

Though a growing number of Americans are Muslim and several American Muslim groups have claimed as many as 7 million adherents, most polls show far smaller counts. According to a profile of the American Muslim population based on data from the CUNY American Religious Identification Survey, there were 1.1 million American Muslims in 2001, or 0.5 percent of the population, up from 0.3 percent in 1990. However, the researchers acknowledged that the current Muslim population may be as high as 2.8 million.

Varying By Degrees

Religious Jews tend to be older, wealthier and more likely to be a Democrat than nonreligious Jews.

Characteristic	Jews by Religion	Jews of No Religion	Jews of Other Religions
Number of Adults	2,930,000	1,120,000	1,470,000
Percent male	49%	52%	45%
Median age	51	44	42
Percent married	59%	45%	59%
Percent of married with Jewish spouse	77%	16%	n/a
Percent college graduate	58%	57%	36%
Percent full-time employed	49%	56%	63%
Percent registered voters	85%	76%	85%
Percent Democrat	55%	41%	28%
Percent who own a home	77%	67%	69%
Median annual household income	$72,000	$58,000	$54,000
Percent in Northeast	43%	26%	20%
Percent in South	26%	31%	36%
Percent in Midwest	10%	9%	13%
Percent in West	21%	34%	31%

Source: CUNY 2001 American Jewish Identity Survey

The Bottom Line

- The vast majority of Americans still identify with an organized religion or religious institution, and a majority (53 percent) see religion as gaining influence in America, according to a March 2002 Gallup poll.

- Although fewer Americans are Christian, and mainstream Protestant faiths are declining, conservative, evangelical and charismatic Christian denominations are on the rise.
- Adherence to minority faiths remains a highly contentious issue, with definitions of Islam and Judaism—and what characterizes their followers—subject to debate. The result is widely varying methods for counting Jews and Muslims and a broad range of population estimates for members of both religions.

Discussion Questions

1. Why is it important to study the demographics of religious groups? Who might use the information in this article and for what purposes?

2. Where would you locate yourself in this article? Do you identify with a particular religion? Were you raised in that religion or did you choose it yourself? How would you answer the questions in the box labeled "The Color of Christianity"? (If you are not a Christian, substitute your own religion in the second item.)

3. Why do you think there has been an overall decrease in people identifying with any religious group and, at the same time, an increase in people identifying with certain types of religious communities?

4. Do you think there has been an increase in the influence of religion in our society in recent years? Is that a good thing or a bad thing, or is it on balance neutral?

32
What's in a Name?

Kendra Hamilton

In almost every decade since the civil rights movement, there has been a flurry of public debate about affirmative action. Many Whites have called it "reverse discrimination" or simply racist. Many people of color claim that they still face discrimination in most areas of life and so argue that affirmative action is still needed. Kendra Hamilton's article "What's in a Name?" adds new data to the discussion. In this article, we find that two eminent researchers, Drs. Bertrand and Mullainathan, published a study in which they argue that people of color still have reason to fear discrimination, specifically in the workplace. Their findings center on the issue of names. Using birth records from Chicago and Boston, they chose "White-sounding" and "Black-sounding" names. For example, "White-sounding names" might be Brad, Matthew, Kristen, or Carrie; while "Black-sounding" names might be Rasheed, Jamal, Aisha, or Tanisha. They then placed these names on nearly 5,000 resumes of varying qualities, which they sent out in response to advertisements for 1,300 jobs that were placed in Chicago and Boston papers. Their findings are remarkable in their pointed measurement of continued discrimination.

In a glimpse of race and class issues, the study found that when applicants' resumes demonstrated a higher income through an indication that the applicant lived in a "better" neighborhood, this benefited those with "White-sounding" names, but not their peers with "Black-sounding names"—"a good address doesn't help African Americans overcome discrimination either." In another example, one that adds gender into the mix, the lowest scoring "Black-sounding" female names were demonstrably lower in the researchers' model than "White-sounding" female names, much more of a gap than that between "White-sounding" and "Black-sounding" male names. Needless to say, the names with the lowest scores of all were "Black-sounding" female names.

Returning to our affirmative action debate, often my students tell me that discrimination is a thing of the past as exemplified by a solid Black middle class. My response to them would be that they could be right, but they should pay heed to the lessons in this article, which make clear that serious and appreciable discrimination still exists in an age of "no more discrimination," even for the most highly qualified, best-educated, and most well-off Blacks.

Thinking of naming your child Keisha or Aisha? How about Rasheed or Tremayne? African American parents across the nation may have to think again, as a recent study has shown that workplace discrimination begins long before the job seeker shows up for an interview.

Indeed, it seems to be in play from the moment the résumé hits the human resource manager's desk.

Dr. Marianne Bertrand, a professor of economics at the University of Chicago, and Dr, Sendhil Mullainathan, MacArthur-winning associate professor of economics at the Massachusetts Institute of Technology, have made a significant contribution to the research literature with their new study, "Are Emily and Brendan More Employable than Lakisha and Jamal? A Field Experiment on Labor Market Discrimination."

With names chosen from birth records in Chicago and Boston, the researchers crafted sets of résumés—some of higher quality, some of lower—labeled them with either "White-sounding" or "Black-sounding" names and sent nearly 5,000 of them out in response to 1,300 jobs advertised in the Chicago and Boston papers.

The response from colleagues as they designed their deceptively simple study was, "'Oh, yes, you'll find a discrimination effect, a reverse discrimination effect,'" Bertrand says.

Instead, they found that résumés with "White-sounding" names—like Jay, Brad, Carrie and Kristen—were 50 percent more likely than those with "Black-sounding" names to receive a callback. The results were striking, holding both for jobs at the lower end of the spectrum—cashier and mailroom clerk positions—and for those at the executive level. Put another way, a White job seeker would have to send out at least 10 résumés to receive a single contact from a potential employer. A Black candidate, meanwhile, would have to send out 15—and this in a "soft" economy with a relatively low rate of new job creation.

The most intriguing—and troubling—aspect of the study was that the discrimination effect held even for candidates with stronger credentials: those who had gone to better schools, or won awards, or had fewer résumé "gaps," periods of at least six months without employment.

"We really thought a higher quality résumé would help the African American candidate—that the employer would put less weight on the names," Bertrand says.

And indeed, improving the résumé quality helped candidates with White-sounding names significantly—their chances of receiving a callback rose 30 percent. But for candidates with Black-sounding names, "we found none of that. If anything, we found the opposite," Bertrand says.

"It was very counterintuitive." she adds. "One imagined employers looking at the names and kind of screening at that stage, not going any further, not even reading the résumé. People in HR (human resources) call that a 'deselection process,' where you see a pile of résumés that you have to get through and do a kind of rapid screen" in order to separate the wheat from the chaff.

"That's exactly how we used to do it," notes Kimberly Wilson, who held a human resources position in a mid-sized social policy research firm in the Washington, D.C., area. It was Wilson's job to cull the stack of resumes—"perhaps around 300" for every position, she says—down to about 20 names that would then be brought before a committee.

"And every time, the committee would be more critical of resumes with Black-sounding or foreign-sounding names. 'Oh, yes, she did a research internship, but it wasn't in health and that's what we're really looking for,'" Wilson says. When the names didn't provide a clue to race, the committee members would often zero in on other data—professional organizations, for example.

"'Oh, he belonged to the Hispanic fellowship group in college,'" she adds, explaining, "I don't even think it was conscious, certainly not in most cases."

Conscious or not, the MIT-UChicago study demonstrates that employers actively discriminate among job candidates on the basis of race. And attempts by African Americans to improve their chances with more education and more skills don't appear to help at all.

In addition, the study showed that:

Adjusting for gender greatly increased the discrimination effect. There was a difference of 3.35 percentage points—or 50 percent—be-

Mean Callback Rates By First Name*

White Female		Black Female		White Male		Black Male	
Name	Mean Callback	Name	Mean Callback	Name	Mean Callback	Name	Mean Callback
Emily	8.3%	Aisha	2.2%	Neil	6.6%	Rasheed	3.0%
Anne	9.0%	Keisha	3.8%	Geoffrey	6.8%	Tremayne	4.3%
Jill	9.3%	Tamika	5.4%	Brett	6.8%	Kareem	4.7%
Allison	9.4%	Lakisha	5.5%	Brendan	7.7%	Darnell	4.8%
Sarah	9.8%	Tanisha	6.3%	Greg	7.8%	Tyrone	5.3%
Meredith	10.6%	Latoya	8.8%	Todd	8.7%	Jamal	6.6%
Laurie	10.8%	Kenya	9.1%	Matthew	9.0%	Hakim	7.3%
Carrie	13.1%	Latonya	9.1%	Jay	13.2%	Leroy	9.4%
Kristen	13.6%	Ebony	10.5%	Brad	15.9%	Jermaine	11.3%

*Notes: (1) Sample: All sent resumes. (2) This table reports callback rates by first name, within each sex/race group, first names are ranked by increasing callback rate.

Source: "Are Emily and Brendan more employable than Lakisha and Jamal? A field experiment on labor market discrimination" by Dr. Marianne Bertrand and Dr. Sendhil Mullainathan.

tween the callback rates for all Whites (10.1 percent) and all Blacks (6.7 percent). But the callback rate for the lowest scoring Black female name, Aisha (2.2 percent) was 6.1 percentage points below that of the lowest scoring White female name, Emily (8.3 percent) and 11.4 percentage points below that of the highest scoring White female name. Indeed, five of the nine Black female names—Aisha, Keisha, Tamika, Lakisha and Tanisha—scored lower than the lowest scoring White female name. By contrast, the racial gap between male names was not nearly so pronounced. The lowest scoring White and Black male names—Neil and Rasheed—were only 3.6 percentage points apart.

Applicants who lived in "better" neighborhoods—"Whiter," more educated, higher income—received more callbacks than those who did not. But again, Whites benefited so much more than Blacks, it was not clear that Blacks benefited at all, suggesting that, despite a widespread societal belief in the stigmatizing effect of a "ghetto" address, a good address doesn't help African Americans overcome discrimination either.

The racial gap in callbacks varied greatly by occupation and industry, but not necessarily in expected ways. The gap between Whites and Blacks for the highest occupational category, the managerial and executive category, was the lowest measured: 3.3 percent. The highest racial gap was seen in the rung below the top level—administrative supervisors, who saw a racial gap of 64 percent. And near the bottom of the ladder, secretaries had the second highest racial gap in callbacks.

The extent of the discrimination is "remarkably uniform" across all occupations and industries. Neither federal contractors—bound by affirmative action rules—nor companies who call themselves "Equal Opportunity Employers" discriminate less than any others, suggesting that the designation may be more or less meaningless. The only exceptions were companies located in Black neighborhoods in Chicago—these discriminated less than other firms.

Placed in the national context—the fact that African Americans are twice as likely to be unemployed as White Americans and that, when employed, they earn 25 percent less—the study seems both an explanation and a reiteration of very bad tidings.

It was certainly greeted as such in Boston and Chicago when the results were released

Racial Gap in Callback Rates by Occupation, Industry*

Panel A: Occupation Breakdown

	% of Ads	Callback rates for White Names	Callback rates for Black Names	Ratio	Difference
Executive & Managerial	14.5%	7.91%	5.95%	1.33	1.96%
Administrative Supervisors	7.7%	9.57%	5.85%	1.64	3.72%
Sales Representatives	15.2%	8.04%	5.09%	1.58	2.95%
Sales Workers, Retail & Personal Services	16.8%	10.46%	7.05%	1.48	3.41%
Secretaries	33.9%	10.49%	6.63%	1.58	3.86%
Clerical Workers, Admin. Support	11.9%	13.75%	9.96%	1.38	3.79%

Panel B: Industry Breakdown

	% of Ads	Callback rates for White Names	Callback rates for Black Names	Ratio	Difference
Manufacturing	8.3%	6.93%	3.96%	1.75	2.97%
Transportation and Communication	3.0%	12.16%	14.86%	0.82	-2.70%
Wholesale and Retail Trade	21.5%	8.76%	5.71%	1.53	3.05%
Finance, Insurance, and Real Estate	8.5%	10.63%	4.35%	2.44	6.28%
Business and Personal Services	26.8%	11.30%	6.71%	1.68	4.59%
Health, Educational and Social Services	15.5%	12.14%	9.50%	1.28	2.64%
Other/Unknown	16.4%	8.71%	6.47%	1.35	2.24%

*Notes:
(1) This table reports callback rates by race and occupation (Panel A) and by race and industry (Panel B). Sample is all sent resumes ($N = 4890$).
(2) The two tests reported in the table are log-likelihood test obtained from two separate probit regressions. In Panel A, we regress the callback dummy on 6 occupation dummies, a black dummy and the interaction of the black dummy with the six occupation dummies. In Panel B, we regress the callback dummy on 7 industry dummies, a black dummy and the interactions of the black dummy with the 7 industry dummies. In each case, the null hypothesis tested is that the interaction term effects are all the same.

Source: "Are Emily and Brendan More Employable Than Lakisha and Jamal? A Field Experiment on Labor Market Discrimination" by Dr. Marianne Betrand and Dr. Sendhil Mullainathan.

earlier this year. They sparked a blizzard of newspaper coverage, not to mention spirited discussions on radio call-in shows.

Bertrand says she has been virtually inundated with phone calls and e-mails—particularly, from "people who in their own lives are carrying out the experiment," she explains. "I've heard from people who were African American and had a very distinct African American name who changed the name on their résumés to a less race-salient name, dumbed down their education and did much better.". . .

"Of course, that was not our point."

Though many media accounts have seized on the name-changing aspect as a possible solution, Bertrand is quite clear that "it seems like an easy way out. The burden should be on the companies, not on the person looking for a job. And to give up your name? When names are such an important part of personal identity—No?"

Nor should the study's findings deter African American job seekers who want to sharpen their skills, says Dr. William Harvey, vice president of the American Council on Education and director of ACE's Office of Minorities in Higher Education.

"Unfortunately, there's nothing in the study that contradicts what we already anecdotally know to be true of the experience of African Americans in the job market. There's nothing surprising here," he says. "So this should not deter those of us being discriminated against from getting as many weapons as possible to add to our arsenals—and one of the most respected weapons is still higher education."

Bertrand adds that she is quite encouraged by the fact that "there's been a huge amount of interest, much more than we expected, from people in training and resource management." She hopes in the future "to use the study as a training device, to kind of illustrate to the HR people that these kinds of biases might be at play, whether they're conscious or subconscious," adding, "What we're hearing from the people in HR who have contacted us is that they want to de-bias the selection process too."

Discussion Questions

1. Do you buy these findings? Why or why not?

2. Do you think Bertrand and Mullainathan's findings would hold if they exchanged "Black-sounding" names for "Latino-sounding" names, especially in light of the reading by Eduardo Bonilla-Silva in this volume?

3. Why do you think the résumés of "Black-sounding" female names were so specifically singled out for negative stigmatization in terms of these research findings?

4. Do you or someone close to you have an ethnic-sounding name? Where does the name come from? How has this impacted your experiences?

33

The Return of the Sweatshop

Edna Bonacich
Richard P. Appelbaum

Would you be surprised to know that when you buy a $100 dress for yourself or someone dear to you from a local shopping center, it is very likely that only $6.00 goes to the actual person who sewed the dress? In this article by Edna Bonacich and Richard Appelbaum, the authors take us on a journey into the history of the American sweatshop, a history that does not end in some far away past but that rubs right up against the present day, finding its current home base in Los Angeles, California. Bonacich and Appelbaum make the convincing argument that the return of sweatshops to the United States has everything to do with the restructuring of "global, flexible capitalism," which has been associated with several significant global processes. Among them are the expansion of free trade through elimination of trade barriers and the insistence by large industrial nations on the rights of their corporations to invest around the world "with a minimization of interference in business practices" by more vulnerable nations with which they and their multinational corporations do business. In addition, global restructuring has meant the decline of the welfare state and an attack on organized labor within the United States. Restructuring has also been associated with the disruption of local economies of less developed nations, which has forced movement of immigrant populations to industrialized nations to survive. Moreover, global restructuring has accelerated the "proletarianization" and immiseration of the world's global "peasantry."

Perhaps the most stunning part of the analysis Bonacich and Appelbaum provide, as if the carefully crafted argument on global restructuring weren't enough, is the discussion of the U.S. apparel industry and how it fits into this new global paradigm, complete with a historical overview that leads inexorably to the city of Los Angeles. This phase of the analysis includes a nicely drawn discussion of how our truly fickle fashion tastes, which change on the turn of a dime, lead to a "risky business" that results in the new growth of the sweatshop itself. Catering to American's fickle tastes, then, means unstable work, poverty, and even abusive working conditions for workers. It is here also that gender, race, and class emerge as significant indicators in the authors' overall analysis. We learn that the apparel industry is itself clearly polarized along class lines with wealthy manufacturers, managers, and real estate owners on one hand, and the poorest and lowest-paid workers on the other. At the same time, the managers and manufacturers are primarily European American, and the garment workers are primarily Latino immigrants. Interestingly, gender is implicated in two interesting ways—the choice of apparel itself and the sweatshop workers. We learn that women's wear is where the "fashion-sensitive sector" of the apparel industry is more concentrated and the sector whose production system is smaller and more likely to feature "contracted-out production units" or sweatshops. Men's wear, in contrast, is produced in larger factories devoted to mass production. In addition, we learn that it is likely that the garment worker is generally a woman working in a small factory or sitting at her own home sewing machine. She epitomizes a gendered workforce toiling for an industry that has created a more effective engine for exploiting workers than those that existed in the nineteenth century.

Our authors wind up this polemical article with a ringing indictment of the apparel industry, which they boldly state is "exploitative at its core," asserting that the suffering of others is much too high a price to pay to satisfy our style and Gap-related needs. The author's arguments are food for thought for American consumers, and in light of their analysis, the old adage that the "customer is always right" takes on a sinister tone.

. . . Where does the money from the sale of a $100 dress actually go? . . . The wholesale cost of a $100 dress made in the United States is about $50; half of the $100 sale price goes to the retailer. Of the $50 wholesale cost, 45 percent, or $22.50, is spent by the manufacturer on the fabric. Twenty-five percent, or $12.50 is profit and overhead for the manufacturer. The remaining 30 percent, or $15, goes to the contractor, and covers both the cost of direct labor and the contractor's other expenses, and profit. Only 6 percent, $6, goes to the person who actually sewed the garment. Furthermore, this individual was more than likely to have been paid by the number of sewing operations performed than by the hour and to have received no benefits of any kind.

Sweatshops have indeed returned to the United States. A phenomenon of the apparel industry considered long past is back, not as a minor aberration, but as a prominent way of doing business. Every once in a while, an especially dramatic story hits the news; an Orange County family is found sewing in their home, where a seven-year-old child works next to his mother. Thai workers in El Monte are found in an apartment complex, held against their will under conditions of semienslavement while earning sub-minimum wages. Kathie Lee Gifford, celebrity endorser of a Wal-Mart label, discovers that her line is being produced in sweatshops both offshore and in the United States and cries in shame on national television. The United States Department of Labor develops a program to make apparel manufacturers take responsibility for sweatshop violations. The President of the United States establishes the Apparel Industry Partnership to see if a solution can be found to the growth of sweatshops here and abroad. The nation is becoming aware that the scourge of sweatshops has returned. . . .

What exactly is a "sweatshop"? A sweatshop is usually defined as a factory or a homework operation that engages in multiple violations of the law, typically the non-payment of minimum or overtime wages and various violations of health and safety regulations. According to this definition, many of the garment factories in Los Angeles are sweatshops. In a sample survey conducted by the United States Department of Labor in January 1998, 61 percent of the garment firms in Los Angeles were found to be violating wage and hour regulations. Workers were underpaid by an estimated $73 million dollars per year.[1] Health and safety violations were not examined in that study, but in a survey completed in 1997, 96 percent of the firms were found to be in violation, 54 percent with deficiencies that could lead to serious injuries or death.

An emphasis merely on violations of the law fails to capture the full extent of what has been happening. In recent years the garment industry has been moving its production offshore to countries where workers earn much lower wages than are paid in the United States. In offshore production, some manufacturers may follow local laws, but the legal standard is so low that the workers, often including young teenagers, live in poverty, although they are working full time. The same problem arises in the United States. Even if a factory follows the letter of the law in every detail, workers may suffer abuse, job insecurity, and poverty. In 1990, according to the United States census, the average garment worker in Los Angeles made only $7,200, less than three-quarters of the poverty-level income for a family of three in that year. Thus we wish to broaden the definition of sweatshops to include factories that fail to pay a "living wage," meaning a wage that enables a family to support itself at a socially defined, decent standard of living.[2] We include in the concept of a living wage the idea that people should be able to afford decent housing, given the local housing market, and that a family should be covered by health insurance. If wages fail to cover these minima, and if families with working members still fall below the official poverty line, they are, we claim, working in sweatshops.

Why are sweatshops returning to the apparel industry a number of decades after they had more or less disappeared? Why have their numbers grown so rapidly, especially in the last two decades of the twentieth century? And why has Los Angeles,[3] in particular, become a center of garment sweatshops?

Global, Flexible Capitalism

The reemergence of apparel industry sweatshops is part of a much broader phenomenon, namely, the restructuring of global capitalism—a phenomenon we refer to as the new global capitalism. Starting in the 1970s, and accelerating rapidly especially in the 1980s and 1990s, the restructuring included a series of complex changes: a decline in the welfare state in most of the developed industrial countries; a growth in multinational corporations and an increase in global production; entry into manufacturing for export by many countries, among them some of the poorest in the world; a rise in world trade and intensification of competition; deindustrialization in the developed countries; a decrease in job security and an increase in part-time work; a rise in immigration from poorer countries to the richer ones; and renewed pressure on what remains of the welfare state.[4]

These changes are all interconnected, and it is difficult to establish a first cause. Combined, they are associated with an effort by capitalists, supported by national governments, to increase profits and push back the effects of egalitarian movements that emerged in the 1960s and 1970s and that achieved some redistributive policies. The new global capitalism is characterized by an effort to let the free market operate with a minimum of government interference. At the same time, nations are themselves promoting the hegemony of the free market and imposing it as a standard for the entire world. . . .

The new global capitalism is often touted for its so-called flexibility.[5] The decades of the 1980s and 1990s have been described as post-Fordist; i.e., we have moved beyond huge, mass-production plants making standardized products on the assembly line to a system in which smaller batches of specialized goods are made for an increasingly diverse consumer market. New systems of production, including contracting out the manufacture of specialized goods and services, and the ability to source goods and services wherever they can most efficiently be provided, enhance this flexibility. It is sometimes argued that the new, flexible production allows for more participation by the workers, by enabling them to develop several skills and encouraging them to use their initiative. Instead of repeating the same boring task, as did the workers on the Fordist assembly line, workers in the new factories may engage in more interesting, well-rounded activities. Critics have pointed out that, while some workers may benefit from the new, flexible production arrangements, others face increased job insecurity, more part-time and temporary work, a greater likelihood of working for subcontractors, and less opportunity for unionization. Flexibility for the employer may lead to the expansion of the contingent labor force, which must shift around to find short-term jobs as they arise.

. . . Even though unions were never popular with business, the major industries, including the apparel industry, came to accept them and accept the fact that they made an important contribution to the well-being of the economy at large.

This view of organized labor has collapsed. Business leaders in the United States now see unions as having pushed the price of American labor too high, thereby limiting the competitiveness of firms that maintain a workforce in this country. Firms in certain industries have increasingly moved offshore to seek out low-wage labor in less developed countries. Business owners and managers also see unions as irrelevant to the new flexible systems of production. Unions grew strong in response to the Fordist production regimes, but with more decentralized systems of production, they are viewed as rigid and unpractical. Besides, argue the owners and managers, more engaged and multiskilled workers no longer need union protection, as they share in a commitment to the firm's goals. Unions interfere with a company's flexibility and therefore hurt everyone, including the firm's employees. . . .

Another significant aspect of the new global economy has been the rise of immigration from the less developed to the industrialized countries. Local economies have been disrupted by the arrival of multinational corporations, and many people see no alternative but to seek a means of survival elsewhere. The involvement of the more developed countries in the economies and governments of the Third World is not a new phenomenon, and it has long been associated with emigration. The countervailing movements of capital and labor in opposite directions have often been noted.[6]

What is new about the recent phase of global capitalism is the accelerated proletarianization of much of the world's remaining peasantry. Young women, in particular, have been drawn into the labor force to become the main workers in plants that engage in manufacturing for export. In many ways they are the ideal workforce, as they frequently lack the experience and alternatives that would enable them to demand higher wages and better treatment. The poor working conditions are exacerbated by political regimes, often supported by the United States, that have restricted the workers' ability to organize and demand change.

The increased exploitation of workers in the Third World has a mirror image in the movement of immigrant workers to the more developed countries. Immigrants come not only because of economic dislocations that arise, in part, from the presence of foreign capital in their homelands, but also because of political struggles that have ensued in connection with the Cold War and its aftermath. A paradox of the new global capitalism is that, although the right of capital to move freely is touted by the supporters of the free market, no such right is afforded labor. Immigration is restricted by state policies. One consequence has been the creation of so-called illegal workers, who are stripped of many basic legal rights. Immigrant workers, especially the undocumented, are more easily exploited than are native workers.

In sum, there has been a shift in the balance of power between capital and labor. Although the working class, including women and people of color, made important gains during the three postwar decades (from the late 1940s through the early 1970s), a backlash began developing in the 1970s and achieved full momentum by the 1980s. This backlash corresponds closely to the "great U-turn" in the United States and other capitalist economies, as a broadly shared postwar rise in living standards came to a halt.[7] Conservative governments in the United States and Eu-

rope have implemented policies that favor capital and the free market over labor and other disadvantaged groups. Even political parties that have traditionally supported the working class, such as the Democrats in the United States and the Labour Party in Britain, have shifted to the right.

The reappearance of sweatshops is a feature of the new global, flexible capitalism. The original sweatshops disappeared with the growth of unions and the development of the welfare state. Today, with both of those institutions weakened, markets have been able to drive down wages and reduce working conditions to substandard levels in many labor-intensive industries, such as electronics, toys, shoes, and sports equipment. Indeed, almost every manufacturing industry and some services are pressed to reduce labor costs by minimizing job stability, by contracting out, by using more contingent (part-time and temporary) workers, by reducing benefits, and by attacking unions. But the apparel industry is leading the way.

The Apparel Industry as a Paradigm

The very word *sweatshop* has its roots in the apparel industry. It is ironic that the apparel industry should be a leader in any trend since, as an old industry, it has remained backward in many areas. Significant advances have been made in certain aspects of production, notably computer-assisted design, computer-assisted grading and marking, and computerized cutting, and there have been innovations in sewing machine technology and in the organization of work flow, but the core production process, namely the sewing of garments, is still low-tech.[8] The primary unit of production continues to be a worker, usually a woman, sitting (or standing) at a sewing machine and sewing together pieces of limp cloth.

Garment production is labor intensive, and, unlike many other industries, it does not require much capital to get into the sewing business. Consequently, sewing factories proliferate and the industry is exceedingly competitive—probably more competitive than most. In some ways the apparel industry is the epitome of free market capitalism because the barriers to entry are so low. Less-developed countries take up apparel production as their first manufacturing industry in their efforts to industrialize. In the shift to global production and manufacturing for export, apparel has been in the vanguard. Clothing firms in the United Stares began to move production offshore to Asia as early as the late 1950s. Today apparel manufacturers in a number of developed countries are opening production facilities and employing workers in almost every country of the world. The result in the United States has been a rise in imports (see Figure 33.1), which started to grow in the 1960s and 1970s and grew at an explosive rate in the 1980s. In 1962 apparel imports totaled $301 million. They had tripled by the end of the decade, to $1.1 billion; increased another fivefold by 1980, to $5.5 billion; and nearly another fourfold by 1990, to $21.9 billion. By 1997, apparel imports totaled $42 billion; they are projected to exceed $50 billion in 1999. According to estimates by the American Apparel Manufacturers Association, imports accounted for 60 percent of the $101 billion wholesale apparel market.[9] Needless to say, this has greatly increased the level of competition within the industry, creating a pressure to lower wages in the United States garment industry to meet the low wages paid overseas. Global production is certainly expanding in other industries, but apparel is the most globalized industry of all.[10] . . .

The return of sweatshops in the United States apparel industry can be partly, but not entirely, attributed to the dramatic rise in offshore production, and the concomitant increase in cheap imports. Much of the industry is driven by fashion, and sales of fashionable garments are highly volatile. The production of apparel is generally a risky business, which discourages heavy capital investment and limits the availability of capital for firms that want to expand or upgrade. The riskiness is augmented by time. Fashion can change quickly. Apparel manufacturers want to be sure that any demand is fully met, but must be wary of overproducing garments that may fall out of fashion. The industry needs to be especially sensitive to changes in consumer taste, to respond quickly to these shifts, and to cease production of dying trends in a timely manner.

Needless to say, the industry tries to mold the fickle consumers' tastes as much as possible, by heavy advertising, by producing fashion shows and magazines, and by publicizing the opinions of pundits who predict and help to determine the trends. Indeed, the industry has considerable internal variation in terms of susceptibility to the fashion dynamic. Some garments, considered to be basics, change only slowly. Basics include most underwear and sleepwear, T-shirts, sweatshirts and sweatpants, denim jeans, and men's shirts and pants. The areas of greatest fashion volatility include women's dresses, skirts and tops, women's bathing suits, and all the traditional basics also can include fashion lines. The Gap made a fortune by turning the basic T-shirt into a personal fashion statement. And denim jeans, when associated with the names of particular designers, have experienced the hot flash of fashion success.

Offshore production usually requires longer waiting times, thereby increasing the risk in making time-sensitive garments. Basics can be planned months in advance without much risk that the garments will go out of fashion. In the United States apparel industry, the production of basics has moved steadily offshore, and highly fashionable apparel is more likely to be made domestically. The distinction is likely to lessen with time as communication and transportation times decrease and as arrangements are made to produce garments in regions closer to their destination market. NAFTA, for example, has led to an enormous growth in Mexico's capacity to produce garments for the United States apparel industry. Because it is much closer to the United States than Asia is, some production has been shifted from Asia to Mexico; and it is possible that the production of more fashion-sensitive garments will also be shifted there. Their proximity also accounts for shifts to the Caribbean and Central America.

The fashion-sensitive sector of the industry is much more concentrated in women's wear than in men's wear, although this may be changing a little. Women in the United States spend twice as much on clothing as do

Figure 33.1
Apparel Imports to the United States, 1962-1997 ($000,000)

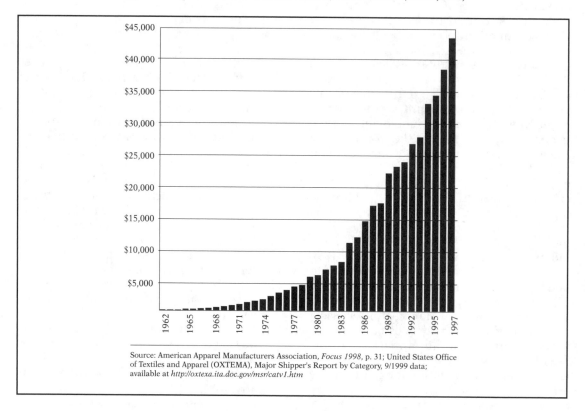

Source: American Apparel Manufacturers Association, *Focus 1998*, p. 31; United States Office of Textiles and Apparel (OXTEMA), Major Shipper's Report by Category, 9/1999 data; available at *http://oxtexa.ita.doc.gov/msr/catv1.htm*

men. The general difference between women's and men's wear has led to a segregation between the two sectors of the industry. For example, the major industry newspaper is called *Women's Wear Daily*. The two major sectors eventually produced two unions: the International Ladies' Garment Workers' Union (ILGWU), which organized workers in the women's sector, and the Amalgamated Clothing and Textile Workers Union (ACTWU), which organized workers in the textile industry and the men's wear sector. The two unions merged in 1995 into UNITE, the Union of Needletrades, Industrial and Textile Employees, probably less because of a convergence between the two types of garment production than because of the loss of membership that each was suffering.

The differences have also led to a divergence in production systems. Men's wear has generally been produced in larger, mass-pro-duction factories, women's wear in smaller, contracted-out production units. Typically, in the production of women's clothing, apparel manufacturers (companies known by the brand names) design and engineer the garments, buy the textiles, and wholesale the completed clothing. The actual production of the garment, the cutting, sewing, laundering, and finishing, are sewing contractors, and they typically receive cut goods that their employees sew. Most garment workers are employed in small, contracting factories, sewing garments for manufacturers, who typically employ several contractors. Contracting out extends at the margins to industrial homework, with a single woman sitting at her home sewing machine, making clothing for a firm that employs her.

The contracting out of apparel production can be seen as an instance of flexible production. It allows apparel manufacturers to deal with fluctuations in fashion and seasons by hiring contractors when they need them and letting them go when they do not. In this respect the apparel industry is at the cutting edge of the new global economy: It has used contracting out for decades and has developed this flexible production system to a fine art. Moreover, the contracting system has been extended to global production. Manufacturers not only employ local contractors, but also often conduct their offshore production through contracting rather than through the ownership of subsidiaries. The lack of fixed assets enables them to move production wherever they can get the best deal in terms of labor cost, taxes and tariffs, environmental regulation, or any other factor that influences the quality and cost of their products.

The virtue of the contracting system for the manufacturers is that they do not need to invest a cent in the factories that actually sew their clothes. Manufacturers engage in arm's-length transactions with their contractors, enabling them to avoid any long-term commitment to a particular contractor or location. The formal commitment lasts only as long as the particular job order. In practice, manufacturers may develop longer-term relationships with a core group of dependable contractors, attempting to ensure that they receive steady work. Nevertheless, the absence of firm ties provides maximum flexibility for manufacturers and the elimination of costly inefficiencies associated with having dependent subsidiaries. Contracting out enables manufacturers to lure only the labor they actually need.

The picture is not quite so rosy from the other side. Contractors, who in the United States and other advanced industrial countries, are often immigrants, must scramble to maintain steady work. And rather than employ a stable workforce, they pass the problems created by flexible production on to their workers. In the United States most garment workers are employed on a piecework basis, so that they are paid only for the work they actually do. If the work is slow, they do not get paid. In offshore production, workers are more likely to receive an hourly wage rather than piece rate, but they are required to produce an arduous daily quota.

Their hours and quotas, like those of piece-rate workers, are determined by the shifting demands of their manufacturers; at the height of the season or if they are producing a hot fashion item, they are required to work long hours. During a lull, they are laid off and go unpaid. . . .

We believe that the way apparel production is organized is a predictor of things to come in many industries and portends the expansion of the sweatshop. One can argue that in the return of the sweatshop we are witnessing a throwback to the earliest phases of the industrial revolution. But it is clear that what is going on is not only "old" but also very new. The apparel industry has managed to combine the latest ideas and technology for the rapid production and distribution of a highly diverse and continually changing product with the oppressive working conditions of the late nineteenth and early twentieth centuries, now coordinated over a global space. Consumers of clothing have never had it so good; the women and men huddled over sewing machines in foreign countries or immigrant enclaves suffer the consequences.

In Figure 33.2 the chief features of the apparel industry and the forces that are leading to the reemergence of sweatshops are summarized. Briefly, the forces are these. Apparel is a fashion-based, seasonal business and is, therefore, highly risky and competitive (1) It is also a low-tech, labor-intensive industry, particularly at the level of production, with low capital requirements and an ease of entry that encourage competitiveness (2) The unpredictability of the industry leads manufacturers to externalize their risk by contracting out the labor to enhance their flexibility (3) The ease of entry means that apparel production is usually the first industry chosen by countries seeking to industrialize (4) The availability of offshore garment factories with low-wage labor encourages United States apparel manufacturers to move some of their production to those facilities, leading to a rise in garment imports into the United States. Contracting out, both locally and abroad, also contributes to the competitive character of the industry (5 and 6).

The highly competitive nature of the apparel industry enables giant retailers to gain power over the manufacturers, a phenomenon that has increased as retailers have consolidated. (7) In turn, the power and consolidation of the retailers adds to the competition between apparel manufacturers, who must jostle for favor with fewer and fewer buyers (8).

The movement of the apparel industry offshore, which is partly encouraged by United States trade and investment policies, combines with interventions by other industries (such as agribusiness) and neoliberal government policies, to create severe economic dislocations among certain segments of the population, especially peasants, but also those in some urban occupations. Coupled with the impact of local wars, many with United States involvement, this dislocation results in a rise in immigration to the United States (9). Because of the low capital requirements for garment contracting, those immigrants with small amounts of capital or limited business experience enter the industry as entrepreneurs. Meanwhile, more impoverished immigrants become available to work in garment factories for low wages.

The reemergence of sweatshops is a product of the confluence of several forces: the availability of immigrant contractors and workers (10), the competition with low-priced imports (11), and the contracting system (12). These developments have all occurred within a context of government policies that support offshore production, contracting out weakened organized labor, and a disenfranchised, immigrant working class (13).

The rise in apparel imports has inevitably led to a decline in jobs in the United States garment industry. Peak employment was reached in the early 1970s; since then, employment has more or less steadily decreased. In 1970 the industry employed 1,364,000 people. By 1980 the number had fallen to 1,264,000. In

Figure 33.2
The Reemergence of Sweatshops in the United States Apparel Industry

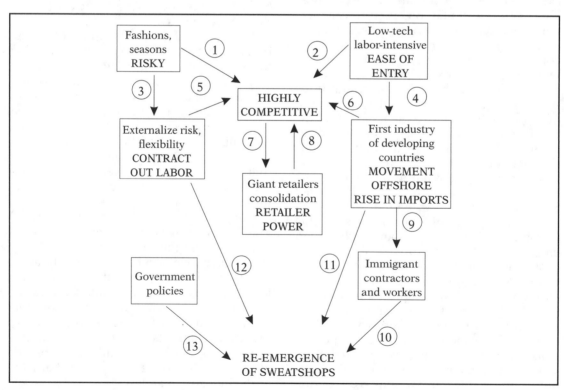

1990 it was 1,036,000, and in 1997, 813,000. Between 1978 and 1998, in almost every state except California, employment in apparel declined. New York, New Jersey, Pennsylvania, and Massachusetts lost over half their apparel jobs.[11] In California, and mostly in Los Angeles, over 50,000 apparel jobs have been added since 1978.

Garment Production in Los Angeles

To the surprise of many people, Los Angeles is the manufacturing center of the nation, with 663,400 manufacturing jobs in 1997. Los Angeles has 5,900 more manufacturing jobs than the second city, Chicago, and over 200,000 more than Detroit, a distant third.[12] Equally surprising is the fact that the apparel industry is the largest manufacturing employer in Los Angeles County, with 122,500 employees enumerated by the Employment Development Department in April 1998. Thus, almost one out of five manufacturing employees in Los Angeles works in the apparel industry. . . .

The Race to the Bottom

The United States is growing more and more unequal, with increasing polarization along race and class lines. In Los Angeles the forces that are shaping inequality in the United States are more sharply focused. The city is characterized by immense wealth, on the one hand, and extreme poverty on the other.[13] A study by a committee of the California legislature found that, between 1989 and 1996, the number of very rich Angelinos, including those with annual incomes over $25 million, doubled, from 165 to 376 individuals, and that, from 1994 to 1996, the numbers of the very poor, those with annual incomes of less that $20,000, grew by 13.5 percent from 2.5 million to 2.9 million people. The authors conclude that there has been a hollowing out of the middle class and that the individuals and families hardest hit by the recession of the early 1990s have been slowest to benefit from the recovery, while the wealthy have benefited strongly.[14] Multimillionaires and even billionaires build mansions in the mountains and canyons and in rich communities such as Beverly Hills and Bel Air, while unemployment soars in the African-American community, and immigrant workers do almost all of the physical labor to eke out a bare survival for themselves and their children. The developments came to a dramatic climax in the so-called riots of April 1992, when all the bitterness of growing inequality in a land of plenty burst out in violent fury.[15]

The apparel industry shows these same extremes. It is an industry in which some people, such as retailers and manufacturers, managers and professionals, bankers and real estate owners, are able to acquire immense wealth. Others, most notably garment workers, are among the poorest, lowest-paid workers in the city. The industry is not only polarized along class lines, it also has a clear racial and ethnic structure and hierarchy. The wealthy at the top are almost all of European extraction. At the bottom, the workers are mainly Latino immigrants, especially from Mexico and Central America, and a minority are Asian immigrants. In the middle are the entrepreneurs who run the contracting shops that employ the workers, and who are mainly immigrants from Asia (and, to a lesser extent, from Mexico and Central America).

Even the phenomenon of Asian middlemen became an issue in the 1992 uprising, as stores owned by Koreans became the target of much of the angry violence. These stores, mainly mom-and-pop operations, came to be seen as the direct oppressors and drainers of African-American and Latino neighborhoods. The situation has parallels in the garment industry. Latino and Asian garment workers come into contact mainly with Asian contractors (among whom Korean immigrants are especially significant) and rarely meet the wealthy whites who are making most of the money generated by their labor.

We must emphasize that the apparel industry is not fundamentally different from other industries in the United States. They all operate on the same principles of private property and competition, and they all demonstrate the same propensity for an increasing accumulation of wealth at the top and growing racial oppression and exploitation at the bottom. Because the apparel industry is one of the worst, it offers a good example of how our society works and how the system produces and reproduces an intensifying polarization by class and race.

In recent years there has been a redistribution of wealth upward, and there is no immediate end in sight. The common justification for this redistribution is the belief that putting wealth in the hands of the rich will lead to greater productive investment, which should benefit everyone. This may sometimes be true, but an important result has been a greater ability by business owners to lower labor's share of the wealth that is produced.

The push for keeping labor costs low comes not only from individual firms or industries but also from the highest levels of finance and government. When wages appear to be climbing, the stock market drops. When unemployment drops, the fear of a tight labor market that will drive up wages has the same effect. The Federal Reserve Bank then raises interest rates in order to keep inflation in check; unemployment is maintained at a so-called acceptable level and wages stagnate.

These abstract economic concepts—the unemployment rate, inflation, and flexibility—have very human faces. A 5- or 6-percent unemployment rate may be good for the economy, but it is dreadful for the individuals and the communities that must endure it in practice. Similarly, the danger of inflation, which never seems to be associated with rising salaries for chief executive officers or excessively high profits, becomes a personal hardship when translated to mean that the earnings of a working family making minimum wage or less should be held where they are. And the much-touted flexibility, which creates a growing army of contingent workers who work in part-time or temporary jobs completely lacking job security, means that many people find it increasingly difficult to plan for any kind of future they can count on. . . .

Notes

1. This figure is arrived at by taking the average back wages owed per factory for ninety days, $3,631, multiplying it by four to get the back wages owed per year, and then by the estimated 5,000 contractors in Los Angeles. This method of calculating was suggested by Gerald Hall of DOL, who at a meeting between the DOL and the Coalition for Garment Workers held on July 9, 1998, also reported the amount collected in back wages, per annum.

2. The Los Angeles City Council passed a living wage ordinance in early 1997: Holders of municipal contracts and firms receiving substantial financial aid from the city must pay their employees at least $7.25 an hour, plus health insurance, or $8.50 an hour without specified benefits. At the time, the state and federal minimum wage was $4.25 an hour. See Jean Merl, "Defiant Mayor Vetoes 'Living Wage' Ordinance," *Los Angeles Times*, 28 March 1997, sec. B, p. 3. The concept of a living wage has emerged in Los Angeles and other cities, where it has become clear that a minimum-wage job without benefits puts a family well below the official poverty level. Those who must labor under such conditions are the working poor.

3. Throughout this book references to Los Angeles indicate the County of Los Angeles, which is the equivalent of the metropolitan area. The City of Los Angeles is only one, though the largest, of a number of cities in the county, which also includes unincorporated areas. References to the city will clearly differentiate it from the county.

4. A large and growing literature treats these developments, for example, David Harvey, *The Condition of Postmodernity* (Cambridge: Blackwell, 1989); Ankie Hoogvelt, *Globalization and the Postcolonial World: The New Political Economy of Development* (Baltimore: Johns Hopkins University Press, 1997); Kim Moody, *Workers in a Lean World* (New York: Verso, 1997); and Beth A. Rubin, *Shifts in the Social Contract: Understanding Change in American Society* (Thousand Oaks Calif.: Pine Forge Press, 1996).

5. See Michael J. Piore and Charles F. Sabel, *The Second Industrial Divide: Possibilities for Prosperity* (New York: Basic Books, 1984) and Joseph B. Pine, *Mass Customization: The New Frontier in Business Competition* (Boston, Mass.: Harvard Business School Press, 1993). For critiques of the "new flexibility," see Harvey, *Condition of Postmodernity*; Alain Lipietz, *Mirages and Miracles: The Crisis of Global Fordism* (London: Verso, 1987); and Richard P. Appelbaum, "Multiculturalism and Flexibility: Some New Directions in Global Capitalism," pp. 297–316 in *Mapping Multi-Culturalism*, ed. by Avery Gordon and Christopher Newfield (Minneapolis: University of Minnesota Press, 1996).

6. Another large literature deals with this topic. See, for example, Saskia Sassen, *The Mobility of Labor and Capital: A Study in International Investment and Labor Flow* (Cambridge: Cambridge University Press, 1988); Paul Ong, Edna Bonacich, and Lucie Cheng, eds., *The New Asian Immigration in Los Angeles and Global Restructuring* (Philadelphia: Temple University Press, 1994).

7. Bennett Harrison and Barry Bluestone, *The Great U-Turn: Corporate Restructuring and the Polarizing of America* (New York: Basic Books, 1990).

8. Kurt Hoffman and Howard Rush, *Micro-Electronics and Clothing: The Impact of Technical Change on a Global Industry* (New York: Praeger, 1988).

9. American Apparel Manufacturers Association, *Focus: An Economic Profile of the Apparel Industry* (Arlington, Va.: AAMA, 1998), 4. The apparel retail market in the United States reached $180 billion in 1997.

10. Imports have also affected the apparel industries of other advanced industrial countries. See Tan M. Taplin and Jonathan Winterton, eds. *Rethinking Global Production: A Comparative Analysis of Restructuring in the Clothing Industry* (Aldershot, England: Ashgate, 1997).

11. American Apparel Manufacturers Association, *Focus 1998* (Arlington, Va.), p. 10. In New York City there has recently been a slight rise in apparel employment. The city's apparel and textile manufacturing employment peaked in the mid-1970s at 250,000, but had dropped to 82,100 by 1996. In 1997 it rose to 84,000. "Rebirth of New York's Apparel Industry," *Apparel Industry Magazine*, March 1998, p. 12.

12. Daniel Taub, "L.A. Beats Out Chicago as No. 1 Manufacturing Center," *Los Angeles Business Journal*, 9 March 1998, p. 5. See also Louis Uchitelle, "The New Faces of U.S. Manufacturing: California's Vision of the Future: Thriving, But with Fewer High-Wage Jobs," *New York Times*, 3 July 1994, sec. 3, p. 1; Jack Kyser, *Manufacturing in Los Angeles* (Los Angeles, Calif.: Economic Development Corp., 1997).

13. Paul M. Ong, *The Widening Divide: Income Inequality and Poverty in Los Angeles* (Los Angeles, Calif.: Graduate School of Architecture and Urban Planning, University of California, Los Angeles, 1989).

14. California Legislature, Assembly Select Committee on the California Middle Class, *The Distribution of Income in California and Los Angeles: A Look at Recent Current Population Survey and State Taxpayer Data* (Sacramento, 1998). The chairman of the committee is Assemblyman Wally Knox.

15. Examples of the growing literature on the restructuring of Los Angeles include: Mike Davis, *City of Quartz: Excavating the Future of Los Angeles* (London: Verso, 1990); Michael J. Dear, H. Eric Schockman, and Greg Hise, eds., *Rethinking Los Angeles* (Thousand Oaks, Calif.: Sage, 1996); Cynthia Hamilton, *Apartheid in an American City: The Case of the Black Community in Los Angeles* (Los Angeles, Calif.: Labor/Community Strategy Center, 1987); Labor/Community Strategy Center, *Reconstructing Los Angeles from the Bottom Up* (Los Angeles, Calif.: Labor/Community Strategy Center, 1993); David Reid, ed. *Sex, Death and God in L.A.* (Berkeley, Calif.: University of California Press, 1994); David Rieff, *Los Angeles: Capital of the Third World* (New York: Simon and Schuster, 1991); Gerry Riposa and Carolyn G. Dersch, eds., *City of Angels* (Dubuque, Iowa: Kendall/Hunt, 1992); Allen J. Scott, *Technopolis: High-Technology Industry and Regional Development in Southern California* (Berkeley, Calif.: University of California Press, 1993); Allen J. Scott and Edward W. Soja, eds., *The City: Los Angeles and Urban Theory at the End of the Twentieth Century* (Berkeley, Calif.: University of California Press, 1996); Edward W. Soja, *Postmodern Geographies; The Reinsertion of Space in Critical Social Theory* (London: Verso, 1989); Edward W. Soja, Rebecca Morales, and Goetz Wolff, "Urban Restructuring: An Analysis of Social and Spatial Change in Los Angeles," *Economic Geography 59* (1983): 195–230; Roger Waldinger and Mehdi Bozorgmehr, eds., *Ethnic Los Angeles* (New York: Russell Sage, 1996).

Discussion Questions

1. What were your thoughts as you read the Bonacich and Appelbaum article? Was it informative? Did it make you angry? Was it confirmation of what you have always thought about the apparel industry? Was it a shock?

2. How do you respond to the authors' suggestion that what is going on in the apparel industry may be a predictor of things to come in other industries, portending the expansion of the sweatshop to the production of other consumer goods? Do you think they are unrealistic or that their point makes sense? Why or why not?

34
Recasting Our Understanding of Gender and Work During Global Restructuring

Jean L. Pyle
Kathryn B. Ward

Several articles in this text put issues of gender, race, and class in international perspective by focusing on globalization. In Section 3, Faye V. Harrison illustrated the impact of global restructuring through the life of one woman in Jamaica. In this section, Angela Y. Davis refers to globalization in relation to the prison industry and Edna Bonacich and Richard P. Applebaum look at its impact on one industry in one city. While they do provide a concrete example from Bangladesh, in this article Jean L. Pyle and Kathryn B. Ward discuss the same issues primarily in general and abstract terms, showing the impact of globalization on the gendered division of labor. Their immediate aim is not to report data from a particular case but to develop a framework within which data from a wide range of cases can be understood. Their ultimate aim is to use that framework to fashion effective strategies for social change and the empowerment of women.

Pyle and Ward first summarize the large-scale or macro-trends in globalization, showing how trade, production, and finance have increasingly come under the control of international and multinational organizations, corporations, and agencies, especially those dealing with markets and seeking profits or debt repayment as opposed to those dealing with human welfare, human rights, and the

environment. The results are that governments are pressured to curtail social services and supports and to try to meet the needs of their populations by attracting multinational corporations, promoting tourism, exporting surplus labor, and adopting microfinance programs. At the same time, trade, production and finance all move from country to country and region to region, seeking the cheapest materials and labor. Women are often preferred as workers as they can be paid less and are considered less likely to be troublemakers than men. The establishment of a factory may temporarily benefit some women and lead their families to become dependent on their earnings. Then, because of new trade agreements or cheaper labor elsewhere, factories move or the work is locally subcontracted, and the women workers are pushed into low-wage work in the unregulated and poorly documented informal sector.

The authors then look at the same phenomena from the inside showing how global production networks populated almost exclusively by women and children have developed in export manufacturing, but also in sex work and domestic work and among recipients of microcredit. In the case of microcredit, very small loans are intended to help women start small enterprises, but it usually takes several years before they can be expected to provide some measure of financial security and meanwhile interest must be paid. The authors note that women often have to migrate to work in factories or become sex or domestic workers. When they work in other countries, they send money home, helping their families and providing their governments with foreign currency. Thus, no one has much motivation to assure that they are safe and secure, that they are not being exploited, and that work they do is legal.

We propose a broad analytic framework for understanding the relationships between globalization, gender and work. This is important, because the way researchers, government officials and development practitioners think about the effects of globalization on the gendered division of labor and the ensuing problems are the fundamental bases upon which to develop effective strategies for change that will reduce gender inequalities and empower women.

We begin by outlining the major trends that characterize the recent period of globalization. Next, we survey the effects of globalization on the gendered division of labor at both macro and micro levels. At the macro level, we trace the effects of the globalization of trade, production and finance on women's roles. We then investigate impacts at a more micro level by looking at four categories of gendered production networks that have grown substantially during the recent period of globalization: export production, sex work, domestic service and microfinance income generation. These four sectors cut across a continuum of household, informal and formal work and illuminate both the problems and the possibilities for change. We analyze the role of governments in these processes. In seeking to satisfy both the demands of international institutions (such as the International Monetary Fund or multinational corporations) and address some of the needs of their citizens, many national governments have been pushed into taking steps that directly or indirectly foster these four types of work.

These gendered global production networks have grown substantially *as a result of* the processes of globalization and major changes in international political economy. We argue there are systemic linkages between the global expansion of production trade and finance on the one hand, and the increase of women in gendered production networks on the other hand, particularly networks that involve informal sector work, lower pay and higher levels of female migration. This broader understanding of the global forces that shape women's lives (and intersection of these global forces with national governments and local conditions) is necessary to develop effective strategies that promote more equal outcomes for women and counter the adverse impacts of globalization on the gendered division of labor.

In the 1990s, the women in development (WID) and gender and development (GAD) discourses broadened to examine the gendered impacts of economic globalization

focusing on the effects of capitalist processes across the entire world—rather than just the so-called developing countries. Feminist economists and sociologists reformulated theories and research methodologies. Some extended their focus to include flows of people internationally in addition to flows of goods, services and capital (Sassen, 2000). Others challenged prevailing theoretical frameworks regarding globalization and work and questioned the impacts of economic globalization on women who vary by location, race, ethnicity and class (Beneria, 1995, 1999; Bandarage, 1997; Pyle, 1999, 2001; Marchand and Runyan, 2000; Sassen, 2000; Bergeron, 2001; Staudt et al., 2001). Many researchers and some policy-makers focused on increasing women's capabilities and began discussion of the risks and rights of women in a globalizing economy (Sen and Grown, 1987; Beneria and Feldman, 1992; Elson, 1995; Summerfield 2001). Important work on gender has been done by institutions such as the United Nations Development Program (UNDP) and UNIFEM (UNDP, 1999; UNIFEM 2000).

Despite these substantive advances, however, most mainstream economists and many sociologists specializing in the study of development, world-systems and globalization have neglected gender and/or the structural causes of gender inequality (Ward, 1993, 1999; Dunaway, 2001). These same economists (more so than sociologists) have been extraordinarily influential in setting international policies. The incomplete understanding of the sources of gender inequality has led, however, to inequitable outcomes for women and can actually undermine economic development (Pyle, 1998). Although some mainstream financial institutions, such as the World Bank, have started promoting gender equality as a means of economic development (King and Mason 2001), they selectively advocate family planning, education and microfinance—strategies that are important but do not address some fundamental sources of inequality. Some researchers have discussed the efforts of feminists to engage with traditional development institutions, including attempts to enter the institutions and change them from within (as 'missionaries'). In so doing, they may bump up against the constraints posed by the bureaucracies and powerful people within them ('mandarins') (for example, see Miller and Razavi, 1998).

Global Trends

The latest period of globalization, the late 1960s/early 1970s to the present, has involved several major trends, as capitalist processes and ideologies spread throughout the world. It has brought both opportunities and problems. The effects are often gendered. First, international financial institutions and most nations have promoted market determination of economic outcomes (versus government involvement in the economy). These include industrialized countries (the US and UK from the early 1980s), developing countries, and former socialist countries in Eastern Europe and Southeast Asia and China. Second, many developing countries have shifted to more open 'export-oriented' production for external trade. Previously many focused on 'import substitution,' the production of essential goods for internal markets (McMichael, 2000).

Third, multinational corporations (MNCs) in manufacturing service and finance sectors have moved into successive tiers of countries over the past three decades and established burgeoning networks of subcontractors (Pyle, 1998 1999). Fourth, since the late 1970s, globalization has also involved structural adjustment policies (SAPs), mandated by the International Monetary Fund (IMF) and World Bank (WB) as a condition for granting loans. SAPs required governments to further open their economies to trade and financial flows (Todaro, 2000), and have often undermined indigenous sustainable development and caused financial instability (Stiglitz, 2002). They have also required austerity measures that have fallen heavily on the poor, particularly women.

These four forms of global restructuring use the language of liberalization and 'free markets.' This perpetuates the myth that subsequent economic outcomes result from competitive markets, where everyone has similar opportunities, and governments have minimal involvement in their economies. However, 20 years of SAPs have led many to

question the rhetoric. Research has shown that all nations and all peoples do not have the same opportunities (UNDP, 1995 1999; World Bank, 2001b, 2002). These forms of global restructuring have resulted from *deliberate* interventions by governments pressured by institutions such as MNCs, the IMF, or the World Trade organization (WTO) and are not 'free market' strategies. This misappropriation of language obscures the realities that these institutions fundamentally concerned with profits or payment of loans dominate countries' economies *and* formulate the mandates to 'open' and 'liberalize' an economy.

Fifth, global power structures have shifted. Institutions focused on markets (MNCs, IMF, WB and WTO) have gained power relative to those centered on people and sustainable human development (the International Labor Organization [ILO], many UN agencies, and nongovernment organizations or NGOs). The WTO, the newest institution in the international power arena, gives increasing support to the interests of MNCs vis-à-vis nations (McMichael, 2000). Formed in relative secrecy by international financial institutions and core governments in the mid-1990s as the successor to the General Agreement on Tariffs and Trade (GAIT), the WTO is an undemocratic, nontransparent organization that can censure nations that promote restrictions to trade (even if the restrictions are designed to protect human rights or the environment). The WTO seeks to extend its control to services via the GATS (General Agreement on Trade in Services).

Resistance has developed to such shifts in power and to the actions of these market-focused institutions. Demonstrations against globalization and the policies of the WTO, WB and IMF surrounded recent meetings of these institutions in Seattle, Washington, DC, Prague, Genoa and Davos. They involved labor organizations, environmentalists and women's and human rights advocates. Gender issues however, have remained at the peripheries of protest documents and websites (Staudt et al., 2001). Some former WB staff have also critiqued these institutions. Former WB chief economist (1997–2000) and 2001 Nobel Laureate Joseph Stiglitz questioned whose interests the WB and IMF really represent and critiqued the misguidedness of their poverty-inducing programs (Stiglitz, 2000, 2001, 2002).

The WB and IMF have been reorienting their focus. Recent WB development reports have advocated poverty reduction and institutional strengthening programs (World Bank, 2001b, 2002). Since the mid-1990s, the WB has also promoted mainstreaming gender concerns. Recent publications stress gender equality as a mechanism for generating development, and acknowledge that gender inequality hinders development (Quisumbing and Maluccio, 1999; Ilahi, 2000). However, the current recommendations of these institutions for reducing poverty and promoting greater gender equality will be difficult to achieve WB and IMF policies from the 1980s onward have decimated countries physical and social infrastructures and their capabilities to meet such goals (Bradshaw et al., 1993; Span, 1994; Buchmann, 1996; Bandarage, 1997; Fall, 1998; Alcaron-Gonzalez and McKinley, 1999). Reduced access to education, health care and income-generating opportunities has diminished women's prospects.

Each of these five trends, and the policies involved at the international, national and corporate levels has effects that shape the gendered division of labor (Lim, L.L. and Oishi, 1996; Bandarage, 1997; Sassen, 2000; Pyle, 2001). We examine the problems these gendered effects present for women.

Globalization and the Gendered Division of Labor

As economic activities become more global, some countries and groups benefit but the hardships of many others increase. Globalization has occurred unevenly and countries have been integrated into the global economy to very different degrees (Bandarage, 1997; McMichael, 2000; Todaro, 2000; UNDP, 1999; World Bank, 2001b). This has resulted in rising inequality and tensions, increasingly considered the flip side of growing reliance on market forces and changes in the international power structure.

We examine the effects of globalization and the prevailing policy framework on the gendered division of labor in two complementary ways. First we consider the impact of the globalization of trade, production and finance and the macroeconomic policies that underlie them on women's roles. This approach helps us understand the processes by which distinctly gendered global production networks have arisen. Second, we examine four of these largely female production networks to show why they have developed and what their effects are on women's work and well-being.

We know that 'gender' has socially constructed components that reflect a society's views regarding appropriate roles for men and women and are reinforced by economic, political, social cultural, and religious institutions. Processes of globalization can undermine existing social constructions of gender or cause them to be more firmly defended (as we have seen with the rise of fundamentalist groups of all faiths and politics). In addition, globalization can combine older and newer views of appropriate gender roles. Global organizations such as MNCs and the IMF use these social constructions to their advantage, citing 'cultural sensitivities,' to restrict choices and access to certain jobs and to pay women less than men.

The Gendered Effects of Globalization of Trade, Production and Finance

Trade. The globalization of trade, under trade regimes such as GATT and the controversial WTO can have divergent effects on women (Fontana and Wood 2000; Durano, 2002; Oxfam, 2002).[1] Such gendered trade effects however have rarely been considered when trade organizations formulate policies. On the one hand, women may benefit from economic globalization if they work in factories producing goods for international trade—as long as they make a living wage and their employer (often an MNC or its subcontractor) remains in their area. On the other hand, in Africa, Latin America and parts of Asia, many women running small enterprises or working in agriculture have been forced out of business by cheaper imports accompanying unequal trade liberalization (Barrientos 1997; Bee, 2000; Dolan, 2001; Schurman, 2001; Preibisch et al. 2002). Alternatively, agricultural women have grappled with the imposition of corporate genetically modified tomatoes (Barndt, 2002). In countries where women have fewer opportunities than men, trade reinforces the traditional gender segregation of work. For example, in sub-Saharan Africa, men were brought into the production of cash crops for export, whereas women remained relegated to subsistence agriculture that feeds their households (Joekes, 1987).

In addition, when developed countries switch trade preferences to other regions, they have ignored the disproportionate impact on women workers in so-called developing countries who became unemployed as a result. Many of these developing countries or industries within them previously had preferential trade status or quotas and/or were highly dependent on export sector earnings. Some women workers in these export sectors had experienced empowerment through their increased access to factory jobs, earnings and more leverage in decision-making in their families. They became disempowered, however, when financiers, buyers and employers shifted their capital, plants and orders. These women have few other economic opportunities beyond work in the informal sector. For example, some of the early Asian garment manufacturers—located in Singapore, Taiwan and South Korea—shifted production to the Caribbean to take advantage of altered trade arrangements and quotas, and pending changes in 2004 MFA agreements (Green 1998).

Many NGOs have urged policy-makers to acknowledge the effects of trade agreements on women and children's livelihoods. The issues are complex. For example, 1994 US legislation banned products produced by child labor and imposed trade policies without consulting relevant NGOs about how poor families would cope without their children's earnings. The idea was to remove children from exploitative working conditions and allow them time to attend school. In order to help support their families, however, many children ended up in even more hazardous occupations without time to obtain an education (Kabeer, 2001).

Production. MNCs have used changes in trade and financial agreements and the Internet to move their production and services around the globe. Much production (apparel, electronics, toys, shoes and sporting goods) and provision of services (data entry, reservations, or business services) have moved internationally, becoming part of the 'global assembly line'. Examples range from data entry in Trinidad and Barbados to Caribbean apparel (Yelvington 1995; Gereffi 1999, 2001; Freeman, 2000), to programming and sales telework in Asia (Hoon et al., 1999; Mitter, 1999; Hafkin and Taggart, 2001; Kelkar, 2002). Many multinational corporations (MNCs) prefer lower-cost women workers, who they believe are unlikely to resist adverse conditions—an example of MNCs using the social construction of gender to their advantage. Women working in MNCs often consider this employment a better option than what is otherwise available (Beek, 2001). However, working conditions can be oppressive—characterized by long hours, a fast pace of work, few breaks, harassment, unsafe and unhealthy workplaces, and no opportunities for advancement (Ward, 1990; Abeywardene et al., 1994; Sivalingam 1994; AMRC, 1998). In addition, such employment is precarious. Since many families have become dependent on their female factory workers they, in turn, are also vulnerable.

When labor costs rise as workers seek to improve their conditions, MNCs combine several strategies to avoid higher costs: automating or using new technologies, suppressing worker demands, moving to other countries with lower labor costs, or establishing subcontracting networks with local manufacturers employing low-paid workers who can be terminated immediately (Pyle 1999). The latter are called more 'flexible' work relations (with the advantage going to the employer). These corporate strategies typically have adverse effects on women's well-being. When corporations automate or relocate, women lose jobs and must eke out income in the informal sector. When MNCs develop subcontracting networks with local factory owners, women produce the goods in small workshops or as home workers (Balakrishnan, 2002). Women undertake informal sector home work because they can combine it with home duties, but this makes organizing among these women workers very difficult. Home work pays much less, is erratic and conditions are even worse than in formal sector jobs, especially in times of global downturns (Bajaj 1999; Chen, M. et al., 1999).[2] Encouraging such subcontracting networks is in the clear interest of MNCs as the goods and services these workers produce are extremely low-cost, meaning that, in essence, informal sector workers subsidize formal sector employment (Portes, 1981).

Research on garment and electronics factories in Asia and other regions that hired new women workers from the 1970s to 1990 but have now closed, suggests that women returned to the household or informal sectors in domestic service and sex work and/or migrated to other countries (Beneria and Roldan, 1987; Ward, 1999; Silvey, 2000; Chen, M. A. et al., 2001; Parrenas, 2001c).

Finance. Financial globalization involves not only foreign direct investment by MNCs, but also buying/selling of stocks, international loans and aid, and links among multinational banks and microfinance organizations. As conditions for loans the IMF and WB typically require countries to adopt SAPs that mandate opening their borders to foreign trade and investment, privatizing state-owned industries and deregulating. They also pressure governments to reduce budget deficits by cutting government employment (often heavily female) and/or by reducing expenditures on social services (Todaro 2000). The IMF argues these policies will increase revenues needed for debt service. The effects of SAPs typically fall heavily on women, however, who try to maintain their families' standards of living despite decreased government expenditures on housing, health, education and food and fuel subsidies. Women take on added household responsibilities and seek additional extra income-earning activities, often in the informal sector to make up the difference. This is another example of an international institution using the social construction of gender roles to its advantage at the expense of the women involved. Across cultures, household responsibilities have been considered 'women's' work. Such obligations have been invisible and unpaid. Women ab-

sorb the costs of the shrinking state supports with larger workloads, higher stress levels and more work-related health hazards.

In servicing their debt, many countries in Latin America and Africa have become net exporters of capital (Bandarage, 1997) to the developed countries. This has required cuts in services to women and their families and less investment in income-generation opportunities in their own economies (Bello, 1994; Ismi 1998; Amin 2002). Thirty-three highly indebted poor countries in Africa paid US$3 in debt service to the North for every US$1 in development assistance (Ambrogi, 1999).

Some developing countries liberalized banking institutions and raised interest rates to attract capital, fueling an economic boom in East Asia. When bankers from developed countries suddenly withdrew their financial capital from East Asia in 1997, they ignored the costs to workers, particularly the most vulnerable—women workers in export factories that closed and migrant workers who were sent home (Nair, 1998; Tauli-Corpuz, 1998; Aslanbeigui and Summerfield 2000; Lim, J. Y., 2000). The IMF response to the East Asian crisis, calling for more liberalization, only made economic conditions worse because the crisis resulted from the extreme mobility of capital rather than debt-laden economies (Stiglitz, 2001, 2002).

Women's voices and lives have remained virtually absent from these policy discussions. Rather than incorporating women into their decisionmaking hierarchy and integrating gender perspectives into development policies, international financial institutions are advocating microfinance (microcredit) to address women's income-generation and poverty reduction needs (Mayoux, 2002). The institutionalization of microfinance through NGOs and state ministries has focused on women because of their putative high rates of repayment, but it rarely reaches the poorest women, e.g., female-headed households. NGOs form small savings and loan groups of women. Participants must save a small amount every week, take tiny loans to establish a small business activity such as raising poultry or crops, sewing or trading—all informal sector activities—and start immediate repayment of their loans.

Although much initial funding came from international donors, this has slowed as donors sought sustainability in microfinance operations (Mayoux, 2002). In seeking financial viability some of the larger NGOs involved in microfinance have started other businesses to finance their operations or established banks and mutual funds. The WB has started connecting multinational banks to NGOs as sources of loan funds (World Bank, 2000a, 2000b, 2001a). When the microfinance women pay interest due, they are often linked with global financial institutions. Such programs do not challenge or change the goals of the global financial system.

In short, although some women have benefited from globalization, many women have fewer choices and less control over their lives due to the spread of market processes and export-oriented development, developed countries' double-standard trade polices, the relentless cost-cutting strategies of MNCs and their production networks and the austerity requirements of financial institutions. Analytical and causal links exist between the spread of MNCs into different areas of the world and the use of SAPs, on the one hand, and increases in women's participation in the informal sector on the other hand. Poverty levels rise. For survival, many women must resort to earning a living as domestics or sex workers or run small businesses using microfinance. Large numbers of women must migrate internationally to find employment, often leaving their 'transnational' families behind (Lim, L. L. and Oishi, 1996; Hochschild, 2000; Hondagneu-Sotelo, 2000; Parrenas, 2001a, 2001b; Siddiqui, 2001).

Gendered Global Production Networks

The second way of looking at the effects of globalization on the gendered division of labor is via examining global production networks that are distinctly gendered (Pyle, 2001). The extent to which such networks have developed and the reasons for their emergence, however, have rarely been a central focus of globalization research. We look *simultaneously* at four gendered sectors that previous researchers have studied separately; sex work, domestic labor, export-oriented

production and microfinance.[3] These sectors typically consist of lower-income jobs or income-generation activities. Women constitute the majority of workers. By analyzing these four sectors together within the context of global changes, we can more fully understand the causal factors involved. We can also see how women move among sectors.

Over the last three decades, increasing numbers of women have become sex workers, maids, workers in export production, or microfinance recipients to earn incomes in the restructured global economy. Many must migrate domestically or internationally to obtain this work (Lim L. L. and Oishi, 1996; Curran and Saguy, 2001; Pyle, 2001). These 'industries' now span the globe, occurring in most areas of the developing world as well as throughout industrialized countries.

Despite their substantial economic importance to their countries, however, women in these sectors remain largely invisible in national income accounts. They are also missing in discussions by international power brokers (IMP, WB leaders) on how to stabilize the international economy and economically troubled nations. In contrast to this invisibility, however, governments and agencies utilize the existence of work in these sectors to their advantage when they create economic development strategies or try to cope with SAPs.

Although researchers have focused on women's roles in export-processing for over 25 years it is only more recently that women's roles in the sex industry as maids or domestics, or as microfinance participants have been more widely examined. This disproportionate attention to women's work in export factories has obscured how such labor constitutes only a small proportion of women's overall work. Many researchers and policy analysts have not recognized that women have always worked (Acevedo 1995; Misra, 2000). Much of women's paid work (as well as unpaid), however, takes place in the informal and household sectors.

Sex and domestic work and microfinance programs are particularly difficult to study because of problems obtaining accurate data regarding the numbers and experiences of women involved in these sectors. Governments do not systematically collect information on them; many activities take place in the underground economy. Research has shown that each sector is typically characterized by low wages, no benefits, long hours, no security, uncertainty and a lack of rights in their workplaces—all of which add to the vulnerability of women workers and constrain their work choices and agency.

Export Workers. Scholars have debated the costs and benefits of export work for women (Tiano, 1994; Ward and Pyle, 1995; Kabeer, 1997, 1999, 2000). Export factories have brought new workers into the labor force from homes, schools, agricultural work or domestic service. In the short run, many women gained wage income, increased mobility and greater power in household decision-making (regarding the timing of marriage, family planning and health care for themselves and their children).[4] Longer-term costs included adverse health effects from factory work and problems finding comparable work if factories close down or move. Some unemployed women have moved into other sectors, informal sector work in the sex industry, domestic service, construction and agriculture.

Sex Workers. The sex industry has grown internationally to provide entertainment and sexual services, often to serve tourists (Sangera, 1997; Kempadoo and Doezema, 1998; Lim, L. L. 1998; Pyle, 2001). International trafficking has become a lucrative industry in which formal and informal organizations move women and children locally and globally. Some women view sex work as another means to support themselves and their families.[5] Many women receive more wages than available in factories or domestic service. Some women and children, however, are drawn into the sex industry involuntarily. Sexual assaults by employers and family members have forced girls and women into sex work, particularly in societies that 'prize' virginity. Some may be deceived into relocating responding to ads and migrating internally and internationally they think, for jobs such as domestic or factory work that turn out to be forced sex work. Others are sold by family members or spouses into sex work.

Many factors have led to increased global sex trafficking (Kempadoo and Doezema, 1998; Raymond et al., 2002). There is a large male demand for sexual services which permeates many civilian societies and is particularly strong where there is a military presence. It is often augmented by racial myths and stereotypes that consider women from other countries more exotic and desirable. Economic policies such as SAPs have a particularly harsh impact on women, pushing many of them into informal sector activities (including sex work) to survive. Many of the most vulnerable are trafficked, especially from the Newly Independent States (NIS) and many developing countries.

Once in the sex industry, many women continue this work because of societal stigma, debts and migration of organized crime agents who constrain their movement into other sectors. The stigma surrounding sex work is so great in some cultures that, even if a woman wants to leave sex work her family members remind her of her past. Part of women's wages from sex work are garnished to repay debts to agents who have trafficked them and are used to pay off police government officials and organized crime. Even though sex workers may not want other women forced into the trade, some, organize for safe and secure working conditions as sex workers.

Domestic Workers. Domestic workers have entered the global economy in migrant worker streams from South and Southeast Asia to other Asian countries and the Middle East, from NIS to other parts of Europe, and from Latin America to North America (Lim L. L. and Oishi, 1996). Women have come to equal or outnumber men in out-migration across Southeast Asia (the Philippines, Indonesia, Thailand and Sri Lanka) (Lim, L. L. and Oishi, 1996).

Many migrant domestic workers move as undocumented workers through illegal recruitment agencies that hold women as debt hostages for their transportation and placement fees. Others enter countries as tourists but work as domestics. Yeoh et al., (1999) found that eight out of 10 Filipinas enter Singapore as tourists but work as domestics. Estimates of women migrant workers—documented and undocumented—exceed 1.5 million and 800,000 women go abroad per year. Government and international agencies can only estimate the total numbers and their remittances to home countries. Undocumented workers receive little protection, if any, from their governments.

Women migrant workers constitute a flexible source of wage labor for their families. As noted by Raghavan (1996: 3) 'the migration is often a family survival strategy in the face of negative effects of the structural adjustment programmes in their home countries'.

Some scholars have traced the global 'nanny chain' where relatively more affluent and educated women domestic workers from poor countries migrate to new industrializing or developed countries to work as domestic workers for middle- and upper-class women who work in formal sector jobs (Chin, 1997; Nair, 1998; Yeoh et al., 1999; Hochschild, 2000; Parrenas, 2000). As migrant workers, female domestic workers typically work (and live) in individual households where they are isolated and subject to employers demands. Their work conditions are unregulated and the problems they encounter include harassment (verbal, physical and sexual), poor living conditions (small quarters and lack of adequate food) and little time off. Conditions vary from country to country. For example, although maids in Hong Kong reported problems, they considered their work better than positions in Singapore or the Middle East (Constable, 1997).

Sending countries have become increasingly dependent on the remittances of migrant maids as they provide substantial amounts of foreign exchange for their home countries. For example, Sri Lankan migrant women remitted 60 billion rupees (US$880 million) from work in the Middle and Far East—60 percent came from registered housemaids (Anon, 1998).

Microfinance. Researchers and advocates have found that microfinance can have positive 'virtuous circle' effects and negative 'feminization of debt' effects on women's lives (Amin, R. et al., 1998; Karim, M. R. and Osada, 1998; Khandker, 1998; Haq, 1999; Rahman, A., 1999b; Kabeer, 2001; Pearl and Phillips, 2001; Khondkar, 2002; Mayoux, 2002; Yunus, 2002). Informally, some critics have called microfinance the welfare pro-

gram of neoliberalism, where women borrow small amounts of money and run small businesses for their survival rather than receiving support from the state (Karides, 2002a, 2002b). For example, development planners in Trinidad assumed that African-Trinidadian women could combine multiple roles of microfinance and caretaking, thereby replacing social safety nets. Microfinance offers few possibilities for larger loans to build enterprises that generate more than subsistence income.

Although the interest rates charged to the women have been lower than money-lenders' rates, additional fees for the group, NGO staff overheads and other expenses have often raised the total costs to participants to relatively high levels (Siddiqui, 2000). Many NGOs have remained outside government regulation over their microfinance operations and business activities, and instead answer to microfinance trade groups and/or donors.

During the early pioneering days of microfinance in Bangladesh, the Grameen Bank and other organizers also provided a variety of social change services such as non-formal education, birth control and business training (Mizan, 1994). The training activities provided were thought to enhance women's human capital as well as social capital (Anderson et al., 2002). Many of these services have been dropped however, because of opposition from religious leaders and shifting priorities. Some have found that credit-plus programs have greater impacts on women than credit alone (Khondkai, 2002; Mahmud, 2002); however, microfinance provides just one component for making changes in women's lives and relationships. Given the lucrative overhead charges, even small NGOs have offered microfinance; however, with less success and lower repayment rates.

The Sectors Together. Since women in these four sectors are present-day workers and also reproduce the next generation of workers, conditions in these gendered production networks affect growth possibilities in the future as well as impact the current economic condition of households and nations.

The economic and political bases underlying the growth in these sectors are critical to understand because solutions to the problems women encounter in all four types of jobs must include recognizing and addressing the underlying causes. We need to examine the reasons why women increasingly work in these sectors and why they often migrate to do so. We also must analyze the institutions and groups with vested interests in having them so employed.

Each of the global trends identified earlier has fostered the increase in women's employment in these four specific sectors. The increased reliance on markets globally the widespread adoption of the export-oriented development strategy and enormous financial flows provide a favorable climate for each of these 'industries.' In addition, the strategies of MNCs and the requirements of SAPs can push women into sectors such as these. Times of economic crises magnify the impacts of these trends and have particularly devastating effects on women-headed households.

Many individuals and households view decisions to become a sex worker, a maid, an export production worker and/or a microfinance participant (or some combination) as rational choices, given the limited options they face within the world economy. A woman (and her household) may consider these types of work (and the needed migration) as a necessary income-earning strategy in spite of the risks associated with such jobs.

The governments' roles in maintaining these sectors are also related to these dimensions of globalization. Many governments have tried to satisfy both the demands of international institutions (such as the IMF, WB or MNCs) and some of the needs of their citizens for income. As a result many national governments have been pushed into taking the following steps that foster these four work sectors:

- Attracting MNCs (this has been the most favored growth strategy and promotes export-processing jobs);

- Promoting their tourism industries (this has been the second most favored

growth sector in the last decade and often leads to sex tourism);

- Exporting surplus labor to other countries (here women typically become maids/domestics or sex workers); and

- Adopting microfinance programs that provide small loans.

Many countries place great economic importance on these four sectors. Governments take actions that support each of these sectors, risky and insecure as they are for women because they provide employment, incomes financial flows and often foreign exchange. Such actions also serve the interests of powerful institutions that national governments have to accommodate. International financial institutions, whose SAPs have pushed women into these sectors, have kept silent about injustices and inequities in such work.

Country Example: Bangladesh

The case of Bangladesh illustrates the importance of these sectors to the nation, the vested interests of the government and the dilemmas that arise. Bangladesh has been one of the poorest countries in the world since its independence in 1971. It remains dependent on donors and their latest structural adjustment liberalization, privatization, or poverty reduction plans. During the 1980s, however, the Bangladeshi government pursued strategies of (1) export-processing in ready-made garments to generate development; (2) promoting the migration of Bangladeshi men and later women to generate foreign revenues and remittances; (3) accommodating NGOs and activists who established microfinance programs that have now spread across the world; and (4) overlooking the widespread trafficking of women. Even so Bangladesh has only started to alleviate poverty; the process is fragile. Progress may be hindered by the country's overwhelming dependence on ready-made garment exports (76 percent of Bangladesh's foreign revenues come from garment exports), changes in trade regimes now and in 2005, and the global economic downturn.

With respect to export-processing, Bangladesh became known for the rapid growth of its exports of ready-made garments. This growth was based on its competitive advantages under the MPA (Multi Fiber Agreement) and the migration of millions of women and girls to work in these factories in Dhaka (Paul-Majumder and Zohir, 1995; Kabeer, 1997, 1999, 2000; Paul-Majumder and Begum, 2000; Feldman, 2001; Kibria, 2001; Ward et al., 2002). The rise of garment industries transformed rural to urban migration as women began migrating to cities. It altered marriage patterns and the socioeconomic position of millions of young women and their families, as young women were sent to work and provide income for their families rather than being married at a very young age. It also generated women's activism (Zaman, 2001). Given the tough and sometimes dangerous working conditions, women garment workers averaged five years of employment before quitting because of impaired health (CAFOD 1998; Karim M. I., 2000).

Bangladeshi garment workers have experienced the rollercoaster of benefits and costs that global restructuring brought to their country through changes in specific trade agreements. Before the US Trade Development Act 2000, the US received 46 percent of its apparel from Bangladesh. This Act, however, gave duty-free access and trade preference to African and Caribbean countries, causing a diversion of garment orders from Bangladesh to these countries (Karim, S., 2001). Many garment factories closed and women workers became unemployed as a result (Rahman M., 2001; Rahman F., 2002).[6] NGOs, such as Karmajibi Nari, and several labor union groups, e.g., BGWUF (Bangladesh Garment Workers Union Federation), have sought to organize women workers around security and working conditions amid changes in the global economy.

To find employment for surplus agricultural labor, the Bangladeshi government promoted the migration of men to the Middle East and Southeast Asian countries such as Malaysia to work in construction and low-wage service sectors. With the downturn of these industries after the Gulf War in the early 1990s some Bangladeshi women entered the international migrant worker circuit, in part to pay off debts (Rahman, A., 1999a; Yeoh et al., 1999). Increasingly, Bangladeshi women engage in short-term migration to the Middle East and Asia for factory work obtained through private employment agencies, while other women migrate unofficially as maids or nurses. Migration agencies have no record of their movements (Siddiqui, 2001). This dynamic is very problematic. Women pursue these options because they provide income-earning opportunities, but can experience rampant abuses (Islam, A. S., 2002). The government has responded to security concerns of migrant women by banning some women's migration for domestic service and nursing work (Islam, T., 1998). This leads to further problems. The country has become dependent on foreign remittances for 25 percent of its foreign exchange and for the support of families who remain in Bangladesh (Hadi, 2001; Siddiqui and Abrar, 2001).[7] Prospects for work opportunities abroad and remittances decreased during the global downturn. Returning women have difficulties finding comparable work (Siddiqui, 2001). Some women migrant workers recently formed a new NGO, the Bangladesh Women Migrant Workers Association, to promote training for women migrants and re-entry among women returnees.

Given the norms of *purdah* (female seclusion) and limited education for females, domestic service has been one of few work options. In urban areas domestic servants consist of younger poor women and recent migrants displaced by natural disasters, homelessness and consequences of SAPs. In addition, middle-persons traffick girls and young women, deceiving poor parents with false promises of marriage, and put these females into domestic service in urban areas and other countries (Hossain, 2000; Khan, 2001). Live-in servants frequently endure harsh working conditions (15–16 hours per day), physical and sexual abuse, and no state regulation of working conditions or wages. Sexually abused servants or daughters have been trafficked or shifted into sex work after they escaped from their homes to the urban areas and on to Pakistan and India (Ward et al., 2002). Sex work and trafficking have a long history in Bangladesh. The government pays intermittent attention to the problems. An NGO, Shoishob, has provided advocacy, late afternoon school programs and outreach workers to many young and older domestic workers.

Providing small loans to millions of women, Bangladesh women's microfinance programs served as models to the rest of the world (Mizan, 1994). Cross-sectional studies suggested that women have high levels of loan repayments, and they reported improved standards of living, decision-making, household income and choices over their fertility, housing and their children's lives (Hashemi et al., 1996; Khandker, 1998; Steele et al., 1998; Kabeer, 2001). Most women wanted larger loans to expand their businesses (Siddiqui, 2000). Members of the NGO microfinance programs needed five to seven years of participation before they began to move from poverty (Khandker, 1998). However, some women became enmeshed in a 'spiral of debt' as some NGOs kept loaning them money to avoid defaults or combining memberships in several microfinance programs (Khan, 2001; 233; Khondkar, 2002; Mayoux 2002). Many women had small rickshaw or sewing businesses that teetered on the edge of solvency with few safety nets.

Meanwhile, many donor and international institutions have questioned the sustainability of the microfinance programs. Some programs have experienced lower repayment rates, owing to multiple microfinance NGOs and dropouts. The Grameen Banks loan repayment rate has dropped to 72 percent (Abedin, 2001). Other microfinance NGOs have little capital and higher default rates of 20–30 percent (Rahman, S. M., 2000; Siddiqui, 2000). From 1998–2000, more program participants have dropped out than joined (Star Business Report, 2001). Some NGOs have responded to dwindling donor funds for microfinance by developing business activities, funded in part through the interest payments of the small loan holders and their savings. The Grameen Bank has stopped accepting donor funds and finances its programs out of deposits and other enterprises such as a mutual fund (Yunus, 2002). The government has proposed taxing and regulating the business activities of microfinance NGOs, but BRAC (an NGO established in Bangladesh in the early 1970s) and others have argued that such businesses provide the ongoing funds for microfinance (Ali, 2002; Islam, M. T., 2002).

Implications and Conclusions

When we see how these four sectors can be implicitly or explicitly central to a country's development strategy, we can understand the magnitude of the problems in devising strategies for change that improve women's lives (and men's and children's). These politically and economically important sectors provide employment and some income for many people. As a result they diminish the social unrest that can accompany severe poverty and undermine or overthrow governments. Although development economists have characterized this informal sector work as a temporary solution during the transition to an industrialized economy, over time, informal income-earning endeavors have become institutionalized in some countries' development plans. Our knowledge of this helps us counteract 'gender-blind' government rhetoric that reliance on work in such sectors is short-term or that governments seek to protect the rights of their citizens.

Governments pay less heed to the concerns of women workers in the widespread MNC subcontracting networks because governments seek to provide hospitable environments to MNCs. Governments have failed to critically examine sex work or domestic employment because income from this work is often essential for the survival of poor families. Women's international migration to work in these sectors provides governments a flow of remittances that women send back to their families. This foreign exchange services the debt or buys imports. Therefore, given the international political economy, the very institution women might seek assistance from in combating the problems of work in these sectors (i.e., their own government) has vested interests in the existence of these industries. We doubt that governments will adopt and enforce policies that address inequities in the gendered division of labor.

Through our analyses, we can see clear linkages between the key global trends discussed earlier, women's increased presence in these sectors and women's disadvantaged status. We can recognize similar issues, problems and concerns across the sectors and develop a more realistic view about the difficulties in organizing for change given the powerful institutions that have vested interests in the existence of these types of jobs (national governments, MNCs, the IMF and WB). Clearly, during this latest period of globalization, institutions on many levels—international and national—have policies that foster the gendered division of labor, where women have jobs with low income and often encounter adverse working conditions.

Given this recasting of gender and work during global restructuring, we can, however, address the problems of the gendered effects of globalization in two ways that can be overlapping and mutually reinforcing: by researching the issues more effectively and by developing creative and realistic broad-based strategies for change that will ensure women's rights and more equality. Within this revised understanding of the global context, we can draw on new developments that provide the basis for positive change for women in the future such as challenges to existing disciplinary paradigms and new multidisciplinary approaches, new concepts (such as caring labor) that are being operationalized, new methodologies (such as gender budgets), and more case studies and multilevel analyses.

Notes

This article draws on a June 2002 presentation by Jean L. Pyle (Pyle, 2002). An earlier version was presented at the 15th World Congress of Sociology/ International Sociological Association, Brisbane, Australia, July 2002. Travel support for Ward was provided in part by an NSF grant to the American Sociological Association. We would like to thank three anonymous reviewers and Joya Misra. In addition, Jean would like to acknowledge the support of the late Susan Smith DeMichele and Kathryn would like to recognize that of the late Rachel Rosenfeld.

1. There is a double standard and cost inefficiency. Developed countries and financial institutions have encouraged developing countries to liberalize and open up their markets while maintaining their own high import tariffs. The costs of these tariffs on goods from developing countries are greater than the foreign aid these developing countries receive from the developed countries.

2. For example, Filipina home workers lost their income-generating activities during the East Asia financial crisis (Pablo, 1999).

3. Pyle (2001) begins this more comprehensive approach by examining three of these sectors together: sex work domestics and export-processing. Ward (1999) added in microfinance and its linkages to international finance and debt.

4. Although wages in some factories may be slightly higher than alternative jobs in Java rural families essentially subsidized MNCs and facilitated lower wages for women workers (Wolf, 1992). This was because the daughters working in factories lived at home, enabling the MNCs to pay them less than subsistence wages.

5. Space does not let us discuss the various positions that differing groups have taken on sex work as work and the 'choice' issue. Readers can consult some of the international websites on sex work: Commercial Sex Information Service, *www.walnet.org/csis/*; on trafficking: Coalition Against Trafficking in Women (CATW) *www.catwinternational.org/* and the Protection Project, *www.protectionproject.org/main2.htm*; or sex trafficking reports (Human Rights Watch 1993; Human Rights Watch-Asia, 1995; Foundation of Women's Forum, 1998; Kempadoo and Doezema, 1998; Coalition Against Trafficking in Women (CATW), 1999; Doezema, 2000; UNIFEM, 1999; Shamim, 2000; US Department of State, 2002).

6. This legislation also added rules of origin for input fabrics and knits that gave preference to US and Caribbean textile and knit producers.

    Although the US granted trade and tariff concessions to allies in the 'war against terrorism', e.g., India and Pakistan, Bangladesh has yet to receive any trade concessions despite stated willingness for US overflights and landing privileges. Ironically the woman prime minister of Bangladesh, Khaleda Zia, has repeatedly stressed that garment factories have led to the 'empowerment' of Bangladeshi women as a rationale for trade concessions. Despite the Bush administration's renewed interest in the position of Afghani women, such pleas for women's empowerment have failed to bring any trade policy changes. Many observers think that the US government has tied gas exports from Bangladesh to trade concessions (Ward et al., 2002).

7. In 2001, remittances constituted US$2 billion, over 4 percent of GDP (UNB, 2002).

References

Abedin S. Z. (2001). 'Recovery Problems Hit Grameen Bank,' *News From Bangladesh*: *http://www.bangladesh-web.com/news/apr/23/ev24n546.htm#541*.

Abeywardene, J., de Alwis, R. Jayasena, A., Jayaweera, S. and Sanmugam, T. (1994). *Export Processing Zones in Sri Lanka: Economic Impact and Social Issues.* Geneva: ILO.

Acevedo L. D. A. (1995). 'Feminist Inroads in the Study of Women's Work and Development,' in C. E. Bose and E. Acosta-Belen (eds.). *Women in the Latin American Development Process* pp. 65–98. Philadelphia, PA: Temple University Press.

Alcaron-Gonzalez, D. and McKinley, T. (1999). 'The Adverse Effects of Structural Adjustment on Working Women in Mexico,' *Latin American Perspectives* 26 (3): 103–101.

Ali, S. (2002). 'Please Leave NGOs Beyond Tax Burden,' *The Daily Star,* at: *www.dailystarnews.com/2000206/2000217/n2061711.htm#BODY2061715.*

Ambrogi, T. (1999). 'Jubilee 2000 and the Campaign for Debt Cancellation; Excerpt of Edited Article from National Catholic Reporter,' *Third World Resurgence* No. 107: July; at: *www.twnside.org.sg/souths/twn/title/thomas-cn.htm.*

Amin, R., Becker, S. and Bayes, A. (1998). 'NGO-Promoted Microcredit Programs and Women's Empowerment in Rural Bangladesh: Quantitative and Qualitative Evidence,' *Journal of Developing Areas* Winter; 221–36.

Amin, S. (2002). 'Africa: Living on the Fringe,' *Monthly Review* 53 (10): 41–50.

AMRC (Asia Monitor Resource Center). (1998). *We in the Zone: Women Workers in Asia's Export Processing Zones* Hong Kong: AMRC.

Anderson C. L., Locker, L. and Nugent, R. A. (2002). 'Microcredit, Social Capital, and Common Pool Resources,' *World Development* 30 (3): 95–105.

Anon. (1998). 'Lessons From the Asian Meltdown,' *Third World Traveler/Multinational Monitor Magazine* (Jan./Feb.); at: *thirdworldtraveler.com/IMF_WB/AsianMeltdown_MNM.html.*

Aslanbeigui, N. and Summerfield, G. (2000). 'The Asian Crisis Gender and the International Financial Architecture,' *Feminist Economics* 6 (3): 81–103.

Bajaj, M. (1999). *Invisible Workers, Visible Contribution: A Study of Homebased Women Workers in Five Sectors across South Asia.* Cambridge, MA: WIEGO; at: *www.wiego.org/main/publi2.shtml.*

Balakrishnan, R., ed. (2002). *The Hidden Assembly Line: Gender Dynamics of Subcontracted Work in a Global Economy.* Bloomfield, CT: Kumarian Press.

Bandarage, A. (1997). *Women, Population and Global Crisis: A Political Economic Analysis.* London: Zed Books.

Barndt, D. (2002). *Tangled Routes: Women, Work, and Globalization on the Tomato Trail.* Lanham, MD: Rowman and Littlefield.

Barrientos, S. (1997). 'The Hidden Ingredient: Female Labour in Chilean Fruit Exports,' *Bulletin of Latin American Research* 16 (1): 71–81.

Bee, A. (2000). 'Globalization, Grapes and Gender: Women's Work in Traditional and Agro-Export Production in Northern Chile,' *The Geographical Journal* 166 (32): 255–65.

Beek, K. A. V. (2001) 'Maquiladoras: Exploitation or Emancipation? An Overview of the Situation of Maquiladora Workers in Honduras,' *World Development* 29 (9): 1553–67.

Bello, W. (1994). 'Global Economic Counterrevolution: (How Northern Economic Warfare Devastates the South),' in K. Danaher (ed.) *50 Years is Enough: The Case Against the World Bank and the International Monetary Fund.* San Francisco: Global Exchange at: *thirdworldtraveler.com/IMF_WB/counterrev_50YIE.html.*

Beneria, L. (1995). 'Toward a Greater Integration of Gender in Economics,' *World Development* 23 (11): 1839–50.

——. (1999). 'Globalization, Gender and the Davos Man,' *Feminist Economics* 5 (3): 61–83.

Beneria, L. and Feldman, S. eds. (1992). *Unequal Burden: Economic Crises, Persistent Poverty, and Women's Work.* Boulder, CO: Westview Press.

Beneria, L. and Roldan, M. (1987). *The Crossroads of Class and Gender.* Chicago, IL: University of Chicago Press.

Bergeron, S. (2001). 'Political Economy Discourses of Globalization and Feminist Politics,' *Signs* 26 (4): 983–1006.

Bradshaw, Y., Noonan, R. Gash, L. and Buchman, Sershen, C. (1993). 'Borrowing against the Future: Children and Third World Indebtedness,' *Social Forces* 71 (3): 629–56.

Buchmann, C. (1996). 'The Debt Crisis, Structural Adjustment and Women's Education,' *International Journal of Comparative Studies* 37 (1/2): 5–30.

CAFOD. (1998). *The Asian Garment Industry and Globalization.* London: CAFOD; at: *www.cafod.org.uk/garment_industry.htm.*

Chen, M., Sebstad, J. and O'Connell, L. (1999). 'Counting the Invisible Workforce: The Case of Homebased Workers,' *World Development* 27 (3): 603–10.

Chen, M. A. Jhabvala, R. and Lund, F. (2001) 'Supporting Workers in the Informal Economy: A Policy Framework,' ILO Task Force on the Informal Economy; at: *www.wiego.org/textonly/publi1.html.*

Chin, C. B. N. (1997) 'Walls of Silence and Late Twentieth Century Representations of the Foreign Female Domestic Worker: The Case of Filipino and Indonesian Female Servants in Malaysia,' *International Migration Review* 31 (2): 353–85.

Coalition Against Trafficking in Women (CATW). (1999). 'Declaration of Rights for Women in Conditions of Sex Trafficking and Prostitution,' *Re/Productions,* at: *www.hsph.harvard.edu/Organizations/healthnet/SAsia/repro2/DECLARATION_OF_RIGHTS_CATW.html.*

Constable, N. (1997). *Maid to Order in Hong Kong: Stories of Filipina Workers.* Ithaca, NY: Cornell University Press.

Curran, S. R. and Saguy, A. C. (2001). 'Migration and Cultural Change: A Role for Gender and Social Networks?' *Journal of International Women's Studies.* June; at: *www.bridgew.edu/DEPTS/ARTSCNCE/JIWS/June0l/Curran.pdf.*

Doezema, J. (2000). 'Loose Women or Lost Women? The Re-Emergence of the Myth of White Slavery in Contemporary Discourses of "Trafficking in Women,"' *Gender Issues* 18 (1): 23–50.

Dolan, C. (2001). 'The "Good Wife": Struggles over Resources in the Kenyan Horticultural Sector.' *The Journal of Development Studies* 37 (3): 39–70.

Dunaway, W. (2001). 'The Double Register of History: Situating the Forgotten Woman and Her Household in Capitalist Commodity Chains,' *Journal of World-Systems Research* VII (1): 2–29, at: *csf.colorado.edu/jwsr.*

Durano, M. F. B. (2002). *Gender Issues in International Trade.* Washington, DC: International Gender and Trade Network; at: *www.genderandtrade.net/Archives/Marina%27s%20paper.htm.*

Elson, D. (1995). 'Male Bias in Macroeconomics: The Case of Structural Adjustment,' in D. Elson (ed.) *Male Bias in the Development Process* pp. 164–190. Manchester: Manchester University Press.

Fall, Y. (1998). 'Promoting Sustainable Human Development Rights for Women in Africa'. *WIDE Bulletin* (Network Women in Development Europe) 9 Feb.; at: *www.twnside.org.sg/souths/twn/title/africa-cn.htm.*

Feldman, S. (2001). 'Exploring Theories of Patriarchy: A Perspective from Contemporary Bangladesh,' *Signs* 26 (4): 1097–1127.

Fontana, M. and Wood, A. (2000). 'Modeling the Effects of Trade on Women, at Work and at Home'. *World Development* 28 (7): 1173–90.

Foundation of Women's Forum. (1998). *Trafficking in Women for the Purpose of Sexual Exploitation.* Stockholm: Foundation of Women's Forum.

Freeman, C. (2000). *High Tech and High Heels in the Global Economy: Women Work, and Pink Collar Identities in the Caribbean.* Durham, NC: Duke University Press.

Gereffi, G. (1999). 'International Trade and Industrial Upgrading in the Apparel Commodity Chain,' *Journal of International Economics* 48 (1): 37–70.

——. (2001). 'Shifting Governance Structures in Global Commodity Chains with Special Reference to the Internet', *The American Behavioral Scientist* 44 (10): 1616–1637.

Green, C. (1998). 'The Asian Connection: The US-Caribbean Apparel Circuit and a New Model of Industrial Relations'. *Latin American Research Review* 33 (3): 7–47.

Hadi, A. (2001). 'International Migration and the Change of Women's Position among the Left-Behind in Rural Bangladesh'. *International Journal of Population Geography* 7 (1): 53–61.

Hafkin, N. and Taggart, N. (2001). *Gender, Information Technology, and Developing Countries: An Analytic Study.* Washington, DC: Academy for Educational Development (AED)/USAID; at: *learnlink.aed.org/Publications/Gender_Book/executive_summary/1gender_foreword.htm.*

Haq, F. (1999). 'Microcredit Reaches More Poor Women'. *South-North Development Monitor*, at: *www.twnside.org.sg/title/micro-cn.htm.*

Hashemi, S., Schuler, S. R. and Riley, A. (1996). 'Rural Credit Programs and Women's Empowerment in Bangladesh,' *World Development* 24 (4): 635–53.

Hochschild, A. R. (2000). 'The Nanny Chain,' *The American Prospect* 32–6.

Hondagneu-Sotelo, P. (2000). 'Feminism and Migration,' *Annals of the American Academy of Political and Social Science* 57: 107–120.

Hoon, C. S., Ng, C. and Mitter, S. (1999). *Teleworking in Malaysia: A Primer.* Maastricht: The United Nations University Institute for New Technologies (UNU/INTECH); at: *www.intech.unu.edu/research/past-research/monitoring-impact-442/monitoring-impact-442.htm.*

Hossain, F. I. (2000). 'A View of Asia's Hapless Children: Save Child Workers,' *Independent*, at: *independent-bangladesh.com/news/aug/25/25082000pd.htm#25082001.*

Human Rights Watch. (1993). *A Modern Form of Slavery Trafficking of Burmese Women and Girls into Brothels in Thailand.* New York: Human Rights Watch.

Human RightsWatch-Asia. (1995). *Rape For Profit: Trafficking of Nepali Girls and Women to India's Brothels.* New York: Human RightsWatch-Asia.

Ilahi, N. (2000). 'The Intra-Household Allocation of Time and Tasks: What Have We Learnt from the Empirical Literature?,' *Gender and Development*, Working Paper Series, No 13; at: *www.worldbank.org/gender/prr.*

Islam, A. S. (2002). 'Migration and Empowerment of Women in Bangladesh,' unpublished master's research paper. Southern Illinois University.

Islam, M. T. (2002). 'Tax the NGOs!,' *The Daily Star*: at: *www.dailystarnews.com/200206/200214/n2061411.htm#BODY2061412.*

Islam, T. (1998). 'Population-Bangladesh: Ban on Export of Nurses Criticised,' *IPS World News*; at: *www.oneworld.org/ips2/aug98/10_18_027.html.*

Ismi, A. (1998). 'Plunder with a Human Face,' *From Z Magazine* Feb.; at: *thirdworldtraveler.com/IMF_WB/PlunderHumanFace.html.*

Joekes, S. (1987). *Women in the World Economy—An Instraw Study.* Oxford: Oxford University Press.

Kabeer, N. (1997). 'Women, Wages and Intra-Household Power Relations in Urban Bangladesh,' *Development and Change* 28: 261–302.

——. (1999). 'Resources Agency Achievements: Reflections on the Measurement of Women's Empowerment,' *Development and Change* 30 (3): 435–64.

——. (2000). *The Power to Choose: Bangladeshi Women and Labour Market Decisions in London and Dhaka.* London: Verso.

——. (2001). 'Conflicts over Credit: Re-Evaluating the Empowerment Potential of Loans to Women in Rural Bangladesh,' *World Development* 29 (1): 63–84.

Karides, M. (2002a). 'Micro-Enterprises: Modernization's Failure and Globalization's Social Safety Net,' unpublished paper: Florida Atlantic University.

——. (2002b). 'Whose Solution Is It? The Expansion of Micro-enterprise Development in the Caribbean Context,' unpublished paper, Florida Atlantic University.

Karim, M. I. (2000). 'Female Migration and Changes in Urban Social Dynamics of Bangladesh,' paper presented at the Urban Futures 2000 International Conference Johannesburg; at: *www.wits.ac.za/fac/arts/urbanf/papers/karim.htm.*

Karim, M. R. and Osada, M. (1998). 'Dropping Out: An Emerging Factor in the Success of Microcredit-Based Poverty Alleviation Programs,' *Developing Economies* 36 (3): 257–288.

Karim, S. (2001). 'Attacks in US Dash Bangladesh's Hopes for Export Recovery,' *The Daily Star*, at: *www.dailystarnews.com/200109/200117/n1091705.htm#BODY1091701*.

Kelkar, G. (2002). 'Special Issue: Women and Digital Divide,' *Gender, Technology and Development* 6 (1).

Kempadoo, K. and Doezema, J. eds. (1998). *Global Sex Workers: Rights, Resistance and Redefinition*. New York: Routledge.

Khan, S. R. (2001). *The Socio-Legal Status of Bangli Women in Bangladesh Dhaka*: UPL.

Khandker, S. (1998). *Fighting Poverty with Microcredit: Experience in Bangladesh*. New York: World Bank/Oxford University Press.

Khondkar, M. (2002). *Women's Empowerment in Bangladesh: Credit is not a Panacea*. London: One World Action; at: *www.oneworldaction.org/genderandmicrofinance.html#asia*.

Kibria, N. (2001). 'Becoming a Garment Worker: The Mobilisation of Women into the Garment Factories of Bangladesh,' in R. Sobhan and N. Khundker (eds.). *Globalisation and Gender: Changing Patterns of Women's Employment in Bangladesh*. Dhaka: UPL/CPD.

King, E. and Mason, A. (2001). *Engendering Development: Through Gender Equality in Rights Resources, Voice*. New York/Washington, DC/New York: Oxford University Press/World Bank.

Lim, J. Y. (2000). 'The Effects of the East Asian Crisis on the Employment of Women and Men: The Philippine Case,' *World Development* 28 (7): 1285–306.

Lim, L. L. ed. (1998). *The Sex Sector: The Economic and Social Bases of Prostitution in Southeast Asia*. Geneva: International Labour Office.

Lim, L. L. and Oishi, N. (1996). *International Labour Migration of Asian Women: Distinctive Characteristics and Policy Concerns*. Geneva: ILO.

McMichael, P. (2000). *Development and Social Change: A Global Perspective*, 2nd ed. Thousand Oaks, CA: Pine Forge.

Mahmud, P. (2002). 'Microcredit: Empowering Women in Bangladesh,' *The Daily Star*, at: *www.dailystarnews.com/200204/200223/n2042309.htm#BODY2042303*.

Marchand, M. and Runyan, A. S. (2000). 'Introduction: Feminist Sightings of Global Restructuring: Conceptualizations and Reconceptualizations,' in M. Marchand and A. S. Runyan (eds.) *Gender and Global Restructuring: Sightings Sites, and Resistance*. pp. 1–22. London: Routledge.

Mayoux, L. (2002). 'Women's Empowerment or Feminisation of Debt? Towards a New Agenda in African Micro-Finance,' paper presented at One World Action Conference London.

Miller, C. and Razavi, S. eds. (1998). *Missionaries and Mandarins: Feminist Engagement with Development Institutions*. London: Intermediate Technology Publications/UNRISD.

Misra, J. (2000). 'Gender and the World-System: Engaging the Feminist Literature on Development,' in T. D. Hall (ed.) *A World-Systems Reader: New Perspectives on Gender, Urbanism, Cultures, Indigenous Peoples and Ecology* pp. 105–130. Lanham, MD: Rowman and Littlefield.

Mitter, S. (1999). *Telework and Teletrade in India: Implications for Employment, Trade and Social Equity*. Maastricht: United Nations University Institute for New Technologies: at: *www.intech.unu.edu/research/past-research/teleworking-india-444/scope-research.pdf*.

Mizan, A. N. (1994). *In Quest of Empowerment: The Grameen Bank Impact on Women's Power and Status*. Dhaka: University Press.

Nair, S. (1998). 'Migrants in a Maelstrom,' *The World Today* March: 66–68.

Oxfam. (2002). *Rigged Rules and Double Standards: Trade, Globalisation and the Fight Against Poverty*. Oxford: Oxfam/Make Trade Fair Campaign; at: *www.maketradefair.com*.

Pablo, A. (1999). 'Invisible Workers Fail to Escape Crisis,' *Businessworld* 8 Feb.

Parrenas, R. S. (2000). 'Migrant Filipina Domestic Workers and the International Division of Reproductive Labor,' *Gender and Society* 14 (4): 560–580.

——. (2001a). 'Mothering from a Distance: Emotions, Gender, and Inter-Generational Relations in Filipino Transnational Families,' *Feminist Studies* 27 (2): 361–390.

——. (2001b). 'Transgressing the Nation-State: The Partial Citizenship and "Imagined (Global) Community" of Migrant Filipina Domestic Workers,' *Signs* 26 (4): 1129–1154.

——. (2001c). *Servants of Globalization: Women Migration and Domestic Work*. Palo Alto, CA: Stanford University Press.

Paul-Majumder, P. and Begum, A. (2000). *The Gender Imbalances in the Export Oriented Garment Industry in Bangladesh*. Policy Research Report on Gender and Development, Working Paper Series, No. 12. Washington, DC: World Bank.

Paul-Majumder, P. and Zohir, S. C. (1995). 'Empowering Women: Wage Employment in the Garment Industry,' *Empowerment* 2: 83–112.

Pearl, D. and Phillips, M. M. (2001). 'Small Change: Bank that Pioneered Loans for the Poor Hits Repayment Snag—"Microcredit" Icon Grameen Faces Questions as Rate of Delinquencies Rises—Mrs Begum's Missing Cow,' *Wall Street Journal* 27 Nov: A1.

Portes, A. (1981). *Labour, Class, and the International System*. London: Academic Press.

Preibisch, K., Herrejon, G. R. and Wiggins, S. (2002). 'Defending Food Security in a Free-Market Economy: The Gendered Dimensions of Restructuring in Rural Mexico,' *Human Organization* 61 (1): 68–79.

Pyle, J. L. (1998). 'Women's Employment and Multinational Corporation Networks,' in N. Stromquist (ed.) *Women in the Third World: An Encyclopedia of Contemporary Issues*, pp. 341–350. New York: Garland.

——. (1999). 'Third World Women and Global Restructuring,' in J. Chafetz (ed.) *Handbook of the Sociol-*

ogy of Gender, pp. 81–104. New York: Kluwer Academic/Plenum Publishers.

——. (2001). 'Sex, Maids, and Export Processing: Risks and Reasons for Gendered Global Production Networks,' *The International Journal of Politics Culture and Society* 15 (1): 55–76.

——. (2002). 'Globalization, Public Policy, and the Gendered Division of Labor,' paper presented at Third International Congress on Women, Work and Health, Stockholm.

Quisumbing, A. R. and Maluccio, J. A. (1999). 'Intrahousehold Allocation and Gender Relations: New Empirical Evidence,' *Gender and Development* Working Paper Series, No 2; at: *www.worldbank.org/gender/prr*.

Raghavan, C. (1996). *Asian Female Migrant Workers Require Protection*. Singapore: Third World Network; at: *www.twnside.org.sg/title/ilo1-cn.htm*.

Rahman, A. (1999a). 'Micro-Credit Initiatives for Equitable and Sustainable Development: Who Pays?,' *World Development* 27 (1): 67–82.

——. (1999b). *Women and Microcredit in Rural Bangladesh*. Boulder, CO: Westview Press.

Rahman, F. (2002). 'Garment Workers and Female Workforce Empowerment in Bangladesh,' paper presented at the meeting of the Midwest Sociological Society, Milwaukee, WI.

Rahman, M. (2001). 'Emerging Concerns in Bangladesh's Export Sector: A Wake Up Call,' *Financial Express* (Dhaka) 30 Nov./Centre for Policy Dialogue; at: *www.cpd-bangladesh.org/art_pro.htm*.

Rahman, S. M. (2000). 'Should the Authorities Oversee Microfinance Plan of NGOs? Pt. 1 & 2,' *The Independent* 2 Feb; at: *independent-bangladesh.com/news/feb/02/02022000pd.htm#A02022002*.

Raymond, J., D'Cunha, J., Dzuhayatin, S. R., Hynes, H. P., Rodriguez, Z. R., and Santos, A. (2002). *A Comparative Study of Women Trafficked in the Migration Process: Patterns Profiles and Health Consequences of Sexual Exploitation in Five Countries (Indonesia, the Philippines, Thailand, Venezuela and the United States)*. Coalition Against Trafficking in Women; at: *action.web.ca/home/catw/attach/CATW%20Comparative%20Study%202002.pdf*.

Sangera, J. (1997). 'In the Belly of the Beast,' discussion paper for the South Asia Regional Consultation on Prostitution, 17–18 February, Bangkok.

Sassen, S. (2000). 'Women's Burden: Counter-Geographies of Globalization and the Feminization of Survival,' *Journal of International Affairs* 53 (2): 503–524.

Schurman, R. (2001). 'Uncertain Gains: Labor in Chile's New Export Sectors,' *Latin American Research Review* 36 (2): 3–29.

Sen, G. and Grown, C. (1987). *Development Crises and Alternative Visions: Third World Women is Perspectives*. New York: Monthly Review Press.

Shamim, I. (2000). 'Trafficking in Women and Children: A Human Rights Concern,' in C. Abrar (ed.) *On the Margin: Refugees, Migrants and Minorities*, pp. 193–208. Dhaka: RMMRU Dhaka University.

Siddiqui, T. (2000). 'Growth and Sustainability of the NGO Sector in Bangladesh,' *bliss Journal* 20 (4): 524–549.

——. (2001). *Transcending Boundaries: Labour Migration of Women from Bangladesh*. Dhaka: University Press.

Siddiqui, T. and Abrar, C. R. (2001). *Migrant Worker Remittances and Micro-Finance in Bangladesh*. Dhaka: ILO/RMMRU.

Silvey, R. M. (2000). 'Stigmatized Spaces: Gender and Mobility under Crisis in South Sulawesi, Indonesia,' *Gender, Place and Culture* 1 (2): 143–161.

Sivalingam, G. (1994). *The Economic and Social Impact of Export Processing Zones: The Case of Malaysia*. Geneva: ILO.

Sparr, P. ed. (1994). *Mortgaging Women's Lives: Feminist Critiques of Structural Adjustment*. London: Zed Books.

Star Business Report. (2001). 'BIDS Study Reveals Net Drop Out in Micro-Credit Receivers 40 pc Rural People Still Depend on Informal Source for Fund,' *The Daily Star*, at: *www.dailystarnews.com/200106/200128/n1062805.htm#BODY1062803*.

Staudt, K., Rai, S. M. and Parpart, J. L. (2001). 'Protesting World Trade Rules: Can We Talk About Empowerment?,' *Signs* 26 (4): 1251–1257.

Steele, F., Amin, S. and Naved, R. T. (1998). *The Impact of an Integrated Micro-Credit Program on Women's Empowerment and Fertility Behavior in Rural Bangladesh*. Working Paper No. 15. New York: Population Council.

Stiglitz, J. (2000). 'The Insider,' *The New Republic* 17/24 April: 56–60.

——. (2001). 'Thanks for Nothing,' *The Atlantic Monthly*, at: *www.theatlantic.com/issues/2001/2010/stiglitz.htm#*.

——. (2002). *Globalization and its Discontents*. New York: Norton.

Summerfield, G., ed. (2001). 'Special Issue on Gender and Development,' *International Journal of Politics, Culture and Society* 15 (1).

Tauli-Corpuz, V. (1998). 'Asia-Pacific Women Grapple with Financial Crisis and Globalisation,' *www.twnside.org.sg/souths/twn/title/grapple-cn.htm*.

Tiano, S. (1994). *Patriarchy on the Line: Labor, Gender, and Ideology in the Mexican Maquila Industry*. Philadelphia, PA: Temple University Press.

Todaro, M. P. (2000). *Economic Development*, 7th edn. Baltimore, MD: Addison-Wesley.

UNB. (2002). 'ADB Foresees Slump in Remittance by Non-Resident Bangladeshis,' *The Independent*; at: *independent-bangladesh.com/news/jan/19/19012002mt.htm#A19012007*.

UNDP (United Nations Development Program). (1995). *Human Development Report 1995: Gender and Human Security*. New York: Oxford University Press.

——. (1999). *Human Development Report 1999: Globalization with a Human Face*. New York: Oxford University Press.

UNIFEM (United Nations Development Fund for Women). (1999). *Trafficking in Women and Children*

Gender Issues Fact Sheet 2. Bangkok: UNIFEM: East and Southeast Asia; at: *www.unifem-eseasia.org/Gendiss/Gendiss2.htm.*

——. (2000). *Progress of the World's Women*. Geneva: UNIFEM.

US Department of State. (2002). *Victims of Trafficking and Violence Protection Act 2000/Trafficking in Persons Report June 2002*. Washington, DC: US Department of State; at: *www.state.gov/documents/organization/10815.pdf.*

Ward, K. ed. (1990). *Women Workers and Global Restructuring*. Ithaca, NY: ILR Press.

——. (1993). 'Reconceptualizing World System Theory to Include Women,' in P. England (ed.) *Theory on Gender/Feminism on Theory* pp. 43–68 New York: Aldine.

——. (1999). 'As The Debt Crisis Turns: Does Finance Have a Gender?,' paper presented at the conference Women and Employment: Linking Local and Global' Illinois State University.

Ward, K. and Pyle, J. L. (1995). 'Gender Industrialization, Transnational Corporations, and Development: An Overview of Trends,' in C. E. Bose and E. Acosta-Belen (eds.) *Women in the Latin American Development Process* pp. 37–64. Philadelphia, PA: Temple University Press.

Ward, K. Das, S. K., Rahman, F., Islam, A. S., Akhter, R. and Kamal, N. (2002). 'The Nari Jibon Project: The Effects of Global Economic Restructuring on Women's Work and Empowerment in Bangladesh,' paper presented at the meetings of the American Sociological Association, Chicago.

Wolf, D. (1992). *Factory Daughters: Gender, Household Dynamics, and Rural Industrialization in Java*. Berkeley: University of California Press.

World Bank. (2000a). *Bangladesh-Poverty Alleviation and Employment Promotion PID Microfinance II*. Washington, DC: World Bank; at: *www.worldbank.org/pics/pid/bd59143.txt.*

——. (2000b). *Empowering the Poor Through Microcredit. The Bangladesh Poverty Alleviation Project*. Washington, DC: World Bank; at: *wbln1018.worldbank.org/sar/sa.nsf/all/1450fc1018a1012fad5479885256865007197cf?opendocument.*

——. (2001a). *Poverty Alleviation Microfinance Project (02) Microfinance II*. Washington, DC: World Bank; at: *worldbank.org/sprojects/Project.asp?pid=P059143.*

——. (2001b). *World Development Report 2000/2001: Attacking Poverty*. Washington, DC: World Bank; at: *www.worldbank.org/poverty/wdr.poverty/.*

——. (2002). *World Development Report 2002. Building Institutions for Markets*. Washington, DC: World Bank; at: *econ.worldbank.org/wdr/2391/.*

Yelvington, K. A. (1995). *Producing Power: Ethnicity Gender, and Glass in a Caribbean Workplace*. Philadelphia, PA: Temple University Press.

Yeoh, B. S. A., Huang, S. and Gonzalez, J. (1999). 'Migrant Female Domestic Workers: Debating the Economic, Social and Political Impacts in Singapore,' *International Migration Review* 33 (1): 114–136.

Yunus, M. (2002). 'A National Strategy for Economic Growth and Poverty Reduction,' *The Daily Star*: at: *www.dailystarnews.com/200206/200227/n2062709.htm#BODY2062701.*

Zaman, H. (2001). 'Paid Work and Socio-Political Consciousness of Garment Workers in Bangladesh,' *Journal of Contemporary Asia* 31 (2): 145.

Discussion Questions

1. Pyle and Ward have outlined the connections between globalization and the gendered division of labor. How can understanding of these connections be used by agencies, government, and individuals to develop strategies for social change and the empowerment of women?

2. Pyle and Ward focus mostly on how globalization affects poor women in poor countries. What impact does it have on the lives of middle-class and wealthy women in poor and rich countries?

3. According to this article, globalization is not a gender-blind or gender-neutral process. What are some of the reasons globalization might have a different impact on women than on men?

4. How might globalization as described by Pyle and Ward contribute to racial or ethnic tensions, especially in the countries most likely to be the host countries for migrant labor? Can you think of specific examples currently in the news?

35

Legal Scholars of Gay Rights Offer Strategies to Combat the 'Apartheid of the Closet'

D. W. Miller

In the United States today, gays and lesbians, regardless of class status, do not enjoy the same rights as heterosexual Americans, especially the benefits surrounding a legal marriage. In this article, D. W. Miller makes a decidedly race- and gender-coded argument in discussing the various strategies used by legal scholars in their struggle against anti-gay discrimination in the United States. The first bit of ammunition used by legal scholars that the author describes is the equal protection clause of the Fourteenth Amendment to the U.S. Constitution, which has been used so effectively to protect the rights of racial and ethnic groups and women from various forms of discrimination. Yet, use of the Fourteenth Amendment or a civil rights-style strategy, Miller notes on the basis of legal scholarship, may have its drawbacks, since protected "classes" such as "race" are largely characterized as "an immutable and conspicuous fact of nature." This argument would leave out gays and lesbians as individuals who could, according to some, arguably "choose" their sexual preference. A second type of legal strategy in legal scholars' arsenal would involve simply relying on the First Amendment, on the grounds that either gay identity is itself a moral conviction much like a religious belief or that gay sexuality is a form of expression covered under constitutional rights to free speech. Drawbacks to these types of strategies include the inference among some policies that what is being punished is not a gay identity but gay conduct, and moreover, that the Supreme Court has only selectively allowed that gay sexuality should be included as a form of expression for which free speech applies. Most fascinating of all legal scholars' approaches is the one whose forum is perhaps the toughest to face—the court of public opinion. Simply enacting laws to outlaw discrimination against racial minorities, the civil rights era has taught us, has not meant an end to racism, Miller suggests, and court decisions with regard to gays and lesbians may not change the hearts and minds of the straight majority either. In all, Miller contends that when it comes to fighting the "apartheid of the closet," whether in the workplace, the marriage bed, the military, the scouting world, or the playground, no one legal strategy suffices and pursuing "cultural change" can mean victories and defeats on both sides.

For a few gay Vermonters like Lois Farnham and Holly Puterbaugh, Independence Day came early this year. On July 1, the pair's pursuit of happiness led them to the city clerk's office in South Burlington, where they became one of the first gay couples in the country to join in a "civil union" akin to marriage.

The women called it the end of a "27-and-a-half-year engagement." It was also the culmination of their civil-rights lawsuit, which had convinced the state's highest court that the Vermont constitution gave them the same rights as heterosexual citizens, including many of the legal benefits of marriage.

In New Jersey, however, James Dale wasn't celebrating. In the same week, the U.S. Supreme Court ended his long fight to resume volunteering as an assistant scoutmaster. The Boy Scouts of America won the right to exclude gay people like Mr. Dale from positions of leadership, on the grounds that they cannot be proper role models for its members. The justices ruled by a vote of 5 to 4 that the Boy Scouts' freedom of association trumps New Jersey's antidiscrimination law.

A modest advance in a small, liberal state. A major disappointment in the very chamber where "separate but equal" lost all legitimacy. It's no wonder that some legal scholars who study gay rights are dissatisfied with the pace of gay liberation.

"There has been tremendous progress," says Evan Gerstmann, an assistant professor of political science at Loyola Marymount University, "but much less than people think." Even today, agrees William N. Eskridge, a law professor at Yale University, gay people suffer an "apartheid of the closet"—a separate set of laws "that are hard to defend on legal grounds, on political grounds, or even on moral grounds."

Some Important Legal Victories

To be sure, the law has become more hospitable to gay rights in recent decades. Dozens of states and localities, for instance, have repealed bans on consensual sodomy or added "sexual orientation" to their antidiscrimination laws. But gay people cannot receive a marriage license, gay soldiers cannot serve openly, and—in some states—gay teachers are forbidden to discuss their orientation in the classroom lest they "promote" homosexuality.

And while the Supreme Court just four years ago protected the political prerogatives of gay people in *Romer v. Evans,* a case that relied on constitutional principles rooted in the civil-rights victories of the 1950s, scholars like Mr. Gerstmann and Mr. Eskridge are not waiting for a replay of the civil-rights revolution in the courts. They urge advocates to fight their battle with other tools, and in other arenas.

The court's ruling in *Romer* seemed like a milestone.

It struck down a voter-approved amendment to Colorado's constitution, Amendment 2, that would have nullified all attempts to add sexual orientation to statewide and local nondiscrimination laws. In its opinion, the court said for the first time that a law that disadvantages gay people cannot stand if it serves no goal more reasonable than indulging the "animus" of the straight majority.

In ruling that way, the court invoked the equal-protection clause of the 14th Amendment, which has long been crucial in protecting black people and other racial and ethnic groups from discriminatory laws and policies. Enacted shortly after the Civil War to shield newly freed slaves from oppression by a white majority, the 14th Amendment says in part that "no state shall deny to any person within its jurisdiction the equal protection of the laws."

Since 1938, the Supreme Court has construed that clause to mean that the government may not pass laws that burden protected, or "suspect," classes of people, unless those laws are narrowly tailored to serve a compelling state interest. Laws subjected to such "strict scrutiny" rarely stand. By the 1970s, the list of suspect classes included categories of race, national origin, alien status, and, as "quasi-suspect," birth legitimacy and gender.

'The Constitutional Underclass'

Having created a powerful tool for protecting minority groups, Mr. Gerstmann argues in *The Constitutional Underclass: Gays, Lesbians, and the Failure of Class-Based Equal Protection* (University of Chicago Press, 1999), the court since the early 1970s has resisted expanding its aegis to include any new groups, including gay people. "Declaring any minority a suspect class," he writes, "is strong medicine, often resulting in the substitution of judicial judgment for democratic decision making in all areas of law affecting the protected group," a substitution the Supreme Court is reluctant to make.

Because of this reluctance, he says, Romer "did very little for gays and lesbians. They still get less protection than racial minorities or women. It was limited to the situation at hand and did not extend gay rights in any way."

That's because the justices neither elevated gay people to the same status as members of racial-minority groups nor declared any general principle for deciding future cases. By holding the law to a standard normally reserved for suspect classes without admitting it was doing so, he writes, "the Court could strike down Amendment 2 without obligating itself to apply a heightened level of scrutiny to any other law disadvantaging gays and lesbians."

That sleight-of-hand is not limited to sexual orientation, he adds. The court has managed to exclude any new groups by fudging the distinction between class and classification. When vulnerable groups such as the poor, the elderly, or gay people, for example, have requested strict scrutiny of laws that burden them as a class, the court has required them to prove they lack political power or share a history of discrimination. Yet it has sided with white plaintiffs—who could never meet that threshold—in striking down affirmative-action programs that impermissibly use race as a classification.

Mr. Gerstmann notes that Amendment 2 supporters claimed gay people wanted local antidiscrimination ordinances to grant them "special rights." As long as the court interprets the 14th Amendment in terms of suspect classes of people, he argues, many Americans will continue to oppose such protections as special rights.

A Matter of Moral Conscience

Dissatisfaction with the prevailing view of equal protection has led legal scholars to offer alternate weapons for advocates' constitutional arsenal. Mr. Gerstmann wants judges to junk class-based analysis of the equal-protection clause altogether. "The judiciary should invoke the Constitution's equal protection not on behalf of classes," he says, but on behalf of rights, such as the right to full political participation or an equal education. That, he says, is how the court wielded the 14th Amendment in *Brown v. Board of Education*, when it declared that segregated schools were inherently unequal.

Even if equal-protection arguments worked, says David A. J. Richards, a professor of law at New York University, he would question the common wisdom of using the civil-rights movement as a model for the advancement of gay rights. That analogy, he argues, implies that sexual orientation could only be constitutionally protected from discrimination if it were, like race, an immutable and conspicuous fact of nature.

While scientists debate the origins of sexual preferences, he says, gay people should secure their rights as a matter of identity and moral conscience. He looks to the First Amendment to protect them, on the grounds of religious toleration.

"Americans, who are very tolerant of almost any religious group, nonetheless are deeply intolerant when it comes to gay and lesbian advocacy," he says. Gay identity is a form of "ethically based conscientious conviction" entitled to equal respect with other forms of convictions, he writes in *Identity and the Case for Gay Rights* (Chicago, 1999). "Yet many laws target just such convictions."

For instance, he argues, the military's Don't Ask, Don't Tell policy claims to punish only homosexual conduct, not homosexual identity. But the military infers such conduct whenever gay soldiers express their sexual identity, such as by declaring "I am gay" or participating in a commitment ceremony with a same-sex partner.

Moreover, he argues, "some forms of legal discrimination against gay people cannot be justified or understood as anything other than sectarian expressions of moral disapproval enacted into law." That, he writes, is exactly what the First Amendment was created to prevent.

Yale's Mr. Eskridge also believes that gay-rights advocates could fashion a stronger shield against certain kinds of discrimination from the First Amendment. He argues that the amendment's guarantee of free speech ought to include the expression of sexuality. In fact, he believes the Supreme Court has already made that interpretation—but only selectively.

As the court has read the First Amendment, he writes in *Gaylaw: Challenging the Apartheid of the Closet* (Harvard University Press, 1999), it has "protected gender-bending literature . . . , assured gay people rights to associate in clubs and college campuses, and protected the right to come out of the closet—but not when the person coming out is a state employee or military person, when the association involves the sale of liquor, or the gender-bending literature is explicitly homoerotic."

If it were applying the First Amendment consistently, he argues, the court would have reinstated a school guidance counselor who was fired after revealing her bisexuality. And it would have protected a gay Naval officer who came out to his superior soon after President Clinton announced his intention to ban discrimination against gay people in the armed forces.

'No Magic Bullet'

Gay-rights litigators say they value the contributions of legal scholars, many of whom help them hone arguments for promising test cases. But they disagree that their legal briefs lack the proper ammunition.

"I don't think the equal-protection clause is useless," says Matthew Coles, a lawyer for the American Civil Liberties Union's Lesbian and Gay Rights Project. "There has been a string of district court cases post-*Romer* that have struck down laws based on 'animus.'" He expects to carry the equal-protection flag into battle against sodomy laws and discrimination in both the workplace and family court.

"We're not looking for a be-all, end-all fix from the courts, certainly not the Supreme Court, because there is no permanent fix," says Beatrice Dohrn, legal director for Lambda Legal Defense and Education Fund, the gay-rights group that took the Boy Scout case to the Supreme Court. "It's much more of a social movement."

"There is no magic bullet in legal discourse, ever," agrees William Rubinstein, a former gay-rights lawyer who teaches law at the University of California at Los Angeles, "We tend to think of *Brown v. Board of Education* as the important watershed" in the civil-rights movement. But even that is now disputed. For one thing, the court took its time in instructing states on how to end legal segregation. For another, he says, "We thought that a lot of racism was legally constructed. But we're still stuck with it."

Gay-rights advocates, he says, can still learn a valuable lesson from the civil-rights era: Don't expect the courts to lead society where it isn't ready to go. In other words, the real battleground is the culture at large. "Court decisions have never been the leading edge for gay rights," says John D'Emilio, a historian in the gender and women's-studies department at the University of Chicago at Illinois. Instead, he says, advocates must keep challenging the straight majority to reconsider its prejudices.

Shifting Legal Ground

The opportunities for such education are everywhere, as the ground under gay rights continues to shift. Some legislatures repeal antisodomy laws, while others refuse to grant gay parents custody of children after divorce. High courts in Hawaii and Alaska rule that their state constitutions require gay marriage, and voters amend them.

That gay advocacy has become so robust, scholars say, is one thing for which judges do deserve some credit. In fact, one of the unheralded victories of the civil-rights era is a string of free-speech cases that bolstered black people's participation in public debate. Since the 1970's, the free expression of gay publications, gay employees, and gay student groups has similarly won favor in the Supreme Court.

"The trick is to combine expression and equality claims," says Nan D. Hunter, a former gay-rights litigator and a professor at the Brooklyn College of Law. That strategy, she says, worked in a recent Utah case in which a high-school teacher was fired as her school's volleyball coach after revealing that she was gay. A federal judge eventually ruled that the school had both violated her free-speech rights and denied her equal protection out of prejudice.

Oddly enough, the pursuit of cultural change turns the logic of victory and defeat upside down.

The Boy Scouts may have won the right to exclude gay leaders like James Dale, but only at the expense of declaring that their objection to homosexuality is a fundamental part of their message. That may cost them members and donations. "The Boy Scouts have taken on a stigma of being antigay," says Ms. Hunter. "It's the kind of case you win even if you lose."

Discussion Questions

1. Miller takes an obvious pro-gay stance in this article. What was your reaction to this line of reasoning? Were you comfortable or uncomfortable with the author's assumptions?

2. How might the experience of gays and lesbians of color be used to create a unique legal strategy against anti-gay discrimination? Does this seem far-fetched?

3. How might the experience of gays and lesbians of color differ from that of White gays and lesbians?

4. Do you think issues for gays and lesbians are also influenced by their respective genders? How so or how not?

36
SES, Race/ Ethnicity, and Health

Melanie L. Johnston

Epidemiologist Melanie L. Johnston looks at the relationship between gender, race/ethnicity, and social class and health. While she finds each of these major variables has an impact, for the most part the influence of socioeconomic status or class is the strongest. Yet there are paradoxes: Despite having comparable socioeconomic status, Hispanic Americans are generally healthier than either African Americans or American Indians. Also, despite their more limited earning power, women are generally healthier than men. Using health, including the occurrence of various diseases and disease-related characteristics and behaviors, and mortality rates as a focus, Johnston's work makes it possible for readers to see the intricate interplay of gender, race/ethnicity, and especially socioeconomic status.

As Johnston points out, race/ethnicity is socially constructed, and there is more genetic variation within various racial/ethnic groups than between them. Thus, the differences in health status observed among the various groups cannot be explained by genetics; they must have what she labels "bio-psycho-social-behavioral" causes. Such causes of relatively poor health may include stressful lives, poor diets, toxic environments, lack of health insurance and access to quality health care, failure to understand health-related issues, feelings of powerlessness, and risky behaviors. Many of these causes are direct or indirect results of limited incomes, individual and community resources, and education.

In discussing why Asian Americans have longer life expectancies than Whites and why Hispanics are healthier than other ethnic

groups with similar incomes, Johnston is careful to note that these generalizations are too broad. Not all Asian Americans are recent immigrants and the category includes some of the most affluent and some of most impoverished groups. Some of the explanations offered for the better health status of Hispanics, for example, the amusingly named salmon bias hypothesis, apply as well to Mexican Americans, who often do return to Mexico when they are old or ill, but they are not relevant for Cuban Americans, who cannot return to Cuba, or Puerto Ricans, who are counted in U.S. statistics whether they are on the mainland or the island. Statistics about American Indians typically reflect only the health status of those living on or near reservations, not those living in cities and towns across the country. The statistics we have leave many questions about health differences unanswered.

Introduction

Class and race/ethnic disparities in health have been well documented. People of lower socioeconomic status (SES) tend to have poorer health, lower levels of life expectancy, earlier onset of disease, and higher mortality rates compared with their wealthier counterparts. African Americans and American Indians share similar health characteristics of low SES populations. Asian Americans and Hispanic Americans tend to be as healthy as Whites. However, the health advantage of Hispanic Americans is considered a paradox given their overall lower levels of SES. This paper discusses SES and race/ethnic differences in health, the wear and tear theory as an explanation for SES differences in health, and the Hispanic mortality paradox. Other factors related to race and SES, such as differences in health behaviors and health care access, are also discussed.

SES and Health

A large body of literature has been shown to document negative health outcomes associated with lower socioeconomic status

(SES). For example, lower SES has been related to a higher prevalence and incidence of most chronic and infectious diseases (Hayward et al. 2000). A negative relationship has also been documented regarding SES and mental distress (Goldstein 1979), depression, and depressive symptoms (Adler et al. 1993). Lower SES has been associated with higher rates of nearly all major causes of morbidity and mortality (Smith 1999), and evidence suggests that this differential between SES and health is widening rather than narrowing (Crimmins and Saito 2001). *Morbidity* is the state of poor health produced by a disease, and *mortality* is the per capita death rate in a population. Overall, the data suggest that there is a linear relationship between SES and health in that there are increasingly better health outcomes as one increases in SES levels (Crimmins and Seeman 2001).

SES is typically measured in terms of education, income, occupation, and the poverty ratio. For example, high school graduates have death rates that are two to three times higher than college graduates (Williams 2004). Furthermore, national studies indicate that low SES adults tend to get sick earlier. In other words, they tend to have levels of illness in their 30s and 40s that are not common in high SES adults until their 60s and 70s (Williams 2004).

However, SES is more than just inadequate financial resources. It is related to several other factors that potentially influence health outcomes. These include social, psychological, and behavioral factors, and life circumstances. Examples of social and psychological mechanisms include access to and use of healthcare, dangerous neighborhoods, the role of social networks/social support, and personal characteristics such as coping ability and level of control (Taylor, Repetti, and Seeman 1997). Behavioral factors include the role of personal health practices such as diet and exercise as well as preventive healthcare. Also, life circumstances are often measured by level of stress, stressful life events, and job characteristics.

Furthermore, much of the variation in SES and health is seen in the later ages (i.e., ages 45–64). In other words, the magnitude of differences in SES and health is greater during the middle to later years. This suggests that the health effects of SES are a result of cumulative processes beginning in early life (Blackwell, Hayward, and Crimmins 2001).

Cumulative Adversity and Later Life Health

Wear and tear theory can help explain the relationship between SES and health. The idea is that cumulative levels of adversity or stress may have deleterious effects on health and longevity (Finch and Seeman 1998) by "wearing out" the body's many basic and interrelated physiological systems. This results in "premature aging" among those of lower SES, with increased risk for nearly all types of negative health outcomes (Seeman and Crimmins 2001). The occurrence of an adverse or stressful event causes the body to release both adrenalin and adrenocortical hormones ("fight or flight response"), which helps the body to survive the immediate crisis (McEwen and Seeman 1999). It is the cumulative exposure to adversity that is experienced among lower SES populations that predisposes them to increased biological risk for poorer health outcomes.

An abundance of research indicates that lower SES individuals report more chronic and acute demands that arise from external and internal environments (Turner, Wheaton, and Lloyd 1995). These demands range across several life domains and are typically measured through questions on self-reported degree of environmental stress (i.e., physical environment characterized by crime, crowding, poor physical amenities, and greater exposure to physical hazards such as industrial and hazardous wastes; occupational environment characterized by inadequate and/or predictable resources, nonexistent/little job security or personal autonomy), social characteristics (sociocultural environment characterized by discrimination and impoverished social and psychological resources), and personal coping ability (individual perceptions of powerlessness, alienation, lack of self-esteem) (Seeman and Crimmins 2001).

Wear and tear theories assume that living organisms are like machines. Due to extended usage, the machine's parts wear out and the machine subsequently breaks down. Similarly, aging is seen as a gradual deterioration of the body (Perlman 1954) due to years of wear and tear. It has been suggested that the risk for poor health is due to the extent of wear and tear on the body over time from more long-term exposures to heightened physiologic activity (the body's response to stress). Biological frailty, as a result of low SES and its associated higher levels of daily stress, can act as a measure of wear and tear.

Interestingly, the wear and tear theory applies to both men and women. However, women appear to be healthier and tend to have a longer life expectancy than men, despite typically lower levels of income. Yet, it has been suggested that women may experience more "stress" over the life course as a result of reduced earning potential. Thus, other factors in addition to SES are responsible for gender differences in health.

Gender Differences in Health

An abundance of research indicates that there are differences in health and disease between men and women (Pinn 2003). Women, in general, tend to be healthier than men. In the U.S., men tend to die younger (an average of 7 years younger), have higher mortality rates from all 15 leading causes of death, are more likely to suffer from 7 out of 10 of the most common infectious diseases, and are more likely to experience severe chronic conditions and fatal diseases (Hellerstedt 2001). There are also gender differences in the ways that diseases manifest, rates at which diseases develop, the course of the disease, and responses to treatment.

Several possible reasons for these gender differences include behavioral differences, social norms, and differences in self-reported health. For example, women are more likely to exercise and use vitamin supplements. Men are more likely to engage in high-risk behaviors, such as smoking, drinking, no seat belt use, drinking and driving, and not getting health screenings. There are also cultural norms about masculinity and femininity as they relate to help-seeking behavior and self-reporting of health status. Men are more likely to lack awareness of medical conditions and are less likely to self-report poor health. Women are more likely to make

health care visits than men. Although differences in the number of visits decline with increased severity of health concerns, men may still be considerably less likely to contact a physician regarding a health problem.

Despite gender differences in health behaviors, economic position, and social class, associations with health are the strongest (Hellerstedt 2001). For example, income levels are typically higher for men than for women, women are more likely to engage in unpaid work, single-adult households headed by women experience greater economic disadvantage, and women are more likely than men to experience poverty at older ages. Few studies have examined gender differences in the cumulative disadvantages of poverty. For example, one study suggested that childhood poverty had a greater effect on young men (aged 23–33 years) and women older than 33 years.

Gender differences in health reflect both behavior and socioeconomic position. However, economic factors typically play a larger role in gender differences in health. Like gender, race/ethnic differences in health are often said to be related to SES. As indicated in the next section, SES plays a large role but is not the sole contributor to race/ethnic disparities in health.

Race/Ethnicity, SES, and Health Status

The health status of U.S. ethnic groups has become an important focus of research due to the rising heterogeneity of the U.S. population and the national goal of reducing racial and ethnic disparities. The majority of studies have focused upon differences in mortality and health between non-Hispanic Whites and other major American ethnic groups, such as African Americans, American Indians, Asian Americans, and Hispanics.

African Americans

In recent years, improvements in economic status of African Americans relative to that of Whites have stagnated (Smith and Welch 1989). Low-income African American families have experienced absolute declines in family income since 1973, and this is associated with worsening health across a number of health status indicators (Williams and Collins 1995). Similarly, the gains in health status of African Americans relative to that of Whites have slowed. In fact, the gap in health status between African Americans and Whites continues to widen (Williams 2004).

On average, African Americans tend to have lower levels of income and education, which are thought to be primary determinants of their poorer health. Life expectancy for African Americans at birth is nearly 7 years shorter than that of White Americans (Rogers, Hummer, and Nam 2000). Further, at age 25, the average White male has a life expectancy of 75 years, while the average African American male can be expected to live until age 71 (Williams 2004). African Americans are more likely to die from most major diseases (Williams 2001), to report higher levels of most diseases and conditions (Hayward et al. 2000), and to experience extraordinary rates of premature aging (Hayward et al. 2000).

As mentioned earlier, the racial gap has been largely attributed to socioeconomic differences and sometimes race is used as an indicator of SES. However, differences in health status associated with race are smaller than those associated with SES (Williams 2004). Also, it has been suggested that adjustments for SES reduce but do not eliminate racial disparities in health as African Americans generally have worse health than Whites within each level of SES (Williams and Collins 1995). For example, national data on infant mortality indicate that for both White and African American women, infant mortality rates go down as years of education increase, yet a very large gap continues to exist between the two races (Williams 2004). Furthermore, it has been suggested that low SES and undereducated White women tend have better health outcomes compared with the most advantaged college educated African American women.

Thus, both race and class interact together to contribute to health inequalities. Although race differences exist independently of class, differences are not typically due to genetics. Recent research indicates that there are more genetic variations within race/ethnic groups than there are between race/ethnic groups. Also, very few genetic differences—which directly relate to health—have been found between races (Cooper 2003; Pearce et al. 2004). Further, since the concept of race is socially constructed, race/ethnic differences in health may reflect the common environment and lifestyle experienced due to the historical and generational effects of polices based on race as well as institutional racism and discrimination (Williams 2003).

Fundamental social causes of disease, such as childhood poverty, inadequate education, marginal employment, low income, and segregated living conditions (Link and Phelan 1995), are more likely to be experienced by African Americans. At every educational level, African Americans receive less income compared with Whites. They also have lower levels of wealth at every level of income and have less purchasing power at a given level of income (Williams 2004). Also, some suggest that differences in health behaviors related to a lack of knowledge may be a partial explanation for poorer health status (Hayward et al. 2000). Part of this is related to a lack of education, but national data also indicate that African Americans receive poorer quality and less intensive medical care than Whites (Williams 2004). For example, a study found that compared with Whites, African Americans (and Hispanics) who had similar severity levels of heart disease were less likely to receive catheterization or bypass surgery (Lehrman 2004). In sum, both current economic status and factors related to economic deprivation over the life course are responsible for poorer health among African Americans.

American Indians

According to the 2000 census, American Indians consist of 1.5 percent of the U.S. population. The general consensus is that the American Indian population experiences significantly poorer health than Whites. This is consistent with data from the Indian Health Services (IHS) (Kington and Nickens 2001). It has also been suggested that the gap between the two races is narrowing. However, data on the health status and health coverage and access of American Indians (including Alaskan natives) are limited due to the population's small numbers and geographical dispersion in the United States (Zuckerman et al. 2004). Much of the data come from the Indian Health Service (IHS), which provides health care services to American Indians who live on or near reservations. Sixty percent of American Indians live on or near reservations, and little is known about the health status of those living in urban areas (Kington and Nickens 2001).

American Indians typically have higher rates of mortality (Zuckerman et al. 2004) and lower rates of life expectancy compared with Whites across the lifespan (Kington and Nickens 2001). Studies on infant mortality indicate that infant mortality rates are 70 percent higher in American Indian populations compared with Whites (DHHS 2004). American Indians are also more likely to suffer from chronic conditions. For example, they have a higher incidence of diabetes. In 2003, 14.5 percent of American Indians seen at IHS were diagnosed with diabetes (DHHS 2004). Also, it has been suggested that heart disease accounts for 20 percent of all deaths in the American Indian population (DHHS 2004).

Like the African American population, poorer health status among the American Indians is related to higher poverty rates and limited access to quality health care compared with Whites. Approximately 49 percent of American Indians have private health care coverage compared with 83 percent of Whites (Zuckerman et al. 2004). Also, 17 percent of American Indians have Medicaid coverage compared with 5 percent of Whites (Schneider and Martinez 1997) and about 48 percent of low-income American Indians are uninsured (Zuckerman et al. 2004). Further, American Indians are more likely to be dissatisfied with their health care and less likely to have a medical or dental visit in a year (Zuckerman et al. 2004).

Asian Americans

Due to high rates of immigration, the Asian American population is the fastest growing and third largest minority population (next to African Americans and Hispanics) in the United States (Markides and Black 1996). Studies comparing Asians with other race/ethnic groups indicate that Asians have a longer life expectancy. The estimated life expectancy, in 1992, of Asian Americans at birth and age 1 was 80.3 years compared with 75.1 years for Whites (Hoyert and Kung 1997).

Overall, Asian Americans tend to have lower mortality from heart disease, cancer, diabetes, liver disease/cirrhosis, pneumonia/influenza, and HIV/AIDS compared with Whites (Williams 2001). These lower mortality rates appear to be indicative of a favorable health status (Hoyert and Kung 1997). For example, Asian Americans also have lower rates of heart disease, cancer, and cardiovascular disease than Whites (Kagawa-Singer, Hikoyeda, and Tanjasiri 1997). However, these comparisons often disguise the diversity that exists within the Asian population. Chinese Americans, Filipinos, and Japanese Americans represent the three largest subgroups among Asian Americans (U.S. Bureau of the Census 1993). The remaining subgroups include the Vietnamese, Koreans, Hawaiians, Samoans, Guamanians, Cambodians, and Hmong. These diverse groups have a different culture, language, and immigration history, which results in variations in health status (Kington and Nickens 2001). For example, 1992 mortality data indicated that in comparison with the U.S. population, certain Asian subgroups such as Japanese, Asian Indians, and Koreans had lower mortality rates or longer life expectancies, while Hawaiians and Samoans had extremely high mortality rates (Hoyert and Kung 1997). Similarly, California data from 1985 to 1990 indicated lower mortality rates for Chinese, Asian Indians, and Japanese (Kington and Nickens 2001).

The general consensus is that some groups of Asian Americans are healthier on average; however, other Asian subgroups have poorer health (Kington and Nickens 2001). The favorable health status of Asian Americans in general may be related to their more advantaged socioeconomic position (Hoyert and Kung 1997). Another potential explanation is the high proportion of immigrants who may be healthier on average than their native-born counterparts (Markides and Black 1996).

Hispanics/Mexican Americans

The majority of studies on the health status of Hispanics have focused on Mexican American mortality rates with the assumption that they would be higher (similar to African Americans) than Whites since their socioeconomic profile includes high unemployment, high levels of poverty, low education, a lower likelihood of having health insurance, and poorer access to health care (Ginzberg 1991). However, the life expectancy of many Mexican Americans is similar to that of Whites (Rogers et al. 1996). Also, local, state, and national data indicate that Hispanics (including Mexican Americans) have lower all-cause mortality rates than Whites, even after controlling for demographic and socioeconomic characteristics (Liao et al. 1998). Hispanics, in general, have a lower mortality than non-Hispanics from a number of conditions including cancer (Sorlie et al. 1993), cardiovascular disease (Sorlie et al. 1993), and chronic obstructive pulmonary disease (Rosenwaike 1987). Although Hispanics have an advantage for some diseases, it has been shown that they are more likely to die from diabetes, liver disease, homicide (Sorlie et al. 1993), cervical cancer (Markides and Coreil 1986), and AIDS (Thiel de Bocanegra, Gany, and Fruchter 1993). Also, Hispanics are more likely to suffer from respiratory problems, infections, pneumonia, influenza, accidents (Markides and Black 1996), and obesity (Winkleby, Garner, and Taylor 1996). It has been suggested that differences in health behaviors do not explain the overall better health of Hispanics (Winkleby, Garner, and Taylor 1996).

The Hispanic Mortality Paradox

The favorable health profile among Hispanics, despite lower levels of SES, has been termed the Hispanic mortality paradox or epidemiological paradox (Abraido-Lanza et al. 1999). Previous research has suggested that their favorable health profile may be a reflection of data artifacts (Palloni and Arias 2004) that create an illusion of better health status. Examples include factors related to migration or being foreign born (Hummer et

al. 1999), also known as the healthy migrant effect and the salmon bias hypothesis. Yet, other research has suggested that certain protective cultural factors may be responsible since one health-enhancing characteristic of the Hispanic lifestyle is the tendency to formulate closer networks compared with their White counterparts (Ramirez de Arellano 1994).

The healthy migrant effect. The foreign-born population currently represents the largest proportion of the total U.S. population since 1930 (Hansen and Farber 1997). According to 2003 estimates, 11.7 percent of Americans are foreign-born. Currently, 53.3 percent of the foreign born are from Latin America, 25 percent from Asia, and 8 percent from other regions around the world (Larsen, 2004). Further, the foreign-born Hispanic ethnic group increased by 53 percent during the 1980s (Hansen and Faber 1997). It is estimated that 47 percent of the Mexican population are foreign-born while 72 percent of Cubans are foreign-born (National Center for Health Statistics 2000).

The healthy migrant effect suggests that the selection of healthy migrants to the United States accounts for the Hispanic paradox (Palloni and Arias 2004). Migrants are typically physically and psychologically healthier than nonmigrants. They may also be healthier than the average individual in the receiving population. Before migration, these migrants are hypothesized to have better health behaviors, family support systems, and health status than their U.S.-born counterparts (Hummer et al. 1999). In contrast, U.S. residents tend to have higher levels of drinking and smoking as well as poorer dietary practices (Scribner 1996).

Foreign-born populations have been shown to exhibit different mortality rates, risk factors for mortality, and health behaviors compared with native-born populations. The foreign-born tend to be healthier (Stephen et al. 1994) and to have lower mortality rates than the U.S. native-born (Fang, Madhavan, and Alderman 1997). The health advantage seems to be greater among the middle-aged and elderly population and exists for both short- and long-term immigrants (Rogers, Hummer, and Nam 2000). It has been suggested that immigrant men and women have significantly lower risks of mortality from cardiovascular diseases, lung and prostate cancer, chronic obstructive pulmonary disease, cirrhosis, pneumonia and influenza, unintentional injuries, and suicide. However, they tend to have higher risks of mortality from stomach and brain cancer and from infectious diseases (Singh and Siahpush 2001).

The health advantage has been found for foreign-born Mexicans, Puerto Ricans, and Cubans. However, other nativity differences also exist in morbidity and cause specific mortality. In a recent study, lower mortality risk in general was found for foreign-born African Americans, foreign-born Hispanics, foreign-born Asians/Pacific Islanders, U.S.-born Asians/Pacific Islanders, U.S.-born Hispanics, and foreign-born Whites, even at equivalent socioeconomic and demographic backgrounds (Singh and Siahpush 2002). In fact, foreign-born Hispanics and foreign-born African Americans experienced 26 percent and 52 percent lower mortality risks that their native-born counterparts. The same study also found that Asians/Pacific Islanders and Hispanic immigrants experienced the lowest risk for mortality in cancer, cardiovascular, respiratory, infectious disease, and injury (Singh and Siahpush 2002). Further, the risks of smoking, obesity, and hypertension were significantly lower for foreign-born populations; however, risk increased with increasing length of U.S. residence (Singh and Siahpush 2002).

The salmon bias effect. The salmon bias effect has been seen among some foreign-born Hispanic subgroups (Palloni and Arias 2004), such as Mexican Americans. Like salmon that return to their place of origin before dying, some immigrants may return to their country of origin after a period of temporary unemployment or illness (Abraido-Lanza et al. 1999). However, the salmon bias effect may not be an adequate explanation for other Hispanic subgroups, such as Cubans and Puerto Ricans. Cubans cannot return to their own country and typically have no desire to do so. Puerto Ricans, on the other hand, are able to access their homeland, but since Puerto Rico is a common-

wealth of the U.S., deaths that occur in Puerto Rico are tabulated in U.S. mortality data (Abraido-Lanza et al. 1999).

Return migration leads to artificially lower mortality rates among Hispanics because there is a reduction in the number of unhealthy persons in the population, thereby leading to the illusion of reduced mortality rates. The salmon bias effect assumes that the returning migrants are typically older and frailer. In contrast, the healthy migrant effect suggests that migration to the United States is more common among the younger and healthier age groups.

Other data artifacts. It has also been suggested that the mortality advantage of Hispanics could be due to other types of data artifacts. For example, there are three other types of data problems: ethnic identification, misreporting of ages, and mismatches of records (Palloni and Arias 2004). Ethnic identification refers to the underreporting of Hispanic origin on U.S. death certificates. Ethnic reporting is based on self-identification and as many as 7 percent of Hispanics are not recorded as Hispanic on death certificates (Rosenberg et al. 1999). The misreporting of ages refers to the tendency of some Hispanic subgroups to overstate their ages, which could lead to a depression in mortality rates at older ages (Palloni and Arias 2004). A mismatch of records is likely to occur when there is limited data available for linking death records to a population. Typically, data such as surnames and social security numbers are used in matching, and mortality rates could be driven down in populations where it is more difficult to obtain identifiers due to the person's legal status or where identifiers are less complete or less reliably recorded. However, there is no source of data that suggests variations in matching rates by ethnic groups.

Protective cultural factors. The cultural hypothesis suggests that the mortality advantage of Hispanics is due to social and cultural factors that differentiate them from other non-Hispanics (Abraido-Lanza et al. 1999). The idea is that culture influences health and lifestyle behaviors, family structure, and social networks (Palloni and Arias 2004). Culture shapes a person's norms and beliefs about family and social obligations, thereby influencing "the propensity to live alone or in extended families, the density of social networks, the amount of social support exchanged and the sense of control and self efficacy" (Palloni and Arias 2004, p. 389). It also shapes health behaviors such as diet, smoking, alcohol consumption, exercise, and the use of preventive medical care (Palloni and Arias 2004).

Research has consistently shown the importance of social support to health, mortality, and mental health (i.e., House, Landis, and Umberson 1988). However, there has been a lack of systematic epidemiological research linking social support to the health of ethnic minorities. Existing research indicates that ethnic minorities experience relatively strong social supports, which may buffer the negative effects of high levels of stress typically experienced by lower SES populations. In 2003, 25 percent of foreign-born households included five or more people (Larsen 2004). In contrast, 12.5 percent of native-born households had five or more people. Furthermore, the foreign-born population was more likely to be married (57.2 percent) compared with the native born population (52.2 percent) (Larsen 2004). Also, the importance of religion and church in strengthening support systems of African Americans (Krause and Wray 1992) as well as Hispanics is well known. Additionally, the significance of family supports as well as the importance of religious values and participation among older Mexican American and other Hispanic groups has been well established (Markides and Black 1996).

The Hispanic mortality paradox and its proposed explanations have been tested in a number of studies (Franzini et al. 2001). Several researchers have found support for the Hispanic paradox and the healthy migrant effect. However, a recent study using the National Health Interview Survey and the National Death Index, by Palloni and Arias (2004), found that the mortality advantage is a characteristic of only foreign-born "other" Hispanics and foreign-born Mexicans. They suggest that the mortality advantage is not "Hispanic" per se as their findings do not apply to Puerto Ricans or Cubans. Further, the mortality advantage appears to be sub-

stantial with 30–50 percent lower mortality rates among the foreign-born "other" Hispanics and foreign-born Mexican Americans. It has been suggested that these findings reflect an increase in life expectancy among these groups, of five to eight years at age 45. Interestingly, return migration effects—or support for the salmon bias hypothesis—was found for foreign-born Mexicans but not "other" Hispanics, while the mortality advantage of the "other" Hispanics persisted after duration of stay and state of residence were accounted for. Finally, no support was found for the cultural hypothesis (Palloni and Arias 2004).

Others also suggest that there is significant variation in the Hispanic mortality paradox. For example, results differ by age, gender, acculturation, and cause of death (Franzini et al. 2001). It has been suggested that data artifacts (including migration) may contribute to but do not fully explain the paradox. It is concluded that the paradox is due to reasons that are multifactorial and social in origin (Franzini, Ribble, and Keddie 2001).

SES, Race, and Other Health Risk Factors

A growing body of literature suggests that risk factors for health outcomes are related to SES and health (Williams 1990). Furthermore, the distribution of resources and risk factors are determined by the conditions under which people live and work. The literature indicates that comparable stressful events, for example, have stronger adverse effects on lower SES individuals (Kessler 1979).

Risk factors related to SES and health, include, for example, health behaviors (smoking, drinking, exercise, diet) and health care utilization (presence of health insurance, regular access and use of health care). The literature suggests that smoking is concentrated among minority and lower SES populations. African American and Hispanic men tend to report a higher prevalence of smoking than Whites. Furthermore, although African Americans tend to start smoking later and smoke fewer cigarettes per day, they are more adversely affected by smoking (Sterling and Weinkam 1989). In fact, there has been a substantial rise in lung cancer incidence among African Americans compared with Whites, and this may be due to the fact that African Americans tend to smoke cigarettes with higher tar content (Williams and Collins 1995).

In contrast, the literature on drinking behavior is mixed. Most research on alcohol indicates either no difference by race or increased consumption among White individuals (Williams and Collins 1995). In terms of exercise, numerous studies have shown that racial minorities exercise less than Whites and engage in less leisure time physical activity (Heath and Smith 1994). Furthermore, there is a lack of recreational facilities or parks in low-income neighborhoods that would enable physical activity among this population (Odoms-Young 2004).

Dietary factors have been associated with onset of chronic disease, and this relationship is particularly differentiated across social class (Sowers 1997). Persons with lower SES in affluent countries tend to be more obese than their higher SES counterparts. Several factors are associated with SES differences in diet, such as the total budget of the economically disadvantaged (which prevents them from buying foods of appropriate quality), the lack of knowledge (due to limited education) required to select and prepare nutritious foods, and the reduced availability of good quality foods at inexpensive prices in poor neighborhoods. The food industry tends to market foods of low quality (with high fat and sugar content) to low income populations. Another factor is increased psychosocial stress among low-income populations, which predisposes them to unhealthy dietary habits (Wamala, Wolk, and Orth-Gomer 1997).

The behavioral aspects of obesity have a strong impact on differences in disease patterns between Whites, African Americans, and Hispanics. Obesity is a risk factor for hypertension, diabetes, and osteoarthritis (Pi-Sunyer 1993), which are more common among African Americans and Hispanics. Both African Americans and Hispanics tend to have higher body mass index than Whites and have greater acceptance of being overweight than Whites (Winkleby, Gardner, and Taylor 1996).

Diet also modifies the incidence of cancer and bio-behavior of tumors (Milner 2002); risk of breast, colon, lung, and liver cancers are frequently associated with dietary patterns. Research has demonstrated the role of fats (Meyer and Gillatt 2002) and obesity (Key et al. 2002) in the onset of cancer, and fiber, fruits and vegetables, antioxidants (e.g., vitamin A, D, E), and certain minerals, such as cadmium and zinc, in the protection against cancer (Meyer and Gillatt 2002). However, inconsistencies in the effect of diet on cancer are not uncommon; they likely reflect the multifactorial and complex nature of cancer, including genetics and other environmental factors (Milner 2002). Furthermore, some suggest that higher rates of cancer among the poor in both rich countries and poor countries reflect the extent of irregularities in food supply (the evolutionary adaptive patterns of food intake) and eating patterns (Potter 1997).

High-fat diets are also associated with higher blood cholesterol concentrations, which is a major risk factor for cardiovascular disease (Kromhout et al. 2002). Heart disease is associated with high-fat diets, high-salt intake, obesity, and body shape (e.g., excessive fat around the abdominal region) (Daniels 2002). Obesity is also often related to diets high in carbohydrates. However, fiber, vitamins A, B6, C, and E, folic acid, zinc, manganese, selenium, copper, and moderate amounts of alcohol (Daniels 2002) appear to be protective against coronary heart disease (Rimm et al. 1998). Further, one study found nutrition-related cardiovascular disease risk factors highly prevalent among older Americans (Erlinger et al. 2000) particularly among African Americans, who tend to benefit more from changes in dietary habits than their White counterparts.

The lack of access to medical and preventive care are considered important determinants of health status among minority populations (Williams and Collins 1995). The literature indicates that there are racial and SES differences in the quantity and quality of medical care. One study found that deaths due to causes that could be avoided by medical intervention accounted for about 1/3 of the excess total death rates of African Americans relative to Whites (Woolhander et al. 1985). Other studies revealed mixed evidence on the contribution of medicine to health status (Adler et al. 1993). However, some suggest that medical care has a greater impact on the health status of African Americans, Hispanics, and lower SES populations than their more advantaged counterparts (Williams 1990). For example, for many diseases and conditions such as hypertension or cancer, the higher incidence rates among African Americans does not account for higher mortality rates. In fact, the higher mortality rates may be due to later initial diagnoses of disease, comorbidity, delays in treatment, and other gaps in quality of care (Williams and Collins 1995). Furthermore, Hispanics tend to have the lowest rates of health insurance coverage, and both Hispanics and African Americans are less likely to be covered by Medicare.

Bio-psycho-social-behavioral models of health outcomes attempt to integrate multiple risk factors in the relationship between SES and health. In accordance with the literature, it is suggested that SES and race work through bio-psycho-social-behavioral and health utilization factors to influence biological mechanisms, which then influence health outcomes. Although there is evidence of reciprocal causal pathways between SES and health outcomes, a common finding is that the pathway from SES to health in contrast to the effect of health on SES is stronger (Mulatu and Schooler 2002).

Conclusion

In conclusion, SES differences in health appear to reflect the cumulative effects of adversity or stress—which tends to exert repeated pressure on physiological regulatory mechanisms. This often leads to an increase in biological frailty or biological risk for poor health. However, SES effects on health are more than just biological and stress-related. SES also regulates access to quality healthcare and knowledge about health behaviors. Race/ethnic differences in health are often said to be related to socioeconomic

levels. However, both race and SES influence health independent of each other and, at the same time, work together to influence health. Furthermore, since *race/ethnicity* is a socially constructed term, it has been suggested that race differences reflect historical policies that served to create the disparities in income, education, and access to adequate health care. The Hispanic mortality paradox appeared to be an anomaly in all of this, and some support has been found for the healthy migrant effect, yet more systematic research is needed to elicit the true explanations for the Hispanic health advantage.

References

Abraido-Lanza, A. F., Dohrenwend, B. P., Ng-Mak, D. S., and Blake Turner, J. (1999). The Latino Mortality Paradox: A Test of the Salmon Bias and Healthy Migrant Hypothesis. *American Journal of Public Health*, 89 (10), 1543–1548.

Adler, N. E., Boyce, W. T., Chesney, M. A., Folkman, S., and Syme, S. L. (1993). Socioeconomic Inequalities in Health: No Easy Solution. *Journal of the American Medical Association*, 269, 3140–3145.

Blackwell, D. L., Hayward, M. D., and Crimmins, E. M. (2001). Does Childhood Health Affect Chronic Morbidity in Later Life? *Social Science and Medicine*, 52, 1269–1284.

Crimmins, E. M., and Saito, Y. (2001). Trends in Disability Free Life Expectancy in the United States, 1970–1990: Gender, Racial, and Educational Differences. *Social Science and Medicine*, 52, 1629–1641.

Crimmins, E. M., and T. E. Seeman. (2001). Integrating Biology Into Demographic Research on Health and Aging with a Focus on the MacArthur Study of Successful Aging. In C. Finch and J. Vaupel (Eds.), *Cells and Surveys: Should Biological Measures Be Included in Social Science Research?* Washington, DC: National Academy Press.

Cooper, R. S. (2003). Race, Genes, and Health—New Wine in Old Bottles? *International Journal of Epidemiology*, 32, 23–25.

Daniels, L. (2002). Diet and Coronary Heart Disease. *Nursing Standard*, 16 (43), 47–52.

Department of Health and Human Services. (2004). Minority Health Disparities at a Glance. *HSS Fact Sheet: July 12, 2004*. Washington, D.C.: U.S. Department of Health and Human Services: The Initiative to Eliminate Racial and Ethnic Disparities in Health.

Erlinger, T. P., Pollac, H., and Appel, L. J. (2000). Nutrition-Related Cardiovascular Risk Factors in Older People: Results from the Third National Health and Nutrition Examination Survey. *American Geriatrics Society*, 48(11), 1486–1489.

Fang, J., Madhavan, S., and Alderman, M. H. (1997). Influence of Nativity on Cancer Mortality Among Black New Yorkers. *Cancer*, 80, 129–135.

Finch, C. E., and Seeman, T. E. (1998). Stress Theories of Aging. Pp. 81–97 in Vern L. Bengtson and K. Warner Schaie (Eds.), *Handbook of the Theories of Aging*. New York: Springer Publishing Company.

Franzini, L., Ribble, J. C., and Keddie, A. M. (2001). Understanding the Hispanic Paradox. *Ethnicity and Disease* 11 (3), 496–518.

Ginzberg, E. (1991). Access to Health Care for Hispanics. *Journal of the American Medical Association*, 265 (2), 238–241.

Goldstein, M. S. (1979). The Sociology of Mental Health and Illness. *Annual Review of Sociology*, 5, 381–409.

Hansen, K. A., and Farber, C. S. (1997). The Foreign-Born Population of the United States: 1996. *Current Population Reports: Population Characteristics*, 420–494.

Hayward, M. D., Crimmins, E. M., Miles, T .P., and Yang, Y. (2000). The Significance of Socioeconomic Status in Explaining the Race Gap in Chronic Health Conditions. *American Sociological Review*, 65, 910–930.

Heath, G. W., and Smith, J. D. (1994). Physical Activity Patterns Among Adults in Georgia: Results from the 1990 Behavioral Risk Factor Surveillance System. *Southern Medical Journal*, 87 (4), 435–439.

Hellerstedt, W. L. (2001). Social Determinants of Gender Differences in Health in the U.S. Presentation at Healthy Generations Conference Series: Women's Reproductive Health—University of Minnesota, Center for Leadership Education in Maternal and Child Public Health, March 14, 2001.

House, J. S., Landis, K. R., and Umberson, D. (1988). Social relationships and health. *Science*, 241, 540–545.

Hoyert, D. L., and Kung, H. C. (1997). Asian or Pacific Islander Mortality, Selected States, 1992. *Monthly Vital Statistics Report*, 14, 46 (1 suppl), 1–63.

Hummer, R. A., Rogers, R. G., Nam, C. B., and LeClere, F. B. (1999). Race/ethnicity, nativity, and U.S. adult mortality. *Social Science Quarterly*, 80 (1), 136–153.

Kagawa-Singer, M., Hikoyeda, N., and Tanjasiri, S. P. (1997). Aging, Chronic Conditions, and Physical Disabilities in Asian and Pacific Islander Americans. In K. S. Markides and M. R. Miranda (Eds.), *Minorities, Aging, and Health*. Thousand Oaks, CA: Sage.

Kessler, R. C. (1979). Stress, social status and psychological distress. *Journal of Health and Social Behavior*, 20, 259–272.

Key, T. J., Allen, N. E., Spencer, E. A., and Travis, R. C. (2002). The effect of diet on risk of cancer. *Lancet*, 360 (9336), 861–868.

Kington, R. S., and Nickens, H. W. (2001). Racial and Ethnic Differences in Health: Recent Trends, Current Patterns, Future Directions. In N. Smelser, W. J. Wilson, and F. Mitchell (Eds.), *America Becoming: Racial Trends and Their Consequences, Volume II*. Washington, DC: National Academy Press.

Krause, N., and Wray, L. A. (1992). Psychosocial Correlates of Health and Illness Among Minority Elders. In E. P. Stanford and F. M. Torres-Gil (Eds.), *Diversity: New Approaches to Ethnic Minority Aging* (pp. 41–52). Amityville, NY: Baywood.

Kromhout, D., Menotti, A., Kesteloot, H., and Sans, S. (2002). Prevention of Coronary Heart Disease by Diet and Lifestyle: Evidence from Prospective Cross-Cultural, Cohort, and Intervention Studies. *Circulation*, 105 (7), 893–898.

Larsen, L. J. (2004). The Foreign-Born Population in the United States: 2003. *Current Population Reports, P20-551*, Washington, DC: U.S. Census Bureau.

Lehrman, S. (2004). Race and Healthcare. *http://www.alternet.org/story/16868/*.

Liao, Y., Cooper, R. S., Cao, G., Durazo-Arvizu, R., Kaufman, J. S., Luke, A., and McGee, D. (1998). Mortality Patterns Among Adult Hispanics: Findings From the NHIS, 1986–1990. *American Journal of Public Health*, 88, 227–32.

Link, B. G., and Phelan, J. (1995). Social Conditions as Fundamental Causes of Disease. *Journal of Health and Social Behavior*, 36, 89–94.

Markides, K. S., and Black, S. A. (1996). Race, Ethnicity, and Aging: The Impact of Inequality. In R. H. Binstock and George, L. K. (Eds.), *Handbook of Aging and the Social Sciences*, 4th ed. Washington, DC: Academic Press.

Markides, K. S., and Coreil, J. (1986). The Health of Hispanics in the Southwestern United States: An Epidemiologic Paradox. *Public Health Reports*, 101, 253–265.

McEwen, B. S., and Seeman, T. (1999). Protective and Damaging Effects of Mediators of Stress. *Annals of the New York Academy of Sciences*, 896, 30–47.

Meyer, J. P., and Gillatt, D. A. (2002). Can Diet Affect Prostate Cancer? *BJU Int.*, 89 (3), 250–254.

Milner, J. A. (2002). Strategies for Cancer Prevention: The Role of Diet. *British Journal of Nutrition*, 87 (Suppl 2), S265–272.

Mulatu, M. S., and Schooler, C. (2002). Causal Connections Between Socio-Economic Status and Health: Reciprocating Effects and Mediating Mechanisms. *Journal of Health and Social Behavior*, 43 (1), 22–41.

National Center for Health Statistics. (1993). Health Promotion and Disease Prevention: United States, 1990. *Vital Health Statistics 10*, 185. Hyattsville, MD: U.S. Dept of Health and Human Services. DHHS publication (PHS) 93–1513.

——. (2000). *Health Outcomes Among Hispanic Subgroups: Data From the National Health Interview Survey, 1992–95*. Hyattsville, MD: U.S. Dept of Health and Human Services. DHHS publication (PHS) 2000–1250.

Odoms-Young, A. M. (2004). Obesity and Poverty. Presentation at Obesity 2004 Conference: Developing Community Strategies for a National Crisis, Case Western Reserve.

Palloni, A., and Arias, E. (2004). Paradox Lost: Explaining the Hispanic Adult Mortality Advantage. *Demography*, 41 (3), 385–415.

Perlman, R. M. (1954). The Aging Syndrome. *Journal of the American Geriatric Society*, 2, 123–129.

Pearce, N., Foliaki, S., Sporle, A., and Cunningham, C. (2004). Genetics, Race, Ethnicity, and Health. *British Medical Journal*, 328: 1070–1072.

Pinn, V. W. (2003). Sex and Gender Factors in Medical Studies: Implications for Health and Clinical Practice. *Journal of the American Medical Association*, 289, 397–400.

Pi-Sunyer, F. X. (1993). Health Implications of Obesity. *American Journal of Clinical Nutrition*, 53, 1595S–1603S.

Potter, J. D. (1997). Diet and Cancer: Possible Explanations for the Higher Risk of Cancer in the Poor. *IARC Scientific Publications*, 138, 265–283.

Ramirez de Arellano, A. B. (1994). The Elderly. In C. W. Molina and M. A. Molina (Eds.), *Latino Health in the U.S.: A Growing Challenge*. Washington, DC: American Public Health Association.

Rimm, E. B., Willett, W., Hu, F. B., Sampson, L., Colditz, G. A., Manson, J. E., Hennekens, C., and Stampfer, M. J. (1998). Folate and Vitamin B6 From Diet and Supplements in Relation to Risk of Coronary Heart Disease Among Women. *Journal of the American Medical Association*, 279 (5), 359–364.

Rogers, R. G., Hummer, R. A., and Nam, C. B. (2000). *Living and Dying in the USA*. San Diego, CA: Academic Press.

Rogers, R. G., Hummer, R. A., Nam, C. B., and Peters, K. (1996). Demographic, Socioeconomic, and Behavioral Factors Affecting Ethnic Mortality by Cause. *Social Forces*, 74, 1419–1438.

Rosenberg, H. M., Maurer, J. D., Sorlie, P. D., Johnson, N. J., MacDorman, M. F., Hoyert, D. L., Spitler, J. F., and Scott, C. (1999). Quality of Death Rates by Race and Hispanic Origin: A Summary of Current Research, 1999. *Vital and Health Statistics*, Series 2 (128). Hyattsville, MD: National Center for Health Statistics.

Rosenwaike, I. (1987). Mortality Differentials Among Persons Born in Cuba, Mexico, and Puerto Rico Residing in the United States, 1979–81. *American Journal of Public Health* 77, 603–606.

Schneider, A., and Martinez, J. (1997). Native Americans and Medicaid: Coverage and Financing Issues. Kaiser Family Foundation (Pub.#2101).

Scribner, R. S. (1996). Paradox as Paradigm: The Health Outcomes of Mexican Americans. *American Journal of Public Health*, 86, 303–304.

Seeman, T. E., and Crimmins, E. M. (2001). Social Environment Effects on Health and Aging: Integrating Epidemiological and Demographic Approaches and Perspectives. *Annals of the New York Academy of Sciences*, 954, 88–117.

Singh, G. K., and Siahpush, M. (2001). All-Cause and Cause-Specific Mortality of Immigrants and Natives in the United States. *American Journal of Public Health*, 91 (3), 392–399.

——. (2002). Ethnic-Immigrant Differentials in Health Behaviors, Morbidity, a Cause Specific Mortality in the United States: An Analysis of Two National Data Bases. *Human Biology*, 74 (1), 83–109.

Smith, J. P. (1999). Healthy Bodies and Thick Wallets: The Dual Relation Between Health and Economic Status. *Journal of Economic Perspectives*, 13, 145–166.

Smith, J. P., and Welch, F. R. (1989). Black Economic Progress After Myrdal, *Journal of Economic Literature* 27, 519–564.

Sorlie, P. D., Backlund, E., Johnson, N. J., and Rogot, E. (1993). Mortality by Hispanic Status in the United States. *Journal of the American Medical Association*, 270, 2464–2468.

Sowers, M. F. (1997). Dietary Factors and SES. John D. and Catherine T. MacArthur Research Network on Socioeconomic Status and Health. *http://www.macses.ucsf.edu/research/allostatic/notebook/diet.html*.

Stephen, E. H., Foote, K., Hendershot, G. E., and Schoenborn, C. A. (1994). Health of the Foreign Born Population: United States, 1989–90. *Advance Data From Vital and Health Statistics* No. 241 (Feb). Hyattsville, MD: National Center for Health Statistics.

Sterling, T. D., and Weinkam, D. (1989). Comparison of Smoking-Related Risk Factors Among Black and White Males. *American Journal of Industrial Medicine*, 15, 319–333.

Taylor, S., Repetti, R., and Seeman, T. (1997). Health Psychology: What Is an Unhealthy Environment and How Does It Get Under the Skin? *Annual Review of Psychology*, 48, 411–447.

Thiel de Bocanegra, H., Gany, F., and Fruchter, R. (1993). Available Epidemiologic Data on New York's Latino Population: A Critical Review of the Literature. *Ethnicity and Disease*, 3, 413–426.

Turner, R. J., Wheaton, B., and Lloyd, D. A. (1995). The Epidemiology of Social Stress. *American Sociological Review*, 60, 104–125.

U.S. Bureau of the Census. (1993). *We, the American Asians*. Washington, DC: U.S. Government Printing Office.

Wamala, S. P., Wolk, A., and Orth-Gomer, K. (1997). Determinants of Obesity in Relation to Socioeconomic Status Among Middle Aged Swedish Women. *Preventive Medicine*, 26 (5 pt 1), 734–744.

Williams, D. R. (1990). Socioeconomic Differentials in Health: A Review and Redirection. *Social Psychology Quarterly*, 53, 31–99.

——. (2001). Racial Variations in Adult Health Status: Patterns, Paradoxes, and Prospects. In N. Smelser, W. J. Wilson and F. Mitchell (Eds.), *America Becoming: Racial Trends and their Consequences*. Washington, DC: National Academy Press.

——. (2003). Racial/Ethnic Discrimination and Health: Findings from Community Studies. *American Journal of Public Health*, 93 (2), 200–208.

——. (2004). The Influence of Socioeconomic Status, Race and Geography on Health Outcomes and Health-care Access. Presented at Inequality Matters Conference. New York University: June 4, 2004.

Williams, D. R., and Collins, C. (1995). U.S. Socioeconomic and Racial Differences in Health: Patterns and Explanations. *Annual Review of Sociology*, 21, 349–386.

Winkleby, M. A., Gardner, C. D., and Taylor, C. B. (1996). The Influence of Gender and Socioeconomic Factors on Hispanic/White Differences in Body Mass Index. *Preventive Medicine*, 25, 203–211.

Woolhandler, S., Himmelstein, D. U., Silber, R., Bader, M., Harnly, M., and Jones, A. A. (1985). Medical Care and Mortality: Racial Differences in Preventable Deaths. *Interntional Journal of Health Services*, 15 (1), 1–22.

Zuckerman, S., Haley, J., Roubideaux, Y., and Lillie-Blanton, M. (2004). Health Service Access, Use, and Insurance Coverage Among American Indians/ Alaska Natives and Whites: What Role Does the Indian Health Service Play? *American Journal of Public Health*, 94 (1), 53–59.

Discussion Questions

1. Women in general have lower earnings than men and often lead stressful lives, for example as single custodial parents, yet they have longer life expectancies and better health than men. What are some of the bio-psycho-social-behavioral factors that might contribute to health and life expectancy differences between women and men?

2. The relationship between diet and exercise and health is well known. Yet millions of American men and women of all racial/ethnic backgrounds are overweight couch potatoes. What are some of the factors that account for this? How are some of these factors related to gender, race/ethnicity, and social class?

3. Many of the immediate correlates of good or poor health are related to individual choices and characteristics such as lifestyles and income, but when we look at the aggregate statistics, it is clear that aspects of social structure and social policy are involved as well. What kinds of social changes could reduce the health disparities among racial/ethnic and economic groups?

4. Assuming that wear-and-tear theories do explain a significant amount of poor health, why would members of some racial/ethnic groups be likely to wear out sooner than members of others?

37

The Illness Experience Among Mexico City's Older Adults

The Effect of Gender, Class, and Race/Ethnicity

Diana Torrez
Roberto Campos-Navarro.
Elia Nora Arganis Juárez

In one of two articles in this volume that focuses on health issues (see also the Johnston
article), Diana Torrez, Roberto Campos-
Navarro, and Elia Nora Arganis Juárez take us
into the homes of elderly Mexicans, conducting in-depth interviews in order to trace the illness experience of these Mexican elders. Torrez
et al. frame their analysis along the central issues of gender, class, and race as they describe
elderly Mexican women and men with little or
no education whose lives are focused on coping
with families living in poverty. The heart of this
analysis is the very words of the respondents
themselves as they describe how they developed their illnesses, the sorts of social supports they rely on, and the treatment strategies
they employ. The respondents describe
"susto"—a folk illness resulting from a sudden
fright—as associated with their current physical symptoms.
   Yet, susto was framed differently by men and
women. Where men associate susto with
work-related accidents, women associate susto
with emotional events, such as family problems. In addition, respondents from lower socioeconomic classes were more likely to pinpoint the causes of their illnesses within a
cultural belief context, while upper-class Mexicans viewed cultural belief descriptions of
illness as "folk myths."
   Treatment approaches to illness were more
varied for women who chose to use medical
prescriptions as well as medicinal plants and
herbs. The authors make the important point
that the elderly Mexican women in the study
were more likely to attend local health programs and presentations, indicative of how
women in Latino culture have historically
taken on the role of treating family illnesses.
Social support seemed impacted by several
factors. In terms of gender, women found networks of support among other women (e.g.,
sisters, daughters, sisters-in-law), while men
either attempted to find work or were assisted
by their children. With regard to class, all of the
respondents were interdependent on family
for economic support. Moreover, the primacy
of the family as the main social support was
indicative of ethnic and cultural belief systems. Torrez, Campos-Navarro, and Arganis
Juárez underscore the notion that illness is
not simply a medical-biological event, but it is
experienced as part of an individual and collective life history that is traced along several
axes, among them gender, class, and race.

In Mexico City, as in much of the developed
world, improvements in the standard of living and increased access to health services
have resulted in significantly decreased rates
of infectious diseases, such as tuberculosis
and diphtheria. Instead, similarly to the
United States, chronic diseases, such as heart
disease and diabetes, have become the leading cause of death. Chronic diseases are diagnosed more often among older adults
(SSA 1994a, 1994b).
   Chronic diseases are experienced and interpreted by individuals as illness, hence the term
"chronic illness." As noted by Fitzpatrick
(1990, 38),

> Today chronic illnesses are the primary
> health problem faced by medicine, the
> longer that an individual lives with his/
> her illness, the longer he/she has to re-in-
> terpret and evaluate his/her symptoms
> and the treatment of these symptoms.

Among older adults, the risk of chronic illness increases as the result of aging as well the social and economic conditions these individuals have faced during their lifetime. At the same time, these older adults enter the retirement phase of their life and transition from a lifetime role of employee to one of pensioned retiree. In this stage individuals begin to experience a change in their social roles and a decrease in their economic resources, which will in turn impact the chronic illness experience (Garcia 1998).

Older adults (age 60+) with limited economic resources often report high rates of co-morbidities, or more than one disease, which increase the likelihood of complications and other problems that may arise from their primary chronic disease. For instance, people with diabetes often report high blood pressure. As a result, these individuals are more likely to experience disability and feel incapacitated by their illness. Further, the treatments offered by the medical profession do not cure, but only offer some level of comfort and allow individuals to manage symptoms and co-exist with their disease. In this way, chronic illness becomes a significant and integral part of the lives of many older adults, an experience that cannot be avoided and must be experienced in its totality. The individual's life and the chronic illness become a unified experience.

Explanatory models of illness must take into account several significant variables that are involved in how disease is interpreted and managed. Disease is a social construction, directly affected by sociohistorical time period as well as the culture in which the disease is discovered. Gender, race/ethnicity, and class, among other relevant variables, play a significant role in understanding how physicians discuss disease with patients, as well as how patients understand the disease process and interpret their experience with illness. Societal values and beliefs, for instance, about a patients' role in acquiring a disease and how gender, race/ethnicity, or class may have contributed to the development of the disease, will affect the patients' illness experience. The explanations and the treatments offered by physicians are also affected by these variables.

Research Methods

This exploratory study allows us to examine the illness experience among a group of older adults with chronic illness. The data for this research project were collected with the assistance of one of Mexico City's Social Security Health Clinics (IMSS)—a family health clinic on the south side of the city. This clinic was selected because it is one of the largest clinics in the city and its patients represented a diversity of occupational backgrounds. The Mexican Social Security System insures employees of private businesses, from small businesses to large corporations. For the purposes of this study, we selected those patients over the age of 60 years who were diagnosed with hypertension, diabetes, and osteoarthritis.

Fifty patients (35 women and 15 men) were randomly selected for this exploratory study. A questionnaire with 85 closed-ended and open-ended questions was administered. The questions probed in the areas of pre-existing conditions, attributed cause of the disease, the signs and symptoms of the disease, complications experienced, and course of treatment pursued. In addition to the questionnaire, the interviewer noted the living conditions of the interviewee. The interviews were conducted in the homes of these individuals.

This sample population ranged between 60 and 75 years of age, the majority had an elementary educational level of attainment or less, and 28 percent of the women were illiterate. In addition, 64 percent of the sample had come to Mexico City as migrants from the central or southern states of Mexico. The majority of the men in this sample received private pensions or were beneficiaries of the Social Security System. Only a small percentage of the men (4 percent) received health services through IMSS as a result of being a dependent of a child. Many of these men still worked at various jobs. The majority of the women were housewives. Some stated that they had worked at various points in their lives. However, the majority received health benefits from IMSS as a result of their husbands or children being the primary beneficiary of IMSS. Despite their chronic illnesses, these women continued to engage in domestic responsibilities in their home and also cared for their grandchildren on a part-time basis in order to help their children.

The majority of the sample can be defined as residing at poverty levels, with an average income of $150 a month. Their living conditions and the services or assistance they received often varied from *colonia* to *colonia*, or neighborhood to neighborhood.

The effect of living with a chronic illness varied depending on the resources the individual had available to him or her. For instance, the composition of the family, number of family members, ages of family members, number of family members who worked, and so on, all affected the illness experience. This was evident from the fact that we encountered both individuals whose lives seemed to have been minimally affected by their chronic illness and others who were unable to continue living their lives as they had prior to developing the disease and who felt quite incapacitated.

In-depth interviews with these individuals allowed us insight into their lives and offered us an understanding of their illness experience. In addition, we were able to note the effect of race, class, and gender on living with and managing chronic illness.

Results

In the section that follows, we present the results of this exploratory study. Five themes emerged from the interview data collected. The findings of the interviews appear, therefore, in five thematic sections.

Previous Life Experiences

Although chronic illnesses are often diagnosed later in life, some older adults who suffered from hypertension, diabetes, and arthritis attributed the cause to events that occurred earlier in their lives. The older adults made reference to a life of poverty and hard work they believed had contributed to the onset of their chronic disease. Martha explained,

This illness (hypertension) is the result of my beginning to work at a very young age. I recall being 6 years old when I was first taken to work at a restaurant, from

four in the morning until eleven at night. I swept the banquet area, washed dishes and ran errands until they came for me in the evening. I earned twenty-five cents a month. Later I married, but my situation did not improve significantly. My husband did not know how to read or write. He worked a lot as a sharecropper, but there were times when he did not make a profit. Since our situation was not improving, we moved to Mexico City.

Those individuals, originally from other states, noted that they had come to Mexico City seeking a better life. These older adults arrived at different stages in their lives, some as infants and others as young married adults. They all noted that they had held various jobs and had lived in different sections of Mexico City. Ruth shared the following:

I am from Puebla, but when I married I went to live in Oriaba (Veracurz). During this time my children were young and since there was no work here, we moved to Mexico City and became squatters.

Jorge noted:

I did not complete elementary school. I worked in the fields as a laborer. After this, I worked in a laminating shop, and also for the government. We lived in the Colonia Anuahac (middle-class neighborhood), but we lost our home. So I mobilized my resources and was able to buy this small house. At first it was quite ugly, but we have fixed it up considerably.

It is evident from these individuals' comments that lower social class was a factor in their decisions to relocate or to accept certain types of employment. It was their jobs and lack of resources that increased their risk to chronic illness as middle-aged and older adults. Although chronic diseases are often associated with old age because of the common onset at this time, for low-income individuals it is more likely to be associated with middle age because the onset of chronic diseases occurs much earlier among this social class.

The Perceived Cause

Although 10 percent of those with chronic illnesses said they did not know the cause of their chronic disease, within the course of the interview it became apparent that older adults attributed the onset of the disease to certain causes. Although the biomedical explanations were accepted, there were certain events in their personal lives that they believed contributed to the onset of the disease. In this vein, it can be noted that one of the fundamental perceived causes of their chronic disease was their social relationships.

For the men, the origin of their health problems was often associated with accidents or unexpected events that occurred at their workplace. For the women, the causes of their chronic diseases were found within their familial relationships and related emotional problems, such as intense anger and worries. For example, Marina said, "I became ill when I became enraged with my husband. That is the source of my health problems." In contrast, Alberto, who experienced a similar chronic illness said, "Before I drove a bus and I had many scares on the highway. I believe this is the source of my illness."

Diabetes is significantly associated with *susto*, a folk illness that is the result of an unexpected, sudden, and frightening event. The men referenced violent events they experienced at their work or work-related accidents that resulted in disease. The women, however, recalled emotional events: rage, suffering, preoccupation, and family problems. In one case, a woman believed that excessive celebration of her church wedding, after cohabitation, was the cause of her disease.

Salvador recalled,

I worked in a bar and these two men with pistols entered the bar at two in the morning. We were assaulted and I ran out of the bar. I was shot. I still have a bullet fragment in my leg. The doctors were never able to remove it completely, and I was told it might cause more damage if they attempted to remove it since it was so small.

Nestor related the following,

I developed diabetes because of a fright I experienced. It all began more than 30 years ago. I lived with my wife on a ranch. One night we saw a light and my wife said to me, "I think they want to kill you," and

I said to her, "Why would they want to kill me?" She replied, "You know there are bad people in this world." I then went to search for the light that appeared to be someone carrying a lamp. As I drew closer, I heard a noise coming from the direction of light, which was moving further away. That is when I noticed that it was not a living person who was there (implying it was someone who had died).

Julieta explained, "I went to visit my daughter who lived in Cancun and I was quite emotionally affected by the Hurricane Gilbert." Another respondent, Mrs. Trinidad, recalled,

I developed diabetes during my 20s. I don't even really remember, but around the death of my mother I began to lose weight. My clothes hung loosely on me. In addition, I began to experience a lot of thirst at night and dizziness.

Hypertension is also associated with fright, worries, and anger, although, in some cases, it is believed to be the result of heredity, fatigue from exercise, dieting to lose weight, or rheumatism. Martina says, "It all began when I begin to diet. I was prescribed some diet pills. I was not hungry and only ate what was on my diet. I did not notice that I was sick, until I went to the doctor."

Gerardo recalled the beginnings of his disease.

I became sick with the earthquake of '85. I worked in a printing shop in the downtown area, and we always began work early. I always had high blood pressure, but it was with the earthquake that it really became a problem. Even though nothing happened, as a result of the earthquake, to the printing shop, I was quite mortified when I went outside the printing shop and saw all the fallen buildings.

Arthritis is associated with the folk belief surrounding the concepts of hot and cold. To be in a situation or circumstance where one is "hot," such as after giving birth or ironing, and then being exposed to cold or humidity can result in disease, according to respondents. Anita related the circumstances she believed caused her arthritis,

My disease began with my last birth. I had taken good care of myself. But I was sent to give birth at La Raza (a speciality hospital). There, I gave birth to my son at 8:00 a.m. At 9:00 a.m., the nurses came in and wanted me to bathe. I told the doctor I did not want to. He told me to tell them I had a cold. I did, but they made me bathe, and there was no hot water, only cold. Ever since then, I have been ill.

Rosa expressed similar ideas. "I believe I became ill because before I washed and ironed, and I believe the coldness crept into my bones."

The comments made by the respondents demonstrate that gender affects the types of relationships formed by men and women, as well as the significance of these relationships on their lives. In addition, ethnicity specifically related to cultural beliefs was also applied in forming an understanding of the origins of chronic illness. For instance, concepts of hot and cold and sudden fright as a result of unexpected events, commonly found in Latino ethnic cultures, were cited as the catalyst in the development of chronic disease.

Ideas Regarding Illness

These individuals were presented with the medical explanations for their diseases, yet we found that they did not have a clear idea of the origins of these diseases. For instance, the respondents often noted that they believed that diabetes was the result of sugar in the blood, thus it was often referred to as "sugar diabetes." Diabetes was perceived as a horrible disease that destroyed the body. Hypertension was viewed as a disease in which the heart worked too hard and the blood pumped too fast. Arthritis was perceived as a disease in which there were clots in the blood and the fingers shrank.

The symptoms that each person described were reconciled with the clinical description of each disease. It was believed that the troubles or discomforts associated with each disease increased with each person's particular problems. That is, social context was considered significant to the illness experience. Additionally, age was viewed as a factor that might not directly affect the disease but, nonetheless, was perceived as a process that resulted in physical decline of the body. The bones were perceived as deteriorating with

age, and for many women, menopause was a time when disease began to take hold, although, they were not clear if this was a coincidence or a cause.

These ideas regarding the origins of the illnesses were ethnicity and class-based. Although the ideas regarding disease and illness were widely found in Latino ethnic cultures, they were more commonly found among the lower classes and rarely among the upper classes. The upper classes were aware of these beliefs regarding the causes of diseases, but they were likely to label them as "old wives tales" or "folk myths." They rarely gave these ideas credence and usually minimized the role of such factors in the onset of disease.

Treatment Utilized

With respect to treatment, these diseases were highly medicalized. Patients most commonly treated their chronic diseases with prescribed medicines obtained through the IMSS clinics. We found that folk treatments were not often used. There was only one instance in our study of a woman who believed her diabetes had been the result of fright and had sought the help of a *curandera,* or folk healer. Medicinal plants and herbs, however, were used frequently, usually as the result of the recommendations of friends or family.

Gender significantly impacted the treatments utilized by respondents to treat chronic illnesses. Women were more likely than men to use medicinal plants and herbs. The primary reason for this was women often shared their "successful outcomes" in treating illnesses with alternative medicines. Older women, therefore, chose to supplement their "medical" treatment with alternative remedies as a result of other women's positive outcomes when utilizing these treatments.

With respect to the support groups or programs offered for their particular chronic disease, 60 percent of the respondents said they had attended a presentation or orientation offered by IMSS, but most said they did not participate. Only 14 percent actually participated in programs sponsored by IMSS, and all of these were women, even though they noted having problems attending as a result of their health, household issues, or grandchild care responsibilities. Women in

Latino ethnic cultures have historically assumed the role of acquiring information that would assist them in treating the illnesses of their families.

These elderly knew their disease was chronic and had no cure. The physicians had brought considerable attention to this aspect of their disease. Jose noted, "The doctor told me that if a physician ever discovered a cure for diabetes, he would become a millionaire and be awarded the Nobel Prize." Even though some of the elderly acknowledged that someday a cure might be found for their particular chronic illness, they did not believe they would benefit from this discovery because of their age.

Social Support

Men and women who lived with their spouses relied on them for assistance. Those who were widowed, approximately 30 percent of respondents, lived with their sons. Nonetheless, we did encounter women who lived by themselves but also had access to some sort of support or assistance. The women who had given birth to numerous children (4 to 13) relied most significantly on the support of other women (daughters primarily, but also sisters, daughter-in-laws, and sister-in-laws) to help them with their domestic responsibilities and also to take them to doctors appointments. The males of the family provided economic resources, but 40 percent of the married women said they did not receive any support from their husbands, only from their children. Although 31 percent of the women said they were married, in actuality, they were separated from their spouses and lived with their children.

The family situation was a significant source of problems for men and women. Although the majority of those interviewed were managing and controlling their chronic disease, they worried about the health status of their spouse. Fully 10 percent of the respondents had a spouse who was experiencing a serious health problem.

Although their children were grown, these elderly continued a preoccupation with their children's social and personal situations. As a result, there was an emotional and economic interdependent relationship among them.

Angeles commented, "One of my daughters left her husband and came to live with me. Now I need to cook for her and I can't continue my diet. I am going to tell her she must return home."

Nicolasa related,

I have a son who drinks and abuses his wife and children. They live with me and I have told him not do to that, but he does not listen to me. I have told his wife to demand he leave the house; perhaps he will change his behavior.

Joaquin explained,

From my two sons, I have only worries. When they were bachelors, they would go to parties on Saturday and not return until Sunday. They would not heed me. Now they are married, and they come to visit when they wish. One of them does offer me support and he does give me some money. The other only brings me problems.

In spite of their illnesses, women continued to carry out their domestic responsibilities and cared for their grandchildren, thereby helping their daughters and daughters-in-law. Men found themselves in different situations. Those who were in better health sought some form of employment to save some money prior to retirement and their projected small pensions. Those who suffered more disabilities relied on the support and assistance of their children.

The relationships with their grandchildren varied, depending on the situation of each family, which was influenced by economic realities and the economic composition of the family. The women who were caring for young grandchildren had close relationships with them. "I love my grandson a lot (a 6-year-old child), he is my companion." When the grandchildren were older, the relationship was transformed into one in which the grandchildren assisted the elders with their health needs, even though they could not always rely on them. Aurora comments, "I have two granddaughters. The youngest gets bored and the other one is married and her husband will not let her help me."

Social support was affected by class, ethnicity, and gender. As a result of the lack of sufficient economic resources on the part of either the respondents or their adult children, an economic interdependent relationship often developed. There were numerous instances where the respondents relied on the informal assistance of their children in their daily lives. However, there were also numerous incidents of respondents providing their children with assistance in the form of child care or housing. Ethnicity also played a role in social support as a result of the belief in Latino ethnic cultures that families have a moral responsibility to provide for their parents or vice versa, if the need arises. In addition, social support was influenced by gender with women relying mainly on women to provide help with day-to-day domestic responsibilities and, in turn, taking care of grandchildren for their daughters and daughters-in-law—underscoring substantial networking relationships among women. Men, on the other hand, sometimes provided economic resources, seeking employment if in good health or relying on the support of their children.

Conclusions

The illness experience is shaped by the life circumstances of the individuals who suffer the chronic diseases. Many other authors have reported similar situations to those found in our interviews. Cohen et. al. (1994), Hernández (1995), and Hunt, Valenzuela, and Pugh (1998) noted that physicians and patients emphasize different aspects of the explanatory disease models. Patients are more likely to emphasize social domains and the impact on their lives, while those in the medical field are more likely to emphasize the pathological aspects and the physical affect of the disease.

Although the majority of older adults accept the biomedical definition of their disease, they come to understand the disease within the framework of their personal lives and the aspects of their lives that are most significant. The illness experience for older adults with chronic diseases is affected by their gender, class, and race/ethnicity. Gender differences in formulating explanations regarding the origins of their disease were evident. Women perceived social relationships to be at the root of their health problems, a reflection of the centrality of these relationships in their lives. Men, however, were more likely to locate the origins of their disease in their work lives, also a reflection of the importance of work in their lives. In addition, it was evident from the interviews that the older adults came to believe that the origin of their disease was rooted in the poverty they experienced and the choices they were often forced to make as a result. These were all individuals in the lower socioeconomic classes who had had little control over their lives and recognized the effect of this on their cumulative health status. Health in "old age" is a result of a lifetime of access or barriers to health service resources. Social class also influenced how diseases were labeled in that upper-class Latinos rarely accepted terminology based in lower-class "folk myths." Finally, Latino ethnic culture shaped the respondents' understanding of the origins of chronic illness, the labeling of specific diseases based on cultural interpretations, and beliefs about moral responsibilities within the family that could also be gender-coded.

It is important to examine the relationship and the representation of the illness experience as well as the modes of treatment in order to better understand the health orientation of each patient. Although chronic disease is biomedically defined, if we are to have an understanding of the experiences of older adults who live with chronic illness, we must understand how they interpret and make sense of the disease in their lives. It is necessary to realize not only that the origins of chronic disease can be found in the personal lives of older adults but also that their present illness experience with the disease continues to be affected by the social dimensions of their personal lives. Physicians may interpret disease utilizing a biomedical model, but for the patients who coexist with the disease, it is transformed into an illness experience that is affected by the social dimensions of their lives. That is, we cannot begin to understand the illness experience of older adults with chronic diseases if we do not place it within the gender, race/ethnicity, and class dimensions of their life experiences.

References

Cohen M. Z., Tripp-Reimer, T., Smith, C., Sorofman, B., and Lively, S. 1994. Explanatory Models of Diabetes: Patient Practitioner Variation. *Social Science and Medicine*, 38 (1), 59–66.

Fitzpatrick, R. 1990. Conceptos Comunes de Enfermedad. En Fitzpatrick, R., Hinton J., Staton Newman, Scambler G., and Thompson, J. *La enfermedad como experiencia* (pp. 19–41). Mèxico. Fondo de Cultura Económica.

García, H. 1998. Sistemas de soporte a la vejez. Apoyos Formales e Informales en el área Metropolitana de Monterrey. En *La Población de México al final del siglo XX*. Hernández, B. H., Menkes, C. (Coordinador), (403–416). Cuernavaca Morelos: CRIM, Sociedad Mexicana de Demografía, UNAM.

Hernández, C. A. 1995. The experience of living with insulin-dependent diabetes: lessons for the diabetes educator. *Diabetes Educator*, 21, 33–37.

Hunt, L. M., Valenzuela, M. A., and Pugh, J. 1998. ¿Por qué me tocó a mi? Mexican American diabetes patients' causal histories and their relationship to treatment behaviors. *Social Science and Medicine*, 46 (8), 959–969.

SSA (Secretar@237a de Salud). 1994a. *Encuesta nacional de enfermedades crónicas*. México.

——. 1994b. "La Transición en salud. Origen, rumbo y destino." México. *Cuadernos de Salud*. Secretaría de Salud: 20–33.

Discussion Questions

1. How might the illness experience of these Mexican elders be similar to or different from that of racial/ethnic minority elderly Americans? How might the illness experience of these Mexican elders be similar to or different from low-income White elderly Americans?

2. Do you think that the illness experience of elderly women from American racial/ethnic groups might resonate with that of these elderly Mexican women?

3. Do you think that Americans have become more accepting of nonmedical treatment strategies? If so, which ones? Do you think Americans have embraced any nonmedical illness causes? If so, which ones?

4. Have you ever used an herbal or medicinal plant remedy to deal with an illness? How did others perceive your choice to treat yourself? How did it work out?

38

White Privilege and Male Privilege

A Personal Account of Coming to See Correspondences Through Work in Women's Studies

Peggy McIntosh

Peggy McIntosh's personal reflection on privilege is a widely reprinted classic. Prior to its publication, discussion of gender, race, and class focused on the disadvantaged position of women, members of racial/ethnic minority groups, working class and poor people, and gay men and lesbians. After this paper was published, scholars began to deal with the implications of the facts that men have gender, White people have race, middle- and upper-class people have socioeconomic status, and straight people have sexuality.

In the paper, McIntosh raises subtle and painful issues. She acknowledges that some men do recognize that women are often ignored in the curriculum and treated unequally by others in everyday life. However, she points out that these same men may ignore the underlying structures that allow men as a category to dominate women as a category. Moreover, they may be willing to include some women in the curriculum or elsewhere, but not at the price of excluding some men to do so. Similar generalizations apply to other dominant/oppressed pairings, such as White people in relation to members of racial or ethnic minority groups, middle-class people in relation to those with lower socioeconomic status, or even people in wealthy nations like the United States in relation to those in developing countries. It is harder to see structural inequality than to see individual acts of prejudice and discrimination, and it is easier to share an unlimited

nonmaterial resource, such as good will, than to redistribute limited material ones, such as economic assets or positions of power.

In this personal account, McIntosh explores her own privileged status by publicly unpacking the "invisible knapsack" we all carry around. The contents form two lists, one representing White privilege and one representing heterosexual privilege. The knapsack contains things she finds (and all other White people or straight people tend to regard as) normal and unremarkable. Some instances of her White privilege are structural, such as being able to rent or purchase a place to live in any area within her means. Others are more individual, such as being able to make a remark or even to use poor manners without her whole race being blamed. Examples of heterosexual privilege include being able to travel with her spouse and talk openly about her social life.

Through work to bring materials and perspectives from Women's Studies into the rest of the curriculum, I have often noticed men's unwillingness to grant that they are overprivileged in the curriculum, even though they may grant that women are disadvantaged. Denials that amount to taboos surround the subject of advantages that men gain from women's disadvantages. These denials protect male privilege from being fully recognized, acknowledged, lessened, or ended.

Thinking through unacknowledged male privilege as a phenomenon with a life of its own, I realized that since hierarchies in our society are interlocking, there was most likely a phenomenon of white privilege that was similarly denied and protected, but alive and real in its effects. As a white person, I realized I had been taught about racism as something that puts others at a disadvantage, but had been taught not to see one of its corollary aspects, white privilege, which puts me at an advantage.

I think whites are carefully taught not to recognize white privilege, as males are taught not to recognize male privilege. So I have begun in an untutored way to ask what it is like to have white privilege. This paper is a partial record of my personal observations and not a scholarly analysis. It is based on my daily experiences within my particular circumstances.

I have come to see white privilege as an invisible package of unearned assets that I can count on cashing in each day, but about which I was "meant" to remain oblivious. White privilege is like an invisible weightless knapsack of special provisions, assurances, tools, maps, guides, codebooks, passports, visas, clothes, compass, emergency gear,' and blank checks.

Since I have had trouble facing white privilege, and describing its results in my life, I saw parallels here with men's reluctance to acknowledge male privilege. Only rarely will a man go beyond acknowledging that women are disadvantaged to acknowledging that men have unearned advantage, or that unearned privilege has not been good for men's development as human beings, or for society's development, or that privilege systems might ever be challenged and *changed*.

I will review here several types or layers of denial that I see at work protecting, and preventing awareness about, entrenched male privilege. Then I will draw parallels, from my own experience, with the denials that veil the facts of white privilege. Finally, I will list forty-six ordinary and daily ways in which I experience having white privilege, by contrast with my African American colleagues in the same building. This list is not intended to be generalizable. Others can make their own lists from within their own life circumstances.

Writing this paper has been difficult, despite warm receptions for the talks on which it is based.[1] For describing white privilege makes one newly accountable. As we in Women's Studies work reveal male privilege and ask men to give up some of their power, so one who writes about having white privilege must ask, "Having described it, what will I do to lessen or end it?"

The denial of men's over privileged state takes many forms in discussions of curriculum change work. Some claim that men must be central in the curriculum because they have done most of what is important or distinctive in life or in civilization. Some recognize sexism in the curriculum but deny that it makes male students seem unduly important in life. Others agree that certain *individual* thinkers are male oriented but deny that there is any *systemic* tendency in disciplinary frameworks or epistemology to overempower men as a group. Those men who do grant that male privilege takes institutionalized and embedded forms are still likely to deny that male hegemony has opened doors for them personally. Virtually all men deny that male overreward alone can explain men's centrality in all the inner sanctums of our most powerful institutions. Moreover, those few who will acknowledge that male privilege systems have overempowered them usually end up doubting that we could dismantle these privilege systems. They may say they will work to improve women's status, in the society or in the university, but they can't or won't support the idea of lessening men's. In curricular terms, this is the point at which they say that they regret they cannot use any of the interesting new scholarship on women because the syllabus is full. When the talk turns to giving men less cultural room, even the most thoughtful and fair-minded of the men I know will tend to reflect, or fall back on, conservative assumptions about the inevitability of present gender relations and distributions of power, calling on precedent or sociobiology and psychobiology to demonstrate that male domination is natural and follows inevitably from evolutionary pressures. Others resort to arguments from "experience" or religion or social responsibility or wishing and dreaming.

After I realized, through faculty development work in Women's Studies, the extent to which men work from a base of unacknowledged privilege, I understood that much of their oppressiveness was unconscious. Then I remembered the frequent charges from women of color that white women whom they encounter are oppressive. I began to understand why we are justly seen as oppressive, even when we don't see ourselves that way. At the very least, obliviousness of one's privileged state can make a person or group irritating to be with. I began to count the ways in which I enjoy unearned skin privilege and have been conditioned into oblivion about its existence, unable to see that it put me "ahead" in any way, or put my people ahead, overrewarding us and yet also paradoxically damaging us, or that it could or should be changed.

My schooling gave me no training in seeing myself as an oppressor, as an unfairly advantaged person, or as a participant in a damaged culture. I was taught to see myself as an individual whose moral state depended on her individual moral will. At school, we were not taught about slavery in any depth; we were not taught to see slaveholders as damaged people. Slaves were seen as the only group at risk of being dehumanized. My schooling followed the pattern which Elizabeth Minnich has pointed out: whites are taught to think of their lives as morally neutral, normative, and average, and also ideal, so that when we work to benefit others, this is seen as work that will allow "them" to be more like "us." I think many of us know how obnoxious this attitude can be in men.

After frustration with men who would not recognize male privilege, I decided to try to work on myself at least by identifying some of the daily effects of white privilege in my life. It is crude work, at this stage, but I will give here a list of special circumstances and conditions I experience that I did not earn but that I have been made to feel are mine by birth, by citizenship, and by virtue of being a conscientious law-abiding "normal" person of goodwill. I have chosen those conditions that I think in my case *attach somewhat more to skin-color privilege* than to class, religion, ethnic status, or geographical location, though these other privileging factors are intricately intertwined. As far as I can see, my Afro-American co-workers, friends, and acquaintances with whom I come into daily or frequent contact in this particular time, place, and line of work cannot count on most of these conditions.

1. I can, if I wish, arrange to be in the company of people of my race most of the time.

2. I can avoid spending time with people whom I was trained to mistrust and who have learned to mistrust my kind or me.

3. If I should need to move, I can be pretty sure of renting or purchasing housing in an area which I can afford and in which I would want to live.

4. I can be reasonably sure that my neighbors in such a location will be neutral or pleasant to me.

5. I can go shopping alone most of the time, fairly well assured that I will not be followed or harassed by store detectives.

6. I can turn on the television or open to the front page of the paper and see people of my race widely and positively represented.

7. When I am told about our national heritage or about "civilization," I am shown that people of my color made it what it is.

8. I can be sure that my children will be given curricular materials that testify to the existence of their race.

9. If I want to, I can be pretty sure of finding a publisher for this piece on white privilege.

10. I can be fairly sure of having my voice heard in a group in which I am the only member of my race.

11. I can be casual about whether or not to listen to another woman's voice in a group in which she is the only member of her race.

12. I can go into a book shop and count on finding the writing of my race represented, into a supermarket and find the staple foods that fit with my cultural traditions, into a hairdresser's shop and find someone who can deal with my hair.

13. Whether I use checks, credit cards, or cash, I can count on my skin color not to work against the appearance that I am financially reliable.

14. I could arrange to protect our young children most of the time from people who might not like them.

15. I did not have to educate our children to be aware of systemic racism for their own daily physical protection.

16. I can be pretty sure that my children's teachers and employers will tolerate them if they fit school and workplace norms; my chief worries about them do not concern others' attitudes toward their race.

17. I can talk with my mouth full and not have people put this down to my color.

18. I can swear, or dress in secondhand clothes, or not answer letters, without having people attribute these choices to the bad morals, the poverty, or the illiteracy of my race.

19. I can speak in public to a powerful male group without putting my race on trial.

20. I can do well in a challenging situation without being called a credit to my race.

21. I am never asked to speak for all the people of my racial group.

22. I can remain oblivious to the language and customs of persons of color who constitute the world's majority without feeling in my culture any penalty for such oblivion.

23. I can criticize our government and talk about how much I fear its policies and behavior without being seen as a cultural outsider.

24. I can be reasonably sure that if I ask to talk to "the person in charge," I will be facing a person of my race.

25. If a traffic cop pulls me over or if the IRS audits my tax return, I can be sure I haven't been singled out because of my race.

26. I can easily buy posters, postcards, picture books, greeting cards, dolls, toys, and children's magazines featuring people of my race.

27. I can go home from most meetings of organizations I belong to feeling somewhat tied in, rather than isolated, out of place, outnumbered, unheard, held at a distance, or feared.

28. I can be pretty sure that an argument with a colleague of another race is more likely to jeopardize her chances for advancement than to jeopardize mine.

29. I can be fairly sure that if I argue for the promotion of a person of another race, or a program centering on race, this is not likely to cost me heavily within my present setting, even if my colleagues disagree with me.

30. If I declare there is a racial issue at hand, or there isn't a racial issue at hand, my race will lend me more credibility for either position than a person of color will have.

31. I can choose to ignore developments in minority writing and minority activist programs, or disparage them, or learn from them, but in any case, I can find ways to be more or less protected from negative consequences of any of these choices.

32. My culture gives me little fear about ignoring the perspectives and powers of people of other races.

33. I am not made acutely aware that my shape, bearing, or body odor will be taken as a reflection on my race.

34. I can worry about racism without being seen as self-interested or self-seeking.

35. I can take a job with an affirmative action employer without having my co-workers on the job suspect that I got it because of my race.

36. If my day, week, or year is going badly, I need not ask of each negative episode or situation whether it has racial overtones.

37. I can be pretty sure of finding people who would be willing to talk with me and advise me about my next steps, professionally.

38. I can think over many options, social, political, imaginative, or professional, without asking whether a person of my race would be accepted or allowed to do what I want to do.

39. I can be late to a meeting without having the lateness reflect on my race.

40. I can choose public accommodation without fearing that people of my race cannot get in or will be mistreated in the places I have chosen.

41. I can be sure that if I need legal or medical help, my race will not work against me.

42. I can arrange my activities so that I will never have to experience feelings of rejection owing to my race.

43. If I have low credibility as a leader, I can be sure that my race is not the problem.

44. I can easily find academic courses and institutions that give attention only to people of my race.

45. I can expect figurative language and imagery in all of the arts to testify to experiences of my race.

46. I can choose blemish cover or bandages in "flesh" color and have them more or less match my skin.

I repeatedly forgot each of the realizations on this list until I wrote it down. For me, white privilege has turned out to be an elusive and fugitive subject. The pressure to avoid it is great, for in facing it I must give up the myth of meritocracy. If these things are true, this is not such a free country; one's life is not what one makes it; many doors open for certain people through no virtues of their own. These perceptions mean also that my moral condition is not what I had been led to believe. The appearance of being a good citizen rather than a troublemaker comes in large part from having all sorts of doors open automatically because of my color.

A further paralysis of nerve comes from literary silence protecting privilege. My clearest memories of finding such analysis are in Lillian Smith's unparalleled *Killers of the Dream* and Margaret Andersen's review of Karen and Mamie Fields' *Lemon Swamp*. Smith, for example, wrote about walking toward black children on the street and knowing they would step into the gutter; Andersen contrasted the pleasure that she, as a white child, took on summer driving trips to the south with Karen Fields' memories of driving in a closed car stocked with all necessities lest, in stopping, her black family should suffer "insult, or worse." Adrienne Rich also recognizes and writes about daily experiences of privilege, but in my observation, white women's writing in this area is far more often on systemic racism than on our daily lives as light-skinned women.[2]

In unpacking this invisible knapsack of white privilege, I have listed conditions of daily experience that I once took for granted, as neutral, normal, and universally available to everybody, just as I once thought of a male-focused curriculum as the neutral or accurate account that can speak for all. Nor did I think of any of these perquisites as bad for the holder. I now think that we need a more finely differentiated taxonomy of privilege, for some of these varieties are only what one would want for everyone in a just society, and others give license to be ignorant, oblivious, arrogant, and destructive. Before proposing some more finely tuned categorization, I will make some observations about the general effects of these conditions on my life and expectations.

In this potpourri of examples, some privileges make me feel at home in the world. Others allow me to escape penalties or dangers that others suffer. Through some, I escape fear, anxiety, insult, injury, or a sense of not being welcome, not being real. Some keep me from having to hide, to be in disguise, to feel sick or crazy, to negotiate each transaction from the position of being an outsider or, within my group, a person who is suspected of having too close links with a dominant culture. Most keep me from having to be angry.

I see a pattern running through the matrix of white privilege, a pattern of assumptions that were passed on to me as a white person. There was one main piece of cultural turf; it was my own turf, and I was among those who could control the turf. I could measure up to the cultural standards and take advantage of the many options I saw around me to make what the culture would call a success of my life. *My skin color was an asset for any move I was educated to want to make.* I could think of myself as "belonging" in major ways and of making-social systems work for me. I could freely disparage, fear, neglect, or be oblivious to anything outside of the dominant cultural forms. Being of the main culture, I could also criticize it fairly freely. My life was reflected back to me frequently enough so that I felt, with regard to my race, if not to my sex, like one of the real people.

Whether through the curriculum or in the newspaper, the television, the economic system, or the general look of people in the streets, I received daily signals and indications that my people counted and that others *either didn't exist or must be trying, not very successfully, to be like people of my race.* I was given cultural permission not to hear voices of people of other races or a tepid cultural tolerance for hearing or acting on such voices. I was also raised not to suffer seriously from anything that darker-skinned people might say about my group, "protected," though perhaps I should more accurately say *prohibited*, through the habits of my economic class and social group, from living in racially mixed groups or being reflective about interactions between people of differing races.

In proportion as my racial group was being made confident, comfortable, and oblivious, other groups were likely being made unconfident, uncomfortable, and alienated. Whiteness protected me from many kinds of hostility, distress, and violence, which I was being subtly trained to visit in turn upon people of color.

For this reason, the word "privilege" now seems to me misleading. Its connotations are too positive to fit the conditions and behaviors which "privilege systems" produce. We usually think of privilege as being a favored state, whether earned, or conferred by birth or luck. School graduates are reminded they are privileged and urged to use their (enviable) assets well. The word "privilege" carries the connotation of being something everyone must want. Yet some of the conditions I have described here work to systemically overempower certain groups. Such privilege simply *confers dominance*, gives permission to control, because of one's race or sex. The kind of privilege that gives license to some people to be, at best, thoughtless and, at worst, murderous should not continue to be referred to as a desirable attribute. Such "privilege" may be widely desired without being in any way beneficial to the whole society.

Moreover, though "privilege" may confer power, it does not confer moral strength. Those who do not depend on conferred dominance have traits and qualities that may never develop in those who do. Just as Women's Studies courses indicate that women survive their political circumstances to lead lives that hold the human race together, so "underprivileged" people of color who are the world's majority have survived their oppression and lived survivors' lives from which the white global minority can and must learn. In some groups, those dominated have actually become strong through *not* having all of these unearned advantages, and this gives them a great deal to teach the others. Members of so-called privileged groups can seem foolish, ridiculous, infantile, or dangerous by contrast.

I want, then, to distinguish between earned strength and unearned power conferred systemically. Power from unearned privilege can look like strength when it is, in fact, permission to escape or to dominate. But not all of the privileges on my list are inevitably damaging. Some, like the expectation that neighbors will be decent to you, or that your race will not count against you in court, should be the norm in a just society and should be considered as the entitlement of everyone. Others, like the privilege not to listen to less powerful people, distort the humanity of the holders as well as the ignored groups. Still others, like finding one's staple foods everywhere, may be a function of being a member of a numerical majority in the population. Others have to do with not having to labor under pervasive negative stereotyping and mythology.

We might at least start by languishing between positive advantages that we can work to spread, to the point where they are not advantages at all but simply part of the normal civic and social fabric, and negative types of advantage that unless rejected will always reinforce our present hierarchies. For example, the positive "privilege" of belonging, the feeling that one belongs within the human circle, as Native Americans say, fosters development and should not be seen as privilege for a few. It is, let us say, an entitlement that none of us should have to earn; ideally it is an *unearned entitlement*. At present, since only a few have it, it is an *unearned advantage* for them. The negative "privilege" that gave me cultural permission not to take darker-skinned Others seriously can be seen as arbitrarily conferred dominance and should not be desirable for anyone. This paper results from a process of coming to see that some of the power that I originally saw as attendant on being a human being in the United States consisted in *unearned advantage* and *conferred dominance*, as well as other kinds of special circumstance not universally taken for granted.

In writing this paper I have also realized that white identity and status (as well as class identity and status) give me considerable power to choose whether to broach this subject and its trouble. I can pretty well decide whether to disappear and avoid and not listen and escape the dislike I may engender in other people through this essay, or interrupt, answer, interpret, preach, correct, criticize, and control to some extent what goes on in reaction to it. Being white, I am given considerable power to escape many kinds of danger or penalty as well as to choose which risks I want to take.

There is an analogy here, once again, with Women's Studies. Our male colleagues do not have a great deal to lose in supporting Women's Studies, but they do not have a great deal to lose if they oppose it either. They simply have the power to decide whether to commit themselves to more equitable distributions of power. They will probably feel few penalties whatever choice they make; they do not seem, in any obvious short-term sense, the ones at risk, though they and we are all at risk because of the behaviors that have been rewarded in them.

Through Women's Studies work I have met very few men who are truly distressed about systemic, unearned male advantage and conferred dominance. And so one question for me and others like me is whether we will be like them, or whether we will get truly distressed, even outraged, about unearned race advantage and conferred dominance and if so, what we will do to lessen them. In any case, we need to do more work in identifying how they actually affect our daily lives. We need more down-to-earth writing by people about these taboo subjects. We need more understanding of the ways in which white "privilege" damages white people, for these are not the same ways in which it damages the victimized. Skewed white psyches are an inseparable part of the picture, though I do not want to confuse the kinds of damage done to the holders of special assets and to those who suffer the deficits. Many, perhaps most, of our white students in the United States think that racism doesn't affect them because they are not people of color; they do not see "whiteness" as a racial identity. Many men likewise think that Women's Studies does not bear on their own existences because they are not female; they do not see themselves as having gendered identities. Insisting on the universal "effects" of "privilege" systems, then, becomes one of our chief tasks, and being more explicit about the *particular* effects in particular contexts is another. Men need to join us in this work.

In addition, since race and sex are not the only advantaging systems at work, we need to similarly examine the daily experience of having age advantage, or ethnic advantage, or physical ability, or advantage related to nationality, religion, or sexual orientation. Professor Marnie Evans suggested to me that in many ways the list I made also applies directly to heterosexual privilege. This is a still more taboo subject than race privilege: the daily ways in which heterosexual privilege makes some persons comfortable or powerful, providing supports, assets, approvals, and rewards to those who live or expect to live in heterosexual pairs. Unpacking that content is still more difficult, owing to the deeper imbeddedness of heterosexual advantage and dominance and stricter taboos surrounding these.

But to start such an analysis I would put this observation from my own experience: the fact that I live under the same roof with a man triggers all kinds of societal assumptions about my worth, politics, life, and values and triggers a host of unearned advantages and powers. After recasting many elements from the original list I would add further observations like these:

1. My children do not have to answer questions about why I live with my partner (my husband).

2. I have no difficulty finding neighborhoods where people approve of our household.

3. Our children are given texts and classes that implicitly support our kind of family unit and do not turn them against my choice of domestic partnership.

4. I can travel alone or with my husband without expecting embarrassment or hostility in those who deal with us.

5. Most people I meet will see my marital arrangements as an asset to my life or as a favorable comment on my likability, my competence, or my mental health.

6. I can talk about the social events of a weekend without fearing most listeners' reactions.

7. I will feel welcomed and "normal" in the usual walks of public life, institutional and social.

8. In many contexts, I am seen as "all right" in daily work on women because I do not live chiefly with women.

Difficulties and dangers surrounding the task of finding parallels are many. Since racism, sexism, and heterosexism are not the same, the advantages associated with them should not be seen as the same. In addition, it is hard to isolate aspects of unearned advantage that derive chiefly from social class, economic class, race, religion, region, sex, or ethnic identity. The oppressions are both distinct and interlocking, as the Combahee River Collective statement of 1977 continues to remind us eloquently.[3]

One factor seems clear about all of the interlocking oppressions. They take both active forms that we can see and embedded forms that members of the dominant group are taught not to see. In my class and place, I did not see myself as racist because I was taught to recognize racism only in individual acts of meanness by members of my group, never in invisible systems conferring racial dominance on my group from birth. Likewise, we are taught to think that sexism or heterosexism is carried on only through intentional, individual acts of discrimination, meanness, or cruelty, rather than in invisible systems conferring unsought dominance on certain groups. Disapproving of the systems won't be enough to change them. I was taught to think that racism could end if white individuals changed their attitudes; many men think sexism can be ended by individual changes in daily behavior toward women. But a man's sex provides advantage for him whether or not he approves of the way in which dominance has been conferred on his group. A "white" skin in the United States opens many doors for whites whether or not we approve of the way dominance has been conferred on us. Individual acts can palliate, but cannot end, these problems. To redesign social systems, we need first to acknowledge their colossal unseen dimensions. The silences and denials surrounding privilege are the key political tool here. They keep the thinking about equality or equity incomplete, protecting unearned advantage and conferred dominance by making these taboo subjects. Most talk by whites about equal opportunity seems to me now to be about equal opportunity to try to get into a position of dominance while denying that *systems* of dominance exist.

Obliviousness about white advantage, like obliviousness about male advantage, is kept strongly inculturated in the United States so as to maintain the myth of meritocracy, the myth that democratic choice is equally available to all. Keeping most people unaware that freedom of confident action is there for just a small number of people props up those in power and serves to keep power in the hands of the same groups that have most of it already. Though systemic change takes many decades, there are pressing questions for me and I imagine for some others like me if we raise our daily consciousness on the perquisites of being light-skinned. What will we do with such knowledge? As we know from watching men, it is an open question whether we will choose to use unearned advantage to weaken invisible privilege systems and whether we will use any of our arbitrarily awarded power to try to reconstruct power systems on a broader base.

Notes

1. This paper was presented at the Virginia Women's Studies Association conference in Richmond in April, 1986, and the American Educational Research Association conference in Boston in October, 1986, and discussed with two groups of participants in the Dodge seminars for Secondary School Teachers in New York and Boston in the spring of 1987.

2. Andersen, Margaret, "Race and the Social Science Curriculum: A Teaching and Learning Discussion" *Radical Teacher*, November, 1984, pp. 17–20. Smith, Lillian, *Killers of the Dream*, New York: W. W. Norton, 1949.

3. "A Black Feminist Statement," The Combahee River Collective, pp 13–22 in G. Hull, P. Scott, B. Smith, Eds., *All the Women Are White, All the Blacks Are Men, But Some of Us Are Brave: Black Women's Studies*, Old Westbury, NY: The Feminist Press, 1982.

Discussion Questions

1. How do the events during and in the immediate aftermath of Hurricane Katrina (see the discussion by Jason DeParle in Section 7) reflect the existence of what McIntosh calls "an invisible package of unearned assets" and a "weightless knapsack of special provisions, assurances, tools, maps, guides, codebooks, passports, visas, clothes, compass, emergency gear, and blank checks" that some Americans have and others lack?

2. McIntosh's paper includes the contents of her knapsacks, two personal lists of privileges. Based on your gender, race/ethnicity, class, and sexual orientation, unpack your knapsack and make your own list remembering that even if you are a member of one or more disadvantaged groups, you are probably a member of at least one advantaged group. Keep in mind that having education beyond high school confers advantage.

3. When McIntosh wrote this paper in 1988, the authors of most of the books and articles that appeared on college and university syllabi and most of the people discussed in classes were middle- and upper-class White men who could be presumed to be heterosexual since no mention was made of their sexual orientation. Has this changed? Thinking about the material you have studied in previous courses and the syllabi for the courses you are currently taking, how well are the less privileged represented?

4. McIntosh suggests that as we look at our lists we should try to distinguish between positive advantages that everyone should have and negative ones that are actually unearned entitlements that no one should have in a just society. Share your list with a few classmates and together begin to make these distinctions. Pick one or two of the negative advantages and discuss how society might work toward eliminating them.

39

White Views of Civil Rights

Color Blindness and Equal Opportunity

Nancy DiTomaso
Rochelle Parks-Yancy
Corinne Post

The central question in "White Views of Civil Rights: Color Blindness and Equal Opportunity," by Nancy DiTomaso, Rochelle Parks-Yancy, and Corinne Post, is this: How can Whites be growing more liberal and less prejudicial in their attitudes about racial equality while being opposed to public policies that are designed to bring about more racial equality? DiTomaso et al. argue that race relations scholars have responded to this seeming inconsistency by either arguing that we have made substantial racial progress or that racism is alive and well but has only become more subtle in nature. These authors make their own attempt at answering this apparent inconsistency by interviewing White men and women from working-class and middle-class backgrounds with regard to their views on racial equality. In this way, the researchers find common ground among their interviewees regardless of gender and class, with race an overarching theme of the interviews.

The researchers' findings are remarkable in that they discover that no inconsistency in fact exists—Whites are becoming more liberal with regard to racial attitudes and they are opposed to public policies that were meant to combat racial equality. How is this possible? The researchers find their answers in the very words of the 246 White interviewees for this study, who in the space of a couple of hours each, manage to claim in one collective breath how nonracist and nonprejudiced they are while vilifying programs like affirmative action. For DiTomaso et al., the meaning is clear—Whites, whether male or female, and whether working-class or middle-class, can have their proverbial cake and eat it too. They manage this in several ways. They compare their own alleged individual, hard-earned efforts to attain jobs with what they believe is the "laziness" and sense of "entitlement" characterizing Blacks who are not doing well in inner cities. They also frame their discussions of racial equality in terms of individual achievements, deflecting attention from structural advantages and group resources that were available to them. They could then, in all sincerity, talk about racial equality, equal opportunity, and their own color blindness in reference to Blacks. What was perhaps most damning were the realities of their individual lives, in their own words. In actuality, while they could only see a personal history of hard work and effort to get and keep work, it became apparent that they had unearned advantage in their work histories practically every step of the way. They were completely blind to the systems of group advantage affecting their own individual lives. These group advantages gave them the luxury to espouse anti-racist, anti-prejudiced jargon, which in turn, had no relation to actual practice.

There are few subjects that generate as much conflict in U.S. history as race relations (Kinder and Sanders 1996), and yet few white Americans think race relations is a topic about them. Gunnar Myrdal made the same point in his famous book, *An American Dilemma* (Myrdal 1996 [1944]: 37): "One can go around for weeks talking to white people in all walks of life and constantly hear about [the racism of other people], yet seldom meeting a person who actually identifies himself with it." Myrdal's point is underlined by Mary Jackman (1994: 137), who argues that racial inequality is reproduced "without active participation by individual whites, and hidden from their view." Thus, when it comes to issues of race, as Jennifer Hochschild notes (1995: 55–71), most white Americans cannot understand "what the fuss is about."

The seeming inconsistency between the pervasive concern about racial conflict and inequality in the country but lack of salience for many white Americans is captured in the controversial statement by Stephen and Abigail Thernstrom (1997:13), who claim: "There is no racism; there is nothing but racism." This seeming inconsistency is also empirically evident in one of the most researched puzzles in the study of race relations, namely, that traditional measures of prejudice suggest a growing liberalization of white racial attitudes, while whites continue to oppose public policies that are intended to bring about greater racial equality (See Bobo 1998; Kinder and Sanders 1996; Kluegel and Smith 1986; Sears 1998; Sniderman and Carmines 1997; Schuman et al. 1997). As a result of these unresolved issues, some scholars argue that there is genuine racial progress (Patterson 1997; Thernstrom and Thernstrom 1997), while others—often with the same evidence—argue that racism has just taken on a new or more subtle form (Bobo et al. 1997; Bonilla-Silva 2001; McConahay 1983; Sears 1988, Sears et al. 2000).

This chapter seeks to shed light on the seeming inconsistency by describing the responses of white interviewees regarding their views on racial inequality. Like Jackman (1994), we argue that one of the reasons that white racial attitudes have puzzled researchers is because they have misunderstood the implications of the commitment whites espouse toward colorblindness, equal opportunity, and individual achievement. In this paper we argue that the ways whites frame racial issues take attention away from issues of power in the reproduction of inequality, and we also argue that they are mischaracterizations of what actually happens in the lives of people who are privileged by race and social position. Our failure to understand these issues reflects insufficient attention to the need for legitimacy in the reproduction of racial inequality (Jost and Major 2001).

First, as Jackman notes (1994: 33–43), the study of race relations still gives primary emphasis to prejudice and/or to racism as the source of conflict among racial groups in the United States. Others have expressed similar views (Blauner 1972; Bonilla-Silva 2001;

Wellman 1993), but despite their calling attention to the institutional or structural processes that reproduce racial inequality, they still insist on labeling these processes as "racism" of one sort or another. In addition to institutional racism (Blauner 1972; Wellman 1993), other new forms of "racism" include: laissez-faire, color-blind, everyday, aversive, modern, and symbolic (Bobo et al. 1997; Bonilla-Silva 2001; Essed 1991; Gaertner and Dovidio 1986; McConahay 1983; Sears 1988). In contrast to these efforts to reinterpret the meaning of racism and to preserve the label of racism toward white attitudes, we argue that one of the characteristics of white privilege (McIntosh 1988; Rothenberg 2002) is that whites do not have to be racists in order for racial inequality to be reproduced. Not only do whites not think of themselves as racists, but they also believe themselves to be part of the solution rather than part of the problem of racial inequality.

Second, we argue that there has been too much emphasis on "equal opportunity" (and by extrapolation on discrimination) in policy discussions about race relations, but there has been insufficient attention given to processes of favoritism or inclusion that help whites (instead of harming blacks and other nonwhites). While some may argue that discrimination and favoritism are different sides of the same coin, discrimination is illegal, whereas favoritism is not (McGinley 1997). In other words, we argue that the advantages that whites enjoy because of their access to social and cultural capital and to economic resources protect whites from having to face "equal opportunity"—that is, the market forces—that they so readily see as the solution to the disadvantage of blacks and other nonwhites.

White advantage, however, is hidden from view, because whites are subject to attribution error (Pettigrew 1979) which leads them to believe that they got ahead because of their own personal characteristics (hard work, effort, and persistence) while they cognitively minimize the situational or contextual factors that may have contributed to their life outcomes. Because of this, many whites can believe themselves to be innocent bystanders vis-à-vis black disadvantage.

Third, the focus on individual achievement rather than group relations has taken attention away from the power relations that exist between groups, a point that has been made by others (Bonilla-Silva 2001; Jackman 1994; Tilly 1998; and Wilson 1998). By thinking of their life outcomes as the result of individual choices and values, whites fail to see the relationship in their own lives to the lives of blacks and other nonwhites (Kluegel and Smith 1986; Spears, Jetten, and Doosje 2001). Jackman and Michael Muha (1984) argue that white emphasis on individualism is part of the strategy for deflecting attention from power issues, while Donald Kinder and Tali Mendelberg (2000: 44–74) argue that individualism is an inherent part at this point in history of "racial resentment." We find that individualism is deeply embedded in the thinking of most Americans, including whites. Whites can easily point to the things they had to do to get to their current places in life, but they do not at the same time as easily recall the group basis of their life outcomes.

In this chapter, we examine how whites talk about civil rights and equal opportunity to explain why whites cannot understand "what the fuss is about" (Hochschild 1995). We argue that the focus whites give to color blindness and to equal opportunity and their belief that individuals are responsible for themselves have allowed whites to accept the premises of the Civil Rights movement and yet to maintain white privilege, in many cases, "without active participation" and "hidden from their view" (Jackman 1994: 137).

Research Methodology

Data for this study come from semistructured interviews with 246 randomly selected whites from three areas of the country: New Jersey, Ohio, and Tennessee. Using the methodology outlined by Michele Lamont (1992, 2000), four zip codes were identified in each region, from which addresses were randomly selected. About a third of the participants in each region who were reached by phone agreed to participate in the study. The target areas were identified based on census data pertaining to their relative regional median income, the area's proportion of non-Hispanic whites, the percentage of the area's population holding managerial jobs, and the percentage of the area's population holding a bachelor's degree.

Participants were restricted to U.S.-born whites between the ages of twenty-five and fifty-five. The sample included approximately equal numbers of men and women and working-class and middle-class respondents in each area, although, reflecting the composition of the areas, there are more middle-class interviewees in New Jersey and more working-class interviewees in Ohio than in the other areas. Class was defined by education, with those having a college education or more being defined as middle class or above, and those with less education being defined as working class (McCall 2001).

Most of the interviews (all done by the first author in the last three years) were conducted in the participant's home and occasionally at a public place or nearby university. The interview included a detailed life history of the respondent, starting with high school, to the present regarding education and jobs, plus questions about self-identity, family, intergroup relations, and views of public policy. The interviews averaged about two hours each, and each interview was transcribed verbatim and then coded for analysis.

This study is qualitative and interpretive. It is both grounded in the qualitative data collected for the study and developed through interaction with the research literature. The purpose of reporting on what the interviewees said is to look for themes or meaning content more than to count how many people said what. For the purposes of this paper, we report on the interviewee responses to questions about "changes that have occurred in access to education and jobs in the last several decades" for African-Americans (separate questions were asked as well about such changes for women and for immigrants). This question was purposely worded so as to avoid the use of the words "equal opportunity" and "affirmative action." The question was asked after the interviewee had described his or her own education and job history. Although there was no explicit question about "color blindness" (i.e., color should not matter), it was a pervasive theme in the interviews. The interviewees were also asked toward the end of the interview what they thought "equal opportunity" should mean and then how they would ensure it, if it were up to them. While there are some differences in the interviews with regard to region, gender, and class, on these particular issues the responses are generally consistent.

Color Blindness

When asked about the "changes that have occurred for blacks over the last several decades," the interviewees generally expressed positive views about the Civil Rights movement and disavowed prejudice, racism, or discrimination on the basis of color, although this was less evident in the Tennessee interviews than in the New Jersey or Ohio interviews. Recurring comments in response to the question about changes for African-Americans in the last several decades were "good," "great," "wonderful," and even "not enough." For example, a middle-class male in Ohio said:

I guess it's about the same, you know. I mean, if people have ability, it doesn't matter what their skin color is or what their gender is. I think they should have the opportunities for education and jobs. I don't think I have any discrimination against groups like that and have no notions that they shouldn't be at school or at certain jobs.

As this interviewee did, most of the interviewees portrayed their own views as supportive of the Civil Right movement and as opposed to "prejudiced people" or to "racists."

When talking about the Civil Rights movement, though, most of the interviewees espoused a general principle of "color blindness." Reflecting these views are claims such as "color shouldn't matter," "skin color is not the way to go," or "a person shouldn't be looked at by the outside, the color of their skin." The interviewees argued that people should be able to do whatever they are capable of and should be chosen on the basis of merit or qualifications rather than for who they are. The notion that outcomes depend on effort and that opportunities should be available based on qualifications or merit largely defines the view of egalitarianism

held by these interviewees. For example, a working-class female from Ohio said: "the person qualified, I don't care what color they are, should get the job." A middle-class male from New Jersey provides another expression of color blindness in a very typical statement: "if someone is qualified, I don't care if they are purple, black, green, or white."

These views appear to serve several functions for the interviewees. It makes the interviewees "good guys." Racism and prejudice are attributed to other abstract people, but the interviewees themselves disavow such views. The standards that the white interviewees express are presumed on their part to be universal and impersonal: those who are qualified deserve to get rewarded, and in their view, people generally get what they deserve. The normative language of color blindness, as others have noted, allows them to direct attention away from the larger patterns of racial inequality in society and places the responsibility for life outcomes on blacks themselves. For example, when the white interviewees commented on the changes that have occurred for blacks with regard to education and jobs, they prefaced the generally supportive comments with statements such as, "if they can do the job" "if they are willing to work hard," "if they have the qualifications." Some interviewees complained that blacks have not taken advantage of the opportunities they have been offered because of the Civil Rights movement.

The language of color blindness also makes civil rights personal (Emerson and Smith 2000). In this sense, the argument that "everyone deserves a chance" removes the white interviewee from having to think of him or herself as unfair (Bonilla-Silva 2001: 137). It conjures up for the interviewee the assurance that he or she has never made a decision about someone based solely on the irrelevant characteristic of race. The emphasis on color blindness allows whites to believe that they are contributing to the elimination of racial problems, that is, by not acknowledging or giving attention to race. Instead, as Myrdal suggested, whites believe race to be an issue only for other people—the "racists"—but they do not include themselves in that category.

Equal Opportunity

The white interviewees in this study frequently argued that everyone deserves an equal opportunity and that no one should be denied opportunity because of "race, creed, or color." For example, a middle-class male from Ohio said: "I think equal opportunity would be to fill jobs and education opportunities without regard to race, gender, age, or anything else." A working-class woman from Ohio said something very similar: "I think everybody should have a chance to try for any job they think they're qualified for." A working-class woman from New Jersey was more explicit. She said: "Equal opportunity is suppose you were black and went for a job. If you are better qualified, you get the job. That's equal opportunity. Too bad on my part."

When it came to their own life experiences, however, many of the interviewees did not themselves rely on equal opportunity. Instead, they sought and accepted special favors, even unsolicited help, and it often made the difference in terms of what they were able to do in their lives. People in then social networks told them about jobs, helped them get jobs, or actually provided jobs. They also provided financial resources and cultural knowledge. In some cases, such help was made available even when the interviewee was clearly not "the best person for the job."

For example, a middle-class male from Ohio said that people should get what they deserve. He also argued that it is not fair if the person with the highest test score is not the one who gets the job. The details of his own life, however, do not conform to these principles. He had flunked out of college, had been fired from jobs, and had failed at several businesses. He even decried the fact that he had never tested his chances in the job market but had instead always relied on the help from family and friends to get jobs. He further reported that his daughter had gotten into law school despite having scores "at the low end of the scale." And regarding himself, he said: "I'm not the greatest student in the world, but I happen to think I'm a pretty good person. If you just looked at my grades, no, I'm not equal to a lot of people. . . . It's more than just my grades, my scores."

Another example can be seen in a working-class man from New Jersey. He was one of the more explicit regarding his negative view of blacks and his opposition to affirmative action. When asked about how he got his own job in the building trades, though, he explained:

> My cousin let my mother know when they were giving out the test, the application for the jobs. So I went down there. And I went to my cousin's job, and I had some of his men on the job put references down for me, because when I went back to the hall, they said how do you know these guys. So I says, well [this fellow], he's my cousin. And he says, all right.

When asked whether knowing when to take the test and having a cousin who could vouch for him helped, he replied, "Yeah, that helps. That helps. But you see, if you don't pass the test, it's not going to help one damn bit."

That is, the interviewees argued that equal opportunity should apply to people in general, but they did not apply it in their own lives. When asked in some interviews about the seeming discrepancy, most of the interviewees minimized or discounted the help that they had received by comments such as: "But that just got me in the door, then I had to prove myself." These attitudes were obviously self-serving, but they are more than that. As Jackman (1994) argues, they also hide or render invisible the privileges that the interviewees have available in their lives. The interviewees in our study, in other words, were subject to attribution errors (Pettigrew 1979), in that they emphasized dispositional or personal characteristics as the basis of their life outcomes while they minimized or forgot to mention the situational or contextual—the structural—advantages of which they were able to avail themselves.

In part because the interviewees were not especially conscious of the help that they had received and in part because they cognitively discounted or minimized it, they primarily constructed an understanding of their life experiences as being the result of their own effort, hard work, and talent. In contrast, many thought of those who had less than they did, and specifically blacks, as being undeserving because, in their view, they had not tried hard enough, gave up too soon, or were not flexible enough. They did not consider that perhaps the absence or lack of the same kind of social resources as they themselves had drawn upon contributed to life outcomes for blacks.

Hence while generally supportive of equal opportunity, many of the interviewees expressed strong opposition to affirmative action. Interestingly, most could not specifically name affirmative action as a policy, but instead, reduced it in their comments to "quotas." The interviewees opposed affirmative action because, they said, the use of policies like affirmative action violated the principle of people being chosen on qualifications or merits without regard to "race, creed, or color." In this regard, a number of the interviewees expressed concern that the government had "gone overboard" and had given extra advantages to blacks in a way that, in their view, harmed whites. Those who raised such issues said that it was not fair because "two wrongs don't make a right."

For example, a middle-class woman from Tennessee said: "I think we find it sometimes going the other direction. We bend over backwards for the minorities and the person that suffers is the white person." Such comments were more frequently heard in the Tennessee interviews, but they occurred in all three regions. The interviewees argued that the policies had done more harm than good and that blacks were getting jobs for which they were not qualified. The white interviewees also expressed concern about lowering standards and about poor attitudes or work habits among blacks hired through affirmative action. Thus despite the generally positive views expressed about the Civil Rights movement and antidiscrimination policies in general, the specific implementation of policies such as affirmative action engendered more negative reactions and even claims about reverse discrimination.

There is another important point, however. The interviewees were also asked later in the interview what they thought equal opportunity should mean if it were up to them. Most said things like: "Best man for the job." For example, a working-class male from Ohio said equal opportunity should mean: "throw color, gender, and everything out. If you're qualified to do the job, then you're qualified." A middle-class male in Tennessee said it should mean: "that the most skilled person gets the job without any other consideration." A middle-class female in New Jersey said: "Equal opportunity means no discrimination against race and creed or your color or whatever."

Despite the claim that equal opportunity should be available to all, when the interviewees were asked as a follow-up how they would ensure that the "best person" got the job, most of the interviewees said that it was not possible. In fact, many did not give a definition of equal opportunity at this point of the interview because they said that it would never be possible to evaluate qualifications without regard to personal ties and employer preferences for whomever they want to hire. In other words, the constant focus on equal opportunity hid the fundamental belief, applied in their own lives, that one cannot eliminate subjective judgment or personal bias in employment decisions.

Individual versus Relational Inequality

In many cases, the interviewees were explicit about their assumptions that no one helped them, even though their life stories suggested otherwise. For example, a working-class male from New Jersey who had been helped into a construction union by his father and then into a more stable job through help from his friends, said when asked whether he earned his place in life: "Did I earn it? Yeah, I worked for what I've got. Definitely. Nobody gave me nothing. Nothing."

Another working-class male, also from New Jersey, received help with every job he had obtained throughout his life. Given his relatively low skills, many of the jobs he got ended with plant closings or layoffs, but he was usually able to find a friend or family member to help him find another one. In one case, a friend also helped him by giving him a copy of the test and answer sheet that he would need to get the job, because he knew that he could not pass the test on his own. Yet, when asked about the reasons for the problems of the inner city, he said: "Bunch of fucking lazy people . . . they think the government owes them something. If you want something . . . you've got to go out and get it. It's not handed to me. . . . They just . . . to me, they're lazy. I mean, point blank. They're looking for the easy way out."

Most of the interviewees assumed that their achievements were due to their own efforts, and they frequently said that people can do whatever they want in life. Others have found that these views are very pervasive in American culture. For example, James Kluegel and Eliot Smith (1986: 23) found that the majority of Americans believe in what they call "the dominant ideology," namely, that "opportunity for economic advancement is widespread," "that individuals are personally responsible for their positions," and that the "system of inequality is . . . equitable and fair" (see also Hochschild 1981).

One of the most important implications of these views for our purposes is that the interviewees (and apparently the population as a whole) do not see any relationship between their own life outcomes and those of others. Even more specifically, they do not see the group basis of their advantages and the relationship between their advantages and others disadvantages. Charles Tilly makes this point as well. He argues that inequality in any society has to be seen with reference to the "cumulative, relational, often unnoticed organizational processes" (Tilly 1998: 35). Tilly further argues that processes such as the opportunity-hoarding evident in these interviews reinforce boundaries between "categorical pairs," maintain inequality, and reproduce it. When jobs are passed among circles of friends, acquaintances, neighbors, and family, then those jobs are effectively taken "out of competition" (or hoarded). The result is to leave many fewer job opportunities that can be competed for among those who are not part of the same networks, friendship circles, or social categories. When the interviewees in my study repeatedly argued that blacks should try harder, prepare themselves more, or believe in themselves, they had in mind the image of themselves as having done it on their own. They did not have in mind their own advantaged lives.

Conclusion

In this chapter, we argue that white racial attitudes must be seen in the context of how whites live their lives. An affirmation of color blindness allows whites to ignore, deny, or disregard any notion that race matters in people's lives. Because the white interviewees in this study constructed an image of themselves as supportive of civil rights in the form of color blindness, they did not need to face the possible conflict that the acknowledgment of the existence of racial inequality might engender.

Intertwined with white views of color blindness is their frequently expressed belief that equal opportunity is the solution to racial (or gender) inequality. To the interviewees, equal opportunity means that the "best person" should get any given job and that jobs should not be set aside for some types of people over others. Yet the majority of the interviewees in this study had gotten their own jobs primarily through the help of family, friends, and acquaintances, and in many examples, the interviewee was presumably not the "best person for the job." When asked about these issues, the interviewees discounted such help with statements such as: "I could do the job; that just got me in the door." In other words, the interviewees themselves did not rely on equal opportunity. Instead, they sought and used advantage.

The whites in our study also espoused beliefs that opportunities are available for blacks and that they just need to take advantage of the opportunities that are already available to them. When they argued that blacks "should do it the way I did," they thought they were holding up as an example their special effort, hard work, and talent rather than the use of the social, economic, and cultural resources that most had in fact used in their own lives. By forgetting or minimizing their own advantages, the white interviewees failed to see any culpability on their part for the outcomes in the lives of blacks. They thought of themselves more as innocent bystanders than as active participants in the creation, maintenance, or reproduction of racial inequality. In this regard, they espoused what Joe Feagin and Hernán Vera (1995: xi) call "sincere fictions."

The white interviewees in this study argued that people get ahead as a result of their own efforts, hard work, and talent, and they generally believe their own life outcomes to be the result of their own efforts as well. The interviewees, however, are subject to attribution errors in giving more emphasis to their individual effort and forgetting or minimizing the structural advantages and economic resources that they had available. We found that the strong individualism expressed by the interviewees enabled them to miss the interconnection between their own lives and the lives of blacks and other nonwhites. By thinking of themselves only as individuals rather than as part of groups whose lives unfold in relationship to other groups in the society, the interviewees were able to hold themselves blameless and to believe that the reasons racial inequality exists—to the extent that they acknowledged that it did—was because of others, especially because of the actions of blacks themselves or because of the unnamed "racists" to which they occasionally referred.

Because their own advantages were not salient or visible to them, the white interviewees espoused a commitment to color blindness and equal opportunity that they did not adhere to in their own lives. The interviewees did not think of themselves as racists and most of them specifically condemned those who held racist views. Instead, because the white interviewees enjoyed the benefits of structural positioning that gave them access to social and cultural capital and economic resources, they could in a sense have the luxury not to be racists. Their belief that prejudice and racism by impersonal but unnamed others are the source of any continued disadvantage for blacks allowed the whites in our study to believe themselves to be blameless regarding racial inequality and not to notice the structural relationships from which they benefited.

As Jackman (1994: 137) argued, by constructing an understanding of life outcomes as the result of impersonal principles like color blindness and of competition and equal opportunity, whites can be "blissfully unaware" of the institutional arrangements that reproduce inequality in their favor "without active participation" and "hidden from view." They can also, as she also argues, "feel quite blameless in the whole affair." This is a good description of what we found in the interviews with whites in this study. The white interviewees were concerned about issues of racial inequality and conflict but they did not think of themselves as participants in bringing these situations about. Further, they thought of themselves as supportive of the solutions, namely, the advocacy of equal opportunity and people getting ahead on their merits, but they were seemingly unaware of the extent to which they gave themselves permission to use advantage from their networks of social resources and of the extent to which they were able to benefit from opportunity-hoarding and other processes by which they obtained structural advantage. With this view of the world and their place in it, whites can continue to be puzzled by the "fuss" that blacks (and other nonwhites) apparently make about the issues of racial inequality.

References

Blauner, Robert. 1972. *Racial Oppression in America.* New York: Harper & Row.

Bobo, Lawrence. 1998. "Race, Interests, and Beliefs about Affirmative Action: Unanswered Questions and New Directions." *American Behavioral Scientist* 41: 985–1003.

Bobo, Lawrence, James Kluegel, and Ryan Smith. 1997. "Laissez-Faire Racism: The Crystallization of a Kinder, Gentler, Antiblack Ideology." Pp. 15–45 in *Racial Attitudes in the 1990s: Continuity and Change,* ed. Stephen Tuch and Jack Martin. Westport, CT: Praeger.

Bonilla-Silva, Eduardo. 2001. *White Supremacy and Racism in the Post-Civil Rights Era.* Boulder, CO: Lynne Rienner.

Emerson, Michael O., and Christian Smith. 2000. *Divided by Faith: Evangelical Religion and the Problem of Race in America.* NY: Oxford University Press.

Feagin, Joe R., and Hernán Vera. 1995. *White Racism: The Basics.* New York: Routledge.

Gaertner, Samuel L., and John F. Dovidio. 1986. "The Aversive From of Racism." Pp. 61–89 in *Prejudice, Discrimination, and Racism,* ed. John F. Dovidio and Samuel L. Gaertner. Orlando, FL: Academic.

Hochschild, Jennifer. 1981. *What's Fair?* Cambridge: Harvard University Press.

——. 1995. *Facing Up to the American Dream: Race, Class and the Soul of the Nation.* Princeton, NJ: Princeton University Press.

Jackman, Mary R. 1994. *The Velvet Glove: Paternalism and Conflict in Gender, Class, and Race Relations.* Berkeley, CA: University of California Press.

Jackman, Mary R., and Michael J. Muha. 1984. "Education and Intergroup Attitudes: Moral Enlightenment, Superficial Democratic Commitment, or Ideological Refinement." *American Sociological Review* 49: 751–769.

Jost, John T. and Brenda Major. 2001. *The Psychology of Legitimacy: Emerging Perspectives on Ideology, Justice, and Intergroup Relations.* Cambridge, UK: Cambridge University Press.

Kinder, Donald R., and Tali Mendelberg. 2000. "Individualism Reconsidered: Principles and Prejudice in Contemporary American Opinion." Pp. 44–47 in *Racialized Politics*, ed. Donald Sears, Jim Sidanius, and Larry Bobo. Chicago: University of Chicago Press.

Kinder, Donald R., and Lynn M. Sanders. 1996. *Divided by Color: Racial Politics and Democratic Ideals.* Chicago: University of Chicago Press.

Kluegel, James R., and Eliot R. Smith. 1986. *Beliefs about Inequality: Americans' Views of What Is and What Ought to Be.* Hawthorne, NY: Aldine de Gruyter.

Lamont, Michele. 1992. *Money, Morals, and Manners.* Chicago: University of Chicago Press.

——. 2000. *The Dignity of Working Men: Morality and the Boundaries of Race, Class, and Immigration.* Cambridge: Harvard University Press, and New York: Russell Sage Foundation.

McCall, Leslie. 2001. *Complex Inequality: Gender, Class, and Race in the New Economy.* New York: Routledge.

McConahay, John B. 1983. "Modern Racism and Modern Discrimination." *Personality and Social Psychology Bulletin* 9: 551–558.

McGinley, A. C. 1997. "The Emerging Cronyism Defense and Affirmative Action: A Critical Perspective on the Distinction between Colorblind and Race-Conscious Decision Making Under Title VII." *Arizona Law Review* 39: 1004–1059.

McIntosh, Peggy. 2001 [1998]. "White Privilege and Male Privilege: A Personal Account of Coming to See Correspondences through Work in Women's Studies." In *Race, Class, and Gender: An Anthology*, ed. Margaret L. Andersen and Patricia Hill Collins. 2001. Belmont, CA: Wadsworth.

Myrdal, Gunnar. 1944. *An American Dilemma: The Negro Problem and Modern Democracy.* New York: Harper.

Patterson, Orlando. 1997. *The Ordeal of Integration: Progress and Resentment an America's "Racial" Crisis.* Washington, DC: Civitas.

Pettigrew, Thomas F. 1979. "The Ultimate Attribution Error." *Personality and Social Psychology Bulletin* 5: 461–476.

Rothenberg, Paula., ed. 2002. *White Privilege: Essential Readings on the Other Side of Racism.* New York: Worth.

Schuman, Howard, Charlotte Steeh, Lawrence Bobo, and Maria Krysan. 1997. *Racial Attitudes in America: Trends and Interpretations.* Cambridge, MA: Harvard University Press.

Sears, David O. 1988. "Symbolic Racism." Pp. 53–84. in *Eliminating Racism: Profiles in Controversy.* eds. Phyllis A. Katz and Dalmas A. Taylor. New York: Plenum.

——. 1998. "Racism and Politics in the United States." Pp. 76–100 in *Confronting Racism: The Problem and the Response*, ed. Jenifer Eberhardt and Susan T. Fiske. Thousand Oaks, CA: Sage.

Sears, David O., Jim Sidanius, and Lawrence Bobo, eds. 2000. *Racialized Politics: The Debate about Racism in America.* Chicago: University of Chicago Press.

Sniderman, Paul M., and Edward G. Carmines. 1997. *Reaching Beyond Race.* Cambridge, MA: Harvard University Press.

Spears, Russell, Jolanda Jetten, and Bertjan Doosje. 2001. "The (Il)legitimacy of Ingroup Bias." Pp. 332–362 in *The Psychology of Legitimacy: Emerging Perspectives on Ideology, Justice, and Intergroup Relations*, ed. John T. Jost and Brenda Major. Cambridge, UK: Cambridge University Press.

Thernstrom, Stephen, and Abigail Thernstrom. 1997. *America in Black and White: One Nation, Indivisible.* New York: Simon and Schuster.

Tilly, Charles. 1998. *Durable Inequality.* Berkeley: University of California Press.

Wellman, David. 1993. *Portraits of White Racism*, 2nd ed., Cambridge, UK: Cambridge University Press.

Wilson, William J. 1998. "The Role of the Environment in the Black-White Test Score Gap." Pp. 501–510 in *The Black-White Test Score Gap*, ed. Christopher Jencks and Meredith Phillips. Washington, DC: The Brookings Institute.

Discussion Questions

1. How did you react to the DiTomaso et al. article? Did it upset you? Did you enjoy it? Why or why not?

2. DiTomaso et al. come to a pretty bold conclusion in this piece. They argue that White Americans enjoy a system of advantages based on race without even needing to be racist. Do you agree with this or disagree with this point?

3. It seemed from the interviews that men and women espoused similar views, while working- and middle-class individuals did as well. Do you think the responses would be different if they had asked poor Whites? Would views be different for poor White men versus women?

4. Did you find yourself agreeing with the White interviewees in the study? If so, when and why?

40

Growing Up White

The Social Geography of Race

Ruth Frankenberg

Ruth Frankenberg is a White feminist who moved to the United States from Great Britain when she was age 21. Her book The Social Construction of Whiteness: White Women, Race Matters, *is based on social history interviews with 30 White women originally from various places in the United States and who were living in California, either in Santa Cruz County or the San Francisco Bay Area, at the time of the interview. When Frankenberg was a graduate student in the 1980s, women of color were beginning to deconstruct the category "women" to show how and why race and class mattered. Her involvement in the feminist movement, and in a social network that was racially diverse and primarily working class, led her to think about what was less often considered, the implications of race and class for White women. In her introduction, she says that "whiteness refers to a set of locations that are historically, socially, politically, and culturally produced and, moreover, are intrinsically linked to unfolding relations of domination."*

*The women interviewed for the study were recruited through organizations and referrals. For example, the woman given the pseudonym Beth, who is described in this reading, was introduced to the author by a mutual friend, and she referred her sister-in-law, who is called Sharon in the book. Employing feminist methodology, Frankenberg did not try to remain completely neutral and anonymous during the interviews. It is not really possible to do so since the interviewees' perceptions of the interviewer are bound to have an influence on their responses. Moreover, she found that dis-*cussing her motives in doing the research or revealing bits of personal information facilitated the interviewing process.

The following interview with Beth Ellison is one of five included in the chapter called "Growing Up White: The Social Geography of Race." Beth was 30 at the time of the interview. She grew up in a middle-class home in segregated neighborhoods in the South. She talks about race as if it is very separate from her childhood and adolescence. Yet, as the interview progresses, it becomes clear that she received mixed messages about race from her family and that racial differences were very clearly part of her environment. She recalls that as a young person, she associated being Black with being poor. She also speaks about having a Black domestic worker in her early childhood home, being in the fifth grade when schools in her community were integrated, being transferred to a segregated private high school as a result of an incident with a Black girl, and her mother's concern about her living in a low-income, racially mixed neighborhood as a young adult. In short, although it is not on the surface of her consciousness, Beth, like most of us, clearly grew up in a context shaped by race and class.

... This book begins with childhood, looking in detail at five white women's descriptions of the places in which they grew up and analyzing them in terms of what I will refer to as the "social geography" of race. *Geography* refers here to the physical landscape—the home, the street, the neighborhood, the school, parts of town visited or driven through rarely or regularly, places visited on vacation. My interest was in how physical space was divided and who inhabited it, and, for my purposes, "who" referred to racially and ethnically identified beings.

The notion of a *social* geography suggests that the physical landscape is peopled and that it is constituted and perceived by means of social rather than natural processes. I thus asked how the women I interviewed conceptualized and related to the people around them. To what extent, for example, did they have relationships of closeness or distance, equality or inequality, with people of color?

What were they encouraged or taught by example to make of the variously "raced" people in their environments? *Racial* social geography, in short, refers to the racial and ethnic mapping of environments in physical and social terms and enables also the beginning of an understanding of the conceptual mappings of self and other operating in white women's lives. . . .

Race was, in fact, lived in as many different ways as there were women I talked with. Nonetheless, patterns emerged as I analyzed the interviews. I clustered the childhood narratives around four types or modes of experience, not because each narrative fell clearly in one or another mode, but because there were enough common threads to make the similarities worth exploring, and because the contrasts between modes were significant enough to require analysis. Of the four modes, one seemed at first to be characterized by an absence of people of color from the narrator's life, but turned out, as I will suggest, to be only "*apparently* all white." Second, there was a racially conflictual mode. Third, there were contexts in which race difference was present, but unremarked, in which race difference functioned as a filter for perception while not always being consciously perceived. Finally, some white women described experiences I have interpreted as quasi-integrated, that is, integrated but not fully so, for reasons that should become clear below. . . .

Beth Ellison: An 'Apparently All-White' Childhood

Many of the women whose childhoods were apparently all white shared suburban middle-class childhoods. Beth, born in 1956, grew up in a white, middle-class, professional suburb in a town in Virginia. Today she describes herself as a feminist. She is an artist who makes a living as a retail worker. Beth said of her childhood:

> I was born in Alabama and spent my real early years in New Orleans. I was five when we moved to Virginia. I remember living in a professional subdivision, our neighbors were all doctors and lawyers. . . . It was a white neighborhood. . . . The only specifically racist thing I remember from growing

up in Virginia was when a Black doctor and his family moved into the neighborhood . . . at that time I guess maybe I was fourteen and I still didn't think about racism . . . I wasn't interested in politics . . . but I vaguely remember neighbors banding together to see if they could keep this family from moving in and I remember thinking that was disgusting, but I was more concerned with my life and being a young teenager.

In the telling of this incident, racism is categorized as "politics," and as separate from daily life as a teenager. Beth's self-description in this sense highlights a key difference between whites' experience of racism and the experience of people of color: racism is frequently pushed to the forefront of consciousness of people of color, as a construct that organizes hardship and discrimination.[1]

The statement that the only *specifically* racist incident was the attempted exclusion of a Black family from the neighborhood suggests a view of racism as limited to willed, concerted activity. Yet the very existence of a neighborhood whose residents are all white itself bespeaks a history of racist structuring of that community. Elements of that history might include both the "redlining" of neighborhoods by realtors to keep Black people from buying property in them and also the economic dimensions of racism that would place affluent neighborhoods beyond the reach of most Black families. The incident that drew Beth's attention to racism was, in short, only the tip of the iceberg.

There *were* Black people not too far away, for Beth says:

> I saw a lot of Black people around . . . on the street and in class and downtown, but I don't remember there being many Black and white people hanging out together, I just don't remember seeing that. And also I didn't pay real close attention to it, either. . . . Now that we're talking about this, I remember seeing a lot of Black people around, and I remember not really hanging out with them . . . it wasn't any kind of conscious decision but it was just not what I did.

With or without a conscious decision, Beth's experience of friendship and community was racially structured in multiple ways.

Beth said that there were no parts of town that she avoided when she was growing up. In her hometown in Virginia, the poorest—and Black—part of town was on the way to the downtown record and bookstores, and Beth traversed it regularly. So, unlike some other women in the "all-white" group, Beth did not perceive people of color as a threat or a group to avoid; rather, their presence or absence was not a salient issue.

If Beth felt no anxiety, however, her mother seemed to oscillate between what Beth called a "humanist" belief in at least a limited integration and the sense that she needed to keep her children apart (and, in her perception, *safe*) from Black children and adults. This is illustrated in Beth's description of school integration, which for her began in fifth grade:

> I would have been about ten when schools were desegregated [in 1965]. I don't remember anyone in my family being upset about it, or my mother trying to withdraw me from school or anything. . . . I was . . . a little bit excited about it because it was something new. . . . My mother tried really hard to be—she's kind of a humanist, so I don't remember her saying anything like "Don't hang out with Black kids."

But later, in high school, Beth was involved in an incident in which she was pushed up against the wall of the gym changing room by a Black girl. This resulted in her parents moving her to a segregated private school. Beth comments:

> We didn't talk about it at the time, but as I look back on it now . . . it seems evident to me that they did this because it wasn't a school where there would be, uh, what they might consider rowdy Black girls for me to have to contend with.

Beth's mother showed a similar ambivalence on the question of residential integration. On the one hand, Beth did not think her mother had taken part in the effort to keep the Black family out of her neighborhood. Her response was very different, however, when Beth, at twenty, moved to a poor, racially mixed part of the same town:

> I do remember my mother being really concerned and I don't know if that's because there were a lot of Black people living there or because it was an extremely poor part of town where you'd be more inclined to be ripped off . . . [but she] wouldn't let my younger brother come visit me.

So Beth grew up in a context in which Black people were the "significant others" of color, and where race and income were intertwined. Being white and middle class meant living somewhere different from Black people. The social distance between white and Black people—which was considerable—was produced and reproduced through the conscious efforts of white people, including Beth's mother and neighbors, and through the more diffuse effects of the interplay of the class structure with racism. White people like Beth's mother deliberated over the permissibility and safety of living in the same terrain as Black people, seemingly projecting their fear or dislike of Black people when they made such decisions.[2] Less visible here are the forms of white people's personal and structural violence toward African Americans that marked both residential and school desegregation and the period of civil rights struggle in general.

In any event, Beth received mixed messages. Her environment was shaped by at least three factors. First, there was a preexisting arrangement of racial segregation and inequality, reproduced, for example, by the all-white private school. Second, Beth's mother's verbal messages about segregation espoused ideas about equality or what Beth called "humanism." Third, and contrasting with her humanism, there were Beth's mother's actions in response to Beth's experiences and choices, which, as Beth tells it, frequently leaned in the direction of segregationism and hostility toward Black people. The result was that, without trying, Beth could continue to live a mostly racially segregated life.

For Beth, the structure of racial inequality was at times simply lived in; at other times, it was both lived and seen. If the consequences for *herself* of a racially structured environment were not always obvious to Beth, however, the impact on others of race and class hierarchy was at times very clear. She said of the two communities she knew well as she was growing up:

Beth: In [the town in Virginia] it seems like it was mostly poor neighborhoods where Black people lived, but there were also a lot of poor white people that lived there too. But in [the town in Alabama], there was a Black part of town and a white part of town. There was the rich part of the white part of town, the middle class, and then the poor white section. And then there was shantytown, and it was literally shacks.

RF: So the shantytown was really the Black part of town?

Beth: Yeah . . . these tiny little shacks that looked like they'd been thrown together out of plywood and two-by-fours. The difference was incredible, because you could drive for one minute in your car and go through rich, beautiful neighborhoods to . . . what looked squalid to me.

Comparing Beth's words here with her memories of her own neighborhood, it is striking that Beth was much more sharply aware of racial *oppression* shaping Black experience than of race *privilege* in her own life. Thus, Beth could be alert to the realities of economic discrimination against Black communities while still conceptualizing her own life as racially neutral—nonracialized, nonpolitical.

For Beth and the other women who grew up in apparently all-white situations, there were in fact at least one or two people of color not too far away. It is in fact conceptually rather than physically that people of color were distant. In this regard, one startling feature of several descriptions of apparently all-white childhoods was the sudden appearance in the narratives of people of color as employees, mainly Black, mainly female, and mainly domestic workers. What is striking here is not the presence of domestic workers as such[3] but the way in which they were talked about. For, oddly, these Black women were not summoned into white women's accounts of their lives by means of questions like "Were there any people of color in your neighborhood?" or "Who lived in your household when you were growing up?" Rather, they arrived previously unheralded, in the context of some other topic.

Black women domestic workers appeared in Beth's narrative when I asked her if she remembered the first time she became conscious of race difference, or conscious that there were Black and white people in the world. Beth responded that her first consciousness of race as a difference was when she was about four years old, when her mother chastised her for referring to a Black woman as a "lady." Here, of course, we are seeing race not just as difference but as hierarchy. Beth said:

> Ever since I was a baby, Black people have been around, the person who taught me to walk was a Black woman, that was a maid for our family . . . pretty much all throughout my childhood, there was a maid around.

She added that, although she had not really noticed at the time, she realized now that when her mother remarried, the family stopped employing anyone to do housework. Thus Black domestic workers, despite involvement in Beth's life on the very intimate level of teaching her to walk, seemed on another level to have been so insignificant as not to have merited mention earlier in our conversation. Nor had she noted their departure from the household after a certain point in her life.

The forgotten and suddenly remembered domestic worker recurred in several of these white, middle-class childhoods. Tamara Green, raised "solidly middle class" in suburban Los Angeles, said:

> I totally forgot until I just started thinking about it—we had housekeepers who, all but one from the time we lived in California, were Latin American, Mexican, Colombian, Honduran, Salvadoran. There was one British Honduran who was Black. And I had a close relationship with one of them.

Why is the story told in this particular way? It may be the status of domestic workers from the standpoint of white middle-class women, or the status of people of color from the purview of a white and middle-class childhood, that made these women invisible and stripped them of subjectivity in the landscapes of childhood.[4] But whether or not it is race per se that determined how the domestic worker of color appeared in the interviews, it is primarily through employer-employee, class-imbalanced relationships that women from apparently all-white homes encountered women of color. If not themselves in positions of clear authority, these white middle-class women must have seen their parents in such positions, able to summon and dismiss the racially different Other at will. It is perhaps in this sense of control and authority that the home was indeed all white, and the neighborhood similarly so. . . .

Conclusion

In all of [the] narratives, landscape and the experience of it were racially structured—whether [the] narratives seemed to be marked predominantly by the presence or the absence of people of color. This is of course not to say that race was the only organizing principle of the social context. Class intersected with race in differentiating [another interviewee's] and Beth's relationships with Black communities and as part of the context for the quasi-integrated experiences of [two other interviewees]. Controls on sexuality link up with racism to create hostility toward relationships between African American men and white women.

Once a person is in a landscape structured by racism, a conceptual mapping of race, of self and others, takes shape, following from and feeding the physical context. Thus, for example, [another interviewee] experienced the term "Anglo" initially without any negative or positive connotation; [another interviewee] both saw through the lens of racial stratification in her own environment *and* did not perceive racial stratification as such. Even the presence or absence of people of color seemed to be as much a social-mental construct as a social-physical one: recall the invisible African American and Latina domestic workers in some apparently all-white homes.

This analysis has some implications for a definition of racism. First of all, it clarifies and makes concrete some of the forms—some subtle, some obvious—that race privilege and racism may take in the lives of white

women: educational and economic inequality, verbal assertions of white superiority, the maintenance of all-white neighborhoods, the "invisibility" of Black and Latina domestic workers, white people's fear of people of color, and the "colonial" notion that the cultures of peoples of color were great only in the past. In this context, it would be hard to maintain the belief that race only affects the lives of people of color. Moreover, racism emerges not only as an ideology or political orientation chosen or rejected at will but also as a system of material relationships with a set of ideas linked to and embedded in those material relations.

The racial structuring of white experience as it emerged in each of these narratives is complex. It is contradictory: the two women most explicitly raised to espouse racist ideas, Beth Ellison and [another interviewee], found moments and situations, however fleeting, in which to question the racist status quo. Conversely, [the two] raised to find ways in which to challenge racism, were nonetheless not outside its reach; racism as well as antiracism shaped their environments, and both women drew at times on white-centered logics in describing and living their lives.

These women's accounts of their environments were also mobile. All [interviewees] indicated in various ways that, with hindsight, they had become more cognizant of the patterning of their earlier experiences: phrases like "now that we're talking about this I remember" and "I was so unaware of cultural difference that" signal both lack of awareness of racism *and* moments of recognition or realization of it. "Experience" emerged here as a complicated concept. As the narratives showed, there are multiple ways in which experiences can be named, forgotten, or remembered through changing conceptual schemata. . . .

Notes

1. See, for example, many of the contributions to Cherríe Moraga and Gloria Anzaldúa, eds., *This Bridge Called My Back: Writings by Radical Women of Color* (Watertown, MA: Persephone, 1981. New York: Kitchen Table Women of Color Press, 1983.

2. Discussion of the decisions Beth's mother made are beyond the scope of this paper since I did not interview her, but only her daughter. However, it is pos-

sible to speculate that, in relation to the Black doctor and his family, a sense of class similarity overrode or mitigated race difference in making Beth's mother feel it acceptable for the family to move in. In contrast, she did not accept Beth's move to a racially mixed neighborhood that was also a low-income area. It is also possible that, for Beth's mother, the presence of one or two Black people did not disrupt her sense of the "whiteness" of the environment, whereas a greater number of Black people, in school or in a neighborhood, was more disturbing.

3. As always, there is an embedded history here, since up until the 1960s as many as half of all Black women in paid employment worked as domestic workers. See, for example, Julianne Malveaux, 1988. "Ain't I a Woman: Differences in the Labor Market Status of Black and White Women," in *Racism and Sexism: An Integrated Study*, ed. Paula S. Rothenberg (New York: St. Martin's, 1988), 76.

4. Judith Rollin's study, *Between Women: Domestics and Their Employees*, (Philadelphia: Temple University Press, 1985) also points to the "invisibility" of Black domestic workers in the contemporary United States (see especially Pp. 207ff).

Discussion Questions

1. Think about your own childhood and adolescence. Is your first impulse like Beth's to describe it as being relatively race- and class-neutral? If so, do you still think of it that way? If not, why not; what made race and/or class more salient for you?

2. Social scientists sometimes speak about "marked" and "unmarked" social categories—ones that we mention and ones we take for granted. Why are White, middle class, and male the unmarked, the ones that seems to be the norm or the expected?

3. Beth calls her mother a "humanist." Frankenberg says she was ambivalent about race and sent Beth mixed messages. What evidence do you see about her mother's racial attitudes in Beth's story? Would you consider her attitudes racist? Why (not)?

4. In Beth's experience Black and White people didn't hang out together. How does the fact that interaction among people of different racial groups is often limited contribute to people who aren't White being seen by White people as "the other" and, thereby, to the social construction of whiteness?

41

Women's Employment Among Blacks, Whites, and Three Groups of Latinas

Do More Privileged Women Have Higher Employment?

Paula England
Carmen Garcia-Beaulieu
Mary Ross

In this article, Paula England, Carmen Garcia-Beaulieu, and Mary Ross frame their arguments decidedly in terms of gender, race, and class as they seek to understand whether women with greater privilege have higher rates of employment. Using demographic measures to ferret out an answer, these researchers conclude that, indeed, White women have the highest levels of employment in comparison with Black women and the three largest subgroups of Latinas in the U.S.—Mexican, Puerto Rican, and Cuban American women. The factors most salient to this fundamental finding involve immigration status, education, and marital status and husband's income, children, age, and region.

Let us take a look at each variable in turn. It will not be surprising to learn that immigrant women have lower levels of employment than those who are native born, which negatively impacted the Latinas in this study—many of whom were immigrants. Education was found to be highly related to employment for all groups in the study regardless of race. In this case, the fact that White women had the highest levels of education, while Mexican women had the lowest, did in fact translate into the largest employment gap between these two groups. Interestingly, though there were substantial differences among these different racial/ethnic groups with regard to marital status and husbands' income, these factors had little explanatory power with regard to ethnic differences in employment and did not deter employment for these groups. Children, on the other hand, did deter employment for all groups. The most significant gap in employment was notably between White and Mexican women, with Mexican fertility ranking highest of all groups. England et al. also suggest from their findings that single women with children may view welfare as a smarter option when weighing lower earnings against child care costs. The factor of age was insignificant as an explanatory variable, for the most part, except in terms of Cuban women, who tended to be older than the others on average, and this only explained a short gap in employment between White and Cuban women. Finally, region did not seem to yield clear results in the analysis despite attempts by the authors to tease out regional concentrations of Puerto Ricans in New York or Cubans in Florida. In sum, the largest gap in employment was between White and Mexican women, largely the result of the fact that there are more immigrants within the Mexican population, lower levels of education, and higher fertility rates among Mexican women.

The authors draw several conclusions. They suggest that the presence of children and not marital status is a major harbinger of gender inequality, with childbearing less likely to be coupled with marriage. These authors also find that the women who have the greatest need for employment are not necessarily the ones employed. In point of fact, it is the women who are the most privileged in terms of race, country of origin, and education who are the most likely to be employed in America. At the same time, women of color are facing lower levels of employment as they face lower rates of marriage and chance of welfare assistance.

In 1890, 40 percent of Black but only 16 percent of white women were in the labor force. By 1950, Black women's participation (38

368

percent) was still way ahead of white women's (29 percent; England 1992). By 1980, Black and white women's employment rates had converged at 47 percent, and both groups had higher employment than Mexican (44 percent) and Puerto Rican (35 percent) women, and 51 percent of Cuban women were employed (calculated from Smith and Tienda 1988, 63). More recent data show that white women are now more likely to be employed than Black women and Latinas (Browne 1999; Corcoran 1999; Corcoran, Heflin, and Reyes 1999). Employment declined substantially for Puerto Rican women (Tienda, Donato, and Cordero-Guzman 1992) and Black mothers with less than high school education (Corcoran 1999) between the 1960s and 1990.

Our analysis will show that in recent (2001) national data, African American women and Latinas (whether of Cuban, Mexican, or Puerto Rican descent) were employed at lower rates than non-Hispanic white women, although the gaps between white women and women of color were small for all groups but Mexican women. In results not shown (but available on request), we did a parallel analysis for 1994 data, when ethnic gaps were larger. Welfare reform, combined with the expansion of the Earned Income Tax Credit, pushed and pulled many poor women of color into employment in the 1990s (Meyer and Rosenbaum 2001), making gaps smaller by 2001. But as our analysis will show, white women still had the highest employment rates by 2001. We find that women with more education are more apt to be employed and that education explains a significant share of race and ethnic group differences in employment. We will show that among women in all racial/ethnic groups except Blacks, immigrants are less likely to be employed than the native born. Our findings, and those of authors who have pointed out the Black-white crossover, point to an emerging reality in which women in more privileged groups on dimensions of race, national origin, or education are more, rather than less, likely to be employed. Our claim is not that they are more privileged because they are employed. For some women who have low potential earnings (for reasons of their skills or discrimination) and would need to pay for child care, employment could make them worse off, especially if it means losing government subsidies, as meager as they are. However, for many women, employment confers benefits not obtainable any other way, and today these benefits go largely to women who are also advantaged on other dimensions. Understandings of how gender intersects with class, race, ethnicity, and national origin must grapple with this new reality.

The scholarly consensus has been that women's employment is deterred by marriage and children in the context of a division of labor that features husbands' specializing in market work and providing income and wives' being responsible for child rearing and household work. We find that the part of this standard gender analysis that remains true is that young children reduce women's employment, although less than in earlier decades (Cohen and Bianchi 1999). But the husband support portion of this view never fit for women of color, immigrants, or many working-class white women who historically have not had the option of being supported by a husband with a family wage. This critique of the standard consensus was made by advocates of intersectionality, a perspective that looks at gender together with race, class, and other vectors of privilege (Higginbotham and Romero 1997). They correctly observed that the lack of husbands with solid incomes, along with lower marriage rates, probably explained Black women's higher employment rates than white women through the 1950s, 1960s, and 1970s. But today, white women, despite being more likely to be married to high-earning men, have higher employment rates than Blacks or Latinas, as we will show. Education has had a positive effect on women's employment at least as far back as 1960 (Spain and Bianchi 1996, 67). But Cohen and Bianchi's (1999) analysis from 1978 to 1998 shows that education became increasingly predictive of women's employment over time, and family factors less so. To the extent that education is indicative of the social class of one's family of origin or one's adult household, this means that women who are privileged on class are now more, not less, likely to be employed. We will document this here with recent data. Thus, today, objective economic need is not the only, and not even the major, factor driving women's employment. Of course, upper-middle-class women may subjectively perceive as much economic need for employment as women with low-earning or no husbands; the former often see their family's consumption is inadequate if it is less than those in their relatively affluent neighborhoods and networks. The earnings of men with no more than a high school education have fallen dramatically in recent decades with economic restructuring, leading to the hypothesis that this may explain some of the increase in women's employment. But this hypothesis does not square with the fact that women with college education, most of whom are married to men with relatively high education and earnings, have increased their employment most dramatically (Chinhui and Murphy 1997). . . .

Data and Method

We use the 2001 Current Population Survey (CPS) Annual Demographic Files (U.S. Bureau of Census 2001). The CPS is a national probability sample of households. We used individuals as the units of analysis, selecting women between the ages of 18 and 65. We compare the three largest subgroups of Latinas with the two largest racial groups, whites and Blacks. We separate out non-Hispanic whites and non-Hispanic Blacks, and among those reported as Hispanic, distinguish those of Mexican, Puerto Rican, or Cuban descent (regardless of race, so that our Latino sample includes some who also identify as Black). Other races (e.g., Asian, Native American) and Hispanics with ancestry from other countries were omitted from our analysis. Although our categories cross-cut race and ethnicity, we use the terms interchangeably below. All analyses are unweighted. Table 41.1 presents the sample sizes and means on all variables for each racial/ethnic group.

Our dependent variable is the number of weeks a woman was employed in the previous year. We chose to use this rather than a simple dichotomy measuring whether the individual was employed at the time of the survey so as to use more detailed information.

We include independent variables hypothesized to explain variation in women's employment. We entered three dummy variables to capture whether a woman is an immigrant and, if so, how recent. The three categories are immigrated to the United States before 1990, immigrated between 1990 and 1997, and immigrated after 1997. The reference category is nonimmigrant. Although people who are born in Puerto Rico and come to the mainland are not, technically speaking, immigrants since they are U.S. citizens, for continuity of terminology across groups, we will refer to them as immigrants to distinguish them from mainland-born women of Puerto Rican descent.

Education is measured with four dummy variables indicating that the woman has completed an advanced degree, completed an undergraduate degree, attended some college, or finished high school, with a reference category of those who did not complete high school. The sample contains women as young as 18; some women in their late teens and 20s are attending college, which is likely to deter employment, so we include a dummy for whether the woman was enrolled in school full-time.

Marital status is captured with two dummy variables: Married and no longer married (divorced or widowed), with a reference category of those never married. We also include a variable for the amount of income a woman's husband earned during the year; for unmarried women, this is 0. We include the number of children younger than 6 that the woman has and the number of children she has between ages 6 and 18 (these are the age categories provided in the publicly available CPS). We distinguish children by age since mothers are more apt to stay home with younger children.

Since CPS data do not include a measure of years of employment experience, which increases across the life cycle with age but also is more continuous in more recent cohorts, we include age to roughly pick up these effects. Because employment opportunities for women may differ by region, and ethnic groups vary in regional concentration, we include dummy variables for the West, North-

Table 41.1
Means on All Variables

	White	Mexican	Puerto Rican	Cuban	Black
Weeks employed	36.01	29.03	30.78	34.34	34.61
Native born (reference)	0.95	0.47	0.50	0.28	0.91
Immigrated before 1990	0.03	0.29	0.38	0.54	0.06
Immigrated from 1990 to 1997	0.01	0.17	0.08	0.13	0.02
Immigrated after 1997	0.01	0.07	0.04	0.06	0.01
Less than high school (reference)	0.08	0.45	0.29	0.16	0.18
High school graduate	0.33	0.28	0.31	0.36	0.35
Some college	0.32	0.20	0.26	0.23	0.32
College graduate	0.19	0.06	0.09	0.16	0.11
Advanced degree	0.08	0.01	0.04	0.08	0.04
Never married (reference)	0.20	0.26	0.30	0.27	0.41
Married, spouse present	0.62	0.57	0.41	0.54	0.32
No longer married	0.18	0.16	0.28	0.20	0.27
Husband's income[a] ($)	38,533	20,958	18,894	30,454	13,991
Number of children younger than 6	0.22	0.45	0.29	0.12	0.25
Number of children 6 to 18	0.52	0.87	0.70	0.40	0.57
Age	41.29	35.65	38.01	41.86	39.40
Age squared	1,868.25	1,413.89	1,598.14	1,928.50	1,718.63
Midwest (reference)	0.27	0.10	0.10	0.02	0.20
Northeast	0.23	0.02	0.61	0.14	0.19
South	0.29	0.30	0.23	0.77	0.54
West	0.22	0.57	0.07	0.07	0.08
Full-time student	0.05	0.05	0.06	0.06	0.05
Sample size	27,570	4,098	726	265	4,160

a. Unmarried women or women with husbands without income enter this average with 0.

east, and South [Midwest is the reference category].

Given the continuous dependent variable, we use ordinary least squares regression to predict weeks worked. However, since weeks worked has a nonnormal distribution, with a large number of women at 0 weeks, in results not shown, we perform a Tobit analysis, and the results are qualitatively similar in terms of associations of variables with employment. For ease of interpretation, we present ordinary least squares results.

We regress weeks worked on dummy variables for ethnic groups (non-Hispanic Blacks, Cubans, Mexicans, and Puerto Ricans, with whites the reference category) and other ex-

planatory variables described above. We then trim all nonsignificant interactions, rerun models, and present results for the coefficients on explanatory variables (other than ethnic dummy variables and interactions with them) in the column labeled "White" in Table 41.2. Coefficients in this column indicate the effect for whites pooled with any ethnic groups whose slope for this variable was not significantly different than whites' (as assessed by the interaction term). The separate columns in Table 41.2 for each group other than whites give the pooled coefficients if the interaction term was not significant and the distinct coefficient for this ethnic group in cases where the interaction terms shows it to

Table 41.2

Coefficients from Ordinary Least Squares Models Predicting Weeks Worked (2001)

	White	Mexican	Puerto Rican	Cuban	Black
Immigration (native born = reference)					
Immigrated before 1990	−0.440	−0.440	−0.440	−0.440	−0.440
Immigrated from 1990 to 1997	−7.143*	−7.143*	−7.143*	−7.143*	0.307[a]
Immigrated after 1997	−16.626*	−7.159a	−16.626*	−16.626*	−7.393[a]
Education (less than high school = reference)					
High school graduate	9.184*	9.184*	9.184*	9.184*	9.184*
Some college	12.304*	12.304*	12.304*	12.304*	12.304*
College graduate	13.200*	13.200*	19.165[a]	13.200*	16.488[a]
Advanced degree	16.587*	16.587*	16.587*	16.587*	16.587*
Marital status (never married = reference)					
Married, spouse present	−0.683	−0.683	−0.683	−0.683	−0.683
No longer married	1.364*	1.364*	1.364*	1.364*	1.364*
Other income					
Husband's income (1,000s)	−0.034*	−0.034*	−0.034*	−0.034*	0.022[a]
Children					
Number of children younger than 6	−6.506*	−6.506*	−6.506*	−6.506*	−3.458[a]
Number of children 6 to 18	−1.892*	−1.892*	−1.892*	−1.892*	−0.584[a]
Control variables					
Age	1.951*	1.951*	1.951*	1.951*	1.951*
Age squared	−0.027*	−0.027*	−0.027*	−0.027*	−0.027*
Region (Midwest = reference)					
Northeast	−2.154*	−2.154*	−2.154*	−2.154*	0.531[a]
South	−2.974*	−2.974*	5.218[a]	−2.974*	1.200[a]
West	−2.852*	−2.852*	−2.852*	−2.852*	−2.852*
Full-time student	−7.189*	−7.189*	−18.140[a]	−7.189*	−16.517[a]

Note: Coefficients from the white model are from the pooled model in which white women were the reference category, after trimming nonsignificant interactions from the model.
a. The group's slope on this variable is significantly different from that of white women. Significance tests are not provided for slopes for individual groups.
Significance of pooled coefficients: *$p < .01$ (two-tailed test).

differ significantly from the coefficient for whites. Where interactions showed that slopes differed by ethnicity, the slope for the group in question was calculated by adding the coefficient on the covariate from the trimmed model (which tells the effect for whites since they are the reference category) to the interaction effect (which tells how different from whites' slope this groups' slope is). Presenting results like this allows us to show group differences in returns only when they are statistically significant.

We use the ethnic-specific means in Table 41.1, together with the regression results in Table 41.2, to decompose ethnic differences in weeks worked between each group of women of color and white women in Table 41.3. We chose white women to serve as the contrast to all groups because they are the largest group, have the most racial/ethnic privilege, and have the highest employment. Regression decomposition takes the difference in means between two groups on a dependent variable and assesses what percentage of that difference is explained by group differences in means on independent variables, on slopes, and on intercepts (and an interaction between slopes and intercepts). We restrict our attention to the portion explained by ethnic group differences in means on independent variables, comparing it to the entire rest of the gap (which may be explained by a combination of slope or intercept differences, or their interaction).[1] To compute the portion of the gap between two groups' average weeks of employment that are explained by group differences in means on an independent variable, we multiply the difference in the groups' means on this independent variable by the slope for this variable. Where the group of women of color had a different slope than white women, Table 41.3 presents the estimate using the slope of the group of women of color; otherwise, the pooled slope is used since it fits both groups.

The decomposition implies this thought experiment, taking the white/Mexican gap as explained by education as an example: Suppose that Mexican women changed their education levels to those white women have, but suppose that the effect of education on their employment (their slopes) remained as observed. How many more weeks of employment per year would they have? What percentage of the gap between their employment and white women's (in weeks per year) would be closed by this change? One interpretive caveat is in order: We will often refer to the coefficients from our regression analysis in Table 41.2 as "effects" of variables because, through inclusion of multiple control variables, we aspire to be estimating causal effects. However, we recognize that coefficients may in some cases mix causal effects with spurious associations (because both employment and the independent variable are affected by a common unmeasured cause). It is also possible that some "in dependent" variables, such as marriage and number of children, are affected by women's employment during the past year, so that we have the causal order reversed. Similarly, when discussing the decomposition results, we will talk about what percentage of ethnic gaps in employment a factor (such as education) "explains." By this we mean that our decomposition shows that if this ethnic gap in an independent variable (e.g., education, number and ages of children, or immigration status) were closed, then given the effects we observe for women of color for this variable, it would close a certain percentage of the employment gap.

This conclusion holds only if the coefficients in the regression are estimates of causal effects.

Results: Explaining Ethnic Differences in Employment

Table 41.1 shows the magnitude of white women's advantage in employment. In 2001, white women had the highest employment, narrowly above Black and Cuban women (less than 2 weeks), but about 6 weeks above Mexican and Puerto Rican women. (In results not shown, we did a parallel analysis for 1994 CPS data to capture the period before welfare reform. In that year, all groups' employment was lower than in 2001, but race gaps were larger, with white women employed 9 weeks more than Mexican, 10 weeks more than Puerto Rican, 4 weeks more than Cuban, and 3 weeks more than Black women. Analyses are available on request.) Below, we present results one explanatory factor at a time, paying attention to what we learn from combining the information from Tables 41.1 through 41.3: How groups are different in their means on each independent variable (see Table 41.1), what net statistical association each variable has with employment (see Table 41.2), and how much of the gap in employment between each group of women of color and white women can be statistically explained by group differences in means on the explanatory factors in each year (see Table 41.3).

Immigration Status

Immigrant women have lower employment levels than native-born women for all ethnic groups except Blacks (see Table 41.2). In 2001, the most recent immigrants (arriving after 1997) averaged 17 weeks less employment, those who arrived between 1990 and 1997 worked 7 weeks less than nonimmigrants, and those who came before 1990 were indistinguishable from nonimmigrants in weeks of employment. Our interpretation of this pattern is that new immigrants lack network connections, English-speaking skills, and/or country-specific experience helpful in getting jobs.

How much of the gap in weeks of employment between white women and women of

Table 41.3

Decomposition of Differences in Average Weeks of Employment Between White Women and Women of Color: Weeks Explained by Group Mean Differences in Independent Variables

	Mexican	Puerto Rican	Cuban	Black
Immigrated before 1990	0.1	0.2	0.3	0.0
Immigrated from 1990 to 1997	1.1	0.5	0.8	0.0[a]
Immigrated after 1997	0.4[a]	0.5	0.9	0.0[a]
Total, immigration	1.7, 25%	1.2, 22%	2.0, 120%	0.0, 2%
High school graduate	0.5	0.1	−0.3	−0.2
Some college	1.5	0.7	1.0	0.0
College graduate	1.8	1.9[a]	0.4	1.4[a]
Advanced degree	1.1	0.7	0.1	0.6
Total, education	4.8, 69%	3.4, 66%	1.1, 68%	1.8, 131%
Married, spouse present	0.0	−0.1	−0.1	−0.2
No longer married	0.0	<0.1	0.0	−0.1
Husband's income (1,000s)	−0.6	−0.7	−0.3	0.5[a]
Total, marital status, and other income	−0.6, −9%	−0.9, −18%	−0.4, −21%	0.2, 15%
Number of children younger than 6	1.5	0.5	−0.7	0.1[a]
Number of children 6 to 18	0.7	0.3	−0.2	0.0[a]
Total, children	2.1, 30%	0.8, 15%	−0.9, −53%	0.1, 9%
Total explained, all variables[b]	7.4, 106%	4.4, 84%	3.3, 200%	1.2, 84%
Actual difference in weeks (from Table 1)	7.0	5.2	1.7	1.4

Notes: (1) Weeks explained are the product of the slope for the group of women of color multiplied by the difference between the mean for white women and this group. The pooled slope is used for this calculation except when the group's own slope is significantly different. (2) The regressions from Table 41.2, including age, age squared, region, and full-time student, are used for purposes of this decomposition.

a. The group slope is different from the pooled slope.

b. Includes portions explained by group mean differences in age, student enrollment, and region. Total for education includes negligible portion for current student enrollment.

color can be explained by immigration? The groups with high proportions of immigrants are the three Latina groups; only 5 percent of whites and 9 percent of Blacks, but 53 percent of Mexicans, 50 percent of Puerto Ricans, and 72 percent of Cubans were immigrants in 2001 (see Table 41.1). Among immigrants, Mexicans are the most and Cubans the least recent, because the largest wave of Cubans came shortly after Castro came to power, whereas Mexican immigration has been continuous and growing. Immigration is an entirely trivial factor in the white/Black employment gap since few of either group are immigrants (see Table 41.3). But presence and recency of immigrants ex-

plains two weeks or 25 percent of the Mexican/white gap (see Table 41.3), one week or 22 percent of the Puerto Rican/white gap, and all of the very small Cuban/white gap. In sum, the greater representation of immigrants among Latinas than whites is an important part of the reason that Latinas, particularly Mexicans and Cubans, have lower employment rates.

Education

Education is related to employment for all groups. In the pooled model, high school graduates have 9 more weeks employment per year than dropouts, those with some college 12 weeks more, college graduates 13 weeks more, and those with advanced degrees 17 weeks more (see Table 41.2). Slopes do not vary by ethnicity, except that Black and Puerto Rican women have higher employment returns to college graduation (see Table 41.2).

How does education affect ethnic differences in employment? Whites have the highest levels of education and Mexicans the lowest (see Table 41.1). Education is important in explaining the employment gap between all groups of women of color and white women. The lower education of Mexicans explains five weeks or 69 percent of their employment gap with whites; for Puerto Ricans, the figure is three weeks or 66 percent; for Cubans, one week or 68 percent; and for Blacks, two weeks, more than the full gap (see Table 41.3). While the general picture is of Black and Puerto Rican women's having less employment because they have less education, given their higher employment returns to college than other groups, an interesting note is that Black and Puerto Rican women who are college graduates actually work a few more weeks per year than white women (not shown).

Marital Status and Husbands' Income

White women are the most likely to be married (62 percent), with Mexican (57 percent) and Cuban (54 percent) women next, and Puerto Rican (41 percent) and Black (32 percent) women having much lower rates (see Table 41.1); husbands' earnings (averaged in at 0 for unmarried women) are much lower for women of color. The older scholarly consensus was that these differences—and the economic need they imply for women to contribute to family support—explained Black women's higher employment in previous decades. But as the regressions show, marriage no longer deters employment for women. There is no significant difference between currently married women and never married women, although divorced and widowed women work 1 more week than those who have never married (these effects apply to all groups; see Table 41.2). Husband's income deters employment for all groups but Blacks, but the magnitude of the difference is trivial (0.3 of a week for each additional $1,000 per

year). Black women are employed trivially more when their husbands earn more. All of these coefficients are too small to be substantively interesting. Given this, it is not surprising that the decompositions in Table 41.3 show little power of marital status and husband's income to explain ethnic differences in employment. Even though ethnic groups differ greatly in the proportion married and in husband's income, the small effects of these factors on employment makes them unimportant in explaining ethnic differentials in employment.

Children

Although marriage and husbands' incomes no longer do much to deter employment, children do deter employment for all ethnic groups. The pooled models show that each child younger than 6 is associated with seven fewer weeks of employment per year, and each child from 6 to 18, with two fewer weeks (see Table 41.2). Blacks show a somewhat smaller (but still significant) deterrent effect than other groups (see Table 41.2). Cuban women have lower fertility than white women, so fertility differences explain none of the employment gap; in fact, the small employment gap would be 53 percent larger if Cuban women had the (higher) fertility of white women (see Table 41.3). In contrast, fertility is crucial to the white/Mexican employment gap, explaining 30 percent of the seven-week gap (see Table 41.3). Black and Puerto Rican women have fertility higher than that of Cubans or whites but lower than that of Mexicans (see Table 41.1). Puerto Rican women's fertility levels relative to white women explain 15 percent of the five-week gap (see Table 41.3). Black women's higher fertility explains less than one week, or 9 percent of the small Black/white gap (see Table 41.3). In results not shown, we interacted children with marriage to see if married women were more likely to forgo employment because of children but found no such consistent pattern. This may be because for single women with low potential earnings, welfare, as meager as it is, may be a better option than their earnings minus child care costs, thus creating a negative effect of children for single women as well.

Age

Age distributions have little to do with ethnic gaps in employment, with one exception. Cubans are older, on average, than other groups because of the large migration after the revolution and their low fertility. Differences in age between Cubans and whites explain about two weeks of the Cuban/white gap (not shown). (The impact of age is included in the total explained in Table 41.3, but is not reported as it had no other effects.)

Region

Results provide no clear message about how groups' different regional distributions affect employment prospects, so we do not show the decomposition for region in Table 41.3 (except that these components are added into totals explained by all independent variables together). In results not shown, we assess whether the concentration of Puerto Ricans in New York and New Jersey or of Cubans in Florida accounts for their lower employment rates. We do not find this to be true; models with dummy variables for each state have similar coefficients to our models with only regional control.

Summary and Conclusion

Our analysis explains all of the large white/Mexican and the small white/Cuban employment gap. In 2001, Mexican women were employed seven weeks less than white women; this gap is explained by the fact that the Mexican population contains more immigrants, especially recent immigrants (two weeks of the gap), has lower education (five weeks), and has higher fertility (two weeks; see Table 41.3). When all factors are added together, the entire gap has been more than explained by these factors, with education being the largest factor by far. Cuban women have a smaller employment gap with white women (three weeks), and all of it is explained by a combination of the older age structure of Cubans (explaining two weeks, not shown), the high proportion of immigrants (two weeks), and slightly lower education (one week). Cuban fertility, being lower than whites,' makes their employment higher than it would be if they had the same fertility rates as whites, so this factor is offsetting (negative one week) rather than contributing to the gap (see Table 41.3). When we say that we have "explained" the ethnic gaps for these groups, we mean that the group differences in mean levels of education, fertility, and immigration status are such that, given the effects of these factors on employment, if the groups of women of color had white women's means, they would have the employment of white women—or even somewhat higher employment in cases where we have explained more than all the gap. In results not shown, but available on request, we performed identical analyses for 1994 data, when ethnic employment gaps were larger. Independent variables other than ethnicity had similar effects to those in 2001, and our decomposition explained 96 percent of the white/Mexican and 93 percent of the white/Cuban employment gaps.

While our decomposition has explained all of whites' employment advantage relative to Mexican and Cuban women, we explain less, although still a large share, of the gap with the most disadvantaged groups, Black and Puerto Rican women. Puerto Rican women worked five weeks less than white women, while the gap for Black women was a trivial one week. Our decomposition explains 84 percent of the gap for each of the two groups relative to white women. For both groups, education is the biggest factor, explaining 66 percent of the white/Puerto Rican gap and all of the (tiny) white/Black gap. Puerto Ricans' higher rate of immigration explains 22 percent of their employment gap with white women. The fact that we cannot explain all of the white/Puerto Rican and white/Black gaps suggests that factors unmeasured in our regressions are affecting Puerto Rican and Black women more than other groups. Some combination of employment discrimination and living in segregated neighborhoods with inferior schools and few jobs, sometimes making welfare the best option for single mothers, undoubtedly contributes to unexplained portions of these gaps.

What do these findings imply for our contemporary understanding of race, gender, and other axes of privilege such as education and being born in the mainland United States? Sociologists often tell a gender story in which women are disadvantaged in the labor market relative to men in part because of a division of labor in marriage in which women do childrearing. Our findings suggest that today, responsibility for children, not marriage, is a lynchpin of gender inequality, at least insofar as it affects employment. And childbearing is less closely coupled with marriage than previously. The higher fertility of Black, Puerto Rican, and especially Mexican women reduces their employment, even while the low marriage rates of Black and Puerto Rican women do little or nothing to encourage their employment. Advocates of an intersectionality perspective have criticized the generic gender account emphasizing marriage and children, pointing out that many Blacks and Latinas need to work for pay because of the unemployment or low wages of men of their race. We agree that scholarship should seek to understand how race, class, and gender intersect, but our findings make clear that the central race/gender interaction is no longer that less privileged women on race and class are more likely to work outside the home. The unquestionably greater need for employment among women of color no longer leads to higher employment rates (albeit at low wages), as it once did.

In recent decades, the rise in women's employment has been greatest among the well educated (Chinhui and Murphy 1997; Cohen and Bianchi 1999). This is one reason that white women, who still have some edge in educational attainment, now have higher employment levels, as our analysis has shown. In the 1970s and 1980s, the most disadvantaged racial and ethnic groups were adversely affected by recent trends toward greater earnings inequality and the drop in demand for labor with workers low in the labor queue for reasons of education or discrimination. It is well known that this negatively affected the earnings of men with low education, especially Black men. But this restructuring made employment more difficult for some groups of women as well, especially women of color with no more than a high school education (Browne 1999; Corcoran 1999; Tienda, Donato, and Cordero-Guzman 1992). While it remains true that many women need employment because they are single or married

to men with modest earnings, it is simply not true today that the women who need jobs the most are most apt to be employed. Women privileged by race, national origin, and education are the most likely to be employed, as our analysis has shown. Some of the employment edge of privileged women is ascriptive (being born in the United States, or the edge of white women over Black and Puerto Rican women that remained unexplained by our models), and some is on achieved criteria such as education or lower fertility.

The past decade has also made it clear that economic and political trends can move the employment of women of color in either direction relative to white women. While some combination of the pressures of welfare reform, the incentives to employment of the Earned Income Tax Credit, and the strong economy of the 1990s increased the employment of women of color more than that of white women in the middle and late 1990s, we would not be surprised if the post-2001 recession is currently reversing those gains. The more general picture of recent trend research is of disproportionate employment losses for men and women toward the bottom of labor queues defined by education or ethnicity. At the same time, all groups share in a retreat from marriage, but less advantaged groups have not delayed their age of childbearing as much as more educated women, so the result is an increased proportion of births outside of marriage, especially among those who do not go to college and particularly among Blacks (Ellwood and Jencks forthcoming; Raley 1996). When we put these realities together with the retrenchment of welfare, we see that women in less privileged racial and ethnic groups are experiencing simultaneous decreases in their chances of employment, marriage, or welfare to provide a decent level of support for themselves and their children. This is the reality that intersectionality studies must grapple with in future research.

Note

1. We focus only on the difference-in-means components because Jones and Kelley (1984) have shown that one cannot distinguish between the portion of the gap explained by group differences in slopes and intercepts; changing the metric on an independent

variable or changing which reference category is used (for a set of dummy variables representing one multiple-category variable) will change how standard formulas apportion the gap between that explained-by intercept and slope differences. Thus, the only clear distinction is between how much of the gap in employment weeks is explained by group differences in means on each variable versus the entirety of the rest of the gap (from differences in slopes and intercepts, taken together). Where group differences in means more than explain the employment gap, it means that intercept and slope differences, together, are more favorable to the employment of women of color than white women.

References

Browne, Irene, ed. 1999. *Race, gender and economic inequality: African American and Latina women in the labor market.* New York: Russell Sage.

Chinhui, Juhn, and Kevin M. Murphy. 1997. Wage inequality and family labor supply. *Journal of Labor Economics* 15: 72–97.

Christopher, Karen. 1996. Explaining the recent employment gap between Black and white women. *Sociological Focus* 29 (3): 263–80.

Cohen, Philip N., and Suzanne M. Bianchi. 1999. Marriage, children, and women's employment: What do we know? *Monthly Labor Review* 122 (December): 22–31.

Cooney, Rosemary S., and Vilma Ortiz. 1983. Nativity, national origin, and Hispanic female participation in the labor force. *Social Sciences Quarterly* 64: 510–23.

Corcoran, Mary. 1999. Black women's economic progress. In *Race, gender and economic inequality: African-American and Latina women in the labor market,* edited by Irene Browne. New York: Russell Sage.

Corcoran, Mary, Colleen M. Heflin, and Belinda I. Reyes. 1999. Latina women in the U.S.: The economic progress of Mexican and Puerto Rican women. In *Race, gender and economic inequality: African-American and Latina women in the labor market,* edited by Irene Browne. New York: Russell Sage.

Ellwood, David T., and Christopher Jencks. Forthcoming. The spread of single parent families in the United States since 1960. In *The future of the family,* edited by Timothy Smeeding, Daniel Patrick Moynihan, and Lee Rainwater. New York: Russell Sage.

England, Paula. 1992. *Comparable worth: Theories and evidence.* Hawthorne, NY: Aldine DeGruyter.

Higginbotham, Elizabeth, and Mary Romero, eds. 1997. *Women and working: Exploring race, ethnicity, and class.* Thousand Oaks, CA: Sage.

Hondagneu-Sotelo, Pierette. 1997. Working "without papers" in the United States: Toward the integration of legal status in frameworks of race, class, and gender. In *Women and working: Exploring race, ethnicity, and class,* edited by Elizabeth Higginbotham and Mary Romero. Thousand Oaks, CA: Sage.

Jones, F. L., and Jonathan Kelley. 1984. Decomposing differences between groups: A cautionary note on measuring discrimination. *Sociological Methods and Research* 12: 323–43.

Kahn, Joan R., and Leslie A. Whittington. 1996. The labor supply of Latinas in the USA: Comparing labor force participation, wages, and hours worked with Anglo and Black women. *Population Research and Policy Review* 15: 45–73.

Meyer, Bruce D., and Dan T. Rosenbaum. 2001. Welfare, the Earned Income Tax Credit, and the labor supply of single mothers. *Quarterly Journal of Economics* 116: 1063–1114.

Pedraza, Silvia. 1991. Women and migration: The social consequences of gender. *Annual Review of Sociology* 17: 303–25.

Prieto, Yolanda. 1978. *Women, work, and change: The case of Cuban women in the U.S.* Latin American Monograph Series, monograph 9. Erie, PA: Northwestern Penn Institute for Latin American Studies, Mercyhurst College.

Raley, R. Kelly. 1996. A shortage of marriageable men? A note on the role of cohabitation in Black-white differences in marriage rates. *American Sociological Review* 61: 973–83.

Reid, Lori. 2002. Occupational segregation, human capital, and motherhood: Black women's higher exit rates from full-time employment. *Gender & Society* 16: 728–47.

Romero, Mary. 2002. *Maid in the U.S.A.* 2d ed. London: Routledge.

Smith, Shelley A., and Marta Tienda. 1988. The doubly disadvantaged: Women of color in the U.S. labor force. In *Women working,* 2d ed., edited by Ann Helton Stromberg and Sirley Harkess. Mountain View, CA: Mayfield.

Spain, Daphne, and Suzanne M. Bianchi. 1996. *Balancing act: Motherhood, marriage, and employment among American women.* New York: Russell Sage.

Stier, Haya, and Marta Tienda. 1992. Family, work and women: The labor supply of Hispanic immigrant wives. *International Migration Review* 26 (4): 1291–1313.

Tienda, Marta, Katharine M. Donato, and Hector Cordero-Guzman. 1992. Schooling, color and the labor force activity of women. *Social Forces* 71 (2): 365–95.

Tienda, Marta, and Jennifer Glass. 1985. Household structure and labor force participation of Black, Hispanic, and white mothers. *Demography* 22 (3): 381–94.

U.S. Bureau of Census. 2001. Current Population Survey: Annual demographic file. MRDF. Washington, DC: U.S. Department of Commerce, Bureau of the Census.

Discussion Questions

1. How do you respond to this article? Did you know about these trends for women of color?

2. How do you think employment trends would look for White men versus men of color? What factors might be involved in that sort of analysis?

3. Why do you think women of color have lower levels of education relative to White women?

4. What sort of solutions to the issues facing women of color might you suggest? Do you think such solutions are being discussed in our current presidential administration? Why or why not?

Reprinted from: Paula England, Carmen Garcia-Beaulieu, and Mary Ross, "Women's Employment Among Blacks, Whites, and Three Groups of Latinas: Do More Privileged Women Have Higher Employment?" In *Gender & Society*, 18 (4), 494–509. Copyright © 2004 by Sage Publications, Inc. Reprinted with permission. ✦

42

Rethinking Official Measures of Poverty

Consideration of Race, Ethnicity, and Gender

Angela Gardner Roux

Who is poor? That question is not as easily answered as you might think. In this article Angela Gardner Roux presents the statistics compiled by the U.S. government. She discusses how the poverty threshold and poverty rates are computed and evaluates their usefulness for the development of social policy. The poverty threshold was created in 1964 and is based on the Consumer Price Index. The federal government uses the threshold, adjusted for family size, to measure rates of poverty. State and local governments use poverty guidelines based on the threshold, sometimes in combination with other factors such as the local cost of living, to determine eligibility and amount of such benefits as public assistance, food stamps, public housing, and free or reduced-price school lunches.

Comparing the poverty rates simultaneously by race or ethnicity and gender, Roux makes a strong case for an intersectional approach. An analysis by race or gender alone would not pick up the fact that although women are more likely to be impoverished than men, the rate of poverty for White women is lower than that for Black or Hispanic men. Poverty rates vary by age, with children and teens in every racial and ethnic category being the most likely to be impoverished and those in the 45–54 age group the least likely. Family composition is important as well. Married couple families are less like to be poor than single households. Families that include members under age 18 are

more likely to be poor than families with no members under 18; this is most dramatically true for single mothers. More than 4 out of 10 households headed by women that include children or teens fall below the poverty threshold.

Overall poverty rates have decreased over time and within specific groups they have sometimes decreased quite dramatically. However, Roux and others are critical of claims that the problem of poverty in the United States has really declined greatly. Loretta Schwartz-Nobel, who told Cathy Lewis' story in Section 2, would certainly not accept the claims. She wrote her first newspaper article on poverty in 1974, her first book was published in 1981, and the hardcover edition of Growing Up Empty: The Hunger Epidemic in America *the book that includes Cathy's story, was published in 2002. After nearly 30 years, she still found dramatic evidence of poverty in rural, urban and even suburban communities.*

Roux and others point out that the policies enacted to reduce poverty assume that giving people jobs will solve the problem. This approach ignores the fact that, even if there were no other factors involved, a minimum wage job will not move a person above the poverty line. When other factors such as the need for childcare and transportation are considered, factors that weigh unevenly on women and members of minority groups, the situation is even more grim. Roux argues for alternative ways of assessing the extent of poverty and alternative solutions for eliminating it.

Official definitions of poverty and political debates about social welfare policy reflect a limited understanding of poverty. These factors have negatively affected all poor people but have been especially detrimental for poor women because their experiences of poverty differ from those of men. Faulty assumptions about the causes of and solutions to poverty, informed in part by official methods of defining and measuring poverty, have been incorporated into social welfare policy. Current poverty policies propose "logical," yet unrealistic, formulas for reducing state aid because they ignore the specific conditions of women's poverty. This chapter will explore the ways in which poverty definitions and measurement have influenced perceptions of poverty that directly and indirectly affect the lives of poor women.

Defining Poverty

A great deal of data exist to describe statistically those living in poverty. Before discussing those who are "in poverty," however, it is necessary to determine what is meant by the term *poverty* itself. The condition is most often defined in terms of material or economic deprivation: a condition of lacking the economic resources necessary to obtain basic needs. Assuming that the cost of basic needs can be accurately estimated, measuring poverty should be a relatively simple matter.

The measurement popularly referred to as the poverty level is the *poverty threshold*, which was created by the Social Security Administration (SSA) in 1964; it takes into account the cost of food, housing, and clothing. Based on the U.S. Department of Agriculture's 1955 Household Food Consumption Survey, several nutritious food plans were constructed to reflect actual consumption patterns. Finding, on average, that food represented one-third of a family's total household expenses, the USDA defined the threshold as the lowest-costing food plan multiplied by three. This calculation established the series of income levels, based on the number of persons in the family unit, which would allow the purchase of basic goods; those with income under the level specified for their family size would be considered to be "in poverty." The current poverty thresholds are not directly based on the "food cost times three" formula. Rather, the Consumer Price Index has been used since 1969 to make yearly adjustments that reflect price increases of basic goods.

Who Is Officially Poor?

The poverty threshold is used by the Census Bureau, which collects information in its annual Current Population Survey to measure and report poverty rates for the United States.[1] After a brief glance at Census Bureau poverty statistics, two points are immediately apparent. First, there is no simple,

singular way to describe poverty in the United States. Second, poverty is not proportionately distributed among racial, ethnic, gender, and age categories. Although the 1997 poverty rate for all people living in the United States was 13.3 percent, poverty rates vary a great deal within and among the Census Bureau's categories of race,[2] sex, and age. The highest poverty rates within each category, respectively, are Hispanic persons (27.1 percent), women (14.9 percent), and those under 18 (19.9 percent); the lowest rates are reported for white persons (11.0 percent), men (11.6 percent), and those aged 45 to 54 (7.2 percent). For a more accurate view of poverty in the United States, these categories should not be considered in isolation from one another. As Table 42.1 demonstrates, the variance in poverty rates is magnified when these three variables are looked at simultaneously, reflecting consistent patterns. Within each race or ethnicity and age category, women's poverty rates are higher than those for men, except for the white, under-18 category, which is 16.1 percent for both sexes. Within each age group, white poverty rates are lower than those for black and Hispanic persons. These data can be used to hypothesize about the impact of gender *and* race or ethnicity on poverty.

There is a significant difference in poverty rates by type of family as well, in terms of race or ethnicity, marital status, and presence of children under 18 in the household. While the poverty rate for all families (10.3 percent) is lower than that for the United States population as a whole (13.3 percent), the rate for single-householder families (27.2 percent) is more than five times that of married-couple families (5.2 percent). Table 42.2 shows that families with children under the age of 18 consistently have the highest poverty rates, across categories of race or ethnicity and family type.

Table 42.3 provides a comparison of poverty rates by the race or ethnicity and gender of the single householder and illustrates that single-female householders have significantly higher rates of poverty on average than single-male householder. The *feminization-of-poverty* theory attributes the higher rates of poverty among women, and especially single

Table 42.1
Poverty Rates by Age, Race/Ethnicity, and Sex, 1997[a]

	All Ages	Under 18	18-24	25-34	35-44	45-54	55-64	65 +
All people	13.3	19.9	17.5	12.1	9.6	7.2	10.0	10.5
Male	11.6	19.7	13.9	8.7	7.6	6.4	8.0	7.0
Female	14.9	20.0	21.1	15.4	11.5	7.9	11.8	13.1
Black	26.5	37.2	28.0	20.9	19.3	13.3	22.1	26.0
Male	23.6	37.0	21.0	12.6	14.4	13.2	19.1	21.8
Female	28.9	37.3	34.1	27.6	23.5	13.5	24.5	28.8
Hispanic	27.1	36.8	25.8	21.9	21.5	15.8	22.0	23.8
Male	24.5	36.5	21.3	16.4	18.3	14.0	17.8	20.3
Female	29.8	37.1	31.0	28.1	24.9	17.5	24.9	26.3
White	11.0	16.1	15.5	10.5	8.0	6.3	8.5	9.0
Male	9.6	16.1	12.6	7.8	6.5	5.5	6.7	5.6
Female	12.4	16.1	18.4	13.1	9.4	7.0	10.3	11.5

Source: U. S. Bureau of the Census (1998), Table 28.2.
[a]Poverty rates for "Asian and Pacific Islander" were not listed for these variables.
United States Bureau of the Census. (1999). *Poverty in the United States: 1987.*

mothers, to a combination of inequitable market conditions that reflect patriarchal assumptions about women's roles as care givers and workers (Goldberg and Kremen 1990). Women are not paid for the work they do within their own homes and are paid less than men for the work they do outside the home due to occupational segregation by gender as well as by race or ethnicity.

Poverty rates are very important because they provide a picture of poverty in the United States and allow social scientists to begin describing the poverty of specific groups. We see that women are more likely to be poor than men are; however, looking at gender alone is too simplistic. The need to include an analysis of race or ethnicity in any discussion of poverty is demonstrated by the significant difference in poverty rates among white, black, and Hispanic women. This fact is emphasized even more by one contradictory pattern observed in Table 42.1. White women's poverty rate (12.4 percent) is lower than that of black (28.9 percent) and Hispanic (29.8 percent) women, which is consistent with the pattern established above for race or ethnicity. White women's poverty rate, however, is *also* lower than that of either

Table 42.2
Percentage of Families Below the Poverty Level by Race and Family Type 1997[a]

	All Families		Married-Couple Families		Single Householder[b]	
	With Children Under 18	With and Without Children Under 18	With Children Under 18	With and Without Children Under 18	With Children Under 18	With and Without Children Under 18
All races	15.7	10.3	7.1	5.2	36.6	27.2
Black	30.5	23.6	9.0	8.0	45.0	37.3
Hispanic	30.4	24.7	21.0	17.4	49.5	41.0
White	13.0	8.4	6.7	4.8	32.7	23.4

Source: U.S. Bureau of the Census (1998), Table C-3.
[a]Poverty rates for "Asian and Pacific Islander" were not listed for these variables.
[b]Single-householder data are calculated from separate male- and female-householder data.
United States Bureau of the Census. (1998). *Poverty in the United States: 1987.*

Table 42.3
1997 Poverty Rates for Single-Householder Families by Race/Ethnicity and Gender [a]

	Single-Male Householder		Single-Female Householder	
	With Children Under 18	With and Without Children Under 18	With Children Under 18	With and Without Children Under 18
All races	18.7	13.0	41.0	31.6
Black	25.6	19.6	46.9	39.8
Hispanic	30.5	21.7	54.2	47.6
White	17.5	11.9	37.6	27.7

Source: U.S. Bureau of the Census (1998), Table C-3.
[a] Poverty rates for "Asian and Pacific Islander" were not listed for these variables.
United States Bureau of the Census. (1998). *Poverty in the United States: 1987.*

black (23.6 percent) or Hispanic men (24.5 percent), which contradicts the pattern for gender. In her critique of the feminization-of-poverty theory, Linda Burnham points out the flaw of focusing on gender to the exclusion of race or ethnicity, by which "the vulnerability of white women to impoverishment is overstated [and] the impoverishment of black men is ignored or underestimated" (1986, 7). Looking at the variables simultaneously allows for a more complex analysis and may help avoid spurious generalizations.

The Uses of Poverty Measures

Aside from providing this statistical landscaping of poverty, the poverty threshold and poverty rates are extremely important in terms of practical consequences for those defined as poor. Both measures play significant roles in public-policy decisions and are used as "evidence" in popular and political debates. First, *poverty guidelines*, which are simplified versions of the poverty threshold, are used to determine income eligibility for several programs that provide some form of assistance to low-income families and individuals.[3] Eligibility for public assistance is not directly tied to the poverty guidelines. Each state establishes its own *need standard*, which reflects the amount of income considered requisite to obtain basic necessities such as food, clothing, and shelter. Need standards vary a great deal among states, with the vast major-

ity being significantly lower than the poverty guidelines.

The reported poverty rates also serve as indicators of "economic well-being" and thus as evidence of whether public-policy changes are needed that would increase or decrease the number of programs and services for the poor. Table 42.4 reports changes in poverty rates for select years since 1959. Based on these statistics, it appears that poverty has declined significantly in the past 38 years for the United States as a whole. Comparing the 1959 and 1997 rates, one might argue that poverty is not nearly the problem today that it has been in the past, despite the fact that, on average, more than 1 out of 10 persons are living in poverty.

Lastly, fluctuations in poverty rates provide "evidence" for policy and program assessment. The Social Security program, which provides income for retired persons, has been credited for much of the reduction in elderly poverty (Marmor, Mashaw, and Harvey 1990). The 1997 poverty rate for persons aged 65 and older (10.5 percent) is less than one-third of the 1959 rate (35.2 percent). No other age group has seen as drastic or as steady a decrease in poverty over this time period. From a sociological perspective, these fluctuations are especially interesting because they provide research opportunities and allow one to draw hypotheses about social and political conditions, including assessments about the impact of social

Table 42.4
Poverty Rates by Race/Ethinicity for Select Years

	1959	1969	1979	1989	1997
All people[a]	22.4	12.1	11.7	12.8	13.3
Asian and Pacific Islander	NA	NA	NA	14.1	14.0
Black	55.1	32.2	31.0	30.7	26.5
Hispanic	NA	NA	21.8	26.2	27.1
White	18.1	9.5	9.0	10.0	11.0
Single-female householder[b]	49.4	38.2	34.9	35.9	35.1
Asian and Pacific Islander	NA	NA	NA	34.6	33.6
Black	70.6	58.2	53.1	49.4	42.8
Hispanic	NA	NA	51.2	50.6	50.9
White	40.2	29.1	25.2	28.1	30.7

Source: United States Bureau of the Census: [a](1998), Table C-1; [b](1999), Table 2.
NA: Rates not available.
United States Bureau of the Census. (1998). *Poverty in the United States: 1987.*

movements on the political and legal structures. Lawrence Powell, Kenneth Branco, and John Williamson (1996) attest to the influence of senior-advocacy groups such as the Grey Panthers and the American Association of Retired Persons (AARP) in creating and maintaining policies that protect the social and economic rights of senior citizens. Many such policies directly reduce the incidence of poverty within this age group. As another example, the decrease in single mothers' poverty after the mid-1960s has been attributed in part to political demands initiated by welfare recipients through the National Welfare Rights Organization (Piven and Cloward 1979). Activists who informed potential recipients of their rights to benefits aided this "relief movement," as did lawyers who obtained entitlement[4] status for Aid to Families with Dependent Children (AFDC). Through a series of legal cases, several "discretionary" practices, used primarily against women of color to deny or terminate AFDC benefits, were determined to be unconstitutional.

Is the Poverty Threshold an Accurate Measure of Poverty?

Social scientists have established that the ways in which poverty is measured and reported have direct and significant consequences for public policy and the lives of individuals. With so much weight resting on the poverty threshold, the accuracy of the measure is crucial. Due to its prevalent use by government agencies, the poverty threshold provides a consistent means of comparing poverty rates among groups and over time. Several methodological issues, however, affect its current efficacy and accuracy.

Although the threshold is adjusted annually to reflect increases in the cost of basic goods, the adjustments have been made on the income levels that were established by the 1964 food-cost-times-three formula. Thus, the "poverty threshold reflects in today's dollars the line that was set some 30 years ago" (Citro and Michael 1995, 25). In 1996 food costs represented approximately one-seventh of household expenditures, rather than one-third, due to changes in consumption patterns and increased standards of living (USGAO 1997, 16). As an *absolute measure* of poverty, the poverty threshold establishes a single standard by which all persons and families in the United States are measured. Families with incomes a few hundred dollars above the poverty threshold would not be counted as officially poor; thus a rigid, and solely financial distinction between "poor" and "nonpoor" is created. Cost-of-living differences by geographic regions or between urban and rural areas, which would include housing, food, and seasonal heating and cooling, are not taken into consideration. The poverty threshold also does not take into account conditions that intensify the economic stress on individual families. Chronic medical conditions, caring for elderly relatives, or the need for child care will increase out-of-pocket expenses and reduce the amount of income available for other necessities.

Lastly, underlying these problems with the poverty threshold is the problem of defining and calculating *income*. The current method includes sources of cash income only[5] and is based on the previous year's income *before* taxes and other payroll deductions are taken out. Annual income figures do not reflect income fluctuations over the course of a year. Seasonal workers and those who suffer from an unexpected illness, injury, or job loss may endure intermittent episodes of poverty during the year, even if their average annual income is not below the poverty threshold.

Women's Poverty

The methodological shortcomings of the poverty threshold should, at least in theory, affect men and women equally. When discussing women's poverty, however, it is not just the accuracy but the *adequacy* of the poverty threshold that needs to be considered. Two factors in particular make women's poverty different from that of men and thus make the poverty threshold's conceptualization of poverty inadequate. First, women carry the larger burden of unpaid caregiving work, whether they are married or single. As mentioned above, the poverty threshold does not include financial costs for ongoing health problems or child care in its calculation of basic needs. While providing for the care of sick or elderly family members and children can put a strain on financial resources for any family, the impact on single-parent families is significantly increased. Because caregiving responsibilities fall disproportionately on women, single mothers will face the greatest difficulty.

> Women often bear the economic as well as the emotional burden of rearing their children. When a couple with children

breaks up, frequently the man becomes single, while the woman becomes a single parent. The poverty rate for households with children has always been greater than that for households that do not have children, and the difference has always been greater for women-maintained households. (Pearce 1990, 267)

Second, women experience discrimination in the labor market, which reduces their ability to earn incomes consistently above the poverty threshold. Mary Stevenson and Elaine Donovan (1996) describe women's labor force participation as a contradictory experience because today a *larger number* of women are working for *longer periods* of their lives, but they are still facing economic difficulties because of inequitable work conditions. Occupational segregation by gender channels men and women into different types of jobs that do not provide equal remuneration in terms of wages, benefits, or respect. . . . Women are often relegated to jobs that mimic their household and caregiving work. This work is *unpaid* in the home and *poorly paid* in the labor market. . . . The AFL-CIO Department of Working Women reports that in 1996, women earned an average of 74 cents on the male dollar (that includes all males), with significant differences among women by race or ethnicity. African American women earned 67 cents, Asian Pacific American women 80 cents, Latinas 58 cents, and white women 75 cents.

In addition to inequitable compensation for their work, women face other difficulties in the labor market. . . . [S]exual harassment creates a physical and emotional barrier for women attempting to obtain or maintain economic independence. The choice between sexual harassment and financial destitution may not be an easy one to make if you are supporting a family. Family obligations also impinge upon women's ability to maintain paid employment outside the home. The financial expense of caring for extended-family members and children is exacerbated for women by the *mental* and *temporal* accountability for negotiating work and family responsibilities. The probability of a sick child or unexpected school closing necessitates a flexible work schedule. Finding part-time, flexible jobs may not be all that difficult for women, but finding such jobs that provide the income and benefits necessary to support a family is another story.

Solutions to Poverty

If women's poverty is different from men's poverty, will the solutions be the same? I pose this question not to be explored here but as a final critique of the poverty threshold that is ideological rather than methodological. The poverty threshold's narrow focus on income reflects beliefs about the solutions to poverty that are, for the most part, untrue for women; namely, that *working* will inevitably end their poverty. The Census Bureau reports poverty rates for three separate work categories: all workers; full-time, year-round; and not full-time, year-round. Among all working women, 7.8 percent are living below the poverty threshold. As might be predicted, the rates for those in the full-time, year-round work category (2.6 percent) are lower than for those not working full-time or year-round (14.5 percent). Within each of the three work categories, black and Hispanic women have poverty rates that are at least double, if not triple, those of white women.

These statistics suggest that although working does increase one's income and reduce economic deprivation, work is not an *absolute* solution for poverty. For example, a full-time, year-round, minimum-wage ($5.15 per hour) service job would gross just $10,712, which is below the poverty threshold even for a family of two. To earn an income above the poverty threshold for a family of four, a single householder, regardless of gender, would have to work at least 62 hours a week at a minimum-wage job. Of course not all jobs are minimum wage, and this example draws upon the worst-case scenario. However, because women are concentrated in lower-paid service jobs, it is quite likely that this scenario will reflect the actual experience of many women (Albelda and Tilly 1997 . . .).

The Poverty Threshold and Social Welfare Policy

Both historic and present-day social welfare policies have incorporated the erroneous belief that poverty is caused primarily by laziness or an unwillingness to work. The complementary belief, that work is the ultimate solution to poverty, has been incorporated as well. Franklin Roosevelt's New Deal legislation in the 1930s established work relief programs along with direct aid to combat the large-scale economic problems of the Depression era. The Social Security Act of 1935 created two categories of permanent income maintenance programs—social insurance and public assistance. Although no work programs were established to provide employment opportunities, amendments made to the SSA since 1935 have increasingly "encouraged" recipients of public assistance to work or at least to participate in work-training programs (Axinn and Levin 1992). The Personal Responsibility and Work Opportunity Reconciliation Act of 1996 (PRWORA), the most recent and most extreme "welfare reform" effort, imposes a 60-month lifetime limit on aid and sets strict work requirements. The PRWORA provisions are especially harsh for women because, as established above, work is neither an absolute nor an effective solution to their poverty. Once again, it is clear how faulty assumptions about poverty disproportionately affect women.

When looking at the impact of the poverty threshold on social-welfare policy, it is important to recognize that the threshold did not *create* the erroneous beliefs about poverty. Likewise, improving the accuracy or adequacy of the poverty threshold as a measure will not necessarily offer a solution to the problem of poverty. The poverty threshold is descriptive, not prescriptive; it defines the criteria by which persons and families will be identified as living in poverty. Nevertheless, it is an important factor to consider when rethinking the problem of poverty.

Overall, the poverty threshold and the resulting poverty rates influence popular understanding of poverty, both in terms of the degree of the problem and the demographic makeup of the poor. Because these standards for measuring and reporting poverty are limited in many ways, the current view of poverty is limited. If income is the only important factor in identifying poverty, and the only basic necessities are food, clothing, and shelter, then improving access to other non-cash resources such as education, child care, and health care is not a relevant issue in poverty discussions. The poverty experiences of many people are minimized or ignored, particularly those of working and married people and single people who do not have children. The limits on the understanding of poverty diminish the potential for poverty policy to be truly responsive to the needs of all poor people.

Developing Alternatives

The criticisms of the current poverty measures are important, but they do not completely negate the value of the poverty threshold and reported poverty rates. Again, because of its consistent use, the poverty threshold provides a good starting point for describing and analyzing poverty in the United States. Even as a low estimate of poverty, the measures provide a uniform point of reference. They identify patterns of economic need and further illustrate patterns of inequality by race or ethnicity, gender, and family type within the population living in poverty. The expectation that a single measure might be an effective, or even adequate, indicator for poverty is unrealistic.

There is much potential, however, for developing a heterogeneous approach to identifying and measuring poverty that would better address the different issues that poor women face. Various governmental and nonprofit agencies regularly collect data that, cumulatively, provide a fuller picture of life conditions for the poor and nonpoor. For example, in their 1998 *Status of Women in the States* report, the Institute for Women's Policy Research (IWPR) demonstrates the possibility of using data from many diverse sources to analyze a problem as complex as gender inequality. Four composite indices were created to assess and compare women's economic, political, and social status in each of the 50 states and the District of Columbia.

The official poverty rate is one indicator used to determine women's *economic autonomy*, which "measures the factors that, in addition to employment and earnings, relate to women's ability to act independently, exercise choice, and control their lives" (IWPR 1998, 21). Other factors include levels of education, access to health insurance, and the percentage of women-owned businesses. Thus, women's economic independence is not conceptualized as merely a matter of having a certain level of income.

The "self-sufficiency standards" created by Wider Opportunities for Women (WOW) provide another model for reconceptualizing and measuring poverty based on a broader definition of basic necessities. The self-sufficiency standards estimate the cost of food, clothing, housing, and health care *plus* the cost of child care and transportation. The last two are "basic necessities" for parents who want or need to maintain full-time employment. The standards recognize the variation in family needs based on the number and age of persons in the household and also reflect cost-of-living differences by geographic location.

The models established by the IWPR and WOW demonstrate the potential for designing quantitative measures for poverty that reflect a more comprehensive understanding of basic living needs as well as a more accurate calculation of their cost. Ideal alternatives would also incorporate qualitative data that testify to the difficulties individual poor people face. Michael Harrington's *The Other America* (1962) drew attention to the degree and conditions of poverty in the 1960s and influenced poverty-policy decisions of the Kennedy and Johnson administrations. Many policy changes have occurred in the 30 years since that time. Ethnographic research exploring the experiences of poor women and people of color, who make up a large percentage of the poor population, may be the key to designing new policies and programs that are more relevant and more responsive to poor people's lives. Books such as Ruth Sidel's *Keeping Women and Children Last* (1996) and Rochelle Lefkowitz and Ann Withorn's *For Crying Out Loud* (1986) provide insight into the lives of poor women and a more extensive awareness of poverty, which one cannot ascertain strictly from poverty rates.

Earlier this discussion mentioned the feminization-of-poverty theory that attributes high rates of poverty for women to labor-market conditions, which reflect patriarchal assumptions about women's traditional caregiving roles. This analysis of official definitions of poverty provides some support for this interpretation, but this theory certainly does not provide the whole picture. Alternative ways of defining poverty must take several situations into account. While it would be difficult, if not impossible, to quantify the fear and exhaustion of living in poverty, how might the serious consideration of such adversity change popular views of the poor? How might poverty policies change if political officials conceded these things: (1) women are not poor *because* they have children; (2) poverty is not a just a problem for single mothers; (3) many people who receive public assistance do work; (4) public-assistance benefits do not provide an adequate level of income; and (5) the cost of public-assistance programs is not imperiling the federal budget (CSWPL 1996)? How might poverty debates become more focused on attacking the problem of poverty rather than attacking those who are poor?

Notes

1. All 1997 poverty rates are taken from the U.S. Bureau of the Census "Historic Poverty Tables" electronic database, or the Current Population Report, *Poverty in the United States*, 1997.

2. The Census Bureau classifies individuals into categories of "race" and "Hispanic origin." "Race" refers to white, black, and Asian and Pacific Islander. Aside from the theoretically problematic issues surrounding the Census Bureau's use of "race," comparing groups by race or ethnicity is difficult because the white category includes persons of Hispanic origin, but the Hispanic origin category includes persons from all three "race" categories. This suggests that all poverty rates for the white category are inflated; for example, only one table distinguishes between the poverty rates for white (11.0 percent) and white, not Hispanic (8.6 percent). Thus, the disparity among the race or ethnicity categories, though significant, is understated. This chapter will use race or ethnicity when referring to the Census Bureau's "race" and Hispanic origin categories.

3. Head Start, the preschool education program for economically disadvantaged children, services those who have incomes at or below 100 percent of the poverty guideline. Other programs use a multiple of the poverty guideline as one criterion in determining eligibility: 130 percent (gross income) for food stamps, 185 percent for the Special Supplemental Nutrition Program for Women, Infants and Children (WIC), 150 percent for the Low-Income Home Energy Assistance Program, and 130 percent for free meals and 185 percent for reduced-price meals under the School Lunch and Breakfast Programs (Citro and Michael 1995, 322).

4. Entitlement programs are those for which the government has established categorical eligibility criteria such as age, disability, income level, and retirement or unemployment status. Anyone who fulfills the criteria is eligible to participate in the program and receive benefits, and the funding of entitlement programs is not a negotiable part of the annual budget; rather, as the cost of providing benefits increases, the funding must also increase.

5. In addition to that earned through employment, pensions, and investments, income includes payments received from the following sources: child support and alimony; SSI, Social Security, and public assistance; unemployment, workers' compensation, and veterans' payments.

References

Albelda, Randy and Chris Tilly. (1997). *Glass Ceilings and Bottomless Pits: Women's Work, Women's Poverty*. Boston: South End.

Axinn, June and Herman Levin. (1992). *Social Welfare: A History of the American Response to Need*. New York: Longman.

Burnham, Linda. (1986). "Has poverty been feminized in black America?" Pp. 69–83 in *For Crying Out Loud: Women's Poverty in the United States*. Rochelle Lefkowitz and Ann Withorn (eds.). New York: Pilgrim.

Center on Social Welfare Policy and Law (CSWPL). (1996). *Welfare Myths: Fact or Fiction? Exploring the Truth About Welfare*. New York: CSWPL

Citro, Constance F. and Robert T. Michael, (eds.). (1995). *Measuring Poverty: A New Approach*. Washington, DC: National Academy.

Dalakea, Joseph and Mary Naifeh. (1998). "U.S. Bureau of the Census, current population report, series P60–201, *Poverty in the United States: 1997*, U.S. Government Printing Office, Washington, DC.

Goldberg, Gertrude Schaffner and Eleanor Kremen. (1990). *The Feminization of Poverty: Only in America?* New York: Praeger.

Harrington, Michael. (1962). *The Other America: Poverty in the United States*. Baltimore, MD: Penguin.

Institute for Women's Policy Research (IWPR). (1998). *Status of Women in the States*. Washington, DC: IWPR.

Lefkowitz, Rochelle and Ann Winthorn (eds.). (1986). *For Crying Out Loud: Women's Poverty in the United States*. New York: Pilgrim.

Marmor, Theodore R., Jerry L. Mashaw, and Philip L. Harvey. (1990). *America's Misunderstood Welfare State: Persistent Myths, Enduring Realities.* New York: Basic.

Pearce, Diane. (1990). "Welfare is not for women: Why the war on poverty cannot conquer the feminization of poverty." Pp. 265–279 in *Women, the State and Welfare.* Linda Gordon (ed.). Madison: University of Wisconsin Press.

Piven, Francis Fox and Richard A. Cloward. (1979). *Poor People's Movements: Why They Succeed, How They Fail.* New York: Vintage.

Powell, Lawrence Alfred, Kenneth J. Branco, and John B. Williamson. (1996). *The Senior Rights Movement: Framing the Policy Debate in America.* New York: Twayne.

Sidel, Ruth. (1996). *Keeping Women and Children Last: America's War on the Poor.* New York: Penguin.

Stevenson, Mary Huff and Elaine Donovan. (1996). "How the U.S. economy creates poverty and inequality." Pp. 67–78 in *For Crying Out Loud: Women's Poverty in the United States,* Second Edition. Diane Dujon and Ann Withorn (eds.). Boston: South End.

U.S. Bureau of the Census (USBC). (1998). *Poverty in the United States, 1997. Current Population Reports,* series P60–201. Washington, DC: U.S. Government Printing Office.

U.S. Bureau of the Census. (Revised, May 24, 1999). "Historical income and poverty tables." Current Population Survey 1997, electronic database. (Accessed July 22, 1999). *http://www.census.gov/hhes/income/histinc/histpovtb.html.*

U.S. General Accounting Office (GAO). (1997). *Poverty Measurement: Issues in Revising and Updating the Official Definition.* Washington, DC: USGAO.

Discussion Questions

1. Consider and respond to the questions Roux asks at the end of the article.

2. What are some of the factors, including those mentioned in the article and others that you can think of, that could account for the fact that members of racial and ethnic minority groups are more likely to be poor than White people?

3. As the statistics in this article show, not all members of racial and ethnic minority groups live below the poverty line and some White people clearly do. What characteristics of individuals, families, and communities are associated with a high probability of not living in poverty?

4. What are some of the reasons women and especially women with children are more likely to be poor than men?

43
Characteristics of the Foreign Born in the United States
Results from Census 2000

Elizabeth Grieco

Elizabeth Grieco summarizes the information about immigration to the United States that is revealed by the 2000 Census, and the facts may surprise many people. We think of the years 1880–1920 as the time when the greatest wave of immigrants came to this country. Indeed, it was during those years that the foreign born made up the largest percentage of the population. The peak year was 1890, when 14.8 percent of the population had been born in another country. However, in terms of numbers, the more than 31.1 million identified by the 2000 Census is the high point in our history.

People leave their home countries for new ones for a variety of reasons. Some, such as the ancestors of many African Americans, were forced to come here as slaves. Some became Americans when the United States annexed or colonized their homes in places as far apart as Mexico and Samoa. Others, such as the Chinese who helped to build the railroad, came as guest workers and decided to stay. Many Europeans came to escape pogroms or totalitarian regimes. Still others came seeking opportunities not open to them as peasants or landless workers in their home countries. From the beginning of our history until the middle of the twentieth century, the largest proportion of foreign born people came from European countries. This has changed. As Grieco reports, in 2000 only 15.8 percent were from Europe while over half (51.7 percent) were from Latin America and more than a quarter (26.4 percent) were from Asia.

According to other data available from the *Migration Information Source* website (www.migrationinformation.org), the median age of those born in other countries has shifted. Prior to 1940, half were under or just slightly above age 40. From 1940–1970, when immigration rates were relatively low, the foreign born population was older, and half were over age 50. Beginning in 1980 when rates began to increase again, the median dropped below age 40. Between 1870 and 1950, there were more men and boys than women and girls among the foreign born. At the high point in 1910, there were more than 131 males for every 100 females. In 1950 the numbers were about equal, and from 1970–1990 there were more women and girls. In 2000 the numbers were about equal again. Women tend to live longer than men, which may account for some of the shift during times when relatively few new members were added to the foreign born population. It would be interesting to know what other factors have contributed to this change in the gender distribution.

December 1, 2002

The United States, a country with a rich immigrant heritage, is experiencing a profound demographic and cultural transformation. The number of immigrants in the US is at its highest point in history, and the rate of immigrant-driven transformation, which began in earnest in the 1960s, is expected to continue to accelerate.

According to the US Census Bureau, the foreign-born population increased from 19.8 million in 1990 to 31.1 million in 2000, representing the largest number of immigrants ever seen in the United States. While the foreign born now account for 11.1 percent of the total population, this figure is still lower than the historic peak of 14.8 percent in 1890. . . . This Spotlight examines some of the demographic, social, and economic characteristics of this important part of the US population.

[See] the bullet points below for more information:

- There are over 31.1 million foreign born in the United States, representing 11.1 percent of the total population.
- Between 1990 and 2000, the foreign-born population increased by 11.3 million people, representing a 57.4 percent increase.

- Of the total foreign born, 42.4 percent arrived between 1990 and 2000.
- The top three countries of birth are Mexico, the Philippines, and India.
- Most of the foreign born are from Latin America.
- The majority of the foreign born describe their race as either white alone or Asian alone.
- Of the total foreign-born population, 45.5 percent are Hispanic or Latino.
- Of the total foreign-born population, 40.3 percent are citizens.
- Among the foreign born, 17.9 percent live in poverty.
- Over four out of every five foreign born speak a language other than English at home.
- Among the foreign born who speak a language other than English at home, 38 percent speak English "very well" while 12.2 percent speak English "not at all."
- Among the foreign born who speak Spanish at home, 52 percent speak English "very well" or "well."

There are over 31.1 million foreign born in the United States, representing 11.1 percent of the total population.

There has been a steady increase in the number and percentage of foreign born in the United States since 1980.

According to the US Census Bureau, there were over 31.1 million foreign born in the United States in 2000, representing 11.1 percent of the total population In 1990, there were 19.8 million foreign born, or 7.9 percent of the total population. In 1980, there were 14.1 million foreign born, or 6.2 percent of the total population.

Between 1990 and 2000, the foreign-born population increased by 11.3 million people, representing a 57.4 percent increase.

The foreign-born population increased at a faster rate between 1990 and 2000 than between 1980 and 1990. Between 1990 and 2000, the foreign-born population increased by 11.3 million, representing a 57.4 percent increase. Between 1980 and 1990, the for-

eign-born population increased by 5.7 million, or by 40.4 percent.

Of the total foreign born, 42.4 percent arrived between 1990 and 2000.

According to Census 2000, of the total foreign born in the United States, 42.4 percent arrived between 1990 and 2000, 27.2 percent arrived between 1980 and 1989, and 30.4 percent arrived before 1980.

Most of the foreign born are from Latin America.

Of the total foreign born in the United States in 2000, 51.7 percent were from Latin America, 26.4 percent from Asia, 15.8 percent from Europe, 2.8 percent from Africa, 2.7 percent from Northern America (including Canada, the United States, Bermuda, Greenland, and St. Pierre and Miquelon), and 0.5 percent from Oceania. Of the 16.1 million foreign born from Latin America, 69.6 percent were from Central America, 18.4 percent from the Caribbean, and 12 percent from South America.

The top three countries of birth are Mexico, the Philippines, and India.

According to Census 2000, of the total foreign born in the United States, 29.5 percent were born in Mexico, 4.4 percent in the Philippines, and 3.3 percent in India. This is followed by 3.2 percent in China (excluding Hong Kong and Taiwan), 3.2 percent in Vietnam, 2.8 percent in Cuba, 2.8 percent in Korea, 2.6 percent in Canada, 2.6 percent in El Salvador, and 2.3 percent in Germany.

The majority of the foreign born describe their race as either white alone or Asian alone.

Of the total foreign born in the United States, the majority reported white alone (43 percent) or Asian alone (22.5 percent) as their race in Census 2000. Additionally, 21.5 percent reported some other race alone, 6.8 percent black or African American alone, 0.4 percent American Indian and Alaska Native alone, 0.2 percent Native Hawaiian and other Pacific Islander alone, and 5.5 percent two or more races.

Of the total foreign-born population, 45.5 percent are Hispanic or Latino.

In the United States, there were 14.2 million foreign born who reported a Hispanic/Latino origin in Census 2000, representing 45.5 percent of the total foreign-born population (31.1 million) and 40.2 percent of the total Hispanic/Latino population (35.2 million).

Of the total foreign-born population, 40.3 percent are citizens.

Census 2000 reported that 40.3 percent of all foreign born in the United States were citizens. By comparison, 40.5 percent of all foreign born in 1990 and 50.5 percent of all foreign born in 1980 were citizens.

Among the foreign born, 17.9 percent live in poverty.

According to Census 2000, among the foreign born for whom poverty status was determined, 17.9 percent had an income in 1999 below poverty level (the poverty threshold for a family of four people was $17,000). Among foreign-born citizens, 10.6 percent lived in poverty, compared with 22.8 percent of foreign-born noncitizens.

Over four out of every five foreign born speak a language other than English at home.

In 2000, of the foreign born five years and over in the United States, 83 percent spoke a language other than English at home. This included 52.3 percent who spoke Spanish, 21.9 percent who spoke other Indo-European languages, 21.6 percent who spoke Asian and Pacific Island languages, and 4.2 percent who spoke other languages.

Among the foreign born who speak a language other than English at home, 38.5 percent speak English 'very well' while 12.2 percent speak English 'not at all.'

In the United States in 2000, of the foreign born five years and over who spoke a language other than English at home, 38.5 percent reported speaking English "very well," 26.3 percent "well," 22.9 percent "not well," and 12.2 percent "not at all."

Among the foreign born who speak Spanish at home, 52 percent speak English 'very well' or 'well.'

According to Census 2000, of the foreign born five years and over in the United States

who spoke Spanish at home, 52 percent spoke English "very well" or "well." By comparison, 82.4 percent of those who spoke other Indo-European languages, 73.7 percent who spoke Asian languages, and 87.4 percent of those who spoke other languages at home reported speaking English "very well" or "well."

Discussion Questions

1. According to the Roux article in this section, 13.3 percent of the U.S. population lives in poverty. Grieco reports that the poverty rate for those who live here but were not born here is 17.9 percent. What might account for this difference?

2. According to this article, 83 percent of the foreign born speak a language other than English at home, and 12.2 percent speak no English at all. Over half of those who speak another language speak Spanish. Given these language statistics, what social policies and actions if any do you think governmental agencies at all levels, schools, and communities should pursue?

3. Looking at the places where today's immigrants come from, why do you think they have come here?

4. Unless you are 100 percent American Indian, Alaskan, or Hawaiian Native someone in your family came from another country. What do you know about your family's immigration history? When did the first person come? Who was the most recent immigrant? Where did they come from and why? Did members of your family come from a single country or more than one? Does your family or given name reflect your origins?

Reprinted from: Elizabeth Grieco, "Characteristics of the Foreign Born in the United States: Results from the Census 2000." Retrieved February 23, 2005 from *http://migrationinformation.org/USfocus*. Originally published on the Migration Information Source *www.migrationinformation.org*, a project of the Migration Policy Institute. ✦

44

Race and Ethnicity

Images of Difference in South Africa[1]

Edwin S. Segal

The word apartheid, *for those nearest my generation, conjures appalling and categorical images of racial strife and brutality, somewhere on a mental continuum between segregation and lynching, and easily encompassing elements of both these two standards of racial inequality. However, for most of my students, born generations later, the word is as foreign and as empty of meaning as the word* typewriter. *Perhaps, this is because apartheid's sickly reign occurred in a geographical and cultural setting halfway across the globe during a time when there was no real sense yet of a "global village." Edwin S. Segal reenters apartheid onto our collective "Google" screens in this new piece of research by taking us back in history and by pivoting our center to South Africa. Segal uses archival data to explore this historical timing and geography to typify the social construction of race within culture and to make manifest race, class, and gender as tools of oppression.*

Segal begins the piece by briefly mapping the easy debunking of a biological stricture and categorization of race. In this way, Segal creates a setting for viewing the biology of race through the lens of culture, essentially rendering it arbitrary, and therefore, toothless. Next, he takes us into the history of the peoples of South Africa, so essential to the reader unfamiliar with the parties involved—Bantu speakers, Khoisan speakers, British, Dutch, Cape Malays, and East Indians from Gujurat. As one can see, this is a complex history racially and otherwise, which the Europeans, collectively, chose to depict as simple and straightforward—"Blacks, Whites, Coloured, and Asians." It is the archival documents Segal utilizes which become the keys to understanding South African cultural views of race—census and other governmental depictions of peoples. These documents say indirectly and even directly what White South Africans believed—that it is easy to create blanket "others," to portray others as inferior, and to treat others with impunity, separating them and keeping them apart from the superior ones à la apartheid, as long as you can point to this as natural. Apartheid would make "others" clearly not part of the power structure, impoverished by a sort of invisible—to Whites—racial intolerance that neatly categorized and grouped millions of men, women, and children over time into clusters of "singing communities," or "historically evolved minorities," depending really only on the whim of arbitrary White classifications. Women and men as groups and as individuals become part of this arbitrary power structure in Segal's rendering as "Black" or "Coloured," depending on the day, the editorial page, or the government counter. Segal notes that even "Miss South Africa" must be enumerated as either "Black" or "Coloured," depending.

Most important perhaps, Segal captures a history that still influences South African sensibilities today as the country remains reflective of and reflective on a painful racial past, even as they seek to carve out a post-apartheid future.

I am concerned here with an imagery of difference. All cultures select characteristics said to typify members of their own societies, as well as members of other groups. These cultural constructs create an enduring background against which interactions take place. In many parts of English-speaking Africa, *race*, *tribe*, and *ethnic group* form a complex of terms with overlapping usage, confused referents, and almost always a biological undertone.

This article rests on the assumption that the reality lying behind the terms "race," "tribe," and "ethnicity" is not at all biological but is entirely social and cultural. The starting point is important because much of everyday discussion proceeds from the very different premise that the social and cultural constructs hide an underlying physical reality. My argument is that the social and cultural forms are the reality with which we must deal. They are neither a false biology nor a false consciousness; they are major elements in the world and in our ability to shape our lives in directions we deem desirable.

A Biological Background

A discussion of race in South Africa, or anywhere else, must begin with the basic statement that data from contemporary biological anthropology make it clear that the concept of race has no support as a description of any physical reality (American Association of Physical Anthropologists 1996). Human biology is everywhere the same, though within it we exhibit physical variations, many of which do seem to cluster within particular human groups.

To be biologically constant, a trait must be genetically based. Most human traits are produced by multiple genes, which means there is considerable difference between a particular external appearance and the several underlying genetic structures. Popular determinations of racial membership are always based on observation of appearances. The result is that the 30,000 genes of the human genome are reduced to only a few phenotypes, whose importance is entirely sociocultural. Since each of the traits usually used as a criterion for racial determination comes in many forms and shades, the dividing lines between groups are arbitrary and based on cultural rather than biological considerations.

Furthermore, the relationships among genes, appearances, and behavior are unclear. We have no evidence that any particular human behavior is directly genetically governed. The most that can be said is that human biology and human culture interact to produce fully functioning human beings.

An examination of the concept of race, as found in any particular society, is actually an examination of the sociocultural creation of race and racial categories and the ways in which it is entwined with local cultures and local ideas about cultures and race. The details of ideas of race and culture vary from culture to culture. There is nothing inevitable about the general concept of race, or its particular form in a particular place. It is as possible for a society to develop a culture that has no concept of race as it is for a culture to develop a concept of race with any number of categories.

Historical Background

From 1948, when it came to power, until 1990, when it began to relinquish political control, South Africa's National Party created and pursued a policy, which it called *apartheid*, with the goal of permanently separating the country's racial groups. To accomplish that goal, the party had to create and define those racial groups. This process was formally begun with passage of the Population Registration Act in 1950, which declared that all people in South Africa had to be properly racially classified. But that legislation only formalized a process that colonial domination had encouraged throughout the nineteenth century and most of the twentieth.

An Office for Race Classification was set up to oversee the process. Classification into groups was carried out using criteria such as outer appearance, general acceptance, and social standing. For example, it defined a "White person" as one who "in appearance is obviously a White person who is generally not accepted as a Coloured person; or is generally accepted as a White person and is not in appearance obviously a white person" (Zegeye, Liebenberg, and Houston 2003, 154). Since some aspects of the profile were of a social nature, reclassifications were a possibility, and a board was established to conduct that process. From 1950 until 1991, when the act was repealed, people in South Africa frequently successfully petitioned the government to have their racial classifications officially changed. Ultimately, *apartheid* foundered on its own internal inconsistencies and incompatibility with the demands of an increasingly industrialized regional power center.

Apartheid's inconsistencies existed on several levels. I am most interested here in assumptions about the nature of race and racial characteristics. These ideas pre-date the National Party by as much as a century and were part and parcel of the ideas and assumptions of both the British and Dutch (or Afrikaner or Boer) colonialists whose struggle created South Africa.

The history of the territory that eventually comes to be known as South Africa begins with a confrontation between Western Europeans and local groups who were culturally and physically very different. They were mostly short and had light brown skin and tightly curled hair. Today, these people are known as speakers of the Khoisan family of languages. Traditionally, they were primarily foragers living on the edges of the Namib-Kalahari desert region and throughout the territory that became South Africa.

The first Europeans came to the southern tip of Africa in the 1650s, not as settlers but to establish a provisioning station for ships belonging to the Dutch East India Company that took the route around the Cape of Good Hope at Africa's southern tip to reach the Dutch East Indies (contemporary Indonesia), India, China, or Southeast Asia. It is not clear that Khoisan-speaking peoples inhabited the area between Table Mountain and the coast. This area is completely taken up by elements of modern Cape Town, and any archaeological evidence is either destroyed or covered over. But it is a good guess that, at the least, Khoisan-speaking peoples came to the Cape to trade with the new arrivals. There is significant evidence that they inhabited the land beyond Table Mountain. Thus, as soon as Europeans moved beyond the narrow confines of the Cape itself, they came in close contact with groups who showed (to seventeenth-century European eyes) more uniformity among themselves than any commonality with the newcomers. At the same time, the southern portion of the continent was also experiencing the southward migration of dark-skinned, cattle-herding, agricultural peoples, who spoke languages in the Bantu family.

From the 1650s onward, much of South African history can be written in terms of competition for land and need for labor. It is unnecessary to detail here the history of the British-Dutch struggles over the country,

which culminated in the Afrikaner Great Trek into the interior in the 1830s and 1840s and the Boer War in 1899–1902. Rather, we need to examine the confrontations among Europeans, Khoisan speakers, and Bantu speakers.

The Dutch East Indies Company established its provisioning station in 1652. The Dutch occupants were, as might be expected in the seventeenth century, largely men, and from the beginning, there were children who would later be called "Coloured"[2] or "mixed race." The Dutch settlers also brought with them slaves from the Dutch-controlled areas of the Malay Peninsula and the East Indies. As is the case with slaves and slave owners everywhere, these too produced Coloured children. They also form the base for a Coloured subgroup, the Cape Malays.

At first, the Dutch (and later other European settlers) acknowledged their Coloured children. In 1656, a few slaves were freed. They moved beyond Table Mountain into the interior to establish farms that would produce the provisions needed by the Cape Colony to fulfill its basic mission. At the same time, more slaves, from Dutch possessions as well as other parts of Africa, were imported into the colony. By 1685, a school was established for the children of Dutch East Indies Company slaves. These children remained slaves, but some effort was made to allow slaves older than age 22 (women) or age 25 (men) to buy their freedom (South Africa History Online 2004).

By 1809, the governor of what had become the British-controlled Cape Colony tried to restrict the use of Khoisan and Coloured labor by European farmers. That effort required restrictions on freedom of movement, resulting in the institution of a pass, or internal passport, system as a device for regulating non-European population movements.

Throughout the first half of the nineteenth century, the British and various Afrikaner groups engaged in a struggle for sovereignty on land taken from the Khoisan- and Bantu-speaking peoples. As well, the British tried to introduce legislation that was said to "ameliorate" the condition of slaves, without freeing them. In 1838, the first effort to write an explicitly racial constitution took place in what eventually became Natal Province, on South Africa's eastern coast. The constitution enshrined a master-slave relationship between Boers and Africans.

By the 1930s, the government of South Africa recognized four basic racial groups: Blacks, Whites, Coloured, and Asian.[3] Although *apartheid*, as a formalized set of governmental policies, would not come into being for another 15 to 20 years, many of the basic structures were created under the British colonial regime and earlier. *Apartheid* and its associated laws and policies were not a new invention of a culturally racist Afrikaner-dominated National Party.

Since the Black population constituted approximately 74 percent of South Africa's population, much of *apartheid* was directed toward them. The laws establishing segregated residential areas, reserved jobs, marital patterns, and internal passports theoretically applied to all groups, but enforcement depended on different levels of power, authority, prestige, and wealth.

Apartheid means "separation" or "apartness." The basic policy was that each racial group should live separately and undergo development in a fashion dictated by the presumed nature of its own culture. This, of course, leads directly to a series of defining questions. Primary among these is the matter of the boundaries between the groups being kept apart and the related rationale for *apartheid*. In large measure, the basic justification lies in a belief that a group's culture is as fixed as its supposed physical characteristics.

An Official Point of View

The sources from which I draw most of my illustrative material are the two series of South African yearbooks. One runs from the union of Dutch and British colonies in 1910 until about 1961, when the Republican constitution was adopted. The other begins in the middle of the 1970s. Since my major focus in this article is on an imagery of difference, I have selected a body of literature whose sole function is expression of public images. This is not the most profound, thoughtful, or intellectually challenging material. It is literature designed to present, rather than create, a public image. This is especially true of the

second series. In the process of presenting that public image of the country, it also presented governmental constructions of the "nature" of different groups.

The first series was published by the Director of Census and Statistics, and its format largely reflects that origin. The largest portion of each volume consists of various statistical compilations and legislative reviews, with a few brief descriptive passages here and there and occasional, longer articles. This series provides a useful platform from which to view the later efforts to shape the imagery more deliberately.

In these volumes, most of the population data are divided simply into Natives, Europeans, Coloureds, and Asiatics (at that point in time, this category was usually subdivided into Indians and Chinese). A few sections (e.g., religious affiliation) are cross-tabulated simply as European and non-European. Although those tables dealing with immigration list a large number of European source countries, these varied origins disappear in all other data. The impression produced is that regardless of origin, Europeans constitute a homogeneous group.

A similar picture is presented of the indigenous population. Throughout this first series of yearbooks there are separate chapters, "Native Affairs." These chapters regularly begin with a simple enumeration phrased as the "number of Natives in the Union at various census dates" (Director of Census and Statistics 1937, 443). Throughout the chapter, divisions within the category "Native" are spoken of entirely in terms of administrative units, and frequently also in terms of consolidating various groups solely for the sake of administrative efficiency. There is no apparent recognition of whether these people see themselves as culturally the same or different.

A Rhetorical Model

By the eve of World War II, a fairly specific way of talking about people had developed. Not surprisingly, it mirrored the characteristics outlined by Hammond and Jablow (1970) in their book dealing with colonial myths about Africa, that is, natives were seen as largely undifferentiated. Further, their cultural characteristics were sometimes admirable, as when they facilitated the spread of Christianity, and sometimes not, as when they posed difficulties for missionaries. However, in either case, these differences were, in the end basically trivial. The real gulf lay between Europeans and Africans, and it was seen as being at once economic, cultural, and genetic.

This approach to viewing the local colonized peoples was also part of the literature of the time written for the popular audience. For example, Junod (1938), a retired missionary, devotes his first chapter to a discussion of biological, cultural, and physical differences and similarities among subSaharan Africans, in general, and Bantu speakers, in particular. Almost all of the rest of the book is devoted to generalized discussions of Bantu cultural features. Although he regularly warns against overgeneralization, and notes that he is largely discussing only one or two groups that he knows well, he regularly draws conclusions about "The Bantu" (sometimes used as a singular and sometimes as a collective noun). This reaches its height in the final two chapters, titled "The Bantu Mind." He begins the final chapter with the question "Is there a Bantu religion?" (p. 124) and comes to the conclusion that

> Bantu religion presents two very different aspects, which can be found . . . all over Bantu Africa. Firstly, the Bantu worship their ancestors and, secondly, they all have a notion of God. Ancestor worship and a vague monotheistic idea are the two manifestations of religion in Bantu Africa. (Junod 1938, 125)

The point here is not to criticize Junod for a mode of thinking now almost 70 years old but, rather, to call attention to it because it expresses part of a way of thinking that continued to be relevant more than half a century later. Up until the 1990s, the images of Black Africans as a single racial group were inextricably entwined with images of eight tribal groups that were so different that they needed to be subjected to different forms of development.

In fact, in this early descriptive literature, a major characteristic of Natives is said to be their inability to transcend tribal and other rivalries. They were seen as being continually split by tribalism and "ancient" tribal antagonisms. A well-known and frequently stated corollary was that Europeans put an end to endemic internecine warfare and that if Europeans were to withdraw their oversight and control too soon, there would be almost immediate reversion to the chaos of intertribal squabbling. The power and persistence of these images can be seen in the fact that during the 1980s and 1990s, as *apartheid* was crumbling and the National Party was relinquishing power, U.S. media regularly portrayed some of the political conflicts among African groups as purely tribal, i.e., between Xhosa and Zulu, rather than political, i.e., between the African National Congress and the Inkhata Freedom Party.

Different Peoples, Different Cultures

By the middle of the 1970s, the South African government was engaged in an effort to reshape the international image of its internal policies. "Segregation" was replaced by "separate development"; "reserves," which had existed throughout the nineteenth century, was replaced by "homelands," with the same boundaries; and "development," though undefined, was said to have different imperatives for culturally different groups of people. The undifferentiated Natives were replaced by eight or nine distinctly different Black tribes, each of which had its own nature and needs. But the laws supporting *apartheid,* as well as their enforcement, continued to be phrased in terms of racial groups. In modern American terms, racial profiling continued to be the dominant feature of South African social life.

The new series of yearbooks, beginning with 1974, reflects the effort to shift into a discussion focusing on cultural diversity, pluralism, and separate development. In the process, it creates its own jargon and continues to treat culture as if it were a racial characteristic.

> Tourists, writers and other commentators often use the cliché "ethnic mosaic" when they describe societies composed of diverse cultural and racial groups. The population structure of the RSA [Republic of South Africa] illustrates this popular con-

cept more strikingly than that of most other countries. (van der Spuy 1974, 123)

The chapter continues to talk in terms of racial and ethnic diversity and the cultural heterogeneity of each of the groups it delineates; but then, when it gets to what the authors term "biogenetic" criteria, there is no change from the categories of a half century earlier.

In terms of racial (biogenetic) criteria, the Whites and Bantu differ substantially, the Whites belonging to the Caucasoid and the Blacks to the Negroid racial division of mankind. The Asians are preponderantly of Indian origin. The Coloureds . . . are a racially mixed group involving the biological confluence of Caucasoid, Asian, Mongoloid, Bushman-Hottentot (Capoid) and Negroid elements. (van der Spuy 1974, 123)

The chapter manages to weave together all the strands already discussed. Blacks consist of nine different peoples; they are a "multinational population." Whites are only culturally heterogeneous with two broad "subcultural entities, speakers of Afrikaans and speakers of English." This leads to the conclusion that

Ethno-demographically, South Africa can thus be divided into a White South Africa and a Bantu South Africa. (van der Spuy 1974, 123)

But even the rhetoric of ethnicity and cultural variation has its limits.

In contradistinction to the Black peoples, the Coloureds and Indians are historically evolved minorities. These minorities differ from the Bantu peoples also in that they do not constitute homogeneous collectivities and thus do not exist as ethnic units or nations. . . . (van der Spuy 1974, 123)

In the period from the establishment of the Union through the first half of the century, it is quite clear that the divisions of the South African population were maintained by the power of law and its enforcement. The initial formal division of land is, after all, the Native Land Act of 1913, which is strengthened by the Group Areas Act of 1950 and the Population Registration Act of 1950. By the 1974 yearbook, a new version of the rhetoric of separation appears, so that in spite of the laws mandating and maintaining ghettos on a large scale, laws of nature are said to be at work.

The traditional combinations in which these groups associate are reflected in the formal classification of the population into Whites, Coloureds, Asians and Bantu. Despite peripheral cross-cultural contact this population structure is largely sustained voluntarily and the resultant pattern of intergroup relations is the function mainly of spontaneous selective association. Basically, therefore, South Africa's ethnic plurality is of a natural order. . . . (van der Spuy 1974, 124)

Finally, while it is said that the Black population consists of several distinct peoples, these have an identity primarily because they are

. . . recognised by the Whites as embryo national communities, "nations-to-be," developing toward independence within their traditional homelands. (van der Spuy 1974, 123)

White guidance was seen as the essential path toward this separate development. The point to be made here is simply that while we can trace a shift from a rhetoric of biological distinction to a rhetoric of cultural diversity, the underlying biological divisions and their assumed innate behavioral correlates do not change. The issue is still a social construction of race.

Other Cultures, Other Groups

Throughout the 1990s and into the first few years of South Africa under a majority government, much of the news media coverage and discussion of South Africa spoke in terms of two major groups, Blacks and Whites. The racial/ethnic dimension is, of course, not quite so simple. In this regard, the rhetorical place of Asians took on some significance. Although demographically small, the Asian population had (and still has) an added significance as a non-Western group, foreign both politically and culturally. To the extent that Britain saw its Indian colonial experiences as providing models for its African ventures (Kirk-Green 1980), importing people who could be expected to "understand" British domination made some sense. The political and economic impact of imported workers was an expansion of the gulf between Europeans and Africans, and an increase in tensions among the already contending groups. Their manifest cultural differences did nothing to alleviate the state of what we might call intergroup relations. At one point, it was even suggested that all Asians would have to be sent back to their countries of origin because they were unassimilable (Davies 1950).

This raises an important question about cultural pluralism and cultural assimilation: Into what cultural fabric could Asians have assimilated? Since, in fact, there was none, the growth and continuation of Indian ethnic distinctiveness and identification is not surprising. This is especially so since most of the people Britain imported came from Gujarat, a single, relatively homogeneous portion of India. Asian cultural distinctiveness allowed both the *apartheid* government and its colonial predecessors to treat them as another racial group.

Similarly, the group usually referred to as Coloured can be seen as a central representative of the difficulty of the issue in the South African context. This group of people is never described as being anything but of "mixed race," implying some sociocultural meaning for a pseudobiological construct. The question of ethnic and cultural distinctiveness is given contradictory treatment. Some of the description even manages to suggest that while they are a new ethnic group, they really lack the cultural distinctiveness that marks English, Bantu, and other Afrikaans speakers. But, even while denying legitimacy to the Coloured population as a group, *apartheid* continued to treat them like a separate racial group.

> Deculturisation and the ravages of three epidemics soon led to the disintegration of the main Hottentot tribes and their subsequent progressive involvement with Negroid and East Indian slaves and White sailors, soldiers and officials in the crystallisation of a new ethnic group—the Cape Coloureds. (van der Spuy 1974, 124)

> But whereas the forebears of the Afrikaners came from nations all belonging to the White race, those of the Coloureds were representative of four different races: Negroids, Khoisan tribes, Whites and Asians. (van der Spuy 1974, 125)

At the same time, there is an interesting effort both to claim them as allies and distance them as people providing charming entertainment.

> In religion, language and general way of life, the Coloureds have always been closely associated with the Whites. Their culture and value orientations are distinctly Western. The homes, food, clothes and other features of the Coloured people's way of life are the same as those of their White neighbours. Differences which do occur are due to regional, educational and socio-economic influences. This does not apply to the Cape Malays, who are Muslims.

> Ninety per cent of all Coloureds are members of some Christian church or other. Only some seven per cent are Muslims. They are therefore the most Christianised non-White population group in the whole of Africa. About 90 percent of the Coloured people speak Afrikaans, while the rest are mainly English-speaking.

> The Coloured people are a singing community, with a natural feeling for rhythm and a strong love of music to which they give expression freely and frequently. The Eoan Group, numerous singing unions, choral societies and orchestras are renowned for their achievements. . . . Their bright rendering of sacred and other songs is a source of delight to all who hear them. (van der Spuy 1974, 144–145)[4]

Given the overt importance of territory and the covert importance of biological identity in the general construction of *apartheid*,[5] the creation of Coloured and Indian Houses of Parliament in 1983 can be interpreted as recognition that the Republic would always contain some "unassimilable" elements.[6]

The Politics of Terminology

Elsewhere I have noted the significance of language and lexicon as an ethnic marker in Malawi (Segal 1991). It is no less so in South

Africa. Again, the fourfold division created by *apartheid* both complicates the discussion and highlights its essential characteristic. During the 1990s, depending on political orientation, the people are called "Coloured" (with or without a set of quotation marks), or "so-called Coloured." By contrast, there is a history of a succession of terms for the majority population: "Native," "Bantu," "Black." As each of these terms was appropriated by the governing authorities, it fell out of favor as a part of more common, everyday language. The process is clearly a form of linguistic resistance.

Although the rhetoric of race and ethnicity is different in the United States, the relatively recent shift in terminology from "Black" to "African American" attempts to set the terms of reference in a cultural heritage-economic opportunity context, similar to that of other "hyphenated Americans." In this regard, it is worth noting that in 1992, Sunday newspapers in Johannesburg described the newly crowned Miss South Africa as the first "Black" Miss South Africa, when all other discussions in the popular media, including other articles in the same papers, placed her as "Coloured," and her runner-up as "Black." In 1993, when 1992's runner-up won, the South African press spoke of her as the second Black Miss South Africa. Ironically, in the United States, where a White South African once observed "everyone is coloured," and "Black" and "Colored" are terms for the same people in different historical periods, the 1993 winner was hailed as the first Black Miss South Africa.

A number of colleagues and informants have suggested that this expanded inclusiveness for "Black" in South Africa had been a growing trend since the 1980s. If so, then populations such as the Coloured and Cape Malay will most assuredly become people in the middle of a contest for their social and cultural allegiance. They will continue to represent, as they do now, the extent to which South Africa is still a racialized society.

Conclusion

I have tried here to sketch the elements of a consistently confused, but enduring, set of public images presented by Europeans of Africans in South Africa. The ways these terms are used and change is part of the process by which South Africa has become a racialized society, that is, a society in which a concept of race is central to the societal debate about the present and future relationships among various groups.

Currently, there are two mainstream models for a concept of race, which, for the sake of simplicity, can be referred to as the biological and the sociological. Both define *race* as a constellation of traits that distinguishes one population from another. The biological approach restricts that constellation to genetic traits and, hence, deals only with clusters of known genetic structures, e.g., blood fractions. The data from this approach tend to indicate that human population clusters are considerably more complex than indicated by classical schemes based solely on appearance.

The sociological approach focuses on a constellation of more or less visible traits, whose boundaries are defined by a society and are assumed by society to have a biological referent. The implication here is that the precise definition of race, in general, and of specific races, in particular, will change from society to society, as well as through history. This, of course, means that there is no objective, universal set of categories for human biological variations based on appearance and clusters of overt traits.

A reading of various documents of the nineteenth and early twentieth centuries will uncover references to the Irish, English, French, or Jewish race, where the context leaves little doubt about the sociocultural reference. However, even here we can hear a concern with type and the sense that there is a clearly demarcated population, a category easily distinguished from all others. These formulations rarely make a distinction between biological and behavioral aspects but regularly assume that all the traits enumerated are, in one way or another, inherent in the group being mentioned.

In the end, human groups and their cultures are conceived of as relatively static. If a group maintains its historically derived patterns and a myth of biological distinctiveness, it is preserving its past and remaining true to type. This sort of categorical thinking lies at the heart of what Pratt (1985) calls the process of "othering."

> The people to be othered are homogenized into a collective "they," which is distilled even further into an iconic "he" (the standardized adult male specimen). This abstracted "he"/"they" is the subject of verbs in a timeless present tense, which characterizes anything "he" is or does not as a particular historical event but as an instance of a pregiven custom or trait. (p. 139)

In this case, the Native/Bantu/Black other seems to carry both no specific traits and any trait. The other becomes whatever is needed at the moment. If the need is for a generalized Bantu or Black society (cf., van der Spuy 1974, 136; Keyter 1990, 60–61), then we can discover that

> The main feature of traditional religion among Blacks is its close connection with the social order. (Keyter 1990, 62)

Otherwise, we can find long-standing ethnic divisions that have survived the *mfecane*[7] (the Zulu expansion in the nineteenth century), European conquest, and all the vicissitudes of history in the nineteenth and twentieth centuries (cf., Keyter 1990, 60). All of these threads have their expression in twentieth-century South African discussions of race, race relations, and racial problems.

This all-purpose other has no identity of its own, and because South African society is so highly racialized, something else also happens. Everyone is placed in some discrete category. What we have here is the effort to establish those categories. We could say that it is a process in which everyone becomes other. This process of self-othering points to the essentially categorical nature of South African society. Such a cultural structure makes it very easy to characterize people as having a sense of rhythm or as being a "singing people" and in this way creating categories based on sociocultural traits treated as if they were innate.

I have tried to emphasize a temporal dimension to racial and ethnic differentiations in South Africa because this is where the parameters constraining contemporary debates are set. The images of racial difference, conflated with images of ethnic difference, created by the imposition of *apartheid* show considerable potential for persisting, as do the patterns of physical and economic difference created by the regime from the middle of the nineteenth century into the last decade of the twentieth. Today, South Africa is not a racist society, but it is a racialized one. Questions of race have a high degree of salience as the government seeks to reshape the society and the cognitive and sociocultural structures it inherited.

Notes

1. The research on which this article is partially based was carried out in 1992 under an Overseas Research Fellowship from the Centre for Science Development, Pretoria, South Africa, which supported a position as visiting scholar at the Institute for Social and Economic Research, Rhodes University, Grahamstown, South Africa. My thanks to both institutions.

2. To avoid confusion, I have adopted the convention of using the South African spelling when referring to a specific population group in that context. For all other uses of the word, I have maintained an American spelling.

3. "Asians" originally applied to imported laborers from China, as well as India. Both were seen as unassimilable groups who had no historic claim to any portion of the country. Eventually, the Chinese-descended people were repatriated, but the Indians were not, probably as a result of Britain's colonial connections with both India and South Africa.

4. This is an interesting statement because the Amharag people of Ethiopia have been Christian for 2,000 years. However, they are Coptic Christians, a group whose existence seems to have been outside the purview of the yearbook authors. There are several interpretations for this curious "mistake," but most of them would slide rapidly into the realm of speculation.

5. By 1993, the government's official statement was that *apartheid* had ended, even though there were many who disputed that claim. In any case neither *apartheid's* physical effects nor its supporting cognitive system seems to have changed as easily as did the laws.

6. As noted earlier, Indians have long been seen as unassimilable; applying this notion to the Coloured population is a matter of inference from the sorts of statements cited here.

7. *Mfecane* means "crushing" in Zulu and Xhosa, the two major Bantu languages of South Africa. It is a reference to the rapid expansion of the Zulu Empire under Chaka in the nineteenth century. As the Zulu expanded, the peoples on their margins were

thrown into a state of social and political chaos. Many fled the region, and many were absorbed by the Zulu.

Works Cited

American Association of Physical Anthropologists. 1996. AAPA Statement on Biological Aspects of Race. *American Journal of Physical Anthropology*, 101, 569–570.

Davies, Horton. 1950. Race-Tensions in South Africa: Formative Factors and Suggested Solutions. *The Hibbert Journal*, XLIX, 118–127.

Director of Census and Statistics. 1937. *Official Yearbook of the Union (of South Africa) and of Basutoland, Bechuanaland Protectorate and Swaziland*. Pretoria: Government Printer.

Hammond, Dorothy, and Alta Jablow. 1970. *The Africa That Never Was: Four Centuries of British Writing About Africa*. New York: Twayne Publishers.

Junod, Henri Philippe. 1938. *Bantu Heritage*. Johannesburg: Hortors Ltd (for the Transvaal Chamber of Mines).

Keyter, Elise, ed. 1990. *South Africa 1989/90: Official Yearbook of the Republic of South Africa*. Pretoria: Government Printer.

Kirk-Green, Anthony H. M. 1980. "Damnosa hereditas": Ethnic Ranking and the Martial Races Imperitive in Africa. Oxford: Oxford University Institute of Commonwealth Studies.

Pratt, Mary Louise. 1985. Scratches on the Face of the Country; or What Mr. Barrow Saw in the Land of the Bushmen. In Henry Louis Gates, Jr. (ed.), *"Race," Writing, and Difference* (pp. 138–162). Chicago: University of Chicago Press.

Segal, Edwin S. 1991. "Tribalism, Ethnicity, and National Unity: Lessons From the Third World," *Innovation in Social Science Research* (Vienna), 4 (2), 245–264.

South African History Online. 2004. *http://www.sahistory.org.za*.

van der Spuy, D. C. (ed.). 1974. *Official Yearbook of the Republic of South Africa*. Pretoria: Government Printer.

Zegeye, A., I. Liebenberg, and G. Houston. 2003. "Resisting Ethnicity From Above: Social Identities and the Deepening of Democracy in South Africa." In Y. Muthien, M. M. Khosa, and B. Magubane (eds.), *Democracy and Governance Review*, Vol. 1 (pp. 151–195). Pretoria: HSRC/Nexus.

Discussion Questions

1. Were you familiar with the term *apartheid* before you read this article? If so, how did you become familiar with the term?

2. Could you draw any parallels between South African and American history in terms of racial classifications and the propensity to "other" groups of people? How so or how not?

3. Do you think most Americans believe that racial categories are real or that they are arbitrary? Why, why not?

4. Does segregation still exist in the United States? Have you ever experienced segregation? If so, explain.

45

The Haves, The Have-Nots

Christopher Reynolds

On this chart Americans have been divided into two equal groups, those who have household incomes above and below the median income of $42,409. The Haves are in the left hand column, the Have Nots in the right. Interpreting the data according to the legend at the top of the chart, we see that the Haves are 34 percent more likely than the national average to read Golf Digest while the Have Nots are 35 percent more likely to read the National Examiner. The Haves drink premium beer and premium coffee, while the Have Nots are more likely to make do with popular brands of beer and coffee. This is a very simple and rough breakdown, since we know from the Roux article in this section that someone working full time at minimum wage would earn less than $11,000 and that there is virtually no upper limit to household income.

Even with this rough breakdown, very real differences in characteristics and habits do emerge. Members of Have Not households tend to be older and to live alone or have very large or very small households; they worry about themselves more and are more likely to feel alone. Haves like to have control over people and resources and, given their incomes, they clearly do control more resources than the Have Nots. It is easy to see that the Haves have and spend more money on travel and leisure and on high-end products. Some of the data, such as those regarding height and weight, may be a bit harder to anticipate or interpret. It is well to remember that data do not speak for themselves. We cannot tell from the data which characteristics are causes, which effects, and which may be the outcome of some third element that is not represented here.

Discussion Questions

1. Place your household, and your parents' household if you now live independently, in the Have or Have Not column. Which of the characteristics listed apply? Are there some that cross over? For example, do you get your caffeine at Starbucks even though you are a Have Not or wear LA Gear shoes even though you are a Have? What factors other than household income account for buying patterns?

2. Look carefully at the age, marital status, and number of people in household information. To what extent does that information help explain income differences? To what extent does income help explain the age, marital status, and household size data?

3. No information about the genders of the household members is reported here. Are there any clues to gender apart from the Haves buying Liz jeans? Would knowing the genders of the household members be useful to you in understanding the findings?

4. Who, apart from sociology students, would be interested in these findings? Why? How might they be used?

Reprinted from: Christopher Reynolds, "The Haves, The Have-Nots." In *American Demographics* 48, June. Copyright © 2004 by Crain Communications. Reprinted with permission. ✦

The Haves
(Household Income Over $45,000)

The Have-Nots
(Household Income Under $45,000)

According to the Census Bureau, the median household income in the U.S. is $42,409. Using this info, we took a look at the divisive issue of income by splitting the country into two groups: household income over $45,000 and under $45,000. Various traits and consumer habits of the two were ranked based on an index. The national average is 100, so an index of 150 means that group would be 50 percent more likely than the average American to exhibit that trait or buy that product.

Age	MRI		
50–54	125	75 or older	179
40–44	119	70–74	155
45–49	119	65–69	141

Marital Status	MRI		
Working parent	126	Widowed	180
Married	120	Separated (legally)	159
Parent (of child currently living with respondent)	114	Respondent is sole parent	148

Number of People in Household	MRI		
Four	126	One	174
Three	116	Seven	120
Five	115	Two	104

Height	SMRB		
6 Feet 2 Inches	132	Under 5 Feet	151
Over 6 Feet 2 Inches	121	5 Feet	118
6 Feet 1 Inch	121	5 Feet 1 Inch	118

Weight	SMRB		
221–230 lbs.	110	Under 100 lbs.	132
191–200 lbs.	108	100–110 lbs.	110
201–210 lbs.	107	171–180 lbs.	110

Opinions (Agree a lot with statement)	SMRB		
Look at work as career not job	120	Worry a lot about myself	145
I like control over people and resources	112	Feel very alone in the world	143
I exercise once a week	111	Enjoy religious TV	135

Car Manufacturer (Most recent purchase)	MRI		
Infiniti	170	Plymouth	136
SAAB	157	Buick	134
Audi	157	Geo	127

Athletic Shoes (Bought in the past 12 months)	MRI		
Asics	151	LA Gear	125
Brooks	146	KSwiss	119
Saucony	138	Airwalk	116

Cigarettes (Smoked in the past 12 months)	MRI		
Capri Lights	125	Newport Lights	157
Marlboro Lights	108	Newport	157
Winston Lights	99	Basic	154

Cell Phone	MRI		
Samsung	145	Audiovox	111
Nextel	139	Ericsson	89
Verizon	129	Nokia	80

Beer (Drank in the past 6 months)	MRI		
Anchor Steam	156	Natural Ice	132
Widmer	156	Busch	126
Pete's Wicked	154	Milwaukee's Best	126

Coffee (Used in the past 6 months)	MRI		
Peet's	162	Sanka	144
Starbucks	149	Folgers	123
Millstone	145	Maxwell House	121

Toothpaste (Used in the past 6 months)	MRI		
Tom's of Maine	131	Pepsodent	134
Crest Multicare	122	Plus+White	133
Rembrandt	120	Close-Up	130

Jeans (Bought in the past 6 months)	SMRB		
Union Bay	136	Sergio Valente	156
Paris Blues	135	Bongo	143
Liz Claiborne	132	Gitano	125

Hometown (Designated Marketing Area)	SR		
Washington, D.C.	129	Charleston/Huntington, WV	152
Bay Area, CA**	122	El Paso, TX	149
Boston, MA	119	Knoxville, TN	143

Magazines (Have read the most recent issue)	SMRB		
Travel & Leisure	136	National Examiner	135
InStyle	134	Star	131
Golf Digest	134	Country Weekly	129

Web Sites* (Visited in March 2004)	CMM		
American Express	117	Community Connect, Inc.	139
Southwest.com	114	Uproar Network	138
Travelocity	114	Columbia House Sites	122

Web Site Categories* (Visited in March 2004)	CMM		
Business/Finance-Online Trading	115	Directories/Resources-Personals	114
Travel-Hotels/Resorts	112	Discussion/Chat	111
Travel-Car Rental	110	Entertainment-Humor	111

Note: *Household Income level split at $40,000 instead of $45,000.

**San Francisco/Oakland/San Jose

Source: Mediamark Research Inc. (MRI), Simmons Market Research Bureau (SMRB), comScore Media Metrix (CMM) and Scarsborough Research (SR).

46
La conciencia de la mestiza/Towards a New Consciousness

Gloria Anzaldúa

Any anthology on gender, race, and class would seem to be incomplete without the groundbreaking work of Chicana feminist lesbian poet and author Gloria Anzaldúa, whose writing has had such a profound impact on Chicana and Chicano writing as well as that of other communities of color and on gay/lesbian writing, as you can see in the reading by Martinez in this volume. The following excerpt from her book Borderlands/La Frontera: The New Mestiza *highlights some of her most important contributions to thinking on the issues of gender, race, and class.*

In this piece, Anzaldúa introduces the mestiza *consciousness, a paradigm shift in thinking that is born in the borderlands or crossroads between different races, classes, and gendered groupings, as well as geographic spaces. She takes her cue from the term* mestiza/o, *which literally implies a mixed heritage. The borderlands have historically been the seat of war, rape, exploitation, domestic violence, enslavement, gay bashing, genocide, and every sort of human predation. Yet, Anzaldúa suggests that it is here in this chaos in the midst of this clash of opposing cultures, groupings, and experiences that the* mestiza *learns new ways of coping with and seeing the world, a* mestiza *consciousness, which embraces all—White and Black, gay and straight, men and women, wealthy and working class, the U.S. and the Mexican side of the border—and envisions a healing of all wounds. Anzaldúa notes that the* mestiza *consciousness takes on all elements in its purview, challenging the sexism of the "macho" male in Chicana/o culture who wounds women, and*

the racism of Whites—"Gringo"—who dehumanized and erased the history of Chicanas/os, while acknowledging the homophobia that plagues both Chicana/o and White culture. At the same time, the mestiza *recognizes that class differences between racial groups can be momentous as she decries the life span of a Mexican farm laborer—56 years old. Finally, Anzaldúa insists that a* mestiza *consciousness must own all its various parts—linking all human blood to a common root—"somos una gente/we are one people." This is precisely her legacy to generations.*

... **J**osé Vasconcelos, Mexican philosopher, *una raza mestiza.* . . . He called it a cosmic race, *la raza cósmica*, a fifth race embracing the four major races of the world.[1] Opposite to the theory of the pure Aryan, and to the policy of racial purity that white America practices, his theory is one of inclusivity. At the confluence of two or more genetic streams, with chromosomes constantly "crossing over," this mixture of races, rather than resulting in an inferior being, provides hybrid progeny, a mutable, more malleable species with a rich gene pool. From this racial, ideological, cultural and biological cross-pollinization, an "alien" consciousness is presently in the making—a new *mestiza* consciousness, *una conciencia de mujer.* It is a consciousness of the Borderlands.

Una lucha de fronteras/A Struggle of Borders

Because I, a *mestiza*,
continually walk out of one culture
and into another,
because I am in all cultures at the same time. . . .

The ambivalence from the clash of voices results in mental and emotional states of perplexity. Internal strife results in insecurity and indecisiveness. The *mestiza's* dual or multiple personality is plagued by psychic restlessness.

In a constant state of mental nepantilism, an Aztec word meaning torn between ways, *la mestiza* is a product of the transfer of the

405

cultural and spiritual values of one group to another. Being tricultural, monolingual, bilingual, or multilingual, speaking a patois, and in a state of perpetual transition, the *mestiza* faces the dilemma of the mixed breed: which collectivity does the daughter of a darkskinned mother listen to?

. . . Cradled in one culture, sandwiched between two cultures, straddling all three cultures and their value systems, *la mestiza* undergoes a struggle of flesh, a struggle of borders, an inner war. Like all people, we perceive the version of reality that our culture communicates. Like others having or living in more than one culture, we get multiple, often opposing messages. The coming together of two self-consistent but habitually incompatible frames of reference[2] causes *un choque,* a cultural collision.

Within us and within *la cultura chicana,* commonly held beliefs of the white culture attack commonly held beliefs of the Mexican culture, and both attack commonly held beliefs of the indigenous culture. Subconsciously, we see an attack on ourselves and our beliefs as a threat and we attempt to block with a counterstance.

But it is not enough to stand on the opposite river bank, shouting questions, challenging patriarchal, white conventions. A counterstance locks one into a duel of oppressor and oppressed; locked in mortal combat, like the cop and the criminal, both are reduced to a common denominator of violence. The counterstance refutes the dominant culture's views and beliefs, and, for this, it is proudly defiant. All reaction is limited by, and dependent on, what it is reacting against. Because the counterstance stems from a problem with authority—outer as well as inner—it's a step towards liberation from cultural domination. But it is not a way of life. At some point, on our way to a new consciousness, we will have to leave the opposite bank, the split between the two mortal combatants somehow healed so that we are on both shores at once and, at once, see through serpent and eagle eyes. Or perhaps we will decide to disengage from the dominant culture, write it off altogether as a lost cause, and cross the border into a wholly new and separate territory. Or we might go another route. The possibilities are numerous once we decide to act and not react.

A Tolerance for Ambiguity

These numerous possibilities leave *la mestiza* floundering in uncharted seas. In perceiving conflicting information and points of view, she is subjected to a swamping of her psychological borders. She has discovered that she can't hold concepts or ideas in rigid boundaries. The borders and walls that are supposed to keep the undesirable ideas out are entrenched habits and patterns of behavior; these habits and patterns are the enemy within. Rigidity means death. Only by remaining flexible is she able to stretch the psyche horizontally and vertically. *La mestiza* constantly has to shift out of habitual formations; from convergent thinking, analytical reasoning that tends to use rationality to move toward a single goal (a Western mode), to divergent thinking,[3] characterized by movement away from set patterns and I goals and toward a more whole perspective, one that includes rather than excludes.

The new *mestiza* copes by developing a tolerance for contradictions, a tolerance for ambiguity. She learns to be an Indian in Mexican culture, to be Mexican from an Anglo point of view. She learns to juggle cultures. She has a plural personality, she operates in a pluralistic mode—nothing is thrust out, the good the bad and the ugly, nothing rejected, nothing abandoned. Not only does she sustain contradictions, she turns the ambivalence into something else.

She can be jarred out of ambivalence by an intense, and often painful, emotional event which inverts or resolves the ambivalence. I'm not sure exactly how. The work takes place underground—subconsciously. It is work that the soul performs. That focal point or fulcrum, that juncture where the *mestiza* stands, is where phenomena tend to collide. It is where the possibility of uniting all that is separate occurs. This assembly is not one where severed or separated pieces merely come together. Nor is it a balancing of opposing powers. In attempting to work out a synthesis, the self has added a third element which is greater than the sum of its severed parts. That third element is a new consciousness—a *mestiza* consciousness—and though it is a source of intense pain, its energy comes from continual creative motion that keeps breaking down the unitary aspect of each new paradigm.

. . . [T]he future will belong to the *mestiza*. Because the future depends on the breaking down of paradigms, it depends on the straddling of two or more cultures. By creating a new mythos—that is, a change in the way we perceive reality, the way we see ourselves, and the ways we behave—*la mestiza* creates a new consciousness.

The work of *mestiza* consciousness is to break down the subject-object duality that keeps her a prisoner and to show in the flesh and through the images in her work how duality is transcended. The answer to the problem between the white race and the colored, between males and females, lies in healing the split that originates in the very foundation of our lives, our culture, our languages, our thoughts. A massive uprooting of dualistic thinking in the individual and collective consciousness is the beginning of a long struggle, but one that could, in our best hopes, bring us to the end of rape, of violence, of war. . . .

Que no se nos olviden los hombres/Let Us Not Forget the Men

. . . "You're nothing but a woman" means you are defective. Its opposite is to be *un macho*. The modern meaning of the word "machismo," as well as the concept, is actually an Anglo invention. For men like my father, being "macho" meant being strong enough to protect and support my mother and us, yet being able to show love. Today's macho has doubts about his ability to feed and protect his family. His "machismo" is an adaptation to oppression and poverty and low self-esteem. It is the result of hierarchical male dominance. The Anglo, feeling inadequate and inferior and powerless, displaces or transfers these feelings to the Chicano by shaming him. In the Gringo world, the Chicano suffers from excessive humility and self-effacement, shame of self and self-deprecation. Around Latinos he suffers from a sense of language

inadequacy and its accompanying discomfort; with Native Americans he suffers from a racial amnesia which ignores our common blood, and from, guilt because the Spanish part of him took their land and oppressed them. He has an excessive compensatory hubris when around Mexicans from the other side. It overlays a deep sense of racial shame.

The loss of a sense of dignity and respect in the macho breeds a false machismo which leads him to put down women and even to brutalize them. Coexisting with his sexist behavior is a love for the mother which takes precedence over that of all others. Devoted son, macho pig. To wash down the shame of his acts, of his very being, and to handle the brute in the mirror, he takes to the bottle, the snort, the needle, and the fist.

***

Though we "understand" the root causes of male hatred and fear, and the subsequent wounding of women, we do not excuse, we do not condone, and we will no longer put up with it. From the men of our race, we demand the admission/acknowledgment/disclosure/testimony that they wound us, violate us, are afraid of us and of our power. We need them to say they will begin to eliminate their hurtful put-down ways. But more than the words, we demand acts. We say to them: We will develop equal power with you and those who have shamed us.

It is imperative that *mestizas* support each other in changing the sexist elements in the Mexican-Indian culture. As long as woman is put down, the Indian and the Black in all of us is put down. The struggle of the *mestiza* is above all a feminist one. . . .

Tenderness, a sign of vulnerability, is so feared that it is showered on women with verbal abuse and blows. Men, even more than women, are fettered to gender roles. Women at least have had the guts to break out of bondage. Only gay men have had the courage to expose themselves to the woman inside them and to challenge the current masculinity. I've encountered a few scattered and isolated gentle straight men, the beginnings of a new breed, but they are confused, and entangled with sexist behaviors that they have not been able to eradicate. We need a new masculinity and the new man needs a movement.

***

Lumping the males who deviate from the general norm with man, the oppressor, is a gross injustice. . . . Being the supreme crossers of cultures, homosexuals have strong bonds with the queer white, Black, Asian, Native American, Latino, and with the queer in Italy, Australia and the rest of the planet. We come from all colors, all classes, all races, all time periods. Our role is to link people with each other—the Blacks with Jews with Indians with Asians with whites with extraterrestrials. It is to transfer ideas and information from one culture to another. Colored homosexuals have more knowledge of other cultures; have always been at the forefront (although sometimes in the closet) of all liberation struggles in this country; have suffered more injustices and have survived them despite all odds. Chicanos need to acknowledge the political and artistic contributions of their queer. People, listen to what your *jotería* is saying.

The *mestizo* and the queer exist at this time and point on the evolutionary continuum for a purpose. We are a blending that proves that all blood is intricately woven together, and that we are spawned out of similar souls.

Somos una gente/We Are One People

. . . **Divided Loyalties.** Many women and men of color do not want to have any dealings with white people. It takes too much time and energy to explain to the downwardly mobile, white middle-class women that its okay for us to want to own "possessions" never having had any nice furniture on our dirt floors or "luxuries" like washing machines. Many feel that whites should help their own people rid themselves of race hatred and fear first. I, for one, choose to use some of my energy to serve as mediator. I think we need to allow whites to be our allies. . . . They will come to see that they are not helping us but following our lead.

Individually, but also as a racial entity, we need to voice our needs. We need to say to white society: We need you to accept the fact that Chicanos are different, to acknowledge your rejection and negation of us. We need you to own the fact that you looked upon us as less than human, that you stole our lands, our personhood, our self-respect. We need you to make public restitution: to say that, to compensate for your own sense of defectiveness, you strive for power over us, you erase our history and our experience because it makes you feel guilty—you'd rather forget your brutish acts. To say you've split yourself from minority groups, that you disown us, that your dual consciousness splits off parts of yourself, transferring the "negative" parts onto us. . . . To say that you are afraid of us, that to put distance between us, you wear the mask of contempt. Admit that Mexico is your double, that she exists in the shadow of this country, that we are irrevocably tied to her. Gringo, accept the doppelganger in your psyche. By taking back your collective shadow the intracultural split will heal. And finally, tell us what you need from us. . . .

El día de la Chicana/The Day of the Chicana

I will not be shamed again
Nor will I shame myself.

I am possessed by a vision: that we Chicanas and Chicanos have taken back or uncovered our true faces, our dignity and self-respect. It's a validation vision.

Seeing the Chicana anew in light of her history, I seek an exoneration, a seeing through the fictions of white supremacy, a seeing of ourselves in our true guises and not as the false racial personality that has been given to us and that we have given to ourselves. I seek our woman's face, our true features, the positive and the negative seen clearly, free of the tainted biases of male dominance. I seek new images of identity, new beliefs about ourselves, our humanity and worth no longer in question. . . .

On December 2nd when my sun goes into my first house, I celebrate *el día de la Chicana y el Chicano*. . . . On that day I bare my soul, make myself vulnerable to friends and family by expressing my feelings. On that day I affirm who we are.

On that day I look inside our conflicts and our basic introverted racial temperament. I identify our needs, voice them. I acknowledge that the self and the race have been wounded. I recognize the need to take care of our personhood, of our racial self. . . .

On that day I say, "Yes, all you people wound us when you reject us. Rejection strips us of self-worth; our vulnerability exposes us to shame. It is our innate identity you find wanting. We are ashamed that we need your good opinion, that we need your acceptance. We can no longer camouflage our needs, can no longer let defenses and fences sprout around us. We can no longer withdraw. To rage and look upon you with contempt is to rage and be contemptuous of ourselves. We can no longer blame you, nor disown the white parts, the male parts, the pathological parts, the queer parts, the vulnerable parts. Here we are weaponless with open arms, with only our magic. Let's try it our way, the *mestiza,* way, the Chicana way, the woman way."

On that day, I search for our essential dignity as a people, a people with a sense of purpose—to belong and contribute to something greater than our pueblo. On that day I seek to recover and reshape my spiritual identity. . . .

El retorno/The Return

. . . I stand at the river, watch the curving, twisting serpent, a serpent nailed to the fence where the mouth of the Rio Grande empties into the Gulf.

I have come back. . . . I shade my eyes and look up. The bone beak of a hawk slowly circling over me, checking me out as potential carrion. In its wane a little bud flickering its wings, swimming sporadically like a fish. In the distance the expressway and the slough of traffic like an irritated sow. The sudden pull in my gut. . . . My land. . . . If I look real hard I can almost see the Spanish fathers who were called "the cavalry of Christ" enter this valley riding their burros, see the clash of cultures commence.

***

. . . This is home, the small towns in the Valley, *los pueblitos* with chicken pens and goats picketed to mesquite shrubs. . . . [O]n the other side of the tracks, junk cars line the front yards of hot pink and lavender-trimmed houses—Chicano architecture we call it, self-consciously. I have missed the TV shows where hosts speak in half and half, and where awards are given in the category of Tex-Mex music. . . .

***

I still feel the old despair when I look at the unpainted, dilapidated, scrap lumber houses consisting mostly of corrugated aluminum. Some of the poorest people in the U.S. live in the Lower Rio Grande Valley, an arid and semi-arid land of irrigated farming, intense sunlight and heat, citrus groves next to chaparral and cactus. I walk through the elementary school I attended so long ago, that remained segregated until recently. I remember how the white teachers used to punish us for being Mexican.

How I love this tragic valley of South Texas, as Ricardo Sánchez calls it; this borderland between the Nueces and the Rio Grande. This land has survived possession and ill-use by five countries: Spain, Mexico, the Republic of Texas, the U.S., the Confederacy, and the U.S. again. It has survived Anglo-Mexican blood feuds, lynchings, burnings, rapes, pillage. . . .

***

"It's been a bad year for corn," my brother, Nune, says. As he talks, I remember my father scanning the sky for a rain that would end the drought, looking up into the sky, day after day, while the corn withered on its stalk. My father has been dead for 29 years, having worked himself to death. The life span of a Mexican farm laborer is 56—he lived to be 38. It shocks me that I am older than he. I, too, search the sky for rain. Like the ancients, I worship the rain god and the maize goddess, but unlike my father I have recovered their names. Now for rain (irrigation) one offers not a sacrifice of blood, but of money. . . .

***

I walk out to the back yard. . . . [Mamá] wants me to help her prune the rose bushes, dig out the carpet grass that is choking them. . . . Here every Mexican grows flowers. If they don't have a piece of dirt, they use car tires, jars, cans, shoe boxes. Roses are the Mexicans favorite flower. I think, how symbolic—thorns and all.

Yes, the Chicano and Chicana have always taken care of growing things and the land. Again I see the four of us kids getting off the school bus, changing into our work clothes, walking into the field with Papi and Mami, all six of us bending to the ground. Below our feet, under the earth lie the watermelon seeds. We cover them with paper plates. . . . The paper plates keep the freeze away. Next day or the next, we remove the plates, bare the tiny green shoots to the elements. They survive and grow, give fruit hundreds of times the size of the seed. We water them and hoe them. We harvest them. The vines dry, rot, are plowed under. Growth, death, decay, birth. The soil prepared again and again, impregnated, worked on. . . .

This land was Mexican once
was Indian always
and is.
And will be again.

Notes

1. This is my own "take off" on José Vasconcelos' idea. Jos Vasconcelos, *La Raza Cósmica: Misión de la Raza Ibero-Americana* (M!xico: Aguilar S.A. de Ediciones, 1961).

2. Arthur Koestler termed this "bisociation." Albert Rothenberg, *The Creative Process in Art, Science, and Other Fields.* Chicago: University of Chicago Press, 1979, 12.

3. In part, I derive my definitions for "convergent" and "divergent" thinking from Rothenberg, 12–13.

Discussion Questions

1. Do you think that being a lesbian adds a dimension to Anzaldúa's writing that you might not find in the writing of other women of color? If so, why or why not?

2. What do you think of the concept of *mestiza* consciousness? Does it seem a worthwhile concept? Did it remind you of other concepts you have learned in other classes?

3. How did you respond to the code-switching or language changes in the piece? Did you like or dislike this writing technique? Why do you think Anzaldúa uses this writing style?

4. Have you known someone who is a *mestiza/o*, that is, someone of mixed blood? If so, what did you learn about their experience?

47

A Place in the Rainbow

Theorizing Lesbian and Gay Culture

Janice M. Irvine

In this article Janice M. Irvine asks questions about who has a place in the rainbow of our—or any—society. She reports the details of a particular controversy that arose over a curriculum proposed for the New York City schools in 1992, but she also raises broad theoretical issues about the nature of cultures. In the past, both social scientists and people on the street thought of "cultures" as entities people were born into; cultures were seen as biological or essential. More contemporary notions, with roots in interdisciplinary fields such as ethnic, cultural, gender, and queer studies, view cultures as social constructions, complexes of shared symbols and identities. Likewise, older definitions of "community" pictured physical locations, while current ideas focus on institutions and relationships. It is easier to see lesbians and gay men as having a culture and being members of communities using the more contemporary definitions.

Current definitions of culture and community make it easier to place those with homosexual identities within them. However, the fit is not perfect because, as Irvine notes and we have seen in the readings by Robb, Seidman, and Ward, "meaning systems within lesbian/gay communities are located along axes of difference, particularly those of race, class, and gender." Lesbians and gay men, people from working- and middle-class backgrounds, White people, and people of color have different experiences and participate to greater or lesser degrees in other cultures and communities. Research represented in this volume and research cited by Irvine makes it clear that

time and place are important factors in shaping both identities and communities.

In recounting the reactions to the Rainbow Curriculum, Irvine reports that some African Americans resented the struggle of lesbians and gays being compared with their struggle for civil rights. One African American parent and teacher asked where gays and lesbians were in the civil rights movement. They were there as they have been in other social movements, but they were not generally open about their sexuality. For example, many people do not know that Bayard Rustin (1912–1987), who was the first field secretary of the Congress of Racial Equality (CORE) and the organizer of the 1963 March on Washington for Jobs and Freedom, was gay. He was asked not to be open about his sexuality for fear it might distract from or discredit his civil rights activities.

In 1992, volatile debates about culture rocked New York City after the introduction of a teacher's guide for a multicultural curriculum in the public schools. Known as the Rainbow curriculum, this guide was unremarkable until key actors discovered brief sections alluding to lesbian and gay families.[1] The ensuing controversy generated national publicity and ultimately contributed to the firing of Schools Chancellor Joseph Fernandez. The Rainbow curriculum is of central importance because the debates over culture, which the curriculum did not initiate but certainly underscored in popular consciousness, continue throughout the country.

The controversy over the Rainbow curriculum is of academic interest to sociologists because of the complicated theoretical concerns it raises about culture, identity, and sexuality. Especially at a time when the term *culture* has achieved popular and widespread usage, opposition to the demands by lesbians and gay men for recognition as a cultural group generates questions about authenticity and definition of culture. What or who is entitled to claim cultural status? How are cultural identities constituted? Are they essential or constructed? What is the role of history, of social agents, and of representation in the invention of cultures? Are some cultures more legitimate than others? Do sexual cultures exist? Adequate answers to these questions necessitate theoretical paradigms that speak to the intersections of culture, sexuality, identities, race, ethnicity, and difference.

Debates about culture certainly constitute a trajectory within the classical sociological theories of Marx, Weber, and Durkheim. Throughout the century, and from a variety of theoretical standpoints, sociologists have examined questions concerning (for example) cultural autonomy, coherence, and consensus. Analysis of culture has recently assumed increasing prominence in sociological theorizing (Alexander and Seidman 1990; Hall and Neitz 1993; Munch and Smelser 1992; Wuthnow 1987). The growing recognition in the discipline of the importance of culture is significant because changing demographic and political factors unceasingly place cultural concerns in the foreground as central to social life. Further, a vibrant discourse typically glossed as "multiculturalism" has facilitated the deployment of the term *culture* in an ever-widening sphere. Yet sociologists have played a minimal role in the exciting advances of cultural and sexuality studies, and sociological theory is inadequate to analyze social events such as the Rainbow controversy.

Certain theoretical frameworks in sociology, such as those of deviance and social problems, have proved to be useful tools whereby some scholars and activists study sexual cultures. Certainly social construction theory, which has its primary roots in sociology, has transformed the history of sexuality. Several factors, however, contribute to sociology's paradigmatic limitations in this area. First, there is no tradition within mainstream sociology of broader inquiry into the study of sexuality. Compared, for example, with historians and anthropologists, few sociologists participate in the burgeoning interdisciplinary field of sexuality studies (for important exceptions see Almaguer 1991; Gagnon 1977; Giddens 1992; Humphries 1974; Irvine 1990, 1994; Luker 1975; Murray 1979, 1992; Plummer 1975, 1981; Seidman 1991, 1992; Simon and Gagnon 1973; Stein 1993, as well as a number of works by historical sociologist Jeffrey Weeks [1979, 1981, 1985, 1991]).

Much of this work is recent. Beyond the absence of a critical canon, this vacuum speaks to a certain illegitimacy within sociology concerning the study of sexuality. This is reinforced materially by the lack of graduate training in the sociology of sexuality and by a dearth of job opportunities for those who might choose to specialize in this area.

Of related concern is sociology's insulation from the interdisciplinary multicultural conversation concerning intersections of race, ethnicity, gender, and sexual identity. Particularly relevant for this paper is the chasm between sociology and lesbian and gay studies. Central to the field of lesbian and gay studies is a range of topics that should hold particular fascination for sociologists: examination of the historical invention of sexual taxonomies and the reciprocal effect of the social organization of sexual communities, as well as inquiry into the origins of sexual cultures, the organization of systems of meaning, and the construction and deconstruction of identities. Whereas lesbians and gay men appear most frequently in sociology as objects of discussion in social problems texts, lesbian and gay studies insist on our subjectivity as social actors and as research agents. Lesbian and gay studies center sexuality as a major social category with important correlates of social organization and behavior rather than relegating it to the status of individual variable.

Using key aspects of the debates about culture that were generated by the Rainbow curriculum, I will highlight how placing lesbian and gay sexual identity in the foreground is essential to this analysis. The application of theoretical perspectives from cultural studies and multicultural studies, in particular lesbian and gay studies and African-American studies, is especially useful in exploring the theoretical implications of pitting racial cultures against sexual cultures, and in the debates over essential and constructed identities. I will examine competing claims about culture by social groups, and will discuss evolving cultural theories among social scientists. To fully contextualize the Rainbow debates, this cultural theory must be located in historical analysis about the invention of racial categories, sexual categories, and the emergence of individual and social identities. The initiative by lesbians and gay men to achieve cultural status in public multicultural education not only is a pivotal moment in lesbian and gay liberation, but also affords the opportunity to further elaborate social theories about culture through an examination of a cultural group actively engaged in its continual reinvention.

Cultures, Multiculturalism, and Sexuality

As the debates over the Rainbow curriculum aptly illustrate, attention to culture, once largely confined within academic discourse, currently occupies a varied and mainstream audience. This shift corresponds to major social changes in structures and consciousness wrought by the many civil rights movements of the last 25 years. Blacks, members of other racial and ethnic groups, women, lesbians and gay men, and disabled people launched legal and social initiatives not only to end discrimination but also to foster recognition of their distinct cultural identities. The richness of recent multicultural awareness is a legacy of these movements. Similarly, the challenges and conflicts generated by multicultural projects rank among the most volatile theoretical and political debates of the late twentieth century.

Much of the sophisticated and engaging new theoretical literature on culture has emerged from those working within cultural studies and in the various ethnic, women's, and lesbian and gay studies programs, as well as from associated independent scholars and activists. In a dialogue that crosses disciplines and identity groups, this scholarship examines a range of questions about the nature, meaning, and practices of culture that should be of great interest to sociologists. As I have noted, some sociologists have traditionally been concerned with issues of culture, race, and ethnicity. Currently, however, and with important exceptions (see, for example, Alba 1990; Collins 1986, 1990; Hall 1989, 1992a, 1992b; Omi and Winant 1986; Stacey and Thorne 1985; Thompson and Tyagi 1993; Waters 1990), sociologists have not yet had a strong voice in articulating the "new cultural politics of difference" (West

1993[a]:18).[2] The proliferation of cultural studies in the United States, as it entails the theorizing of culture in the deeply political context of day-to-day negotiations of race, ethnicity, gender, and sexuality, has been cross-disciplinary or even antidisciplinary, resulting in a number of independent academic centers of cultural studies (Hall 1992a; Nelson [et al.] 1992). Sociologists have produced little of this cultural studies scholarship.[3]

As Seidman (1990) has aptly observed, sociological inquiries into culture are not simply theoretical, but are central to negotiations of everyday life. This suggests that sociologists may want to attend to the new discursive formulations deployed by scholars who are theorizing the daily complications of culture and multiculturalism as they are articulated and experienced within existing and contested relations of power.

The educational system has proved to be a central location in which the complexities of culture are manifested daily. Schools have been the site of extensive conflict and debate. This is not surprising because educational institutions are primary vehicles for the transmission of culture (Bouidieu 1968). On all levels of the system, historically marginalized groups have sought to destabilize the hegemonic notion of a homogeneous and inclusive "American culture" (Hu-DeHart 1993: 8) and to gain recognition for their own diverse histories, traditions, and identities. The first disruptions started at the university level in the late 1960s, when student protesters demanded the establishment of ethnic and women's studies programs. Multicultural curricula are now being implemented in primary and secondary schools across the country, in a climate of both enthusiasm and opposition.

In multicultural educational systems, schools become the site not simply for cultural assertion and socialization, but also for the active invention of culture. Students do not passively learn about cultures and identities, but participate in ongoing adoption and reformulation of traditional cultural identities, logics, and strategies. As Lubiano suggests, education is a site where "people think themselves into being" (Thompson and Tyagi 1993: xxxi). Representation in multicultural curricula is crucial for the visibility and legitimacy it affords to a cultural group, but also for that group's continual reinvigoration. Increasingly, too, multicultural programs are becoming sites not only for the support of cultural identities, but also for destabilizing discussions of the limitations of identity politics and of reified notions of identity (West 1993a).

This power of multicultural education forms the basis for controversies such as the Rainbow curriculum, where lesbians and gay men seek to be included in public school curricula. The fierce and widely publicized battle waged over this curriculum resonated across the country, becoming a benchmark contest over sexuality education more generally. These cultural debates assumed discursive parameters which were made possible only through the intellectual and political achievements of several decades of lesbian/gay liberation. At a moment during which multicultural education is increasingly prominent, it was inevitable that lesbians and gay men would begin initiatives to secure for their own communities a place in these curricula.

Opposition to the Rainbow curriculum is illustrative both of popular ideas about the nature of culture, and of the varied faces of homophobia. Critics refused to acknowledge that lesbian and gay men constitute a culture, and instead adamantly insisted that homosexuals were deviant, immoral individuals who pose a threat to children. This individualizing strategy supported the contention that lesbians and gay men simply live an aberrant lifestyle rather than constituting a legitimate cultural identity. Culture, in the view of the critics, is a status available only to those born into groups with a history and a shared set of practices. It is an essential and consistent identity. This formulation of culture fostered one of the most pernicious aspects of the Rainbow debates: the pitting of racial groups against lesbians and gay men.[4]

Critics of the idea of a lesbian/gay culture deployed a simple but powerful tactic to argue that it should be excluded from the multicultural curriculum. They compared the allegedly stable and indisputable cultural categories of race and ethnicity with the purportedly ridiculous and fictive notion of lesbian/gay culture "They want to teach my kid that being gay fits in with being Italian and Puerto Rican!" one parent cried (Tabor 1992). Some African-American critics were incensed by comparisons of lesbian and gay politics and culture to the black civil rights movement. At one community school board meeting, a parent and teacher said:

> Years of being thrown in jail for demonstrating against racism and being sprayed by fire hoses taught me something. I ask you where was the gay community when school children died in Mobile, Alabama? Where was the gay community when many of us were beaten at a lunch counter? Is this the only way we can be included in the curriculum? To allow the gay community to piggyback off our achievement? (D'Angelo 1992).

For others, the outrage was fueled by the contention that, unlike blacks or (presumably) members of other racial groups, lesbians and gay men have no common cultural symbols or artifacts Olivia Banks (1993), the chair of the curriculum committee of School Board 29, was vehement during a *60 Minutes* broadcast on the Rainbow curriculum:

> How dare they compare themselves to the blacks, who've had to struggle . . . for over 250-some years? They have no special language, no special clothing, no special food, no special dress-wear, so what . . . makes them a culture? They don't fit into any definition of what a culture is. They are using the racial issue as a way to open doors. How dare they?

When Ed Bradley suggested that lesbians and gay men have a minority identity, Banks fumed, "You're doing it again. You're putting a sexual orientation on the same level of a race, and that's unacceptable to this person sitting here."

Much popular opposition to the idea that lesbians and gay men constitute a culture rests on an important subtextual insistence that we are all born with and into culture. In this model, race and ethnicity become the quintessentially authentic cultures. Lingering traces of biologism from the social sciences are entrenched in mainstream thought, and cast race as a fixed and natural essence. As explanatory systems, these racial beliefs, which fuse physiological and social differences, function as "amateur biology" (Omi and Winant 1986: 62). From this perspective, one's social location in a racial culture is secured at birth, and, as Banks implies above, allows one entry into a stable system of shared language, dress, clothing, and other cultural signifiers.

The conviction that cultural status is biologically and generationally transmitted inevitably excludes lesbians and gay men, who cannot make such claims.[5] As illustrated above, critics greet the suggestion of a lesbian and gay culture not simply with opposition, but with the fear that such recognition would somehow diminish their social position or erode whatever legitimacy they have managed to garner from years of civil rights efforts.[6] Ironically, however, the establishment of multicultural education in public schools, and of university programs such as black studies, was itself the outcome of protracted efforts, much like those now undertaken by lesbians and gay men, to transform the educational system into a set of institutions more aware and more responsive to the cultures of ethnic and racial groups (Blassingame 1971; Ford 1973).

This discursive positioning of racial/ethnic cultures against lesbian/gay cultures in such a volatile mainstream debate invites an examination of the important scholarship on both racial and sexual cultures. Ironically, as we shall see, opponents of the Rainbow curriculum are promulgating rigidly essential definitions of race at a moment when theorists are destabilizing those ideas by asserting the socially and historically constructed nature of racial categories. Similarly, lesbian and gay scholarship has detailed the important historical transformation of structures and meaning from homosexuality as an individual, deviant sexual act, to a personal social identity, to a complex and sophisticated cultural group. In many ways, then, social theorists of race and of sexuality have been engaged in parallel endeavors of placing both race and sexual identity in the foreground as social categories while rejecting false universalisms and ahistorical essentialisms. Further, in deconstructing racial and sexual categories, these theorists have been insistent

that all cultures are historically contingent and invented, including dominant cultures such as those of whites and heterosexuals.

Lesbian and Gay Cultures, Communities, and Identities

The Rainbow controversy aptly reveals the binarisms rending contemporary society: the idea of a positive lesbian/gay culture worthy of recognition and respect is coterminous with the specter of the deviant, individual homosexual. Lesbian/gay movements throughout the century have sought to erase the stigma of individual sickness and perversion, institutionalized by law, medicine, and science. As the Rainbow debates indicate, these efforts to transform social meanings from homosexual to gay (Herdt 1992; Weinberg 1972)—that is, from individual, pathological behavior to a rich and distinctive cultural system—have been only partially successful Rainbow opponents, such as the highly visible right-wing organizer Mary Cummins, were strategically canny in framing the debate as exclusively about the (typically male) sexually deviant individual. Cummins described the curriculum as "aimed at promoting acceptance of sodomy." When questioned by reporter Ed Bradley (1993), she insisted, "What is homosexuality except sodomy? . . . There's no difference. Homosexuals are sodomists."

Cultures emerge in a historical, political, and economic context. Cummins's comment, therefore, and a full understanding of the shift from individual homosexual behavior to gay cultural identity, require an examination of the social production of sexual identities. Proponents of the idea of lesbian/gay culture base their arguments on a body of important historical literature about lesbians and gay men as social actors engaged in the active invention of communities and in the transformation of social meanings of same-sex sexual behavior. The shift from the individual sodomist to the lesbian and gay cultural subject occurred in the context of social, political, and economic changes over the course of many decades, including (as we will see) the intellectual activities of sociologists. In addition, academic research produced by lesbians and gay men concerning their cultural status has been shaped by the evolving theoretical perspectives on the nature and definitions of culture within the social sciences, particularly anthropology.

Our current ideas about sexual identity rest on deep and fundamental changes in the social organization of sexuality that date to the late nineteenth century. Historians cite that period as an era during which dominant sexual meanings shifted from a familial and reproductive orientation to a focus on sexuality as vital to individual happiness and emotional intimacy (D'Emilio and Freedman 1988; Foucault 1978; Weeks 1981). Our modern preoccupation with sexuality as a cornerstone of personality and a prerequisite for fulfillment is a decidedly recent phenomenon. This shift is important in understanding the genuine instability of current notions that there are distinct heterosexual and homosexual persons. The organization of individual identity around sexual feelings and behaviors would have been unthinkable before the last century.

A related historical development in the organization of sexual identities was the emergence of the legal, and particularly the medical, professions as central institutions in the regulation of sexuality. Although homosexual activity was subject to sodomy laws in England before 1885, historians emphasize that those laws were directed against specific acts, not particular categories of people (Weeks 1979, 1981). Acts of sodomy committed between women and men were as vulnerable to prosecution as were those between men and men. Beginning in 1885, however, the laws began to target sexual acts between men; at that time, as a result of new medical discourses, homosexuality was increasingly defined as an internal, individual trait. The idea of a deviant, homosexual person was given a public face, in part, by highly publicized trials such as that of Oscar Wilde at the end of the century.

The invention of medical categories of sexual identities in the late nineteenth century was one artifact of the wider expansion of the emerging cultural authority of the medical profession over issues of health, illness, and (increasingly) sexuality (Irvine

1990; Starr 1982). Physicians were consolidating their power to regulate and define large areas of human experience, even those, as later critics would note, which fell outside the bounds of their training and expertise (Conrad and Schneider 1992; Friedson 1970; Zola 1972). The rise of physicians as the new "moral entrepreneurs" ensured the application of the medical model as the dominant explanatory framework for behavior considered different (Becker 1963). As with sexual identity, the medicalization of "deviance" locates its origins within the individual. As with homosexuality, this medicalization stipulates a cause that is anatomical, physiological, or psychological.

Whereas religion and the law previously had taken note of *acts* of sodomy, the new medical discourse recognized a distinct kind of sexual *person*. Beginning in the 1860s, a variety of terms to describe this new individual emerged, including *invert*, *urning*, and *homosexual*. The year 1892 marks some of the earliest textual appearances of the word *homosexual* (Halperin 1990; Katz 1990). By this time a heterosexual character, variously defined, began to appear in the medical discourse as well (Katz 1990).

Historians have differed on the significance of medical labeling: did it create a subculture that organized around the new concept of homosexual identity, or was medicalization a response to, and an attempt to define and control, preexisting sexual communities (Chauncey 1982 and 1989; D'Emilio and Freedman 1988; Faderman 1981; Newton 1984; Smith-Rosenberg 1985)? Although evidence indicates that the determinative role of medical literature in shaping homosexual activity and identity was limited, medicalization shifted the locus of moral authority to the medicopsychiatric profession, and much early research focused on descriptive and etiological studies of this new individual. The newly medicalized condition was variously conceptualized as a disease or, as by Havelock Ellis, an anomaly akin to color blindness. Whatever the specific diagnosis, homosexuality was seen as an individual condition, and appropriate interventions were subject to the current theories and treatment modalities of medicine and psychiatry.

One hundred years since their invention, the categories of homosexuality and heterosexuality have achieved the status of assumed knowledge; the idea that there are distinct heterosexual and homosexual persons forms the centerpiece of the sexual wisdom of our society. An important factor in the persistence of ideas about fixed sexual identity derives from the cultural activities of lesbians and gay men themselves: it must be reemphasized that medical discourse did not create categories of sexuality out of whole cloth, but was partially responding to the nascent social organization of groups of people who were beginning to coalesce and identify around their sexual interests and behaviors. Indeed, the last hundred years have witnessed the rapid and transformative development of social worlds of lesbian and gay men, particularly since World War II (D'Emilio 1983).

The social organization of lesbians and gay men has centered around the shared experience of transgressive sexuality, which has been variously defined throughout the century. Certainly legal sanctions and the medicopsychiatric consensus of homosexual pathology shaped early social networks. The stigma of perversion tainted the collective consciousness, even if some individual members refused to internalize that stigma. Pervasive social attitudes that homosexuals were bizarre, criminal, or sick were reinforced by, and contributed to, a crushing isolation and invisibility. Secrecy was an institutional tyranny rather than an individual prerogative; the closet became "the defining structure for gay oppression in this century" (Sedgwick 1993: 48). In this context, the early lesbian and gay world sought a transformation of social definitions from individual homosexual behavior to a social identity and, significantly, from a "spoiled identity" (Goffman 1963) to one of respect and value. This process much later would prompt lesbians and gay men to seek recognition for their own identities and culture within multicultural curricula such as the Rainbow.

This rearticulation of sociosexual meanings has been a complex process proceeding on many fronts. The political initiatives of the lesbian/gay movement have been pivotal in challenging both individual and institutional structures of oppression (see, for example, D'Emilio 1983; Duberman, Vicinus, and Chauncey 1989; Weeks 1979). These efforts, of course, have been shaped by a range of broader social influences, such as social and demographic changes wrought by World War II, the impact of McCarthyism, the rise of religious fundamentalism, and the emergence of liberation movements organized around race and gender.

Academic research and scholarship also helped create an intellectual climate conducive to the redefinition of sexual meaning systems. For example, Alfred Kinsey's (1948, 1953) research challenged the widespread notion that gay people were a distinct and pathological set of individuals, and suggested that everyone had the "capacity" for homosexuality. Although the gay visibility engendered by the Kinsey reports contributed to a cultural panic that fed McCarthyism, it also helped consolidate a growing 1950s homophile movement (Irvine 1990). New sociological theories also supported the efforts of this movement. In particular, deviance theory, which underwent a radical postwar transformation, provided an intellectual infrastructure for new definitions of sexual identities (see D'Emilio 1983). The work of Erving Goffman (1963), Howard Becker (1963), and Joseph Gusfield (1955), for example, was instrumental in shifting the theoretical view of deviance from that of a quality located within the individual person or act to that of a historically specific status created by social censure.

This sociological deviance theory of the 1960s was in radical opposition to the psychoanalytic discourse on homosexuality Irving Bieber and Charles Socarides rose to prominence at that time with their oedipal and preoedipal theories of the pathological development of homosexuality. Socarides claimed that psychoanalysis could cure up to 50 percent of "strongly motivated obligatory homosexuals" (see Bayer 1981: 37). On the other hand, the interactionist model of deviance facilitated a definition of lesbians and gay men simply as rule breakers rather than as essentially flawed individuals. In Becker's terms, lesbians and gay men were "outsiders" who had been labeled deviant.

Becker's observation that the deviant identity becomes the defining one, and therefore that outsiders create distinct social worlds, was particularly relevant to the social organization of lesbians and gay men: this century has witnessed the formation of elaborate collectivities of lesbian and gay life organized around erotic identity. These networks, however, have become increasingly expansive, with sexuality less explicitly in the foreground. With the elaboration of this complex social world has come disagreement about how to characterize it. Is it a lifestyle enclave (Bellah et al. 1985), a community (D'Emilio 1983; Kennedy and Davis 1993; Murray 1979), a culture (Altman 1982; Bronski 1984; Ferguson 1990; Herdt 1992; Weeks 1979), an ethnicity (Epstein 1987), or nationalism (Duggan 1992; Newton 1993)?

Yet the idea of culture has gained popular and widespread currency as an often loosely defined signifier of shared identity. Much of the intellectual debate among lesbian and gay scholars has concerned the question of cultural status; the discourse has followed theoretical advances in the social sciences, particularly anthropology and cultural studies, on the definition of culture. Until the late 1950s, behaviorism dominated the social sciences, and culture was defined as patterns of behavior, actions, and customs (D'Andrade 1984; Shweder 1984). This notion still retains popular credibility, as evidenced by Rainbow curriculum opponent Olivia Banks's earlier charge that gay people lack unique food or clothing.

As the behaviorist paradigm eroded across the disciplines, ideas about culture shifted. Anthropologists argued that culture is constituted by shared information, knowledge, or symbols—that is, through Geertz's popular notion of "webs of significance" (Geertz 1973: 5). As we will see, this definition introduced complexity not only for gay people but for other cultural groups as well, because it brought to the foreground problems of cultural unity and of how extensively knowledge and symbols are shared within social groups.

The literature on lesbian and gay social organization, until very recently, addressed these two concepts of culture: that of patterns of behavior and customs, and that of shared symbolic systems. With some exceptions (Browning 1993; Ferguson 1990; Grover 1988), there is consensus that lesbians and gay men constitute a community with a distinct culture. This has been argued on a number of fronts. Murray (1979), for example, examined changes in social science definitions of community, from that of a discrete entity to that of a process, and pointed out the lack of a well-defined and agreed-upon definition. Nevertheless, from his studies of Toronto and San Francisco (Murray 1992), he argued that the gay community meets all of the "modes of social relations" inherent in the various definitions of communities. Historians have detailed the elaborate array of social institutions as evidence of a gay community (D'Emilio 1983; Weeks 1979). These include churches, health and counseling clinics, newspapers and other media, sports teams, theater companies, travel agencies, and much more. As lesbian and gay history becomes more articulated, it is clear that community institutions (for example, the urban lesbian bar before Stonewall) were instrumental in supporting not only relationships but identity (Kennedy and Davis 1993). These studies highlight the important dialectical relationship between community and identity.

In the debate about lesbian/gay culture, it is perhaps less complicated, although by no means easy, to bring the behavioral aspects of culture into the foreground. Thus, in reply to Banks's remark on the Rainbow curriculum that gay people share no common artifacts, a gay man retorted, "We do have a culture. We do have our own literature. We have our own artworks. We have music that would be identifiable to lesbian and gay people" (Madson 1993: 6). Weeks (1979) has described a substantial gay argot as evidence of a culture; Bronski (1984) has discussed gay male sensibility in movies, theater, opera, and pornography. Altman (1982) noted an issue of the *Soho News* in which quiche and Perrier are designated as "the gay food." Clothing is an important cultural signifier, especially for a group whose members need help in recognizing each other. Kennedy and Davis (1993) have described how lesbians in the 1940s and 1950s learned to dress in ways that would both reinforce their sexual identity and signal it to other lesbians.

It has been possible to identify behavioral signifiers of lesbian/gay culture, but it is more difficult to argue the existence of shared symbolic systems of knowledge or information. Bronski offered perhaps the most comprehensive argument with his early, important formulation of the gay (male) sensibility; this formulation, although historically situated, assumes a somewhat determinist aspect. Some of the new anthropological scholarship is more successful in empirically describing the construction of historically specific lesbian and gay communities, with complex systems of cultural meanings (Kennedy and Davis 1993; Newton 1993). These studies reveal how meaning systems within lesbian/gay communities are located along axes of difference, particularly those of race, class, and gender. Although knowledge and symbols may be shared, such a process is inevitably partial and fragmented.

The inability to conclusively demonstrate shared symbolic systems among lesbians and gay men speaks not to the absence of cultural status but to the inadequacy of theory that totalizes culture. In a discussion of "warring factions" among the organizers of the 1993 lesbian and gay march on Washington, Goldstein stated, "Anyone who knows the gay community is aware that it stands for many things, some quite contradictory" (1993). Cultural theory is increasingly rejecting earlier perspectives that highlighted unity in favor of the recognition of internal contradiction and multiplicity. As Clifford notes, "If 'culture' is not an object to be described, neither is it a unified corpus of symbols and meanings that can be definitively interpreted. Culture is contested, temporal, and emergent" (1986:19). New theoretical articulations of culture and identity have had important implications for the activism and scholarship of all social groups.

Destabilizing Theory

Contemporary debates about culture and identities, as they are enacted in popular discourse such as that concerning the Rainbow curriculum, are infused with notions such as permanence, tradition, and (often implicitly) the imperative for a biological essence. Racial categories almost uniformly meet such criteria; their allegedly stable boundaries are policed by biological markers. On the other hand, sexual identity (read "homosexuality") is found wanting. Critics charge that at its best, the lesbian/gay community is a random group of individuals who have perversely chosen a deviant lifestyle. At its worst, it is a random group which must seduce vulnerable others in order to perpetuate itself. Not surprisingly, this charge can inspire a strategy on the part of some lesbians and gay men of asserting biological origins for their sexuality in the belief that essentialism is a precondition for legitimacy. Emerging multicultural theoretical and political initiatives problematize all of these areas of assumed knowledge, such as the immutability of culture, the construction and meaning of racial and sexual identities, the stability of social categories, and the nature and politics of difference.

These disruptions of the "common sense" arose from the synergistic power of social construction theory (with roots in symbolic interactionism), poststructuralist theory, cultural studies, and multicultural studies as represented by African-American and ethnic studies, women's studies, and lesbian and gay studies or queer theory. These theories have been both shaped and informed by political movements organized around race, ethnicity, gender, and sexuality.[7] In the briefest summary, these critical theories challenge the idea of fixed or essential social identities and raise a persistent question about the historical and political circumstances under which subjectivities are continually recreated. Identities and social categories are recognized as fluid and unstable, but also as multiple and internally contradictory. Narratives of social location therefore must account for the intersectionality of identities. The impulse to destabilize assumed social knowledge is common to these theories.

Poststructuralism and lesbian/gay studies have not necessarily eliminated earlier ideas about culture, but have enlarged and decentered them. If, as some theorists have suggested (e. g., Alexander 1992), culture is a meaningful set of symbolic patterns that can be read as a text, poststructuralism insists that there will be multiple interpretations of such readings, as of texts. Dimensions of culture, whether values, shared language or slang, geography, subjective beliefs, or symbolic systems, are not universal, deterministic, or static. Cultural artifacts, subjectivities, and identities are more fragmented and divided. These theories call into question the nature and meaning of all cultural groups by challenging the authenticity of any one culture, by suggesting that the meaning of culture will vary historically and contextually, and by observing that cultural identifications are multiple and overlapping.

Because the categories of race and sexual identity were so frequently positioned in opposition to each other in mainstream debates over the Rainbow curriculum, it is instructive to recognize scholarship that questions the authenticity of an essentially racial culture and identity. Critical race theorists have deployed the insight that identity does not reflect an essential self in arguing that race and ethnicity are constituted not in biology, but in ongoing social and political processes. This is a powerfully radical theoretical challenge in light of the seemingly very visible and immutable quality of race, as compared with the seeming invisibility of sexual identity. Skin color, Stuart Hall (1989, 1992b) argues, has nothing to do with blackness "People are all sorts of colors. The question is whether you are *culturally, historically, politically* Black" (1989:15). Rather than an objective, natural category, race is an unstable "complex of social meanings constantly being transformed by political struggle" (Omi and Winant 1986: 68). Race, then, is an identity that people are not born with but must assume in an ongoing process of identification.

The indeterminacy of biology and the construction of racial identities inform a range of painful narratives by critical race theorists about skin color, passing, and the impact of cruel and oppressive racial meanings generated both by the dominant culture and in communities of color (for some recent examples see Carter 1993; Dent 1992; Loury 1993; McKnight 1993; Njeri 1993; Russell, Wilson, and Hall 1992; for an analysis of the social construction of whiteness, see Frankenberg 1993). The conviction that racial identity is a process, but also (significantly) that it is a choice, is thematic to these accounts. As Carter insists, "Race is a claim. A choice. A decision" (1993: 79). Yet he goes on to acknowledge the impact of external social institutions and meanings:

> Oh, it is imposed, too. The society tells us: "You are black because we say so." Skin color is selected as one of many possible characteristics of morphology used for sorting. Never mind the reasons. It is simply so. It is not, however, logically entailed (1993: 79).

These critical theories therefore challenge racial essentialism, emphasize the process of individual identification, and analyze the social, political, and economic process of racial formation (Omi and Winant 1986). They historicize the process by which skin color became the basis for the invention of racial categories, and the ways in which these categories mapped new identities not only for persons of color, but also for whites. Inevitably these theories complicate any simple notions of stable and monolithic racial cultures and communities.

Lesbian and gay studies, informed by social construction theory and most recently by queer theory, have undertaken a similar intellectual project. This field has placed sexuality in the foreground as a category which, like gender and race, must be central to social analyses. Social construction theory, which denies the existence of a natural, biological sexuality, has provided the infrastructure for research on the production, organization, and regulation of sexuality. Constructionists argue that sexual acts, identities, and communities are imbued with meaning through social and historical processes; indeed, sexual desire itself may well be socially constructed (Vance 1991). Lesbian and gay scholarship examines the historical invention of sexual identities and communities, the ways in which power is infused and deployed through sexual categories, and the complicated relationships between sexuality and other social categories such as gender, race, and class. (Although it is impossible to cite all of this scholarship, some important works include Beam 1986; Chauncey 1982; D'Emilio 1983; D'Emilio and Freedman 1988; Duberman et al. 1989; Foucault 1978; Hull, Scott, and Smith 1982; Jackson 1993; Katz 1976; Kennedy and Davis 1993; Lorde 1988; Peterson 1992; Rubin 1975, 1984; Weeks 1979, 1981, 1985, 1991.)

Queer theory builds on social constructionism to further dismantle sexual identities and categories. Drawing on postmodern critiques, the new theoretical deployment of queerness recognizes the instabilities of traditional oppositions such as lesbian/gay and heterosexual. Queerness is often used as an inclusive signifier for lesbian, gay, bisexual, transgender, drag, straights who pass as gay (Powers 1993), and any permutation of sex/gender dissent (see de Lauretis 1991; Doty 1993; Duggan 1992). It is an encompassing identity that simultaneously challenges and resists the calcification of identities and categories. Also, the use of the term *queer* is not unanimously celebrated; some scholars question the historiographic usefulness of deconstructing a marginal identity at a critical moment of activism and scholarship (Penn 1993).[8] Foremost, however, among the tasks of a queer project are challenges to seemingly stable categories—lesbianism and gayness as well as the heterosexuality.

Together, the overlapping intellectual projects of postmodernism, cultural studies, critical race theories, and lesbian/gay studies and queer theory serve as powerful challenges to traditional notions of culture and identity. Cultures cannot be understood simply as a static and historically consistent aggregate of shared practices or knowledge. Rather, they are dynamic processes which, as Clifford notes, "do not hold still for their portraits" (1986:10). Further, critical theories emphasize that cultures, as the construction of social categories on the basis of physiological characteristics or sexual expression, are products of human agency. Cultures are social inventions, not biological inevitabilities. None is more authentic than another.

These deconstructions, however, do not suggest that cultures are so amorphous and so diffuse that they defy social analysis. Nor do they imply that identities are so fluid as to be easily tried on and shrugged off, thus becoming culturally and individually meaningless. Rather, they insist on a recognition of the paradoxes of culture and identity: we need cultural identities for social location, even while we must maintain continual awareness of their constructed nature; social movements simultaneously challenge and reinforce the importance and meanings of identities. In the women's movement, this dilemma has been articulated by Ann Snitow as the "recurring feminist divide"—that is, the imperative to "build the identity 'woman' and give it solid political meaning and the need to tear down the very category 'woman' and dismantle its all-too-solid history" (1989: 205). Similarly, gay social historian Jeffrey Weeks speaks of sexual identities as "necessary fictions" (1991: viii), a term that neatly encompasses the paradox. Finally, Stuart Hall describes an "ethnicity of the margins, of the periphery" (1992b: 258), which supports the recognition that we all speak from a particular social and historical standpoint without being contained by that position. This recurrent tension demands fuller articulation in both our theories and our politics.

Back to the Rainbow: Sociology and Theory

This review of historical and theoretical scholarship on the invention of racial and sexual cultures and identities highlights its centrality to analyses of debates such as those over the Rainbow curriculum. The arguments that only racial/ethnic groups have culture, while lesbians and gay men are aberrant individuals, can be understood only through the theoretical lenses of new African-American scholarship on the social construction of race and of literature by lesbian and gay scholars on the historical invention of culture and sexual identity. These theories suggest that all cultures are constructed and unstable; none have more authenticity than others. In addition, the insights of lesbian and gay theory—that sexuality is a major social category giving rise to structures of inequality and patterns of discrimination and invisibility—are obviously crucial to this analysis.

The enterprises of lesbian and gay studies and of African-American and ethnic studies concern the invention of racial and sexual cultures. Yet they also address other central aspects of the Rainbow debates, such as the construction of self and identities, the instability, multiplicity, and dynamism of cultures, and the limitations of essentialized identities. Further, any effective analysis of the volatile and often destructive debates about the Rainbow curriculum also must untangle the complicated relations of power and difference in the clash of separate and overlapping cultural identifications. For example, gay people were pitted against people of color; thus, complex permutations of racism and homophobia were triggered. Often silenced in the debate were lesbians and gay men of color.

In this area of power, difference, and multiple identifications, programs such as cultural studies, ethnic studies, women's studies, and lesbian and gay studies are developing important theory. Beyond a recognition of the invention of cultures lies its day-to-day working out, the discursive formations (Jackson 1993) in which meanings are constituted through fluid negotiations of race, gender, sexual identity, and other social categories. We need theory that affords an understanding of our structural and interpersonal positions as they are configured through power and difference. Also, scholars and activists are engaged in the complicated practice of theorizing and historicizing cultural identities within a simultaneous awareness of their fragility. These dialogues could be central to sociology.

Several themes raised by current popular debates about culture might concern us as theorists while we develop more fully the idea of culture, and of sexual cultures, as deployed and manifested among people without "inherent" shared identities. As we explore the specific processes by which all cultures are constructed, we must articulate more clearly the complexities of social construction theory and must clarify common misunderstandings.[9] Further questions for sociologists concern the complications inherent in cultures and identities that are constructed around seemingly biological categories such as race, ethnicity, and gender. How can we understand and reconcile the needs of some people, often generated by legal and political strategizing, to more deeply essentialize such categories, even while others, through historical and social research, are demonstrating their radically constructed nature? In these debates, how does scientific inquiry function to reinforce particular ideologies about culture and identity? Can the histories of other oppressed groups seeking to achieve political rights and cultural legitimacy yield insights into recent attempts to biologize sexual identity more fully? Is it inevitable, in a context of deprivation and marginality, that different cultural groups will compete for status and resources? Finally, given that individuals have multiple subject positions, can we more fully develop theories that give voice to inter sectional identities (Crenshaw 1992) rather than forcing people to choose one standpoint, such as race, over another, such as sexual identity or gender?

It is reasonable to expect that sociologists, for whom the study of social groups is the central task, would theorize these cultural dilemmas. Yet to do so, sociological theory must be more responsive to the insights of lesbian and gay and other multicultural theorists, placing social categories such as sexuality and race in the foreground in the context of power and difference. In 1992 Richard Perry wrote an article titled "Why Do Multiculturalists Ignore Anthropologists?" His argument, among others, was that anthropologists have much to offer multicultural scholars outside the discipline about the study of cultures. This point is well taken, and certainly can be made about the potential contributions of sociologists as well. On the other hand, an equally pertinent question is "Why have the traditional disciplines, sociology among them, not enthusiastically engaged in the important historical and theoretical work of multicultural groups such as lesbian and gay studies?" Sexuality and culture will continue to be central social issues; as such, they are central to our discipline as well.

Notes

1. Designed as a guide for teachers, the Rainbow curriculum contained lessons on the artifacts, folk songs, and holidays of other cultures. It was based on the premise that children could be taught basic lessons in mathematics, grammar, and reading by using the games, songs and dances indigenous to a wide range of cultures.

   The controversy over the curriculum centered on brief sections, in fact merely six entries in a 443-page document, which discussed lesbian and gay families. One section noted, "The issues surrounding family may be very sensitive for children. Teachers should be aware of varied family structures including two-parent or single-parent households, gay or lesbian parents, divorced parents, adoptive parents, and guardians or foster parents. Children must be taught to acknowledge the positive aspects of each type of household and the importance of love and care in family living." It went on to say that children growing up in families headed by heterosexuals "may be experiencing contact with lesbians/gays for the first time . . . teachers of first graders have an opportunity to give children a healthy sense of identity at an early age. Classes should include references to lesbians/gay people in all curricular areas. Educators have the potential to help increase the tolerance and acceptance of the lesbian/gay community and to decrease the staggering number of hate crimes perpetrated against them." The curriculum emphasized the recognition of lesbian/gay culture; nowhere was there any mention of sex.

2. Sociological theory has certainly informed cultural studies, particularly in Britain. Sociologist Stuart Hall (1990) describes the formation of the Centre for Cultural Studies at the University of Birmingham by a handful of scholars who were marginal to academic life. He notes how sociologists attacked their work even while these new cultural theorists "raided" sociology and other traditional disciplines for theory, which they then rearticulated. Cultural studies served as a challenge to traditional sociology. As Hall notes, they took the risk of saying to sociologists "that what they say sociology is, is not what it is. We had to teach what we thought a kind of sociology that would be of service to people studying culture would be something we could not get from self-designated sociologists" (1990: 16).

3. For example, an examination of the list of contributors to the proceedings of a large international conference on cultural studies, held in 1990 reveals very few sociologists. See Grossberg, Nelson and Treichler (1992).

4. This is a complicated dynamic that is impossible to fully explore in this article. Although homophobia in certain communities of color certainly contributed to these tensions and formulations, opponents in certain historically racist, white, working-class sections of Queens and Brooklyn inflamed fears and misunderstandings by distorting the curriculum and appealing to anxieties of racial groups they had previously ignored. In a complicated and often ignored role in the debates were lesbians and gay men of color.

5. Some lesbians and gay men, however, are developing political strategies for legitimacy based on the alleged and unproved biological origins of homosexuality.

6. Not only people of color are voicing this threat. For example, Dolores Ayling of Concerned Parents for Educational Accountability (a religious right group that organized to oppose the curriculum) spoke of the outrage at the fact that sexual orientation is included in the Rainbow curriculum in a way that detracts from the authenticity of race as a cultural category (personal conversation, April 14, 1993). Many of these white advocates had not previously been noted for their vigorous support of communities of color.

7. See J. L. Newton (1989) for a discussion of how early feminist politics articulated current postmodernist critiques such as the absence of a "universal humanity," the cultural construction of subjectivity, and the interaction of representation and social relations. See Hall (1992a) for an examination of the role of feminism and critical race theories in shaping cultural studies.

8. This concern about the dismantling of the categories "lesbian" and "gay" echoes those expressed by other scholars regarding postmodern critiques of identity. Some theorists have noted how the critique of stable identities and of authoritative experience has emerged at precisely a moment of increasing subjectivity, visibility, and production of knowledge among historically marginalized groups such as women, lesbians and gay men, and people of color. Similarly, the important recognitions of the limitations of identity politics as an expression of static, homogeneous, and essential self-groupings have been coterminous with a vital activism among such groups. See, for example, de Lauretis (199[1]).

9. Misconceptions about social construction theory have most typically arisen from its use in the area of sexuality. Expansion and clarification are important because of the widespread relevance of constructionism for theorizing issues of culture and identity. First, the constructionist analysis is often mistakenly glossed as one which insists that individual sexual desires and directions are learned and not inborn. Yet constructionism goes far beyond the familiar nature-nurture debates. Social construction theory does not simply speak about the origins of sexuality, but examines the attribution of meaning to sexual desires, behaviors, and communities. Further, it challenges the notion that

there is any historical or cross-cultural consistency to sexual acts, beliefs, or practices. Second, to suggest that sexuality is socially constructed is not to say that it is a fluid, changeable process open to intentional redefinition" (Epstein 1987: 22). Social constructionists have not fully theorized the ways in which sexual desires, feelings, and beliefs are mediated by sociocultural factors and, in many people, result in deeply felt inclinations that may then be socialized into sexual identities. This theoretical gap should not be misconstrued as a suggestion that "constructedness" implies a superficial and easily unlearned sexuality. These misconceptions simply highlight areas in which sociologists might articulate social construction theory more fully, particularly in the relationships among social ideologies, individual desires and experiences, and individual and social identities. See Vance (1991) for an excellent theoretical clarification of social constructionism.

References

Alba, Richard D. 1990. *Ethnic Identity: The Transformation of White America*. New Haven: Yale University Press.

Alexander, Jeffrey C. 1992. "The Promise of a Cultural Sociology: Technological Discourse and the Sacred and Profane Information Machine." Pp. 293–223 in *Theory of Culture*, edited by Richard Munch and Neil J. Smelser. Berkeley: University of California Press.

Alexander, Jeffrey C. and Steven Seidman. 1990. *Culture and Society: Contemporary Debates*. Cambridge, UK: Cambridge University Press.

Almaguer, Tomas. 1991 "Chicano Men: A Cartography of Homosexual Identity and Behavior," *differences* 3 (2): 75–100.

Altman, Dennis. 1982. *The Homosexualization of America*. Boston: Beacon.

Banks, Olivia. 1993. *The Rainbow Curriculum: 60 Minutes*. April 4.

Bayer, Richard. 1981. *Homosexuality and American Psychiatry: The Politics of Diagnosis*. New York: Basic Books.

Beam, Joseph 1986. *In the Life: A Gay Black Anthology*. Boston: Alyson.

Becker, Howard. 1963. *Outsiders Studies in the Sociology of Deviance*. New York: Free Press.

Bellah, Robert N., Richard Madsen, William M. Sullivan, Ann Swidler, and Steven T. Tipton. 1985. *Habits of the Heart*. Berkeley: University of California Press.

Blassingame, John. 1971. *New Perspectives on Black Studies*. Chicago: University of Illinois Press.

Bourdieu, Pierre. 1968. "Outline of a Theory of Art Perception." *International Social Science Journal* 2 (4): 589–612.

Bradley, Ed. 1993. *The Rainbow Curriculum: 60 Minutes*. April 4.

Bronski, Michael. 1984. *Culture Clash: The Making of Gay Sensibility*. Boston: South End Press.

Browning, Frank. 1993. *The Culture of Desire: Paradox and Perversity in Gay Lives Today*. New York: Crown.

Carter, Stephen I. 1993. "The Black Table, the Empty Seat and the Tie." Pp. 55–79 in *Lure and Loathing: Essays on Race Identify, and the Ambivalence of Assimilation*, edited by Gerald Early. New York: Penguin.

Chauncey, George, Jr. 1982. "From Sexual Inversion to Homosexuality: Medicine and the Changing Conceptualization of Female Deviance." *Salmagundi* 58–59: 114–46.

——. 1989. "Christian Brotherhood or Sexual Perversion? Homosexual Identities and the Construction of Sexual Boundaries in the World War I Era" Pp. 294–317 in *Hidden from History: Reclaiming the Gay and Lesbian Past*, edited by Martin Dubennan, Martha Vicinus, and George Chauncey, Jr. New York: Penguin.

Clifford, James. 1986. "Introduction: Partial Truths." Pp. 1–26 in *Writing Culture: The Poetics and Politics of Ethnography*, edited by James Clifford and George E. Marcus. Berkeley: University of California Press.

Collins, Patricia Hill. 1986. "Learning from the Outsider Within: The Sociological Significance of Black Feminist Thought." *Social Problems* 33: S14–S32.

——. 1990. *Black Feminist Thought: Knowledge Consciousness and the Politics of Empowerment*. Boston: Unwin Hyman.

Conrad, Peter and Joseph Schneider. 1992. *Deviance and Medicalization: From Badness to Sickness*. Philadelphia: Temple University Press.

Crenshaw, Kimberley. 1992. "Whose Story Is It, Anyway? Feminist and Antiracist Appropriations of Anita Hill." Pp. 402–440 in *Race-ing Justice, En-gendering Power: Essays on Anita Hill, Clarence Thomas, and the Construction of Social Reality*, edited by Toni Morrison. New York: Pantheon.

D'Andrade, Roy G. 1984. "Cultural Meaning Systems." Pp. 88–119 in *Culture Theory: Essays on Mind, Self and Emotion*, edited by Richard A. Shweder and Robert A. LeVine. Cambridge: Cambridge University Press.

D'Angelo, Laura. 1992. "Repercussions Continue after School Board Vote." *Stolen Island Sunday Advance*, September 6.

de Lauretis, Teresa. 1991. "Queer Theory: Lesbian and Gay Sexualities." *differences* 3: iii–xviii.

D'Emilio, John. 1983. *Sexual Politics, Sexual Communities: The Making of a Homosexual Minority in the United States, 1940–1970*. Chicago: University of Chicago Press.

D'Emilio, John and Estelle Freedman. 1988. *Intimate Matters: A History of Sexuality in America*. New York: Harper and Row.

Dent, Gina. 1992. *Black Popular Culture*. Seattle: Bay Press.

Doty, Alexander. 1993. *Making Things Perfectly Queer: Interpreting Mass Culture*. Minneapolis: University of Minnesota Press.

Duberman, Martin, Martha Vicinus, and George Chauncey, Jr. 1989. *Hidden from History: Re-*

claiming the Gay and Lesbian Past. New York: Penguin Books.

Duggan, Lisa. 1992. "Making It Perfectly Queer" *Socialist Review* 22: 11–32.

Epstein, Steven. 1987. "Gay Politics, Ethnic Identity: The Limits of Social Constructionism." *Socialist Review* (93–94): pages 9–54.

Faderman, Lillian. 1981. *Surpassing the Love of Men.* New York: Morrow.

Ferguson, Ann. 1990. "Is There a Lesbian Culture?" Pp. 63–88 in *Lesbian Philosophies and Cultures,* edited by Jeffner Allen. Albany: SUNY Press.

Ford, Nick Aaron. 1973. *Black Studies: Threat-or-Challenge.* Port Washington, NY: Kennikat.

Foucault, Michel. 1978. *The History of Sexuality: An Introduction.* Vol. 1. New York: Vintage.

Frankenberg, Ruth. 1993. *White Women, Race Matters: The Social Construction of Whiteness.* Minneapolis: University of Minnesota Press.

Friedson, Eliot. 1970. *Profession of Medicine: A Study of the Sociology of Applied Knowledge.* New York: Harper & Row.

Gagnon, John. 1977. *Human Sexualities.* Glenview, IL: Scott Foresman.

Gagnon, John and William Simon. 1973. *Sexual Conduct: The Social Sources of Human Sexuality.* Chicago: Aldine.

Geertz, Clifford. 1973. *The Interpretation of Cultures.* New York: Basic Books.

Giddens, Anthony. 1992. *The Transformation of Intimacy: Sexuality, Love and Eroticism in Modern Societies.* Stanford: Stanford University Press.

Goffman, Erving. 1963. *Stigma: Notes on the Management of Spoiled Identity.* New York: Simon and Schuster.

Goldstein, Richard. 1993. "Faith, Hope, and Sodomy: Gay Liberation Embarks on a Vision Quest" *Village Voice,* June 29, pp. 21–31.

Grossberg, Lawrence, Gary Nelson and Paula Treichler, eds. 1992. *Cultural Studies.* New York: Routledge.

Grover, Jan Z. 1988. "AIDS: Keywords." Pp. 17–30 in *AIDS Cultural Analysis: Cultural Activism,* edited by Douglas Crimp. Cambridge, MA: Mil Press.

Gusfield, Joseph R. 1955. *Symbolic Crusade.* Urbana: University of Illinois Press.

Hall, John R. and Mary Jo Neitz. 1993. *Culture: Sociological Perspectives.* Englewood Cliffs, NJ: Prentice-Hall.

Hall, Stuart. 1989. "Ethnicity: Identity and Difference" *Radical America.* 23: 9–20.

——. 1990. "The Emergence of Cultural Studies and the Crisis of the Humanities." October (Summer): 11–23.

——. 1992a. "Cultural Studies and Its Theoretical Legacies." Pp. 277–294 in *Cultural Studies* edited by Lawrence Grossberg, Cary Nelson, and Paula Treichler. New York: Routledge.

——. 1992b. "New Ethnicities" Pp. 252–259 in *'Race' Culture and Difference* edited by James Donald and Ali Rattansi. London: Sage.

Halperin, David. 1990. *One Hundred Years of Homosexuality.* New York: Routledge.

Herdt, Gilbert. 1992. *Gay Culture in America: Essays from the Field.* Boston: Beacon.

Hu-DeHart, Evelyn. 1993. "Rethinking America: The Practice and Politics of Muiticulturalism in Higher Education." Pp. 3–17 in *Beyond a Dream Deferred: Multicultural Education and the Politics of Excellence,* edited by Becky W. Thompson and Sangeeta Tyagi. Minneapolis: University of Minnesota Press.

Hull, Gloria, Patricia Bell Scott, and Barbara Smith. 1982. *All the Women Are White, All the Blacks Are Men, But Some of Us Are Brave.* Westbury, NY: Feminist Press.

Humphries, Laud. 1974. *Tearoom Trade: Impersonal Sex in Public Places.* Chicago: Aldine.

Irvine, Janice M. 1990. *Disorders of Desire: Sex and Gender in Modern American Sexology.* Philadelphia: Temple University Press.

——. 1994. *Sexual Cultures and the Construction of Adolescent Identities.* Philadelphia: Temple University Press.

Jackson, Earl, Jr. 1993. "The Responsibility of and to Differences: Theorizing Race and Ethnicity in Lesbian and Gay Studies" Pp. 131–161 in *Beyond a Dream Deferred: Multicultural Education and the Politics of Excellence,* edited by Becky W. Thompson and Sangeeta Tyagi. Minneapolis: University of Minnesota Press.

Katz, Jonathan. 1976. *Gay American History.* New York: Crowell.

——. 1990. "The Invention of Heterosexuality." *Socialist Review* 21: 7–34.

Kennedy, Elizabeth Lapovsky and Madeline D. Davis. 1993. *Boots of Leather, Slippers of Gold: The History of a Lesbian Community.* New York: Routledge.

Kinsey, Alfred C., Wardell B. Pomeroy, Clyde E. Martin, and Paul H. Gebhard. 1948. *Sexual Behavior in the Human Male.* Philadelphia: Saundeis.

——. 1953. *Sexual Behavior in the Human Female.* New York: Pocket Books.

Lorde, Audre. 1988. *A Burst of Light.* Ithaca: Firebrand Books.

Loury, Glenn C. 1993. "Free at Last? A Personal Perspective on Race and Identity in America." Pp. 1–12 in *Lure and Loathing: Essays on Race Identity, and the Ambivalence of Assimilation,* edited by Gerald Early. New York: Penguin.

Luker, Kristen. 1975. *Taking Chances: Abortion and the Decision Not to Contracept.* Berkeley: University of California Press.

Madson, Ron. 1993. *The Rainbow Curriculum: 60 Minutes.* April 4.

McKnight, Reginald. 1993. "Confessions of a Wannabe Negro." Pp. 95–112 in *Lure and Loathing: Essays on Race, Identity, and the Ambivalence of Assimilation,* edited by Gerald Early. New York: Penguin.

Munch, Richard and Neil J. Smelser. 1992. *Theory of Culture.* Berkeley: University of California Press.

Murray, Stephen O. 1979. "The Institutional Elaboration of a Quasi-Ethnic Community." *International Review of Modern Sociology* 9: 165–177.

——. 1992. "Components of Gay Community in San Francisco." Pp. 107–146 in *Gay Culture in America: Essays from the Field*, edited by Gilbert Herdt. Boston: Beacon.

Nelson, Cary, et al. 1992. "Cultural Studies: An Introduction." Pp. 1–16 in *Cultural Studies*, edited by Lawrence Grossberg, Cary Nelson, Paula Treichler. New York: Routledge.

Newton, Esther. 1984. "The Mythic Mannish Lesbian: Radclyffe Hall and the New Woman." *Signs* 9: 556–575.

——. 1993. *Cherry Grove: Pleasure Island, Gay and Lesbian U.S.A., 1930s–1980s*. Boston: Beacon.

Njeri, Itabari. 1993. "Sushi and Grits: Ethnic Identity and Conflict in a Newly Multicultural America." Pp. 13–40 in *Lure and Loathing: Essays on Race Identity, and the Ambivalence of Assimilation*, edited by Gerald Early. New York: Penguin.

Omi, Michael and Howard Winant. 1986. *Racial Formation in the United States from the 1960s to the 1980s*. New York: Routledge.

Penn, Donna. 1993. "If It Walks like a Dyke, Talks like a Dyke, It Must Be a Dyke?" Unpublished paper.

Perry, Richard J. 1992. "Why Do Multiculturalists Ignore Anthropologists?" *Chronicle of Higher Education*, March 4, pp. A52.

Peterson, John. 1992. "Black Men and Their Same-Sex Desires and Behaviors." Pp. 147–164 in *Gay Culture in American Essays from the Field*, edited by Gilbert Herdt. Boston: Beacon.

Plummer, Kenneth. 1975. *Sexual Stigma: An Interactionist Account*. London: Routledge.

——. 1981. *The Making of the Modern Homosexual*. London: Hutchinson.

Powers, Ann. 1993. "Queer in the Streets, Straight in the Sheets" *Village Voice*. June 29, p. 24.

Rubin, Gayle. 1975. "The Traffic in Women: Notes on the Political Economy of Sex." Pp. 157–210 in *Toward an Anthropology of Women*, edited by R. Reiter. New York: Monthly Review Press.

——. 1984. "Thinking Sex." Pp. 267–319 in *Pleasure and Danger: Exploring Female Sexuality*, edited by Carole S. Vance. Boston: Routledge.

Russell, Kathy, Midge Wilson, and Ronald Hall. 1992. *The Color Complex: The Politics of Skin Color among African Americans*. New York: Harcourt Brace Jovanovich.

Sedgwick, Eve Kosofsky. 1993. "Epistemology of the Closet." Pp. 45–61 in *The Lesbian and Gay Studies Reader*, edited by Henry Abelove, Michele Aina Barale, and David M. Halperin. New York: Routledge.

Seidman, Steven. 1990. "Substantive Debates." Pp. 217–235 in *Culture and Society*, edited by Jeffrey Alexander and Steven Seidman. New York: Cambridge University Press.

——. 1991. *Romantic Longings: Love in America, 1830–1980*. New York: Routledge.

——. 1992. *Embattled Eros: Sexual Politics and Ethics in Contemporary America*. New York: Routledge.

Shweder, Richard A. 1984. "Anthropology's Romantic Rebellion against the Enlightenment, or There's More to Thinking Than Reason and Evidence." Pp.

27–66 in *Culture Theory: Essays on Mind Self, and Emotion*, edited by Richard A. Shweder and Robert A. LeVine. New York: Cambridge University Press.

Simon, William and John Gagnon. 1973. *Sexual Conduct*. Chicago: Aldine.

Smith-Rosenberg, Carroll. 1985. *Disorderly Conduct: Visions of Gender in Victorian America*. New York: Knopf.

Snitow, Ann. 1989. "Pages from a Gender Diary Dissent ()." 205–224.

Stacey, Judith and Barry Thorne. 1985. "The Missing Feminist Revolution in Sociology." *Social Problems* 32: 301–316.

Starr, Paul. 1982. *The Social Transformation of American Medicine*. New York: Basic Books.

Stein, Arlene. 1993. *Sisters, Sexperts, and Queers*. New York: Plume.

Tabor, Mary W. 1992. "S.I. Drops Gay Issues from Student Guide." *New York Times*. June 9.

Thompson, Becky W. and Sangeeta Tyagi. 1993. *Beyond a Dream Deferred: Multicultural Education and the Politics of Excellence*. Minneapolis: University of Minnesota Press.

Vance, Carole S. 1991. "Anthropology Rediscovers Sexuality: A Theoretical Comment." *Social Science and Medicine* 33: 875–884.

Waters, Mary C. 1990. *Ethnic Options: Choosing Identities in America*. Berkeley: University of California Press.

Weeks, Jeffrey. 197[9]. *Coming Out: Homosexual Politics in Britain from the Nineteenth Century to the Present*. London: Quartet Books.

——. 1981. *Sex, Politics and Society: The Regulation of Sexuality since 1800*. London: Longman.

——. 1985. *Sexuality and Its Discontents: Meanings, Myths and Modern Sexualities*. London: Routledge.

——. 1991. *Against Nature: Essays in History, Sexuality and Identity*. London: Rivers Oram.

Weinberg, George. 1972. *Society and the Healthy Homosexual*. New York: St. Martin's.

West, Cornel. 1993a. "The New Cultural Politics of Difference." Pp. 18–40 in *Beyond a Dream Deferred: Multicultural Education and the Politics of Excellence*, edited by Becky W. Thompson and Sangeeta Tyagi. Minneapolis: University of Minnesota Press.

——. 1993b. *Race Matters*. Boston: Beacon.

Wuthnow, Robert. 1987. *Meaning and Moral Order: Explorations in Cultural Analysis*. Berkeley: University of California Press.

Zola, Irving K. 1972. "Medicine as an Institution of Social Control." *Sociological Review* 20: 487–504.

Discussion Questions

1. This article was published in 1994. Irvine criticizes sociology for ignoring the study of the intersections of race, gender, class, and sexuality. Based on what you have read in this volume and the material you have studied in this course, do you think sociology is still

open to this criticism? Cite examples to support your position.

2. In the years since this article was written, some of the symbols of gay culture or examples of gay sensibility have become part of popular or mass culture. Give some examples of this. Do you think this has reduced, increased, or had no effect on homophobia?

3. Would you object to or support the Rainbow Curriculum being introduced in the schools in your community? Why?

4. Irvine herself asks a number of important questions in the next to last paragraph of the article. One is: "Is it inevitable, in a context of deprivation and marginality, that different cultural groups will compete for status and resources?" Based on this and other readings in this volume, how would you answer that question?

Reprinted from: Janice M. Irvine, "A Place in the Rainbow: Theorizing Lesbian and Gay Culture." In *Sociological Theory*, 12 (2), pp. 232–248. Copyright © 1994 by the American Sociological Association. Reprinted with permission. ✦

48
Women of Color on the Front Line

Celene Krauss

While most of us might associate environmental activism with the work of national organizations headed by White middle-class males, Celene Krauss pivots the center of this discussion to the grass-roots community level environmental activism of working-class White, Black, and American Indian women. What is immediately telling about Krauss' study is her careful grounding in feminist modes of analysis. She wants the reader to know that while dominant ideologies might separate the "public" sphere of politics and power from the "private" sphere of family and home, she wishes to firmly debunk the separation by arguing that, in fact, the experience of everyday life in the home is fundamentally linked to politics and public policy. Therefore, Krauss focuses on the subjective experience of her respondents, allowing the everyday experiences of these working-class women to tell the tale of their solid environmental activism. Gender and class issues, then, become the framework for Krauss' analysis, while race becomes identifiable as a dependent variable of sorts.

Krauss first identifies why all these working-class women became grassroots environmental activists. The answer: their love for their children and their families. In fact, the women maintained that it was because they were caring mothers that they became politically active—a clear overturning of the public-private argument. In addition, as working-class women, their experience was based in extended family/community resource networks, not isolated nuclear, middle-class constructs of family, which made neighborhoods and communities fundamental to their survival. From this perspective, it was essentially the lives of their children and families and their whole way of life that were at stake when it came to toxic dump-

ing in their communities. It was on the axis of race that their stories differed.

White working-class women told stories of marrying young and wanting nothing more than to be good wives and mothers. These women came to the table with a fundamental trust in government. Indeed, these women told Krauss they initially believed that they need only inform the government of the facts and this would take care of everything. Over time, these women learned to distrust what they came to see as a government influenced by corporate interests. While class issues framed a lot of their initial activist arguments—critique of corporate government—issues of gender would also come to frame their growth as role models to their children and as wives who wished to alter relationships with their spouses.

Black working-class women, on the other hand, brought none of White women's initial trust in government to the table. Having experienced racist government policies, these women simply saw the toxic dumping issue as one more racist issue to counter—environmental racism. These women also viewed environmental activism within a context of historical and contemporary activism around issues of civil rights, housing, crime, and employment. Moreover, these women underscored their disillusionment with traditional environmental causes, arguing that while environmental groups were often fighting to save parks, they were fighting to save their own children.

While American Indian working class women, like Black women, shared a distrust of government based on racist policies and framed their activism around issues of environmental racism, unique themes emerged from their discussion of activism which differed from both Whites and Blacks. American Indian women described environmental racism from the context of deeply rooted fears of past genocidal practices. In addition, American Indian women grounded their understanding of activism in their experience as women in key tribal leadership positions. Moreover, these women viewed their womanhood as central to a connection with the land—Mother Earth—and did not separate their value for their tribal sovereignty from this essential value for the land.

Toxic waste disposal is a central focus of women's grass-roots environmental activism. Toxic waste facilities are predominantly sited in working-class and low-income communities and communities of color, reflecting the disproportionate burden placed on these communities by a political economy of growth that distributes the costs of economic growth unequally. Spurred by the threat that toxic wastes pose to family health and community survival, female grass-roots activists have assumed the leadership of community environmental struggles. As part of a larger movement for environmental justice, they constitute a diverse constituency, including working-class housewives and secretaries, rural African American farmers, urban residents, Mexican American farm workers, and Native Americans.

These activists attempt to differentiate themselves from what they see as the white, male, middle-class leadership of many national environmental organizations. Unlike the more abstract, issue-oriented focus of national groups, women's focus is on environmental issues that grow out of their concrete, immediate experiences. Female blue-collar activists often share a loosely defined ideology of environmental justice and a critique of dominant social institutions and mainstream environmental organizations, which they believe do not address the broader issues of inequality underlying environmental hazards. At the same time, these activists exhibit significant diversity in their conceptualization of toxic waste issues, reflecting different experiences of class, race, and ethnicity.

This [essay] looks at the ways in which different working-class women formulate ideologies of resistance around toxic waste issues and the process by which they arrive at a concept of environmental justice. Through an analysis of interviews, newsletters, and conference presentations, I show the voices of white, African American, and Native American female activists and the resources that inform and support their protests. What emerges is an environmental discourse that is mediated by subjective experiences and interpretations and rooted in the political truths women construct out of their identities as housewives, mothers, and members of communities and racial and ethnic groups.

The Subjective Dimension of Grass-Roots Activism

Grass-roots protest activities have often been trivialized, ignored, and viewed as self-interested actions that are particularistic and parochial, failing to go beyond a single-issue focus. This view of community grass-roots protests is held by most policymakers as well as by many analysts of movements for progressive social change.

In contrast, the voices of blue-collar women engaged in protests regarding toxic waste issues tell us that single-issue protests are about more than the single issue. They reveal a larger world of power and resistance, which in some measure ends up challenging the social relations of power. This challenge becomes visible when we shift the analysis of environmental activism to the experiences of working-class women and the subjective meanings they create around toxic waste issues.

In traditional sociological analysis, this subjective dimension of protest has often been ignored or viewed as private and individualistic. Feminist theory, however, helps us to see its importance. For feminists, the critical reflection on the everyday world of experience is an important subjective dimension of social change. Feminists show us that experience is not merely a personal, individualistic concept. It is social. People's experiences reflect where they fit in the social hierarchy. Thus, blue-collar women of differing backgrounds interpret their experiences of toxic waste problems within the context of their particular cultural histories, starting from different assumptions and arriving at concepts of environmental justice that reflect broader experiences of class and race.

Feminist theorists also challenge a dominant ideology that separates the "public" world of policy and power from the "private" and personal world of everyday experience. By definition, this ideology relegates the lives and concerns of women relating to home and family to the private, nonpolitical arena, leading to invisibility of their grass-roots protests about issues such as toxic wastes. As Ann Bookman has noted in her important study of working-class women's community struggles, women's political-activism in general, and working-class political life at the community level in particular, remain "peripheral to the historical record . . . where there is a tendency to privilege male political activity and labor activism."[1] The women's movement took as its central task the reconceptualization of the political itself, critiquing this dominant ideology and constructing a new definition of the political located in the everyday world of ordinary women rather than in the world of public policy. Feminists provide a perspective for making visible the importance of particular, single-issue protests regarding toxic wastes by showing how ordinary women subjectively link the particulars of their private lives with a broader analysis of power in the public sphere.

Social historians such as George Rudé have pointed out that it is often difficult to understand the experience and ideologies of resistance because ordinary working people appropriate and reshape traditional beliefs embedded within working-class culture, such as family and community. This point is also relevant for understanding the environmental protests of working-class women. Their protests are framed in terms of the traditions of motherhood and family; as a result, they often appear parochial or even conservative. As we shall see, however, for working-class women, these traditions become the levers that set in motion a political process, shaping the language and oppositional meanings that emerge and providing resources for social change.

Shifting the analysis of toxic waste issues to the subjective experience of ordinary women makes visible a complex relationship between everyday life and the larger structures of public power. It reveals the potential for human agency that is hidden in a more traditional sociological approach and provides us with a means of seeing "the sources of power which subordinated groups have created."[2]

The analysis presented in this [essay] is based on the oral and written voices of women involved in toxic waste protests. Interviews were conducted at environmental conferences such as the First National People of Color Environmental Leadership Summit, Washington, DC, 1991, and the World Women's Congress for a Healthy Planet, Miami, Florida, 1991, and by telephone. Additional sources include conference presentations, pamphlets, books, and other written materials that have emerged from this movement. This research is part of an ongoing comparative study that will examine the ways in which experiences of race, class, and ethnicity mediate women's environmental activism. Future research includes an analysis of the environmental activism of Mexican American women in addition to that of the women discussed here.

Toxic Waste Protests and the Resource of Motherhood

Blue-collar women do not use the language of the bureaucrat to talk about environmental issues. They do not spout data or marshal statistics in support of their positions. In fact, interviews with these women rarely generate a lot of discussion about the environmental problem per se. But in telling their stories about their protest against a landfill or incinerator, they ultimately tell larger stories about their discovery or analysis of oppression. Theirs is a political, not a technical, analysis.

Working-class women of diverse racial and ethnic backgrounds identify the toxic waste movement as a women's movement, composed primarily of mothers. Says one woman who fought against an incinerator in Arizona and subsequently worked on other anti-incinerator campaigns throughout the state, "Women are the backbone of the grass-roots groups; they are the ones who stick with it, the ones who won't back off." By and large, it is women, in their traditional role as mothers, who make the link between toxic wastes and their children's ill health. They discover the hazards of toxic contamination: multiple miscarriages, birth defects, cancer deaths, and so on. This is not surprising, as the gender-based division of labor in a capitalist society gives working-class women the responsibility for the health of their children.

These women define their environmental protests as part of the work that mothers do. Cora Tucker, an African American activist who fought against uranium mining in Virginia and who now organizes nationally, says:

> It's not that I don't think that women are smarter, [she laughs] but I think that we are with the kids all day long. If Johnny gets a cough and Mary gets a cough, we try to discover the problem.

Another activist from California sums up this view: "If we don't oppose an incinerator, we're not doing our work as mothers."

For these women, family serves as a spur to action, contradicting popular notions of family as conservative and parochial. Family has a very different meaning for these women than it does for the middle-class nuclear family. Theirs is a less privatized, extended family that is open, permeable, and attached to community. This more extended family creates the networks and resources that enable working-class communities to survive materially given few economic resources. The destruction of working-class neighborhoods by economic growth deprives blue-collar communities of the basic resources of survival; hence the resistance engendered by toxic waste issues. Working-class women's struggles over toxic waste issues are, at root, issues about survival. Ideologies of motherhood, traditionally relegated to the private sphere, become political resources that working-class women use to initiate and justify their resistance. In the process of protest, working-class women come to reject the dominant ideology, which separates the public and private arenas.

Working-class women's extended network of family and community serves as the vehicle for spreading information and concern about toxic waste issues. Extended networks of kinship and friendship become political resources of opposition. For example, in one community in Detroit, women discovered patterns of health problems while attending Tupperware parties. Frequently, a mother may read about a hazard in a newspaper, make a tentative connection between her own child's ill health and the pollutant, and start telephoning friends and family, developing an informal health survey. Such a discovery process is rooted in what Sarah Ruddick has called the everyday practice of mothering.[3] Through their informal networks, they compare notes and experiences and develop an oppositional knowledge used to resist the dominant knowledge of experts and the decisions of government and corporate officials.

These women separate themselves from "mainstream" environmental organizations, which are seen as dominated by white, middle-class men and concerned with remote issues. Says one woman from Rahway, New Jersey: "The mainstream groups deal with safe issues. They want to stop incinerators to save the eagle, or they protect trees for the owl. But we say, what about the people?"

Another activist implicitly criticizes the mainstream environmental groups when she says of the grass-roots Citizens' Clearinghouse for Hazardous Wastes:

> Rather than oceans and lakes, they're concerned about kids dying. Once you've had someone in your family who has been attacked by the environment—I mean who has had cancer or some other disease—you get a keen sense of what's going on.

It is the traditional, "private" women's concerns about home, children, and family that provide the initial impetus for blue-collar women's involvement in issues of toxic waste. The political analyses they develop break down the public-private distinction of dominant ideology and frame a particular toxic waste issue within broader contexts of power relationships.

The Role of Race, Ethnicity, and Class

Interviews with white, African American, and Native American women show that the starting places for and subsequent development of their analyses of toxic waste protests are mediated by issues of class, race, and ethnicity.

White working-class women come from a culture in which traditional women's roles center on the private arena of family. They often marry young; although they may work out of financial necessity, the primary roles from which they derive meaning and satisfaction are those of mothering and taking care of family. They are revered and supported for fulfilling the ideology of a patriarchal family. And these families often reflect a strong belief in the existing political system. The narratives of white working-class women involved in toxic waste issues are filled with the process by which they discover the injustice of their government, their own insecurity about entering the public sphere of politics, and the constraints of the patriarchal family, which, ironically prevent them from becoming fully active in the defense of their family, especially in their protest. Their narratives are marked by a strong initial faith in "their" government, as well as a remarkable transformation as they become disillusioned with the system. They discover "that they never knew what they were capable of doing in defense of their children."

For white working-class women, whose views on public issues are generally expressed only within family or among friends, entering a more public arena to confront toxic waste issues is often extremely stressful. "Even when I went to the PTA," says one activist, "I rarely spoke. I was so nervous." Says another: "My views have always been strong, but I expressed them only in the family. They were not for the public." A strong belief in the existing political system is characteristic of these women's initial response to toxic waste issues. Lois Gibbs, whose involvement in toxic waste issues started at Love Canal, tells us, "I believed if I had a problem I just had to go to the right person in government and he would take care of it."

Initially, white working-class women believe that all they have to do is give the government the facts and then problem will be taken care of. They become progressively disenchanted with what they view as the violation or their rights and the injustice of a system that allows their children and family to die. In the process, they develop a perspective of environmental justice rooted in issues of class, the attempt to make democracy real, and a critique of the corporate state. Says one activist who fought the siting of an incinerator in Sumter County, Alabama: "We need to stop letting economic development be the true God and religion of this country. We have to prevent big money from influencing our government."

A recurring theme in the narratives of these women is the transformation of their beliefs about government and power. Their politicization is rooted in the deep sense of violation, betrayal, and hurt they feel when they find that their government will not protect their families. Lois Gibbs sums up this feeling well:

> I grew up in a blue-collar community. We were very into democracy. There is something about discovering that democracy isn't democracy as we know it. When you lose faith in your government, it's like finding out your mother was fooling around on your father. I was very upset. It almost broke my heart because I really believed in the system. I still believe in the system, only now I believe that democracy is of the people and by the people, that people have to move it, it ain't gonna move by itself.

Echoes of this disillusionment are heard from white blue-collar women throughout the country. One activist relates:

> We decided to tell our elected officials about the problems of incineration because we didn't think they knew. Surely if they knew that there was a toxic waste dump in our county they would stop it. I was politically naïve. I was real surprised because I live in an area that's like the Bible Belt of the South. Now I think the God of the United States is really economic development, and that has got to change.

Ultimately, these women become aware of the inequities of power as it is shaped by issues of class and gender. Highly traditional values of democracy and motherhood remain central to their lives. But in the process of politicization through their work on toxic waste issues, these values become transformed into resources of opposition that enable women to enter the public arena and challenge its legitimacy. They justify their resistance as a way to make democracy real and to protect their children.

White blue-collar women's stories are stories of transformations; transformations into more self-confident and assertive women; into political activists who challenge the existing system and feel powerful in that challenge; into wives and mothers who establish new relationships with their spouses (or get divorced) and new, empowering relationships with their children as they provide role models of women capable of fighting for what they believe in.

African American working-class women begin their involvement in toxic waste protests from a different place. They bring to their protests a political awareness that is grounded in race and that shares none of the white blue-collar women's initial trust in democratic institutions. These women view government with mistrust, having been victims of racist policies throughout their lives. Individual toxic waste issues are immediately framed within a broader political context and viewed as environmental racism. Says an African American activist from Rahway, New Jersey:

> When they sited the incinerator for Rahway, I wasn't surprised. All you have to do is look around my community to know that we are a dumping ground for all kinds of urban industrial projects that no one else wants. I knew this was about environmental racism the moment that they proposed the incinerator.

An African American woman who fought the siting of a landfill on the South Side of Chicago reiterates this view: "My community is an all-black community isolated from everyone. They don't care what happens to us." She describes her community as a "toxic doughnut":

> We have seven landfills. We have a sewer treatment plant. We have the Ford Motor Company. We have a paint factory. We have numerous chemical companies and steel mills. The river is just a few blocks away from us and is carrying water so highly contaminated that they say it would take seventy-five years or more before they can clean it up.

This activist sees her involvement in toxic waste issues as a challenge to traditional stereotypes of African American women. She says, "I'm here to tell the story that all people in the projects are not lazy and dumb!"

Some of these women share experiences of personal empowerment through their involvement in toxic waste issues. Says one African American activist:

> Twenty years ago I couldn't do this because I was so shy I had to really know you to talk with you. Now I talk. Sometimes I think I talk too much. I waited until my fifties to go to jail. But it was well worth it. I never went to no university or college, but I'm going in there and making speeches.

However, this is not a major theme in the narratives of female African American activists, as it is in those of white blue-collar women. African American women's private work as mothers has traditionally extended to a more public role in the local community as protectors of the race. As a decade of African American feminist history has shown, African American women have historically played a central role in community activism and in dealing with issues of race and economic injustice. They receive tremendous status and recognition from their community. Many women participating in toxic waste protests have come out of a history of civil rights activism, and their environmental protests, especially in the South, develop through community organizations born during the civil rights movement. And while the visible leaders are often male, the base of the organizing has been led by African American women, who, as Cheryl Townsend Gilkes has written, have often been called "race women," responsible for the "racial uplift" of their communities.[4]

African American women perceive that traditional environmental groups only peripherally relate to their concerns. As Cora Tucker relates:

> This white woman from an environmental group asked me to come down to save a park. She said that they had been trying to get black folks involved and that they won't come. I said, "Honey, it's not that they aren't concerned, but when their babies are dying in their arms they don't give a damn about a park." I said, "They want to save their babies. If you can help them save their babies, then in turn they can help you save your park." And she

said, "But this is a real immediate problem." And I said, "Well, these people's kids dying is immediate."

Tucker says that white environmental groups often call her or the head of the NAACP at the last minute to participate in an environmental rally because they want to "include" African Americans. But they exclude African Americans from the process of defining the issues in the first place. What African American communities are doing is changing the agenda.

Because the concrete experience of African Americans' lives is the experience and analysis of racism, social issues are interpreted and struggled with within this context. Cora Tucker's story of attending a town board meeting shows that the issue she deals with is not merely the environment but also the disempowerment she experiences as an African American woman. At the meeting, white women were addressed as Mrs. So-and-So by the all-white, male board. When Mrs. Tucker stood up, however, she was addressed as "Cora":

> One morning I got up and I got pissed off and I said, "What did you call me?" He said, "Cora," and I said, "The name is Mrs. Tucker." And I had the floor until he said "Mrs. Tucker." He waited five minutes before he said "Mrs. Tucker." And I held the floor I said, "I'm Mrs. Tucker," I said, "Mr. Chairman, I don't call you by your first name and I don't want you to call me by mine. My name is Mrs. Tucker. And when you want me, you call me Mrs. Tucker." It's not that—I mean it's not like you gotta call me Mrs. Tucker, but it was the respect.

In discussing this small act of resistance as an African American woman, Cora Tucker is showing how environmental issues may be about corporate and state power, but they are also about race. For female African American activists, environmental issues are seen as reflecting environmental racism and linked to other social justice issues, such as jobs, housing, and crime. They are viewed as part of a broader picture of social inequity based on race. Hence, the solution articulated in a vision of environmental justice is a civil rights vision—rooted in the everyday

experience of racism. Environmental justice comes to mean the need to resolve the broad social inequities of race.

The narratives of Native American women are also filled with the theme of environmental racism. However, their analysis is laced with different images. It is a genocidal analysis rooted in the Native American cultural identification, the experience of colonialism, and the imminent endangerment of their culture. A Native American woman from North Dakota, who opposed a landfill, says:

> Ever since the white man came here, they keep pushing us back, taking our lands, pushing us onto reservations. We are down to 3 percent now, and I see this as just another way for them to take our lands, to completely annihilate our races. We see that as racism.

Like that of the African American women, these women's involvement in toxic waste protests is grounded from the start in race and shares none of the white blue-collar women's initial belief in the state. A Native American woman from southern California who opposed a landfill on the Rosebud Reservation in South Dakota tells us:

> Government did pretty much what we expected them to do. They supported the dump. People here fear the government. They control so many aspects of our life. When I became involved in opposing the garbage landfill, my people told me to be careful. They said they annihilate people like me.

Another woman involved in the protest in South Dakota describes a government official's derision of the tribe's resistance to the siting of a landfill:

> If we wanted to live the life of Mother Earth, we should get a tepee and live on the Great Plains and hunt buffalo.

Native American women come from a culture in which women have had more empowered and public roles than is the case in white working-class culture. Within the Native American community, women are revered as nurturers. From childhood, boys and girls learn that men depend on women for their survival. Women also play a central role in the decision-making process within the tribe. Tribal council membership is often equally divided between men and women; many women are tribal leaders and medicine women. Native American religions embody a respect for women as well as an ecological ethic based on values such as reciprocity and sustainable development: Native Americans pray to Mother Earth, as opposed to the dominant culture's belief in a white, male, Anglicized representation of divinity.

In describing the ways in which their culture integrates notions of environmentalism and womanhood, one woman from New Mexico says:

> We deal with the whole of life and community; we're not separated, we're born into it—you are it. Our connection as women is to the Mother Earth, from the time of our consciousness. We're not environmentalists. We're born into the struggle of protecting and preserving our communities. We don't separate ourselves. Our lifeblood automatically makes us responsible; we are born with it. Our teaching comes from a spiritual base. This is foreign to our culture. There isn't even a word for dioxin in Navajo.

In recent years, Native American lands have become common sites for commercial garbage dumping. Garbage and waste companies have exploited the poverty and lack of jobs in Native American communities and the fact that Native American lands, as sovereign nation territories, are often exempt from local environmental regulations. In discussing their opposition to dumping, Native American women ground their narratives in values about land that are inherent in the Native American community. They see these projects as violating tribal sovereignty and the deep meaning of land, the last resource they have. The issue, says a Native American woman from California, is

> protection of the land for future generations, not really as a mother, but for the health of the people, for survival. Our tribe bases its sovereignty on our land base, and if we lose our land base, then we will be a lost people. We can't afford to take this trash and jeopardize our tribe.

> If you don't take care of the land, then the land isn't going to take care of you. Because everything we have around us involves Mother Earth. If we don't take care of the land, what's going to happen to us?

In the process of protest, these women tell us, they are forced to articulate more clearly their cultural values, which become resources of resistance in helping the tribe organize against a landfill. While many tribal members may not articulate an "environmental" critique, they well understand the meaning of land and their religion of Mother Earth, on which their society is built.

Conclusion

The narratives of white, African American, and Native American women involved in toxic waste protests reveal the ways in which their subjective, particular experiences lead them to analyses of toxic waste issues that extend beyond the particularistic issue to wider worlds of power. Traditional beliefs about home, family, and community provide the impetus for women's involvement in these issues and become a rich source of empowerment as women reshape traditional language and meanings into an ideology of resistance. These stories challenge traditional views of toxic waste protests as parochial, self-interested, and failing to go beyond a single-issue focus. They show that single-issue protests are ultimately about far more and reveal the experiences of daily life and resources that different groups use to resist. Through environmental protests, these women challenge, in some measure, the social relations of race, class, and gender.

These women's protests have different beginning places, and their analyses of environmental justice are mediated by issues of class and race. For white blue-collar women, the critique of the corporate state and the realization of a more genuine democracy are central to a vision of environmental justice. The definition of environmental justice that they develop becomes rooted in the issue of class. For women of color, it is the link between race and environment, rather than between class and environment, that characterizes definitions of environmental justice.

African American women's narratives strongly link environment justice to other social justice concerns, such as jobs, housing, and crime. Environmental justice comes to mean the need to resolve the broad social inequities of race. For Native American women, environmental justice is bound up with the sovereignty of the indigenous peoples.

In these women's stories, their responses to particular toxic waste issues are inextricably tied to the injustice they feel as mothers, as working-class women, as African Americans, and as Native Americans. They do not talk about their protests in terms of single issues. Thus, their political activism has implications far beyond the visible, particularistic concern of a toxic waste dump site or the siting of a hazardous waste incinerator.

Notes

1. Sandra Morgen, "'It's the Whole Power of the City Against Us!': The Development of Political Consciousness in a Women's Health Care Coalition," in *Women and the Politics of Empowerment*, eds. Ann Bookman and Sandra Morgen (Philadelphia: Temple University Press, 1988), p. 97.

2. Sheila Rowbotham, *Women's Consciousness, Man's World* (New York: Penguin, 1973).

3. See Sara Ruddick, *Maternal Thinking: Towards a Politics of Peace* (New York Ballantine, 1989).

4. Cheryl Townsend Gilkes, "Building in Many Places: Multiple Commitments and Ideologies in Black Women's Community Work," in *Women and the Politics of Empowerment*, op. cit.

Discussion Questions

1. How did you respond to Krauss' analysis? What did you like or dislike about Krauss' article?

2. How do you think the experience of Mexican American women's stories of environmental activism might differ from the stories Krauss outlines in this analysis?

3. Does it surprise you that White working class women would be so naïve with regard to the government response to toxic dumping? Why or why not?

4. Have you ever participated in any grassroots activism? Why or why not? What did you participate in?

49
Angry Women Are Building

Issues and Struggles Facing American Indian Women Today

Paula Gunn Allen

The numbers have increased in the two decades since Paula Gunn Allen wrote this chapter. According to the 2000 U.S. Census, the population of those who selected American Indian or Alaskan Native as their only racial/ethnic identity was just shy of 2.5 million. If we add those who selected American Indian or Alaskan Native plus one or more other racial/ethnic categories, the number is well over 2.6 million, slightly more than one percent of the total population. Many other Americans selected a different primary race/ethnicity but indicated that they too had some Indian ancestry. The numbers have increased, but the problems about which she writes angrily and eloquently have not disappeared. American Indian women and communities still suffer from unemployment, poor health, and physical, emotional, and substance abuse. Their physical and cultural survival is still not assured.

Gunn Allen alludes to the history of the relationship between the U.S. government and indigenous peoples. In the eighteenth and nineteenth centuries, land they traditionally occupied was taken from them and they were forced onto reservations where some could carry out only modified forms of their traditional cultures. Later, policies intended to foster assimilation, such as sending children to boarding schools where they were forbidden to use their tribal languages and could not learn or carry out cultural traditions and relocating families to urban communities far from their reservations, were put in place. Although a few tribes today are gaining wealth by operating casinos, for the most part, reservation life is characterized by the lack of material resources and employment and the ready availability of alcohol. Moreover, as Gunn Allen notes, the media, popular culture, and even school texts have depicted American Indian men "as bloodthirsty savages devoted to treating women cruelly." Many of the men have come to believe, and some to act out, this image of themselves and their traditions. Thus, the women are compelled to resist forces from within and without their communities to ensure survival.

The central issue that confronts American Indian women throughout the hemisphere is survival, *literal survival*, both on a cultural and biological level. According to the 1980 census, population of American Indians is just over one million. This figure, which is disputed by some American Indians, is probably a fair estimate, and it carries certain implications.*

Some researchers put our pre-contact population at more than 45 million, while others put it at around 20 million. The U.S. government long put it at 450,000—a comforting if imaginary figure, though at one point it was put at around 270,000. If our current population is around one million; if, as some researchers estimate, around 25 percent of Indian women and 10 percent of Indian men in the United States have been sterilized without informed consent; if our average life expectancy is, as the best-informed research presently says, 55 years; if our infant mortality rate continues at well above national standards; if our average unemployment for all segments of our population—male, female, young, adult, and middle-aged—is between 60 and 90 percent; if the U.S. government continues its policy of termination, relocation, removal, and assimilation along with the destruction of wilderness, reservation land, and its resources, and severe curtailment of hunting, fishing, timber harvesting and water-use rights—then existing tribes are facing the threat of extinction which for several hundred tribal groups has already become fact in the past five hundred years.

437

In this nation of more than 200 million, the Indian people constitute less than one-half of one per cent of the population.** In a nation that offers refuge, sympathy, and billions of dollars in aid from federal and private sources in the form of food to the hungry, medicine to the sick, and comfort to the dying, the indigenous subject population goes hungry, homeless, impoverished, cut out of the American deal, new, old, and in between. Americans are daily made aware of the worldwide slaughter of native peoples such as the Cambodians, the Palestinians, the Armenians, the Jews—who constitute only a few groups faced with genocide in this century. . . . The American Indian people are in a situation comparable to the imminent genocide in many parts of the world today. The plight of our people north and south of us is no better; to the south it is considerably worse. Consciously or unconsciously, deliberately, as a matter of national policy, or accidentally as a matter of "fate," *every single government,* right, left, or centrist in the western hemisphere is consciously or subconsciously dedicated to the extinction of those tribal people who live within its borders.

Within this geopolitical channel house, American Indian women struggle on every front for the survival of our children, our people, our self-respect, our value systems, and our way of life. The past five hundred years testify to our skill at waging this struggle: for all the varied weapons of extinction pointed at our heads, we endure.

We survive war and conquest; we survive colonization, acculturation, assimilation; we survive beating, rape, starvation, mutilation, sterilization, abandonment, neglect, death of our children, our loved ones, destruction of our land, our homes, our past, and our future. We survive, and we do more than just survive. We bond, we care, we fight, we teach, we nurse, we bear, we feed, we earn, we laugh, we love, we hang in there, no matter what.

Of course, some, many of us, just give up. Many are alcoholics, many are addicts. Many abandon the children, the old ones. Many commit suicide. Many become violent, go insane. Many go "white" and are never seen or heard from again. But enough hold on to their traditions and their ways so that even after almost five hundred brutal years, we endure. And we even write songs and poems, make paintings and drawings that say "We walk in beauty. Let us continue."

Currently our struggles are on two fronts: physical survival and cultural survival. For women this means fighting alcoholism and drug abuse (our own and that of our husbands, lovers, parents, children);[1] poverty; affluence—a destroyer of people who are not traditionally socialized to deal with large sums of money; rape, incest, battering by Indian men; assaults on fertility and other health matters by the Indian Health Service and the Public Health Service; high infant mortality due to substandard medical care, nutrition, and health information; poor educational opportunities or education that takes us away from our traditions, language, and communities; suicide, homicide, or similar expressions of self-hatred; lack of economic opportunities; substandard housing; sometimes violent and always virulent racist attitudes and behaviors directed against us by an entertainment and educational system that wants only one thing from Indians: our silence, our invisibility, and our collective death.

A headline in the *Navajo Times* . . . reported that rape was the number one crime on the Navajo reservation. In a professional mental health journal of the Indian Health Services, Phyllis Old Dog Cross reported that incest and rape are common among Indian women seeking services and that their incidence is increasing. "It is believed that at least 80 percent of the Native Women seen at the regional psychiatric service center (five state area) have experienced some sort of sexual assault."[2] Among the forms of abuse being suffered by Native American women, Old Dog Cross cites a recent phenomenon, something called "training." This form of gang rape is "a punitive act of a group of males who band together and get even or take revenge on a selected woman."[3]

These and other cases of violence against women are powerful evidence that the status of women within the tribes has suffered grievous decline since contact, and the decline has increased in intensity in recent years. The amount of violence against women, alcoholism, and violence, abuse, and neglect by women against their children and their aged relatives have all increased. These social ills were virtually unheard of among most tribes fifty years ago, popular American opinion to the contrary. As Old Dog Cross remarks:

Rapid, unstable and irrational change was required of the Indian people if they were to survive. Incredible loss of all that had meaning was the norm. Inhuman treatment, murder, death, and punishment was a typical experience for all the tribal groups and some didn't survive.

The dominant society devoted its efforts to the attempt to change the Indian into a white-Indian. No inhuman pressure to effect this change was overlooked. These pressures included starvation, incarceration and enforced education. Religious and healing customs were banished.

In spite of the years of oppression, the Indian and the Indian spirit survived. Not, however, without adverse effect. One of the major effects was the loss of cultured values and the concomitant loss of personal identity. The Indian was taught to be ashamed of being Indian and to emulate the non-Indian. In short, "white was right." For the Indian male, the only route to be successful, to be good, to be right, and to have an identity was to be as much like the white man as he could.[4]

Often it is said that the increase of violence against women is a result of various sociological factors such as oppression, racism, poverty, hopelessness, emasculation of men, and loss of male self-esteem as their own place within traditional society has been systematically destroyed by increasing urbanization, industrialization, and institutionalization, but seldom do we notice that for the past forty to fifty years, American popular media have depicted American Indian men as blood-thirsty savages devoted to treating women cruelly. While traditional Indian men seldom did any such thing—and in fact among most tribes abuse of women was simply unthinkable, as was abuse of children or the aged—the lie about "usual" male Indian behavior seems to have taken root and now bears its brutal and bitter fruit.

Image casting and image control constitute the central process that American Indian women must come to terms with, for on that control rests our sense of self, our claim to a past and to a future that we define and that we build. Images of Indians in media and educational materials profoundly influence how we act, how we relate to the world and to each other, and how we value ourselves. They also determine to a large extent how our men act toward us, toward our children, and toward each other. The popular American media image of Indian people as savages with no conscience, no compassion, and no sense of the value of human life and human dignity was hardly true of the tribes—however true it was of the invaders. But as Adolf Hitler noted a little over fifty years ago, if you tell a lie big enough and often enough, it will be believed. Evidently, while Americans and people all over the world have been led into a deep and unquestioned belief that American Indians are cruel savages, a number of American Indian men have been equally deluded into internalizing that image and acting on it. Media images, literary images, and artistic images, particularly those embedded in popular culture, must be changed before Indian women will see much relief from the violence that destroys so many lives.

To survive culturally, American Indian women must often fight the United States government, the tribal governments, women and men of their tribe or their urban community who are virulently misogynist or who are threatened by attempts to change the images foisted on us over the centuries by whites. The colonizers' revisions of our lives, values, and histories have devastated us at the most critical level of all—that of our own minds, our own sense of who we are.

Many women express strong opposition to those who would alter our life supports, steal our tribal lands, colonize our cultures and cultural expressions, and revise our very identities. We must strive to maintain tribal status; we must make certain that the tribes continue to be legally recognized entities, sovereign nations within the larger United States, and we must wage this struggle in many ways—political, educational, literary, artistic, individual, and communal. We are doing all we can: as mothers and grandmothers; as family members and tribal members; as professionals, workers, artists, shamans, leaders, chiefs, speakers, writers, and organizers, we daily demonstrate that we have no intention of disappearing, of being silent, or of quietly acquiescing in our extinction.

Notes

1. It is likely, say some researchers, that fetal alcohol syndrome, which is serious among many Indian groups, will be so serious among the White Mountain Apache and the Pine Ridge Sioux that if present trends continue, by the year 2000 some people estimate that almost one-half of all children born on those reservations will in some way be affected by FAS. (Michael Dorris, Native American Studies, Dartmouth College, private conversation. Dorris has done extensive research into the syndrome as it affects native populations in the United States as well as in New Zealand.)

2. Phyllis Old Dog Cross, "Sexual Abuse, a New Threat to the Native American Woman: An Overview," *Listening Post: A Periodical of the Mental Health Programs of Indian Health Services*, vol. 6, no 2 (April 1982), p. 18.

3. Old Dog Cross, p. 18.

4. Old Dog Cross, p. 20.

Editor's Notes

*The 1995 population is over two million.
**In 2000, this figure was one percent.

Discussion Questions

1. With what images of American Indians did you grow up? Where did those images come from? TV and movies? Textbooks? Parents? Were they all negative images? Were they all stereotypes depicting all Indian nations as pretty much the same?

2. What kinds of relationships does Gunn Allen see between Native American men and women today? How does she account for those relationships? Do you think she thinks the situation can be fixed? Do you?

3. Gunn Allen believes that it is important for American Indians to secure and maintain their tribal status and to resist assimilation. What is her reason for these views? Do you agree?

4. When you respond to the U.S. Census, which racial/ethnic category or categories do you select? Now that it is possible to identify yourself as a person with multiple ancestries, do you do so? Are you primarily American Indian, Alaskan Native, or Native Hawaiian? If not, to your knowledge, do you have any American Indian ancestry?

50

The Political Is Personal

The Influence of White Supremacy on White Antiracists' Personal Relationships

Eileen O'Brien

Eileen O'Brien focuses this article on what she calls "antiracists"—people who acknowledge that racism still exists and who work to combat inequality. O'Brien is particularly interested in how White antiracists negotiate their interpersonal relationships with Whites and people of color, arguing that issues of empathy and autonomy come to the fore for White antiracists in a society that is still dealing with issues of racism and white supremacy. In this regard, O'Brien defines her terms for the reader in a larger context. O'Brien argues that White antiracists must strive for true empathy with people of color that is beyond false empathy. False empathy occurs when White antiracists are genuinely interested in challenging issues that concern people color, but ultimately believe that they, White people, know best what people of color really need. False empathy often stems from Whites' lack of understanding of day-to-day issues for people of color. The White antiracist, O'Brien argues, must ultimately strive for autonomy with other Whites, which means development of a White antiracist identity and the ability to extend true empathy to Whites regardless of whether they are antiracists or not. In O'Brien's analysis, race is the backdrop for the study, while class and gender become apparent in the lived experiences of the individual respondents.

To study White antiracists, O'Brien conducted 30 in-depth interviews with 15 men and 15 women from two antiracist groups, fo-cusing on these respondents' relationships with people of color, on the one hand, and their relationships to other Whites, on the other.

In terms of White antiracists' relationships with people of color, O'Brien found that it was easy to find examples of false empathy and defensiveness when White antiracists came into contact with people of color. In one example of a confrontation between two young men—a White antiracist and a Black man—the White antiracist became defensive and, O'Brien suggests, lost the chance to develop a potential relationship with the young man of color. Interestingly, one of O'Brien's young male activists of color's response to a question about White antiracist false empathy emphasized the class-based attitude of the Whites in this interaction—middle-class Whites upbraiding people of color for not being radical enough when they themselves were not really risking anything. Yet O'Brien also found that when White antiracists committed to a relationship with people of color and were willing to get beyond defensiveness to work together, this could mean a lasting relationship. In fact, O'Brien stresses that those White antiracists who have achieved true empathy recognize that they must stay accountable to people of color since their own ways of knowing might lead them away from issues for people of color.

In terms of White antiracists' relationships with White people, O'Brien found that initially antiracist Whites went though a period of "White-avoiding," feeling disgusted with the history of White treatment of people of color. This has meant, for some White antiracists, avoiding White people for years. Interestingly, according to O'Brien, this does not win them friends among people of color who interpret White antiracist avoidance of Whites as judgmental and arrogant. At the same time, O'Brien stresses that part of the issue is that White antiracists lack White role models, not because they did not exist historically but because there tends to be either silence in reference to White antiracists or a tendency to demonize them—a sure way to discourage other Whites from joining the struggle for equality. O'Brien emphasizes that White antiracists must make the difficult journey toward autonomy by staying connected to other Whites. These relationships, she stresses, will not survive if the White *antiracist behaves with arrogance, self-righ-teousness, or judgment, but connections should be maintained to effectively come full circle and authentically further the cause of antiracism by challenging real White contributions to racism.*

Whites and people of color in the United States are separated by a vast "perception gap"—whites feel that racism ended in the 1960s and see people of color as complaining or overreacting, while people of color see continued racial discrimination (Steinhorn and Diggs-Brown 2000). This perception gap means that substantial white support for antiracist policies is lacking. Because whites are a majority in numbers and power in this nation, the "conversion" of whites to anti-racism is a crucial part of the larger political struggle for human rights. Yet we seldom hear about whites who have taken the step to anti-racism. This step is a substantial one, far from simply being nonracist. Joe Barndt writes: "Nonracists try to deny that the prison exists. Antiracists work for the prison's eventual de-struction" (1991:65). Whereas nonracists merely profess tolerant attitudes and think everyone should be treated equally, anti-racists not only acknowledge that not every-one is treated equally but work "daily [and] vigilantly" (hooks 1995:1581) to combat this inequality.

Recently writers have been engaged in the process of describing what this antiracist path might look like. Paul Kivel (1996) ad-vises whites to become "allies" of people of color, while Noel Ignatiev and John Garvey (1994) suggest a "race traitor" stance, where one refuses to partake in the "white club" of privileges accorded to those who appear "white" in our society. Anthologies such as *Off White* (Fine et al. 1997) and *Critical White Studies* (Delgado and Stefancic 1997) offer perspectives on how whites can challenge the centrality of whiteness, thereby upset-ting the very foundation of racism in North American culture. However, there has been little empirical analysis of white antiracists themselves, and nothing to my knowledge has been written on how taking such a politi-cal stance affects the *interpersonal relation-*

ships of these whites. In this analysis, I will demonstrate how whites' relationships with people of color and their relationships with other whites are impacted by their commit-ments to being antiracist. In particular, I will argue that just because whites have dedi-cated their lives to antiracism does not mean that they exhibit *empathy* in their relation-ships with people of color, nor does it mean that they have developed the *autonomy* of a secure white identity that enables them to in-teract with other whites. Indeed, empathy and autonomy are so difficult to achieve for white antiracists because of the pervasive-ness of white supremacy and racism.

Joe Feagin and Hernán Vera (1995) found that what set white antiracists apart from the general white population was their ability to empathize with people of color. For whites, developing empathy means having to step across that perception gap, grasping the ex-tent to which racism still exists, and validat-ing the experiences of people of color. Be-cause white denial about modern racism is so pervasive, we might expect that people of color would instantly bond to those few whites who are actually antiracist. However, this is seldom the case. During my first pre-sentation of some of my research on white antiracists, one African-American woman re-sponded: "those are the people I don't trust." My first instinct was to clarify who my sample was—perhaps she had not understood that I was studying white *antiracists*, not white rac-ists. Yet she assured me she had not mis-spoken. Indeed, this woman echoes the sen-timents of many African-Americans, including 1960s activists such as Dick Greg-ory and Malcolm X, who said they preferred a white bigot to a white liberal because at least the former was under no false pretenses of being well-intentioned. Three decades later, Richard Delgado developed the con-cept of false empathy to explain how well-in-tentioned whites can actually do more harm than good without realizing it:

> False empathy is worse than none at all, worse than indifference. It makes you overconfident, so that you can easily harm the intended beneficiary. You are apt to be paternalistic, thinking you know what the other really wants or needs. You

can easily substitute your own goal for his. You visualize what you would want if you were he, when your experiences and needs are radically different. (Delgado 1996: 31)

Because white antiracists can easily fall into the behavior that Delgado describes above, people of color often choose to keep their distance until a white antiracist has earned their trust. Hence white antiracists face the challenge of establishing *empathy*, rather than false empathy, when creating relationships with people of color.

Empathy is often more easily achieved by those who have a secure racial identity. Janet Helms (1990) has developed a stage theory of racial identity development, noting that both whites and people of color go through parallel but not identical six-stage processes. For whites, the first three stages (contact, disintegration, reintegration) represent those who are ignorant about racism, due to either lack of exposure or limited exposure without fully understanding. The second three (pseudo-independence, immersion-emersion, autonomy) represent a journey "toward a nonracist white identity" (Jones and Carter 1996: 7). Beverly Tatum (1992, 1994) has observed that for whites, pseudo-independence is often characterized by avoidance of other whites. That is, once they become aware of racism and accept that it exists, it may seem like their only option is associating with predominantly people of color since most whites do not share their newfound perspective. Viewing whites as the primary perpetrators of racism, they may feel that in order to be good antiracists they must stay away from other whites. It also may be uncomfortable for them to connect with whites who are not antiracist, because they would face the daunting task of educating them. Pseudo-independents believe themselves to be confident as white antiracists, yet they are confident in this identity only around those who already agree with them—usually people of color. Whites typically emerge out of this stage when they are able to discover white antiracist role models. This search for others like them is part of the immersion-emersion stage, and once they have successfully incorporated this acceptance of a white antiracist

identity as part of their self-concept, they reach autonomy (Helms's final stage).

Helms's racial identity theory has direct implications for white antiracists' personal relationships with other whites. If whites are in the pseudo-independence stage, their political stance of antiracism may be intact, but their personal relationships with other whites could be either suffering or nonexistent. They may sever ties with white people who have previously meant a lot to them or miss out on opportunities to connect with whites who are not necessarily antiracist but still could be receptive to their point of view. On the other hand, if they have reached autonomy, they should be more likely to extend empathy to other whites whether or not they are antiracist. They may even use those relationships with whites as opportunities to share an antiracist perspective. Hence, in moving towards empathy and autonomy, white antiracists create the greatest possibilities for successful *inter*racial and *intra*racial relationships.

This movement, however, is not easy in today's white-supremacist/racist society. In contrast with older traditional definitions of racism which focus on attitudes and behaviors, modern racism is often less overt and barely detectable to most whites. It is reproduced in the everyday normal functioning of society, resulting in countless material advantages or "privileges" for whites (Bonilla-Silva 2001; Feagin 2000). This system does not change simply because individual whites become antiracist. Even white antiracists carry white-supremacist expectations about the everyday dynamics of their lives. For one thing, it is less imperative for whites to have to consider alternative perspectives when embarking upon a course of action, whereas for people of color such considerations are much more common for reasons of survival. It is under this context that white false empathy occurs—even though they may mean well by suggesting solutions for racism, they may not stop to consider alternatives because it has not been in their everyday experience to have to do so.

Another everyday privilege of whiteness is that whites assume or expect that they will be trusted and taken seriously. However, all of these privileges flow much more smoothly to whites who support the dominant color-blind ideology. Once they challenge this ideology, their fellow whites are not automatically receptive to them. Another privilege is for them to withdraw into supportive communities and not face that challenge with other non-antiracist whites (the choice against autonomy).

In these ways, then, their movement towards empathy with people of color and autonomy with other whites is a direct struggle against white supremacy. It is a struggle to translate a political commitment (to antiracism) into one's personal relationships—that everyday realm where white supremacy is reproduced.

Methods

The data analyzed in this chapter are part of a larger research project on white antiracist activists which utilized a multiple method strategy of interviews, participant observation, and archival analysis of organizational literature of two major antiracist groups: Anti-Racist Action (ARA) and the People's Institute for Survival and Beyond (PISB). Here I draw primarily from thirty in-depth interviews collected between 1996 and 1999 using a purposive snowball sampling technique. The sample is split evenly with respect to gender (fifteen women and fifteen men), and a variety of ages are represented (10 are age 30 or under, 17 are between the ages of 31 and 60, and three are over age 60). The interviewees also represent different regions of North America. Two interviewees reside in Toronto, two reside west of the Mississippi River (in North Dakota and Arizona), and the rest are from east of the Mississippi River in the United States—nine from the Midwest (Ohio, Illinois, and Michigan), five from the Northeast (Massachusetts, New York, and Washington DC), five from the Southeast (Florida and North Carolina), and seven from Louisiana.

About half of the sample consists of members of ARA or PISB, and the other half represent other organizations or were not part of any organization. Elsewhere (O'Brien 2001), I have focused more specifically on the differences between these two organizations,

since each group has distinct foci and methods of action, but here I focus on the influence of organizational ideology only as it is relevant to personal relationship development. I also quote some activists of color who have been interviewed about their perceptions of white antiracists.

Relationships with People of Color

Journeys to Empathy

Delgado (1996) and Feagan and Vera (1995) emphasize the importance of moving from false empathy to empathy for whites. Yet false empathy can be common for those in these early stages of antiracism. Jason, a young white antiracist, displayed an example of false empathy as he described an incident at the Lollapalooza tour (a concert event) where he was "tabling" for his antiracist organization (distributing newsletters and brochures and signing people up for the mailing list).

> There was a table almost beside us . . . who were in MTV's Choose or Lose thing, the voter registration drive. There was probably about 15 to 20 people staffing it, and they were all black people. And when they were setting up, [we asked them] "Oh who are you guys with?" [they said] "MTV's Choose or Lose," and I was like, "Oh that's pretty cool." And one of the people there asked us who we were with, and we said "Anti Racist Action" and I heard a snicker. [laughs] Like that. And my guard just went up, and I was like, "what was that for?" I almost wanted to say to him, "You should be working with us, rather than working for MTV!"

Here Jason faced a common situation for white antiracists, where credibility as whites doing antiracist work needs to be established in order to foster trusting relationships with people of color. When Jason sensed his credibility was being challenged, rather than reaching out to establish that credibility, he became defensive and assumed a paternalistic attitude toward this black young man, implying he himself knew better than this person of color how his activist energies should be spent. This type of false empathy prevented a potential relationship between the two young men from developing. Had the two of them talked openly, a white person might have learned how important lack of voter registration has been to black freedom struggles both historically and currently, and a black person might have learned about a white young man who put his life on the line to challenge police brutality. Yet this did not occur.

It might be useful to contrast this account with a viewpoint from Lorenzo, an activist of color, who faced a similar situation in organizing a campus-wide coalition against racism:

> I saw a lot of whites that talked the talk, but never really sort of gave up their white supremacy beliefs, whether conscious or unconscious. And for example when we were pushing a particular agenda, these folks came behind and tried to tell us how to basically organize and how to proceed in the movement. . . . These are the folks, in terms of practical matters were middle class, settled, nothing would happen to them and still they sort of chastised us because in their estimation we were not radical enough and they wanted us to be more radical. I was like, "look, this is not a revolution, this is a very restricted struggle here and the conditions are not such to be aspiring for a revolution.". . . I'm talking about socialist folks who claim to be on our side, but in truth were more interested in telling us how to run the movement.

Here we can begin to understand what it might feel like for a person of color to try and interact with white antiracists who perceive him as "not radical enough." Being told what to do by white people, whether they claimed to be antiracist or not, for him felt like just another manifestation of white supremacy.

Rosalind, another white antiracist, a bit older than Jason, who struggled with her tendency to adopt a paternalistic attitude towards people of color, described a maturation process. She was beginning to try to understand why people of color might opt for different methods of antiracism and community organizing from those she would have them select:

> I still sort of feel like I'm beating my head against the wall when I try to work with [African-American community]. I don't know how much you know about them,

but they are unusual about being pretty far along in self-determination and community empowerment in terms of [a] really oppressed community. But I've been very frustrated in the partnership areas. They'll demand that we meet and work together, and then they won't [pause] they won't do it! And I understand the[ir] resistance to doing it. So I'm not as impatient with that as I used to be, but it's still real frustrating.

Like Jason, Rosalind revealed her frustration that people of color do not necessarily choose to do their community organizing with *her* (predominantly white) antiracist group. Yet unlike Jason, she expressed some willingness to understand the reasoning behind these African-Americans decisions. Both Jason and Rosalind demonstrated that false empathy is an easy pattern to fall into and that it takes a conscious effort to resist it.

Part of the journey to empathy for whites is facing the historical atrocities committed by whites against people of color and realizing that the distrust of whites that people of color may have is grounded in a long history. White antiracists who grasp this reality may be more likely to wait out the initial distrust and work towards forming relationships with people of color. Pam explained:

> A white antiracist is looked at very skeptically from the community of color, and *rightfully so*. . . . Until that person, that group, whatever gets to know an individual and understand why [they are antiracist], I think, their skepticism—I can't condemn them for that. If a white person comes around, there's gotta be a reason why they're doing something that they're doing. Why did the army men give all those warm blankets to the Indians that were infected with smallpox? They gave those blankets to those people for a reason, they wanted to get rid of them! So why am I doing something then? Do I wanna get inside so I can find out the inner workings of the community so I can destroy it, or am I a curiosity-seeker, or do I really want to help? So I think people of color should look at white antiracists a little questionably at first and until they realize that this person's OK. They have *every reason* for being skeptical.

While earlier Rosalind stated that she "understand[s] the resistance" of people of color to working with antiracist whites, here Pam elaborated on the source of that resistance, described it, and seemed truly empathic. Rather than exhibiting false empathy, Pam spoke from a place of wanting to understand where people of color were coming from, even though in condoning those actions she condoned some treatment of her as a white person that could be uncomfortable for her.

One of the many unfortunate consequences of racism is that truly intimate interracial relationships are difficult to form. White antiracists are not exempt from this consequence. Those who approach their relationships with people of color with false empathy probably will not be successful in building lasting interracial relationships. Those who strive for empathy have no less of a thorny road to travel. They must persevere in the face of rejection. But their openness to facing constructive criticism without becoming defensive is exactly what their allies of color may desire. Lorenzo, the activist of color quoted earlier in this section, explained this perspective:

> Whites obviously feel afraid of many of us minorities thinking that we're not going to trust them, that we're not really going to be on their side, and this and that. That fear . . . has a limited basis in reality because my impression of the situation is that, if you walk the walk, after the first encounter or two when I see or we see that you are on our side you become a brother, OK? But anyway, because many people are not willing to expose themselves and be vulnerable to misunderstandings, which is part of the game, then they develop a shield and never really go beyond sort of appearances and always remain sort of aloof. That sense of aloofness has always been an issue in developing true interracial organizations and struggles. So you need to break those barriers and the only way is by making mistakes, by saying silly things occasionally, and then getting mad and then learning and then sort of getting smart and then moving on.

This vulnerability to face one's own mistakes and willingness to learn and grow from them is the first step to building authentic relationships with people of color.

Authentic Relationships and Accountability

As whites learn how to develop empathy, rather than false empathy, with people of color, they begin to develop meaningful relationships with them. While most whites may go through their entire lives thinking they have a token "black friend," in actuality this person may be nothing more than an acquaintance who does not feel comfortable sharing his or her thoughts about racial matters with this white "friend." Whites have a history of *rereading* or *looping* (Rosenblum and Travis 1996) upon being told about instances of discrimination—that is, they will tend to suggest that the tellers were either overreacting or perhaps provoked the incident themselves. Such behavior obviously thwarts the establishment of empathy. When these interracial relationships can survive discussions that confront racism head-on, "authentic relationships" are established, according to PISB. In a similar vein of Delgado's (1996) discussion of false empathy, PISB assert that well-intentioned white antiracists may be doing more harm than good if they do not have "accountability" to people of color through these authentic relationships. Hence, interracial relationships are not just sites of personal connection but also are crucial to ensuring effective activism. David, an organizer and trainer with PISB, addressed why the concept of accountability is important for whites:

> There's got to be *accountability* to oppressed peoples . . . otherwise, even though we [whites] would claim to be antiracist, we'd change the subject. We would, by the very nature of what it means to be white, if all of us get into a room talking, and meeting, and doing whatever, if we're not held *accountable*, the forces will take us off course. And we will either start fighting with each other on the things that white folks fall out with each other on, or we would begin to take over the study of what it means to be white in a way that doesn't mesh with peoples of color's reality.

For white antiracist activists, the method for keeping oneself in check is not adherence to some abstract code of ethics or to a board of directors; rather it is in interpersonal relationships that accountability is sustained. The personal is indeed political, as one's political action is inspired and adjusted by the personal connection of authentic relationships.

These dynamics come into play more specifically in white antiracists' lives. PISB member Kendra described the tenacity and commitment that goes into sustaining authentic relationships, even when being held accountable causes humiliation and pain:

> The first year that I was working in relation to the community I worked in [an African-American community] . . . I was very excited about their model of organizing and I wrote two articles about it, and had them published. And I had passed them around the community beforehand, and stuff, but when it came out, [pause] it was a shock to people . . . this was not what they expected. And they felt used, and they felt abused, and they felt that their lives had been taken from them and put in a book and by someone they trusted—it really breached the trust that we had very, very deeply. . . . So I had to sit down with the community, and talk about it. And the people were *really* angry at me, and I made a commitment that I was going to accept responsibility. . . . What I've learned [from this] is an understanding that, to really make the change happen that needs to happen in this world, it's gonna take commitment and staying in there and hanging in there when things get difficult.

Although the concepts of authentic relationships and accountability are unique to PISB, other white antiracists who are not members of that organization also rely on their personal relationships with people of color to keep them vigilant on their antiracist journeys. Angela, for example, found herself challenged about her white privilege during a heated argument with her African-American partner about how they celebrated Christmas:

> [My partner] said, "Look, we cannot resolve this until we start talking about the class part of this." And that of course intrigued me enough to sort of keep me in there. . . . She began to explain to me, "we do Christmas the way you did it . . . you take weeks and weeks to do it. . . . And I grew up in a situation where I was working and my mother was working and my father was working up until the afternoon of Christmas Eve. And our tradition was always running up to Woolworth's and getting gifts for each other.". . . I devote three to four weeks leading up to it . . . but some of the way that I can do that is really about my privilege, and I had a mom at home and aunts living right next door to me, I had the advantage and the privilege I guess of some sorts of making that happen and making it possible.

White supremacy encroached upon the most intimate relationship in Angela's life. The way she approached the holiday season was embedded in her privilege in a way she had not recognized until her African-American partner pointed it out to her. A common denominator in these situations of accountability is that the white antiracists resisted acting out of defensiveness or false empathy. They remained open to a person of color's interpretation of racism and their own role in it, and strove to use that information to inspire their own further growth as an antiracist. In these cases, empathy is achieved, and interpersonal relationships become potential sites of social change.

Another activist of color, Vanessa, explained what she is looking for in those white antiracists whom she can truly trust, and it resembles what Kendra and Angela described above:

> I look for that self-analysis. . . . I look for a willingness to take whatever criticisms I may have without being defensive. Sort of accepting that and [being] willing to have the conversation that that might be true. Not to be caught up in yes I do or no I don't or this person does it more. A willingness to work on solutions from both parties about whatever the behavior is.

Vanessa does not only look at how whites respond to her, she also looks at how they respond to their white "peers," the issue to which I now turn.

Relationships with Other Whites

Being 'Disgusted' with Whites

The literature on white racial identity development acknowledges that whites may go through a period of abhorrence of whiteness when first committing to antiracism (Tatum 1992, 1994). Although not using the language of these stages, the white antiracist respondents in this study agree that it was a "progression" on their journey to move out of a pseudo-independence, or white-avoiding, stage. Mike, for example, stated:

> I've seen a lot of white people go through this. They get real disgusted with white culture, because when you become aware of the reality of what has been done by the white collective, it's kind of disgusting. I personally went through a process where there was very few [white] people that I wanted to be around . . . I just wasn't wanting to be around most of the people that had been my support system. And that was real disappointing for a long time, it put me in a real difficult place. And that's progressed to the point where I understand that . . . there's work for me to do within the white community.

As Mike pointed out, one moves beyond this avoidance of whites by coming to understand the importance of bringing other whites to awareness. But this progression is sometimes not an easy one. Nancy's progression was at least 30 years in the making, dating back to the 1960s and extending into the 1990s. She recalled:

> I think from the earliest times I thought it was unjust and I wanted to be part of the solution. I didn't understand how to be a part of that solution within the white community—at all! I mean, even when Malcolm started saying go back to your own community, I was like, you don't know where I come from! [laughs] . . . because we knew we couldn't go home, I mean our parents would never speak to us again. . . . But then on the other hand, I'm showing absolute respect for what he meant by that, so I'm not trying to make light of that. . . . I've learned over the years how much I have to do to be willing to come back and work in the white community and work on antiracism with white people. . . . And that was the hardest trip I've ever had to make . . . was from living very, very comfortably in African-American neighborhoods, and living with my friends, and surrounded by predominantly African-American culture

and stuff, to saying it is my responsibility, if I mean that sincerely, to make this move and work with white people.

Nancy spent most of her adult life avoiding whites. She lived comfortably in black neighborhoods, worshipping in black churches, and being an activist in predominantly black political organizations. Indeed "the hardest trip [she] ever had to make" was reestablishing significant personal attachments to other whites and accepting that as part of her antiracist work.

This "pseudo-independent" behavior is not perceived favorably by people of color, and hence it alienates whites not only from other whites but from people of color as well. Interestingly, both activists of color quoted in the previous section mentioned their perceptions of white antiracists who separate themselves as the "good whites" from other white peers. Both Lorenzo and Vanessa perceived this behavior as arrogant and judgmental:

> Humility is something that white people need big time, because even in this antiracist organization I have found that many of them develop this notion that I am better than anybody. Some of them develop the belief that they are better than the average white because they're "beyond" and then some of them believe they're better than us because they "understand."

> Often times I find white antiracist workers a bit judging. I think that they set themselves above their white peers. I think that often this marker of antiracism gets worn as a banner that yeah, I'm down with the black people, the colored people, the "whatever" people.

While the more obvious consequence of pseudo-independent behavior is the lack of relationships with other whites, a latent consequence is that the alliances whites forge with people of color based upon that premise will not be solid either.

David, quoted previously, drew upon the PISB philosophy as he explained the difficulty of but necessity for antiracist whites to maintain relationships with other whites:

The [People's] Institute would later talk to me about how important it would be for me to maintain my relationship with my family and thus model, [or] attempt to model, how other whites must always keep the connection, must not write each other off, must try to keep from being split all the time in the many ways that white folks split themselves and divide themselves from each other. . . . Who had resisted this construct of race who were white? Who had stood against it? What were their names? What did they look like? They're invisible in history. We would hear about other peoples being in-visible-ized, but those whites who stood against it, with one or two exceptions, were not there either. . . . None of us got here on our own, we all stand on the shoulders of others.

A major source of the difficulty in moving out of the "pseudo-independent" stage is the lack of white antiracist role models (Tatum 1992, 1994). It is not that they never existed; rather, there is a historical silence about them. Malcolm X pointed out there was a reason behind the silencing and/or discrediting of white antiracists. If we were told that white people like John Brown (who was executed for inciting a slave rebellion) were lunatics instead of heroes, then whites would be less likely to break the status quo and join in the struggle.

The effects of this silence are political and personal. Whites not only lose out on opportunities to advance antiracism but also decrease their capability for intimate connections with other whites. Nowhere was this more evident than in the story of Nancy's relationship with her white son:

My biggest disappointment is that I didn't understand well enough about dealing with whiteness to make the life of my white son [long pause]—I wasn't able to give him the tools that he needed to understand the complicated world that he was living in racially. . . . He always knew that I valued black culture, and blackness, and that I valued societal change. He grew up a kid who always chose black friends. . . . I don't think I was ever the kind of person who bashed people. But I didn't know how to make him feel really good about being a white person and an

antiracist and a resistor. I didn't help him to have a positive [pause] white identity or male identity. I sort of thought if you're white and male in this culture, every-thing's positive. . . . But . . . he didn't want to be like those white men. It took me years before I realized that I had ill-equipped him. . . . We're just learning how to deal with ourselves as white people and be proud of ourselves by choosing role models who are white that we can be like.

White antiracists face unique challenges in developing and maintaining interpersonal relationships with other whites. The political divide-and-conquer strategies which define racism as a "black issue" about which whites should have no concern keep us from seeing the long history of whites who *have* been concerned and lived lives dedicated to that concern. Yet these politics trickle down and have a very personal impact on people's lives. Although white antiracists may find it easier to connect with people of color, the "hardest trip" but most necessary trip may be the one towards autonomy, in which they maintain their connections with other whites.

Staying Connected to Other Whites

As with their journeys to true empathy with people of color, these white antiracists also described journeys to greater openness to other whites as they continued their work. Paul, a teacher, described his movement from separating himself from other whites to a more nonjudgmental attitude that allowed him to connect more with others:

I can tend to get excited about things and tend to become evangelistic. And so I was the person at the school, once I began to see it, I was talking about it, and I knew that I was quickly getting marginalized. And so a lot of the work for me has been, how do I do this work holding people with love that I'm working with and not be judgmental?

At some point Paul began to realize that becoming "marginalized" would not ultimately help him do his antiracist work effectively. Mac discussed a similar evolution in his own work, and explained in more detail the practical implications of staying connected for further antiracism:

> I'm a real practical person and I don't try to convince anyone beyond the amount I think I can. . . . I am more skilled as a revolutionary now than I was when I believed that every time somebody said "nigger" I had to throw a fit. I don't have to do anything, except whatever is the most effective right then to get them closer to fixing it. So, if shutting your mouth and walking out is the smartest thing—well, actually, if any other choice will create more harm than good—then your responsibility as a revolutionary is to shut your mouth, smile, act like you didn't hear it, and move on, because we have to win. We can't be just making stands in the abstract and being unpopular. We have to get people's ideas to change, and ranting sometimes pushes them the other way.

Both Mac and Paul realized that behaving in an aggressively self-righteous way with other whites was not the best way to "get people's ideas to change."

Maintaining relationships with other whites means that white antiracists are not just "preaching to the choir," or spending time only with whites who agree with them, as pseudo-independents would. They are increasing the span of the lives that they touch, by maintaining those connections. They are continually challenging other whites to question the ways in which they unknowingly contribute to racism. In this way, they further their goal of fighting racism through their interpersonal relationships. However, as the above quotes point out, this goal cannot be met by becoming angry and indignant at every turn. This presents a special challenge when dealing with family members, since people often are more likely to be candid and emotional in familial settings. Kendra recounted one such challenge in the following anecdote:

> One night I was sitting at the dinner table with my [black] husband, and my [white] stepmother, and my little daughter, and we needed some napkins. And my little brother was in the other room and I said, "[Name], will you grab me a napkin?" Then [he] came into the room with a roll of paper towels. And my mother says,

> "[Name], there's napkins in there, come on, let's eat like the white folks." [pause] And [laughs] [my husband] and I are looking at her, you know? And she's like, "Oh, I'm so sorry, I'm so sorry," and she said, "Oh, I spent too many years hanging around your father." So she was blaming it on him and [laughs] I said, "Well, that wasn't him, that was *you, you* said that!" [laughs] . . . If [my husband] had wanted to get up and walk out, we would've. But . . . I don't think it would have changed her. I think that having her realize that she had just hurt someone who's a member of our family, who she says she loves and respects, made more of a difference. And if I had, on my own, gotten up and stormed out of the house, I don't think I would have helped, it would have hurt more. And I think it would have been arrogant of me. If [my husband] had just said, "I cannot sit at the table with this woman," I would have left. . . . But it was like he took it with a certain grace and sense of humor, and I think I had an obligation to do the same thing. And I don't think she says stuff like that anymore.

Rather than making a scene, Kendra spoke of her concern for effectiveness and success when se said, "I don't think it would have changed her," and "I don't think it would have helped, it would have hurt more." Additionally, like Paul and Mac, she referred to minimizing the self-righteous attitude when she remarked that it would have been "arrogant" for her to storm out of the house in retaliation. Kendra selected a course of action that still called a racist comment into question without disrupting the family dinner, and without severing her relationship with her stepmother.

In using her husband's reaction as a guide, Kendra was practicing accountability to people of color as discussed previously. Often, a person of color will not want to "make a scene" when racism occurs because it happens so often that they would not have the energy to endure every such "scene." In becoming indignant in such situations, as if speaking for the person of color, whites can lapse into the false empathy that Delgado (1996) describes. In actuality, people of color may view nonresponse to a racist situation as most appropriate, especially when action

Chapter 50 ✦ *The Political Is Personal*   451

could detain them or put them in danger. Having not lived their lives with such regular possibilities of danger looming, whites may be unaware of these kinds of considerations. This is when accountability to people of color can be especially useful, even lifesaving. The practices of accountability to people of color and of maintaining connection to other whites came together effectively in Kendra's example. Indeed, one activist of color quoted previously, Vanessa, asserted that how white antiracists respond to their white peers is the most important criterion for her in determining whether she can truly have an authentic relationship with that person:

> Call your peers to the table! My main quest would be that this is all good and great, but we would get along even better if I saw you sticking your neck out there, calling your own folks to the table. Not in a condescending way, not in a way that says you're better than they are, but really call them to the table to have the discussion.

Conclusion

"Condescending," "arrogant," and "judgmental" are just some of the adjectives used to describe white antiracists throughout these interviews. Yet it is crucial that these barriers to empathy and autonomy are understood not as personality shortcomings but as collective inheritances that whites as a group receive under white supremacy. Hence, increasing the number of whites who are politically committed to antiracism will not alone eradicate racism. As Eduardo Bonilla-Silva aptly points out, the focus on a struggle between the "good whites" and "bad whites" misses the point, since white supremacy is continually reproduced in the "everyday rituals" of society (2001: 196). White antiracists must not only cease being prejudiced and discriminatory and fight racist institutional practices, but they must also tend to their everyday interactions with others, where white supremacy also resides.

False empathy as a barrier to white antiracists' relationships with people of color is not a problem of these whites' personal prejudices. Rather, under white supremacy, whites have been trained to not have to take into consideration "other" worldviews, so any strategy they propose for ending racism may unintentionally come across as arrogant to people of color who have had to adopt a "double consciousness" to survive. Further, whites have had the privilege of being judged solely as individuals and hence expect that. Those white antiracists who struggle for empathic relationships with people of color not only strive to reduce personal prejudice and discrimination but humble themselves to alternative interpretations of their actions, understanding that they occupy a privileged position in white supremacy that has little to do with their individual convictions.

Beyond their relationships with people of color, it may seem surprising that white antiracists' relationships with other whites are also constrained by white supremacy. Yet indeed, we see here how the choice either to separate from other whites or to relate to them only with arrogant admonitions (in the "good white/bad white" model) further perpetuates racism, even though no overt act of antiblack discrimination is taking place. The individualistic orientation to life that is a white privilege gives whites the idea that they can be one-man or one-woman islands of political antiracism and still be effective in their work. Ironically, Helms has named her most developed stage of white identity "autonomy," which refers to someone who maintains a subversive antiracist ideology despite the pressures to conform to the dominant ideology. One cannot maintain this orientation if constantly cut off from those who hold the dominant ideology, whether through avoidance or arrogance. If being antiracist means challenging the modern existence of racism, then white antiracists must continue to be present in those "everyday rituals" of white supremacy if they expect to interrupt it effectively. This means that remaining connected to other whites is a decisively antiracist act both personal and political.

In describing true white antiracism as "daily [and] vigilant," bell hooks (1995: 158) understood the pervasiveness of white supremacy. Only antiracism which struggles against these everyday manifestations of white supremacy in the most personal and intimate of relationships can be effective in today's "new racist" society.

References

Barndt, Joseph. 1991. *Dismantling Racism: The Continuing Challenge to White America*. Minneapolis, MN: Augsberg Fortress.

Bonilla-Silva, Eduardo. 2001. *White Supremacy and Racism in the Post-Civil Rights Era*. Boulder, CO: Lynne Rienner.

Delgado, Richard. 1996. *The Coming Race War?* New York: New York University Press.

Delgado, Richard, and Jean Stefancic, eds. 1997. *Critical White Studies: Looking behind the Mirror*. Philadelphia: Temple University Press.

Feagin, Joe R. 2000. *Racist America: Roots, Current Realities, and Future Reparations*. New York: Routledge.

Feagin, Joe R., and Hernán Vera. 1995. *White Racism: The Basics*. New York: Routledge.

Fine, Michelle, Lois Weis, Linda C. Powell, and L. Mun Wong, eds. 1997. *Off White: Readings on Race, Power, and Society*. New York: Routledge.

Helms, Janet E., ed. 1990. *Black and White Racial Identity: Theory, Research and Practice*. New York: Greenwood.

hooks, bell. 1995. *Killing Rage: Ending Racism*. New York: Henry Holt.

Ignatiev, Noel, and John Garvey, eds. 1993–1994. *Race Traitor*. Published at Box 603, Cambridge, MA 02140.

Jones, James M., and Robert T. Carter. 1996. "Racism and White Racial Identity: Merging Realities." Pp. 1–23 in *Impacts of Racism on White Americans*, ed. Benjamin P. Bowser and Raymond G. Hunt. Thousand Oaks, CA: Sage.

Kivel, Paul. 1996. *Uprooting Racism: How White People Can Work for Racial Justice*. Gabriola Island, BC: New Society.

O'Brien, Eileen. 2001. *Whites Confront Racism: Antiracists and Their Paths to Action*. Boulder, CO: Rowman and Littlefield.

Rosenblum, Karen E., and Toni-Michelle C. Travis. 1996. *The Meaning of Difference: American Constructions of Race, Sex and Gender, Social Class, and Sexual Orientation*. New York: McGraw Hill.

Steinhorn, Leonard, and Barbara Diggs-Brown. 2000. *By the Color of Our Skin: The Illusion of Integration and the Reality of Race*. New York: Plume Books.

Tatum, Beverly Daniel. 1992. "Talking about Race, Learning about Racism: The Application of Racial Identity Development Theory in the Classroom." *Harvard Educational Review* 62: 1–24.

——. 1994. "Teaching White Students about Racism: The Search for White Allies and the Restoration of Hope." *Teachers College Record* 95: 462–476.

Discussion Questions

1. This article stresses the importance of White antiracism and strategies for this stance. How do you respond to the article and to the author's obvious political stance?

2. How did you respond to the findings on White antiracist's behavior toward people of color and White people? Did it surprise you that White antiracists go through a White-avoiding phase?

3. How do you think this analysis might have been different if it had been conducted with Latinos/as, Asian Americans, or American Indians? Do you think there would have been any subtle or overt differences?

4. Does your personal experience resonate in any way with the respondents, either White or Black, in this study? How or how not?

51

'If It Wasn't for the Women . . .'

African American Women, Community Work, and Social Change

Cheryl Townsend Gilkes

In this article, Cheryl Townsend Gilkes used oral histories and observation to learn how African American women's community work contributed to social change. She defines community work as the work that people do outside their homes and apart from their paid work. The kinds of work she has in mind are forms of creative social conflict and reflect the double consciousness that thinkers like W. E. B. DuBois and Gloria Anzaldúa wrote about (see Martinez in Section 1 and Anzaldúa in this section). The women she interviewed formed organizations, led protests, and taught others necessary school and work skills, but also how to organize and lead.

Gilkes' work shows the integration and interdependence of community institutions. Factories, unions, jails, schools, polling places, banks, churches, hospitals, social clubs, and sanitation departments are all related and are all potential arenas for social action. Her work also shows how effective working-class women with minimal resources can be and how members of the working and middle classes can contribute to social change. She notes that this important work was done separately from, differently from, and occasionally with opposition from men. Yet the work was for the advancement of the race, not of individuals or of women only.

Many sociologists who studied the relationships between dominant and subordinate racial-ethnic groups in the 1960s and 1970s stress the creative ways in which individuals and groups enable communities to articulate their own needs and challenge oppressive structures in the wider society (Morris 1984). Other sociologists, such as Stanford Lyman (1972), emphasize the historical experience of racial-ethnic groups in the data used for sociological interpretation. The Civil Rights Movement, the Black Power Movement, and the American Indian Movement, along with diverse movements within Asian American, Puerto Rican, and Chicano communities, challenged sociologists to explore historically rooted conflicts over power, labor, economic resources, and the appropriate strategies for achieving social change (Blauner 1972; Wilson 1973; Gilkes 1980).

Creative social conflict is inevitable and necessary if racial-ethnic, gender, and class inequities are to be eliminated and social justice achieved. When enterprising, caring members of oppressed communities become involved in public affairs, their actions often contribute to a creative cultural process that is a force for social change. This [paper] is about an aspect of that creative cultural process: enterprising women in African American communities who shape social change through their community work.

Women are vital to the creative cultural process of social change African American women and their community work highlight the importance of a group's history and culture to the process of social change The rise of the women's liberation movement and public concern about African American women, their families, and their position in the labor force (Cade 1970; King 1987; Gilkes 1990) generated a particular interest in their roles in the process of social change. Along with Asian American, Native American, and Latina women, African American women's work outside the home was recognized as a distinctive component in their family roles. Community work is part of this work outside the home. It is labor these women perform in addition to work in the household and the labor force.[1]

This [paper] describes the contemporary expression, historical foundations, and persistent activities of the community work of African American women. Community work includes a wide range of diverse tasks performed to confront and challenge racism as a total system. This work has historical foundations, and a historical perspective helps to highlight the areas of activity common to the work at different time periods. Community work consists of the women's activities to combat racism and empower their communities to survive, grow, and advance in a hostile society. The totality of their work is an emergent dynamic, interactive model of social action in which community workers discover and explore oppressive structures, challenge many different structures and practices that keep their communities powerless and disadvantaged, and then build, maintain, and strengthen institutions within their community. These institutions become the basis for the community's political culture. The women generate an alternative organization and a set of commitments to group interests that are the basic elements of "community." They work for the community that they themselves re-create and sustain, a mutually reinforcing process.

During the late 1970s in a Northeastern city I gathered oral histories and observed the community activities of 25 African American women whom other African Americans had identified as those "who have worked hard for a long time for change in the Black community."[2] As these women talked about the ways in which they became involved in community work and the different kinds of organizations and activities in which they participated, I learned about the very intricate and diverse ways in which people make social change. I also learned about the many ways in which women experience racial oppression. Their family roles made them acutely conscious not only of their own deprivations but also of the suffering of their children and the men in their lives. Their insightful and enterprising responses to these many kinds of suffering led to their prominence in the community. They were responsible for maintaining a dynamic community life to create social change and an adaptive family system

to foster survival in a hostile environment. Through community and family, these women generated a set of values and a social organization that persistently challenged and changed American society.

Community Work

Women in American society are expected to be good managers. They organize and coordinate diverse schedules and activities within their families, and among the organizations and institutions with which family members are involved. Work outside the home is often added to this responsibility. African American women usually work, manage their families, and, if they are community workers, participate in the struggles between the communities and the dominant society.

James Blackwell's (1985) definition of the African American community helps us to understand the context of their work. Blackwell argues that the community, although diverse, is held together by both internal and external forces. It is "a highly diversified set of interrelated structures and aggregates of people who are held together by the forces of white oppression and racism. Unity within the black community is a function of the strategies developed to combat white racism and to strengthen black social, economic, and political institutions for group survival and advancement" (1985: xi).

Community work consists of all tasks contained in strategies to combat racial oppression and to strengthen African American social, economic, and political institutions in order to foster group survival, growth, and advancement. Community work is focused on internal development and external challenge, and creates ideas enabling people to think about change. It is the work that opens doors to elected and appointed positions in the political power struggle, and demands and creates jobs in local labor markets and the larger economic system. Community work also focuses on changing ideas, stereotypes, and images that keep a group perpetually stigmatized. Sometimes this is done by demanding different textbooks in the schools or publicly criticizing newspapers and other media. At the same time, community workers may insist, rightly or wrongly, that community members change their behavior to avoid being treated in terms of prevailing stereotypes. Community work is a constant struggle, and it consists of everything that people do to address oppression in their own lives, suffering in the lives of others, and their sense of solidarity or group kinship.

Women participate in every part of a community's experience of racial oppression. Racial oppression is a phenomenon that not only singles out African Americans because of their heritage and color but also places the entire community in a colonial relationship, a relationship of powerlessness and dependency, within a dominant and dominating society. Robert Blauner (1972) calls this "internal colonialism," and it involves the subordination of an entire group of people in order to take away its land, to capture its labor, or to do both. Colonized people must be excluded from the political process and, by law, have few if any, citizenship rights. Because the primary purpose of the group is to labor unceasingly for someone else, the other dimensions of its cultural life, such as family life, health, education, and religion, become difficult, if not impossible, to pursue.

During slavery African Americans had their children and spouses sold away from them. Their family lives were repeatedly disrupted and invaded by the sexual terrorism that was part of slavery. Teaching slaves to read and write in the antebellum South was illegal. During the last decades of slavery, religious worship outside of the supervision of white people was illegal as well. The health of African Americans was constantly threatened by the violence of white slave owners, through beatings and overwork. Because they were legally nonpersons, emancipation left African Americans overwhelmingly landless and still dependent upon white landowners for a livelihood. Political powerlessness through violence and denial of the vote increased that dependence. Racist stereotypes, ideologies, and actions continued to justify the dominant group's actions and the continued subordination of another group.[3] Racial oppression is a total phenomenon that combines cultural humiliation and destruction, political subordination, and economic exploitation to maintain a hierarchy that limits the life chances of a group of people.

The economic needs and organization of the society change. Slavery was abolished in 1865; African Americans moved to northern cities in large numbers during World Wars I and II; the Civil Rights Movement did away with Jim Crow laws. However, the racist hierarchy retained a life and meaning that survived massive changes in economic, legal, political, and social institutions. Although slavery ended, the society learned to associate low-paying, dirty work with Black people and higher-paying, clean work with White people. Contemporary racial stereotypes and media images perpetuate those images rooted in slavery.

Community work confronts this totality. Everett Hughes (1971: 313) suggested that an important way to conceptualize "work" is to view it as a "bundle of several tasks." Racial oppression takes up more time and creates extra work, or more "bundles of tasks," for members of a victimized group.[4] People working for and with their communities involve themselves in activities surrounding the problems associated with jobs: labor union activities, creating access to jobs, teaching strategies to fight specific problems in work settings, and seeking legislation to protect occupations where group members are concentrated. One community worker had worked for the Urban League early in her career. She described recruiting other African American women for newly created jobs during World War II by visiting churches and women's clubs. She then organized discussion groups in order to teach these women how to confront the racial harassment they would encounter in unions and factories. Another woman described in great detail the way her women's club of the 1920s and 1930s taught fellow domestic workers how to demand the full wages their White female employers had promised. That same women's club, in the 1960s and 1970s, was involved in administering job training programs for homemakers *at the same time* they were lobbying for protective legislation for household workers. Community workers involved themselves in activities that confronted ideas as well as structures within and outside the community.

Education is a case in point. Issues of self-image and self-esteem are related to educational success at the same time that employment discrimination and racist attitudes in the educational system account for the lack of African American teachers. Educational failure locks many members of the community out of the economic system at the same time that political powerlessness through gerrymandering accounts for the lack of access to low-skilled but high-paying municipal jobs. One woman who had been quite prominent in challenging the public educational system talked about the importance of self-esteem for African American students. Another woman, an elected official, displayed publications she used for raising the racial self-esteem of teenagers and described the workshops she gave for parents in order to reduce the sense of intimidation they felt when confronting White teachers. Each of these problems presents a different "bundle of tasks," yet they are all manifestations of the totality of racial oppression.

Each woman interviewed described diverse and intricate daily schedules that reflected the complexity and connectedness of the social, political, and economic problems that pervade everyday life in minority communities. One woman, for example, described getting a group of adolescent males assigned to early morning jobs, going to court as a character witness for a teenager, meeting with a board of directors in another part of the city, and coordinating a public demonstration against that same board of directors before leaving for the meeting. While levels of confrontation and activity often vary, community work persistently rejects racial oppression as a normal and natural feature of human experience. Community work, encompassing issues of challenge as well as survival, is perhaps more complicated than the racial oppression that gives rise to it.

Historical Foundations

Community workers' expectations and obligations represent a historical role. These women, through their public participation on so many levels, claim a prominent place in the community's history. This historical prominence often provides levels of prestige and influence unmatched in the lives of White women of similar class backgrounds.[5] All of the women were connected in some way to earlier generations of organizations, activists, and confrontations. What becomes visible to outsider observers as "social movements" are the most dramatic dimensions of an intergenerational tradition of community work. Bernice Johnson Reagon (1982: 82–83) emphasizes this continuity:

> If we understand that we are talking about a struggle that is hundreds of years old, then we must acknowledge a continuance: that to be Black women is to move forward the struggle for the kind of space in this society that will make sense for our people. It is different today. Things have changed. The search for high levels of humanity and space to be who we know we are is the same. And if we can make sense of our people in this society, we will go a long way in making sense for the rest of the peoples who also live and suffer here.

The historical continuity of community work depends upon an intricate fit between many kinds of organizations and people. All of the women worked within traditional and nationally recognized groups, such as churches, the National Association for the Advancement of Colored People (NAACP), the Urban League, the Student Non-Violent Coordinating Committee (SNCC), the Young Women's Christian Association (YWCA), the National Association of Colored Women's Clubs, and the National Council of Negro Women. At the same time they formed local organizations that specialized in problems of job training, drug addiction, city services, welfare rights, or public education. People in the community actively encouraged these community workers to be leaders and, once the women responded to a community need, they organized whatever was necessary to see an activity through.

Such activities were not possible without intergenerational connections. When interviewing I asked the women to identify their heroes and heroines. These women identified specific women within the local community as well as such notables as Mary

McLeod Bethune. One woman remembered very clearly being impressed when Mrs. Bethune spoke at a local church for the Women's Day service. Several women identified Mrs. Burns,[6] who was also interviewed as their heroine and local sponsor. One said, "I walked to Mrs. Burns when I was nine months old!" This elderly community worker identified Mrs. Bethune as a coworker in the National Association of Colored Women. Older community workers, as heroines and sponsors, were the critical connection to earlier generations of community workers or "Race" women. These women who remembered Mary McLeod Bethune and Mary Church Terrell, not only as "heroines" but also as living role models in club work and church work, were the links to an unbroken tradition of community work or working for "the Race" that could be traced directly to antebellum communities, both slave and free.

Working for "the Race" began during slavery. Within the slave community, women not only played key roles in the development of family, education, and religion but also developed a women's network that was a foundation of strength, leaders, and mutual aid (White 1985; Webber 1978). Deborah Gray White (1985) names midwives, nurses, and religious leaders as critical sources of survival. One religious leader, a prophet named Sinda, preaching the imminent end of the world, precipitated a strike by an entire plantation labor force. African American women in Northern free communities built churches and developed abolitionist, literary, mutual-aid, and missionary societies that provided poor-relief and insurance benefits for their communities (Perkins 1981; Sterling 1984). Women such as Maria Stewart and Frances Ellen Watkins Harper were militant anti-slavery crusaders and public lecturers. Stewart was the first woman of any race in the United States to lecture publicly and leave manuscripts that are still extant (Giddings 1984; Richardson 1987), and Harper was the first female public lecturer that many women, Black or White, ever saw and heard (Sterling 1984).

After emancipation, church women and teachers organized schools and churches throughout the South. Since male ministers also worked as teachers, male and female educators (preachers and teachers) became the vital source of leaders. With the rise of Jim Crow laws, women's public activism outside the church emerged in the form of an anti-lynching movement under the leadership of Ida B. Wells Barnett. This movement was the basis for the formation of the National Association of Colored Women, whose motto was "Lifting as We Climb." That club movement explored and confronted the way in which racism threatened or distorted every aspect of life.

In order to provide the leadership essential for their communities, African American women insisted upon their organizational autonomy while addressing their efforts to the condition of the entire community. In 1895, Josephine St. Pierre Ruffin wrote:

> Our woman's movement is a woman's movement in that it is led and directed by women for the good of women and men, for the benefit of all humanity. . . . We want, we ask the active interest of our men: . . . we are not alienating or withdrawing we are only coming to the front, willing to join any others in the same work and inviting others to join us. (Davis 1933: 19)

The importance of these women's clubs was evident in the interview with the elderly community workers, who described these organizations as places where they learned to lead and administer, and where they organized to win elections in organizations seemingly dominated by men, such as the NAACP and the Urban League.[7] The oldest surviving national African American political organizations are women's organizations whose founders and members also participated in organizing the NAACP, the Urban League,[8] the Association for the Study of Afro-American Life and History, and every other national African American organization. Emerging as one of the prominent leaders during the Depression, Mary McLeod Bethune created the National Council of Negro Women as a lobby for civil rights and working women. The clubs served as training stations for both middle-class and lower-class women leaders.

Several observers in the late nineteenth and early twentieth centuries noted the prestige associated with women's public participation and work for "the Race" (Perkins 1981; Lerner 1972). In urban communities, mothers clubs were organized to deal with childbirth at home, housework, and child care. As children grew older, these clubs became scholarship clubs. Clubs for the protection, cultural "uplift," and mutual aid of household workers were formed. Carter Woodson (1930) identified the significant role of washerwomen in financing and building associations that developed into the major Black insurance companies. He argued that this was one of many examples of the way in which African American working women not only supported their families but also contributed to the possibility of economic self-sufficiency in the entire community. Through such community work, Maggie Lena Walker became the first woman of any color to be a bank president in the United States (Brown 1989; Giddings 198[4]).

W. E. B. Du Bois (1975) observed that the club movement, lacking money as a resource, made its most substantial contribution through the web of affiliations it built, connecting and empowering Black people across class and status lines:

> . . . the women of America who are doing humble but on the whole the most effective work in the social uplift of the lowly, not so much by money as by personal contact, are the colored women. Little is said or known about it but in thousands of churches and social clubs, in missionary societies and fraternal organizations, in unions like the National Association of Colored Women, these workers are founding and sustaining orphanages and old folk homes; distributing personal charity and relief; visiting prisoners; helping hospitals; teaching children; and ministering to all sorts of needs. (1975: 273)

The organizational history of these women is central to African American protest and survival history. They and their organizations have provided the space where contemporary community workers work as directors, managers, social workers, elected politicians, and advocates.

Because of the efforts of community workers, ideas and strategies change. People reflect on their successes and failures, and as new problems arise, these reflections contribute to new solutions or a change in ideology. Black Power activists, for instance, often accused older members of the community of complacency, accommodations, and do-nothingness. One community worker described a confrontation in which "young militants" challenged Mrs. Burns concerning what she had done for the community "lately," implying that she was an accommodationist and represented an old and useless style of leadership. Mrs. Burns reportedly replied, "I was out raising scholarship money to send you to college so you could come back here and give me sass!" When interviewed, Mrs. Burns mentioned things that she would have done differently in light of the logic of the Black Power Movement; she also named things that she was currently doing differently because of her own reflections on history. She told of one encounter with a Black federal official whom she lectured concerning his being used by his agency to steal ideas from her club rather than empowering the club to be the agency's subcontractor to teach the ideas to others. She claimed her feistiness came from her own reflections on a conflict during the 1920s when she accused another activist of "bringing Jim Crow" to her city by campaigning to build a Black hospital. Mrs. Burns conceded, in light of the late 1960s and early 1970s arguments for community control, that he had been right and she, although her view had prevailed then, had been wrong.

Discovery, Challenge, and Development: An Emergent Model of Community Work

The totality of racial oppression and the diversity of African American communities combine to make the tasks of community work so varied as almost to defy any kind of classification. Community work comprises both responses to and catalysts for change. Successful or not, it is the effort to make things better and to eliminate the problems and structures that make life difficult. Community work is the persistent effort across time to close the gap between Black and White life chances. The work is both immediate and long term, and its effects are cumulative. There is, however, an emergent model of action that is present in all of this. It is a model of discovery, challenge, and development that represents a multifaceted model of resistance.

Discovery that there is a problem is the first critical step. Community workers observe, discover, and explore the effects of oppressive practices and structures in their own and others' lives. They are the critical connection between the abrasions of personal experience and the social and political contexts that shape experience. It can be the simple act of sending one's daughter to the mailbox that leads to critical discovery. Describing this as the impetus for her neighborhood association, one worker said, "And simply because we wanted to get together and do things for the community and get the streets cleaned up and the garbage picked up and wanted a mailbox installed on the corner, things like that . . . and then we branched out into other things."

Personal discovery does not lead immediately to community action. The discovery process is complex and involves communicating with others about the reality and nature of community problems. Another worker, a Southern migrant whose community work addressed drug problems and public education, told of her "discovery" of school problems when comparing her son's homework with that of his cousin, who attended school in another, predominantly White, neighborhood. She went on to talk about the problem of transforming personal discovery into collective action, particularly in the North:

A lot is like shadow boxing. The problem is there, but you can't quite see it. We cover them a lot. But down South everything is out in the open. You knew where you stood and everybody knew where the line was drawn, and actually you could deal with it better than here. First you've got to find the problem, then you've got to pull it out from under the covers, and then if somebody says it is a problem. . . . I

remember when I came to Hamptonville I thought there was discrimination in the schools *then*. . . when my kids were in school. We [she and her sister-in-law] were discussing our children's work from school one day, and I looked at my son and his cousin [who were] in the same grade, and the entire curriculum was different. And I said "What is this!" You know, they were in the same grade, and why is this curriculum so different . . . so when I questioned these things, I was really put down; I was bringing discrimination from the South. So I really kept quiet but I've been looking at this thing for a long time.

The activity of discovery and exploration often overlaps with challenge, since discovery itself is subversive. The actions that follow from discovery challenge oppressive structures and practices in a variety of ways. Challenge begins when community workers raise questions among their kin and neighbors, and eventually organize some kind of action. In order to do this they must argue, obstruct, organize, teach, lecture, demonstrate, sue, write letters, and so on. They communicate in such a way that they create a critical speech community around the problem—a group of people who share a point of view on a problem, acknowledging that it exists and that it is something on which public action is necessary.

These initial acts of challenge sometimes emerge into full-blown social movements. At other times, discovery and small-scale actions in one area—welfare rights, for instance—will bring a community worker to the attention of others and involve her in a related but quite different social movement. One woman, describing her involvement on the board of directors of a large human services agency outside of her neighborhood and her own community work focus, said, "The director of the program was having some trouble. . . . She knew that I had raised Hell over in [one neighborhood], so she figured that she needed some raised over in [another neighborhood]."

At the same time they are organizing confrontations with oppressive forces outside the community, community workers address needs within their communities that enable people to resist oppression and participate meaningfully in community life. In the struggle for voting rights, for example, civil rights organizations confronted voter registrars throughout the South with demonstrations and registration campaigns at the same time workers like Septima Clark organized schools to teach African Americans how to read and take the tests (Morris 1984). This is the task of internal development, the building and maintenance of organizations and institutions indigenous to the community.

One elected official argued that the most important problem African Americans faced was internal control: ". . . the way they can't have control over their lives. Although I am not a separatist, I feel as though until we can get into the mainstream of this society . . . we are going to be third- or fourth-class citizens." Trained in elementary education, she surprised me when she told me that she had no intention of teaching children. "I felt that even though I worked with a parents' group, that because I wasn't a teacher, no one took my words very seriously, and I decided that I was going to become a teacher, not to work in the classroom but to work with parents." For some community workers, internal development was so critical, it became their full-time vocation. They either found jobs in agencies that permitted them to do such work or they organized their own agencies.

In a society in which "integration" has become the dominant theme in the politics of race, internal community development can often be very controversial, implying separatism and inter-racial hostility. Mrs. Burns experienced such a conflict and found herself, fifty years later, an advocate for the kind of community control she had earlier labeled "bringing Jim Crow." Because of the power of the dominant society, failure to build and maintain community institutions is a problem. Carter Woodson (1933) labeled it "miseducation" and suggested that it could be solved by building alternative institutions. In my own research, community workers called this activity "building Black-oriented institutions."

What has been labeled a "retreat from integration" is actually the discovery of the internal development that was sometimes accomplished in disadvantaged, segregated, Southern schools. Because education was viewed as something akin to a religious mission, African American teachers, especially after 1915, taught African American history in Southern schools at least durng the month of February. Aware of the aspirations of many fathers and mothers for their daughters' college educations, and also aware of the grim realities that governed women's opportunities, these teachers often insisted that their students learn classical subjects alongside trades and business subjects. In effect they refused to compound limited social opportunities with inflexible educational policies, now called tracking. Since Southern states made it illegal for White teachers to teach Black children, those children were inadvertently provided with important role models. Although African American teachers in segregated schools could be very assimilationist and Anglocentric in their outlook and thinking, their commitment to the community made a real difference. The teachers believed in and supported the students, who, in turn, observed educated African American women and men in positions of leadership.

The activities of discovery, challenge, and development are interrelated and together represent a tradition of resistance. This model of social action must be seen as dynamic and interactive. The women are agents of this tradition of resistance as both volunteers and professionals. Their persistent refusal to accept the discomfort of racial oppression is the conflicted connection between the individual and the society that contributes to the emergence of a social force for change. Commenting that "revolutions happen in the funniest ways," one worker whose agency specialized in developing women for jobs and finding jobs for women said:

> It just started on a physical level. It really just shocked me that I was going to be physically inconvenienced for the simple reason that I was Black. You know? It was that simple, because I was Black. There were certain things that I was not going to be able to get physically, that was going to create conditions of security and warmth and feeling good.

The diversity of their work again points to the totality of the pressure on African Americans as a group. When one accounts for the full range of the women's work, it becomes apparent that every question raised about the source of community afflictions contains the seeds of rebellion and social change.

Conclusion: If It Wasn't For the Women . . .

African American women's community work connects many "small pieces" of community life and contributes to the process of empowerment. The centrality of their work points to the need to examine the importance of women in any community resisting racial oppression. Racial oppression is a complex and interconnected phenomenon that shapes the lives of women and men. Most women of color are trapped in the worst and dirtiest sectors of the female labor market, providing the sole support of their families or supplementing the wages of their husbands who are similarly trapped in male markets. Their families are not accorded the institutional and ideological supports that benefit White families. Additionally, African American, Asian, Latina, and Native American women also do community work. They find their historical role organized around the nurturance and defense and advancement of an oppressed public family. Women in a variety of community settings now and historically have demonstrated that it is safe to parallel the oft-repeated statement of African American church women that "If it wasn't for the women, you wouldn't have a church," to say, "If it were not for women of color, African American, Asian, Latino, and Native peoples would have far fewer alternatives and resources to maintain themselves and challenge a hostile social system."

African American women, and by extension Asian American, Native American, and Latina women, highlight the importance of women and their work for the creation of a just and more equitable society. Women bring three perspectives to community work that make them particularly rebellious. First, their consciousness is shaped by their experience in the society, especially in the labor force. Second, they see men's suffering and feel its effects in their own lives. These women observe and experience the effects of racism on the men of their community along with the effects of that racism in their own lives. The third and perhaps most important source of discontent is the effect of racial oppression in the lives of their children. Combating the damage to their children and attempting to fashion a more inclusive future for them was stated as the most important motivation for involvement. Community workers got involved "through my kids." It is in their roles as the principal caretakers of children that racial-ethnic women pose the largest political threat to the dominant society. Women and their children are the core around which group solidarity is constructed. Community workers are, in the words of Sadie Daniels, "women builders." Community work derives its character from the shared nature of the problems confronting all members of the community. The depths and complexities of racial oppression cannot be grasped without a thorough understanding of its expression in the lives of women and their children.

Although perspectives on women's roles are becoming a prominent part of the social science canon, this development has not incorporated the complex historical roles of women in powerless communities. These women must confront a politics that involves more than the politics implied by race or class or gender. When viewing the creative role of women in the simultaneous processes of social change and community survival, one must conclude that if it wasn't for the women, racially oppressed communities would not have the institutions, organizations, strategies, and ethics that enable the group not only to survive or to maintain itself as an integral whole, but also to develop in an alien, hostile, oppressive situation and to challenge it. In spite of their powerlessness, African American women and women of color generally have a dramatic impact within and beyond their communities. The translation of this historical role into real power and social justice is the ultimate goal of community work.

Notes

1. The data for this chapter are taken from my larger study, "Living and Working in a World of Trouble: The Emergent Career of the Black Woman Community Worker." Similar studies of the Chinese American community (Yap 1983) and the Puerto Rican community (Uriarte-Gaston 1988) also identify the critical role of women community workers.

2. Earlier versions of this paper were presented to the Center for Research on Women, Memphis State University, Summer Research Institutes, 1983 and 1986.

3. Substantial insights for this discussion of racial oppression and internal colonialism are drawn from collaborative work with Bonnie Thornton Dill, Evelyn Nakano Glenn, Elizabeth Higginbotham, and Ruth Zambrana sponsored by the Interuniversity Working Group on Gender, Race, and Class.

4. The importance of the extra time and work cannot be overstated. Bettylou Valentine (1978), discussing the expanded time budgets of ghettoized African Americans, considers this to be part of the social cost of their combined poverty and racial oppression. She not only identifies "hustling" as the legal and extralegal strategies that Blackston residents used to produce and augment income, she also means the term to apply to the extra work, the extra hustle, that must be packed into each day because of poverty and racial oppression.

5. When I first began this research, people assumed I would be studying the African American equivalent of the Junior League. Although the 23 women who were employed full-time were in middle-class occupations, their class origins were as diverse as those of the larger community. Women with poor and working-class origins had usually experienced their upward mobility in the process of acquiring more education in order [to] qualify for positions in human services that allowed them to do community work full-time, both as volunteers and as professionals. Calling it "going up for the oppressed," I explore this special kind of upward mobility in an earlier article (Gilkes 1983).

6. A pseudonym.

7. One Urban League consultant stated that women emerged as presidents of local Urban League and NAACP chapters as often as men, although they did not preside over the national bodies. She concluded that the role of women as local Urban League presidents combined with their roles in Urban League Guilds (women's clubs that raised money for the Urban League) showed the importance of the unacknowledged power of women in community affairs.

8. The Urban League was formed through the merger of two organizations, one male and one female.

References

Balbus, Isaac. 1977. *The Dialectics of Legal Repression: Black Rebels Before the American Criminal Courts.* New Brunswick, NJ: Transaction Books.

Blackwell, James. 1985. *The Black Community: Diversity and Unity.* Second edition. New York: Harper & Row.

Blauner, Robert. 1972. *Racial Oppression in America.* New York: Harper & Row.

Brown, Elsa Barkley. 1989. "Womanist Consciousness: Maggie Lena Walker and the Independent Order of Saint Luke." *Signs: Journal of Women in Culture and Society* 14 (3): 610–633.

Cade, Toni, ed. 1970. *The Black Woman: An Anthology.* New York: Signet.

Cesaire, Aime, 1972. *Discourse on Colonialism.* New York: Monthly Review Press (First published 1955).

Davis, Angela. 1971. "Reflections on the Black Woman's Role in the Community of Slaves." *Black Scholar* 3 (4): 2–15.

———. 1981. *Women, Race, and Class.* New York: Random House.

Davis, Elizabeth Lindsey. 1933. *Lifting as They Climb: A History of the National Association of Colored Women.* Washington, DC: Moorland-Springam Research Center.

Deloria, Vine. 1970. *We Talk, You Listen: New Tribes, New Turf.* New York: Dell.

Du Bois, W. E. B. 1975. *The Gift of Black Folk: Negroes in the Making of America* (1924). Millwood, NY: Kraus-Thompson Organization.

Edelman, Marian Wright. 1987. *Families in Peril: An Agenda for Social Change.* Cambridge, MA: Harvard University Press.

Faris, Robert E. L. 1967. *Chicago Sociology, 1920–1932.* Chicago: University of Chicago Press.

Giddings, Paula. 1984. *When and Where I Enter: The Impact of Black Women on Race and Sex in America.* New York: William Morrow.

Gilkes, Cheryl Townsend. 1979. "Living and Working in a World of Trouble: The Emergent Career of the Black Woman Community Worker." Ph.D. dissertation, Northeastern University.

———. 1980. "The Sources of Conceptual Revolutions in the Field of Race Relations." Pp. 7–31 in David Claerbaut, ed., *New Directions in Ethnic Studies: Minorities in America.* San Francisco: Century Twenty-One.

———. 1983. "Going up for the Oppressed: The Career Mobility of Black Women Community Workers." *Journal of Social Issues* 39 (3):115–139.

———. 1990. "'Liberated to Work Like Dogs': Labeling Black Women and Their Work." Pp. 165–188 in Hildreth Y. Grossman and Nia Lane Chester, eds., *The Experience and Meaning of Work in Women's Lives.* Hillsdale, NJ: Lawrence Erlbaum Associates.

Hughes, Everett C. 1963. "Race Relations and the Sociological Imagination." *American Sociological Review* 28 (6): 879–890.

———. 1971. *The Sociological Eye: Selected Papers on Work, Self, and the Study of Society.* Chicago: Aldine-Atherton.

King, Mary. 1987. *Freedom Song: A Personal Story of the 1960s Civil Rights Movement.* New York: William Morrow.

Lerner, Gerda. 1972. *Black Women in White America: A Documentary History.* New York: Vintage Books.

Lyman, Stanford. 1972. *The Black American in Sociological Thought: A Failure of Perspective.* New York: G. P. Putnam.

Marable, Manning. 1983. *How Capitalism Underdeveloped Black America: Problems in Race, Political Economy and Society.* Boston: South End Press.

Morris, Aldon. 1984. *The Origins of the Civil Rights Movement: Black Communities Organizing for Change.* New York: Free Press.

Perkins, Linda. 1981. "Black Women and Racial 'Uplift' Prior to Emancipation." Pp. 317–334 in Filomina Chioma Steady, ed., *The Black Woman Cross-Culturally.* Cambridge, MA: Schenkman.

Reagon, Bernice Johnson. 1982 "My Black Mothers and Sisters or on Beginning a Cultural Autobiography." *Feminist Studies* 8 (1): 81–96.

——. 1986. "African Diaspora Women: The Making of Cultural Workers." *Feminist Studies* 12 (1): 77–90.

Richardson, Marilyn, ed. 1987. *Maria Stewart, America's First Black Woman Political Writer: Essays and Speeches.* Bloomington: Indiana University Press.

Sterling, Dorothy. 1984. *We Are Your Sisters: Black Women in the Nineteenth Century.* New York: W. W. Norton.

Uriarte-Gaston, Miren. 1988. "Organizing for Survival: The Emergence of a Puerto Rican Community." Ph. D. dissertation, Boston University.

Valentine, Bettylou. 1978. *Hustling and Other Hard Work: Life Styles in the Ghetto.* New York: Free Press.

Webber, Thomas L. 1978. *Deep like the Rivers: Education in the Slave Quarter Community, 1831–1865.* New York: W. W. Norton.

White, Deborah Gray. 1985. *Ar'n't I a Woman? Female Slaves in the Plantation South.* New York: W. W. Norton.

Wilson, William Julius. 1973. *Power, Racism and Privilege: Race Relations in Theoretical and Sociohistorical Perspectives.* New York: Macmillan.

Woodson, Carter G. 1930. "The Negro Washerwoman." *Journal of Negro History* 15 (3): 269–277.

——. 1933. *The Mis-Education of the Negro.* New York: Associated Publishers.

Yap, Stacey Guat Hong. 1983. "Gather Your Strength, Sisters: The Emergence of Chinese Women Community Workers." Ph. D. dissertation, Boston University.

Discussion Questions

1. What do you think Gilkes means by "if it wasn't for the women"? She implies that social change would not have occurred in oppressed communities without women's contributions. How does she support that position?

2. Does the community work done by women differ from that done by men? If so, what might account for the difference? The paid work of working-class people differs from that of middle-class people. Does their community work differ too? How and why?

3. This reading contains a model of community work. What are the elements of that model?

4. Are you involved in community work of any sort? Are your activities directed toward social change or toward keeping some aspects of the community the way they are? How did you get involved? If school and other responsibilities are keeping you too busy right now, what sort of community work do you think you might be involved in at some later date?

52

Liberia's Female Warriors

Fierce, Feared

Glenn McKenzie

In this piece, Glenn McKenzie focuses on the experiences of the all-female Women's Artillery Commandos of Liberia, Africa. The all-female commando units headed by leaders such as Black Diamond (mentioned in the article) are part of a larger rebel movement against strongman Charles Taylor and his brutal forces, notorious for their proclivity for rape and pillaging. It is in the stories of the female rebels that McKenzie's article sheds light on African women in the midst of civil war—stories on gender, class, and race.

According to McKenzie, one of the reasons these Liberian women have joined the rebel forces and taken up arms is having been victims of or witnesses of sexual assault—a sexualized brutal reminder of gendered tyranny. In addition, Taylor's fighters seem to think nothing of capturing and enslaving young women to meet their domestic needs—condemning these women to a class-based hell of servitude. At the same time, this Liberian male brutality is aimed at Liberian females and so depredations are visited on the women of one's own racial-cultural group—a reminder of patriarchal power at home.

Yet, it is the women's resistance to all of these forms of oppression which is the most remarkable part of McKenzie's article. McKenzie notes that the women are trained along with the men and are perfectly capable of standing up to Taylor's men—intimidating men who are physically larger. In addition, the female rebel fighters are also quite capable of standing up to male rebel fighters who have not learned to treat women fairly, as they have been known to shoot rapist officers and successfully repel unwanted advances by their male peers. Interestingly, it is even believed by some men who have fought against them, McKenzie notes, that all-female units have their own unique strengths above and beyond those of the men, evidently able to fight for considerably longer stretches than men.

Finally, McKenzie reports that Black Diamond and her female commandos, while willing and able to continue the fighting as long as may be necessary, ultimately want to return to life as free women and hope to shape a world better than the one they came from.

Her uniform is a red beret, spaghetti-strap halter top and black jeans. Her weapons are Kalashnikov AK-47s and mortars.

Black Diamond, 22, is a Liberian rebel commander—known by her nom de guerre and feared by friends and foes alike in a war-shattered nation where women and girls are more likely to be victims than avengers.

Whether blasting mortar rounds at enemy troops or slapping down armed looters, she and her all-female Womens' Artillery Commandos fight for revenge, they say, against wrongs by Liberia's brutal government forces.

They don't have to fight for respect; they've already got it.

"Fire you! Fire you!" Black Diamond snarled one day this month at armed men lugging sacks of grain in a looting spree she and her fighters, many in earrings and lipstick, had been ordered to stop.

Astonished

She blasted her rifle inches over the head of a muscular looter who was slow to drop his weapon, then struck him in the chest with a lightning-fast fist and screamed in his face.

The man—nearly twice her size—fell backward, astonished and cowering.

Black Diamond said later at the rebel stronghold of Tubmanburg, 40 miles from Monrovia, "Women can fight the same as men. Some women more than men."

"They are trained like we are. They are the same," confirmed Ranger One, commander of an all-male unit.

Asked about the women's much-touted ferocity, Ranger One replied that he would never marry a female fighter "because it's risky to my life."

Liberia has a history of women in arms in its 14 years of conflict under Charles Taylor.

In the 1989–96 civil war, which Taylor launched, his own faction had female artillery units renowned for their bravery and accuracy. Some senior female commanders took posts in Liberia's armed forces when Taylor won the presidency in 1997.

When Liberia's main rebel movement took up arms four years ago, Black Diamond and many other women were among the first to join. Their mission was to unseat Taylor, whose unsalaried, undisciplined fighters made raping and looting a perk of service in Liberia's armed forces.

"Operation Pay Yourself," the soldiers called it.

Black Diamond's mother was killed in the civil war, though she refuses to say how or when. Other relatives fled their homes in the capital Monrovia, for neighboring Guinea.

"Yes," Black Diamond said when asked if she had suffered at the hands of Taylor's vicious troops. "No," she said, looking down, when asked to elaborate.

"If I explain all that, I will cry," she growled, her lower lip trembling slightly. "No more raping," she added, in a mumble.

Liberian Health Minister Peter Coleman, a surgeon and therapist, has encountered a number of female fighters in the years of near constant warfare.

Many told him they were motivated by rage after they or their relatives were sexually assaulted. Others took up arms after being captured to perform domestic and sexual services for male fighters.

"When you think of cooks and sex slaves, it is preferable for many to fight, even if you could be killed," the health minister said.

Others join because "you see other girls in action, they look good and you want to just join them."

Rebel factions prize their female officers because they are "more disciplined than the men. They don't get drunk and they take their mission very seriously," Coleman said.

"I saw a woman shoot another officer because he raped a woman," he said. "She could not tolerate it. Everyone was afraid of her."

Government militias—which also have female fighters—say women are among their most feared opponents.

"They have powers that men don't have. They will not stop when others stop," said a government officer, who identified himself only as Powell.

Male rebel commanders treat the women as equals.

Although physically weaker than the men, "I will show you I don't want you to have me the way you want to have me," Black Diamond said of unwanted advances by male counterparts.

When rebels marched from the jungle to the capital in June, Black Diamond and her commandoes marched, too.

When Taylor fell, forced out by the rebels and international pressure, Black Diamond and her unit celebrated.

After West African peacekeepers and U.S. Marines deployed to secure Monrovia's port, Black Diamond and her unit withdrew to their headquarters in a ramshackle cement-block, tin-roof house in Tubmanburg.

There, the women await orders, ready to relaunch war. "[I]f our chairman orders it," Black Diamond said. "I am not tired. Only Charles Taylor is tired."

She hopes peace will hold so she and her commandoes can return to civilian life—"something even better" than what they left behind.

"If you go to school, you go to school. If you do business, you do business," Black Diamond said, but quickly shrugged off talk of her postwar dreams.

"The time has not come to say."

Discussion Questions

1. What do you think of Black Diamond and her all-female rebel units? Does their experience in any way resonate with your own? Do you find them heroic or ludicrous or something in between? Why or why not?

2. Often research on gender, race, and class finds a historically rooted bigotry toward

women of color as not as refined and "lady-like" as European-women. Some of these bigoted views describe women of color as bestial and animal-like. Do you think this article plays into this view or challenges it? Why or why not?

3. If this article was about all-female Irish units, British units, or German units, do you think you would have had the same reaction to the piece? Why or why not?

4. Do you think that women can be as effective soldiers as men? Do you think women should be part of combat units? Why or why not?

5. Do you know a woman in the military? Is she a friend or family member? What has been her experience in the military? Has she seen any combat?

Reprinted from: Glenn McKenzie, "Liberia's Female Warriors—Fierce, Feared." In the *Minneapolis Star Tribune*, (August 30) pp. A1, A21. Copyright © 2003 by the Associated Press. Reprinted by permission. ✦

53
The Heterosexual Questionnaire

Martin Rochlin

George Herbert Mead (1863–1931) is considered a founder of social psychology. He taught that the ability to take the role of the other was a crucial component of the development of the self. The author of this questionnaire owes a great deal to Mead. Anyone, gay or straight, who has heard the questions straight people typically ask gay people will recognize what Martin Rochlin has done here. Isn't this just a phase? Why do you have to flaunt it? What do you do in bed? Have you considered therapy?

In some ways this questionnaire is just a playful opportunity for the straight majority to reverse roles with the gay and lesbian minority. However, some of the questions demand a little more reflection. Because we think of heterosexuality as "normal," we don't often ask what might have "caused" it or when someone decided she or he was not gay. Many social and life scientists believe that we should not be looking for a unique "cause," whether biological, psychological, or sociocultural, for homosexuality but rather that the same theories ought to explain all varieties of sexuality.

1. What do you think caused your heterosexuality?

2. When and how did you decide you were a heterosexual?

3. Is it possible that your heterosexuality is just a phase you may grow out of?

4. Is it possible that your heterosexuality stems from a neurotic fear of others of the same sex?

5. If you have never slept with a person of the same sex, is it possible that all you need is a good Gay lover?

6. Do your parents know that you are straight? Do your friends and/or roommate(s) know? How did they react?

7. Why do you insist on flaunting your heterosexuality? Can't you just be who you are and keep it quiet?

8. Why do heterosexuals place so much emphasis on sex?

9. Why do heterosexuals feel compelled to seduce others into their lifestyle?

10. A disproportionate majority of child molesters are heterosexual. Do you consider it safe to expose children to heterosexual teachers?

11. Just what do men and women do in bed together? How can they truly know how to please each other, being so anatomically different?

12. With all the societal support marriage receives, the divorce rate is spiraling. Why are there so few stable relationships among heterosexuals?

13. Statistics show that lesbians have the lowest incidence of sexually transmitted diseases. Is it really safe for a woman to maintain a heterosexual lifestyle and run the risk of disease and pregnancy?

14. How can you become a whole person if you limit yourself to compulsive, exclusive heterosexuality?

15. Considering the menace of overpopulation, how could the human race survive if everyone were heterosexual?

16. Could you trust a heterosexual therapist to be objective? Don't you feel s/he might be inclined to influence you in the direction of her/his own leanings?

17. There seem to be very few happy heterosexuals. Techniques have been developed that might enable you to change if you really want to. Have you considered trying aversion therapy?

18. Would you want your child to be heterosexual, knowing the problems that s/he would face?

Discussion Questions

1. How did reading these questions make you feel? Uncomfortable? Embarrassed? Amused? Angry? What did you want to say? "Right on"? "Come off it"? "Get over it"? Share your thoughts with someone else in the class.

2. This questionnaire has been widely circulated on the Internet. In fact, I initially used it in classes without knowing who wrote it or where it was published. What kinds of websites would you expect to find it on? Why do you think it has been circulated so widely?

3. Have you read or heard any recent discussions of the causes of sexual orientation? What theory or theories were being presented? What kind of evidence was offered? Did the discussions focus only on one type of sexual orientation or did they attempt to account for sexuality in general?

4. There are no explicit references to race or class and only one, regarding lesbians and sexually transmitted diseases and pregnancy, to gender in this questionnaire. Can you suggest some additional questions that might reflect race- or class-based assumptions about gay or straight individuals? For example, you might ask why many people assume that gay people have more disposable income than straight people.

54
Race Lessons

Dalton Conley

When reading this piece by Dalton Conley, it is easy to slip into the sense that one is reading from a novel. Yet, for all the quality of good storytelling this chapter evinces, Conley is actually quite deftly navigating us through the empirical territory of race, class, gender, and even a smattering of religion for good measure, with seemingly little effort. What reads like a novel for the audience, then, is actually a carefully crafted analysis.

In Dalton Conley's world, race, gender, class, and religion weave in and out of the story and examples are everywhere present. Conley notes that he and his sister, whose experiences make up the piece, are made to understand that they are not like everyone else in their school playground—they are not Black. Even in this setting and at such young ages, it is clear that the other children understand the privileges of race as the Black girls fight to trade their Black Barbies for his sister's White one—read the "real" Barbie. Conley and his sister, who are Jewish, are forced to celebrate all the Christian holidays at the local federally subsidized Head Start school for poor kids. At Christmas, Santa doles out boy dolls for boys and girl dolls for girls—appropriate gender-coded toys—even after his sister has asked for a Big Wheel—a toy fashioned for discovery and independence. Conley's sister will also learn that when she wants to be like her Black friends—to wear her hair in cornrows, it will be unacceptable and mocked, and she will retaliate by mocking Black hair as well, retreating into her straight, blonde White girlhood. In the school, the principal states flat out to Conley's mother that there is no place for her son—he is White in a world of Black, Puerto Rican, and Chinese students. She chooses the "Black class," and in this environment, Conley learns the rules of in-class jokes—jokes about welfare casually stated in a setting where welfare is familiar to the students. Conley also learns that all of his classmates are subject to corporal punishment from the teacher except himself—the Black teacher will not cross the racial divide to punish a White student. Conley develops a twitching and blinking series of idiosyncratic movements, mainly based on knowing that, unlike his Black and Puerto Rican counterparts, he is not receiving any punishment or discipline at all while his fellow classmates bleed after blows from the yardstick. Eventually, Conley's mother will take her son out of the school altogether and move him into schools with middle- and upper-class children—mainly White. The losers, Conley notes, were the local schools, filled with boys and girls of color.

Learning race is like learning a language. First we try mouthing all sounds. Then we learn which are not words and which have meaning to the people around us. Likewise, for my sister and me, the first step in our socialization was being taught that we weren't black. Like a couple of boot camp trainees, we had first to be stripped of any illusions we harbored of being like the other kids, then be built back up in whiteness.

My sister, Alexandra, started getting the message as early as age two. She and I attended nursery school courtesy of the federally subsidized Head Start program. One of the Great Society initiatives that seemed to parallel our lives, Head Start was the result of a decade of research showing that the educational deficits poor kids faced in high school could be traced back to their preschool years—that is, to the time when they were with their parents at home. Never mind what this implied about certain people's parenting practices; the answer was to provide poor kids with day care where they would get at least one nutritious meal a day and be exposed to educational toys. Head Start even had a government-mandated commencement day to get us accustomed to the idea of graduating so it wouldn't seem strange by the time we reached high school. We had to make our own caps and gowns out of crepe paper.

Despite the nominal separation of church and state, our local program first met in the basement of a local church before moving to the community center of the Bernard Baruch houses on the other side of Columbia Street. Likewise, our Head Start celebrated all Christian holidays. Each December Santa Claus came bounding in with a bag of presents and a series of "Ho! Ho! Hos!" so enthusiastic and deep in tone that they scared us and shook the cubbyholes where we stored our things each morning. Then he would sit down and balance each kid on his knee as if he were the ventriloquist and we the wooden dummies.

"And have you been a naughty girl or a nice girl?" he asked my sister when her turn came one particular year.

"I want a Big Wheel," she responded, her manner as rehearsed as Santa's.

It didn't matter what they asked for; everyone got dolls. The boys got boy dolls, and the girls got girl dolls. In line with the consciousness of the times, the teachers had made sure that the dolls were ethnically appropriate. The other kids' dolls looked like black versions of Ken and Barbie, while my sister ended up with the only white doll in her class. All the figures were generic knockoffs, probably bought from a street vendor in Chinatown; in fact, the black dolls looked exactly like the white one, but with a coat of brown paint on their bodies and hair. Nonetheless, when the other kids saw that Alexandra had a real Barbie, they stampeded her, begging, pleading, and demanding that she trade with them. She clutched the doll to her chest as girls and even boys tried to pry it from her.

"Black is beautiful!" the teachers screamed over the din of crying and yelling.

"We want Barbie!" the kids yelled back in unison.

Finally, one kid pulled hard at the white doll's legs and broke the toy in half. Evidently satisfied that she had secured at least a piece of Barbie, she scurried off to a corner to dress up the half-doll. Eventually my sister got the other half back and willingly traded her white doll for one in the black style. She was content. All she wanted was a doll with long hair that she could comb.

At some point that same week, our grandparents called to wish us a Happy Chanukah. My sister recounted the Barbie events to my grandmother, who, in turn, told her the story of King Solomon and the baby. "Two women each said that the baby was hers," she explained slowly, enunciating each syllable to my sister who, at that stage in her development, paid eager attention to anything involving babies. "King Solomon told them that he would cut the baby in half and then each could have part of it." She explained that one of the women broke down crying, offering the baby to the other woman. "'You are the true mother,' the King told this one," Grandma recounted as our grandfather breathed not quite silently on the other phone extension, as was his custom.

"Do you know how he knew?" Grandma then asked, trying to pry the moral of the story out of Alexandra. "What would you say if King Solomon said that to you about your baby?"

"I would take the top half," my sister explained. "So I could brush her hair."

In the family annals, my sister's answer to the King Solomon question was what got told and retold; the issue of black beauty, the other kids' desperation for the white doll, and the idea that a "real" Barbie could only be white was left for the parents of the other children to sort out. It wasn't our problem; after all, we *were* the color of Barbie.

The next year everyone got black dolls whether they liked it or not. And since they had long hair, my sister was happy.

By the time she was six years old, Alexandra had tired of combing and brushing and wanted to do more advanced hair things. All her friends now had cornrows, and my sister begged my mother to braid some for her, too. Alexandra's best friend, Adoonie, lived in the building across from ours in the complex. She and my sister spent hours envying each other's hair. Adoonie wanted blond locks that looked like Farrah Fawcett's, while my sister wanted the cornrows that made Adoonie fit in with the rest of the kids in the playground. My sister got particularly jealous each month when Adoonie and her mother unbraided and cleaned her cornrows with witch hazel, then rebraided them so neatly that they looked like rows of stitches on some machine-knitted sweater. The whole procedure took hours, and since Adoonie was an only child she and her mother could spend an entire leisurely day on the endeavor. It was pure mother-daughter time, something Alexandra craved in the face of her competition with me for parental attention.

"Please, can you do my hair like Doonie's?" she'd plead with our mother every so often, trying to braid her own hair to demonstrate the technique. "Please, please, please!" My mother, who couldn't draw, knit, or cornrow a straight line, told Alexandra that her hair type wouldn't work for that style but was beautiful in its own right.

"I don't care; I want my hair like Doonie's— like everybody's," Alexandra pouted. Ellen wiped the tears from her face and spent a good portion of the next hour brushing my sister's hair in the mirror. After a couple more episodes like this one, Alexandra finally let go of the dream of cornrows. But the next year the movie *10* came out, making Bo Derek famous. At first all the little girls thought Bo Derek, with her cornrowed hair and tropical tan, must be black. They wanted to grow their own cornrows longer so that they, like Bo Derek, could have the best of both worlds: long hair and tight braids along their scalp.

Then one of the older girls told the group that Bo Derek was actually white, a revelation that left the younger ones feeling confused, hurt, and betrayed. My sister, however, was joyous; now she, too, could have the cornrows she had, up till then, been denied because of her race. When she brought home this piece of information, our mother had no choice but to relent and braid Alexandra's hair as best she could, putting in black, red, and orange African beads as my sister requested. It was all to no avail. The braids frayed, and the beads didn't stand out against her chestnut hair; rather, they looked like colored gnats or lice that had infested her scalp. My sister was not entirely satisfied with my mother's effort, but she wanted to show Adoonie nonetheless, so she rushed out to the playground to find her.

"Yo, excuse me, miss," an older girl said and laughed, "someone left some twine on your head."

"Is that some cornrows?" another asked, stopping from her jump-rope counting game. "Looks more like wheat to me."

"Oh, snap," added a third, cracking up.

Alexandra started crying and ran back into the pitted brick building. When Adoonie found her upstairs, she tried to console her. "My mother will do your braids for you if you like." She stroked my sister's head as she spoke softly to her. "Won't that be nice, wouldn't you like that?"

"Forget it," Alexandra said as she unwound the cornrows, which had already started to unbraid themselves as if they, too, didn't like how the experiment had turned out. "I don't want the stupid cornrows. They're stupid." At this comment, Adoonie cried and ran off. From then on Alexandra only wanted long blond hair, straight as could be, taking comfort in the cultural value of her whiteness.

It didn't take more than one or two messages like this to drive home the meaning of race to my sister. Race was not something mutable, like a freckle or a hairstyle; it defined who looked like whom, who was allowed to be in the group—and who wasn't. But for Alexandra and me, race was turned inside-out. Notwithstanding the Barbie incident, the cornrows, and the images we saw on television, we had no idea that we belonged to the majority group, the privileged one. We merely thought we didn't belong.

That began to change for me when I started at the local public school, across Pitt Street on the other side of the housing complex. By then I had learned that I was white and other people around me weren't, but I had yet to understand what that difference meant. I had yet to learn the privileges that attended whiteness. One month in public school would fix that.

On the first day of classes that fall, the principal called my mother and me into his office. "Mrs. Cone-ly," he said in a heavy Puerto Rican accent, "can I speak with you for a moment?" The school was Public School 4, the Mini School, named for its diminutive size. However, the moniker reflected nothing about the size of the classes. There were only three, each of them overcrowded with about forty students.

"We do not have a class for your son," the principal told my mother, looking down and smiling at me; I remember staring, transfixed, at his snakeskin boots, feeling as if they might slither around the floor of his office if I took my eyes off them. "You see," he continued, "there is the black and Puerto Rican classes." The words *Puerto Rican* stood out from the rest; they seemed to spring naturally from his mouth, whereas the English words dropped out like stillborns. "And then there is the Chinese class. . .," he trailed off, as if he regretted the Chinese class. "There have been many Chinese that come here now." They were coming from an ever-expanding Chinatown, which had crept into the other side of the school district.

My mother didn't quite follow him. She wondered whether the fact that the principal did not speak English too well meant I would learn Spanish in this school. I remember only his attire, every detail of it. Over his snakeskin boots he wore a beige polyester suit and matching tie. The jacket had many buttons, so that it looked more like a shirt than the upper half of a suit.

"So, which class do you prefer?" he asked, fingering one of the buttons.

It now dawned on my mother that school desegregation did not necessarily mean classroom desegregation. She still had not answered the principal, who now took it upon himself to explain further. "You see," he added, "there is no white class." He now reclined, crossed his arms, and smiled, content that he had finally gotten his point across.

"I suppose we'll take the black class," she said, trying to guess which one my father would have chosen. In this instance, the choices our race gave us were made quite explicit—by a government institution, no less.

I found myself in a crowded classroom with paint peeling from the walls and plaster falling from the ceiling. The teacher was a black woman with a slender frame but a booming voice. She normally taught fourth or fifth grade and wasn't too happy about being stuck with us first-graders. She paced across the front of the room, intermittently drawing on the blackboard to illustrate what she was saying. Sometimes she would write out big words, forgetting that most of us could not read much more than the alphabet or words like "cat." When not drawing on the board, she compulsively brushed chalk residue off her hands and dress. Nevertheless, as each day wore on the layer of chalk dust covering her got progressively deeper, giving her skin a ghost-like quality, as if she were fading away—along with our attention—during the afternoon hours.

As if to compensate for her weakening skin tone and our waning concentration, she grew stricter by the hour. In the mornings we could get away with whispering or fidgeting in our seats. But by one p.m., any peep or audible rustle meant a whack across the knuckles with a yardstick. For everybody but me, that is.

"Yo, your momma been on welfare so long," my classmate Earl whispered to me, "her face's on food stamps." He gave a low five to the boy seated in front of him, checking first to see that the teacher was still turned toward the blackboard. However, he did not take account of the fact that her hearing improved after the lunch hour.

"Up here right now, Earl," she said. She stood akimbo, fists balled up.

Earl marched up slowly, staring at his sneakers, face down and Afro up, as if it offered protection. It didn't. She took his hands and whacked them three times with the thin edge of the ruler. I felt myself leap off the seat with each whack, as if the ruler were a lever and I were sitting on the other end of it. My spine and head stayed still, but the rest of me moved upward. Then I started to blink, and my cheeks began to twitch. Earl did not flinch or yelp in the least.

He turned around and walked back to his desk with a stoicism that exceeded his age. When he passed by my seat on the way back to his place, I stared down as he had in the presence of the teacher, unable to look him in the eyes. I remember catching a glimpse of his bloodied knuckles, where his brown skin had parted to reveal the scarlet flesh underneath. I fantasized about being beaten myself, digging the graphite tip of my number-two pencil into my skin. Then I released the pressure, trying to share the sense of relief I imagined Earl felt after his punishment was over. At lunch Earl asked if he could sit next to me. I nodded. Still looking down, I tensed up and twitched, waiting for his blow. It never came. He offered me his Tater Tots. As if he could read my mind, he said, "Aw, she's alright; don't worry about her."

Over the weeks, every kid received this form of corporal punishment, boys and girls alike. Some kids, Earl among them, suffered the ruler's blows so often that their knuckles scabbed and then scarred over into rough keloid skin. I was the only one who escaped the yardstick—and not, I knew even at the time, because I was particularly well behaved. Everyone involved, teacher and students, took it for granted that a black teacher would never cross the racial line to strike a white student. The other kids never resented me for this; on the contrary, they were quite cheerful toward me. I even tried to get into fights in that school, fights I knew I would lose; I wanted to feel the relief of being struck. But Earl, one of the largest kids in the school, took it upon himself to protect me. By the end of my first term there, my mother noticed that I was twitching and blinking compulsively—not just during classroom hours, and not just from the image of the yardstick striking Earl's knuckles. There was something else bothering me. Each day I came home from school trembling and immediately ran to the bathroom to relieve myself. My mother also noticed that my Fruit-of-the-Loom underwear and even some of my Toughskin jeans were urine-stained. She asked me why I didn't go to the bathroom at school.

"If you go to the bathroom," I said, nodding my head to emphasize the seriousness of what I was saying, "they cut off your pee-pee."

"No, they don't cut off your pee-pee," she answered, stroking my head as it jerked repeatedly to the side in one of my many new tics.

"Yes," I nodded exuberantly, quite sure of what I was saying, appearing almost happy at the horrible possibility I was describing. Only when I was deeply engrossed in or completely certain of something did my tics disappear. "If you go to the bathroom, they cut off your pee-pee." I now said it as if I were exasperated at having to explain something so obvious. This was the first time that I used the term *they* to describe the collective other, the same *they* who would commit countless crimes throughout my childhood but a different *they* from those who made the rules for school, set policy on busing, and decided how much rent we paid or how many food stamps we received.

Wanting to get to the bottom of my tics and my reluctance to use the restroom at school, my mother made an appointment with the principal. This time his clothing had changed dramatically. He wore the same gray snakeskin boots, but over them hung not a friendly beige suit but rather a black, urbane one with a matching silk shirt. His tie, which bore a picture of Bugs Bunny, stood in sharp contrast to the gangsterish shirt and jacket. He sat on the edge of his desk, one foot swinging back and forth slowly, as if he were trying to hypnotize my mother. His head motion added to this effect. He nodded rhythmically, as if he were checking out her body. She was wearing her favorite denim jacket with mother-of-pearl buttons, though she could not fasten them across her ample chest. She had sewn a Navajo bead design on the back to force some strange truce between cowboys and Indians in her clothing.

"Does the teacher hit Dalton?" she asked. She had already asked me, and I had said no—but I twitched when I answered the question.

"Oh, no," he answered. "In fact," he added, "Dalton is the only student that is not hit."

Bingo! thought my mother, realizing I had told her the truth. "That must be it," she said to the principal. "That's why he's twitching."

"So you want him to receive physical discipline as well, then?" the principal asked, as if this were the logical conclusion to their conversation. His boots had stopped moving and were now clamped against the side of his desk for balance as he leaned toward her.

"No, no," she said, pushing her glasses back up her nose, as was her habit. She asked whether something could be done to prevent the other kids from being struck.

"No, Mrs. Cone-ly," he explained in a tone that was simultaneously sympathetic and exasperated. He explained that the other parents had requested that their children be physically disciplined. "We knew that white parents spoil their kids," he said, "so she doesn't strike Dalton."

The Puerto Rican class had a Puerto Rican teacher who also hit the students, so the solution that the principal and my mother worked out was to switch me to the Chinese class. The teacher there did not use corporal punishment. Though growing rapidly, the local Asian population was still comparatively small, so the class had the added benefit of having fewer students than the others. I transferred in during the first week of the spring semester. Half the lessons were taught in English, the other half in Chinese. I liked the friendly dynamics of the class and felt challenged by my language handicap. My linguistic disadvantage compensated for the fact that by some error, I had been switched from my first-grade class into kindergarten.

"When I call out your name, stand up," the teacher said during roll call on my first day. "If you have an American name, tomorrow I will tell you your name in Chinese. If you have a Chinese name, tomorrow I will tell you your name in English." I was excited by the prospect of being renamed and merging into the group, of which I was the only non-ethnically Chinese member. The next morning the instructor came in and started the roll call again. This time she read off two names for everyone.

"John," she said. "Jiang. Jaili, Julie." Then she got to me. "Dalton," she said. "Dalton," she repeated.

I was crushed. She announced that she could not find a translation for my name. Of course, at the time I didn't know that none of these name pairs were actual translations, that there was no straightforward way to convert names from a tonal, character-based language to English. Nonetheless, to make me feel better she said my name once again in the second tone, so that it went up in pitch in the latter syllable. She made the entire class repeat it in her Cantonese accent. They did. Instead of feeling better, though, I felt singled out by this attention.

To make matters worse, the next day we went through our birthdays. I found out that everyone else had been born in the year of the dog, 1970, while I—the ostensible first-grader among them—was born in the year of the rooster, 1969. The kids chuckled to themselves, but their laughter did not wound me the way the snaps of some of the black kids had. This, I would later realize, captured the essential difference between race and ethnicity. It would have seemed absurd if the black teacher had tried to integrate me into that class. Racial groupings were about domination and struggles for power; what's more, race barriers were taken as both natural and insurmountable.

But in the Chinese class, eventually I began to feel I was part of the student community. My Chinese language skills improved, and my black hair grew longer and straighter—as if I were unconsciously trying to assimilate—so that by the end of the first month my mother confessed she could not pick me out instantly when she came to walk me home from school.

While life was for the most part more comfortable for me in the Chinese class, I made no real friends there, no one that I saw after school. Most of the kids lived west of the school, on the other side of the district, and were picked up promptly at three o'clock by their grandparents, who generally spoke no English and shepherded them home by their wrists. I must have already started to segregate myself culturally, since it never even crossed my mind to invite any of the kids home with me after school. At the same time, I had lost touch with most of my friends from the black class, who lived scattered among the housing projects and tenements of my neighborhood.

After I switched classes my tics gradually disappeared, and I no longer held my urine all day. My mother asked me if I was, in fact, going to the bathroom at school. "Yes," I responded. "Now they no cut off your pee-pee." My diction had taken on a Chinese rhythm. She laughed, relieved that I had resolved my fears. But soon afterward she read a very disturbing story in the *Daily News*. "Castrator Caught," the headline read. The story went on to explain how several students had lost their genitals in the P.S. 4 bathroom. An angry crowd had finally apprehended this child molester and beaten him to death on Delancey Street. I had been right all along.

My parents decided that enough was enough. When the semester ended I was once again yanked from my class, this time bound for another school altogether. That didn't work out either. But then my mother learned from a friend that the Board of Education did not require much in the way of proof of one's address to verify a child's school district. She could tell them she lived in the Empire State Building and, as long as she could get mail there and respond to immunization notices, lice alerts, and other school correspondence, no one would ever be the wiser. It was even the case, she learned, that after October 1 she could switch my address back to the projects and, since the school year would already be under way, the Board of Education could not force me to return to my local school. What's more, once October rolled around, my adopted school was legally required—thanks to the liberal New York State courts—to send a bus to pick me up and take me home.

A small group of enterprising parents from the neighborhood had enough cross-town contacts to take advantage of these loopholes. They spent the first month of each academic year carting their kids across town on the subway or the M14 bus to schools in well-endowed districts; once the October 1 deadline came, a yellow school bus would swoop into the projects, rounding up the fortunate kids. Each year the dance would begin anew. The schools that were inundated with us "ghetto" kids didn't mind the arrangement, since we took funds with us wherever we went. Title I of the Elementary and Secondary Education Act of 1965, one of the cornerstones of Lyndon Johnson's Great Society, provided federal funds for students from economically distressed areas, be they the dirt farms of eastern Kentucky or the dirt-colored buildings of the Lower East Side. Title I kids, as we were called, benefited by getting better educations, while the schools themselves won out financially. The losers in the arrangement were the local schools, which lost not only funding but also the students whose parents enjoyed the most "social capital," that is, connections.

The *they* who made up these policies were, on the surface, quite different in character from the *they* who stole car radios or cut off the peckers of my classmates at the Mini School. The Board of Education, the state welfare agency, and all the other *theys* who set the rules of our lives seemed obsessed with laws and regulations. They wrote them, implemented them, followed them, and in some cases were actually composed of them and nothing more. Beneath the surface, however, these state behemoths were no different in nature from the spirits who stole; they were just as arbitrary, random, and mysterious. One rule said you had to go to school where you lived; another said that where you "lived" was your choice. One law gave extra money to underfunded school districts; another took it away and gave it to better-off districts. It seemed possible to get whatever you wanted as long as you knew the magic words and when to say them. It was through such a spell that I was propelled off the life trajectory shared by the other neighborhood kids and catapulted into New York City's middle and upper classes. My life chances had just taken a turn for the better, but my sense of the order of things—that is, the pecking order of race and class—was about to be stood on its head.

By the time I left the Mini School I had learned what the concept of race meant. I now knew that, based on the color of my skin, I would be treated a certain way, whether that entailed not getting rapped across the knuckles, not having a name like everyone else, or not having the same kind of hair as my best friend. Some kids got unique treatment for being taller or heavier than everyone else, but being whiter than everyone else was a different matter altogether. Teachers usually did a good job of ignoring the fact that one kid was shorter than another or another was fatter, but it was they, not the other students, who made my skin color an issue. The kids had only picked up on the adult cues and then reinterpreted them. Moreover, height, weight, and other physical characteristics were relative states. But being white was constructed as a matter of kind, not degree. Either you were black, or you weren't. Some of the kids in my original first-grade class were *blancitos*—lighter-skinned Puerto Ricans—but that didn't mean that they got rapped on the knuckles any softer than the darker-skinned kids. Once you weren't a *blanco*, it didn't matter what your skin color was in P.S. 4.

At my new school, the name of the game was class. That brought a whole new set of rules. And it would take me a while to learn them.

Discussion Questions

1. Did you enjoy Conley's style of writing the piece, more like a novel or story? Why or why not? Have you read any other social science work that has been similar? If so, what was it?

2. Why do the Black girls so desperately want White Barbies and see only these particular Barbies as authentic? Do you think this Barbie story says anything about elements of gender and race combined?

3. What were the most salient structural aspects in the article, that is, the parts involving institutional settings and practices that dovetailed with issues of race, class, gender, or religion?

4. Have you had any similar experiences that resonate with the Conley article? If so, describe them.

55

Lunch With My 'Enemy'

Exploring the Roots of Ethnic Strife

Amitava Kumar

Professor Amitava Kumar and his "enemy," Mr. Jagdish Barotia (not his real name), are both Hindus and members of the growing Indian immigrant community. The fact that there is tension and hostility, a sense of enmity between them, illustrates the fact that factions exist within as well as between minority communities. Mr. Barotia sees Professor Kumar as a traitor to the cause of Hindu nationalism, based on his writings and the fact that his wife comes from a Pakistani Muslim family. Professor Kumar explains the tensions, at least in part, on class differences. While he was born in a rural area, Kumar is now part of the urban, English-speaking elite, while Barotia is working class and closer to his rural roots.

On the surface it is easy to dismiss Barotia as a member of a lunatic fringe. He is a member of a political party that admires Hitler, yet he is linked in the United States with a radical and violent Zionist group, and he believes that Muslims are somehow implicated not only in the events of 9/11 but also in the assassination of JFK. Sitting in a modest restaurant in Queens, the borough of New York City that is home to many recent immigrant groups, eating pakora (fried vegetables) and nan (flat bread), he makes bigoted and wildly inaccurate statements about the Prophet Muhammed and Islam and enthusiastically and approvingly discusses violent riots in which Hindus murdered and raped Muslims.

Kumar is more reflective than Barotia. He wonders what separates the writer from the rioter. While he believes in co-existence with Muslims and sees common activities, includ-ing sports and romance, as personal ways of working toward peace, he acknowledges that longstanding class-related problems in India provide some justification for Barotia's passion-filled resentment. He also acknowledges that he himself grew up with prejudice against Muslims.

This article raises a number of issues that go beyond the meeting between Kumar and Barotia or even the specific tensions between Hindus and Muslims. New immigrant groups make welcome (e.g., wonderful food, new and different art forms) and unwelcome (e.g., hostilities based on religion, class, and, though not mentioned in this particular article, gender) contributions to the American scene. They draw our attention to and raise funds for causes about which we have been previously and blissfully unaware. They post new insights and new forms of hate literature on the Internet, and they combine with and clash with groups that were already here. These new groups and their issues tie the United States to the wider world and obligate us to expand the scope of matters that concern us.

M<small>r.</small> Barotia was talking to someone when he opened the door. Speaking into the phone that he held in his left hand, he gave me his right fist, which I couldn't quite decide whether to touch or to hold. He said to the person on the phone, *"Haan, haan, we will sit down and talk about it."*

The apartment, with the sunlight falling on the bulky white furniture, some of it covered with transparent plastic, was clean and bright, especially after the darkness of the corridor outside with its musty carpeting. I was happy that I had gotten so far. I had spoken to Mr. Barotia for the first time only the previous week. On the phone he had called me a *haraami*, which means bastard in Hindi, and, after clarifying that he didn't mean this abuse only for me, but for everyone else who was like me, he had also called me a *kutta*, a dog.

Although I had had no idea of Jagdish Barotia's identity till recently (and that is not his real name), I had wanted to meet him for well over two years. I wanted to meet face to

477

face a man who thought I was his enemy, to see if I could understand why he hated me so much, and why he seemed to hate other people who were different from him. My name had appeared on a "black list" put on a Web site in the year 2000 (a previous version of the site called it a "hit list") that belongs to a group called Hindu Unity—Mr. Barotia says he is a supporter—which presented links to other rightwing Hindu groups. My name was on a list of individuals who were regarded as enemies of a Hindu India. There was special anger for people like me, who were Hindus but, in the minds of the list's organizers, traitors to Hindutva, the ideology of a resurgent, anti-left, ultranationalistic Hindu cause.

The summer after the site was established, *The New York Times* published a report on the alliance that Hindu Unity had formed with Rabbi Meir Kahane's group. This is how the article began: "A Web site run by militant Hindus in Queens and Long Island was recently shut down by its service provider because of complaints that it advocated hatred and violence toward Muslims. But a few days later, the site was back on the Internet. The unlikely rescuers were some radical Jews in Brooklyn who are under investigation for possible ties to anti-Arab terrorist organizations in Israel." The Zionist organization and the Hindutva group had come together in New York City against what they considered their common enemy, Islam.

The news story had mentioned that Hindu Unity was a secretive group. It had been difficult for the reporter to meet the men who ran the Web site. I had sent several e-mail messages to the address provided on the site—the address where one was supposed to write and report the names of the enemies of Hindus—but no one had responded to my requests for an interview. Then, while I was having lunch at an Indian restaurant with a leader of the Overseas Friends of the Bharatiya Janata Party, Mr. Barotia's name came up. The BJP is the right-wing Hindu party in power in Delhi; the Overseas Friends is an umbrella organization of Hindu groups outside India, zealously presenting to anyone who cares to listen the details of what they regard as the menace of minorities (that

is, non-Hindus) in India. When I told the man that I'd like to meet Mr. Barotia, he gave me his phone number and, just as casually, mentioned that he understood that Mr. Barotia had been instrumental in establishing the Web site for Hindu Unity. . . .

Half an hour later, I was on the phone with Mr. Barotia. When I gave him my name, he recognized it and his voice lost its warmth. He told me that he had read an article of mine describing a visit to Pakistan, and he asked me to confirm what he knew about me, that I had married a Muslim. When I replied that I had, he said, "You have caused me a lot of pain." I didn't know what to say. It was then, after I told him I wanted to meet him, that he called me a bastard and a dog. He also said that people like me were not secular, we were actually confused. We would learn our lesson, he said, when the Muslim population increased in India, and the Muslims came after us and chopped our legs off.

I guess I could say that I felt his pain when he said that he didn't understand what had happened to the Hindu children, how it had come to be that they were surrounded by so much darkness. I told him that I was not a child anymore, but I sounded like one when I said that Mr. Barotia invited me to his home, saying that he was sure that after he had talked to me and given me "all the facts," I would change my mind about Muslims. . . . The Internet was a gift to Mr. Barotia's views. It made him a bette long-distance nationalist. He said, "If the Hindus will be saved, it wil be because of the Internet. I send out an e-mail and am able to talk at once to 5,000 Hindus." And so it was that less than a week later, I took the train to Elmhurst, Queens, to meet Mr. Barotia.

In the summer of 1999, when India and Pakistan were engaged in a conflict near Kargil, in Kashmir, I had gotten married. In the days leading up to my wedding, I often told myself that the marriage was unusually symbolic: I was doing my bit to help bring peace to more than a billion people living in the subcontinent, because I am an Indian Hindu and the woman I was about to marry, Mona, is a Pakistani Muslim.

The wedding took place in June, and it was hot when I drove from my home in

Pennsylvania up to Toronto, where Mona's parents had recently moved from Karachi. Driving home alone after the wedding (Mona had stayed behind with her family for a few days because they were returning to Pakistan), past Niagara Falls, where I had heard that honeymooners often go, I felt good about myself for marrying "the enemy." The thought gave me a small thrill. I began to compose in my mind a brief newspaper editorial about how my marriage had opened a new track for people-to-people diplomacy.

Every day in Toronto the news bulletins had brought to us the war in Kashmir. But we had other preoccupations. Along with Mona's brothers and father, I would wake up at 5 in the morning to watch India and Pakistan fighting it out on the cricket fields in England, where the World Cup tournament was being played. A day before our wedding, India beat Pakistan in the match in Manchester. During that match, one lone spectator had held a sign, "Cricket for Peace." Watching the match on television, I wondered whether I too could walk around with a placard hung from my neck, saying "Marriage for Peace." The article I eventually wrote for an Indian newspaper was what first brought me to Mr. Barotia's attention. We became enemies.

At least, that is how he thinks of his relationship to me. We hardly know each other. The issue is not personal; it is political. After reading my articles about my marriage and, later, my visit to Pakistan, Mr. Barotia denounced me as an enemy of India. I went to meet him in his apartment in Queens because I wanted a dialogue with him. I also wanted to see his face. I found the idea of a faceless enemy unbearable. That wasn't a psychological problem so much as a writer's problem. I wanted detail and voice. Mr. Barotia had said to me on the phone that the Hindu rioters in Gujarat, who burned, raped, or slaughtered more than a thousand Muslims earlier that year had taught the Indian minorities a lesson they would never forget. I wanted to meet Mr. Barotia so that I could ask him about the process through which he had come to think of Muslims as the enemy. I did ask him, but his response revealed little to me that was new.

Nevertheless, our meeting was a discovery because it made me think not simply of our differences but also our similarities. What is it that divides the writer from the rioter? The answer is not clear or simple. There could be more in common between the two than either might imagine—a vast hinterland of cultural memory and shared prejudice, for example. Was it an excess of sympathy on my part—or, on the contrary, too little of it—that made it difficult, if not impossible, for me to draw a plainly legible line between a man in a mob and myself?

Mr. Barotia was short and had a round face, with gray eyebrows. He put on a pair of gold-rimmed spectacles after I told him that I doubted his statement that we had met before. Mr. Barotia touched his glasses and frowned. He said, "But your face looks familiar." I suddenly thought of the Hindu Unity Web site, where my photograph had appeared, picked up from my newspaper pieces. Perhaps that was the reason why Mr. Barotia thought that he had seen me before. He had seen my face on the site's so-called black list, along with my name and address. But I couldn't bring myself to tell him that. Instead, I drank the tea that I was offered. And then Mr. Barotia began to tell me about what he called "the poison of Islam."

The litany of complaints was familiar and quickly wearying. Mr. Barotia began with the names of all the Indian male film stars who were Muslim and married to Hindu women. "Sharmila Tagore is now Ayesha Begum, and that pimp Amir Khan is married to a Hindu girl. Her name is Gauri." These women had been forced to convert, he said, and now Muslims were having sex with them, thereby defiling them. . . .

Soon, it became clear that Mr. Barotia was going to buy me lunch. We walked to an Indian diner about 10 minutes away, in Jackson Heights. Mr. Barotia behaved like a friendly host, urging me to try the different dishes, putting bits of warm nan on my plate. He ate with gusto, refilling his plate several times, and as I looked at him, his shirt front flecked with the food he had dropped there, I saw him as a contented, slightly tired old man who was perhaps getting ready to take an afternoon nap. Earlier, Mr. Barotia had told me that because the Hindus had killed so many Muslims earlier that year in Gujarat, a change had come about. "We have created fear," he boasted. *"Yeh garmi jo hai, main India mein phaila doonga.* This heat that is there, I will spread it in India. And those who write against us, their fingers will be cut." But, for now, he was quietly staffing pakoras into his mouth: a retired immigrant worker eating in a cheap immigrant restaurant.

Mr. Barotia had told me earlier that day that he had come to the United States in 1972. For 25 years he had worked as a legal secretary in Manhattan—the BJP man in the restaurant the previous week had told me that Mr. Barotia had been "a typist," and I had seen from the gesture of his hand that he was being dismissive. Mr. Barotia said that he had gotten along well with his colleagues at work and they treated him as "a partner in the firm," and one of them had even called him after the attacks of September 11 to say: "Jagdish, we thought you were obsessed with Muslims. But you were right."

During lunch, Mr. Barotia told me that I was ungrateful if I forgot how Hindu warriors had saved our motherland. He must have gotten to me because when he asked me why I believed in coexistence with Muslims, I said a phrase in Hindi that essentially meant "we are Nehru's bastards." It was an admission of guilt, of illegitimacy, as if Nehru, the socialist first prime minister of India, had done something wrong in being a liberal, and those of us who believed in his vision of an inclusive India were his ill-begotten offspring. Nehru is often accused by his detractors of having been a profligate person, and my remark had granted him a certain promiscuity. But the more serious charge hidden in my comment was that the former prime minister had produced a polity that was the result of a miscegenation with the West.

I was being disingenuous—and so was Mr. Barotia. Our lives and our histories, with or without Nehru, were tied up with links with the wider world. I am an Indian writer who writes in English. Mr. Barotia's parent party, the RSS, had been inspired by the Nazis and revered a German man, Hitler. Today, Mr.

Barotia is a fan of the Internet. We both live and work in the United States. We are both struggling, each in our way, to be *like* Nehru, whose eclecticism was exceptional. But Nehru was also exemplary because, unlike many of his Hindu compatriots, he had an unwavering belief that Hindu-Muslim conflict had nothing to do with tradition but was a modern phenomenon, which could be corrected by means of enlightened policy.

In the train, flipping over some of the papers that Mr. Barotia had given me, I began to read. . . .

As I read the following words, it was as if I could hear Mr. Barotia's hectoring voice. His interest in alliteration had not been evident to me before, but it didn't distract me from his real interest in producing a phony history and linking it to language. "As the history of Muhammed goes, he was a serial rapist, a serial murderer, a chronic criminal, a treacherous terrorist who was banished by his family and the society of his times," Mr. Barotia wrote. He followed a little later with a bogus disquisition on the etymology of the name for Muslims. The Prophet, in order to avenge the lack of respect shown him, founded "gangs of powerful youth (Muscle Men), offering them girls of their choice, food and wine." And "the illiterate Muhammed mispronounced the word 'Muscle Man' as 'Musalman.' Over a period of time, this mispronunciation became an accepted pronunciation!" The 10-page text ended with a question not about September 11 but an earlier unresolved crime that is still an obsession for many conspiracy theorists in America and to which Mr. Barotia was only giving a new twist: "Who was behind the planning, plotting and planting the Death of the Dearest JFK?" The answer: "It was ISLAM, ISLAM and ISLAM, the ever valiant villain."

There are various things that could be said about Mr. Barotia. One would be that he is a fringe element that gives a dangerous edge to an increasingly powerful and mainstream ideology in the subcontinent. His political affiliation is with the party that rules now in New Delhi, although it is in retreat in parts of India. Mr. Barotia is also a member of the group that claims success in raising money in the West—including investments made by expatriate Indians, allegedly to the tune of $4 billion—to support the Indian government after economic sanctions had been imposed on India following its nuclear tests in 1998.

But what interests me, as a writer, are the words that Mr. Barotia uses. Their violence and ferocity—their absoluteness compromised and made vulnerable in different ways—carry the threat most visible in the rhetoric of rioters in India today. That rhetoric leaves no place for the middle-class gentility of Nehruvian liberalism. Indeed, its incivility is a response to the failures of the idealism represented by the likes of Nehru and Gandhi. Mr. Barotia's voice is the voice of the lumpen that knows it is lumpen no longer. It almost has the legitimacy of being the voice of the people, which it is not and its aggressiveness is born from its own sense that it is pitched in battle against those who held power for too long.

I am not sure whether I would ever, or for long, envy Mr. Barotia's passion, but I find myself sympathetic to his perception that the English-speaking elite of India has not granted the likes of him a proper place under the Indian flag. Once that thought enters my head, I am uneasily conscious of the ways in which I found myself mocking Mr. Barotia's bigotry by noticing his ungrammatical English. Like Mr. Barotia, I was born in the provinces and grew up in small towns. For me, the move to the city meant that I learned English and embraced secular, universal rationality and liberalism. Mr. Barotia remained truer to his roots and retained his religion as well as a narrower form of nationalism that went with it. It seemed to me that his insecurity about his background took the form of fanaticism—a land of revenge on big-city intellectuals. I do not envy him his changes, but I can't think of those changes without a small degree of tenderness.

There is another reason why Mr. Barotia's words hold my attention. His stories about heroism and betrayal share something with the fantasy world of my own childhood, whose half-understood atmosphere of rumor and prejudice was a part not of a private universe but a largely public one. What Mr. Barotia and I share in some deep way is the language of memory—that well from which we have drawn, like water, our collective stories. After my meeting with Mr. Barotia, I thought of a particular incident from my childhood and wondered whether he, too, had similar memories, linking him and me, all of us, to all the bigots of the world.

My memory concerned a dead lizard. I must have been 5 or 6 at the time. The lizards, the *girgit*, were everywhere. In the small garden outside our home in Patna, they would creep out of the hedge and sun themselves on the metal gate. (Many years later, in a mall near Washington, I saw the lizards being sold as pets, and was reminded of my childhood fear of them.) These lizards were yellow or brown, their thin bodies scaly, and many of them had bloated red sacs under then chins. Although I was scared of the lizards, I also wanted to kill them. I often daydreamed about killing one by throwing a stone at it when it wasn't looking. I would try to imagine what its pale exposed belly would look like when it fell though the air, from the gate to the ground.

A boy who was a year ahead of me in school actually killed one of them, bringing it to me in a plastic bag. It was he who told me that the lizards were Muslim. He pointed out the sacs under then chins and said that they used to be beards. Here is the story he told:

During the riots that accompanied the partition of India in 1947, the Muslims were running scared of the Hindus. If the Hindus found the Muslims, they would murder them. If the Hindus did not kill the Muslims first, the Muslims would instead butcher the Hindus with their swords. Or they would take the Hindus to the new county, Pakistan, where the Hindus would be converted and become trapped forever. One day, the Hindus saw a bearded Muslim running away. They caught him and were about to chop off his head. The man was a coward. In order to save his life, he pointed with his beard toward the well where other Muslims were hiding. Because of this act of treachery, that man was turned into a lizard with a sac under his chin. That is why when we Hindus look at those lizards, they bob their heads as if they are pointing toward a well.

Discussion Questions

1. In this article Professor Kumar refers to the hostility between Hindus and Muslims. He says that some people see this hostility as traditional and probably irreconcilable but that Nehru, the first prime minister of India, saw it as modern and correctable. Do you know anything about the history of India and Pakistan? Is the name of Nehru familiar to you? Related issues crop up in the news frequently. If your knowledge is very limited, use the Internet or other sources to get enough information to make sense of this and articles you might read in the future.

2. Are you or any members of your class of Indian or Pakistani origin? Do you personally know any Indian or Pakistani people? If the answer is "yes," did that influence your reaction to this article? How?

3. Professor Kumar is not a rioter or a supporter of those who advocate the use of violence to achieve social change. What steps could he take in response to the activities of Mr. Barotia and his organization?

4. Thinking about the broader issues raised by this article, can you name other recent immigrant groups that have been active in raising funds, shaping public opinion, or trying to influence U.S. policy toward their countries of origin? Is your reaction to their efforts generally positive, negative, or neutral? Why?

56

'New Racism,' Color-Blind Racism, and the Future of Whiteness in America

Eduardo Bonilla-Silva

In this article, Eduardo Bonilla-Silva directs our attention to the privilege of Whiteness through the lens of what he calls the "new racism"—the version of racism most salient in a postmodern world. While Bonilla-Silva defines Whiteness as "embodied racial power," and "the visible uniform of the dominant racial group," he wants to explore how Whiteness will play out in the twenty-first century. Bonilla-Silva, then, captures racial- and class-centered issues, with gender always implied as part of the story in the everyday experiences of people of color.

Bonilla-Silva begins by discussing the nature of the "new racism." Instead of utilizing overtly racially discriminatory Jim Crow practices, the "new racism" is covert and accomplishes the same task under the cover of legality. Instead of simply forcing segregation, for example, the "new racism" tactic is to deny available housing to Blacks in certain areas of the city. Studies indicate, Bonilla-Silva suggests, that Blacks are not allowed to see as many apartments, are quoted higher rental prices, and are steered to specific neighborhoods—practices Whites do not generally experience. He also points out several well-known studies on everyday discrimination faced by Black men and women, whether middle class or low income. For example, Lawrence Otis-Graham writes

about taking friends to New York's best restaurants and receiving worse than questionable service as Black men and women—being mistaken for restaurant employees or seated in the worst seats. In fact, according to Bonilla-Silva, lower-income Blacks may not encounter as many of these acts of everyday discrimination since they have fewer opportunities to interact with Whites, whether in posh restaurants, board rooms, or classrooms.

Next, he discusses the concept of "color-blind racism," which he argues undergirds the "new racism." Instead of Jim Crow racial ideology, developed out of beliefs in the moral and intellectual inferiority of Black people, "color-blind racism" enters as the new racial ideology for the young century framed in terms of abstract liberalism and naturalization, according to Bonilla-Silva. Abstract liberalism, he suggests, adheres to a liberal rhetoric of equality while denying past and contemporary discrimination, which in effect denies equal opportunity to racial groups. (This is reminiscent of respondents in the DiTomaso et al. study in this volume). Naturalization, which adheres to a liberal rhetoric, is all about making issues such as de facto segregation seem like "the way it is;" that is, part of the natural way Whites and Blacks live, denying any socioeconomic and structural discrimination involved. In this regard, Bonilla-Silva quotes a White couple, both of whom explain the lack of racial integration in their neighborhood by describing the segregation as natural.

Bonilla-Silva then describes the Latin-Americanization of Whiteness. In this section, he wishes to convey the cartography of American Whiteness, which he believes will move toward a more triracial model as in Latin America. In this model, the top group in the hierarchy would be "Whites," followed by the middle level of "Honorary Whites," and the bottom level of the "Collective Black." Bonilla-Silva posits that such a schema makes sense when we consider the decreasing size of the White population in America, a demographic transition that he likens to Latin America and the Caribbean in the sixteenth and seventeenth centuries. He also presents data that presages the emergence of the triracial hierarchy. One piece of this data describes racial assimilation through marriage, where children of mixed

White-Asian and White-Latino unions are more likely to be considered White in classifications. This is juxtaposed with children of Black fathers and White mothers, who are much less likely to be classified as White. In this case, race trumps all gendered relationships.

Finally, Bonilla-Silva concludes with a discussion of the political implications of the new racial paradigm he has presented along with the sorts of strategies that might be used to challenge these new issues in the world of race relations. One strategy, he suggests, is sending out testers who are matched in all characteristics except race to investigate claims of discrimination in housing, banking, retail shopping, and employment.

In most postmodern writing, whiteness is regarded as an identity, a performance, a mere cultural construct, or is framed as a moral problem. In sharp contrast, we anchored [the] volume [in which this chapter originally appears] on the idea that whiteness is the foundational category of "white supremacy" (Mills 1997). *Whiteness, then, in all of its manifestations, is embodied racial power.* Whether expressed in militant (e.g., the Klan) or tranquil fashion (e.g., most members of the white middle class) and whether actors deemed "white" are cognizant of it, *whiteness is the visible uniform of the dominant racial group.* Therefore all actors socially regarded as "white"—and, as I shall argue later, as "near white"—receive systemic privileges by virtue of wearing the white—or virtually white—outfit, whereas those regarded as nonwhite are denied those privileges.[1] This explains, for instance, why "not-yet-white" ethnic immigrants (Roediger 2002) historically strove to become white as well as why immigrants of color always attempt to distance themselves from dark identities (blackness) when they enter the United States' racial polity (Bonilla-Silva 1997, Bonilla-Silva and Lewis 1999).

The authors in [the original] volume have addressed various aspects of whiteness as embodied racial power (e.g., whiteness in neighborhoods, whiteness by class, whiteness among biracials, whiteness in certain professions, whiteness among Latinos, etc.). In this chapter I attempt to explain how whiteness survives in a country that proclaims to be "beyond race" and to forecast how whiteness will play out in the twenty-first century. First, I discuss the nature of the "new racism"—the racial structure (specific set of social arrangements and practices that produce and reproduce a racial order) that replaced Jim Crow in the 1960s and 1970s. I follow this with a description of the basic contours of "color-blind racism," or the racial ideology that bonds the "new racism." After explaining the structural and ideological context for whiteness in post-civil rights America, I suggest in the next section that whiteness will undergo a major transformation in the twenty-first century and become Latin America-like. I conclude this chapter with an analysis of the political implications of the "new racism," color-blind racism, and the Latin-Americanization of whiteness and offer various strategies to challenge them.

Now You See it, Now You Don't: Post-Civil Rights White Supremacy

Although whites' common sense on racial matters ("We used to have a lot of racism, but things are so much better today!") is not totally without foundation (e.g., traditional forms of racial discrimination and exclusion as well as Jim Crow-based racist beliefs have decreased in significance), it is ultimately false. A number of researchers have documented the manifold subtle yet systematic ways in which racial privilege is reproduced in the United States (Feagin 2000; R. C. Smith 1995). I have labeled this new, kinder and gentler, white supremacy as the "new racism" and have argued that it is the main force behind contemporary racial inequality (Bonilla-Silva 2001; Bonilla-Silva and Lewis 1999).

Although the "new racism" seems to be racism lite, it is as effective as slavery and Jim Crow in maintaining the racial status quo. The central elements of this new structure are: (1) the increasingly *covert* nature of racial discourse and practices; (2) the avoidance of racial terminology and the ever-growing claim by whites that they experience "reverse racism"; (3) the invisibility of most mechanisms to reproduce racial inequality;

(4) the incorporation of "safe minorities" (e.g., Clarence Thomas, Condeleeza Rice, or Colin Powell) to signify the nonracialism of the polity; and (5) the rearticulation of some racial practices characteristic of the Jim Crow period of race relations. In what follows, I explain why this "new racism" emerged and succinctly, because of space constraints, discuss how it operates in the area of social interaction (for a full discussion on how it works in other areas, see Bonilla-Silva 2001).

Why a 'New Racism'?

Systems of racial domination, which I have labeled elsewhere as "racialized social systems" (Bonilla-Silva 1997, 2001; Bonilla-Silva and Lewis, 1999) are not static. Much like capitalism and patriarchy, they change due to external and internal pressures. The racial apartheid that blacks and other people of color experienced in the United States from the 1860s until the 1960s was predicated on (1) keeping them in rural areas, mostly in the South; (2) maintaining them as agricultural workers; and (3) excluding them from the political process. However, as people of color successfully challenged their socioeconomic position by migrating initially from rural areas to urban areas in the South and later to the North and West, by pushing themselves by whatever means necessary into nonagricultural occupations (Tuttle 1970), and by developing political organizations and movements such Garveyism, the NAACP, CORE, La Raza Unida Party, Brown Berets, and SNCC (Payne 1995; Montejano 1987), the infrastructure of apartheid began to crumble.

Among the external factors leading to the abolition of the Jim Crow racial order, the most significant were the participation of people of color in World Wars I and II, which patently underscored the contradiction between fighting for freedom abroad and lacking it at home; the Cold War, which made it a necessity to eliminate overt discrimination at home in order to sell the United States as the champion of democracy; and a number of judicial decisions, legislative acts, and presidential decrees that have transpired since the forties.

These demographic, social, political, and economic factors and the actions of various racial minority groups made change almost inevitable. But ripe conditions are not enough to change any structural order. Hence the racial order had to be directly challenged if it was going to be effectively transformed. That was the role fulfilled by the Civil Rights movement and the other forms of mass protest by blacks that took place in the sixties and seventies (Payne 1995). Organized and spontaneous challenges (e.g., the over three-hundred racial riots in the 1960s) were the catalysts that brought down Jim Crow white supremacy.

'New Racism' in Social Interaction

Despite the real progress that the abolition of most of the formal, overt, and humiliating practices associated with Jim Crow represented, this did not mean the end of practices to reproduce racial hierarchy. Instead, new racism practices have replaced Jim Crow ones in all areas of life. In terms of social interaction among the races in neighborhoods, schools, stores, and other areas, whites and minorities (but blacks in particular) have very limited and regimented interactions.

Yet the way in which racial inequality is reproduced in this area is vastly different from how it was reproduced in the past. For instance, residential segregation today, which is almost as high as it was forty years ago (Lewis Mumford Center 2001; Yinger 1995), is no longer accomplished through clearly discriminatory practices, such as real-estate agents employing outright refusal or subterfuge to avoid renting or selling to minority customers, federal government redlining policies, antiminority insurance and lending practices, and racially restrictive covenants on housing deeds (Massey and Denton 1993). In contrast, in the face of equal housing laws and other civil rights legislation, covert behaviors and strategies have largely replaced Jim Crow practices and have maintained the same outcome—separate communities. For example, housing audits indicate that blacks are denied available housing from 35 percent to 75 percent of the time, depending on the city in question (Smith 1995; Yinger 1995). These housing studies have shown that, when paired with similar white counterparts, minorities are likely to be shown fewer apartments, be quoted higher rents, or offered worse conditions, and be steered to specific neighborhoods (Galster 1990a, 1990b; Turner, Struyk, and Yinger 1991).

In the realm of everyday life, several recent works have attempted to examine the experiences blacks, have with discrimination (S. Collins 1997; Feagin and Sikes 1994). In his interviews of middle-class blacks who have supposedly "made it," Ellis Cose (1995 [1993]) repeatedly discovered a sense among these "successful blacks" that they were being continually blocked and constrained (see also Hochschild 1995). Cose cites the cases of a trade association vice president who is kept is charge of "minority affairs," a law partner always viewed as a "*black* litigator," a prominent journalist who is demoted for pointing out how race affects news reporting, and a law professor at Georgetown who is embarrassed by Harvard in a recruitment effort (Chapter I, Cose 1995 [1993]. The same pattern was evident in Sharon Collins's work in the Chicago area).

In 1981 Howard Schuman and his colleagues replicated a 1950 study of restaurants in New York's Upper East Side and found a substantial amount of discrimination remained (Schuman et al. 1983). Similar to the housing audits, the discrimination was of a subtle nature. Lawrence Otis-Graham reports in his book *Member of the Club* (1995) that in ten of New York's best restaurants he and his friends visited, they were stared at, mistaken for restaurant workers, seated in terrible spots, and buffered so as to avoid proximity to whites in most of them. He reports that they were treated reasonably well in only two of the ten restaurants. The suits recently filed against Denny's, Shoney's, and the International House of Pancakes suggest that discrimination in restaurants is experienced by blacks of all class backgrounds (Feagin and Sikes 1994).

The existence of everyday discrimination is also confirmed by existing survey data. For instance, one study found that 38 percent of blacks report discrimination as a result of being unfairly fired or denied a promotion, 37 percent report harassment by the police, and 32 percent report not being hired for a job (Forman, Williams, and Jackson 1997). Similar to other studies, the rates of discrimination reported by blacks on any single item were quite modest (see also Bobo and Suh 2000; Sigelman and Welch 1991). However, a shift to the question of how many blacks have experienced at least one form of discrimination in their lifetime provides some intriguing results (they were asked about six different types): 70 percent of blacks report experiencing at least one form of major discrimination in their lifetime (Forman, Williams, and Jackson 1997). Students of color on predominantly white college campuses have also reported extensive patterns of daily discrimination (Feagin, Vera and Imani 1996).

Joe Feagin and Melvin Sikes (1994) also document the dense network of discriminatory practices confronted by middle-class blacks in everyday life. Although they correctly point out that blacks face discriminatory practices that range from overt and violent to covert and gentle, the latter seem to be prevalent. In public spaces the discriminatory behavior described by black interviewees included poor service, special requirements applied only to them, surveillance in stores, being ignored at retail stores selling expensive commodities, receiving the worst accommodations in restaurants or hotels, being constantly confused with menial workers, along with the usual but seemingly less frequent epithets and overtly racist behavior (see Chapter 2 in Feagin and Sikes 1994).

Moreover, many of these patterns experienced by middle-income blacks are more apparent only because they have at least secured access to previously inaccessible social space. For low-income racial minorities, these lands of experiences with daily discrimination are perhaps less rampant because they are, for the most part, physically excluded from white environs (neighborhoods, board meetings, classrooms, etc.; however, see my arguments about light-skinned Latinos and many Asians below). For example, in a study of families in several different school communities, low-income Latino families reported very little racial discrimination because they had contact primarily with other low-income Latinos in their neighborhoods and in the workplace. Discrimination was most apparent in those moments when these parents had to interact with large public institutions, where they reported rampant disrespect and disregard if not explicit racism (Fine and Weis 1998). Tyrone Forman and colleagues also found a similar pattern in their study of African-Americans in the Detroit metropolitan area. That is, blacks who have attended college or received a college degree report experiencing more discrimination than those who have not (Forman, Williams, and Jackson 1997).

This almost invisible racial structure maintains the "wages of whiteness" (Du Bois 1969) at the social, economic, political, and even psychological levels. By hiding their racial motif, new racism practices have become the present-day Trojan horse of white power.

Color-Blind Racism: How Whites Justify Contemporary Racial Inequality

If Jim Crow's racial structure has been replaced by a "new racism," what happened to Jim Crow racial ideology? What happened to beliefs about minorities' mental, moral, and intellectual inferiority?—to the idea that "it is the [blacks'] own fault that he is a lower-caste . . . a lower-class man" or the assertion that blacks' lack initiative, are shiftless, and have no sense of time; in short, what happened to the basic claim that minorities (but again, blacks in particular) are subhuman? (Dollard 1949: 372). Social analysts of all stripes agree that most whites no longer subscribe to these tenets in a traditional, straightforward fashion. However, this does not mean the "end of racism," as a few conservative commentators have suggested (D'Souza 1995; Thernstrom and Thernstrom 1997). Instead, a new powerful racial ideology[2] has emerged that combines elements of liberalism with culturally based antiminority views to justify the contemporary racial order: color-blind racism. Yet this new ideology is a curious one. Although it engages, as all such ideologies do, in "blaming the victim," it does so in a very indirect

"now you see it, now you don't" style that matches perfectly the character of the "new racism." In this section, I discuss briefly its central frames with examples drawn from in-depth interviews conducted as part of the 1997 Survey of College Students' Social Attitudes and the 1998 Detroit Area Study (DAS henceforth)[3] and from the material presented by some of the authors in this volume (for a full discussion of all the features of this ideology, see Bonilla-Silva 2003).

The Frames of Color-Blind Racism

Color-blind racism has four central frames, namely, *abstract liberalism, naturalization, cultural racism,* and *minimization of racism.* I illustrate here the first two frames and explain how whites use them to defend and, ultimately, justify contemporary racial inequality.

Abstract Liberalism: Unmasking Reasonable Racism. When minorities were slaves, contract laborers, or *"braceros,"* the principles of liberalism and humanism were not extended to them. Today whites believe minorities are part of the body-politic but extend the ideas associated with liberalism in an *abstract* and *decontextualized* manner ("I am all for equal opportunity, that's why I oppose affirmative action") that ends up rationalizing racially unfair situations. An archetypal example of how whites use this frame to oppose racial fairness is Sue, a college student in a Southern University. When asked if minority students should be provided unique opportunities to be admitted into universities, Sue stated:

> I don't think that they should be provided with unique opportunities. I think that they should have the same opportunities as everyone else. You know, it's up to them to meet the standards and whatever that's required for entrance into universities or whatever. I don't think that just because they're a minority that they should, you know, not meet the requirements, you know.

Sue, like most whites in contemporary America, ignores the effects of past and contemporary discrimination on the social, economic, and educational status of minorities. Therefore, by supporting equal opportunity for everyone without a concern for the savage racial inequalities between whites and minorities, her stance safeguards white privilege.

Naturalization: Decoding the Meaning of 'That's the Way It Is.' A frame that has not yet been brought to the fore by social scientists is whites' naturalization of race-related matters. Whites invoke this frame mostly when discussing school or neighborhood matters to explain the limited contact between whites and minorities and to justify whites' preference for whites as significant others. The word "natural" or the phrase "that's the way it is" is often interjected, to normalize events or actions that could otherwise be interpreted as racially motivated (residential segregation) or racist (preference for whites as friends and partners). For instance, Bill, a manager in a manufacturing firm, explained the limited level of school integration as follows:

> Bill: I don't think it's anybody's fault. Because people tend to group with their own people. Whether it's white or black or upper-middle-class or lower-class or, you know, upper-class, you know, Asians. People tend to group with their own. Doesn't mean if a black person moves into your neighborhood, they shouldn't go to your school. They should and you should mix and welcome them and everything else, but you can't force people together. If people want to be together, they should intermix more.

> Interviewer: OK. So the lack of mixing is really just kind of an individual lack of desire?

> Bill: Well, individuals, it's just the way it is. You know, people group together for lots of different reasons: social, religious. Just as animals in the wild, you know. Elephants group together, cheetahs group together. You bus a cheetah into an elephant herd because they should mix? You can't force that [laughs].

Bill's crude, unflattering, and unfitting metaphor comparing racial segregation to the separation of species, however, is not the only way of using the naturalization frame. Many whites naturalize in a gentler fashion. For instance, Steve and Jan Hadley, two of the respondents cited [in an article] by Johnson and Shapiro . . . explain their lack of racial mix in their neighborhood and in the schools their children attended as follows:

> Steve: No, I mean, it, it just happened. So, um.

> Tan: No, it's just, it's based on the churches, you know, the four churches that own the school and—

> Steve: Yeah, and, they, they're from the south county are also so, and there just are, there aren't many blacks.

> Jan: Unless they are part of the bussing program, and you will find that in the public school system, but not in the private sector. So. And that's, I mean, that's not a problem as far as I'm—see, we have black friends, but it just happens to work out that way.

Despite whites' belief that residential and school segregation, friendship, and attraction are natural, raceless occurrences, social scientists have documented how racial considerations affect all these issues. For example, residential segregation is created by white buyers searching for white neighborhoods and aided by realtors, bankers, and sellers. As white neighborhoods develop, white schools follow—an outcome that further contributes to the process of racial isolation. Socialized in a "white habitus" (Bonilla-Silva 2003) and influenced by our Eurocentric culture, it is no wonder whites' interpret their racialized choices for white significant others as "natural." All these "choices" are the "natural" consequences of a white socialization process.

Although this frame seems to contradict the color-blind script, it is in fact used to deflate charges of racism. If someone argues that whites go to school, live with, befriend, and date other whites, whites can say "It's a natural thing" and that all groups do it. Hence something that presumably everybody does "naturally" is something that is "beyond race."

The Latin-Americanization of Whiteness in the United States

What will be the cartography of whiteness in twenty-first-century America? Who will be "white" and who will be "nonwhite"? Will the traditional (albeit always somewhat porous) lines of whiteness and nonwhiteness remain or will they be reconfigured? In what follows I suggest that whiteness will shed its traditional garb and slip into Latin American-like clothes. Specifically, I argue that the United States will develop a triracial system with "whites" at the top, an intermediary group of "honorary whites"—similar to the coloreds in South Africa—and a nonwhite group or the "collective black" at the bottom (see Figure 56.1). In addition, as is the case in Latin America and the Caribbean, I expect the color logic of white supremacy to become more salient. "Shade discrimination" (Kinsbrunner 1996), or preference for people who are light-skinned, will become a more important factor in all kinds of social transactions.

There are multiple reasons why I posit that whiteness will become Latin-Americanized. The most basic one is demographic-political in nature. The white population, which has always been a numerical majority in the country—with a few notable exceptions during some historical junctures in some regions—is decreasing in size and by the middle of this century may have become a numerical minority (see Table 56.1). This rapid darkening of America is creating a situation similar to that of many Latin American and Caribbean countries in the sixteenth and seventeenth centuries (e.g., Puerto Rico, Cuba, and Venezuela), or of South American countries such as Argentina, Chile, and Uruguay in the late eighteenth and early nineteenth centuries. In both historical periods, white elites realized their countries were becoming majority nonwhite and devised a number of strategies (unsuccessful in the former and successful in the latter) to whiten their population and preserve racial power (Helg 1990). Although whitening the population through immigration or by classifying many newcomers as white (Gans 1999b; Warren and Twine 1997) is a possible solution to the new American dilemma, a more plausible one is to create an intermediate racial group to buffer racial conflict, allow some newcomers into the white racial strata, and incorporate most immigrants of color into a new bottom strata.

Figure 56.1
Preliminary Map of Triracial System in the United States[1]

"Whites"

Whites
New Whites (Russians, Albanians, etc.)
Assimilated light-skinned Latinos
Some multiracials
Assimilated (urban) Native Americans
A few Asian-origin people

"Honorary Whites"

Light-skinned Latinos
Japanese-Americans
Korean-Americans
Asian Indians
Chinese-Americans
Middle Eastern Americans
Most multiracials

"Collective Black"

Filipinos
Vietnamese
Hmong
Laotians
Dark-skinned Latinos
Blacks
New West Indian and African immigrants
Reservation-bound Native Americans

1. This is a heuristic rather than an analytical device, Hence not all groups are included, and the position of a few groups may change.

Even though Latin-Americanization will not fully materialize for several more decades, many social trends that correspond to the emerging stratification order are already evident. For example, the standing of the groups in Figure 56.1 in terms of income, education, wealth, occupations, and even social prestige largely follows the expected patterns. Hence in general terms, whites have higher income, education, and better occupations than "honorary whites," who in turn have a higher standing than members of the collective black in all those areas.

If these groups develop significant status differences, those differences should be reflected in their consciousness. Specifically, if my Latin-Americanization thesis is accurate, whites should be making distinctions among "honorary whites" and the "collective black" (exhibiting a more positive outlook

Table 56.1
Projected Population of the United States by Race and Ethnicity (%) in 2020, 2045, 2070, and 2100

	2020	2045	2070	2100
Whites	63.8	54.5	46.8	40.3
Latinos	17.0	23.1	28.6	33.3
Blacks	12.0	13.2	13.2	13.0
Asians	5.7	8.4	10.6	12.6
Native Americans	0.8	0.8	0.8	0.7

Source: U.S. Census Bureau, Population Projections Branch. Maintained by: Laura K. Yax (Population Division). Last revised: August 02, 2002 at 01:55:31 PM. Available from *http://eire.census.gov/popest/estimates.php*.

toward "honorary whites" than toward members of the "collective black"). Similarly, "honorary whites" should exhibit attitudes toward the "collective black" similar to those of whites (see them as "inferior," etc.). Finally, members of the "collective black" should exhibit a less coherent and more disarticulated racial consciousness than in the past,[4] as is the case of the subordinated caste in Latin America and the Caribbean (Hanchard 1994; Twine 1998).

Although assessing some of these matters is very problematic as few data sets include information on skin tone, the available data are very suggestive as they mostly fit my Latin-Americanization thesis. For example, various surveys on Latinos confirm that they tend to self-identify as "white." However, the proportion varies tremendously by groups in a manner that is congruent with my expectations. Whereas over 75 percent of Cubans, Argentines, Chileans, and Venezuelans identify as white, fewer than 45 percent of dark-skinned or Indian-looking Latinos such as Puerto Ricans, Salvadorans, and Dominicans do so (Rodriguez 2000). In line with this finding, data from the Latino National Political Survey reveal that Mexicans and Puerto Ricans—two groups primarily composed of people who will belong to the "collective black"—are more likely than Cubans—a group that will mostly be comprised of "honorary whites"—to be sympathetic toward blacks. More significantly, the degree of closeness toward blacks *was greater* among those Latinos

who self-identify as black while those who self-identify as white who were more sympathetic toward whites and Asians (Forman, Martinez, and Bonilla-Silva unpublished).

Various studies have documented that Asians tend to hold antiblack and anti-Latino attitudes. For instance, Lawrence Bobo and associates (1995) found that Chinese residents of Los Angeles expressed negative racial attitudes toward blacks. One Chinese resident stated: "Blacks in general seem to be overly lazy" and another asserted: "Blacks have a definite attitude problem" (Bobo et al. 1995: 78; see also Bobo and Johnson 2000). Studies of Korean shopkeepers in various locales have found that over 70 percent of them hold antiblack attitudes (Weitzer 1997; Yoon 1997; Min 1996). In a more recent study of Asians (Chinese, Koreans, and Japanese) in Los Angeles (Bobo and Johnson 2000), Asians were more likely than even whites to hold antiblack and anti-Latino views. In line with this finding and with my thesis, they held more positive views about whites than about Latinos and blacks. Not surprisingly, as the racial attitudes of whites and Asians are converging, their views on racial policies are too. For example, in a recent poll in California, 78 percent of blacks and 66 percent of Latinos supported maintaining affirmative action, but only 27 percent of whites and 49 percent of Asians did so (Hajnal and Baldassare 2001). Similarly, as the views of Asians and whites converge, their political allegiances may too. The same recent study in California found that Latinos and blacks register mostly as Democrats, while Asians lean slightly toward the Democratic Party and whites split their party allegiances.

If groups develop status differences and translate them to their consciousness, they should also show signs of behavioral and associational patterns consistent with their new position. Whites should exhibit a clear preference for associating with "honorary whites" and vice versa. "Honorary whites" should not favor mingling with members of the "collective black" but members of the "collective black" should favor associating with members who are higher in the racial order. The rates of interracial marriage (the bulk of it is with whites) tend to fit the Latin-Americanization expectations. Whereas 93 percent of whites and blacks marry within-group, 70 percent of Latinos and Asians do so and only 33 percent of Native Americans marry Native Americans (Moran 2001:103). More significantly, when one disentangles the generic terms "Asians" and "Latinos," the data fit the Latin-Americanization thesis even more closely. For example, among Latinos, the groups that potentially include more members of the "honorary white" category, such as Cubans, Mexicans, Central Americans, and South Americans, have higher rates of intermarriage than the groups that have more individuals belonging to the "collective black" category, such as Puerto Ricans and Dominicans (Gilbertson et al. 1996). Although interpreting the Asian-American outmarriage patterns is very complex (groups such as Filipinos and Vietnamese have higher-than-expected rates in part due to the Vietnam War and the military bases in the Philippines), it is worth pointing out that the highest outmarriage rate belongs to Japanese-Americans and Chinese (the Asian overclass) (Kitano and Daniels 1995) and the lowest to Southeast Asians.

Data on racial assimilation through marriage ("whitening") show that the children of Asian-white and Latino-white unions are more likely to be classified as white than the children of black-white unions. Hence whereas only 22 percent of the children of black fathers and white mothers are classified as white, the children of similar unions between whites and Asians are twice as likely

to be classified as white (Waters 1997). For Latinos, the data fit my thesis even closer, as Latinos of Cuban, Mexican, and South American origin have high rates of exogamy compared to Puerto Ricans and Dominicans (Gilbertson et al. 1996). This may reflect the fact that these latter groups have far more dark-skinned members, which would limit their chances for outmarriage in a highly racialized marriage market.

Repercussions of Latin Americanization for the Future of Whiteness in America

With some trepidation, given the data limitations I have pointed out, I suggest that the Latin Americanization of race relations in the United States is already under way. If this is the case, what will be the repercussions for whiteness? First, the category white, which has always been fluid, as evidenced by the fact that over the last two hundred years it has incorporated "ethnic" groups such as Irish, Jews, Italians, Polish, Greeks, and so on, will undergo a major transformation. The white category will *darken* and include unexpected company as a segment of the "multiracial" community joins its ranks (Rockquemore 2002, 2003). "Whites" will also include assimilated light-skinned Latinos (Barry Alvarez, the football coach at the University of Wisconsin, Lauro Cavazos, former secretary of education under Reagan, etc.), some well-to-do assimilated Asians, and maybe even a few "blacks" who "marry up" (Ward Connelly, Tiger Woods, etc.).

Second, Latin-Americanization will force a reshuffling of *all* ethnic identities. Certain "ethnic" claims may dissipate (or, in some cases, decline in significance) as mobility will increasingly be seen as based on (1) whiteness or near-whiteness; and (2) intermarriage with whites (this seems to be the case among many Japanese-Americans, particularly those who have intermarried). This dissipation of ethnicity will not be limited to "honorary whites," as members of the "collective black" strata strive to position themselves higher on the new racial totem pole based on degrees of proximity or closeness to whiteness. Will Vietnamese, Filipinos, and other members of the Asian, underclass coalesce with blacks and dark-skinned Latinos or will they try to distance themselves from them and struggle to emphasize their "Americanness"?

Third, whiteness will have a new ally in near-whiteness. "Honorary whites" will do the bulk of the dirty work to preserve white supremacy as they will think their fate is tied to whites. Two incidents reported by Norman Matloff in an op-ed piece in the *San Francisco Chronicle* (1997) are examples of things to come:

> In the newsletter of the Oakland chapter of the Organization of Chinese Americans, editor Peter Eng opined: "Chinese-Americans will need to separate and distance ourselves from other ethnic immigrant groups" and suggested that Latino immigration was a burden to society.

> Elaine Kim, a Korean-American UC Berkeley professor, has written that a major Latino organization suggested to her [actually to Korean community activist Bong-Huan Kim—added by Matloff] that Asians and Latinos work together against blacks in an Oakland redistricting proposal. And an Asian/Latino coalition is suing Oakland, claiming it awards too many city contracts to black-owned firms.

Lastly, the space for contesting whiteness and white supremacy will be drastically reduced, as is the case all over Latin America. As the mantra of "We are all Americans" becomes part of the fabric of the United States, traditional racial politics will become harder to maintain. Activists trying to organize in the future around the "we" versus "them" dynamic will be declared "racist" and accused of trying to divide the "long and hard-fought national unity."

How To Fight Whiteness and White Supremacy in the Twenty-First Century

How can we organize to fight a racial structure that is almost invisible, an ideology that denies being racial, and a whiteness that will be stretched out and be seemingly "inclusive"[?] In what follows, I outline a political strategy to fight the three heads of postmodern white supremacy in the United States.

The first head of contemporary white supremacy is the "new racism." I argued that because post-1960s racial practices tend to be covert, subtle, institutional, and apparently nonracial, white privilege is maintained in a "now you see it, now you don't fashion." Furthermore, because systemic advantage is less dependent on virulent actions by individual actors,[5] the average white person does not see "racism" or is less likely than ever to understand minorities' complaints. Instead, whites believe the passage of civil rights legislation leveled the playing field and thus regard any talk about racism as an "excuse" used by minorities to avoid dealing with the real problems in their communities. The filler for whites' racial narratives comes from the second head of postmodern white supremacy, color-blind racism or the dominant post-civil rights racial ideology.

I have suggested elsewhere that the task for progressive social scientists and activists fighting contemporary white supremacy and color-blind racism is to unmask the racial character of many of these practices and accompanying beliefs; to make visible what remains invisible (Bonilla-Silva 2001). To this effect, we can follow the lead of the department of Housing and Urban Development, which has developed the audit strategy of sending out testers evenly matched on all characteristics except race to investigate claims of housing discrimination. This strategy can be used by researchers and activists alike in a variety of venues: banks, retail stores, jobs, and so on.

Another strategy that may prove useful is to do undercover work on racial affairs. Investigative news shows such as *Prime Time, 20/20,* and others have used this technique quite successfully to document discrimination. Lawrence Otis-Graham used this strategy for gathering data for his book *Member of the Club* (1995). Otis-Graham, who is a black lawyer, worked at a private golf club as a waiter and showed that elite whites talk about race in an old-fashioned manner when they are in the comfort of their (almost) all-white environments. We can use this technique in an even more effective manner if white progressives do the undercover work.

Yet uncovering these new racism practices and documenting the whiteness of color blindness, as important as this is, will not lead to a major change unless we can organize a new Civil Rights movement. The task at hand is to demand what whites do not want to give us: *equality of results*. Equal opportunity is not equal if the groups in competition do not have similar foundations (e.g., levels of income, education, etc.) and if some groups still suffer from discrimination. This new movement should demand proportional representation in everything. If blacks and Latinos represent 25 percent of the nation, that should be their proportion among lawyers, doctors, and engineers as well as among people in the nations' prisons. How to achieve this (reparations, affirmative action, a Marshall-like program?) is a matter to be fought and discussed by this new Civil Rights movement (for details, see Bonilla-Silva 2001).

I have left the last head for the end—the Latin-Americanization of whiteness—because I believe this will be the hardest one to slay. Why? Because if whiteness becomes Latin American-like, then race will disappear from the social radar, and contesting racial issues will be an extremely difficult thing to do (How can we fight something that is not *socially* accepted as real?). That said, my point is that race relations will become Latin American-*like*, not *exactly like* in Latin America. Hence, for example, the black-white fracture will remain in place, albeit in a changed format. Similarly, the deep racism experienced by dark-skinned Latinos will also form part of the future. Lastly, the discrimination that Asian-Americans have experienced will not dissipate totally in years to come.

Therein lies the weakness of the emerging triracial order and the possibilities for challenging Latin American-like whiteness. Members of the "collective black" must be the backbone of the new Civil Rights movement as they are the ones who will remain literally "at the bottom of the well." However, if they want to be successful, they must wage, in coalition with progressive Asian and Latino organizations, a concerted effort to politicize the segments I label "honorary whites" and make them aware of the *honorary* character of their status. As Dr. Moses Seenarine

(1999), professor and a South-Asian-Indian organizer, recently put it:

> as long as a particular minority community continue to exclude others, they themselves will be excluded. As long as one group discriminates and are prejudiced to those who are poorer or "blacker" than themselves and their communities, they continue to reinforce and maintain the system of white racism. It is of no use of Indo-Caribbeans trying to distance themselves from Africans, or for South Asians distancing themselves from Indo-Caribbeans and Africans, because ultimately, these groups are all considered "black" by the dominant whites. Instead of excluding others, all "Indian-looking" peoples should build alliances with each other, and with African, Latino and other minority groups, to prevent racism in all of our communities.

This is the way out of the new quandary. We need to short-circuit the belief in near-whiteness as the solution to status differences and create a coalition of all "people of color" and their white allies. If the Latin-American model of race prevails and "pigmentocracy" crystallizes, we will all scramble for the meager wages that near-whiteness will provide to all who are willing to play the "we are all American" game.

Notes

1. Although the profitability of whiteness varies by class and gender (e.g., elite white men earn more than poor white women), *all* actors socially designated as "white" receive a better deal—more social, economic, political, and psychological benefits—than their nonwhite equivalents. Hence, poor white men do better than poor black men, poor white women than poor black women, and so on.

2. By racial ideology I mean the racially based frameworks used by actors to explain and justify (dominant race) or challenge (subordinate races) the racial status quo. I have suggested that it can be operationalized as comprised of frames, style, and racial stories (see Bonilla-Silva 2001, 2003). In this chapter I discuss only its frames.

3. I was the principal investigator in these two projects. For details on these projects, see Bonilla-Silva and Forman (2000) and Bonilla-Silva (2001).

4. This new disarticulated consciousness will reflect (1) the effects of a triracial order, which blunts the "us" versus "them" racial dynamic; and (2) the fact that members of the "collective black" can expect some real degree of racial (and class) mobility

through association and marriage with lighter-skinned people.

5. Most whites, unlike during slavery and Jim Crow, need not take direct action for "keeping minorities in their place." By just following the post-1960s white script (i.e., living in white neighborhoods, sending their children to white schools, and associating primarily with whites) they help produce the geopolitical and cultural conditions needed for white supremacy.

References

Bobo, Lawrence, and Devon Johnson. 2000. "Racial Attitudes in a Prismatic Metropolis: Mapping Identity, Stereotypes, Competition, and Views on Affirmative Action." Pp. 81–166 in *Prismatic Metropolis*, ed. Lawrence Bobo, Melvin Oliver, and James Johnson, and Abel Valenzuela. New York: Russell Sage Foundation.

Bobo, Lawrence, and Susan Suh. 2000. "Surveying Racial Discrimination: Analyses from a Multiethnic Labor Market." Pp. 523–560 in *Prismatic Metropolis: Inequality in Los Angeles*, ed. Lawrence Bobo, Melvin Oliver, James Johnson Jr., and Abel Valenzuela Jr. New York: Russell Sage.

Bobo, Lawrence, Camille Zubrinsky, James Johnson Jr., and Melvin Oliver. 1995. "Work Orientation, Job Discrimination, and Ethnicity." *Research in the Sociology of Work* 5: 45–85.

Bonacich, Edna. 1980. "Class Approaches to Ethnicity and Race." *The Insurgent Sociologist* 10 (2): 9–24.

Bonilla-Silva, Eduardo. 1997. "Rethinking Racism: Toward a Structural Interpretation." *American Sociological Review* 62: 465–480.

———. 2000. "'This Is a White Country': The Racial Ideology of the Western Nations of the World-System." *Sociological Inquiry* 70: 188–214.

———. 2001. *White Supremacy and Racism in the Post-Civil Rights Era*. Boulder, CO: Lynne Rienner.

———. 2003. *Racism without Racists: Color Blind Racism and the Persistence of Racial Inequality in the Unites States*. Boulder, CO: Rowman and Littlefield.

Bonilla-Silva, Eduardo, and Amanda Lewis. 1999. "The New Racism: Toward an Analysis of the U.S. Racial Structure, 1960s–1990." In *Race, Ethnicity and Nationality in the United States: Toward the Twenty-First Century*, ed. Paul Wong. Boulder, CO: Westview.

Collins, Sharon. 1997. *Black Corporate Executives: The Making and Breaking of the Black Middle Class*. Philadelphia, PA: Temple University Press.

Cose, Ellis. 1995 [1993]. *The Rage of a Privileged Class*. New York: HarperCollins.

Dollard, John. 1949. *Caste and Class in a Southern Town*. New York: Harper.

D'Souza, Dinesh. 1995. *The End of Racism*. New York: Free Press.

Du Bois, W. E. B. 1969 [1920]. *Darkwater*. New York: Schocken.

Feagin, Joe R. 2000. *Racist America: Roots, Current Realities, and Future Reparations*. New York: Routledge.

Feagin, Joe R., and Melvin P. Sikes. 1994. *Living with Racism: The Black Middle-Class Experience*. Boston, MA: Beacon.

Feagin, Joe R., Hernán Vera, and Nikitah Imani. 1996. *The Agony of Education: Black Students at White Colleges and Universities*. New York: Routledge.

Fine, Michelle, and Lois Weis. 1998. *The Unknown City*. Boston, MA: Beacon.

Forman, Tyrone, A., Gloria Martinez, and Eduardo Bonilla-Silva. Unpublished. "Latino's Perceptions of Blacks and Asians: Testing the Immigrant Hypothesis."

Forman, Tyrone, David Williams, and James Jackson. 1997. "Race, Place, and Discrimination." *Perspectives on Social Problems* 9: 231–261.

Galster, George C. 1990a. "Racial Steering by Real Estate Agents: Mechanisms and Motives." *The Review of Black Political Economy* 18 (Spring): 39–61.

———. 1990b. "Racial Steering in Urban Housing Markets: A Review of the Audit Evidence." *Review of Black Political Economy* 48 (3): 105–129.

Gans, Herbert. 1999. "The Possibility of a New Racial Hierarchy in the Twenty-First Century United State." Pp. 371–390 in *The Cultural Territories of Race*, ed. Michelle Lamont. Chicago, IL: University of Chicago Press.

Gilbertson, Greta, Joseph P. Kitzpatrick, and Lijun Yang. 1996. "Hispanic Outmarriage in New York City: New Evidence from 1991." *International Migration Review* 30: 445–450.

Hajnal, Zoltan, and Mark Baldassare. 2001. *Finding Common Ground: Racial and Ethnic Attitudes in California*. San Francisco, CA: Public Policy Institute of California.

Hanchard, Michael G. 1994. *Orpheus and Power*. Princeton, NJ: Princeton University Press.

Helg, Aline. 1990. "Race in Argentina and Cuba, 1880–1930: Theory, Policies, and Popular Reaction." Pp. 37–61 in *The Idea of Race in Latin America, 1870–1940*, ed. Richard Graham. Austin, TX: University of Texas Press.

Heller, Zoe. 2001. "When All Else Fails, Tell Her She Has Got Lumpy Thighs." *Daily Telegraph* August 4, 2001: 23.

Helms, Janet E., ed. 1990. *Black and White Racial Identity: Theory, Research and Practice*. New York: Greenwood.

———. 1994. "Racial Identity and Career Assessment." *Journal of Career Assessment* 2: 199–209.

———. 1996. "Toward a Methodology for Measuring and Assessing Racial as Distinguished from Ethnic Identity." Pp. 143–192 in *Multicultural Assessment in Counseling and Clinical Psychology*, ed. Gargi R. Sadowsky and James C. Impara. Lincoln, NE: University of Nebraska Press.

Henry, Charles. 1980. "Black-Chicano Coalitions: Possibilities and Problems." *Western Journal of Black Studies* 4: 222–232.

Henry, Charles, and Carlos Munoz. 1991. "Ideological and Interest Linkages in California Rainbow Politics." In *Racial and Ethnic Politics in California*, ed. Byron O. Jackson and Michael B. Preston. Berkeley, CA: IGS Press.

Herrnstein, Richard J., and Charles Murray. 1994. *The Bell Curve: Intelligence and Class Structure in American Life*. New York: Free Press.

Hickman, Christine B. 1997. "The Devil and the One Drop Rule: Racial Categories, African Americans, and the U.S. Census." *Michigan Law Review* 95: 1163–1265.

Higginbotham, A. Leon, Jr. 1978. *In the Matter of Color: Race and the American Legal Process—The Colonial Period*. New York: Oxford University Press.

——. 1996. *Shades of Freedom: Racial Politics and Presumptions of the American Legal Process*. New York: Oxford University Press.

Hochschild, Jennifer. 1995. *Facing Up to the American Dream: Race, Class and the Soul of the Nation*. Princeton, NJ: Princeton University Press.

Kinsbrunner, Jay. 1996. *Not of Pure Blood: The Free People of Color and Racial Prejudice in Nineteenth-Century Puerto Rico*. Durham, NC: Duke University Press.

Kitano, Harry H. L., and Roger Daniels. 1995. *Asian Americans: Emerging Minorities*. Upper Saddle River, NJ: Prentice Hall.

Lewis Mumford Center. 2001. "Ethnic Diversity Grows, Neighborhood Integration Lags Behind." Report by Lewis Mumford Center. Albany, NY: University of Albany. Available from *http://mumford1.dyndns.org/cen2000/WholePop/WPreport/MumfordReport.pdf*

Massey, Douglas S., and Nancy A. Denton. 1993. *American Apartheid: Segregation and the Making of the Underclass*. Cambridge, MA: Harvard University Press.

Matloff, Norman. 1997. "Asians, Blacks, and Intolerance." *San Francisco Chronicle*. (May 20).

Mills, Charles. 1997. *The Racial Contract*. Ithaca, NY: Cornell University Press.

Min, Pyong Gap. 1996. *Caught in the Middle: Korean Communities in New York and Los Angeles*. Berkeley, CA: University of California Press.

Montejano, David. 1987. *Anglos and Mexicans in the Making of Texas, 1836–1986*. Austin, TX: University of Texas Press.

Moran, Rachel. 2001. *Interracial Intimacy*. Chicago, IL: University of Chicago Press.

Otis-Graham, L. 1995. *Member of the Club: Reflections on Life in a Racially Polarized World*. New York: Harper Collins.

Payne, Charles. 1995. *I've Got the Light of Freedom*. Berkeley, CA: University of California Press.

Rockquemore, Kerry Ann. 2002. "Negotiating the Color Line: The Gendered Process of Racial Identity Construction among Black/White Biracial Women." *Gender & Society* 16: 485–503.

——. 2003. "Socially Embedded Identities: Theories, Typologies, and Processes of Racial Identity among Biracials." *The Sociological Quarterly*.

Rodriguez, Clara. 2000. *Changing Race: Latinos, the Census, and the History or Ethnicity in the United States*. New York: New York University Press.

Roediger, David R. 2002. *Colored White: Transcending the Racial Past*. Berkeley, CA: University of California Press.

Schuman, H., E. Singer, R. Donovan, and C. Sellitz. 1983. "Discriminatory Behavior in New York Restaurants." *Social Indicators* 13: 69–83.

Seenarine, Moses. 1999. "South Asians and Indo-Caribbeans Confronting Racism in the US." *Cricket Int'l*.

Sigelman, Lee, and Susan Welch. 1991. *Black Americans' Views of Racial Inequality*. New York: Cambridge University Press.

Smith, Robert Charles. 1995. *Racism in the Post-Civil Rights Era*. Albany, NY: State University of New York Press.

Thernstrom, Stephen, and Abigail Thernstrom. 1997. *America in Black and White: One Nation, Indivisible*. New York: Simon and Schuster.

Turner, Margery A., Raymond Struyk, and John Yinger. 1991. *The Housing Discrimination Study*. Washington, DC: The Urban Institute.

Tuttle, William M., Jr. 1970. *Race Riot: Chicago in the Red Summer of 1919*. New York: Atheneum.

Twine, France Winddance. 1998. *Racism in a Racial Democracy: The Maintenance of White Supremacy in Brazil*. New Brunswick, NJ: Rutgers University Press.

Warren, Jonathan, and France Winddance Twine. 1997. "White Americans, the New Minority? Non-Blacks and the Ever-Expanding Boundaries of Whiteness." *Journal of Black Studies* 28: 200–218.

Waters, Mary C. 1997. "Prepared Testimony of Professor Mary C. Waters, Department of Sociology, Harvard University." House Committee on Government Reform and Oversight, Subcommittee on Government Management, Information, and Technology. Washington, DC: Federal News Service.

Weitzer, Ronald. 1997. "Racial Prejudice among Korean Merchants in African-American Neighborhoods." *The Sociological Quarterly* 38: 587–606.

Yinger, J. Milton. 1995. *Closed Doors, Opportunities Lost: The Continuing Costs of Housing Discrimination*. New York: Russell Sage.

Yoon, In-jin. 1997. *On My Own: Korean Businesses and Race Relations in America*. Chicago, IL: University of Chicago Press.

Discussion Questions

1. How do you respond to Bonilla-Silva's paradigm of the "new racism," "color-blind racism," and the Latin-Americanization of the United States? Do you agree with his position, disagree, are undecided? Why or why not?

2. In Bonilla-Silva's paradigm, gender is secondary to race. Do you think that gender could be made a stronger part of the paradigm when we look at the treatment of women of color?

3. What was your response to research presented by Bonilla-Silva, such as the treatment of Blacks in New York's finest

restaurants? Did you know that such treatment is still common even in relation to successful Blacks?

4. Do you think the strategies Bonilla-Silva suggested in this chapter would be effective in dealing with the "new racism"? What other strategies might be used to deal with the "new racism"?

57

Buried Alive

The Concept of Race in Science

Troy Duster

In this article, sociologist Troy Duster notes that discarding the concept of "race" has great appeal to a wide range of people. Let me cite only a few examples. Folks on the right would like to discard race since it would serve their interests to do away with affirmative action and similar race-based initiatives. Those on the left believe inequities are better explained by class differences and so discarding race would not offend this camp either. Those in the center would be happy to discard race since they believe a colorblind society would be a fairer society. Academic disciplines likewise join this fray. Scholars in the social sciences propose that race, like gender and sexual orientation, is socially constructed; while those in the humanities argue that all categories to which people may be assigned are temporary and fluctuating. Even natural scientists have something to add, arguing that the Human Genome Project, which demonstrates that social categories do not map exactly with biological reality, is proof that we should abandon "race." However, Duster who has been considering the ethical, legal, and social implications of the Human Genome Project for several years, disagrees.

Duster says we cannot simply make race go away because we want it to. Instead, we now have the complex task of figuring out the relationship between the social and the biological. In the article, he discusses some well-known if imperfect correlations between race/ethnicity and genetic diseases such as Tay-Sachs among Ashkenazic Jews, sickle cell anemia among African Americans of West African heritage, and cystic fibrosis among Americans of Northern European descent. Genes for each of these conditions are more prevalent among people with common ancestry, but not entirely absent in other populations. He notes that there are eco-nomic, social, and ethical dimensions to be considered. The first "ethnic drug," BiDil, is intended to treat heart disease among African Americans, but would it work for everyone who is considered to be African American? Would giving it only to African Americans ignore the fact that it might actually benefit some Whites or Asians? Moreover, would market forces dictate that gene-based pharmacological research focus on drugs for large segments of the population or segments most likely to be able to afford expensive therapies and neglect others? For example, would attention be directed toward drugs for Whites ignoring the needs of groups like the Zuni, who are at risk for cystic fibrosis from a different mutation than Northern European Whites?

Duster leaves readers with a great deal to think about. He says that our "major task . . . is to analyze how and under what circumstances we use the concept of race" (p. 499). However, the issues he raises actually go well beyond the concept of "race" as we usually think of it. Different segments of society have vested interests in how we view race/ethnicity, gender, and sexual orientation. The biological and social sciences can provide some perspectives, but their findings can be used for economic and political ends and may have differing impacts on various portions of the population.

In the last decade, many Americans have urged that the concept of race be abandoned, purged from our public discourse, rooted out of medicine, and exiled from science. Indeed, there is something of a bandwagon of publicly expressed sentiment that we should get rid of the idea of race altogether, and some unlikely allies are riding on that bandwagon.

In politics, left-leaning analysts have long advocated a heavier emphasis on class than on race, because they see economic forces as more fundamental for explaining how societies stratify their members. But in recent years, we have also heard a crescendoing clamor from those on the right who would like to end affirmative action—both in the workplace and in educational admissions policies. For somewhat different reasons, a cadre of political centrists finds the idea (and ideal) of a colorblind society quite attractive. Equating colorblindness with fairness and justice, they object to practices like racial profiling by the police and racial redlining by the banks.

Thus the motives for getting rid of race range from wishing to solidify entrenched privilege to trying to dislodge it, and from thinking that racial discrimination is a thing of the past to believing that the only way to get rid of persistent racist practices is to jettison the concept of race.

Much of academe is on board the "do away with race" bandwagon. In the humanities, increasing numbers of postmodernists and poststructuralists are arguing for alternative narratives of ever-shifting human taxonomies, and that trend dovetails conveniently with those academics in the social sciences who are repeating the mantra that race is merely a social construct. However, the feat that has done the most in the last few years to direct the media's attention and the public's imagination to the idea of getting rid of race is the sequencing of the human genetic code—and the rhetoric that has accompanied it.

A lot of hope is being expressed these days about the potential power of human genetics. People are excited not just about the prospects for delivering drugs that are customized to individual patients' genes but also about the use of DNA for the exculpation of the innocent on death row. In addition, they hear predictions that the findings from the Human Genome Project will lay to rest, once and for all, the myth that race has a biological basis. However, people can easily confuse high expectations of legal and medical developments in genetics with dreams of new social views of race. Can science rescue us from race and its diabolical Siamese twin, racism?

J. Craig Venter—the head of Celera Genomics, the private company involved in sequencing the human genome—and many others have said that race is not a scientific concept. However, before we leap to the conclusion that only the scientifically uninformed persist in believing in the existence of race, we should pay attention to a series of developments within molecular biology and its practical uses that not only complicate that picture, but subvert the idea that we can easily separate scientific from racial thinking.

The central rationale behind the Human Genome Project is the promise of improved health. The government used that rationale to justify spending more than $2 billion on the project, and many biotechnology companies will ultimately succeed or fail based on the degree to which they can fulfill that promise. The project did not promise only abstract theoretical advances in science. The advances in human genetics about which we hear so much in the media are trumpeted precisely because of their potential practical applications.

But in medicine, categories are rarely discrete; they often overlap. Thus, we should hardly expect genetics to deliver pharmaceuticals to us in neat and tidy packages designed only for Group A, pharmaceuticals that would never work on Group B.

It will come as no surprise to anyone knowledgeable about human genetics that in the United States, for example, there are African-Americans with cystic fibrosis, a genetic disorder that impairs breathing capacity, which is found mainly in persons of northern European descent. And of course there are whites in America with sickle cell anemia, a genetic disorder of the blood found mainly in people of West African descent. But the existence of exceptions does not negate the practicality of acknowledging a pattern.

The story begins to crystallize with the cost-benefit calculation of testing for genetic disorders. We have known for at least a half-century that many genetic disorders are distributed in the population in less-than-random fashion, primarily because of cultural rules about mate selection, as well as geographic proximity. Any group comprising people who for many centuries have mated within their group may be at greater risk of certain genetic disorders. Americans of Ashkenazic Jewish descent have a greater risk of developing Tay-Sachs disease—a genetic disorder that causes degeneration of the neurological system in early childhood—than members of other groups do; and, as noted above, the same is true of Americans of northern European descent and cystic fibrosis, and Americans of West African descent and sickle cell anemia. So far, no issue of race here.

Over the years, we have developed genetic tests to detect whether a person is a carrier of the genes for one of those diseases. Knowing that Ashkenazic Jews are more likely to have Tay-Sachs disease than gentiles whose ancestors came from the same part of Europe, we do not typically test gentiles for the disease. The problem is that, with some genetic disorders, like cystic fibrosis, no single gene is responsible for the condition; hundreds of mutations can cause it. In the last decade, for example, we have learned that Americans of northern European descent are more likely than other Americans to have a particular mutation involved in cystic fibrosis, labeled DF508. However, a very different mutation puts the Zuni Indians at an equal risk of developing cystic fibrosis.

Now we come to two striking features of the story. First, the genetic test that has been developed detects only the DF508 mutation. There is no genetic test for the Zuni mutation. Second, and vital to the story, the DF508 test is not equally sensitive in the different groups that we associate with the social categories of white, Asian, and black. The test detects over 90 percent of the mutations in whites, but only about 70 percent in blacks and less than 30 percent in Asians.

We should not be surprised by those differences. In 1995, Unesco issued a statement on race, which said that race has no utility as a concept in the biological sciences and suggested that race is not a valid concept for any scientific work. Yet only two years after the publication of that statement, an article appeared in the American Journal of Human Genetics titled "Ethnic-Affiliation Estimation by Use of Population-Specific DNA Markers," Mark D. Shriver, of the University of Pittsburgh, and his co-authors reported that, after a search of the literature and unpublished data, they had identified genetic markers that, when used in combination with other markers, allow "robust ethnic-af-

filiation estimation" for members of the major groups in the U.S. population.

Indeed, the new pharmacogenomics asserts unequivocally that different races respond differently to certain drugs. For instance, in a 1999 article in Science, William E. Evans and Mary V. Relling, of the University of Tennessee, claim that "all pharmacogenetic polymorphisms studied to date differ in frequency among ethnic and racial groups." That finding may not be based on thoughtfully controlled studies of different populations, but it helps explain the recent announcement that the Food and Drug Administration has issued a "letter of approvability" for NitroMed, a pharmaceutical company, to try to market what the Financial Times called "the first 'ethnic' drug," BiDil. It is a drug specifically designed to treat heart disease in African-Americans, who are twice as likely as white people to suffer heart failure. This is a social time bomb, dangerous even in the hands of well-intentioned persons who have not thought carefully about what it would mean to market such a drug.

It is certain that some whites would benefit from it, and some blacks would not. The "one drop of blood" rule is biologically absurd, but it still colors the thinking of many people, including some biological scientists and pharmacogenomicists.

A larger issue is represented by the fact that nobody is developing pharmaceuticals or genetic tests for groups like the Zuni. Although the first "ethnic drug" to reach the market is aimed exclusively at African-Americans, it is very likely that most drugs will be aimed at groups with the money to buy them—and the numbers to make that money add up. Biotechnology companies are in business to turn a profit. It would have been politically difficult to start with a drug aimed exclusively at whites, but once the foot is in the door, we can anticipate which direction the rest of the body will go.

It is both naive and futile to try to abolish the concept of race with a series of ex cathedra pronouncements from the government, scientists flushed with pride in the latest genetic discoveries, humanities professors brimming with insights about alternative discursive narrative, or social scientists retelling yet again the socially constructed nature of all human taxonomies.

The French try to solve the problem of race by looking the other way. But does anyone really believe that just because the French don't count the numbers of Tunisians, Algerians, and sub-Saharan blacks in their midst, they do not discriminate in housing and employment against the members of those groups?

The major task for Americans is to analyze how and under what circumstances we use the concept of race. We can and should refer to race when we consider it as part of a complex interaction of social forces and biological feedback loops. The current budget of the National Institutes of Health quite properly sets aside a substantial amount of money for a study of health disparities between whites and other ethnic and racial groups. It is important for us to understand why, for example, the rate of prostate cancer is approximately twice as high among African-American males aged 50 to 70 as it is among white males of comparable age. Is it because African-Americans are more likely than whites to live near toxic-waste dumps? Or to eat different foods? Or to have "one drop" of "other" blood?

It is a mistake to discard race just because racial categories do not map exactly onto biological processes. But it is also a mistake to uncritically accept old racial classifications when we study medical treatments. The task is to determine how the social meaning of race can affect biological outcomes like varying rates of cancer and heart failure. Burying the concept of race can seem very appealing in the short term. But in practical applications, race remains very much alive.

Discussion Questions

1. Duster asks whether science can rescue us from race and the evils of racism. Based on this article and other readings, how would you respond to that question?

2. Many of the readings in this volume implicitly or explicitly adopt the social science view that race, gender, and sexual orientation are socially constructed. Did reading this article cause you question or modify that view?

3. The editors of this volume explicitly take an intersectional perspective, claiming that race, gender, and class should not be viewed individually, but in relationship to one another. Does this article challenge or support that perspective? Explain.

4. Now that the human genome has been mapped, do you think it would be a good thing or a bad thing for the pharmaceutical industry to concentrate its research on drugs for specific ethnic groups? Work with other students to develop a list of pro and con arguments on this issue.

Reprinted from: Troy Duster, "Buried Alive: The Concept of Race in Science." The *Chronicle of Higher Education*, 48 (3), pp. B11, 2p. Copyright © 2001 by Troy Duster. Published by the *Chronicle of Higher Education*. Reprinted by permission of the author. ✦

58
Playing in the Gender Transgression Zone

Race, Class, and Hegemonic Masculinity in Middle Childhood

C. Shawn McGuffey
B. Lindsay Rich

Who would have thought that you could see gender relations so strikingly within the interactions of 5–12 year olds? C. Shawn McGuffey and B. Lindsay Rich take us to a summer camp with children in this age group—middle childhood—to uncover what gendered negotiations are already at play at this age. In addition, the authors want us to understand that gender is not the only salient variable at play but also racial, class, sexual, and age variables. The authors most want us to consider the territory where boys and girls transgress gender codes for masculinity and femininity and either expand or maintain existing gender boundaries—the transgender zone.

McGuffey and Rich first describe the concept of "hegemonic masculinity," which overlays the entire piece and conveys gender relations as they are predominantly done in our culture, that is, a privileging of masculine over feminine qualities. Next the researchers enter the bounded world of the camp, noting how boys and girls structure their interactions. McGuffey and Rich find that boys create a hierarchical interactional structure, resolving conflicts with aggression, name-calling, and even exclusion of others. In this gendered grouping,

a high value is placed on being competitive, unemotional, and getting attention. Boys at this young age are already objectifying women. Interestingly, among boys in this age group, race and class were not as salient as gender in the structure of the hierarchy, since Black or socioeconomically disadvantaged boys could be found at the highest levels of the hierarchy.

Girls, on the other hand, do not stress hierarchy but organize themselves in small groups defined by age group where conflicts are dealt with through social manipulation and exclusion. Aggression among girls is not physical but, nonetheless, can leave emotional scars. Girls groups centered on emotional intimacy and the ideal of being "nice." While niceness was relative, all girl groups placed an emphasis on it. Interestingly, among the girls, both class and race were salient variables. With regard to class, girl groupings were marked by clear class affiliations with different girl cliques focused around neighborhood or school affiliations. At the same time, African American girls, unlike White girls, often grouped together despite age differences and were more clearly assertive than White girls. Older African American girls facilitated activities among the entire group of Black girls with input from the younger ones, stressing a communal approach to making decisions as opposed to a hierarchical method.

It is in the "gender transgression zone," perhaps, that McGuffey and Rich take their article to the next level. It is here that boys patrol boys and maintain hegemonic masculinity by rejecting, ostracizing, and even abusing any boy who transgresses into "sissy" behavior using clear homophobic messages. Boys also patrol the zone with regard to girls, who are either marginalized (made to feel inadequate) or masculinized (made into yet another boy). Tellingly for these 5–12 year olds, girls are not welcome in the world of the boy unless they sacrifice their femininity. In the transgender zone, girls learn the limitation of their power relative to boys. Girls also tended to back girls who stood up to boys regardless of any other social markers—race, class, or age—a remarkable case of "girl solidarity." In addition, girls were much more understanding of boys who transgressed within the zone, welcoming so-called sissies into their play groups as long as they were "nice."

One of the most interesting moments in the reading is the final section on how high-status boys can directly change the contours of the gender transgression zone. In this case, the highest status boy, Adam, learns to like and master a "girl" game, opening the door for other boys to engage in what was formerly a girl-only form of play without stigma. Here also hegemonic masculinity rears its head as the boys turn the game itself into an opportunity for male sexual swaggering.

By now, R. W. Connell's concept of "hegemonic masculinity" has wide currency among students of gender.[1] The concept implies that there is a predominant way of doing gender relations (typically by men and boys, but not necessarily limited to men and boys) that enforces the gender order status quo: It elevates the general social status of masculine over feminine qualities and privileges some masculine qualities over others. The notion that "masculinities" and "femininities" exist and can be interrogated as negotiated realities allows us to further our understanding about the larger gender order in which they are embedded.

We want to caution, however, against the temptation to over generalize the concept of hegemonic masculinity. To do so runs the risk of glossing the modalities, both historical and social-spatial (in terms of class, ethnoracial, sexual, and age variations), in which hegemonic masculinity emerges. We believe that hegemonic masculinity, while having general qualities as a form of social power, may take on many valences and nuances, depending on the social setting and the social actors involved. Connell (1987, 1995, 36–37) is himself careful to make the sorts of qualifications we make here while similarly claiming the general analytic utility of the concept. We agree with advocates of the concept that it indeed gives us great theoretical leverage and explanatory power toward clarifying and refining how and why men's dominance works at higher levels of social organization, perhaps even at the global level (Connell 1995; Hawkesworth 1997). In this article, we provide evidence of how hegemonic masculinity is manifest in middle childhood play and used to re-create a gender order among children wherein the larger social relations of men's dominance are learned, employed, reinforced, and potentially changed. Specifically, we present and discuss the results of a preliminary participant observation study of microlevel processes of gender boundary negotiation in middle childhood (ages 5–12).

Providing empirical evidence about the ways in which boys and girls negotiate gender relations within specific social contexts can further understanding about why gender relations take the forms they do in childhood. Using the concept of hegemonic masculinity as a heuristic tool, we decided to focus on how gender relations—specifically, the enactment of masculine hegemony within these relations—were "done" (West and Zimmerman 1987). We eschew the notion that men and women (or boys and girls) merely enact "sex roles" as handed-down scripts. Rather, while acknowledging structural gender socialization implied by the concept of role, we focus on the ways in which the relations between girls and boys are negotiated (Connell 1987, 1995; Messner 1998).

There are at least two important reasons for this focus when studying children. First, even when "gender roles" are "visible" to and internalized by kids, the meanings attached to them are partly context specific and negotiable. Second, the relative status of gender-typed behaviors implied by conceptualizing multiple, contested forms of masculinity or femininity is a dynamic, historical process that must be continually created or re-created; it happens most palpably at the microlevel, in face-to-face social interactions of individuals and small groups. Connell (1995, 65), borrowing from Kosik (1976), uses the term *onto-formative* to capture the emergent process through which social agents actually create or re-create gender dynamics in, during, and through social interaction. Thus, we want to emphasize the context-bound nature of hegemonic masculinity as a style of gender domination that emerges in this specific middle-childhood context.

A substantial amount of research has been dedicated to studying how boys and girls both segregate and organize themselves within the same gender groupings. Barrie Thorne (1994), for instance, has documented numerous examples of boys organizing themselves in larger, hierarchical groups and occupying more space than their female counterparts. While Thorne asserts that children in middle childhood "use the frame of play as a guise for often serious, gender-related messages" (5), few have explored the power dynamics of gender boundary negotiations as they are "played out" in childhood.

We analyze the process of gender boundary negotiation by focusing on the intersection of gender-segregated activities. Since boys and girls tend to organize themselves into gender-homogeneous groups, they are generally aware that their sphere of "gender-appropriate" activities has boundaries. When they transgress these bounds, they enter a contested area that we refer to as the "gender transgression zone" (GTZ). Since gender identity is a "continual process whereby meanings are attributed by and to individuals through social interaction" (Bird 1996, 122), this contentious area is extremely consequential to the development of children. In the GTZ, gender boundaries are constantly being negotiated. Therefore, it is in the GTZ that we should expect to find continuities, as well as changes, in the construction of "gendered" activities and thus the definition of what is hegemonically masculine and what is "other," typically defined as "effeminate." Related research has demonstrated that an important, if not the central, criterion for defining one's masculinity is to distance oneself from anything feminine (e.g., Bird 1996; McCreary 1994).[2]

Considering the importance of the GTZ as the social location where hegemonic notions of gender are challenged and defended, who ultimately decides the rules of negotiation in the GTZ and how? The evidence from this study suggests that high-status boys control the rules of the game in the GTZ. By learning and enforcing hegemonic masculinity (in this setting, the dominant boys' style stresses emotional detachment, competition and rivalry, public attention-getting for victories, and the sexual objectification of females),

high-status boys control gender boundaries within the GTZ.

After describing the setting, sample, and method of data collection, our argument develops by first analyzing the principle of homosocial organization among the boys in a status hierarchy and the homosocial organizational strategies of girls in non-hierarchical small cliques. Using the notion of "gender patrolling," we discuss how heterosocial "playing" occurs in the GTZ and show how the dominant high-status boys exercise hegemony through patrolling. Finally, we examine how the GTZ is (re)produced and how it is changed.

Setting, Sample, and Method

The results reported here are the product of discussions we had during and after the first author observed and participated an average of seven hours daily in these processes as a camp counselor at a children's summer camp in a mid-sized southeastern city. This participant observation was carried out over a period of nine weeks in the summer of 1996, involving a total of approximately 315 hours. The camp itself serves a fairly broad range of families, both in terms of class standing and ethnoracial characteristics. Camp registration forms indicated the household income and racial identification of each child participating in the program. Most children came from middle- to lower-middle-class families, with some poor children attending who were aided by a limited number of scholarships to help pay camp fees. The ethnoracial composition of the sample was as follows: 67 percent white, 25 percent African American, 5 percent Asian or Asian American, and the remaining 3 percent comprising various multiethnic, Arabic, and Latino peoples. These percentages are precise approximations because although there was some turnover in children over the weeks (about 20 percent each two-week session), it had very little impact on the ethnoracial composition. The camp averaged 77 participants per week—ages 5 to 12—with approximately 80 percent of those enrolled returning each week. The gender composition of the children held quite steady throughout the nine weeks at 54 percent girls, 46 percent boys.

The routine of this summer camp was heavily marked by a lot of "playing." Although each day differed depending on the daily field trip, campers arrived at approximately 8:00 a.m. and had free time—unorganized play in which they could participate in a variety of activities from board games to basketball—until 8:30. At this time, the children were organized into four age groups (5–6, 7–8, 9–10, 11–12) in which counselors informed the campers of the day's activities. The camp had three large areas of play that sponsored assorted games and activities (e.g., prison ball, field hockey, and kick ball) and an arts and crafts facility. The four groups participated in each of the four activities on a rotating basis. Around noon, the participants had lunch and soon after loaded the buses for the daily field trip. Field trips included outings to the local pool, planetarium, parks, and numerous other places. Depending on when the children returned to the campsite, the camp resumed its age-ranked rotation or played large games that included the participation of all campers. Five-thirty until close was always designated free time. During free time, lunch, snack, and field trips, children were free to interact with children from other age groups. In sum, this summer camp typically involved the children in plenty of play activity, most of which was not organized on a gender-segregated basis.

As a counselor, the first author supervised the children's activities and assisted in the daily functioning of the site. He kept a daily log of findings, based on notes taken throughout the day and detailed recollections of gender play and interactions, with many verbatim quotes. These logs were systematized and typed up every evening after work. Once a week, we had extensive discussions based on these accumulating logs, relating the concrete activities and events of the camp to our evolving formulations and theoretical understandings. Early on in this process, we decided that particular attention should be placed on how and where gender boundaries were created and how they were transgressed. We made the methodological

decision to be vigilant to both homosocial transgression (i.e., children engaging in gender-inappropriate activities among members of the same gender) and to heterosocial transgression (i.e., boys or girls engaging in gender-inappropriate activities among members of the other gender). We believe that this aided tremendously in allowing us to narrow the observational target and increase the quality of the data collected. In addition to participant observation, the first author interviewed 22 of the children and six parents near the end of the summer to gain insight into the ways children and parents constructed meanings around the observed gendering processes. Finally, when we refer to specific children in this study, we designate ethnoracial, gender, and age distinctions as follows: W = White, B = Black, A = Asian, B = Boy, G = Girl, and a number representing the age of the child. For example, an African American girl who is 7 years old will be represented as (BG7). If a child is of another racial category other than white, black, or Asian, his or her specific classification will be marked accordingly.

Organization of Homosocial Status Systems

When examined as two separate social groups, boys and girls organize themselves differently based on distinct systems of valuing. We must reiterate that masculinity and femininity are not bipolar or opposites but are rather "separate and relatively independent dimensions" (Absi-Semaan, Crombie, and Freeman 1993, 188). Gender is a social construction that is constantly being modified as individuals mature. What may be gender appropriate at one stage in life may be gender inappropriate at a later stage. Boys, for example, are free to touch each other affectionately in early middle childhood, but this is subsequently stigmatized, with a few exceptions (such as victory celebrations). As "independent dimensions," one can develop a clearer view of masculinity and femininity by studying how they differ in context to intragender (homosocial) relations and then how they interact in intergender (heterosocial) relations. Homosocial relationships—nonsexual attractions held by members of the same sex—define how heterosocial relationships are maintained. Thus, it is essential to understand how boys and girls organize themselves within each homosocial group to understand how they negotiate boundaries between the two (Bird 1996).[3]

Structural Formation of Boys in Middle Childhood

Boys in middle childhood organize themselves in a definite hierarchical structure in which the high-status boys decide what is acceptable and valued—that which is hegemonically masculine—and what is not. A boy's rank in the hierarchy is chiefly determined by his athletic ability. Researchers have identified sports as a central focus in boys' development (Fine 1992; Messner 1992, 1994). Boys in this context were observed using words such as *captain, leader,* and various other ranking references, even when they were not playing sports. Messner (1994, 209) explains the attraction of sports in hegemonic masculinity as a result of young males finding the "rulebound structure of games and sports to be a psychologically 'safe' place in which [they] can get (nonintimate) connection with others within a context that maintains clear boundaries, distance, and separation from others." Sharon Bird (1996) identifies three characteristics in maintaining hegemonic masculinity: emotional detachment, competitiveness, and the sexual objectification of women, in which masculinity is thought of as different from and better than femininty. As another essential feature of hegemonic masculinity, we want to add to these characteristics the ability to draw attention to one's self. Because hegemony is sustained publicly, being able to attract positive attention to one's self is vital. The recognition a boy receives from his public performance of masculinity allows him to maintain his high status and/or increase his rank in the hierarchy.

Conflicts and disagreements in the boys' hierarchy are resolved by name-calling and teasing, physical aggression, and exclusion from the group. These forms of aggression structure and maintain the hierarchy by subordinating alternate propositions and iden-

tities that threaten hegemonic masculinity. Although direct and physical aggression are the most physically damaging, the fear of being exiled from the group is the most devastating since the hierarchy confirms masculinity and self worth for many young boys. According to Kaufman (1995, 16), the basis for a hegemonic masculinity is "unconsciously rooted before the age of six" and "is reinforced as the child develops." Lower-status boys adhere to the hegemonic rules as established by the top boys even if they do not receive any direct benefits from the hierarchy within the homosocial context. The overwhelming majority of boys support hegemonic masculinity in relation to subordinated masculinities and femininities because it not only gives boys power over an entire sex (i.e., girls), but it also gives them the opportunity to acquire power over members of their own sex. This helps maintain the hierarchical frame by always giving boys—even low-status boys—status and power over others. Connell (1987, 183) states that hegemonic masculinity "is always constructed in relation to various subordinated masculinities as well as in relation to women." Connell (1995, 79) describes this pan-masculine privilege over girls and women as the "patriarchal dividend." Hegemonic masculinity is publicly used to sustain the power of high-status boys over subordinate boys and boys over girls.

Emotional detachment, competitiveness, and attention arousal could be witnessed in any game of basketball. High-status boys in our study generally performed the best and always distinguished themselves after scoring points. Three high-status boys demonstrate this particularly well. After scoring, Adam[4] (WB11) usually jumped in the air, fist in hand, and shouted either, "In your face!" or "You can't handle this!" Brian's (BB11) style consisted of a little dance followed by, "It's all good and it's all me!" Darell (BB11) also had a shuffle he performed and ended his routine with, "You can't handle my flow!" or "Pay attention and take notes on how a real 'G' [man] does it." These three are also the most aggressive, oftentimes running over their own teammates. By constantly displaying their athletic superiority, these high-status boys are validating their position and maintaining separation from lower-status boys. Most boys usually did some "attention getting" as well when they scored.

The sexual objectification of women can easily be seen in boys' homosocial interactions. Sexually degrading remarks by boys about women and girls at the pool were common; harassment by young boys occasionally occurred. In one instance at a nearby swimming pool, an adolescent girl, approximately 16 years old, was on her stomach sunbathing with the top portion of her bikini unfastened. Adam (WB11)—the highest-ranked boy—walked over to the young lady and asked if he could put some tanning lotion on her back. After she refused his offer, Adam—with a group of boys urging him on—poured cold water on her back, causing her to instinctually raise up and reveal her breasts. While he was being disciplined, the other boys cheered him on, and Adam smiled with pride. In "The Dirty Play of Little Boys," Gary Fine (1992, 137) argues that "given the reality that many talkers have not reached puberty, we can assume that their sexual interests are more social than physiological. Boys wish to convince their peers that they are sexually mature, active, and knowledgeable" and, we might add, definitely heterosexual.

Despite the fact that there were definite racial and class differences in the boys' hierarchy, these factors had surprisingly little consequence for rankings in the power structure. Black and/or economically disadvantaged boys were just as likely to hold high positions of authority as their white and/or middle-class counterparts. Though a white middle-class boy (Adam) was the highest-ranked youth in the boys' hierarchy, two poor Black youths (Brian and Darrel) held the second and third positions in the hierarchy. Furthermore, when Adam went on a two-week vacation with his family, Darrel surpassed Brian and assumed the alpha position in the boys' social order. Nonetheless, upon his return, Adam reasserted his dominance in the group.

Structural Formation of Girls in Middle Childhood

Girls' homosocial organizational forms are distinct from boys. The tendency toward a single hierarchy, for example, is quite rare. Social aggression (e.g., isolating a member of the group) is used to mark boundaries of femininity. These boundaries do not seem to involve a singular notion of hegemonic femininity with which to subordinate other forms or to heighten public notice of a higher-status femininity. Girls' boundaries are less defined than boys'. The girls in our study generally organized themselves in small groups ranging from two to four individuals. These groups, nonetheless, usually had one girl who was of higher status than the other girls in the clique. The highest-status girl was generally the one considered the most sociable and the most admired by others in the immediate clique as well as others in the camp. Much as Luria and Thorne (1994, 52) observed, the girls were connected by shifting alliances. Girls deal with personal conflicts by way of exclusion from the group and social manipulation. Social manipulation includes gossiping, friendship bartering, and indirectly turning the group against an individual. Contrary to the findings of many sociologists and anthropologists who only characterize aggression in physical aspects, we—like Kaj Bjorkqvist (1994) in "Sex Differences in Physical, Verbal, and Indirect Aggression"—found that girls display just as much aggression as boys but in different ways. When Elaine (WG8), for example, would not share her candy with her best friends Brandi (WG8) and Darlene (WG7), Brandi and Darlene proclaimed that Elaine could no longer be their friend. Elaine then joined another group of girls. This is quite representative of what happens when one girl is excluded from a clique. To get back at Brandi and Darlene, Elaine told her new "best friends" that Brandi liked Kevin (biracial B11) and that Darlene urinated on herself earlier that day. This soon spread throughout the camp, and Darlene and Brandi were teased for the rest of the day, causing them to cry. As Bjorkqvist (1994, 180) suggests, there is no reason to believe that girls are any less aggressive than boys. In fact, social manipulation may be more damaging than physical aggression because though physical wounds heal, gossip and group exclusion can persist eternally (or at least until the end of summer).

Unlike the boys who perform or comply with a predominant form of masculinity, no such form of hegemonic femininity was observed. Connell (1987) explains the lack of a hegemonic form of femininity as the result of the collective subordination of women to the men's homosocial hierarchy. According to Connell, since power rests in the men's (boys') sphere, there is no reason to form power relations over other women (girls). Hence, "no pressure is set up to negate or subordinate other forms of femininity in the way hegemonic masculinity must negate other masculinities" (Connell 1987, 187). Girls were inclined to gather in different groups, or cliques, reflective of various ways to define femininity; they gathered with those who defined their girlhood on the same terms. Just as Ann Beutel and Margaret Marini (1995, 436) discovered in their work, "Gender and Values," girls in our study also formed girl cliques "characterized by greater emotional intimacy, self-disclosure, and supportiveness." Intimacy helps ensure faithfulness to the group. All the girl groups—regardless of racial makeup, socioeconomic background, or age differences—had an idea of being "nice," which enhanced clique solidarity. Various girls were asked to give a definition of what it meant to be nice: "Nice just means, you know, helping each other out" (BG12); "Nice just means doing the right thing" (BG7); "Nice means getting along" (WG11). Despite this notion of being nice, however, being nice in one group may be seen as being mean in another. In some groups, for example, it was considered nice for one girl to ask another if the former could have some of the other's chips at lunch. In others, though, this was considered rude; the nice, or proper, conduct was to wait until one was offered some chips. Nice was relative to the particular group. Being nice among the girls observed in this study generally entailed sharing, the aversion of physical and direct aggression, and the avoidance of selfish acts.

The organization of African American girls was somewhat unique. As mentioned, campers were divided into four age groups. In each age group, there were no more than four or five Black girls. Within these age groups, African American girls had the same structural patterns as Caucasians—small cliques of two to four in which a person may drift from clique to clique at a given time. There were no problems with the Black girls mixing with the white girls in age groups or organized activities.

During times when the campers were not restricted to specific groups (e.g., snack time, most field trips, at the pool, group games, and free time), however, the preponderance of African American girls gravitated to each other, despite age differences. This differs from previous research that notes that children in middle childhood associate with near-aged members (Absi-Semaan, Crombie, and Freeman 1993; Andersen 1993; Beutel and Marini 1995; Block 1984; Curran and Renzetti 1992; Luria and Thorne 1994). The first author also visited another camp with similar demographics and observed a similar lack of age segregation among African American girls. African American girls formed larger groups and occupied more space than white girls.

In general, Black girls were more assertive and therefore less likely to be bothered by boys. A loose hierarchy formed in which the older girls made most of the decisions for the younger ones in the group. This hierarchy was by no means hegemonic as in the boys' hierarchy. Rather, this hierarchy used a communal approach to decision making, with the older girls working to facilitate activities for the group. This process was illustrated every day as this group of girls decided which activity they would participate in at free time. The oldest girls—Brittany (BG11), Alexia (BG12), and Melanie (BG11)—would give options such as arts and crafts, checkers, basketball, and jump roping for the group to choose from. After considering all the options—taking into account what they had played the day before, the time left to participate in the activity, and the consensus of the group—the older girls indirectly shifted the focus to a particular activity that seldom received objection from the younger girls in the clique.

To make sense of our findings regarding the African American girl clique, we compared our field notes to Marjorie Harness Goodwin's (1994) "Social Differentiation and Alliance Formation in an African-American Children's Peer Group," a study that observed Black girls organizing larger coalitions than the relatively small associations typical of white girls. Goodwin's study, nonetheless, revealed age segregation. We believe cross-age interaction was prominent with the African American girls in our study because they were in the minority, whereas Black girls were a majority in Goodwin's sample. This minority ethnoracial/gender status may have contributed to undercutting the typical age divisions among the Black girls. Since Black and white boys did not exhibit such racial segregation in the boys' hierarchy, we do not believe ethnoracial differences directly account for the separation of Black and white girls. Because the Black girls tended to be more assertive as a whole, they gravitated toward one another, despite age differences. In addition, the racial connection allowed this girl peer group to foster and reinforce its own assertive, yet nurturing, characteristics

in an environment where these attributes might otherwise be eclipsed. In other words, by pulling together, they created a clique that supports their culture of femininity.

Moreover, whereas the boys displayed little class segregation, the girls were clearly marked by class affiliations. Girls usually formed groups with other girls from their neighborhood. Most of the girls in a clique knew each other as neighbors or schoolmates. Even when girls switched groups or bartered for friendship, they often did so along class lines. This was especially evident in unstructured activities in which children could freely choose to associate with whomever they wanted (e.g., snack time and free time). The data here suggest that class and racial distinctions are more salient for girls than boys in middle childhood.

The Gender Transgression Zone

How do boys and girls negotiate boundaries in the GTZ? This area of activity—where boys and girls conduct heterosocial relations in hopes of either expanding or maintaining current gender boundaries in child culture—is where gender transgression takes place. A boy playing hand-clapping games (e.g., patty cake) or a girl com-

Figure 58.1
The Gender Transgression Zone and Its Boundaries

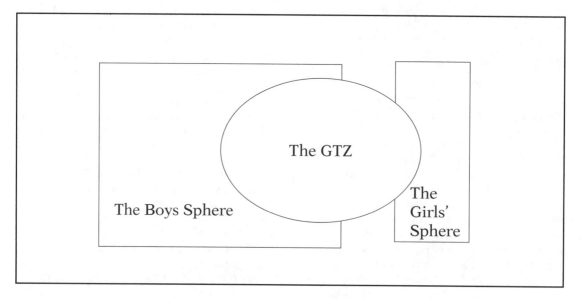

pleting an obstacle course that is designed to determine one's "manliness" are instances of transgression that occur in this zone. Figure 58.1 illustrates the areas of discussion for the rest of the article.

The left rectangle represents the boys' sphere of gender-appropriate activity, the right rectangle represents the girls' sphere, and the central oval represents the GTZ. The right rectangle, the bounds of femininity, is purposely drawn smaller; although girls have a wider range of possible normative femininities than the narrower hegemonic form of masculinity predominant among boys, girls control fewer resources and retain less power. The GTZ extends farther into the masculine realm because girls cross over more than boys and receive fewer sanctions for gender deviations. This figure, nonetheless, is not static. Since gender is continually (re)structured and (re)shaped, these boundaries are constantly shifting and challenged.

Hegemonic Masculinity in the Gender Transgression Zone

Boys spend the majority of their time trying to maintain current gender boundaries. It is through the enforcement of gender boundaries that boys construct their social status. High-status boys are especially concerned with gender maintenance because they have the most to lose. By maintaining gender boundaries, top boys secure resources for themselves—such as playing area, social prestige/status, and power. The social prestige procured by high-status boys causes lower-status boys and girls to grant deference to high-ranked boys. If a high-ranked boy insults a lower-status boy or interrupts girls' activities, he is much less likely to be socially sanctioned by boys or girls. The position of lower-status boys in the hierarchy prevents them from challenging the higher-ranked boy's authority, while the collective subordination of girls to boys inhibits much dissension from girls. Connell (1987, 187) would likely suggest that girls' deference to high-status boys is an adaptive strategy to "the global dominance of heterosexual men."

To young children, "masculinity is power" (Kaufman 1995, 16). As a social construction, then, masculinity is maintained through a hegemonic process that excludes femininity and alternate masculinities. Hence, in the GTZ, boys seldom accept deviant boys or girls. Just as boys actively participate in the maintenance of the hegemonic hierarchy by using name-calling, physical aggression, and exclusion to handle personal conflicts, these same tactics are used to handle gender transgressors. The GTZ, then, is where hegemonic masculinity flexes its social muscle.

Boys Patrolling Boys in the GTZ

High-status boys maximize the influence of hegemonic masculinity and minimize gender transgressors by identifying social deviants and labeling them as outcasts. A continuous process occurs of homosocial patrolling and stigmatizing anomalies. Boys who deviate are routinely chastised for their aberrant behavior. Two examples of this process are particularly obvious. Joseph (WB7) is a seven-year-old who is recognized as a "cry baby." He is not very coordinated and gets along better with girls than boys. Because Joseph is so young, he is not directly affected by the full scrutiny of the solidified form of hegemonic masculinity. His age still allows him the luxury of displaying certain behaviors (e.g., crying) that are discredited in subsequent stages of middle childhood. Although the first author did not observe any kids in Joseph's own age group calling Joseph names, many older boys figure that he will "probably be gay when he grows up," as stated by Daniel (WB10). Fewer of the older boys associate with Joseph during free time, and he is not allowed around the older boys as are some of the other more "hegemonically correct" younger boys.

Phillip (WB10) was rejected by all the boys, which, in turn, aided in the maintenance of hegemonic masculinity. Phillip acted rather feminine and looked feminine as well. He lacked coordination, was small in stature, and had shoulder-length hair. Phillip often played with girls and preferred stereotypically feminine activities (e.g., jump rope). It was not uncommon to hear him being referred to as a faggot, fag, or gay. He was the ultimate pariah in the boys' sphere. He was constantly rejected from all circles of boys but got along quite fine with girls. His untouchable status was exemplified clearly in two instances. First, during a game of trains and tunnels—which requires partners linking arms—all players voluntarily paired up with same-sex companions except Phillip. As parents came to pick up their children, however, cross-gendered pairs began to form. This caused little disruption. However, there came a point when a hegemonically masculine boy, Sean (WB9), should have paired up with Phillip. Upon finding out who his new partner would be, Sean violently rejected Phillip. Sean was told that if he did not accept Phillip as his partner, he would have to sit out the rest of the game. Sean screamed, "I don't care if I have to sit out the whole summer 'cause I'm not going to let that faggot touch me!" In another situation during an arts and crafts activity, Phillip finished early. When kids finished early, the staff usually asked them to help an individual who was having problems. Usually everyone accepted help. However, when Phillip attempted to assist Markus (WB9), Markus rejected him harshly. Nonetheless, Markus did accept help from Karen (WG10). Phillip threatened a boy's masculinity because Phillip had been labeled homosexual; receiving help from a girl in this particular area is nonthreatening. If Joseph's behavior continues, we expect that he will experience the same harsh rejections that Phillip received. By stigmatizing Joseph and rejecting Phillip, homophobia emerges as a cautionary tale in the GTZ that deters other boys from deviating from the norm out of fear of rejection.

The boys in our case study used Joseph and Phillip to represent what would happen to other boys who transgressed the bounds of hegemonic masculinity. If a boy started slipping from gender-appropriate activities, then other boys would simply associate him with one of the two pariahs, Joseph or Phillip, or call him a fag to get him back in the hegemonic group. The boys devalue homosexuality; the threat of being labeled gay is used as a control mechanism to keep boys conforming to the norms of hegemonic mas-

culinity. Gregory Lehne (1992, 389) says that the fear of being labeled gay "is a threat used by societies and individuals to enforce social conformity in the male role, and maintain social control . . . used in many ways to encourage certain types of male behavior and to define the limits of 'acceptable' masculinity." Talk of faggots and gays is also used to help define a boy's own masculinity.[5] By negatively talking about gays and excluding members who are presumed homosexual, individual boys are defining their own heterosexuality, while collectively they are endorsing hegemonic masculinity. Because most of these boys are not sexually mature or knowledgeable, many do not have an accurate conception of homosexuality (or, for that matter, heterosexuality) at this age. Gay bashing is another way boys can separate themselves from gender-deviant behavior.

Boys Patrolling Girls in the GTZ

Just as it is important for boys to patrol their own sex, it is equally important for boys to monitor the activities of girls and to keep them out of the boys' domain. If girls entered the boys' sphere in substantial numbers, the hegemonic hierarchy would be jeopardized. Girls who enter the boys' realm, therefore, are made to feel inadequate by the boys. The few girls who do succeed in the boys' sphere, nevertheless, are either marginalized or adopted into boys' middle-childhood culture (masculinized). Marginalization or masculinization depends on the girl's overall athletic prowess and emotional detachment while in the boys' sphere. This is illustrated by the following incident.

During one of the camp field trips, campers went to a university athletic training center. During the tennis rotation, Adrianne (WG10) was put with three boys. Adrianne, who took tennis lessons, was ignored by the boys. While the boys were arguing over the proper way to hit a backhand, Adrianne sat quietly on the sideline. When one boy finally asked her if she knew how to hit a backhand, she shook her head no. The first author knew this was incorrect because Adrianne had explained to him the proper way to hit a backhand earlier that day. Therefore, the first author asked Adrianne why she responded no.

She replied, "When you're with boys, sometimes it's better to pretend like you don't know stuff because they're going to ignore you or tell you you're wrong."

Marginalization also occurs when girls meet some, but not all, of the requirements of hegemonic masculinity. The group of African American girls, for example, was marginalized. Many were just as assertive, and two were more athletic than some boys of high status. Yet, these girls remained marginal, retaining too many feminine characteristics, such as expressive acts of emotion when comforting teammates when they performed poorly in an activity. When a group of boys was asked why they did not associate with these girls who were more athletic than many of the boys in the hierarchy, Adam replied, "They're just different. I don't know about them. That whole group of them are just different. They're all weird."

Girl masculinization occurs when boys dissociate a girl from her feminine gender. The best example of a girl being adopted into a hegemonic masculine identity is Patricia (WG11). She is very athletic and can outplay many boys in basketball, the game that seemed to most signify one's masculinity at this site.[6] She also remained emotionally detached while interacting with boys. One time at the playground, Adam (WB11) created an obstacle course that he contended proved whether or not one was a "man." Some of the "manhood" tests were very dangerous—such as balancing on the rails of a high overhang—and had to be stopped. Each boy who completed a task successfully received applause and high fives. Those who did not complete successfully were laughed at because, according to the other boys, they were not "men." There was one catch to this test of masculinity—Patricia. She completed the numerous tasks faster and better than many of the boys. She did not get the screams of jubilation and high fives as did the other boys at first. As she proved her "manhood," however, she began to be accepted by the boys. By the end of the tests, Patricia was proclaimed a "man." About eight weeks later, when the first author asked a group of boys why Patricia was accepted as a member of their group, Adam, the apparent spokesman

for the hierarchy, said, "Well, Patricia is not really a girl. Technically she is, but not really. I mean, come on, she acts like a boy most of the time. She even passed the 'manhood' test, remember?" Though this reveals Patricia's acceptance into the boys' hierarchy, she had to forfeit her feminine gender. As Thorne (1994) recognizes, girls who successfully transgress into the boys' activities under boys' terms do not challenge stereotypical gender norms. Hence, Patricia's participation in boys' activities "does little to challenge existing arrangements" (Thorne 1994, 333).

Hegemonic masculinity in middle childhood maintains itself in regards to girls in the GTZ. Girls are not welcome into the boys' sphere, which occupies more space. If girls partially meet standards, they are marginalized and thought of as "weird." In a way, they are almost degendered. Girls who fit all hegemonic requirements (tomboys) are conceptualized as masculine, or a boy/man. This reasoning is especially disturbing because masculinity is not only maintaining and defining itself, but it is also defining femininity.

Femininity in the Gender Transgression Zone

As previously stated, girls find various forms of femininity acceptable, despite how different the form may be from their own. With this in mind, one can understand that while some girls do not challenge gender boundaries, those who do are not stigmatized by other girls. To test this observation, a group of girls (who were stereotypically "gender appropriate") were asked during lunch one day their views about the behavior of various girls who transgressed into the boys' sphere. Speaking of Patricia (WG11)—the girl who was proclaimed a "man"—Melissa (WG11) said, "She's pretty nice," and Lucia (WG9) added, "Yeah, she's pretty cool. . . . She just likes to do different stuff! There's nothing wrong with that." They were then asked about the various members of the Black girl clique, and Melissa responded, "They're nice to [us]." When the girls were specifically asked if there was anything wrong with the way these gender transgressors behaved, Melissa and Lucia simply said no. Even Robin (WG10), who was not completely comfortable with the actions of these transgressors, replied, "I guess not. They just have their own way of acting. I just don't think it's very lady-like acting." As one can see, gender transgression is virtually accepted among even gender-traditional girls. Nevertheless, girls deal with clique deviants—those who are not "nice" relative to the clique's definition—just as they handle personal conflicts: exclusion from a particular group and social manipulation.

Girls Patrolling Girls in the GTZ

As girls get older, they recognize the higher value that society puts on masculine traits as well as the resources accumulated in the boys' sphere. Girls also see masculinity as power (Connell 1987). With increasing encouragement from the larger society (parents, teachers, and other pro-feminist role models), many girls attempt to access these resources as they mature. It should be noted, however, that high-status girls in these small groups also have social power in their cliques. The highest-ranked girl largely dictated who was gossiped about and who would be banished from the group. Yet, girls' resources were limited in comparison to their masculine-gendered playmates because their resources did not extend much further than their small clique. Interestingly, girls who dare to participate in the boys' realm not only avoid stigmatization from most girls but are often praised by other girls if they succeed in the boys' sphere. For the most part, girls only receive restrictions from the prime agents of hegemonic masculinity at play—boys. Though girls' relations generally consist of small, intimate groupings when dealing with each other, large group affiliation and support seem to be the gender strategy when girls transgress onto traditional boys' turf. This was observed frequently throughout the summer.

Whenever a girl beat a boy in an athletic event, girls, as a collectivity, cheered them on despite age differences. During a Connect Four contest, Travis (WB9), the champion, was bragging about winning—especially when he beat girls. He would say, "It only takes me two minutes to beat girls," and "Girls aren't a challenge." This changed, however, when Corisa (BG6) started to play. Corisa beat Travis four times in a row. Girls of all ages rallied behind Corisa. For the duration of the day, girls praised Corisa, and some even introduced their parents to Corisa in admiration. One introduction went as follows: "Mommy, this is Corisa. She beats boys in Connect Four." Thorne (1994) also observed similar reactions in her work when a girl beat up a boy. Thorne writes, "[A] ripple of excitement moved among the girls, including me; I think it gave us a sense that one of our kind could resist and even herself exert dominance over boys" (p. 133).

The best example of group solidarity in resistance to boys' dominance was provided one day when leaving the swimming pool. Molly (WG9)—whose eyes were irritated by chlorine and was basically walking to the locker room with her eyes closed—accidentally entered the boys locker room while the campers were changing. Many of the boys laughed at her and ridiculed Molly for her mistake. Brian (BB11) said, "She just wanted to look at our private stuff," and Thomas (WB12) called her a "slut." Molly started to cry. Girls, however, came to Molly's rescue. While Molly's immediate clique comforted her, the other girls scared off boys who attempted to harass Molly for the rest of the day. Crysta (BG9) and Brittany (BG11) were the most effective protectors. This was surprising because even though Molly and Crysta were in the same age group, they did not get along, and Brittany—who is in the oldest group—to the best of our knowledge, had never even talked to Molly. As a gender strategy, girls—regardless of age, class, or racial differences—united together to combat the dominance of boys.

Girls Patrolling Boys in the GTZ

Without a uniform or constant form of femininity, girls were more lenient to both girls and boys when either ventured into the GTZ. Girls accepted Joseph and Phillip, both gender-deviant boys, into all their activities without a problem. These boys, nevertheless, had to adhere to the same principles of "niceness" as did the girls. If the boys did not, they were punished in the same manner as girls—exclusion and social manipulation. When Joseph (WB7) did not share his "Now and Later" candy during lunch one day with the group of girls he was eating with, he soon found himself eating alone and the subject of much gossip in the girls' sphere.

'Alphas Rule! Others Drool!' Or How High-Status Boys Direct Change in the GTZ

The top-ranked boys in the hierarchy direct the actions of all the boys who aspire to hegemonic masculinity (or are, at least, complicit with it). High-status boys are primarily concerned with maintaining gender boundaries to retain status and all the luxuries that are a result of being hegemonically masculine. Dominant boys make decisions for the group and can manipulate the other boys to sustain high-status and its privileges. Examples of status privileges include being picked first for teams, getting first dibs on other people's lunches, being allowed to cut in line, and being freed by other males during prison ball—a game similar to dodge ball—with no reciprocal obligation to free low- or middle-status boys.

High-status boys have the unique power of negotiating gender boundaries by accepting, denying, or altering gender codes. The power of high-status boys to alter gender boundaries was strikingly borne out by a series of events that, for weeks, redefined a feminine gender-stereotyped activity, hand-clapping games, into a hegemonically masculine one. This example of the defeminization (and thus, from the hegemonic standpoint, destigmatization of girls' behavior) illustrates the ruling dynamic of gender relations in the GTZ. In this camp, boys who even entertained the notion of playing hand-clapping games were confronted, ridiculed, and/or excluded by proponents of hegemonic masculinity.

Here is how the defeminization occurred. One day, right before the closing of the camp, Adam—the highest-ranked boy—was the only boy left waiting for his mother to pick him up. Four girls remained as well and were performing the *Rockin' Robin* hand-clap-

ping routine. When one of the girls left, one of the three remaining girls asked Adam if he would like to learn the routine. He angrily replied, "No, that's girly stuff!" Having been a camp counselor for three years, the first author knows every clapping routine from *Bo Bo See Aut In Totin* to *Miss Susie's Steamboat*. He, therefore, volunteered. The girls were amazed that he knew so many of what they referred to as "their" games. After a while, only two girls remained and *Rockin' Robin* requires four participants. Surprisingly, Adam asked to learn. Before he left, Adam had learned the sequence and was having a good time.

We believe that Adam transgressed for three reasons. One, all the other boys were gone, so there were no relevant or important (to him) witnesses to his transgression. Thorne (1994, 54) repeatedly states that witnesses hinder gender deviance: "Teasing makes cross-gender interaction risky, increases social distance between girls and boys, and has the effect of making and policing gender boundaries." Second, Adam saw the first author participate freely in an activity that was previously reserved for girls. Third, as the highest-ranked boy, Adam has a certain degree of freedom that allows him to transgress with little stigmatization. Thorne asserts that the highest-status boy in a hierarchy has "extensive social leeway" (p. 123) since his masculinity is rarely questioned. The next day, Adam was seen perfecting the routine he learned the day before. Many of the boys looked curiously and questioned why Adam was partaking in such an activity. Soon after, other boys started playing, and boys and girls were interacting heterosocially in what was formerly defined as a "girls-only" activity. Cross-gendered hand-clapping games continued for the rest of the summer and remained an area in which both girls and boys could come together. Defeminization occurred because Adam—the highest-status boy—set the standard and affirmed this type of entertainment as acceptable for boys. This incident supports our view that high-status boys control gender negotiations by showing that gender boundaries can be modified if someone of high status changes the standard of hegemonic masculinity.

To make hand-clapping more masculine, nonetheless, the first author documented boys changing the verses of the most popular hand-clapping game, *Rockin' Robin*, to further defeminize the activity. One of the original verses is "All the little birdies on J-Bird Street like to hear the robin go tweet, tweet, tweet." The boys changed this to 'All the little birdies on J-Bird Street like to hear robin say eat my meat!" About a month later, the first author discovered another altered verse from the boys. They changed "Brother's in jail waiting for bail" to "Brother's in jail raising hell!" Since these verses were not condoned at the camp—though we are sure the children used them out of the hearing distance of counselors—girls cleverly modified one of the profane verses by singing, "Brother's in jail raising H-E- double hockey sticks!" This, too, the boys picked up and started applying as their own. Hand-clapping games moved from the girls' sphere to the GTZ. Defeminization of hand clapping exposes the constant fluctuation and restructuring of gender norms in childhood play.

Boys in middle childhood organize themselves in a definite hierarchy that is run by high-status boys in accordance with the hegemonic form of masculinity that they embody and police in the GTZ. Boys are not accepting of deviant boys or girls. Gender deviants are handled by teasing and name-calling, marginalization and exclusion from the group, and physical aggression. High-status boys, though, have the unique power to negotiate gender boundaries by either accepting, denying, or altering gender codes. Girls who enter the boys' realm are made to feel inadequate by the boys. Those girls who do succeed in the boys' sphere, nevertheless, are either marginalized from or masculinized into boys' middle-childhood culture. They are forced to leave their femininity behind if they want to cross the border fully. Therefore, no feminization of hegemonic masculinity is allowed. As can be seen in the hand-clapping phenomenon, the redefinition entails defeminization.

Conclusion

The findings of this preliminary research suggest that hegemonic masculinity in middle childhood not only regulates boys' homosocial boundaries but also controls the rules of gender negotiation and transgression for both boys and girls. The foundation of the boys' hierarchy is based on an idea of supremacy. The top boys rule the hierarchy and manipulate it so that it preserves their position and thus their higher status. Hegemonic masculinity is public and is used to sustain the power of high-status boys over subordinate boys and over girls. The overwhelming majority of boys support hegemonic masculinity because it gives power over the other sex. It also gives them the opportunity to acquire power over members of their own sex. We argue that our data support the claim that even though most boys do not directly enjoy the benefits of hegemonic masculinity as do higher-status boys (because that status is restricted to a few), they express complicity with the hegemonic regime because the gender order ensures them social status over girls.

On the other side of the gender divide, girls, realizing the power that is retained in the boys' sphere, have an incentive to transgress into boys' territory with few sanctions from their own homosocial sphere. Thus, those who successfully transgress boys' boundaries receive communal support from other girls, even when they are not in the same intimate association or clique. To combat the invasion of gender transgressors, high-status boys handle gender deviants by name-calling, exclusion from the group, and physical aggression. High-status boys lead their army of lower-status, complicit boys—using the social construction of hegemonic masculinity to unite them—against intruders. High-status boys use aggressive, athletic, and boastful behavior to display and sustain their position. By keeping the lower strata of the hierarchy intact—by way of internal struggles for ascendancy in the boys' hierarchy and the constant subordination of gender deviants—high-status boys continue their reign by continually defining what is masculine, what is feminine, and reserving the authority to sanction all gender transgressions in hopes of sustaining valued resources and social prestige.

This study reveals that race and class intersect with gender in complicated ways for boys and girls. Boys revealed little to no racial or class segregation in the hegemonic hierarchy. Boys of various racial and class designations held positions of high authority in the power structure. This is likely attributable to the unstructured nature of the day camp. Free of the institutionally discriminatory practices of the larger social world, a boy had considerable opportunities for upward mobility in the hierarchy since social achievement was chiefly based on athletic ability. Conversely, girls often separated on racial and class divisions. Since white girls formed smaller associations based on pre-camp friendships from their neighborhoods and school, class and race had visible consequences for girls' cliques. Similar to Goodwin's (1994) research, African American girls formed a larger group during non-age-specific activities and occupied more space than their white counterparts. In addition, a girl's status largely depended on her relationships with others (or other children's perceptions of her). Consequently, boys tended to have more chances to improve their social status relative to girls due to boys' connection to hegemonic masculinity. The actions of hegemonically masculine boys and the collective insurgence of gender-transgressive girls and their supporters are potentially important sources of change in the gender order of childhood. Further research might look for variations in the types of behaviors manifest in the GTZ and in the characteristics of hegemonic masculinity within other domains of childhood.

Notes

1. To the best of our knowledge this concept was first set out in his book *Gender and Power* (Connell 1987, 183–188).

2. The pre-Oedipal psychodynamics of this process are detailed in Chodorow (1978).

3. Bird (1996) explains how homosocial interactions maintain gender boundaries among adult men. Beutel and Marini (1995) discuss the contrasting value systems of males and females.

4. The names of children in this study are pseudonyms.

5. This may be part and parcel of what McCreary (1994) refers to as the universal avoidance of femininity: Homophobia may be a rejection of the "abnormality" of being attracted to boys (i.e., being "girlish").

6. At the other site that the first author visited, football was the most masculinizing athletic activity.

References

Absi-Semaan, N. G. Crombie and C. Freeman. 1993. Masculinity and femininity in middle childhood: Developmental and factor analyses. *Sex Roles* 28 (3/4): 187–206.

Andersen, Margaret L. 1993. *Thinking about women.* New York: Macmillan.

Beutel, Ann M., and Margaret M. Marini. 1995. Gender and values. *American Sociological Review* 60 (3): 436–438.

Bird, Sharon R. 1996. Welcome to the men's club: Homosociality and the maintenance of hegemonic masculinity. *Gender & Society* 10 (2): 120–32.

Bjorkqvist, Kaj. 1994. Sex differences in physical verbal, and indirect aggression: A review of recent research. *Sex Roles* 30 (3/4): 177–88.

Block, Jeanne H. 1984. *Sex role identity and ego development.* San Francisco: Jossey-Bass.

Chodorow, Nancy. 1978. *The reproduction of mothering: Psychoanalysis and the sociology of gender.* Berkeley: University of California Press.

Connell, R. W. 1987. *Gender & power.* Stanford, CA: Stanford University Press.

———. 1995. *Masculinities.* Berkeley: University of California Press.

Curran, Daniel J., and Claire E. Renzetti. 1992. *Women, men, and society* 2d ed. Needham Heights, MA: Allyn & Bacon.

Fine, Gary Alan. 1992. The dirty play of little boys. In *Men's lives* edited by Michael S. Kimmel and Michael A. Messner. New York: Macmillan.

Goodwin, Marjorie Harness. 1994. Social differentiation and alliance formation in an African-American children's peer group. In *Gender Roles through the Life Span*, edited by Michael R. Stevenson. Muncie, IN: Ball State University.

Hawkesworth, Mary. 1997. Confounding gender. *Signs: Journal of Women in Culture and Society* 22 (3): 649–86.

Kaufman, Michael. 1995. The construction of masculinity and the triad of men's violence. In *Men's lives* edited by Michael Kimmel and Michael Messner. New York: Macmillan.

Kosik, Karel. 1976. *Dialectics of the concrete: A study on problems of man and the world.* Dordrecht, the Netherlands: D. Reidel.

Lehne, Gregory K. 1992. Homophobia among men: Supporting and defining the male role. In *Men's lives*, edited by Michael S. Kimmel and Michael Messner. New York: Macmillan.

Luria, Zella and Barrie Thorne. 1994. Sexuality and gender in children's daily worlds." In *Sociology: Windows on society*, edited by John W. Heeren and Marylee Mason. Los Angeles: Roxbury.

McCreary, Donald R. 1994. The male role and avoiding femininity." *Sex Roles* 31 (9): 517–32.

Messner, Michael A. 1992. *Power At play: Sports and the problem of masculinity*. Boston: Beacon.

——. 1994. The meaning of success: The athletic experience and the development of male identity." In *Sociology: Windows on society*, edited by John W. Heeren and Marylee Mason. Los Angeles: Roxbury.

——. 1998. The limits of "the male sex role": An analysis of the men's liberation and men's rights movements discourse." *Gender & Society* 12 (3): 255–76.

Thorne, Barrie. 1994. *Gender play: Girls and boys in school*. New Brunswick, NJ: Rutgers University Press.

West, Candace, and Don H. Zimmerman. 1987. Doing gender." *Gender & Society* 1 (2): 125–51.

Discussion Questions

1. Is it difficult to believe that such young children have already learned the rules of gendered behavior? Why or why not?

2. Do you think the dynamics would have been different if we added Latino boys and girls to the mix? How or how not?

3. What was most fascinating to you about the article? What was the least interesting part of the article for you? Why?

4. Have you observed the sort of behavior in boys and girls that McGuffey and Rich describe? If so, where did you observe this behavior? Was it different or similar to the experiences described by these authors?

5. Why do you think race and class were more salient for girls than they were for boys?

59
Puerto Rican Wannabes

Sexual Spectacle and the Marking of Race, Class, and Gender Boundaries

Amy C. Wilkins

In this article, Amy C. Wilkins explores the nature of racial/ethnic and social class boundaries among teens and young adults and shows how gender and sexual behavior are used to define and structure them. She gathered her data through interviews and informal conversations with young Puerto Rican, Black, and White people in western Massachusetts but tells us that the ideas and relationships she explores go well beyond these particular groups in this particular place and time. The interviewees include males and females, wannabes and nonwannabes. Gender, race/ethnicity, and class are embedded not only in the background and characteristics of each interviewee but also in their discourse.

White girls contrast themselves and their behavior to those of wannabes who are also actually White girls. White boys are attracted to the wannabes yet want to save them from the choices they have made. Both boys and girls of color are concerned with authenticity. They see the role-playing of the wannabes as a caricature of their culture and, therefore, embarrassing. The girls, who are in sexual competition with the wannabes, refer to them as "sluts" and "trash." The boys date them as a way to get sex without having to make commitments. In that way they express their masculinity and gain status among their peers while maintaining the appearance of solidarity with girls of color.

Those labeled "wannabes" by others do not use the term. Jaclyn, Kelli, and Shari establish their authenticity by referring to ways their gender, class status, or experiences at school or work cause them to identify with people of color and to be attracted to men of color. Because each is concerned about being seen as a genuine, if honorary, member of the community of color, their discourse includes disparaging comments about each other. Any solidarity among them is tenuous, making it even more important to be accepted as not "other."

On the surface this article is about White girls who have adopted certain appearances, attitudes, and behavior in order to date Black and Puerto Rican men and join communities of color. It is about them and about the attitudes of White, Black, and Puerto Rican youth toward them. Beneath that surface, it is about the social construction of race/ethnicity and gender. It shows how elements of popular culture, in this case, hip hop music and fashions, are incorporated into that construction and how both the performance of race/ethnicity, gender, and class and the reactions to that performance vary by those same characteristics. It is also about identity and belonging and community and how fluid these things can be.

The "Puerto Rican wannabe" is a caricature of racial, class, and gender inauthenticity drawn by "authentic" white, Puerto Rican, and Black kids. In this study, I interviewed both wannabes and nonwannabes to explore the symbol of the wannabe in the ongoing construction of race, class, and gender categories. By challenging the boundaries of racially designated, but also classed and gendered, categories, the wannabe provides a symbol onto which other young people project their own stereotypes, anxieties, and desires. While wannabes have their own stories to tell, these stories should not be read as the truth but instead as another version of the negotiation of ethnic, class, and gender meanings. Together, these stories unveil the persistence and the fragility of ethnic, class, and gender identities and underline the centrality of sexuality in both bolstering and undermining them.

"Puerto Rican wannabe" is a label applied to a particular kind of white girl in a particu-

517

lar geographical context and a particular historical moment. While her label might be local, her iconography is not. She is seen across the United States in adolescent and now young adult cultural lore, popping up frequently as a "wigger"—a "white nigger." Like the wigger, the stereotypical Puerto Rican wannabe rejects white middle-class cultural style, adopting an urban presentation of self associated with people of color. She wears hip-hop clothes and Puerto Rican hairstyles, drinks malt liquor, and smokes Newports. She adopts an attitude, acting tough and engaging in verbal and physical fights. And perhaps most important, she dates and has sex with Black and Puerto Rican men.

The wannabe's violation of whiteness fascinates and alarms. As the "wannabe" label—used by nonwannabes but not by wannabes themselves—implies, her appropriation of nonwhite behavior is contested, exposing struggles over ethnic categories. Part of this struggle revolves around the wannabe's enactment of a stereotypical presentation of Puerto Rican femininity, one that is simultaneously desired and degraded. This presentation feeds on the historical association of women of color with exotic sexuality (e.g., Mink 1990; Tolman 1996). The label "Puerto Rican wannabe" perpetuates the association of Puerto Rican femininity with behavior deemed morally undesirable by both whites and people of color. She rejects this label, positioning her self as racially authentic.

The wannabe continually slips back and forth between a chosen and an imposed identity. While she attempts to choose a more fluid racial identity, others hold her accountable to their more fixed interpretations of who she is. In this struggle, racial authenticity becomes a key category of expression and interpretation. Used to determine racial eligibility, the criteria for authenticity are necessarily slippery, molded to accommodate the ends of the person employing the criteria.

The Puerto Rican wannabe is symbolically loaded because she violates understandings about appropriate gender and (middle) classed behavior for white young women, understandings that are grounded in "proper" race-specific sexual conduct. In this article, I argue that interpretations of sexual behavior are critical to marking classed gender and racial boundaries. Puerto Rican wannabes delineate and efface ethnic boundaries through their sexual transgressions: Their preference for interracial dating and their "inappropriate," nonwhite sexual self-presentations. In turn, nonwannabes, both girls and boys, use the wannabes sexual transgressions as a foil against which they construct and negotiate their own classed race and gender locations.

The class status of the wannabes is an open question. In the interviews I conducted, wannabes are alternatively imagined as fallen middle-class white girls or as poor white girls. Perhaps there are some of both. More likely, the inability to articulate their class location is a reflection of the larger American inability to articulate class. Regardless, imagined class matters. Class is used to validate or invalidate the wannabes' claims to racial crossing and, in turn, to bolster each person's own claims to moral, intellectual, or cultural superiority. The white youth in my study seem to inflexibly conflate class and race assuming that whiteness means middle class-ness. The youth of color, on the other hand, are more open to the possibility of variation in the class location of the wannabes but assume that whiteness automatically confers a set of class privileges.

Although the wannabes objective class location is ambiguous, these various narratives make clear that the Puerto Rican wannabe presentation is concomitantly a racial violation and a middle-class violation. Moreover, this violation is inherently gendered. Puerto Rican wannabes are not behaving like proper white middle-class young women. While these violations cross a number of behavioral categories, they are grounded most firmly in the wannabes' perceived rejection of appropriate white, middle-class, feminine sexual conduct, both through the choice of nonwhite dating partners and through the presentation of explicitly sexualized selves.

Sexuality and the Construction of Race, Class, and Gender

While gender and race continue to be popularly understood as biological categories, social constructionist arguments have gained a steady footing. This position holds that gender and race are flexible categories, able to shift and change form in different contexts and across time. Scholars have documented the contours of some of these metamorphoses, providing a clear picture of the effects of structural forces on the meanings and boundaries of gender and racial categories (e.g., Laqueur 1990; Nagel 1996; Omi and Winant 1986). But gender and race, as well as class, meanings are not just produced at the macro level; they are ongoing, local productions (Butler 1990; West and Fenstermaker 1995). Moreover, gender, race, and class categories intersect (Anderson and Hill Collins 1992), generating hierarchies both between and within categories.

Contemporary social, economic, and political changes make this a moment in which category negotiations are particularly intense. The mass influx of Latino and Asian immigrants, the increasing class heterogeneity of traditional raced groups, and the increase in the ethnically mixed population are forcing a reconfiguration of the U.S. racial structure. The presence of these groups complicates the straightforward deployment of race as a biological category, propelling both specific ethnic groups and U.S. society more generally to rethink the criteria for racial membership.

For many white, middle-class Americans, these changes have replaced overt racism with a logic of cultural inferiority that blames the disadvantaged socioeconomic position of many Blacks and Latinos on their behaviors (Bobo, Kluegel, and Smith 1997), allowing whites to perceive themselves as "color-blind" (Frankenberg 1993) even while they resuscitate racial stereotypes. At the same time, however, hip-hop culture has gained social ascendance. Emerging out of the Black urban experience of persistent socioeconomic and racial oppression, hip-hop music has captured the imaginations of white, middle-class, suburban kids (Kelley 1997; Rose 1994). The widespread consumption of hip-hop has given (mostly male) Blacks widespread cultural power in the form of coolness—even while white men capture most of its profit.

Latinos occupy the unstable borderland between Blackness and whiteness. As some middle-class Puerto Ricans draw a line around authentic island culture, pushing out hybrid cultural forms that integrate island elements with hip-hop culture, they make salient the importance of class to racial constructions. For example, New York-born Puerto Ricans, who are overwhelmingly poor, are often dismissed as inauthentic with the derisive label "Nuyorican" (Lao 1997; Negrón-Muntaner 1997). For some Puerto Ricans, this tension entails choosing between a "Spanish" identity and a Black identity. The Black identity carries more status in the currency of cool but often also requires the shifting of community allegiance.

Historical studies indicate the importance of sexuality as a mechanism for delineating racial membership in U.S. society. In their transition from Negro to (almost) white, for example, the Mississippi Chinese ended their sexual and marital relationships with Negro women, cutting off ties with both Negro kin and any Chinese who violated this proscription (Loewen 1971). Similarly, the Irish claim to whiteness depended on sexual separation from Blacks enacted both by cutting off sexual relations with Blacks and by bringing their sexual behavior in line with Anglo standards (Roediger 1991).

The ethnic hierarchies created by sexuality are gendered. Historically and contemporarily, the assumption of insatiable, exotic sexuality—in contrast to the "pure" sexuality of white women—has been used to justify the degradation of women of color. At the same time, women of color have used their own sexual restraint to position themselves above "loose" white women (Espiritu 2001). As Nagel (2000, 109) argued, this use of sexual hierarchies "reinforce[s] and re-establish[es] sexual [and] gender hegemony." By resurrecting the moral superiority of the virginal woman, ethnic communities place much of the responsibility for maintaining the community's sexual integrity on women. For example, both Das Gupta (1997) and Espiritu

(2001) documented the ways that women's ethnic membership as Indians and as Filipinas in the United States is tied to a particular, restrictive performance of gender, enacted through sexual behavior aimed at intraethnic familial reproduction and devotion. These studies make clear that ethnic violations can occur both when a woman has sex across an ethnic border and when she has the wrong kind of sex.

My study combines the insights of these various strands of analysis. I use local youth and young adults to document empirically the ongoing production and negotiation of racial identities. I demonstrate the particular combinations of race, class, and gender boundary marking produced by and around the Puerto Rican wannabe. And I explore the critical role of sexuality in producing classed, raced, and gendered identities and boundaries.

The Study

I began my study with an unfocused interview with Carrie, a white middle-class girl. It was in this interview that the concept of the wannabe emerged. I was immediately fascinated, both by Carrie's palpable and uncharacteristic contempt and by the distinction she made between the behavior of the wannabes and my own relationship with a Puerto Rican man. My conversation with Carrie propelled my desire to explore the wannabes from a variety of perspectives. I thus pursued interviews with young people occupying a range of backgrounds. However, the constant policing of race, class, and gender borders made the interviews difficult to arrange. My original contacts—the white middle-class youth whose social locations were most like mine—were eager to talk to me about Puerto Rican wannabes, but youth of color were reluctant to talk to me at all. To them, I learned, I was "that (white) lady." I was able to secure interviews when the initial contact was made through a Puerto Rican: My boyfriend or one of my friends. Once they established my legitimacy, I successfully attained trust and rapport with my informants: indeed, they were frequently delighted to educate me on both their terminol-

ogy (e.g., "kicking it") and their dating norms. These interviews, moreover, tended to generate at least one more contact. My luck was not so good with wannabes themselves, whose responses to my conversational attempts ranged from cordially cold to rude. Six months after my first attempt to talk to a wannabe, I convinced one to talk to me. She, in turn, introduced me to the other two wannabes in this study.

The sample that I compiled, then, is a convenience sample. At the time of the study, my informants ranged from 14-year-old ninth graders to 22-year-olds. Young people are a useful group for this study for a number of reasons. First, they are in a transitory life stage popularly associated with identity phases. Their identity experiments are less directly encumbered by concerns about career or family formation. The intensity of their identity negotiations thus provides rich material for understanding the construction of gender, race, and class. Second, the wannabe is a phenomenon of young people, emerging in part out of the recent extension of hip-hop to suburban youth culture. When I mention the wannabe to young people, I do not need to explain her the way I must to older adults. For all the participants in the study, the wannabe is a salient symbol of transgression.

I conducted 21 formal interviews (and multiple casual conversations) with adolescents and young adults representing a wide range of race, gender, and class positions (see Table 59.1). Interviewees determined their own racial/ethnic categorization. I determined class by parental occupation and residential location. I designated class as ambiguous when class markers conflicted. For example, Mani's mother is low income, but his father and stepfather (with whom he lived for a number of years) are middle class. Although the formal interviews took place at prearranged times and places, they were really informal conversations, loosely guided topically by me but given specific form by the participants. On average, those conversations lasted an hour and a half but several lasted much longer, and I had multiple interviews with three of my contacts. I taped and transcribed interviews and recorded field notes as soon as possible after casual conversations.

I conducted my research in Amherst and Northampton, two college towns in the Pioneer Valley of western Massachusetts. The towns and cities in the valley seep into each other; thus, the social circles I investigated cross town borders, flowing between Northampton and Amherst and pushing outward into, and pulling in from, the neighboring cities of Holyoke and Springfield. In Amherst and Northampton, gentrification, rising housing costs, and a declining visible white working-class culture abet the appearance of widespread affluence. The increasing invisibility of economic hardship in Amherst and Northampton pushes low-income kids to look to the broader community for both a model of low-income membership

and validation of their relative poverty. In Amherst and Northampton, as well as Holyoke and Springfield, Puerto Rican median household income is well below that of both whites and Blacks. Objectively the most impoverished group in the area, Puerto Ricans are also the symbol of poverty. Thus, interpretations of Puerto Rican culture and low-income culture intertwine: To be poor is to be Puerto Rican.

White Middle-Class Youth: "And Then There's Those 'Other' Girls"

The stories white middle-class girls and boys tell about Puerto Rican wannabes are racialized tales of good (white) girls gone bad. Puerto Rican wannabes used to be proper white middle-class girls, and then

Table 59.1
Characteristics of Sample Population

Pseudonym	Gender	Race	Class	Age
Bryan	Male	White	Middle	18
Carrie	Female	White	Middle	16
Claudia	Female	Puerto Rican	Low Income	15
Courtney	Female	White	Middle	16
Danielle	Female	White	Middle	17
Eric	Male	White	Middle	17
Hadley	Male	Black	Middle	21
Imani	Female	Black	Low Income	14
Jaclyn	Female	White wannabe	Low Income	22
Jennifer	Female	Black	Low Income	14
Jose	Male	Puerto Rican	Low Income	17
Kelli	Female	White wannabe	Ambiguous	22
Laura	Female	White	Middle	17
Maddie	Female	White	Middle	15
Mani	Male	Puerto Rican	Ambiguous	21
Mariella	Female	Puerto Rican	Middle	15
Mark	Male	White	Middle	18
Nia	Female	"Brown"	Low Income	14
Nora	Female	Puerto Rican/White	Low Income	14
Rafi	Male	Puerto Rican	Low Income	21
Shari	Female	White wannabe	Middle	22

they changed. Now they are too loud, too tough, and "too proud of their sexuality." At once victims and bitches, the wannabes are scrutinized by the white middle-class girls I interviewed with both concern and contempt. Ironically, the strands of concern, rooted in while middle-class feminist discourse, strip the wannabes of agency, presenting them as insecure dupes, exploited by their Puerto Rican boyfriends. The strands of anger, on the other hand, suggest that the wannabes deliberately reject the behaviors of white middle-class femininity. The white middle-class boys in my study add the desire to "save [the wannabes] from themselves" to the girls' mix of concern and contempt.

By constructing tales of fallen white middle-class girls, these young people point to the intersection of class, ethnicity, and gender. Carrie describes wannabes as "obnoxious, yell[ing] obscene things." Laura paints a more detailed portrait: "Wannabes are so fucking annoying, loud, obnoxious, bitchy, always fighting—'oh, I'll kick your ass.'" They "hate school," skipping classes and "com[ing] across as academically ignorant because of the way they speak" (the Puerto Rican version of Ebonics) and smoking Newports (a brand of cigarettes associated with people of color) in the bathroom at school. Laura sees this "fuck the world attitude" as a show. She describes wannabes as "loving the image." "Maybe they do come from really good middle-American homes and don't like that because that's not dramatic enough or something." She presents the wannabes as having diverged from an otherwise uncluttered path to college and successful white womanhood.

Bryan tells a more specific transformation tale about Kim—"the biggest Puerto Rican wannabe in [Northampton High] School." Kim "was the whitest white girl . . . rich as hell, nice cashmere clothes, almost a dork." Now she's living with her Puerto Rican boyfriend, seven months pregnant, dealing cocaine and marijuana, and "has about one thousand dollars worth of gold on her body." Kim's style shift crystallizes the symbolism of clothes. While both cashmere clothes and gold jewelry demonstrate consumption, cashmere clothes are associated with taste and restraint (both sexual, because cashmere is unrevealing, and financial, because cashmere is a quality investment), while the gold jewelry is linked to the stereotypically flashy, unwise spending of the poor. Giving up cashmere in favor of gold symbolizes Kim's rejection of her parents' money, the rejection of their cultural capital and the rejection of white male approval.

In all the white youth versions of the wannabes' transformation, the biggest transgressions involve sex. Eric explains that wannabes change the "way they speak, think, and act," "warping their style" and "who they are" to "attract a certain kind of guy." They thus have sex with the wrong kind of guys ("older guys who appear to be drug dealers," according to Carrie) and have sex in the wrong way ("unprotected sex with [their] boyfriend[s] and risk pregnancy because [they] don't give a shit" according to Laura). Moreover, they do not hide their interest in sex or tone down their own sexualized self-presentations. Instead they openly grind (rub their pelvises into their partners' pelvises) at school dances, dress in tight clothes, and wear dark makeup.

The white middle-class girls I interviewed interpret this shocking display of sexuality as both victimization and deviance. On one hand, the wannabes are victims of sexually predatory and emotionally abusive Puerto Rican boys who take advantage of their insecurities. Repeatedly describing wannabes as "insecure" and "lost," Courtney contends that they need "something to fit into," and so they become "wrapped up" in their Puerto Rican boyfriends. On the other hand, they are openly violating race and gender rules for sexual behavior. Wannabes are "seen as more sexual than other *white* girls. They're more open—they talk about it. They're proud. . . . They seem like *typical* boys—sex is an accomplishment" (emphasis added).

Frequently, the strands entangle in the story, tying victimization and deviance into a morally suspect knot, as in Courtney's description of the wannabes relationships. The Puerto Rican boyfriends "make [the wannabes] feel good about themselves" but not because they respect them. Instead they make them "feel wanted and loved" by "getting mad at the girls for talking to other guys." Not only are they "seen as becoming their boyfriends," Laura contends, but "they let guys talk them into whatever they want them to do," which includes unwanted sex and unsafe sex. Wannabes "have sex with boys to make them happy." "Puerto Rican guys don't want to have safe sex ever. Two girls got pregnant and had abortions."

The braid these girls weave displaces the threat of sexual victimization onto the wannabes. By alternatively seeing the wannabes as sexual deviants and as victims of a particular (race, class, and age-coded) kind of man, these girls draw a net of safety around themselves: It will not happen to us because we know better. They simultaneously draw on both liberal feminist precepts of adolescent girls' self-actualization and traditional understandings of white middle-class girls sexual restraint to position themselves as morally and politically superior and as sexually safer.

The middle-class white boys I interviewed have a different relationship to the wannabes' sexuality. Attracted to the exotic hypersexuality they associate with the Puerto Rican wannabes, these boys use redemption narratives to justify their sexual pursuit. They present it as their responsibility to try to "save [the wannabes] from themselves." According to Eric, the conversion to the "gangster lifestyle" is a "cry for help." The "tough girl thing," he tells me, is attractive to some white boys who "think they can be revolutionary; they're out to break the girl, break some secret code or some such shit." Eric admits to being attracted to tough girls himself when they show "they have a weakness in them."

Bryan too is attracted to Kim, despite (or because of) her flagrant sexual violations. He first cheated on his ex-girlfriend with her and then went on a personal crusade "to get her back" while she was hospitalized after an illegal abortion. Kim "didn't want to come back." But Bryan's friend Mark, another Northampton senior, did redeem his girlfriend Julie from wannabehood. Mark clearly sees himself as a good influence in white middle-class terms.

She was considered a bad—you know—she snuck out of her house to go to [a roller skating rink]. . . . She knew she was headed in the wrong direction and hanging out in the wrong crowd. She was still getting As, so it wasn't totally ruining her life.

These kids depend on racist tropes of Puerto Rican femininity and masculinity to make sense of the wannabes behavior and to give emotional weight to their concerns. The boys in my study more directly condemn the wannabes for what they see as a perplexing choice of a lesser status. "If you're Puerto Rican," Bryan says, "you're already on a lower [level], not only to teachers but to peers." These girls, on the other hand, want to see themselves as colorblind, explaining that they "hate how [they are] sucked into stereotyping." Laura, in particular, pushes the violation of liberal middle-class racial codes onto the wannabes. "Wannabes," she complains,

Are taking the stereotype of Puerto Ricans and making it something they want to be. They're trying to be something they're not. . . . They seem so ignorant about what it means to be Puerto Rican, what the group really is. . . . People like that make it hard because they glorify these stereotypes by dressing up like that, and that makes me even more mad.

Explicitly constructing themselves in opposition to the wannabes, these girls situate themselves as "together," authentic white girls making individual choices. Indeed, in a historical period characterized by widespread unemployment, increasing poverty, rising numbers of single-parent families, and the persistence of gender discrimination, it is perhaps important for these girls to see themselves as psychologically advantaged, as emerging strong and intact from the minefield of female-adolescence, as making the right choices, as having the self-esteem and integrity required for career and financial success. At the same time, this construction veils both the race and the class advantages that allow them to see themselves as authentic individuals and the future limitations to individual success they are likely to experience as women. Moreover, it perpetuates a narrow vision of proper sexual conduct for girls.

These boys' comments similarly assume that white kids, regardless of economic circumstance or of gender, have equal access to the privilege of whiteness. Moreover, the boys' deployment of the romantic hero discourse signals the persistence of racial and gender hierarchies. They both desire the exotic and dangerous wannabes and want to tame them. The wannabes offer the boys a chance to reassert their gender and racial dominance as protectors.

Youth of Color: 'Don't Think Just Because You Know Spanish You're Already Puerto Rican'

Claudia and Imani, low-income; Puerto Rican and Black, respectively; ninth-grade girls at Amherst High School, say that white girls hope that by hanging out with Puerto Rican and Black people, some of their coolness will rub off on them. They speak Spanish, copy clothing and hairstyles, try to act tough—all to try to fit in. But it does not work. They try too hard and it backfires. Imani explains,

> They're trying to be down, and it's just like they try to be around you so much that it irritates you. 'Cause it's just not them. For them to be Puerto Rican, you know what I'm saying? You can be friends, but for them to try so hard it's just not working for them because they're taking it too far.

Claudia complains most vehemently about Candy, who has nicknamed herself "Miss Puertorriqueña," and Tina, who insists on speaking Spanish even when Claudia initiates a conversation in English:

> She was like getting on my nerves all the time. . . . I'm all the time talking to her in English and she would just bust out talking to me in Spanish and things like that, and she just started getting too much into my business and I was just like, yo, I need to push this to the side, so she got kicked to the side.

Similarly, Nia a low-income, self-identified "Brown" (her mother is white; her father is

Black) Amherst 10th-grader, expresses disgust with white girls who tout symbols of Puerto Rican or Black ethnic pride (e.g., wearing a Puerto Rican flag): "Why are you trying to be down with a culture that's not yours?"

The boys of color I interviewed weave an account that sounds very much like the stories told by the girls. According to Rafi, a Puerto Rican on the edge of the Amherst gangster scene, wannabes are "people with no identity who want to adapt something they think is cool." Wannabes may think they are "down;" but listening to hip-hop, smoking "blunts" (marijuana rolled in cigar wrappers), and drinking "forties" (40-ounce cans of malt liquor marketed to and associated with poor Blacks) does not make them any less white. So Rafi rhetorically asks them, "Why don't you act like who you really are?"

The wannabes are dismissed alternatively on biological and cultural grounds. They are condemned both for not acting white and for performing Puerto Rican-ness inadequately. As Rafi says,

> [Wannabes think that by] acting Puerto Rican . . . they can pretty much just look down on people . . . . More of an attitude they never had, and they somehow fucking changed and they think they're bad and they want to fight. *Because she's white and she acts like that, people look down on her. That's the only reason.* (emphasis added).

But while Rafi trivializes the wannabes' loneliness because he sees it as racially inauthentic, Claudia scoffs at the wannabes' passivity. "[Tina] got beat up by a Puerto Rican, and she let the girl beat her up, and Puerto Ricans don't let nobody just beat them up." Candy's unwillingness to spar verbally with Claudia provokes a similar response: "Us Puerto Ricans, we don't shut up by nobody, you know what I'm saying? You dis us, we'll dis you right back and things like that. With [Candy], she'll stay quiet." Nia, too, contends that the wannabes are not "as hard [tough] as they think they are."

To the kids of color, wannabes behavior is more than just inauthentic: It is embarrassing. "They're like a disgrace to [Puerto Rican] culture or something," Nia comments. Hadley, who is Black, similarly explains, "They're acting all ghetto. They're not acting like us and participating in the mainstream life-style. And it gives the connotation that being Puerto Rican is being ghetto." Rafi adds, "It's fucked up because it gives us a bad image."

By participating in behaviors associated with the urban poor and calling them Puerto Rican, the wannabes perpetuate negative stereotypes about people of color. Moreover, wannabes are seen as sacrificing white privilege in favor of Puerto Rican coolness. This trade is degrading because it implies that Puerto Ricans and Blacks devalue ambition and mainstream socioeconomic success, disparaging the efforts of those Puerto Ricans and Blacks who seek upward mobility. Thus, at least for these boys of color, white people are occasionally allowed to cross if they "do school and everything," that is, if they do not throw away the (classed) resources of whiteness by "try[ing] too hard."

Underlying all of these accounts is anxiety over racial solidarity. The symbol of Black and Puerto Rican pride most frequently invoked by these kids is coolness. The more relaxed attitude associated with "chillin" and the mass popularity of Black and Puerto Rican cultural forms allow these youth of color to think of themselves as more interesting, as more desirable, or as having more fun than white youth. In the absence of traditional routes to socioeconomic success, coolness provides both an alternative definition of success and a point of ethnic pride around which solidarity can be built. Coolness is thus both a psychological and a political resource.

To maintain the boundaries of coolness, girls and boys of color struggle with the meaning of race, concurrently invoking biological and cultural definitions. This struggle is most visible in the tension between race and class, as they sometimes contest the association of Puerto Ricans and Blacks with ghetto behavior, while they also frequently use ghetto behavior as a symbol of Puerto Rican and Black ethnicity. These complicated constructions reflect a more widespread anxiety about personal and collective strategies for success. Variously recognizing the constraints on their opportunities, these kids develop multiple alliances,

pushing for solidarity while sometimes seeking status through individual and collective differentiation. They thus employ "strategic essentialism" (Spivak, cited in Hall 1992) to claim the distinctiveness and exclusivity of their cultural space while they also make room for their own exceptionality (and thus chances of individual upward mobility) by challenging the biological bases of race.

While the youth of color invoke similar critiques of the wannabes' consumption of Black and Puerto Rican culture, the accounts diverge around the issue of sexuality. For the girls of color, stories of the wannabes' improper sexual behavior are the chief medium through which they express both derision and embarrassment. Nia, in particular, castigates the wannabes as sluts: "You hear all the rumors and you know they're true because you see all the hickeys and stuff." "Guys talk about all the things she's done with them—willingly." "They wear all these hootchy mama [slutty] things." "They're just walking down with their five kids and their attitude—makes them look low class, like trash."

Nia's indictment depicts the mutual constitution of ethnicity, class, and gender. Her description of Christine, a wannabe, highlights this interrelationship:

> She's always been a little Betty Boop or something. . . . Then she started sleeping around with all these guys. She thought she was pregnant this year. Her voice is so annoying. [I] don't look at her when she's talking—speaking Ebonics and stuff. All ghetto. . . . I hate her walk—it's nasty. She sticks her chest out, holds her hands out, and she has an attitude on her face, like she's all tough or something.

Rejecting the physical presentation and restrained sexuality associated with middle-class white femininity, Christine adopts a class- and gender-specific Puerto Rican-ness or Blackness. Nia differentiates her own brownness from Christine's ghetto attitude and flamboyant sexuality. Her disgust and anger stem, in part, from her recognition that Christine's race-marked behavior limits Nia's ability to submerge her own stigmatized ethnic and class position.

Like Nia, Claudia and Imani use sexual behavior to draw a boundary between themselves and the wannabes. Tina they tell me, does not know the rules of the Puerto Rican and Black dating game. She "gives it up too soon," talks to too many boys, and does not wait for a commitment (in the form of being asked out) before she acts on her physical desire. "She's a fool.... That's what makes people talk junk about her," Claudia says, "all the boys want her for is just that, you know." While Claudia and Imani call Tina a fool for not knowing the game, Claudia ridicules Candy for knowing it too well. "She tries to be a player, like most Puerto Ricans are players, and she's just like trying to play them or whatever." Imani and Claudia use their own relative sexual restraint to position themselves as more socially skilled, and thus more authentically Puerto Rican, than are Tina and Candy.

At the same time, this line allows the girls to construct themselves as both good and smart in opposition to the feminine transgressions of the wannabes. Tina is a "fool" who gets "used" because she is too easy. Candy "tries to be a player," but Claudia "ain't." Imani and Claudia play the game right; they both capitalize on whatever their (authentic) ethnicity can provide them with (coolness, pride) and maintain whatever gendered power they can within their social network (by playing the boys right so they do not get used, for example). Nia also emphasizes the authenticity of her Brownness by distinguishing herself both from the false pride (attitude) and hootchy behavior of wannabes and (more ambivalently) from the ghetto preoccupations of other kids of color. These girls of color, then, both concretely and symbolically reject the wannabes' attempts at solidarity.

The boys share the girls' contempt with the girls over the wannabes perceived unrestrained sexuality. However, unlike the girls, who are often in sexual competition with the wannabes, many of the boys establish sexual and romantic relationships with them. The boys compensate for this possible cross-racial alliance by using sexuality to racially differentiate wannabes and girls of color. This strategy allows boys of color to preserve both their solidarity with girls of color and their sexual access to wannabes.

These boys portray wannabes as a sexual opportunity to be exploited but not taken seriously. "People say they're easy," Rafi tells me,

> And they [Puerto Rican and Black boys] can get away with a lot more stuff, like fucking around. [White girls] are more naïve than other girls. They usually put up with a lot more stuff. People call them suckers half the time.

By seeing wannabes as offering easy sexual access without commitment boys of color can use them to gain status in their own social networks. Mani, another Amherst Puerto Rican, explains that sex with Puerto Rican girls both compromises the girls' purity and ensnares the boys in obligatory relationships. In contrast, sex with wannabes provides the boys with a chance to prove their masculinity (interpreted as virility and promiscuity) without tarnishing girls of color.

The appeal of this possibility rests on, perpetuates, and reconstructs a double standard. First, the equation of masculinity with sexual prowess and femininity with sexual restraint makes the boys' sexual conquests status producing in the first place. It also provides the impetus to preserve the sexual virtue of Puerto Rican and Black girls. These behaviors then reinvigorate the sexual line that divides "proper" boys from "proper" girls. The second double standard (bad girls do and good girls do not) bolsters and is bolstered by the drive to keep girls of color pure. But by having sex with the wannabes instead, the boys of color also invert the racial hierarchy that is inscribed on the madonna/whore dichotomy. Historically, white men have preserved the virtue of white women by using women of color sexually. This practice, in addition, served as both a bodily reminder of racial subordination and a justification of that subordination by constructing women of color as sexually other. By using wannabes as disposable, exploitable sexual objects, boys of color turn white girls into whores the same way white men have turned women of color into whores. Blackness and Puerto Rican-ness triumph over whiteness, but this reversal of the racial hierarchy depends on the maintenance of a gender hierarchy that positions men over women and good women over bad women. To participate in this racial triumph, then, girls of color must buy into their own sexual subordination.

Dismissing the wannabes as fake and untrustworthy exonerates the young men's exploitative treatment of them. It also maintains the symbolic transposition of the hierarchy between (white) wannabes and girls of color, whose (perhaps similar) behavior is read as racially consistent and thus not fake, leaving solidarity between boys and girls of color at least partially intact. (It is important to remember that this work deals with the construction of meaning, not with actual behavior. Thus, I am not arguing here that boys of color actually treat girls of color in a nonexploitative fashion, only that they construct them as being both sexually and racially different from the wannabes.) At the same time, this construction leaves little room for a boy of color to take a wannabe seriously if he wants to. Hadley's jokes about Rafi's wannabe ex-girlfriends make salient this limitation. The policing of this norm both limits the wannabes' ability to claim Puerto Rican-ness through interracial dating and illustrates the strength of their threat.

Puerto Rican Wannabes: 'There's a Lot of White Girls Who Give Some White Girls a Bad Name'

Jaclyn prides herself on her ability to pass as Puerto Rican, but she rejects and resents the label "Puerto Rican wannabe," describing herself instead as someone who "dates interracially" as a "lifestyle." In addition to her highly stylized self-presentation designed to attract men of color, Jaclyn, now 22, structures her social life so that most of the men she meets are Black or Latino. She attends Black fraternity parties at a nearby university, Black and Latino nightclubs in Springfield and Boston, and basketball games at the park where the people of color hang out.

Jaclyn initially naturalizes her attraction to Black men, arguing that people are just attracted to who they are attracted to. Her ar-

gument about the naturalness of her dating choices is repeated by Kelli and Shari. Kelli contends that she is "more comfortable" in majority Black settings, while Shari says, "That's what I'm attracted to, you know I think I just like their skin." Both Kelli and Shari, like Jaclyn, suggest that they have more in common with Black and Puerto Rican men because of their love for hip-hop music.

Jaclyn expands this analysis, however, building an explanation of her dating pattern that rests not only on shared interests but also on shared experiences.

> I mean, dating Black men is not this fad that a lot of people think it is: you know a lot of people think it's about being cool and about being down and because hip-hop is considered cool that everybody wants to do it. It's not about that. At all. It's about experiences and understanding and having different perspective and really being able to passionately feel with somebody else because you have felt similar things. . . . Like poverty. Like prejudice—because I'm a woman.

By claiming a shared experience of oppression, Jaclyn's justification of her involvement with Black men replicates the distinctions between authentic and unauthentic participation in Black culture made by the youth of color. She uses her class disadvantage to locate herself organically in the community.

Kelli and Shari advance similar if less elaborate, and less explicitly class-based, arguments. Kelli contends that as an Amherst High School athlete, she was a member of the "popular group," a group comprising mostly Black kids. And Shari claims that her friends are primarily Puerto Ricans because those are the people she used to work with. While Kelli suggests a natural fit because of her athleticism, however, Shari uniquely portrays herself as having changed, as having integrated into her existing environment by adopting a convincing Puerto Rican accent (although she does not speak Spanish), by learning to cook Puerto Rican food, and by becoming "more feminine." Shari's transformation is dramatized by her move from racially homogeneous New Hampshire to the Valley and by her "biracial" infant, whose father is Puerto Rican.

While these women's accounts share similar elements, the women do not claim alliances with each other. Indeed, Jaclyn's strategy depends on distancing herself from other, "embarrassing" white women. Like the non-wannabe girls in the study, she uses the trope, but not the label, of the wannabe as a foil against which she positions herself as authentic and deserving: Unlike other white women who date Black men just to be rebellious, she is genuinely concerned with racial oppression and Black culture. Unlike other white women who "try too hard," exaggerating symbols of hip-hop culture and coming across as fake, she exhibits only those aspects of hip-hop culture that come naturally to her. And unlike other white women who date and sleep with any Black men who come their way, she is "not easy," shelving her sexual desire until she feels she has earned the respect of her partner.

Jaclyn's stories echo the contempt of both the middle-class white girls and the girls of color, but their tone is more intimate. These are stories told about women who are ostensibly her friends. These are stories told not about the other but about women who are like her, about women she tries to turn into the other as a means of erasing her own otherness.

At our first, six-hour meeting, Jaclyn gossiped about Kelli, with whom she and I had just had dinner, and with whom she has an on-again/off-again friendship. The two women engage with each other with warmth and humor. Indeed, Jaclyn invited Kelli to join us for dinner on the basis of their social similarities. Yet Jaclyn quickly indicates that she perceives their similarities to be merely superficial. Unlike her own genuine location in the Black and Latino subculture, Kelli is "fake." As the three of us were talking, for example, Jaclyn pointed out to me how Kelli's accent shifted when she began talking on the phone to her Black friends. Kelli "tries too hard." To further illustrate this point, Jaclyn tells a story about a recent dinner the women had with two semiprofessional basketball players:

And Andrew goes "Where are you from?" and she goes, "Amherst." He goes "Oh, no, before that," and he said, "Like from the South somewhere," and she's like—you know she got really offended because you could tell it was so fake and he was trying to tell her it was fake without saying it—you know, just blunt and right out, "Hey, you're really fake," and uh, it was just really bothering me.

Kelli's behavior calls attention to her position as a racial outsider, as a white woman in a Black social world, and thus, by extension, also highlights Jaclyn's whiteness. Kelli is "embarrassing" not because she exaggerates racial stereotypes, as the youth of color suggest, but because her exaggeration reminds people that she is performing.

Jaclyn is additionally embarrassed by Kelli's too open display of sexual desire. As she says, "There's a lot of white girls [who] give some white girls a bad name, and it's true. Because Black men think that white girls are easy."

The way Kelli carries herself if she drinks too much in a club is extremely humiliating. And they all look at her like that horny easy white girl. And I'm there with her. And I'm there *with* her, you know.

Like the Filipina women in Espiritu's (2001) study, Jaclyn separates herself from the improper sexuality associated with white women to establish her (cross-)ethnic legitimacy.

Jaclyn's strategy is multifaceted. Rather than collapsing the boundaries between racial categories, Jaclyn uses her class location to naturalize her location on the Black and Latino side of the boundary while concurrently using her behavior to suggest that she has earned her status as a racial insider. Because she relies on distancing herself from the "humiliating" behavior of other white girls, Jaclyn necessarily resurrects the racial boundary. She thus becomes an exceptional case, allowed to cross because of her (self-described) exemplary (and thus unfake) behavior.

Jaclyn's strategy is a sensible response to limited mobility. Without the educational opportunities and the cultural capital of the white middle class, Jaclyn has little chance of being a successful participant in white middle-class culture. Skilled in the Black and Puerto Rican culture she grew up around, she uses her personal resources (intelligence, beauty, assertiveness) to claim a place in it. Her efforts provide her with the status of notoriety, of desirability, of coolness, but these benefits incur considerable costs.

Jaclyn's legitimacy in the Black/Latino subculture depends on her ability to attract Black and Puerto Rican men both as sexual partners and as potential mates. The first task requires physical labor, the second, emotional labor. Her physical attractiveness is time consuming and expensive. Moreover, her strategy of neutralizing her white otherness forces her to play the madonna/whore card: Jaclyn puts considerable effort into managing her sexual reputation, by postponing her own sexual satisfaction and limiting interactions between former and current sexual or romantic partners and by separating herself from embarrassing, "easy," white women. For Jaclyn, restrained sexuality is a means of naturalizing her (cross-)racial membership. She uses her emotional investment in Black and Puerto Rican men to position herself as a logical member of her community. By espousing the conflation of emotional intimacy and sexuality she adds weight to her interracial relationships. But her commitment to racial crossing comes at the expense of her friendships with other wannabes. Over time, not surprisingly, her stories reveal a pattern of disrupted and competitive friendships—a pattern that is both destabilizing and isolating.

Conclusion

The contentions that race, class, and gender are both performative and intersecting are by now staples of feminist work. This study gives empirical flesh to these theories by using the spectacle of the Puerto Rican wannabe to demonstrate the tense coproduction of race, gender, and class. As the "wannabe" label implies, her acquisition of a transgressive racial identity is contested; it is validated, repudiated, and reshaped through an ongoing process of negotiation between herself and her peers. This negotiation process is critical to the individual success of the wannabes strategy as well as to its political impact.

The wannabe's identity production uses gender and class performances to shift the wannabe's racial location. This process makes clear that while gender, race, and class are always coconstructed, they are not constructed in equivalent ways. In this case, the salience of racial language makes race the category of acknowledged negotiation. But the explicit transgression of racial categories does not mean that they are the only ones at stake. Indeed, profound class anxiety pervades this study but is displaced onto race; outrage over racial violations almost always expresses alarm about what the wannabes strategy means for long-term class mobility.

Gender operates differently from either race or class. The wannabe manipulates her gender performance as a means of crossing racial boundaries. This strategy pushes against the constraints of white girlhood, giving her access to behaviors and a pool of potential sexual partners she was disallowed as a (proper) white girl. Her performance and its interpretations are then used to shuffle racialized femininities. However, this shuffling of gender meanings operates within an unacknowledged (and thus unchallenged) system of dichotomous, heterosexual gender identities and thus reinforces gender boundaries. Moreover, even the struggles over gender meanings involve differently racialized girls laying claim to conventional notions of privileged femininity rather than challenges to femininity's narrow and restrictive definition.

The wannabes' access to cross-racial membership is predicated on their subscription to restrained heterosexuality. And they are not alone. In this study, sexual restraint is the primary criterion for evaluating feminine performance in every racial category. Girls' ability to access stable racial identities rests on the perception of their sexuality as properly contained. Girls who violate (or are perceived to violate) the convention of restrained sexuality are deraced, pushed out of whiteness but unaccepted by Blackness, Puerto Rican-ness or (at least some of) their fellow wannabes. While wannabehood does allow white girls to shift their pool or potential sexual partners, then, it does not open up "the discourse of desire" (Fine 1988) for wannabes or for other girls. This particular

use of sexuality to establish racial membership and to shape racial identities leaves
women disempowered in heterosexual relationships and prevents girls from establishing sexual agency. Whether girls are able to
create spaces that allow unrestricted sexual
desire is an open question.

In *Gender Trouble,* Butler (1990) theorizes
that cross-gender performances destabilize
dichotomous gender categories by exposing
the performativity of gender. Like the drag
queen, the Puerto Rican wannabe exposes
the performativity of categories through her
spectacle. As Butler's argument suggests, her
performance destabilizes racial categories,
adding elasticity to their boundaries and
molding their content. Here, however, it is
racial rather than gender categories that are
being destabilized. Moreover that racial
destabilization rests on stable heteronormative and hierarchical gender categories. In the case of the wannabe, then, the
radical potential of racial destabilization is
blunted by its reinscription of inequality between men and women as well as between
women. As one of many contemporary spectacles, the Puerto Rican wannabe gives us insight into one way race, gender, and class
categories construct each other. The critical
insight is not that boundaries are in flux but
rather that fluctuations on one boundary
construct and deconstruct other boundaries.
The task ahead, then, is to specify the variety
of circumstances in which categories are
used to stabilize and destabilize each other.

References

Anderson, Margaret and Patricia Hill Collins. 1992.
Race, Class and Gender: An anthology. Belmont, CA:
Wadsworth.

Bobo, Lawrence, James R. Kluegel and Ryan A. Smith.
1997. Laissez-faire racism: The crystallization of a
kinder gentler antiblack ideology. In *Racial attitudes in the 1990s: Continuity and change* edited by
Steven Tuch and Jack Martin. Westport, CT:
Praeger.

Butler, Judith. 1990. *Gender trouble: Feminism and the
subversion of identity.* New York: Routledge.

Das Gupta, Monisha 1997. "What is Indian about
you?": A gendered transnational approach to ethnicity. *Gender & Society* 11 (5): 572–96.

Espiritu, Yen Le. 2001. "We don't sleep around like white
girls do: Family, culture, and gender in Filipina
American lives. *Signs: Journal of Women in Culture
and Society* 26 (2): 415–40.

Fine, Michelle. 1988. Sexuality, schooling, and adolescent females: The missing discourse of desire. *Harvard Educational Review* 58 (1): 29–53.

Frankenberg, Ruth. 1993. *White women, race matters:
The social construction of whiteness.* Minneapolis:
University of Minnesota Press.

Hall, Stuart. 1992. What is this "Black" in Black popu-
lar culture? In *Black popular culture: A project by
Michelle Wallace,* edited by G. Dent. Seattle, WA:
Bay.

Kelley, Robin D. G. 1997. Playing for keeps: Pleasure
and profit on the postindustrial playground. In *The
home that race built,* edited by Wahneema Lubiano.
New York: Vintage.

Lao, Augustin. 1997. Islands at the crossroads: Puerto
Ricanness traveling between the translocal nation
and the global city. In *Puerto Rican jam: Essays on
culture and politics,* edited by Frances
Negrón-Muntaner and Ramon Grosfoguel. Minneapolis: University of Minnesota Press.

Laqueur, Thomas. 1990. *Making sex: Body and gender
from the Greeks to Freud.* Cambridge, MA: Harvard
University Press.

Loewen, James. 1971. *The Mississippi Chinese: Between Black and White.* Cambridge, MA: Harvard
University Press.

Mink, Gwendolyn. 1990. The lady and the tramp: Gender, race, and the origins of the American welfare
state. In *Women, the state, and welfare,* edited by
Linda Gordon. Madison: University of Wisconsin
Press.

Nagel, Joane. 1996. *American Indian ethnic renewal:
Red power and the resurgence of identity and culture.*
New York: Oxford.

——. 2000. Ethnicity and sexuality. *Annual Review of
Sociology* 26: 107–133.

Negrón-Muntaner, Frances. 1997. English only jamás
but Spanish only cuidado: Language and nationalism in contemporary Puerto Rico. In *Puerto Rican
jam: Essays on culture and politics,* edited by Frances Negrón-Muntaner and Ramon Grosfoguel.
Minneapolis: University of Minnesota Press.

Omi, Michael and Howard Winant. 1996. *Racial formations in the United Stales: From the 1960s to the
1980s.* New York: Routledge.

Roediger, David R. 1991. *The wages of whiteness: Race
amd the making of the American working class.* New
York: Verso.

Rose, Tricia. 1994. *Black noise: Rap music and Black
culture in contemporary America.* Middletown, CT:
Wesleyan.

Tolman, Deborah. 1996. Adolescent girls' sexuality:
Debunking the myth of the urban girl. In *Urban
girls: Resisting stereotypes, creating identities,* edited
by Bonnie J. Ross Leadbeater and Niobe Way. New
York: New York University Press.

West, Candace, and Sarah Fenstermaker. 1995. Doing
difference. Gender & Society 9 (1): 8–37.

Discussion Questions

1. Do you think the wannabes described
    and interviewed in this article have

"*mestiza* consciousnesses" as that concept is discussed by Anzaldúa or that they resemble the White anti-racists described by O'Brien (see Section 6 for both articles)? Explain your answer.

2. Do you think it is possible for someone from a different background to become authentically part of a racial/ethnic community? What are some of the factors that might be relevant? Is color necessarily a barrier that cannot be overcome?

3. Heterosexual activity is central to the thinking and behavior of everyone interviewed for this article, but it plays different roles for boys and girls; Puerto Ricans, Blacks, and Whites; and wannabes and nonwannabes. It is also used as a marker of social class. Discuss the ways in which sexuality is shown in this arti-cle to be important in the construction of race/ethnicity, gender, and class.

4. Do you know anyone who might be called a "wannabe?"—not necessarily a Puerto Rican wannabe, but someone who identifies with and tries to be a member of a group other than his or her own? How did you explain the person's behavior to yourself before reading this article? Has this article changed your opinion in any way or given you any insight into your own reactions?

Reprinted from: Amy C. Wilkins, "Puerto Rican Wannabes: Sexual Spectacle and the Marking of Race, Class, and Gender Boundaries." *Gender & Society*, 18 (1), 103–121. Copyright © 2004 by Sociologists for Women and Society. Reprinted by permission of Sage Publications, Inc. ✦

60

All Men Are *Not* Created Equal

Asian Men in U.S. History

Yen Le Espiritu

In *"All Men are Not Created Equal: Asian Men in U.S. History,"* Yen Le Espiritu uncovers the little known history of Asian men in America and the intricacies of gender, race, and class that dominated their experiences. Espiritu argues that while a feminist tenet might well be solidarity among women in the face of patriarchy, this conception is shortsighted, to say the least, when factors such as race and class are combined with gender. Specifically, she suggests that Asian men have not traditionally reaped the rewards of patriarchal power, but on the contrary, have been relegated to "feminine" tasks and forced to serve not only the categorical White male oppressor but the White female as well.

Espiritu draws our attention to three time periods which exemplify her thesis. In the first period, which precedes World War II, the shortage of women coupled with a closed labor market for noncitizens, relegated Chinese, Japanese, and also Filipino men to limited employment opportunities as domestics, laundry workers, or cooks. Immigration policies and labor conditions, then, had both racial and gender implications, Espiritu emphasizes, effectively emasculating generations of Asian men. She shares a quote from a Japanese domestic servant that underscores his unequal relationship to both the White master and White mistress of the house—patriarchy is not shared equally by all men. The responses of Asian men to this racial, class, and gendered order were varied, according to Espiritu, with some denigrating Asian women—reasserting patriarchal relations at least in the home sphere, and others bringing their domestic talents home to negotiate new

gendered divisions of labor in the home with their wives.

The second period in U.S. history Espiritu describes is during the wartime internment of Japanese Americans. In this case, an interned class of people divided over gendered and generational lines. She describes Japanese internment in terms of its disruption of the classic patriarchal role of the Japanese father as breadwinner and decision maker for the family. Internment broke these lines of authority. Women gained more power and independence, and children were also given more latitude and independence. In fact, the second generation Nisei children were given more power than their parents and were eligible to vote and hold positions of stature in the camps. This meant a total break with the past of the Issei immigrant parental authority, especially the father. Further, all things Japanese were denigrated in the camps, rendering Japanese racial status inferior to imminent Americanization of the second generation. She argues that these changes were devastating to Nisei men who, even when returned to their original American homes, had lost their farms and businesses. One gets the sense, from Espiritu's reading of this history, that a generation of men simply did not recover from the wartime internment of their families.

Finally, Espiritu discusses the contemporary scene for Asian Americans. Here she debunks the "model minority myth"—the belief that the majority of Asian Americans hold degrees and lucrative jobs—by describing a spectrum of Asian American economic realities. That is, some Asian Americans may hold advanced degrees and earn relatively high incomes, but others may have the lowest paying jobs in the secondary labor sector. Many Asian Americans, especially immigrants, have limited English skills, education, and job skills, she emphasizes. In the case of those Asian Americans who lack skills and education, it is the women who are more likely to be employed, according to Espiritu, because the manufacturing jobs males have historically held have moved overseas, while the low-paying garment industry and canning jobs that employ women remain. She stresses that it is the employers racist and patriarchal beliefs that play a part here as Asian women are perceived as suited for routine work and as a group that can afford to *work for less. These employment variations have meant a loss of status and power among Asian men, a challenge to their patriarchal authority. This has resulted in domestic abuse and depression among Asian men. Espiritu highlights the dilemma here and the intersectionality of the oppression of Asian American men along race, class, and gender lines. Specifically, she notes that working-class Asian American men of color find that racism and classism limits their access to economic opportunities, and this, in turn, limits their gendered authority in the home.*

In all, Espiritu wishes to emphasize that sexism alone fails to grasp the picture for people of color who must also contend with issues of racism and classism—clearly, not all men are created equal.

Today, virtually every major metropolitan market across the United States has at least one Asian American female newscaster. In contrast, there is a nearly total absence of Asian American men in anchor positions (Hamamoto, 1994, p. 245; Fong-Torres, 1995). This gender imbalance in television news broadcasting exemplifies the racialization of Asian American manhood: Historically, they have been depicted as either asexual or hypersexual; today, they are constructed to be less successful, assimilated, attractive, and desirable than their female counterparts (Espiritu, 1996, pp. 95–98). The exclusion of Asian men from Eurocentric notions of the masculine reminds us that not all men benefit—or benefit equally—from a patriarchal system designed to maintain the unequal relationship that exists between men and women. The feminist mandate for gender solidarity tends to ignore power differentials among men, among women, and between white women and men of color. This exclusive focus on gender bars traditional feminists from recognizing the oppression of men of color: the fact that there are men, and not only women, who have been "feminized" and the fact that some white middle-class women hold cultural power and class power over certain men of color (Cheung, 1990, pp. 245–246; Wiegman, 1991, p. 311). Presenting race and gender as

relationally constructed, King-Kok Cheung (1990) exhorted white scholars to acknowledge that, like female voices, "the voices of many men of color have been historically silenced or dismissed" (p. 246). Along the same line, black feminists have referred to "racial patriarchy"—a concept that calls attention to the white/patriarch master in U.S. history and his dominance over the black male as well as the black female (Gaines, 1990, p. 202).

Throughout their history in the United States, Asian American men, as immigrants and citizens of color, have faced a variety of economic, political, and ideological racism that have assaulted their manhood. During the pre-World War II period, racialized and gendered immigration policies and labor conditions emasculated Asian men, forcing them into womanless communities and into "feminized" jobs that had gone unfilled due to the absence of women. During World War II, the internment of Japanese Americans stripped Issei (first generation) men of their role as the family breadwinner, transferred some of their power and status to the U.S.-born children, and decreased male dominance over women. In the contemporary period, the patriarchal authority of Asian immigrant men, particularly those of the working class, has also been challenged due to the social and economic losses that they suffered in their transition to life in the United States. As detailed below, these three historically specific cases establish that the material existences of Asian American men have historically contradicted the Eurocentric, middle-class constructions of manhood.

Asian Men in Domestic Service

Feminist scholars have argued accurately that domestic service involves a three-way relationship between privileged white men, privileged white women, and poor women of color (Romero, 1992). But women have not been the only domestic workers. During the pre-World War II period, racialized and gendered immigration policies and labor conditions forced Asian men into "feminized" jobs such as domestic service, laundry work, and food preparation.[1] Due to their noncitizen status, the closed labor market, and the shortage of women, Asian immigrant men, first Chinese and later Japanese, substituted to some extent for female labor in the American West. David Katzman (1978) noted the peculiarities of the domestic labor situation in the West in this period: "In 1880, California and Washington were the only states in which a majority of domestic servants were men" (p. 55).

At the turn of the twentieth century, lacking other job alternatives, many Chinese men entered into domestic service in private homes, hotels, and rooming houses (Daniels, 1988, p. 74). Whites rarely objected to Chinese in domestic service. In fact, through the 1900s, the Chinese houseboy was the symbol of upper-class status in San Francisco (Glenn, 1986, p. 106). As late as 1920, close to 50 percent of the Chinese in the United States were still occupied as domestic servants (Light, 1972, p. 7). Large numbers of Chinese also became laundrymen, not because laundering was a traditional male occupation in China, but because there were very few women of any ethnic origin—and thus few washerwomen—in gold-rush California (Chan, 1991, pp. 33–34). Chinese laundrymen thus provided commercial services that replaced women's unpaid labor in the home. White consumers were prepared to patronize a Chinese laundryman because as such he "occupied a status which was in accordance with the social definition of the place in the economic hierarchy suitable for a member of an 'inferior race'" (cited in Siu, 1987, p. 21). In her autobiographical fiction *China Men*, Maxine Hong Kingston presents her father and his partners as engaged in their laundry business for long periods each day—a business considered so low and debased that, in their songs, they associate it with the washing of menstrual blood (Goellnicht, 1992, p. 198). The existence of the Chinese houseboy and launderer—and their forced "bachelor" status—further bolstered the stereotype of the feminized and asexual or homosexual Asian man. Their feminization, in turn, confirmed their assignment to the state's labor force which performed "women's work."

Japanese men followed Chinese men into domestic service. By the end of the first decade of the twentieth century, the U.S. Immigration Commission estimated that 12,000 to 15,000 Japanese in the western United States earned a living in domestic service (Chan, 1991, pp. 39–40). Many Japanese men considered housework beneath them because in Japan only lower-class women worked as domestic servants (Ichioka, 1988, p. 24). Studies of Issei occupational histories indicate that a domestic job was the first occupation for many of the new arrivals; but unlike Chinese domestic workers, most Issei eventually moved on to agricultural or city trades (Glenn, 1986, p. 108). Filipino and Korean boys and men likewise relied on domestic service for their livelihood (Chan, 1991, p. 40). In his autobiography *East Goes West*, Korean immigrant writer Younghill Kang (1937) related that he worked as a domestic servant for a white family who treated him "like a cat or a dog" (p. 66).

Filipinos, as stewards in the U.S. Navy, also performed domestic duties for white U.S. naval officers. During the 94 years of U.S. military presence in the Philippines, U.S. bases served as recruiting stations for the U.S. armed forces, particularly the navy. Soon after the United States acquired the Philippines from Spain in 1898, its navy began actively recruiting Filipinos—but only as stewards and mess attendants. Barred from admissions to other ratings, Filipino enlistees performed the work of domestics, preparing and serving the officers' meals, and caring for the officers' galley, wardroom, and living spaces. Ashore, their duties ranged from ordinary housework to food services at the U.S. Naval Academy hall. Unofficially, Filipino stewards also have been ordered to perform menial chores such as walking the officers' dogs and acting as personal servants for the officers' wives (Espiritu, 1995, p. 16).

As domestic servants, Asian men became subordinates of not only privileged white men but also privileged white women. The following testimony from a Japanese house servant captures this unequal relationship:

immediately the ma'am demanded me to scrub the floor. I took one hour to finish. Then I had to wash windows. That was very difficult job for me. Three windows for another hour! . . . The ma'am taught me how to cook. . . . I was sitting on the kitchen chair and thinking what a change of life it was. The ma'am came into the kitchen and was so furious! It was such a hard work for me to wash up all dishes, pans, glasses, etc., after dinner. When I went into the dining room to put all silvers on sideboard, I saw the reflection of myself on the looking glass. In a white coat and apron! I could not control my feelings. The tears so freely flowed out from my eyes, and I buried my face with my both arms (quoted in Ichioka, 1988, pp. 25–26).

The experiences of Asian male domestic service workers demonstrate that not all men benefit equally from patriarchy. Depending on their race and class, men experience gender differently. While male domination of women may tie all men together, men share unequally in the fruits of this domination. For Asian American male domestic workers, economic and social discriminations locked them into an unequal relationship with not only privileged white men but also privileged white women (Kim, 1990, p. 74).

The racist and classist devaluation of Asian men had gender implications. The available evidence indicates that immigrant men reasserted their lost patriarchal power in racist America by denigrating a weaker group: Asian women. In *China Men*, Kingston's immigrant father, having been forced into "feminine" subject positions, lapses into silence, breaking the silence only to utter curses against women (Goellnicht, 1992, pp. 200–201). Kingston (1980) traces her father's abuse of Chinese women back to his feeling of emasculation in America: "We knew that it was to feed us you had to endure demons and physical labor" (p. 13). On the other hand, some men brought home the domestic skills they learned on the jobs. Anamaria Labao Cabato relates that her Filipino-born father, who spent 28 years in the navy as a steward, is "one of the best cooks around" (Espiritu, 1995, p. 143). Leo Sicat, a retired U.S. Navy man, similarly reports that "we learned how to cook in the Navy, and we brought it home. The Filipino women are very fortunate because the husband does the cooking. In our household, I do the cooking, and my wife does the washing" (Espiritu, 1995, p. 108). Along the same line, in some instances, the

domestic skills which men were forced to learn in their wives' absence were put to use when husbands and wives reunited in the United States. The history of Asian male domestic workers suggests that the denigration of women is only one response to the stripping of male privilege. The other is to institute a revised domestic division of labor and gender relations in the families.

Changing Gender Relations: The Wartime Internment of Japanese Americans

Immediately after the bombing of Pearl Harbor, the incarceration of Japanese Americans began. On the night of 7 December 1941, working on the principle of guilt by association, the Federal Bureau of Investigation (FBI) began taking into custody persons of Japanese ancestry who had connections to the Japanese government. On 19 February 1942, President Franklin Delano Roosevelt signed Executive Order 9066, arbitrarily suspending civil rights of U.S. citizens by authorizing the "evacuation" of 120,000 persons of Japanese ancestry into concentration camps, of whom approximately 50 percent were women and 60 percent were U.S.-born citizens (Matsumoto, 1989, p. 116).

The camp environment—with its lack of privacy, regimented routines, and new power hierarchy—inflicted serious and lasting wounds on Japanese American family life. In the crammed 20-by-25-foot "apartment" units, tensions were high as men, women, and children struggled to recreate family life under very trying conditions. The internment also transformed the balance of power in families: husbands lost some of their power over wives, as did parents over children. Until the internment, the Issei man had been the undisputed authority over his wife and children: he was both the breadwinner and the decision-maker for the entire family. Now "he had no rights, no home, no control over his own life" (Houston and Houston, 1973, p. 62). Most important, the internment reverted the economic roles—and thus the status and authority—of family members. With their means of livelihood cut off indefinitely, Issei men lost their role as breadwinners. Despondent over the loss of almost everything they had worked so hard to acquire, many Issei men felt useless and frustrated, particularly as their wives and children became less dependent on them. Daisuke Kitagawa (1967) reports that in the Tule Lake relocation center, "the [Issei] men looked as if they had suddenly aged in ten years They lost the capacity to plan for their own futures, let alone those of their sons and daughters" (p. 91).

Issei men responded to this emasculation in various ways. By the end of three years' internment, formerly enterprising, energetic Issei men had become immobilized with feelings of despair, hopelessness, and insecurity. Charles Kikuchi remembers his father—who "used to be a perfect terror and dictator"—spending all day lying on his cot: "He probably realizes that he no longer controls the family group and rarely exerts himself so that there is little family conflict as far as he is concerned" (Modell, 1973, p. 62). But others, like Jeanne Wakatsuki Houston's father, reasserted their patriarchal power by abusing their wives and children. Stripped of his roles as the protector and provider for his family, Houston's father "kept pursuing oblivion through drink, he kept abusing Mama, and there seemed to be no way out of it for anyone. You couldn't even run" (Houston and Houston, 1973, p. 61). The experiences of the Issei men underscore the intersections of racism and sexism—the fact that men of color live in a society that creates sex-based norms and expectations (i.e., man as breadwinner) which racism operates simultaneously to deny (Crenshaw, 1989, p. 155).

Camp life also widened the distance and deepened the conflict between the Issei and their U.S.-born children. At the root of these tensions were growing cultural rifts between the generations as well as a decline in the power and authority of the Issei fathers. The cultural rifts reflected not only a general process of acculturation, but were accelerated by the degradation of everything Japanese and the simultaneous promotion of Americanization in the camps (Chan, 1991, p. 128; see also Okihiro, 1991, pp. 229–232). The younger Nisei also spent much more time away from their parents' supervision. As a consequence, Issei parents gradually lost

their ability to discipline their children, whom they seldom saw during the day. Much to the chagrin of the conservative parents, young men and women began to spend more time with each other unchaperoned—at the sports events, the dances, and other school functions. Freed from some of the parental constraints, the Nisei women socialized more with their peers and also expected to choose their own husbands and to marry for "love"—a departure from the old customs of arranged marriage (Matsumoto, 1989, p. 117). Once this occurred, the prominent role that the father plays in marriage arrangements—and by extension in their children's lives—declined (Okihiro, 1991, p. 231).

Privileging U.S. citizenship and U.S. education, War Relocation Authority (WRA) policies regarding camp life further reverted the power hierarchy between the Japan-born Issei and their U.S.-born children. In the camps, only Nisei were eligible to vote and to hold office in the Community Council; Issei were excluded because of their alien status. Daisuke Kitagawa (1967) records the impact of this policy on parental authority:

> In the eyes of young children, their parents were definitely inferior to their grown-up brothers and sisters, who as U.S. citizens could elect and be elected members of the Community Council. For all these reasons many youngsters lost confidence in, and respect for, their parents (p. 88).

Similarly, the WRA salary scales were based on English-speaking ability and on citizenship status. As a result, the Nisei youths and young adults could earn relatively higher wages than their fathers. This shift in earning abilities eroded the economic basis for parental authority (Matsumoto, 1989, p. 116).

At war's end in August 1945, Japanese Americans had lost much of the economic ground that they had gained in more than a generation. The majority of Issei women and men no longer had their farms, businesses, and financial savings; those who still owned property found their homes dilapidated and vandalized and their personal belongings stolen or destroyed (Broom and Riemer, 1949). The internment also ended Japanese American concentration in agriculture and small businesses. In their absence, other groups had taken over these ethnic niches. This loss further eroded the economic basis of parental authority since Issei men no longer had businesses to hand down to their Nisei sons (Broom and Riemer, 1949, p. 31). Historian Roger Daniels (1988) declared that by the end of World War II, "the generational struggle was over: the day of the Issei had passed" (p. 286). Issei men, now in their sixties, no longer had the vigor to start over from scratch. Forced to find employment quickly after the war, many Issei couples who had owned small businesses before the war returned to the forms of manual labor in which they began a generation ago. Most men found work as janitors, gardeners, kitchen helpers, and handymen; their wives toiled as domestic servants, garment workers, and cannery workers (Yanagisako, 1987, p. 92).

Contemporary Asian America: The Disadvantaged

Relative to earlier historical periods, the economic pattern of contemporary Asian America is considerably more varied, a result of both the postwar restructured economy and the 1965 Immigration Act.[2] The dual goals of the 1965 Immigration Act—to facilitate family reunification and to admit educated workers needed by the U.S. economy—have produced two distinct chains of emigration from Asia: one comprising the relatives of working-class Asians who had immigrated to the United States prior to 1965; the other of highly trained immigrants who entered during the late 1960s and early 1970s (Liu, Ong, and Rosenstein, 1991). Given their dissimilar backgrounds, Asian Americans "can be found throughout the income spectrum of this nation" (Ong, 1994, p. 4). In other words, today's Asian American men both join whites in the well-paid, educated, white collar sector of the workforce *and* join Latino immigrants in lower-paying secondary sector jobs (Ong and Hee, 1994). This economic diversity contradicts the model minority stereotype—the common belief that most Asian American men are college educated and in high-paying professional or technical jobs.

The contemporary Asian American community includes a sizable population with limited education, skills, and English-speaking ability. In 1990, 18 percent of Asian men and 26 percent of Asian women in the United States, age 25 and over, had less than a high school degree. Also, of the 4.1 million Asians 5 years and over, 56 percent did not speak English "very well" and 35 percent were linguistically isolated (U.S. Bureau of the Census, 1993, Table 2). The median income for those with limited English was $20,000 for males and $15,600 for females; for those with less than a high school degree, the figures were $18,000 and $15,000, respectively. Asian American men and women with both limited English-speaking ability and low levels of education fared the worst. For a large portion of this disadvantaged population, even working full-time, full-year brought in less than $10,000 in earnings (Ong and Hee, 1994, p. 45).

The disadvantaged population is largely a product of immigration: Nine tenths are immigrants (Ong and Hee, 1994). The majority enter as relatives of the pre-1956 working-class Asian immigrants. Because immigrants tend to have socioeconomic backgrounds similar to those of their sponsors, most family reunification immigrants represent a continuation of the unskilled and semiskilled Asian labor that emigrated before 1956 (Liu, Ong, and Rosenstein, 1991). Southeast Asian refugees, particularly the second-wave refugees who arrived after 1978, represent another largely disadvantaged group. This is partly so because refugees are less likely to have acquired readily transferable skills and are more likely to have made investments (in training and education) specific to the country of origin (Chiswick, 1979; Montero, 1980). For example, there are significant numbers of Southeast Asian military men with skills for which there is no longer a market in the United States. In 1990, the overall economic status of the Southeast Asian population was characterized by unstable, minimum-wage employment, welfare dependency, and participation in the informal economy (Gold and Kibria, 1993). These economic facts underscore the danger of lumping all Asian Americans together because many Asian men do not share in the relatively favorable socio-economic outcomes attributed to the "average" Asian American.

Lacking the skills and education to catapult them into the primary sector of the economy, disadvantaged Asian American men and women work in the secondary labor market—the labor-intensive, low-capital service, and small manufacturing sectors. In this labor market, disadvantaged men generally have fewer employment options than women. This is due in part to the decline of male-occupied manufacturing jobs and the concurrent growth of female-intensive industries in the United States, particularly in service, micro electronics, and apparel manufacturing. The garment industry, microelectronics, and canning industries are top employers of immigrant women (Takaki, 1989, p. 427; Mazumdar, 1989, p. 19; Villones, 1989, p. 176; Hossfeld, 1994, pp. 71–72). In a study of Silicon Valley (California's famed high-tech industrial region) Karen Hossfeld (1994) reported that the employers interviewed preferred to hire immigrant women over immigrant men for entry-level, operative jobs (p. 74). The employers' "gender logic" was informed by the patriarchal and racist beliefs that women can afford to work for less, do not mind dead-end jobs, and are more suited physiologically to certain kinds of detailed and routine work. As Linda Lim (1983) observes, it is the "*comparative disadvantage* of women in the wage-labor market that gives them a comparative advantage vis-á-vis men in the occupations and industries where they are concentrated—so-called female ghettoes of employment" (p. 78). A white male production manager and hiring supervisor in a California Silicon Valley assembly shop discusses his formula for hiring:

> Just three things I look for in hiring [entry-level, high-tech manufacturing operatives]: small, foreign and female. You find those three things and you're pretty much automatically guaranteed the right kind of workforce. These little foreign gals are grateful to be hired—very, very grateful—no matter what (Hossfeld, 1994 p. 65).

Refugee women have also been found to be more in demand than men in secretarial, clerical, and interpreter jobs in social service work. In a study of Cambodian refugees in Stockton, California, Shiori Ui (1991) found that social service agency executives preferred to hire Cambodian women over men when both had the same qualifications. One executive explained his preference, "It seems that some ethnic populations relate better to women than men. Another thing is that the pay is so bad" (cited in Ui, 1991, p. 169). As a result, in the Cambodian communities in Stockton, it is often women—and not men—who have greater economic opportunities and who are the primary breadwinners in their families (Ui, 1991, p. 171).

Due to the significant decline in the economic contributions of Asian immigrant men, women's earnings comprise an equal or greater share of the family income. Because the wage each earns is low, only by pooling incomes can a husband and wife earn enough to support a family (Glenn, 1983, p. 42). These shifts in resources have challenged the patriarchal authority of Asian men. Men's loss of status and power—not only in the public but also in the domestic arena—places severe pressure on their sense of well-being. Responding to this pressure, some men accepted the new division of labor in the family (Ui, 1991, pp. 170–173), but many others resorted to spousal abuse and divorce (Lira, 1989, p. 68). A Korean immigrant man describes his frustrations over changing gender roles and expectations:

> In Korea [my wife] used to have breakfast ready for me. She didn't do it any more because she said she was too busy getting ready to go to work. If I complained she talked back at me, telling me to fix my own breakfast. . . . I was very frustrated about her, started fighting and hit her (Yim, 1978, quoted in Mazumdar, 1989, p. 18).

Loss of status and power has similarly led to depression and anxieties in Hmong males. In particular, the women's ability—and the men's inability—to earn money for households "has undermined severely male omnipotence" (Irby and Pon, 1988, p. 112). Male unhappiness and helplessness can be detected in the following joke told at a family picnic, "When we get on the plane to go back to Laos, the first thing we will do is beat up the women!" The joke—which generated laughter by both men and women—drew upon a combination of "the men's unemployability, the sudden economic value placed on women's work, and men's fear of losing power in their families" (Donnelly, 1994, pp. 74–75). As such, it highlights the interconnections of race, class, and gender—the fact that in a racist and classist society working-class men of color have limited access to economic opportunities and thus limited claim to patriarchal authority.

Conclusion

A central task in feminist scholarship is to expose and dismantle the stereotypes that traditionally have provided ideological justifications for women's subordination. But to conceptualize oppression only in terms of male dominance and female subordination is to obscure the centrality of classism, racism, and other forms of inequality in U.S. society (Stacey and Thorne, 1985, p. 311). The multiplicities of Asian men's lives indicate that ideologies of manhood and womanhood have as much to do with class and race as they have to do with sex. The intersections of race, gender, and class mean that there are also hierarchies among women and among men and that some women hold power over certain groups of men. The task for feminist scholars, then, is to develop paradigms that articulate the complicity among these categories of oppression, that strengthen the alliance between gender and ethnic studies, and that reach out not only to women, but also to men, of color.

Notes

1. One of the most noticeable characteristics of pre-World War II Asian America was a pronounced shortage of women. During this period, U.S. immigration policies barred the entry of most Asian women. America's capitalist economy also wanted Asian male workers but not their families. In most instances, families were seen as a threat to the efficiency and exploitability of the workforce and were actively prohibited.

2. The 1965 Immigration Act ended Asian exclusion and equalized immigration rights for all nationalities. No longer constrained by exclusion laws, Asian immigrants began arriving in much larger numbers than ever before. In the 1980s Asia was the largest source of U.S. legal immigrants, accounting for 40 percent to 47 percent of the total influx (Min, 1995, p. 12).

References

Broom, Leonard and Ruth Riemer. 1949. *Removal and Return: The Socio-Economic Effects of the War on Japanese Americans.* Berkeley: University of California Press.

Chan, Sucheng. 1991. *Asian Americans: An Interpretive History.* Boston: Twayne.

Cheung, King-Kok. 1990. "The Woman Warrior Versus the Chinaman Pacific: Must a Chinese American Critic Choose Between Feminism and Heroism?" Pp. 234–251 in *Conflicts in Feminism,* edited by Marianne Hirsch and Evelyn Fox Keller. New York and London: Routledge.

Chiswick, Barry. 1979. "The Economic Progress of Immigrants: Some Apparently Universal Patterns." Pp. 357–399 in *Contemporary Economic Problems* edited by W. Fellner. Washington, DC: American Enterprise Institute.

Crenshaw, Kimberlee. 1989. "Demarginalizing the Intersection of Race and Sex: A Black Feminist Critique of Antidiscrimination Doctrine, Feminist Theory and Antiracist Politics." In *University of Chicago Legal Forum: Feminism in the Law: Theory, Practice, and Criticism* (pp. 139–167). Chicago: University of Chicago Press.

Daniels, Roger. 1988. *Asian America: Chinese and Japanese in the United States Since 1850.* Seattle: University of Washington Press.

Donnelly, Nancy D. 1994. *Changing Lives of Refugee Hmong Women.* Seattle: Washington University Press.

Espiritu, Yen Le. 1995. *Filipino American Lives.* Philadelphia: Temple University Press.

Espiritu, Yen Le. 1996. *Asian American Women and Men: Labor, Laws, and Love.* Thousand Oaks, CA: Sage.

Fong-Torres, Ben. 1995. "Why Are There No Male Asian Anchormen on TV?" Pp. 208–211 in *Men's, Lives* 3rd ed., edited by Michael S. Kimmel and Michael A. Messner. Boston: Allyn and Bacon.

Gaines Jane. 1990. "White Privilege and Looking Relations: Race and Gender in Feminist Film Theory." Pp. 197–214 in *Issues in Feminist Film Criticism,* edited by Patricia Erens. Bloomington: Indiana University Press.

Glenn, Evelyn Nakano. 1983. "Split Household, Small Producer and Dual Wage Earner: An Analysis of Chinese-American Family Strategies." *Journal of Marriage and the Family.* February: 35–46.

——. 1986. *Issei, Nisei, War Bride: Three Generations of Japanese American Women at Domestic Service.* Philadelphia: Temple University Press.

Goellnicht, Donald C. 1992. "Tang Ao in America: Male Subject Positions in China Men." Pp. 191–212 in *Reading the Literatures of Asian America,* edited by

Shirley Geok-lin-Lim and Amy Ling. Philadelphia: Temple University Press.

Gold, Steve and Nazli Kibria. 1993. "Vietnamese Refugees and Blocked Mobility." *Asian and Pacific Migration Review* 2: 27–56.

Hamamoto Darrell. 1994. *Monitored Peril: Asian Americans and the Politics of Representation*. Minneapolis: University of Minnesota Press.

Hossfeld, Karen J. 1994. "Hiring Immigrant Women: Silicon Valley's 'Simple Formula.'" Pp. 65–93 in *Women of Color in U.S. Society*, edited by Maxine Baca Zinn and Bonnie Thornton Dill. Philadelphia: Temple University Press.

Houston, Jeanne Wakatsuki and James D. Houston. 1973. *Farewell to Manzanar*. San Francisco: Houghton Mifflin.

Ichioka, Yuji. 1988. *The Issei: The World of the First Generation Japanese Immigrants, 1885–1924*. New York: The Free Press.

Irby, Charles and Ernest M. Pon. 1988. "Confronting New Mountains: Mental Health Problems among Male Hmong and Mien Refugees." *Amerasia Journal* 14: 109–118.

Kang, Younghill. 1937. *East Goes West*. New York: C. Scribner's Sons.

Katzman, David. 1978. "Domestic Service: Women's Work." Pp. 377–391 in *Women Working: Theories and Fans in Perspective*, edited by Ann Stromberg and Shirley Harkess. Palo Alto: Mayfield.

Kim, Elaine. 1990. "'Such Opposite Creatures': Men and Women in Asian American Literature." *Michigan Quarterly Review*, 68–93.

Kingston, Maxine Hong. 1980. *China Men*. New York: Knopf.

Kitagawa, Daisuke. 1967. *Issei and Nisei: The Internment Years*. New York: Seabury Press.

Kitano, Harry H. L. 1991. "The Effects of the Evacuation on the Japanese Americans." Pp. 151–162 in *Japanese Americans. From Relocation to Redress*, edited by Roger Daniels, Sandra C. Taylor, and Harry Kitano. Seattle: University of Washington Press.

Light, Ivan. 1972. *Ethnic Enterprise in America: Business and Welfare Among Chinese, Japanese, and Blacks*. Berkeley and Los Angeles: University of California Press.

Lim, Linda. Y. C. 1983. "Capitalism, Imperialism, and Patriarchy: The Dilemma of Third-World Women Workers in Multinational Factories." Pp. 70–91 in *Women, Men, and the International Division of Labor*, edited by June Nash and Maria Patricia Fernandez-Kelly. Albany: State University of New York.

Liu, John, Paul Ong, and Carolyn Rosenstein. 1991. "Dual Chain Migration: Post-1965 Filipino Immigration to the United States." *International Migration Review* 25 (3): 487–513.

Luu, Van. 1989. "The Hardships of Escape for Vietnamese Women." Pp. 60–72 in *Making Waves: An Anthology of Writings by and about Asian American Women*, edited by Asian Women United of California. Boston: Beacon Press.

Matsumoto, Valerie. 1989. "Nisei Women and Resettlement During World War II." Pp. 115–126 in *Making Waves: An Anthology of Writings by and about Asian American Women*, edited by Asian Women United of California. Boston: Beacon Press.

Mazumdar, Sucheta. 1989. "General Introduction: A Woman-Centered Perspective on Asian American History." Pp. 1–22 in *Making Waves: An Anthology by and about Asian American Women*, edited by Asian Women United of California. Boston: Beacon Press.

Min, Pyong Gap. 1995. "Korean Americans." Pp. 199–231 in *Asian Americans: Contemporary Trends and Issues*, edited by Pyong Gap Min. Thousand Oaks, CA: Sage.

Modell, John, ed. 1973. *The Kikuchi Diary: Chronicle from an American Concentration Camp*. Urbana: University of Illinois Press.

Montero, Darrell. 1980. *Vietnamese Americans: Patterns of Settlement and Socioeconomic Adaptation in the United States*. Boulder, CO: Westview.

Okihiro, Gary Y. 1991. *Cane Fires: The Anti-Japanese Movement in Hawaii, 1865–1945*. Philadelphia: Temple University Press.

Ong, Paul. 1994. "Asian Pacific Americans and Public Policy." Pp. 1–9 in *The State of Asian Pacific America Economic Diversity, Issues, & Policies*, edited by Paul Ong. Los Angeles: LEAP Asian Pacific American Public Policy Institute and UCLA Asian American Studies Center.

Ong, Paul and Suzanne Hee. 1994. "Economic Diversity." Pp. 31–56 in *The State of Asian Pacific America: Economic Diversity, Issues, & Policies*, edited by Paul Ong. Los Angeles: LEAP Asian Pacific American Public Policy Institute and UCLA Asian American Studies Center.

Romero, Mary. 1992. *Maid in the USA*. New York: Routledge.

Siu, Paul. 1987. *The Chinese Laundryman: A Study in Social Isolation*. New York: New York University Press.

Stacey, Judith and Barrie Thorne. 1985. "The Missing Feminist Revolution in Sociology." *Social Problems* 32: 301–316.

Takaki, Ronald. 1989. *Strangers from a Different Shore: A History of Asian Americans*. Boston: Little Brown.

Ui, Shiori. 1991. "'Unlikely Heroes': The Evolution of Female Leadership in a Cambodian Ethnic Enclave." Pp. 161–177 in *Ethnography Unbound: Power and Resistance in the Modern Metropolis*, edited by Michael Burawoy et al. Berkeley: University of California Press.

U.S. Bureau of the Census. 1993. *We the American Asians*. Washington, DC: U.S. Government Printing Office.

Villones, Rebecca. 1989. "Women in the Silicon Valley." Pp. 172–176 in *Making Waves: An Anthology of Writings by and about Asian American Women*, edited by Asian Women United of California. Boston: Beacon Press.

Wiegman, Robyn. 1991. "Black Bodies/American Commodities: Gender, Race, and the Bourgeois Ideal in Contemporary Film." Pp. 308–328 in *Unspeakable Images: Ethnicity and the American Cinema*, edited by Lester Friedman. Urbana and Chicago: University of Illinois Press.

Yanagisako, Sylvia Junko. 1987. "Mixed Metaphors: Native and Anthropological Models of Gender and Kinship Domains." Pp. 86–118 in *Gender and Kinship: Essays Toward a Unified Analysis,* edited by Jane Fishburne Collier and Sylvia Junko Yanagisako. Stanford: Stanford University Press.

Discussion Questions

1. What elements in African American or Latino history might resonate with Espiritu's arguments about Asian American men? Have African American men and Latinos also dealt with periods in the histories of their communities that have threatened their manhood? If so, describe these periods briefly.

2. If this article were written about women of color in relation to White women, do you think you would find levels of inequality in this context? How so?

3. Were you aware of the periods of history that Espiritu described in relation to Asian American men? If so, which period(s)? Do you think these histories are commonly discussed in U.S. high schools? Why or why not?

4. What stereotypes of Asian American men have you seen in the media? Describe them.

Reprinted from: Yen Le Espiritu, "All Men Are *Not* Created Equal: Asian Men in U.S. History." In *Men's Lives,* 5th ed., M. S. Kimmel and M. A. Messner (eds.), pp. 33–41, published by Allyn and Bacon. Copyright © 2001 by Yen Le Espiritu. Reprinted with permission. ✦

61
LGBT Parents and Their Children

Kristin E. Joos

Sociologists for Women in Society (SWS), an organization of sociologists and sociology students, publishes the journal Gender & Society, from which two of the articles in this section are reprinted, and Network News, a quarterly newsletter. In keeping with its mission to apply sociological knowledge and research skills to further the understanding of the way gender functions in society, fact sheets on important social issues are compiled periodically and published in Network News. Once published, they are available for use by those interested in the subject matter. To learn more about SWS and its publications, check out its website (www.socwomen.org) or look for issues of Gender & Society in your library.

In this fact sheet, Kristin E. Joos reviews the research reported in peer-reviewed sociology and psychology journals to summarize what we know about lesbian, gay, bisexual, and transgendered (LGBT) parents and their children. Contrary to what some people may believe or fear, the studies show that LGBT parents are pretty much like other parents, and despite the additional challenges they face, LGBT families are pretty much like other families. One really positive finding is that children raised in LGBT households tend to be more tolerant than their peers. An October 17, 2005, presentation to the American Academy of Pediatrics by Ellen Perrin, MD, professor of pediatrics at Tufts University reaches similar conclusions. Summaries of her presentation were posted on the Internet by AAP (www.aap.org) and WebMD (http://www.webmd.com).

While both this fact sheet and Perrin's presentation are based on reviews of systematically gathered empirical evidence, Joos acknowledges that the conclusions we can draw from the existing research are incomplete for two reasons.

One is that members of the current generation of LGBT parents are really the first who have been able to live their family lives and raise their children openly. The second reason is that it is difficult to obtain representative samples of LGBT individuals and families. Those represented in the studies we currently have are, overwhelmingly, urban, White, and affluent. Data on poor and working-class families, rural residents, and LGBT people of the whole range of racial and ethnic groups that make up American society are needed.

After summarizing what we do and do not know about LGBT parents and their children, Joos provides many useful resources, including the supportive position on LGBT parenting adopted by the American Psychological Association in 1976 and the websites where similar statements by other professional groups can be found; the policies regarding custody and adoption by LGBT individuals and couples in various states of the United States and in other nations; the means of contacting a wide range of organizations with an interest in the subject; and relevant journal references, websites and films. The information in this fact sheet is relevant as individuals and couples make decisions about whether to become parents or to work out custody arrangements; as schools, social service agencies, and other institutions serve children and families with different compositions; and as legislatures and judicial systems make laws and rulings that affect the fates of families and children. As I write this, a legislator in one midwestern state has proposed banning women who are not heterosexually married from receiving assistance, such as artificial insemination, to conceive. Moreover, two judges in that same state have ruled differently on the right of a lesbian couple to adopt a baby, although the baby's biological mother explicitly chose them to be her child's adoptive parents.

Introduction

The image of family has been long upheld as a singular notion of a mother, a father, and children. Yet according to the U.S. Census 2000,[1] this form of heterosexual nuclear family represents just a minority (fewer than

24 percent) of households in the U.S. Though the idealized image persists, there is much diversity in families today: single parents, child-free couples, parents who adopt or are foster parents, multiracial couples and their children, stepfamilies, etc. Parents who are lesbian, gay, bisexual, or transgender and their children are contributing to this societal shift that is broadening the traditional and idealized notion of family.

In 1990 *Newsweek*[2] referred to the growing number of lesbian and gay people becoming parents as a "gayby boom." While this term is used in the popular media, in academia LGBT people who raise children have often been labeled as "same-sex parents" or "alternative families."[3] Contemporary scholars are more commonly using the terms "LGBT families" or "Queer families," or stating more specifically, "lesbian and gay parents and their children." Regardless of how these families are referred to, they are becoming increasingly visible and are challenging definitions of what it means to be a family. According to one of the most respected experts in this field, Judith Stacey, "Gay and lesbian families represent such a new, embattled, visible, and necessarily self-conscious genre of kinship that they help to expose the widening gap between the complex reality of contemporary family forms and the dated family ideology that still undergirds most public rhetoric, policy, and law concerning families."[4]

The grassroots gay liberation movement of the 1960s–70s led to an increase in the acceptability of LGBT identities. Yet it was not until this past decade that "having a family" was an option available to lesbian and gay individuals and couples. Policies and laws are now being challenged in the nation's and world's courts because the existing legislation does not accurately represent the needs of LGBT families today. Although there has been progress, there has also been backlash. Laws vary from state to state and county to county. Some courts represent these families fairly, while others persist in denying their legitimacy as well as their very existence.

Because courts have historically been unfair to LGBT persons and families, social scientists have played a major role in building the case that LGBT families are valid and their children are not adversely affected by their upbringing. Over the course of the past 30 years, a number of studies have been conducted by family sociologists, psychologists, and other scholarly researchers. No evidence exists to demonstrate that lesbian and gays are unfit as parents or that their children are psychologically or physically harmed by having lesbian, gay, bisexual, or transgender parents.

What We Know About LGBT Parents and Their Children[5]
What Do LGBT Families Look Like?

Similar to heterosexual families, there is no singular LGBT family form because the makeup of all families varies greatly. Not only do differences exist in terms of family relations, sizes, and forms, there is also diversity in terms of race/ethnicity, socioeconomic status, political affiliation, physical ability, religious tradition, etc. Some examples of LGBT family forms include a gay male couple who foster or adopt one or more children, or a lesbian couple who visit a sperm bank to create a child. Much of the earliest research on LGBT parents and families involved a lesbian woman or gay man who was in a heterosexual marriage. After divorcing (often coinciding with their "coming out"), they negotiated custody with their former spouse. LGBT families also include single gay fathers and single lesbian mothers who are single by choice or after the death of a partner. Some LGBT families consist of combinations of LGBT people who raise children as platonic co-parents. Again, there is no one family form in either heterosexual or LGBT families.

How Many Families Are Headed by LGBT Parent(s)?

There is little consensus among experts as to the prevalence of LGBT parents and their children. Estimates have varied greatly, ranging from 1–20 million children in the United States under the age of 18 who have one or more gay or lesbian parents. An accurate number is, understandably, difficult to calculate. LGBT families are often invisible and for some, it is still unsafe for them to be "out." A widely accepted statistic of 6 million children was first introduced in 1987.[6] While social climate has changed dramatically in nearly two decades, the most frequently cited number has remained static. Most recently, a meta-analysis of 21 existing studies conducted by family sociologists Judith Stacey and Timothy Biblarz explained that 1–12 percent of all children in the U.S. under age 18 have one or more lesbian, gay, or bisexual parents. According to analyses of Census 2000,[7] 1 in 3 lesbian couples and 1 in 5 gay male couples have at least one child under the age of 18 in their household.

What Are the Research Conclusions About LGBT Parents and Their Children?

Historically, assumptions that LGBT parents were unfit threatened their right to raise children. All of the existing social research studies (appearing in rigorously peer reviewed journals such as *Journal of Marriage and the Family, American Journal of Sociology,* and *Child Development,* as outlined in the meta-analyses listed in the Major Research Articles section below) dispute this notion, instead asserting that LGBT individuals and couples are just as fit and effective as heterosexual parents; their children are also just as healthy and well-adjusted as other children. In main aspects, families headed by LGBT individuals and couples show few significant differences from other families. They spend much of their everyday lives engaged in typical parenting activities such as getting the kids ready for school, arranging extra curricular activities, struggling to juggle the demands of work and family life, etc.

An Overview of the Existing Research Indicates That There Are Also No Significant Differences on the Following Dimensions:

- Gay and lesbian parents are comparable to heterosexual parents in the areas of mental health, self-esteem, approaches and skills related to parenting, as well as ability and commitment to parenting.

- Unlike the persistent myths portraying LGBT individuals as sexual predators, they are actually no more likely than heterosexuals to abuse their children.

- Children of LGBT parents are likely to develop gender-roles that are much like those of children raised by heterosexuals, with some exceptions, as explained in "advantages" below.

- Multiple measures of children's psychological well-being and social adjustment (e.g., self-esteem, anxiety, depression, behavioral problems, performance in school and extracurricular activities, IQ, ability to make friends, sociability and quality of relationships with peers and intimates, etc.) indicate no difference compared with their peers.

- Children with lesbian mothers develop closer relationships to their mother's new female partner when compared to the level of closeness that children of single heterosexual mothers report having with their mother's new male partner.

- Lesbian co-parents are more egalitarian in terms of parenting and family responsibilities than are heterosexual couples.

Advantages: Positive Outcomes Experienced by LGBT Parents and Their Children:

- While there is an assumption that children raised by LGBT parents lack relationships and positive role models with adults of a gender other than that of their parent(s), research suggests the contrary. Same sex parents provide their children with a wide array of role models from both genders.

- LGBT parents are somewhat more nurturing and tolerant than heterosexual parents.

- Children of LGBT parent(s) are more openminded, less prejudiced, and express a greater sense of social responsibility than their peers.

- Daughters of lesbian mothers have higher self-esteem and aspire to future careers and occupations outside of those typically considered to be roles for women, such as nursing or teaching. In fact, they are more likely to aspire to be doctors, engineers, and astronauts than are daughters of heterosexual mothers.

- Sons of lesbian mothers are less physically aggressive, more caring, and more capable of communicating their feelings. They have higher levels of self-esteem and aspire to a wider range of career opportunities than do sons of heterosexual mothers.

Challenges Faced by LGBT Parents and Their Children:

- LGBT parents who come out of a heterosexual marriage experience more difficulty arranging custody visits than do heterosexual parents; yet the children benefit from more contact with their non-custodial parent than do children of divorced heterosexual parents.

- Young adults of LGBT parents are more likely to experience stigma from their peers regarding their own sexuality than are the kids of heterosexual parents.

- Current federal and state legislation both in the United States and internationally pose a challenge for many families. See tables below.

- Overcoming legal discrimination and social prejudice are difficulties faced by many LGBT parents and their children. Not only are LGBT families largely culturally invisible, they often struggle to deal with homophobia and heterosexism.

Are Children of LGBT Parents More Likely to Grow Up to Be LGBT Themselves?

Evidence from the existing studies are unclear regarding this question.

- More than 30 published studies that compare the children of LGBT parent(s) with those of heterosexual parents indicate that there are no significant differences in terms of gender identity and sexual orientation (see Johnson & O'Connor 2002, Patterson 1995, and Laird 1993).

- The one study that followed children of LGBT parents until adulthood found no difference in the proportion of those

identifying as LGBT compared to the general population. However, children of lesbian mothers were more likely to have considered the possibility of having a same-sex relationship or to have experienced one (see Golombok and Tasker 1996).

- Children raised in LGBT families express greater openness to homosexuality or bisexuality, reducing risk of denial or self-loathing for those children who may question their sexuality. According to Stacey, "It seems likely that growing up with gay parents should reduce a child's reluctance to acknowledge, accept, or act upon same-sex sexual desires if they experience them. Because the first generation of children parented by self-identified lesbians or gay men is just now reaching adulthood, it is too soon to know if the finding in that one study will prove to be generally true" (Interview with Stacey on *www.lethimstay.com*).

What We Do Not Know About LGBT Parenting and Children

The above reported findings are derived from meta-analyses of more than a hundred studies on LGBT parents and their children by social science scholars (see footnote 5 . . .). The majority of these studies are based on small scale, self-selected, convenience samples. Oftentimes participants are active in LGBT family organizations, resulting in an oversampling of a few children's voices. They are disproportionately urban, white, and affluent. Early research on lesbian and gay parenting emerged in the late 1970s and early 1980s to "test" whether lesbian women or gay men were "fit" parents in custody cases. These studies tended to come from a "deviance" perspective, comparing LGBT families to the assumed heteronormative "ideal." As Stacey and Biblarz explain, "the predominant research designs place the burden of proof on lesbigay parents to demonstrate that they are not less successful or less worthy than heterosexual parents" (2001, 162). Future studies must not assume that differences indicate deficiencies. Additionally, future studies need to examine all types of

LGBT families; the majority of existing studies involve the children of lesbian mothers with few including the children of gay dads. In particular, future studies will need to fill the void by examining families under-represented in the current research, including emerging family formations such as intentional families of lesbian and gay individuals and couples, as well as bisexual and transgender parents. To date, there exists only one longitudinal study and no large-scale surveys. Long term, large-scale qualitative and quantitative research is both costly and time consuming, yet such studies are needed. Finally, we need more research that involves samples that more accurately reflect the diversity of LGBT families in terms of race, ethnicity, income, level of education, and geographic location.

Position Statements of Major Organizations and Associations

For almost 30 years experts and major professional associations have asserted that there is nothing deviant or pathological about LGBT sexual orientations. Recently many researchers, professors, physicians, psychologists and other experts have voiced their support for LGBT parents and families. In the interest of space, only the position statement of the American Psychological Association is included in this factsheet. Other organizations make similar assertions that may be obtained through their websites, as linked below.

American Psychological Association (1976). APA Council of Representatives adopted the following position on parenting: "The sex, gender identity or sexual orientation of natural or prospective adoptive or foster parents should not be the sole or primary variable considered in custody or placement cases." *http://www.apa.org/pi/lgbc/policy/statements.html#2* Child Welfare League of America (1988) *http://www.cwla.org/articles/cv0201gayadopt.htm* American Bar Association (1995) *http://www.abanet.org/leadership/2003/journal/112.pdf* North American Council on Adoptable Children (1998) *http://www.nacac.org/pub_statements.html#gay* American Academy of Pediatrics (2002) *http://*

www.aafp.org/policy/020008.html American Academy of Family Physicians (2002) *http://www.aafp.org/fpr/assembly2002/1017/7.html* American Psychiatric Association (2002) *http:/www.psych.org/archives/200214.pdf* American Psychoanalytic Association (2002) *http://apsa-co.org/ctf/cgli/parenting.htm*

U.S. State Policies & Legislation

Custody and Visitation States that have not been found to discriminate against sexual orientation in custody/visitation rulings: Alaska, California, D.C., Delaware, Illinois, Maine, Maryland, Massachusetts, Minnesota, Nebraska, New Jersey, New Mexico, New York, Ohio, Oklahoma, Oregon, Pennsylvania, Rhode Island, South Carolina, Vermont, Washington, Wisconsin
Adoption: Same-sex States granting same-sex couple adoption: California, D.C., Illinois, Massachusetts, New Jersey, New York, Pennsylvania, Rhode Island, Vermont, Washington, Wisconsin
States recognizing same-sex second parent adoption: California, D.C., Massachusetts, New Jersey, New York, Pennsylvania, Vermont, Wisconsin
States allowing lesbian and gay individuals to adopt: Alaska, California, Colorado, Connecticut, D.C., Delaware, Illinois, Maryland, Massachusetts, Michigan, Minnesota, New Hampshire, New Jersey, New Mexico, New York, Ohio, Oregon, Pennsylvania, Rhode Island, Tennessee, Vermont, Washington, Wisconsin
Compiled from information at HRC FamilyNet at http://www.hrc.org/familynet/parenting_laws.asp. Retrieved October 1, 2003.

International laws

Australia. Many states within Australia have extended legal recognition provided to unmarried opposite sex couples to same-sex couples, though most ban gay/lesbian adoption.

Belgium. In 2003, Belgium began recognizing same-sex couples equally in marriage, but stipulates that only couples from countries that allow same-sex marriages can be married under the law and does not allow same-sex married couples to adopt children together.

Canada. In 2003, Ontario and British Columbia began granting marriage to same-sex couples. All Canadian territories allow gay and lesbian adoption.

Denmark. In 1989, the Danish Parliament approved a law that allows same-sex couples to enter into registered partnerships, granting most of the rights of married couples to same-sex couples and allowing partnership adoption.

Europe. In September 2003, the European Parliament urged the fifteen member countries of the European Union to extend full marriage and adoption rights to same-sex couples.

Germany. On December 1, 2000, the German Parliament began recognizing registered partnership status for same-sex couples, allowing some adoption and joint parenting rights.

Netherlands. In 2001, the Netherlands became the first country to extend marriage rights to same-sex couples and allow two women or two men to jointly adopt a child.

New Zealand. Unmarried same-sex couples can make an individual application to adopt a child but expect a certain level of discrimination.

Norway. Norway has a registered partnership system, but maintains that only married heterosexual couples are permitted to adopt.

South Africa. On September 10, 2003 South Africa became the first African country to let same sex couples legally adopt children.

Sweden. In February 2003 Swedish legislators let same-sex couples who are registered in a legal partnership be joint adoptive parents of children adopted in the country or abroad. One of the partners also is able to adopt the child of another.

Switzerland. Registered partners can receive most benefits available to married couples, but cannot adopt or co-parent.

United Kingdom. The House of Commons passed the Adoption of Children Bill allowing lesbian and gay couples to apply for adoption in 2002.

- *Legal World Survey.* (n.d.). Retrieved on October 1, 2003, from The International Lesbian and Gay Association Web site: *http://www.ilga.org*

- *Laws Worldwide* (n.d.). Retrieved October 1, 2003, from Gay Law Net Web site: *http://www.gaylawnet.com*

- *Annual Report of the European Parliament.*(September 5, 2003). Retrieved October 1, 2003, from the European Parliament Web site: *http://www.europarl.eu.int*

Resources:

There are numerous resources for scholars wishing to study LGBT parenting issues as well as LGBT persons who are or are planning to become parents. Below is a list of major national and international organizations, key research articles, books, websites, films, educational curricula, and other resources such as magazines and family events.

Organizations:

Family Pride Coalition

The mission of the Family Pride Coalition is to advance the well-being of lesbian, gay, bisexual and transgendered parents and their families through mutual support, community collaboration, and public understanding. *http://www.familypride.org, info@familypride.org,* Phone: (202) 331-5015

Children of Lesbians and Gays Everywhere (COLAGE)

COLAGE (Children of Lesbian and Gays Everywhere) is a well-respected and influential youth-led national organization that offers support and activism by and for people with LGBT parents. Our mission is to engage, connect and empower people to make the world a better place for all children of LGBT parents and families. *http://www.colage.org, info@colage.org,* Phone: (415) 861-5437

Our Family Coalition

Our Family Coalition protects the civil rights and well being of families with lesbian, gay, bisexual and transgender members through education, advocacy, social networking and grassroots community organizing. *http://www.ourfamily.org,* Phone: (415) 981-1960

Parents, Families, and Friends of Lesbians and Gays (PFLAG)

PFLAG promotes the health and well-being of gay, lesbian, bisexual and transgendered persons, their families and friends through support to cope with an adverse society, education to enlighten an ill-informed public, and advocacy to end discrimination and to secure equal civil rights. PFLAG provides opportunity for dialogue about sexual orientation and gender identity, and acts to create a society that is healthy and respectful of human diversity. *http://www.pflag.org, info@pflag.org,* Phone: (202) 467-8180

Family Net: Human Flights Campaign (HRC)

HRC Family Net provides information and resources about adoption, civil unions, coming out, custody and visitation, donor insemination, family law, families of origin, marriage, money, parenting, religion, schools, senior health and housing state laws and legislation, straight spouses, transgender and workplace issues. *http://www.hrc.org/familynet/index.asp, familynet@hrc.org,* Phone: (202) 628-4160

National Gay and Lesbian Task Force (NGLTF)

NGLTF is the national progressive organization working for the civil rights of gay, lesbian, bisexual and transgender people, with the vision and commitment to building a powerful political movement. *http://www.ngltf.org, info@ngltf.org,* Phone: (212) 604-9830

American Civil Liberties Union (ACLU), Lesbian & Gay Rights

The American Civil Liberties Union (ACLU) is our nation's guardian of liberty, working daily in courts, legislatures and communities to defend and preserve the individual rights and liberties guaranteed to all people in this country by the Constitution and laws of the U.S. *http://www.aclu.org/LesbianGayRights/ LesbianGayRightsmain.cfm,* Phone: (212) 519-2500

Major Research Articles:

Allen, K. R., Demo, D. H. (1995). "The Families of Lesbians and Gay Men: A New Frontier in Family Research," *Journal of Marriage and the Family,* 57: 111–127.

Allen, Mike and Nancy Burrell. (1996). "Comparing the Impact of Homosexual and Heterosexual Parents on Children: Meta-Analysis of Existing Research." *Journal of Homosexuality* 32: 19–35.

Bozett, F. W. (ed.) (1987). *Gay and Lesbian Parents.* New York: Praeger.

Golombok, Susan and Fiona Tasker. (1996). "Do Parents Influence the Sexual Orientation of Their Children? Findings From a Longitudinal Study of Lesbian Families." *Developmental Psychology* 32: 3–11.

Johnson, Suzanne M. and Elizabeth O'Connor. (2002). *The Gay Baby Boom: The Psychology of Gay Parenthood.* New York: New York University Press.

Laird, Joan. (1993). "Lesbian and Gay Families." In *Normal Family Processes* 2nd ed., edited by F. Walsh. New York: Guilford Press.

Patterson, C. J. (1995). "Summary of research findings." In *Lesbian and Gay Parenting: A Resource for Psychologists* (pp. 1–12). Washington, D.C.: American Psychological Association. Retrieved October 1, 2003, from the American Psychological Association, Public Interest Dictorate Web site: *http://www.apa.org/pi/parent.html*

Patterson, Charlotte J. and Lisa V. Freil. 2000. "Sexual Orientation and Fertility." In *Infertility in the Modern: World-Biosocial Perspectives,* edited by G. Bentley and N. Mascie-Taylor. Cambridge, England: Cambridge University Press.

Stacey, Judith. (2003). "Gay and Lesbian Families: Queer like Us" in Mason, Skolink, and Sugarman, eds., *All Our Families: New Policies for a New Century.* Oxford: Oxford University Press.

Stacey, Judith and Timothy Biblarz. (April 2001). (How) Does the Sexual Orientation of Parents Matter? *American Sociological Review,* 66: 159–183 *http://www.asanet.org/pubs/stacey.pdf*

Why it's Wrong: The Social Science Case, A Conversation with Professor Judith Stacey. Retrieved October 1, 2003, from the ACLU Lesbian & Gay Rights Project, Let Him Stay Web site: *http://www.lethimstay.com/ wrong_socscience_expert.html*

Books about LGBT Families and Parenting:

Andrews, Nancy. (1994). *Family: A Portrait of Gay and Lesbian America.* San Francisco: Harper Collins.

Bernstein, Mary. (2001). *Queer Families, Queer Politics.* New York: Columbia University Press.

Boenke, Mary, ed. (1999). *Trans Forming Families—Real Stories about Transgendered Loved One.* New Castle: Oak Knoll Press.

Carrington, Christopher. (1999). *No Place Like Home: Relationships and Family Life among Lesbians and Gay Men.* Chicago: University of Chicago Press.

Drucker, Jane and Howard Schulweis. (2001). *Lesbian and Gay Families Speak Out: Understanding the Joys and Challenges of Diverse Family Life.* Boulder, CO: Perseus Publishing.

Galluccio, Jon. (2001). *An American Family.* New York: St. Martin's Press.

Garner, Abigail. (2004). *Families Like Mine: Children of Gay Parents Tell It Like It Is.* New York: Harper Collins.

Gillespie, Peggy, ed. (1999). *Love Makes a Family: Portraits of Lesbian, Gay, Bisexual, and Transgender Parents and Their Families.* Amherst: University of Massachusetts Press.

Green, Jesse. (1998). *The Velveteen Father.* New York: Ballantine Books.

Howey, Noelle and Ellen Samuels, eds. (2000). *Out of the Ordinary: Essays on Growing Up with Gay, Lesbian, and Trans-gender Parents.* New York: St Martin's Press.

Lehr, Valerie. (1999). *Queer Family Values: Debunking the Myth of the Nuclear Family (Queer Politics, Queer Theories)*. Philadelphia: Temple Press University.

Moraga, Cherie. (1997). *Waiting in the Wings: Portrait of a Queer Motherhood*. Ann Arbor: Firebrand Books.

Savage, Dan. (2000). *The Kid: What Happened After My Boyfriend and I Decided to Go Get Pregnant: An Adoption Story*. New York: Plume.

Stacey, Judith. (1990). *Brave New Families: Stories of Domestic Upheaval in Late-Twentieth-Century America*. Berkeley: University of California Press.

Sullivan, Richard T., ed. (1999). *Queer Families, Common Agendas: Gay People, Lesbians, and Family Values*. San Francisco: Haworth Press Inc.

Weston, Kath. (1997). *Families We Choose*. New York: Columbia University Press.

Willhoite, Michael. (1999). *Daddy's Roommate*. Los Angeles: Alyson Books.

Websites:

In addition to the websites, of the organizations mentioned above there are other sites on the internet that provide much important information and resources and are a place for members of LGBT families to connect.

ProudParenting.com serves as an online portal for gay, lesbian, bisexual and transgender parents and their families worldwide.

FamiliesLikeMine.com a web site dedicated to decreasing isolation for people who have parents who are LGBT, and bringing voice to the experiences of these families. This site was created by Abigail Gainer, a lifetime advocate for LGBT families because she comes from one herself.

ACLU's "Let Him Stay" a web site of the ACLU Lesbian & Gay Rights Project is a resource for LGBT parents and families who experience anti-gay discrimination and provides extensive information about the legal, social science, and public policy cases in support of LGBT parenting. *http://www.lethimstay.com/wrong_socscience__expert.html*

TheGaybyBoom.com a network to help LGBT persons find resources and professionals for family planning and family-living.

Parents Place on gay.com *http://content.gay.com/channels/home/parents*

Transfamily *http://www.transfamily.org*

Transparentcy *http://www.geocities.com/transparentcy*

Videos:

Daddy & [Papa] Exploring the growing phenomenon of gay fatherhood and its impact on American culture. *http://www.daddyandpapa.com*

Our House: A very real documentary about kids of gay and lesbian parents. Our House is the first national television documentary about kids of lesbian and gay parents. It profiles the children of five different families in a frank exploration of what it means to grow up with gay or lesbian parents. Produced and directed by Meema Spadola, daughter of a lesbian mom. *http://www.sugarpictures.com/Films/OurHouse.html*

No Dumb Questions: A documentary about three sisters and their transgendered aunt. *http://www.nodumbquestions.com*

Both of My Moms' Names Are Judy: Children of Lesbians and Gays Speak Out, produced by The Lesbian and Gay Parents Association, presents a diverse group of children (ages 7–11) who have lesbian and gay parents. In candid interviews, they talk about who's in their families, how it feels to be teased about their parents, how classroom silence about homosexuality affects them, and what they would like to see change. Phone (415) 387-9336 or e-mail *lgpasf@aol.com* for more information.

Educational curricula about diverse families: That's a Family. *http://www.womedia.org/press/kits/taf_kit.html*

Challenging Homophobia in Schools: A K–12 Resource, by the Gay and Lesbian Educators. K–12 resources for educators, counselors and administrators to aid in the support of, and education about, lesbian, gay; bisexual, and transgender youth and families. *http://www.galebc.org*

Opening Doors: Education Issues for LGBT Parents, By the Education Committee of Family Pride Coalition *http://www.familypride.org/store/commerce.cgi?product=new%20schools*

Talking to Children About Our Families, By Margie Brickley and Aimee Gelnaw for the Family Pride Coalition *http://www.hrc.org/familynet/documents/2c19b.pdf*

Other:
Magazines:

And Baby *http://www.andbabymag.com/*

In the Family *http://www.inthefamily.com/*

Gay Parent magazine *http://www.gayparentmag.com*

Family Week *http://www.familypride.org/events/familyweek2003.htm*

Summer Camps for Kids With LGBT Parents and LGBT Families:

http://www.colage.org/summer_camps.html

Art Exhibit:

Love Makes a Family
The photo-text exhibit celebrates families of every kind, including adoptive families, foster families, multiracial families, physically challenged families, lesbian and gay parented families, inter-faith families, multi-generational families and more. *http://www.lovemakesafamily.org/*

Book Publishing:

Two Lives Press
Two Lives is a complete resource center for lesbian, gay, bisexual and transgendered parents and their children. Our mission is to publish quality books for children in alternative families and to provide

information to the LGBT family community through our Web site. *http://www.twolives.com/*

Notes

1. Simmons, Tavia and Grade O'Neill "Households and Families: 2000." U.S. Census Bureau, Washington, DC, *www.census.gov*, September 2001. p. 4. *http://www.census.gov/prod/2001pubs/c2kbr01-8.pdf*

2. Salholz, Eloise. (1990, March 12). "The Future of Gay America." *Newsweek*, 23.

3. "Alternative families" is limiting because it presumes that research will be presented in a defensive stance, setting heterosexual families as the standard to which LGBT parents and their children should be compared. "Same-sex parents" is problematic because it excludes a significant population of LGBT parents, specifically lesbian mothers or gay fathers who are single by choice or circumstance, as well as combinations of gay men and lesbian women who are co-parenting together.

4. See Stacey, 2003, 143.

5. The findings reported in this fact sheet were obtained from meta-analyses of psychological and sociological studies published in respected, peer-reviewed academic journals. The earliest such meta-analyses appeared almost 20 years ago, in 1985 by Bozett. Currently, Patterson is working on an updated review of the literature, forthcoming later this year. A list of the meta-analyses, major reviews of the literature, and other key articles are listed in the "major research articles" section of this factsheet.

6. "ABA Annual Meeting Provides Forum for Family Law Experts." (August 25, 1987). 13 Family Law Report (BNA) 1512.

7. Simmons, Tavia and O'Connell, Martin. "Married-Couple and Unmarried-Partner Households: 2000." U.S. Census Bureau. Washington, DC, *www.census.gov*, February 2003. p. 10. *http://www.census.gov/prod/2003pubs/censr-5.pdf*.

Discussion Questions

1. If you were a social worker making a recommendation about whether a certain couple were suitable foster or adoptive parents, what factors would you consider? Would the sexual orientation of the couple be one of those factors? Why (not)?

2. Look at the research findings about LGBT families reported in this fact sheet. Which ones surprised you or seemed counter-intuitive to you? Why?

3. Think about the diversity of families. Joos reports that most of the research is based on data collected from urban families that are White and affluent. Would you expect the findings to be different if we had data on different kinds of families? Joos does not discuss lesbian and gay households separately except to report that fewer gay men than lesbians are raising children. Would you expect differences in same-sex families depending on the sex of the parents?

4. Check out at least one of the resource websites Joos lists or read one of the research articles she cites. Write a brief statement about what you learned and note anything that surprised you.

62
Color-Blind Racism and Post-Feminism

The Contemporary Politics of Inequality

Abby L. Ferber

Abby Ferber opens her article "Color-Blind Racism and Post-Feminism: The Contemporary Politics of Inequality" by positing a fundamental paradox within American culture—we are a people who believe in equality and "liberty and justice for all"; yet we are still in a land where racial and gender inequality are far from being footnotes in our "land of opportunity" gilded history books. In fact, Ferber suggests, although the civil rights and the women's liberation movements resulted in positive strides, people of color and women in America today still continue to face contemporary discrimination. Like Bonilla-Silva and DiTomaso in this volume, Ferber states clearly for her readers that the general American public firmly denies the existence of contemporary racial discrimination with subtle rhetoric designed to minimize the realities still faced by people of color. Moreover, she insists that public discourse also denies the realities of gender discrimination by fixating on a supposed dawn of equal rights for women. Ferber, then, takes two paradigms on inequality—"color-blind racism" and "post-feminism"—finding the common ground in each and exploring their intersectional overlap in terms of gender, race, and class.

Ferber begins by reminding her readers of the entrenched levels of gendered and racial inequality she finds in the United States. She starts by mapping disturbing statistics on rape and unpaid domestic labor, on the wage gap, domestic violence, and homicide. These are the gendered litany that American women continue to face, Ferber insists. She then looks at the landscape of racial inequality in America. This place is dotted with poverty, incredibly low net wealth, unemployment, and low wages, as well as appalling levels of discrimination in healthcare, housing, educational institutions, and the list goes on and on. Ferber follows up these findings with a disturbing discussion of White perceptions that indicate gross ignorance with regard to the working lives of people of color—Whites believe that Whites will be the victims of job discrimination; however, it is Blacks who experience job discrimination in reality. In this segregated landscape, Ferber tells us, few Whites even come into contact with Blacks.

It is from this platform that Ferber frames her central theoretical paradigms. She first defines color-blind racism in the terms used by Bonilla-Silva in this volume, which are laced with abstract liberalism and naturalization, as well as cultural racism and minimization of racism, among other tenets of this concept. From the standpoint of color-blind racism, racial discrimination is a thing of the past in the wake of legal advances—now people naturally live in segregated neighborhoods, Blacks and Latinos/as fail to succeed because they lack a work ethic, and people of color need to stop their whining and get over the chips on their shoulders. Second, Ferber defines post-feminism as an alleged time of equal rights for women, necessitating no more concerns about discrimination along gender lines. Ferber then takes Bonilla-Silva's four ideological elements for color-blind racism and demonstrates how these same elements are used to justify gender inequality. From the standpoint of post-feminism, sexism is a thing of the past since women choose to work part-time for low wages, have equal job opportunities by law, are just naturally more likely to be home taking care of children or to take on nurturing jobs, and, of course, are naturally more likely to be less competitive than men. Never mind that women have similar skills and levels of education; they are relegated to the "pink-collar" via some alleged women's culture.

Interestingly, Ferber notes, both color-blind racism and post-feminism, have emerged in a time of backlash in response to real or imag-

ined advancement by people of color as well as women. And both, she suggests, act as a defense of the "culture of privilege" for Whites and men who seek to preserve their dominance along racial, gender, and class lines.

Finally, Ferber stresses that to deal with such ideologies—color-blind racism and post-feminism—we must espouse an intersectional approach. That is, the discourses of each ideology overlap along race, gender, and class lines and underscore the common ground of oppression.

The Reality of Inequality

I have long been interested in understanding the paradox of widespread race and gender inequality in this land supposedly dedicated to equality. Although the U.S. is supposed to be the home of opportunity for all, we have far to go to achieve that dream. The civil rights and women's movements have made great strides in advancing equality under the law; however, the reality remains that women and people of color face ongoing discrimination and oppression. In this chapter, I examine two recent ideologies that have sprung up to justify and rationalize this inequality: color-blind racism and post-feminism. These two perspectives have been explored in detail by many scholars; however, I argue that we should not continue to explore them in isolation from each other but, instead, embrace an intersectional approach and examine the ways in which they interact and reinforce one another. These two ideologies work together, and we need to address both at the same time if we are to advance the cause of social justice.

Before focusing on these ideologies, it is important to keep in mind that both gender and racial oppression remain entrenched in the United States. Women face terrifying levels of violence: Between 24–45 percent of women in the United States have been raped or the victim of attempted rape. A woman is battered every 15 seconds in the United States, and the number one cause of injury to women in the United States is domestic violence. One-third of all females who are murdered are killed by their husbands or boyfriends, and murder is the leading cause of death for pregnant women (Kimmel 2000; Women's Action Coalition 1993). Half of all homeless women and children are homeless because they are fleeing domestic violence. At home, women continue to perform the vast majority of unpaid domestic labor (see for example, Aguirre and Baker 2000; Freedman 2002; Hammer 2002; Women's Action Coalition 1993). Further, women on average earn only 73 percent of what men earn, and in many occupations, the wage gap has widened in recent years (Armas 2003). Around the world, rural women own only 1 percent of all land but head 25 percent of all households. Sex trafficking, quickly becoming the world's largest growth industry, has been dubbed "the slavery of the twenty-first century" by the *New York Times* (Kristof 2005).

Looking at racial inequality, the landscape is just as dismal. Blacks and dark-skinned racial minorities are three times more likely to be poor than whites, earn 40 percent less than whites, and have one-tenth the net wealth of whites (Bonilla-Silva 2003). Even with the exact same levels of education, people of color are much more likely to face unemployment and lower wages than whites. Sociologist Joe Feagin has meticulously documented ongoing discrimination in health care, the criminal justice system, housing, educational institutions, insurance industries, employment (including hiring, career advancement, and pay), and in other institutions, leading him to conclude that "being black means living with racial oppression from cradle to grave" (Feagin 2001, 173; Feagin, Vera, and Batur 2001).

Law professor Patricia Williams muses, "How can it be that so many well-meaning white people have never thought about race when so few blacks pass a single day without being reminded of it?" (Williams 1997, 28). The answer, I believe, is that few people of privilege realize the extent to which inequality is still pervasive. It is not uncommon to hear people argue that "if blacks and other minorities would just stop thinking about the past, work hard, and complain less (particularly about racial discrimination), then

Americans of all hues could 'all just get along'" (Bonilla-Silva 2003, 1).

Many white people believe that discrimination against people of color is a thing of the past. For example, white people generally believe that whites are actually more likely to face job discrimination than people of color. When asked whether African-Americans or whites were at greater risk of discrimination at work, respondents named whites twice as often; and two-thirds to four-fifths of whites surveyed thought it likely that less qualified African Americans won jobs or promotions over more qualified whites. The *reality*, however, is that few whites experience job discrimination. Only 5–12 percent of whites actually believe their race has cost them a job or promotion, compared with 36 percent of African Americans. Further, studies of discrimination complaints filed with the EEOC find that less than 2 percent of all cases reaching the courts charge reverse discrimination, and almost all end up dismissed by the courts for lack of merit (Pincus 2003; Reskin 1998).

Segregated housing and increasingly segregated schools result in many white people having very little opportunity to get to know people of color in their daily lives. Only 2 percent of white people have a black neighbor (Williams 1997). The images we see on television and in the movie theaters are too often the *only* images we have of people different from ourselves.

Color-Blind Racism and Post-Feminism

Ignorance thus remains a serious threat to continued progress. Too many people believe these problems have been solved and are behind us. In terms of race, sociologists and other scholars have labeled this phenomenon "*color-blind racism*." Color-blind racism is a recent phenomenon that denies the reality of race and racial inequality in American life.

According to sociologist Eduardo Bonilla-Silva (2003), color-blind racism consists of four ideological elements:

1. *Abstract liberalism* weds political liberalism (such as the ideal of equal opportunity, the belief that progress can be secured through legislative and public policy changes) to economic liberalism (the ideology that sees individuals as free, rational human beings, making their own choices, unfettered by the social world around them). According to this philosophy, legal changes have already been made, discriminatory practices are now against the law, and all people have equal opportunity to succeed. Therefore, if anyone is not successful, it is a result of their own poor choices (sociologists call this blaming the victim).

2. *Naturalization* justifies racial processes as naturally occurring rather than the product of social forces. For example, from this perspective, people simply *choose* to live near, work with, and marry people of the same race.

3. *Cultural racism* argues that it is not racism but cultural differences between racial groups that explain inequality. For example, the myth that blacks and Latina/os do not value education and hard work is often offered to explain inequality in the workplace.

4. *Minimization of racism* defines discrimination as a thing of the past (in other words, get over it!).

Just how widespread are these views? According to the National Opinion Research Center, over half of white respondents believe that blacks are more likely to prefer to live on welfare than support themselves. "A majority of whites still stereotype black people as violence-prone, inclined to live on welfare, and disinclined to hard work, and a substantial majority still stereotype black Americans as unintelligent" (Feagin, Vera and Batur 2001, 188).

I have found the concept of color-blind racism extremely useful for understanding the predominant ways we approach race and race relations today. However, this approach is not limited to our understanding of race. Indeed, I find the current discourses on gender are remarkably similar.

Many gender scholars have observed a shift in the ways in which we talk about gender and feminism. It is common today for journalists and conservative commentators to argue that we have moved beyond the need for feminism and have entered the "post-feminist" phase (see for example, Sommers 1994; Paglia 1994; Rogers and Garrett 2002). According to the advocates of post-feminism, men and women now have equal opportunities. The first and second phases of the women's movement accomplished their goals: Women now have the right to vote, are protected from discrimination, and have the same rights as men. For example, women can no longer legally be excluded from occupations simply because they are women, fired because they get pregnant, or denied credit cards and home loans in their own names. Some commentators even argue that the push for equality has gone too far, arguing that men are now victims of feminist frenzy. Just as the advocates of color-blind racism believe that racial inequality is a thing of the past, and that further attempts to remedy inequality lead to "reverse discrimination" against whites, we see similar arguments about gender.

It is true that legislative and policy reforms have contributed to greater equality for women. While we certainly should not underestimate the significance of these monumental accomplishments, we are still a far way off from saying that the problem of gender inequality has been solved, and the discourse of post-feminism threatens further progress.

The four frames of color-blind ideology also operate to justify gender oppression. Abstract liberalism works to argue that women's status today is a product of their own choices. We are told that more women simply choose to work temporary or part time jobs, or choose less demanding careers so that they can spend more time with their children. Women have the same opportunities as men, by law, and therefore, if women are more likely to be found in low-paying, part-time jobs, it must be because of their own choosing.

Naturalization works in much the same way. Job segregation and the persistent wage gap are explained away with the argument that women are just naturally better caretakers and thus more likely to be found in the home, responsible for childcare and housework. Further, as an extension of women's caregiving natures, they are more likely to pursue careers in nursing, teaching, day care, or social work than men, knowing that these jobs pay significantly less compared with male careers requiring similar skills and education levels. Cultural differences are also invoked to rationalize gender inequality. Men and women are seen as partaking in two separate cultures: women's culture is caring, altruistic, peaceful, and values connections to others; men's is aggressive, individualistic, and profit-oriented, we are told.

Lastly, post-feminism also minimizes discrimination and sexism, dismissing them as a thing of the past. Any differences between men and women today are seen as a result of men's and women's different natures, and the choices men and women make. Both color-blind racism and post-feminism are inherently unsociological, ignoring the vast body of literature that examines the ways in which the social institutions of schooling, work, and the family (to name but a few) shape and constrain all of our choices and opportunities (a few good examples include Crittenden 2001; Lewis 2003; Van Ausdale and Feagin 2001).

Backlash and the Justification of Inequality

Both color-blind ideology and post-feminism lead to the conclusion that "we've done all we can; that's just the way it is." We should stop trying to change people's seemingly "essential" natures.

Both of these perspectives need to be examined within a broader framework of political backlash against the social movements of the 1960s and 1970s, including the women's, civil rights, and gay and lesbian movements, which challenge longstanding inequalities.

According to Coppock, Haydon, and Richter, "the proclamation of 'post-feminism' has occurred at precisely the same moment as acclaimed feminist studies demonstrate that not only have women's real advancements been limited, but also that there has been a backlash against feminism of international significance" (Coppock, Haydon, and Richter 1995, 3). The concept of post-feminism itself is part of this backlash, levied to argue that feminism is no longer necessary and to dismiss contemporary feminists as radical man-haters, without considering the scholarship and research that continues to document widespread discrimination, violence, and inequality.

Similarly, Bonilla-Silva argues that color-blind racism "has become a formidable political tool for the maintenance of the racial order [serving] as the ideological armor for a covert and institutionalized system [of racial oppression] in the post-Civil Rights era." Bonilla-Silva 2003, 3). Both post-feminism and color-blind racism are part of the defense of a culture of privilege I have described elsewhere (Ferber 2003). This culture of privilege seeks to naturalize inequality and preserve race, gender, and class privilege. In an era where inequality has been interrogated and policies implemented to attempt to level the playing field, many people feel their privileged positions are being threatened. Numerous white supremacist and men's rights organizations have recruited disgruntled white men who feel under attack. This perspective is extremely harmful and distorts the reality of race and gender relations today. It should not be surprising, however, that many people embrace this view, relieved of any guilt or responsibility and comforted by its justification of inequality.

An Intersectional Approach

If we are to understand and respond to these ideologies, we must embrace an intersectional approach, which examines the overlap and interconnections among discourses of race, gender, and class. Color-blind racism and post-feminism are two sides of the same coin, and focusing on only one or the other seriously limits the extent to which we can successfully argue against these distortions of the reality of inequality.

It is time that anti-racist scholars and activists and feminist scholars and activists joined forces. So long as either color-blind racism or post-feminism remains intact, it will be used to support the other. For example, the belief that legal obstacles to equality

have been removed is used to justify *both* race and gender inequality today as the product of the poor choices of individuals, rather than a system of institutionalized oppression. When we hear the very same arguments offered to explain both racial and gender inequality, it gives them more legitimacy; the more familiar the arguments are, the more they feel intuitively right to people.

Not only do these two ideologies work to simultaneously support each, neither can be fully understood alone. For example, in my research on the white supremacist movement, I have found that the naturalization of gender differences is frequently used to justify the naturalization of racial differences, and vice versa. White supremacist authors argue that one reason the white race is superior is *because* of the unparalleled beauty of its women. On the other hand, they argue for the superiority of men over women, because women are the breeders of the race, whose reproductive capacities *must* be controlled by men. They embrace both racial and gender hierarchies to argue for the inherent superiority of white men (Ferber 1998; 2004). Neither race nor gender ideologies can be fully understood in isolation from the other.

We need to understand post-feminism and color-blind racism not only in relation to each other but also as two strands of a broader, comprehensive ideology explaining away inequality and trying to justify oppression and privilege. They are both part and parcel of a broad ideology of backlash that reinforces the belief that the United States is a meritocracy, where all people have equal opportunities to succeed and achieve the American dream. If we simply work hard, we will succeed, or so we are told. This perspective justifies and reinforces *class* inequality as well. As Gregory Mantsios argues, class is perhaps the most invisible axis of inequality in the United States (Mantsios 2003). Once we shift our focus to the broader ideology itself, and examine the many ways in which it manifests itself, we can see the ways in which it is used to justify many different forms of inequality and is not limited to just race or gender.

It is only by adopting an intersectional approach, which examines the ways in which race, gender, and other systems of inequality interact and intersect, as part of what Patricia Hill Collins calls a "matrix of privilege and oppression," that we can fully comprehend and work to develop successful strategies for combating any and all forms of oppression (Collins 2003).

References

Aguirre Jr., Adalberto, and David V. Baker. 2000. *Structured inequality in the United States.* Upper Saddle River, NJ: Prentice Hall.

Armas, Genaro C. 2003. "Women in top jobs, but not for top pay." *Denver Post.* March 25.

Bonilla-Silva, Eduardo. 2003. *Racism without racists: Color-blind racism and the persistence of racial inequality in the United States.* Lanham, MD: Rowman and Littlefield.

Collins, Patricia Hill. 2003. "Toward a new vision." In *Privilege: A reader*, pp. 331–348. Boulder, CO: Westview.

Coppock, Vicki, Deena Haydon, and Ingrid Richter. 1995. *The illusions of 'Post-feminism.'* London: Taylor and Francis.

Crittenden, Ann. 2001. *The price of motherhood: Why the most important job in the world is still the least valued.* New York: Henry Holt.

Feagin, Joe R. 2001. *Racist America: Roots, current realities, and future reparations.* New York: Routledge.

Feagin, Joe R., Hernán Vera, and Pinar Batur. 2001. *White racism*, 2nd ed. New York: Routledge.

Ferber, Abby L. 1998. *White man falling: Race, gender, and white supremacy.* Lanham, MD: Rowman and Littlefield.

——. 2003. "Defending the culture of privilege." In *Privilege: A reader*, pp. 319–330. Boulder, CO: Westview.

——. 2004. *Home-grown hate: Gender and organized racism.* New York: Routledge.

Freedman, Estelle B. 2002. *No turning back: The history of feminism and the future of women.* New York: Ballantine Books.

Hammer, Rhonda. 2002. *Antifeminism and family terrorism: A critical feminist perspective.* Lanham, MD: Rowman and Littlefield.

Kimmel, Michael S. 2000. *The gendered society.* Oxford: Oxford University Press.

Kristof, Nicholas D. 2005. "Cambodia, where sex traffickers are king." *New York Times.* Section A, page 15. January 15.

Lewis, Amanda. 2003. *Race in the schoolyard: Negotiating the color line in classrooms and communities.* New Brunswick, NJ: Rutgers University Press.

Mantsios, Gregory. 2003. "Class in America." In *Privilege: A reader*, pp. 33–50. Boulder, CO: Westview.

Paglia, Camille. 1994. *Vamps and tramps: New essays.* New York: Vintage.

Pincus, Fred L. 2003. *Reverse discrimination: Dismantling the myth.* Boulder, CO: Lynne Rienner.

Reskin, Barbara. 1998. *The realities of affirmative action in employment.* Washington, DC: American Sociological Association.

Rogers, Mary F., and C. D. Garrett. 2002. *Who's afraid of women's studies? Feminism in everyday life.* Walnut Creek, CA: Alta Mira Press.

Sommers, Christina Hoff. 1994. *Who stole feminism? How women have betrayed women.* New York: Touchstone.

Van Ausdale, Debra, and Joe R. Feagin. 2001. *The first R: How children learn race and racism.* 2001. Lanham, MD: Rowman and Littlefield.

Williams, Patricia. 1997. *Seeing a color-blind future: The paradox of race.* New York: Noonday Press.

Women's Action Coalition. 1993. *WAC stats: The facts about women.* New York: The New Press.

Discussion Questions

1. You have already been introduced to the concept of "color-blind racism" if you had a chance to read the Bonilla-Silva article in this volume. What do you think of the concept of post-feminism? Do you think it is a fair approach to describing gender relations in the U.S.? Why or why not?

2. Although color-blind racism deals with race and post-feminism deals with gender, neither of these terms deals specifically with issues for women of color whose experiences straddle these two worlds. If we were to add issues for women of color to Ferber's paradigm, what ideological term might best fit their experience of multiple oppressions?

3. Do you think systematic racism and sexism still exist? Why or why not?

4. Does Ferber's article resonate with your own personal experience? If so, how or how not?

63
Systems of Oppression
Ten Principles

Vasilikie Demos
Anthony J. Lemelle, Jr.
with Solomon Gashaw

In this essay, which is based on materials being developed for a forthcoming book, Vasilikie Demos and Anthony J. Lemelle, Jr., in collaboration with Solomon Gashaw, enumerate ten principles that characterize any System of Oppression (SOP). These authors recognize that Americans and those who come to our shores from other lands share the American Dream of social mobility. They also recognize that there are structural barriers that keep some people from realizing the Dream. As their simple but elegant diagram shows, society is stratified in multiple ways, most especially by race, class, gender, and sexuality. Principles of oppression operate to limit the options of people who are poor, people of color, women, and sexual minorities. Yet, as we see here and in other readings, these oppressed social categories are not homogeneous and members of them are not without agency. They can and do act individually and collectively to alter their situations.

This essay states in the relatively abstract language of sociological theory what most of the others in the volume have shown. Oppression is not something that occurs naturally or by chance. It is socially constructed, historically rooted, based on the unequal distribution of power, and supported by ideology. It is at once pervasive, invisible, and dynamic. SOPs are jointly maintained by the oppressors and the oppressed and they intersect so that they can only be separated for purposes of analysis. Rather than attempt to spell out the dynamics of each principle fully in a few pages, the au-

thors provide definitions and illustrations to help readers understand and think about each of the ten principles. They show how oppression can take the form of unspeakably horrible acts such as lynching and seemingly trivial acts such as telling sexual jokes among friends. They show how SOPs are reinforced by institutions such as the media and religion and how they can be resisted by the use of language that affirms what others deride, as in the slogan "Black Is Beautiful."

Many people place the blame for their plight on those who fail to get ahead, who work all their lives at minimum wage jobs or are forced to rely on public assistance. They point to others who have gone if not from rags to riches, at least from near poverty to relative comfort. They advocate one-step solutions such as getting a job—any job—or claim to be color-blind and admonish others to be as well. This essay suggests that oppression is real, systematic, and deeply rooted in our social structure. If that is the case, it will take more than workfare programs or not caring what color a person is to end oppression. It will take societal action that addresses and engages multiple institutions. At the same time, because both oppressor and oppressed participate in SOPs, it will also require individuals to participate in various forms of social action or what Gilkes (see Section 6) calls "community work."

"You have been with me a week, Arthur," he said. "Yes, sir," said Dodger, looking up inquiringly. "I hope you are satisfied with me?" "Yes, I think I may say I am. You don't seem to be afraid of work." Dodger felt proud of his success, and put away the fifteen dollars with a feeling of satisfaction. He found that he could live for eight dollars a week, and he began to lay by seven dollars a week with the view of securing funds sufficient to take him back to New York. (Alger n.d.; Kanfer 2000)

The "American Dream" is deeply embedded in American culture. Although variously envisioned from the nineteenth to the twenty-first centuries, the dream has remained essentially the same: In America, through hard work, honesty, sacrifice, and persistence, a person from the lowest rungs of society can individually earn her or his way to prosperity and well-being. According to the dream, failure to succeed and prosper in the United States is the fault of the individual, and poor people are viewed as too lazy to better themselves.

The American Dream is easy for many, especially the privileged, to comprehend. Everyone knows someone who has "made it." They can point to the individual born a child of poverty who worked her way through college attending classes at night and who is now a successful attorney with a six-figure income, or to the hip hop artist who came out of the projects and through sheer perseverance is now an international star, or to the immigrant who began selling hot dogs on the street and is now a multimillionaire.

What is often difficult to understand is how people can work two and three jobs, and still remain unable to get ahead. How can some individuals realize the American Dream and many more not? We acknowledge that people have the potential to change their circumstances for the better, that, for example, by taking one's education seriously, studying hard, and obtaining a college or university degree, one can advance oneself materially. We acknowledge that some individuals are born with unusual talent or are born into families with contacts or wealth.

Such people can work hard with talent or networks and move from their status of origin to higher positions in society. The American Dream of success is possible. It is a reality that attracts immigrants from all over the world to the United States.

There is, however, another reality that operates alongside the American Dream. This is a structural reality. It is that reality that we call a "system of oppression" (SOP), a reality that explains why certain types of people are better able to realize the American Dream than other types. We have identified ten SOP principles that provide an understanding of social structural differences in peoples' well-being. By so doing, we are also identifying the fault lines of an SOP, and possibilities for human agency. We maintain there are actual social structural barriers to some peoples' striving for success, but we also maintain that individuals are not completely powerless and that people can and do resist structural impediments, sometimes with relative success. Figure 63.1 is a graphic representation of our conceptualized logic.

We begin with a discussion of the contemporary study of social inequality and the place of an SOP in that study. This is followed by a discussion of the ten SOP principles.

Figure 63.1
Conceptualization of a System of Oppression (SOP)

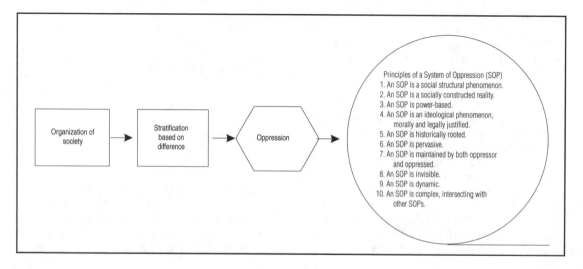

Social Stratification and SOP

Traditionally, the concepts of "class," "status," and "party" have been the lynchpins of social stratification research, but in the last fifteen to twenty years, a major change has occurred in the area of social stratification or structured social inequality. For many contemporary scholars (Andersen and Collins 2004; Brewer 1996; Feagin and Vera 2001; Glenn 2002; Kuumba and Ajanaku 1996; Lemelle 1995; Omi and Winant 1994; Romero 1992), "class" remains an important concept. The concepts of "status" and "party" are less important than are those of "race," "gender," and "sexuality."

Studies of class, race, gender, and sexuality as single dimensions of stratification or as intersecting ones have proliferated to the degree that we know a great deal about these bases of social inequality. We are at a point where it is feasible and helpful to develop a synthesis of our knowledge. The ten SOP principles we identify are derived from this new body of work. We use the term SOP to discuss the "basic four" dimensions of inequality because we believe they most accurately convey the "sense" of the research.

We look to Marilyn Frye's (2004) classic article on oppression for our understanding of the term SOP. Frye makes two critical points relevant to our own thinking. First, she explains that *oppression* means to "press" (2004, 175). It is a force outside the individual and requires resistance if it is to be offset. Second, though Frye's main concern is with the concept of oppression, through the metaphor of the bird cage she provides an understanding of oppression as a system as well as an understanding of why oppression is difficult to see. She points out that when one comes very close to the bird cage and sees only one of the wires, it is difficult to understand why the bird cannot escape. One understands why the bird cannot fly out by moving further away and by seeing the crisscrossing of wires as a "unitary whole" that is, after all, a cage.

Ten SOP Principles

(1) *An SOP is a social structural phenomenon.* As a social structure, an SOP consists of a stable set of social relationships. It is organized by rules of rights and obligations that are expected as normal lines of behavior in social situations. An SOP is characterized by institutionalized relations from the micro level of individuals interacting with other individuals to the macro level of public policies and societal practices.

In the United States, the distribution of people among institutions of higher education fall into a very clear socioeconomic pattern with the upper class disproportionately represented in the Ivy League, and the lower classes disproportionately represented in community colleges. Because education is a major vehicle for upward mobility, unequal access to institutions of higher learning constitutes a systemic barrier to the poor. It is an example of how class systematically limits the life chances of some people and facilitates the life chances of others. Indeed, some social scientists (Luttrell 2003; Bowles and Gintis 1976) observe that education in America operates to maintain social inequality as it reproduces it.

(2) *An SOP is a socially constructed reality.* The norms, laws, and formal policies of a society are developed by human beings. When individuals join together as members of a group to develop public and social policies, they are often selected for group membership based upon their experience and work with the group's issue. Often individuals are asked to work with groups based upon their mindset, worldview, or value commitments. In bureaucratic organizations, these groups are usually formed as committees. But such group formations happen throughout the society and could include groups such as the entering freshman class of a university or the entering class at the police academy. In fact, as societies become more advanced, they develop written and verbal exams to test individuals to help decision makers select the people with "the right stuff" to do the job expected of them. The criteria for establishing what is or is not "the right stuff" do not exist outside of individuals who come together to create criteria and methods of evaluating specific criterion. For this reason, many sociologists stress that important social decisions are socially constructed. By this they mean that individuals with worldviews and

values come together in some socially organized way to make the social rules. These rules have rights and obligations attached to them.

The social construction of oppression can be exemplified by considering gender oppression in a more complicated way. The expected roles for someone who is Black, lesbian, and female are not the same as the expected roles for someone who is Black, heterosexual, and female. Women are less powerful than men in the society, they are often stigmatized because of their bodies and its functions, and they are regular targets of symbolic and physical abuse from males. Lesbian and Black women must endure even more structural oppression in their daily lives. To see this on one dimension we need to merely think about the norm of compulsory heterosexuality and think about a woman who does not solicit or expect being hit on by men in public social space. It is just assumed by most males in the society that they have a right to approach women who they find attractive. In many social situations, women who ignore or express disinterest in male romantic advances open themselves up for various forms of symbolic violence, including shunning, gesturing, and verbal forms of violence. The French intellectual Michel Foucault (1979) named these forms of violence the microphysics of violence. The microphysics of violence refers to cruel sanctioning of individuals based on their inability or unwillingness to behave in expected socially constructed ways. Many citizens feel they have a right to "act out" abuse on individuals because they are different.

(3) *An SOP is power-based.* By definition, *oppression* involves power. There are many kinds of power. "Power over," arguably the type of greatest interest in the social sciences, is hierarchal and involves one or more individuals or groups dominating other individuals or groups. Power over, particularly in the form of authority, is a critical feature of an SOP. Authority, the basis of a stable social order, is presented as naturalized in an SOP. In a stable society, people generally "obey the law" because they assume "that's the way things should be."

Power over is not a zero-sum proposition. When people question their "taken-for-granted" social world or "how things are," they feel "empowered" to challenge authority. Using their own power, as a large body of people or with their own weapons, they present a challenge to the status quo.

In the southern part of the United States, the Jim Crow system separating Blacks and Whites in public facilities such as buses, restaurants, drinking fountains, schools, and hotels survived into the middle of the 1960s. When as a part of the civil rights movement, Blacks questioned their relegation to what constituted secondary and inferior accommodations, they challenged the status quo and the authority of state governments as well as the federal government to keep them out of the superior public accommodations that were available only to Whites. Their challenge to authority initially took the form of nonviolent protest—the use of moral power. Black students sat at lunch counters designated for Whites only day after day to confront White owners morally about their refusal to treat them as equal human beings and serve them.

(4) *An SOP is an ideological phenomenon, morally and legally justified.* Ideology is a set of powerful ideas that justifies a social order in legal and nonlegal as well as in written and spoken terms. Ideology involves direct and explicit communication justifying inequality. One example of ideology is the way many contemporary religious leaders have defined gay men and lesbians as sinners. Ideology also involves indirect and implicit communication justifying inequality. Sexual jokes, for example, typically feature women as targets and play on the idea of women's inferiority to men. The informal settings in which sexual jokes are told among friends provide a license for the telling and social pressure to "get it," to laugh, and hence to "go along" with the message conveyed.

Oppressed groups aware of the power of ideology have challenged the dominant ideology and have developed their own. American Indians have staged protests against the use of their symbols by mainstream society to name sports teams, observing that the use represents a theft and conveys a stereotypic image of them. The queer movement is in part an attempt to take language used against gay men and lesbians and turn it into language used for them. Just as the slogan "Black Is Beautiful" was used to counter mainstream ideology, so gay men and lesbians use the term "queer" to counter the negative connotation associated with mainstream use of the term. The women's movement in its fight against domestic violence uses the slogan "Take Back the Night" to identify the yearly event publicizing this issue and to counter the idea that women should not go out at night by the idea that the streets should be made safe for women.

(5) *An SOP is historically rooted.* The existential basis of human life is time and place. History, the intersection of time and place, provides meaning for a system of oppression. The song "Strange Fruit," made famous by the great blues singer Billie Holiday, speaks directly to the complexity of southern racism in the early part of the twentieth century. It uses the metaphor of the sweet magnolia tree to describe a scene in which Black bodies hang from trees that drip blood. The song tells of the lynching of Black men that took place throughout the United States, but primarily in the South at the end of the nineteenth century and in the early part of the twentieth century.

"Strange Fruit" refers to a history of racism in which gender and sexuality play critical parts. White men lynched Black men because they suspected them of having sexual relations with "their" White women. The historical record reveals that while a sexual relationship between White women and Black men was taboo, White men, often in their role as slave holders, showed no hesitation in taking a Black slave woman as a mistress.

(6) *An SOP is pervasive.* As a system, oppression is more than an isolated phenomenon. Oppression or its effects are found throughout the society, socially and geographically. The heterosexist assumption that sexuality between a man and a woman is *natural,* and, thus, morally correct, underlies every institution in American society, including religion and politics. Sexuality between same-gendered individuals is stigmatized and has great economic and social consequences.

For example, the legal definition of *marriage* in the United States has become a social issue not only with religious groups but also political bodies that maintain marriage between people of the same gender is immoral. In so far as legalized marriage carries with it specific spousal rights, including inheritance and medical benefits, same-gendered people in a stable sexual relationship are denied these rights of marriage.

Heterosexism pervades the geopolitical terrain of American society. Nationally, the mass media broadcasts heterosexism directly through political and religious leaders who make statements, and indirectly through over-saturation of heterosexist imagery and sound bites. Local communities, too, reinforce heterosexism and negatively sanction homosexuality through gossip and confrontation, ranging from name calling to tolerance of hate crimes directed toward gay men, lesbians, and transsexual and transgendered persons.

The societal pervasiveness of oppression creates a great deal of hardship for individuals as they go from one institution to another and as they travel from one geographical place to another. Yet, its pervasiveness can paradoxically be used to challenge it. While heterosexism is pervasive, its form and the extent of its effects vary by localities. In New York City, the Stonewall Inn was known as a gay bar that was frequently raided by police enforcing the law against homosexuality. When in 1969, the gay clientele actively fought the police, the gay liberation movement was born and spread throughout the United States as gay men, lesbians, and transgendered and transsexual people challenged the society's understanding of homosexuality as deviant and the way they were treated in their local communities.

(7) *An SOP is maintained by both oppressor and oppressed.* Antonio Gramsci's (1999) notion of hegemony can help us understand how oppression is reproduced both by the victim and the oppressor. Hegemony is the ability of a dominant group to project its image and ideology or world outlook as all-inclusive, leading the subordinate group to voluntarily assimilate the worldview of the dominant group. Institutions such as schools,

the media, and so forth are institutional centers for the operation of hegemony. They are the conduit through which the condition of domination is transmitted and blended into the popular or mass culture. Ideas such as the American Dream, human rights, and multi-culturalism are framed to appeal to subordinate groups who are taught to believe they are included in every aspect of American life.

Cultural critic bell hooks (1992) suggested in one analysis of pop culture icon and vocal artist Madonna that she had internalized structural sexism and this resulted in Madonna presenting herself in ways that demean women. In one example, Madonna wore little girl's clothes in a major magazine spread. She bent over a swing with her rear end centered in the photograph. The photograph presents Madonna as juvenile and passive. The imagery implies that women are not intelligent and their primary social role is as sexual objects for men. This imagery is exactly what many feminists worked for years to transform since it results in women being labeled as "bimbos" and regarded as "sex objects." In the 1990s, this line of research became particularly prominent. Researchers (see, Lemelle 1996) asked why oppressed groups buy into ideas and behaviors that are designed to oppress them. One answer was that cultural hegemony, or cultural authority, accounted for the internalization of self-fulfilling prophecies. The folkways, mores, norms, and values of the dominant group in society become diffused in the society, and these oppressive socially constructed cultural elements are internalized by individuals. Powerful groups have more privilege in the SOP, and they have greater control over symbols and images, thereby enabling them to sustain their interpretation of role expectations. Some sociologists (see, Collins 1990) refer to this as "controlling images."

(8) *An SOP is invisible.* Oppression is often invisible to dominant groups who do not have contact with the oppressed. Michael Harrington (1963) in his book, *The Other America*, brought poverty to the attention of an America that believed in the affluence of all Americans. He noted the poor were invisible to the nonpoor. They were hidden outside the view of the typical middle- and upper-class American in such places as inner cities and the picturesque mountains of Appalachia. Writing at a time before Medicare and Medicaid, he pointed to the problem of poverty among the elderly—a problem that could not easily be identified because the elderly tended to remain indoors, unseen by younger people in the society.

An SOP is made invisible, also, because of the tendency of the privileged to "blame the victim." In their classic book, *Regulating the Poor*, Francis Fox Piven and Richard Cloward (1993) argued that federal assistance to the poor is liberally given in times of political unrest to prevent turmoil created by masses of impoverished people, but that in times of political stability, assistance is stigmatized as a "hand-out." Politicians proclaim that the solution to poverty is paid employment, even in a setting in which there is no work available or the work does not pay a living wage. To the extent poverty can be blamed on the poor, the problem can be contained and no systemic solution is sought. Further, to the extent the poor can be persuaded that they are to blame for their plight, they will feel too ashamed to ask for the assistance to which they are entitled by law, and their oppression becomes invisible.

(9) *An SOP is dynamic.* While a SOP is a social structural phenomenon and has stability, it is also changing, adapting to shifting circumstances. Its historical course is such that what appears as oppression in one place and time disappears in another place and time, often to be replaced by another form of oppression.

The dynamic quality of racism is demonstrated by the history of such "White" ethnic groups as Italians, Slovaks, and Jews. As noted by Noel Ignatiev (1995) and David R. Roediger (2005), when the mass migration from Central, Eastern, and Southern Europe as well as Ireland to the United States occurred in the latter part of the nineteenth and the early twentieth centuries, the immigrants were subjects of racism. Within a context of a nation-state that had been populated primarily by White Anglo-Saxon Protestants (WASPs), the "new" immigrants were considered "other than" White or Caucasian. They were targets of such hate groups as the Ku Klux Klan and were considered enough of a threat to the country that their entry was virtually curtailed by the passage of immigration laws in 1920 and 1924. By the beginning of the 1950s, however, the United States had changed. The first and second generations of immigrants from the turn of the century had become assimilated "White ethnics" and were no longer treated as racially inferior.

(10) *An SOP is complex, intersecting with other SOPs.* The principles have been described as discrete entities. In reality, it is often difficult to differentiate the presence of one from the other. One may ask: how is ideology differentiated from power? or is not the dynamic aspect of an SOP a part of the historical aspect? These questions have merit. Our purpose in delineating the ten principles, which in reality overlap, is to draw attention to multiple aspects of a system of oppression. It is our intent that the principles be used by first identifying those that best apply to an actual situation. These can then be used as guides to the application of the other principles.

Theoretically, an SOP can be visualized in its pure form, that is, as operating without the influence of other SOPs. In reality, no one human being is a part of just one SOP. A woman and a man are not simply their genders. They occupy a number of other places in society, including class, race, and sexuality places. In addition, as pointed out by the third wave of the women's movement, all men are not powerful over all women, and all women are not essentially the same, just as all men are not the same.

An intersected approach is theoretically and pragmatically necessary for an understanding of actual oppression. This approach, as defined by sociologist Patricia Hill Collins (1998) and others, provides a view of oppression that is nuanced. For example, the issue of priority for White women concerned with population control has been that of the right to abortion; by contrast, for Native American and Black women (Davis 1983; Roberts 1997), it has been enforced sterilization. Abortion rights and the right to have children are both reproductive issues relevant to women's concerns. Thus, both are feminist issues, but the focus on one as opposed to the other has the effect of alienating a large segment of women.

Analysis and Action

We believe that successful action follows theory. Our purpose in theoretically identifying the ten SOP principles is to provide a tool for the elimination of oppression. Before acting to change social life, we must have a clear conceptualization of what we wish to change. The ten principles taken together necessarily define the theoretical reality of a SOP. They form an "ideal type," an intellectual tool for the analysis of actual oppression. In using such a tool, it is not necessary to find the applicability of each characteristic; rather, a sufficient analysis can be made using a subset of the characteristics. The applicability of each SOP principle or combination of principles will vary according to the actual manifestation of oppression and the analyzer's orientation. Finally, by identifying the ten SOP principles, we provide ten different points of entry for deconstructing oppression. The principles are dialectical: each implies a means for the elimination of oppression.

References

Alger, Jr. Horatio. N.D. *Adrift in New York.* Akron, OH: The Saalfield Publishing Co.

Andersen, Margaret L., and Patricia Hill Collins, eds. 2004. *Race, Class, and Gender,* (5th ed.). Belmont, CA: Wadsworth.

Bowles, Samuel, and Herbert Gintis. 1976. *Schooling in Capitalist America: Educational Reform and the Contradictions of Economic Life.* New York: Basic Books.

Brewer, Rose. 1996. "Gender Studies in Sociology: Race, Class Formation, and African American Girls." Pp. 157–187 in *Theory, Methods, and Praxis, Advances in Gender Research, Vol. 1,* edited by Marcia Texler Segal and Vasilikie Demos. Greenwich, CT: JAI Press.

Collins, Patricia Hill. 1990. *Black Feminist Thought.* Boston: Unwin Hyman.

———. 1998. *Fighting Words: Black Women in the Search for Justice.* Minneapolis: University of Minnesota Press.

Davis, Angela Y. 1983. *Women, Race, & Class.* New York: Vintage.

Feagin, Joe R., and Hernán Vera. 2001. Liberation Sociology. Boulder, CO: Westview.

Foucault, Michel. 1979. *Discipline & Punish: The Birth of the Prison.* New York: Vintage.

Frye, Marilyn. 2004. "Oppression." Pp. 174–178 in *Race, Class, and Gender in the United States,* edited by Paula S. Rothenberg. New York: Worth.

Glenn, Evelyn Nakano. 2002. *Unequal Freedom.* Cambridge, MA: Harvard University Press.

Gramsci, A. 1999. *The Gramsci Reader: Selected Writings.* London: Lawrence & Wishart.

Harrington, Michael. 1963. *The Other America: Poverty in the United States.* Baltimore, MD: Penguin.

hooks, bell. 1992. *Black Looks: Race and Representation.* Boston: South End Press.

Ignatiev, Noel. 1995. *How the Irish Became White.* New York: Routledge.

Kanfer, Stefan. 2000. "Horatio Alger: The Moral of the Story." *City Journal,* 10, 4. Retrieved April 2, 2005 (*http://www.city-journal.org/html/10_4_urban-ites-the_moral.html*).

Kuumba M. Bahati, and Femi Ajanaku. 1996. "Women's Liberation Research: Methodological Strategies for Social Change." Pp. 189–212 in *Theory, Methods, and Praxis, Advances in Gender Research, Vol.1,* edited by Marcia Texler Segal and Vasilikie Demos. Greenwich, CT: JAI Press.

Lemelle, Anthony J. 1995. *Black Male Deviance.* Westport, CT: Praeger.

——. 1996. "The Other Cyborgs: African-American Male Role and Feminist Theory." Pp. 157–187 in *Theory, Methods, and Praxis, Advances in Gender Research, Vol. 1,* edited by Marcia Texler Segal and Vasilikie Demos. Greenwich, CT: JAI Press.

Luttrell, Wendy. 2003. *Pregnant Bodies, Fertile Minds: Gender, Race, and the Schooling of Pregnant Teens.* New York: Routledge.

Omi, Michael, and Howard Winant. 1994. *Racial Formation in America,* (2nd ed.). New York: Routledge.

Piven, Frances Fox, and Richard A. Cloward. 1993. *Regulating the Poor: The Functions of Public Welfare.* New York: Vintage.

Roberts, Dorothy. 1997. *Killing the Black Body: Race, Reproduction, and the Meaning of Liberty.* New York: Vintage.

Roediger, David R. 2005. *How America's Immigrants Became White: The Strange Journey from Ellis Island to the Suburbs.* New York: Basic Books.

Romero, Mary. 1992. *Maid in the U.S.A.* New York: Routledge.

Discussion Questions

1. Select one of the SOP principles from this article and, using materials from other readings in this volume, show more fully how it operates in society.

2. Discuss the role of ideology in maintaining and in challenging oppression.

3. The authors of this essay discuss each of the 10 principles of SOPs separately, but claim that all the principles actually intersect (Principle 10). In a brief essay, show how at least two of the principles intersect.

4. Did you find any of the 10 principles difficult to understand or to accept? Is there one that you would like clarification of or more examples of or one that you would contest? Write a brief note to the authors or the editors explaining your response to that principle. If all the principles seemed perfectly clear and you accepted them all, write about one that gave you new insight into inequality in our society.

64

Broken Levees, Unbroken Barriers

Jason DeParle

The stormy days in New Orleans, Louisiana, in August of 2005 will not be forgotten. Hurricane Katrina hit the Louisiana and Mississippi coasts, bringing a natural disaster of inestimable proportions—one of the worst in our country's history. The nation is truly still reeling from this tragedy as I write this introduction. Yet, the story of Katrina's stormy days will not likely be remembered for broken levees alone but for broken promises. In the social contract America has with its citizens, we hold it to be self-evident that all men, women, and children are endowed with certain inalienable rights—life and liberty, certainly, and the pursuit of happiness. The story of New Orleans in the wake of Katrina raises issues for us as Americans, issues Jason DeParle seeks to pinpoint with a question about race, and class, and America—what happens to a race deferred?

What is most telling about the story of hurricane Katrina, DeParle tells us his readers, is the literal way the hurricane underscored the unequal divide in the community of New Orleans. This divide fractured along well-grooved paths in this community—one Black and one White, one poor and one middle class to affluent—as obvious as the segregated communities of Lake Pontchartrain and inner-city New Orleans. Interestingly, DeParle juxtaposes two men in this article—a White man named David Duke, a former Klansman, who won more than half of the White votes in Louisiana in his bid for governor, and a Black man, C. Ray Nagin, from a poor area of town, who is now New Orleans mayor, weeping in the face of an unresponsive federal government.

The truth is, the White people could afford to get out, while the Black people were limited by the simple turned deadly lack of access to a household car. While DeParle does not mention it, the most vulnerable to Katrina were Black women with children—a reminder of gendered dynamics relative to race and class. DeParle notes that this is a tragedy among many for poor Black communities nationwide, for example, where heat waves in Chicago kill hundreds and Blacks die at higher rates compared with Whites of similar age because of their relative social isolation from populated parts of town.

Interestingly, one blogger writes, according to DeParle, that New Orleans is yet another Hotel Rwanda. How telling. If the tragedy of New Orleans is a sign of things to come, the inner cities of this country will continue to be, like Rwanda, places where race and class divisions can fast become a matter of life and death.

The white people got out. Most of them, anyway. If television and newspaper images can be deemed a statistical sample, it was mostly black people who were left behind. Poor black people, growing more hungry, sick and frightened by the hour as faraway officials counseled patience and warned that rescues take time.

What a shocked world saw exposed in New Orleans last week wasn't just a broken levee. It was a cleavage of race and class, at once familiar and startlingly new, laid bare in a setting where they suddenly amounted to matters of life and death. Hydrology joined sociology throughout the story line, from the settling of the flood-prone city, where well-to-do white people lived on the high ground, to its frantic abandonment.

The pictures of the suffering vied with reports of marauding, of gunshots fired at rescue vehicles and armed bands taking over the streets. The city of quaint eccentricity—of King Cakes, Mardi Gras beads and nice neighbors named Tookie—had taken a Conradian turn.

In the middle of the delayed rescue, the New Orleans mayor, C. Ray Nagin, a local boy made good from a poor, black ward, burst into tears of frustration as he denounced slow moving federal officials and called for martial law.

Even people who had spent a lifetime studying race and class found themselves slack-jawed.

"This is a pretty graphic illustration of who gets left behind in this society—in a literal way," said Christopher Jencks, a sociologist glued to the televised images from his office at Harvard. Surprised to have found himself surprised, Mr. Jencks took to thinking out loud, "Maybe it's just an in-the-face version of something I already knew," he said. "All the people who don't get out, or don't have the resources, or don't believe the warning are African-American."

"It's not that it's at odds with the way I see American society," Mr. Jencks said. "But it's at odds with the way I want to see American society."

Last week it was how others saw American society, too, in images beamed across the globe. Were it not for the distinctive outlines of the Superdome, the pictures of hovering rescue helicopters might have carried a Somalian dateline. The Sri Lankan ambassador offered to help raise foreign aid.

Anyone who knew New Orleans knew that danger lurked behind the festive front. Let the good times roll, the tourists on Bourbon Street were told. Yet in every season, someone who rolled a few blocks in the wrong direction wound up in the city morgue.

Unusually poor (27.4 percent below the poverty line in 2000), disproportionately black (over two-thirds), the Big Easy is also disproportionately murderous—with a rate that was for years among the country's highest.

Once one of the most mixed societies, in recent decades, the city has become unusually segregated, and the white middle class is all but gone, moved north across Lake Pontchartrain or west to Jefferson Parish—home of David Duke, the one-time Klansman who ran for governor in 1991 and won more than half of the state's white vote.

Shortly after I arrived in town two decades ago as a fledgling reporter, I was dispatched to cover a cheerleading tryout, and I asked a grinning, half-drunk accountant where he was from, city or suburb. "White people don't live in New Orleans," he answered with a where-have-you-been disdain.

For those who loved it, its glories as well as its flaws, last week brought only heartbreak. So much of New Orleans, from its music and its food to its architecture, had shown a rainbow society at its best, even as everyone knew it was more complicated than that.

"New Orleans, first of all, is both in reality and in rhetoric an extraordinarily successful multicultural society," said Philip Carter, a developer and retired journalist whose roots in the city extend back more at least four generations. "But is also a multicultural society driven by race and class, and all this has been exposed by these stormy days. The people of our community are pitted against each other across the barricades of race and class that six months from now may be [the] last remaining levees in New Orleans."

No one was immune, of course. With 80 percent of the city under water, tragedy swallowed the privilege[d] and poor, and traveled spread across racial lines.

But the divides in the city were evident in things as simple as access to a car. The 35 percent of black households that didn't have one, compared with just 15 percent among whites.

"The evacuation plan was really based on people driving out," said Craig E. Colten, a geologist at Louisiana State University and an expert on the city's vulnerable topography. "They didn't have buses. They didn't have trains."

As if to punctuate the divide, the water especially devastated the Ninth Ward, among [the] city's poorest and lowest lying.

"Out West, there is a saying that water flows to money," Mr. Colten said. "But in New Orleans, water flows away from money. Those with resources who control where the drainage goes have always chosen to live on the high ground. So the people in the low areas were hardest hit."

Outrage grew as the week wore on, among black politicians who saw the tragedy as a reflection of a broader neglect of American cities, and in the blogosphere.

"The real reason no one is helping is because of the color of these people!" wrote "myfan88" on the Flickr blog. "This is Hotel Rwanda all over again."

"Is this what the pioneers of the civil rights movement fought to achieve, a society where many black people are as trapped and isolated by their poverty as they were by legal segregation laws?" wrote Mark Naison, director of the urban studies program at Fordham, on another blog.

One question that could not be answered last week was whether, put to a similar test, other cities would fracture along the same lines.

At one level, everything about New Orleans appears sui generis, not least its location below sea level. Many New Orleanians don't just accept the jokes about living in a Banana Republic. They spread them.

But in a quieter catastrophe, the 1995 heat wave that killed hundreds of Chicagoans, blacks in comparable age groups as whites died at higher rates—in part because they tended to live in greater social isolation, in depopulated parts of town. As in New Orleans, space intertwined with race.

And the violence? Similarly shocking scenes had erupted in Los Angeles in 1992, after the acquittal of white police officers charged with beating a black man, Rodney King. Newark, Detroit, Washington—all burned in the race riots of the 1960's. It was for residents of any major city, watching the mayhem, to feel certain their community would be immune.

With months still to go just to pump out the water that covers the city, no one can be sure how the social fault lines will rearrange. But with white flight a defining element of New Orleans in the recent past, there was already the fear in the air this week that the breached levee would leave a separated society further apart.

"Maybe we can build the levees back," said Mr. Carter. "But that sense of extreme division by class and race is going to long survive the physical reconstruction of New Orleans."

Discussion Questions

1. What is the lesson about race and class that we can learn from the tragedy of hurricane Katrina?

2. How does the aftermath of Katrina teach us anything about solutions to racial and class divides?

3. Can you think of other events or tragedies that have highlighted race, class, and gender divides in our country?

4. Where were you when Katrina hit the Gulf Coast? What were you thinking as this tragedy unfolded?